G000160659

Paul's Parallels

Paul's Parallels

An Echoes Synopsis

By

Patricia Elyse Terrell

NEW YORK • LONDON

2009

The Continuum International Publishing Group Inc
80 Maiden Lane, New York, NY 10038

The Continuum International Publishing Group Ltd
The Tower Building, 11 York Road, London SE1 7NX

www.continuumbooks.com

Copyright © 2009 by Patricia Elyse Terrell

The Scripture quotations contained herein are from the King James Version, copyright © 2005 by Cambridge University on behalf of Her Majesty, the Queen of England, and are used by permission. All rights reserved.

All rights reserved. No part of this book may be reproduced, stored in a retrieval system, or transmitted, in any form or by any means, electronic, mechanical, photocopying, recording, or otherwise, without the written permission of the publishers.

Library of Congress Cataloging-in-Publication Data

A catalog record for this book is available from the Library of Congress.

Printed in the United States of America

ISBN 9780567027450

Paul's Parallels is dedicated to
the New Testament Seminar of Oxford University

Brief Contents

Detailed Contents

PAULINE EPISTLES: SECTION II

Foreword

Christopher C. Rowland

Dean Ireland Professor of the Exegesis of Holy Scripture, Oxford University

The writings of Paul contained in the New Testament have had an extraordinary influence on the history of Christianity. The effects of a remarkable, driven, and much-maligned person, in his own lifetime, are still very much with us. How are we to understand these, sometimes, complex texts for ourselves? Centuries of tradition and the received wisdom of Christian churches inevitably condition the ways in which we read Paul's letters. If we want to try and understand for ourselves, we need to engage with these texts in ways which can open the background and the ways in which Paul dealt with the small groups of fellow-believers, whose lives were changed by their engagement with this itinerant preacher, by relating them to other texts from antiquity. This will mean primarily texts from the Bible, though historical scholarship has over the last two hundred years done much to also provide analogies from contemporary literature, whether Jewish, Greek or Roman.

When we try and make sense of what we read, we find ourselves drawing analogies from our own experience, or from what we have been taught in order to understand what lies before. This is just as true of reading the Bible. I can understand Paul's letters better by knowing what else he said, or what other passages may have inspired him in what he said, or even what others who were Christians at the same time as him said about similar issues. The opening up of the meaning of texts by use of parallel material is at the heart of what we mean by exegesis, the interpretation, or exposition, of texts. Unlike most of us, Paul carried the Bible in his head and that meant for him what we now know as the Old Testament, or at least parts of it (we cannot be exactly sure what was regarded as Holy Scripture in Paul's day). That meant that he couldn't help himself picking on words or phrases to say what he wanted to say, even when he wasn't consciously and deliberately quoting Scripture. It's something like what happens to us when we find ourselves quoting a familiar passage such as "Sufficient unto the day is the evil thereof" (Matthew 6:34). Biblical phraseology and ideas are the furniture of Paul's thought and language in ways which are rare in the modern world, though this doesn't mean that he is always deliberately quoting the Bible—far from it, so much as having his mental furniture furnished with its words and themes.

What Patricia Terrell's book does is offer an innovative contribution to enable us to understand the context of Paul within the Bible and thereby inform the ways in which we can better understand his writings. Of course, the parallels will not explain Paul's thoughts for us, but they will do three things. First of all, we have a tool which will enable us to do the interpretative job ourselves and not rely on what the experts tell us is the case. Secondly, by giving us analogous passages we shall be better informed about the wider biblical context. Thirdly, and, in my view, most importantly, the method of this book gives us an example of how we should go about biblical interpretation: looking for analogies is at the heart of how we go about finding meaning in texts. It isn't just other biblical passages which provide analogies to Paul (or other parts of the Bible), for we may find that analogies from our contemporary world may illuminate the Bible and shed light on its impact. It can do this as much by way of differences between the Bible and our world as close parallels. Either way it will remind us that the analogical method is the way in which we go about making sense of a particular passage, and this book will be of assistance in helping us do just that.

Abbreviations

JEWISH WRITINGS (originally in Hebrew dialects), Canonical Order

Genesis	Gen	Proverbs	Prov
Exodus	Ex	Ecclesiastes	Eccl
Leviticus	Lev	Song of Songs	Sg
Numbers	Num	Wisdom	Wis
Deuteronomy	Dt	Sirach	Sir
Joshua	Jos	Isaiah	Is
Judges	Jdg	Jeremiah	Jer
Ruth	Ru	Lamentations	Lam
1 Samuel	1 Sam	Baruch	Bar
2 Samuel	2 Sam	Ezekiel	Ezek
1 Kings	1 Kgs	Daniel	Dan
2 Kings	2 Kgs	Hosea	Hos
1 Chronicles	1 Chr	Joel	Joel
2 Chronicles	2 Chr	Amos	Amos
Ezra	Ezr	Obadiah	Ob
Nehemiah	Neh	Jonah	Jon
Tobit	Tb	Micah	Mic
Judith	Jdt	Nahum	Nah
Esther	Est	Habakkuk	Hb
1 Maccabees	1 Mac	Zephaniah	Zep
2 Maccabees	2 Mac	Haggai	Hg
Job	Job	Zechariah	Zach
Psalms	Ps(s)	Malachi	Mal

NEW TESTAMENT (Apostolic writings were originally in Greek), Canonical Order

Matthew	Mt	1 Timothy	1 Tim
Mark	Mk	2 Timothy	2 Tim
Luke	Lk	Titus	Tit
John	Jn	Philemon	Phlm
Acts of the Apostles	Acts	Hebrews	Heb
Romans	Rom	James	Jas
1 Corinthians	1 Cor	1 Peter	1 Pet
2 Corinthians	2 Cor	2 Peter	2 Pet
Galatians	Gal	1 John	1 Jn
Ephesians	Eph	2 John	2 Jn
Philippians	Phil	3 John	3 Jn
Colossians	Col	Jude	Jud
1 Thessalonians	1 Thes	Revelation	Rev
2 Thessalonians	2 Thes		

NON-CANONICAL TEXTS, Date Ordering

Lost Sayings of Q	Q-Quelle	40–80 AD	Fayyum Fragment	Fayyum	70–200 AD
Didache	Did	50–120 AD	Epistle of Barnabas	EpisBar	80–120 AD
Gospel of Thomas	GThom	50–140 AD	Papyrus Egerton	PEger	80–120 AD
Oxyrhynchus	Oxy	50–140 AD	1 Clement	1 Clem	80–140 AD
Epistle of James	EpisJas	70–100 AD	Gospel of Egyptians	GEgyp	80–150 AD
Gospel of Peter	GPet	70–160 AD	Gospel of Hebrews	GHeb	80–150 AD

Flavius Josephus	Josephus	93 AD
Apocalypse of Peter	ApocPet	100–150 AD
Protoevangelium James	PJas	100–150 AD
Gospel of Ebionites	GEbi	100–160 AD
Gospel of Nazoreans	GNaz	100–160 AD
Ignatius of Antioch	Igna	105–115 AD
Polycarp	Polycp	110–140 AD
Gospel of Mary	Gos Ma	120–180 AD
2 Apocalypse of James	2 ApocJas	120–180 AD
2 Clement	2 Clem	130–160 AD
Gospel of Judas	GosJud	130–170 AD
Infancy Gospel of James	In Jas	140–170 AD
Infancy Gospel of Thomas	In Thom	140–170 AD
Justin Martyr	Jus	150–160 AD
Acts of Pilate	Act Pi	150–400 AD
Irenaeus	Iren	175–185 AD
1 Apocalypse of James	1 ApocJas	180–250 AD
Gospel of Philip	Gos Phil	180–250 AD
Clement	Clem	182–202 AD
Origen	Ori	203–250 AD

Introduction

Who Is Paul?

St. Paul, an apostle and the founder of several original Christian churches, was a key figure in teaching and demonstrating the power of Jesus' revelation for the Greek Gentiles who would become believers.

Paul's birth name was Saul. He was named after the first leader of Israel and was born a Jew and a Roman citizen. His early years reveal only that he trained under the finest Jewish scholar of his time, Gamaliel. As a gifted religious man, Paul wished to protect his Jewish faith from bad teachings and believing Christians to be heretical, he persecuted many. The chronology of St. Paul's life suggests, but has not confirmed, that he may have been present when Jesus was crucified, as an antagonist, and that Saul stood over the stoning of St. Stephen, the first Christian martyr. Shortly after Stephen's death, Saul underwent a dramatic transformation. As he and his party were traveling to Damascus, they saw a flash of lightening and heard thunderous sounds from heaven. It blinded Saul, but God instructed Ananias, a Christian, to go to him and pray for his eyes to be opened. Ananias did not want to go because he heard Saul was zealous in eliminating Christianity, but he went because God commanded it. In fact, Saul regained his sight and a new name—Paul. When God gave Saul a new name, as he had done with others, it signified Paul belonged to God.

Paul's miracle opened his eyes to the truth of Jesus' message and he zealously pursued the new Way. Paul went into the desert for ten years in order to familiarize himself with all that Jesus said and did. Then Paul began evangelizing Jews explaining all that Jesus taught, but they would not hear him so he opened the Word to Greeks, also known as Gentiles or Hellenists. He journeyed from Israel, across present-day Turkey (known as East Greece), and throughout Greece. The Hellenists received the news with joy and several churches began in the Eastern Mediterranean regions. Many of Paul's letters were named after those churches.

Luke, the evangelist, traveled extensively with Paul and wrote a gospel about Jesus as well as a sequel, Acts of the Apostles, which recorded the history of Peter's and Paul's Christian vocations. In narrative form, Luke's gospel illustrated Jesus Christ's message. The book of Acts testified to the fact that Jesus' Resurrection made the "acts of the Holy Spirit" available to all believers. Paul wrote letters advising his church congregations even before Luke or any of the evangelists raised a pen. Those letters, often called epistles, are a major part of the New Testament.

Paul's Letters and Written Testimony

Purpose of the Letters to the Churches

In the first century, Paul wrote epistles (letters) in the local Greek vernacular to particular congregations. They were circulated among Christian communities, just as we read them today. Scholars believe his letters developed an understanding of the Christian faith according to the needs of each Church. In them, he also argued venomously against false teachings that crept into his communities, usually generated by religious Jews, anti-Christian sects, and men claiming divine knowledge from different sources.

Paul wanted to tell others how to live so they might experience the fullness of God's promise—in a language they could understand. It was apparent in reading the epistles that Paul analyzed his own life and struggled with his own attitudes and former ways. His boasting turned to meekness over time and trial. Paul went through a process of change from following Judaism to Christianity that involved strict lifestyle behavioral guidelines, but he continued to reiterate deep faith *in* and *of* Jesus [*pistou christou*] as the centrifugal force.

Christian Transition from Jewish Law *to Jewish* Principles

The book of "Acts" explained that Paul had to confront the Christian leaders in Jerusalem because the apostles had reverted to practicing Jewish Law way beyond the pale of Jesus' teaching. Paul convinced Peter and James, leaders of the council that was emerging in the Jerusalem church, that Gentiles should not be required to observe Jewish practices because it compromised the Christian doctrine, which asked one to live a Christlike lifestyle. The Jerusalem council was impressed by the faith of Gentile converts as well as the swift spread of Christianity so they blessed Paul and his companions as they set forth on missionary journeys.

Commissioning Paul and Jesus' disciples for mission ultimately became the new basis for the rites of ordination (Holy Orders). In Jewish law, leadership was inherited through the Levitical bloodline. With the Resurrection of Jesus, the Holy Spirit initiated a new order of priesthood and the deaconate. The power of Jesus' anointing flowed through the Good News preached by apostolic ministry and this post-Resurrection Christian faith was recorded in the New Testament.

Transmission of the Faith

Paul knew and, therefore, influenced the apostles through discussions, travel, and friendship. They ate and drank together, comparing important milestones about what marked Christian principles. Paul's enlightenment experience combined with a great education made him a more articulate spokesperson earlier than any of the others. By the end of Paul's lifetime, many of the patterns of persecution, humiliation, and sacrifice seen in Jesus' life and ministry were echoed in Paul's own Christian walk. Jesus had indeed passed the baton, so to speak, and Paul was wise to see that all of civilization could be transformed by the Christian faith.

Like Judaism, Christianity was passed from generation to generation by oral tradition. The writing materials to make the scrolls for the Jewish temple were very expensive and not many Jews possessed holy writ in their homes. St. Paul could afford to put his thoughts into writing, which enabled Christian oral tradition a legacy of written records. Years later, St. Luke, a Gentile who was an educated and eloquent Greek physician, documented Jesus' life, death, and resurrection. Truly grateful for the Christian life, he also authored a type of history of the Holy Spirit in the "Acts of the Apostles." Matthew's written version was longer and, as a repentant tax collector, he still had resources to evangelize Jesus' ministry—with a Jewish accent. Mark was Paul's first missionary companion. He became Peter's scribe and may have borrowed bits from conversations with Paul for the gospel of "Mark." Mark's was a shorter gospel and it is possible that writing materials were just too dear for a fisherman, that is, Peter. Paul shared ideas with fellow believers that they used later in their own written testimonies. Could Paul be the "Q" source hypothesized for the synoptic gospels? That answer must be reserved for another project.

Holy texts spanned the corridors of time. It is part of their authenticity. It is a "living word" that seeps into natural thought processes. Scripture flowed effortlessly from the lips and writings of devoted Christians. Often called saints, their autographs contained continual scripture citations—the higher the number of citations, the greater one's endowment of holiness.

New Testament Collection of Writings

Oral tradition over the millennia held to a high level accountability for transmitting Holy Writ. The Hebrew language was itself a holy vessel. The translation of the Jewish sacred texts into Greek formulated the *Septuagint*. In bearing God's Word, the Greek was sacred. Texts took many forms. Some were written in small cursive letters (minuscule), while others had all capital letters (uncial). Writing materials included papyrus (woven reeds), dried sheep or animal skins, which were rolled into scrolls, or bound into a codex—all were catalogued copies of copies (no originals survived).

The dating and geography of the New Testament writings are not certain, but Paul began writing them about fifteen years after Jesus was crucified. A scribe assisted Paul, which was typical for the early Mediterranean era.

In the collection of Paul's writings, Paul speaks of "ευαγγηλιον" (*euangelion*) as the "gospel of God" or the "gospel of Christ" and sometimes he wrote "my gospel" or "our gospel." His letters were an early gospel occasioned by situations in which new Christians needed his attention. Paul's *euangelion* was a collection of expressions and the growing pains of early church communities adopting a Christian lifestyle. It was his particular style of communicating Christ's message. The epistles were written prior to the four gospels and were a *bona fide* interpretation of the gospel of God through Paul's lens and experience. His letters were placed in the Bible directly *following* Matthew, Mark, Luke, John, and Luke's Acts of the Apostles. The epistles were arranged by length. The Epistle to the Romans was longest so it was the first and it was the most mature of Paul's writings.

The Greek New Testament is not only a composition of writings by several authors, but Paul's epistles came from discoveries of fragmented documents found at several locations, over centuries, usually in Greek. Each fragment was identified by the family name of the discoverer or the place from which it was excavated. Bruce Metzger's and Kurt Aland's *Greek New Testament* has annotations about specific fragments that assist textual critics with fragment details and variances. From a textual criticism point-of-view, Paul's parallels are really "echoes" affirming established traditions and principles, without an exact replication of wording, such as is seen in the synoptic gospels.

Purpose and Organization of *Paul's Parallels*

Highlights

Paul's Parallels is the first and only New Testament resource text in tables format presenting Paul's verses first, followed by a row of parallels, echoes, or like-minded quotes from Old and New Testament resources as well as other recently translated extant biblical materials. The passages are cited in full.

The King James Bible (KJB) is the English translation or version (KJV) of choice since it was accessible while remaining closest to the original biblical languages, according to Alister McGrath, Laurence Vance, Herman Hanko, and numerous KJV experts. The KJV, with rights retained by the Crown of the United Kingdom, lends its 400-year old authenticity to this Pauline exposition.

This master of the epistolary writings gives a verse-by-verse demonstration of Paul's thoughts, his ethic, and his actions that were picked up by later Christian writers as well as copied by pseudo-Pauline admirers. It delineates some as distinctively Christian while others remained only in Paul's writing.

The Apostle Paul is the most written about personality in the New Testament and this text provides an instant reference for all of St. Paul's writings. It is a valuable time-saver and a perfect desktop tool.

St. Paul, *Acts of the Apostles*

In Section I, Paul's life and ministry from Luke's "Acts of the Apostles" offers a sacred, factual, eyewitness account (Lk 1:2–4). This provides the reader with a chrono-historical context for cross-evaluation with Paul's letters, assisted by a table showing Luke's and Paul's overlapping accounts. Luke focused on Christian eternal values so Luke's first-century history is presented differently than that of a twenty-first-century historian. Another notable variance is the attention given to Jesus' exact words in Luke's gospel vis-à-vis his tendency to paraphrase speeches in Acts.

The Acts Section is exclusive to Paul's story alone. The "theme" of each verse appears in the first column next to the verse itself, recited in full. Analogous citations were aligned in a columnar format. Documenting the Lukan *in situ* history of Paul's ministry in the same book as the epistles allows the reader to instantly give a context to the particular message, while investigating serious textual, literary, or genre types, as well as other theological characteristics. Without losing one's place, the mind can reflect upon Paul's conversion, his change of heart and mind, Paul's audience, his living situation, and lifestyle to connect the overall picture to the epistle. There remain unresolved time-place discrepancies in the reports given by Luke's "Acts" and what is known about Paul's epistles. Here are two differing styles of writing, whose authors complement Christian goals.

Pauline Epistles

The section featuring Paul's letters ordered the writings canonically, that is by length, rather than chronology. The New Testament canon is: Romans, 1 Corinthians, 2 Corinthians, Galatians, Ephesians, Philippians, Colossians, 1 Thessalonians, 2 Thessalonians, 1 Timothy, 2 Timothy, Titus, and Philemon. Romans, 1 and 2 Corinthians, Galatians, Philippians, Colossians, 1 and 2 Thessalonians, and Philemon have strong internal and external attestation as to their Pauline authorship. Ephesians, 1 and 2 Timothy, and Titus were close imitations of Paul's writing, which was normative during that era for one who was admired and revered. These pseudo-Pauline documents were faithful to the Christian teachings and were canonical on that basis, long before the modern critical methods. Above each table is a reference giving the date, geography, or environment affecting the verse.

This book was designed to make the Pauline comparisons readily accessible in English. The table contains full citations. Each row begins with a "theme" offering a simple theology for the verse or pericope to which it applies. Paul's verse appears next to other biblical resources. Columnar order is: Matthew, Mark, Luke (including Luke-Acts), John (including 1, 2, 3 John), Paul (including pseudo-Paul), New Testament (Hebrews, James, 1 and 2 Peter, Jude, and Revelation), Jewish Writings (including 1, 2 Maccabees, and Josephus), and Other (general or more recently translated biblical resources).

Church Fathers and Roman historians collected meaningful texts and some were outside the canon. In this volume one may find: Lost Sayings of Q (Quelle, 40–80 AD), Didache (50–120 AD), Gospel of Thomas (50–140 AD), Oxyrhynchus (50–140 AD), Epistle of James (70–100 AD), Gospel of Peter (70–160 AD), Fayyum Fragment (70–200 AD), Epistle of Barnabas (80–120 AD), 1 Clement (80–140 AD), Gospel of the Egyptians (80–150 AD), Gospel of Hebrews (80–150 AD), Christian Sibyllines (80–250 AD), Flavius Josephus (93 AD), Apocalypse of Peter (100–150 AD), Gospel of the Ebionites (100–160 AD), Gospel of the Nazoreans (100–160 AD), Ignatius of Antioch (105–115 AD), Polycarp (110–140 AD), Gospel of Mary (120–180 AD), 2 Apocalypse of James (120–180 AD), 2 Clement (130–160 AD), Gospel of Judas (130–170 AD), Infancy Gospel of James (140–170 AD), Infancy Gospel of Thomas (140–170 AD), Justin Martyr (150–60 AD), Acts of Pilate (150–400 AD), Irenaeus (175–185 AD), 1 Apocalypse of James (180–250 AD), Gospel of Philip (180–250 AD), Clement (182–202 AD), and Origen (203–250 AD).

As Jesus' message reverberated across cultures and ages, the Greek rendition, often taught as "classic," was supplemented when Jerome made an official Latin translation for the Catholic Church, known as the "Vulgate" (cf. vulgar or common language of the community). Latin was only for the eyes of educated, tonsured clerics who wanted to protect the official Church interpretation. Translating the Bible so ordinary people could understand it was only a few generations away. Today, Bibles can be found in a myriad of languages. Current translations often emphasize a smoother reading over exact translation.

English Translations

This volume is for English readers. While the *King James Bible* was the version authorized by royal decree, it was the successor to several good English translations.

Tyndale (1525)
Coverdale (1535)
The Matthew Bible (1539)
The Great Bible (1539)
Geneva Bible (1560)
The Bishop's Bible (1568)
King James (1611)

King James Version

The King James Bible (KJB) serves the purposes of this reference text because it is in English, very closely translated from the original Greek New Testament fragments, and it was polished over the years. (This is not to say KJV improved on the scripture itself.) The King James Bible is a distinguished literary masterpiece. It was a Shakespearean resource. Families that could afford only one book usually owned a Bible and one learned English from the King James Bible.

The meaning of English words and colloquialisms on England's side of the pond varies from American English. Early English used double vowels and consonants, "e" ended many words, "u" appeared in place of "v", -eth [and -ith] identified a singular thou (second person), like a child's lisp, and "s" represented a plural "you," just to name a few.

Alister McGrath explained certain "politically correct" factors. "Thereof" was used to avoid "its" or the masculine gender possessive pronoun. "Church" was not to be translated "congregation" or *ecclesia*. YHWH (Tetragrammaton) was rendered as LORD (caps), or LORD GOD; Adonai YHWH was "Lord YHWH" and Jesus is "Lord."

There is a glossary at the back of *Paul's Parallels and Echoes*, informed by the 1828 version of Webster's dictionary to assist the reader in finding the meaning intended by England's translators. The glossary offers a basic definition and this author presumed the reader could differentiate and cross reference a given word to its use as a pronoun, noun, verb, etc.

The King James project is widely used today since it made a monumental impact on society at its appointed time in history.

King James' Family

King James was devoted to creating a Bible that was accessible in English, precisely accurate, and readable in the translation, and some of his motivations were political. The 1603 historical vortex of the coronation of James framed many changes. The crown passed from the Tudors to the Stewarts. His mother, Mary Stewart, Queen of Scots, was an avid defender of Roman Catholicism, and her cousin Elizabeth Tudor, Queen of England, was the descendant of Henry VIII who protested papal authority and, hence, was a Protestant. After Elizabeth's death, James VI of Scotland was crowned King James I of England and inherited a land needing unification. England had extremely diverse English dialects arising from Norman and Anglo-Saxon Germanic invaders, the French tongues from William the Conqueror's court as well as an aristocratic group that the Middle Ages fiefdom linguistically separated from its serfs. England did not want any more invading rulers. While the Church of England practiced the faith according to its Catholic heritage, it had replaced the Roman "Papa" or Pope with England's own monarch, which created a schism, drawing its own orthodoxy under a magnifying glass. The Puritans asked the Realm to justify itself biblically and King James wanted to protect his authority from the counterproductive "comments" in the notes section of the most popular English Bible of the day, the Geneva Bible, which was widely read among Protestants.

Commissioning the King James Bible

Hence, King James established a commission to collaborate on the King James Bible (i.e., KJB; or, KJV, King James Version). It consisted of fifty-four well-educated members working at Westminster, Cambridge, and Oxford, forty-seven of whom remained actively engaged in the translations. Specific mandates were followed to retain the highest authenticity, including preserving large portions (80 percent) of the existing Tyndale translation because it was so well done. The groups consulted sources from Greek, Latin, Hebrew, Aramaic, French, German, Italian, Spanish, Latin, as well as requesting interpretative affirmations from ordained priests. Six groups performed the majority of the work. Genesis to 2 Kings was translated at Westminster by Lancelot Andrewes, William Bedwell, Francis Burleigh, Richard Clarke, Jeffrey King, John Layfield, John Overall, Hadrian Saravia, Richard Thomson, and Robert Tighe. 1 Chronicles to the Song of Solomon was translated at Cambridge by Roger Andrews, Andrew Bing, Lawrence Chaderton, Francis Dillingham, Thomas Harrison, Edward Lively, John Richardson, and Robert Spaulding. The Oxford scholars translating Isaiah to Malachi were Richard Brett, Daniel Fairclough, John Harding, Thomas Holland, Richard Kilby, John Rainolds [Reynolds], and Miles Smith. The Gospels, Acts of the Apostles, and John's Revelation were completed by Oxford's George Abbot, Richard Eedes, John Harmar, John Peryn, Ralph Ravens, Thomas Ravis, Sir Henry Savile, and Giles Tomson. Westminster was given the Epistles, with translations by William Barlow, William Dakins, Roger Fenton, Ralph Hutchenson, Robert Rabbet, Thomas Sanderson, and John Spencer. Cambridge translated the Apocrypha with John Aglionby, Richard Bancroft, Thomas Bilson, John Bois, William Brantwaite, Andrew Downes, John Duport, Leonard Hutton, Jeremiah Radcliffe, John Ward, and Samuel Ward steering the helm. Exact translations, in some cases, would render the texts awkwardly. The experts read the Bible aloud to obtain the highest degree of resonance and dignity. The translations were examined by two other commissions and, finally, by Archbishop Laud, Canterbury. John Miles explained in the KJB Preface that it was a "revision" of the earlier English Bible. This project sought unity for the Church of England and the nation.

The King James Bible was published in 1611 and became the Authorized Version. By the eighteenth century, several misprints begged for corrected editions until Oxford's Benjamin Blayney achieved the 1769 Authorized Version, which was The English translation for about 250 years. The Apocrypha was placed in the English Bible between the Old and New Testaments, except where certain interests excluded the Apocrypha all together, for financial expediency as well as to limit the Bible to canonical books. Since the 1950s, a variety of English translations were published and circulated. The KJV had a more conservative style, with a few expressions that are archaic to readers from the twenty-first century, but it retained a rhythm *in English* that has been listened to and remembered for over two and a half centuries.

Cambridge University Press represents the British Crown's publication rights for the King James Bible (KJB or KJV). In 2005, Cambridge modernized the spelling of the King James Version. Adopting the KJV for *Paul's Parallels* guaranteed a high quality, well accepted English translation that honored the original languages.

FEATURES

- This is the *first* and *only* New Testament reference text featuring all of the Pauline and Pseudo-Pauline writings in the first column of a tables format cross-referencing parallel, echoing, and the most up-to-date translated like-minded biblical studies texts—side-by-side and cited in full.
- *It is a desktop resource* for theology teachers and professors, literary and early history researchers, ministry and seminary professionals, students of Christianity and biblical studies, as well as anyone researching the most written about personality in the biblical world—that is, the Apostle Paul.
- *Until this book featuring Paul's verses in the primary field, writers favored gospel verses as the focal point,* in part due to the primacy of Jesus' exemplary life, but also because scholarly interests during those decades held to the intrigues of synoptic comparisons. Mining synoptic textual similarities has many resources, but interests change and grow. One who was concerned about chronological matters, while researching Paul, needed a more complete composition to study. Leading with Paul's verses reveals that Paul worked through the challenges of "articulating the inarticulate" in full view of the apostles.
- *This approach to scriptural research offers a new perspective to New Testament studies* because Paul's themes, his theology, his interpretation of Jesus' teachings, and his imitation of Christ become *an independent focal point* and, from this book, it is clear he influences a sea of later writings, including the gospels and copyists.
- *New research, theses, dissertations, books, articles, and literature of all types will result due to this new perspective featuring Paul's initiating influence.* Extracting Paul's verses from the "opponents theses" in which much of the writing is cast, allows Christian

themes to breathe. One may view Paul as a natural person who is in the process of being converted from a rough, legalistic, religious personality into a little Jesus (also seen in Luke's "Acts").

- *This book liberates Paul from positioning behind the gospel writers so researchers can study ways in which Paul shaped gospel scholarship* [because he wrote before the evangelists]. *This reference book cites Paul first and lets chronology speak for itself.*
- *Paul made scholarly contributions* to the gospel writers, which can be tested through this material. The educated Jewish Pharisee, Paul, showed the gospel writers which Jewish material mattered and ways to organize it.
- *Paul informed readers about aspects of his journey that ultimately led to the holy mysteries intended for all humankind.* Paul's descriptions seem peculiar, but one who ventures into the holy life will recognize the meaning when it happens—this is a real phenomenon and the particulars can be teased out using this book. Paul's life, ministry, revelatory faith experiences, and their articulation preceded gospel authorship. Paul taught the evangelists how to better express Jesus' demonstration of the holy mysteries through his own enlightenment.
- A *theme is enunciated for each verse* and its biblical complements to guide the reader and keep him/her focused on the subject.
- *The tables format points out the major themes Paul makes use of in converting the Gentiles* throughout his missionary journeys—these are plain and repetitive. Professional missionaries can be reassured of their methods and current activities in light of Paul's missionary activities as guided by the Holy Spirit.
- *This book is a seminal reference text* for teachers, professors, students, theologians, seminarians, religion teachers, pastors, ministers, priests, and any biblical studies researcher.
- Every student and researcher of Pauline and Pseudo-Pauline literature has the *fingertip ability to see how verses relate to one another and the frequency of citation.*
- *Theology teachers and students as well as ministers preparing sermons have a clear reference about where Paul's life and ministry echoed Jesus' own experiences, without having to backtrack from the gospel parallels*—to find the Pauline precedents.
- *Readers can quickly view the biblical sources that supported Paul's proclamation* [from whom/where he derived his positions].
- *The reader can see who cited Paul,* including ardent pseudo-Pauline enthusiasts and, perhaps, the evangelists who wrote the gospels much later than Paul.
- *Pseudo-Pauline texts quickly show cross-references to Paul's original recitations*—and other supporting resources.
- *Theologians and ministers can easily and competently organize Paul's words and events into a more reliable historical sequence* (Paul's epistles were sequenced by length, not date). Corinthians and Philippians were composed of fragments from differing time periods; this resource recognized that the project must be done carefully and with integrity, examining each verse. The format offers researchers more opportunity to organize Paul's texts into a historical sequence because Paul's verses and themes are independent.
- *The researcher who energetically endeavors to sequence Paul's spiritual growth, Christian awareness, and transformation will find this reference invaluable* in developing a more accurate timeline of Paul's experiences and psychological development—research with credibility.
- The reader can develop *new Pauline systematic theology techniques* using this resource.
- *This reference text allows the reader to explore* the impact Paul made upon the gospel writers and his co-workers in Christ.
- *This book relieves the researcher of laboriously searching* through concordances and biblical notes to cross-reference Paul's verses with supporting information.
- *The book is intellectually and linguistically accessible* using the King James translation because KJV is closest to the original Greek New Testament writings, according to KJV experts Alister McGrath, Laurence Vance, Herman Hanko, and others.
- *Preachers see the Christian experience through Paul's eyes,* as one who imitated Jesus' lifestyle, encountered God, and wrote about the resulting events—this creates many *new preaching possibilities.*
- *This reference text has a universal audience* for those interested in the Bible and the Apostle Paul. Like all biblical resources, accessibility to this material depends on its translation into other modern languages

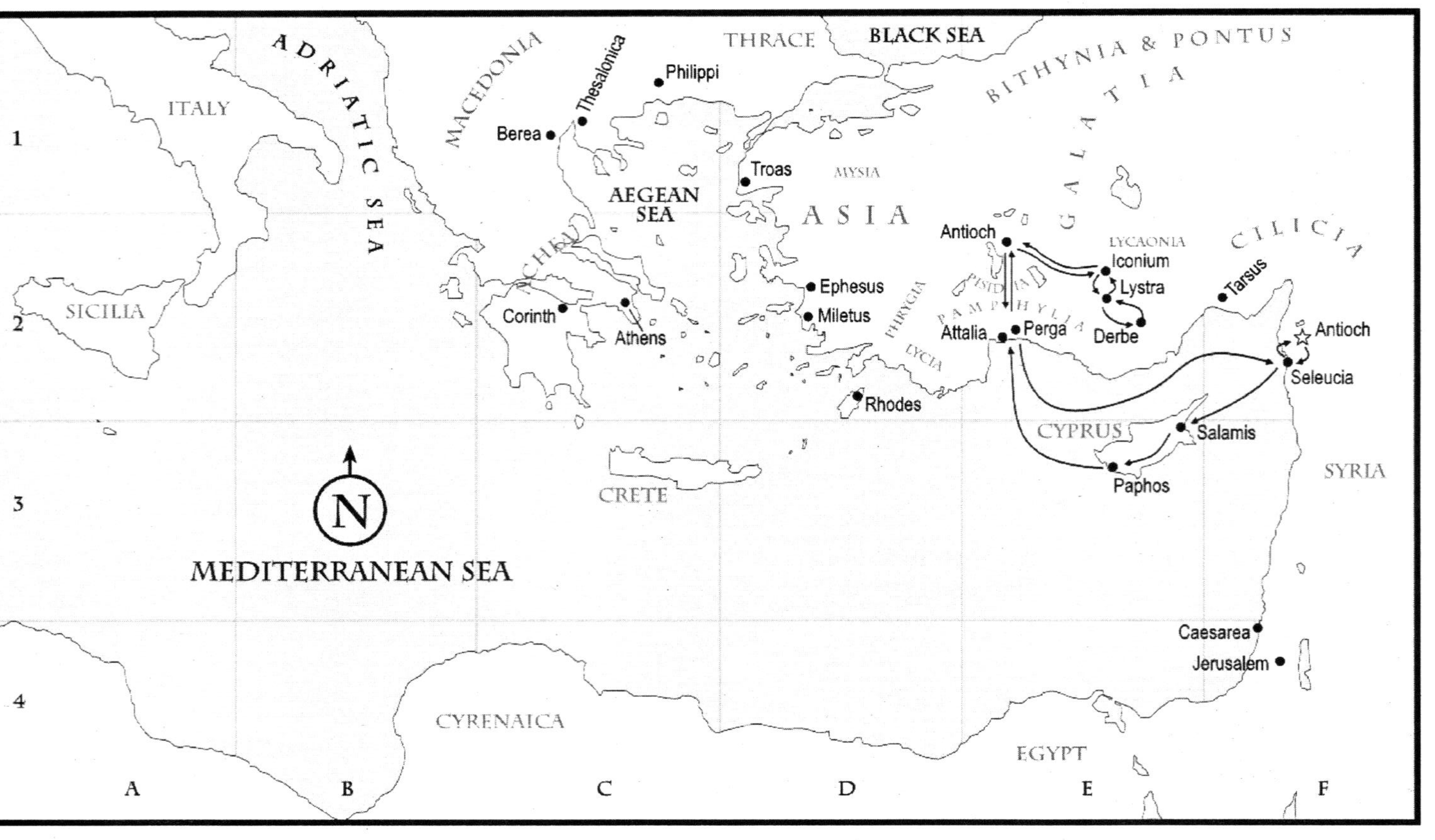

Paul's First Missionary Journey

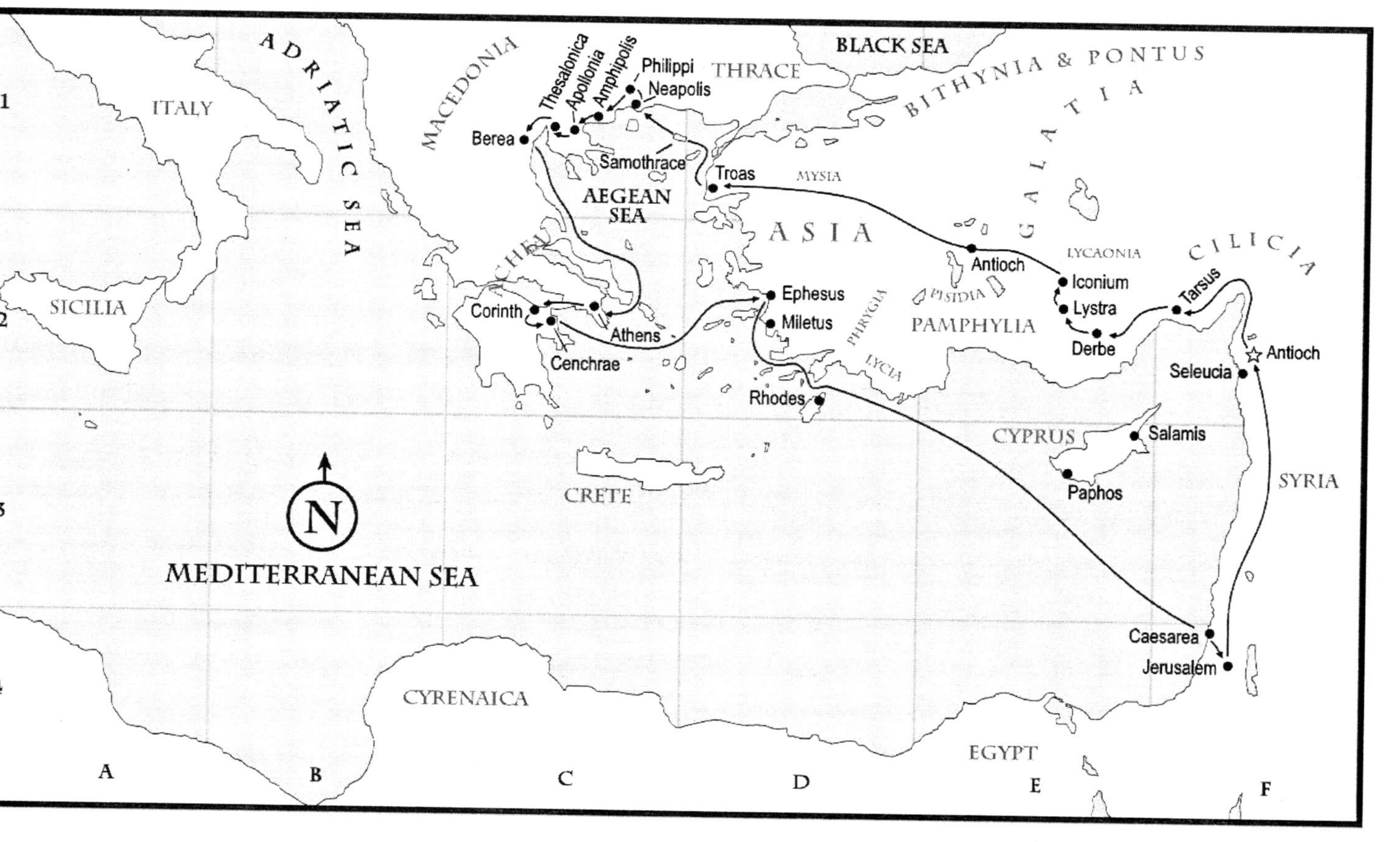

Paul's Second Missionary Journey

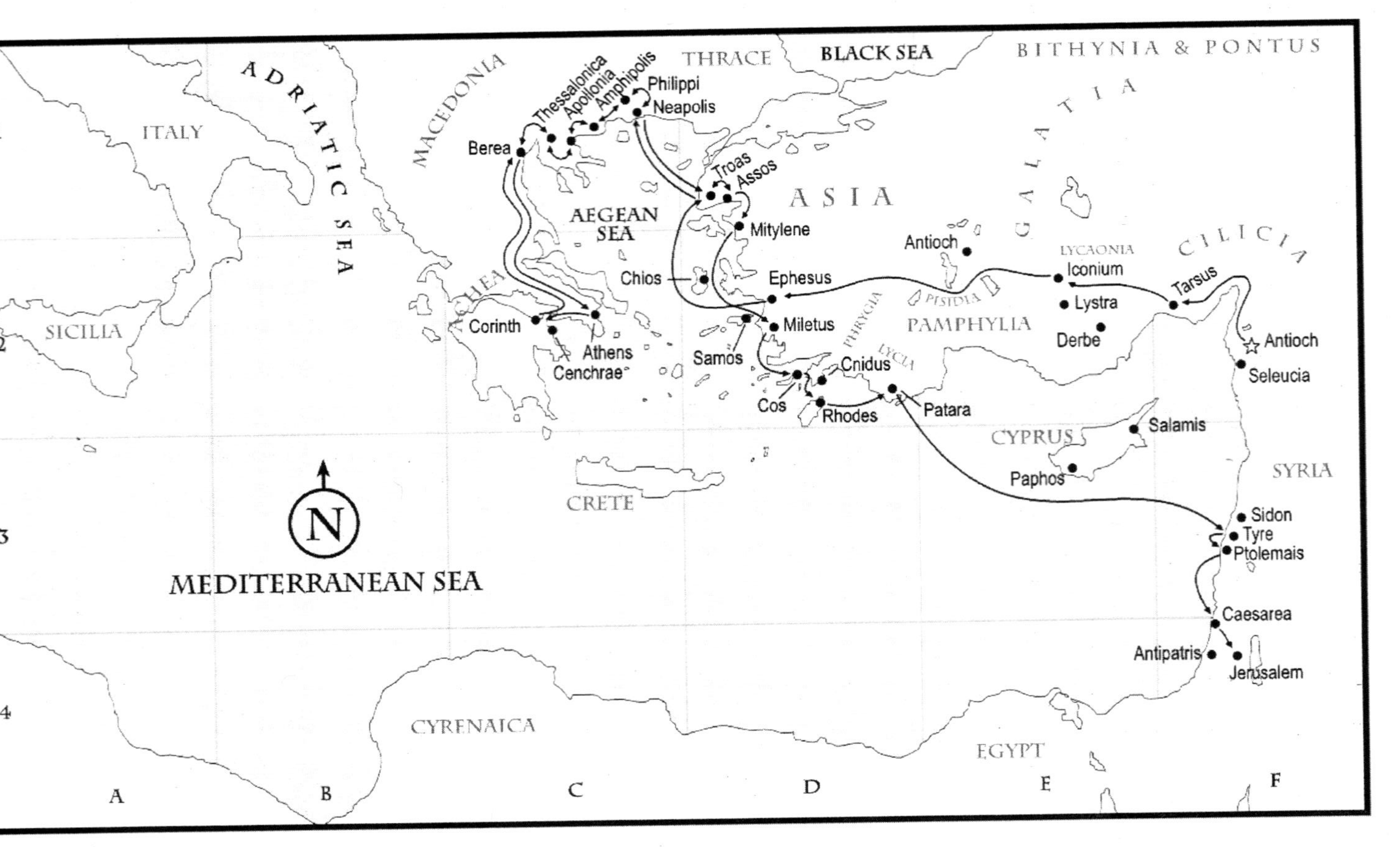

Paul's Third Missionary Journey

Cover Map. Map of the Ancient World Known to Paul, the Apostles, and the Early Christian Communities

ACTS OF THE APOSTLES: SECTION I

Identifying Missionary Journeys in Acts and the Epistles

Verse	Acts	Verse	Epistle
9:1–22	Damascus	Gal 1:17c	Conversion near Damascus
		Gal 1: 17b	To Arabia
		Gal 1:17c	Return to Damascus (3 years)
9:23–25	Flight from Damascus	2 Cor 11:32–33	Flight from Damascus
9:26–29	To Jerusalem	Gal 1:18–20	To Jerusalem
9:30	Caesarea and Tarsus	Gal 1:21–22	Regions of Syria and Cilicia
11:26	Antioch		
11:29–30, 12:25	Jerusalem		
13:1–4a	Mission 1—Antioch		
13:4b–12	Seleucia, Salamis, Cyprus		
13:13–14:25	South Galatia	Phil 4:15	Churches evangelized prior to Macedonian Philippi
14:26–28	Antioch		
15:1–12	Jerusalem	Gal 2:1	Up to Jerusalem for Council
15:35	Antioch—Mission 2	Gal 2:11–14	Antioch encounter
15:41	Syria and Cilicia		
16:1-5	South Galatia		
16:6	Phrygia, N. Galatia	1 Cor 16:1 Gal 4:13	Galatia evangelized first
16:7–10	Mysia, Troas		
16:11–40	Philippi	1 Thes 2:2 2 Cor 11:9	Philippi Macedonia
17:1–9	Amphipolis, Apollonia, Thessalonica	1 Thes 2:2 1 Thes 3:6 Phil 4:15–16	Thessalonica
17:10–14	Beroea		
17:15–34	Athens	1 Thes 3:1 1 Thes 2:17–18	Athens
18:1–18a	Corinth for 18 months	2 Cor 1:19 2 Cor 11:7–9	Evangelization of Corinth
18:5	Silas and Timothy return from Macedonia	1 Thes 3:6 1 Thes 1:1	Timothy arrives in Corinth accompanied by Silvanus
18:18b	Paul departs at Cenchreae		
18:19–21	Priscilla and Aquila remain at Ephesus		
18:17	Priscilla and Aquila send Apollos to Achaia [Greece]	1 Cor 16:12	While in Ephesus, Paul urges Apollos to got to Corinth
18:22a	Paul goes to Caesarea Maritima		
18:22b	Paul to Jerusalem		
18:22c	Paul in Antioch		
18:23	Mission 3– North Galatia and Phrygia	Gal 4:13	Second visit to North Galatia

Verse	Acts	Verse	Epistle
19:1–20 19:20–31	3 years at Ephesus At Ephesus 25 months (calendar difference)	1 Cor 16:1-8	Ephesus
		1 Cor 1:11 1 Cor 16:17 1 Cor 7:1	Visit Chloe, Stephanas and others. Bring letter to Paul at Ephesus
		1 Cor 15:32 2 Cor 1:8	Paul in prison
		1 Cor 4:17 1 Cor 16:10	Timothy sent to Corinth
		2 Cor 13:2	Paul visits Corinth second time and is disheartened. He returns to Ephesus
		2 Cor 2:13	Titus sent to Corinth with letter expressing Paul's grief
19:21	Visit Macedonia, Achaia [Greece], Jerusalem, Rome	1 Cor 16:3 2 Cor 1:15–16	Visit Macedonia, Corinth, Jerusalem-Judea
		2 Cor 2:12	Troas
20:1b	Macedonia	2 Cor 2:13 2 Cor 7:5 2 Cor 9:2b-4 2 Cor 7:6	To Macedonia Arrival of Titus
		2 Cor 7:16–17 Rom 15:19	Titus goes ahead to Corinth Illyricum
20:2–3	3 months in Greece [Achaia]	Rom 16:26 Rom 16:1 2 Cor 13:1	Achaia [Greece] Third visit to Corinth by Paul
20:3 20:3b–6a	Paul leaves toward Syria via Macedonia and Philippi		
20:6b–12	Troas		
20:15c–38	Miletus		
21:7–14	Tyre, Ptolemais, Caesarea		
21:15–23:30	Jerusalem	Rom 15:22–27	Planned visits to Jerusalem, Rome, Spain
23:31–26:32	Caesarea		
27:1–28:14	To Rome	Rom 15:22–27	Planned visits to Jerusalem, Rome, Spain
28:15–31	Rome		

*Joseph A. Fitzmyer, S.J., *Paul and His Theology: A Brief Sketch* (Englewood Cliffs, NJ: Prentice-Hall, 1989), 3–8.

Paul's Parallels: An Echoes Synopsis

ACTS 1–8—Luke's biblical history gives accounts of the Holy Spirit's activities after Jesus' ascension. First, Peter's wonders are discussed, then Paul's evangelical mission that develops the church community and institution. Verses from Acts 1:1–2:13 introduce the Holy Spirit as the gift that flowed through Jesus' Resurrection to guide Christian life toward the Kingdom of Heaven. Paul's first appearance is when he is persecuting the church at Stephen's stoning in Acts 7:51–8:3

ACTS 1:1–2—Promise of the Spirit (1:1–5)

Theme	ACTS	Mt	Mk
Prologue.1	**1:1–2** [1]The former treatise have I made, O Theophilus, of all that Jesus began both to do and teach[2]Until the day in which he was taken up, after that he through the Holy Ghost had given commandments unto the apostles whom he had chosen:	**28:19–20** [19]Go ye therefore, and teach all nations, baptizing them in the name of the Father, and of the Son, and of the Holy Ghost: [20]Teaching them to observe all things whatsoever I have commanded you: and, lo, I am with you always, even unto the end of the world. Amen.	**1:1** [1]The beginning of the gospel of Jesus Christ, the Son of God;

ACTS 1:1–2—Promise of the Spirit (1:1–5) (*continued*)

Theme	ACTS	Paul
(*Cont.*) **Prologue.1**	**1:1–2 (above)**	**1 Tim 3:16 (Pseudo)** [16]And without controversy great is the mystery of godliness: God was manifest in the flesh, justified in the Spirit, seen of angels, preached unto the Gentiles, believed on in the world, received up into glory.

Lk

1:1–4

1Forasmuch as many have taken in hand to set forth in order a declaration of those things which are most surely
believed among us,2Even as they delivered them unto us, which from the beginning were eyewitnesses, and ministers
of the word;3It seemed good to me also, having had perfect understanding of all things from the very first, to write unto
thee in order, most excellent Theophilus,4That thou mightest know the certainty of those things, wherein thou hast
been instructed.

24:44–49

44And he said unto them, These are the words which I spake unto you, while I was yet with you, that all things must be
fulfilled, which were written in the law of Moses, and in the prophets, and in the psalms, concerning me. 45Then opened
he their understanding, that they might understand the scriptures, 46And said unto them, Thus it is written, and thus it
behoved Christ to suffer, and to rise from the dead the third day: 47And that repentance and remission of sins should be
preached in his name among all nations, beginning at Jerusalem. 48And ye are witnesses of these things. 49And, behold,
I send the promise of my Father upon you: but tarry ye in the city of Jerusalem, until ye be endued with power from on
high.

Jn

15:27

27And ye also shall
bear witness,
because ye have
been with me from
the beginning.

20:22

22And when he
had said this, he
breathed on them,
and saith unto
them, Receive ye
the Holy Ghost:

Other

Josephus, Against Apion, 1.1.1–3

1I suppose that by my books of the Antiquity of the Jews, most excellent Epaphroditus, have made it evident to those who peruse them, that our Jewish nation is of very great antiquity, and had a distinct subsistence of its own originally; as also, I have therein declared how we came to inhabit this country wherein we now live. Those Antiquities contain the history of five thousand years, and are taken out of our sacred books, but are translated by me into the Greek tongue. However, since I observe a considerable number of people giving ear to the reproaches that are laid against us by those who bear ill-will to us, and will not believe what I have written concerning the antiquity of our nation, while they take it for a plain sign that our nation is of a late date, because they are not so much as vouchsafed a bare mention by the most famous historiographers among the Grecians. I therefore have thought myself under an obligation to write somewhat briefly about these subjects, in order to convict those that reproach us of spite and voluntary falsehood, and to correct the ignorance of others, and withal to instruct all those who are desirous of knowing the truth of what great antiquity we really are. As for the witnesses whom I shall produce for the proof of what I say, they shall be such as are esteemed to be of the greatest reputation for truth, and the most skillful in the knowledge of all antiquity by the Greeks themselves. I will also show, that those who have written so reproachfully and falsely about us are to be convicted by what they have written themselves to the contrary. I shall also endeavor to give an account of the reasons why it hath so happened, that there have not been a great number of Greeks who have made mention of our nation in their histories. I will, however, bring those Grecians to light who have not omitted such our history, for the sake of those that either do not know them, or pretend not to know them already. *(Continued)*

Acts 1:1–2 continued on next page

ACTS 1:1–2—Promise of the Spirit (1:1–5) (*continued*)

Theme	ACTS	Other
(*Cont.*) **Prologue.1**	**1:1–2** (above)	**Josephus, Against Apion (*continued*)** [2]And now, in the first place, I cannot but greatly wonder at those men, who suppose that we must attend to none but Grecians, when we are inquiring about the most ancient facts, and must inform ourselves of their truth from them only, while we must not believe ourselves nor other men; for I am convinced that the very reverse is the truth of the case. I mean this, if we will not be led by vain opinions, but will make inquiry after truth from facts themselves; for they will find that almost all which concerns the Greeks happened not long ago; nay, one may say, is of yesterday only. I speak of the building of their cities, the inventions of their arts, and the description of their laws; and as for their care about the writing down of their histories, it is very near the last thing they set about. However, they acknowledge themselves so far, that they were the Egyptians, the Chaldeans, and the Phoenicians (for I will not now reckon ourselves among them) that have preserved the memorials of the most ancient and most lasting traditions of mankind; for almost all these nations inhabit such countries as are least subject to destruction from the world about them; and these also have taken especial care to have nothing omitted of what was [remarkably] done among them; but their history was esteemed sacred, and put into public tables, as written by men of the greatest wisdom they had among them. But as for the place where the Grecians inhabit, ten thousand destructions have overtaken it, and blotted out the memory of former actions; so that they were ever beginning a new way of living, and supposed that every one of them was the origin of their new state. It was also late, and with difficulty, that they came to know the letters they now use; for those who would advance their use of these letters to the greatest antiquity pretend that they learned them from the Phoenicians and from Cadmus; yet is nobody able to demonstrate that they have any writing preserved from that time, neither in their temples, nor in any other time. However, there is not any writing which the Greeks agree to he genuine among them ancienter than Homer's Poems, who must plainly he confessed later than the siege of Troy; nay, the report goes, that even he did not leave his poems in writing, but that their memory was preserved in songs, and they were put together afterward, and that this is the reason of such a number of variations as are found in them. As for those who set themselves about writing their histories, I mean such as Cadmus of Miletus, and Acusilaus of Argos, and any others that may be mentioned as succeeding Acusilaus, they lived but a little while before the Persian expedition into Greece. But then for those that first introduced philosophy, and the consideration of things celestial and divine among them, such as Pherceydes the Syrian, and Pythagoras, and Thales, all with one consent agree, that they learned what they knew of the Egyptians and Chaldeans, and wrote but little And these are the things which are supposed to be the oldest of all among the Greeks; and they have much ado to believe that the writings ascribed to those men are genuine. [3]How can it then be other than an absurd thing, for the Greeks to be so proud, and to vaunt themselves to be the only people that are acquainted with antiquity, and that have delivered the true accounts of those early times after an accurate manner? Nay, who is there that cannot easily gather from the Greek writers themselves, that they knew but little on any good foundation when they set to write, but rather wrote their histories from their own conjectures? Accordingly, they confute one another in their own books to purpose, and are not ashamed to give us the most contradictory accounts of the same things; and I should spend my time to little purpose, if I should pretend to teach the Greeks that which they know better than I already, what a great disagreement there is between Hellanicus and Acusilaus about their genealogies; in how many eases Acusilaus corrects Hesiod: or after what manner Ephorus demonstrates Hellanicus to have told lies in the greatest part of his history; as does Timeus in like manner as to Ephorus, and the succeeding writers do to Timeus, and all the later writers do to Herodotus nor could Timeus agree with Antiochus and Philistius, or with Callias, about the Sicilian History, no more than do the several writers of the Athide follow one another about the Athenian affairs; nor do the historians the like, that wrote the Argolics, about the affairs of the Argives. And now what need I say any more about particular cities and smaller places, while in the most approved writers of the expedition of the Persians, and of the actions which were therein performed, there are so great differences? Nay, Thucydides himself is accused of some as writing what is false, although he seems to have given us the exactest history of the affairs of his own time.

ACTS 1:1–2—Promise of the Spirit (1:1–5) (*continued*)

Theme	ACTS	Other
(*Cont.*) **Prologue.1**	**1:1–2** **(above)**	**Josephus, Wars 2.1.1** Now there was about this time Jesus, a wise man if it be lawful to call him a man, for he was a doer of wonders, A Teacher of such men as receive the truth with pleasure. He drew many after him both of the Jews and the Gentiles. He was the Christ. When Pilate, at the suggestion of the principal men among us, had condemned him to the cross, those that loved him at the first did not forsake him, for he appeared to them alive again the third day, as the divine prophets had foretold these and then thousand other wonderful things about him, and the tribe of Christians, so named from him, are not extinct at this day. **Philo, On the Life of Moses, 1.1.1–4** [1]I have conceived the idea of writing the life of Moses, who, according to the account of some persons, was the lawgiver of the Jews, but according to others only an interpreter of the sacred laws, the greatest and most perfect man that ever lived, having a desire to make his character fully known to those who ought not to remain in ignorance respecting him, [2]for the glory of the laws which he left behind him has reached over the whole world, and has penetrated to the very furthest limits of the universe; and those who do really and truly understand him are not many, perhaps partly out of envy, or else from the disposition so common to many persons of resisting the commands which are delivered by lawgivers in different states, since the historians who have flourished among the Greeks have not chosen to think him worthy of mention, [3]the greater part of whom have both in their poems and also in their prose writings, disparaged or defaced the powers which they have received through education, composing comedies and works full of Sybaritish profligacy and licentiousness to their everlasting shame, while they ought rather to have employed their natural endowments and abilities in preserving a record of virtuous men and praiseworthy lives, so that honourable actions, whether ancient or modern, might not be buried in silence, and thus have all recollection of them lost, while they might shine gloriously if duly celebrated; and that they might not themselves have seemed to pass by more appropriate subjects, and to prefer such as were unworthy of being mentioned at all, while they were eager to give a specious appearance to infamous actions, so as to secure notoriety for disgraceful deeds. [4]But I disregard the envious disposition of these men, and shall proceed to narrate the events which befell him, having learnt them both from those sacred scriptures which he has left as marvellous memorials of his wisdom, and having also heard many things from the elders of my nation, for I have continually connected together what I have heard with what I have read, and in this way I look upon it that I am acquainted with the history of his life more accurately than other people. [**Yonge's full title, A Treatise on the Life of Moses or On the Theology and Prophetic Office of Moses, Book I.] **GThom** The Coptic Gospel of Thomas. These are the secret sayings which the living Jessu [Jesus] spoke and which Didymos Judas Thomas wrote down. **In Thom 1:1** [1]I, Thomas the Israelite, make this report to all of you, my brothers among the Gentiles, that you may know the magnificent childhood activities of your Lord Jesus Christ—all that he did after being born in our country. The beginning is as follows:

ACTS 1:4–8—Promise of the Spirit (1:1–5)

Theme	ACTS	Mt	Mk
Jesus instructs disciples on resurrection and departure	**1:4–8** [4]And, being assembled together with them, commanded them that they should not depart from Jerusalem, but wait for the promise of the Father, which, saith he, ye have heard of me. [5]For John truly baptized with water; but ye shall be baptized with the Holy Ghost not many days hence. When they therefore were come together, they asked of him, saying, Lord, wilt thou at this time restore again the kingdom to Israel? [7]And he said unto them, It is not for you to know the times or the seasons, which the Father hath put in his own power. [8]But ye shall receive power, after that the Holy Ghost is come upon you: and ye shall be witnesses unto me both in Jerusa- lem, and in all Judaea, and in Samaria, and unto the uttermost part of the earth. **11:16** [16]Then remembered I the word of the Lord, how that he said, John indeed baptized with water; but ye shall be baptized with the Holy Ghost.	**3:11** [11]I indeed baptize you with water unto repentance: but he that cometh after me is mightier than I, whose shoes I am not worthy to bear: he shall baptize you with the Holy Ghost, and with fire:	**1:8** [8]I indeed have baptized you with water: but he shall baptize you with the Holy Ghost.

Lk

3:16

[16]John answered, saying unto them all, I indeed baptize you with water; but one mightier than I cometh, the latchet of whose shoes I am not worthy to unloose: he shall baptize you with the Holy Ghost and with fire:

9:22

[22]Saying, The Son of man must suffer many things, and be rejected of the elders and chief priests and scribes, and be slain, and be raised the third day.

9:44

[44]Let these sayings sink down into your ears: for the Son of man shall be delivered into the hands of men.

9:45

[45]But they understood not this saying, and it was hid from them, that they perceived it not: and they feared to ask him of that saying.

17:25

[25]But first must he suffer many things, and be rejected of this generation.

18:31–33

[31]Then he took unto him the twelve, and said unto them, Behold, we go up to Jerusalem, and all things that are written by the prophets concerning the Son of man shall be accomplished.[32]For he shall be delivered unto the Gentiles, and shall be mocked, and spitefully entreated, and spitted on:[33]And they shall scourge him, and put him to death: and the third day he shall rise again.

18:34

[34]And they understood none of these things: and this saying was hid from them, neither knew they the things which were spoken.

22:22

[22]And truly the Son of man goeth, as it was determined: but woe unto that man by whom he is betrayed!

24:6–8

[6]He is not here, but is risen: remember how he spake unto you when he was yet in Galilee,[7]Saying, The Son of man must be delivered into the hands of sinful men, and be crucified, and the third day rise again.[8]And they remembered his words,

24:25–27

[25]Then he said unto them, O fools, and slow of heart to believe all that the prophets have spoken:**[26]Ought not Christ to have suffered these things, and to enter into his glory?** [27]And beginning at Moses and all the prophets, he expounded unto them in all the scriptures the things concerning himself.

24:44–49

[44]And he said unto them, These are the words which I spake unto you, while I was yet with you, that all things must be fulfilled, which were written in the law of Moses, and in the prophets, and in the psalms, concerning me.[45]Then opened he their understanding, that they might understand the scriptures, [46]And said unto them, Thus it is written, and thus it behoved Christ to suffer, and to rise from the dead the third day:[47]And that repentance and remission of sins should be preached in his name among all nations, beginning at Jerusalem. [48]And ye are witnesses of these things.[49]And, behold, I send the promise of my Father upon you: but tarry ye in the city of Jerusalem, until ye be endued with power from on high.

Acts 1:4–8 continued on next page

ACTS 1:4–8—Promise of the Spirit (1:1–5) (*continued*)

Theme	ACTS	Jn
(*Cont.*) **Jesus instructs his disciples on resurrection and departure**	**1:4–8 (above)** **11:16 (above)**	**1:26** [26]John answered them, saying, I baptize with water: but there standeth one among you, whom ye know not; **14:16** [16]And I will pray the Father, and he shall give you another Comforter, that he may abide with you for ever; **17:26** [26]And I have declared unto them thy name, and will declare it: that the love wherewith thou hast loved me may be in them, and I in them. **20:19–23** [19]Then the same day at evening, being the first day of the week, when the doors were shut where the disciples were assembled for fear of the Jews, came Jesus and stood in the midst, and saith unto them, Peace be unto you. [20]And when he had so said, he showed unto them his hands and his side. Then were the disciples glad, when they saw the Lord. [21]Then said Jesus to them again, Peace be unto you: as my Father hath sent me, even so send I you. [22]And when he had said this, he breathed on them, and saith unto them, Receive ye the Holy Ghost: [23]Whose soever sins ye remit, they are remitted unto them; and whose soever sins ye retain, they are retained. **20:24–29** [24]But Thomas, one of the twelve, called Didymus, was not with them when Jesus came. [25]The other disciples therefore said unto him, We have seen the Lord. But he said unto them, Except I shall see in his hands the print of the nails, and put my finger into the print of the nails, and thrust my hand into his side, I will not believe. [26]And after eight days again his disciples were within, and Thomas with them: then came Jesus, the doors being shut, and stood in the midst, and said, Peace be unto you. [27]Then saith he to Thomas, Reach hither thy finger, and behold my hands; and reach hither thy hand, and thrust it into my side: and be not faithless, but believing. [28]And Thomas answered and said unto him, My Lord and my God. [29]Jesus saith unto him, Thomas, because thou hast seen me, thou hast believed: blessed are they that have not seen, and yet have believed.

ACTS 1:5—Promise of the Spirit (1:1–5)

Theme	ACTS	Mt	Lk
Baptism by John the Baptist and by the Holy Spirit	**1:5** [5]For John truly baptized with water; but ye shall be baptized with the Holy Ghost not many days hence. **11:16** [16]Then remembered I the word of the Lord, how that he said, John indeed baptized with water; but ye shall be baptized with the Holy Ghost.	**1:15** [15]And Eliud begat Eleazar; and Eleazar begat Matthan; and Matthan begat Jacob; **3:11** [11]I indeed baptize you with water unto repentance: but he that cometh after me is mightier than I, whose shoes I am not worthy to bear: he shall baptize you with the Holy Ghost, and with fire:	**3:16** [16]John answered, saying unto them all, I indeed baptize you with water; but one mightier than I cometh, the latchet of whose shoes I am not worthy to unloose: he shall baptize you with the Holy Ghost and with fire: **6:43–44** [43]For a good tree bringeth not forth corrupt fruit; neither doth a corrupt tree bring forth good fruit. [44]For every tree is known by his own fruit. For of thorns men do not gather figs, nor of a bramble bush gather they grapes.

Paul	Other
Eph 1:13 (Pseudo) [13]In whom ye also trusted, after that ye heard the word of truth, the gospel of your salvation: in whom also after that ye believed, ye were sealed with that holy Spirit of promise,	**ActPil 14.1** [1]Now a certain priest named Phinees and Addas a teacher and Aggaeus (Ogias Copt., Egias lat.) a Levite came down from Galilee unto Jerusalem and told the rulers of the synagogue and the priests and the Levites, saying: We saw Jesus and his disciples sitting upon the mountain which is called Mamilch (Mambre or Malech lat., Mambrech Copt.), and he said unto his disciples: Go into all the world and preach unto every creature (the whole creation): he that believeth and is baptized shall be saved, and he that disbelieveth shall be condemned. [And these signs shall follow upon shall be condemned. [And these signs shall follow upon them that believe: in my name they shall cast out devils, they shall speak with new tongues, they shall take up serpents and if they drink any deadly thing it shall not hurt them: they shall lay hands upon the sick and they shall recover.] And while Jesus yet spake unto his disciples we saw him taken up into heaven. (Early Christian texts website, ActPil, GNicodemus) **Ign, Smyr 3.2** [2]For I know that after His resurrection also He was still possessed of flesh, and I believe that He is so now. When, for instance, He came to those who were with Peter, He said to them, "Lay hold, handle Me, and see that I am not an incorporeal spirit." And immediately they touched Him, and believed, being convinced both by His flesh and spirit. For this cause also they despised death, and were found its conquerors. And after his resurrection He did eat and drink with them, as being possessed of flesh, although spiritually He was united to the Father. **Q-Quelle** Preaching of John: Acts 1:4-8; [Mt 3:7-10], Mt 3:11-12/Mk 1:7-8/[Lk 3:7-9 (QS4)], Lk 3:15-18 (QS 5)

Jn	Paul
1:26 [26]John answered them, saying, I baptize with water: but there standeth one among you, whom ye know not; **8:39** [39]They answered and said unto him, Abraham is our father. Jesus saith unto them, If ye were Abraham's children, ye would do the works of Abraham.	**Eph 1:13 (Pseudo)** [13]In whom ye also trusted, after that ye heard the word of truth, the gospel of your salvation: in whom also after that ye believed, ye were sealed with that holy Spirit of promise,

Acts 1:5 continued on next page

ACTS 1:5—Promise of the Spirit (1:1–5) (*continued*)

Theme	ACTS	Other
(*Cont.*) **Baptism by John the Baptist and by the Holy Spirit**	**1:5 (above)** **11:16 (above)**	**1 ApocJas** It is the Lord who spoke with me: "See now the completion of my redemption. I have given you a sign of these things, James, my brother. For not without reason have I called you my brother, although you are not my brother materially. And I am not ignorant concerning you; so that when I give you a sign—know and hear." "Nothing existed except Him-who-is. He is unnameable and ineffable. I myself am also unnameable, from Him-who-is, just as I have been given a number of names—two from Him-who-is. And I, I am before you. . . . The Lord said, "James, he who spoke concerning this scripture had a limited understanding. I, however, shall reveal to you what has come forth from him who has no number. I shall give a sign concerning their number. As for what has come forth from him who has no measure, I shall give a sign concerning their measure.". . . The Lord said, ". . .unnumbered hosts. Him-who-is, however, has been given [. . .] on account of [. . .] Him-who-is [. . .] they are unnumbered. If you want to give them a number now, you will not be able to do so until you cast away from your blind thought, this bond of flesh which encircles you. And then you will reach Him-who-is. And you will no longer be James; rather you are the One-who-is. And all those who are unnumbered will all have been named.". . . You walked in mud, and your garments were not soiled, and you have not been buried in their filth, and you have not been caught. . . . And I was not like them, but I clothed myself with everything of theirs. . . . There is in me forgetfulness, yet I remember things that are not theirs. . . . There is in me [. . . .], and I am in their [. . .]. [. . .] knowledge [. . .] not in their sufferings [. . .]. But I have become afraid before them, since they rule. For what will they do? What will I be able to say? Or what word will I be able to say that I may escape them?" The Lord said, "James, I praise your understanding and your fear. If you continue to be distressed, do not be concerned for anything else except your redemption. For behold, I shall complete this destiny upon this earth as I have said from the heavens. And I shall reveal to you your redemption.". . . The Lord said, "James, after these things I shall reveal to you everything, not for your sake alone but for the sake of the unbelief of men, so that faith may exist in them. For a multitude will attain to faith and they will increase in [. . .]. . . .But now I shall go. Remember the things I have spoken and let them go up before you." James said, "Lord, I shall hasten as you have said." The Lord said farewell to him and fulfilled what was fitting. . . . The Lord said to him, "James, behold, I shall reveal to you your redemption. . . . They are to inherit these things and the understanding of him who [. . .] exalts. And they are to receive [. . .] through him from his intellect. Now, the younger of them is greater. And may these things remain hidden in him until he comes to the age of seventeen years [. . .] beginning [. . .] through them. They will pursue him exceedingly, since they are from his [. . .] companions. He will be proclaimed through them, and they will proclaim this word. Then he will become a seed of [. . .]." . . James said, "I am satisfied [. . .] and they are [. . .] my soul. . . . Yet another thing I ask of you: who are the seven women who have been your disciples? And behold all women bless you. I also am amazed how powerless vessels have become strong by a perception which is in them." The Lord said, "You [. . .] well [. . .] a spirit of [. . .], a spirit of thought, a spirit of counsel of a [. . .], a spirit [. . .] a spirit of knowledge [. . .] of their fear. [. . .] when we had passed through the breath of this archon who is named Adonaios [. . .] him and [. . .] he was ignorant [. . .] when I came forth from him, he remembered that I am a son of his. He was gracious to me at that time as his son. And then, before <I> appeared here, <he> cast them among this people. And from the place of heaven the prophets [. . .]." . . . James said, "Rabbi, [. . .] I [. . .] all together [. . .] in them especially [. . .]." The Lord said, "James, I praise you [. . .] walk upon the earth [. . .] the words while he [. . .] on the [. . .]. For cast away from you the cup which is bitterness. For some from [. . .] set themselves against you. For you have begun to understand their roots from beginning to end. Cast away from yourself all lawlessness. And beware lest they envy you. When you speak these words of this perception, encourage these four: Salome and Mariam and Martha and Arsinoe [. . .] since he takes some [. . .] to me he is [. . .] burnt offerings and [. . .]. But I [. . .] not in this way; but [. . .] first-fruits of the [. . .] upward [. . .] so that the power of God might appear. The perishable has gone up to the imperishable and the female element has attained to this male element." . . . James said, "Rabbi, into these three (things), then, has their [. . .] been cast. For they have been reviled, and they have been persecuted [. . .]. Behold [. . .] everything [. . .] from anyone [. . .]. For you have received [. . .] of knowledge. And [. . .] that what is the [. . .] go [. . .] you will find [. . .]. (*Continued*)

ACTS 1:5—Promise of the Spirit (1:1–5) (*continued*)

Theme	ACTS	Other
(*Cont.*) **Baptism by John the Baptist and by the Holy Spirit**	**1:5** (above) **11:16** (above)	**1 ApocJas (*continued*)** But I shall go forth and shall reveal that they believed in you, that they may be content with their blessing and salvation, and this revelation may come to pass." . . . And he went at that time immediately and rebuked the twelve and cast out of them contentment concerning the way of knowledge [. . .]. [. . .]. And the majority of them [. . .] when they saw, the messenger took in [. . .]. The others [. . .] said, "[. . .] him from this earth. For he is not worthy of life." These, then, were afraid. They arose, saying, "We have no part in this blood, for a just man will perish through injustice" James departed so that [. . .] look [. . .] for we [. . .] him. The Apocalypse of James **GEbi 2 and 3** [2]For by chopping off the genealogies of Matthew they made their gospel begin as we indicated before, with the words: "And so in the days of Herod, King of Judea, when Caiaphas was high priest, a certain one named John came baptizing a baptism of repentance in the Jordan River." (Epiphanius, Panarion, 30, 14, 3) [3]And so John was baptizing, and Pharisees came to him and were baptized, as was all of Jerusalem. John wore a garment of camel hair and a leather belt around his waist; and his food was wild honey that tasted like manna, like a cake cooked in oil. (Epiphanius, Panarion, 30, 13, 4-5) **Q-Quelle** Preaching of John: Acts 1:5/[Mt 3:7-10], Mt 3:11-12/ [Mk 1:7-8]/[Lk 3:7-9 (QS4)], Lk 3:15-18 (QS5); Fruits: Acts 1:5/[Mt 7:15-20, 12:33-35]/Lk 6:43-45 (QS13/[Thom 45])

ACTS 1:7—Ascension of Jesus (1:6–12)

Theme	ACTS	Mt
Only God knows eschatology	**1:7** [7]And he said unto them, It is not for you to know the times or the seasons, which the Father hath put in his own power.	**24:36** [36]But of that day and hour knoweth no man, no, not the angels of heaven, but my Father only.

ACTS 1:9–11—Ascension of Jesus (1:6–12)

Theme	ACTS	Mk	Lk	Jn	Paul
Heavenly ascent	**1:9–11** [9]And when he had spoken these things, while they beheld, he was taken up; and a cloud received him out of their sight. [10]And while they looked steadfastly toward heaven as he went up, behold, two men stood by them in white apparel; [11]Which also said, Ye men of Galilee, why stand ye gazing up into heaven? this same Jesus, which is taken up from you into heaven, shall so come in like manner as ye have seen him go into heaven.	**16:19** [19]So then after the Lord had spoken unto them, he was received up into heaven, and sat on the right hand of God.	**24:51** [51]And it came to pass, while he blessed them, he was parted from them, and carried up into heaven.	**20:17** [17]Jesus saith unto her, Touch me not; for I am not yet ascended to my Father: but go to my brethren, and say unto them, I ascend unto my Father, and your Father; and to my God, and your God.	**Eph 4:8–10 (Pseudo)** [8]Wherefore he saith, When he ascended up on high, he led captivity captive, and gave gifts unto men. [9](Now that he ascended, what is it but that he also descended first into the lower parts of the earth? [10]He that descended is the same also that ascended up far above all heavens, that he might fill all things.)

ACTS 2:13—Coming of Spirit (2:1–13)

Theme	ACTS	Paul
Effects of the Spirit	**2:13** [13]Others mocking said, These men are full of new wine.	**1 Cor 14:23** [33]For God is not the author of confusion, but of peace, as in all churches of the saints.

Paul
1 Thes 5:1–2 [1]But of the times and the seasons, brethren, ye have no need that I write unto you. [2]For yourselves know perfectly that the day of the Lord so cometh as a thief in the night.

NT	Jewish Writings	Other
1 Pet 3:22 [22]Who is gone into heaven, and is on the right hand of God; angels and authorities and powers being made subject unto him. **Rev 1:7** [7]Behold, he cometh with clouds; and every eye shall see him, and they also which pierced him: and all kindreds of the earth shall wail because of him. Even so, Amen.	**2 Kgs 2:11** [11]And it came to pass, as they still went on, and talked, that, behold, there appeared a chariot of fire, and horses of fire, and parted them both asunder; and Elijah went up by a whirlwind into heaven.	**ActPil 14:1** [1]Now a certain priest named Phinees and Addas a teacher and Aggaeus (Ogias Copt., Egias lat.) a Levite came down from Galilee unto Jerusalem and told the rulers of the synagogue and the priests and the Levites, saying: We saw Jesus and his disciples sitting upon the mountain which is called Mamilch (Mambre or Malech lat., Mambrech Copt.), and he said unto his disciples: Go into all the world and preach unto every creature (the whole creation): he that believeth and is baptized shall be saved, and he that disbelieveth shall be condemned. [And these signs shall follow upon shall be condemned. [And these signs shall follow upon them that believe: in my name they shall cast out devils, they shall speak with new tongues, they shall take up serpents and if they drink any deadly thing it shall not hurt them: they shall lay hands upon the sick and they shall recover.] And while Jesus yet spake unto his disciples we saw him taken up into heaven.

ACTS 7:51–52—Stephen accuses Jews of not recognizing Jesus. Martyred. Church persecuted. Saul/Paul appears in NT history (7:51–8:3)

Theme	ACTS	Mt
Killing God's messengers	**7:51–52** [51]Ye stiffnecked and uncircumcised in heart and ears, ye do always resist the Holy Ghost: as your fathers did, so do ye. [52]Which of the prophets have not your fathers persecuted? and they have slain them which showed before of the coming of the Just One; of whom ye have been now the betrayers and murderers:	**5:3–12** [3]Blessed are the poor in spirit: for theirs is the kingdom of heaven. [4]Blessed are they that mourn: for they shall be comforted. [5]Blessed are the meek: for they shall inherit the earth. [6]Blessed are they which do hunger and thirst after righteousness: for they shall be filled. [7]Blessed are the merciful: for they shall obtain mercy. [8]Blessed are the pure in heart: for they shall see God. [9]Blessed are the peacemakers: for they shall be called the children of God. [10]Blessed are they which are persecuted for righteousness' sake: for theirs is the kingdom of heaven. [11]Blessed are ye, when men shall revile you, and persecute you, and shall say all manner of evil against you falsely, for my sake. [12]Rejoice, and be exceeding glad: for great is your reward in heaven: for so persecuted they the prophets which were before you. **23:4** [4]For they bind heavy burdens and grievous to be borne, and lay them on men's shoulders; but they themselves will not move them with one of their fingers. **23:13** [13]But woe unto you, scribes and Pharisees, hypocrites! for ye shut up the kingdom of heaven against men: for ye neither go in yourselves, neither suffer ye them that are entering to go in. **23:29–31** [29]Woe unto you, scribes and Pharisees, hypocrites! because ye build the tombs of the prophets, and garnish the sepulchres of the righteous, [30]And say, If we had been in the days of our fathers, we would not have been partakers with them in the blood of the prophets. [31]Wherefore ye be witnesses unto yourselves, that ye are the children of them which killed the prophets. **23:32–36** [32]Fill ye up then the measure of your fathers. [33]Ye serpents, ye generation of vipers, how can ye escape the damnation of hell? [34]Wherefore, behold, I send unto you prophets, and wise men, and scribes: and some of them ye shall kill and crucify; and some of them shall ye scourge in your synagogues, and persecute them from city to city: [35]That upon you may come all the righteous blood shed upon the earth, from the blood of righteous Abel unto the blood of Zacharias son of Barachias, whom ye slew between the temple and the altar. [36]Verily I say unto you, All these things shall come upon this generation.

Lk	NT
6:20–26	**1 Pet 4:15–16**
[20]And he lifted up his eyes on his disciples, and said, Blessed be ye poor: for yours is the kingdom of God. [21]Blessed are ye that hunger now: for ye shall be filled. Blessed are ye that weep now: for ye shall laugh. [22]Blessed are ye, when men shall hate you, and when they shall separate you from their company, and shall reproach you, and cast out your name as evil, for the Son of man's sake. [23]Rejoice ye in that day, and leap for joy: for, behold, your reward is great in heaven: for in the like manner did their fathers unto the prophets. [24]But woe unto you that are rich! for ye have received your consolation. [25]Woe unto you that are full! for ye shall hunger. Woe unto you that laugh now! for ye shall mourn and weep. [26]Woe unto you, when all men shall speak well of you! for so did their fathers to the false prophets.	[15]But let none of you suffer as a murderer, or as a thief, or as an evildoer, or as a busybody in other men's matters. [16]Yet if any man suffer as a Christian, let him not be ashamed; but let him glorify God on this behalf.
11:45–54	
[45]Then answered one of the lawyers, and said unto him, Master, thus saying thou reproachest us also. [46]And he said, Woe unto you also, ye lawyers! for ye lade men with burdens grievous to be borne, and ye yourselves touch not the burdens with one of your fingers. [47]Woe unto you! for ye build the sepulchres of the prophets, and your fathers killed them. [48]Truly ye bear witness that ye allow the deeds of your fathers: for they indeed killed them, and ye build their sepulchres. [49]Therefore also said the wisdom of God, I will send them prophets and apostles, and some of them they shall slay and persecute: [50]That the blood of all the prophets, which was shed from the foundation of the world, may be required of this generation; [51]From the blood of Abel unto the blood of Zacharias, which perished between the altar and the temple: verily I say unto you, It shall be required of this generation. [52]Woe unto you, lawyers! for ye have taken away the key of knowledge: ye entered not in yourselves, and them that were entering in ye hindered. [53]And as he said these things unto them, the scribes and the Pharisees began to urge him vehemently, and to provoke him to speak of many things: [54]Laying wait for him, and seeking to catch something out of his mouth, that they might accuse him.	
13:33–34	
[33]Nevertheless I must walk to day, and to morrow, and the day following: for it cannot be that a prophet perish out of Jerusalem. [34]O Jerusalem, Jerusalem, which killest the prophets, and stonest them that are sent unto thee; how often would I have gathered thy children together, as a hen doth gather her brood under her wings, and ye would not!	

Acts 7:51–52 continued on next page

ACTS 7:51–52—Stephen accuses Jews of not recognizing Jesus. Martyred. Church persecuted. Saul/Paul appears in NT history (7:51–8:3) (*continued*)

Theme	Acts	Jewish Writings
(*Cont.*) **Killing God's messengers**	**7:51–52 (above)**	**Gen 4:8** [8]And Cain talked with Abel his brother: and it came to pass, when they were in the field, that Cain rose up against Abel his brother, and slew him. **2 Chr 24:20–21** [20]And the Spirit of God came upon Zechariah the son of Jehoiada the priest, which stood above the people, and said unto them, Thus saith God, Why transgress ye the commandments of the LORD, that ye cannot prosper? because ye have forsaken the LORD, he hath also forsaken you. [21]And they conspired against him, and stoned him with stones at the commandment of the king in the court of the house of the LORD. **Ps 126:1–2** [1]When the LORD turned again the captivity of Zion, we were like them that dream. [2]Then was our mouth filled with laughter, and our tongue with singing: then said they among the heathen, The LORD hath done great things for them. **Zech 1:1–6** [1]In the eighth month, in the second year of Darius, came the word of the LORD unto Zechariah, the son of Berechiah, the son of Iddo the prophet, saying, [2]The LORD hath been sore displeased with your fathers. [3]Therefore say thou unto them, Thus saith the LORD of hosts; Turn ye unto me, saith the LORD of hosts, and I will turn unto you, saith the LORD of hosts. [4]Be ye not as your fathers, unto whom the former prophets have cried, saying, Thus saith the LORD of hosts; Turn ye now from your evil ways, and from your evil doings: but they did not hear, nor hearken unto me, saith the LORD. [5]Your fathers, where are they? and the prophets, do they live for ever? [6]But my words and my statutes, which I commanded my servants the prophets, did they not take hold of your fathers? and they returned and said, Like as the LORD of hosts thought to do unto us, according to our ways, and according to our doings, so hath he dealt with us.

ACTS 7:53—Stephen accuses Jews of not recognizing Jesus. Martyred. Church persecuted. Saul/Paul appears in NT history (7:51–8:3)

Theme	ACTS	Paul
Serving the law	**7:53** [53]Who have received the law by the disposition of angels, and have not kept it.	**Gal 3:19** [19]Wherefore then serveth the law? It was added because of transgressions, till the seed should come to whom the promise was made; and it was ordained by angels in the hand of a mediator.

Other

PJas 24:1–4

[1]The priests acme out a the time of the greeting, but Zacharias did not come out to meet them with his blessings, as was customary. The priests stood , waiting to greet Zacharias with a prayer and to glorify the Most High. [2] When he did not come everyone grew afraid. One of them took courage, entered the sanctuary, and saw blood congealed beside the altar of the Lord. And he heard a voice, "Zacharias has been murdered, and his blood will not be wiped away until his avenger comes." When he heard this word he was afraid and went outside to report to the priests what he had seen and heard. [3] Taking courage they entered and saw what had happened, and the paneling around and the temple cried out aloud; and they ripped their clothes from top to bottom. They did not find his body, but they found his blood turned to stone. They left in fear, and reported to all the people that Zacharias had been murdered. [4] After three days the priests decided to put someone in his place, and the lot fell to Simeon. For this is the one who learned from a revelation of the Holy Spirit that he would not see death until he should see the messiah in the flesh.

GNaz 17

[17]In the Gospel which the Nazarenes use, instead of "son of Barachias" we have found written "son of Joiada." (Jerome, Commentary on Matthew 4 [on Matthew 23:35])

GThom 39

[39]Jesus said, "The pharisees and the scribes have taken the keys of knowledge (gnosis) and hidden them. They themselves have not entered, nor have they allowed to enter those who wish to. You, however, be as wise as serpents and as innocent as doves."

GThom 54

[54]Jesus said, "Blessed are the poor for yours is the kingdom of heaven."

GThom 68–69

[68]Jesus said, "Blessed are you when you are hated and persecuted. Wherever you have been persecuted they will find no place." [69] Jesus said, "Blessed are they who have been persecuted within themselves. It is they who have come to truly know the father. Blessed are the hungry for the belly of him who desires will be filled."

GThom 102

[102]Jesus said, "Woe to the Pharisees, for they are like a dog sleeping in the manger of oxen, for neither does he eat or does he let the oxen eat."

Q-Quelle

Beatitudes: Acts 7:51-52/Mt 5:3-12/Lk 6:20b-23 (QS8); Against Pharisees: Acts 7:51-52/[Mt 23:4-36]/[Mk 7:1-9]/Lk 11:37-54 (QS 34[Thom 39:1/89/102]); Lament over Jerusalem: Acts 7:51-52/[Mt 23:37-39]/Lk 13:34-35 (QS49)

NT

Heb 2:2

[2]For if the word spoken by angels was stedfast, and every transgression and disobedience received a just recompense of reward;

ACTS 7:54—Stephen accuses Jews of not recognizing Jesus. Martyred. Church persecuted. Saul/Paul appears in NT history (7:51–8:3)

Theme	ACTS	Mt	Mk
Holy people rejected; God saves	**7:54** [54]When they heard these things, they were cut to the heart, and they gnashed on him with their teeth. **7:58a** [58]And cast him out of the city. **10:36–38** [36]He brought them out, after that he had showed wonders and signs in the land of Egypt, and in the Red sea, and in the wilderness forty years. [37]This is that Moses, which said unto the children of Israel, A prophet shall the Lord your God raise up unto you of your brethren, like unto me; him shall ye hear. [38]This is he, that was in the church in the wilderness with the angel which spake to him in the mount Sina, and with our fathers: who received the lively oracles to give unto us:	**13:53–58** [53]And it came to pass, that when Jesus had finished these parables, he departed thence. [54]And when he was come into his own country, he taught them in their synagogue, insomuch that they were astonished, and said, Whence hath this man this wisdom, and these mighty works? [55]Is not this the carpenter's son? is not his mother called Mary? and his brethren, James, and Joses, and Simon, and Judas? [56]And his sisters, are they not all with us? Whence then hath this man all these things? [57]And they were offended in him. But Jesus said unto them, A prophet is not without honour, save in his own country, and in his own house. [58]And he did not many mighty works there because of their unbelief.	**6:1–6** [1]And he went out from thence, and came into his own country; and his disciples follow him. [2]And when the sabbath day was come, he began to teach in the synagogue: and many hearing him were astonished, saying, From whence hath this man these things? and what wisdom is this which is given unto him, that even such mighty works are wrought by his hands? [3]Is not this the carpenter, the son of Mary, the brother of James, and Joses, and of Juda, and Simon? and are not his sisters here with us? And they were offended at him. [4]But Jesus said unto them, A prophet is not without honour, but in his own country, and among his own kin, and in his own house. [5]And he could there do no mighty work, save that he laid his hands upon a few sick folk, and healed them. [6]And he marvelled because of their unbelief. And he went round about the villages, teaching.

Lk	Jn	Jewish Writings	Other
4:16–30 16 And he came to Nazareth, where he had been brought up: and, as his custom was, he went into the synagogue on the sabbath day, and stood up for to read. 17 And there was delivered unto him the book of the prophet Esaias. And when he had opened the book, he found the place where it was written, 18 The Spirit of the Lord is upon me, because he hath anointed me to preach the gospel to the poor; he hath sent me to heal the brokenhearted, to preach deliverance to the captives, and recovering of sight to the blind, to set at liberty them that are bruised, 19 To preach the acceptable year of the Lord. 20 And he closed the book, and he gave it again to the minister, and sat down. And the eyes of all them that were in the synagogue were fastened on him. 21 And he began to say unto them, This day is this scripture fulfilled in your ears. 22 And all bare him witness, and wondered at the gracious words which proceeded out of his mouth. And they said, Is not this Joseph's son? 23 And he said unto them, Ye will surely say unto me this proverb, Physician, heal thyself: whatsoever we have heard done in Capernaum, do also here in thy country. 24 And he said, Verily I say unto you, No prophet is accepted in his own country. 25 But I tell you of a truth, many widows were in Israel in the days of Elias, when the heaven was shut up three years and six months, when great famine was throughout all the land; 26 But unto none of them was Elias sent, save unto Sarepta, a city of Sidon, unto a woman that was a widow. 27 And many lepers were in Israel in the time of Eliseus the prophet; and none of them was cleansed, saving Naaman the Syrian. 28 And all they in the synagogue, when they heard these things, were filled with wrath, 29 And rose up, and thrust him out of the city, and led him unto the brow of the hill whereon their city was built, that they might cast him down headlong. 30 But he passing through the midst of them went his way. **4:43** 43 And he said unto them, I must preach the kingdom of God to other cities also: for therefore am I sent. **7:22** 22 Then Jesus answering said unto them, Go your way, and tell John what things ye have seen and heard; how that the blind see, the lame walk, the lepers are cleansed, the deaf hear, the dead are raised, to the poor the gospel is preached.	**1:45** 45 Philip findeth Nathanael, and saith unto him, We have found him, of whom Moses in the law, and the prophets, did write, Jesus of Nazareth, the son of Joseph. **4:44** 44 For Jesus himself testified, that a prophet hath no honour in his own country. **6:4** 4 And the passover, a feast of the Jews, was nigh. **8:59** 59 Then took they up stones to cast at him: but Jesus hid himself, and went out of the temple, going through the midst of them, and so passed by.	**Is 61:1–2** 1 The Spirit of the Lord GOD is upon me; because the LORD hath anointed me to preach good tidings unto the meek; he hath sent me to bind up the brokenhearted, to proclaim liberty to the captives, and the opening of the prison to them that are bound; 2 To proclaim the acceptable year of the LORD, and the day of vengeance of our God; to comfort all that mourn;	**GThom 31** 31 Jesus said, "No prophet is accepted in his own village; no physician heals those who know him." **Q-Quelle** John's Ques/ Jesus' Answ: Acts 7:54/[Mt 11:2-6]/Lk 7:18-23 (QS16)

ACTS 7:55–56—Stephen accuses Jews of not recognizing Jesus. Martyred. Church persecuted. Saul/Paul appears in NT history (7:51–8:3)

Theme	Acts	Mt
Righteous death; deliverance	**7:55–56** [55]But he, being full of the Holy Ghost, looked up stedfastly into heaven, and saw the glory of God, and Jesus standing on the right hand of God, [56]And said, Behold, I see the heavens opened, and the Son of man standing on the right hand of God.	**22:41–46** [41]While the Pharisees were gathered together, Jesus asked them, [42]Saying, What think ye of Christ? whose son is he? They say unto him, The Son of David. [43]He saith unto them, How then doth David in spirit call him Lord, saying, [44]The LORD said unto my Lord, Sit thou on my right hand, till I make thine enemies thy footstool? [45]If David then call him Lord, how is he his son? [46]And no man was able to answer him a word, neither durst any man from that day forth ask him any more questions.
	2:34–35 [34]I have seen, I have seen the affliction of my people which is in Egypt, and I have heard their groaning, and am come down to deliver them. And now come, I will send thee into Egypt. [35]This Moses whom they refused, saying, Who made thee a ruler and a judge? the same did God send to be a ruler and a deliverer by the hand of the angel which appeared to him in the bush.	**24:30** [30]And then shall appear the sign of the Son of man in heaven: and then shall all the tribes of the earth mourn, and they shall see the Son of man coming in the clouds of heaven with power and great glory. **26:57–58** [57]And they that had laid hold on Jesus led him away to Caiaphas the high priest, where the scribes and the elders were assembled. [58]But Peter followed him afar off unto the high priest's palace, and went in, and sat with the servants, to see the end. **26:59–68** [59]Now the chief priests, and elders, and all the council, sought false witness against Jesus, to put him to death; [60]But found none: yea, though many false witnesses came, yet found they none. At the last came two false witnesses, [61]And said, This fellow said, I am able to destroy the temple of God, and to build it in three days. [62]And the high priest arose, and said unto him, Answerest thou nothing? what is it which these witness against thee? [63]But Jesus held his peace. And the high priest answered and said unto him, I adjure thee by the living God, that thou tell us whether thou be the Christ, the Son of God. [64]Jesus saith unto him, Thou hast said: nevertheless I say unto you, Hereafter shall ye see the Son of man sitting on the right hand of power, and coming in the clouds of heaven. [65]Then the high priest rent his clothes, saying, He hath spoken blasphemy; what further need have we of witnesses? behold, now ye have heard his blasphemy. [66]What think ye? They answered and said, He is guilty of death. [67]Then did they spit in his face, and buffeted him; and others smote him with the palms of their hands, [68]Saying, Prophesy unto us, thou Christ, Who is he that smote thee?

Mk

12:34

[34]And when Jesus saw that he answered discreetly, he said unto him, Thou art not far from the kingdom of God. And no man after that durst ask him any question.

12:35–37

[35]And Jesus answered and said, while he taught in the temple, How say the scribes that Christ is the Son of David? [36]For David himself said by the Holy Ghost, The LORD said to my Lord, Sit thou on my right hand, till I make thine enemies thy footstool. [37]David therefore himself calleth him Lord; and whence is he then his son? And the common people heard him gladly.

13:26

[26]And then shall they see the Son of man coming in the clouds with great power and glory.

14:53–54

[53]And they led Jesus away to the high priest: and with him were assembled all the chief priests and the elders and the scribes. [54]And Peter followed him afar off, even into the palace of the high priest: and he sat with the servants, and warmed himself at the fire.

14:55–65

[55]And the chief priests and all the council sought for witness against Jesus to put him to death; and found none. [56]For many bare false witness against him, but their witness agreed not together. [57]And there arose certain, and bare false witness against him, saying, [58]We heard him say, I will destroy this temple that is made with hands, and within three days I will build another made without hands. [59]But neither so did their witness agree together. [60]And the high priest stood up in the midst, and asked Jesus, saying, Answerest thou nothing? what is it which these witness against thee? [61]But he held his peace, and answered nothing. Again the high priest asked him, and said unto him, Art thou the Christ, the Son of the Blessed? [62]And Jesus said, I am: and ye shall see the Son of man sitting on the right hand of power, and coming in the clouds of heaven. [63]Then the high priest rent his clothes, and saith, What need we any further witnesses? [64]Ye have heard the blasphemy: what think ye? And they all condemned him to be guilty of death. [65]And some began to spit on him, and to cover his face, and to buffet him, and to say unto him, Prophesy: and the servants did strike him with the palms of their hands.

Lk

20:41–44

[41]And he said unto them, How say they that Christ is David's son? [42]And David himself saith in the book of Psalms, The LORD said unto my Lord, Sit thou on my right hand, [43]Till I make thine enemies thy footstool. [44]David therefore calleth him Lord, how is he then his son?

21:27

[27]And then shall they see the Son of man coming in a cloud with power and great glory.

22:54b–65

And Peter followed afar off. [55]And when they had kindled a fire in the midst of the hall, and were set down together, Peter sat down among them. [56]But a certain maid beheld him as he sat by the fire, and earnestly looked upon him, and said, This man was also with him. [57]And he denied him, saying, Woman, I know him not. [58]And after a little while another saw him, and said, Thou art also of them. And Peter said, Man, I am not. [59]And about the space of one hour after another confidently affirmed, saying, Of a truth this fellow also was with him: for he is a Galilaean. [60]And Peter said, Man, I know not what thou sayest. And immediately, while he yet spake, the cock crew. [61]And the Lord turned, and looked upon Peter. And Peter remembered the word of the Lord, how he had said unto him, Before the cock crow, thou shalt deny me thrice. [62]And Peter went out, and wept bitterly. [63]And the men that held Jesus mocked him, and smote him. [64]And when they had blindfolded him, they struck him on the face, and asked him, saying, Prophesy, who is it that smote thee? [65]And many other things blasphemously spake they against him.

Acts 7:55–56 continued on next page

ACTS 7:55–56—Stephen accuses Jews of not recognizing Jesus. Martyred. Church persecuted. Saul/Paul appears in NT history (7:51–8:3) (*continued*)

Theme	ACTS	Lk	Jn
(*Cont.*) **Righteous death; deliverance**	**7:55–56** **(above)** **2:34–35** **(above)**	**(*Continued*)** **22:66–71** [66]And as soon as it was day, the elders of the people and the chief priests and the scribes came together, and led him into their council, saying, [67]Art thou the Christ? tell us. And he said unto them, If I tell you, ye will not believe: [68]And if I also ask you, ye will not answer me, nor let me go. [69]Hereafter shall the Son of man sit on the right hand of the power of God. [70]Then said they all, Art thou then the Son of God? And he said unto them, Ye say that I am. [71]And they said, What need we any further witness? for we ourselves have heard of his own mouth.	**2:19** [19]Jesus answered and said unto them, Destroy this temple, and in three days I will raise it up. **7:40–44** [40]Many of the people therefore, when they heard this saying, said, Of a truth this is the Prophet. [41]Others said, This is the Christ. But some said, Shall Christ come out of Galilee? [42]Hath not the scripture said, That Christ cometh of the seed of David, and out of the town of Bethlehem, where David was? [43]So there was a division among the people because of him. [44]And some of them would have taken him; but no man laid hands on him. **18:13–14** [13]And led him away to Annas first; for he was father in law to Caiaphas, which was the high priest that same year. [14]Now Caiaphas was he, which gave counsel to the Jews, that it was expedient that one man should die for the people. **18:19–24** [19]The high priest then asked Jesus of his disciples, and of his doctrine. [20]Jesus answered him, I spake openly to the world; I ever taught in the synagogue, and in the temple, whither the Jews always resort; and in secret have I said nothing. [21]Why askest thou me? ask them which heard me, what I have said unto them: behold, they know what I said. [22]And when he had thus spoken, one of the officers which stood by struck Jesus with the palm of his hand, saying, Answerest thou the high priest so? [23]Jesus answered him, If I have spoken evil, bear witness of the evil: but if well, why smitest thou me? [24]Now Annas had sent him bound unto Caiaphas the high priest.

Paul	Jewish Writings	Other
1 Cor 15:20–28 20But now is Christ risen from the dead, and become the first-fruits of them that slept. 21For since by man came death, by man came also the resurrection of the dead. 22For as in Adam all die, even so in Christ shall all be made alive. 23But every man in his own order: Christ the first-fruits; afterward they that are Christ's at his coming. 24Then cometh the end, when he shall have delivered up the kingdom to God, even the Father; when he shall have put down all rule and all authority and power. 25For he must reign, till he hath put all enemies under his feet. 26The last enemy that shall be destroyed is death. 27For he hath put all things under his feet. But when he saith all things are put under him, it is manifest that he is excepted, which did put all things under him. 28And when all things shall be subdued unto him, then shall the Son also himself be subject unto him that put all things under him, that God may be all in all.	**Lev 24:16** 16And he that blasphemeth the name of the LORD, he shall surely be put to death, and all the congregation shall certainly stone him: as well the stranger, as he that is born in the land, when he blasphemeth the name of the LORD, shall be put to death. **2 Sam 7:12–16** 12Then Samuel took a stone, and set it between Mizpeh and Shen, and called the name of it Ebenezer, saying, Hitherto hath the LORD helped us. 13So the Philistines were subdued, and they came no more into the coast of Israel: and the hand of the LORD was against the Philistines all the days of Samuel. 14And the cities which the Philistines had taken from Israel were restored to Israel, from Ekron even unto Gath; and the coasts thereof did Israel deliver out of the hands of the Philistines. And there was peace between Israel and the Amorites. 15And Samuel judged Israel all the days of his life. 16And he went from year to year in circuit to Bethel, and Gilgal, and Mizpeh, and judged Israel in all those places. **Ps 89:3–4** 3Thy people shall be willing in the day of thy power, in the beauties of holiness from the womb of the morning: thou hast the dew of thy youth. 4The LORD hath sworn, and will not repent, Thou art a priest for ever after the order of Melchizedek. **Ps 110:1** 1The LORD said unto my Lord, Sit thou at my right hand, until I make thine enemies thy footstool. **Dan 7:13–14** 13I saw in the night visions, and, behold, one like the Son of man came with the clouds of heaven, and came to the Ancient of days, and they brought him near before him. 14And there was given him dominion, and glory, and a kingdom, that all people, nations, and languages, should serve him: his dominion is an everlasting dominion, which shall not pass away, and his kingdom that which shall not be destroyed.	**GPet 3** 3Standing there was Joseph, a friend of both Pilate and the Lord; when they knew that they were about to crucify him, he came to Pilate and asked for the Lord's body for burial. **GPet 9** 9Others standing there were spitting in his face; some slapped his cheeks; others were beating him with a reed; and some began to flog him, saying, "This is how we should honor the Son of God!" **GThom 71** 71Jesus said, " I shall [destroy this] house, and no one shall be able to build it [. . .]"

ACTS 7:59—Stephen accuses Jews of not recognizing Jesus. Martyred. Church persecuted. Saul/Paul appears in NT history (7:51–8:3) (*continued*)

Theme	Acts	Mt
Holy death/ Passion	**7:59** 59 And they stoned Stephen, calling upon God, and saying, Lord Jesus, receive my spirit.	**27:45–56** 45 Now from the sixth hour there was darkness over all the land unto the ninth hour. 46 And about the ninth hour Jesus cried with a loud voice, saying, Eli, Eli, lama sabachthani? that is to say, My God, my God, why hast thou forsaken me? 47 Some of them that stood there, when they heard that, said, This man calleth for Elias. 48 And straightway one of them ran, and took a sponge, and filled it with vinegar, and put it on a reed, and gave him to drink. 49 The rest said, Let be, let us see whether Elias will come to save him. 50 Jesus, when he had cried again with a loud voice, yielded up the ghost. 51 And, behold, the veil of the temple was rent in twain from the top to the bottom; and the earth did quake, and the rocks rent; 52 And the graves were opened; and many bodies of the saints which slept arose, 53 And came out of the graves after his resurrection, and went into the holy city, and appeared unto many. 54 Now when the centurion, and they that were with him, watching Jesus, saw the earthquake, and those things that were done, they feared greatly, saying, Truly this was the Son of God. 55 And many women were there beholding afar off, which followed Jesus from Galilee, ministering unto him: 56 Among which was Mary Magdalene, and Mary the mother of James and Joses, and the mother of Zebedee's children.

<table>
<tr><th>Mk</th><th>Lk</th></tr>
<tr><td rowspan="4">15:33–41

[33]And when the sixth hour was come, there was darkness over
the whole land until the ninth hour. [34]And at the ninth hour Jesus
cried with a loud voice, saying, Eloi, Eloi, lama sabachthani?
which is, being interpreted, My God, my God, why hast thou
forsaken me? [35]And some of them that stood by, when they heard
it, said, Behold, he calleth Elias. [36]And one ran and filled a sponge
full of vinegar, and put it on a reed, and gave him to drink, saying,
Let alone; let us see whether Elias will come to take him down.
[37]And Jesus cried with a loud voice, and gave up the ghost. [38]And
the veil of the temple was rent in twain from the top to the bot-
tom. [39]And when the centurion, which stood over against him,
saw that he so cried out, and gave up the ghost, he said, Truly this
man was the Son of God. [40]There were also women looking on afar
off: among whom was Mary Magdalene, and Mary the mother of
James the less and of Joses, and Salome; [41](Who also, when he was
in Galilee, followed him, and ministered unto him;) and many
other women which came up with him unto Jerusalem.</td><td>8:1–3

[1]And it came to pass afterward, that he went throughout every city and
villa[3]</td></tr>
<tr><td>23:36

[36]And the soldiers also mocked him, coming to him, and offering him
vinegar.</td></tr>
<tr><td>23:44–49

[44]And it was about the sixth hour, and there was a darkness over all the
earth until the ninth hour. [45]And the sun was darkened, and the veil
of the temple was rent in the midst. [46]And when Jesus had cried with
a loud voice, he said, Father, into thy hands I commend my spirit: and
having said thus, he gave up the ghost. [47]Now when the centurion saw
what was done, he glorified God, saying, Certainly this was a righteous
man. [48]And all the people that came together to that sight, beholding
the things which were done, smote their breasts, and returned. [49]And all
his acquaintance, and the women that followed him from Galilee, stood
afar off, beholding these things.</td></tr>
<tr><td>23:55

[55]And the women also, which came with him from Galilee, followed
after, and beheld the sepulchre, and how his body was laid.</td></tr>
</table>

Acts 7:59 continued on next page

ACTS 7:59—Stephen accuses Jews of not recognizing Jesus. Martyred. Church persecuted. Saul/Paul appears in NT history (7:51–8:3) (*continued*)

Theme	Acts	Jn
(*Cont.*) **Holy death/ Passion**	**7:59** **(above)**	**19:25–37** [25]Now there stood by the cross of Jesus his mother, and his mother's sister, Mary the wife of Cleophas, and Mary Magdalene. [26]When Jesus therefore saw his mother, and the disciple standing by, whom he loved, he saith unto his mother, Woman, behold thy son! [27]Then saith he to the disciple, Behold thy mother! And from that hour that disciple took her unto his own home. [28]After this, Jesus knowing that all things were now accomplished, that the scripture might be fulfilled, saith, I thirst. [29]Now there was set a vessel full of vinegar: and they filled a sponge with vinegar, and put it upon hyssop, and put it to his mouth. [30]When Jesus therefore had received the vinegar, he said, It is finished: and he bowed his head, and gave up the ghost. [31]The Jews therefore, because it was the preparation, that the bodies should not remain upon the cross on the sabbath day, (for that sabbath day was an high day,) besought Pilate that their legs might be broken, and that they might be taken away. [32]Then came the soldiers, and brake the legs of the first, and of the other which was crucified with him. [33]But when they came to Jesus, and saw that he was dead already, they brake not his legs: [34]But one of the soldiers with a spear pierced his side, and forthwith came there out blood and water. [35]And he that saw it bare record, and his record is true: and he knoweth that he saith true, that ye might believe. [36]For these things were done, that the scripture should be fulfilled, A bone of him shall not be broken. [37]And again another scripture saith, They shall look on him whom they pierced.

Jewish Writings	Other
Ps 22:1 [1]My God, my God, why hast thou forsaken me? why art thou so far from helping me, and from the words of my roaring? **Ps 31:5** [5]O God, thou knowest my foolishness; and my sins are not hid from thee. **Ps 38:11** [11]My lovers and my friends stand aloof from my sore; and my kinsmen stand afar off. **Ps 69:1** [1]Save me, O God; for the waters are come in unto my soul.	**ActPil 11:1–3a** [1]And it was about the sixth hour, and there was darkness over the land until the ninth hour, for the sun was darkened: and the veil of the temple was rent asunder in the midst. And Jesus called with a loud voice and said: Father, baddach ephkid rouel, which is interpreted: Into thy hands I commend my spirit. And having thus said he gave up the ghost. And when the centurion saw what was done, he glorified God, saying: This man was righteous. And all the multitudes that had come to the sight, when they beheld what was done smote their breasts and returned. [2]But the centurion reported unto the governor the things that had come to pass: and when the governor and his wife heard, they were sore vexed, and neither ate nor drank that day. And Pilate sent for the Jews and said unto them: Did ye see that which came to pass? But they said: There was an eclipse of the sun after the accustomed sort. [3]And his acquaintance had stood afar off, and the women which came with him from Galilee, beholding these things. (Roberts-Donaldson, ActPil, GNicodemus) **GPet 5** [5]Herod said, "Brother Pilate, even if no one had asked for him we would have buried him, since the Sabbath is dawning. For it is written in the law that the sun must not set on one who is killed." And he delivered him to the people the day before the Feast of Unleavened Bread. **GPet 7** [7]They clothed him in purple and sat him on a judges seat, saying give a righteous judgment, O King of Israel!" **GPet 15–20** [15]It was noon and darkness came over all of Judea. They were disturbed and upset that the sun may have already set while he was still alive: for their Scripture says that the sun must not set on one who has been killed. [16]One of them said, "Give him gall mixed with vinegar to drink." And they made the mixture and gave it to him to drink. [17]Thus they brought all things to fulfillment and completed all their sins on their heads. [18]But many were wandering around with torches, thinking that it was night; and they stumbled about. [19]And the Lord cried out, "My power, O power, you have left me behind! When he said, this, he was taken up. [20]At that time the curtain of the temple in Jerusalem was ripped in half. **GPet 25** [25]Then the Jews, he elders realized how much evil they had done to themselves and began beating their breasts, saying, "Woe to us because of your sins. The judgment and the end of Jerusalem are near."

ACTS 7:60—Stephen accuses Jews of not recognizing Jesus. Martyred. Church persecuted. Saul/Paul appears in NT history (7:51–8:3)

Theme	Acts	Mt	Mk
Holy death/ Passion	**7:60** [60]And he kneeled down, and cried with a loud voice, Lord, lay not this sin to their charge. And when he had said this, he fell asleep.	**27:33–44** [33]And when they were come unto a place called Golgotha, that is to say, a place of a skull, [34]They gave him vinegar to drink mingled with gall: and when he had tasted thereof, he would not drink. [35]And they crucified him, and parted his garments, casting lots: that it might be fulfilled which was spoken by the prophet, They parted my garments among them, and upon my vesture did they cast lots. [36]And sitting down they watched him there; [37]And set up over his head his accusation written, THIS IS JESUS THE KING OF THE JEWS. [38]Then were there two thieves crucified with him, one on the right hand, and another on the left. [39]And they that passed by reviled him, wagging their heads, [40]And saying, Thou that destroyest the temple, and buildest it in three days, save thyself. If thou be the Son of God, come down from the cross. [41]Likewise also the chief priests mocking him, with the scribes and elders, said, [42]He saved others; himself he cannot save. If he be the King of Israel, let him now come down from the cross, and we will believe him. [43]He trusted in God; let him deliver him now, if he will have him: for he said, I am the Son of God. [44]The thieves also, which were crucified with him, cast the same in his teeth. **27:47–48** [47]Some of them that stood there, when they heard that, said, This man calleth for Elias. [48]And straightway one of them ran, and took a sponge, and filled it with vinegar, and put it on a reed, and gave him to drink.	**15:22–32** [22]And they bring him unto the place Golgotha, which is, being interpreted, The place of a skull. [23]And they gave him to drink wine mingled with myrrh: but he received it not. [24]And when they had crucified him, they parted his garments, casting lots upon them, what every man should take. [25]And it was the third hour, and they crucified him. [26]And the superscription of his accusation was written over, THE KING OF THE JEWS. [27]And with him they crucify two thieves; the one on his right hand, and the other on his left. [28]And the scripture was fulfilled, which saith, And he was numbered with the transgressors. [29]And they that passed by railed on him, wagging their heads, and saying, Ah, thou that destroyest the temple, and buildest it in three days, [30]Save thyself, and come down from the cross. [31]Likewise also the chief priests mocking said among themselves with the scribes, He saved others; himself he cannot save. [32]Let Christ the King of Israel descend now from the cross, that we may see and believe. And they that were crucified with him reviled him. **15:35–36** [35]And some of them that stood by, when they heard it, said, Behold, he calleth Elias. [36]And one ran and filled a sponge full of vinegar, and put it on a reed, and gave him to drink, saying, Let alone; let us see whether Elias will come to take him down.

Lk	Jn	Jewish Writings
22:29–30 29And I appoint unto you a kingdom, as my Father hath appointed unto me; 30That ye may eat and drink at my table in my kingdom, and sit on thrones judging the twelve tribes of Israel. **23:33–43** 33And when they were come to the place, which is called Calvary, there they crucified him, and the malefac- tors, one on the right hand, and the other on the left. 34Then said Jesus, Father, forgive them; for they know not what they do. And they parted his raiment, and cast lots. 35And the people stood beholding. And the rulers also with them derided him, saying, He saved others; let him save himself, if he be Christ, the chosen of God. 36And the soldiers also mocked him, coming to him, and offering him vinegar, 37And saying, If thou be the king of the Jews, save thyself. 38And a superscription also was written over him in letters of Greek, and Latin, and Hebrew, THIS IS THE KING OF THE JEWS. 39And one of the malefactors which were hanged railed on him, saying, If thou be Christ, save thyself and us. 40But the other answering rebuked him, saying, Dost not thou fear God, seeing thou art in the same condemnation? 41And we indeed justly; for we receive the due reward of our deeds: but this man hath done nothing amiss. 42And he said unto Jesus, Lord, remember me when thou comest into thy kingdom. 43And Jesus said unto him, Verily I say unto thee, To day shalt thou be with me in paradise.	**19:17–24** 19And Pilate wrote a title, and put it on the cross. And the writing was, JESUS OF NAZARETH THE KING OF THE JEWS. 20This title then read many of the Jews: for the place where Jesus was crucified was nigh to the city: and it was written in Hebrew, and Greek, and Latin. 21Then said the chief priests of the Jews to Pilate, Write not, The King of the Jews; but that he said, I am King of the Jews. 22Pilate answered, What I have written I have written. 23Then the soldiers, when they had cruci- fied Jesus, took his garments, and made four parts, to every soldier a part; and also his coat: now the coat was without seam, woven from the top throughout. 24They said therefore among themselves, Let us not rend it, but cast lots for it, whose it shall be: that the scripture might be fulfilled, which saith, They parted my raiment among them, and for my vesture they did cast lots. These things therefore the soldiers did. **19:28–30** 28After this, Jesus knowing that all things were now accomplished, that the scripture might be fulfilled, saith, I thirst. 29Now there was set a vessel full of vinegar: and they filled a sponge with vinegar, and put it upon hyssop, and put it to his mouth. 30When Jesus therefore had received the vinegar, he said, It is finished: and he bowed his head, and gave up the ghost.	**Ps 22:7** 7All they that see me laugh me to scorn: they shoot out the lip, they shake the head, saying, **Ps 22:8** 8He trusted on the LORD that he would deliver him: let him deliver him, seeing he delighted in him. **Ps 22:18** 18They part my gar- ments among them, and cast lots upon my vesture. **Ps 69:21** 21They gave me also gall for my meat; and in my thirst they gave me vinegar to drink.

Acts 7:60 continued on next page

ACTS 7:60—Stephen accuses Jews of not recognizing Jesus. Martyred. Church persecuted. Saul/Paul appears in NT history (7:51–8:3) (*continued*)

Theme	Acts	Other
(*Cont.*) **Holy death/ Passion**	**7:60 (above)**	**ActPil 10:1–2** [1]And Jesus went forth of the judgement hall and the two malefactors with him. And when they were come to the place they stripped him of his garments and girt him with a linen cloth and put a crown of thorns about his head: likewise also they hanged up the two malefactors. But Jesus said: Father forgive them, for they know not what they do. And the soldiers divided his garments among them. And the people stood looking upon him, and the chief priests and the rulers with them derided him, saying: He saved others let him save himself: if he be the son of God [let him come down from the cross]. And the soldiers also mocked him, coming and offering him vinegar with gall; and they said: If thou be the King of the Jews, save thyself. And Pilate after the sentence commanded his accusation to be written for a title in letters of Greek and Latin and Hebrew according to the saying of the Jews: that he was the King of the Jews. [2]And one of the malefactors that were hanged [by name Gestas] spake unto him, saying: If thou be the Christ, save thyself, and us. But Dysmas answering rebuked him, saying: Dost thou not at all fear God, seeing thou art in the same condemnation? and we indeed justly, for we receive the due reward of our deeds; but this man hath done nothing amiss. And he said unto Jesus: Remember me, Lord, in thy kingdom. And Jesus said unto him: Verily, verily, I say unto thee, that today thou shalt be (art) with me in paradise. (Roberts-Donaldson, ActPil, GNicodemus) **GPet 4** [4]Pilate sent word to Herod, asking for the body. **GPet 5** [5]Herod said, "Bother Pilate, even if no one had asked for him we would have buried him since the Sabbath is dawning. For it is written in the Law that the sun must not set on one who has been killed." And he delivered him over to the people the day before the Feast of the Unleavened Bread. **GPet 10–14** [10]They brought forth two evildoers and crucified the Lord Between them. But he was silent as if he had no pain. [11]When they had set the cross upright, they wrote an inscription: "This is the King of Israel." [12]Putting his clothes in front of them they divided them up and cast a lot for them [13]But one of the evildoers reviled them, "We have suffered like this for the evil things we did; but this one the Savior of the people—what wrong has he done tot you?" [14]They became angry at him and ordered that his legs be broken, so that he would die in torment. **GPet 16** [16]One of them said, "Give him gall mixed with vinegar to drink." And they made the mixture and gave it to him to drink. **GThom 71** [71]Jesus said, " I shall [destroy this] house, and no one shall be able to build it [. . .]" **Q-Quelle** Precedence: Acts 7:60/[Mt 19:28]/[Mk10:41-45]/Lk 22:28-30 (QS62)

ACTS 8–12:24—Paul's transition, conversion, God speaks, signs of ministry

ACTS 8:1—Saul/Paul persecutes Church

Theme	ACTS
Saul/Paul persecutes church	**8:1** [1]And Saul was consenting unto his death. And at that time there was a great persecution against the church which was at Jerusalem; and they were all scattered abroad throughout the regions of Judaea and Samaria, except the apostles. **22:20** [20]And when the blood of thy martyr Stephen was shed, I also was standing by, and consenting unto his death, and kept the raiment of them that slew him.

ACTS 8:3—Saul/Paul persecutes Church

Theme	ACTS	Paul
Saul/Paul persecutes church	**8:3** [3]As for Saul, he made havock of the church, entering into every house, and haling men and women committed them to prison. **9:1, 13** [1]And Saul, yet breathing out threatenings and slaughter against the disciples of the Lord, went unto the high priest,. . . [13]Then Ananias answered, Lord, I have heard by many of this man, how much evil he hath done to thy saints at Jerusalem: **22:4** [4]And I persecuted this way unto the death, binding and delivering into prisons both men and women. **26:9–11** [9]I verily thought with myself, that I ought to do many things contrary to the name of Jesus of Nazareth. [10]Which thing I also did in Jerusalem: and many of the saints did I shut up in prison, having received authority from the chief priests; and when they were put to death, I gave my voice against them. [11]And I punished them oft in every synagogue, and compelled them to blaspheme; and being exceedingly mad against them, I persecuted them even unto strange cities.	**1 Cor 5:9** [9]I wrote unto you in an epistle not to company with fornicators: **Gal 1:13** [13]For ye have heard of my conversation in time past in the Jews' religion, how that beyond measure I persecuted the church of God, and wasted it:

Saul/Paul's Conversion 9:1–19

ACTS 9:1–2—Saul/Paul's persecution of Church, leading to conversion (9:1–19)

Theme	ACTS
Saul/Paul seeks to destroy Christians	**9:1–2** [1]And Saul, yet breathing out threatenings and slaughter against the disciples of the Lord, went unto the high priest, [2]And desired of him letters to Damascus to the synagogues, that if he found any of this way, whether they were men or women, he might bring them bound unto Jerusalem. **9:14** [14]And here he hath authority from the chief priests to bind all that call on thy name. **26:10** [10]Which thing I also did in Jerusalem: and many of the saints did I shut up in prison, having received authority from the chief priests; and when they were put to death, I gave my voice against them.

ACTS 9:1—Saul/Paul's persecution of the Church, leading to conversion (9:1–19)

Theme	ACTS	Paul
Saul/Paul persecutes church	**9:1** [1]And Saul, yet breathing out threatenings and slaughter against the disciples of the Lord, went unto the high priest, **8:3** [3]As for Saul, he made havock of the church, entering into every house, and haling men and women committed them to prison. **9:13** [13]Then Ananias answered, Lord, I have heard by many of this man, how much evil he hath done to thy saints at Jerusalem: **22:4** [4]And I persecuted this way unto the death, binding and delivering into prisons both men and women.	**1 Cor 15:9** [9]For I am the least of the apostles, that am not meet to be called an apostle, because I persecuted the church of God. **Gal 1:13–14** [13]For ye have heard of my conversation in time past in the Jews' religion, how that beyond measure I persecuted the church of God, and wasted it: [14]And profited in the Jews' religion above many my equals in mine own nation, being more exceedingly zealous of the traditions of my fathers.

ACTS 9:3—Saul/Paul's conversion (9:1–19)

Theme	ACTS	Paul
Saul/Paul's encounter with light	**9:3** [3]And as he journeyed, he came near Damascus: and suddenly there shined round about him a light from heaven:	**1 Cor 9:1** [1]Am I not an apostle? am I not free? have I not seen Jesus Christ our Lord? are not ye my work in the Lord? **Gal 1:16** [16]To reveal his Son in me, that I might preach him among the heathen; immediately I conferred not with flesh and blood:

ACTS 9:4—Saul/Paul's conversion (9:1–19)

Theme	ACTS
Jesus speaks to Saul/Paul	**9:4** [4]And he fell to the earth, and heard a voice saying unto him, Saul, Saul, why persecutest thou me? **22:6** [6]And it came to pass, that, as I made my journey, and was come nigh unto Damascus about noon, suddenly there shone from heaven a great light round about me. **26:14** [14]And when we were all fallen to the earth, I heard a voice speaking unto me, and saying in the Hebrew tongue, Saul, Saul, why persecutest thou me? it is hard for thee to kick against the pricks.

ACTS 9:5—Saul/Paul's conversion (9:1–19)

Theme	ACTS	Mt
Paul strikes out against Jesus	**9:5** [5]And he said, Who art thou, Lord? And the Lord said, I am Jesus whom thou persecutest: it is hard for thee to kick against the pricks. **22:8** [8]And I answered, Who art thou, Lord? And he said unto me, I am Jesus of Nazareth, whom thou persecutest. **26:15** [15]And I said, Who art thou, Lord? And he said, I am Jesus whom thou persecutest.	**25:40** [40]And the King shall answer and say unto them, Verily I say unto you, Inasmuch as ye have done it unto one of the least of these my brethren, ye have done it unto me.

ACTS 9:6—Saul/Paul's conversion (9:1–19)

Theme	ACTS
Reconciliation	**9:6** [6]And he trembling and astonished said, Lord, what wilt thou have me to do? And the Lord said unto him, Arise, and go into the city, and it shall be told thee what thou must do. **22:1** [1]Men, brethren, and fathers, hear ye my defence which I make now unto you. **26:16** [16]And now why tarriest thou? arise, and be baptized, and wash away thy sins, calling on the name of the Lord.

ACTS 9:7—Saul/Paul's conversion (9:1–19)

Theme	ACTS
Hearing the voice of God	**9:7** [7]And the men which journeyed with him stood speechless, hearing a voice, but seeing no man. **22:9** [9]And they that were with me saw indeed the light, and were afraid; but they heard not the voice of him that spake to me. **26:13–14** [13]At midday, O king, I saw in the way a light from heaven, above the brightness of the sun, shining round about me and them which journeyed with me. [14]And when we were all fallen to the earth, I heard a voice speaking unto me, and saying in the Hebrew tongue, Saul, Saul, why persecutest thou me? it is hard for thee to kick against the pricks.

ACTS 9:8—Saul/Paul's conversion (9:1–19)

Theme	ACTS
Saul/Paul struck blind	**9:8** [8]And Saul arose from the earth; and when his eyes were opened, he saw no man: but they led him by the hand, and brought him into Damascus. **22:12–16** [12]And one Ananias, a devout man according to the law, having a good report of all the Jews which dwelt there, [13]Came unto me, and stood, and said unto me, Brother Saul, receive thy sight. And the same hour I looked up upon him. [14]And he said, The God of our fathers hath chosen thee, that thou shouldest know his will, and see that Just One, and shouldest hear the voice of his mouth. [15]For thou shalt be his witness unto all men of what thou hast seen and heard. [16]And now why tarriest thou? arise, and be baptized, and wash away thy sins, calling on the name of the Lord.

ACTS 9:10–19—Saul/Paul's conversion (9:1–19)

Theme	ACTS
Vision of Ananias to visit Saul/Paul	**9:10–19** [10]And there was a certain disciple at Damascus, named Ananias; and to him said the Lord in a vision, Ananias. And he said, Behold, I am here, Lord. [11]And the Lord said unto him, Arise, and go into the street which is called Straight, and inquire in the house of Judas for one called Saul, of Tarsus: for, behold, he prayeth, [12]And hath seen in a vision a man named Ananias coming in, and putting his hand on him, that he might receive his sight. [13]Then Ananias answered, Lord, I have heard by many of this man, how much evil he hath done to thy saints at Jerusalem: [14]And here he hath authority from the chief priests to bind all that call on thy name. [15]But the Lord said unto him, Go thy way: for he is a chosen vessel unto me, to bear my name before the Gentiles, and kings, and the children of Israel: [16]For I will show him how great things he must suffer for my name's sake. [17]And Ananias went his way, and entered into the house; and putting his hands on him said, Brother Saul, the Lord, even Jesus, that appeared unto thee in the way as thou camest, hath sent me, that thou mightest receive thy sight, and be filled with the Holy Ghost. [18]And immediately there fell from his eyes as it had been scales: and he received sight forthwith, and arose, and was baptized. [19]And when he had received meat, he was strengthened. Then was Saul certain days with the disciples which were at Damascus. **22:12–16** [12]And one Ananias, a devout man according to the law, having a good report of all the Jews which dwelt there, [13]Came unto me, and stood, and said unto me, Brother Saul, receive thy sight. And the same hour I looked up upon him. [14]And he said, The God of our fathers hath chosen thee, that thou shouldest know his will, and see that Just One, and shouldest hear the voice of his mouth. [15]For thou shalt be his witness unto all men of what thou hast seen and heard. [16]And now why tarriest thou? arise, and be baptized, and wash away thy sins, calling on the name of the Lord.

ACTS 9:11—Saul/Paul's conversion (9:1–19)

Theme	ACTS
Ananias sent	**9:11** [11]And the Lord said unto him, Arise, and go into the street which is called Straight, and inquire in the house of Judas for one called Saul, of Tarsus: for, behold, he prayeth, **21:39** [39]But Paul said, I am a man which am a Jew of Tarsus, a city in Cilicia, a citizen of no mean city: and, I beseech thee, suffer me to speak unto the people.

ACTS 9:14—Saul/Paul's conversion (9:1–19)

Theme	ACTS	Paul
Authority of chief priests	**9:14** [14]And here he hath authority from the chief priests to bind all that call on thy name. **9:1–2** [1]And Saul, yet breathing out threatenings and slaughter against the disciples of the Lord, went unto the high priest, [2]And desired of him letters to Damascus to the synagogues, that if he found any of this way, whether they were men or women, he might bring them bound unto Jerusalem. **26:10** [10]Which thing I also did in Jerusalem: and many of the saints did I shut up in prison, having received authority from the chief priests; and when they were put to death, I gave my voice against them.	**1 Cor 1:2** [2]Unto the church of God which is at Corinth, to them that are sanctified in Christ Jesus, called to be saints, with all that in every place call upon the name of Jesus Christ our Lord, both theirs and ours: **2 Tim 2:22 (Pseudo)** [22]Flee also youthful lusts: but follow righteousness, faith, charity, peace, with them that call on the Lord out of a pure heart.

ACTS 9:15—Saul/Paul's conversion (9:1–19)

Theme	ACTS
Paul chosen by God to serve Gentiles	**9:15** [15]But the Lord said unto him, Go thy way: for he is a chosen vessel unto me, to bear my name before the Gentiles, and kings, and the children of Israel: **22:15** [15]For thou shalt be his witness unto all men of what thou hast seen and heard. **26:1** [1]Then Agrippa said unto Paul, Thou art permitted to speak for thyself. Then Paul stretched forth the hand, and answered for himself: **27:24** [24]Saying, Fear not, Paul; thou must be brought before Caesar: and, lo, God hath given thee all them that sail with thee.

Paul preaches in Damascus (9:20–22)

Paul visits Jerusalem 9:23–30

ACTS 9:24–25—Paul visits Jerusalem (9:23–30)

Theme	ACTS	Paul
Plot to harm Saul/Paul	**9:24–25** [24]But their laying await was known of Saul. And they watched the gates day and night to kill him. [25]Then the disciples took him by night, and let him down by the wall in a basket.	**2 Cor 11:32–33** [32]In Damascus the governor under Aretas the king kept the city of the Damascenes with a garrison, desirous to apprehend me: [33]And through a window in a basket was I let down by the wall, and escaped his hands.

ACTS 9:26–27—Paul visits Jerusalem (9:23–30)

Theme	ACTS	Paul
Saul/Paul's defense to apostles	**9:26–27** [26]And when Saul was come to Jerusalem, he assayed to join himself to the disciples: but they were all afraid of him, and believed not that he was a disciple. [27]But Barnabas took him, and brought him to the apostles, and declared unto them how he had seen the Lord in the way, and that he had spoken to him, and how he had preached boldly at Damascus in the name of Jesus.	**Gal 1:18** [18]Then after three years I went up to Jerusalem to see Peter, and abode with him fifteen days.

ACTS 9:30—Paul visits Jerusalem (9:23–30)

Theme	ACTS
Sending Saul/Paul	**9:30** [30]Which when the brethren knew, they brought him down to Caesarea, and sent him forth to Tarsus. **11:25** [25]Then departed Barnabas to Tarsus, for to seek Saul:

Church at Peace (9:31)

ACTS 11:19—Church at Antioch—Barnabas finds Paul of Tarsus (11:19–26)

Theme	ACTS
Word for Jews travels to Gentiles	**11:19** [19]Now they which were scattered abroad upon the persecution that arose about Stephen travelled as far as Phenice, and Cyprus, and Antioch, preaching the word to none but unto the Jews only. **18:1–4** [1]After these things Paul departed from Athens, and came to Corinth; [2]And found a certain Jew named Aquila, born in Pontus, lately come from Italy, with his wife Priscilla; (because that Claudius had commanded all Jews to depart from Rome:) and came unto them. [3]And because he was of the same craft, he abode with them, and wrought: for by their occupation they were tentmakers. [4]And he reasoned in the synagogue every sabbath, and persuaded the Jews and the Greeks.

Agabus predicts famine—Barnabas and Saul take relief money to Judea (11:27)

ACTS 12:24–15:35 First Missionary Journey

ACTS 12:25—First Mission of Barnabas and Paul (12:25–33)

Theme	ACTS
Earliest missions	**12:25** [25]And Barnabas and Saul returned from Jerusalem, when they had fulfilled their ministry, and took with them John, whose surname was Mark. **11:29–30** [29]Then the disciples, every man according to his ability, determined to send relief unto the brethren which dwelt in Judaea: [30]Which also they did, and sent it to the elders by the hands of Barnabas and Saul.

ACTS 13:10—First Mission—Cyprus (13:4–12)

Theme	ACTS
Perversion of the righteous way	**13:10** [10]And said, O full of all subtlety and all mischief, thou child of the devil, thou enemy of all righteousness, wilt thou not cease to pervert the right ways of the Lord? **1:5** [5]For John truly baptized with water; but ye shall be baptized with the Holy Ghost not many days **2:38** [38]Then Peter said unto them, Repent, and be baptized every one of you in the name of Jesus Christ for the remission of sins, and ye shall receive the gift of the Holy Ghost. **11:16** [16]Then remembered I the word of the Lord, how that he said, John indeed baptized with water; but ye shall be baptized with the Holy Ghost. **13:24–25** [24]When John had first preached before his coming the baptism of repentance to all the people of Israel. [25]And as John fulfilled his course, he said, Whom think ye that I am? I am not he. But, behold, there cometh one after me, whose shoes of his feet I am not worthy to loose. **13:47** [47]For so hath the Lord commanded us, saying, I have set thee to be a light of the Gentiles, that thou shouldest be for salvation unto the ends of the earth. **19:1–7** [1]And it came to pass, that, while Apollos was at Corinth, Paul having passed through the upper coasts came to Ephesus: and finding certain disciples, [2]He said unto them, Have ye received the Holy Ghost since ye believed? And they said unto him, We have not so much as heard whether there be any Holy Ghost. [3]And he said unto them, Unto what then were ye baptized? And they said, Unto John's baptism. [4]Then said Paul, John verily baptized with the baptism of repentance, saying unto the people, that they should believe on him which should come after him, that is, on Christ Jesus. [5]When they heard this, they were baptized in the name of the Lord Jesus. [6]And when Paul had laid his hands upon them, the Holy Ghost came on them; and they spake with tongues, and prophesied. [7]And all the men were about twelve. hence. **26:20** [20]But showed first unto them of Damascus, and at Jerusalem, and throughout all the coasts of Judaea, and then to the Gentiles, that they should repent and turn to God, and do works meet for repentance. **28:28** [28]Be it known therefore unto you, that the salvation of God is sent unto the Gentiles, and that they will hear it.

Mt
1:15
[15]And Eliud begat Eleazar; and Eleazar begat Matthan; and Matthan begat Jacob;
3:1–12
[1]In those days came John the Baptist, preaching in the wilderness of Judaea, [2]And saying, Repent ye: for the kingdom of heaven is at hand. [3]For this is he that was spoken of by the prophet Esaias, saying, The voice of one crying in the wilderness, Prepare ye the way of the Lord, make his paths straight. [4]And the same John had his raiment of camel's hair, and a leathern girdle about his loins; and his meat was locusts and wild honey. [5]Then went out to him Jerusalem, and all Judaea, and all the region round about Jordan, [6]And were baptized of him in Jordan, confessing their sins.[7]But when he saw many of the Pharisees and Sadducees come to his baptism, he said unto them, O generation of vipers, who hath warned you to flee from the wrath to come? [8]Bring forth therefore fruits meet for repentance: [9]And think not to say within yourselves, We have Abraham to our father: for I say unto you, that God is able of these stones to raise up children unto Abraham. [10]And now also the axe is laid unto the root of the trees: therefore every tree which bringeth not forth good fruit is hewn down, and cast into the fire. [11]I indeed baptize you with water unto repentance: but he that cometh after me is mightier than I, whose shoes I am not worthy to bear: he shall baptize you with the Holy Ghost, and with fire: [12]Whose fan is in his hand, and he will thoroughly purge his floor, and gather his wheat into the garner; but he will burn up the chaff with unquenchable fire.
7:19
[19]Every tree that bringeth not forth good fruit is hewn down, and cast into the fire.
11:10
[10]For this is he, of whom it is written, Behold, I send my messenger before thy face, which shall prepare thy way before thee.
14:3–4
[3]For Herod had laid hold on John, and bound him, and put him in prison for Herodias' sake, his brother Philip's wife. [4]For John said unto him, It is not lawful for thee to have her.

Acts 13:10 continued on next page

ACTS 13:10—First Mission—Cyprus (13:4–12) (*continued*)

Theme	ACTS	Mk
(*Cont.*) **Perversion of the righteous way**	**13:10** (above) **1:5** (above) **2:38** (above) **11:16** (above) **13:10** (above) **13:24–25** (above) **13:47** (above) **19:1–7** (above) **26:20** (above) **28:28** (above)	**1:2–8** 2As it is written in the prophets, Behold, I send my messenger before thy face, which shall prepare thy way before thee. 3The voice of one crying in the wilderness, Prepare ye the way of the Lord, make his paths straight. 4John did baptize in the wilderness, and preach the baptism of repentance for the remission of sins. 5And there went out unto him all the land of Judaea, and they of Jerusalem, and were all baptized of him in the river of Jordan, confessing their sins. 6And John was clothed with camel's hair, and with a girdle of a skin about his loins; and he did eat locusts and wild honey; 7And preached, saying, There cometh one mightier than I after me, the latchet of whose shoes I am not worthy to stoop down and unloose. 8I indeed have baptized you with water: but he shall baptize you with the Holy Ghost. **1:15** 15And saying, The time is fulfilled, and the kingdom of God is at hand: repent ye, and believe the gospel. **2:8** 8And immediately when Jesus perceived in his spirit that they so reasoned within themselves, he said unto them, Why reason ye these things in your hearts?

Lk

1:76

76 And thou, child, shalt be called the prophet of the Highest: for thou shalt go before the face of the Lord to prepare his
ways;

2:30–32

30 For mine eyes have seen thy salvation, 31 Which thou hast prepared before the face of all people; 32 A light to lighten the
Gentiles, and the glory of thy people Israel.

3:1–20

1 Now in the fifteenth year of the reign of Tiberius Caesar, Pontius Pilate being governor of Judaea, and Herod being
tetrarch of Galilee, and his brother Philip tetrarch of Ituraea and of the region of Trachonitis, and Lysanias the tetrarch
of Abilene, 2 Annas and Caiaphas being the high priests, the word of God came unto John the son of Zacharias in the
wilderness. 3 And he came into all the country about Jordan, preaching the baptism of repentance for the remission of
sins; 4 As it is written in the book of the words of Esaias the prophet, saying, The voice of one crying in the wilderness,
Prepare ye the way of the Lord, make his paths straight. 5 Every valley shall be filled, and every mountain and hill shall
be brought low; and the crooked shall be made straight, and the rough ways shall be made smooth; 6 And all flesh shall
see the salvation of God. 7 Then said he to the multitude that came forth to be baptized of him, O generation of vipers,
who hath warned you to flee from the wrath to come? 8 Bring forth therefore fruits worthy of repentance, and begin not
to say within yourselves, We have Abraham to our father: for I say unto you, That God is able of these stones to raise up
children unto Abraham. 9 And now also the axe is laid unto the root of the trees: every tree therefore which bringeth not
forth good fruit is hewn down, and cast into the fire. 10 And the people asked him, saying, What shall we do then? 11 He
answereth and saith unto them, He that hath two coats, let him impart to him that hath none; and he that hath meat,
let him do likewise. 12 Then came also publicans to be baptized, and said unto him, Master, what shall we do? 13 And he
said unto them, Exact no more than that which is appointed you. 14 And the soldiers likewise demanded of him, saying,
And what shall we do? And he said unto them, Do violence to no man, neither accuse any falsely; and be content with
your wages. 15 And as the people were in expectation, and all men mused in their hearts of John, whether he were the
Christ, or not; 16 John answered, saying unto them all, I indeed baptize you with water; but one mightier than I cometh,
the latchet of whose shoes I am not worthy to unloose: he shall baptize you with the Holy Ghost and with fire: 17 Whose
fan is in his hand, and he will thoroughly purge his floor, and will gather the wheat into his garner; but the chaff he will
burn with fire unquenchable. 18 And many other things in his exhortation preached he unto the people. 19 But Herod
the tetrarch, being reproved by him for Herodias his brother Philip's wife, and for all the evils which Herod had done,
20 Added yet this above all, that he shut up John in prison.

6:43–44

43 For a good tree bringeth not forth corrupt fruit; neither doth a corrupt tree bring forth good fruit. 44 For every tree is
known by his own fruit. For of thorns men do not gather figs, nor of a bramble bush gather they grapes.

7:27

27 This is he, of whom it is written, Behold, I send my messenger before thy face, which shall prepare thy way before thee.

13:31

31 The same day there came certain of the Pharisees, saying unto him, Get thee out, and depart hence: for Herod will
kill thee.

23:8

8 And when Herod saw Jesus, he was exceeding glad: for he was desirous to see him of a long season, because he had
heard many things of him; and he hoped to have seen some miracle done by him.

Acts 13:10 continued on next page

ACTS 13:10—First Mission—Cyprus (13:4–12) (*continued*)

Theme	ACTS	Jn	Jewish Writings
(*Cont.*) **Perversion of the righteous way**	**13:10** **(above)** **1:5** **(above)** **2:38** **(above)** **11:16** **(above)** **13:10** **(above)** **13:24–25** **(above)** **13:47** **(above)** **19:1–7** **(above)** **26:20** **(above)** **28:28** **(above)**	**1:19–28** [19]And this is the record of John, when the Jews sent priests and Levites from Jerusalem to ask him, Who art thou? [20]And he confessed, and denied not; but confessed, I am not the Christ. [21]And they asked him, What then? Art thou Elias? And he saith, I am not. Art thou that prophet? And he answered, No. [22]Then said they unto him, Who art thou? that we may give an answer to them that sent us. What sayest thou of thyself? [23]He said, I am the voice of one crying in the wilderness, Make straight the way of the Lord, as said the prophet Esaias. [24]And they which were sent were of the Pharisees. [25]And they asked him, and said unto him, Why baptizest thou then, if thou be not that Christ, nor Elias, neither that prophet? [26]John answered them, saying, I baptize with water: but there standeth one among you, whom ye know not; [27]He it is, who coming after me is preferred before me, whose shoe's latchet I am not worthy to unloose. [28]These things were done in Bethabara beyond Jordan, where John was baptizing. **1:31–32** [31]And I knew him not: but that he should be made manifest to Israel, therefore am I come baptizing with water. [32]And John bare record, saying, I saw the Spirit descending from heaven like a dove, and it abode upon him. **8:39** [38]I speak that which I have seen with my Father: and ye do that which ye have seen with your father.	**2 Kgs 1:8** [8]And they answered him, He was an hairy man, and girt with a girdle of leather about his loins. And he said, It is Elijah the Tishbite. **Is 40:3** [3]The voice of him that crieth in the wilderness, Prepare ye the way of the LORD, make straight in the desert a highway for our God. **Mal 3:1a** [1]Behold, I will send my messenger, and he shall prepare the way before me: and the Lord, whom ye seek, shall suddenly come to his temple, even the messenger of the covenant, whom ye delight in: behold, he shall come, saith the LORD of hosts.

Other

1 ApocJas

It is the Lord who spoke with me: "See now the completion of my redemption. I have given you a sign of these things, James, my brother. . . .know and hear. . . . James, he who spoke concerning this scripture had a limited understanding. I, however, shall reveal to you what has come forth from him who has no number. I shall give a sign concerning their number. As for what has come forth from him who has no measure, I shall give a sign concerning their measure. . . .you will not be able to do so until you cast away from your blind thought, this bond of flesh which encircles you. And then you will reach Him-who-is. And you will no longer be James; rather you are the One-who-is. And all those who are unnumbered will all have been named." [James said,], "Rabbi, in what way shall I reach Him-who-is, since all these powers and these hosts are armed against me?" He said to me, "These powers are not armed against you specifically, but are armed against another. It is against me that they are armed. And they are armed with other powers. But they are armed against me in judgment. They did not give [. . .] to me in it [. . .] through them [. . .]. In this place [. . .] suffering, I shall [. . .]. He will [. . .] and I shall not rebuke them. But there shall be within me a silence and a hidden mystery. But I am fainthearted before their anger." James said, "Rabbi, if they arm themselves against you, then is there no blame? [The Lord] "You have come with knowledge, that you might rebuke their forgetfulness. You have come with recollection, that you might rebuke their ignorance. . . .But I was concerned because of you. For you descended into a great ignorance, but you have not been defiled by anything in it. For you descended into a great mindlessness, and your recollection remained. . . .You walked in mud, and your garments were not soiled, and you have not been buried in their filth, and you have not been caught. . . .And I was not like them, but I clothed myself with everything of theirs. . .There is in me forgetfulness, yet I remember things that are not theirs. . .There is in me [. . . .], and I am in their [. . .]. James said, "Rabbi, how, after these things, will you appear to us again? After they seize you, and you complete this destiny, you will go up to Him-who-is." The Lord said, "James, after these things I shall reveal to you everything, not for your sake alone but for the sake of the unbelief of men, so that faith may exist in them. For a multitude will attain to faith and they will increase in [. . .]. And after this I shall appear for a reproof to the archons. And I shall reveal to them that he cannot be seized. If they seize him, then he will overpower each of them. But now I shall go. Remember the things I have spoken and let them go up before you." James said, "Lord, I shall hasten as you have said." The Lord said farewell to him and fulfilled what was fitting. When James heard of his suffering and was much distressed, they awaited the sign of his coming. And he came after several days. And James was walking upon the mountain which is called "Gaugelan", with his disciples, who listened to him because they had been distressed, and he was [. . .] a comforter, saying, "This is [. . .] second [. . .]" Then the crowd dispersed, but James remained [. . .] prayer [. . .], as was his custom. And the Lord appeared to him. Then he stopped (his) prayer and embraced him. He kissed him, saying, "Rabbi, I have found you! I have heard of your sufferings, which you endured. And I have been much distressed. My compassion you know. Therefore, on reflection, I was wishing that I would not see this people. They must be judged for these things that they have done. For these things that they have done are contrary to what is fitting". . . The Lord said, "James, do not be concerned for me or for this people. I am he who was within me. Never have I suffered in any way, nor have I been distressed. And this people has done me no harm. But this (people) existed as a type of the archons, and it deserved to be destroyed through them. But [. . .] the archons, [. . .] who has [. . .] but since it [. . .] angry with [. . .] The just [. . .] is his servant. Therefore your name is "James the Just". You see how you will become sober when you see me. And you stopped this prayer. Now since you are a just man of God, you have embraced me and kissed me. Truly I say to you that you have stirred up great anger and wrath against yourself. But (this has happened) so that these others might come to be."

Acts 13:10 continued on next page

ACTS 13:10—First Mission—Cyprus (13:4–12) (*continued*)

Theme	ACTS	Other
(*Cont.*) **Perversion of the righteous way**	**13:10 (above)** **1:5 (above)** **2:38 (above)** **11:16 (above)** **13:10 (above)** **13:24–25 (above)** **13:47 (above)** **19:1–7 (above)** **26:20 (above)** **28:28 (above)**	**GEbi 2 and 3** [2]For by chopping off the genealogies of Matthew they made their gospel begin as we indicated before, with the words: "And so in the days of Herod, King of Judea, when Caiaphas was high priest, a certain one named John came baptizing a baptism of repentance in the Jordan River." (Epiphanius, Panarion, 30, 14, 3) [3]And so John was baptizing, and Pharisees came to him and were baptized, as was all of Jerusalem. John wore a garment of camel hair and a leather belt around his waist; and his food was wild honey that tasted like manna, like a cake cooked in oil. (Epiphanius, Panarion, 30, 13, 4-5) **Q-Quelle** Preaching of John: Acts 13:10/Mt 3:7-10, Mt 3:11-12/Mk 1:7-8/Lk 3:7-9(QS4), Lk 3:15-18 (QS5); Fruits: Acts 13:10/[Mt 7:15-20, 12:33-35]/Lk 6:43-45 (QS13/[Thom 45]); Jesus' witness to John: Acts 13:10/[Rom 8:28-29]/Mt 11:7-19, [Mt 21:31-32]/Lk 7:24-35 (QS 17[Thom 74/46]), [Lk 16:16 (QS56)]

ACTS 13:13—Paul at Antioch and Pisidin (13:13–15)

Theme	ACTS
Mission	**13:13** [13]Now when Paul and his company loosed from Paphos, they came to Perga in Pamphylia: and John departing from them returned to Jerusalem. **15:38** [38]But Paul thought not good to take him with them, who departed from them from Pamphylia, and went not with them to the work.

ACTS 13:17—Paul's address in the synagogue (13:16–43)

Theme	ACTS	Jewish Writings
Role of Jewish heritage	**13:17** [17]The God of this people of Israel chose our fathers, and exalted the people when they dwelt as strangers in the land of Egypt, and with an high arm brought he them out of it.	**Ex 6:1, 6** [1]Then the LORD said unto Moses, Now shalt thou see what I will do to Pharaoh: for with a strong hand shall he let them go, and with a strong hand shall he drive them out of his land. . . . [6]Wherefore say unto the children of Israel, I am the LORD, and I will bring you out from under the burdens of the Egyptians, and I will rid you out of their bondage, and I will redeem you with a stretched out arm, and with great judgments: **Ex 12:51** [51]And it came to pass the selfsame day, that the LORD did bring the children of Israel out of the land of Egypt by their armies.

ACTS 13:19—Paul's address in the synagogue (13:16–43)

Theme	ACTS	Jewish Writings
Apportion land to Jews	**13:19** [19]And when he had destroyed seven nations in the land of Chanaan, he divided their land to them by lot.	**Dt 7:1** [1]When the LORD thy God shall bring thee into the land whither thou goest to possess it, and hath cast out many nations before thee, the Hittites, and the Girgashites, and the Amorites, and the Canaanites, and the Perizzites, and the Hivites, and the Jebusites, seven nations greater and mightier than thou; **Jos 14:1–2** [1]And these are the countries which the children of Israel inherited in the land of Canaan, which Eleazar the priest, and Joshua the son of Nun, and the heads of the fathers of the tribes of the children of Israel, distributed for inheritance to them. [2]By lot was their inheritance, as the LORD commanded by the hand of Moses, for the nine tribes, and for the half tribe.

ACTS 13:20—Paul's address in the synagogue (13:16–43)

Theme	ACTS	NT	Jewish Writings
Judges rule Israel	**13:20** [20]And after that he gave unto them judges about the space of four hundred and fifty years, until Samuel the prophet.	**Jud 2:16** [16]Nevertheless the LORD raised up judges, which delivered them out of the hand of those that spoiled them.	**1 Sam 3:20** [20]And all Israel from Dan even to Beersheba knew that Samuel was established to be a prophet of the LORD.

ACTS 13:21—Paul's address in the synagogue (13:16–43)

Theme	ACTS	Jewish Writings
Jews ask for a king	**13:21** [21]And afterward they desired a king: and God gave unto them Saul the son of Cis, a man of the tribe of Benjamin, by the space of forty years.	**1 Sam 8:5, 19** [5]And said unto him, Behold, thou art old, and thy sons walk not in thy ways: now make us a king to judge us like all the nations.... [19]Nevertheless the people refused to obey the voice of Samuel; and they said, Nay; but we will have a king over us; **1 Sam 9:16** [16]To morrow about this time I will send thee a man out of the land of Benjamin, and thou shalt anoint him to be captain over my people Israel, that he may save my people out of the hand of the Philistines: for I have looked upon my people, because their cry is come unto me. **1 Sam 10:1, 20–21, 24** [1]Then Samuel took a vial of oil, and poured it upon his head, and kissed him, and said, Is it not because the LORD hath anointed thee to be captain over his inheritance?... [20]And when Samuel had caused all the tribes of Israel to come near, the tribe of Benjamin was taken. [21]When he had caused the tribe of Benjamin to come near by their families, the family of Matri was taken, and Saul the son of Kish was taken: and when they sought him, he could not be found.... [24]And Samuel said to all the people, See ye him whom the LORD hath chosen, that there is none like him among all the people? And all the people shouted, and said, God save the king. **1 Sam 11:15** [15]And all the people went to Gilgal; and there they made Saul king before the LORD in Gilgal; and there they sacrificed sacrifices of peace offerings before the LORD; and there Saul and all the men of Israel rejoiced greatly.

ACTS 13:22—Paul's address in the synagogue (13:16–43)

Theme	ACTS	Jewish Writings
God anoints David king	**13:22** [22]And when he had removed him, he raised up unto them David to be their king; to whom also he gave testimony, and said, I have found David the son of Jesse, a man after mine own heart, which shall fulfil all my will.	**1 Sam 13:14** [14]But when they departed from Perga, they came to Antioch in Pisidia, and went into the synagogue on the sabbath day, and sat down. **1 Sam 16:12–13** [12]And he sent, and brought him in. Now he was ruddy, and withal of a beautiful countenance, and goodly to look to. And the LORD said, Arise, anoint him: for this is he. [13]Then Samuel took the horn of oil, and anointed him in the midst of his brethren: and the Spirit of the LORD came upon David from that day forward. So Samuel rose up, and went to Ramah. **Ps 89:20–21** [20]I have found David my servant; with my holy oil have I anointed him: [21]With whom my hand shall be established: mine arm also shall strengthen him.

ACTS 13:23—Paul's address in the synagogue (13:16–43)

Theme	ACTS	Mt	Lk
Prophesy of Jesus' birth	**13:23** [23]Of this man's seed hath God according to his promise raised unto Israel a Saviour, Jesus:	**2:1–12** [1]The book of the generation of Jesus Christ, the son of David, the son of Abraham. [2]Abraham begat Isaac; and Isaac begat Jacob; and Jacob begat Judas and his brethren; [3]And Judas begat Phares and Zara of Thamar; and Phares begat Esrom; and Esrom begat Aram; [4]And Aram begat Aminadab; and Aminadab begat Naasson; and Naasson begat Salmon; [5]And Salmon begat Booz of Rachab; and Booz begat Obed of Ruth; and Obed begat Jesse; [6]And Jesse begat David the king; and David the king begat Solomon of her that had been the wife of Urias; [7]And Solomon begat Roboam; and Roboam begat Abia; and Abia begat Asa; [8]And Asa begat Josaphat; and Josaphat begat Joram; and Joram begat Ozias; [9]And Ozias begat Joatham; and Joatham begat Achaz; and Achaz begat Ezekias; [10]And Ezekias begat Manasses; and Manasses begat Amon; and Amon begat Josias; [11]And Josias begat Jechonias and his brethren, about the time they were carried away to Babylon: [12]And after they were brought to Babylon, Jechonias begat Salathiel; and Salathiel begat Zorobabel;	**2:15–20** [15]For he shall be great in the sight of the Lord, and shall drink neither wine nor strong drink; and he shall be filled with the Holy Ghost, even from his mother's womb. [16]And many of the children of Israel shall he turn to the Lord their God. [17]And he shall go before him in the spirit and power of Elias, to turn the hearts of the fathers to the children, and the disobedient to the wisdom of the just; to make ready a people prepared for the Lord. [18]And Zacharias said unto the angel, Whereby shall I know this? for I am an old man, and my wife well stricken in years. [19]And the angel answering said unto him, I am Gabriel, that stand in the presence of God; and am sent to speak unto thee, and to show thee these glad tidings. [20]And, behold, thou shalt be dumb, and not able to speak, until the day that these things shall be performed, because thou believest not my words, which shall be fulfilled in their season. **2:51** [51]And he went down with them, and came to Nazareth, and was subject unto them: but his mother kept all these sayings in her heart. **19:38** [38]Saying, Blessed be the King that cometh in the name of the Lord: peace in heaven, and glory in the highest.

Jewish Writings	Other
2 Sam 7:12–16 [12]And when thy days be fulfilled, and thou shalt sleep with thy fathers, I will set up thy seed after thee, which shall proceed out of thy bowels, and I will establish his kingdom. [13]He shall build an house for my name, and I will establish the throne of his kingdom for ever. [14]I will be his father, and he shall be my son. If he commit iniquity, I will chasten him with the rod of men, and with the stripes of the children of men: [15]But my mercy shall not depart away from him, as I took it from Saul, whom I put away before thee. [16]And thine house and thy kingdom shall be established for ever before thee: thy throne shall be established for ever. **Is 11:1** [1]And there shall come forth a rod out of the stem of Jesse, and a Branch shall grow out of his roots:	**In Thom 11:2c** [2]And she kept to herself the mysterious deeds she saw him do **In Thom 19:5a** [5]Jesus got up from there and followed his mother and he was obedient to his parents.

ACTS 13:24–25—Paul's address in the synagogue (13:16–43)

Theme	ACTS
John Baptist less than Christ	**13:24–25** 24When John had first preached before his coming the baptism of repentance to all the people of Israel. 25And as John fulfilled his course, he said, Whom think ye that I am? I am not he. But, behold, there cometh one after me, whose shoes of his feet I am not worthy to loose. **1:5** 5For John truly baptized with water; but ye shall be baptized with the Holy Ghost not many days hence. **2:28** 28Thou hast made known to me the ways of life; thou shalt make me full of joy with thy countenance. **2:38** 38Then Peter said unto them, Repent, and be baptized every one of you in the name of Jesus Christ for the remission of sins, and ye shall receive the gift of the Holy Ghost. **11:16** 16Then remembered I the word of the Lord, how that he said, John indeed baptized with water; but ye shall be baptized with the Holy Ghost. **13:10** 10And said, O full of all subtlety and all mischief, thou child of the devil, thou enemy of all righteousness, wilt thou not cease to pervert the right ways of the Lord? **13:47** 47For so hath the Lord commanded us, saying, I have set thee to be a light of the Gentiles, that thou shouldest be for salvation unto the ends of the earth. **19:17** 17And this was known to all the Jews and Greeks also dwelling at Ephesus; and fear fell on them all, and the name of the Lord Jesus was magnified. **26:20** 20And some of them were men of Cyprus and Cyrene, which, when they were come to Antioch, spake unto the Grecians, preaching the Lord Jesus.

Mt

1:15

[15]And Eliud begat Eleazar; and Eleazar begat Matthan; and Matthan begat Jacob;

3:1–12

[1]In those days came John the Baptist, preaching in the wilderness of Judaea, [2]And saying, Repent ye: for the kingdom of heaven is at hand. [3]For this is he that was spoken of by the prophet Esaias, saying, The voice of one crying in the wilderness, Prepare ye the way of the Lord, make his paths straight. [4]And the same John had his raiment of camel's hair, and a leathern girdle about his loins; and his meat was locusts and wild honey. [5]Then went out to him Jerusalem and all Judaea, and all the region round about Jordan, [6]And were baptized of him in Jordan, confessing their sins. [7]But when he saw many of the Pharisees and Sadducees come to his baptism, he said unto them, O generation of vipers, who hath warned you to flee from the wrath to come? [8]Bring forth therefore fruits meet for repentance: [9]And think not to say within yourselves, We have Abraham to our father: for I say unto you, that God is able of these stones to raise up children unto Abraham. [10]And now also the axe is laid unto the root of the trees: therefore every tree which bringeth not forth good fruit is hewn down, and cast into the fire. [11]I indeed baptize you with water unto repentance: but he that cometh after me is mightier than I, whose shoes I am not worthy to bear: he shall baptize you with the Holy Ghost, and with fire: [12]Whose fan is in his hand, and he will thoroughly purge his floor, and gather his wheat into the garner; but he will burn up the chaff with unquenchable fire.

7:19

[19]Every tree that bringeth not forth good fruit is hewn down, and cast into the fire.

11:10

[10]For this is he, of whom it is written, Behold, I send my messenger before thy face, which shall prepare thy way before thee.

14:3–4

[3]For Herod had laid hold on John, and bound him, and put him in prison for Herodias' sake, his brother Philip's wife. [4]For John said unto him, It is not lawful for thee to have her.

Mk

1:2–8

[2]As it is written in the prophets, Behold, I send my messenger before thy face, which shall prepare thy way before thee. [3]The voice of one crying in the wilderness, Prepare ye the way of the Lord, make his paths straight. [4]John did baptize in the wilderness, and preach the baptism of repentance for the remission of sins. [5]And there went out unto him all the land of Judaea, and they of Jerusalem, and were all baptized of him in the river of Jordan, confessing their sins. [6]And John was clothed with camel's hair, and with a girdle of a skin about his loins; and he did eat locusts and wild honey; [7]And preached, saying, There cometh one mightier than I after me, the latchet of whose shoes I am not worthy to stoop down and unloose. [8]I indeed have baptized you with water: but he shall baptize you with the Holy Ghost.

1:7

[7]And preached, saying, There cometh one mightier than I after me, the latchet of whose shoes I am not worthy to stoop down and unloose.

1:15

[15]And saying, The time is fulfilled, and the kingdom of God is at hand: repent ye, and believe the gospel.

2:8

[8]And immediately when Jesus perceived in his spirit that they so reasoned within themselves, he said unto them, Why reason ye these things in your hearts?

6:17–18

[17]For Herod himself had sent forth and laid hold upon John, and bound him in prison for Herodias' sake, his brother Philip's wife: for he had married her. [18]For John had said unto Herod, It is not lawful for thee to have thy brother's wife.

Acts 13:24–25 continued on next page

ACTS 13:24–25—Paul's address in the synagogue (13:16–43) (*continued*)

Theme	ACTS	Lk
(*Cont.*) **John Baptist less than Christ**	**13:24–25 (above)** **1:5 (above)** **2:28 (above)** **2:38 (above)** **11:16 (above)** **13:10 (above)** **13:47 (above)** **19:17 (above)** **26:20 (above)**	**1:76** 76And thou, child, shalt be called the prophet of the Highest: for thou shalt go before the face of the Lord to prepare his ways; **2:30–32** 30For mine eyes have seen thy salvation, 31Which thou hast prepared before the face of all people; 32A light to lighten the Gentiles, and the glory of thy people Israel. **3:1–20** 1Now in the fifteenth year of the reign of Tiberius Caesar, Pontius Pilate being governor of Judaea, and Herod being tetrarch of Galilee, and his brother Philip tetrarch of Ituraea and of the region of Trachonitis, and Lysanias the tetrarch of Abilene, 2Annas and Caiaphas being the high priests, the word of God came unto John the son of Zacharias in the wilderness. 3And he came into all the country about Jordan, preaching the baptism of repentance for the remission of sins; 4As it is written in the book of the words of Esaias the prophet, saying, The voice of one crying in the wilderness, Prepare ye the way of the Lord, make his paths straight. 5Every valley shall be filled, and every mountain and hill shall be brought low; and the crooked shall be made straight, and the rough ways shall be made smooth; 6And all flesh shall see the salvation of God. 7Then said he to the multitude that came forth to be baptized of him, O generation of vipers, who hath warned you to flee from the wrath to come? 8Bring forth therefore fruits worthy of repentance, and begin not to say within yourselves, We have Abraham to our father: for I say unto you, That God is able of these stones to raise up children unto Abraham. 9And now also the axe is laid unto the root of the trees: every tree therefore which bringeth not forth good fruit is hewn down, and cast into the fire. 10And the people asked him, saying, What shall we do then? 11He answereth and saith unto them, He that hath two coats, let him impart to him that hath none; and he that hath meat, let him do likewise. 12Then came also publicans to be baptized, and said unto him, Master, what shall we do? 13And he said unto them, Exact no more than that which is appointed you. 14And the soldiers likewise demanded of him, saying, And what shall we do? And he said unto them, Do violence to no man, neither accuse any falsely; and be content with your wages. 15And as the people were in expectation, and all men mused in their hearts of John, whether he were the Christ, or not; 16John answered, saying unto them all, I indeed baptize you with water; but one mightier than I cometh, the latchet of whose shoes I am not worthy to unloose: he shall baptize you with the Holy Ghost and with fire: 17Whose fan is in his hand, and he will thoroughly purge his floor, and will gather the wheat into his garner; but the chaff he will burn with fire unquenchable. 18And many other things in his exhortation preached he unto the people. 19But Herod the tetrarch, being reproved by him for Herodias his brother Philip's wife, and for all the evils which Herod had done, 20Added yet this above all, that he shut up John in prison. **6:43–44** 43For a good tree bringeth not forth corrupt fruit; neither doth a corrupt tree bring forth good fruit. 44For every tree is known by his own fruit. For of thorns men do not gather figs, nor of a bramble bush gather they grapes. **7:27** 27This is he, of whom it is written, Behold, I send my messenger before thy face, which shall prepare thy way before thee. **13:6–9** 6He spake also this parable; A certain man had a fig tree planted in his vineyard; and he came and sought fruit thereon, and found none. 7Then said he unto the dresser of his vineyard, Behold, these three years I come seeking fruit on this fig tree, and find none: cut it down; why cumbereth it the ground? 8And he answering said unto him, Lord, let it alone this year also, till I shall dig about it, and dung it: 9And if it bear fruit, well: and if not, then after that thou shalt cut it down. **13:31** 31The same day there came certain of the Pharisees, saying unto him, Get thee out, and depart hence: for Herod will kill thee. **23:8** 8And when Herod saw Jesus, he was exceeding glad: for he was desirous to see him of a long season, because he had heard many things of him; and he hoped to have seen some miracle done by him.

Jn

1:19–28

19 And this is the record of John, when the Jews
sent priests and Levites from Jerusalem to ask
him, Who art thou? 20 And he confessed, and
denied not; but confessed, I am not the Christ.
21 And they asked him, What then? Art thou Elias?
And he saith, I am not. Art thou that prophet?
And he answered, No. 22 Then said they unto him,
Who art thou? that we may give an answer to
them that sent us. What sayest thou of thyself?
23 He said, I am the voice of one crying in the
wilderness, Make straight the way of the Lord, as
said the prophet Esaias. 24 And they which were
sent were of the Pharisees. 25 And they asked him,
and said unto him, Why baptizest thou then, if
thou be not that Christ, nor Elias, neither that
prophet? 26 John answered them, saying, I baptize
with water: but there standeth one among you,
whom ye know not; 27 He it is, who coming after
me is preferred before me, whose shoe's latchet
I am not worthy to unloose. 28 These things were
done in Bethabara beyond Jordan, where John
was baptizing.

1:31–32

31 And I knew him not: but that he should be made
manifest to Israel, therefore am I come baptizing
with water. 32 And John bare record, saying, I saw
the Spirit descending from heaven like a dove,
and it abode upon him.

8:39

39 They answered and said unto him, Abraham
is our father. Jesus saith unto them, If ye were
Abraham's children, ye would do the works of
Abraham.

Acts 13:24–25 continued on next page

ACTS 13:24–25—Paul's address in the synagogue (13:16–43) (*continued*)

Theme	ACTS	Jewish Writings
(*Cont.*) **John Baptist less than Christ**	**13:24–25** (above) **1:5** (above) **2:28** (above) **2:38** (above) **11:16** (above) **13:10** (above) **13:47** (above) **19:17** (above) **26:20** (above)	**2 Kgs 1:8** [8]And they answered him, He was an hairy man, and girt with a girdle of leather about his loins. And he said, It is Elijah the Tishbite. **Is 40:3–6** [3]The voice of him that crieth in the wilderness, Prepare ye the way of the LORD, make straight in the desert a highway for our God. [4]Every valley shall be exalted, and every mountain and hill shall be made low: and the crooked shall be made straight, and the rough places plain: [5]And the glory of the LORD shall be revealed, and all flesh shall see it together: for the mouth of the LORD hath spoken it. [6]The voice said, Cry. And he said, What shall I cry? All flesh is grass, and all the goodliness thereof is as the flower of the field:

Other

1 ApocJas

It is the Lord who spoke with me: "See now the completion of my redemption. I have given you a sign of these things, James, my brother. For not without reason have I called you my brother, although you are not my brother materially. And I am not ignorant concerning you; so that when I give you a sign—know and hear." . . . "Nothing existed except Him-who-is. He is unnameable and ineffable. I myself am also unnameable, from Him-who-is, just as I have been given a number of names—two from Him-who-is. And I, I am before you. Since you have asked concerning femaleness, femaleness existed, but femaleness was not first. And it prepared for itself powers and gods. But it did not exist when I came forth, since I am an image of Him-who-is. But I have brought forth the image of him so that the sons of Him-who-is might know what things are theirs and what things are alien (to them). Behold, I shall reveal to you everything of this mystery. For they will seize me the day after tomorrow. But my redemption will be near." . . . James said, "Rabbi, you have said, 'they will seize me.' But I, what can I do?" He said to me, "Fear not, James. You too will they seize. But leave Jerusalem. For it is she who always gives the cup of bitterness to the sons of light. She is a dwelling place of a great number of archons. But your redemption will be preserved from them. So that you may understand who they are and what kinds they are, you will [. . .]. And listen. They are not [. . .] but archons [. . .]. These twelve [. . .] down [. . .] archons [. . .] upon his own hebdomad." . . . James said, "Rabbi, are there then twelve hebdomads and not seven as there are in the scriptures?" The Lord said, "James, he who spoke concerning this scripture had a limited understanding. I, however, shall reveal to you what has come forth from him who has no number. I shall give a sign concerning their number. As for what has come forth from him who has no measure, I shall give a sign concerning their measure" . . . James said, "Rabbi, behold then, I have received their number. There are seventy-two measures!" The Lord said, "These are the seventy-two heavens, which are their subordinates. These are the powers of all their might; and they were established by them; and these are they who were distributed everywhere, existing under the authority of the twelve archons. The inferior power among them brought forth for itself angels and unnumbered hosts. Him-who-is, however, has been given [. . .] on account of [. . .] Him-who-is [. . .] they are unnumbered. If you want to give them a number now, you will not be able to do so until you cast away from your blind thought, this bond of flesh which encircles you. And then you will reach Him-who-is. And you will no longer be James; rather you are the One-who-is. And all those who are unnumbered will all have been named." . . . [James said,], "Rabbi, in what way shall I reach Him-who-is, since all these powers and these hosts are armed against me?" He said to me, "These powers are not armed against you specifically, but are armed against another. It is against me that they are armed. And they are armed with other powers. But they are armed against me in judgment. They did not give [. . .] to me in it [. . .] through them [. . .]. In this place [. . .] suffering, I shall [. . .]. He will [. . .] and I shall not rebuke them. But there shall be within me a silence and a hidden mystery. But I am fainthearted before their anger." James said, "Rabbi, if they arm themselves against you, then is there no blame?" . . . You have come with knowledge, that you might rebuke their forgetfulness. You have come with recollection, that you might rebuke their ignorance. . . . But I was concerned because of you. For you descended into a great ignorance, but you have not been defiled by anything in it. . . . For you descended into a great mindlessness, and your recollection remained. . . . You walked in mud, and your garments were not soiled, and you have not been buried in their filth, and you have not been caught. . . . And I was not like them, but I clothed myself with everything of theirs. . . . There is in me forgetfulness, yet I remember things that are not theirs. . . . There is in me [. . . .], . . . and I am in their [. . .]. [. . .] knowledge [. . .] not in their sufferings [. . .]. But I have become afraid before them, since they rule. For what will they do? What will I be able to say? Or what word will I be able to say that I may escape them?" The Lord said, "James, I praise your understanding and your fear. If you continue to be distressed, do not be concerned for anything else except your redemption. For behold, I shall complete this destiny upon this earth as I have said from the heavens. And I shall reveal to you your redemption."

GEbi 2 and 3

[2]For by chopping off the genealogies of Matthew they made their gospel begin as we indicated before, with the words: "And so in the days of Herod, King of Judea, when Caiaphas was high priest, a certain one named John came baptizing a baptism of repentance in the Jordan River." (Epiphanius, Panarion, 30, 14, 3) [3]And so John was baptizing, and Pharisees came to him and were baptized, as was all of Jerusalem. John wore a garment of camel hair and a leather belt around his waist; and his food was wild honey that tasted like manna, like a cake cooked in oil. (Epiphanius, Panarion, 30, 13, 4-5)

Q-Quelle

Preaching of John: Acts 13:24-25/Mt 3:7-10, 3:11-12/ [Mk 1:7-8]/Lk 3:7-9(QS4), Lk 3:15-18 (QS5); Fruits: Acts 13:24-25/Mt 7:15-20, [Mt 12:33-35]/Lk 6:43-45 (QS13/[Thom 45]); Jesus' witness to John: Acts 13:24-25/Mt 11:7-19, [Mt 21:31-32]/Lk 7:24-35 (QS 17[Thom 74/46]), [Lk 16:16 (QS56)]

ACTS 13:28—Paul's address in the synagogue (13:16–43)

Theme	ACTS	Mt	Mk
Death sentence	**13:28** [28]And though they found no cause of death in him, yet desired they Pilate that he should be slain.	**27:20** [20]But the chief priests and elders persuaded the multitude that they should ask Barabbas, and destroy Jesus. **27:22–23** [22]Pilate saith unto them, What shall I do then with Jesus which is called Christ? They all say unto him, Let him be crucified. [23]And the governor said, Why, what evil hath he done? But they cried out the more, saying, Let him be crucified.	**15:13–14** [13]And they cried out again, Crucify him. [14]Then Pilate said unto them, Why, what evil hath he done? And they cried out the more exceedingly, Crucify him.

ACTS 13:29—Paul's address in the synagogue (13:16–43)

Theme	ACTS	Mt	Mk
Burial	**13:29** [29]And when they had fulfilled all that was written of him, they took him down from the tree, and laid him in a sepulchre.	**27:59–60** [59]And when Joseph had taken the body, he wrapped it in a clean linen cloth, [60]And laid it in his own new tomb, which he had hewn out in the rock: and he rolled a great stone to the door of the sepulchre, and departed.	**15:46** [46]And he bought fine linen, and took him down, and wrapped him in the linen, and laid him in a sepulchre which was hewn out of a rock, and rolled a stone unto the door of the sepulchre.

ACTS 13:30—Paul's address in the synagogue (13:16–43)

Theme	ACTS
Jesus raised from dead	**13:30** [30]But God raised him from the dead: **2:24** [24]Whom God hath raised up, having loosed the pains of death: because it was not possible that he should be holden of it. **2:32** [32]This Jesus hath God raised up, whereof we all are witnesses. **3:15** [15]And killed the Prince of life, whom God hath raised from the dead; whereof we are witnesses. **4:10** [10]Be it known unto you all, and to all the people of Israel, that by the name of Jesus Christ of Nazareth, whom ye crucified, whom God raised from the dead, even by him doth this man stand here before you whole. **17:31** [31]Because he hath appointed a day, in the which he will judge the world in righteousness by that man whom he hath ordained; whereof he hath given assurance unto all men, in that he hath raised him from the dead.

Lk	Jn
23:4 [4]Then said Pilate to the chief priests and to the people, I find no fault in this man. **23:14–15** [14]Said unto them, Ye have brought this man unto me, as one that perverteth the people: and, behold, I, having examined him before you, have found no fault in this man touching those things whereof ye accuse him: [15]No, nor yet Herod: for I sent you to him; and, lo, nothing worthy of death is done unto him. **23:21–23** [21]But they cried, saying, Crucify him, crucify him. [22]And he said unto them the third time, Why, what evil hath he done? I have found no cause of death in him: I will therefore chastise him, and let him go. [23]And they were instant with loud voices, requiring that he might be crucified. And the voices of them and of the chief priests prevailed.	**19:4–6** [4]Pilate therefore went forth again, and saith unto them, Behold, I bring him forth to you, that ye may know that I find no fault in him. [5]Then came Jesus forth, wearing the crown of thorns, and the purple robe. And Pilate saith unto them, Behold the man! [6]When the chief priests therefore and officers saw him, they cried out, saying, Crucify him, crucify him. Pilate saith unto them, Take ye him, and crucify him: for I find no fault in him. **19:15** [15]But they cried out, Away with him, away with him, crucify him. Pilate saith unto them, Shall I crucify your King? The chief priests answered, We have no king but Caesar.

Lk	Jn
23:53 [53]And he took it down, and wrapped it in linen, and laid it in a sepulchre that was hewn in stone, wherein never man before was laid.	**19:38** [38]And after this Joseph of Arimathaea, being a disciple of Jesus, but secretly for fear of the Jews, besought Pilate that he might take away the body of Jesus: and Pilate gave him leave. He came therefore, and took the body of Jesus. **19:41–42** [41]Now in the place where he was crucified there was a garden; and in the garden a new sepulchre, wherein was never man yet laid. [42]There laid they Jesus therefore because of the Jews' preparation day; for the sepulchre was nigh at hand.

ACTS 13:31—Paul's address in the synagogue (13:16–43)

Theme	ACTS	Mt	Mk
Jesus' post-resurrection appearances	**13:31** [31]And he was seen many days of them which came up with him from Galilee to Jerusalem, who are his witnesses unto the people. **1:3** [3]To whom also he showed himself alive after his passion by many infallible proofs, being seen of them forty days, and speaking of the things pertaining to the kingdom of God. **1:8** [8]But ye shall receive power, after that the Holy Ghost is come upon you: and ye shall be witnesses unto me both in Jerusalem, and in all Judaea, and in Samaria, and unto the uttermost part of the earth. **10:39** [39]And we are witnesses of all things which he did both in the land of the Jews, and in Jerusalem; whom they slew and hanged on a tree. **10:41** [41]Not to all the people, but unto witnesses chosen before of God, even to us, who did eat and drink with him after he rose from the dead.	**28:8–10** [8]And they departed quickly from the sepulchre with fear and great joy; and did run to bring his disciples word. [9]And as they went to tell his disciples, behold, Jesus met them, saying, All hail. And they came and held him by the feet, and worshipped him. [10]Then said Jesus unto them, Be not afraid: go tell my brethren that they go into Galilee, and there shall they see me. **28:16–20** [16]Then the eleven disciples went away into Galilee, into a mountain where Jesus had appointed them. [17]And when they saw him, they worshipped him: but some doubted. [18]And Jesus came and spake unto them, saying, All power is given unto me in heaven and in earth. [19]Go ye therefore, and teach all nations, baptizing them in the name of the Father, and of the Son, and of the Holy Ghost: [20]Teaching them to observe all things whatsoever I have commanded you: and, lo, I am with you alway, even unto the end of the world. Amen.	**16:9** [9]Now when Jesus was risen early the first day of the week, he appeared first to Mary Magdalene, out of whom he had cast seven devils. **16:12–20** [12]After that he appeared in another form unto two of them, as they walked, and went into the country. [13]And they went and told it unto the residue: neither believed they them. [14]Afterward he appeared unto the eleven as they sat at meat, and upbraided them with their unbelief and hardness of heart, because they believed not them which had seen him after he was risen. [15]And he said unto them, Go ye into all the world, and preach the gospel to every creature. [16]He that believeth and is baptized shall be saved; but he that believeth not shall be damned. [17]And these signs shall follow them that believe; In my name shall they cast out devils; they shall speak with new tongues; [18]They shall take up serpents; and if they drink any deadly thing, it shall not hurt them; they shall lay hands on the sick, and they shall recover.[19]So then after the Lord had spoken unto them, he was received up into heaven, and sat on the right hand of God. [20]And they went forth, and preached every where, the Lord working with them, and confirming the word with signs following. Amen.

Lk

24:13–53

[13]And, behold, two of them went that same day to a village called Emmaus, which was from Jerusalem about threescore
furlongs. [14]And they talked together of all these things which had happened. [15]And it came to pass, that, while they
communed together and reasoned, Jesus himself drew near, and went with them. [16]But their eyes were holden that
they should not know him. [17]And he said unto them, What manner of communications are these that ye have one to
another, as ye walk, and are sad? [18]And the one of them, whose name was Cleopas, answering said unto him, Art thou
only a stranger in Jerusalem, and hast not known the things which are come to pass there in these days? [19]And he said
unto them, What things? And they said unto him, Concerning Jesus of Nazareth, which was a prophet mighty in deed
and word before God and all the people: [20]And how the chief priests and our rulers delivered him to be condemned
to death, and have crucified him. [21]But we trusted that it had been he which should have redeemed Israel: and beside
all this, to day is the third day since these things were done. [22]Yea, and certain women also of our company made us
astonished, which were early at the sepulchre; [23]And when they found not his body, they came, saying, that they had
also seen a vision of angels, which said that he was alive. [24]And certain of them which were with us went to the sepulchre, and found it even so as the women had said: but him they saw not. [25]Then he said unto them, O fools, and slow of
heart to believe all that the prophets have spoken: [26]Ought not Christ to have suffered these things, and to enter into
his glory? [27]And beginning at Moses and all the prophets, he expounded unto them in all the scriptures the things concerning himself. [28]And they drew nigh unto the village, whither they went: and he made as though he would have gone
further. [29]But they constrained him, saying, Abide with us: for it is toward evening, and the day is far spent. And he
went in to tarry with them. [30]And it came to pass, as he sat at meat with them, he took bread, and blessed it, and brake,
and gave to them. [31]And their eyes were opened, and they knew him; and he vanished out of their sight. [32]And they said
one to another, Did not our heart burn within us, while he talked with us by the way, and while he opened to us the
scriptures? [33]And they rose up the same hour, and returned to Jerusalem, and found the eleven gathered together, and
them that were with them, [34]Saying, The Lord is risen indeed, and hath appeared to Simon. [35]And they told what things
were done in the way, and how he was known of them in breaking of bread. [36]And as they thus spake, Jesus himself
stood in the midst of them, and saith unto them, Peace be unto you. [37]But they were terrified and affrighted, and supposed that they had seen a spirit. [38]And he said unto them, Why are ye troubled? and why do thoughts arise in your
hearts? [39]Behold my hands and my feet, that it is I myself: handle me, and see; for a spirit hath not flesh and bones, as ye
see me have. [40]And when he had thus spoken, he showed them his hands and his feet. [41]And while they yet believed not
for joy, and wondered, he said unto them, Have ye here any meat? [42]And they gave him a piece of a broiled fish, and of
an honeycomb. [43]And he took it, and did eat before them. [44]And he said unto them, These are the words which I spake
unto you, while I was yet with you, that all things must be fulfilled, which were written in the law of Moses, and in the
prophets, and in the psalms, concerning me. [45]Then opened he their under-standing, that they might understand the
scriptures, [46]And said unto them, Thus it is written, and thus it behoved Christ to suffer, and to rise from the dead the
third day: [47]And that repentance and remission of sins should be preached in his name among all nations, beginning at
Jerusalem. [48]And ye are witnesses of these things. [49]And, behold, I send the promise of my Father upon you: but tarry
ye in the city of Jerusalem, until ye be endued with power from on high. [50]And he led them out as far as to Bethany, and
he lifted up his hands, and blessed them. [51]And it came to pass, while he blessed them, he was parted from them, and
carried up into heaven. [52]And they worshipped him, and returned to Jerusalem with great joy: [53]And were continually
in the temple, praising and blessing God. Amen.

Acts 13:31 continued on next page

ACTS 13:31—Paul's address in the synagogue (13:16–43) (*continued*)

Theme	ACTS	Jn
(*Cont.*) Jesus' post-resurection appearances	**13:31 (above)**	**20:11–29** [11]But Mary stood without at the sepulchre weeping: and as she wept, she stooped down, and looked into the sepulchre, [12]And seeth two angels in white sitting, the one at the head, and the other at the feet, where the body of Jesus had lain. [13]And they say unto her, Woman, why weepest thou? She saith unto them, Because they have taken away my Lord, and I know not where they have laid him. [14]And when she had thus said, she turned herself back, and saw Jesus standing, and knew not that it was Jesus. [15]Jesus saith unto her, Woman, why weepest thou? whom seekest thou? She, supposing him to be the gardener, saith unto him, Sir, if thou have borne him hence, tell me where thou hast laid him, and I will take him away. [16]Jesus saith unto her, Mary. She turned herself, and saith unto him, Rabboni; which is to say, Master. [17]Jesus saith unto her, Touch me not; for I am not yet ascended to my Father: but go to my brethren, and say unto them, I ascend unto my Father, and your Father; and to my God, and your God. [18]Mary Magdalene came and told the disciples that she had seen the Lord, and that he had spoken these things unto her. [19]Then the same day at evening, being the first day of the week, when the doors were shut where the disciples were assembled for fear of the Jews, came Jesus and stood in the midst, and saith unto them, Peace be unto you. [20]And when he had so said, he showed unto them his hands and his side. Then were the disciples glad, when they saw the Lord. [21]Then said Jesus to them again, Peace be unto you: as my Father hath sent me, even so send I you. [22]And when he had said this, he breathed on them, and saith unto them, Receive ye the Holy Ghost: [23]Whose soever sins ye remit, they are remitted unto them; and whose soever sins ye retain, they are retained. [24]But Thomas, one of the twelve, called Didymus, was not with them when Jesus came. [25]The other disciples therefore said unto him, We have seen the Lord. But he said unto them, Except I shall see in his hands the print of the nails, and put my finger into the print of the nails, and thrust my hand into his side, I will not believe. [26]And after eight days again his disciples were within, and Thomas with them: then came Jesus, the doors being shut, and stood in the midst, and said, Peace be unto you. [27]Then saith he to Thomas, Reach hither thy finger, and behold my hands; and reach hither thy hand, and thrust it into my side: and be not faithless, but believing. [28]And Thomas answered and said unto him, My Lord and my God. [29]Jesus saith unto him, Thomas, because thou hast seen me, thou hast believed: blessed are they that have not seen, and yet have believed. **21:1–23** [1]After these things Jesus showed himself again to the disciples at the sea of Tiberias; and on this wise showed he himself. [2]There were together Simon Peter, and Thomas called Didymus, and Nathanael of Cana in Galilee, and the sons of Zebedee, and two other of his disciples. [3]Simon Peter saith unto them, I go a fishing. They say unto him, We also go with thee. They went forth, and entered into a ship immediately; and that night they caught nothing. [4]But when the morning was now come, Jesus stood on the shore: but the disciples knew not that it was Jesus. [5]Then Jesus saith unto them, Children, have ye any meat? They answered him, No. [6]And he said unto them, Cast the net on the right side of the ship, and ye shall find. They cast therefore, and now they were not able to draw it for the multitude of fishes. [7]Therefore that disciple whom Jesus loved saith unto Peter, It is the Lord. Now when Simon Peter heard that it was the Lord, he girt his fisher's coat unto him, (for he was naked,) and did cast himself into the sea. [8]And the other disciples came in a little ship; (for they were not far from land, but as it were two hundred cubits,) dragging the net with fishes. [9]As soon then as they were come to land, they saw a fire of coals there, and fish laid thereon, and bread. [10]Jesus saith unto them, Bring of the fish which ye have now caught. [11]Simon Peter went up, and drew the net to land full of great fishes, an hundred and fifty and three: and for all there were so many, yet was not the net broken. [12]Jesus saith unto them, Come and dine. And none of the disciples durst ask him, Who art thou? knowing that it was the Lord. [13]Jesus then cometh, and taketh bread, and giveth them, and fish likewise. [14]This is now the third time that Jesus showed himself to his disciples, after that he was risen from the dead. [15]So when they had dined, Jesus saith to Simon Peter, Simon, son of Jonas, lovest thou me more than these? He saith unto him, Yea, Lord; thou knowest that I love thee. He saith unto him, Feed my lambs. [16]He saith to him again the second time, Simon, son of Jonas, lovest thou me? He saith unto him, Yea, Lord; thou knowest that I love thee. He saith unto him, Feed my sheep. [17]He saith unto him the third time, Simon, son of Jonas, lovest thou me? Peter was grieved because he said unto him the third time, Lovest thou me? And he said unto him, Lord, thou knowest all things; thou knowest that I love thee. Jesus saith unto him, Feed my sheep. [18]Verily, verily, I say unto thee, When thou wast young, thou girdedst thyself, and walkedst whither thou wouldest: but when thou shalt be old, thou shalt stretch forth thy hands, and another shall gird thee, and carry thee

ACTS 13:31—Paul's address in the synagogue (13:16–43) (*continued*)

Theme	ACTS	Jn
(*Cont.*) Jesus' post-resurection appearances	13:31 (above)	**21:1–23 (*continued*)** whither thou wouldest not. [19]This spake he, signifying by what death he should glorify God. And when he had spoken this, he saith unto him, Follow me. [20]Then Peter, turning about, seeth the disciple whom Jesus loved following; which also leaned on his breast at supper, and said, Lord, which is he that betrayeth thee? [21]Peter seeing him saith to Jesus, Lord, and what shall this man do? [22]Jesus saith unto him, If I will that he tarry till I come, what is that to thee? follow thou me. [23]Then went this saying abroad among the brethren, that that disciple should not die: yet Jesus said not unto him, He shall not die; but, If I will that he tarry till I come, what is that to thee?

ACTS 13:33—Paul's address in the synagogue (13:16–43)

Theme	ACTS	Jewish Writings
Jesus is Son of God	**13:33** [33]God hath fulfilled the same unto us their children, in that he hath raised up Jesus again; as it is also written in the second psalm, Thou art my Son, this day have I begotten thee.	**Ps 2:7** [7]I will declare the decree: the LORD hath said unto me, Thou art my Son; this day have I begotten thee.

ACTS 13:34—Paul's address in the synagogue (13:16–43)

Theme	ACTS	Jewish Writings
Jesus raised after 3 days	**13:34** [34]And as concerning that he raised him up from the dead, now no more to return to corruption, he said on this wise, I will give you the sure mercies of David.	**Is 55:3** [3]Incline your ear, and come unto me: hear, and your soul shall live; and I will make an everlasting covenant with you, even the sure mercies of David.

ACTS 13:35—Paul's address in the synagogue (13:16–43)

Theme	ACTS	Jewish Writings
Holy ones see no corruption	**13:35** [35]Wherefore he saith also in another psalm, Thou shalt not suffer thine Holy One to see corruption.	**Ps 16:10** [10]For thou wilt not leave my soul in hell; neither wilt thou suffer thine Holy One to see corruption.

ACTS 13:36—Paul's address in the synagogue (13:16–43)

Theme	ACTS	Jewish Writings
David's body decays	**13:36** [36]For David, after he had served his own generation by the will of God, fell on sleep, and was laid unto his fathers, and saw corruption: **2:29** [29]Men and brethren, let me freely speak unto you of the patriarch David, that he is both dead and buried, and his sepulchre is with us unto this day.	**1 Kgs 2:10** [10]So David slept with his fathers, and was buried in the city of David.

ACTS 13:39—Paul's address in the synagogue (13:16–43)

Theme	ACTS	Paul
Justification	**13:39** [39]And by him all that believe are justified from all things, from which ye could not be justified by the law of Moses.	**Rom 3:20** [20]Therefore by the deeds of the law there shall no flesh be justified in his sight: for by the law is the knowledge of sin.

ACTS 13:41—Paul's address in the synagogue (13:16–43)

Theme	ACTS	NT
Belief	**13:41** [41]Behold, ye despisers, and wonder, and perish: for I work a work in your days, a work which ye shall in no wise believe, though a man declare it unto you.	**Heb 1:5** [5]For unto which of the angels said he at any time, Thou art my Son, this day have I begotten thee? And again, I will be to him a Father, and he shall be to me a Son?

Paul's address to Gentiles 13:44–52

ACTS 13:46—Paul's address to Gentiles (13:44–52)

Theme	ACTS	Paul
Preach Good News	**13:46** [46]Then Paul and Barnabas waxed bold, and said, It was necessary that the word of God should first have been spoken to you: but seeing ye put it from you, and judge yourselves unworthy of everlasting life, lo, we turn to the Gentiles. **3:26** [26]Unto you first God, having raised up his Son Jesus, sent him to bless you, in turning away every one of you from his iniquities.	**Rom 1:16** [16]For I am not ashamed of the gospel of Christ: for it is the power of God unto salvation to every one that believeth; to the Jew first, and also to the Greek.

ACTS 13:47—Paul's address to Gentiles (13:44–52)

Theme	ACTS
Salvation for the Gentiles/ mission	**13:47** 47 For so hath the Lord commanded us, saying, I have set thee to be a light of the Gentiles, that thou shouldest be for salvation unto the ends of the earth. **1:5** 5 For John truly baptized with water; but ye shall be baptized with the Holy Ghost not many days hence. **2:38** 38 Then Peter said unto them, Repent, and be baptized every one of you in the name of Jesus Christ for the remission of sins, and ye shall receive the gift of the Holy Ghost. **11:16** 16 Then remembered I the word of the Lord, how that he said, John indeed baptized with water; but ye shall be baptized with the Holy Ghost. **13:10** 10 And said, O full of all subtlety and all mischief, thou child of the devil, thou enemy of all righteousness wilt thou not cease to pervert the right ways of the Lord? **13:24–25** 24 When John had first preached before his coming the baptism of repentance to all the people of Israel. 25 And as John fulfilled his course, he said, Whom think ye that I am? I am not he. But, behold, there cometh one after me, whose shoes of his feet I am not worthy to loose. **18:6** 6 And when they opposed themselves, and blasphemed, he shook his raiment, and said unto them, Your blood be upon your own heads; I am clean: from henceforth I will go unto the Gentiles. **19:1–7** 1 And it came to pass, that, while Apollos was at Corinth, Paul having passed through the upper coasts came to Ephesus: and finding certain disciples, 2 He said unto them, Have ye received the Holy Ghost since ye believed? And they said unto him, We have not so much as heard whether there be any Holy Ghost. 3 And he said unto them, Unto what then were ye baptized? And they said, Unto John's baptism. 4 Then said Paul, John verily baptized with the baptism of repentance, saying unto the people, that they should believe on him which should come after him, that is, on Christ Jesus. 5 When they heard this, they were baptized in the name of the Lord Jesus. 6 And when Paul had laid his hands upon them, the Holy Ghost came on them; and they spake with tongues, and prophesied. 7 And all the men were about twelve. **26:20** 20 But showed first unto them of Damascus, and at Jerusalem, and throughout all the coasts of Judaea, and then to the Gentiles, that they should repent and turn to God, and do works meet for repentance. **26:23** 23 That Christ should suffer, and that he should be the first that should rise from the dead, and should show light unto the people, and to the Gentiles. **28:28** 28 Be it known therefore unto you, that the salvation of God is sent unto the Gentiles, and that they will hear it.

Mt

1:15

15 And Eliud begat Eleazar; and Eleazar begat Matthan; and Matthan begat Jacob;

3:1–12

1 In those days came John the Baptist, preaching in the wilderness of Judaea, 2 And saying, Repent ye: for the kingdom
of heaven is at hand. 3 For this is he that was spoken of by the prophet Esaias, saying, The voice of one crying in the
wilderness, Prepare ye the way of the Lord, make his paths straight. 4 And the same John had his raiment of camel's
hair, and a leathern girdle about his loins; and his meat was locusts and wild honey. 5 Then went out to him Jerusalem,
and all Judaea, and all the region round about Jordan, 6 And were baptized of him in Jordan, confessing their sins. 7 But
when he saw many of the Pharisees and Sadducees come to his baptism, he said unto them, O generation of vipers, who
hath warned you to flee from the wrath to come? 8 Bring forth therefore fruits meet for repentance: 9 And think not to
say within yourselves, We have Abraham to our father: for I say unto you, that God is able of these stones to raise up
children unto Abraham. 10 And now also the axe is laid unto the root of the trees: therefore every tree which bringeth
not forth good fruit is hewn down, and cast into the fire. 11 I indeed baptize you with water unto repentance: but he that
cometh after me is mightier than I, whose shoes I am not worthy to bear: he shall baptize you with the Holy Ghost, and
with fire: 12 Whose fan is in his hand, and he will thoroughly purge his floor, and gather his wheat into the garner; but he
will burn up the chaff with unquenchable fire.

7:19

19 Every tree that bringeth not forth good fruit is hewn down, and cast into the fire.

10:1

1 And when he had called unto him his twelve disciples, he gave them power against unclean spirits, to cast them out,
and to heal all manner of sickness and all manner of disease.

10:9–14

9 Provide neither gold, nor silver, nor brass in your purses, 10 Nor scrip for your journey, neither two coats, neither shoes,
nor yet staves: for the workman is worthy of his meat. 11 And into whatsoever city or town ye shall enter, inquire who in
it is worthy; and there abide till ye go thence. 12 And when ye come into an house, salute it. 13 And if the house be worthy,
let your peace come upon it: but if it be not worthy, let your peace return to you. 14 And whosoever shall not receive you,
nor hear your words, when ye depart out of that house or city, shake off the dust of your feet.

11:10

10 For this is he, of whom it is written, Behold I send my messenger before thy face, which shall prepare thy way before
thee.

14:3–4

3 For Herod had laid hold on John, and bound him, and put him in prison for Herodias' sake, his brother Philip's wife.
4 For John said unto him, It is not lawful for thee to have her.

Acts 13:47 continued on next page

ACTS 13:47—Paul's address to Gentiles (13:44–52) (*continued*)

Theme	Acts	Mk
(*Cont.*) **Salvation for the Gentiles/ mission**	**13:47** (above) **1:5** (above) **2:38** (above) **11:16** (above) **13:10** (above) **13:24–25** (above) **18:6** (above) **19:1–7** (above) **26:20** (above) **26:23** (above) **28:28** (above)	**1:2–8** [2]As it is written in the prophets, Behold, I send my messenger before thy face, which shall prepare thy way before thee. [3]The voice of one crying in the wilderness, Prepare ye the way of the Lord, make his paths straight. [4]John did baptize in the wilderness, and preach the baptism of repentance for the remission of sins. [5]And there went out unto him all the land of Judaea, and they of Jerusalem, and were all baptized of him in the river of Jordan, confessing their sins. [6]And John was clothed with camel's hair, and with a girdle of a skin about his loins; and he did eat locusts and wild honey; [7]And preached, saying, There cometh one mightier than I after me, the latchet of whose shoes I am not worthy to stoop down and unloose. [8]I indeed have baptized you with water: but he shall baptize you with the Holy Ghost. **1:15** [15]And saying, The time is fulfilled, and the kingdom of God is at hand: repent ye, and believe the gospel. **2:8** [8]And immediately when Jesus perceived in his spirit that they so reasoned within themselves, he said unto them, Why reason ye these things in your hearts? **3:6** [6]And the Pharisees went forth, and straightway took counsel with the Herodians against him, how they might destroy him. **3:14–15** [14]And he ordained twelve, that they should be with him, and that he might send them forth to preach, [15]And to have power to heal sicknesses, and to cast out devils: **6:7–13** [7]And Solomon begat Roboam; and Roboam begat Abia; and Abia begat Asa; [8]And Asa begat Josaphat; and Josaphat begat Joram; and Joram begat Ozias; [9]And Ozias begat Joatham; and Joatham begat Achaz; and Achaz begat Ezekias; [10]And Ezekias begat Manasses; and Manasses begat Amon; and Amon begat Josias; [11]And Josias begat Jechonias and his brethren, about the time they were carried away to Babylon: [12]And after they were brought to Babylon, Jechonias begat Salathiel; and Salathiel begat Zorobabel; [13]And Zorobabel begat Abiud; and Abiud begat Eliakim; and Eliakim begat Azor;

Lk

1:76

[76]And thou, child, shalt be called the prophet of the Highest: for thou shalt go before the face of the Lord to prepare his ways;

1:80

[80]And the child grew, and waxed strong in spirit, and was in the deserts till the day of his showing unto Israel.

2:30–32

[30]For mine eyes have seen thy salvation, [31]Which thou hast prepared before the face of all people; [32]A light to lighten the Gentiles, and the glory of thy people Israel.

2:39–40

[39]And when they had performed all things according to the law of the Lord, they returned into Galilee, to their own city Nazareth. [40]And the child grew, and waxed strong in spirit, filled with wisdom: and the grace of God was upon him.

2:52

[52]And Jesus increased in wisdom and stature, and in favour with God and man.

3:16

[16]John answered, saying unto them all, I indeed baptize you with water; but one mightier than I cometh, the latchet of whose shoes I am not worthy to unloose: he shall baptize you with the Holy Ghost and with fire:

6:43–44

[43]For a good tree bringeth not forth corrupt fruit; neither doth a corrupt tree bring forth good fruit. [44]For every tree is known by his own fruit. For of thorns men do not gather figs, nor of a bramble bush gather they grapes.

7:27

[27]This is he, of whom it is written, Behold, I send my messenger before thy face, which shall prepare thy way before thee.

9:1–6

[1]Then he called his twelve disciples together, and gave them power and authority over all devils, and to cure diseases. [2]And he sent them to preach the kingdom of God, and to heal the sick. [3]And he said unto them, Take nothing for your journey, neither staves, nor scrip, neither bread, neither money; neither have two coats apiece. [4]And whatsoever house ye enter into, there abide, and thence depart. [5]And whosoever will not receive you, when ye go out of that city, shake off the very dust from your feet for a testimony against them. [6]And they departed, and went through the towns, preaching the gospel, and healing every where.

10:11

[11]Even the very dust of your city, which cleaveth on us, we do wipe off against you: notwithstanding be ye sure of this, that the kingdom of God is come nigh unto you.

12:6

[6]Are not five sparrows sold for two farthings, and not one of them is forgotten before God?

13:31

[31]The same day there came certain of the Pharisees, saying unto him, Get thee out, and depart hence: for Herod will kill thee.

22:35–36

[35]And he said unto them, When I sent you without purse, and scrip, and shoes, lacked ye any thing? And they said, Nothing. [36]Then said he unto them, But now, he that hath a purse, let him take it, and likewise his scrip: and he that hath no sword, let him sell his garment, and buy one.

23:8

[8]And when Herod saw Jesus, he was exceeding glad: for he was desirous to see him of a long season, because he had heard many things of him; and he hoped to have seen some miracle done by him.

Acts 13:47 continued on next page

ACTS 13:47—Paul's address to Gentiles (13:44–52) (*continued*)

Theme	Acts	Jn
(*Cont.*) **Salvation for the Gentiles/ Mission**	**13:47 (above)** **1:5 (above)** **2:38 (above)** **11:16 (above)** **13:10 (above)** **13:24–25 (above)** **18:6 (above)** **19:1–7 (above)** **26:20 (above)** **26:23 (above)** **28:28 (above)**	**1:19–28** [19]And this is the record of John, when the Jews sent priests and Levites from Jerusalem to ask him, Who art thou? [20]And he confessed, and denied not; but confessed, I am not the Christ. [21]And they asked him, What then? Art thou Elias? And he saith, I am not. Art thou that prophet? And he answered, No. [22]Then said they unto him, Who art thou? that we may give an answer to them that sent us. What sayest thou of thyself? [23]He said, I am the voice of one crying in the wilderness, Make straight the way of the Lord, as said the prophet Esaias. [24]And they which were sent were of the Pharisees. [25]And they asked him, and said unto him, Why baptizest thou then, if thou be not that Christ, nor Elias, neither that prophet? [26]John answered them, saying, I baptize with water: but there standeth one among you, whom ye know not; [27]He it is, who coming after me is preferred before me, whose shoe's latchet I am not worthy to unloose. [28]These things were done in Bethabara beyond Jordan, where John was baptizing. **1:31–32** [31]And I knew him not: but that he should be made manifest to Israel, therefore am I come baptizing with water. [32]And John bare record, saying, I saw the Spirit descending from heaven like a dove, and it abode upon him. **8:39** [39]They answered and said unto him, Abraham is our father. Jesus saith unto them, If ye were Abraham's children, ye would do the works of Abraham.

Jewish Writings

Ex 13:2–12

2Sanctify unto me all the firstborn, whatsoever openeth the womb among the children of Israel, both of man and of
beast: it is mine. 3And Moses said unto the people, Remember this day, in which ye came out from Egypt, out of the
house of bondage; for by strength of hand the LORD brought you out from this place: there shall no leavened bread be
eaten. 4This day came ye out in the month Abib. 5And it shall be when the LORD shall bring thee into the land of the
Canaanites, and the Hittites, and the Amorites, and the Hivites, and the Jebusites, which he sware unto thy fathers to
give thee, a land flowing with milk and honey, that thou shalt keep this service in this month. 6Seven days thou shalt eat
unleavened bread, and in the seventh day shall be a feast to the LORD. 7Unleavened bread shall be eaten seven days;
and there shall no leavened bread be seen with thee, neither shall there be leaven seen with thee in all thy quarters.
8And thou shalt shew thy son in that day, saying, This is done because of that which the LORD did unto me when I
came forth out of Egypt. 9And it shall be for a sign unto thee upon thine hand, and for a memorial between thine eyes,
that the LORD's law may be in thy mouth: for with a strong hand hath the LORD brought thee out of Egypt. 10Thou
shalt therefore keep this ordinance in his season from year to year. 11And it shall be when the LORD shall bring thee
into the land of the Canaanites, as he sware unto thee and to thy fathers, and shall give it thee, 12That thou shalt set
apart unto the LORD all that openeth the matrix, and every firstling that cometh of a beast which thou hast; the males
shall be the LORD's.

Ex 13:15

15And it came to pass, when Pharaoh would hardly let us go, that the LORD slew all the firstborn in the land of Egypt,
both the firstborn of man, and the firstborn of beast: therefore I sacrifice to the LORD all that openeth the matrix,
being males; but all the firstborn of my children I redeem.

Lev 12:6

6And when the days of her purifying are fulfilled, for a son, or for a daughter, she shall bring a lamb of the first year for
a burnt offering, and a young pigeon, or a turtledove, for a sin offering, unto the door of the tabernacle of the congregation, unto the priest:...

Lev 12:8

8And if she be not able to bring a lamb, then she shall bring two turtles, or two young pigeons; the one for the burnt
offering, and the other for a sin offering: and the priest shall make an atonement for her, and she shall be clean.

2 Kgs 1:8

8And they answered him, He was an hairy man, and girt with a girdle of leather about his loins. And he said, It is Elijah
the Tishbite.

Is 40:3–6

3The voice of him that crieth in the wilderness, Prepare ye the way of the LORD, make straight in the desert a highway
for our God. 4Every valley shall be exalted, and every mountain and hill shall be made low: and the crooked shall
be made straight, and the rough places plain: 5And the glory of the LORD shall be revealed, and all flesh shall see it
together: for the mouth of the LORD hath spoken it. 6The voice said, Cry. And he said, What shall I cry? All flesh is
grass, and all the goodliness thereof is as the flower of the field

Is 49:6

**6And he said, It is a light thing that thou shouldest be my servant to raise up the tribes of Jacob, and to restore
the preserved of Israel: I will also give thee for a light to the Gentiles, that thou mayest be my salvation unto the
end of the earth.**

Is 52:10

10The LORD hath made bare his holy arm in the eyes of all the nations; and all the ends of the earth shall see the salvation of our God.

Mal 3:1a

1Behold, I will send my messenger, and he shall prepare the way before me:

Acts 13:47 continued on next page

ACTS 13:47—Paul's address to Gentiles (13:44–52) (*continued*)

Theme	Acts	Other
(*Cont.*) **Salvation for the Gentiles/ Mission**	**13:47 (above)** **1:5 (above)** **2:38 (above)** **11:16 (above)** **13:10 (above)** **13:24–25 (above)** **18:6 (above)** **19:1–7 (above)** **26:20 (above)** **26:23 (above)** **28:28 (above)**	**1 ApocJas** It is the Lord who spoke with me: "See now the completion of my redemption. I have given you a sign of these things, James, my brother. For not without reason have I called you my brother, although you are not my brother materially. And I am not ignorant concerning you; so that when I give you a sign—know and hear." "But I have brought forth the image of him so that the sons of Him-who-is might know what things are theirs and what things are alien (to them). Behold, I shall reveal to you everything of this mystery. For they will seize me the day after tomorrow. But my redemption will be near. . . ". . .you will not be able to do so until you cast away from your blind thought, this bond of flesh which encircles you. And then you will reach Him-who-is. And you will no longer be James; rather you are the One-who-is. And all those who are unnumbered will all have been named." "You walked in mud, and your garments were not soiled, and you have not been buried in their filth, and you have not been caught. "And I was not like them, but I clothed myself with everything of theirs. There is in me forgetfulness, yet I remember things that are not theirs. . . .do not be concerned for anything else except your redemption. For behold, I shall complete this destiny upon this earth as I have said from the heavens. And I shall reveal to you your redemption." "James, after these things I shall reveal to you everything, not for your sake alone but for the sake of the unbelief of men, so that faith may exist in them. For a multitude will attain to faith and they will increase in [. . .]. they are from his [. . .] companions. He will be proclaimed through them, and they will proclaim this word. Then he will become a seed of [. . .]." James said, "I am satisfied [. . .] and they are [. . .] my soul. first-fruits of the [. . .] upward [. . .] so that the power of God might appear. The perishable has gone up to the imperishable and the female element has attained to this male element." James said, "Rabbi, into these three (things), then, has their [. . .] been cast. For they have been reviled, and they have been persecuted [. . .]. Behold [. . .] everything [. . .] from anyone [. . .]. For you have received [. . .] of knowledge. And [. . .] that what is the [. . .] go [. . .] you will find [. . .]. But I shall go forth and shall reveal that they believed in you, that they may be content with their blessing and salvation, and this revelation may come to pass."

ACTS 13:47—Paul's address to Gentiles (13:44–52) (*continued*)

Theme	Acts	Other
(*Cont.*) **Salvation for the Gentiles/ Mission**	**13:47 (above)** **1:5 (above)** **2:38 (above)** **11:16 (above)** **13:10 (above)** **13:24–25 (above)** **18:6 (above)** **19:1–7 (above)** **26:20 (above)** **26:23 (above)** **28:28 (above)**	**GEbi 2 and 3** [2]For by chopping off the genealogies of Matthew they made their gospel begin as we indicated before, with the words: "And so in the days of Herod, King of Judea, when Caiaphas was high priest, a certain one named John came baptizing a baptism of repentance in the Jordan River." (Epiphanius, Panarion, 30, 14, 3) [3]And so John was baptizing, and Pharisees came to him and were baptized, as was all of Jerusalem. John wore a garment of camel hair and a leather belt around his waist; and his food was wild honey that tasted like manna, like a cake cooked in oil. (Epiphanius, Panarion, 30, 13, 4-5) **PJas 24:4** [4]After three days the priests decided to put someone in his place, and the lot fell to Simeon. For this is the one who learned form a revelation of the Holy Spirit that he would not see death until he could see the messiah in the flesh. **In Thom 19:5b** [5]But his mother kept to herself all these things that had happened. **Q-Quelle** Commissioning of the 70: Acts 13:51/Mt 9:37-38, Mt 10:7-16/Lk 10:2-12 (QS 20/[Thom 13; 14.2]); Commissioning of the 12: Acts 13:51/Mt 10:1, 10:7-11, 10:14/Mk 6:6b-13/Lk 9:1-6; Whoever hears you hears me: Acts 13:51/Mt 10:40/[Lk 10:13-15 (QS22)]; Jesus' witness to John: Acts 13:51/Mt 11:7-19, 21:31-32/Lk 7:24-35 (QS 17[Thom 74, 46] QS 18)

ACTS 13:51—Paul's address to Gentiles (13:44–52)

Theme	Acts	Mt
Mission and opposition	**13:51** [51]But they shook off the dust of their feet against them, and came unto Iconium. **18:6** [6]And when they opposed themselves, and blasphemed, he shook his raiment, and said unto them, Your blood be upon your own heads; I am clean: from henceforth I will go unto the Gentiles.	**9:35–38** [35]And Jesus went about all the cities and villages, teaching in their synagogues, and preaching the gospel of the kingdom, and healing every sickness and every disease among the people. [36]But when he saw the multitudes, he was moved with compassion on them, because they fainted, and were scattered abroad, as sheep having no shepherd. [37]Then saith he unto his disciples, The harvest truly is plenteous, but the labourers are few; [38]Pray ye therefore the Lord of the harvest, that he will send forth labourers into his harvest. **10:5–15** [5]These twelve Jesus sent forth, and commanded them, saying, Go not into the way of the Gentiles, and into any city of the Samaritans enter ye not: [6]But go rather to the lost sheep of the house of Israel. [7]And as ye go, preach, saying, The kingdom of heaven is at hand. [8]Heal the sick, cleanse the lepers, raise the dead, cast out devils: freely ye have received, freely give. [9]Provide neither gold, nor silver, nor brass in your purses, [10]Nor scrip for your journey, neither two coats, neither shoes, nor yet staves: for the workman is worthy of his meat. [11]And into whatsoever city or town ye shall enter, inquire who in it is worthy; and there abide till ye go thence. [12]And when ye come into an house, salute it. [13]And if the house be worthy, let your peace come upon it: but if it be not worthy, let your peace return to you. [14]And whosoever shall not receive you, nor hear your words, when ye depart out of that house or city, shake off the dust of your feet. [15]Verily I say unto you, It shall be more tolerable for the land of Sodom and Gomorrha in the day of judgment, than for that city. **10:14** [14]And whosoever shall not receive you, nor hear your words, when ye depart out of that house or city, shake off the dust of your feet. **10:16** [16]Behold, I send you forth as sheep in the midst of wolves: be ye therefore wise as serpents, and harmless as doves. **10:40** [40]He that receiveth you receiveth me, and he that receiveth me receiveth him that sent me. **11:20** [20]Then began he to upbraid the cities wherein most of his mighty works were done, because they repented not:

ACTS 13:51—Paul's address to Gentiles (13:44–52) (*continued*)

Theme	Acts	Jn
(*Cont.*) **Mission and opposition**	**13:51 (above)** **18:6 (above)**	**4:35** [35]Say not ye, There are yet four months, and then cometh harvest? behold, I say unto you, Lift up your eyes, and look on the fields; for they are white already to harvest. **5:23** [23]That all men should honour the Son, even as they honour the Father. He that honoureth not the Son honoureth not the Father which hath sent him. **12:44–45** [44]Jesus cried and said, He that believeth on me, believeth not on me, but on him that sent me. [45]And he that seeth me seeth him that sent me. **15:23** [23]He that hateth me hateth my Father also.

Mk	Lk
6:7–13 [6]And he marvelled because of their unbelief. And he went round about the villages, teaching. [7]And he called unto him the twelve, and began to send them forth by two and two; and gave them power over unclean spirits; [8]And commanded them that they should take nothing for their journey, save a staff only; no scrip, no bread, no money in their purse: [9]But be shod with sandals; and not put on two coats. [10]And he said unto them, In what place soever ye enter into an house, there abide till ye depart from that place. [11]And whosoever shall not receive you, nor hear you, when ye depart thence, shake off the dust under your feet for a testimony against them. Verily I say unto you, It shall be more tolerable for Sodom and Gomorrha in the day of judgment, than for that city. [12]And they went out, and preached that men should repent. [13]And they cast out many devils, and anointed with oil many that were sick, and healed them. **9:37** [37]Whosoever shall receive one of such children in my name, receiveth me: and whosoever shall receive me, receiveth not me, but him that sent me.	**1:76** [76]And thou, child, shalt be called the prophet of the Highest: for thou shalt go before the face of the Lord to prepare his ways; **3:4** [4]As it is written in the book of the words of Esaias the prophet, saying, The voice of one crying in the wilderness, Prepare ye the way of the Lord, make his paths straight. **7:27** [27]This is he, of whom it is written, Behold, I send my messenger before thy face, which shall prepare thy way before thee. **9:1–6** [1]Then he called his twelve disciples together, and gave them power and authority over all devils, and to cure diseases. [2]And he sent them to preach the kingdom of God, and to heal the sick. [3]And he said unto them, Take nothing for your journey, neither staves, nor scrip, neither bread, neither money; neither have two coats apiece. [4]And whatsoever house ye enter into, there abide, and thence depart. [5]And whosoever will not receive you, when ye go out of that city, shake off the very dust from your feet for a testimony against them. [6]And they departed, and went through the towns, preaching the gospel, and healing every where. **9:48** [48]And said unto them, Whosoever shall receive this child in my name receiveth me: and whosoever shall receive me receiveth him that sent me: for he that is least among you all, the same shall be great. **9:51–52** [50]And Jesus said unto him, Forbid him not: for he that is not against us is for us. [51]And it came to pass, when the time was come that he should be received up, he stedfastly set his face to go to Jerusalem, **10:11** [11]Even the very dust of your city, which cleaveth on us, we do wipe off against you: notwithstanding be ye sure of this, that the kingdom of God is come nigh unto you. **22:35–36** [35]And he said unto them, When I sent you without purse, and scrip, and shoes, lacked ye any thing? And they said, Nothing. [36]Then said he unto them, But now, he that hath a purse, let him take it, and likewise his scrip: and he that hath no sword, let him sell his garment, and buy one.

Other
2 Clem 5:2 [2]For the Lord says, "You will be like sheep in the midst of wolves." **GThom 14** [14]Jesus said, "If you fast, you will give rise to sin for yourselves; and if you pray, you will be condemned; and if you give alms, you will do harm to your spirits. When you go into any land and walk about in the districts, if they receive you, eat what they set before you, and heal the sick among them. For what goes into your mouth will not defile you, but that which issues from your mouth—it is that which will defile you." **GThom 73** [73]Jesus said, "The harvest is great but the laborers are few. Beseech the lord, therefore, to send out laborers to the harvest." **Q-Quelle** Commissioning of the 70: Acts 13:51/Mt 9:37-38, Mt 10:7-16/Lk 10:2-12 (QS 20/[Thom 13; 14.2]); Commissioning of the 12: Acts 13:51/Mt 10:1, 10:7-11, 10:14/Mk 6:6b-13/Lk 9:1-6; Whoever hears you hears me: Acts 13:51/Mt 10:40/[Lk 10:13-15 (QS22)]; Jesus' witness to John: Acts 13:51/Mt 11:7-19, 21:31-32/Lk 7:24-35 (QS 17[Thom 74, 46] QS 18)

ACTS 14:3—Paul and Barnabas at Iconium (14:1–20)

Theme	Acts	Mk
Signs and wonders as evidence of ministry	**14:3** [3]Long time therefore abode they speaking boldly in the Lord, which gave testimony unto the word of his grace, and granted signs and wonders to be done by their hands.	**16:17–20** [17]And these signs shall follow them that believe; In my name shall they cast out devils; they shall speak with new tongues; [18]They shall take up serpents; and if they drink any deadly thing, it shall not hurt them; they shall lay hands on the sick, and they shall recover. [19]So then after the Lord had spoken unto them, he was received up into heaven, and sat on the right hand of God. [20]And they went forth, and preached every where, the Lord working with them, and confirming the word with signs following. Amen.

ACTS 14:5—Paul and Barnabas at Iconium (14:1–20)

Theme	Acts	Paul
Assaulted by unbelievers	**14:5** [5]And when there was an assault made both of the Gentiles, and also of the Jews with their rulers, to use them despitefully, and to stone them,	**2 Tim 3:11 (Pseudo)** [11]Persecutions, afflictions, which came unto me at Antioch, at Iconium, at Lystra; what persecutions I endured: but out of them all the Lord delivered me.

ACTS 14:11—Paul and Barnabas at Iconium (14:1–20)

Theme	Acts
Mistaking Paul for Greek gods	**14:11** [11]And when the people saw what Paul had done, they lifted up their voices, saying in the speech of Lycaonia, The gods are come down to us in the likeness of men. **28:6** [6]Howbeit they looked when he should have swollen, or fallen down dead suddenly: but after they had looked a great while, and saw no harm come to him, they changed their minds, and said that he was a god.

ACTS 14:15—Paul and Barnabas at Iconium (14:1–20)

Theme	Acts	Jewish Writings
Turn to living God	**14:15** [15]And saying, Sirs, why do ye these things? We also are men of like passions with you, and preach unto you that ye should turn from these vanities unto the living God, which made heaven, and earth, and the sea, and all things that are therein: **3:12** [12]And when Peter saw it, he answered unto the people, Ye men of Israel, why marvel ye at this? or why look ye so earnestly on us, as though by our own power or holiness we had made this man to walk? **10:26** [26]But Peter took him up, saying, Stand up; I myself also am a man.	**Ex 20:11** [11]For in six days the LORD made heaven and earth, the sea, and all that in them is, and rested the seventh day: wherefore the LORD blessed the sabbath day, and hallowed it. **Ps 146:6** [6]Which made heaven, and earth, the sea, and all that therein is: which keepeth truth for ever:

ACTS 14:16—Paul and Barnabas at Iconium (14:1–20)

Theme	ACTS
Ignorance of God	**14:16** [16]Who in times past suffered all nations to walk in their own ways. **17:30** [30]And the times of this ignorance God winked at; but now commandeth all men every where to repent:

ACTS 14:17—Paul and Barnabas at Iconium (14:1–20)

Theme	ACTS	Jewish Writings
God leaves witness	**14:17** [17]Nevertheless he left not himself without witness, in that he did good, and gave us rain from heaven, and fruitful seasons, filling our hearts with food and gladness.	**Wis 13:1** [1]Surely vain are all men by nature, who are ignorant of God, and could not out of the good things that are seen know him that is: neither by considering the works did they acknowledge the workmaster;

ACTS 14:19–20—Paul and Barnabas at Iconium (14:1–20)

Theme	ACTS	Paul
Jews challenge Paul's ministry	**14:19–20** [19]And there came thither certain Jews from Antioch and Iconium, who persuaded the people, and, having stoned Paul, drew him out of the city, supposing he had been dead. [20]Howbeit, as the disciples stood round about him, he rose up, and came into the city: and the next day he departed with Barnabas to Derbe.	**2 Cor 11:25** [25]Thrice was I beaten with rods, once was I stoned, thrice I suffered shipwreck, a night and a day I have been in the deep; **2 Tim 3:11 (Pseudo)** [11]Persecutions, afflictions, which came unto me at Antioch, at Iconium, at Lystra; what persecutions I endured: but out of them all the Lord delivered me.

End of First Mission 14:21–28

ACTS 14:22—End of First Mission (14:21–28)

Theme	ACTS	Paul
Encouraged to continue in faith	**14:22** [22]Confirming the souls of the disciples, and exhorting them to continue in the faith, and that we must through much tribulation enter into the kingdom of God.	**1 Thes 3:3** [3]That no man should be moved by these afflictions: for yourselves know that we are appointed thereunto.

ACTS 14:26—End of First Mission (14:21–28)

Theme	ACTS
Commended to the work of God	**14:26** [26]And thence sailed to Antioch, from whence they had been recommended to the grace of God for the work which they fulfilled. **13:1–3** [1]Now there were in the church that was at Antioch certain prophets and teachers; as Barnabas, and Simeon that was called Niger, and Lucius of Cyrene, and Manaen, which had been brought up with Herod the tetrarch, and Saul. [2]As they ministered to the Lord, and fasted, the Holy Ghost said, Separate me Barnabas and Saul for the work whereunto I have called them. [3]And when they had fasted and prayed, and laid their hands on them, they sent them away.

ACTS 15:1–4—Council of Jerusalem, guidelines for Christian converts (15:1–12)

Theme	ACTS	Paul
Council at Jerusalem	**15:1–4** [1]And certain men which came down from Judaea taught the brethren, and said, Except ye be circumcised after the manner of Moses, ye cannot be saved. [2]When therefore Paul and Barnabas had no small dissension and disputation with them, they determined that Paul and Barnabas, and certain other of them, should go up to Jerusalem unto the apostles and elders about this question. [3]And being brought on their way by the church, they passed through Phenice and Samaria, declaring the conversion of the Gentiles: and they caused great joy unto all the brethren. [4]And when they were come to Jerusalem, they were received of the church, and of the apostles and elders, and they declared all things that God had done with them.	**Gal 2:1–9** [1]Then fourteen years after I went up again to Jerusalem with Barnabas, and took Titus with me also. [2]And I went up by revelation, and communicated unto them that gospel which I preach among the Gentiles, but privately to them which were of reputation, lest by any means I should run, or had run, in vain. [3]But neither Titus, who was with me, being a Greek, was compelled to be circumcised: [4]And that because of false brethren unawares brought in, who came in privily to spy out our liberty which we have in Christ Jesus, that they might bring us into bondage: [5]To whom we gave place by subjection, no, not for an hour; that the truth of the gospel might continue with you. [6]But of these who seemed to be somewhat, (whatsoever they were, it maketh no matter to me: God accepteth no man's person:) for they who seemed to be somewhat in conference added nothing to me: [7]But contrariwise, when they saw that the gospel of the uncircumcision was committed unto me, as the gospel of the circumcision was unto Peter; [8](For he that wrought effectually in Peter to the apostleship of the circumcision, the same was mighty in me toward the Gentiles:) [9]And when James, Cephas, and John, who seemed to be pillars, perceived the grace that was given unto me, they gave to me and Barnabas the right hands of fellowship; that we should go unto the heathen, and they unto the circumcision.

ACTS 15:1—Council of Jerusalem, guidelines for Christian converts (15:1–12)

Theme	ACTS	Paul	Jewish Writings
Christians and circumcision	**15:1** [1]And certain men which came down from Judaea taught the brethren, and said, Except ye be circumcised after the manner of Moses, ye cannot be saved.	**Gal 5:2** [2]Behold, I Paul say unto you, that if ye be circumcised, Christ shall profit you nothing.	**Lev 12:3** [3]And in the eighth day the flesh of his foreskin shall be circumcised.

ACTS 15:7—Council of Jerusalem, guidelines for Christian converts (15:1–12)

Theme	ACTS
Peter defends Gentile conversion	**15:7** [7]And when there had been much disputing, Peter rose up, and said unto them, Men and brethren, ye know how that a good while ago God made choice among us, that the Gentiles by my mouth should hear the word of the gospel, and believe. **10:27–43** [27]And as he talked with him, he went in, and found many that were come together. [28]And he said unto them, Ye know how that it is an unlawful thing for a man that is a Jew to keep company, or come unto one of another nation; but God hath showed me that I should not call any man common or unclean. [29]Therefore came I unto you without gainsaying, as soon as I was sent for: I ask therefore for what intent ye have sent for me? [30]And Cornelius said, Four days ago I was fasting until this hour; and at the ninth hour I prayed in my house, and, behold, a man stood before me in bright clothing, [31]And said, Cornelius, thy prayer is heard, and thine alms are had in remembrance in the sight of God. [32]Send therefore to Joppa, and call hither Simon, whose surname is Peter; he is lodged in the house of one Simon a tanner by the sea side: who, when he cometh, shall speak unto thee. [33]Immediately therefore I sent to thee; and thou hast well done that thou art come. Now therefore are we all here present before God, to hear all things that are commanded thee of God. [34]Then Peter opened his mouth, and said, Of a truth I perceive that God is no respecter of persons: [35]But in every nation he that feareth him, and worketh righteousness, is accepted with him. [36]The word which God sent unto the children of Israel, preaching peace by Jesus Christ: (he is Lord of all:) [37]That word, I say, ye know, which was published throughout all Judaea, and began from Galilee, after the baptism which John preached; [38]How God anointed Jesus of Nazareth with the Holy Ghost and with power: who went about doing good, and healing all that were oppressed of the devil; for God was with him. [39]And we are witnesses of all things which he did both in the land of the Jews, and in Jerusalem; whom they slew and hanged on a tree: [40]Him God raised up the third day, and showed him openly; [41]Not to all the people, but unto witnesses chosen before of God, even to us, who did eat and drink with him after he rose from the dead. [42]And he commanded us to preach unto the people, and to testify that it is he which was ordained of God to be the Judge of quick and dead. [43]To him give all the prophets witness, that through his name whosoever believeth in him shall receive remission of sins.

ACTS 15:8—Council of Jerusalem, guidelines for Christian converts (15:1–12)

Theme	ACTS
God sees the heart	**15:8** [8]And God, which knoweth the hearts, bare them witness, giving them the Holy Ghost, even as he did unto us; **10:44–48** [44]While Peter yet spake these words, the Holy Ghost fell on all them which heard the word. [45]And they of the circumcision which believed were astonished, as many as came with Peter, because that on the Gentiles also was poured out the gift of the Holy Ghost. [46]For they heard them speak with tongues, and magnify God. Then answered Peter, [47]Can any man forbid water, that these should not be baptized, which have received the Holy Ghost as well as we? [48]And he commanded them to be baptized in the name of the Lord. Then prayed they him to tarry certain days.

ACTS 15:9—Council of Jerusalem, guidelines for Christian converts (15:1–12)

Theme	ACTS
Hearts purified in faith	**15:9** [9]And put no difference between us and them, purifying their hearts by faith. **10:34–35** [34]Then Peter opened his mouth, and said, Of a truth I perceive that God is no respecter of persons: [35]But in every nation he that feareth him, and worketh righteousness, is accepted with him.

ACTS 15:10—Council of Jerusalem, guidelines for Christian converts (15:1–12)

Theme	ACTS	Mt	Paul	Other
Jesus' yoke is easy	**15:10** [10]Now therefore why tempt ye God, to put a yoke upon the neck of the disciples, which neither our fathers nor we were able to bear?	**23:4** [4]For they bind heavy burdens and grievous to be borne, and lay them on men's shoulders; but they themselves will not move them with one of their fingers.	**Gal 5:1** [1]Stand fast therefore in the liberty wherewith Christ hath made us free, and be not entangled again with the yoke of bondage.	**Q-Quelle** Against Pharisees: Acts 15:10/Mt 23:4-36/[Mk 7:1-9]/[Lk 11:37-54]

ACTS 15:11—Council of Jerusalem, guidelines for Christian converts (15:1–12)

Theme	ACTS	Paul
Saved by grace	**15:11** [11]But we believe that through the grace of the Lord Jesus Christ we shall be saved, even as they.	**Gal 2:16** [16]Knowing that a man is not justified by the works of the law, but by the faith of Jesus Christ, even we have believed in Jesus Christ, that we might be justified by the faith of Christ, and not by the works of the law: for by the works of the law shall no flesh be justified. **Eph 2:5–8 (Pseudo)** [5]Even when we were dead in sins, hath quickened us together with Christ, (by grace ye are saved;) [6]And hath raised us up together, and made us sit together in heavenly places in Christ Jesus: [7]That in the ages to come he might show the exceeding riches of his grace in his kindness toward us through Christ Jesus. [8]For by grace are ye saved through faith; and that not of yourselves: it is the gift of God:

Paul is given apostolic letter for converts (15:22–29)

ACTS 15:28–29—Paul is given apostolic letter for converts (15:22–29)

Theme	ACTS	Jewish Writings
Basic rules	**15:28–29** [28]For it seemed good to the Holy Ghost, and to us, to lay upon you no greater burden than these necessary things; [29]That ye abstain from meats offered to idols, and from blood, and from things strangled, and from fornication: from which if ye keep yourselves, ye shall do well. Fare ye well. **15:19–20** [19]Wherefore my sentence is, that we trouble not them, which from among the Gentiles are turned to God: [20]But that we write unto them, that they abstain from pollutions of idols, and from fornication, and from things strangled, and from blood.	**Gen 9:4** [4]But flesh with the life thereof, which is the blood thereof, shall ye not eat. **Lev 3:17** [17]It shall be a perpetual statute for your generations throughout all your dwellings, that ye eat neither fat nor blood. **Lev 17:10–14** [10]And whatsoever man there be of the house of Israel, or of the strangers that sojourn among you, that eateth any manner of blood; I will even set my face against that soul that eateth blood, and will cut him off from among his people. [11]For the life of the flesh is in the blood: and I have given it to you upon the altar to make an atonement for your souls: for it is the blood that maketh an atonement for the soul. [12]Therefore I said unto the children of Israel, No soul of you shall eat blood, neither shall any stranger that sojourneth among you eat blood. [13]And whatsoever man there be of the children of Israel, or of the strangers that sojourn among you, which hunteth and catcheth any beast or fowl that may be eaten; he shall even pour out the blood thereof, and cover it with dust. [14]For it is the life of all flesh; the blood of it is for the life thereof: therefore I said unto the children of Israel, Ye shall eat the blood of no manner of flesh: for the life of all flesh is the blood thereof: whosoever eateth it shall be cut off.

Apostolic letter received at Antioch (15:30–35)

ACTS 15:38

Theme	ACTS
Paul refuses Barnabas	**15:38** [38]But Paul thought not good to take him with them, who departed from them from Pamphylia, and went not with them to the work. **13:13** [13]Now when Paul and his company loosed from Paphos, they came to Perga in Pamphylia: and John departing from them returned to Jerusalem.

Paul and Barnabas separate (15:36–41)

ACTS 15:40—18:23 Second Missionary Journey

ACTS 16:1—Paul in Lyconia (Ref. Timothy) (16:1–5)

Theme	ACTS	Paul
Discipleship of Timothy	**16:1** [1]Then came he to Derbe and Lystra: and, behold, a certain disciple was there, named Timotheus, the son of a certain woman, which was a Jewess, and believed; but his father was a Greek:	**1 Tim 1:2 (Pseudo)** [2]Unto Timothy, my own son in the faith: Grace, mercy, and peace, from God our Father and Jesus Christ our Lord. **2 Tim 1:5 (Pseudo)** [5]When I call to remembrance the unfeigned faith that is in thee, which dwelt first in thy grandmother Lois, and thy mother Eunice; and I am persuaded that in thee also.

ACTS 16:2—Paul in Lyconia (Ref. Timothy) (16:1–5)

Theme	ACTS	Paul
Mission reports	**16:2** [2]Which was well reported of by the brethren that were at Lystra and Iconium.	**Phil 2:20** [20]For I have no man likeminded, who will naturally care for your state.

Paul—Phrygia, Galatia, Mysia (Holy Spirit blocks Asia and Bithyara (16:6–10)

Paul—Troas, Samothrace, Neopolis, Philippi, Lydia's place, Baptisms (16:11–15)

ACTS 16:22–23—Paul, a Roman citizen, imprisoned without due rights

Theme	ACTS	Paul
Opposition to mission	**16:22–23** [22]And the multitude rose up together against them: and the magistrates rent off their clothes, and commanded to beat them. [23]And when they had laid many stripes upon them, they cast them into prison, charging the jailor to keep them safely:	**2 Cor 11:25** [25]Thrice was I beaten with rods, once was I stoned, thrice I suffered shipwreck, a night and a day I have been in the deep; **Phil 1:30** [30]Having the same conflict which ye saw in me, and now hear to be in me. **1 Thes 2:2** [2]But even after that we had suffered before, and were shamefully entreated, as ye know, at Philippi, we were bold in our God to speak unto you the gospel of God with much contention.

Paul heals woman of fortune telling; he is imprisoned, then released 16:25–40

ACTS 16:37—Asks for respectful treatment (16:25–40)

Theme	ACTS
Prison and Roman law	**16:37** [37]But Paul said unto them, They have beaten us openly uncondemned, being Romans, and have cast us into prison; and now do they thrust us out privily? nay verily; but let them come themselves and fetch us out. **22:25** [25]And as they bound him with thongs, Paul said unto the centurion that stood by, Is it lawful for you to scourge a man that is a Roman, and uncondemned?

ACTS 16:38—Authorities fearful (16:25–40)

Theme	ACTS
Authorities feared Roman law	**16:38** [38]And the serjeants told these words unto the magistrates: and they feared, when they heard that they were Romans. **22:29** [29]Then straightway they departed from him which should have examined him: and the chief captain also was afraid, after he knew that he was a Roman, and because he had bound him.

Paul—Thessalonica 17:1–9

ACTS 17:1—Paul at Thessalonica (17:1–9)

Theme	ACTS	Paul
Mission at Thessalonica	**17:1** [1]Now when they had passed through Amphipolis and Apollonia, they came to Thessalonica, where was a synagogue of the Jews:	**1 Thes 2:1–2** [1]For yourselves, brethren, know our entrance in unto you, that it was not in vain: [2]But even after that we had suffered before, and were shamefully entreated, as ye know, at Philippi, we were bold in our God to speak unto you the gospel of God with much contention.

ACTS 17:3—Paul at Thessalonica (17:1–9)

Theme	ACTS	Lk
Christ must suffer	**17:3** [3]Opening and alleging, that Christ must needs have suffered, and risen again from the dead; and that this Jesus, whom I preach unto you, is Christ. **3:18** [18]But those things, which God before had showed by the mouth of all his prophets, that Christ should suffer, he hath so fulfilled.	**24:25–26** [25]Then he said unto them, O fools, and slow of heart to believe all that the prophets have spoken: [26]Ought not Christ to have suffered these things, and to enter into his glory? **24:46** [46]And said unto them, Thus it is written, and thus it behoved Christ to suffer, and to rise from the dead the third day:

ACTS 17:5—Paul at Thessalonica (17:1–9)

Theme	ACTS	Paul
Jewish envy	**17:5** [5]But the Jews which believed not, moved with envy, took unto them certain lewd fellows of the baser sort, and gathered a company, and set all the city on an uproar, and assaulted the house of Jason, and sought to bring them out to the people.	**Rom 16:21** [21]Timotheus my workfellow, and Lucius, and Jason, and Sosipater, my kinsmen, salute you.

ACTS 17:7—Paul at Thessalonica (17:1–9)

Theme	ACTS	Lk	Jn
King of earth is not king of heaven	**17:7** [7]Whom Jason hath received: and these all do contrary to the decrees of Caesar, saying that there is another king, one Jesus.	**23:2** [2]And they began to accuse him, saying, We found this fellow perverting the nation, and forbidding to give tribute to Caesar, saying that he himself is Christ a King.	**19:12–15** [12]And from thenceforth Pilate sought to release him: but the Jews cried out, saying, If thou let this man go, thou art not Caesar's friend: whosoever maketh himself a king speaketh against Caesar. [13]When Pilate therefore heard that saying, he brought Jesus forth, and sat down in the judgment seat in a place that is called the Pavement, but in the Hebrew, Gabbatha. [14]And it was the preparation of the passover, and about the sixth hour: and he saith unto the Jews, Behold your King! [15]But they cried out, Away with him, away with him, crucify him. Pilate saith unto them, Shall I crucify your King? The chief priests answered, We have no king but Caesar.

Paul—Berea 17:10–15

ACTS 17:11—Paul at Berea (17:10–15)

Theme	ACTS	Jn
Receiving the Word	**17:11** [11]These were more noble than those in Thessalonica, in that they received the word with all readiness of mind, and searched the scriptures daily, whether those things were so.	**5:39** [39]Search the scriptures; for in them ye think ye have eternal life: and they are they which testify of me.

ACTS 17:14—Paul at Berea (17:10–15)

Theme	ACTS	Paul
Dispersing ministers	**17:14** [14]And then immediately the brethren sent away Paul to go as it were to the sea: but Silas and Timotheus abode there still.	**1 Thes 3:1–2** [1]Wherefore when we could no longer forbear, we thought it good to be left at Athens alone; [2]And sent Timotheus, our brother, and minister of God, and our fellowlabourer in the gospel of Christ, to establish you, and to comfort you concerning your faith:

Paul—Athens 17:16–21

ACTS 17:19—Paul at Athens (17:16–21)

Theme	ACTS	Paul
Hearing the Word	**17:19** [19]And they took him, and brought him unto Areopagus, saying, May we know what this new doctrine, whereof thou speakest, is?	**1 Cor 1:22** [22]For the Jews require a sign, and the Greeks seek after wisdom:

Paul's speech at Aeropagus 17:22–34

ACTS 17:24—Paul's speech at Aeropagus (17:22–34)

Theme	ACTS
God is Lord over heaven and earth	**17:24** [24]God that made the world and all things therein, seeing that he is Lord of heaven and earth, dwelleth not in temples made with hands; **7:48–50** [48]Howbeit the most High dwelleth not in temples made with hands; as saith the prophet, [49]Heaven is my throne, and earth is my footstool: what house will ye build me? saith the Lord: or what is the place of my rest? [50]Hath not my hand made all these things?

ACTS 17:27—Paul's speech at Aeropagus (17:22–34)

Theme	ACTS	Paul
Need to seek the Lord	**17:27** [27]That they should seek the Lord, if haply they might feel after him, and find him, though he be not far from every one of us:	**Rom 1:19** [19]Because that which may be known of God is manifest in them; for God hath showed it unto them.

Jewish Writings
Gen 1:1
[1]In the beginning God created the heaven and the earth.
1 Kgs 8:27
[27]But will God indeed dwell on the earth? behold, the heaven and heaven of heavens cannot contain thee; how much less this house that I have builded?
Is 42:5
[5]Thus saith God the LORD, he that created the heavens, and stretched them out; he that spread forth the earth, and that which cometh out of it; he that giveth breath unto the people upon it, and spirit to them that walk therein:

Jewish Writings
Wis 13:6
[6]But yet for this they are the less to be blamed: for they peradventure err, seeking God, and desirous to find him.
Jer 23:23
[23]Am I a God at hand, saith the LORD, and not a God afar off?

ACTS 17:29—Paul's speech at Aeropagus (17:22–34)

Theme	ACTS	Paul
God's Way is wiser than that of humans	**17:29** [29]Forasmuch then as we are the offspring of God, we ought not to think that the Godhead is like unto gold, or silver, or stone, graven by art and man's device. **19:26** [26]Moreover ye see and hear, that not alone at Ephesus, but almost throughout all Asia, this Paul hath persuaded and turned away much people, saying that they be no gods, which are made with hands:	**Rom 1:22–23** [22]Professing themselves to be wise, they became fools, [23]And changed the glory of the uncorruptible God into an image made like to corruptible man, and to birds, and fourfooted beasts, and creeping things.

ACTS 17:31—Paul's speech at Aeropagus (17:22–34)

Theme	ACTS
Judgment	**17:31** [31]Because he hath appointed a day, in the which he will judge the world in righteousness by that man whom he hath ordained; whereof he hath given assurance unto all men, in that he hath raised him from the dead. **10:42** [42]And he commanded us to preach unto the people, and to testify that it is he which was ordained of God to be the Judge of quick and dead.

Paul—Corinth 18:1–11

ACTS 18:2—Paul at Corinth (18:1–11)

Theme	ACTS	Paul
Gathering workers	**18:2** [2]And found a certain Jew named Aquila, born in Pontus, lately come from Italy, with his wife Priscilla; (because that Claudius had commanded all Jews to depart from Rome:) and came unto them.	**Rom 16:3** [3]Greet Priscilla and Aquila my helpers in Christ Jesus:

Jewish Writings

Is 40:18–20

[18]To whom then will ye liken God? or what likeness will ye compare unto him? [19]The workman melteth a graven image, and the goldsmith spreadeth it over with gold, and casteth silver chains. [20]He that is so impoverished that he hath no oblation chooseth a tree that will not rot; he seeketh unto him a cunning workman to prepare a graven image, that shall not be moved.

Is 44:10–17

[10]Who hath formed a god, or molten a graven image that is profitable for nothing? [11]Behold, all his fellows shall be ashamed: and the workmen, they are of men: let them all be gathered together, let them stand up; yet they shall fear, and they shall be ashamed together. [12]The smith with the tongs both worketh in the coals, and fashioneth it with hammers, and worketh it with the strength of his arms: yea, he is hungry, and his strength faileth: he drinketh no water, and is faint. [13]The carpenter stretcheth out his rule; he marketh it out with a line; he fitteth it with planes, and he marketh it out with the compass, and maketh it after the figure of a man, according to the beauty of a man; that it may remain in the house. [14]He heweth him down cedars, and taketh the cypress and the oak, which he strengtheneth for himself among the trees of the forest: he planteth an ash, and the rain doth nourish it. [15]Then shall it be for a man to burn: for he will take thereof, and warm himself; yea, he kindleth it, and baketh bread; yea, he maketh a god, and worshippeth it; he maketh it a graven image, and falleth down thereto. [16]He burneth part thereof in the fire; with part thereof he eateth flesh; he roasteth roast, and is satisfied: yea, he warmeth himself, and saith, Aha, I am warm, I have seen the fire: [17]And the residue thereof he maketh a god, even his graven image: he falleth down unto it, and worshippeth it, and prayeth unto it, and saith, Deliver me; for thou art my god.

ACTS 18:6—Paul at Corinth (18:1–11)

Theme	ACTS	Mt
Mission and opposition	**18:6** [6]And when they opposed themselves, and blasphemed, he shook his raiment, and said unto them, Your blood be upon your own heads; I am clean: from henceforth I will go unto the Gentiles. **13:51** [51]But they shook off the dust of their feet against them, and came unto Iconium.	**9:35–38** [35]And all that dwelt at Lydda and Saron saw him, and turned to the Lord. [36]Now there was at Joppa a certain disciple named Tabitha, which by interpretation is called Dorcas: this woman was full of good works and almsdeeds which she did. [37]And it came to pass in those days, that she was sick, and died: whom when they had washed, they laid her in an upper chamber. [38]And forasmuch as Lydda was nigh to Joppa, and the disciples had heard that Peter was there, they sent unto him two men, desiring him that he would not delay to come to them. **10:5–15** [5]And now send men to Joppa, and call for one Simon, whose surname is Peter: [6]He lodgeth with one Simon a tanner, whose house is by the sea side: he shall tell thee what thou oughtest to do. [7]And when the angel which spake unto Cornelius was departed, he called two of his household servants, and a devout soldier of them that waited on him continually; [8]And when he had declared all these things unto them, he sent them to Joppa. [9]On the morrow, as they went on their journey, and drew nigh unto the city, Peter went up upon the housetop to pray about the sixth hour: [10]And he became very hungry, and would have eaten: but while they made ready, he fell into a trance, [11]And saw heaven opened, and a certain vessel descending unto him, as it had been a great sheet knit at the four corners, and let down to the earth: [12]Wherein were all manner of fourfooted beasts of the earth, and wild beasts, and creeping things, and fowls of the air. [13]And there came a voice to him, Rise, Peter; kill, and eat. [14]But Peter said, Not so, Lord; for I have never eaten any thing that is common or unclean. [15]And the voice spake unto him again the second time, What God hath cleansed, that call not thou common. **10:16** [16]This was done thrice: and the vessel was received up again into heaven. **10:40** [40]Him God raised up the third day, and showed him openly; **11:20** [20]And some of them were men of Cyprus and Cyrene, which, when they were come to Antioch, spake unto the Grecians, preaching the Lord Jesus. **18:5** [5]And when Silas and Timotheus were come from Macedonia, Paul was pressed in the spirit, and testified to the Jews that Jesus was Christ. **27:24–25** [24]When Pilate saw that he could prevail nothing, but that rather a tumult was made, he took water, and washed his hands before the multitude, saying, I am innocent of the blood of this just person: see ye to it. [25]Then answered all the people, and said, His blood be on us, and on our children.

Mk
3:14–15
[14]And he ordained twelve, that they should be with him, and that he might send them forth to preach, [15]And to have power to heal sicknesses, and to cast out devils:
6:7–13
[7]And he called unto him the twelve, and began to send them forth by two and two; and gave them power over unclean spirits; [8]And commanded them that they should take nothing for their journey, save a staff only; no scrip, no bread, no money in their purse: [9]But be shod with sandals; and not put on two coats. [10]And he said unto them, In what place soever ye enter into an house, there abide till ye depart from that place. [11]And whosoever shall not receive you, nor hear you, when ye depart thence, shake off the dust under your feet for a testimony against them. Verily I say unto you, It shall be more tolerable for Sodom and Gomorrha in the day of judgment, than for that city. [12]And they went out, and preached that men should repent. [13]And they cast out many devils, and anointed with oil many that were sick, and healed them.
9:37
[37]Whosoever shall receive one of such children in my name, receiveth me: and whosoever shall receive me, receiveth not me, but him that sent me.

Acts 18:6 continued on next page

ACTS 18:6—Paul at Corinth (18:1–11) (*continued*)

Theme	ACTS	Lk
(*Cont.*) **Mission and opposition**	**18:6** (above) **13:51** (above)	**1:76** [76]And thou, child, shalt be called the prophet of the Highest: for thou shalt go before the face of the Lord to prepare his ways; **3:4** [4]As it is written in the book of the words of Esaias the prophet, saying, The voice of one crying in the wilderness, Prepare ye the way of the Lord, make his paths straight. **7:27** [27]This is he, of whom it is written, Behold, I send my messenger before thy face, which shall prepare thy way before thee. **9:1–6** [1]Then he called his twelve disciples together, and gave them power and authority over all devils, and to cure diseases. [2]And he sent them to preach the kingdom of God, and to heal the sick. [3]And he said unto them, Take nothing for your journey, neither staves, nor scrip, neither bread, neither money; neither have two coats apiece. [4]And whatsoever house ye enter into, there abide, and thence depart. [5]And whosoever will not receive you, when ye go out of that city, shake off the very dust from your feet for a testimony against them. [6]And they departed, and went through the towns, preaching the gospel, and healing every where. **9:48** [48]And said unto them, Whosoever shall receive this child in my name receiveth me: and whosoever shall receive me receiveth him that sent me: for he that is least among you all, the same shall be great. **9:51–52** [51]And it came to pass, when the time was come that he should be received up, he stedfastly set his face to go to Jerusalem, [52]And sent messengers before his face: and they went, and entered into a village of the Samaritans, to make ready for him. **10:10–11** But into whatsoever city ye enter, and they receive you not, go your ways out into the streets of the same, and say,[11]Even the very dust of your city, which cleaveth on us, we do wipe off against you: notwithstanding be ye sure of this, that the kingdom of God is come nigh unto you. **22:35–36** [35]And he said unto them, When I sent you without purse, and scrip, and shoes, lacked ye any thing? And they said, Nothing. [36]Then said he unto them, But now, he that hath a purse, let him take it, and likewise his scrip: and he that hath no sword, let him sell his garment, and buy one.

ACTS 18:7—Paul at Corinth (18:1–11)

Theme	ACTS
Firm in the Faith	**18:7** [7]And he departed thence, and entered into a certain man's house, named Justus, one that worshipped God, whose house joined hard to the synagogue. **13:46–47** [46]Then Paul and Barnabas waxed bold, and said, It was necessary that the word of God should first have been spoken to you: but seeing ye put it from you, and judge yourselves unworthy of everlasting life, lo, we turn to the Gentiles. [47]For so hath the Lord commanded us, saying, I have set thee to be a light of the Gentiles, that thou shouldest be for salvation unto the ends of the earth. **28:28** [28]Be it known therefore unto you, that the salvation of God is sent unto the Gentiles, and that they will hear it.

Jn	Other
4:35 [35]Say not ye, There are yet four months, and then cometh harvest? behold, I say unto you, Lift up your eyes, and look on the fields; for they are white already to harvest. **5:23** [23]That all men should honour the Son, even as they honour the Father. He that honoureth not the Son honoureth not the Father which hath sent him. **12:44–45** [44]Jesus cried and said, He that believeth on me, believeth not on me, but on him that sent me. [45]And he that seeth me seeth him that sent me. **12:48** [48]He that rejecteth me, and receiveth not my words, hath one that judgeth him: the word that I have spoken, the same shall judge him in the last day. **13:20** [20]Verily, verily, I say unto you, He that receiveth whomsoever I send receiveth me; and he that receiveth me receiveth him that sent me. **15:23** [23]He that hateth me hateth my Father also.	**2 Clem 5:2** [5:2]For the Lord says, "You will be like sheep in the midst of wolves." **GThom 14** [14]Jesus said, "If you fast, you will give rise to sin for yourselves; and if you pray, you will be condemned; and if you give alms, you will do harm to your spirits. When you go into any land and walk about in the districts, if they receive you, eat what they set before you, and heal the sick among them. For what goes into your mouth will not defile you, but that which issues from your mouth—it is that which will defile you." **GThom 73** [73]Jesus said, "The harvest is great but the laborers are few. Beseech the lord, therefore, to send out laborers to the harvest." **Q-Quelle** Commissioning of the 70: Acts 18:6/Mt 9:37-38, Mt 10:7-16/Lk 10:2-12 (QS 20/[Thom 13; 14.2]); Commissioning of the 12: Acts 18:6/Mt 10:1, 10:7-11, 10:14/Mk 6:6b-13/Lk 9:1-6; Whoever hears you hears me: Acts 18:6/Mt 10:40/Lk 10:13-15 (QS22); Jesus' witness to John: Acts 18:6/Mt 11:7-19, 21:31-32/Lk 7:24-35 (QS 17[Thom 74, 46] QS 18)

ACTS 18:8—Paul at Corinth (18:1–11)

Theme	ACTS	Paul
Faith in the Lord	**18:8** [8]And Crispus, the chief ruler of the synagogue, believed on the Lord with all his house; and many of the Corinthians hearing believed, and were baptized.	**1 Cor 1:14** [14]I thank God that I baptized none of you, but Crispus and Gaius;

ACTS 18:9–10—Paul at Corinth (18:1–11)

Theme	ACTS	Jewish Writings
Jesus' presence with believer	**18:9–10** [9]Then spake the Lord to Paul in the night by a vision, Be not afraid, but speak, and hold not thy peace: [10]For I am with thee, and no man shall set on thee to hurt thee: for I have much people in this city.	**Jer 1:8** [8]Be not afraid of their faces: for I am with thee to deliver thee, saith the LORD. **Jer 1:18** [18]For, behold, I have made thee this day a defenced city, and an iron pillar, and brazen walls against the whole land, against the kings of Judah, against the princes thereof, against the priests thereof, and against the people of the land.

Jews accuse Paul before Gallio (18:12–17)

Paul—Cenchreae, Ephesus, Caesarea, Syrian Antioch, Galatia, Phrygia 18:18–23

ACTS 18:18—Paul at Cenchreae, Ephesus, Caesarea, Syrian Antioch, Galatia, Phrygia (18:18–23)

Theme	ACTS	Jewish Writings
Ritual purification	**18:18** [18]And Paul after this tarried there yet a good while, and then took his leave of the brethren, and sailed thence into Syria, and with him Priscilla and Aquila; having shorn his head in Cenchrea: for he had a vow. **21:24** [24]Them take, and purify thyself with them, and be at charges with them, that they may shave their heads: and all may know that those things, whereof they were informed concerning thee, are nothing; but that thou thyself also walkest orderly, and keepest the law.	**Num 6:18** [18]And the Nazarite shall shave the head of his separation at the door of the tabernacle of the congregation, and shall take the hair of the head of his separation, and put it in the fire which is under the sacrifice of the peace offerings.

ACTS 18:24—20:6 Third Missionary Journey

ACTS 18:24—Early in Paul's Third Missionary Journey

Theme	ACTS	Paul
Faith in scriptures	**18:24** [24]And a certain Jew named Apollos, born at Alexandria, an eloquent man, and mighty in the scriptures, came to Ephesus.	**1 Cor 1:12** [12]Now this I say, that every one of you saith, I am of Paul; and I of Apollos; and I of Cephas; and I of Christ.

Paul at Ephesus 19:1–12

ACTS 19:1–7—Paul at Ephesus (19:1–12)

Theme	ACTS	Mt	Mk
Repent and baptism of the Holy Spirit	**19:1–7** 1And it came to pass, that, while Apollos was at Corinth, Paul having passed through the upper coasts came to Ephesus: and finding certain disciples, 2He said unto them, Have ye received the Holy Ghost since ye believed? And they said unto him, We have not so much as heard whether there be any Holy Ghost. 3And he said unto them, Unto what then were ye baptized? And they said, Unto John's baptism. 4Then said Paul, John verily baptized with the baptism of repentance, saying unto the people, that they should **believe on him which should come after him, that is, on Christ Jesus.** 5When they heard this, they were baptized in the name of the Lord Jesus. 6And when Paul had laid his hands upon them, the Holy Ghost came on them; and they spake with tongues, and prophesied. 7And all the men were about twelve. **1:5** 1Now there were in the church that was at Antioch certain prophets and teachers; as Barnabas, and Simeon that was called Niger, and Lucius of Cyrene, and Manaen, which had been brought up with Herod the tetrarch, and Saul. 2As they ministered to the Lord, and fasted, the Holy Ghost said, Separate me Barnabas and Saul for the work whereunto I have called them. 3And when they had fasted and prayed, and laid their hands on them, they sent them away.4So they, being sent forth by the Holy Ghost, departed unto Seleucia; and from thence they sailed to Cyprus. 5And when they were at Salamis, they preached the word of God in the synagogues of the Jews: and they had also John to their minister. **2:38** 38Then Peter said unto them, Repent, and be baptized every one of you in the name of Jesus Christ for the remission of sins, and ye shall receive the gift of the Holy Ghost. **8:15–17** 15But that on the good ground are they, which in an honest and good heart, having heard the word, keep it, and bring forth fruit with patience. 16No man, when he hath lighted a candle, covereth it with a vessel, or putteth it under a bed; but setteth it on a candlestick, that they which enter in may see the light. 17For nothing is secret, that shall not be made manifest; neither any thing hid, that shall not be known and come abroad. **11:16** 16Then remembered I the word of the Lord, how that he said, John indeed baptized with water; but ye shall be baptized with the Holy Ghost. **13:10** 10And said, O full of all subtlety and all mischief, thou child of the devil, thou enemy of all righteousness, wilt thou not cease to pervert the right ways of the Lord? **13:47** 47For so hath the Lord commanded us, saying, I have set thee to be a light of the Gentiles, that thou shouldest be for salvation unto the ends of the earth. **26:20** 20But showed first unto them of Damascus, and at Jerusalem, and throughout all the coasts of Judaea, and then to the Gentiles, that they should repent and turn to God, and do works meet for repentance. **28:28** 28Be it known therefore unto you, that the salvation of God is sent unto the Gentiles, and that they will hear it.	**1:10** 10And Ezekias begat Manasses; and Manasses begat Amon; and Amon begat Josias; **1:15** 15And Eliud begat Eleazar; and Eleazar begat Matthan; and Matthan begat Jacob; **14:3–4** 3For Herod had laid hold on John, and bound him, and put him in prison for Herodias' sake, his brother Philip's wife. 4For John said unto him, It is not lawful for thee to have her.	**1:2–8** 2Abraham begat Isaac; and Isaac begat Jacob; and Jacob begat Judas and his brethren; 3And Judas begat Phares and Zara of Thamar; and Phares begat Esrom; and Esrom begat Aram; 4And Aram begat Aminadab; and Aminadab begat Naasson; and Naasson begat Salmon; 5And Salmon begat Booz of Rachab; and Booz begat Obed of Ruth; and Obed begat Jesse; 6And Jesse begat David the king; and David the king begat Solomon of her that had been the wife of Urias; 7And Solomon begat Roboam; and Roboam begat Abia; and Abia begat Asa; 8And Asa begat Josaphat; and Josaphat begat Joram; and Joram begat Ozias; **1:15** 15And Eliud begat Eleazar; and Eleazar begat Matthan; and Matthan begat Jacob;

ACTS 19:1–7—Paul at Ephesus (19:1–12)

Theme	ACTS	Lk
(*Cont.*) Repent and baptism of the Holy Spirit	**19:1–7 (above)** **1:5 (above)** **2:38 (above)** **8:15–17 (above)** **10:44–46 (above)** **11:16 (above)** **13:10 (above)** **13:47 (above)** **26:20 (above)** **28:28 (above)**	**1:76** 76 And thou, child, shalt be called the prophet of the Highest: for thou shalt go before the face of the Lord to prepare his ways; **3:1–20** 1 Now in the fifteenth year of the reign of Tiberius Caesar, Pontius Pilate being governor of Judaea, and Herod being tetrarch of Galilee, and his brother Philip tetrarch of Ituraea and of the region of Trachonitis, and Lysanias the tetrarch of abilene, 2 Annas and Caiaphas being the high priests, the word of God came unto John the son of Zacharias in the wilderness. 3 And he came into all the country about Jordan, preaching the baptism of repentance for the remission of sins; 4 As it is written in the book of the words of Esaias the prophet, saying, The voice of one crying in the wilderness, Prepare ye the way of the Lord, make his paths straight. 5 Every valley shall be filled, and every mountain and hill shall be brought low; and the crooked shall be made straight, and the rough ways shall be made smooth; 6 And all flesh shall see the salvation of God. 7 Then said he to the multitude that came forth to be baptized of him, O generation of vipers, who hath warned you to flee from the wrath to come? 8 Bring forth therefore fruits worthy of repentance, and begin not to say within yourselves, We have Abraham to our father: for I say unto you, That God is able of these stones to raise up children unto Abraham. 9 And now also the axe is laid unto the root of the trees: every tree therefore which bringeth not forth good fruit is hewn down, and cast into the fire. 10 And the people asked him, saying, What shall we do then? 11 He answereth and saith unto them, He that hath two coats, let him impart to him that hath none; and he that hath meat, let him do likewise. 12 Then came also publicans to be baptized, and said unto him, Master, what shall we do? 13 And he said unto them, Exact no more than that which is appointed you. 14 And the soldiers likewise demanded of him, saying, And what shall we do? And he said unto them, Do violence to no man, neither accuse any falsely; and be content with your wages. 15 And as the people were in expectation, and all men mused in their hearts of John, whether he were the Christ, or not; 16 John answered, saying unto them all, I indeed baptize you with water; but one mightier than I cometh, the latchet of whose shoes I am not worthy to unloose: he shall baptize you with the Holy Ghost and with fire: 17 Whose fan is in his hand, and he will thoroughly purge his floor, and will gather the wheat into his garner; but the chaff he will burn with fire unquenchable. 18 And many other things in his exhortation preached he unto the people. 19 But Herod the tetrarch, being reproved by him for Herodias his brother Philip's wife, and for all the evils which Herod had done, 20 Added yet this above all, that he shut up John in prison. **6:43–44** 43 For a good tree bringeth not forth corrupt fruit; neither doth a corrupt tree bring forth good fruit. 44 For every tree is known by his own fruit. For of thorns men do not gather figs, nor of a bramble bush gather they grapes. **7:27** 27 This is he, of whom it is written, Behold, I send my messenger before thy face, which shall prepare thy way before thee. **13:6–9** 6 He spake also this parable; A certain man had a fig tree planted in his vineyard; and he came and sought fruit thereon, and found none. 7 Then said he unto the dresser of his vineyard, Behold, these three years I come seeking fruit on this fig tree, and find none: cut it down; why cumbereth it the ground? 8 And he answering said unto him, Lord, let it alone this year also, till I shall dig about it, and dung it: 9 And if it bear fruit, well: and if not, then after that thou shalt cut it down. **13:31** 31 The same day there came certain of the Pharisees, saying unto him, Get thee out, and depart hence: for Herod will kill thee. **23:8** 8 And when Herod saw Jesus, he was exceeding glad: for he was desirous to see him of a long season, because he had heard many things of him; and he hoped to have seen some miracle done by him.

Jn	Jewish Writings
1:3 [3]All things were made by him; and without him not anything made that was made **1:31–32** [31]And I knew him not: but that he should be made manifest to Israel, therefore am I come baptizing with water. [32]And John bare record, saying, I saw the Spirit descending from heaven like a dove, and it abode upon him. **8:39** [39]They answered and said unto him, Abraham is our father. Jesus saith unto them, If ye were Abraham's children, ye would do the works of Abraham.	**1 Kgs 1:8** [8]But Zadok the priest, and Benaiah the son of Jehoiada, and Nathan the prophet, and Shimei, and Rei, and the mighty men which belonged to David, were not with Adonijah. **Is 40:3–6** [3]The voice of him that crieth in the wilderness, Prepare ye the way of the LORD, make straight in the desert a highway for our God. [4]Every valley shall be exalted, and every mountain and hill shall be made low: and the crooked shall be made straight, and the rough places plain: [5]And the glory of the LORD shall be revealed, and all flesh shall see it together: for the mouth of the LORD hath spoken it. [6]The voice said, Cry. And he said, What shall I cry? All flesh is grass, and all the goodliness thereof is as the flower of the field:

Acts 19:1–7 continued on next page

ACTS 19:1–7—Paul at Ephesus (19:1–12) (*continued*)

Theme	ACTS	Other
(*Cont.*) Baptism of the Holy Spirit (variation of supra)	**19:1–7 (above)** **1:5 (above)** **2:38 (above)** **8:15–17 (above)** **10:44–46 (above)** **11:16 (above)** **13:10 (above)** **13:47 (above)** **26:20 (above)** **28:28 (above)**	**1 ApocJas** It is the Lord who spoke with me: "See now the completion of my redemption. I have given you a sign of these things, James, my brother. For not without reason have I called you my brother, although you are not my brother materially. And I am not ignorant concerning you; so that when I give you a sign—know and hear. Nothing existed except Him-who-is. He is unnameable and ineffable. I myself am also unnameable, from Him-who-is, just as I have been given a number of names—two from Him-who-is.. . .so that the sons of Him-who-is might know what things are theirs and what things are alien (to them). Behold, I shall reveal to you everything of this mystery.. . . As for what has come forth from him who has no measure, I shall give a sign concerning their measure. . .has been given [. . .] on account of [. . .] Him-who-is [. . .] they are unnumbered. If you want to give them a number now, you will not be able to do so until you cast away from your blind thought, this bond of flesh which encircles you. And then you will reach Him-who-is. And you will no longer be James; rather you are the One-who-is. And all those who are unnumbered will all have been named. You walked in mud, and your garments were not soiled, and you have not been buried in their filth, and you have not been caught. . . . ". . .do not be concerned for anything else except your redemption. For behold, I shall complete this destiny upon this earth as I have said from the heavens. And I shall reveal to you your redemption." . . . But I shall call upon the imperishable knowledge, which is Sophia who is in the Father (and) who is the mother of Achamoth. Achamoth had no father nor male consort, but she is female from a female. She produced you without a male, since she was alone (and) in ignorance as to what lives through her mother because she thought that she alone existed. But I shall cry out to her mother. And then they will fall into confusion (and) will blame their root and the race of their mother. But you will go up to what is yours [. . .] you will [. . .] the Pre-existent One." . . . "They are a type of the twelve disciples and the twelve pairs, [. . .] Achamoth, which is translated 'Sophia'. And who I myself am, (and) who the imperishable Sophia (is) through whom you will be redeemed, and (who are) all the sons of Him-who-is—these things they have known and have hidden within them. You are to hide <these things> within you, and you are to keep silence. . . . James said, "I am satisfied [. . .] and they are [. . .] my soul. Yet another thing I ask of you: who are the seven women who have been your disciples? And behold all women bless you. I also am amazed how powerless vessels have become strong by a perception which is in them." The Lord said, "You [. . .] well [. . .] a spirit of [. . .], a spirit of thought, a spirit of counsel of a [. . .], a spirit [. . .] a spirit of knowledge [. . .] of their fear. [. . .] when we had passed through the breath of this archon who is named Adonaios [. . .] him and [. . .] he was ignorant [. . .] when I came forth from him, he remembered that I am a son of his. He was gracious to me at that time as his son. And then, before <I> appeared here, <he> cast them among this people. And from the place of heaven the prophets [. . .]." . . .James said, "Rabbi, [. . .] I [. . .] all together [. . .] in them especially [. . .]." The Lord said, "James, I praise you [. . .] walk upon the earth [. . .] the words while he [. . .] on the [. . .]. For cast away from you the cup which is bitterness. For some from [. . .] set themselves against you. For you have begun to understand their roots from beginning to end. Cast away from yourself all lawlessness. And beware lest they envy you. When you speak these words of this perception, encourage these four: Salome and Mariam and Martha and Arsinoe [. . .] since he takes some [. . .] to me he is [. . .] burnt offerings and [. . .]. But I [. . .] not in this way; but [. . .] first-fruits of the [. . .] upward [. . .] so that the power of God might appear. The perishable has gone up to the imperishable and the female element has attained to this male element. . . . "But I shall go forth and shall reveal that they believed in you, that they may be content with their blessing and salvation, and this revelation may come to pass." **GEbi 2 and 3** [2]For by chopping off the genealogies of Matthew they made their gospel begin as we indicated before, with the words: "And so in the days of Herod, King of Judea, when Caiaphas was high priest, a certain one named John came baptizing a baptism of repentance in the Jordan River." (Epiphanius, Panarion, 30, 14, 3) [3]And so John was baptizing, and Pharisees came to him and were baptized, as was all of Jerusalem. John wore a garment of camel hair and a leather belt around his waist; and his food was wild honey that tasted like manna, like a cake cooked in oil. (Epiphanius, Panarion, 30, 13, 4-5)

ACTS 19:1–7—Paul at Ephesus (19:1–12) (*continued*)

Theme	ACTS	Other
(*Cont.*) Baptism of the Holy Spirit (variation of supra)	19:1–7 (above) 1:5 (above) 2:38 (above) 8:15–17 (above) 10:44–46 (above) 11:16 (above) 13:10 (above) 13:47 (above) 26:20 (above) 28:28 (above)	(*Continued*) **Q-Quelle** Preaching of John: Acts 19:1-7/[Mt 3:7-10, Mt 3:11-12]/Mk 1:7-8/Lk 3:7-9, Lk 3:15-18 (QS5); Fruits: Acts 19:1-7/ [Mt 7:15-20, 12:33-35]/Lk 6:43-45 (QS13/Thom 45]); Jesus' witness to John: Acts 19:1-7/ [Mt 11:7-19, 21:31-32]/Lk 7:24-35 (QS 17)/[Thom 74, 46] (QS18), [Lk 16:16 (QS 56)]

ACTS 19:4—Paul at Ephesus (19:1–12)

Theme	ACTS	Mt
Baptism, in general	**19:4** [4]Then said Paul, John verily baptized with the baptism of repentance, saying unto the people, that they should believe on him which should come after him, that is, on Christ Jesus. **1:5** [5]For John truly baptized with water; but ye shall be baptized with the Holy Ghost not many days hence. **11:16** [16]Then remembered I the word of the Lord, how that he said, John indeed baptized with water; but ye shall be baptized with the Holy Ghost. **13:24–25** [24]When John had first preached before his coming the baptism of repentance to all the people of Israel. [25]And as John fulfilled his course, he said, Whom think ye that I am? I am not he. But, behold, there cometh one after me, whose shoes of his feet I am not worthy to loose. **19:1–7** [1]And it came to pass, that, while Apollos was at Corinth, Paul having passed through the upper coasts came to Ephesus: and finding certain disciples, [2]He said unto them, Have ye received the Holy Ghost since ye believed? And they said unto him, We have not so much as heard whether there be any Holy Ghost. [3]And he said unto them, Unto what then were ye baptized? And they said, Unto John's baptism. [4]Then said Paul, John verily baptized with the baptism of repentance, saying unto the people, that they should believe on him which should come after him, that is, on Christ Jesus. [5]When they heard this, they were baptized in the name of the Lord Jesus. [6]And when Paul had laid his hands upon them, the Holy Ghost came on them; and they spake with tongues, and prophesied. [7]And all the men were about twelve.	**3:1–12** [1]In those days came John the Baptist, preaching in the wilderness of Judaea, [2]And saying, Repent ye: for the kingdom of heaven is at hand. [3]For this is he that was spoken of by the prophet Esaias, saying, The voice of one crying in the wilderness, Prepare ye the way of the Lord, make his paths straight. [4]And the same John had his raiment of camel's hair, and a leathern girdle about his loins; and his meat was locusts and wild honey. [5]Then went out to him Jerusalem, and all Judaea, and all the region round about Jordan, [6]And were baptized of him in Jordan, confessing their sins. [7]But when he saw many of the Pharisees and Sadducees come to his baptism, he said unto them, O generation of vipers, who hath warned you to flee from the wrath to come? [8]Bring forth therefore fruits meet for repentance: [9]And think not to say within yourselves, We have Abraham to our father: for I say unto you, that God is able of these stones to raise up children unto Abraham. [10]And now also the axe is laid unto the root of the trees: therefore every tree which bringeth not forth good fruit is hewn down, and cast into the fire. [11]I indeed baptize you with water unto repentance: but he that cometh after me is mightier than I, whose shoes I am not worthy to bear: he shall baptize you with the Holy Ghost, and with fire: [12]Whose fan is in his hand, and he will thoroughly purge his floor, and gather his wheat into the garner; but he will burn up the chaff with unquenchable fire. **7:19** [19]Every tree that bringeth not forth good fruit is hewn down, and cast into the fire.

ACTS 19:12—Paul at Ephesus (19:1–12)

Theme	ACTS	Lk
Holiness heals	**19:12** [12]So that from his body were brought unto the sick handkerchiefs or aprons, and the diseases departed from them, and the evil spirits went out of them. **5:15–16** [15]Insomuch that they brought forth the sick into the streets, and laid them on beds and couches, that at the least the shadow of Peter passing by might overshadow some of them. [16]There came also a multitude out of the cities round about unto Jerusalem, bringing sick folks, and them which were vexed with unclean spirits: and they were healed every one.	**8:44–47** [44]Came behind him, and touched the border of his garment: and immediately her issue of blood stanched. [45]And Jesus said, Who touched me? When all denied, Peter and they that were with him said, Master, the multitude throng thee and press thee, and sayest thou, Who touched me? [46]And Jesus said, Somebody hath touched me: for I perceive that virtue is gone out of me. [47]And when the woman saw that she was not hid, she came trembling, and falling down before him, she declared unto him before all the people for what cause she had touched him, and how she was healed immediately.

Mk	Lk	Other
1:4 [4]And Aram begat Aminadab; and Aminadab begat Naasson; and Naasson begat Salmon; **1:8** [8]I indeed have baptized you with water: but he shall baptize you with the Holy Ghost. **1:15** [15]And Eliud begat Eleazar; and Eleazar begat Matthan; and Matthan begat Jacob;	**3:16** [16]John answered, saying unto them all, I indeed baptize you with water; but one mightier than I cometh, the latchet of whose shoes I am not worthy to unloose: he shall baptize you with the Holy Ghost and with fire:	**GEbi 2 and 3** [2]For by chopping off the genealogies of Matthew they made their gospel begin as we indicated before, with the words: "And so in the days of Herod, King of Judea, when Caiaphas was high priest, a certain one named John came baptizing a baptism of repentance in the Jordan River." [3]And so John was baptizing, and Pharisees came to him and were baptized, as was all of Jerusalem. John wore a garment of camel hair and a leather belt around his waist; and his food was wild honey that tasted like manna, like a cake cooked in oil. (Epiphanius, Panarion, 30, 13, 4-5) **Q-Quelle** Preaching of John: Acts 19:4/Mt 3:7-10, Mt 3:11-12/ Mk 1:7-8/[Lk 3:7-9], Lk 3:15-18 (QS5); Fruits: Acts 19:4/Mt 7:15-20, [12:33-35]/[Lk 6:43-45 (QS13/ Thom 45])

Paul's name confessed by evil spirits during exorcism (19:13–20)

ACTS 19:21—Paul's name confessed by evil spirits during exorcism (19:13–20)

Theme	ACTS	Paul
Paul's destination is Rome	**19:21** [21]After these things were ended, Paul purposed in the spirit, when he had passed through Macedonia and Achaia, to go to Jerusalem, saying, After I have been there, I must also see Rome. **23:11** [11]And the night following the Lord stood by him, and said, Be of good cheer, Paul: for as thou hast testified of me in Jerusalem, so must thou bear witness also at Rome.	**Rom 1:13** [13]Now I would not have you ignorant, brethren, that oftentimes I purposed to come unto you, (but was let hitherto,) that I might have some fruit among you also, even as among other Gentiles. **Rom 15:22–32** [22]For which cause also I have been much hindered from coming to you. [23]But now having no more place in these parts, and having a great desire these many years to come unto you; [24]Whensoever I take my journey into Spain, I will come to you: for I trust to see you in my journey, and to be brought on my way thitherward by you, if first I be somewhat filled with your company. [25]But now I go unto Jerusalem to minister unto the saints. [26]For it hath pleased them of Macedonia and Achaia to make a certain contribution for the poor saints which are at Jerusalem. [27]It hath pleased them verily; and their debtors they are. For if the Gentiles have been made partakers of their spiritual things, their duty is also to minister unto them in carnal things. [28]When therefore I have performed this, and have sealed to them this fruit, I will come by you into Spain. [29]And I am sure that, when I come unto you, I shall come in the fulness of the blessing of the gospel of Christ. [30]Now I beseech you, brethren, for the Lord Jesus Christ's sake, and for the love of the Spirit, that ye strive together with me in your prayers to God for me; [31]That I may be delivered from them that do not believe in Judaea; and that my service which I have for Jerusalem may be accepted of the saints; [32]That I may come unto you with joy by the will of God, and may with you be refreshed. [33]Now the God of peace be with you all. Amen.

Paul's plans (19:21–22)

ACTS 19:26—Ephesus' idols silversmiths retaliate against Paul's teachings (19:23–40)

Theme	ACTS
Idols cannot serve God's purposes	**19:26** [26]Moreover ye see and hear, that not alone at Ephesus, but almost throughout all Asia, this Paul hath persuaded and turned away much people, saying that they be no gods, which are made with hands: **17:29** [29]Forasmuch then as we are the offspring of God, we ought not to think that the Godhead is like unto gold, or silver, or stone, graven by art and man's device.

Paul—Macedonia and Greece 20:1–3

ACTS 20:1—Paul at Macedonia and Greece (20:1–3)

Theme	ACTS	Paul
Mission in Macedonia	**20:1** [1]And after the uproar was ceased, Paul called unto him the disciples, and embraced them, and departed for to go into Macedonia.	**1 Cor 16:1, 4** [1]Now concerning the collection for the saints, as I have given order to the churches of Galatia, even so do ye. . . . [4]And if it be meet that I go also, they shall go with me.

Paul—Troas 20:4–6

ACTS 20:4—Paul at Troas (20:4–6)

Theme	ACTS	Paul
Paul's mission and authenticity	**20:4** [4]And there accompanied him into Asia Sopater of Berea; and of the Thessalonians, Aristarchus and Secundus; and Gaius of Derbe, and Timotheus; and of Asia, Tychicus and Trophimus.	**Rom 16:21** [21]The salutation of me Paul with mine own hand.

ACTS 20:5—Paul at Troas (20:4–6)

Theme	ACTS	Paul
Paul's companions	**20:5** [5]These going before tarried for us at Troas. **21:29** [29](For they had seen before with him in the city Trophimus an Ephesian, whom they supposed that Paul had brought into the temple.)	**2 Tim 4:20 (Pseudo)** [20]Erastus abode at Corinth: but Trophimus have I left at Miletum sick.

ACTS 20:6–28:31 Paul's return to Palestine, trial and voyage to Rome to stand before Caesar

ACTS 20:7–12—Paul restores life of Euticus (20:7–12)

Theme	ACTS	Mt	Mk	Lk
God's power to raise the dead	**20:7–12** [7]And upon the first day of the week, when the disciples came together to break bread, Paul preached unto them, ready to depart on the morrow; and continued his speech until midnight. [8]And there were many lights in the upper chamber, where they were gathered together. [9]And there sat in a window a certain young man named Eutychus, being fallen into a deep sleep: and as Paul was long preaching, he sunk down with sleep, and fell down from the third loft, and was taken up dead. [10]And Paul went down, and fell on him, and embracing him said, Trouble not yourselves; for his life is in him. [11]When he therefore was come up again, and had broken bread, and eaten, and talked a long while, even till break of day, so he departed. [12]And they brought the young man alive, and were not a little comforted.	**9:24** [24]He said unto them, Give place: for the maid is not dead, but sleepeth. And they laughed him to scorn.	**5:39** [39]And when he was come in, he saith unto them, Why make ye this ado, and weep? the damsel is not dead, but sleepeth.	**7:11–17** [11]And it came to pass the day after, that he went into a city called Nain; and many of his disciples went with him, and much people. [12]Now when he came nigh to the gate of the city, behold, there was a dead man carried out, the only son of his mother, and she was a widow: and much people of the city was with her. [13]And when the Lord saw her, he had compassion on her, and said unto her, Weep not. [14]And he came and touched the bier: and they that bare him stood still. And he said, Young man, I say unto thee, Arise. [15]And he that was dead sat up, and began to speak. And he delivered him to his mother. [16]And there came a fear on all: and they glorified God, saying, That a great prophet is risen up among us; and, That God hath visited his people. [17]And this rumour of him went forth throughout all Judaea, and throughout all the region round about. **8:52** [52]And all wept, and bewailed her: but he said, Weep not; she is not dead, but sleepeth.

Paul—Miletus (20:13–16)

Paul—Speech at Ephesus 20:17–38

ACTS 20:23—Paul's speech at Ephesus (20:17–38)

Theme	ACTS
Witness and suffering	**20:23** [23]Save that the Holy Ghost witnesseth in every city, saying that bonds and afflictions abide me. **9:16** [16]For I will shew him how great things he must suffer for my name's sake.

ACTS 20:24—Paul's speech at Ephesus (20:17–38)

Theme	ACTS	Paul
Gospel testimony	**20:24** [24]But none of these things move me, neither count I my life dear unto myself, so that I might finish my course with joy, and the ministry, which I have received of the Lord Jesus, to testify the gospel of the grace of God.	**2 Tim 4:7 (Pseudo)** [7]I have fought a good fight, I have finished my course, I have kept the faith:

Jewish Writings

1 Kgs 17:17–24

[17]And it came to pass after these things, that the son of the woman, the mistress of the house, fell sick; and his sickness
was so sore, that there was no breath left in him. [18]And she said unto Elijah, What have I to do with thee, O thou man
of God? art thou come unto me to call my sin to remembrance, and to slay my son? [19]And he said unto her, Give me thy
son. And he took him out of her bosom, and carried him up into a loft, where he abode, and laid him upon his own bed.
[20]And he cried unto the LORD, and said, O LORD my God, hast thou also brought evil upon the widow with whom I
sojourn, by slaying her son? [21]And he stretched himself upon the child three times, and cried unto the LORD, and said,
O LORD my God, I pray thee, let this child's soul come into him again. [22]And the LORD heard the voice of Elijah; and
the soul of the child came into him again, and he revived. [23]And Elijah took the child, and brought him down out of the
chamber into the house, and delivered him unto his mother: and Elijah said, See, thy son liveth. [24]And the woman said
to Elijah, Now by this I know that thou art a man of God, and that the word of the LORD in thy mouth is truth.

2 Kgs 4:30–37

[30]And the mother of the child said, As the LORD liveth, and as thy soul liveth, I will not leave thee. And he arose, and
followed her. [31]And Gehazi passed on before them, and laid the staff upon the face of the child; but there was neither
voice, nor hearing. Wherefore he went again to meet him, and told him, saying, The child is not awaked. [32]And when
Elisha was come into the house, behold, the child was dead, and laid upon his bed. [33]He went in therefore, and shut the
door upon them twain, and prayed unto the LORD. [34]And he went up, and lay upon the child, and put his mouth upon
his mouth, and his eyes upon his eyes, and his hands upon his hands: and he stretched himself upon the child; and
the flesh of the child waxed warm. [35]Then he returned, and walked in the house to and fro; and went up, and stretched
himself upon him: and the child sneezed seven times, and the child opened his eyes. [36]And he called Gehazi, and said,
Call this Shunammite. So he called her. And when she was come in unto him, he said, Take up thy son. [37]Then she went
in, and fell at his feet, and bowed herself to the ground, and took up her son, and went out.

ACTS 20:28—Paul's speech at Ephesus (20:17–38)

Theme	ACTS	Jn	NT
Faithfulness challenged	**20:28** [28]Take heed therefore unto yourselves, and to all the flock, over which the Holy Ghost hath made you overseers, to feed the church of God, which he hath purchased with his own blood.	**21:15–17** [15] So when they had dined, Jesus saith to Simon Peter, Simon, son of Jonas, lovest thou me more than these? He saith unto him, Yea, Lord; thou knowest that I love thee. He saith unto him, Feed my lambs. [16] He saith to him again the second time, Simon, son of Jonas, lovest thou me? He saith unto him, Yea, Lord; thou knowest that I love thee. He saith unto him, Feed my sheep. [17] He saith unto him the third time, Simon, son of Jonas, lovest thou me? Peter was grieved because he said unto him the third time, Lovest thou me? And he said unto him, Lord, thou knowest all things; thou knowest that I love thee. Jesus saith unto him, Feed my sheep.	**1 Pet 5:2** [2] Feed the flock of God which is among you, taking the oversight thereof, not by constraint, but willingly; not for filthy lucre, but of a ready mind;

ACTS 20:29—Paul's speech at Ephesus (20:17–38)

Theme	ACTS	Jn
Wolves in the flock	**20:29** [29]For I know this, that after my departing shall grievous wolves enter in among you, not sparing the flock.	**Jn 10:12** [12]But he that is an hireling, and not the shepherd, whose own the sheep are not, seeth the wolf coming, and leaveth the sheep, and fleeth: and the wolf catcheth them, and scattereth the sheep.

ACTS 20:30—Paul's speech at Ephesus (20:17–38)

Theme	ACTS	Mt	Jn	NT	Other
Beware false teachings	**20:30** [30]Also of your own selves shall men arise, speaking perverse things, to draw away disciples after them.	**7:15** [15]Beware of false prophets, which come to you in sheep's clothing, but inwardly they are ravening wolves.	**1 Jn 2:18–19** [18]Little children, it is the last time: and as ye have heard that antichrist shall come, even now are there many antichrists; whereby we know that it is the last time. [19]They went out from us, but they were not of us; for if they had been of us, they would no doubt have continued with us: but they went out, that they might be made manifest that they were not all of us.	**2 Pet 2:1–3** [1]But there were false prophets also among the people, even as there shall be false teachers among you, who privily shall bring in damnable heresies, even denying the Lord that bought them, and bring upon themselves swift destruction. [2]And many shall follow their pernicious ways; by reason of whom the way of truth shall be evil spoken of. [3]And through covetousness shall they with feigned words make merchandise of you: whose judgment now of a long time lingereth not, and their damnation slumbereth not.	**Q-Quelle** Fruits: Acts 20:30/Mt 7:15-20, [Mt 12:33-35]/ [Lk 6:43-45]

ACTS 20:31—Paul's speech at Ephesus (20:17–38)

Theme	ACTS	Paul
Sincerity with care	**20:31** [31]Therefore watch, and remember, that by the space of three years I ceased not to warn every one night and day with tears.	**1 Thes 2:11** [11]As ye know how we exhorted and comforted and charged every one of you, as a father doth his children,

ACTS 20:34—Paul's speech at Ephesus (20:17–38)

Theme	ACTS	Paul
Laboring for provisions	**20:34** [34]Yea, ye yourselves know, that these hands have ministered unto my necessities, and to them that were with me.	**1 Cor 4:12** [12]And labour, working with our own hands: being reviled, we bless; being persecuted, we suffer it: **1 Thes 2:9** [9]For ye remember, brethren, our labour and travail: for labouring night and day, because we would not be chargeable unto any of you, we preached unto you the gospel of God. **2 Thes 3:8** [8]Neither did we eat any man's bread for nought; but wrought with labour and travail night and day, that we might not be chargeable to any of you:

ACTS 20:35—Paul's speech at Ephesus (20:17–38)

Theme	ACTS	Jewish Writings
Laboring for others	**20:35** [35]I have showed you all things, how that so labouring ye ought to support the weak, and to remember the words of the Lord Jesus, how he said, It is more blessed to give than to receive.	**Sir 4:31** [31]Let not thine hand be stretched out to receive, and shut when thou shouldest repay.

Paul—Kos, Rhodes, Patara, Phoenicia, Syria-Tyre (21:1–6)

Paul—Ptolemais and Caesarea 21:7–14

ACTS 21:8—Paul, Ptolemais and Caesarea (21:7–14)

Theme	ACTS
Chosen for ministry	**21:8** [8]And the next day we that were of Paul's company departed, and came unto Caesarea: and we entered into the house of Philip the evangelist, which was one of the seven; and abode with him. **6:5** [5]And the saying pleased the whole multitude: and they chose Stephen, a man full of faith and of the Holy Ghost, and Philip, and Prochorus, and Nicanor, and Timon, and Parmenas, and Nicolas a proselyte of Antioch: **8:5–6** [5]Then Philip went down to the city of Samaria, and preached Christ unto them. [6]And the people with one accord gave heed unto those things which Philip spake, hearing and seeing the miracles which he did.

ACTS 21:11—Paul, Ptolemais and Caesarea (21:7–14)

Theme	ACTS
Prophesy of suffering	**21:11** [11]And when he was come unto us, he took Paul's girdle, and bound his own hands and feet, and said, Thus saith the Holy Ghost, So shall the Jews at Jerusalem bind the man that owneth this girdle, and shall deliver him into the hands of the Gentiles. **11:28** [28]And there stood up one of them named Agabus, and signified by the Spirit that there should be great dearth throughout all the world: which came to pass in the days of Claudius Caesar. **20:23** [23]Save that the Holy Ghost witnesseth in every city, saying that bonds and afflictions abide me.

ACTS 21:13—Paul, Ptolemais and Caesarea (21:7–14)

Theme	ACTS	Mt	Mk	Lk
Sacrifices come with serving God	**21:13** [13]Then Paul answered, What mean ye to weep and to break mine heart? for I am ready not to be bound only, but also to die at Jerusalem for the name of the Lord Jesus. **19:15–16** [15]And the evil spirit answered and said, Jesus I know, and Paul I know; but who are ye? [16]And the man in whom the evil spirit was leaped on them, and overcame them, and prevailed against them, so that they fled out of that house naked and wounded.	**26:30–35** [30]And when they had sung an hymn, they went out into the mount of Olives. [31] Then saith Jesus unto them, All ye shall be offended because of me this night: for it is written, I will smite the shepherd, and the sheep of the flock shall be scattered abroad. [32]But after I am risen again, I will go before you into Galilee. [33]Peter answered and said unto him, Though all men shall be offended because of thee, yet will I never be offended. [34]Jesus said unto him, Verily I say unto thee, That this night, before the cock crow, thou shalt deny me thrice. [35]Peter said unto him, Though I should die with thee, yet will I not deny thee. Likewise also said all the disciples.	**14:26–31** [26]And when they had sung an hymn, they went out into the mount of Olives. [27]And Jesus saith unto them, All ye shall be offended because of me this night: for it is written, I will smite the shepherd, and the sheep shall be scattered. [28]But after that I am risen, I will go before you into Galilee. [29]But Peter said unto him, Although all shall be offended, yet will not I. [30]And Jesus saith unto him, Verily I say unto thee, That this day, even in this night, before the cock crow twice, thou shalt deny me thrice. [31]But he spake the more vehemently, If I should die with thee, I will not deny thee in any wise. Likewise also said they all.	**22:31–34** [31]And the Lord said, Simon, Simon, behold, Satan hath desired to have you, that he may sift you as wheat: [32]But I have prayed for thee, that thy faith fail not: and when thou art converted, strengthen thy brethren. [33]And he said unto him, Lord, I am ready to go with thee, both into prison, and to death. [34]And he said, I tell thee, Peter, the cock shall not crow this day, before that thou shalt thrice deny that thou knowest me. **22:39** [39]And he came out, and went, as he was wont, to the mount of Olives; and his disciples also followed him. **22:54b-62** And Peter followed afar off. [55]And when they had kindled a fire in the midst of the hall, and were set down together, Peter sat down among them. [56]But a certain maid beheld him as he sat by the fire, and earnestly looked upon him, and said, This man was also with him. [57]And he denied him, saying, Woman, I know him not. [58]And after a little while another saw him, and said, Thou art also of them. And Peter said, Man, I am not. [59]And about the space of one hour after another confidently affirmed, saying, Of a truth this fellow also was with him: for he is a Galilaean. [60]And Peter said, Man, I know not what thou sayest. And immediately, while he yet spake, the cock crew. [61] And the Lord turned, and looked upon Peter. And Peter remembered the word of the Lord, how he had said unto him, Before the cock crow, thou shalt deny me thrice. [62]And Peter went out, and wept bitterly.

Jn	Jewish Writings	Other
11:16 [16]Then said Thomas, which is called Didymus, unto his fellow disciples, Let us also go, that we may die with him. **13:36–38** [36]Simon Peter said unto him, Lord, whither goest thou? Jesus answered him, Whither I go, thou canst not follow me now; but thou shalt follow me afterwards. [37]Peter said unto him, Lord, why cannot I follow thee now? I will lay down my life for thy sake. [38]Jesus answered him, Wilt thou lay down thy life for my sake? Verily, verily, I say unto thee, The cock shall not crow, till thou hast denied me thrice. **16:32** [32]Behold, the hour cometh, yea, is now come, that ye shall be scattered, every man to his own, and shall leave me alone: and yet I am not alone, because the Father is with me. **18:1** [1]When Jesus had spoken these words, he went forth with his disciples over the brook Cedron, where was a garden, into the which he entered, and his disciples.	**Zech 13:7** [7]Awake, O sword, against my shepherd, and against the man that is my fellow, saith the LORD of hosts: smite the shepherd, and the sheep shall be scattered: and I will turn mine hand upon the little ones.	**Fayyum Frag** . . .while he was going out, he said, "This night you will all fall away, as it is written, 'I will strike the shepherd, and the sheep will be scattered." When Peter said, "Even though all, not I," Jesus said, "Before the cock crows twice, you will this deny me three times. [PViennaG 2325 Sayings Parallels, #463]

ACTS 21:14—Paul, Ptolemais and Caesarea (21:7–14)

Theme	ACTS	Mt
God's will	**21:14** [14]And when he would not be persuaded, we ceased, saying, The will of the Lord be done.	**6:10** [10]Thy kingdom come. Thy will be done in earth, as it is in heaven. **26:36** [36]Then cometh Jesus with them unto a place called Gethsemane, and saith unto the disciples, Sit ye here, while I go and pray yonder. **26:37–38** [37]And he took with him Peter and the two sons of Zebedee, and began to be sorrowful and very heavy. [38]Then saith he unto them, My soul is exceeding sorrowful, even unto death: tarry ye here, and watch with me. **26:39** [39]And he went a little further, and fell on his face, and prayed, saying, O my Father, if it be possible, let this cup pass from me: nevertheless not as I will, but as thou wilt. **26:40–41** [40]And he cometh unto the disciples, and findeth them asleep, and saith unto Peter, What, could ye not watch with me one hour? [41]Watch and pray, that ye enter not into temptation: the spirit indeed is willing, but the flesh is weak. **26:42** [42]He went away again the second time, and prayed, saying, O my Father, if this cup may not pass away from me, except I drink it, thy will be done. **26:43** [43]And he came and found them asleep again: for their eyes were heavy. **26:44** [44]And he left them, and went away again, and prayed the third time, saying the same words. **26:45–46** [45]Then cometh he to his disciples, and saith unto them, Sleep on now, and take your rest: behold, the hour is at hand, and the Son of man is betrayed into the hands of sinners. [46]Rise, let us be going: behold, he is at hand that doth betray me.

Mk	Lk	Jn
14:32 [32]And they came to a place which was named Gethsemane: and he saith to his disciples, Sit ye here, while I shall pray. **14:33–34** [33]And he taketh with him Peter and James and John, and began to be sore amazed, and to be very heavy; [34]And saith unto them, My soul is exceeding sorrowful unto death: tarry ye here, and watch. **14:35–36** [35]And he went forward a little, and fell on the ground, and prayed that, if it were possible, the hour might pass from him. [36]And he said, Abba, Father, all things are possible unto thee; take away this cup from me: nevertheless not what I will, but what thou wilt. **14:37–38** [37]And he cometh, and findeth them sleeping, and saith unto Peter, Simon, sleepest thou? couldest not thou watch one hour? [38]Watch ye and pray, lest ye enter into temptation. The spirit truly is ready, but the flesh is weak. **14:39** [39]And again he went away, and prayed, and spake the same words. **14:40** [40]And when he returned, he found them asleep again, (for their eyes were heavy,) neither wist they what to answer him. **14:41–42** [41]And he cometh the third time, and saith unto them, Sleep on now, and take your rest: it is enough, the hour is come; behold, the Son of man is betrayed into the hands of sinners. [42]Rise up, let us go; lo, he that betrayeth me is at hand.	**22:39** [39]And he came out, and went, as he was wont, to the mount of Olives; and his disciples also followed him. **22:40–42** [40]And when he was at the place, he said unto them, Pray that ye enter not into temptation. [41]And he was withdrawn from them about a stone's cast, and kneeled down, and prayed, [42]Saying, Father, if thou be willing, remove this cup from me: nevertheless not my will, but thine, be done. **22:45–46** [45]And when he rose up from prayer, and was come to his disciples, he found them sleeping for sorrow, [46]And said unto them, Why sleep ye? rise and pray, lest ye enter into temptation.	**12:27** [27]Now is my soul troubled; and what shall I say? Father, save me from this hour: but for this cause came I unto this hour. **18:1** [1]When Jesus had spoken these words, he went forth with his disciples over the brook Cedron, where was a garden, into the which he entered, and his disciples. **18:11** [11]Then said Jesus unto Peter, Put up thy sword into the sheath: the cup which my Father hath given me, shall I not drink it?

Paul and James at Jerusalem 21:15–26

ACTS 21:23–27—Paul and James at Jerusalem (21:15–26)

Theme	ACTS
Godly practices for Gentile converts	**21:23–27** [23]Do therefore this that we say to thee: We have four men which have a vow on them [24]Them take, and purify thyself with them, and be at charges with them, that they may shave their heads: and all may know that those things, whereof they were informed concerning thee, are nothing; but that thou thyself also walkest orderly, and keepest the law. [25]As touching the Gentiles which believe, we have written and concluded that they observe no such thing, save only that they keep them-selves from things offered to idols, and from blood, and from strangled, and from fornication. [26]Then Paul took the men, and the next day purifying himself with them entered into the temple, to signify the accomplishment of the days of purification, until that an offering should be offered for every one of them. [27]And when the seven days were almost ended, the Jews which were of Asia, when they saw him in the temple, stirred up all the people, and laid hands on him, **18:18** [18]And Paul after this tarried there yet a good while, and then took his leave of the brethren, and sailed thence into Syria, and with him Priscilla and Aquila; having shorn his head in Cenchrea: for he had a vow.

ACTS 21:25—Paul and James at Jerusalem (21:15–26)

Theme	ACTS
Gentile observances	**21:25** [25]As touching the Gentiles which believe, we have written and concluded that they observe no such thing, save only that they keep themselves from things offered to idols, and from blood, and from strangled, and from fornication. **15:19–20, 28–29** [19]Wherefore my sentence is, that we trouble not them, which from among the Gentiles are turned to God: [20]But that we write unto them, that they abstain from pollutions of idols, and from fornication, and from things strangled, and from blood. . . . [28]For it seemed good to the Holy Ghost, and to us, to lay upon you no greater burden than these necessary things; [29]That ye abstain from meats offered to idols, and from blood, and from things strangled, and from fornication: from which if ye keep yourselves, ye shall do well. Fare ye well.

Jewish Writings

Num 6:1–21

[1]And the LORD spake unto Moses, saying, [2]Speak unto the children of Israel, and say unto them, When either man
or woman shall separate themselves to vow a vow of a Nazarite, to separate themselves unto the LORD: [3]He shall
separate himself from wine and strong drink, and shall drink no vinegar of wine, or vinegar of strong drink, neither
shall he drink any liquor of grapes, nor eat moist grapes, or dried. [4]All the days of his separation shall he eat nothing
that is made of the vine tree, from the kernels even to the husk. [5]All the days of the vow of his separation there shall
no razor come upon his head: until the days be fulfilled, in the which he separateth himself unto the LORD, he shall
be holy, and shall let the locks of the hair of his head grow. [6]All the days that he separateth himself unto the LORD
he shall come at no dead body. [7]He shall not make himself unclean for his father, or for his mother, for his brother, or
for his sister, when they die: because the consecration of his God is upon his head. [8]All the days of his separation he
is holy unto the LORD. [9]And if any man die very suddenly by him, and he hath defiled the head of his consecration;
then he shall shave his head in the day of his cleansing, on the seventh day shall he shave it. [10]And on the eighth day he
shall bring two turtles, or two young pigeons, to the priest, to the door of the tabernacle of the congregation: [11]And the
priest shall offer the one for a sin offering, and the other for a burnt offering, and make an atonement for him, for that
he sinned by the dead, and shall hallow his head that same day. [12]And he shall consecrate unto the LORD the days of
his separation, and shall bring a lamb of the first year for a trespass offering: but the days that were before shall be lost,
because his separation was defiled. [13]And this is the law of the Nazarite, when the days of his separation are fulfilled: he
shall be brought unto the door of the tabernacle of the congregation: [14]And he shall offer his offering unto the LORD,
one he lamb of the first year without blemish for a burnt offering, and one ewe lamb of the first year without blemish for
a sin offering, and one ram without blemish for peace offerings, [15]And a basket of unleavened bread, cakes of fine flour
mingled with oil, and wafers of unleavened bread anointed with oil, and their meat offering, and their drink offerings.
[16]And the priest shall bring them before the LORD, and shall offer his sin offering, and his burnt offering: [17]And he
shall offer the ram for a sacrifice of peace offerings unto the LORD, with the basket of unleavened bread: the priest
shall offer also his meat offering, and his drink offering. [18]And the Nazarite shall shave the head of his separation at the
door of the tabernacle of the congregation, and shall take the hair of the head of his separation, and put it in the fire
which is under the sacrifice of the peace offerings. [19]And the priest shall take the sodden shoulder of the ram, and one
unleavened cake out of the basket, and one unleavened wafer, and shall put them upon the hands of the Nazarite, after
the hair of his separation is shaven: [20]And the priest shall wave them for a wave offering before the LORD: this is holy
for the priest, with the wave breast and heave shoulder: and after that the Nazarite may drink wine. [21]This is the law
of the Nazarite who hath vowed, and of his offering unto the LORD for his separation, beside that his hand shall get:
according to the vow which he vowed, so he must do after the law of his separation.

ACTS 21:26—Paul and James at Jerusalem (21:15–26)

Theme	ACTS
Ritual sanctification	**21:26** [26]Then Paul took the men, and the next day purifying himself with them entered into the temple, to signify the accomplishment of the days of purification, until that an offering should be offered for every one of them.

Paul arrested at the Temple 21:27–40

ACTS 21:28—Paul arrested at the Temple (21:27–40)

Theme	ACTS	Paul
Accusing Paul of apostasy	**21:28** [28]Crying out, Men of Israel, help: This is the man, that teacheth all men every where against the people, and the law, and this place: and further brought Greeks also into the temple, and hath polluted this holy place.	**Rom 15:31** [31]That I may be delivered from them that do not believe in Judaea; and that my service which I have for Jerusalem may be accepted of the saints;

ACTS 21:36—Paul arrested at the Temple (21:27–40)

The	ACTS	Mt
Trial	**21:36** [36]For the multitude of the people followed after, crying, Away with him. **3:13–15** [13]The God of Abraham, and of Isaac, and of Jacob, the God of our fathers, hath glorified his Son Jesus; whom ye delivered up, and denied him in the presence of Pilate, when he was determined to let him go. [14]But ye denied the Holy One and the Just, and desired a murderer to be granted unto you; [15]And killed the Prince of life, whom God hath raised from the dead; whereof we are witnesses. **22:22** [22]And they gave him audience unto this word, and then lifted up their voices, and said, Away with such a fellow from the earth: for it is not fit that he should live.	**27:1–2** [12]And when he was accused of the chief priests and elders, he answered nothing. **27:11–14** [11]And Jesus stood before the governor: and the governor asked him, saying, Art thou the King of the Jews? And Jesus said unto him, Thou sayest. [12]And when he was accused of the chief priests and elders, he answered nothing. [13]Then said Pilate unto him, Hearest thou not how many things they witness against thee? [14]And he answered him to never a word; insomuch that the governor marvelled greatly. **27:15–26** [15]Now at that feast the governor was wont to release unto the people a prisoner, whom they would. [16]And they had then a notable prisoner, called Barabbas. [17]Therefore when they were gathered together, Pilate said unto them, Whom will ye that I release unto you? Barabbas, or Jesus which is called Christ? [18]For he knew that for envy they had delivered him. [19]When he was set down on the judgment seat, his wife sent unto him, saying, Have thou nothing to do with that just man: for I have suffered many things this day in a dream because of him. [20]But the chief priests and elders persuaded the multitude that they should ask Barabbas, and destroy Jesus. [21]The governor answered and said unto them, Whether of the twain will ye that I release unto you? They said, Barabbas. [22]Pilate saith unto them, What shall I do then with Jesus which is called Christ? They all say unto him, Let him be crucified. [23]And the governor said, Why, what evil hath he done? But they cried out the more, saying, Let him be crucified. [24]When Pilate saw that he could prevail nothing, but that rather a tumult was made, he took water, and washed his hands before the multitude, saying, I am innocent of the blood of this just person: see ye to it. [25]Then answered all the people, and said, His blood be on us, and on our children. [26]Then released he Barabbas unto them: and when he had scourged Jesus, he delivered him to be crucified.

Paul

1 Cor 9:20

20And unto the Jews I became as a Jew, that I might gain the Jews; to them that are under the law, as under the law, that I might gain them that are under the law;

Mk

15:1–5

1And straightway in the morning the chief priests held a consultation with the elders and scribes and the whole council, and bound Jesus, and carried him away, and delivered him to Pilate. 2And Pilate asked him, Art thou the King of the Jews? And he answering said unto him, Thou sayest it. 3And the chief priests accused him of many things: but he answered nothing. 4And Pilate asked him again, saying, Answerest thou nothing? behold how many things they witness against thee. 5But Jesus yet answered nothing; so that Pilate marvelled.

15:6–15

6Now at that feast he released unto them one prisoner, whomsoever they desired. 7And there was one named Barabbas, which lay bound with them that had made insurrection with him, who had committed murder in the insurrection. 8And the multitude crying aloud began to desire him to do as he had ever done unto them. 9But Pilate answered them, saying, Will ye that I release unto you the King of the Jews? 10For he knew that the chief priests had delivered him for envy. 11But the chief priests moved the people, that he should rather release Barabbas unto them. 12And Pilate answered and said again unto them, What will ye then that I shall do unto him whom ye call the King of the Jews? 13And they cried out again, Crucify him. 14Then Pilate said unto them, Why, what evil hath he done? And they cried out the more exceedingly, Crucify him.15And so Pilate, willing to content the people, released Barabbas unto them, and delivered Jesus, when he had scourged him, to be crucified.

Lk

23:1–7

1And the whole multitude of them arose, and led him unto Pilate. 2And they began to accuse him, saying, We found this fellow perverting the nation, and forbid-ding to give tribute to Caesar, saying that he himself is Christ a King. 3And Pilate asked him, saying, Art thou the King of the Jews? And he answered him and said, Thou sayest it. 4Then said Pilate to the chief priests and to the people, I find no fault in this man. 5And they were the more fierce, saying, He stirreth up the people, teaching through-out all Jewry, beginning from Galilee to this place. 6When Pilate heard of Galilee, he asked whether the man were a Galilaean. 7And as soon as he knew that he belonged unto Herod's jurisdiction, he sent him to Herod, who himself also was at Jerusalem at that time.

23:13–25

13And Pilate, when he had called together the chief priests and the rulers and the people, 14Said unto them, Ye have brought this man unto me, as one that perverteth the people: and, behold, I, having examined him before you, have found no fault in this man touching those things whereof ye accuse him: 15No, nor yet Herod: for I sent you to him; and, lo, nothing worthy of death is done unto him. 16I will therefore chastise him, and release him. 17(For of necessity he must release one unto them at the feast.) 18And they cried out all at once, saying, Away with this man, and release unto us Barabbas: 19(Who for a certain sedition made in the city, and for murder, was cast into prison.) 20Pilate therefore, willing to release Jesus, spake again to them. 21But they cried, saying, Crucify him, crucify him. 22And he said unto them the third time, Why, what evil hath he done? I have found no cause of death in him: I will therefore chastise him, and let him go. 23And they were instant with loud voices, requiring that he might be crucified. And the voices of them and of the chief priests prevailed. 24And Pilate gave sentence that it should be as they required. 25And he released unto them him that for sedition and murder was cast into prison, whom they had desired; but he delivered Jesus to their will.

Acts 21:36 continued on next page

ACTS 21:36—Paul arrested at the Temple (21:27–40) (*continued*)

Theme	ACTS	Jn
(*Cont.*) Trial	21:36 (above) 3:13–15 (above) 22:22 (above)	**18:28–19:16** [28]Then Peter said, Lo, we have left all, and followed thee. [29]And he said unto them, Verily I say unto you, There is no man that hath left house, or parents, or brethren, or wife, or children, for the kingdom of God's sake, [30]Who shall not receive manifold more in this present time, and in the world to come life everlasting. [31]Then he took unto him the twelve, and said unto them, Behold, we go up to Jerusalem, and all things that are written by the prophets concerning the Son of man shall be accomplished. [32]For he shall be delivered unto the Gentiles, and shall be mocked, and spitefully entreated, and spitted on: [33]And they shall scourge him, and put him to death: and the third day he shall rise again. [34]And they understood none of these things: and this saying was hid from them, neither knew they the things which were spoken. [35]And it came to pass, that as he was come nigh unto Jericho, a certain blind man sat by the way side begging: [36]And hearing the multitude pass by, he asked what it meant. [37]And they told him, that Jesus of Nazareth passeth by. [38]And he cried, saying, Jesus, thou Son of David, have mercy on me. [39]And they which went before rebuked him, that he should hold his peace: but he cried so much the more, Thou Son of David, have mercy on me. [40]And Jesus stood, and commanded him to be brought unto him: and when he was come near, he asked him, [41]Saying, What wilt thou that I shall do unto thee? And he said, Lord, that I may receive my sight. [42]And Jesus said unto him, Receive thy sight: thy faith hath saved thee. [43]And immediately he received his sight, and followed him, glorifying God: and all the people, when they saw it, gave praise unto God. (19) [1]And Jesus entered and passed through Jericho. [2]And, behold, there was a man named Zacchaeus, which was the chief among the publicans, and he was rich. [3]And he sought to see Jesus who he was; and could not for the press, because he was little of stature. [4]And he ran before, and climbed up into a sycamore tree to see him: for he was to pass that way. [5]And when Jesus came to the place, he looked up, and saw him, and said unto him, Zacchaeus, make haste, and come down; for to day I must abide at thy house. [6]And he made haste, and came down, and received him joyfully. [7]And when they saw it, they all murmured, saying, That he was gone to be guest with a man that is a sinner. [8]And Zacchaeus stood, and said unto the Lord; Behold, Lord, the half of my goods I give to the poor; and if I have taken any thing from any man by false accusation, I restore him fourfold. [9]And Jesus said unto him, This day is salvation come to this house, forsomuch as he also is a son of Abraham. [10]For the Son of man is come to seek and to save that which was lost. [11]And as they heard these things, he added and spake a parable, because he was nigh to Jerusalem, and because they thought that the kingdom of God should immediately appear. [12]He said therefore, A certain nobleman went into a far country to receive for himself a kingdom, and to return. [13]And he called his ten servants, and delivered them ten pounds, and said unto them, Occupy till I come. [14]But his citizens hated him, and sent a message after him, saying, We will not have this man to reign over us. [15]And it came to pass, that when he was returned, having received the kingdom, then he commanded these servants to be called unto him, to whom he had given the money, that he might know how much every man had gained by trading. [16]Then came the first, saying, Lord, thy pound hath gained ten pounds.

ACTS 21:38—Paul arrested at Temple (21:27–40)

Theme	ACTS
Accusations of disloyalty	**21:38** [38]Art not thou that Egyptian, which before these days madest an uproar, and leddest out into the wilderness four thousand men that were murderers? **5:36–37** [36]For before these days rose up Theudas, boasting himself to be somebody; to whom a number of men, about four hundred, joined themselves: who was slain; and all, as many as obeyed him, were scattered, and brought to nought. [37]After this man rose up Judas of Galilee in the days of the taxing, and drew away much people after him: he also perished; and all, even as many as obeyed him, were dispersed.

Other

ActPil 3:2

[2]And Pilate went in again into the judgement hall and called Jesus apart and said unto him: Art thou the King of the Jews? Jesus answered and said to Pilate: Sayest thou this thing of thyself, or did others tell it thee of me? Pilate answered Jesus: Am I also a Jew? thine own nation and the chief priests have delivered thee unto me: what hast thou done? Jesus answered: My kingdom is not of this world; for if my kingdom were of this world, my servants would have striven that I should not be delivered to the Jews: but now is my kingdom not from hence. Pilate said unto him: Art thou a king, then? Jesus answered him: Thou sayest that I am a king; for this cause was I born and am come, that every one that is of the truth should hear my voice. Pilate saith unto him: What is truth? Jesus saith unto him: Truth is of heaven. Pilate saith: Is there not truth upon earth? Jesus saith unto Pilate: Thou seest how that they which speak the truth are judged of them that have authority upon earth.

ActPil 4:4–5

[4]Pilate saith unto them: Take ye him and avenge yourselves of him in what manner ye will. The Jews say unto Pilate: We will that he be crucified. Pilate saith: He deserveth not to be crucified. [5]Now as the governor looked round about upon the multitude of the Jews which stood by, he beheld many of the Jews weeping, and said: Not all the multitude desire that he should be put to death. The elder of the Jews said: To this end have the whole multitude of us come Hither, that he should be put to death. Pilate saith to the Jews: Wherefore should he die? The Jews said: Because he called himself the Son of God, and a king.

ActPil 9:4–5

[4]And when Pilate heard these words he was afraid. And Pilate silenced the multitude, because they cried still, and said unto them: So, then, this is he whom Herod sought? The Jews say: Yea, this is he. And Pilate took water and washed his hands before the sun, saying: I am innocent of the blood of this just man: see ye to it. Again the Jews cried out: His blood be upon us and upon our children. [5]Then Pilate commanded the veil to be drawn before the judgement-seat whereon he sat, and saith unto Jesus: Thy nation hath convicted thee (accused thee) as being a king: therefore have I decreed that thou shouldest first be scourged according to the law of the pious emperors, and thereafter hanged upon the cross in the garden wherein thou wast taken: and let Dysmas and Gestas the two malefactors be crucified with thee.

GNaz 20

[20]Barabbas. . . is interpreted in the so-called Gospel according to the Hebrews as "son of their teacher."

GPet 1.1–2

[1]. . .but none of the Jews washed his hands, nor did Herod or any of his judges. Since they did not wish to wash, Pilate stood up. [2]The king Herod ordered the Lord to be taken away and said to them, "Do everything that I ordered you to do to him."

Paul speaks of his life as a zealous Jew and his radical conversion 22:1–21

ACTS 22:3—Paul speaks of his life as a zealous Jew and his radical conversion (22:1–21)

Theme	ACTS	Paul
Paul's claim to Jewish heritage	**22:3** [3]I am verily a man which am a Jew, born in Tarsus, a city in Cilicia, yet brought up in this city at the feet of Gamaliel, and taught according to the perfect manner of the law of the fathers, and was zealous toward God, as ye all are this day. **5:34** [34]Then stood there up one in the council, a Pharisee, named Gamaliel, a doctor of the law, had in reputation among all the people, and commanded to put the apostles forth a little space; **26:4–5** [4]My manner of life from my youth, which was at the first among mine own nation at Jerusalem, know all the Jews; [5]Which knew me from the beginning, if they would testify, that after the most straitest sect of our religion I lived a Pharisee.	**2 Cor 11:22** [22]Are they Hebrews? so am I. Are they Israelites? so am I. Are they the seed of Abraham? so am I. **Gal 1:13–14** [13]For ye have heard of my conversation in time past in the Jews' religion, how that beyond measure I persecuted the church of God, and wasted it: [14]And profited in the Jews' religion above many my equals in mine own nation, being more exceedingly zealous of the traditions of my fathers. **Phil 3:5–6** [5]Circumcised the eighth day, of the stock of Israel, of the tribe of Benjamin, an Hebrew of the Hebrews; as touching the law, a Pharisee; [6]Concerning zeal, persecuting the church; touching the righteousness which is in the law, blameless.

ACTS 22:4—Paul speaks of his life as a zealous Jew and his radical conversion (22:1–21)

Theme	ACTS	Paul
Paul persecuted Christians	**22:4** [4]And I persecuted this way unto the death, binding and delivering into prisons both men and women. **8:3** [3]As for Saul, he made havock of the church, entering into every house, and haling men and women committed them to prison. **9:1–2** [1]And Saul, yet breathing out threatenings and slaughter against the disciples of the Lord, went unto the high priest, [2]And desired of him letters to Damascus to the synagogues, that if he found any of this way, whether they were men or women, he might bring them bound unto Jerusalem. **22:19** [19]And I said, Lord, they know that I imprisoned and beat in every synagogue them that believed on thee: **26:9–11** [9]I verily thought with myself, that I ought to do many things contrary to the name of Jesus of Nazareth. [10]Which thing I also did in Jerusalem: and many of the saints did I shut up in prison, having received authority from the chief priests; and when they were put to death, I gave my voice against them. [11]And I punished them oft in every synagogue, and compelled them to blaspheme; and being exceedingly mad against them, I persecuted them even unto strange cities.	**Phil 3:6** [6]Concerning zeal, persecuting the church; touching the righteousness which is in the law, blameless.

ACTS 22:6—Paul speaks of his life as a zealous Jew and his radical conversion (22:1–21)

Theme	ACTS	Paul
Paul's Damascus conversion	**22:6** [6]And it came to pass, that, as I made my journey, and was come nigh unto Damascus about noon, suddenly there shone from heaven a great light round about me. **9:3** [3]And as he journeyed, he came near Damascus: and suddenly there shined round about him a light from heaven: **26:13** [13]At midday, O king, I saw in the way a light from heaven, above the brightness of the sun, shining round about me and them which journeyed with me.	**1 Cor 15:8** [8]And last of all he was seen of me also, as of one born out of due time.

ACTS 22:7—Paul speaks of his life as a zealous Jew and his radical conversion (22:1–21)

Theme	ACTS
Jesus speaks to Paul at Damascus	**22:7** [7]And I fell unto the ground, and heard a voice saying unto me, Saul, Saul, why persecutest thou me? **9:4** [4]And he fell to the earth, and heard a voice saying unto him, Saul, Saul, why persecutest thou me? **26:14** [14]And when we were all fallen to the earth, I heard a voice speaking unto me, and saying in the Hebrew tongue, Saul, Saul, why persecutest thou me? it is hard for thee to kick against the pricks.

ACTS 22:8—Paul speaks of his life as a zealous Jew and his radical conversion (22:1–21)

Theme	ACTS	Mt
Paul inquires of God at Damascus	**22:8** [8]And I answered, Who art thou, Lord? And he said unto me, I am Jesus of Nazareth, whom thou persecutest. **9:5** [5]And he said, Who art thou, Lord? And the Lord said, I am Jesus whom thou persecutest: it is hard for thee to kick against the pricks. **26:15** [15]And I said, Who art thou, Lord? And he said, I am Jesus whom thou persecutest.	**25:40** [40]And the King shall answer and say unto them, Verily I say unto you, Inasmuch as ye have done it unto one of the least of these my brethren, ye have done it unto me.

ACTS 22:9—Paul speaks of his life as a zealous Jew and his radical conversion (22:1–21)

Theme	ACTS
Paul and the light from heaven	**22:9** [9]And they that were with me saw indeed the light, and were afraid; but they heard not the voice of him that spake to me. **9:7** [7]And the men which journeyed with him stood speechless, hearing a voice, but seeing no man. **26:13–14** [13]At midday, O king, I saw in the way a light from heaven, above the brightness of the sun, shining round about me and them which journeyed with me. [14]And when we were all fallen to the earth, I heard a voice speaking unto me, and saying in the Hebrew tongue, Saul, Saul, why persecutest thou me? it is hard for thee to kick against the pricks.

ACTS 22:11—Paul speaks of his life as a zealous Jew and his radical conversion (22:1–21)

Theme	ACTS
Paul blinded	**22:11** [11]And when I could not see for the glory of that light, being led by the hand of them that were with me, I came into Damascus. **9:8** [8]And Saul arose from the earth; and when his eyes were opened, he saw no man: but they led him by the hand, and brought him into Damascus.

ACTS 22:12–16—Paul speaks of his life as a zealous Jew and his radical conversion (22:1–21)

Theme	ACTS
Paul receives his sight	**22:12–16** [12]And one Ananias, a devout man according to the law, having a good report of all the Jews which dwelt there, [13]Came unto me, and stood, and said unto me, Brother Saul, receive thy sight. And the same hour I looked up upon him. [14]And he said, The God of our fathers hath chosen thee, that thou shouldest know his will, and see that Just One, and shouldest hear the voice of his mouth. [15]For thou shalt be his witness unto all men of what thou hast seen and heard. [16]And now why tarriest thou? arise, and be baptized, and wash away thy sins, calling on the name of the Lord. **9:10–19** [10]And there was a certain disciple at Damascus, named Ananias; and to him said the Lord in a vision, Ananias. And he said, Behold, I am here, Lord. [11]And the Lord said unto him, Arise, and go into the street which is called Straight, and inquire in the house of Judas for one called Saul, of Tarsus: for, behold, he prayeth, [12]And hath seen in a vision a man named Ananias coming in, and putting his hand on him, that he might receive his sight. [13]Then Ananias answered, Lord, I have heard by many of this man, how much evil he hath done to thy saints at Jerusalem: [14]And here he hath authority from the chief priests to bind all that call on thy name. [15]But the Lord said unto him, Go thy way: for he is a chosen vessel unto me, to bear my name before the Gentiles, and kings, and the children of Israel: [16]For I will show him how great things he must suffer for my name's sake. [17]And Ananias went his way, and entered into the house; and putting his hands on him said, Brother Saul, the Lord, even Jesus, that appeared unto thee in the way as thou camest, hath sent me, that thou mightest receive thy sight, and be filled with the Holy Ghost. [18]And immediately there fell from his eyes as it had been scales: and he received sight forthwith, and arose, and was baptized. [19]And when he had received meat, he was strengthened. Then was Saul certain days with the disciples which were at Damascus.

ACTS 22:19—Paul speaks of his life as a zealous Jew and his radical conversion (22:1–21)

Theme	ACTS
Paul persecuted Christians	**22:19** [19]And I said, Lord, they know that I imprisoned and beat in every synagogue them that believed on thee: **8:3** [3]As for Saul, he made havock of the church, entering into every house, and haling men and women committed them to prison. **9:1–2** [1]And Saul, yet breathing out threatenings and slaughter against the disciples of the Lord, went unto the high priest, [2]And desired of him letters to Damascus to the synagogues, that if he found any of this way, whether they were men or women, he might bring them bound unto Jerusalem. **22:4–5** [4]And I persecuted this way unto the death, binding and delivering into prisons both men and women. [5]As also the high priest doth bear me witness, and all the estate of the elders: from whom also I received letters unto the brethren, and went to Damascus, to bring them which were there bound unto Jerusalem, for to be punished. **26:9–11** [9]I verily thought with myself, that I ought to do many things contrary to the name of Jesus of Nazareth. [10]Which thing I also did in Jerusalem: and many of the saints did I shut up in prison, having received authority from the chief priests; and when they were put to death, I gave my voice against them. [11]And I punished them oft in every synagogue, and compelled them to blaspheme; and being exceedingly mad against them, I persecuted them even unto strange cities.

ACTS 22:20—Paul speaks of his life as a zealous Jew and his radical conversion (22:1–21)

Theme	ACTS
Paul at Stephen's stoning	**22:20** [20]And when the blood of thy martyr Stephen was shed, I also was standing by, and consenting unto his death, and kept the raiment of them that slew him. **7:58** [58]And cast him out of the city, and stoned him: and the witnesses laid down their clothes at a young man's feet, whose name was Saul. **8:1** [1]And Saul was consenting unto his death. And at that time there was a great persecution against the church which was at Jerusalem; and they were all scattered abroad throughout the regions of Judaea and Samaria, except the apostles.

ACTS 22:21—Paul speaks of his life as a zealous Jew and his radical conversion (22:1–21)

Theme	ACTS	Paul
Paul called to serve Gentiles	**22:21** [21]And he said unto me, Depart: for I will send thee far hence unto the Gentiles. **9:15** [15]But the Lord said unto him, Go thy way: for he is a chosen vessel unto me, to bear my name before the Gentiles, and kings, and the children of Israel: **26:15** [15]And I said, Who art thou, Lord? And he said, I am Jesus whom thou persecutest.	**Gal 2:7–9** [7]But contrariwise, when they saw that the gospel of the uncircumcision was committed unto me, as the gospel of the circumcision was unto Peter; [8](For he that wrought effectually in Peter to the apostleship of the circumcision, the same was mighty in me toward the Gentiles:) [9]And when James, Cephas, and John, who seemed to be pillars, perceived the grace that was given unto me, they gave to me and Barnabas the right hands of fellowship; that we should go unto the heathen, and they unto the circumcision.

Paul imprisoned; Paul released due to Roman citizenship 22:22–29

ACTS 22:22—Paul imprisoned. Paul released due to Roman citizenship (22:22–29)

Theme	ACTS	Lk	Jn
People martyred Jesus	**22:22** [22]And they gave him audience unto this word, and then lifted up their voices, and said, Away with such a fellow from the earth: for it is not fit that he should live. **21:36** [36]For the multitude of the people followed after, crying, Away with him.	**23:18** [18]And they cried out all at once, saying, Away with this man, and release unto us Barabbas:	**19:15** [15]But they cried out, Away with him, away with him, crucify him. Pilate saith unto them, Shall I crucify your King? The chief priests answered, We have no king but Caesar.

ACTS 22:25—Paul imprisoned. Paul released due to Roman citizenship (22:22–29)

Theme	ACTS
Paul's defense from scourging	**22:25** [25]And as they bound him with thongs, Paul said unto the centurion that stood by, Is it lawful for you to scourge a man that is a Roman, and uncondemned? **16:37** [37]But Paul said unto them, They have beaten us openly uncondemned, being Romans, and have cast us into prison; and now do they thrust us out privily? nay verily; but let them come themselves and fetch us out.

Paul's trial before the Sanhedrin 22:30–23:11

ACTS 23:1—Paul's trial before the Sanhedrin (22:30–23:11)

Theme	ACTS
Clear conscience	**23:1** [1]And Paul, earnestly beholding the council, said, Men and brethren, I have lived in all good conscience before God until this day. **24:16** [16]And herein do I exercise myself, to have always a conscience void of offence toward God, and toward men.

ACTS 23:3—Paul's trial before the Sanhedrin (22:30–23:11)

Theme	ACTS	Mt	Jewish Writings	Other
Under God's wrath	**23:3** [3]Then said Paul unto him, God shall smite thee, thou whited wall: for sittest thou to judge me after the law, and commandest me to be smitten contrary to the law? **9:5** [5]And he said, Who art thou, Lord? And the Lord said, I am Jesus whom thou persecutest: it is hard for thee to kick against the pricks. **26:15** [15]And I said, Who art thou, Lord? And he said, I am Jesus whom thou persecutest.	**23:27** [27]Woe unto you, scribes and Pharisees, hypocrites! for ye are like unto whited sepulchres, which indeed appear beautiful outward, but are within full of dead men's bones, and of all uncleanness.	**Ezek 13:10–15** [10]Because, even because they have seduced my people, saying, Peace; and there was no peace; and one built up a wall, and, lo, others daubed it with untempered mortar: [11]Say unto them which daub it with untempered mortar, that it shall fall: there shall be an overflowing shower; and ye, O great hailstones, shall fall; and a stormy wind shall rend it. [12]Lo, when the wall is fallen, shall it not be said unto you, Where is the daubing wherewith ye have daubed it? [13]Therefore thus saith the Lord GOD; I will even rend it with a stormy wind in my fury; and there shall be an overflowing shower in mine anger, and great hailstones in my fury to consume it. [14]So will I break down the wall that ye have daubed with untempered mortar, and bring it down to the ground, so that the foundation thereof shall be discovered, and it shall fall, and ye shall be consumed in the midst thereof: and ye shall know that I am the LORD. [15]Thus will I accomplish my wrath upon the wall, and upon them that have daubed it with untempered mortar, and will say unto you, The wall is no more, neither they that daubed it;	**Q-Quelle** Against Pharisees: Acts 23:3/ Mt 23:4-36/ [Mk 7:1-9]/ [Luke 11:37-54 (QS 34{Thom 39:1, 89, 102])]

ACTS 23:5—Paul's trial before the Sanhedrin (22:30–23:11)

Theme	ACTS	Jewish Writings
Assaut against authority	**23:5** [5]Then said Paul, I wist not, brethren, that he was the high priest: for it is written, Thou shalt not speak evil of the ruler of thy people.	**Ex 22:27** [27]Her princes in the midst thereof are like wolves ravening the prey, to shed blood, and to destroy souls, to get dishonest gain.

ACTS 23:6—Paul's trial before the Sanhedrin (22:30–23:11)

Theme	ACTS	Paul
Paul was a Pharisee	**23:6** [6]But when Paul perceived that the one part were Sadducees, and the other Pharisees, he cried out in the council, Men and brethren, I am a Pharisee, the son of a Pharisee: of the hope and resurrection of the dead I am called in question. **24:15, 21** [15]And have hope toward God, which they themselves also allow, that there shall be a resurrection of the dead, both of the just and unjust. . . . [21]Except it be for this one voice, that I cried standing among them, Touching the resurrection of the dead I am called in question by you this day. **26:5** [5]Which knew me from the beginning, if they would testify, that after the most straitest sect of our religion I lived a Pharisee.	**Phil 3:5** [5]Circumcised the eighth day, of the stock of Israel, of the tribe of Benjamin, an Hebrew of the Hebrews; as touching the law, a Pharisee;

ACTS 23:8—Paul's trial before the Sanhedrin (22:30–23:11)

Theme	ACTS	Mt	Lk
Sadducees say...	**23:8** [8]For the Sadducees say that there is no resurrection, neither angel, nor spirit: but the Pharisees confess both	**22:23** [23]The same day came to him the Sadducees, which say that there is no resurrection, and asked him,	**20:27** [27]Then came to him certain of the Sadducees, which deny that there is any resurrection; and they asked him,

ACTS 23:11—Paul's trial before the Sanhedrin (22:30–23:11)

Theme	ACTS
Paul's call	**23:11** [11]And the night following the Lord stood by him, and said, Be of good cheer, Paul: for as thou hast testified of me in Jerusalem, so must thou bear witness also at Rome. **19:21** [21]After these things were ended, Paul purposed in the spirit, when he had passed through Macedonia and Achaia, to go to Jerusalem, saying, After I have been there, I must also see Rome.

Paul transferred to Caesarea 23:12–35

ACTS 23:27—Paul transferred to Caesarea (23:12–35)

Theme	ACTS
Paul shielded in circumstances	**23:27** [27]This man was taken of the Jews, and should have been killed of them: then came I with an army, and rescued him, having understood that he was a Roman. **21:30–34** [30]And when Paul would have entered in unto the people, the disciples suffered him not. [31]And certain of the chief of Asia, which were his friends, sent unto him, desiring him that he would not adventure himself into the theatre. [32]Some therefore cried one thing, and some another: for the assembly was confused; and the more part knew not wherefore they were come together. [33]And they drew Alexander out of the multitude, the Jews putting him forward. And Alexander beckoned with the hand, and would have made his defence unto the people. [34]But when they knew that he was a Jew, all with one voice about the space of two hours cried out, Great is Diana of the Ephesians. **22:27** [27]Then the chief captain came, and said unto him, Tell me, art thou a Roman? He said, Yea.

ACTS 23:29—Paul transferred to Caesarea (23:12–35)

Theme	ACTS
Government will not judge religious law	**23:29** [29]Whom I perceived to be accused of questions of their law, but to have nothing laid to his charge worthy of death or of bonds. **18:14–15** [14]And when Paul was now about to open his mouth, Gallio said unto the Jews, If it were a matter of wrong or wicked lewdness, O ye Jews, reason would that I should bear with you: [15]But if it be a question of words and names, and of your law, look ye to it; for I will be no judge of such matters. **25:18–19** [18]Against whom when the accusers stood up, they brought none accusation of such things as I supposed: [19]But had certain questions against him of their own superstition, and of one Jesus, which was dead, whom Paul affirmed to be alive.

Paul's trial before Felix 24:1–23

ACTS 24:5—Paul's trial before Felix (24:1–23)

Theme	ACTS	Lk
Charges of sedition	**24:5** [5]For we have found this man a pestilent fellow, and a mover of sedition among all the Jews throughout the world, and a ringleader of the sect of the Nazarenes: **24:14** [14]But this I confess unto thee, that after the way which they call heresy, so worship I the God of my fathers, believing all things which are written in the law and in the prophets:	**23:2** [2]And they began to accuse him, saying, We found this fellow perverting the nation, and forbidding to give tribute to Caesar, saying that he himself is Christ a King.

ACTS 24:6—Paul's trial before Felix (24:1–23)

Theme	ACTS	Paul
Paul riles Jews and makes defense	**24:6** [6]Who also hath gone about to profane the temple: whom we took, and would have judged according to our law. **21:28** [28]Crying out, Men of Israel, help: This is the man, that teacheth all men every where against the people, and the law, and this place: and further brought Greeks also into the temple, and hath polluted this holy place.	**Phil 3:5** [5]Circumcised the eighth day, of the stock of Israel, of the tribe of Benjamin, an Hebrew of the Hebrews; as touching the law, a Pharisee;

ACTS 24:15—Paul's trial before Felix (24:1–23)

Theme	ACTS	Jn	Jewish Writings
Resurrection of just and unjust	**24:15** [15]And have hope toward God, which they themselves also allow, that there shall be a resurrection of the dead, both of the just and unjust.	**5:28–29** [28]Marvel not at this: for the hour is coming, in the which all that are in the graves shall hear his voice, [29]And shall come forth; they that have done good, unto the resurrection of life; and they that have done evil, unto the resurrection of damnation.	**Dan 12:2** [2]And many of them that sleep in the dust of the earth shall awake, some to everlasting life, and some to shame and everlasting contempt.

ACTS 24:16—Paul's trial before Felix (24:1–23)

Theme	ACTS
Good conscience	**24:16** [16]And herein do I exercise myself, to have always a conscience void of offence toward God, and toward men. **23:1** [1]And Paul, earnestly beholding the council, said, Men and brethren, I have lived in all good conscience before God until this day.

ACTS 24:17—Paul's trial before Felix (24:1–23)

Theme	ACTS	Paul
Doing good for others	**24:17** [17]Now after many years I came to bring alms to my nation, and offerings. **24:16** [16]And herein do I exercise myself, to have always a conscience void of offence toward God, and toward men.	**Rom 15:25–26** [25]But now I go unto Jerusalem to minister unto the saints. [26]For it hath pleased them of Macedonia and Achaia to make a certain contribution for the poor saints which are at Jerusalem. **Gal 2:10** [10]Only they would that we should remember the poor; the same which I also was forward to do.

ACTS 24:19–20—Paul's trial before Felix (24:1–23)

Theme	ACTS	Mt	Jewish Writings	Other
God only honors sanctified religious leaders	**24:19–20** [19]Who ought to have been here before thee, and object, if they had ought against me. [20]Or else let these same here say, if they have found any evil doing in me, while I stood before the council, **21:26–30** [26]Then Paul took the men, and the next day purifying himself with them entered into the temple, to signify the accomplishment of the days of purification, until that an offering should be offered for every one of them. [27]And when the seven days were almost ended, the Jews which were of Asia, when they saw him in the temple, stirred up all the people, and laid hands on him, [28]Crying out, Men of Israel, help: This is the man, that teacheth all men every where against the people, and the law, and this place: and further brought Greeks also into the temple, and hath polluted this holy place. [29](For they had seen before with him in the city Trophimus an Ephesian, whom they supposed that Paul had brought into the temple.) [30]And all the city was moved, and the people ran together: and they took Paul, and drew him out of the temple: and forthwith the doors were shut.	**23:27** [27]Woe unto you, scribes and Pharisees, hypocrites! for ye are like unto whited sepulchres, which indeed appear beautiful outward, but are within full of dead men's bones, and of all uncleanness.	**Ezek 13:10–15** [10]Because, even because they have seduced my people, saying, Peace; and there was no peace; and one built up a wall, and, lo, others daubed it with untempered mortar: [11]Say unto them which daub it with untempered mortar, that it shall fall: there shall be an overflowing shower; and ye, O great hailstones, shall fall; and a stormy wind shall rend it. [12]Lo, when the wall is fallen, shall it not be said unto you, Where is the daubing wherewith ye have daubed it? [13]Therefore thus saith the Lord GOD; I will even rend it with a stormy wind in my fury; and there shall be an overflowing shower in mine anger, and great hailstones in my fury to consume it. [14]So will I break down the wall that ye have daubed with untempered mortar, and bring it down to the ground, so that the foundation thereof shall be discovered, and it shall fall, and ye shall be consumed in the midst thereof: and ye shall know that I am the LORD. [15]Thus will I accomplish my wrath upon the wall, and upon them that have daubed it with untempered mortar, and will say unto you, The wall is no more, neither they that daubed it;	**Q-Quelle** Against Pharisees: Acts 24:19-20/ Mt 23:4-36/ [Mk 7:1-9]/ Lk 11:37-54 (QS 34 [Thom 39.1, 89, 102)]

ACTS 24:21—Paul's trial before Felix (24:1–23)

Theme	ACTS
Resurrection and the Pharisees	**24:21** [21]Except it be for this one voice, that I cried standing among them, Touching the resurrection of the dead I am called in question by you this day. **23:6** [6]But when Paul perceived that the one part were Sadducees, and the other Pharisees, he cried out in the council, Men and brethren, I am a Pharisee, the son of a Pharisee: of the hope and resurrection of the dead I am called in question. **24:15** [15]And have hope toward God, which they themselves also allow, that there shall be a resurrection of the dead, both of the just and unjust.

Felix delays Paul's trial. He left Paul in prison when succeeded by Porcius Festus (24:12–27)

Paul before King Agrippa 25:13–27

ACTS 25:14—Paul before King Agrippa (25:13–27)

Theme	ACTS
Paul and Felix	**25:14** [14]And when they had been there many days, Festus declared Paul's cause unto the king, saying, There is a certain man left in bonds by Felix: **24:27** [27]But after two years Porcius Festus came into Felix' room: and Felix, willing to show the Jews a pleasure, left Paul bound.

ACTS 25:18–19—Paul before King Agrippa (25:13–27)

Theme	ACTS
Paul's testimony	**25:18–19** [18]Against whom when the accusers stood up, they brought none accusation of such things as I supposed: [19]But had certain questions against him of their own superstition, and of one Jesus, which was dead, whom Paul affirmed to be alive. **18:14–15** [14]And when Paul was now about to open his mouth, Gallio said unto the Jews, If it were a matter of wrong or wicked lewdness, O ye Jews, reason would that I should bear with you: [15]But if it be a question of words and names, and of your law, look ye to it; for I will be no judge of such matters. **23:29** [29]Whom I perceived to be accused of questions of their law, but to have nothing laid to his charge worthy of death or of bonds.

King Agrippa hears Paul 26:1–23

ACTS 26:5—King Agrippa hears Paul (26:1–23)

Theme	ACTS	Paul
Paul, a Pharisee	**26:5** [5]Which knew me from the beginning, if they would testify, that after the most straitest sect of our religion I lived a Pharisee.	**2 Cor 11:22** [22]Are they Hebrews? so am I. Are they Israelites? so am I. Are they the seed of Abraham? so am I. **Gal 1:13–14** [13]For ye have heard of my conversation in time past in the Jews' religion, how that beyond measure I persecuted the church of God, and wasted it: [14]And profited in the Jews' religion above many my equals in mine own nation, being more exceedingly zealous of the traditions of my fathers. **Phil 3:5–6** [5]Circumcised the eighth day, of the stock of Israel, of the tribe of Benjamin, an Hebrew of the Hebrews; as touching the law, a Pharisee; [6]Concerning zeal, persecuting the church; touching the righteousness which is in the law, blameless.

ACTS 26:6–8—King Agrippa hears Paul (26:1–23)

Theme	ACTS
Paul on trial	**26:6–8** [6]And now I stand and am judged for the hope of the promise made of God unto our fathers: [7]Unto which promise our twelve tribes, instantly serving God day and night, hope to come. For which hope's sake, king Agrippa, I am accused of the Jews. [8]Why should it be thought a thing incredible with you, that God should raise the dead? **23:6** [6]But when Paul perceived that the one part were Sadducees, and the other Pharisees, he cried out in the council, Men and brethren, I am a Pharisee, the son of a Pharisee: of the hope and resurrection of the dead I am called in question. **24:15** [15]And have hope toward God, which they themselves also allow, that there shall be a resurrection of the dead, both of the just and unjust. . . . **24:21** [21]Except it be for this one voice, that I cried standing among them, Touching the resurrection of the dead I am called in question by you this day. **28:20** [20]For this cause therefore have I called for you, to see you, and to speak with you: because that for the hope of Israel I am bound with this chain.

ACTS 26:9–11—King Agrippa hears Paul (26:1–23)

Theme	ACTS	Paul
Paul persecuted the Church	**26:9–11** [9]I verily thought with myself, that I ought to do many things contrary to the name of Jesus of Nazareth. [10]Which thing I also did in Jerusalem: and many of the saints did I shut up in prison, having received authority from the chief priests; and when they were put to death, I gave my voice against them. [11]And I punished them oft in every synagogue, and compelled them to blaspheme; and being exceedingly mad against them, I persecuted them even unto strange cities. **8:3** [3]As for Saul, he made havock of the church, entering into every house, and haling men and women committed them to prison. **9:1–2** [1]And Saul, yet breathing out threatenings and slaughter against the disciples of the Lord, went unto the high priest, [2]And desired of him letters to Damascus to the synagogues, that if he found any of this way, whether they were men or women, he might bring them bound unto Jerusalem. **22:19** [19]And I said, Lord, they know that I imprisoned and beat in every synagogue them that believed on thee:	**Phil 3:6** [6]Concerning zeal, persecuting the church; touching the righteousness which is in the law, blameless.

ACTS 26:10—King Agrippa hears Paul (26:1–23)

Theme	ACTS
Jewish authority to persecute	**26:10** [10]Which thing I also did in Jerusalem: and many of the saints did I shut up in prison, having received authority from the chief priests; and when they were put to death, I gave my voice against them. **9:14** [14]And here he hath authority from the chief priests to bind all that call on thy name.

ACTS 26:13–14—King Agrippa hears Paul (26:1–23)

Theme	ACTS
Paul's testimony of faith	**26:13–14** [13]At midday, O king, I saw in the way a light from heaven, above the brightness of the sun, shining round about me and them which journeyed with me. [14]And when we were all fallen to the earth, I heard a voice speaking unto me, and saying in the Hebrew tongue, Saul, Saul, why persecutest thou me? it is hard for thee to kick against the pricks. **9:3–4** [3]And as he journeyed, he came near Damascus: and suddenly there shined round about him a light from heaven: [4]And he fell to the earth, and heard a voice saying unto him, Saul, Saul, why persecutest thou me? **9:7** [7]And the men which journeyed with him stood speechless, hearing a voice, but seeing no man. **22:6–7** [6]And it came to pass, that, as I made my journey, and was come nigh unto Damascus about noon, suddenly there shone from heaven a great light round about me. [7]And I fell unto the ground, and heard a voice saying unto me, Saul, Saul, why persecutest thou me?

ACTS 26:15—King Agrippa hears Paul (26:1–23)

Theme	ACTS	Mt
Paul testifies about Damascus experience	**26:15** [15]And I said, Who art thou, Lord? And he said, I am Jesus whom thou persecutest. **9:5** [5]And he said, Who art thou, Lord? And the Lord said, I am Jesus whom thou persecut-est: it is hard for thee to kick against the pricks. **22:8** [8]And I answered, Who art thou, Lord? And he said unto me, I am Jesus of Nazareth, whom thou persecutest.	**25:40** [40]And the King shall answer and say unto them, Verily I say unto you, Inasmuch as ye have done it unto one of the least of these my brethren, ye have done it unto me.

ACTS 26:16—King Agrippa hears Paul (26:1–23)

Theme	ACTS	Jewish Writings
Paul called to Gentile ministry	**26:16** [16]But rise, and stand upon thy feet: for I have appeared unto thee for this purpose, to make thee a minister and a witness both of these things which thou hast seen, and of those things in the which I will appear unto thee; **9:6** [6]And he trembling and astonished said, Lord, what wilt thou have me to do? And the Lord said unto him, Arise, and go into the city, and it shall be told thee what thou must do. **22:10** [10]And I said, What shall I do, Lord? And the Lord said unto me, Arise, and go into Damascus; and there it shall be told thee of all things which are appointed for thee to do.	**Ezek 2:1** [1]And he said unto me, Son of man, stand upon thy feet, and I will speak unto thee.

ACTS 26:17—King Agrippa hears Paul (26:1–23)

Theme	ACTS	Jewish Writings
Sending	**26:17** [17]Delivering thee from the people, and from the Gentiles, unto whom now I send thee,	**Jer 1:7** [7]But the LORD said unto me, Say not, I am a child: for thou shalt go to all that I shall send thee, and whatsoever I command thee thou shalt speak.

ACTS 26:18—King Agrippa hears Paul (26:1–23)

Theme	ACTS	Paul	Jewish Writings
Opening blind eyes	**26:18** [18]To open their eyes, and to turn them from darkness to light, and from the power of Satan unto God, that they may receive forgiveness of sins, and inheritance among them which are sanctified by faith that is in me.	**Col 1:13** [13]Who hath delivered us from the power of darkness, and hath translated us into the kingdom of his dear Son:	**Is 42:7, 16** [7]To open the blind eyes, to bring out the prisoners from the prison, and them that sit in darkness out of the prison house. . . . [16]And I will bring the blind by a way that they knew not; I will lead them in paths that they have not known: I will make darkness light before them, and crooked things straight. These things will I do unto them, and not forsake them. **Is 61:1 (see LXX)** [1]The Spirit of the Lord GOD is upon me; because the LORD hath anointed me to preach good tidings unto the meek; he hath sent me to bind up the brokenhearted, to proclaim liberty to the captives, and the opening of the prison to them that are bound;

ACTS 26:20—King Agrippa hears Paul (26:1–23)

Theme	ACTS
Word to Jews first, then Gentiles	**26:20**
	[20]But showed first unto them of Damascus, and at Jerusalem, and throughout all the coasts of Judaea, and then to the Gentiles, that they should repent and turn to God, and do works meet for repentance.
	1:5
	[5]For John truly baptized with water; but ye shall be baptized with the Holy Ghost not many days hence.
	2:38
	[28]Thou hast made known to me the ways of life; thou shalt make me full of joy with thy countenance.
	11:16
	[16]Then remembered I the word of the Lord, how that he said, John indeed baptized with water; but ye shall be baptized with the Holy Ghost.
	13:10
	[10]And said, O full of all subtlety and all mischief, thou child of the devil, thou enemy of all righteousness, wilt thou not cease to pervert the right ways of the Lord?
	13:24–25
	[24]When John had first preached before his coming the baptism of repentance to all the people of Israel. [25]And as John fulfilled his course, he said, Whom think ye that I am? I am not he. But, behold, there cometh one after me, whose shoes of his feet I am not worthy to loose.
	13:47
	[47]For so hath the Lord commanded us, saying, I have set thee to be a light of the Gentiles, that thou shouldest be for salva- tion unto the ends of the earth.
	19:1–7
	[1]And it came to pass, that, while Apollos was at Corinth, Paul having passed through the upper coasts came to Ephesus: and finding certain disciples, [2]He said unto them, Have ye received the Holy Ghost since ye believed? And they said unto him, We have not so much as heard whether there be any Holy Ghost. [3]And he said unto them, Unto what then were ye baptized? And they said, Unto John's baptism. [4]Then said Paul, John verily baptized with the baptism of repentance, say- ing unto the people, that they should believe on him which should come after him, that is, on Christ Jesus. [5]When they heard this, they were baptized in the name of the Lord Jesus. [6]And when Paul had laid his hands upon them, the Holy Ghost came on them; and they spake with tongues, and prophesied. [7]And all the men were about twelve.
	28:28
	[28]Be it known therefore unto you, that the salvation of God is sent unto the Gentiles, and that they will hear it.

Mt	Mk
1:15 [15]And Eliud begat Eleazar; and Eleazar begat Matthan; and Matthan begat Jacob; **3:1–12** [1]In those days came John the Baptist, preaching in the wilderness of Judaea, [2]And saying, Repent ye: for the kingdom of heaven is at hand. [3]For this is he that was spoken of by the prophet Esaias, saying, The voice of one crying in the wilderness, Prepare ye the way of the Lord, make his paths straight. [4]And the same John had his raiment of camel's hair, and a leathern girdle about his loins; and his meat was locusts and wild honey. [5]Then went out to him Jerusalem, and all Judaea, and all the region round about Jordan, [6]And were baptized of him in Jordan, confessing their sins. [7]But when he saw many of the Pharisees and Sadducees come to his baptism, he said unto them, O generation of vipers, who hath warned you to flee from the wrath to come? [8]Bring forth therefore fruits meet for repentance: [9]And think not to say within your-selves, We have Abraham to our father: for I say unto you, that God is able of these stones to raise up children unto Abraham. [10]And now also the axe is laid unto the root of the trees: therefore every tree which bringeth not forth good fruit is hewn down, and cast into the fire. [11]I indeed baptize you with water unto repentance: but he that cometh after me is mightier than I, whose shoes I am not worthy to bear: he shall baptize you with the Holy Ghost, and with fire: [12]Whose fan is in his hand, and he will thoroughly purge his floor, and gather his wheat into the garner; but he will burn up the chaff with unquenchable fire. **7:19** [19]Every tree that bringeth not forth good fruit is hewn down, and cast into the fire. **11:10** [10]For this is he, of whom it is written, Behold, I send my messenger before thy face, which shall prepare thy way before thee. **14:3–4** [3]For Herod had laid hold on John, and bound him, and put him in prison for Herodias' sake, his brother Philip's wife. [4]For John said unto him, It is not lawful for thee to have her.	**1:2–8** [2]As it is written in the prophets, Behold, I send my messenger before thy face, which shall prepare thy way before thee. [3]The voice of one crying in the wilderness, Prepare ye the way of the Lord, make his paths straight. [4]John did baptize in the wilderness, and preach the baptism of repentance for the remission of sins. [5]And there went out unto him all the land of Judaea, and they of Jerusalem, and were all baptized of him in the river of Jordan, confessing their sins. [6]And John was clothed with camel's hair, and with a girdle of a skin about his loins; and he did eat locusts and wild honey; [7]And preached, saying, There cometh one mightier than I after me, the latchet of whose shoes I am not worthy to stoop down and unloose. [8]I indeed have baptized you with water: but he shall baptize you with the Holy Ghost. **1:15** [15]And saying, The time is fulfilled, and the kingdom of God is at hand: repent ye, and believe the gospel. **6:17–18** [17]For Herod himself had sent forth and laid hold upon John, and bound him in prison for Herodias' sake, his brother Philip's wife: for he had married her. [18]For John had said unto Herod, It is not lawful for thee to have thy brother's wife.

Acts 26:20 continued on next page

ACTS 26:20—King Agrippa hears Paul (26:1–23) (*continued*)

Theme	ACTS	Lk
(*Cont.*) **Word to Jews first, then Gentiles**	**26:20 (above)** **1:5 (above)** **2:38 (above)** **11:16 (above)** **13:10 (above)** **13:24–25 (above)** **13:47 (above)** **19:1–7 (above)** **28:28 (above)**	**1:76** [76]And thou, child, shalt be called the prophet of the Highest: for thou shalt go before the face of the Lord to prepare his **2:30–32** [30]For mine eyes have seen thy salvation, [31]Which thou hast prepared before the face of all people; [32]A light to lighten the Gentiles, and the glory of thy people Israel. **3:1–20** [1]Now in the fifteenth year of the reign of Tiberius Caesar, Pontius Pilate being governor of Judaea, and Herod being tetrarch of Galilee, and his brother Philip tetrarch of Ituraea and of the region of Trachonitis, and Lysanias the tetrarch of Abilene, [2]Annas and Caiaphas being the high priests, the word of God came unto John the son of Zacharias in the wilderness. [3]And he came into all the country about Jordan, preaching the baptism of repentance for the remission of sins; [4]As it is written in the book of the words of Esaias the prophet, saying, The voice of one crying in the wilderness, Prepare ye the way of the Lord, make his paths straight. [5]Every valley shall be filled, and every mountain and hill shall be brought low; and the crooked shall be made straight, and the rough ways shall be made smooth; [6]And all flesh shall see the salvation of God. [7]Then said he to the multitude that came forth to be baptized of him, O generation of vipers, who hath warned you to flee from the wrath to come? [8]Bring forth therefore fruits worthy of repentance, and begin not to say within yourselves, We have Abraham to our father: for I say unto you, That God is able of these stones to raise up children unto Abraham. [9]And now also the axe is laid unto the root of the trees: every tree therefore which bringeth not forth good fruit is hewn down, and cast into the fire. [10]And the people asked him, saying, What shall we do then? [11]He answereth and saith unto them, He that hath two coats, let him impart to him that hath none; and he that hath meat, let him do likewise. [12]Then came also publicans to be baptized, and said unto him, Master, what shall we do? [13]And he said unto them, Exact no more than that which is appointed you. [14]And the soldiers likewise demanded of him, saying, And what shall we do? And he said unto them, Do violence to no man, neither accuse any falsely; and be content with your wages. [15]And as the people were in expectation, and all men mused in their hearts of John, whether he were the Christ, or not; [16]John answered, saying unto them all, I indeed baptize you with water; but one mightier than I cometh, the latchet of whose shoes I am not worthy to unloose: he shall baptize you with the Holy Ghost and with fire: [17]Whose fan is in his hand, and he will thoroughly purge his floor, and will gather the wheat into his garner; but the chaff he will burn with fire unquenchable. [18]And many other things in his exhortation preached he unto the people. [19]But Herod the tetrarch, being reproved by him for Herodias his brother Philip's wife, and for all the evils which Herod had done, [20]Added yet this above all, that he shut up John in prison. ways; **6:43–44** [43]For a good tree bringeth not forth corrupt fruit; neither doth a corrupt tree bring forth good fruit. [44]For every tree is known by his own fruit. For of thorns men do not gather figs, nor of a bramble bush gather they grapes. **7:27** [27]This is he, of whom it is written, Behold, I send my messenger before thy face, which shall prepare thy way before thee. **13:6–9** [6]He spake also this parable; A certain man had a fig tree planted in his vineyard; and he came and sought fruit thereon, and found none. [7]Then said he unto the dresser of his vineyard, Behold, these three years I come seeking fruit on this fig tree, and find none: cut it down; why cumbereth it the ground? [8]And he answering said unto him, Lord, let it alone this year also, till I shall dig about it, and dung it: [9]And if it bear fruit, well: and if not, then after that thou shalt cut it down. **13:31** [31]The same day there came certain of the Pharisees, saying unto him, Get thee out, and depart hence: for Herod will kill thee. **23:8** [8]And when Herod saw Jesus, he was exceeding glad: for he was desirous to see him of a long season, because he had heard many things of him; and he hoped to have seen some miracle done by him.

Jn

1:19–28

[19]And this is the record of John,
when the Jews sent priests and
Levites from Jerusalem to ask him,
Who art thou? [20]And he confessed,
and denied not; but confessed, I am
not the Christ. [21]And they asked
him, What then? Art thou Elias?
And he saith, I am not. Art thou
that prophet? And he answered,
No. [22]Then said they unto him,
Who art thou? that we may give an
answer to them that sent us. What
sayest thou of thyself? [23]He said, I
am the voice of one crying in the
wilderness, Make straight the way
of the Lord, as said the prophet
Esaias. [24]And they which were sent
were of the Pharisees. [25]And they
asked him, and said unto him, Why
baptizest thou then, if thou be not
that Christ, nor Elias, neither that
prophet? [26]John answered them, saying, I baptize with water: but there
standeth one among you, whom ye
know not; [27]He it is, who coming
after me is preferred before me,
whose shoe's latchet I am not worthy
to unloose. [28]These things were done
in Bethabara beyond Jordan, where
John was baptizing.

1:31–32

[31]And I knew him not: but that he
should be made manifest to Israel,
therefore am I come baptizing with
water. [32]And John bare record, saying, I saw the Spirit descending from
heaven like a dove, and it abode
upon him.

8:39

[39]They answered and said unto him,
Abraham is our father. Jesus saith
unto them, If ye were Abraham's
children, ye would do the works of
Abraham.

Acts 26:20 continued on next page

ACTS 26:20—King Agrippa hears Paul (26:1–23) (*continued*)

Theme	ACTS	Jewish Writings
(*Cont.*) **Word to Jews first, then Gentiles**	**26:20 (above)** **1:5 (above)** **2:38 (above)** **11:16 (above)** **13:10 (above)** **13:24–25 (above)** **13:47 (above)** **19:1–7 (above)** **28:28 (above)**	**2 Kgs 1:8** [8]And they answered him, He was an hairy man, and girt with a girdle of leather about his loins. And he said, It is Elijah the Tishbite. **Is 40:3–6** [3]The voice of him that crieth in the wilderness, Prepare ye the way of the LORD, make straight in the desert a highway for our God. [4]Every valley shall be exalted, and every mountain and hill shall be made low: and the crooked shall be made straight, and the rough places plain: [5]And the glory of the LORD shall be revealed, and all flesh shall see it together: for the mouth of the LORD hath spoken it. [6]The voice said, Cry. And he said, What shall I cry? All flesh is grass, and all the goodliness thereof is as the flower of the field: **Mal 3:1a** [1]Behold, I will send my messenger, and he shall prepare the way before me:

Other

1 ApocJas

[Lord] "Nothing existed except Him-who-is. He is unnameable and ineffable. I myself am also unnameable, from Him-who-is, just as I have been given a number of names—two from Him-who-is. And I, I am before you. . . .But I have brought forth the image of him so that the sons of Him-who-is might know what things are theirs and what things are alien (to them). Behold, I shall reveal to you everything of this mystery. . . .I, however, shall reveal to you what has come forth from him who has no number. I shall give a sign concerning their number. As for what has come forth from him who has no measure, I shall give a sign concerning their measure. James, I praise your understanding and your fear. If you continue to be distressed, do not be concerned for anything else except your redemption. For behold, I shall complete this destiny upon this earth as I have said from the heavens. And I shall reveal to you your redemption." . . . James said, "Rabbi, how, after these things, will you appear to us again? After they seize you, and you complete this destiny, you will go up to Him-who-is." . . . The Lord said, "James, after these things I shall reveal to you everything, not for your sake alone but for the sake of the unbelief of men, so that faith may exist in them. For a multitude will attain to faith and they will increase in [. . .]. And after this I shall appear for a reproof to the archons. But I shall call upon the imperishable knowledge, which is Sophia who is in the Father (and) who is the mother of Achamoth. Achamoth had no father nor male consort, but she is female from a female. She produced you without a male, since she was alone (and) in ignorance as to what lives through her mother because she thought that she alone existed. But I shall cry out to her mother. And then they will fall into confusion (and) will blame their root and the race of their mother. But you will go up to what is yours [. . .] you will [. . .] the Pre-existent One. They will pursue him exceedingly, since they are from his [. . .] companions. He will be proclaimed through them, and they will proclaim this word. Then he will become a seed of [. . .]." . . . James said, "I am satisfied [. . .] and they are [. . .] my soul. Yet another thing I ask of you: who are the seven women who have been your disciples? And behold all women bless you. I also am amazed how powerless vessels have become strong by a perception which is in them." . . . The Lord said, "You [. . .] well [. . .] a spirit of [. . .], a spirit of thought, a spirit of counsel of a [. . .], a spirit [. . .] a spirit of knowledge [. . .] of their fear. [. . .] when we had passed through the breath of this archon who is named Adonaios [. . .] him and [. . .] he was ignorant [. . .] when I came forth from him, he remembered that I am a son of his. He was gracious to me at that time as his son. And then, before <I> appeared here, <he> cast them among this people. And from the place of heaven the prophets [. . .]." . . . James said, "Rabbi, [. . .] I [. . .] all together [. . .] in them especially [. . .]." The Lord said, "James, I praise you [. . .] walk upon the earth [. . .] the words while he [. . .] on the [. . .]. For cast away from you the cup which is bitterness. For some from [. . .] set themselves against you. For you have begun to understand their roots from beginning to end.

GEbi 2 and 3

[2]For by chopping off the genealogies of Matthew they made their gospel begin as we indicated before, with the words: "And so in the days of Herod, King of Judea, when Caiaphas was high priest, a certain one named John came baptizing a baptism of repentance in the Jordan River." [3]And so John was baptizing, and Pharisees came to him and were baptized, as was all of Jerusalem. John wore a garment of camel hair and a leather belt around his waist; and his food was wild honey that tasted like manna, like a cake cooked in oil. (Epiphanius, Panarion, 30, 13, 4-5)

Q-Quelle

Preaching of John: Acts 26:20/Mt 3:7-10, Mt 3:11-12/Mk 1:7-8/Lk 3:7-9(QS4), Lk 3:15-18 (QS5); Fruits: Acts 26:20/ Mt 7:15-20 [Mt 12:33-35]/Lk 6:43-45 (QS13/[Thom 45]; Jesus' witness to John: Acts 26:20/Mt 11:7-19, [Mt 21:31-32]/Lk 7:24-35 (QS 17[Thom 74/46]), [Lk 16:16 (QS56)]

ACTS 26:23—King Agrippa hears Paul (26:1–23)

Theme	ACTS	Lk
The Christ suffers and rises	**26:22–23** [22] But those things, which God before had shewed by the mouth of all his prophets, that Christ should suffer, he hath so fulfilled. [23] That Christ should suffer, and that he should be the first that should rise from the dead, and should show light unto the people, and to the Gentiles. **3:18** [18] But those things, which God before had showed by the mouth of all his prophets, that Christ should suffer, he hath so fulfilled.	**2:32** [32] A light to lighten the Gentiles, and the glory of thy people Israel. **2:52** [52] And Jesus increased in wisdom and stature, and in favour with God and man. **24:26–27, 44–47** [26] Ought not Christ to have suffered these things, and to enter into his glory? [27] And beginning at Moses and all the prophets, he expounded unto them in all the scriptures the things concerning himself. . . . [44] And he said unto them, These are the words which I spake unto you, while I was yet with you, that all things must be fulfilled, which were written in the law of Moses, and in the prophets, and in the psalms, concerning me. [45] Then opened he their understanding, that they might understand the scriptures, [46] And said unto them, Thus it is written, and thus it behoved Christ to suffer, and to rise from the dead the third day: [47] And that repentance and remission of sins should be preached in his name among all nations, beginning at Jerusalem.

Agrippa finds no fault with Paul and wants to free him 26:24–32

ACTS 26:32—Agrippa finds no fault with Paul and wants to free him (26:24–32)

Theme	ACTS
Paul appeals to Caesar	**26:32** [32] Then said Agrippa unto Festus, This man might have been set at liberty, if he had not appealed unto Caesar. **25:11–12** [11] For if I be an offender, or have committed any thing worthy of death, I refuse not to die: but if there be none of these things whereof these accuse me, no man may deliver me unto them. I appeal unto Caesar. [12] Then Festus, when he had conferred with the council, answered, Hast thou appealed unto Caesar? unto Caesar shalt thou go

Paul	Jewish Writings
1 Cor 15:20–23	**Lev 12:6, 8**
[20]But now is Christ risen from the dead, and become the firstfruits of them that slept. [21]For since by man came death, by man came also the resurrection of the dead. [22]For as in Adam all die, even so in Christ shall all be made alive. [23]But every man in his own order: Christ the firstfruits; afterward they that are Christ's at his coming.	[6]And when the days of her purifying are fulfilled, for a son, or for a daughter, she shall bring a lamb of the first year for a burnt offering, and a young pigeon, or a turtledove, for a sin offering, unto the door of the tabernacle of the congregation, unto the priest: [8]And if she be not able to bring a lamb, then she shall bring two turtles, or two young pigeons; the one for the burnt offering, and the other for a sin offering: and the priest shall make an atonement for her, and she shall be clean. **Is 42:6** [6]I the LORD have called thee in righteousness, and will hold thine hand, and will keep thee, and give thee for a covenant of the people, for a light of the Gentiles; **Is 49:6** [6]And he said, It is a light thing that thou shouldest be my servant to raise up the tribes of Jacob, and to restore the preserved of Israel: I will also give thee for a light to the Gentiles, that thou mayest be my salvation unto the end of the earth.

Paul departs for Rome under Julias (Cohort Augustus), Adramyttium, Sidon, Cyprus, Cilicia, Pamphylia, Myra, Lycia 27:1–5

ACTS 27:2—Paul departs for Rome under Julias (Cohort Augustus), Adramyttium, Sidon, Cyprus, Cilicia, Pamphylia, Myra, Lycia (27:1–5)

Theme	ACTS
Paul's mission trips	**27:2** [2]And entering into a ship of Adramyttium, we launched, meaning to sail by the coasts of Asia; one Aristarchus, a Macedonian of Thessalonica, being with us. **19:29** [29]And the whole city was filled with confusion: and having caught Gaius and Aristarchus, men of Macedonia, Paul's companions in travel, they rushed with one accord into the theatre. **20:4** [4]And there accompanied him into Asia Sopater of Berea; and of the Thessalonians, Aristarchus and Secundus; and Gaius of Derbe, and Timotheus; and of Asia, Tychicus and Trophimus. **20:9** [9]And there sat in a window a certain young man named Eutychus, being fallen into a deep sleep: and as Paul was long preaching, he sunk down with sleep, and fell down from the third loft, and was taken up dead.

Alexandrian ship—Cnidus, Salome, Fair Havens, Lasea, storm at sea 27:6–44

ACTS 27:9—Alexandrian ship—Cnidus, Salome, Fair Havens, Lasea, storm at sea (27:6–44)

Theme	ACTS	Jewish Writings
Jewish fasting	**27:9** [9]Now when much time was spent, and when sailing was now dangerous, because the fast was now already past, Paul admonished them,	**Lev 16:29–31** [29]And this shall be a statute for ever unto you: that in the seventh month, on the tenth day of the month, ye shall afflict your souls, and do no work at all, whether it be one of your own country, or a stranger that sojourneth among you: [30]For on that day shall the priest make an atonement for you, to cleanse you, that ye may be clean from all your sins before the LORD. [31]It shall be a sabbath of rest unto you, and ye shall afflict your souls, by a statute for ever.

ACTS 27:24—Alexandrian ship—Cnidus, Salome, Fair Havens, Lasea, storm at sea (27:6–44)

Theme	ACTS
Paul to testify in Rome	**27:24** [24]Saying, Fear not, Paul; thou must be brought before Caesar: and, lo, God hath given thee all them that sail with thee. **23:11** [11]And the night following the Lord stood by him, and said, Be of good cheer, Paul: for as thou hast testified of me in Jerusalem, so must thou bear witness also at Rome.

ACTS 27:34—Alexandrian ship—Cnidus, Salome, Fair Havens, Lasea, storm at sea (27:6–44)

Theme	ACTS	Mt
Signs and end times	**27:34** [34]Wherefore I pray you to take some meat: for this is for your health: for there shall not an hair fall from the head of any of you. **4:5–8** [5]And it came to pass on the morrow, that their rulers, and elders, and scribes, [6]And Annas the high priest, and Caiaphas, and John, and Alexander, and as many as were of the kindred of the high priest, were gathered together at Jerusalem. [7]And when they had set them in the midst, they asked, By what power, or by what name, have ye done this? [8]Then Peter, filled with the Holy Ghost, said unto them, Ye rulers of the people, and elders of Israel,	**10:16–23** [16]Behold, I send you forth as sheep in the midst of wolves: be ye therefore wise as serpents, and harmless as doves. [17]But beware of men: for they will deliver you up to the councils, and they will scourge you in their synagogues; [18]And ye shall be brought before governors and kings for my sake, for a testimony against them and the Gentiles. **[19]But when they deliver you up, take no thought how or what ye shall speak: for it shall be given you in that same hour what ye shall speak. [20]For it is not ye that speak, but the Spirit of your Father which speaketh in you.** [21]And the brother shall deliver up the brother to death, and the father the child: and the children shall rise up against their parents, and cause them to be put to death. **[22]And ye shall be hated of all men for my name's sake: but he that endureth to the end shall be saved.** [23]But when they persecute you in this city, flee ye into another: for verily I say unto you, Ye shall not have gone over the cities of Israel, till the Son of man be come. **10:26–33** [26]Fear them not therefore: for there is nothing covered, that shall not be revealed; and hid, that shall not be known. [27]What I tell you in darkness, that speak ye in light: and what ye hear in the ear, that preach ye upon the housetops. [28]And fear not them which kill the body, but are not able to kill the soul: but rather fear him which is able to destroy both soul and body in hell. [29]Are not two sparrows sold for a farthing? and one of them shall not fall on the ground without your Father. **[30]But the very hairs of your head are all numbered.** [31]Fear ye not therefore, ye are of more value than many sparrows. [32]Whosoever therefore shall confess me before men, him will I confess also before my Father which is in heaven. [33]But whosoever shall deny me before men, him will I also deny before my Father which is in heaven. **12:32** [32]And whosoever speaketh a word against the Son of man, it shall be forgiven him: but whosoever speaketh against the Holy Ghost, it shall not be forgiven him, neither in this world, neither in the world to come. **24:3–14** [3]And as he sat upon the mount of Olives, the disciples came unto him privately, saying, Tell us, when shall these things be? and what shall be the sign of thy coming, and of the end of the world? [4]And Jesus answered and said unto them, Take heed that no man deceive you. [5]For many shall come in my name, saying, I am Christ; and shall deceive many. [6]And ye shall hear of wars and rumours of wars: see that ye be not troubled: for all these things must come to pass, but the end is not yet. [7]For nation shall rise against nation, and kingdom against kingdom: and there shall be famines, and pestilences, and earthquakes, in divers places. [8]All these are the beginning of sorrows. [9]Then shall they deliver you up to be afflicted, and shall kill you: and ye shall be hated of all nations for my name's sake. [10]And then shall many be offended, and shall betray one another, and shall hate one another. [11]And many false prophets shall rise, and shall deceive many. [2]And because iniquity shall abound, the love of many shall wax cold. [13]But he that shall endure unto the end, the same shall be saved. [14]And this gospel of the kingdom shall be preached in all the world for a witness unto all nations; and then shall the end come. **24:23–26** [23]Then if any man shall say unto you, Lo, here is Christ, or there; believe it not. [24]For there shall arise false Christs, and false prophets, and shall show great signs and wonders; insomuch that, if it were possible, they shall deceive the very elect. [25]Behold, I have told you before. [26]Wherefore if they shall say unto you, Behold, he is in the desert; go not forth: behold, he is in the secret chambers; believe it not.

Acts 27:34 continued on next page

ACTS 27:34—Alexandrian ship—Cnidus, Salome, Fair Havens, Lasea, storm at sea (27:6–44) (*continued*)

Theme	ACTS	Mk
(*Cont.*) **Signs and end times**	**27:34 (above)** **4:5–8 (above)**	**3:28–29** 28 And they answered, John the Baptist: but some say, Elias; and others, One of the prophets. 29 And he saith unto them, But whom say ye that I am? And Peter answereth and saith unto him, Thou art the Christ. **4:21–23** 21 And he said unto them, Is a candle brought to be put under a bushel, or under a bed? and not to be set on a candlestick? 22 For there is nothing hid, which shall not be manifested; neither was any thing kept secret, but that it should come abroad. 23 If any man have ears to hear, let him hear. **8:38** 38 Whosoever therefore shall be ashamed of me and of my words in this adulterous and sinful generation; of him also shall the Son of man be ashamed, when he cometh in the glory of his Father with the holy angels. **13:3–13** 3 And as he sat upon the mount of Olives over against the temple, Peter and James and John and Andrew asked him privately, 4 Tell us, when shall these things be? and what *shall be* the sign when all these things shall be fulfilled? 5 And Jesus answering them began to say, Take heed lest any *man* deceive you: 6 For many shall come in my name, saying, I am *Christ*; and shall deceive many. 7 And when ye shall hear of wars and rumours of wars, be ye not troubled: for *such things* must needs be; but the end *shall* not *be* yet. 8 For nation shall rise against nation, and kingdom against kingdom: and there shall be earthquakes in divers places, and there shall be famines and troubles: these *are* the beginnings of sorrows. 9 But take heed to yourselves: for they shall deliver you up to councils; and in the synagogues ye shall be beaten: and ye shall be brought before rulers and kings for my sake, for a testimony against them. 10 And the gospel must first be published among all nations. 11 But when they shall lead *you*, and deliver you up, take no thought beforehand what ye shall speak, neither do ye premeditate: but whatsoever shall be given you in that hour, that speak ye: for it is not ye that speak, but the Holy Ghost. 12 Now the brother shall betray the brother to death, and the father the son; and children shall rise up against *their* parents, and shall cause them to be put to death. 13 And ye shall be hated of all *men* for my name's sake: but he that shall endure unto the end, the same shall be saved. And he saith unto the man which had the withered hand, Stand forth. **13:21–23** 21 And then if any man shall say to you, Lo, here is Christ; or, lo, he is there; believe him not: 22 For false Christs and false prophets shall rise, and shall show signs and wonders, to seduce, if it were possible, even the elect. 23 But take ye heed: behold, I have foretold you all things.

Lk

8:16–17

[16]No man, when he hath lighted a candle, covereth it with a vessel, or putteth it under a bed; but setteth it on a candlestick, that they which enter in may see the light. [17]For nothing is secret, that shall not be made manifest; neither any thing hid, that shall not be known and come abroad.

9:26

[26]For whosoever shall be ashamed of me and of my words, of him shall the Son of man be ashamed, when he shall come in his own glory, and in his Father's, and of the holy angels.

12:1–12

[1]In the mean time, when there were gathered together an innumerable multitude of people, insomuch that they trode one upon another, he began to say unto his disciples first of all, Beware ye of the leaven of the Pharisees, which is hypocrisy. [2]For there is nothing covered, that shall not be revealed; neither hid, that shall not be known. [3]Therefore whatsoever ye have spoken in darkness shall be heard in the light; and that which ye have spoken in the ear in closets shall be proclaimed upon the housetops. [4]And I say unto you my friends, Be not afraid of them that kill the body, and after that have no more that they can do. [5]But I will forewarn you whom ye shall fear: Fear him, which after he hath killed hath power to cast into hell; yea, I say unto you, Fear him. [6]Are not five sparrows sold for two farthings, and not one of them is forgotten before God? [7]But even the very hairs of your head are all numbered. Fear not therefore: ye are of more value than many sparrows. [8]Also I say unto you, Whosoever shall confess me before men, him shall the Son of man also confess before the angels of God: [9]But he that denieth me before men shall be denied before the angels of God. [10]And whosoever shall speak a word against the Son of man, it shall be forgiven him: but unto him that blasphemeth against the Holy Ghost it shall not be forgiven. **[11]And when they bring you unto the synagogues, and unto magistrates, and powers, take ye no thought how or what thing ye shall answer, or what ye shall say: [12]For the Holy Ghost shall teach you in the same hour what ye ought to say.**

12:7

[7]But even the very hairs of your head are all numbered. Fear not therefore: ye are of more value than many sparrows.

12:24

[24]Consider the ravens: for they neither sow nor reap; which neither have storehouse nor barn; and God feedeth them: how much more are ye better than the fowls?

17:23

[23]And they shall say to you, See here; or, see there: go not after them, nor follow them.

19:44

[44]And shall lay thee even with the ground, and thy children within thee; and they shall not leave in thee one stone upon another; because thou knewest not the time of thy visitation.

21:5–19

[5]And as some spake of the temple, how it was adorned with goodly stones and gifts, he said, [6]As for these things which ye behold, the days will come, in the which there shall not be left one stone upon another, that shall not be thrown down. [7]And they asked him, saying, Master, but when shall these things be? and what sign will there be when these things shall come to pass? [8]And he said, Take heed that ye be not deceived: for many shall come in my name, saying, I am Christ; and the time draweth near: go ye not therefore after them. [9]But when ye shall hear of wars and commotions, be not terrified: for these things must first come to pass; but the end is not by and by. [10]Then said he unto them, Nation shall rise against nation, and kingdom against kingdom: [11]And great earthquakes shall be in divers places, and famines, and pestilences; and fearful sights and great signs shall there be from heaven. [12]But before all these, they shall lay their hands on you, and persecute you, delivering you up to the synagogues, and into prisons, being brought before kings and rulers for my name's sake. [13]And it shall turn to you for a testimony. **[14]Settle it therefore in your hearts, not to meditate before what ye shall answer: [15]For I will give you a mouth and wisdom, which all your adversaries shall not be able to gainsay nor resist.** [16]And ye shall be betrayed both by parents, and brethren, and kinsfolks, and friends; and some of you shall they cause to be put to death. [17]And ye shall be hated of all men for my name's sake. **[18]But there shall not an hair of your head perish.** [19]In your patience possess ye your souls.

Jn

14:26

[26]But the Comforter, which is the Holy Ghost, whom the Father will send in my name, he shall teach you all things, and bring all things to your remembrance, whatsoever I have said unto you.

15:18–21

[18]If the world hate you, ye know that it hated me before it hated you. [19]If ye were of the world, the world would love his own: but because ye are not of the world, but I have chosen you out of the world, therefore the world hateth you. [20]Remember the word that I said unto you, The servant is not greater than his lord. If they have persecuted me, they will also persecute you; if they have kept my saying, they will keep yours also. [21]But all these things will they do unto you for my name's sake, because they know not him that sent me.

16:2

[2]They shall put you out of the synagogues: yea, the time cometh, that whosoever killeth you will think that he doeth God service.

Acts 27:34 continued on next page

ACTS 27:34—Alexandrian ship—Cnidus, Salome, Fair Havens, Lasea, storm at sea (27:6–44) (*continued*)

Them	ACT	Other
(*Cont.*) **Signs and end times**	27:34 (above) 4:5–8 (above)	**2 Clem 3:2** [2]For even he himself says, "I will acknowledge before my Father the one who acknowledges me before others." **GThom 6** [6]His disciples questioned him and said to him, "Do you want us to fast? How shall we pray? Shall we give alms? What diet shall we observe? Jesus said, "Do not tell lies, and do not do what you hate, for all things are plain in the sight of heaven. For nothing hidden will not become manifest, and nothing covered will remain without being uncovered. " **GThom 33** [33]Jesus said, "Preach form your housetops that which you will hear in your ear. Fro no one lights a lamp and puts it under a bushel, nor does he put it in a hidden place, but rather he sets it upon a lamp-stand so that everyone who enters and leaves will see its light." **GThom 44** [44]Jesus said, "Whoever blasphemes against the father will be forgiven, and whoever blasphemes against the son will be forgiven, but whoever blasphemes against the holy spirit will not be forgiven either on earth or in heaven." **Q-Quelle** Anxiety: Acts 27:34/[Mt 6:25-34]/Lk 12:22-31 (QS 39 [Thom 36])/[Mt 9:37-38]; Commissioning of the 70: Acts 27:34/Mt 10:7-16/[Lk 10:1-12(QS 20/[Thom 73; 14:2]/[Lk 10:1-12(QS 20,21)]; Assistance of HS: Acts 27:34/ [Mt 10:19-20]/[Mk 13:11]/Lk 12:11-12 (QS37)/[Thom 44], [Lk 21:14-15]; Fearless Confession: Acts 27:34/Mt 10:26-33/Lk 12:2-9 (QS 35 Thom [5:2], 6, 33, [36, 37], 44; Sin against the HS: Acts 27:34/Mt 12:31-32/[Mk 3:29-30]/Lk 12:10 (QS37)/[Thom 44]; Day of SOM: Acts 27:34/Mt 24:23, 24:26-27 [Mt 10:39, 24:17-18, 24:28,24:37-39, 24:40-41/[Mk 13:19-23, 13:14-16], Lk 17:22-37 (QS 60/[Thom 3, 51,61,113])

ACTS 27:35—Alexandrian ship—Cnidus, Salome, Fair Havens, Lasea, storm at sea (27:6–44)

Theme	ACTS	Mt
Signs and feeding the masses	**27:35** [35]And when he had thus spoken, he took bread, and gave thanks to God in presence of them all: and when he had broken it, he began to eat.	**9:36** [36]But when he saw the multitudes, he was moved with compassion on them, because they fainted, and were scattered abroad, as sheep having no shepherd. **14:15–21** [15]And when it was evening, his disciples came to him, saying, This is a desert place, and the time is now past; send the multitude away, that they may go into the villages, and buy themselves victuals. [16]But Jesus said unto them, They need not depart; give ye them to eat. [17]And they say unto him, We have here but five loaves, and two fishes. [18]He said, Bring them hither to me. [19]And he commanded the multitude to sit down on the grass, and took the five loaves, and the two fishes, and looking up to heaven, he blessed, and brake, and gave the loaves to his disciples, and the disciples to the multitude. [20]And they did all eat, and were filled: and they took up of the fragments that remained twelve baskets full. [21]And they that had eaten were about five thousand men, beside women and children. **15:15–21** [15]Then answered Peter and said unto him, Declare unto us this parable. [16]And Jesus said, Are ye also yet without understanding? [17]Do not ye yet understand, that whatsoever entereth in at the mouth goeth into the belly, and is cast out into the draught? [18]But those things which proceed out of the mouth come forth from the heart; and they defile the man. [19]For out of the heart proceed evil thoughts, murders, adulteries, fornications, thefts, false witness, blasphemies: [20]These are the things which defile a man: but to eat with unwashen hands defileth not a man. [21]Then Jesus went thence, and departed into the coasts of Tyre and Sidon **15:22–23** [22]And, behold, a woman of Canaan came out of the same coasts, and cried unto him, saying, Have mercy on me, O Lord, thou Son of David; my daughter is grievously vexed with a devil. [23]But he answered her not a word. And his disciples came and besought him, saying, Send her away; for she crieth after us. **26:26** [26]And as they were eating, Jesus took bread, and blessed it, and brake it, and gave it to the disciples, and said, Take, eat; this is my body.

ACTS 27:35—Alexandrian ship—Cnidus, Salome, Fair Havens, Lasea, storm at sea (27:6–44) (*continued*)

Theme	ACTS	Mk
(*Cont.*) **Signs and feeding the masses**	27:35 (above)	**6:35–44** [35]And when the day was now far spent, his disciples came unto him, and said, This is a desert place, and now the time is far passed: [36]Send them away, that they may go into the country round about, and into the villages, and buy themselves bread: for they have nothing to eat. [37]He answered and said unto them, Give ye them to eat. And they say unto him, Shall we go and buy two hundred pennyworth of bread, and give them to eat? [38]He saith unto them, How many loaves have ye? go and see. And when they knew, they say, Five, and two fishes. [39]And he commanded them to make all sit down by companies upon the green grass. [40]And they sat down in ranks, by hundreds, and by fifties. [41]And when he had taken the five loaves and the two fishes, he looked up to heaven, and blessed, and brake the loaves, and gave them to his disciples to set before them; and the two fishes divided he among them all. [42]And they did all eat, and were filled. [43]And they took up twelve baskets full of the fragments, and of the fishes. [44]And they that did eat of the loaves were about five thousand men. **8:1–10** [1]In those days the multitude being very great, and having nothing to eat, Jesus called his disciples unto him, and saith unto them, [2]I have compassion on the multitude, because they have now been with me three days, and have nothing to eat: [3]And if I send them away fasting to their own houses, they will faint by the way: for divers of them came from far. [4]And his disciples answered him, From whence can a man satisfy these men with bread here in the wilderness? [5]And he asked them, How many loaves have ye? And they said, Seven. [6]And he commanded the people to sit down on the ground: and he took the seven loaves, and gave thanks, and brake, and gave to his disciples to set before them; and they did set them before the people. [7]And they had a few small fishes: and he blessed, and commanded to set them also before them. [8]So they did eat, and were filled: and they took up of the broken meat that was left seven baskets. [9]And they that had eaten were about four thousand: and he sent them away. [10]And straightway he entered into a ship with his disciples, and came into the parts of Dalmanutha. **14:22** [22]And as they did eat, Jesus took bread, and blessed, and brake it, and gave to them, and said, Take, eat: this is my body.

Lk	Jn	Jewish Writings
9:12–17 [12]And when the day began to wear away, then came the twelve, and said unto him, Send the multitude away, that they may go into the towns and country round about, and lodge, and get victuals: for we are here in a desert place. [13]But he said unto them, Give ye them to eat. And they said, We have no more but five loaves and two fishes; except we should go and buy meat for all this people. [14]For they were about five thousand men. And he said to his disciples, Make them sit down by fifties in a company. [15]And they did so, and made them all sit down. [16]Then he took the five loaves and the two fishes, and looking up to heaven, he blessed them, and brake, and gave to the disciples to set before the multitude. [17]And they did eat, and were all filled: and there was taken up of fragments that remained to them twelve baskets. **22:19** [19]And he took bread, and gave thanks, and brake it, and gave unto them, saying, This is my body which is given for you: this do in remembrance of me **24:30** [30]And it came to pass, as he sat at meat with them, he took bread, and blessed it, and brake, and gave to them.	**6:1–15** [1]After these things Jesus went over the sea of Galilee, which is the sea of Tiberias. [2]And a great multitude followed him, because they saw his miracles which he did on them that were diseased. [3]And Jesus went up into a mountain, and there he sat with his disciples. [4]And the passover, a feast of the Jews, was nigh. [5]When Jesus then lifted up his eyes, and saw a great company come unto him, he saith unto Philip, Whence shall we buy bread, that these may eat? [6]And this he said to prove him: for he himself knew what he would do. [7]Philip answered him, Two hundred pennyworth of bread is not sufficient for them, that every one of them may take a little. [8]One of his disciples, Andrew, Simon Peter's brother, saith unto him, [9]There is a lad here, which hath five barley loaves, and two small fishes: but what are they among so many? [10]And Jesus said, Make the men sit down. Now there was much grass in the place. So the men sat down, in number about five thousand. [11]And Jesus took the loaves; and when he had given thanks, he distributed to the disciples, and the disciples to them that were set down; and likewise of the fishes as much as they would. [12]When they were filled, he said unto his disciples, Gather up the fragments that remain, that nothing be lost. [13]Therefore they gathered them together, and filled twelve baskets with the fragments of the five barley loaves, which remained over and above unto them that had eaten. [14]Then those men, when they had seen the miracle that Jesus did, said, This is of a truth that prophet that should come into the world. [15]When Jesus therefore perceived that they would come and take him by force, to make him a king, he departed again into a mountain himself alone.	**2 Kgs 4:42–44** [42]And there came a man from Baalshalisha, and brought the man of God bread of the firstfruits, twenty loaves of barley, and full ears of corn in the husk thereof. And he said, Give unto the people, that they may eat. [43]And his servitor said, What, should I set this before an hundred men? He said again, Give the people, that they may eat: for thus saith the LORD, They shall eat, and shall leave thereof. [44]So he set it before them, and they did eat, and left thereof, according to the word of the LORD.

Winter at Malta after shipwreck 28:1–10

ACTS 28:6—Winter at Malta after shipwreck (28:1–10)

Theme	ACTS
People mistake Paul for a god	**28:6** [6]Howbeit they looked when he should have swollen, or fallen down dead suddenly: but after they had looked a great while, and saw no harm come to him, they changed their minds, and said that he was a god. **14:11** [11]And when the people saw what Paul had done, they lifted up their voices, saying in the speech of Lycaonia, The gods are come down to us in the likeness of men.

Syracuse, Rhegium, Puteoli, Rome with free-house (28:11–16)

Testimony to the Jews at Rome 28:17–31

ACTS 28:17—Testimony to the Jews at Rome (28:17–31)

Theme	ACTS	Jewish Writings
Jewish religious practices	**28:17** [17]And it came to pass, that after three days Paul called the chief of the Jews together: and when they were come together, he said unto them, Men and brethren, though I have committed nothing against the people, or customs of our fathers, yet was I delivered prisoner from Jerusalem into the hands of the Romans. **24:12–13** [12]And they neither found me in the temple disputing with any man, neither raising up the people, neither in the synagogues, nor in the city: [13]Neither can they prove the things whereof they now accuse me. **25:8** [8]While he answered for himself, Neither against the law of the Jews, neither against the temple, nor yet against Caesar, have I offended any thing at all.	**Lev 16:29–31** [29]And this shall be a statute for ever unto you: that in the seventh month, on the tenth day of the month, ye shall afflict your souls, and do no work at all, whether it be one of your own country, or a stranger that sojourneth among you: [30]For on that day shall the priest make an atonement for you, to cleanse you, that ye may be clean from all your sins before the LORD. [31]It shall be a sabbath of rest unto you, and ye shall afflict your souls, by a statute for ever.

ACTS 28:18—Testimony to the Jews at Rome (28:17–31)

Theme	ACTS
Actions do not deserve death	**28:18** [18]Who, when they had examined me, would have let me go, because there was no cause of death in me. **23:29** [29]Whom I perceived to be accused of questions of their law, but to have nothing laid to his charge worthy of death or of bonds. **25:25** [25]But when I found that he had committed nothing worthy of death, and that he himself hath appealed to Augustus, I have determined to send him. **26:31–32** [31]And when they were gone aside, they talked between themselves, saying, This man doeth nothing worthy of death or of bonds. [32]Then said Agrippa unto Festus, This man might have been set at liberty, if he had not appealed unto Caesar.

ACTS 28:19—Testimony to the Jews at Rome (28:17–31)

Theme	ACTS
Appeal to Caesar	**28:19** [19]But when the Jews spake against it, I was constrained to appeal unto Caesar; not that I had ought to accuse my nation of. **25:11** [11]For if I be an offender, or have committed any thing worthy of death, I refuse not to die: but if there be none of these things whereof these accuse me, no man may deliver me unto them. I appeal unto Caesar.

ACTS 28:20—Testimony to the Jews at Rome (28:17–31)

Theme	ACTS
Pharisee's hope for Israel and resurrection	**28:20** [20]For this cause therefore have I called for you, to see you, and to speak with you: because that for the hope of Israel I am bound with this chain. **23:6** [6]But when Paul perceived that the one part were Sadducees, and the other Pharisees, he cried out in the council, Men and brethren, I am a Pharisee, the son of a Pharisee: of the hope and resurrection of the dead I am called in question. **24:15** [15]And have hope toward God, which they themselves also allow, that there shall be a resurrection of the dead, both of the just and unjust. **24:21** [21]Except it be for this one voice, that I cried standing among them, Touching the resurrection of the dead I am called in question by you this day. **26:6–8** [6]And now I stand and am judged for the hope of the promise made of God unto our fathers: [7]Unto which promise our twelve tribes, instantly serving God day and night, hope to come. For which hope's sake, king Agrippa, I am accused of the Jews. [8]Why should it be thought a thing incredible with you, that God should raise the dead?

ACTS 28:22—Testimony to the Jews at Rome (28:17–31)

Theme	ACTS
Testimony about the "Way"	**28:22** [22]But we desire to hear of thee what thou thinkest: for as concerning this sect, we know that every where it is spoken against. **24:5, 14** [5]For we have found this man a pestilent fellow, and a mover of sedition among all the Jews throughout the world, and a ringleader of the sect of the Nazarenes:. . . [14]But this I confess unto thee, that after the way which they call heresy, so worship I the God of my fathers, believing all things which are written in the law and in the prophets:

ACTS 28:25–28—Testimony to the Jews at Rome (28:17–31)

Theme	ACTS	Mt	Mk
Word given to the Gentiles and parables	**28:25–28** [25]And when they agreed not among themselves, they departed, after that Paul had spoken one word, Well spake the Holy Ghost by Esaias the prophet unto our fathers, [26]Saying, Go unto this people, and say, Hearing ye shall hear, and shall not understand; and seeing ye shall see, and not perceive: [27]For the heart of this people is waxed gross, and their ears are dull of hearing, and their eyes have they closed; lest they should see with their eyes, and hear with their ears, and understand with their heart, and should be converted, and I should heal them. [28]Be it known therefore unto you, that the salvation of God is sent unto the Gentiles, and that they will hear it.	**13:10–17** [10]And the disciples came, and said unto him, Why speakest thou unto them in parables? [11]He answered and said unto them, Because it is given unto you to know the mysteries of the kingdom of heaven, but to them it is not given. [12]For whosoever hath, to him shall be given, and he shall have more abundance: but whosoever hath not, from him shall be taken away even that he hath. [13]Therefore speak I to them in parables: because they seeing see not; and hearing they hear not, neither do they understand. [14]And in them is fulfilled the prophecy of Esaias, which saith, By hearing ye shall hear, and shall not understand; and seeing ye shall see, and shall not perceive: [15]For this people's heart is waxed gross, and their ears are dull of hearing, and their eyes they have closed; lest at any time they should see with their eyes, and hear with their ears, and should understand with their heart, and should be converted, and I should heal them. [16]But blessed are your eyes, for they see: and your ears, for they hear. [17]For verily I say unto you, That many prophets and righteous men have desired to see those things which ye see, and have not seen them; and to hear those things which ye hear, and have not heard them. **25:29** [29]For unto every one that hath shall be given, and he shall have abundance: but from him that hath not shall be taken away even that which he hath.	**4:10–12** [10]And when he was alone, they that were about him with the twelve asked of him the parable. [11]And he said unto them, Unto you it is given to know the mystery of the kingdom of God: but unto them that are without, all these things are done in parables: [12]That seeing they may see, and not perceive; and hearing they may hear, and not understand; lest at any time they should be converted, and their sins should be forgiven them. **4:25** [25]For he that hath, to him shall be given: and he that hath not, from him shall be taken even that which he hath.

ACTS 28:26—Testimony to the Jews at Rome (28:17–31)

Theme	ACTS	Mt	Mk	Lk
Faithful hearing and seeing	**28:26** [26]Saying, Go unto this people, and say, Hearing ye shall hear, and shall not understand; and seeing ye shall see, and not perceive:	**13:14–15** [14]And in them is fulfilled the prophecy of Esaias, which saith, By hearing ye shall hear, and shall not understand; and seeing ye shall see, and shall not perceive: [15]For this people's heart is waxed gross, and their ears are dull of hearing, and their eyes they have closed; lest at any time they should see with their eyes, and hear with their ears, and should understand with their heart, and should be converted, and I should heal them.	**4:12** [12]That seeing they may see, and not perceive; and hearing they may hear, and not understand; lest at any time they should be converted, and their sins should be forgiven them.	**8:10** [10]And he said, Unto you it is given to know the mysteries of the kingdom of God: but to others in parables; that seeing they might not see, and hearing they might not understand.

Lk	Jn	Jewish	Other
8:9–10 [8]And other fell on good ground, and sprang up, and bare fruit a hundredfold. And when he had said these things, he cried, He that hath ears to hear, let him hear. [9]And his disciples asked him, saying, What might this parable be? [10]And he said, Unto you it is given to know the mysteries of the kingdom of God: but to others in parables; that seeing they might not see, and hearing they might not understand. **8:18** [18]Take heed therefore how ye hear: for whosoever hath, to him shall be given; and whosoever hath not, from him shall be taken even that which he seemeth to have. **10:23–24** [23]And he turned him unto his disciples, and said privately, Blessed are the eyes which see the things that ye see: [24]For I tell you, that many prophets and kings have desired to see those things which ye see, and have not seen them; and to hear those things which ye hear, and have not heard them. **19:26** [26]For I say unto you, That unto every one which hath shall be given; and from him that hath not, even that he hath shall be taken away from him.	**12:40** [40]He hath blinded their eyes, and hardened their heart; that they should not see with their eyes, nor understand with their heart, and be converted, and I should heal them.	**Is 6:9–10** [9]And he said, Go, and tell this people, Hear ye indeed, but understand not; and see ye indeed, but perceive not. [10]Make the heart of this people fat, and make their ears heavy, and shut their eyes; lest they see with their eyes, and hear with their ears, and understand with their heart, and convert, and be healed.	**GThom 38** [33]Jesus said, "Many times have you desired to hear these words, which I am saying to you, and you have no one else to hear them from. There will be days when you look for me and will not find me." **GThom 41** [41]Jesus said, "Whoever has something in his hand will receive more, and whoever has nothing will be deprived of the little he has." **Q-Quelle** Thanks and blessings/ disciples: Acts 28:25-28/[Mt 11:25-27, 13:16-17]/Lk 10:21-24 (QS 25); Parable of Pounds: Acts 28:25-28/ [Mt 25:14-30]/Lk 19:11-27 (QS41)

Jn	Paul	Jewish Writings	Other
12:40 [40]He hath blinded their eyes, and hardened their heart; that they should not see with their eyes, nor understand with their heart, and be converted, and I should heal them.	**Rom 11:8** [8](According as it is written, God hath given them the spirit of slumber, eyes that they should not see, and ears that they should not hear;) unto this day.	**Is 6:9–10** [9]And he said, Go, and tell this people, Hear ye indeed, but understand not; and see ye indeed, but perceive not. [10]Make the heart of this people fat, and make their ears heavy, and shut their eyes; lest they see with their eyes, and hear with their ears, and understand with their heart, and convert, and be healed.	**Q-Quelle** Thanks and blessings/disciples: Acts 28:26/Mt 11:25-27, Mt 13:16-17] /Lk 10:21-24 (QS 25)

ACTS 28:28—Testimony to the Jews at Rome (28:17–31)

Theme	ACTS	Mt
Salvation for Gentiles	**28:28** [28]Be it known therefore unto you, that the salvation of God is sent unto the Gentiles, and that they will hear it. **1:5** [5]For John truly baptized with water; but ye shall be baptized with the Holy Ghost not many days hence. **2:38** [38]Then Peter said unto them, Repent, and be baptized every one of you in the name of Jesus Christ for the remission of sins, and ye shall receive the gift of the Holy Ghost. **11:16** [16]Then remembered I the word of the Lord, how that he said, John indeed baptized with water; but ye shall be baptized with the Holy Ghost. **13:10** [10]And said, O full of all subtlety and all mischief, thou child of the devil, thou enemy of all righteousness, wilt thou not cease to pervert the right ways of the Lord? **13:24–25** [24]When John had first preached before his coming the baptism of repentance to all the people of Israel. [25]And as John fulfilled his course, he said, Whom think ye that I am? I am not he. But, behold, there cometh one after me, whose shoes of his feet I am not worthy to loose. **13:46–47** [46]Then Paul and Barnabas waxed bold, and said, It was necessary that the word of God should first have been spoken to you: but seeing ye put it from you, and judge yourselves unworthy of everlasting life, lo, we turn to the Gentiles.[47]For so hath the Lord commanded us, saying, I have set thee to be a light of the Gentiles, that thou shouldest be for salvation unto the ends of the earth. **18:6** [6]And the Lord said, Hear what the unjust judge saith. **19:17** [17]And this was known to all the Jews and Greeks also dwelling at Ephesus; and fear fell on them all, and the name of the Lord Jesus was magnified. **26:20** [20]But showed first unto them of Damascus, and at Jerusalem, and throughout all the coasts of Judaea, and then to the Gentiles, that they should repent and turn to God, and do works meet for repentance.	**1:15** [15]And Eliud begat Eleazar; and Eleazar begat Matthan; and Matthan begat Jacob **11:10** [10]For this is he, of whom it is written, Behold, I send my messenger before thy face, which shall prepare thy way before thee. **14:3–4** [3]For Herod had laid hold on John, and bound him, and put him in prison for Herodias' sake, his brother Philip's wife. [4]For John said unto him, It is not lawful for thee to have her.;

Mk	Lk	Jn
1:2–8 2 As it is written in the prophets, Behold, I send my messenger before thy face, which shall prepare thy way before thee. 3 The voice of one crying in the wilderness, Prepare ye the way of the Lord, make his paths straight. 4 John did baptize in the wilderness, and preach the baptism of repentance for the remission of sins. 5 And there went out unto him all the land of Judaea, and they of Jerusalem, and were all baptized of him in the river of Jordan, confessing their sins. 6 And John was clothed with camel's hair, and with a girdle of a skin about his loins; and he did eat locusts and wild honey; 7 And preached, saying, There cometh one mightier than I after me, the latchet of whose shoes I am not worthy to stoop down and unloose. 8 I indeed have baptized you with water: but he shall baptize you with the Holy Ghost. **1:15** 15 And saying, The time is fulfilled, and the kingdom of God is at hand: repent ye, and believe the gospel.	**2:30–32** 30 For mine eyes have seen thy salvation, 31 Which thou hast prepared before the face of all people; 32 A light to lighten the Gentiles, and the glory of thy people Israel. **3:6** 6 And all flesh shall see the salvation of God. **6:43–44** 43 For a good tree bringeth not forth corrupt fruit; neither doth a corrupt tree bring forth good fruit. 44 For every tree is known by his own fruit. For of thorns men do not gather figs, nor of a bramble bush gather they grapes. **7:27** 27 This is he, of whom it is written, Behold, I send my messenger before thy face, which shall prepare thy way before thee. **12:6** 6 Are not five sparrows sold for two farthings, and not one of them is forgotten before God? **13:31** 31 The same day there came certain of the Pharisees, saying unto him, Get thee out, and depart hence: for Herod will kill thee. **23:8** 8 And when Herod saw Jesus, he was exceeding glad: for he was desirous to see him of a long season, because he had heard many things of him; and he hoped to have seen some miracle done by him.	**1:19–28** 19 And this is the record of John, when the Jews sent priests and Levites from Jerusalem to ask him, Who art thou? 20 And he confessed, and denied not; but confessed, I am not the Christ. 21 And they asked him, What then? Art thou Elias? And he saith, I am not. Art thou that prophet? And he answered, No. 22 Then said they unto him, Who art thou? that we may give an answer to them that sent us. What sayest thou of thyself? 23 He said, I am the voice of one crying in the wilderness, Make straight the way of the Lord, as said the prophet Esaias. 24 And they which were sent were of the Pharisees. 25 And they asked him, and said unto him, Why baptizest thou then, if thou be not that Christ, nor Elias, neither that prophet? 26 John answered them, saying, I baptize with water: but there standeth one among you, whom ye know not; 27 He it is, who coming after me is preferred before me, whose shoe's latchet I am not worthy to unloose. 28 These things were done in Bethabara beyond Jordan, where John was baptizing. **1:31–32** 31 And I knew him not: but that he should be made manifest to Israel, therefore am I come baptizing with water. 32 And John bare record, saying, I saw the Spirit descending from heaven like a dove, and it abode upon him. **8:39** 39 They answered and said unto him, Abraham is our father. Jesus saith unto them, If ye were Abraham's children, ye would do the works of Abraham.

Acts 28:28 continued on next page

ACTS 28:28—Testimony to Jews at Rome (28:17–31) (*continued*)

Theme	ACTS	Jewish Writings
(*Cont.*) **Salvation for Gentiles**	**28:28 (above)** **1:5 (above)** **2:38 (above)** **11:16 (above)** **13:10 (above)** **13:24–25 (above)** **13:47 (above)** **18:6 (above)** **19:17 (above)** **26:20 (above)**	**Ex 13:2** [2]Sanctify unto me all the firstborn, whatsoever openeth the womb among the children of Israel, both of man and of beast: it is mine.
		Ex 13:12 [12]That thou shalt set apart unto the LORD all that openeth the matrix, and every firstling that cometh of a beast which thou hast; the males shall be the LORD'S.
		Ex 13:15 [15]And it came to pass, when Pharaoh would hardly let us go, that the LORD slew all the firstborn in the land of Egypt, both the firstborn of man, and the firstborn of beast: therefore I sacrifice to the LORD all that openeth the matrix, being males; but all the firstborn of my children I redeem.
		Lev 12:8 [8]And if she be not able to bring a lamb, then she shall bring two turtles, or two young pigeons; the one for the burnt offering, and the other for a sin offering: and the priest shall make an atonement for her, and she shall be clean.
		2 Kgs 1:8 [1]Then Moab rebelled against Israel after the death of Ahab. [2]And Ahaziah fell down through a lattice in his upper chamber that was in Samaria, and was sick: and he sent messengers, and said unto them, Go, inquire of Baalzebub the god of Ekron whether I shall recover of this disease. [3]But the angel of the LORD said to Elijah the Tishbite, Arise, go up to meet the messengers of the king of Samaria, and say unto them, Is it not because there is not a God in Israel, that ye go to inquire of Baalzebub the god of Ekron? [4]Now therefore thus saith the LORD, Thou shalt not come down from that bed on which thou art gone up, but shalt surely die. And Elijah departed. [5]And when the messengers turned back unto him, he said unto them, Why are ye now turned back? [6]And they said unto him, There came a man up to meet us, and said unto us, Go, turn again unto the king that sent you, and say unto him, Thus saith the LORD, Is it not because there is not a God in Israel, that thou sendest to inquire of Baalzebub the god of Ekron? therefore thou shalt not come down from that bed on which thou art gone up, but shalt surely die. [7]And he said unto them, What manner of man was he which came up to meet you, and told you these words? [8]And they answered him, He was an hairy man, and girt with a girdle of leather about his loins. And he said, It is Elijah the Tishbite.
		Ps 67:2 [2]That thy way may be known upon earth, thy saving health among all nations.
		Is 40:3–6 [3]The voice of him that crieth in the wilderness, Prepare ye the way of the LORD, make straight in the desert a highway for our God. [4]Every valley shall be exalted, and every mountain and hill shall be made low: and the crooked shall be made straight, and the rough places plain: [5]And the glory of the LORD shall be revealed, and all flesh shall see it together: for the mouth of the LORD hath spoken it. [6]The voice said, Cry. And he said, What shall I cry? All flesh is grass, and all the goodliness thereof is as the flower of the field:
		Is 40:5 (See LXX) [5]And the glory of the LORD shall be revealed, and all flesh shall see it together: for the mouth of the LORD hath spoken it.
		Is 49:6 [6]And he said, It is a light thing that thou shouldest be my servant to raise up the tribes of Jacob, and to restore the preserved of Israel: I will also give thee for a light to the Gentiles, that thou mayest be my salvation unto the end of the earth.
		Is 52:10 [10]The LORD hath made bare his holy arm in the eyes of all the nations; and all the ends of the earth shall see the salvation of our God.

Other

1 ApocJas

It is the Lord who spoke with me: "... But I have brought forth the image of him so that the sons of Him-who-is might know what things are theirs and what things are alien (to them). Behold, I shall reveal to you everything of this mystery. For they will seize me the day after tomorrow. But my redemption will be near." ... [James said,], "Rabbi, in what way shall I reach Him-who-is, since all these powers and these hosts are armed against me?" He said to me, "These powers are not armed against you specifically, but are armed against another. It is against me that they are armed. And they are armed with other powers. But they are armed against me in judgment. They did not give [...] to me in it [...] through them [...]. In this place [...] suffering, I shall [...]. He will [...] and I shall not rebuke them. But there shall be within me a silence and a hidden mystery. But I am fainthearted before their anger." James said, "Rabbi, if they arm themselves against you, then is there no blame?" ... You have come with knowledge, that you might rebuke their forgetfulness. You have come with recollection, that you might rebuke their ignorance. ...But I was concerned because of you. For you descended into a great ignorance, but you have not been defiled by anything in it. ... For you descended into a great mindlessness, and your recollection remained. You walked in mud, and your garments were not soiled, and you have not been buried in their filth, and you have not been caught. ... And I was not like them, but I clothed myself with everything of theirs.

The Lord said, "James, I praise your understanding and your fear. If you continue to be distressed, do not be concerned for anything else except your redemption. For behold, I shall complete this destiny upon this earth as I have said from the heavens. And I shall reveal to you your redemption."

[James] "Therefore, on reflection, I was wishing that I would not see this people. They must be judged for these things that they have done. For these things that they have done are contrary to what is fitting." The Lord said, "James, do not be concerned for me or for this people. I am he who was within me. Never have I suffered in any way, nor have I been distressed. And this people has done me no harm. But this (people) existed as a type of the archons, and it deserved to be destroyed through them. But [...] the archons, [...] who has [...] but since it [...] angry with [...] The just [...] is his servant. Therefore your name is "James the Just"...you have embraced me and kissed me. Truly I say to you that you have stirred up great anger and wrath against yourself. But (this has happened) so that these others might come to be." James said, "I am satisfied [...] and they are [...] my soul. Yet another thing I ask of you: who are the seven women who have been your disciples? And behold all women bless you. I also am amazed how powerless vessels have become strong by a perception which is in them." The Lord said, "You [...] well [...] a spirit of [...], a spirit of thought, a spirit of counsel of a [...], a spirit [...] a spirit of knowledge [...] of their fear. [...] when we had passed through the breath of this archon who is named Adonaios [...] him and [...] he was ignorant [...] when I came forth from him, he remembered that I am a son of his. He was gracious to me at that time as his son. And then, before <I> appeared here, <he> cast them among this people. And from the place of heaven the prophets [...]." But I shall go forth and shall reveal that they believed in you, that they may be content with their blessing and salvation, and this revelation may come to pass." And he went at that time immediately and rebuked the twelve and cast out of them contentment concerning the way of knowledge [...]. [...]. And the majority of them [...] when they saw, the messenger took in [...]. The others [...] said, "[...] him from this earth. For he is not worthy of life." These, then, were afraid. They arose, saying, "We have no part in this blood, for a just man will perish through injustice" James departed so that [...] look [...] for we [...] him.

GEbi 2 and 3

[2]For by chopping off the genealogies of Matthew they made their gospel begin as we indicated before, with the words: "And so in the days of Herod, King of Judea, when Caiaphas was high priest, a certain one named John came baptizing a baptism of repentance in the Jordan River." (Epiphanius, Panarion, 30, 14, 3) [3] And so John was baptizing, and Pharisees came to him and were baptized, as was all of Jerusalem. John wore a garment of camel hair and a leather belt around his waist; and his food was wild honey that tasted like manna, like a cake cooked in oil. (Epiphanius, Panarion, 30, 13, 4-5)

In Thom 19:5b

[5]But his mother kept to herself all these things that had happened.

Q-Quelle

Preaching of John: Acts 28:28/[Mt 3:7-10, 3:11-12]/Mk 1:7-8/[Lk 3:7-9 (QS4), Lk 3:15-18 (QS 5)]; Fruit: Acts 28:28/ [Mt 7:15-20, 12:33-35]/Lk 6:43-45 (QS 13[Thom 45]); Jesus' witness to John: Acts 28:28/ [Mt 11:7-19, 21:31-32]/Lk 7:24-35 (QS 17[Thom 74,46]); Fearless confession: Acts 28:28/ [Mt 10:26-33]/Lk 12:2-9 (QS 35[Thom 5:2, 6:3, 33:1], QS36, QS 37 [Thom 44])

PAULINE EPISTLES:
SECTION II

Paul's Parallels: An Echoes Synopsis

ROMANS

Paul writes 56–58 CE, with a fully mature faith

ADDRESS 1:1–5

ROMANS 1:1—Address (1:1–5) 56–58 CE

Theme	ROM	Lk	Paul
Paul's call to be an apostle	**1:1** [1]Paul, a servant of Jesus Christ, called to be an apostle, separated unto the gospel of God,	**Acts 9:15** [15]But the Lord said unto him, Go thy way: for he is a chosen vessel unto me, to bear my name before the Gentiles, and kings, and the children of Israel: **Acts 13:2** [2]As they ministered to the Lord, and fasted, the Holy Ghost said, Separate me Barnabas and Saul for the work whereunto I have called them.	**1 Cor 1:1** [1]Paul, called to be an apostle of Jesus Christ through the will of God, and Sosthenes our brother, **Gal 1:1** [1]Paul, an apostle, (not of men, neither by man, but by Jesus Christ, and God the Father, who raised him from the dead;) **Gal 1:15** [15]But when it pleased God, who separated me from my mother's womb, and called me by his grace, **Phil 1:1** [1]Paul and Timotheus, the servants of Jesus Christ, to all the saints in Christ Jesus which are at Philippi, with the bishops and deacons: **Tit 1:1 (Pseudo)** [1]Paul, a servant of God, and an apostle of Jesus Christ, according to the faith of God's elect, and the acknowledging of the truth which is after godliness;

ROMANS 1:2—Address (1:1–5) 56–58 CE

Theme	ROM	Paul
Promise in the gospel	**1:2** [2](Which he had promised afore by his prophets in the holy scriptures,) **16:25–26** [25]Now to him that is of power to stablish you according to my gospel, and the preaching of Jesus Christ, according to the revelation of the mystery, which was kept secret since the world began, [26]But now is made manifest, and by the scriptures of the prophets, according to the commandment of the everlasting God, made known to all nations for the obedience of faith	**Tit 1:2 (Pseudo)** [2]In hope of eternal life, which God, that cannot lie, promised before the world began;

NT
Jas 1:1
[1]James, a servant of God and of the Lord Jesus Christ, to the twelve tribes which are scattered abroad, greeting.

ROMANS 1:3–4—Address (1:1–5): Jewish inheritance, 56–58 CE

Theme	ROM	Mt	Mk
Son of God: Son of David (human)	**1:3–4** [3]Concerning his Son Jesus Christ our Lord, which was made of the seed of David according to the flesh; [4]And declared to be the Son of God with power, according to the spirit of holiness, by the resurrection from the dead: **1:7** [7]To all that be in Rome, beloved of God, called to be saints: Grace to you and peace from God our Father, and the Lord Jesus Christ. **8:3** [3]For what the law could not do, in that it was weak through the flesh, God sending his own Son in the likeness of sinful flesh, and for sin, condemned sin in the flesh: **8:15** [15]For ye have not received the spirit of bondage again to fear; but ye have received the Spirit of adoption, whereby we cry, Abba, Father. **10:9** [9]That if thou shalt confess with thy mouth the Lord Jesus, and shalt believe in thine heart that God hath raised him from the dead, thou shalt be saved.	**21:33–44** [33]Hear another parable: There was a certain householder, which planted a vineyard, and hedged it round about, and digged a winepress in it, and built a tower, and let it out to husbandmen, and went into a far country: [34]And when the time of the fruit drew near, he sent his servants to the husbandmen, that they might receive the fruits of it. [35]And the husbandmen took his servants, and beat one, and killed another, and stoned another. [36]Again, he sent other servants more than the first: and they did unto them likewise. [37]But last of all he sent unto them his son, saying, They will reverence my son. [38]But when the husbandmen saw the son, they said among themselves, This is the heir; come, let us kill him, and let us seize on his inheritance. [39]And they caught him, and cast him out of the vineyard, and slew him. [40]When the lord therefore of the vineyard cometh, what will he do unto those husbandmen? [41]They say unto him, He will miserably destroy those wicked men, and will let out his vineyard unto other husbandmen, which shall render him the fruits in their seasons. [42]Jesus saith unto them, Did ye never read in the scriptures, The stone which the builders rejected, the same is become the head of the corner: this is the Lord's doing, and it is marvellous in our eyes? [43]Therefore say I unto you, The kingdom of God shall be taken from you, and given to a nation bringing forth the fruits thereof. [44]And whosoever shall fall on this stone shall be broken: but on whomsoever it shall fall, it will grind him to powder.	**14:36** [36]And he said, Abba, Father, all things are possible unto thee; take away this cup from me: nevertheless not what I will, but what thou wilt.

Jn	Paul
1 Jn 2:18–23	**Gal 4:4,6**
[18]Little children, it is the last time: and as ye have heard that antichrist shall come, even now are there many antichrists; whereby we know that it is the last time. [19]They went out from us, but they were not of us; for if they had been of us, they would no doubt have continued with us: but they went out, that they might be made manifest that they were not all of us. [20]But ye have an unction from the Holy One, and ye know all things. [21]I have not written unto you because ye know not the truth, but because ye know it, and that no lie is of the truth. [22]Who is a liar but he that denieth that Jesus is the Christ? He is antichrist, that denieth the Father and the Son. [23]Whosoever denieth the Son, the same hath not the Father: (but) he that acknowledgeth the Son hath the Father also.	[4]Who gave himself for our sins, that he might deliver us from this present evil world, according to the will of God and our Father:. . . [6]I marvel that ye are so soon removed from him that called you into the grace of Christ unto another gospel: **Col 2:8–19** [8]Beware lest any man spoil you through philosophy and vain deceit, after the tradition of men, after the rudiments of the world, and not after Christ. [9]For in him dwelleth all the fulness of the Godhead bodily. [10]And ye are complete in him, which is the head of all principality and power: [11]In whom also ye are circumcised with the circumcision made without hands, in putting off the body of the sins of the flesh by the circumcision of Christ: [12]Buried with him in baptism, wherein also ye are risen with him through the faith of the operation of God, who hath raised him from the dead. [13]And you, being dead in your sins and the uncircumcision of your flesh, hath he quickened together with him, having forgiven you all trespasses; [14]Blotting out the handwriting of ordinances that was against us, which was contrary to us, and took it out of the way, nailing it to his cross; [15]And having spoiled principalities and powers, he made a show of them openly, triumphing over them in it. [16]Let no man therefore judge you in meat, or in drink, or in respect of an holyday, or of the new moon, or of the Sabbath days: [17]Which are a shadow of things to come; but the body is of Christ. [18]Let no man beguile you of your reward in a voluntary humility and worshipping of angels, intruding into those things which he hath not seen, vainly puffed up by his fleshly mind, [19]And not holding the Head, from which all the body by joints and bands having nourishment ministered, and knit together, increaseth with the increase of God.

Romans 1:3–4 continued on next page

ROMANS 1:3–4—Address (1:1–5): Jewish inheritance, 56–58 CE (*continued*)

Theme	ROM	Jewish Writings
(*Cont.*) Son of God: Son of David (human)	**1:3–4 (above) 1:7 (above) 8:3 (above) 8:15 (above)**	**Dan 7** 1In the first year of Belshazzar king of Babylon Daniel had a dream and visions of his head upon his bed: then he wrote the dream, and told the sum of the matters. 2Daniel spake and said, I saw in my vision by night, and, behold, the four winds of the heaven strove upon the great sea. 3And four great beasts came up from the sea, diverse one from another. 4The first was like a lion, and had eagle's wings: I beheld till the wings thereof were plucked, and it was lifted up from the earth, and made stand upon the feet as a man, and a man's heart was given to it. 5And behold another beast, a second, like to a bear, and it raised up itself on one side, and it had three ribs in the mouth of it between the teeth of it: and they said thus unto it, Arise, devour much flesh. 6After this I beheld, and lo another, like a leopard, which had upon the back of it four wings of a fowl; the beast had also four heads; and dominion was given to it. 7After this I saw in the night visions, and behold a fourth beast, dreadful and terrible, and strong exceedingly; and it had great iron teeth: it devoured and brake in pieces, and stamped the residue with the feet of it: and it was diverse from all the beasts that were before it; and it had ten horns. 8I considered the horns, and, behold, there came up among them another little horn, before whom there were three of the first horns plucked up by the roots: and, behold, in this horn were eyes like the eyes of man, and a mouth speaking great things. 9I beheld till the thrones were cast down, and the Ancient of days did sit, whose garment was white as snow, and the hair of his head like the pure wool: his throne was like the fiery flame, and his wheels as burning fire. 10A fiery stream issued and came forth from before him: thousand thousands ministered unto him, and ten thousand times ten thousand stood before him: the judgment was set, and the books were opened. 11I beheld then because of the voice of the great words which the horn spake: I beheld even till the beast was slain, and his body destroyed, and given to the burning flame. 12As concerning the rest of the beasts, they had their dominion taken away: yet their lives were prolonged for a season and time. 13I saw in the night visions, and, behold, one like the Son of man came with the clouds of heaven, and came to the Ancient of days, and they brought him near before him. 14And there was given him dominion, and glory, and a kingdom, that all people, nations, and languages, should serve him: his dominion is an everlasting dominion, which shall not pass away, and his kingdom that which shall not be destroyed. 15I Daniel was grieved in my spirit in the midst of my body, and the visions of my head troubled me. 16I came near unto one of them that stood by, and asked him the truth of all this. So he told me, and made me know the interpretation of the things. 17These great beasts, which are four, are four kings, which shall arise out of the earth. 18But the saints of the most High shall take the kingdom, and possess the kingdom for ever, even for ever and ever. 19Then I would know the truth of the fourth beast, which was diverse from all the others, exceeding dreadful, whose teeth were of iron, and his nails of brass; which devoured, brake in pieces, and stamped the residue with his feet; 20And of the ten horns that were in his head, and of the other which came up, and before whom three fell; even of that horn that had eyes, and a mouth that spake very great things, whose look was more stout than his fellows. 21I beheld, and the same horn made war with the saints, and prevailed against them; 22Until the Ancient of days came, and judgment was given to the saints of the most High; and the time came that the saints possessed the kingdom. 23Thus he said, The fourth beast shall be the fourth kingdom upon earth, which shall be diverse from all kingdoms, and shall devour the whole earth, and shall tread it down, and break it in pieces. 24And the ten horns out of this kingdom are ten kings that shall arise: and another shall rise after them; and he shall be diverse from the first, and he shall subdue three kings. 25And he shall speak great words against the most High, and shall wear out the saints of the most High, and think to change times and laws: and they shall be given into his hand until a time and times and the dividing of time. 26But the judgment shall sit, and they shall take away his dominion, to consume and to destroy it unto the end. 27And the kingdom and dominion, and the greatness of the kingdom under the whole heaven, shall be given to the people of the saints of the most High, whose kingdom is an everlasting kingdom, and all dominions shall serve and obey him. 28Hitherto is the end of the matter. As for me Daniel, my cogitations much troubled me, and my countenance changed in me: but I kept the matter in my heart.

ROMANS 1:3–4—Address (1:1–5): Jewish inheritance, 56–58 CE (*continued*)

Theme	ROM	Mt	Mk	Lk
Son of God: Sent from heaven (variation of supra)	**1:3–4 (above)** **1:7 (above)** **8:3 (above)** **8:15 (above)**	**23:34** [34]Wherefore, behold, I send unto you prophets, and wise men, and scribes: and some of them ye shall kill and crucify; and some of them shall ye scourge in your synagogues, and persecute them from city to city:	**12:1–22** [1]And he began to speak unto them by parables. A certain man planted a vineyard, and set an hedge about it, and digged a place for the winefat, and built a tower, and let it out to husbandmen, and went into a far country. [2]And at the season he sent to the husbandmen a servant, that he might receive from the husbandmen of the fruit of the vineyard. [3]And they caught him, and beat him, and sent him away empty. [4]And again he sent unto them another servant; and at him they cast stones, and wounded him in the head, and sent him away shamefully handled. [5]And again he sent another; and him they killed, and many others; beating some, and killing some. [6]Having yet therefore one son, his wellbeloved, he sent him also last unto them, saying, They will reverence my son. [7]But those husbandmen said among themselves, This is the heir; come, let us kill him, and the inheritance shall be ours. [8]And they took him, and killed him, and cast him out of the vineyard. [9]What shall therefore the lord of the vineyard do? he will come and destroy the husbandmen, and will give the vineyard unto others. [10]And have ye not read this scripture; The stone which the builders rejected is become the head of the corner: [11]This was the Lord's doing, and it is marvellous in our eyes? [12]And they sought to lay hold on him, but feared the people: for they knew that he had spoken the parable against them: and they left him, and went their way. [13]And they send unto him certain of the Pharisees and of the Herodians, to catch him in his words. [14]And when they were come, they say unto him, Master, we know that thou art true, and carest for no man: for thou regardest not the person of men, but teachest the way of God in truth: Is it lawful to give tribute to Caesar, or not? [15]Shall we give, or shall we not give? But he, knowing their hypocrisy, said unto them, Why tempt ye me? bring me a penny, that I may see it. [16]And they brought it. And he saith unto them, Whose is this image and superscription? And they said unto him, Caesar's. [17]And Jesus answering said unto them, Render to Caesar the things that are Caesar's, and to God the things that are God's. And they marvelled at him. [18]Then come unto him the Sadducees, which say there is no resurrection; and they asked him, saying, [19]Master, Moses wrote unto us, If a man's brother die, and leave his wife behind him, and leave no children, that his brother should take his wife, and raise up seed unto his brother. [20]Now there were seven brethren: and the first took a wife, and dying left no seed. [21]And the second took her, and died, neither left he any seed: and the third likewise. [22]And the seven had her, and left no seed: last of all the woman died also.	**20:9–19** [9]Then began he to speak to the people this parable; A certain man planted a vineyard, and let it forth to husbandmen, and went into a far country for a long time. [10]And at the season he sent a servant to the husbandmen, that they should give him of the fruit of the vineyard: but the husbandmen beat him, and sent him away empty. [11]And again he sent another servant: and they beat him also, and entreated him shamefully, and sent him away empty. [12]And again he sent a third: and they wounded him also, and cast him out. [13]Then said the lord of the vineyard, What shall I do? I will send my beloved son: it may be they will reverence him when they see him. [14]But when the husbandmen saw him, they reasoned among themselves, saying, This is the heir: come, let us kill him, that the inheritance may be ours. [15]So they cast him out of the vineyard, and killed him. What therefore shall the lord of the vineyard do unto them? [16]He shall come and destroy these husbandmen, and shall give the vineyard to others. And when they heard it, they said, God forbid. [17]And he beheld them, and said, What is this then that is written, The stone which the builders rejected, the same is become the head of the corner? [18]Whosoever shall fall upon that stone shall be broken; but on whomsoever it shall fall, it will grind him to powder. [19]And the chief priests and the scribes the same hour sought to lay hands on him; and they feared the people: for they perceived that he had spoken this parable against them. **Acts 13:33** [33]God hath fulfilled the same unto us their children, in that he hath raised up Jesus again; as it is also written in the second psalm, Thou art my Son, this day have I begotten thee.

Romans 1:3–4 continued on next page

ROMANS 1:3–4—Address (1:1–5): Jewish inheritance, 56–58 CE (*continued*)

Theme	ROM	Paul	Jewish	Other
(*Cont.*) **Son of God: Sent from heaven (variation of supra)**	**1:3–4 (above)** **1:7 (above)** **8:3 (above)** **8:15 (above)**	**Phil 3:10** [10]That I may know him, and the power of his resurrection, and the fellowship of his sufferings, being made conformable unto his death;	**Is 45:23** [23]I have sworn by myself, the word is gone out of my mouth in righteousness, and shall not return, That unto me every knee shall bow, every tongue shall swear.	**Q-Quelle** Against Pharisees: Rom 1:3-4/Mt 23:4-36/[Mk 7:1-9]/[Lk 11:37-54 (QS 34 [Thom 39:1, 89, 102])]

ROMANS 1:3–4—Address (1:1–5): Jewish inheritance, 56–58 CE (*continued*)

Theme	ROM	Mt	Lk
Son of God: Image/form (variation of supra)	**1:3–4 (above)** **1:7 (above)** **8:3 (above)** **8:15 (above)**	**11:19** [19]The Son of man came eating and drinking, and they say, Behold a man gluttonous, and a winebibber, a friend of publicans and sinners.	**7:35** [35]But wisdom is justified of all her children. **11:49** [49]Therefore also said the wisdom of God, I will send them prophets and apostles, and some of them they shall slay and persecute:

Paul	Other
Phil 2:5–8 [5]Let this mind be in you, which was also in Christ Jesus: [6]Who, being in the form of God, thought it not robbery to be equal with God: [7]But made himself of no reputation, and took upon him the form of a servant, and was made in the likeness of men: [8]And being found in fashion as a man, he humbled himself, and became obedient unto death, even the death of the cross. **Col 1:15–16** [15]Who is the image of the invisible God, the firstborn of every creature: **[16]For by him were all things created, that are in heaven, and that are in earth, visible and invisible, whether they be thrones, or dominions, or principalities, or powers: all things were created by him, and for him:**	**Q-Quelle** Jesus' witness to John: Rom 1:3-4/Col 1:15-16/Mt 11:7-19,[21:31-32]/Lk 7:24-35 (QS 17 [Thom 74,46]), [Lk 16:16 (QS 56)]; Against Pharisees: Rom 1:3-4/Col 1:15-16/[Mt 23:4-36][Mk 7:1-9]/Lk 11:37-54 (QS 34 [Thom 39:1, 89, 102])

ROMANS 1:3—Address (1:1–5): Jewish inheritance, 56–58 CE

Theme	ROM
Jesus' human birth and life	**1:3** [3]Concerning his Son Jesus Christ our Lord, which was made of the seed of David according to the flesh;
	1:31 [31]Without understanding, covenantbreakers, without natural affection, implacable, unmerciful:
	4:21–25 [21]And being fully persuaded that, what he had promised, he was able also to perform. [22]And therefore it was imputed to him for righteousness. [23]Now it was not written for his sake alone, that it was imputed to him; [24]But for us also, to whom it shall be imputed, if we believe on him that raised up Jesus our Lord from the dead; [25]Who was delivered for our offences, and was raised again for our justification.
	Ch 5 [1]Therefore being justified by faith, we have peace with God through our Lord Jesus Christ: [2]By whom also we have access by faith into this grace wherein we stand, and rejoice in hope of the glory of God. [3]And not only so, but we glory in tribulations also: knowing that tribulation worketh patience; [4]And patience, experience; and experience, hope: [5]And hope maketh not ashamed; because the love of God is shed abroad in our hearts by the Holy Ghost which is given unto us. [6]For when we were yet without strength, in due time Christ died for the ungodly. [7]For scarcely for a righteous man will one die: yet peradventure for a good man some would even dare to die. [8]But God commendeth his love toward us, in that, while we were yet sinners, Christ died for us. [9]Much more then, being now justified by his blood, we shall be saved from wrath through him. [10]For if, when we were enemies, we were reconciled to God by the death of his Son, much more, being reconciled, we shall be saved by his life. [11]And not only so, but we also joy in God through our Lord Jesus Christ, by whom we have now received the atonement. [12]Wherefore, as by one man sin entered into the world, and death by sin; and so death passed upon all men, for that all have sinned: [13](For until the law sin was in the world: but sin is not imputed when there is no law. [14]Nevertheless death reigned from Adam to Moses, even over them that had not sinned after the similitude of Adam's transgression, who is the figure of him that was to come. [15]But not as the offence, so also is the free gift. For if through the offence of one many be dead, much more the grace of God, and the gift by grace, which is by one man, Jesus Christ, hath abounded unto many. [16]And not as it was by one that sinned, so is the gift: for the judgment was by one to condemnation, but the free gift is of many offences unto justification. [17]For if by one man's offence death reigned by one; much more they which receive abundance of grace and of the gift of righteousness shall reign in life by one, Jesus Christ.) [18]Therefore as by the offence of one judgment came upon all men to condemnation; even so by the righteousness of one the free gift came upon all men unto justification of life. [19]For as by one man's disobedience many were made sinners, so by the obedience of one shall many be made righteous. [20]Moreover the law entered, that the offence might abound. But where sin abounded, grace did much more abound: [21]That as sin hath reigned unto death, even so might grace reign through righteousness unto eternal life by Jesus Christ our Lord.
	9:5 [5]Whose are the fathers, and of whom as concerning the flesh Christ came, who is over all, God blessed for ever. Amen.
	15:3 [3]For even Christ pleased not himself; but, as it is written, The reproaches of them that reproached thee fell on me.

Mt	Mk
1:1 [1]The book of the generation of Jesus Christ, the son of David, the son of Abraham. **1:17** [17]So all the generations from Abraham to David are fourteen generations; and from David until the carrying away into Babylon are fourteen generations; and from the carrying away into Babylon unto Christ are fourteen generations. **1:20–21** [20]But while he thought on these things, behold, the angel of the Lord appeared unto him in a dream, saying, Joseph, thou son of David, fear not to take unto thee Mary thy wife: for that which is conceived in her is of the Holy Ghost. [21]And she shall bring forth a son, and thou shalt call his name JESUS: for he shall save his people from their sins. **2:5–6** [5]And they said unto him, In Bethlehem of Judaea: for thus it is written by the prophet, [6]And thou Bethlehem, in the land of Juda, art not the least among the princes of Juda: for out of thee shall come a Governor, that shall rule my people Israel. **2:15** [15]And was there until the death of Herod: that it might be fulfilled which was spoken of the Lord by the prophet, saying, Out of Egypt have I called my son. **19:8** [8]He saith unto them, Moses because of the hardness of your hearts suffered you to put away your wives: but from the beginning it was not so.	**10:6** [6]But from the beginning of the creation God made them male and female **12:35** [36]For David himself said by the Holy Ghost, The LORD said to my Lord, Sit thou on my right hand, till I make thine enemies thy footstool.

Romans 1:3 continued on next page

ROMANS 1:3—Address (1:1–5): Jewish inheritance, 56–58 CE (*continued*)

Theme	ROM	Lk	Jn
(Cont.) **Jesus' human birth and life**	**1:3 (above)** **1:31 (above)** **4:21–25 (above)** **Ch 5 (above)** **9:5 (above)** **15:3 (above)**	**1:32** [32]He shall be great, and shall be called the Son of the Highest: and the Lord God shall give unto him the throne of his father David: **1:35** [35]And the angel answered and said unto her, The Holy Ghost shall come upon thee, and the power of the Highest shall overshadow thee: therefore also that holy thing which shall be born of thee shall be called the Son of God. **1:57** [57]Now Elisabeth's full time came that she should be delivered; and she brought forth a son. **1:69** [69]And hath raised up an horn of salvation for us in the house of his servant David; **2:4** [4]And Joseph also went up from Galilee, out of the city of Nazareth, into Judaea, unto the city of David, which is called Bethlehem; (because he was of the house and lineage of David:) **2:6–7** [6]And so it was, that, while they were there, the days were accomplished that she should be delivered. [7]And she brought forth her firstborn son, and wrapped him in swaddling clothes, and laid him in a manger; because there was no room for them in the inn. **2:11** [11]For unto you is born this day in the city of David a Saviour, which is Christ the Lord. **2:22–24** [22]And when the days of her purification according to the law of Moses were accomplished, they brought him to Jerusalem, to present him to the Lord; [23](As it is written in the law of the Lord, Every male that openeth the womb shall be called holy to the Lord;) [24]And to offer a sacrifice according to that which is said in the law of the Lord, A pair of turtledoves, or two young pigeons. **Acts 13:22–23** [22]And when he had removed him, he raised up unto them David to be their king; to whom also he gave testimony, and said, I have found David the son of Jesse, a man after mine own heart, which shall fulfil all my will. [23]Of this man's seed hath God according to his promise raised unto Israel a Saviour, Jesus:	**7:42** [42]Hath not the scripture said, That Christ cometh of the seed of David, and out of the town of Bethlehem, where David was?

Paul

1 Cor 15:27

[27]For he hath put all things under his feet. But when he saith all things are put under him, it is manifest that he is excepted, which did put all things under him.

1 Cor 15:49

[49]And as we have borne the image of the earthy, we shall also bear the image of the heavenly.

2 Cor 3:18

[18]But we all, with open face beholding as in a glass the glory of the Lord, are changed into the same image from glory to glory, even as by the Spirit of the Lord.

Gal 4:4

[4]But when the fulness of the time was come, God sent forth his Son, made of a woman made under the law.

Gal 4:14

[14]And my temptation which was in my flesh ye despised not, nor rejected; but received me as an angel of God, even as Christ Jesus.

Phil 2

[1]If there be therefore any consolation in Christ, if any comfort of love, if any fellowship of the Spirit, if any bowels and mercies, [2]Fulfil ye my joy, that ye be likeminded, having the same love, being of one accord, of one mind. [3]Let nothing be done through strife or vainglory; but in lowliness of mind let each esteem other better than themselves. [4]Look not every man on his own things, but every man also on the things of others. [5]Let this mind be in you, which was also in Christ Jesus: [6]Who, being in the form of God, thought it not robbery to be equal with God: [7]But made himself of no reputation, and took upon him the form of a servant, and was made in the likeness of men: [8]And being found in fashion as a man, he humbled himself, and became obedient unto death, even the death of the cross. [9]Wherefore God also hath highly exalted him, and given him a name which is above every name: [10]That at the name of Jesus every knee should bow, of things in heaven, and things in earth, and things under the earth; [11]And that every tongue should confess that Jesus Christ is Lord, to the glory of God the Father. [2]Wherefore, my beloved, as ye have always obeyed, not as in my presence only, but now much more in my absence, work out your own salvation with fear and trembling. [13]For it is God which worketh in you both to will and to do of his good pleasure. [14]Do all things without murmurings and disputings: [15]That ye may be blameless and harmless, the sons of God, without rebuke, in the midst of a crooked and perverse nation, among whom ye shine as lights in the world; [16]Holding forth the word of life; that I may rejoice in the day of Christ, that I have not run in vain, neither laboured in vain. [17]Yea, and if I be offered upon the sacrifice and service of your faith, I joy, and rejoice with you all. [18]For the same cause also do ye joy, and rejoice with me. [19]But I trust in the Lord Jesus to send Timotheus shortly unto you, that I also may be of good comfort, when I know your state. [20]For I have no man likeminded, who will naturally care for your state. [21]For all seek their own, not the things which are Jesus Christ's. [22]But ye know the proof of him, that, as a son with the father, he hath served with me in the gospel. [23]Him therefore I hope to send presently, so soon as I shall see how it will go with me. [24]But I trust in the Lord that I also myself shall come shortly. [25]Yet I supposed it necessary to send to you Epaphroditus, my brother, and companion in labour, and fellowsoldier, but your messenger, and he that ministered to my wants. [26]For he longed after you all, and was full of heaviness, because that ye had heard that he had been sick. [27]For indeed he was sick nigh unto death: but God had mercy on him; and not on him only, but on me also, lest I should have sorrow upon sorrow. [28]I sent him therefore the more carefully, that, when ye see him again, ye may rejoice, and that I may be the less sorrowful. [29]Receive him therefore in the Lord with all gladness; and hold such in reputation: [30]Because for the work of Christ he was nigh unto death, not regarding his life, to supply your lack of service toward me.

Phil 2:7

[7]But made himself of no reputation, and took upon him the form of a servant, and was made in the likeness of men:

Col 3:10

[10]And have put on the new man, which is renewed in knowledge after the image of him that created him:

2 Tim 2:8 (Pseudo)

[8]Remember that Jesus Christ of the seed of David was raised from the dead according to my gospel:

Romans 1:3 continued on next page

ROMANS 1:3—Address (1:1–5): Jewish inheritance, 56–58 CE (*continued*)

Theme	ROM	NT
(*Cont.*) **Jesus' human birth and life**	**1:3** (above) **Ch 5** (above)	**Rev 22:16** [16]I, Jesus, have sent My angel to testify to you these things in the churches. I am the Root and the Offspring of David, the Bright and Morning Star."

Jewish Writings	Other
Gen 1:28	**Q-Quelle**
[28]And God blessed them, and God said unto them, Be fruitful, and multiply, and replenish the earth, and subdue it: and have dominion over the fish of the sea, and over the fowl of the air, and over every living thing that moveth upon the earth. **2 Sam 7** [1] And it came to pass, when the king sat in his house, and the LORD had given him rest round about from all his enemies; [2] That the king said unto Nathan the prophet, See now, I dwell in an house of cedar, but the ark of God dwelleth within curtains. [3] And Nathan said to the king, Go, do all that is in thine heart; for the LORD is with thee. [4] And it came to pass that night, that the word of the LORD came unto Nathan, saying, [5] Go and tell my servant David, Thus saith the LORD, Shalt thou build me an house for me to dwell in? [6] Whereas I have not dwelt in any house since the time that I brought up the children of Israel out of Egypt, even to this day, but have walked in a tent and in a tabernacle. [7] In all the places wherein I have walked with all the children of Israel spake I a word with any of the tribes of Israel, whom I commanded to feed my people Israel, saying, Why build ye not me an house of cedar? [8] Now therefore so shalt thou say unto my servant David, Thus saith the LORD of hosts, I took thee from the sheepcote, from following the sheep, to be ruler over my people, over Israel: [9] And I was with thee whithersoever thou wentest, and have cut off all thine enemies out of thy sight, and have made thee a great name, like unto the name of the great men that are in the earth. [10] Moreover I will appoint a place for my people Israel, and will plant them, that they may dwell in a place of their own, and move no more; neither shall the children of wickedness afflict them any more, as beforetime, [11] And as since the time that I commanded judges to be over my people Israel, and have caused thee to rest from all thine enemies. Also the LORD telleth thee that he will make thee an house. [12] And when thy days be fulfilled, and thou shalt sleep with thy fathers, I will set up thy seed after thee, which shall proceed out of thy bowels, and I will establish his kingdom. [13] He shall build an house for my name, and I will stablish the throne of his kingdom for ever. [14] I will be his father, and he shall be my son. If he commit iniquity, I will chasten him with the rod of men, and with the stripes of the children of men: [15] But my mercy shall not depart away from him, as I took it from Saul, whom I put away before thee. [16] And thine house and thy kingdom shall be established for ever before thee: thy throne shall be established for ever. [17] According to all these words, and according to all this vision, so did Nathan speak unto David. [18] Then went king David in, and sat before the LORD, and he said, Who am I, O Lord GOD? and what is my house, that thou hast brought me hitherto? [19] And this was yet a small thing in thy sight, O Lord GOD; but thou hast spoken also of thy servant's house for a great while to come. And is this the manner of man, O Lord GOD? [20] And what can David say more unto thee? for thou, Lord GOD, knowest thy servant. [21] For thy word's sake, and according to thine own heart, hast thou done all these great things, to make thy servant know them. [22] Wherefore thou art great, O LORD God: for there is none like thee, neither is there any God beside thee, according to all that we have heard with our ears. [23] And what one nation in the earth is like thy people, even like Israel, whom God went to redeem for a people to himself, and to make him a name, and to do for you great things and terrible, for thy land, before thy people, which thou redeemedst to thee from Egypt, from the nations and their gods? [24] For thou hast confirmed to thyself thy people Israel to be a people unto thee for ever: and thou, LORD, art become their God. [25] And now, O LORD God, the word that thou hast spoken concerning thy servant, and concerning his house, establish it for ever, and do as thou hast said. [26] And let thy name be magnified for ever, saying, The LORD of hosts is the God over Israel: and let the house of thy servant David be established before thee. [27] For thou, O LORD of hosts, God of Israel, hast revealed to thy servant, saying, I will build thee an house: therefore hath thy servant found in his heart to pray this prayer unto thee. [28] And now, O Lord GOD, thou art that God, and thy words be true, and thou hast promised this goodness unto thy servant: [29] Therefore now let it please thee to bless the house of thy servant, that it may continue for ever before thee: for thou, O Lord GOD, hast spoken it: and with thy blessing let the house of thy servant be blessed for ever.	Jesus' witness to John: Rom 1:3/Gal 4:4/[Mt 11:7-19, 21:31-32]/[Lk 7:24-35 (QS 17 [Thom 46, 74], QS 18)], [Lk 16:16 (QS 56)]

ROMANS 1:5—Address (1:1–5): Jewish inheritance, 56–58 CE

Theme	ROM	Mt
Commissioning	**1:5** [5]By whom we have received grace and apostleship, for obedience to the faith among all nations, for his name: **15:15** [15]Nevertheless, brethren, I have written the more boldly unto you in some sort, as putting you in mind, because of the grace that is given to me of God, **15:18** [18]For I will not dare to speak of any of those things which Christ hath not wrought by me, to make the Gentiles obedient, by word and deed,	**28:16–20** [16]Then the eleven disciples went away into Galilee, into a mountain where Jesus had appointed them. [17]And when they saw him, they worshipped him: but some doubted. [18]And Jesus came and spake unto them, saying, All power is given unto me in heaven and in earth. [19]Go ye therefore, and teach all nations, baptizing them in the name of the Father, and of the Son, and of the Holy Ghost: [20]Teaching them to observe all things whatsoever I have commanded you: and, lo, I am with you alway, even unto the end of the world. Amen.

ROMANS 1:6—Jewish inheritance, 56–58 CE

Theme	ROM	Paul
Calling	**1:6** [6]Among whom are ye also the called of Jesus Christ:	**1 Cor 1:9** [9]God is faithful, by whom ye were called unto the fellowship of his Son Jesus Christ our Lord.

Lk	Paul
24:44–49 44 And he said unto them, These are the words which I spake unto you, while I was yet with you, that all things must be fulfilled, which were written in the law of Moses, and in the prophets, and in the psalms, concerning me. 45 Then opened he their understanding, that they might understand the scriptures, 46 And said unto them, Thus it is written, and thus it behoved Christ to suffer, and to rise from the dead the third day: 47 And that repentance and remission of sins should be preached in his name among all nations, beginning at Jerusalem. 48 And ye are witnesses of these things. 49 And, behold, I send the promise of my Father upon you: but tarry ye in the city of Jerusalem, until ye be endued with power from on high. **Acts 9:15** 15 But the Lord said unto him, Go thy way: for he is a chosen vessel unto me, to bear my name before the Gentiles, and kings, and the children of Israel: **Acts 26:16–18** 16 But rise, and stand upon thy feet: for I have appeared unto thee for this purpose, to make thee a minister and a witness both of these things which thou hast seen, and of those things in the which I will appear unto thee; 17 Delivering thee from the people, and from the Gentiles, unto whom now I send thee, 18 To open their eyes, and to turn them from darkness to light, and from the power of Satan unto God, that they may receive forgiveness of sins, and inheritance among them which are sanctified by faith that is in me.	**Gal 1:16** 16 To reveal his Son in me, that I might preach him among the heathen; immediately I conferred not with flesh and blood: **Gal 2:7, 9** 7 But contrariwise, when they saw that the gospel of the uncircumcision was committed unto me, as the gospel of the circumcision was unto Peter;... 9 And when James, Cephas, and John, who seemed to be pillars, perceived the grace that was given unto me, they gave to me and Barnabas the right hands of fellowship; that we should go unto the heathen, and they unto the circumcision.

ROMANS 1:7—Jewish inheritance, 56–58 CE

Theme	ROM	Paul	Jewish Writings
Being called to sainthood	**1:7** [7]To all that be in Rome, beloved of God, called to be saints: Grace to you and peace from God our Father, and the Lord Jesus Christ.	**1 Cor 1:2–3** [2]Unto the church of God which is at Corinth, to them that are sanctified in Christ Jesus, called to be saints, with all that in every place call upon the name of Jesus Christ our Lord, both theirs and ours: [3]Grace be unto you, and peace, from God our Father, and from the Lord Jesus Christ. **2 Cor 1:1–2** [1]Paul, an apostle of Jesus Christ by the will of God, and Timothy our brother, unto the church of God which is at Corinth, with all the saints which are in all Achaia: [2]Grace be to you and peace from God our Father, and from the Lord Jesus Christ.	**Num 6:25–26** [25]The LORD make his face shine upon thee, and be gracious unto thee: [26]The LORD lift up his countenance upon thee, and give thee peace.

ROMANS 1:8—Jewish inheritance, 56–58 CE

Theme	ROM	Paul
Commissioning	**1:8** [8]First, I thank my God through Jesus Christ for you all, that your faith is spoken of throughout the whole world. **16:19** [19]For your obedience is come abroad unto all men. I am glad therefore on your behalf: but yet I would have you wise unto that which is good, and simple concerning evil.	**1 Thes 1:8** [8]For from you sounded out the word of the Lord not only in Macedonia and Achaia, but also in every place your faith to God-ward is spread abroad; so that we need not to speak any thing.

ROMANS 1:9—Jewish inheritance, 56–58 CE

Theme	ROM	Paul
Serving God	**1:9** [9]For God is my witness, whom I serve with my spirit in the gospel of his Son, that without ceasing I make mention of you always in my prayers;	**2 Cor 1:23** [23]Moreover I call God for a record upon my soul, that to spare you I came not as yet unto Corinth. **Eph 1:16** [16]Cease not to give thanks for you, making mention of you in my prayers; **Phil 1:8** [8]For God is my record, how greatly I long after you all in the bowels of Jesus Christ. **1 Thes 1:1** [1]Paul, and Silvanus, and Timotheus, unto the church of the Thessalonians which is in God the Father and in the Lord Jesus Christ: Grace be unto you, and peace, from God our Father, and the Lord Jesus Christ. **1 Thes 2:5, 10** [5]For neither at any time used we flattering words, as ye know, nor a cloak of covetousness; God is witness:... [10]Ye are witnesses, and God also, how holily and justly and unblameably we behaved ourselves among you that believe: **2 Tim 1:3 (Pseudo)** [3]I thank God, whom I serve from my forefathers with pure conscience, that without ceasing I have remembrance of thee in my prayers night and day;

ROMANS 1:10—Jewish inheritance, 56–58 CE

Theme	ROM
Commissioning	**1:10** [10]Making request, if by any means now at length I might have a prosperous journey by the will of God to come unto you. **15:23, 32** [23]But now having no more place in these parts, and having a great desire these many years to come unto you;... [32]That I may come unto you with joy by the will of God, and may with you be refreshed.

GOSPEL REDEEMS HUMANKIND (1:16–3:20)

ROMANS 1:16—Gospel redeems humankind (1:16–3:20), 56–58 CE

Theme	ROM	Mk	Lk
Gospel to the Jew first, and also to the Greek	**1:16** [16]For I am not ashamed of the gospel of Christ: for it is the power of God unto salvation to every one that believeth; to the Jew first, and also to the Greek.	**8:36, 38** [36]For what shall it profit a man, if he shall gain the whole world, and lose his own soul? [38]Whosoever therefore shall be ashamed of me and of my words in this adulterous and sinful generation; of him also shall the Son of man be ashamed, when he cometh in the glory of his Father with the holy angels.	**Acts 3:26** [26]Unto you first God, having raised up his Son Jesus, sent him to bless you, in turning away every one of you from his iniquities. **Acts 13:46** [46]Then Paul and Barnabas waxed bold, and said, It was necessary that the word of God should first have been spoken to you: but seeing ye put it from you, and judge yourselves unworthy of everlasting life, lo, we turn to the Gentiles.

ROMANS 1:17—Gospel redeems humankind (1:16–3:20), 56–58 CE

Theme	ROM
Righteousness in/of Jesus	**1:17** [17]For therein is the righteousness of God revealed from faith to faith: as it is written, The just shall live by faith. **3:21–22** [21]But now the righteousness of God without the law is manifested, being witnessed by the law and the prophets; [22]Even the righteousness of God which is by faith of Jesus Christ unto all and upon all them that believe: for there is no difference: **3:26** [26]To declare, I say, at this time his righteousness: that he might be just, and the justifier of him which believeth in Jesus. **4:6** [6]Even as David also describeth the blessedness of the man, unto whom God imputeth righteousness without works,

Paul	Jewish Writings
1 Cor 1:16 [16]And I baptized also the household of Stephanas: besides, I know not whether I baptized any other. **1 Cor 1:18** [18]For the preaching of the cross is to them that perish foolishness; but unto us which are saved it is the power of God. **1 Cor 1:24** [24]But unto them which are called, both Jews and Greeks, Christ the power of God, and the wisdom of God. **1 Cor 2:9** [9]But as it is written, Eye hath not seen, nor ear heard, neither have entered into the heart of man, the things which God hath prepared for them that love him. **Phil 1:20** [20]According to my earnest expectation and my hope, that in nothing I shall be ashamed, but that with all boldness, as always, so now also Christ shall be magnified in my body, whether it be by life, or by death. **Phil 3:7–11** [7]But what things were gain to me, those I counted loss for Christ. [8]Yea doubtless, and I count all things but loss for the excellency of the knowledge of Christ Jesus my Lord: for whom I have suffered the loss of all things, and do count them but dung, that I may win Christ, [9]And be found in him, not having mine own righteousness, which is of the law, but that which is through the faith of Christ, the righteousness which is of God by faith: [10]That I may know him, and the power of his resurrection, and the fellowship of his sufferings, being made conformable unto his death; [11]If by any means I might attain unto the resurrection of the dead.	**Ps 119:46** [46]I will speak of thy testimonies also before kings, and will not be ashamed.

Paul	NT
Gal 2:16 [16]Knowing that a man is not justified by the works of the law, but by the faith of Jesus Christ, even we have believed in Jesus Christ, that we might be justified by the faith of Christ, and not by the works of the law: for by the works of the law shall no flesh be justified. **Gal 3:11** [11]But that no man is justified by the law in the sight of God, it is evident: for, The just shall live by faith. **Gal 3:22** [22]But the scripture hath concluded all under sin, that the promise by faith of Jesus Christ might be given to them that believe. **Phil 3:9** [9]So then they which be of faith are blessed with faithful Abraham.	**Heb 2:4** [4]God also bearing them witness, both with signs and wonders, and with divers miracles, and gifts of the Holy Ghost, according to his own will? **Heb 10:38** [38]Now the just shall live by faith: but if any man draw back, my soul shall have no pleasure in him.

ROMANS 1:18—Gospel redeems humankind (1:16–3:20), 56–58 CE

Theme	ROM	Paul
God's wrath and hard hearts	**1:18** [18]For the wrath of God is revealed from heaven against all ungodliness and unrighteousness of men, who hold the truth in unrighteousness; **2:5, 8–9** [5]But after thy hardness and impenitent heart treasurest up unto thyself wrath against the day of wrath and revelation of the righteous judgment of God;. . . [8]But unto them that are contentious, and do not obey the truth, but obey unrighteousness, indignation and wrath, [9]Tribulation and anguish, upon every soul of man that doeth evil, of the Jew first, and also of the Gentile;	**Eph 5:6 (Pseudo)** [6]Let no man deceive you with vain words: for because of these things cometh the wrath of God upon the children of disobedience. **Col 3:6** [6]For which things' sake the wrath of God cometh on the children of disobedience:

ROMANS 1:19–32—Gospel redeems humankind (1:16–3:20), 56–58 CE

Theme	ROM
God is above all creation	**1:19–32** [19]Because that which may be known of God is manifest in them; for God hath showed it unto them. [20]For the invisible things of him from the creation of the world are clearly seen, being understood by the things that are made, even his eternal power and Godhead; so that they are without excuse: [21]Because that, when they knew God, they glorified him not as God, neither were thankful; but became vain in their imaginations, and their foolish heart was darkened. [22]Professing themselves to be wise, they became fools, [23]And changed the glory of the uncorruptible God into an image made like to corruptible man, and to birds, and fourfooted beasts, and creeping things. [24]Wherefore God also gave them up to uncleanness through the lusts of their own hearts, to dishonour their own bodies between themselves: [25]Who changed the truth of God into a lie, and worshipped and served the creature more than the Creator, who is blessed for ever. Amen. [26]For this cause God gave them up unto vile affections: for even their women did change the natural use into that which is against nature: [27]And likewise also the men, leaving the natural use of the woman, burned in their lust one toward another; men with men working that which is unseemly, and receiving in themselves that recompense of their error which was meet. [28]And even as they did not like to retain God in their knowledge, God gave them over to a reprobate mind, to do those things which are not convenient; [29]Being filled with all unrighteousness, fornication, wickedness, covetousness, maliciousness; full of envy, murder, debate, deceit, malignity; whisperers, [30]Backbiters, haters of God, despiteful, proud, boasters, inventors of evil things, disobedient to parents, [31]Without understanding, covenantbreakers, without natural affection, implacable, unmerciful: [32]Who knowing the judgment of God, that they which commit such things are worthy of death, not only do the same, but have pleasure in them that do them.

ROMANS 1:20—Gospel redeems humankind (1:16–3:20), 56–58 CE

Theme	ROM	Lk
Created order testifies to God's wonder	**1:20** [20]For the invisible things of him from the creation of the world are clearly seen, being under-stood by the things that are made, even his eternal power and Godhead; so that they are without excuse:	**Acts 14:17** [17]Nevertheless he left not himself without witness, in that he did good, and gave us rain from heaven, and fruitful seasons, filling our hearts with food and gladness. **Acts 17: 25–28** [25]Neither is worshipped with men's hands, as though he needed any thing, seeing he giveth to all life, and breath, and all things; [26]And hath made of one blood all nations of men for to dwell on all the face of the earth, and hath determined the times before appointed, and the bounds of their habitation; [27]That they should seek the Lord, if haply they might feel after him, and find him, though he be not far from every one of us: [28]For in him we live, and move, and have our being; as certain also of your own poets have said, For we are also his offspring.

Jewish Writings
Is 66:15
[15]For, behold, the LORD will come with fire, and with his chariots like a whirlwind, to render his anger with fury, and his rebuke with flames of fire.

Lk	Jewish Writings
Acts 14:15–17	**Wis 13:19**
[15]And saying, Sirs, why do ye these things? We also are men of like passions with you, and preach unto you that ye should turn from these vanities unto the living God, which made heaven, and earth, and the sea, and all things that are therein: [16]Who in times past suffered all nations to walk in their own ways. [17]Nevertheless he left not himself without witness, in that he did good, and gave us rain from heaven, and fruitful seasons, filling our hearts with food and gladness.	[19]And for gaining and getting, and for good success of his hands, asketh ability to do of him, that is most unable to do any thing.
Act 17:23–29	
[23]For as I passed by, and beheld your devotions, I found an altar with this inscription, TO THE UNKNOWN GOD. Whom therefore ye ignorantly worship, him declare I unto you. [24]God that made the world and all things therein, seeing that he is Lord of heaven and earth, dwelleth not in temples made with hands; [25]Neither is worshipped with men's hands, as though he needed any thing, seeing he giveth to all life, and breath, and all things; [26]And hath made of one blood all nations of men for to dwell on all the face of the earth, and hath determined the times before appointed, and the bounds of their habitation; [27]That they should seek the Lord, if haply they might feel after him, and find him, though he be not far from every one of us: [28]For in him we live, and move, and have our being; as certain also of your own poets have said, For we are also his offspring. [29]Forasmuch then as we are the offspring of God, we ought not to think that the Godhead is like unto gold, or silver, or stone, graven by art and man's device.	

Jewish Writings
Job 12:7–9
[7]But ask now the beasts, and they shall teach thee; and the fowls of the air, and they shall tell thee: [8]Or speak to the earth, and it shall teach thee: and the fishes of the sea shall declare unto thee. [9]Who knoweth not in all these that the hand of the LORD hath wrought this?
Ps 8:4
[4]What is man, that thou art mindful of him? and the son of man, that thou visitest him?
Ps 19:2
[2]Day unto day uttereth speech, and night unto night showeth knowledge.
Sir 17:7–9
[7]Withal he filled them with the knowledge of understanding, and shewed them good and evil. [8] He set his eye upon their hearts, that he might shew them the greatness of his works. [9] He gave them to glory in his marvellous acts for ever, that they might declare his works with under-standing.
Is 40:26
[26]Lift up your eyes on high, and behold who hath created these things, that bringeth out their host by number: he calleth them all by names by the greatness of his might, for that he is strong in power; not one faileth.

ROMANS 1:21—Gospel redeems humankind (1:16–3:20), 56–58 CE

Theme	ROM	Paul
Walking in vanity	**1:21** [21]Because that, when they knew God, they glorified him not as God, neither were thankful; but became vain in their imaginations, and their foolish heart was darkened.	**Eph 4:17–18 (Pseudo)** [17]This I say therefore, and testify in the Lord, that ye henceforth walk not as other Gentiles walk, in the vanity of their mind, [18]Having the understanding darkened, being alienated from the life of God through the ignorance that is in them, because of the blindness of their heart:

ROMANS 1:22—Gospel redeems humankind (1:16–3:20), 56–58 CE

Theme	ROM	Lk	Paul	Jewish Writings
Wise become foolish	**1:22** [22]Professing themselves to be wise, they became fools,	**Acts 17:29–30** [29]Forasmuch then as we are the offspring of God, we ought not to think that the God-head is like unto gold, or silver, or stone, graven by art and man's device. [30]And the times of this ignorance God winked at; but now commandeth all men every where to repent:	**1 Cor 1:19–21** [19]For it is written, I will destroy the wisdom of the wise, and will bring to nothing the understanding of the prudent. [20]Where is the wise? where is the scribe? where is the disputer of this world? hath not God made foolish the wisdom of this world? [21]For after that in the wisdom of God the world by wisdom knew not God, it pleased God by the foolishness of preaching to save them that believe.	**Wis 13:1–9** [1]Surely vain are all men by nature, who are ignorant of God, and could not out of the good things that are seen know him that is: neither by considering the works did they acknowledge the workmaster; [2] But deemed either fire, or wind, or the swift air, or the circle of the stars, or the violent water, or the lights of heaven, to be the gods which govern the world. [3] With whose beauty if they being delighted took them to be gods; let them know how much better the Lord of them is: for the first author of beauty hath created them. [4] But if they were astonished at their power and virtue, let them understand by them, how much mightier he is that made them. [5] For by the greatness and beauty of the creatures proportionably the maker of them is seen. [6] But yet for this they are the less to be blamed: for they peradventure err, seeking God, and desirous to find him. [7] For being conversant in his works they search him diligently, and believe their sight: because the things are beautiful that are seen. [8] Howbeit neither are they to be pardoned. [9] For if they were able to know so much, that they could aim at the world; how did they not sooner find out the Lord thereof? **Is 5:21** [21]Woe unto them that are wise in their own eyes, and prudent in their own sight! **Jer 10:14** [14]Every man is brutish in his knowledge: every founder is con-founded by the graven image: for his molten image is falsehood, and there is no breath in them.

ROMANS 1:23—Gospel redeems humankind (1:16–3:20), 56–58 CE

Theme	ROM	Jewish Writings
Corrupt images	**1:23** [23]And changed the glory of the uncorruptible God into an image made like to corruptible man, and to birds, and four-footed beasts, and creeping things.	**Dt 4:15–19** [15]Take ye therefore good heed unto yourselves; for ye saw no manner of similitude on the day that the LORD spake unto you in Horeb out of the midst of the fire: [16]Lest ye corrupt yourselves, and make you a graven image, the similitude of any figure, the likeness of male or female, [17]The likeness of any beast that is on the earth, the likeness of any winged fowl that flieth in the air, [18]The likeness of any thing that creepeth on the ground, the likeness of any fish that is in the waters beneath the earth: [19]And lest thou lift up thine eyes unto heaven, and when thou seest the sun, and the moon, and the stars, even all the host of heaven, shouldest be driven to worship them, and serve them, which the LORD thy God hath divided unto all nations under the whole heaven. **Ps 106:20** [20]Thus they changed their glory into the similitude of an ox that eateth grass. **Wis 11:15** [15]But for the foolish devices of their wickedness, wherewith being deceived they worshipped serpents void of reason, and vile beasts thou didst send a multitude of unreasonable beasts upon them for vengeance; **Wis 12:24** [24]For they went astray very far in the ways of error, and held them for gods, which even among the beasts of their enemies were despised, being deceived, as children of no understanding. **Wis 13:10–19** [10]But miserable are they, and in dead things is their hope, who call them gods, which are the works of men's hands, gold and silver, to shew art in, and resemblances of beasts, or a stone good for nothing, the work of an ancient hand. [11]Now a carpenter that felleth timber, after he hath sawn down a tree meet for the purpose, and taken off all the bark skillfully round about, and hath wrought it handsomely, and made a vessel thereof fit for the service of man's life; [12]And after spending the refuse of his work to dress his meat, hath filled himself; [13]And taking the very refuse among those which served to no use, being a crooked piece of wood, and full of knots, hath carved it diligently, when he had nothing else to do, and formed it by the skill of his understanding, and fashioned it to the image of a man; [14]Or made it like some vile beast, laying it over with vermilion, and with paint colouring it red, and covering every spot therein; [15]And when he had made a convenient room for it, set it in a wall, and made it fast with iron: [16]For he provided for it that it might not fall, knowing that it was unable to help itself; for it is an image, and hath need of help: [17]Then maketh he prayer for his goods, for his wife and children, and is not ashamed to speak to that which hath no life. [18]For health he calleth upon that which is weak: for life prayeth to that which is dead; for aid humbly beseecheth that which hath least means to help: and for a good journey he asketh of that which cannot set a foot forward: [19]And for gaining and getting, and for good success of his hands, asketh ability to do of him, that is most unable to do any thing. **Jer 2:11** [11]Hath a nation changed their gods, which are yet no gods? but my people have changed their glory for that which doth not profit.

ROMANS 1:24—Gospel redeems humankind (1:16–3:20), 56–58 CE

Theme	ROM	Lk	Paul
False images	**1:24** [24]Wherefore God also gave them up to uncleanness through the lusts of their own hearts, to dishonour their own bodies between themselves:	**Acts 7:41–42** [41]And they made a calf in those days, and offered sacrifice unto the idol, and rejoiced in the works of their own hands. [42]Then God turned, and gave them up to worship the host of heaven; as it is written in the book of the prophets, O ye house of Israel, have ye offered to me slain beasts and sacrifices by the space of forty years in the wilderness?	**Eph 4:19 (Pseudo)** [19]Who being past feeling have given themselves over unto lasciviousness, to work all uncleanness with greediness.

ROMANS 1:25—Gospel redeems humankind (1:16–3:20), 56–58 CE

Theme	ROM
Worshipping idols, not God	**1:25** [25]Who changed the truth of God into a lie, and worshipped and served the creature more than the Creator, who is blessed for ever. Amen. **9:5** [5]Whose are the fathers, and of whom as concerning the flesh Christ came, who is over all, God blessed for ever. Amen.

ROMANS 1:27—Gospel redeems humankind (1:16–3:20), 56–58 CE

Theme	ROM	Paul
Sexual abomination	**1:27** [27]And likewise also the men, leaving the natural use of the woman, burned in their lust one toward another; men with men working that which is unseemly, and receiving in themselves that recompense of their error which was meet.	**1 Cor 6:9** [9]Know ye not that the unrighteous shall not inherit the kingdom of God? Be not deceived: neither fornicators, nor idolaters, nor adulterers, nor effeminate, nor abusers of themselves with mankind, **1 Tim 1:10 (Pseudo)** [10]For whoremongers, for them that defile themselves with mankind, for menstealers, for liars, for perjured persons, and if there be any other thing that is contrary to sound doctrine;

Jewish Writings

Wis 12:25

[25]Therefore unto them, as to children without the use of reason, thou didst send a judgment to mock them.

Wis 14:22–31

[22]Moreover this was not enough for them, that they erred in the knowledge of God; but whereas they lived in the great war of ignorance, those so great plagues called they peace. [23]For whilst they slew their children in sacrifices, or used secret ceremonies, or made revellings of strange rites; [24]They kept neither lives nor marriages any longer undefiled: but either one slew another traiterously, or grieved him by adultery. [25]So that there reigned in all men without exception blood, manslaughter, theft, and dissimulation, corruption, unfaithfulness, tumults, perjury, [26]Disquieting of good men, forgetfulness of good turns, defiling of souls, changing of kind, disorder in marriages, adultery, and shameless uncleanness. [27]For the worshipping of idols not to be named is the beginning, the cause, and the end, of all evil. [28]For either they are mad when they be merry, or prophesy lies, or live unjustly, or else lightly forswear themselves. [29]For insomuch as their trust is in idols, which have no life; though they swear falsely, yet they look not to be hurt. [30]Howbeit for both causes shall they be justly punished: both because they thought not well of God, giving heed unto idols, and also unjustly swore in deceit, despising holiness. [31]For it is not the power of them by whom they swear: but it is the just vengeance of sinners, that punisheth always the offence of the ungodly.

Jewish Writings

Jer 13:25–27

[25]This is thy lot, the portion of thy measures from me, saith the LORD; because thou hast forgotten me, and trusted in falsehood. [26]Therefore will I discover thy skirts upon thy face, that thy shame may appear. [27]I have seen thine adulteries, and thy neighings, the lewdness of thy whoredom, and thine abominations on the hills in the fields. Woe unto thee, O Jerusalem! wilt thou not be made clean? when shall it once be?

Jewish Writings

Lev 18:22

[22]Thou shalt not lie with mankind, as with womankind: it is abomination.

Lev 20:13

[13]If a man also lie with mankind, as he lieth with a woman, both of them have committed an abomination: they shall surely be put to death; their blood shall be upon them.

Wis 14:26

[26]Disquieting of good men, forgetfulness of good turns, defiling of souls, changing of kind, disorder in marriages, adultery, and shameless uncleanness.

ROMANS 1:29–31—Gospel redeems humankind (1:16–3:20), 56–58 CE

Theme	ROM	Mt	Mk
Unrighteous heart	**1:29–31** [29]Being filled with all unrighteousness, fornication, wickedness, covetousness, maliciousness; full of envy, murder, debate, deceit, malignity; whisperers, [30]Backbiters, haters of God, despiteful, proud, boasters, inventors of evil things, disobedient to parents, [31]Without understanding, covenantbreakers, without natural affection, implacable, unmerciful: **13:13** [13]Let us walk honestly, as in the day; not in rioting and drunkenness, not in chambering and wantonness, not in strife and envying.	**15:19** [19]For out of the heart proceed evil thoughts, murders, adulteries, fornications, thefts, false witness, blasphemies:	**7:21–22** [21]For from within, out of the heart of men, proceed evil thoughts, adulteries, fornications, murders, [22]Thefts, covetousness, wickedness, deceit, lasciviousness, an evil eye, blasphemy, pride, foolishness:

ROMANS 1:32—Gospel redeems humankind (1:16–3:20), 56–58 CE

Theme	ROM	Lk	Paul
Bad behavior	**1:32** [32]Who knowing the judgment of God, that they which commit such things are worthy of death, not only do the same, but have pleasure in them that do them.	**Acts 8:1** [1]And Saul was consenting unto his death. And at that time there was a great persecution against the church which was at Jerusalem; and they were all scattered abroad throughout the regions of Judaea and Samaria, except the apostles.	**2 Thes 2:12** [11]And for this cause God shall send them strong delusion, that they should believe a lie:

ROMANS Ch 2—Gospel redeems humankind (1:16–3:20), 56–58 CE

Theme	ROM
Do good and do not judge	**Ch 2** [1]Therefore thou art inexcusable, O man, whosoever thou art that judgest: for wherein thou judgest another, thou condemnest thyself; for thou that judgest doest the same things. [2]But we are sure that the judgment of God is according to truth against them which commit such things. [3]And thinkest thou this, O man, that judgest them which do such things, and doest the same, that thou shalt escape the judgment of God? [4]Or despisest thou the riches of his goodness and forbearance and longsuffering; not knowing that the goodness of God leadeth thee to repentance? [5]But after thy hardness and impenitent heart treasurest up unto thyself wrath against the day of wrath and revelation of the righteous judgment of God; [6]Who will render to every man according to his deeds: [7]To them who by patient continuance in well doing seek for glory and honour and immortality, eternal life: [8]But unto them that are contentious, and do not obey the truth, but obey unrighteousness, indignation and wrath, [9]Tribulation and anguish, upon every soul of man that doeth evil, of the Jew first, and also of the Gentile; [10]But glory, honour, and peace, to every man that worketh good, to the Jew first, and also to the Gentile: [11]For there is no respect of persons with God. [12]For as many as have sinned without law shall also perish without law: and as many as have sinned in the law shall be judged by the law; [13](For not the hearers of the law are just before God, but the doers of the law shall be justified. [14]For when the Gentiles, which have not the law, do by nature the things contained in the law, these, having not the law, are a law unto themselves: [15]Which show the work of the law written in their hearts, their conscience also bearing witness, and their thoughts the mean while accusing or else excusing one another;) [16]In the day when God shall judge the secrets of men by Jesus Christ according to my gospel. [17]Behold, thou art called a Jew, and restest in the law, and makest thy boast of God, [18]And knowest his will, and approvest the things that are more excellent, being instructed out of the law; [19]And art confident that thou thyself art a guide of the blind, a light of them which are in darkness, [20]An instructor of the foolish, a teacher of babes, which hast the form of knowledge and of the truth in the law. [21]Thou therefore which teachest another, teachest thou not thyself? thou that preachest a man should not steal, dost thou steal? [22]Thou that sayest a man should not commit adultery, dost thou commit adultery? thou that abhorrest idols, dost thou commit sacrilege? [23]Thou that makest thy boast of the law, through breaking the law dishonourest thou God? [24]For the name of God is blasphemed among the Gentiles through you, as it is written. [25]For circumcision verily profiteth, if thou keep the law: but if thou be a breaker of the law, thy circumcision is made uncircumcision. [26]Therefore if the uncircumcision keep the righteousness of the law, shall not his uncircumcision be counted for circumcision? [27]And shall not uncircumcision which is by nature, if it fulfil the law, judge thee, who by the letter and circumcision dost transgress the law? [28]For he is not a Jew, which is one outwardly; neither is that circumcision, which is outward in the flesh: [29]But he is a Jew, which is one inwardly; and circumcision is that of the heart, in the spirit, and not in the letter; whose praise is not of men, but of God

Paul	Other
Gal 5:19–21 [19]Now the works of the flesh are manifest, which are these; Adultery, fornication, uncleanness, lascivious- ness, [20]Idolatry, witchcraft, hatred, variance, emulations, wrath, strife, seditions, heresies, [21]Envyings, murders, drunkenness, revellings, and such like: of the which I tell you before, as I have also told you in time past, that they which do such things shall not inherit the kingdom of God. **2 Tim 3:2–4 (Pseudo)** [2]For men shall be lovers of their own selves, covetous, boasters, proud, blasphemers, disobedient to parents, unthankful, unholy, [3]Without natural affection, trucebreakers, false accusers, incontinent, fierce, despisers of those that are good, [4]Traitors, heady, highminded, lovers of pleasures more than lovers of God;	**Q-Quelle** Anxiety: Rom 1:29-31/Gal 5:19-21/[Mt 6:25-34]/[Lk 12:22-32 (QS 39 [Thom 36])]

Mt
10:15 [15]Verily I say unto you, It shall be more tolerable for the land of Sodom and Gomorrha in the day of judgment, than for that city. **11:20–24** [20]Then began he to upbraid the cities wherein most of his mighty works were done, because they repented not: [21]Woe unto thee, Chorazin! woe unto thee, Bethsaida! for if the mighty works, which were done in you, had been done in Tyre and Sidon, they would have repented long ago in sackcloth and ashes. [22]But I say unto you, It shall be more tolerable for Tyre and Sidon at the day of judgment, than for you. [23]And thou, Capernaum, which art exalted unto heaven, shalt be brought down to hell: for if the mighty works, which have been done in thee, had been done in Sodom, it would have remained until this day. [24]But I say unto you, That it shall be more tolerable for the land of Sodom in the day of judgment, than for thee. **12:41–42** [41]The men of Nineveh shall rise in judgment with this generation, and shall condemn it: because they repented at the preaching of Jonas; and, behold, a greater than Jonas is here. [42]The queen of the south shall rise up in the judgment with this generation, and shall condemn it: for she came from the uttermost parts of the earth to hear the wisdom of Solomon; and, behold, a greater than Solomon is here.

Romans Ch 2 continued on next page

ROMANS Ch 2—Gospel redeems humankind (1:16–3:20), 56–58 CE (*continued*)

Theme	ROM	Mt
(*Cont.*) **Do good and do not judge**	**Ch 2** **(above)**	***(continued)*** **Ch 23** [1]Then spake Jesus to the multitude, and to his disciples, [2]Saying, The scribes and the Pharisees sit in Moses' seat: [3]All therefore whatsoever they bid you observe, that observe and do; but do not ye after their works: for they say, and do not. [4]For they bind heavy burdens and grievous to be borne, and lay them on men's shoulders; but they themselves will not move them with one of their fingers. [5]But all their works they do for to be seen of men: they make broad their phylacteries, and enlarge the borders of their garments, [6]And love the uppermost rooms at feasts, and the chief seats in the synagogues, [7]And greetings in the markets, and to be called of men, Rabbi, Rabbi. [8]But be not ye called Rabbi: for one is your Master, even Christ; and all ye are brethren. [9]And call no man your father upon the earth: for one is your Father, which is in heaven. [10]Neither be ye called masters: for one is your Master, even Christ. [11]But he that is greatest among you shall be your servant. [12]And whosoever shall exalt himself shall be abased; and he that shall humble himself shall be exalted. [13]But woe unto you, scribes and Pharisees, hypocrites! for ye shut up the kingdom of heaven against men: for ye neither go in yourselves, neither suffer ye them that are entering to go in. [14]Woe unto you, scribes and Pharisees, hypocrites! for ye devour widows' houses, and for a pretence make long prayer: therefore ye shall receive the greater damnation. [15]Woe unto you, scribes and Pharisees, hypocrites! for ye compass sea and land to make one proselyte, and when he is made, ye make him twofold more the child of hell than yourselves. [16]Woe unto you, ye blind guides, which say, Whosoever shall swear by the temple, it is nothing; but whosoever shall swear by the gold of the temple, he is a debtor! [17]Ye fools and blind: for whether is greater, the gold, or the temple that sanctifieth the gold? [18]And, Whosoever shall swear by the altar, it is nothing; but whosoever sweareth by the gift that is upon it, he is guilty. [19]Ye fools and blind: for whether is greater, the gift, or the altar that sanctifieth the gift? [20]Whoso therefore shall swear by the altar, sweareth by it, and by all things thereon. [21]And whoso shall swear by the temple, sweareth by it, and by him that dwelleth therein. [22]And he that shall swear by heaven, sweareth by the throne of God, and by him that sitteth thereon. [23]Woe unto you, scribes and Pharisees, hypocrites! for ye pay tithe of mint and anise and cummin, and have omitted the weightier matters of the law, judgment, mercy, and faith: these ought ye to have done, and not to leave the other undone. [24]Ye blind guides, which strain at a gnat, and swallow a camel. [25]Woe unto you, scribes and Pharisees, hypocrites! for ye make clean the outside of the cup and of the platter, but within they are full of extortion and excess. [26]Thou blind Pharisee, cleanse first that which is within the cup and platter, that the outside of them may be clean also. [27]Woe unto you, scribes and Pharisees, hypocrites! for ye are like unto whited sepulchres, which indeed appear beautiful outward, but are within full of dead men's bones, and of all uncleanness. [28]Even so ye also outwardly appear righteous unto men, but within ye are full of hypocrisy and iniquity. [29]Woe unto you, scribes and Pharisees, hypocrites! because ye build the tombs of the prophets, and garnish the sepulchres of the righteous, [30]And say, If we had been in the days of our fathers, we would not have been partakers with them in the blood of the prophets. [31]Wherefore ye be witnesses unto yourselves, that ye are the children of them which killed the prophets. [32]Fill ye up then the measure of your fathers. [33]Ye serpents, ye generation of vipers, how can ye escape the damnation of hell? [34]Wherefore, behold, I send unto you prophets, and wise men, and scribes: and some of them ye shall kill and crucify; and some of them shall ye scourge in your synagogues, and persecute them from city to city: [35]That upon you may come all the righteous blood shed upon the earth, from the blood of righteous Abel unto the blood of Zacharias son of Barachias, whom ye slew between the temple and the altar. [36]Verily I say unto you, All these things shall come upon this generation. [37]O Jerusalem, Jerusalem, thou that killest the prophets, and stonest them which are sent unto thee, how often would I have gathered thy children together, even as a hen gathereth her chickens under her wings, and ye would not! [38]Behold, your house is left unto you desolate. [39]For I say unto you, Ye shall not see me henceforth, till ye shall say, Blessed is he that cometh in the name of the Lord.

Lk	Other
10:12–15	**Q-Quelle**
[12]But I say unto you, that it shall be more tolerable in that day for Sodom, than for that city. [13]Woe unto thee, Chorazin! woe unto thee, Bethsaida! for if the mighty works had been done in Tyre and Sidon, which have been done in you, they had a great while ago repented, sitting in sack-cloth and ashes. [14]But it shall be more tolerable for Tyre and Sidon at the judgment, than for you. [15]And thou, Capernaum, which art exalted to heaven, shalt be thrust down to hell. **11:31–32** [31]The queen of the south shall rise up in the judgment with the men of this generation, and condemn them: for she came from the utmost parts of the earth to hear the wisdom of Solomon; and, behold, a greater than Solomon is here. [32]The men of Nineve shall rise up in the judgment with this generation, and shall condemn it: for they repented at the preaching of Jonas; and, behold, a greater than Jonas is here.	Commissioning of the 70: Rom Ch 2/[Mt 9:37-38], Mt 10:7-16/ Lk 10:1-12 (QS 20/ [Thom 73; 14.1] QS 21); Woes on Galilee: Rom Ch 2/Mt 11:20-24/Lk 10:12 (QS 21), Lk 10:13-15(QS 22); Sign of Jonah: Rom Ch 2/Mt 12:38-42, [Mt 16:1-4]/[Mk 8:11-12]/[Lk 11:16 (QS 28 [Thom 35])], Lk 11:29-32 (QS 32)]; Against Pharisees: Rom Ch 2/ [Mt 23:4-36]/[Mk7:1-9]/[Lk 11:37-54 (QS 34 [Thom 39:1, 89, 102])]

ROMANS 2:1—Gospel redeems humankind (1:16–3:20), 56–58 CE

Theme	ROM	Mt
Self condemnation	**2:1** [1]Therefore thou art inexcusable, O man, whosoever thou art that judgest: for wherein thou judgest another, thou condemnest thyself; for thou that judgest doest the same things.	**7:1–2** [1]Judge not, that ye be not judged. [2]For with what judgment ye judge, ye shall be judged: and with what measure ye mete, it shall be measured to you again.

ROMANS 2:3—Gospel redeems humankind (1:16–3:20), 56–58 CE

Theme	ROM	Jewish Writings
Personal blindness	**2:3** [3]And thinkest thou this, O man, that judgest them which do such things, and doest the same, that thou shalt escape the judgment of God?	**Wis 6:15–16** [15]To think therefore upon her is perfection of wisdom: and whoso watcheth for her shall quickly be without care. [16]For she goeth about seeking such as are worthy of her, sheweth herself favourably unto them in the ways, and meeteth them in every thought.

ROMANS 2:4—Gospel redeems humankind (1:16–3:20), 56–58 CE

Theme	ROM
Long-suffering and reward	**2:4** [4]Or despisest thou the riches of his goodness and forbearance and long-suffering; not knowing that the goodness of God leadeth thee to repentance? **3:25–26** [25]Whom God hath set forth to be a propitiation through faith in his blood, to declare his righteousness for the remission of sins that are past, through the forbearance of God; [26]To declare, I say, at this time his righteousness: that he might be just, and the justifier of him which believeth in Jesus. **9:22** [22]What if God, willing to show his wrath, and to make his power known, endured with much longsuffering the vessels of wrath fitted to destruction:

ROMANS 2:5—Gospel redeems humankind (1:16–3:20), 56–58 CE

Theme	ROM	Lk	NT
Day of wrath	**2:5** [5]But after thy hardness and impenitent heart treasurest up unto thyself wrath against the day of wrath and revelation of the righteous judgment of God;	**Acts 7:51** [51]Ye stiffnecked and uncircumcised in heart and ears, ye do always resist the Holy Ghost: as your fathers did, so do ye.	**Rev 6:17** [17]For the great day of his wrath is come; and who shall be able to stand? **Rev 11:18** [18]And the nations were angry, and thy wrath is come, and the time of the dead, that they should be judged, and that thou shouldest give reward unto thy servants the prophets, and to the saints, and them that fear thy name, small and great; and shouldest destroy them which destroy the earth.

Other
Q-Quelle
Judging: Rom 2:1/Mt 7:1-5, [12:36-37, 15:14, 10:24-25]/[Mk4;24-25]/[Lk 6:37-42 (QS 10, 11[Thom 34])]

NT	Jewish Writings
2 Pet 3:9	**Wis 11:23**
[9]The Lord is not slack concerning his promise, as some men count slackness; but is longsuffering to us-ward, not willing that any should perish, but that all should come to repentance.	[23]But thou hast mercy upon all; for thou canst do all things, and winkest at the sins of men, because they should amend.
2 Pet 3:15	**Wis 15:1**
[15]And account that the longsuffering of our Lord is salvation; even as our beloved brother Paul also according to the wisdom given unto him hath written unto you;	[1]But thou, O God, art gracious and true, longsuffering, and in mercy ordering all things,

Jewish Writings
Ex 33:3
[3]Unto a land flowing with milk and honey: for I will not go up in the midst of thee; for thou art a stiffnecked people: lest I consume thee in the way.

ROMANS 2:6—Gospel redeems humankind (1:16–3:20), 56–58 CE

Theme	ROM	Mt
All are judged	**2:6** [6]Who will render to every man according to his deeds:	**7:21–27** [21]Not every one that saith unto me, Lord, Lord, shall enter into the kingdom of heaven; but he that doeth the will of my Father which is in heaven. [22]Many will say to me in that day, Lord, Lord, have we not prophesied in thy name? and in thy name have cast out devils? and in thy name done many wonderful works? [23]And then will I profess unto them, I never knew you: depart from me, ye that work iniquity. [24]Therefore whosoever heareth these sayings of mine, and doeth them, I will liken him unto a wise man, which built his house upon a rock: [25]And the rain descended, and the floods came, and the winds blew, and beat upon that house; and it fell not: for it was founded upon a rock. [26]And every one that heareth these sayings of mine, and doeth them not, shall be likened unto a foolish man, which built his house upon the sand: [27]And the rain descended, and the floods came, and the winds blew, and beat upon that house; and it fell: and great was the fall of it. **13:24–30** [24]Another parable put he forth unto them, saying, The kingdom of heaven is likened unto a man which sowed good seed in his field: [25]But while men slept, his enemy came and sowed tares among the wheat, and went his way. [26]But when the blade was sprung up, and brought forth fruit, then appeared the tares also. [27]So the servants of the householder came and said unto him, Sir, didst not thou sow good seed in thy field? from whence then hath it tares? [28]He said unto them, An enemy hath done this. The servants said unto him, Wilt thou then that we go and gather them up? [29]But he said, Nay; lest while ye gather up the tares, ye root up also the wheat with them. [30]Let both grow together until the harvest: and in the time of harvest I will say to the reapers, Gather ye together first the tares, and bind them in bundles to burn them: but gather the wheat into my barn. **13:47–50** [47]Again, the kingdom of heaven is like unto a net, that was cast into the sea, and gathered of every kind: [48]Which, when it was full, they drew to shore, and sat down, and gathered the good into vessels, but cast the bad away. [49]So shall it be at the end of the world: the angels shall come forth, and sever the wicked from among the just, [50]And shall cast them into the furnace of fire: there shall be wailing and gnashing of teeth. **24:26–27** [26]Wherefore if they shall say unto you, Behold, he is in the desert; go not forth: behold, he is in the secret chambers; believe it not. [27]**For as the lightning cometh out of the east, and shineth even unto the west; so shall also the coming of the Son of man be.** **24:37–39** [37]But as the days of Noe were, so shall also the coming of the Son of man be. [38]For as in the days that were before the flood they were eating and drinking, marrying and giving in marriage, until the day that Noe entered into the ark, [39]And knew not until the flood came, and took them all away; so shall also the coming of the Son of man be. **25:31–46** [31]When the Son of man shall come in his glory, and all the holy angels with him, then shall he sit upon the throne of his glory: [32]And before him shall be gathered all nations: and he shall separate them one from another, as a shepherd divideth his sheep from the goats: [33]And he shall set the sheep on his right hand, but the goats on the left. [34]Then shall the King say unto them on his right hand, Come, ye blessed of my Father, inherit the kingdom prepared for you from the foundation of the world: [35]For I was an hungered, and ye gave me meat: I was thirsty, and ye gave me drink: I was a stranger, and ye took me in: [36]Naked, and ye clothed me: I was sick, and ye visited me: I was in prison, and ye came unto me.

Mk
9:42–48
[42]And whosoever shall offend one of these little ones that believe in me, it is better for him that a millstone were hanged about his neck, and he were cast into the sea. [43]And if thy hand offend thee, cut it off: it is better for thee to enter into life maimed, than having two hands to go into hell, into the fire that never shall be quenched: [44]Where their worm dieth not, and the fire is not quenched. [45]And if thy foot offend thee, cut it off: it is bet- ter for thee to enter halt into life, than having two feet to be cast into hell, into the fire that never shall be quenched: [46]Where their worm dieth not, and the fire is not quenched. [47]And if thine eye offend thee, pluck it out: it is better for thee to enter into the kingdom of God with one eye, than having two eyes to be cast into hell fire: [48]Where their worm dieth not, and the fire is not quenched.

ROMANS 2:6—Gospel redeems humankind (1:16–3:20), 56–58 CE (*continued*)

Theme	ROM	Lk
(*Cont.*) **All are judged by God**	**2:6** **(above)**	**6:46–49** [46]And why call ye me, Lord, Lord, and do not the things which I say? [47]Whosoever cometh to me, and heareth my sayings, and doeth them, I will show you to whom he is like: [48]He is like a man which built an house, and digged deep, and laid the foundation on a rock: and when the flood arose, the stream beat vehemently upon that house, and could not shake it: for it was founded upon a rock. [49]But he that heareth, and doeth not, is like a man that without a foundation built an house upon the earth; against which the stream did beat vehemently, and immediately it fell; and the ruin of that house was great.
		13:25–27 [25]When once the master of the house is risen up, and hath shut to the door, and ye begin to stand without, and to knock at the door, saying, Lord, Lord, open unto us; and he shall answer and say unto you, I know you not whence ye are: [26]Then shall ye begin to say, We have eaten and drunk in thy presence, and thou hast taught in our streets. [27]But he shall say, I tell you, I know you not whence ye are; depart from me, all ye workers of iniquity.
		16:19–31 [19]There was a certain rich man, which was clothed in purple and fine linen, and fared sumptuously every day: [20]And there was a certain beggar named Lazarus, which was laid at his gate, full of sores, [21]And desiring to be fed with the crumbs which fell from the rich man's table: moreover the dogs came and licked his sores. [22]And it came to pass, that the beggar died, and was carried by the angels into Abraham's bosom: the rich man also died, and was buried; [23]And in hell he lift up his eyes, being in torments, and seeth Abraham afar off, and Lazarus in his bosom. [24]And he cried and said, Father Abraham, have mercy on me, and send Lazarus, that he may dip the tip of his finger in water, and cool my tongue; for I am tormented in this flame. [25]But Abraham said, Son, remember that thou in thy lifetime receivedst thy good things, and likewise Lazarus evil things: but now he is comforted, and thou art tormented. [26]And beside all this, between us and you there is a great gulf fixed: so that they which would pass from hence to you cannot; neither can they pass to us, that would come from thence. [27]Then he said, I pray thee therefore, father, that thou wouldest send him to my father's house: [28]For I have five brethren; that he may testify unto them, lest they also come into this place of torment. [29]Abraham saith unto him, They have Moses and the prophets; let them hear them. [30]And he said, Nay, father Abraham: but if one went unto them from the dead, they will repent. [31]And he said unto him, If they hear not Moses and the prophets, neither will they be persuaded, though one rose from the dead.
		17:22–34 [22]And he said unto the disciples, The days will come, when ye shall desire to see one of the days of the Son of man, and ye shall not see it. [23]And they shall say to you, See here; or, see there: go not after them, nor follow them. [24]For as the lightning, that lighteneth out of the one part under heaven, shineth unto the other part under heaven; so shall also the Son of man be in his day. [25]But first must he suffer many things, and be rejected of this generation. [26]And as it was in the days of Noe, so shall it be also in the days of the Son of man. [27]They did eat, they drank, they married wives, they were given in marriage, until the day that Noe entered into the ark, and the flood came, and destroyed them all. [28]Likewise also as it was in the days of Lot; they did eat, they drank, they bought, they sold, they planted, they builded; [29]But the same day that Lot went out of Sodom it rained fire and brimstone from heaven, and destroyed them all. [30]Even thus shall it be in the day when the Son of man is revealed. [31]In that day, he which shall be upon the housetop, and his stuff in the house, let him not come down to take it away: and he that is in the field, let him likewise not return back. [32]Remember Lot's wife. [33]Whosoever shall seek to save his life shall lose it; and whosoever shall lose his life shall preserve it. [34]I tell you, in that night there shall be two men in one bed; the one shall be taken, and the other shall be left. [35]Two women shall be grinding together; the one shall be taken, and the other left. [36]Two men shall be in the field; the one shall be taken, and the other left. [37]And they answered and said unto him, Where, Lord? And he said unto them, Wheresoever the body is, thither will the eagles be gathered together.

ROMANS 2:6—Gospel redeems humankind (1:16–3:20), 56–58 CE (*continued*)

Theme	ROM	Jn	Paul	Jewish Writings	Other
(*Cont.*) **All are judged by God**	**2:6 (above)**	**5:29** [29]And shall come forth; they that have done good, unto the resurrection of life; and they that have done evil, unto the resurrection of damnation.	**1 Cor 3:12–15** [12]Now if any man build upon this foundation gold, silver, precious stones, wood, hay, stubble; [13]Every man's work shall be made manifest: for the day shall declare it, because it shall be revealed by fire; and the fire shall try every man's work of what sort it is. [14]If any man's work abide which he hath built thereupon, he shall receive a reward. [15]If any man's work shall be burned, he shall suffer loss: but he himself shall be saved; yet so as by fire. **1 Cor 4:4** [4]For I know nothing by myself; yet am I not hereby justified: but he that judgeth me is the Lord. **1 Cor 5:2** [2]And ye are puffed up, and have not rather mourned, that he that hath done this deed might be taken away from among you. **2 Cor 5:10** [10]Yet not altogether with the fornicators of this world, or with the covetous, or extortioners, or with idolaters; for then must ye needs go out of the world.	**Ps 62:12** [12]Also unto thee, O Lord, belongeth mercy: for thou renderest to every man according to his work. **Prov 24:12** [12]If thou sayest, Behold, we knew it not; doth not he that pondereth the heart consider it? and he that keepeth thy soul, doth not he know it? and shall not he render to every man according to his works? **Sir 16:14** [14]Make way for every work of mercy: for every man shall find according to the measure he gives	**Q-Quelle** Exclusion from the Kingdom of God: Rom 2:6/1 Cor 4:1-5/[Mt 7:13-14], Mt 7:22-23, [Mt 8:11-12, 19:30]/Lk 13:22-30 (QS47, 48); House on a Rock: Rom 2:6/1 Cor 4:1-5/Mt 7:21-27 /Lk 6:46-49(QS 14); Day of SOM: Rom 2:6/[Mt 10:39, 24:17-18, 23], 24:26-27, 37-39, [Mt 24:28, 40-41]/[Mk 13:14-16, 19-23]/Lk 17:22-37 (QS 60 [Thom 3, 51, 61, 113]); Warning Against Offenses: Rom 2:6/[Mt 18:6-7]/Mk 9:42/[Lk 17:1-3a (QS 57, 58)]/[Mt 7:21-27]/Lk 6:46-49 (QS 14)

ROMANS 2:8—Gospel redeems humankind (1:16–3:20), 56–58 CE

Theme	ROM	Paul
Wrath and fire	**2:8** [8]But unto them that are contentious, and do not obey the truth, but obey unrighteousness, indignation and wrath,	**2 Thes 1:8** [8]In flaming fire taking vengeance on them that know not God, and that obey not the gospel of our Lord Jesus Christ:

ROMANS 2:10—Gospel redeems humankind (1:16–3:20), 56–58 CE

Theme	ROM
Goodness brings peace	**2:10** [10]But glory, honour, and peace, to every man that worketh good, to the Jew first, and also to the Gentile: **1:16** [16]For I am not ashamed of the gospel of Christ: for it is the power of God unto salvation to every one that believeth; to the Jew first, and also to the Greek. **3:9** [9]What then? are we better than they? No, in no wise: for we have before proved both Jews and Gentiles, that they are all under sin;

ROMANS 2:11—Gospel redeems humankind (1:16–3;20), 56–58 CE

Theme	ROM	Lk	Paul
Equality among persons	**2:11** [11]For there is no respect of persons with God.	**Acts 10:34** [34]Then Peter opened his mouth, and said, Of a truth I perceive that God is no respecter of persons:	**Gal 2:6** [6]But of these who seemed to be somewhat, (whatsoever they were, it maketh no matter to me: God accepteth no man's person:) for they who seemed to be somewhat in conference added nothing to me: **Eph 6:9 (Pseudo)** [9]And, ye masters, do the same things unto them, forbearing threatening: knowing that your Master also is in heaven; neither is there respect of persons with him. **Col 3:25** [25]But he that doeth wrong shall receive for the wrong which he hath done: and there is no respect of persons.

ROMANS 2:12—Gospel redeems humankind (1:16–3:20), 56–58 CE

Theme	ROM
Judged by law	**2:12** [12]For as many as have sinned without law shall also perish without law and as many as have sinned in the law shall be judged by the law; **3:19** [19]Now we know that what things soever the law saith, it saith to them who are under the law: that every mouth may be stopped, and all the world may become guilty before God.

ROMANS 2:13—Gospel redeems humankind (1:16–3:20), 56–58 CE

Theme	ROM	Mt	Lk
Hearers and doers of the Word	**2:13** [13](For not the hearers of the law are just before God, but the doers of the law shall be justified.	**7:21** [21]Not every one that saith unto me, Lord, Lord, shall enter into the kingdom of heaven; but he that doeth the will of my Father which is in heaven.	**6:46–49** [46]And why call ye me, Lord, Lord, and do not the things which I say? [47]Whosoever cometh to me, and heareth my sayings, and doeth them, I will show you to whom he is like: [48]He is like a man which built an house, and digged deep, and laid the foundation on a rock: and when the flood arose, the stream beat vehemently upon that house, and could not shake it: for it was founded upon a rock. [49]But he that heareth, and doeth not, is like a man that without a foundation built an house upon the earth; against which the stream did beat vehemently, and immediately it fell; and the ruin of that house was great. **8:21** [21]And he answered and said unto them, My mother and my brethren are these which hear the word of God, and do it.

ROMANS 2:14—Gospel redeems humankind (1:16–3:20), 56–58 CE

Theme	ROM	Lk
Natural Righteousness	**2:14** [14]For when the Gentiles, which have not the law, do by nature the things contained in the law, these, having not the law, are a law unto themselves:	**Acts 10:35** [35]But in every nation he that feareth him, and worketh righteousness, is accepted with him.

NT	Jewish Writings
1 Pet 1:17	**Dt 10:17**
[17]And if ye call on the Father, who without respect of persons judgeth according to every man's work, pass the time of your sojourning here in fear:	[17]For the LORD your God is God of gods, and Lord of lords, a great God, a mighty, and a terrible, which regardeth not persons, nor taketh reward: **2 Chr 19:7** [7]Wherefore now let the fear of the LORD be upon you; take heed and do it: for there is no iniquity with the LORD our God, nor respect of persons, nor taking of gifts. **Sir 35:12–13** [12] Do not think to corrupt with gifts; for such he will not receive: and trust not to unrighteous sacrifices; for the Lord is judge, and with him is no respect of persons. [13] He will not accept any person against a poor man, but will hear the prayer of the oppressed.

Jn	NT	Other
1 Jn 3:7	**Jas 1:22–25**	**Q-Quelle**
[7]Little children, let no man deceive you: he that doeth righteousness is righteous, even as he is righteous.	[22]But be ye doers of the word, and not hearers only, deceiving your own selves. [23]For if any be a hearer of the word, and not a doer, he is like unto a man beholding his natural face in a glass: [24]For he beholdeth himself, and goeth his way, and straightway forgetteth what manner of man he was. [25]But whoso looketh into the perfect law of liberty, and continueth therein, he being not a forgetful hearer, but a doer of the work, this man shall be blessed in his deed.	House on Rock: Rom 2:13/Mt 7:21-27/Lk 6:46-49 (QS 14)

ROMANS 2:16—Gospel redeems humankind (1:16–3:20), 56–58 CE

Theme	ROM	Mk
Piety in private	**2:16** [16]In the day when God shall judge the secrets of men by Jesus Christ according to my gospel. **2:28–29** [28]For he is not a Jew, which is one outwardly; neither is that circumcision, which is outward in the flesh: [29]But he is a Jew, which is one inwardly; and circumcision is that of the heart, in the spirit, and not in the letter; whose praise is not of men, but of God	**4:22** [22]For there is nothing hid, which shall not be manifested; neither was any thing kept secret, but that it should come abroad.

ROMANS 2:17—Gospel redeems humankind (1:16–3:20), 56–58 CE

Theme	ROM	Paul
Obedience to God's law	**2:17** [17]Behold, thou art called a Jew, and restest in the law, and makest thy boast of God,	**Phil 3:4–6** [4]Though I might also have confidence in the flesh. If any other man thinketh that he hath whereof he might trust in the flesh, I more: [5]Circumcised the eighth day, of the stock of Israel, of the tribe of Benjamin, an Hebrew of the Hebrews; as touching the law, a Pharisee; [6]Concerning zeal, persecuting the church; touching the righteousness which is in the law, blameless.

ROMANS 2:18—Gospel redeems humankind (1:16–3:20), 56–58 CE

Theme	ROM	Paul
Right actions	**2:18** [18]And knowest his will, and approvest the things that are more excellent, being instructed out of the law;	**Phil 1:10** [10]That ye may approve things that are excellent; that ye may be sincere and without offence till the day of Christ;

ROMANS 2:19—Gospel redeems humankind (1:16–3:20), 56–58 CE

Theme	ROM	Mt	Lk
Critiques of Judaism	**2:19** [19]And art confident that thou thyself art a guide of the blind, a light of them which are in darkness,	**15:14** [14]Let them alone: they be blind leaders of the blind. And if the blind lead the blind, both shall fall into the ditch. **23:16** [16]Woe unto you, ye blind guides, which say, Whosoever shall swear by the temple, it is nothing; but whosoever shall swear by the gold of the temple, he is a debtor!	**6:39** [39]And he spake a parable unto them, Can the blind lead the blind? shall they not both fall into the ditch? **11:52** [52]Woe unto you, lawyers! for ye have taken away the key of knowledge: ye entered not in yourselves, and them that were entering in ye hindered.

Lk	Paul
8:17	**1 Cor 4:5**
[17]For nothing is secret, that shall not be made manifest; neither any thing hid, that shall not be known and come abroad. **Acts 10:42** [42]And he commanded us to preach unto the people, and to testify that it is he which was ordained of God to be the Judge of quick and dead. **Acts 17:31** [31]Because he hath appointed a day, in the which he will judge the world in righteousness by that man whom he hath ordained; whereof he hath given assurance unto all men, in that he hath raised him from the dead.	[5]Therefore judge nothing before the time, until the Lord come, who both will bring to light the hidden things of darkness, and will make manifest the counsels of the hearts: and then shall every man have praise of God. **1 Cor 14:25** [25]And thus are the secrets of his heart made manifest; and so falling down on his face he will worship God, and report that God is in you of a truth.

Jewish Writings
Is 48:1–2
[1]Hear ye this, O house of Jacob, which are called by the name of Israel, and are come forth out of the waters of Judah, which swear by the name of the LORD, and make mention of the God of Israel, but not in truth, nor in righteousness. [2]For they call themselves of the holy city, and stay themselves upon the God of Israel; The LORD of hosts is his name. **Mic 3:11** [11]The heads thereof judge for reward, and the priests thereof teach for hire, and the prophets thereof divine for money: yet will they lean upon the LORD, and say, Is not the LORD among us? none evil can come upon us.

Paul	Other
Gal 2:17	**Q- Quelle**
[17]But if, while we seek to be justified by Christ, we ourselves also are found sinners, is therefore Christ the minister of sin? God forbid.	Judging: Rom 2:19/[Mt 7:1-5, 12:36-37], Mt 15:14, [10:24-25]/[Mk 4:24-25]/Lk 6:37-42(QS 10); Against Pharisees: Rom 2:19/Mt 23:4-36/[Mk 7:1-9]/Lk 11:37-54 (QS 34 [Thom 39:1, 89, 102]); Beatitudes: Rom 2:19/Gal 2:17/[Mt 5:3-12/Lk 6:20b-23] (QS 8 [Thom 54,68,69]); Agreement with Accuser: Rom 2:19/Gal 2:17/[Mt 5:25-26]/[Lk 12:57-59]; Sound eye: Rom 2:19/Gal 2:17/[Mt 6:22-23]/[Lk 11:34-36 (QS 33 [Thom 33:2])]

ROMANS 2:20—Gospel redeems humankind (1:16–3:20), 56–58 CE

Theme	ROM	Paul
Foolish and wise teachers	**2:20** [20]An instructor of the foolish, a teacher of babes, which hast the form of knowledge and of the truth in the law.	**2 Tim 3:15 (Pseudo)** [15]And that from a child thou hast known the holy scriptures, which are able to make thee wise unto salvation through faith which is in Christ Jesus.

ROMANS 2:21—Gospel redeems humankind (1:16–3:20), 56–58 CE

Theme	ROM	Mt
Practicing teachings	**2:21** [21]Thou therefore which teachest another, teachest thou not thyself? thou that preachest a man should not steal, dost thou steal?	**23:3–4** [3]All therefore whatsoever they bid you observe, that observe and do; but do not ye after their works: for they say, and do not. [4]For they bind heavy burdens and grievous to be borne, and lay them on men's shoulders; but they themselves will not move them with one of their fingers.

ROMANS 2:24—Gospel redeems humankind (1:16–3:20), 56–58 CE

Theme	ROM	NT	Jewish Writings
Not respecting God's name	**2:24** [24]For the name of God is blasphemed among the Gentiles through you, as it is written.	**2 Pet 2:2** [2]And many shall follow their pernicious ways; by reason of whom the way of truth shall be evil spoken of.	**Is 52:5** [5]Now therefore, what have I here, saith the LORD, that my people is taken away for nought? they that rule over them make them to howl, saith the LORD; and my name continually every day is blasphemed. **Ezek 36:20** [20]And when they entered unto the heathen, whither they went, they profaned my holy name, when they said to them, These are the people of the LORD, and are gone forth out of his land.

ROMANS 2:25–29—Gospel redeems humankind (1:16–3:20), 56–58 CE

Theme	ROM
Circumcision	**2:25–29** [25]For circumcision verily profiteth, if thou keep the law: but if thou be a breaker of the law, thy circumcision is made uncircumcision. [26]Therefore if the uncircumcision keep the righteousness of the law, shall not his uncircumcision be counted for circumcision? [27]And shall not uncircumcision which is by nature, if it fulfil the law, judge thee, who by the letter and circumcision dost transgress the law? [28]For he is not a Jew, which is one outwardly; neither is that circumcision, which is outward in the flesh: [29]But he is a Jew, which is one inwardly; and circumcision is that of the heart, in the spirit, and not in the letter; whose praise is not of men, but of God

Jewish Writings	Other
Ps 50:16–21	**Q-Quelle**
[16]But unto the wicked God saith, What hast thou to do to declare my statutes, or that thou shouldest take my covenant in thy mouth? [17]Seeing thou hatest instruction, and castest my words behind thee. [18]When thou sawest a thief, then thou consentedst with him, and hast been partaker with adulterers. [19]Thou givest thy mouth to evil, and thy tongue frameth deceit. [20]Thou sittest and speakest against thy brother; thou slanderest thine own mother's son. [21]These things hast thou done, and I kept silence; thou thoughtest that I was altogether such an one as thyself: but I will reprove thee, and set them in order before thine eyes.	Against Pharisees: Rom 2:21/ Mt 23:4-36/[Mk 7:1-9]/[Lk 11:37-54 (QS 34 [Thom 39:1, 89, 102])]

Jewish Writings
Jer 4:4
[4]Circumcise yourselves to the LORD, and take away the foreskins of your heart, ye men of Judah and inhabitants of Jerusalem: lest my fury come forth like fire, and burn that none can quench it, because of the evil of your doings.
Jer 9:24–25
[24]But let him that glorieth glory in this, that he understandeth and knoweth me, that I am the LORD which exercise lovingkindness, judgment, and righteousness, in the earth: for in these things I delight, saith the LORD. [25]Behold, the days come, saith the LORD, that I will punish all them which are circumcised with the uncircumcised;

ROMANS 2:25—Gospel redeems humankind (1:16–3:20), 56–58 CE

Theme	ROM	Paul
Circumcision	**2:25**	**1 Cor 7:19**
	[25]For circumcision verily profiteth, if thou keep the law: but if thou be a breaker of the law, thy circumcision is made uncircumcision.	[19]Circumcision is nothing, and uncircumcision is nothing, but the keeping of the commandments of God. **Gal 5:3** [3]For I testify again to every man that is circumcised, that he is a debtor to do the whole law.

ROMANS 2:26—Gospel redeems humankind (1:16–3:20), 56–58 CE

Theme	ROM	Paul
Circumcision	**2:26**	**Gal 5:6**
	[26]Therefore if the uncircumcision keep the righteousness of the law, shall not his uncircumcision be counted for circumcision?	[6]For in Jesus Christ neither circumcision availeth any thing, nor uncircumcision; but faith which worketh by love.

ROMANS 2:28—Gospel redeems humankind (1:16–3:20), 56–58 CE

Theme	ROM	Jn
Circumcision	**2:28**	**7:24**
	[28]For he is not a Jew, which is one outwardly; neither is that circumcision, which is outward in the flesh:	[24]Judge not according to the appearance, but judge righteous judgment. **8:15** [15]Ye judge after the flesh; I judge no man. **8:39** [39]They answered and said unto him, Abraham is our father. Jesus saith unto them, If ye were Abraham's children, ye would do the works of Abraham.

ROMANS 2:29—Gospel redeems humankind (1:16–3:20), 56–58 CE

Theme	ROM	Paul	Jewish Writings
Circumcision	**2:29**	**1 Cor 4:5**	**Dt 30:6**
	[29]But he is a Jew, which is one inwardly; and circumcision is that of the heart, in the spirit, and not in the letter; whose praise is not of men, but of God.	[5]Therefore judge nothing before the time, until the Lord come, who both will bring to light the hidden things of darkness, and will make manifest the counsels of the hearts: and then shall every man have praise of God. **2 Cor 10:18** [18]For not he that commendeth himself is approved, but whom the Lord commendeth. **Col 2:11** [11]In whom also ye are circumcised with the circumcision made without hands, in putting off the body of the sins of the flesh by the circumcision of Christ:	[6]And the LORD thy God will circumcise thine heart, and the heart of thy seed, to love the LORD thy God with all thine heart, and with all thy soul, that thou mayest live. **Jer 4:4** [4]Circumcise yourselves to the LORD, and take away the foreskins of your heart, ye men of Judah and inhabitants of Jerusalem: lest my fury come forth like fire, and burn that none can quench it, because of the evil of your doings. **Jer 9:25** [25]Behold, the days come, saith the LORD, that I will punish all them which are circumcised with the uncircumcised;

ROMANS 3:2—Gospel redeems humankind (1:16–3:20), 56–58 CE

Theme	ROM	Jewish Writings
Israel was God's first trust	**3:2** [2]Much every way: chiefly, because that unto them were committed the oracles of God. **9:4** [4]Who are Israelites; to whom pertaineth the adoption, and the glory, and the covenants, and the giving of the law, and the service of God, and the promises;	**Dt 4:7–8** [7]For what nation is there so great, who hath God so nigh unto them, as the LORD our God is in all things that we call upon him for? [8]And what nation is there so great, that hath statutes and judgments so righteous as all this law, which I set before you this day? **Ps 103:7** [7]He made known his ways unto Moses, his acts unto the children of Israel. **Ps 147:19–20** [19]He showeth his word unto Jacob, his statutes and his judgments unto Israel. [20]He hath not dealt so with any nation: and as for his judgments, they have not known them. Praise ye the LORD.

ROMANS 3:3—Gospel redeems humankind (1:16–3:20), 56–58 CE

Theme	ROM	Jewish Writings	Paul
Israel and not Israel	**3:3** [3]For what if some did not believe? shall their unbelief make the faith of God without effect? **9:6** [6]Not as though the word of God hath taken none effect. For they are not all Israel, which are of Israel: **11:1** [1]I say then, Hath God cast away his people? God forbid. For I also am an Israelite, of the seed of Abraham, of the tribe of Benjamin. **11:29** [29]For the gifts and calling of God are without repentance.	**Ps 89:30–37** [30]If his children forsake my law, and walk not in my judgments; [31]If they break my statutes, and keep not my commandments; [32]Then will I visit their transgression with the rod, and their iniquity with stripes. [33]Nevertheless my lovingkindness will I not utterly take from him, nor suffer my faithfulness to fail. [34]My covenant will I not break, nor alter the thing that is gone out of my lips. [35]Once have I sworn by my holiness that I will not lie unto David. [36]His seed shall endure for ever, and his throne as the sun before me. [37]It shall be established for ever as the moon, and as a faithful witness in heaven. Selah	**2 Tim 2:13 (Pseudo)** [13]If we believe not, yet he abideth faithful: he cannot deny himself.

ROMANS 3:4—Gospel redeems humankind (1:16–3:20), 56–58 CE

Theme	ROM	Jewish Writings
Truth and lies	**3:4** [4]God forbid: yea, let God be true, but every man a liar; as it is written, That thou mightest be justified in thy sayings, and mightest overcome when thou art judged.	**Ps 51:6** [6]Behold, thou desirest truth in the inward parts: and in the hidden part thou shalt make me to know wisdom. **Ps 116:11** [11]I said in my haste, All men are liars.

ROMANS 3:5—Gospel redeems humankind (1:16–3:20), 56–58 CE

Theme	ROM	Jewish Writings
Righteous and unrighteous	**3:5** [5]But if our unrighteousness commend the righteousness of God, what shall we say? Is God unrighteous who taketh vengeance? (I speak as a man) **9:14** [14]What shall we say then? Is there unrighteousness with God? God forbid.	**Job 34:12–17** [12]Yea, surely God will not do wickedly, neither will the Almighty pervert judgment. [13]Who hath given him a charge over the earth? or who hath disposed the whole world? [14]If he set his heart upon man, if he gather unto himself his spirit and his breath; [15]All flesh shall perish together, and man shall turn again unto dust. [16]If now thou hast understanding, hear this: hearken to the voice of my words. [17]Shall even he that hateth right govern? and wilt thou condemn him that is most just?

ROMANS 3:8—Gospel redeems humankind (1:16–3:20), 56–58 CE

Theme	ROM	Paul
Paul's anti-nomianism	**3:8** [8]And not rather, (as we be slanderously reported, and as some affirm that we say,) Let us do evil, that good may come? whose damnation is just. **6:1** [1]What shall we say then? Shall we continue in sin, that grace may abound?	**1 Cor 6:12** [12]All things are lawful unto me, but all things are not expedient: all things are lawful for me, but I will not be brought under the power of any. **1 Cor 7:19** [19]Circumcision is nothing, and uncircumcision is nothing, but the keeping of the commandments of God.

ROMANS 3:9—Gospel redeems humankind (1:16–3:20), 56–58 CE

Theme	ROM	Jewish Writings
Jesus is for Jews and Gentiles	**3:9** [9]What then? are we better than they? No, in no wise: for we have before proved both Jews and Gentiles, that they are all under sin; **1:18–2:25** [18]For the wrath of God is revealed from heaven against all ungodliness and unrighteousness of men, who hold the truth in unrighteousness; [19]Because that which may be known of God is manifest in them; for God hath showed it unto them. [20]For the invisible things of him from the creation of the world are clearly seen, being understood by the things that are made, even his eternal power and Godhead; so that they are without excuse: [21]Because that, when they knew God, they glorified him not as God, neither were thankful; but became vain in their imaginations, and their foolish heart was darkened. [22]Professing themselves to be wise, they became fools, [23]And changed the glory of the uncorruptible God into an image made like to corruptible man, and to birds, and fourfooted beasts, and creeping things. [24]Wherefore God also gave them up to uncleanness through the lusts of their own hearts, to dishonour their own bodies between themselves: [25]Who changed the truth of God into a lie, and worshipped and served the creature more than the Creator, who is blessed for ever. Amen. [26]For this cause God gave them up unto vile affections: for even their women did change the natural use into that which is against nature: [27]And likewise also the men, leaving the natural use of the woman, burned in their lust one toward another; men with men working that which is unseemly, and receiving in themselves that recompense of their error which was meet. [28]And even as they did not like to retain God in their knowledge, God gave them over to a reprobate mind, to do those things which are not convenient; [29]Being filled with all unrighteousness, fornication, wickedness, covetousness, maliciousness; full of envy, murder, debate, deceit, malignity; whisperers, [30]Backbiters, haters of God, despiteful, proud, boasters, inventors of evil things, disobedient to parents, [31]Without understanding, covenantbreakers, without natural affection, implacable, unmerciful: [32]Who knowing the judgment of God, that they which commit such things are worthy of death, not only do the same, but have pleasure in them that do them. **2** [1]Therefore thou art inexcusable, O man, whosoever thou art that judgest: for wherein thou judgest another, thou condemnest thyself; for thou that judgest doest the same things. [2]But we are sure that the judgment of God is according to truth against them which commit such things. [3]And thinkest thou this, O man, that judgest them which do such things, and doest the same, that thou shalt escape the judgment of God? [4]Or despisest thou the riches of his goodness and forbearance and longsuffering; not knowing that the goodness of God leadeth thee to repentance? [5]But after thy hardness and impenitent heart treasurest up unto thyself wrath against the day of wrath and revelation of the righteous judgment of God; [6]Who will render to every man according to his deeds: [7]To them who by patient continuance in well doing seek for glory and honour and immortality, eternal life: [8]But unto them that are contentious, and do not obey the truth, but obey unrighteousness, indignation and wrath, [9]Tribulation and anguish, upon every soul of man that doeth evil, of the Jew first, and also of the Gentile; [10]But glory, honour, and peace, to every man that worketh good, to the Jew first, and also to the Gentile: [11]For there is no respect of persons with God. [12]For as many as have sinned without law shall also perish without law: and as many as have sinned in the law shall be judged by the law; [13](For not the hearers of the law are just before God, but the doers of the law shall be justified. [14]For when the Gentiles, which have not the law, do by nature the things contained in the law, these, having not the law, are a law unto themselves: [15]Which show the work of the law written in their hearts, their conscience also bearing witness, and their thoughts the mean while accusing or else excusing one another;) [16]In the day when God shall judge the secrets of men by Jesus Christ according to my gospel. [17]Behold, thou art called a Jew, and restest in the law, and makest thy boast of God, [18]And knowest his will, and approvest the things that are more excellent, being instructed out of the law; [19]And art confident that thou thyself art a guide of the blind, a light of them which are in darkness, [20]An instructor of the foolish, a teacher of babes, which hast the form of knowledge and of the truth in the law. [21]Thou therefore which teachest another, teachest thou not thyself? thou that preachest a man should not steal, dost thou steal? [22]Thou that sayest a man should not commit adultery, dost thou commit adultery? thou that abhorrest idols, dost thou commit sacrilege? [23]Thou that makest thy boast of the law, through breaking the law dishonourest thou God? [24]For the name of God is blasphemed among the Gentiles through you, as it is written. [25]For circumcision verily profiteth, if thou keep the law: but if thou be a breaker of the law, thy circumcision is made uncircumcision. **3:23** [23]For all have sinned, and come short of the glory of God;	**Sir 8:5** [5]Reproach not a man that turneth from sin, but remember that we are all worthy of punishment.

ROMANS 3:10–11—Gospel redeems humankind (1:16–3:20), 56–58 CE

Theme	ROM	Jewish Writings
None are righteous	**3:10–11** [10]As it is written, There is none righteous, no, not one: [11]There is none that understandeth, there is none that seeketh after God.	**Ps 14:1–3** [1]The fool hath said in his heart, There is no God. They are corrupt, they have done abominable works, there is none that doeth good. [2]The LORD looked down from heaven upon the children of men, to see if there were any that did understand, and seek God. [3]They are all gone aside, they are all together become filthy: there is none that doeth good, no, not one. **Ps 53:2–4** [3]Every one of them is gone back: they are altogether become filthy; there is none that doeth good, no, not one. [4]Have the workers of iniquity no knowledge? who eat up my people as they eat bread: they have not called upon God. **Eccl 7:20** [20]For there is not a just man upon earth, that doeth good, and sinneth not.

ROMANS 3:13—Gospel redeems humankind (1:16–3:20), 56–58 CE

Theme	ROM	Jewish Writings
Inner wickedness	**3:13** [13]Their throat is an open sepulchre; with their tongues they have used deceit; the poison of asps is under their lips:	**Ps 5:10** [10]Destroy thou them, O God; let them fall by their own counsels; cast them out in the multitude of their transgressions; for they have rebelled against thee. **Ps 140:4** [4]Keep me, O LORD, from the hands of the wicked; preserve me from the violent man; who have purposed to overthrow my goings.

ROMANS 3:14—Gospel redeems humankind (1:16–3:20), 56–58 CE

Theme	ROM	Jewish Writings
Mouth is grave	**3:14** [14]Whose mouth is full of cursing and bitterness:	**Ps 10:7** [7]His mouth is full of cursing and deceit and fraud: under his tongue is mischief and vanity.

ROMANS 3:15–17—Gospel redeems humankind (1:16–3:20), 56–58 CE

Theme	ROM	Jewish Writings
Corrupt ways	**3:15–17** [15]Their feet are swift to shed blood: [16]Destruction and misery are in their ways: [17]And the way of peace have they not known:	**Prov 1:16** [16]For their feet run to evil, and make haste to shed blood. **Is 59:7–8** [7]Their feet run to evil, and they make haste to shed innocent blood: their thoughts are thoughts of iniquity; wasting and destruction are in their paths. [8]The way of peace they know not; and there is no judgment in their goings: they have made them crooked paths: whosoever goeth therein shall not know peace.

ROMANS 3:18—Gospel redeems humankind (1:16–3:20), 56–58 CE

Theme	ROM	Jewish Writings
Fear of God	**3:18** [18]There is no fear of God before their eyes.	**Ps 36:2** [2] For he flattereth himself in his own eyes, until his iniquity be found to be hateful.

ROMANS 3:19—Gospel redeems humankind (1:16–3:20), 56–58 CE

Theme	ROM
Law and sin	**3:19** [19]Now we know that what things soever the law saith, it saith to them who are under the law: that every mouth may be stopped, and all the world may become guilty before God. **7:7** [7]What shall we say then? Is the law sin? God forbid. Nay, I had not known sin, but by the law: for I had not known lust, except the law had said, Thou shalt not covet.

ROMANS 3:20—Gospel redeems humankind (1:16–3:20), 56–58 CE

Theme	ROM	Paul	Jewish Writings
Law brings knowledge of sin	**3:20** [20]Therefore by the deeds of the law there shall no flesh be justified in his sight: for by the law is the knowledge of sin. **7:7** [7]What shall we say then? Is the law sin? God forbid. Nay, I had not known sin, but by the law: for I had not known lust, except the law had said, Thou shalt not covet.	**Gal 2:16** [16]Knowing that a man is not justified by the works of the law, but by the faith of Jesus Christ, even we have believed in Jesus Christ, that we might be justified by the faith of Christ, and not by the works of the law: for by the works of the law shall no flesh be justified.	**Ps 143:2** [2]And enter not into judgment with thy servant: for in thy sight shall no man living be justified.

JUSTIFIED BY FAITH (3:21–5:21)

ROMANS 3:21–26—Justified by faith (3:21–5:21), 56–58 CE

Theme	ROM	Mt	Mk
Salvation by grace	**3:21–26** [21]But now the righteousness of God without the law is manifested, being witnessed by the law and the prophets; [22]Even the righteousness of God which is by faith of Jesus Christ unto all and upon all them that believe: for there is no difference: [23]For all have sinned, and come short of the glory of God; [24]Being justified freely by his grace through the redemption that is in Christ Jesus: [25]Whom God hath set forth to be a propitiation through faith in his blood, to declare his righteousness for the remission of sins that are past, through the forbearance of God; [26]To declare, I say, at this time his righteousness: that he might be just, and the justifier of him which believeth in Jesus.	**9:13** [13]But go ye and learn what that meaneth, I will have mercy, and not sacrifice: for I am not come to call the righteous, but sinners to repentance. **16:21** [21]From that time forth began Jesus to show unto his disciples, how that he must go unto Jerusalem, and suffer many things of the elders and chief priests and scribes, and be killed, and be raised again the third day.	**2:17** [17]When Jesus heard it, he saith unto them, They that are whole have no need of the physician, but they that are sick: I came not to call the righteous, but sinners to repentance. **8:31** [31]And he began to teach them, that the Son of man must suffer many things, and be rejected of the elders, and of the chief priests, and scribes, and be killed, and after three days rise again.

Lk	Paul	Other
5:32 [32]I came not to call the righteous, but sinners to repentance. **9:22** [22]Saying, The Son of man must suffer many things, and be rejected of the elders and chief priests and scribes, and be slain, and be raised the third day. **Ch 15** [1]Then drew near unto him all the publicans and sinners for to hear him. [2]And the Pharisees and scribes murmured, saying, This man receiveth sinners, and eateth with them. [3]And he spake this parable unto them, saying, [4]What man of you, having an hundred sheep, if he lose one of them, doth not leave the ninety and nine in the wilderness, and go after that which is lost, until he find it? [5]And when he hath found it, he layeth it on his shoulders, rejoicing. [6]And when he cometh home, he calleth together his friends and neighbours, saying unto them, Rejoice with me; for I have found my sheep which was lost. [7]I say unto you, that likewise joy shall be in heaven over one sinner that repenteth, more than over ninety and nine just persons, which need no repentance. [8]Either what woman having ten pieces of silver, if she lose one piece, doth not light a candle, and sweep the house, and seek diligently till she find it? [9]And when she hath found it, she calleth her friends and her neighbours together, saying, Rejoice with me; for I have found the piece which I had lost. [10]Likewise, I say unto you, there is joy in the presence of the angels of God over one sinner that repenteth. [11]And he said, A certain man had two sons: [12]And the younger of them said to his father, Father, give me the portion of goods that falleth to me. And he divided unto them his living. [13]And not many days after the younger son gathered all together, and took his journey into a far country, and there wasted his substance with riotous living. [14]And when he had spent all, there arose a mighty famine in that land; and he began to be in want. [15]And he went and joined himself to a citizen of that country; and he sent him into his fields to feed swine. [16]And he would fain have filled his belly with the husks that the swine did eat: and no man gave unto him. [17]And when he came to himself, he said, How many hired servants of my father's have bread enough and to spare, and I perish with hunger! [18]I will arise and go to my father, and will say unto him, Father, I have sinned against heaven, and before thee, [19]And am no more worthy to be called thy son: make me as one of thy hired servants. [20]And he arose, and came to his father. But when he was yet a great way off, his father saw him, and had compassion, and ran, and fell on his neck, and kissed him. [21]And the son said unto him, Father, I have sinned against heaven, and in thy sight, and am no more worthy to be called thy son. [22]But the father said to his servants, Bring forth the best robe, and put it on him; and put a ring on his hand, and shoes on his feet: [23]And bring hither the fatted calf, and kill it; and let us eat, and be merry: [24]For this my son was dead, and is alive again; he was lost, and is found. And they began to be merry. [25]Now his elder son was in the field: and as he came and drew nigh to the house, he heard music and dancing. [26]And he called one of the servants, and asked what these things meant. [27]And he said unto him, Thy brother is come; and thy father hath killed the fatted calf, because he hath received him safe and sound. [28]And he was angry, and would not go in: therefore came his father out, and entreated him. [29]And he answering said to his father, Lo, these many years do I serve thee, neither transgressed I at any time thy commandment: and yet thou never gavest me a kid, that I might make merry with my friends: [30]But as soon as this thy son was come, which hath devoured thy living with harlots, thou hast killed for him the fatted calf. [31]And he said unto him, Son, thou art ever with me, and all that I have is thine. [32]It was meet that we should make merry, and be glad: for this thy brother was dead, and is alive again; and was lost, and is found. **19:10** [10]For the Son of man is come to seek and to save that which was lost. **23:34** [34]Then said Jesus, Father, forgive them; for they know not what they do. And they parted his raiment, and cast lots. **23:43** [43]And Jesus said unto him, Verily I say unto thee, To day shalt thou be with me in paradise.	**1 Cor 1:23** [23]But we preach Christ crucified, unto the Jews a stumblingblock, and unto the Greeks foolishness; **1 Cor 15:3** [3]For I delivered unto you first of all that which I also received, how that Christ died for our sins according to the scriptures; **Gal 6:14** [14]But God forbid that I should glory, save in the cross of our Lord Jesus Christ, by whom the world is crucified unto me, and I unto the world.	**Q-Quelle** Lost Sheep: Rom 3:21-26;[Mt 18:12-14]/Lk 15:1-7 (QS 54 [Thom 107]); Precedence: Rom 3:21-26/Gal 6:14/[Mt 19:28]/[Mk 10:41-45]/[Lk 22:28-30 (QS 62)

ROMANS 3:21—Justified by faith (3:21–5:21), 56–58 CE

Theme	ROM	Lk
Witness of the law	**3:21** [21]But now the righteousness of God without the law is manifested, being witnessed by the law and the prophets;	**Acts 10:43** [43]To him give all the prophets witness, that through his name whosoever believeth in him shall receive remission of sins.

ROMANS 3:22—Justified by faith (3:21–5:21), 56–58 CE

Theme	ROM
Faith and the righteous	**3:22** [22]Even the righteousness of God which is by faith of Jesus Christ unto all and upon all them that believe: for there is no difference: **1:17** [17]For therein is the righteousness of God revealed from faith to faith: as it is written, The just shall live by faith.

ROMANS 3:23—Justified by faith (3:21–5:21), 56–58 CE

Theme	ROM
All have sinned	**3:23** [23]For all have sinned, and come short of the glory of God; **3:9** [9]What then? are we better than they? No, in no wise: for we have before proved both Jews and Gentiles, that they are all under sin; **5:12** [12]Wherefore, as by one man sin entered into the world, and death by sin; and so death passed upon all men, for that all have sinned:

Jewish Writings
Is 51:6–8
[6]Lift up your eyes to the heavens, and look upon the earth beneath: for the heavens shall vanish away like smoke, and the earth shall wax old like a garment, and they that dwell therein shall die in like manner: but my salvation shall be for ever, and my righteousness shall not be abolished. [7]Hearken unto me, ye that know righteousness, the people in whose heart is my law; fear ye not the reproach of men, neither be ye afraid of their revilings. [8]For the moth shall eat them up like a garment, and the worm shall eat them like wool: but my righteousness shall be for ever, and my salvation from generation to generation.

Paul
Gal 2:16
[16]Knowing that a man is not justified by the works of the law, but by the faith of Jesus Christ, even we have believed in Jesus Christ, that we might be justified by the faith of Christ, and not by the works of the law: for by the works of the law shall no flesh be justified.
Phil 3:9
[9]And be found in him, not having mine own righteousness, which is of the law, but that which is through the faith of Christ, the righteousness which is of God by faith:

ROMANS 3:24—Justified by faith (3:21–5:21), 56–58 CE

Theme	ROM	Mt	Mk
Justified by grace	**3:24** [24]Being justified freely by his grace through the redemption that is in Christ Jesus: **5:1–2** [1]Therefore being justified by faith, we have peace with God through our Lord Jesus Christ: [2]By whom also we have access by faith into this grace wherein we stand, and rejoice in hope of the glory of God. **6:14** [14]For sin shall not have dominion over you: for ye are not under the law, but under grace.	**20:28** [28]Even as the Son of man came not to be ministered unto, but to minister, and to give his life a ransom for many.	**10:45** [45]For even the Son of man came not to be ministered unto, but to minister, and to give his life a ransom for many.

ROMANS 3:24—Justified by faith (3:21–5:21), 56–58 CE (*continued*)

Theme	ROM	Paul
(*Cont.*) **Justified by grace**	**3:24 (above)** **5:1–2 (above)** **6:14 (above)**	**1 Cor 10** [1]Moreover, brethren, I would not that ye should be ignorant, how that all our fathers were under the cloud, and all passed through the sea; [2]And were all baptized unto Moses in the cloud and in the sea; [3]And did all eat the same spiritual meat; [4]And did all drink the same spiritual drink: for they drank of that spiritual Rock that followed them: and that Rock was Christ. [5]But with many of them God was not well pleased: for they were overthrown in the wilderness. [6]Now these things were our examples, to the intent we should not lust after evil things, as they also lusted. [7]Neither be ye idolaters, as were some of them; as it is written, The people sat down to eat and drink, and rose up to play. [8]Neither let us commit fornication, as some of them committed, and fell in one day three and twenty thousand. [9]Neither let us tempt Christ, as some of them also tempted, and were destroyed of serpents. [10]Neither murmur ye, as some of them also murmured, and were destroyed of the destroyer. [11]Now all these things happened unto them for ensamples: and they are written for our admonition, upon whom the ends of the world are come. [12]Where-fore let him that thinketh he standeth take heed lest he fall. [13]There hath no temptation taken you but such as is common to man: but God is faithful, who will not suffer you to be tempted above that ye are able; but will with the temptation also make a way to escape, that ye may be able to bear it. [14]Wherefore, my dearly beloved, flee from idolatry. [15]I speak as to wise men; judge ye what I say. [16]The cup of blessing which we bless, is it not the communion of the blood of Christ? The bread which we break, is it not the communion of the body of Christ? [17]For we being many are one bread, and one body: for we are all partakers of that one bread. [18]Behold Israel after the flesh: are not they which eat of the sacrifices partakers of the altar? [19]What say I then? that the idol is any thing, or that which is offered in sacrifice to idols is any thing? [20]But I say, that the things which the Gentiles sacrifice, they sacrifice to devils, and not to God: and I would not that ye should have fellowship with devils. [21]Ye cannot drink the cup of the Lord, and the cup of devils: ye cannot be partakers of the Lord's table, and of the table of devils. [22]Do we provoke the Lord to jealousy? are we stronger than he? [23]All things are lawful for me, but all things are not expedient: all things are lawful for me, but all things edify not. [24]Let no man seek his own, but every man another's wealth. [25]Whatsoever is sold in the shambles, that eat, asking no question for conscience sake: [26]For the earth is the Lord's, and the fulness thereof. [27]If any of them that believe not bid you to a feast, and ye be disposed to go; whatsoever is set before you, eat, asking no question for conscience sake. [28]But if any man say unto you, This is offered in sacrifice unto idols, eat not for his sake that showed it, and for conscience sake: for the earth is the Lord's, and the fulness thereof: [29]Conscience, I say, not thine own, but of the other: for why is my liberty judged of another man's conscience? [30]For if I by grace be a partaker, why am I evil spoken of for that for which I give thanks? [31]Whether therefore ye eat, or drink, or whatsoever ye do, do all to the glory of God. [32]Give none offence, neither to the Jews, nor to the Gentiles, nor to the church of God: [33]Even as I please all men in all things, not seeking mine own profit, but the profit of many, that they may be saved. **2 Cor 5:21** [21]For he hath made him to be sin for us, who knew no sin; that we might be made the righteousness of God in him. **Gal 3:13** [13]Christ hath redeemed us from the curse of the law, being made a curse for us: for it is written, Cursed is every one that hangeth on a tree: **Gal 3:23–5:1** [23]But before faith came, we were kept under the law, shut up unto the faith which should afterwards be revealed. [24]Wherefore the law was our schoolmaster to bring us unto Christ, that we might be justified by faith. [25]But after that faith is come, we are no longer under a schoolmaster. [26]For ye are all the children of God by faith in Christ Jesus. [27]For as many of you as have been baptized into Christ have put on Christ. [28]There is neither Jew nor Greek, there is neither bond nor free, there is neither male nor female: for ye are all one in Christ Jesus. [29]And if ye be Christ's, then are ye Abraham's seed, and heirs according to the promise.

Romans 3:24 continued on next page

ROMANS 3:24—Justified by faith (3:21–5:21), 56–58 CE (*continued*)

Theme	ROM	Paul
(*Cont.*) Justified by grace	**3:24 (above)** **5:1–2 (above)** **6:14 (above)**	(*Continued*) **Gal 3:23–5:1** **4** 1Now I say, That the heir, as long as he is a child, differeth nothing from a servant, though he be lord of all; 2But is under tutors and governors until the time appointed of the father. 3Even so we, when we were children, were in bondage under the elements of the world: 4But when the fulness of the time was come, God sent forth his Son, made of a woman, made under the law, 5To redeem them that were under the law, that we might receive the adoption of sons. 6And because ye are sons, God hath sent forth the Spirit of his Son into your hearts, crying, Abba, Father. 7Wherefore thou art no more a servant, but a son; and if a son, then an heir of God through Christ. 8Howbeit then, when ye knew not God, ye did service unto them which by nature are no gods. 9But now, after that ye have known God, or rather are known of God, how turn ye again to the weak and beggarly elements, whereunto ye desire again to be in bondage? 10Ye observe days, and months, and times, and years. 11I am afraid of you, lest I have bestowed upon you labour in vain. 12Brethren, I beseech you, be as I am; for I am as ye are: ye have not injured me at all. 13Ye know how through infirmity of the flesh I preached the gospel unto you at the first. 14And my temptation which was in my flesh ye despised not, nor rejected; but received me as an angel of God, even as Christ Jesus. 15Where is then the blessedness ye spake of? for I bear you record, that, if it had been possible, ye would have plucked out your own eyes, and have given them to me. 16Am I therefore become your enemy, because I tell you the truth? 17They zealously affect you, but not well; yea, they would exclude you, that ye might affect them. 18But it is good to be zealously affected always in a good thing, and not only when I am present with you. 19My little children, of whom I travail in birth again until Christ be formed in you, 20I desire to be present with you now, and to change my voice; for I stand in doubt of you. 21Tell me, ye that desire to be under the law, do ye not hear the law? 22For it is written, that Abraham had two sons, the one by a bondmaid, the other by a freewoman. 23But he who was of the bondwoman was born after the flesh; but he of the freewoman was by promise. 24Which things are an allegory: for these are the two covenants; the one from the mount Sinai, which gendereth to bondage, which is Agar. 25For this Agar is mount Sinai in Arabia, and answereth to Jerusalem which now is, and is in bondage with her children. 26But Jerusalem which is above is free, which is the mother of us all. 27For it is written, Rejoice, thou barren that bearest not; break forth and cry, thou that travailest not: for the desolate hath many more children than she which hath an husband. 28Now we, brethren, as Isaac was, are the children of promise. 29But as then he that was born after the flesh persecuted him that was born after the Spirit, even so it is now. 30Nevertheless what saith the scripture? Cast out the bondwoman and her son: for the son of the bondwoman shall not be heir with the son of the freewoman. 31So then, brethren, we are not children of the bondwoman, but of the free. **5** 1Stand fast therefore in the liberty wherewith Christ hath made us free, and be not entangled again with the yoke of bondage. **Eph 1:7 (Pseudo)** 7In whom we have redemption through his blood, the forgiveness of sins, according to the riches of his grace; **Eph 2:8 (Pseudo)** 8For by grace are ye saved through faith; and that not of yourselves: it is the gift of God: **Tit 3:7 (Pseudo)** 7That being justified by his grace, we should be made heirs according to the hope of eternal life.

ROMANS 3:24—Justified by faith (3:21–5:21), 56–58 CE (*continued*)

Theme	ROM	Jewish Writings
(*Cont.*) **Justified by grace**	**3:24 (above)** **5:1–2 (above)** **6:14 (above)**	**Ex 15:13** [13]Thou in thy mercy hast led forth the people which thou hast redeemed: thou hast guided them in thy strength unto thy holy habitation. **Ex 25:16–21** [16]And thou shalt put into the ark the testimony which I shall give thee. [17]And thou shalt make a mercy seat of pure gold: two cubits and a half shall be the length thereof, and a cubit and a half the breadth thereof. [18]And thou shalt make two cherubims of gold, of beaten work shalt thou make them, in the two ends of the mercy seat. [19]And make one cherub on the one end, and the other cherub on the other end: even of the mercy seat shall ye make the cherubims on the two ends thereof. [20]And the cherubims shall stretch forth their wings on high, covering the mercy seat with their wings, and their faces shall look one to another; toward the mercy seat shall the faces of the cherubims be. [21]And thou shalt put the mercy seat above upon the ark; and in the ark thou shalt put the testimony that I shall give thee. **Lev 1:4** [4]And he shall put his hand upon the head of the burnt offering; and it shall be accepted for him to make atonement for him. **Lev 4–5** **4**[1]And the LORD spake unto Moses, saying, [2]Speak unto the children of Israel, saying, If a soul shall sin through ignorance against any of the commandments of the LORD concerning things which ought not to be done, and shall do against any of them: [3]If the priest that is anointed do sin according to the sin of the people; then let him bring for his sin, which he hath sinned, a young bullock without blemish unto the LORD for a sin offering. [4]And he shall bring the bullock unto the door of the tabernacle of the congregation before the LORD; and shall lay his hand upon the bullock's head, and kill the bullock before the LORD. [5]And the priest that is anointed shall take of the bullock's blood, and bring it to the tabernacle of the congregation: [6]And the priest shall dip his finger in the blood, and sprinkle of the blood seven times before the LORD, before the veil of the sanctuary. [7]And the priest shall put some of the blood upon the horns of the altar of sweet incense before the LORD, which is in the tabernacle of the congregation; and shall pour all the blood of the bullock at the bottom of the altar of the burnt offering, which is at the door of the tabernacle of the congregation. [8]And he shall take off from it all the fat of the bullock for the sin offering; the fat that covereth the inwards, and all the fat that is upon the inwards, [9]And the two kidneys, and the fat that is upon them, which is by the flanks, and the caul above the liver, with the kidneys, it shall he take away, [10]As it was taken off from the bullock of the sacrifice of peace offerings: and the priest shall burn them upon the altar of the burnt offering. [11]And the skin of the bullock, and all his flesh, with his head, and with his legs, and his inwards, and his dung, [12]Even the whole bullock shall he carry forth without the camp unto a clean place, where the ashes are poured out, and burn him on the wood with fire: where the ashes are poured out shall he be burnt. [13]And if the whole congregation of Israel sin through ignorance, and the thing be hid from the eyes of the assembly, and they have done somewhat against any of the commandments of the LORD concerning things which should not be done, and are guilty; [14]When the sin, which they have sinned against it, is known, then the congregation shall offer a young bullock for the sin, and bring him before the tabernacle of the congregation. [15]And the elders of the congregation shall lay their hands upon the head of the bullock before the LORD: and the bullock shall be killed before the LORD. [16]And the priest that is anointed shall bring of the bullock's blood to the tabernacle of the congregation: [17]And the priest shall dip his finger in some of the blood, and sprinkle it seven times before the LORD, even before the veil. [18]And he shall put some of the blood upon the horns of the altar which is before the LORD, that is in the tabernacle of the congregation, and shall pour out all the blood at the bottom of the altar of the burnt offering, which is at the door of the tabernacle of the congregation. [19]And he shall take all his fat from him, and burn it upon the altar. [20]And he shall do with the bullock as he did with the bullock for a sin offering, so shall he do with this: and the priest shall make an atonement for them, and it shall be forgiven them. [21]And he shall carry forth the bullock without the camp, and burn him as he burned the first bullock: it is a sin offering for the congregation. [22]When a ruler hath sinned, and done somewhat through ignorance against any of the commandments of the LORD his God concerning things which should not be done, and is guilty; [23]Or if his sin, wherein he hath sinned, come to his knowledge; he shall bring his offering, a kid of the goats, a male without blemish: [24]And he shall lay his hand upon the head of the goat, and kill it in the place where they kill the burnt offering before the LORD: it is a sin offering. [25]And the priest shall take of the blood of the sin offering with his finger, and put it upon the horns of the altar of burnt offering, and shall pour out his

Romans 3:24 continued on next page

ROMANS 3:24—Justified by faith (3:21–5:21), 56–58 CE (*continued*)

Theme	ROM	Jewish Writings
(*Cont.*) **Justified by grace**	**3:24 (above)** **5:1–2 (above)** **6:14 (above)**	(*continued*) **Lev 4–5** blood at the bottom of the altar of burnt offering. [26]And he shall burn all his fat upon the altar, as the fat of the sacrifice of peace offerings: and the priest shall make an atonement for him as concerning his sin, and it shall be forgiven him. [27]And if any one of the common people sin through ignorance, while he doeth somewhat against any of the commandments of the LORD concerning things which ought not to be done, and be guilty; [28]Or if his sin, which he hath sinned, come to his knowledge: then he shall bring his offering, a kid of the goats, a female without blemish, for his sin which he hath sinned. [29]And he shall lay his hand upon the head of the sin offering, and slay the sin offering in the place of the burnt offering. [30]And the priest shall take of the blood thereof with his finger, and put it upon the horns of the altar of burnt offering, and shall pour out all the blood thereof at the bottom of the altar. [31]And he shall take away all the fat thereof, as the fat is taken away from off the sacrifice of peace offerings; and the priest shall burn it upon the altar for a sweet savour unto the LORD; and the priest shall make an atonement for him, and it shall be forgiven him. [32]And if he bring a lamb for a sin offering, he shall bring it a female without blemish. [33]And he shall lay his hand upon the head of the sin offering, and slay it for a sin offering in the place where they kill the burnt offering. [34]And the priest shall take of the blood of the sin offering with his finger, and put it upon the horns of the altar of burnt offering, and shall pour out all the blood thereof at the bottom of the altar: [35]And he shall take away all the fat thereof, as the fat of the lamb is taken away from the sacrifice of the peace offerings; and the priest shall burn them upon the altar, according to the offerings made by fire unto the LORD: and the priest shall make an atonement for his sin that he hath committed, and it shall be forgiven him. **5** [1]And if a soul sin, and hear the voice of swearing, and is a witness, whether he hath seen or known of it; if he do not utter it, then he shall bear his iniquity. [2]Or if a soul touch any unclean thing, whether it be a carcase of an unclean beast, or a carcase of unclean cattle, or the carcase of unclean creeping things, and if it be hidden from him; he also shall be unclean, and guilty. [3]Or if he touch the uncleanness of man, whatsoever uncleanness it be that a man shall be defiled withal, and it be hid from him; when he knoweth of it, then he shall be guilty. [4]Or if a soul swear, pronouncing with his lips to do evil, or to do good, whatsoever it be that a man shall pronounce with an oath, and it be hid from him; when he knoweth of it, then he shall be guilty in one of these. [5]And it shall be, when he shall be guilty in one of these things, that he shall confess that he hath sinned in that thing: [6]And he shall bring his trespass offering unto the LORD for his sin which he hath sinned, a female from the flock, a lamb or a kid of the goats, for a sin offering; and the priest shall make an atonement for him concerning his sin. [7]And if he be not able to bring a lamb, then he shall bring for his trespass, which he hath committed, two turtledoves, or two young pigeons, unto the LORD; one for a sin offering, and the other for a burnt offering. [8]And he shall bring them unto the priest, who shall offer that which is for the sin offering first, and wring off his head from his neck, but shall not divide it asunder: [9]And he shall sprinkle of the blood of the sin offering upon the side of the altar; and the rest of the blood shall be wrung out at the bottom of the altar: it is a sin offering. [10]And he shall offer the second for a burnt offering, according to the manner: and the priest shall make an atonement for him for his sin which he hath sinned, and it shall be forgiven him. [11]But if he be not able to bring two turtledoves, or two young pigeons, then he that sinned shall bring for his offering the tenth part of an ephah of fine flour for a sin offering; he shall put no oil upon it, neither shall he put any frankincense thereon: for it is a sin offering. [12]Then shall he bring it to the priest, and the priest shall take his handful of it, even a memorial thereof, and burn it on the altar, according to the offerings made by fire unto the LORD: it is a sin offering. [13]And the priest shall make an atonement for him as touching his sin that he hath sinned in one of these, and it shall be forgiven him: and the remnant shall be the priest's, as a meat offering. [14]And the LORD spake unto Moses, saying, [15]If a soul commit a trespass, and sin through ignorance, in the holy things of the LORD; then he shall bring for his trespass unto the LORD a ram without blemish out of the flocks, with thy estimation by shekels of silver, after the shekel of the sanctuary, for a trespass offering: [16]And he shall make amends for the harm that he hath done in the holy thing, and shall add the fifth part thereto, and give it unto the priest: and the priest shall make an atonement for him with the ram of the trespass offering, and it shall be forgiven him. [17]And if a soul sin, and commit any of these things which are forbidden to be done by the commandments of the LORD; though he wist it not, yet is he guilty, and shall bear his iniquity. [18]And he shall bring a ram without blemish out of the flock, with thy estimation, for a trespass offering, unto the priest: and the priest shall make an atonement for him concerning his ignorance wherein he erred and wist it not, and it shall be forgiven him. [19]It is a trespass offering: he hath certainly trespassed against the LORD. **Is 41:14** [14]Fear not, thou worm Jacob, and ye men of Israel; I will help thee, saith the LORD, and thy redeemer, the Holy One of Israel.

Other
Q-Quelle
Precedence: Rom 3:24/[1 Cor 10]/[Gal 3:23-5:1]/[Mt 19:28]/ Mk 10:41-45 /[Lk 22:28-30 (QS 62)]

ROMANS 3:25—Justified by faith (3:21–5:21), 56–58 CE

Theme	ROM	Lk	Jn	NT
Atonement	**3:25** [25]Whom God hath set forth to be a propitiation through faith in his blood, to declare his righteousness for the remission of sins that are past, through the forbearance of God; **8:3** [3]For what the law could not do, in that it was weak through the flesh, God sending his own Son in the likeness of sinful flesh, and for sin, condemned sin in the flesh:	**Acts 17:31** [31]Because he hath appointed a day, in the which he will judge the world in righteousness by that man whom he hath ordained; whereof he hath given assurance unto all men, in that he hath raised him from the dead.	**4:10** [10]Jesus answered and said unto her, If thou knewest the gift of God, and who it is that saith to thee, Give me to drink; thou wouldest have asked of him, and he would have given thee living water.	**Heb 9:5** [5]And over it the cherubims of glory shadowing the mercyseat; of which we cannot now speak particularly.

ROMANS 3:27—Justified by faith (3:21–5:21), 56–58 CE

Theme	ROM	Paul
Law of faith	**3:27** [27]Where is boasting then? It is excluded. By what law? of works? Nay: but by the law of faith. **8:2** [2]For the law of the Spirit of life in Christ Jesus hath made me free from the law of sin and death.	**1 Cor 1:29–31** [29]That no flesh should glory in his presence. [30]But of him are ye in Christ Jesus, who of God is made unto us wisdom, and righteousness, and sanctification, and redemption: [31]That, according as it is written, He that glorieth, let him glory in the Lord.

ROMANS 3:28—Justified by faith (3:21–5:21), 56–58 CE

Theme	ROM	Paul
Justified by faith	**3:28** [28]Therefore we conclude that a man is justified by faith without the deeds of the law. **5:1** [1]Therefore being justified by faith, we have peace with God through our Lord Jesus Christ:	**Gal 2:16** [16]Knowing that a man is not justified by the works of the law, but by the faith of Jesus Christ, even we have believed in Jesus Christ, that we might be justified by the faith of Christ, and not by the works of the law: for by the works of the law shall no flesh be justified.

ROMANS 3:29—Justified by faith (3:21–5:21), 56–58 CE

Theme	ROM
God of all	**3:29** [29]Is he the God of the Jews only? is he not also of the Gentiles? Yes, of the Gentiles also: **10:12** [12]For there is no difference between the Jew and the Greek: for the same Lord over all is rich unto all that call upon him.

Jewish Writings

Lev 16:12–15

[12]And he shall take a censer full of burning coals of fire from off the altar
before the LORD, and his hands full of sweet incense beaten small, and
bring it within the veil: [13]And he shall put the incense upon the fire before
the LORD, that the cloud of the incense may cover the mercy seat that is
upon the testimony, that he die not: [14]And he shall take of the blood of the
bullock, and sprinkle it with his finger upon the mercy seat eastward; and
before the mercy seat shall he sprinkle of the blood with his finger seven
times. [15]Then shall he kill the goat of the sin offering, that is for the people,
and bring his blood within the veil, and do with that blood as he did with
the blood of the bullock, and sprinkle it upon the mercy seat, and before
the mercy seat:

ROMANS 3:30—Justified by faith (3:21–5:21), 56–58 CE (54–58CE)

Theme	ROM	Paul	NT
One God	**3:30** [30]Seeing it is one God, which shall justify the circumcision by faith, and uncircumcision through faith.	**Gal 3:20** [20]Now a mediator is not a mediator of one, but God is one.	**Jas 2:19** [19]Thou believest that there is one God; thou doest well: the devils also believe, and tremble. **Jas 4:11–12** [11]Speak not evil one of another, brethren. He that speaketh evil of his brother, and judgeth his brother, speaketh evil of the law, and judgeth the law: but if thou judge the law, thou art not a doer of the law, but a judge. [12]There is one lawgiver, who is able to save and to destroy: who art thou that judgest another?

ROMANS 3:31—Justified by faith (3:21–5:21), 56–58 CE

Theme	ROM	Mt	Lk
Jesus fulfilled law: mercy, not sacrifice	**3:31** [31]Do we then make void the law through faith? God forbid: yea, we establish the law. **7:4–6** [4]Wherefore, my brethren, ye also are become dead to the law by the body of Christ; that ye should be married to another, even to him who is raised from the dead, that we should bring forth fruit unto God. [5]For when we were in the flesh, the motions of sins, which were by the law, did work in our members to bring forth fruit unto death. [6]But now we are delivered from the law, that being dead wherein we were held; that we should serve in newness of spirit, and not in the oldness of the letter. **8:4** [4]That the righteousness of the law might be fulfilled in us, who walk not after the flesh, but after the Spirit.	**5:17** [17]Think not that I am come to destroy the law, or the prophets: I am not come to destroy, but to fulfil. **9:13** [13]But go ye and learn what that meaneth, I will have mercy, and not sacrifice: for I am not come to call the righteous, but sinners to repentance. **12:7** [7]But if ye had known what this meaneth, I will have mercy, and not sacrifice, ye would not have condemned the guiltless.	**10:25–27** [25]And, behold, a certain lawyer stood up, and tempted him, saying, Master, what shall I do to inherit eternal life? [26]He said unto him, What is written in the law? how readest thou? [27]And he answering said, Thou shalt love the Lord thy God with all thy heart, and with all thy soul, and with all thy strength, and with all thy mind; and thy neighbour as thyself.

Jewish Writings
Dt 6:4
[4]Hear, O Israel: The LORD our God is one LORD:

Paul	Jewish Writings
Rom 13:10 [10]Love worketh no ill to his neighbour: therefore love is the fulfilling of the law. **Rom 15:9–12** [9]And that the Gentiles might glorify God for his mercy; as it is written, For this cause I will confess to thee among the Gentiles, and sing unto thy name. [10]And again he saith, Rejoice, ye Gentiles, with his people. [11]And again, Praise the Lord, all ye Gentiles; and laud him, all ye people. [12]And again, Esaias saith, There shall be a root of Jesse, and he that shall rise to reign over the Gentiles; in him shall the Gentiles trust. **Gal 5:14** [14]For all the law is fulfilled in one word, even in this; Thou shalt love thy neighbour as thyself.	**Hos 6:6** [6]For I desired mercy, and not sacrifice; and the knowledge of God more than burnt offerings.

ROMANS Ch 4—Justified by faith (3:21–5:21), 56–58 CE

Theme	ROM
Jesus fulfilled faith of Abraham	**Ch 4** 1 What shall we say then that Abraham our father, as pertaining to the flesh, hath found? 2 For if Abraham were justified by works, he hath whereof to glory; but not before God. 3 For what saith the scripture? Abraham believed God, and it was counted unto him for righteousness. 4 Now to him that worketh is the reward not reckoned of grace, but of debt. 5 But to him that worketh not, but believeth on him that justifieth the ungodly, his faith is counted for righteousness. 6 Even as David also describeth the blessedness of the man, unto whom God imputeth righteousness without works, 7 Saying, Blessed are they whose iniquities are forgiven, and whose sins are covered. 8 Blessed is the man to whom the Lord will not impute sin. 9 Cometh this blessedness then upon the circumcision only, or upon the uncircumcision also? for we say that faith was reckoned to Abraham for righteousness. 10 How was it then reckoned? when he was in circumcision, or in uncircumcision? Not in circumcision, but in uncircumcision. 11 And he received the sign of circumcision, a seal of the righteousness of the faith which he had yet being uncircumcised: that he might be the father of all them that believe, though they be not circumcised; that righteousness might be imputed unto them also: 12 And the father of circumcision to them who are not of the circumcision only, but who also walk in the steps of that faith of our father Abraham, which he had being yet uncircumcised. 13 For the promise, that he should be the heir of the world, was not to Abraham, or to his seed, through the law, but through the righteousness of faith. 14 For if they which are of the law be heirs, faith is made void, and the promise made of none effect: 15 Because the law worketh wrath: for where no law is, there is no transgression. 16 Therefore it is of faith, that it might be by grace; to the end the promise might be sure to all the seed; not to that only which is of the law, but to that also which is of the faith of Abraham; who is the father of us all, 17 (As it is written, I have made thee a father of many nations,) before him whom he believed, even God, who quickeneth the dead, and calleth those things which be not as though they were. 18 Who against hope believed in hope, that he might become the father of many nations, according to that which was spoken, So shall thy seed be. 19 And being not weak in faith, he considered not his own body now dead, when he was about an hundred years old, neither yet the deadness of Sarah's womb: 20 He staggered not at the promise of God through unbelief; but was strong in faith, giving glory to God; 21 And being fully persuaded that, what he had promised, he was able also to perform. 22 And therefore it was imputed to him for righteousness. 23 Now it was not written for his sake alone, that it was imputed to him; 24 But for us also, to whom it shall be imputed, if we believe on him that raised up Jesus our Lord from the dead; 25 Who was delivered for our offences, and was raised again for our justification. **Rom 9** 1 I say the truth in Christ, I lie not, my conscience also bearing me witness in the Holy Ghost, 2 That I have great heaviness and continual sorrow in my heart. 3 For I could wish that myself were accursed from Christ for my brethren, my kinsmen according to the flesh: 4 Who are Israelites; to whom pertaineth the adoption, and the glory, and the covenants, and the giving of the law, and the service of God, and the promises; 5 Whose are the fathers, and of whom as concerning the flesh Christ came, who is over all, God blessed for ever. Amen. 6 Not as though the word of God hath taken none effect. For they are not all Israel, which are of Israel: 7 Neither, because they are the seed of Abraham, are they all children: but, In Isaac shall thy seed be called. 8 That is, They which are the children of the flesh, these are not the children of God: but the children of the promise are counted for the seed. 9 For this is the word of promise, At this time will I come, and Sarah shall have a son. 10 And not only this; but when Rebecca also had conceived by one, even by our father Isaac; 11 (For the children being not yet born, neither having done any good or evil, that the purpose of God according to election might stand, not of works, but of him that calleth;) 12 It was said unto her, The elder shall serve the younger. 13 As it is written, Jacob have I loved, but Esau have I hated. 14 What shall we say then? Is there unrighteousness with God? God forbid. 15 For he saith to Moses, I will have mercy on whom I will have mercy, and I will have compassion on whom I will have compassion. 16 So then it is not of him that willeth, nor of him that runneth, but of God that showeth mercy. 17 For the scripture saith unto Pharaoh, Even for this same purpose have I raised thee up, that I might show my power in thee, and that my name might be declared throughout all the earth. 18 Therefore hath he mercy on whom he will have mercy, and whom he will he hardeneth. 19 Thou wilt say then unto me, Why doth he yet find fault? For who hath resisted his will? 20 Nay but, O man, who art thou that repliest against God? Shall the thing formed say to him that formed it, Why hast thou made me thus? 21 Hath not the potter power over the clay, of the same lump to make one vessel unto honour, and another unto dishonour? 22 What if God, willing to show his wrath, and to make his power known, endured with much longsuffering the vessels of wrath fitted to destruction: 23 And that he might make known the riches of his glory on the vessels of mercy, which he had afore prepared unto glory, 24 Even us, whom he hath called, not of the Jews only, but also of the Gentiles? 25 As he saith also in Osee, I will call them my people, which were not my people; and her beloved, which was not beloved. 26 And it shall come to pass, that in the place where it was said unto them, Ye are not my people; there shall they be called

ROMANS Ch 4—Justified by faith (3:21–5:21), 56–58 CE (*continued*)

Theme	ROM
(Cont.) **Jesus fulfilled faith of Abraham**	***(continued)*** **Rom 9** the children of the living God. 27Esaias also crieth concerning Israel, Though the number of the children of Israel be as the sand of the sea, a remnant shall be saved: 28For he will finish the work, and cut it short in righteousness: because a short work will the Lord make upon the earth. 29And as Esaias said before, Except the Lord of Sabaoth had left us a seed, we had been as Sodoma, and been made like unto Gomorrha. 30What shall we say then? That the Gentiles, which followed not after righteousness, have attained to righteousness, even the righteousness which is of faith. 31But Israel, which followed after the law of righteousness, hath not attained to the law of righteousness. 32Wherefore? Because they sought it not by faith, but as it were by the works of the law. For they stumbled at that stumblingstone; 33As it is written, Behold, I lay in Sion a stumblingstone and rock of offence: and whosoever believeth on him shall not be ashamed. **Rom 11** 1I say then, Hath God cast away his people? God forbid. For I also am an Israelite, of the seed of Abraham, of the tribe of Benjamin. 2God hath not cast away his people which he foreknew. Wot ye not what the scripture saith of Elias? how he maketh intercession to God against Israel, saying, 3Lord, they have killed thy prophets, and digged down thine altars; and I am left alone, and they seek my life. 4But what saith the answer of God unto him? I have reserved to myself seven thousand men, who have not bowed the knee to the image of Baal. 5Even so then at this present time also there is a remnant according to the election of grace. 6And if by grace, then is it no more of works: otherwise grace is no more grace. But if it be of works, then is it no more grace: otherwise work is no more work. 7What then? Israel hath not obtained that which he seeketh for; but the election hath obtained it, and the rest were blinded 8(According as it is written, God hath given them the spirit of slumber, eyes that they should not see, and ears that they should not hear;) unto this day. 9And David saith, Let their table be made a snare, and a trap, and a stumblingblock, and a recompense unto them: 10Let their eyes be darkened, that they may not see, and bow down their back alway. 11I say then, Have they stumbled that they should fall? God forbid: but rather through their fall salvation is come unto the Gentiles, for to provoke them to jealousy. 12Now if the fall of them be the riches of the world, and the diminishing of them the riches of the Gentiles; how much more their fulness? 13For I speak to you Gentiles, inasmuch as I am the apostle of the Gentiles, I magnify mine office: 14If by any means I may provoke to emulation them which are my flesh, and might save some of them. 15For if the casting away of them be the reconciling of the world, what shall the receiving of them be, but life from the dead? 16For if the firstfruit be holy, the lump is also holy: and if the root be holy, so are the branches. 17And if some of the branches be broken off, and thou, being a wild olive tree, wert grafted in among them, and with them partakest of the root and fatness of the olive tree; 18Boast not against the branches. But if thou boast, thou bearest not the root, but the root thee. 19Thou wilt say then, The branches were broken off, that I might be grafted in. 20Well; because of unbelief they were broken off, and thou standest by faith. Be not highminded, but fear: 21For if God spared not the natural branches, take heed lest he also spare not thee. 22Behold therefore the goodness and severity of God: on them which fell, severity; but toward thee, goodness, if thou continue in his goodness: otherwise thou also shalt be cut off. 23And they also, if they abide not still in unbelief, shall be grafted in: for God is able to graft them in again. 24For if thou wert cut out of the olive tree which is wild by nature, and wert grafted contrary to nature into a good olive tree: how much more shall these, which be the natural branches, be grafted into their own olive tree? 25For I would not, brethren, that ye should be ignorant of this mystery, lest ye should be wise in your own conceits; that blindness in part is happened to Israel, until the fulness of the Gentiles be come in. 26And so all Israel shall be saved: as it is written, There shall come out of Sion the Deliverer, and shall turn away ungodliness from Jacob: 27For this is my covenant unto them, when I shall take away their sins. 28As concerning the gospel, they are enemies for your sakes: but as touching the election, they are beloved for the fathers' sakes. 29For the gifts and calling of God are without repentance. 30For as ye in times past have not believed God, yet have now obtained mercy through their unbelief: 31Even so have these also now not believed, that through your mercy they also may obtain mercy. 32For God hath concluded them all in unbelief, that he might have mercy upon all. 33O the depth of the riches both of the wisdom and knowledge of God! how unsearchable are his judgments, and his ways past finding out! 34For who hath known the mind of the Lord? or who hath been his counselor? 35Or who hath first given to him, and it shall be recompensed unto him again? 36For of him, and through him, and to him, are all things: to whom be glory for ever. Amen.

ROMANS 4:1—Justified by faith (3:21–5:21), 56–58 CE

Theme	ROM	Paul
Abraham's faith	**4:1** [1]What shall we say then that Abraham our father, as pertaining to the flesh, hath found?	**Gal 3:6–9** [6]Even as Abraham believed God, and it was accounted to him for righteousness. [7]Know ye therefore that they which are of faith, the same are the children of Abraham. [8]And the scripture, foreseeing that God would justify the heathen through faith, preached before the gospel unto Abraham, saying, In thee shall all nations be blessed. [9]So then they which be of faith are blessed with faithful Abraham.

ROMANS 4:3—Justified by faith (3:21–5:21), 56–58 CE

Theme	ROM	Paul	NT	Jewish Writings
Abraham believed God	**4:3** [3]For what saith the scripture? Abraham believed God, and it was counted unto him for righteousness.	**Gal 3:6** [6]Even as Abraham believed God, and it was accounted to him for righteousness.	**Jas 2:14** [14]What doth it profit, my brethren, though a man say he hath faith, and have not works? can faith save him? **Jas 2:20–24** [20]But wilt thou know, O vain man, that faith without works is dead? [21]Was not Abraham our father justified by works, when he had offered Isaac his son upon the altar? [22]Seest thou how faith wrought with his works, and by works was faith made perfect? [23]And the scripture was fulfilled which saith, Abraham believed God, and it was imputed unto him for righteousness: and he was called the Friend of God. [24]Ye see then how that by works a man is justified, and not by faith only.	**Gen 15:6** [6]And he believed in the LORD; and he counted it to him for righteousness.

ROMANS 4:4—Justified by faith (3:21–5:21), 56–58 CE

Theme	ROM
Grace, not works	**4:4** [4]Now to him that worketh is the reward not reckoned of grace, but of debt. **11:6** [6]And if by grace, then is it no more of works: otherwise grace is no more grace. But if it be of works, then is it no more grace: otherwise work is no more work.

ROMANS 4:7–8—Justified by faith (3:21–5:21), 56–58 CE

Theme	ROM	Jewish Writings
God's forgiveness	**4:7–8** [7]Saying, Blessed are they whose iniquities are forgiven, and whose sins are covered. [8]Blessed is the man to whom the Lord will not impute sin.	**Ps 32:1–2** [1]essed is he whose transgression is forgiven, whose sin is covered. [2]Blessed is the man unto whom the LORD imputeth not iniquity, and in whose spirit there is no guile.

ROMANS 4:9—Justified by faith (3:21–5:21), 56–58 CE

Theme	ROM
Righteousness of Abraham	**4:9** [9]Cometh this blessedness then upon the circumcision only, or upon the uncircumcision also? for we say that faith was reckoned to Abraham for righteousness. **4:3** [3]For what saith the scripture? Abraham believed God, and it was counted unto him for righteousness.

ROMANS 4:11—Justified by faith (3:21–5:21), 56–58 CE

Theme	ROM	Paul	Jewish Writings
Sign of circumcision	**4:11** [11]And he received the sign of circumcision, a seal of the righteousness of the faith which he had yet being uncircumcised: that he might be the father of all them that believe, though they be not circumcised; that righteousness might be imputed unto them also:	**Gal 3:6–8** [6]Even as Abraham believed God, and it was accounted to him for righteousness. [7]Know ye therefore that they which are of faith, the same are the children of Abraham. [8]And the scripture, foreseeing that God would justify the heathen through faith, preached before the gospel unto Abraham, saying, In thee shall all nations be blessed.	**Gen 17:10–11** [10]This is my covenant, which ye shall keep, between me and you and thy seed after thee; Every man child among you shall be circumcised. [11]And ye shall circumcise the flesh of your foreskin; and it shall be a token of the covenant betwixt me and you.

ROMANS 4:13—Justified by faith (3:21–5:21), 56–58 CE

Theme	ROM	Paul	Jewish Writings
Heir of righteousness	**4:13** [13]For the promise, that he should be the heir of the world, was not to Abraham, or to his seed, through the law, but through the righteousness of faith.	**Gal 3:16–18** [16]Now to Abraham and his seed were the promises made. He saith not, And to seeds, as of many; but as of one, And to thy seed, which is Christ. [17]And this I say, that the covenant, that was confirmed before of God in Christ, the law, which was four hundred and thirty years after, cannot disannul, that it should make the promise of none effect. [18]For if the inheritance be of the law, it is no more of promise: but God gave it to Abraham by promise. **Gal 3:29** [29]And if ye be Christ's, then are ye Abraham's seed, and heirs according to the promise.	**Gen 12:7** [7]And the LORD appeared unto Abram, and said, Unto thy seed will I give this land: and there builded he an altar unto the LORD, who appeared unto him. **Gen 18:18** [18]Seeing that Abraham shall surely become a great and mighty nation, and all the nations of the earth shall be blessed in him? **Gen 22:17–18** [17]That in blessing I will bless thee, and in multiplying I will multiply thy seed as the stars of the heaven, and as the sand which is upon the sea shore; and thy seed shall possess the gate of his enemies; [18]And in thy seed shall all the nations of the earth be blessed; because thou hast obeyed my voice. **Sir 44:21** [21]Therefore he assured him by an oath, that he would bless the nations in his seed, and that he would multiply him as the dust of the earth, and exalt his seed as the stars, and cause them to inherit from sea to sea, and from the river unto the utmost part of the land

ROMANS 4:14—Justified by faith (3:21–5:21), 56–58 CE

Theme	ROM	Paul
Law voids faith	**4:14** [14]For if they which are of the law be heirs, faith is made void, and the promise made of none effect:	**Gal 3:18** [18]For if the inheritance be of the law, it is no more of promise: but God gave it to Abraham by promise.

ROMANS 4:15—Justified by faith (3:21–5:21), 56–58 CE (54–58CE)

Theme	ROM	Paul
Law works wrath	**4:15** [15]Because the law worketh wrath: for where no law is, there is no transgression. **3:20** [20]Therefore by the deeds of the law there shall no flesh be justified in his sight: for by the law is the knowledge of sin. **5:13** [13](For until the law sin was in the world: but sin is not imputed when there is no law. **7:8** [8]But sin, taking occasion by the commandment, wrought in me all manner of concupiscence. For without the law sin was dead.	**Gal 3:19** [19]Wherefore then serveth the law? It was added because of transgressions, till the seed should come to whom the promise was made; and it was ordained by angels in the hand of a mediator.

ROMANS 4:16—Justified by faith (3:21–5:21), 56–58 CE

Theme	ROM	Paul	Jewish Writings
Promise to all, by grace	**4:16** [16]Therefore it is of faith, that it might be by grace; to the end the promise might be sure to all the seed; not to that only which is of the law, but to that also which is of the faith of Abraham; who is the father of us all,	**Gal 3:7–9** [7]Know ye therefore that they which are of faith, the same are the children of Abraham. [8]And the scripture, foreseeing that God would justify the heathen through faith, preached before the gospel unto Abraham, saying, In thee shall all nations be blessed. [9]So then they which be of faith are blessed with faithful Abraham.	**Sir 44:19** [19]Abraham was a great father of many people: in glory was there none like unto him;

ROMANS 4:17—Justified by faith (3:21–5:21), 56–58 CE

Theme	ROM	NT	Jewish Writings
Abraham, Father of many nations	**4:17** [17](As it is written, I have made thee a father of many nations,) before him whom he believed, even God, who quickeneth the dead, and calleth those things which be not as though they were.	**Heb 11:19** [19]Accounting that God was able to raise him up, even from the dead; from whence also he received him in a figure.	**Gen 17:5** [5]Neither shall thy name any more be called Abram, but thy name shall be Abraham; for a father of many nations have I made thee. **Is 48:13** [13]Mine hand also hath laid the foundation of the earth, and my right hand hath spanned the heavens: when I call unto them, they stand up together.

ROMANS 4:18—Justified by faith (3:21–5:21), 56–58 CE

Theme	ROM	Jewish Writings
Father of many nations	**4:18** [18]Who against hope believed in hope, that he might become the father of many nations, according to that which was spoken, So shall thy seed be.	**Gen 15:5** [5]And he brought him forth abroad, and said, Look now toward heaven, and tell the stars, if thou be able to number them: and he said unto him, So shall thy seed be.

ROMANS 4:19–20—Justified by faith (3:21–5:21), 56–58 CE

Theme	ROM	NT	Jewish Writings
Heir by faith	**4:19–20** [19]And being not weak in faith, he considered not his own body now dead, when he was about an hundred years old, neither yet the deadness of Sarah's womb: [20]He staggered not at the promise of God through unbelief; but was strong in faith, giving glory to God;	**Heb 11:11** [11]Through faith also Sarah herself received strength to conceive seed, and was delivered of a child when she was past age, because she judged him faithful who had promised.	**Gen 17:17** [17]Then Abraham fell upon his face, and laughed, and said in his heart, Shall a child be born unto him that is an hundred years old? and shall Sarah, that is ninety years old, bear?

ROMANS 4:21—Justified by faith (3:21–5:21), 56–58 CE

Theme	ROM	Lk	Jewish Writings
Belief in the Promise	**4:21** [21]And being fully persuaded that, what he had promised, he was able also to perform.	**1:37** [37]For with God nothing shall be impossible.	**Gen 18:14** [14]Is any thing too hard for the LORD? At the time appointed I will return unto thee, according to the time of life, and Sarah shall have a son.

ROMANS 4:22—Justified by faith (3:21–5:21), 56–58 CE

Theme	ROM	Jewish Writings
Faith as righteousness	**4:22** [22]And therefore it was imputed to him for righteousness.	**Gen 15:6** [6]And he believed in the LORD; and he counted it to him for righteousness.

ROMANS 4:24—Justified by faith (3:21–5:21), 56–58 CE

Theme	ROM	NT
Faith to raise the dead	**4:24** [24]But for us also, to whom it shall be imputed, if we believe on him that raised up Jesus our Lord from the dead; **10:9** [9]That if thou shalt confess with thy mouth the Lord Jesus, and shalt believe in thine heart that God hath raised him from the dead, thou shalt be saved.	**1 Pet 1:21** [21]Who by him do believe in God, that raised him up from the dead, and gave him glory; that your faith and hope might be in God.

ROMANS 4:25—Justified by faith (3:21–5:21), 56–58 CE

Theme	ROM	Mt	Mk	Lk
Sacrifice pleasing to God (betrayal)	**4:25** [25]Who was delivered for our offences, and was raised again for our justification. **8:11** [11]But if the Spirit of him that raised up Jesus from the dead dwell in you, he that raised up Christ from the dead shall also quicken your mortal bodies by his Spirit that dwelleth in you. **15:3** [3]For even Christ pleased not himself; but, as it is written, The reproaches of them that reproached thee fell on me. **15:32** [32]That I may come unto you with joy by the will of God, and may with you be refreshed.	**27:44** [44]The thieves also, which were crucified with him, cast the same in his teeth.	**15:32** [32]Let Christ the King of Israel descend now from the cross, that we may see and believe. And they that were crucified with him reviled him.	**22:53** [53]When I was daily with you in the temple, ye stretched forth no hands against me: but this is your hour, and the power of darkness.

ROMANS Ch 5—Justified by faith (3:21–5:21), 56–58 CE

Theme	ROM
Jesus knew no sin and overcame temptation	**Ch 5** [1]Therefore being justified by faith, we have peace with God through our Lord Jesus Christ: [2]By whom also we have access by faith into this grace wherein we stand, and rejoice in hope of the glory of God. [3]And not only so, but we glory in tribulations also: knowing that tribulation worketh patience; [4]And patience, experience; and experience, hope: [5]And hope maketh not ashamed; because the love of God is shed abroad in our hearts by the Holy Ghost which is given unto us. [6]For when we were yet without strength, in due time Christ died for the ungodly. [7]For scarcely for a righteous man will one die: yet peradventure for a good man some would even dare to die. [8]But God commendeth his love toward us, in that, while we were yet sinners, Christ died for us. [9]Much more then, being now justified by his blood, we shall be saved from wrath through him. [10]For if, when we were enemies, we were reconciled to God by the death of his Son, much more, being reconciled, we shall be saved by his life. [11]And not only so, but we also joy in God through our Lord Jesus Christ, by whom we have now received the atonement. [12]Wherefore, as by one man sin entered into the world, and death by sin; and so death passed upon all men, for that all have sinned: [13](For until the law sin was in the world: but sin is not imputed when there is no law. [14]Nevertheless death reigned from Adam to Moses, even over them that had not sinned after the similitude of Adam's transgression, who is the figure of him that was to come. [15]But not as the offence, so also is the free gift. For if through the offence of one many be dead, much more the grace of God, and the gift by grace, which is by one man, Jesus Christ, hath abounded unto many. [16]And not as it was by one that sinned, so is the gift: for the judg- ment was by one to condemnation, but the free gift is of many offences unto justification. [17]For if by one man's offence death reigned by one; much more they which receive abundance of grace and of the gift of righteousness shall reign in life by one, Jesus Christ.) [18]Therefore as by the offence of one judgment came upon all men to condemnation; even so by the righteousness of one the free gift came upon all men unto justification of life. [19]For as by one man's disobedience many were made sinners, so by the obedience of one shall many be made righteous. [20]Moreover the law entered, that the offence might abound. But where sin abounded, grace did much more abound: [21]That as sin hath reigned unto death, even so might grace reign through righteousness unto eternal life by Jesus Christ our Lord.

Paul	NT	Jewish Writings
1 Cor 15:17 [17] And if Christ be not raised, your faith is vain; ye are yet in your sins. **2 Cor 4:11** [11]For if that which is done away was glorious, much more that which remaineth is glorious. **Gal 2:20** [20]I am crucified with Christ: nevertheless I live; yet not I, but Christ liveth in me: and the life which I now live in the flesh I live by the faith of the Son of God, who loved me, and gave himself for me. **Col 3:13** [13]Forbearing one another, and for-giving one another, if any man have a quarrel against any: even as Christ forgave you, so also do ye.	**1 Pet 1:3** [3]Blessed be the God and Father of our Lord Jesus Christ, which according to his abundant mercy hath begotten us again unto a lively hope by the resurrection of Jesus Christ from the dead,	**Ps 69:9** [9]For the zeal of thine house hath eaten me up; and the reproaches of them that reproached thee are fallen upon me. **Is 53:4–5** [4]Surely he hath borne our griefs, and carried our sorrows: yet we did esteem him stricken, smitten of God, and afflicted. [5]But he was wounded for our transgressions, he was bruised for our iniquities: the chastisement of our peace was upon him; and with his stripes we are healed. **Is 53:12** [12]Therefore will I divide him a portion with the great, and he shall divide the spoil with the strong; because he hath poured out his soul unto death: and he was numbered with the transgressors; and he bare the sin of many, and made intercession for the transgressors.

Mt	Mk	Lk
3:13–15 [13]Then cometh Jesus from Galilee to Jordan unto John, to be baptized of him. [14]But John forbad him, saying, I have need to be baptized of thee, and comest thou to me? [15]And Jesus answering said unto him, Suffer it to be so now: for thus it becometh us to fulfil all righteousness. Then he suffered him. **4:1–11** [1]Then was Jesus led up of the Spirit into the wilderness to be tempted of the devil. [2]And when he had fasted forty days and forty nights, he was afterward an hungered. [3]And when the tempter came to him, he said, If thou be the Son of God, command that these stones be made bread. [4]But he answered and said, It is written, Man shall not live by bread alone, but by every word that proceedeth out of the mouth of God. [5]Then the devil taketh him up into the holy city, and setteth him on a pinnacle of the temple, [6]And saith unto him, If thou be the Son of God, cast thyself down: for it is written, He shall give his angels charge concerning thee: and in their hands they shall bear thee up, lest at any time thou dash thy foot against a stone. [7]Jesus said unto him, It is written again, Thou shalt not tempt the Lord thy God. [8]Again, the devil taketh him up into an exceeding high mountain, and showeth him all the kingdoms of the world, and the glory of them; [9]And saith unto him, All these things will I give thee, if thou wilt fall down and worship me. [10]Then saith Jesus unto him, Get thee hence, Satan: for it is written, Thou shalt worship the Lord thy God, and him only shalt thou serve. [11]Then the devil leaveth him, and, behold, angels came and ministered unto him.	**1:12– 13** [12]And immediately the Spirit driveth him into the wilderness. [13]And he was there in the wilderness forty days, tempted of Satan; and was with the wild beasts; and the angels ministered unto him.	**4:1–13** [1]And Jesus being full of the Holy Ghost returned from Jordan, and was led by the Spirit into the wilderness, [2]Being forty days tempted of the devil. And in those days he did eat nothing: and when they were ended, he afterward hungered. [3]And the devil said unto him, If thou be the Son of God, command this stone that it be made bread. [4]And Jesus answered him, saying, It is written, That man shall not live by bread alone, but by every word of God. [5]And the devil, taking him up into an high mountain, showed unto him all the kingdoms of the world in a moment of time. [6]And the devil said unto him, All this power will I give thee, and the glory of them: for that is delivered unto me; and to whomsoever I will I give it. [7]If thou therefore wilt worship me, all shall be thine. [8]And Jesus answered and said unto him, Get thee behind me, Satan: for it is written, Thou shalt worship the Lord thy God, and him only shalt thou serve. [9]And he brought him to Jerusalem, and set him on a pinnacle of the temple, and said unto him, If thou be the Son of God, cast thyself down from hence: [10]For it is written, He shall give his angels charge over thee, to keep thee: [11]And in their hands they shall bear thee up, lest at any time thou dash thy foot against a stone. [12]And Jesus answering said unto him, It is said, Thou shalt not tempt the Lord thy God. [13]And when the devil had ended all the temptation, he departed from him for a season.

Romans Ch 5 continued on next page

ROMANS Ch 5—Justified by faith (3:21–5:21), 56–58 CE (*continued*)

Theme	ROM	Jn	Paul
(*Cont.*) **Jesus knew no sin and overcame temptation**	**Ch 5 (above)**	**7:18** [18]He that speaketh of himself seeketh his own glory: but he that seeketh his glory that sent him, the same is true, and no unrighteousness is in him. **8:46** [46]Which of you convinceth me of sin? And if I say the truth, why do ye not believe me?	**1 Cor 7:5** [5]Defraud ye not one the other, except it be with consent for a time, that ye may give yourselves to fasting and prayer; and come together again, that Satan tempt you not for your incontinency. **1 Cor 10:1–13** [1]Moreover, brethren, I would not that ye should be ignorant, how that all our fathers were under the cloud, and all passed through the sea; [2]And were all baptized unto Moses in the cloud and in the sea; [3]And did all eat the same spiritual meat; [4]And did all drink the same spiritual drink: for they drank of that spiritual Rock that followed them: and that Rock was Christ. [5]But with many of them God was not well pleased: for they were overthrown in the wilderness. [6]Now these things were our examples, to the intent we should not lust after evil things, as they also lusted. [7]Neither be ye idolaters, as were some of them; as it is written, The people sat down to eat and drink, and rose up to play. [8]Neither let us commit fornication, as some of them committed, and fell in one day three and twenty thousand. [9]Neither let us tempt Christ, as some of them also tempted, and were destroyed of serpents. [10]Neither murmur ye, as some of them also murmured, and were destroyed of the destroyer. [11]Now all these things happened unto them for ensamples: and they are written for our admonition, upon whom the ends of the world are come. [12]Wherefore let him that thinketh he standeth take heed lest he fall. [13]There hath no temptation taken you but such as is common to man: but God is faithful, who will not suffer you to be tempted above that ye are able; but will with the temptation also make a way to escape, that ye may be able to bear it. **2 Cor 11:14** [14]And no marvel; for Satan himself is transformed into an angel of light. **2 Cor 12:7–10** [7]And lest I should be exalted above measure through the abundance of the revelations, there was given to me a thorn in the flesh, the messenger of Satan to buffet me, lest I should be exalted above measure. [8]For this thing I besought the Lord thrice, that it might depart from me. [9]And he said unto me, My grace is sufficient for thee: for my strength is made perfect in weakness. Most gladly therefore will I rather glory in my infirmities, that the power of Christ may rest upon me. [10]Therefore I take pleasure in infirmities, in reproaches, in necessities, in persecutions, in distresses for Christ's sake: for when I am weak, then am I strong. **Gal 6:1** [1]Brethren, if a man be overtaken in a fault, ye which are spiritual, restore such an one in the spirit of meekness; considering thyself, lest thou also be tempted. **Phil 2:5–11** [5]Let this mind be in you, which was also in Christ Jesus: [6]Who, being in the form of God, thought it not robbery to be equal with God: [7]But made himself of no reputation, and took upon him the form of a servant, and was made in the likeness of men: [8]And being found in fashion as a man, he humbled himself, and became obedient unto death, even the death of the cross. [9]Wherefore God also hath highly exalted him, and given him a name which is above every name: [10]That at the name of Jesus every knee should bow, of things in heaven, and things in earth, and things under the earth; [11]And that every tongue should confess that Jesus Christ is Lord, to the glory of God the Father. **1 Thes 3:5** [5]For this cause, when I could no longer forbear, I sent to know your faith, lest by some means the tempter have tempted you, and our labour be in vain.

Other
Q-Quelle
Temptations: Rom Ch 5/Mt 4:1-11/Lk 4:1-13 (QS 6)

ROMANS 5:1—Justified by faith (3:21–5:21), 56–58 CE

Theme	ROM	Paul
Justified by faith	**5:1** [1]Therefore being justified by faith, we have peace with God through our Lord Jesus Christ: **3:24–28** [24]Being justified freely by his grace through the redemption that is in Christ Jesus: [25]Whom God hath set forth to be a propitiation through faith in his blood, to declare his righteousness for the remission of sins that are past, through the forbearance of God; [26]To declare, I say, at this time his righteousness: that he might be just, and the justifier of him which believeth in Jesus. [27]Where is boasting then? It is excluded. By what law? of works? Nay: but by the law of faith. [28]Therefore we conclude that a man is justified by faith without the deeds of the law.	**Gal 2:16** [16]Knowing that a man is not justified by the works of the law, but by the faith of Jesus Christ, even we have believed in Jesus Christ, that we might be justified by the faith of Christ, and not by the works of the law: for by the works of the law shall no flesh be justified.

ROMANS 5:2—Justified by faith (3:21–5:21), 56–58 CE

Theme	ROM	Paul
Faith by grace	**5:2** [2]By whom also we have access by faith into this grace wherein we stand, and rejoice in hope of the glory of God.	**Eph 2:18 (Pseudo)** [18]For through him we both have access by one Spirit unto the Father. **Eph 3:12 (Pseudo)** [12]In whom we have boldness and access with confidence by the faith of him.

ROMANS 5:4—Justified by faith (3:21–5:21), 56–58 CE

Theme	ROM	Paul	NT
Enduring qualities	**5:4** [4]And patience, experience; and experience, hope:	**2 Cor 12:9–10** [9]And he said unto me, My grace is sufficient for thee: for my strength is made perfect in weakness. Most gladly therefore will I rather glory in my infirmities, that the power of Christ may rest upon me. [10]Therefore I take pleasure in infirmities, in reproaches, in necessities, in persecutions, in distresses for Christ's sake: for when I am weak, then am I strong.	**Jas 1:2–4** [2]My brethren, count it all joy when ye fall into divers temptations; [3]Knowing this, that the trying of your faith worketh patience. [4]But let patience have her perfect work, that ye may be perfect and entire, wanting nothing. **1 Pet 1:5–7** [5]Who are kept by the power of God through faith unto salvation ready to be revealed in the last time. [6]Wherein ye greatly rejoice, though now for a season, if need be, ye are in heaviness through manifold temptations: [7]That the trial of your faith, being much more precious than of gold that perisheth, though it be tried with fire, might be found unto praise and honour and glory at the appearing of Jesus Christ: **1 Pet 4:12–14** [12]Beloved, think it not strange concerning the fiery trial which is to try you, as though some strange thing happened unto you: [13]But rejoice, inasmuch as ye are partakers of Christ's sufferings; that, when his glory shall be revealed, ye may be glad also with exceeding joy. [14]If ye be reproached for the name of Christ, happy are ye; for the spirit of glory and of God resteth upon you: on their part he is evil spoken of, but on your part he is glorified.

ROMANS 5:5—Justified by faith (3:21–5:21), 56–58 CE

Theme	ROM	Jewish Writings
Love and hope	**5:5** [5]And hope maketh not ashamed; because the love of God is shed abroad in our hearts by the Holy Ghost which is given unto us. **8:14–16** [14]For as many as are led by the Spirit of God, they are the sons of God. [15]For ye have not received the spirit of bondage again to fear; but ye have received the Spirit of adoption, whereby we cry, Abba, Father. [16]The Spirit itself beareth witness with our spirit, that we are the children of God:	**Ps 22:5–6** [5]They cried unto thee, and were delivered: they trusted in thee, and were not confounded. [6]But I am a worm, and no man; a reproach of men, and despised of the people. **Ps 25:20** [20]O keep my soul, and deliver me: let me not be ashamed; for I put my trust in thee.

ROMANS 5:6—Justified by faith (3:21–5:21), 56–58 CE

Theme	ROM	Paul
Cross heals weak	**5:6** [6]For when we were yet without strength, in due time Christ died for the ungodly.	**1 Cor 1:23–24** [23]But we preach Christ crucified, unto the Jews a stumblingblock, and unto the Greeks foolishness; [24]But unto them which are called, both Jews and Greeks, Christ the power of God, and the wisdom of God. **2 Cor 12:9–10** [9]And he said unto me, My grace is sufficient for thee: for my strength is made perfect in weakness. Most gladly therefore will I rather glory in my infirmities, that the power of Christ may rest upon me. [10]Therefore I take pleasure in infirmities, in reproaches, in necessities, in persecutions, in distresses for Christ's sake: for when I am weak, then am I strong. **2 Cor 13:4** [4]For though he was crucified through weakness, yet he liveth by the power of God. For we also are weak in him, but we shall live with him by the power of God toward you.

ROMANS 5:8—Justified by faith (3:21–5:21), 56–58 CE

Theme	ROM	Jn
Christ died for sinners	**5:8** [8]But God commendeth his love toward us, in that, while we were yet sinners, Christ died for us.	**3:16** [16]For God so loved the world, that he gave his only begotten Son, that whosoever believeth in him should not perish, but have everlasting life. **1 Jn 4:10, 19** [10]Herein is love, not that we loved God, but that he loved us, and sent his Son to be the propitiation for our sins. . . . [19]We love him, because he first loved us.

ROMANS 5:9—Justified by faith (3:21–5:21), 56–58 CE

Theme	ROM	Paul
Saved from wrath	**5:9** [9]Much more then, being now justified by his blood, we shall be saved from wrath through him. **1:18** [18]For the wrath of God is revealed from heaven against all ungodliness and unrighteousness of men, who hold the truth in unrighteousness;	**1 Thes 1:10** [10]And to wait for his Son from heaven, whom he raised from the dead, even Jesus, which delivered us from the wrath to come.

ROMANS 5:10—Justified by faith (3:21–5:21), 56–58 CE

Theme	ROM
Reconciled through Jesus' death	**5:10** [10]For if, when we were enemies, we were reconciled to God by the death of his Son, much more, being reconciled, we shall be saved by his life. **8:7–8** [7]Because the carnal mind is enmity against God: for it is not subject to the law of God, neither indeed can be. [8]So then they that are in the flesh cannot please God.

ROMANS 5:12—Justified by faith (3:21–5:21), 56–58 CE

Theme	ROM
Humanity inherited original sin	**5:12** [12]Wherefore, as by one man sin entered into the world, and death by sin; and so death passed upon all men, for that all have sinned: **3:19, 23** [19] Now we know that what things soever the law saith, it saith to them who are under the law: that every mouth may be stopped, and all the world may become guilty before God. . . . [23] For all have sinned, and come short of the glory of God;

Other
Q-Quelle
Lord's Prayer: Rom 5:9/1 Thes 1:10/[Mt 6:9-13]/[Lk 11:1-4 (QS 26)]; Parable of Mustard Seed: Rom 5:9/1 Thes 1:10/ [Mt 13:31-32]/ [Mk 4:30-3]2[/Lk 13:18-19 (QS 46 [Thom 20, 96])]

Paul

2 Cor 5:18

18 And all things are of God, who hath reconciled us to himself by Jesus Christ, and hath given to us the ministry of reconciliation;

Col 1:21–22

21 And you, that were sometime alienated and enemies in your mind by wicked works, yet now hath he reconciled
22 In the body of his flesh through death, to present you holy and unblameable and unreproveable in his sight

Jewish Writings

Gen 2:17

17 But of the tree of the knowledge of good and evil, thou shalt not eat of it: for in the day that thou eatest thereof thou shalt surely die.

Gen 3:1–19

1 Now the serpent was more subtil than any beast of the field which the LORD God had made. And he said unto the woman, Yea,
hath God said, Ye shall not eat of every tree of the garden? 2 And the woman said unto the serpent, We may eat of the fruit of the trees
of the garden: 3 But of the fruit of the tree which is in the midst of the garden, God hath said, Ye shall not eat of it, neither shall ye
touch it, lest ye die. 4 And the serpent said unto the woman, Ye shall not surely die: 5 For God doth know that in the day ye eat thereof,
then your eyes shall be opened, and ye shall be as gods, knowing good and evil. 6 And when the woman saw that the tree was good
for food, and that it was pleasant to the eyes, and a tree to be desired to make one wise, she took of the fruit thereof, and did eat, and
gave also unto her husband with her; and he did eat. 7 And the eyes of them both were opened, and they knew that they were naked;
and they sewed fig leaves together, and made themselves aprons. 8 And they heard the voice of the LORD God walking in the garden
in the cool of the day: and Adam and his wife hid themselves from the presence of the LORD God amongst the trees of the garden.
9 And the LORD God called unto Adam, and said unto him, Where art thou? 10 And he said, I heard thy voice in the garden, and I was
afraid, because I was naked; and I hid myself. 11 And he said, Who told thee that thou wast naked? Hast thou eaten of the tree, whereof
I commanded thee that thou shouldest not eat? 12 And the man said, The woman whom thou gavest to be with me, she gave me of the
tree, and I did eat. 13 And the LORD God said unto the woman, What is this that thou hast done? And the woman said, The serpent
beguiled me, and I did eat. 14 And the LORD God said unto the serpent, Because thou hast done this, thou art cursed above all cattle,
and above every beast of the field; upon thy belly shalt thou go, and dust shalt thou eat all the days of thy life: 15 And I will put enmity
between thee and the woman, and between thy seed and her seed; it shall bruise thy head, and thou shalt bruise his heel. 16 Unto the
woman he said, I will greatly multiply thy sorrow and thy conception; in sorrow thou shalt bring forth children; and thy desire shall
be to thy husband, and he shall rule over thee. 17 And unto Adam he said, Because thou hast hearkened unto the voice of thy wife, and
hast eaten of the tree, of which I commanded thee, saying, Thou shalt not eat of it: cursed is the ground for thy sake; in sorrow shalt
thou eat of it all the days of thy life; 18 Thorns also and thistles shall it bring forth to thee; and thou shalt eat the herb of the field; 19 In
the sweat of thy face shalt thou eat bread, till thou return unto the ground; for out of it wast thou taken: for dust thou art, and unto
dust shalt thou return.

Wis 2:24

24 Never-theless through envy of the devil came death into the world: and they that do hold of his side do find it.

ROMANS 5:13—Justified by faith (3:21–5:21), 56–58 CE

Theme	ROM
Law reveals sin, no law, no sin	**5:13** [13](For until the law sin was in the world: but sin is not imputed when there is no law. **4:15** [15]Because the law worketh wrath: for where no law is, there is no transgression.

ROMANS 5:14—Justified by faith (3:21–5:21), 56–58 CE

Theme	ROM	Paul
Death and salvation	**5:14** [14]Nevertheless death reigned from Adam to Moses, even over them that had not sinned after the similitude of Adam's transgression, who is the figure of him that was to come.	**1 Cor 15:21** [21]For since by man came death, by man came also the resurrection of the dead.

ROMANS 5:18—Justified by faith (3:21–5:21), 56–58 CE

Theme	ROM	Paul
Resurrection of Christ brings life	**5:18** [18]Therefore as by the offence of one judgment came upon all men to condemnation; even so by the righteousness of one the free gift came upon all men unto justification of life.	**1 Cor 15:21–22** [21]For since by man came death, by man came also the resurrection of the dead. [22]For as in Adam all die, even so in Christ shall all be made alive.

ROMANS 5:19—Justified by faith (3:21–5:21), 56–58 CE

Theme	ROM	Paul	Jewish Writings
Jesus' obedience brings righteousness	**5:19** [19]For as by one man's disobedience many were made sinners, so by the obedience of one shall many be made righteous.	**Phil 2:8–9** [8]And being found in fashion as a man, he humbled himself, and became obedient unto death, even the death of the cross. [9]Wherefore God also hath highly exalted him, and given him a name which is above every name:	**Is 53:11** [11]He shall see of the travail of his soul, and shall be satisfied: by his knowledge shall my righteous servant justify many; for he shall bear their iniquities.

ROMANS 5:20—Justified by faith (3:21–5:21), 56–58 CE

Theme	ROM	Paul
Grace greater than offence	**5:20** [20]Moreover the law entered, that the offence might abound. But where sin abounded, grace did much more abound: **4:15** [15]Because the law worketh wrath: for where no law is, there is no transgression. **7:7–8** [7]What shall we say then? Is the law sin? God forbid. Nay, I had not known sin, but by the law: for I had not known lust, except the law had said, Thou shalt not covet. [8]But sin, taking occasion by the commandment, wrought in me all manner of concupiscence. For without the law sin was dead.	**Gal 3:19** [19]Wherefore then serveth the law? It was added because of transgressions, till the seed should come to whom the promise was made; and it was ordained by angels in the hand of a mediator.

ROMANS 5:21—Justified by faith (3:21–5:21), 56–58 CE

Theme	ROM
Wages of sin is death; righteous live	**5:21** [21]That as sin hath reigned unto death, even so might grace reign through righteousness unto eternal life by Jesus Christ our Lord. **6:23** [23]For the wages of sin is death; but the gift of God is eternal life through Jesus Christ our Lord.

LIVING THE CHRISTIAN LIFE (6:1–8:39)

ROMANS 6:1—Living the Christian life (6:1–8:39), 56–58 CE

Theme	ROM
Does sin bring grace	**6:1** [1]What shall we say then? Shall we continue in sin, that grace may abound? **3:5–8** [5] But if our unrighteousness commend the righteousness of God, what shall we say? Is God unrighteous who taketh vengeance? (I speak as a man) [6] God forbid: for then how shall God judge the world? [7] For if the truth of God hath more abounded through my lie unto his glory; why yet am I also judged as a sinner? [8] And not rather, (as we be slanderously reported, and as some affirm that we say,) Let us do evil, that good may come? whose damnation is just.

ROMANS 6:2—Living the Christian life (6:1–8:39), 56–58 CE

Theme	ROM	NT
Suffering ceases sin	**6:2** [2]God forbid. How shall we, that are dead to sin, live any longer therein?	**1 Pet 4:1** [1]Forasmuch then as Christ hath suffered for us in the flesh, arm yourselves likewise with the same mind: for he that hath suffered in the flesh hath ceased from sin;

ROMANS 6:3–4—Living the Christian life (6:1–8:39), 56–58 CE

Theme	ROM	Mt	Mk	Lk
Baptism into Christ's death	**6:3–4** [3]Know ye not, that so many of us as were baptized into Jesus Christ were baptized into his death? [4]Therefore we are buried with him by baptism into death: that like as Christ was raised up from the dead by the glory of the Father, even so we also should walk in newness of life.	**16:24** [24]Then said Jesus unto his disciples, If any man will come after me, let him deny himself, and take up his cross, and follow me. **20:22–23** [22]But Jesus answered and said, Ye know not what ye ask. Are ye able to drink of the cup that I shall drink of, and to be baptized with the baptism that I am baptized with? They say unto him, We are able. [23]And he saith unto them, Ye shall drink indeed of my cup, and be baptized with the baptism that I am baptized with: but to sit on my right hand, and on my left, is not mine to give, but it shall be given to them for whom it is prepared of my Father.	**8:34** [34]And when he had called the people unto him with his disciples also, he said unto them, Whosoever will come after me, let him deny himself, and take up his cross, and follow me. **10:38** [38]But Jesus said unto them, Ye know not what ye ask: can ye drink of the cup that I drink of? and be baptized with the baptism that I am baptized with?	**9:23** [23]And he said to them all, If any man will come after me, let him deny himself, and take up his cross daily, and follow me. **12:50** [50]But I have a baptism to be baptized with; and how am I straitened till it be accomplished!

ROMANS 6:5—Living the Christian life (6:1–8:39), 56–58 CE

Theme	ROM	Paul
Likeness of death and resurrection	**6:5** [5]For if we have been planted together in the likeness of his death, we shall be also in the likeness of his resurrection:	**Phil 3:10–11** [10]That I may know him, and the power of his resurrection, and the fellowship of his sufferings, being made conformable unto his death; [11]If by any means I might attain unto the resurrection of the dead. **2 Tim 2:11 (Pseudo)** [11]It is a faithful saying: For if we be dead with him, we shall also live with him:

ROMANS 6:6—Living the Christian life (6:1–8:39), 56–58 CE

Theme	ROM	Paul
Old man crucified, sin destroyed	**6:6** [6]Knowing this, that our old man is crucified with him, that the body of sin might be destroyed, that henceforth we should not serve sin.	**Gal 5:24** [24]And they that are Christ's have crucified the flesh with the affections and lusts. **Gal 6:14** [14]But God forbid that I should glory, save in the cross of our Lord Jesus Christ, by whom the world is crucified unto me, and I unto the world. **Eph 4:22–23 (Pseudo)** [22]That ye put off concerning the former conversation the old man, which is corrupt according to the deceitful lusts; [23]And be renewed in the spirit of your mind;

Paul	NT	Other
Gal 2:19 [19]For I through the law am dead to the law, that I might live unto God. **Gal 3:27** [27]For as many of you as have been baptized into Christ have put on Christ. **Col 2:8–12** [8]Beware lest any man spoil you through philosophy and vain deceit, after the tradition of men, after the rudiments of the world, and not after Christ. [9]For in him dwelleth all the fulness of the Godhead bodily. [10]And ye are complete in him, which is the head of all principality and power: [11]In whom also ye are circumcised with the circumcision made without hands, in putting off the body of the sins of the flesh by the circumcision of Christ: [12]Buried with him in baptism, wherein also ye are risen with him through the faith of the operation of God, who hath raised him from the dead.	**1 Pet 3:21–22** [21]The like figure whereunto even baptism doth also now save us (not the putting away of the filth of the flesh, but the answer of a good conscience toward God,) by the resurrection of Jesus Christ: [22]Who is gone into heaven, and is on the right hand of God; angels and authorities and powers being made subject unto him.	**Q-Quelle** Divisions in Households: Rom 6:3-4/[1 Cor 10:16]/Gal 2:18-19/[Phil 3:7-11]/[Mt 10:34-36]/Lk 12:49-53 (QS 43 [Thom 16])

ROMANS 6:8—Living the Christian life (6:1–8:39), 56–58 CE

Theme	ROM	Paul	Other
Dead with Christ, live with Him	**6:8** [8]Now if we be dead with Christ, we believe that we shall also live with him:	**1 Thes 4:17** [17]Then we which are alive and remain shall be caught up together with them in the clouds, to meet the Lord in the air: and so shall we ever be with the Lord.	**Q-Quelle** Divisions in Households: Rom 6:8/[1 Cor 10:16]/[Gal 2:18-19]/[Mt 10:34-36]/[Lk 12:49-53 (QS 43 [Thom 16])]

ROMANS 6:9—Living the Christian life (6:1–8:39), 56–58 CE

Theme	ROM	Lk	Paul	NT
Being raised, ends death	**6:9** [9]Knowing that Christ being raised from the dead dieth no more; death hath no more dominion over him.	**Acts 13:34** [34]And as concerning that he raised him up from the dead, now no more to return to corruption, he said on this wise, I will give you the sure mercies of David.	**1 Cor 15:26** [26]The last enemy that shall be destroyed is death. **2 Tim 1:10 (Pseudo)** [10]But is now made manifest by the appearing of our Saviour Jesus Christ, who hath abolished death, and hath brought life and immortality to light through the gospel:	**Rev 1:18** [18]I am he that liveth, and was dead; and, behold, I am alive for evermore, Amen; and have the keys of hell and of death.

ROMANS 6:10—Living the Christian life (6:1–8:39), 56–58 CE

Theme	ROM	NT
Sacrifice ends condemnation	**6:10** [10]For in that he died, he died unto sin once: but in that he liveth, he liveth unto God.	**Heb 9:26–28** [26]For then must he often have suffered since the foundation of the world: but now once in the end of the world hath he appeared to put away sin by the sacrifice of himself. [27]And as it is appointed unto men once to die, but after this the judgment: [28]So Christ was once offered to bear the sins of many; and unto them that look for him shall he appear the second time without sin unto salvation. **1 Pet 3:18** [18]For Christ also hath once suffered for sins, the just for the unjust, that he might bring us to God, being put to death in the flesh, but quickened by the Spirit:

ROMANS 6:11—Living the Christian life (6:1–8:39), 56–58 CE

Theme	ROM	Paul	NT
Be alive in Christ	**6:11** [11]Likewise reckon ye also yourselves to be dead indeed unto sin, but alive unto God through Jesus Christ our Lord.	**2 Cor 5:15** [15]And that he died for all, that they which live should not henceforth live unto themselves, but unto him which died for them, and rose again.	**1 Pet 2:24** [24]Who his own self bare our sins in his own body on the tree, that we, being dead to sins, should live unto righteousness: by whose stripes ye were healed.

ROMANS 6:12—Living the Christian life (6:1–8:39), 56–58 CE

Theme	ROM	Jewish Writings
Turn from sin	**6:12** [12]Let not sin therefore reign in your mortal body, that ye should obey it in the lusts thereof.	**Gen 4:7** [7]If thou doest well, shalt thou not be accepted? and if thou doest not well, sin lieth at the door. And unto thee shall be his desire, and thou shalt rule over him.

ROMANS 6:13—Living the Christian life (6:1–8:39), 56–58 CE

Theme	ROM	Paul
Keep members from sin	**6:13** [13]Neither yield ye your members as instruments of unrighteousness unto sin: but yield yourselves unto God, as those that are alive from the dead, and your members as instruments of righteousness unto God. **12:1** [1]I beseech you therefore, brethren, by the mercies of God, that ye present your bodies a living sacrifice, holy, acceptable unto God, which is your reasonable service.	**Eph 2:5 (Pseudo)** [5]Even when we were dead in sins, hath quickened us together with Christ (by grace ye are saved) **Eph 5:14 (Pseudo)** [14]Wherefore he saith, Awake thou that sleepest, and arise from the dead, and Christ shall give thee light. **Col 3:5** [5]Mortify therefore your members which are upon the earth; fornication, uncleanness, inordinate affection, evil concupiscence, and covetousness, which is idolatry:

ROMANS 6:14—Living the Christian life (6:1–8:39), 56–58 CE

Theme	ROM	Paul	Jn
No sin under grace	**6:14** [14]For sin shall not have dominion over you: for ye are not under the law, but under grace.	**Gal 5:18** [18]But if ye be led of the Spirit, ye are not under the law.	**1 Jn 3:6** [6]Whosoever abideth in him sinneth not: whosoever sinneth hath not seen him, neither known him.

ROMANS 6:15—Living the Christian life (6:1–8:39), 56–58 CE

Theme	ROM
Shall we sin?	**6:15** [15]What then? shall we sin, because we are not under the law, but under grace? God forbid. **5:17, 21** [17]For if by one man's offence death reigned by one; much more they which receive abundance of grace and of the gift of righteousness shall reign in life by one, Jesus Christ.). . . [21]That as sin hath reigned unto death, even so might grace reign through righteousness unto eternal life by Jesus Christ our Lord.

ROMANS 6:16–18—Living the Christian life (6:1–8:39), 56–58 CE

Theme	ROM	Jn
Sin to death; obedience to righteous	**6:16–18** [16]Know ye not, that to whom ye yield yourselves servants to obey, his servants ye are to whom ye obey; whether of sin unto death, or of obedience unto righteousness? [17]But God be thanked, that ye were the servants of sin, but ye have obeyed from the heart that form of doctrine which was delivered you. [18]Being then made free from sin, ye became the servants of righteousness.	**8:32–36** [32]And ye shall know the truth, and the truth shall make you free. [33]They answered him, We be Abraham's seed, and were never in bondage to any man: how sayest thou, Ye shall be made free? [34]Jesus answered them, Verily, verily, I say unto you, Whosoever committeth sin is the servant of sin. [35]And the servant abideth not in the house for ever: but the Son abideth ever. [36]If the Son therefore shall make you free, ye shall be free indeed.

ROMANS 6:16—Living the Christian life (6:1–8:39), 56–58 CE

Theme	ROM	Jn	NT
Obey death of righteousness	**6:16** [16]Know ye not, that to whom ye yield yourselves servants to obey, his servants ye are to whom ye obey; whether of sin unto death, or of obedience unto righteousness?	**8:31–34** [31]Then said Jesus to those Jews which believed on him, If ye continue in my word, then are ye my disciples indeed; [32]And ye shall know the truth, and the truth shall make you free. [33]They answered him, We be Abraham's seed, and were never in bondage to any man: how sayest thou, Ye shall be made free? [34]Jesus answered them, Verily, verily, I say unto you, Whosoever committeth sin is the servant of sin.	**2 Pet 2:19** [19]While they promise them liberty, they themselves are the servants of corruption: for of whom a man is overcome, of the same is he brought in bondage.

ROMANS 6:20—Living the Christian life (6:1–8:39), 56–58 CE

Theme	ROM	Jn
Servant of sin or right	**6:20** [20]For when ye were the servants of sin, ye were free from righteousness.	**8:34** [34]Jesus answered them, Verily, verily, I say unto you, Whosoever committeth sin is the servant of sin.

ROMANS 6:21—Living the Christian life (6:1–8:39), 56–58 CE

Theme	ROM	Jewish Writings
Fruit versus shame	**6:21** [21]What fruit had ye then in those things whereof ye are now ashamed? for the end of those things is death. **8:6** [6]For to be carnally minded is death; but to be spiritually minded is life and peace. **8:13** [13]For if ye live after the flesh, ye shall die: but if ye through the Spirit do mortify the deeds of the body, ye shall live.	**Prov 12:28** [28]In the way of righteousness is life; and in the pathway thereof there is no death. **Ezek 16:61** [61]Then thou shalt remember thy ways, and be ashamed, when thou shalt receive thy sisters, thine elder and thy younger: and I will give them unto thee for daughters, but not by thy covenant. **Ezek 16:63** [63]That thou mayest remember, and be confounded, and never open thy mouth any more because of thy shame, when I am pacified toward thee for all that thou hast done, saith the Lord GOD.

ROMANS 6:22—Living the Christian life (6:1–8:39), 56–58 CE

Theme	ROM	NT
Fruit unto holiness	**6:22** [22]But now being made free from sin, and become servants to God, ye have your fruit unto holiness, and the end everlasting life.	**1 Pet 1:9** [9]Receiving the end of your faith, even the salvation of your souls.

ROMANS 6:23—Living the Christian life (6:1–8:39), 56–58 CE

Theme	ROM	Paul	NT	Jewish Writings
Wages of sin is death	**6:23** [23]For the wages of sin is death; but the gift of God is eternal life through Jesus Christ our Lord.	**Gal 6:7–9** [7]Be not deceived; God is not mocked: for whatsoever a man soweth, that shall he also reap. [8]For he that soweth to his flesh shall of the flesh reap corruption; but he that soweth to the Spirit shall of the Spirit reap life everlasting. [9]And let us not be weary in well doing: for in due season we shall reap, if we faint not.	**Jas 1:15** [15]Then when lust hath conceived, it bringeth forth sin: and sin, when it is finished, bringeth forth death.	**Gen 2:17** [17]But of the tree of the knowledge of good and evil, thou shalt not eat of it: for in the day that thou eatest thereof thou shalt surely die.

ROMANS 7:1–4—Living the Christian life (6:1–8:39), 56–58 CE

Theme	ROM	Mt	Mk	Lk
Marriage example for church and Christ	**7:1–4** [1]Know ye not, brethren, (for I speak to them that know the law,) how that the law hath dominion over a man as long as he liveth? [2]For the woman which hath an husband is bound by the law to her husband so long as he liveth; but if the husband be dead, she is loosed from the law of her husband. [3]So then if, while her husband liveth, she be married to another man, she shall be called an adulteress: but if her husband be dead, she is free from that law; so that she is no adulteress, though she be married to another man. [4]Wherefore, my brethren, ye also are become dead to the law by the body of Christ; that ye should be married to another, even to him who is raised from the dead, that we should bring forth fruit unto God.	**2:1–4** [1]Now when Jesus was born in Bethlehem of Judaea in the days of Herod the king, behold, there came wise men from the east to Jerusalem, [2]Saying, Where is he that is born King of the Jews? for we have seen his star in the east, and are come to worship him. [3]When Herod the king had heard these things, he was troubled, and all Jerusalem with him. [4]And when he had gathered all the chief priests and scribes of the people together, he demanded of them where Christ should be born. **9:15** [15]And Jesus said unto them, Can the children of the bridechamber mourn, as long as the bridegroom is with them? but the days will come, when the bridegroom shall be taken from them, and then shall they fast. **25:1–13** [1]Then shall the kingdom of heaven be likened unto ten virgins, which took their lamps, and went forth to meet the bridegroom. [2]And five of them were wise, and five were foolish. [3]They that were foolish took their lamps, and took no oil with them: [4]But the wise took oil in their vessels with their lamps. [5]While the bridegroom tarried, they all slumbered and slept. [6]And at midnight there was a cry made, Behold, the bridegroom cometh; go ye out to meet him. [7]Then all those virgins arose, and trimmed their lamps. [8]And the foolish said unto the wise, Give us of your oil; for our lamps are gone out. [9]But the wise answered, saying, Not so; lest there be not enough for us and you: but go ye rather to them that sell, and buy for yourselves. [10]And while they went to buy, the bridegroom came; and they that were ready went in with him to the marriage: and the door was shut. [11]Afterward came also the other virgins, saying, Lord, Lord, open to us. [12]But he answered and said, Verily I say unto you, I know you not. [13]Watch therefore, for ye know neither the day nor the hour wherein the Son of man cometh.	**2:1** [1]And again he entered into Capernaum after some days; and it was noised that he was in the house.	**5:34** [34]And he said unto them, Can ye make the children of the bridechamber fast, while the bridegroom is with them? **12:36** [36]And ye yourselves like unto men that wait for their lord, when he will return from the wedding; that when he cometh and knocketh, they may open unto him immediately.

ROMANS 7:2—Living the Christian life (6:1–8:39), 56–58 CE

Theme	ROM	Paul
Example of husband and wife	**7:2** [2]For the woman which hath an husband is bound by the law to her husband so long as he liveth; but if the husband be dead, she is loosed from the law of her husband.	**1 Cor 7:39** [39]The wife is bound by the law as long as her husband liveth; but if her husband be dead, she is at liberty to be married to whom she will; only in the Lord.

Paul	Jewish Writings	Other
1 Cor 7:39	**Gen 2**	**Q-Quelle**
[39]The wife is bound by the law as long as her husband liveth; but if her husband be dead, she is at liberty to be married to whom she will; only in the Lord. **Eph 5:24–33 (Pseudo)** [24]Therefore as the church is subject unto Christ, so let the wives be to their own husbands in every thing. [25]Husbands, love your wives, even as Christ also loved the church, and gave himself for it; [26]That he might sanctify and cleanse it with the washing of water by the word, [27]That he might present it to himself a glorious church, not having spot, or wrinkle, or any such thing; but that it should be holy and without blemish. [28]So ought men to love their wives as their own bodies. He that loveth his wife loveth himself. [29]For no man ever yet hated his own flesh; but nourisheth and cherisheth it, even as the Lord the church: [30]For we are members of his body, of his flesh, and of his bones. [31]For this cause shall a man leave his father and mother, and shall be joined unto his wife, and they two shall be one flesh. [32]This is a great mystery: but I speak concerning Christ and the church. [33]Nevertheless let every one of you in particular so love his wife even as himself; and the wife see that she reverence her husband.	[1]Thus the heavens and the earth were finished, and all the host of them. [2]And on the seventh day God ended his work which he had made; and he rested on the seventh day from all his work which he had made. [3]And God blessed the seventh day, and sanctified it: because that in it he had rested from all his work which God created and made. [4]These are the generations of the heavens and of the earth when they were created, in the day that the LORD God made the earth and the heavens, [5]And every plant of the field before it was in the earth, and every herb of the field before it grew: for the LORD God had not caused it to rain upon the earth, and there was not a man to till the ground. [6]But there went up a mist from the earth, and watered the whole face of the ground. [7]And the LORD God formed man of the dust of the ground, and breathed into his nostrils the breath of life; and man became a living soul. [8]And the LORD God planted a garden eastward in Eden; and there he put the man whom he had formed. [9]And out of the ground made the LORD God to grow every tree that is pleasant to the sight, and good for food; the tree of life also in the midst of the garden, and the tree of knowledge of good and evil. [10]And a river went out of Eden to water the garden; and from thence it was parted, and became into four heads. [11]The name of the first is Pison: that is it which compasseth the whole land of Havilah, where there is gold; [12]And the gold of that land is good: there is bdellium and the onyx stone. [13]And the name of the second river is Gihon: the same is it that compasseth the whole land of Ethiopia. [14]And the name of the third river is Hiddekel: that is it which goeth toward the east of Assyria. And the fourth river is Euphrates. [15]And the LORD God took the man, and put him into the garden of Eden to dress it and to keep it. [16]And the LORD God commanded the man, saying, Of every tree of the garden thou mayest freely eat: [17]But of the tree of the knowledge of good and evil, thou shalt not eat of it: for in the day that thou eatest thereof thou shalt surely die. [18]And the LORD God said, It is not good that the man should be alone; I will make him an help meet for him. [19]And out of the ground the LORD God formed every beast of the field, and every fowl of the air; and brought them unto Adam to see what he would call them: and whatsoever Adam called every living creature, that was the name thereof. [20]And Adam gave names to all cattle, and to the fowl of the air, and to every beast of the field; but for Adam there was not found an help meet for him. [21]And the LORD God caused a deep sleep to fall upon Adam, and he slept: and he took one of his ribs, and closed up the flesh instead thereof; [22]And the rib, which the LORD God had taken from man, made he a woman, and brought her unto the man. [23]And Adam said, This is now bone of my bones, and flesh of my flesh: she shall be called Woman, because she was taken out of Man. [24]Therefore shall a man leave his father and his mother, and shall cleave unto his wife: and they shall be one flesh. [25]And they were both naked, the man and his wife, and were not ashamed.	Watchful and faithful: Rom 7:1-4/Eph 5:24-33/[Mt 24:42-51]/Lk 12:35-48 (QS 41 [Thom 21:3, 103], QS 42)

ROMANS 7:5—Living the Christian life (6:1–8:39), 56–58 CE

Theme	ROM
Death in fleshly ways	**7:5** [5]For when we were in the flesh, the motions of sins, which were by the law, did work in our members to bring forth fruit unto death. **6:21** [21]What fruit had ye then in those things whereof ye are now ashamed? for the end of those things is death. **8:6, 13** [6]For to be carnally minded is death; but to be spiritually minded is life and peace. . . . [13]For if ye live after the flesh, ye shall die: but if ye through the Spirit do mortify the deeds of the body, ye shall live.

ROMANS 7:6—Living the Christian life (6:1–8:39), 56–58 CE

Theme	ROM	Paul
Delivered from law	**7:6** [6]But now we are delivered from the law, that being dead wherein we were held; that we should serve in newness of spirit, and not in the oldness of the letter. **8:2** [2]For the law of the Spirit of life in Christ Jesus hath made me free from the law of sin and death.	**2 Cor 3:6** [6]Who also hath made us able ministers of the new testament; not of the letter, but of the spirit: for the letter killeth, but the spirit giveth life.

ROMANS 7:7—Living the Christian life (6:1–8:39), 56–58 CE

Theme	ROM	Jewish Writings
Is law sin?	**7:7** [7]What shall we say then? Is the law sin? God forbid. Nay, I had not known sin, but by the law: for I had not known lust, except the law had said, Thou shalt not covet. **3:20** [20]Therefore by the deeds of the law there shall no flesh be justified in his sight: for by the law is the knowledge of sin.	**Ex 20:17** [17]Thou shalt not covet thy neighbour's house, thou shalt not covet thy neighbour's wife, nor his manservant, nor his maidservant, nor his ox, nor his ass, nor any thing that is thy neighbour's. **Dt 5:21** [21]Neither shalt thou desire thy neighbour's wife, neither shalt thou covet thy neighbour's house, his field, or his manservant, or his maidservant, his ox, or his ass, or any thing that is thy neighbour's.

ROMANS 7:8—Living the Christian life (6:1–8:39), 56–58 CE

Theme	ROM	Paul
Law wrought sin	**7:8** [8]But sin, taking occasion by the commandment, wrought in me all manner of concupiscence. For without the law sin was dead. **5:13, 20** [13](For until the law sin was in the world: but sin is not imputed when there is no law. . . . [20]Moreover the law entered, that the offence might abound. But where sin abounded, grace did much more abound:	**1 Cor 4:15** [15]For though ye have ten thousand instructors in Christ, yet have ye not many fathers: for in Christ Jesus I have begotten you through the gospel. **1 Cor 15:56** [56]The sting of death is sin; and the strength of sin is the law.

ROMANS 7:10—Living the Christian life (6:1–8:39), 56–58 CE

Theme	ROM	Jewish Writings
Law revealed sin	**7:10** [10]And the commandment, which was ordained to life, I found to be unto death.	**Lev 18:5** [5]Ye shall therefore keep my statutes, and my judgments: which if a man do, he shall live in them: I am the LORD.

ROMANS 7:11—Living the Christian life (6:1–8:39), 56–58 CE

Theme	ROM	NT	Jewish Writings
Blinded by sin	**7:11** [11]For sin, taking occasion by the commandment, deceived me, and by it slew me.	**Heb 3:13** [13]But exhort one another daily, while it is called Today; lest any of you be hardened through the deceitfulness of sin.	**Gen 3:13** [13]And the LORD God said unto the woman, What is this that thou hast done? And the woman said, The serpent beguiled me, and I did eat.

ROMANS 7:12—Living the Christian life (6:1–8:39), 56–58 CE

Theme	ROM	Mt	Lk	Paul
Jesus fulfills law **Living in love fulfills law**	**7:12** [12]Wherefore the law is holy, and the commandment holy, and just, and good. **8:4** [4]That the righteousness of the law might be fulfilled in us, who walk not after the flesh, but after the Spirit. **12:8–10** [8]Or he that exhorteth, on exhortation: he that giveth, let him do it with simplicity; he that ruleth, with diligence; he that showeth mercy, with cheerfulness. [9]Let love be without dissimulation. Abhor that which is evil; cleave to that which is good. [10]Be kindly affectioned one to another with brotherly love; in honour preferring one another;	**5:17–20** [17]Think not that I am come to destroy the law, or the prophets: I am not come to destroy, but to fulfil. [18]For verily I say unto you, Till heaven and earth pass, one jot or one tittle shall in no wise pass from the law, till all be fulfilled. [19]Whosoever therefore shall break one of these least commandments, and shall teach men so, he shall be called the least in the kingdom of heaven: but whosoever shall do and teach them, the same shall be called great in the kingdom of heaven. [20]For I say unto you, That except your righteousness shall exceed the righteousness of the scribes and Pharisees, ye shall in no case enter into the kingdom of heaven.	**24:44** [44]And he said unto them, These are the words which I spake unto you, while I was yet with you, that all things must be fulfilled, which were written in the law of Moses, and in the prophets, and in the psalms, concerning me.	**2 Cor 3** [1]Do we begin again to commend ourselves? or need we, as some others, epistles of commendation to you, or letters of commendation from you? [2]Ye are our epistle written in our hearts, known and read of all men: [3]Forasmuch as ye are manifestly declared to be the epistle of Christ ministered by us, written not with ink, but with the Spirit of the living God; not in tables of stone, but in fleshy tables of the heart. [4]And such trust have we through Christ to God-ward: [5]Not that we are sufficient of ourselves to think any thing as of ourselves; but our sufficiency is of God; [6]Who also hath made us able ministers of the new testament; not of the letter, but of the spirit: for the letter killeth, but the spirit giveth life. [7]But if the ministration of death, written and engraven in stones, was glorious, so that the children of Israel could not stedfastly behold the face of Moses for the glory of his countenance; which glory was to be done away: [8]How shall not the ministration of the spirit be rather glorious? [9]For if the ministration of condemnation be glory, much more doth the ministration of righteousness exceed in glory. [10]For even that which was made glorious had no glory in this respect, by reason of the glory that excelleth. [11]For if that which is done away was glorious, much more that which remaineth is glorious. [12]Seeing then that we have such hope, we use great plainness of speech: [13]And not as Moses, which put a veil over his face, that the children of Israel could not stedfastly look to the end of that which is abolished: [14]But their minds were blinded: for until this day remaineth the same veil untaken away in the reading of the old testament; which veil is done away in Christ. [15]But even unto this day, when Moses is read, the veil is upon their heart. [16]Nevertheless when it shall turn to the Lord, the veil shall be taken away. [17]Now the Lord is that Spirit: and where the Spirit of the Lord is, there is liberty. [18]But we all, with open face beholding as in a glass the glory of the Lord, are changed into the same image from glory to glory, even as by the Spirit of the Lord. **2 Cor 5:14** [14]For the love of Christ constraineth us; because we thus judge, that if one died for all, then were all dead: **1 Tim 1:8 (Pseudo)** [8]But we know that the law is good, if a man use it lawfully;

Jewish Writings	Other
Jer 31	**Q-Quelle**
[1]At the same time, saith the LORD, will I be the God of all the families of Israel, and they shall be my people. [2]Thus saith the LORD, The people which were left of the sword found grace in the wilderness; even Israel, when I went to cause him to rest. [3]The LORD hath appeared of old unto me, saying, Yea, I have loved thee with an everlasting love: therefore with lovingkindness have I drawn thee. [4]Again I will build thee, and thou shalt be built, O virgin of Israel: thou shalt again be adorned with thy tabrets, and shalt go forth in the dances of them that make merry. [5]Thou shalt yet plant vines upon the mountains of Samaria: the planters shall plant, and shall eat them as common things. [6]For there shall be a day, that the watchmen upon the mount Ephraim shall cry, Arise ye, and let us go up to Zion unto the LORD our God. [7]For thus saith the LORD; Sing with gladness for Jacob, and shout among the chief of the nations: publish ye, praise ye, and say, O LORD, save thy people, the remnant of Israel. [8]Behold, I will bring them from the north country, and gather them from the coasts of the earth, and with them the blind and the lame, the woman with child and her that travaileth with child together: a great company shall return thither. [9]They shall come with weeping, and with supplications will I lead them: I will cause them to walk by the rivers of waters in a straight way, wherein they shall not stumble: for I am a father to Israel, and Ephraim is my firstborn. [10]Hear the word of the LORD, O ye nations, and declare it in the isles afar off, and say, He that scattered Israel will gather him, and keep him, as a shepherd doth his flock. [11]For the LORD hath redeemed Jacob, and ransomed him from the hand of him that was stronger than he. [12]Therefore they shall come and sing in the height of Zion, and shall flow together to the goodness of the LORD, for wheat, and for wine, and for oil, and for the young of the flock and of the herd: and their soul shall be as a watered garden; and they shall not sorrow any more at all. [13]Then shall the virgin rejoice in the dance, both young men and old together: for I will turn their mourning into joy, and will comfort them, and make them rejoice from their sorrow. [14]And I will satiate the soul of the priests with fatness, and my people shall be satisfied with my goodness, saith the LORD. [15]Thus saith the LORD; A voice was heard in Ramah, lamentation, and bitter weeping; Rahel weeping for her children refused to be comforted for her children, because they were not. [16]Thus saith the LORD; Refrain thy voice from weeping, and thine eyes from tears: for thy work shall be rewarded, saith the LORD; and they shall come again from the land of the enemy. [17]And there is hope in thine end, saith the LORD, that thy children shall come again to their own border. [18]I have surely heard Ephraim bemoaning himself thus; Thou hast chastised me, and I was chastised, as a bullock unaccustomed to the yoke: turn thou me, and I shall be turned; for thou art the LORD my God. [19]Surely after that I was turned, I repented; and after that I was instructed, I smote upon my thigh: I was ashamed, yea, even confounded, because I did bear the reproach of my youth. [20]Is Ephraim my dear son? is he a pleasant child? for since I spake against him, I do earnestly remember him still: therefore my bowels are troubled for him; I will surely have mercy upon him, saith the LORD. [21]Set thee up waymarks, make thee high heaps: set thine heart toward the highway, even the way which thou wentest: turn again, O virgin of Israel, turn again to these thy cities. [22]How long wilt thou go about, O thou backsliding daughter? for the LORD hath created a new thing in the earth, A woman shall compass a man. [23]Thus saith the LORD of hosts, the God of Israel; As yet they shall use this speech in the land of Judah and in the cities thereof, when I shall bring again their captivity; The LORD bless thee, O habitation of justice, and mountain of holiness. [24]And there shall dwell in Judah itself, and in all the cities thereof together, husbandmen, and they that go forth with flocks. [25]For I have satiated the weary soul, and I have replenished every sorrowful soul. [26]Upon this I awaked, and beheld; and my sleep was sweet unto me. [27]Behold, the days come, saith the LORD, that I will sow the house of Israel and the house of Judah with the seed of man, and with the seed of beast. [28]And it shall come to pass, that like as I have watched over them, to pluck up, and to break down, and to throw down, and to destroy, and to afflict; so will I watch over them, to build, and to plant, saith the LORD. [29]In those days they shall say no more, The fathers have eaten a sour grape, and the children's teeth are set on edge. [30]But every one shall die for his own iniquity: every man that eateth the sour grape, his teeth shall be set on edge. [31]Behold, the days come, saith the LORD, that I will make a new covenant with the house of Israel, and with the house of Judah: [32]Not according to the covenant that I made with their fathers in the day that I took them by the hand to bring them out of the land of Egypt; which my covenant they brake, although I was an husband unto them, saith the LORD: [33]But this shall be the covenant that I will make with the house of Israel; After those days, saith the LORD, I will put my law in their inward parts, and write it in their hearts; and will be their God, and they shall be my people. [34]And they shall teach no more every man his neighbour, and every man his brother, saying, Know the LORD: for they shall all know me, from the least of them unto the greatest of them, saith the LORD: for I will forgive their iniquity, and I will remember their sin no more. [35]Thus saith the LORD, which giveth the sun for a light by day, and the ordinances of the moon and of the stars for a light by night, which divideth the sea when the waves thereof roar; The LORD of hosts is his name: [36]If those ordinances depart from before me, saith the LORD, then the seed of Israel also shall cease from being a nation before me for ever. [37]Thus saith the LORD; If heaven above can be measured, and the foundations of the earth searched out beneath, I will also cast off all the seed of Israel for all that they have done, saith the LORD. [38]Behold, the days come, saith the LORD, that the city shall be built to the LORD from the tower of Hananeel unto the gate of the corner. [39]And the measuring line shall yet go forth over against it upon the hill Gareb, and shall compass about to Goath. [40]And the whole valley of the dead bodies, and of the ashes, and all the fields unto the brook of Kidron, unto the corner of the horse gate toward the east, shall be holy unto the LORD; it shall not be plucked up, nor thrown down any more for ever.	Concerning the Law: Rom 7:12/Mt 5:18, [Mt 11:12-13]/ [Lk 16:16-17 (QS 56)]

ROMANS 7:13—Living the Christian life (6:1–8:39), 56–58 CE

Theme	ROM
Law worketh death	**7:13** [13]Was then that which is good made death unto me? God forbid. But sin, that it might appear sin, working death in me by that which is good; that sin by the commandment might become exceeding sinful. **4:15** [15]Because the law worketh wrath: for where no law is, there is no transgression. **5:20** [20]Moreover the law entered, that the offence might abound. But where sin abounded, grace did much more abound:

ROMANS 7:14—Living the Christian life (6:1–8:39), 56–58 CE

Theme	ROM	Jewish Writings
Law is spiritual, flesh is sold to sin	**7:14** [14]For we know that the law is spiritual: but I am carnal, sold under sin. **8:7–8** [7]Because the carnal mind is enmity against God: for it is not subject to the law of God, neither indeed can be. [8]So then they that are in the flesh cannot please God.	**Ps 51:7** [7]Purge me with hyssop, and I shall be clean: wash me, and I shall be whiter than snow.

ROMANS 7:18—Living the Christian life (6:1–8:39), 56–58 CE

Theme	ROM	Paul	Jewish Writings
Flesh has no good thing	**7:18** [18]For I know that in me (that is, in my flesh,) dwelleth no good thing: for to will is present with me; but how to perform that which is good I find not.	**Phil 2:13** [13]For it is God which worketh in you both to will and to do of his good pleasure.	**Gen 6:5** [5]And God saw that the wickedness of man was great in the earth, and that every imagination of the thoughts of his heart was only evil continually.

ROMANS 7:23—Living the Christian life (6:1–8:39), 56–58 CE

Theme	ROM	Paul	NT
Law in body wars with the mind	**7:23** [23]But I see another law in my members, warring against the law of my mind, and bringing me into captivity to the law of sin which is in my members.	**Gal 5:17** [17]For the flesh lusteth against the Spirit, and the Spirit against the flesh: and these are contrary the one to the other: so that ye cannot do the things that ye would.	**1 Pet 2:11** [11]Dearly beloved, I beseech you as strangers and pilgrims, abstain from fleshly lusts, which war against the soul;

ROMANS 7:25—Living the Christian life (6:1–8:39), 56–58 CE

Theme	ROM	Paul
Mind serves God	**7:25** [25]I thank God through Jesus Christ our Lord. So then with the mind I myself serve the law of God; but with the flesh the law of sin.	**1 Cor 15:57** [57]But thanks be to God, which giveth us the victory through our Lord Jesus Christ.

ROMANS 8:2—Living the Christian life (6:1–8:39), 56–58 CE

Theme	ROM
Freedom in sonship	**8:2** [2]For the law of the Spirit of life in Christ Jesus hath made me free from the law of sin and death. **Rom 6** [1]What shall we say then? Shall we continue in sin, that grace may abound? [2]God forbid. How shall we, that are dead to sin, live any longer therein? [3]Know ye not, that so many of us as were baptized into Jesus Christ were baptized into his death? [4]Therefore we are buried with him by baptism into death: that like as Christ was raised up from the dead by the glory of the Father, even so we also should walk in newness of life. [5]For if we have been planted together in the likeness of his death, we shall be also in the likeness of his resurrection: [6]Knowing this, that our old man is crucified with him, that the body of sin might be destroyed, that henceforth we should not serve sin. [7]For he that is dead is freed from sin. [8]Now if we be dead with Christ, we believe that we shall also live with him: [9]Knowing that Christ being raised from the dead dieth no more; death hath no more dominion over him. [10]For in that he died, he died unto sin once: but in that he liveth, he liveth unto God. [11]Likewise reckon ye also yourselves to be dead indeed unto sin, but alive unto God through Jesus Christ our Lord. [12]Let not sin therefore reign in your mortal body, that ye should obey it in the lusts thereof. [13]Neither yield ye your members as instruments of unrighteousness unto sin: but yield yourselves unto God, as those that are alive from the dead, and your members as instruments of righteousness unto God. [14]For sin shall not have dominion over you: for ye are not under the law, but under grace. [15]What then? shall we sin, because we are not under the law, but under grace? God forbid. [16]Know ye not, that to whom ye yield yourselves servants to obey, his servants ye are to whom ye obey; whether of sin unto death, or of obedience unto righteousness? [17]But God be thanked, that ye were the servants of sin, but ye have obeyed from the heart that form of doctrine which was delivered you. [18]Being then made free from sin, ye became the servants of righteousness. [19]I speak after the manner of men because of the infirmity of your flesh: for as ye have yielded your members servants to uncleanness and to iniquity unto iniquity; even so now yield your members servants to righteousness unto holiness. [20]For when ye were the servants of sin, ye were free from righteousness. [21]What fruit had ye then in those things whereof ye are now ashamed? for the end of those things is death. [22]But now being made free from sin, and become servants to God, ye have your fruit unto holiness, and the end everlasting life. [23]For the wages of sin is death; but the gift of God is eternal life through Jesus Christ our Lord. **Rom 7** [1]Know ye not, brethren, (for I speak to them that know the law,) how that the law hath dominion over a man as long as he liveth? [2]For the woman which hath an husband is bound by the law to her husband so long as he liveth; but if the husband be dead, she is loosed from the law of her husband. [3]So then if, while her husband liveth, she be married to another man, she shall be called an adulteress: but if her husband be dead, she is free from that law; so that she is no adulteress, though she be married to another man. [4]Wherefore, my brethren, ye also are become dead to the law by the body of Christ; that ye should be married to another, even to him who is raised from the dead, that we should bring forth fruit unto God. [5]For when we were in the flesh, the motions of sins, which were by the law, did work in our members to bring forth fruit unto death. [6]But now we are delivered from the law, that being dead wherein we were held; that we should serve in newness of spirit, and not in the oldness of the letter. [7]What shall we say then? Is the law sin? God forbid. Nay, I had not known sin, but by the law: for I had not known lust, except the law had said, Thou shalt not covet. [8]But sin, taking occasion by the commandment, wrought in me all manner of concupiscence. For without the law sin was dead. [9]For I was alive without the law once: but when the commandment came, sin revived, and I died. [10]And the commandment, which was ordained to life, I found to be unto death. [11]For sin, taking occasion by the commandment, deceived me, and by it slew me. [12]Wherefore the law is holy, and the commandment holy, and just, and good. [13]Was then that which is good made death unto me? God forbid. But sin, that it might appear sin, working death in me by that which is good; that sin by the commandment might become exceeding sinful. [14]For we know that the law is spiritual: but I am carnal, sold under sin. [15]For that which I do I allow not: for what I would, that do I not; but what I hate, that do I. [16]If then I do that which I would not, I consent unto the law that it is good. [17]Now then it is no more I that do it, but sin that dwelleth in me. [18]For I know that in me (that is, in my flesh,) dwelleth no good thing: for to will is present with me; but how to perform that which is good I find not. [19]For the good that I would I do not: but the evil which I would not, that I do. [20]Now if I do that I would not, it is no more I that do it, but sin that dwelleth in me. [21]I find then a law, that, when I would do good, evil is present with me. [22]For I delight in the law of God after the inward man: **[23]But I see another law in my members, warring against the law of my mind, and bringing me into captivity to the law of sin which is in my members. [24]O wretched man that I am! who shall deliver me from the body of this death? [25]I thank God through Jesus Christ our Lord. So then with the mind I myself serve the law of God; but with the flesh the law of sin.**

Paul
2 Cor 3:17 [17]Now the Lord is that Spirit: and where the Spirit of the Lord is, there is liberty. **Gal 3:21–26** [21]Is the law then against the promises of God? God forbid: for if there had been a law given which could have given life, verily righteousness should have been by the law. [22]But the scripture hath concluded all under sin, that the promise by faith of Jesus Christ might be given to them that believe. [23]But before faith came, we were kept under the law, shut up unto the faith which should afterwards be revealed. [24]Wherefore the law was our schoolmaster to bring us unto Christ, that we might be justified by faith. [25]But after that faith is come, we are no longer under a schoolmaster. [26]For ye are all the children of God by faith in Christ Jesus. **Gal 4:5** [5]To redeem them that were under the law, that we might receive the adoption of sons.

ROMANS 8:3—Living the Christian life (6:1–8:39), 56–58 CE

Theme	ROM	Lk	Jn
God sent son in flesh	**8:3** [3]For what the law could not do, in that it was weak through the flesh, God sending his own Son in the likeness of sinful flesh, and for sin, condemned sin in the flesh:	**Acts 13:38** [38]Be it known unto you therefore, men and brethren, that through this man is preached unto you the forgiveness of sins: **Acts 15:10** [10]Now therefore why tempt ye God, to put a yoke upon the neck of the disciples, which neither our fathers nor we were able to bear?	**Jn 3:16–17** [16]For God so loved the world, that he gave his only begotten Son, that whosoever believeth in him should not perish, but have everlasting life. [17]For God sent not his Son into the world to condemn the world; but that the world through him might be saved. **1 Jn 4:9** [9]In this was manifested the love of God toward us, because that God sent his only begotten Son into the world, that we might live through him.

ROMANS 8:4—Living the Christian life (6:1–8:39), 56–58 CE

Theme	ROM	Paul
Walk after the Spirit	**8:4** [4]That the righteousness of the law might be fulfilled in us, who walk not after the flesh, but after the Spirit.	**Gal 5:16–25** [16]This I say then, Walk in the Spirit, and ye shall not fulfil the lust of the flesh. [17]For the flesh lusteth against the Spirit, and the Spirit against the flesh: and these are contrary the one to the other: so that ye cannot do the things that ye would. [18]But if ye be led of the Spirit, ye are not under the law. [19]Now the works of the flesh are manifest, which are these; Adultery, fornication, uncleanness, lasciviousness, [20]Idolatry, witchcraft, hatred, variance, emulations, wrath, strife, seditions, heresies, [21]Envyings, murders, drunkenness, revellings, and such like: of the which I tell you before, as I have also told you in time past, that they which do such things shall not inherit the kingdom of God. [22]But the fruit of the Spirit is love, joy, peace, longsuffering, gentleness, goodness, faith, [23]Meekness, temperance: against such there is no law. [24]And they that are Christ's have crucified the flesh with the affections and lusts. [25]If we live in the Spirit, let us also walk in the Spirit.

Paul	NT	Other
2 Cor 5:21 [21]For he hath made him to be sin for us, who knew no sin; that we might be made the righteousness of God in him. **Gal 3:13** [13]Christ hath redeemed us from the curse of the law, being made a curse for us: for it is written, Cursed is every one that hangeth on a tree: **Gal 4:4** [4]But when the fulness of the time was come, God sent forth his Son, made of a woman, made under the law, **Phil 2:7** [7]But made himself of no reputation, and took upon him the form of a servant, and was made in the likeness of men: **Col 1:22** [22]In the body of his flesh through death, to present you holy and unblameable and unreproveable in his sight:	**Heb 2:17** [17]Wherefore in all things it behoved him to be made like unto his brethren, that he might be a merciful and faithful high priest in things pertaining to God, to make reconciliation for the sins of the people.	**Q-Quelle** Jesus' witness to John: Rom 8:3/Gal 4:4/[Col 1:15-16]/[Mt 11:7-19, 21:31-32]/[Lk 7:24-35 (QS 17 [Thom 46, 74], QS 18), Lk 16:16 (QS 56)]; Against Pharisees: Rom 8:3/Gal 4:4/[Mt 23:4-36]/[Mk 7:1-9]/[Lk 11:37-54 (QS 34 [Thom 39:1, 89, 102])]

ROMANS 8:6—Living the Christian life (6:1–8:39), 56–58 CE

Theme	ROM	Mt	Mk	Lk
Living in the Spirit of God	**8:6** [6]For to be carnally minded is death; but to be spiritually minded is life and peace. **6:21** [21]What fruit had ye then in those things whereof ye are now ashamed? for the end of those things is death. **7:5** [5]For when we were in the flesh, the motions of sins, which were by the law, did work in our members to bring forth fruit unto death. **8:13** [13]For if ye live after the flesh, ye shall die: but if ye through the Spirit do mortify the deeds of the body, ye shall live. **8:16** [16]The Spirit itself beareth witness with our spirit, that we are the children of God:	**3:11** [11]I indeed baptize you with water unto repentance: but he that cometh after me is mightier than I, whose shoes I am not worthy to bear: he shall baptize you with the Holy Ghost, and with fire: **3:13** [13]Then cometh Jesus from Galilee to Jordan unto John, to be baptized of him.	**8:34** [34]And when he had called the people unto him with his disciples also, he said unto them, Whosoever will come after me, let him deny himself, and take up his cross, and follow me. **10:39** [39]And they said unto him, We can. And Jesus said unto them, Ye shall indeed drink of the cup that I drink of; and with the baptism that I am baptized withal shall ye be baptized:	**3:15** [15]And as the people were in expectation, and all men mused in their hearts of John, whether he were the Christ, or not; **4:18** [18]The Spirit of the Lord is upon me, because he hath anointed me to preach the gospel to the poor; he hath sent me to heal the brokenhearted, to preach deliverance to the captives, and recovering of sight to the blind, to set at liberty them that are bruised, **Acts 1:5** [5]For John truly baptized with water; but ye shall be baptized with the Holy Ghost not many days hence. **Acts 2:38–39** [38]Then Peter said unto them, Repent, and be baptized every one of you in the name of Jesus Christ for the remission of sins, and ye shall receive the gift of the Holy Ghost. [39]For the promise is unto you, and to your children, and to all that are afar off, even as many as the Lord our God shall call. **Acts 10:38** [38]How God anointed Jesus of Nazareth with the Holy Ghost and with power: who went about doing good, and healing all that were oppressed of the devil; for God was with him.

Jn	Paul	Other
1:33 [33]And I knew him not: but he that sent me to baptize with water, the same said unto me, Upon whom thou shalt see the Spirit descending, and remaining on him, the same is he which baptizeth with the Holy Ghost.	**1 Cor 10:2** [2]And were all baptized unto Moses in the cloud and in the sea; **1 Cor 12:13** [13]For by one Spirit are we all baptized into one body, whether we be Jews or Gentiles, whether we be bond or free; and have been all made to drink into one Spirit. **2 Cor 1:21–22** [21]For after that in the wisdom of God the world by wisdom knew not God, it pleased God by the foolishness of preaching to save them that believe. [22]For the Jews require a sign, and the Greeks seek after wisdom **Gal 3:26–27** [26]For ye are all the children of God by faith in Christ Jesus. [27]For as many of you as have been baptized into Christ have put on Christ. **Gal 4:6** [6]And because ye are sons, God hath sent forth the Spirit of his Son into your hearts, crying, Abba, Father. **Gal 6:8** [8]For he that soweth to his flesh shall of the flesh reap corruption; but he that soweth to the Spirit shall of the Spirit reap life everlasting.	**Q-Quelle** Preaching of John: Rom 8:6/[Mt 3:7-10], Mt 3:11-12/[Mk 1:7-8]/Lk 3:15-18 (QS 5)]

ROMANS 8:7—Living the Christian life (6:1–8:39), 56–58 CE

Theme	ROM	NT
Carnal mind at enmity with God	**8:7** [7]Because the carnal mind is enmity against God: for it is not subject to the law of God, neither indeed can be. **5:10** [10]For if, when we were enemies, we were reconciled to God by the death of his Son, much more, being reconciled, we shall be saved by his life.	**Jas 4:4** [4]Ye adulterers and adulteresses, know ye not that the friendship of the world is enmity with God? whosoever therefore will be a friend of the world is the enemy of God.

ROMANS 8:8—Living the Christian life (6:1–8:39), 56–58 CE

Theme	ROM	Jn
Flesh is not Godly	**8:8** [8]So then they that are in the flesh cannot please God.	**1 Jn 2:16** [16]For all that is in the world, the lust of the flesh, and the lust of the eyes, and the pride of life, is not of the Father, but is of the world.

ROMANS 8:9—Living the Christian life (6:1–8:39), 56–58 CE

Theme	ROM	Paul
In the Spirit	**8:9** [9]But ye are not in the flesh, but in the Spirit, if so be that the Spirit of God dwell in you. Now if any man have not the Spirit of Christ, he is none of his.	**1 Cor 3:16** [16]Know ye not that ye are the temple of God, and that the Spirit of God dwelleth in you?

ROMANS 8:10—Living the Christian life (6:1–8:39), 56–58 CE

Theme	ROM	Paul	NT
Spirit is life	**8:10** [10]And if Christ be in you, the body is dead because of sin; but the Spirit is life because of righteousness.	**Gal 2:20** [20]I am crucified with Christ: nevertheless I live; yet not I, but Christ liveth in me: and the life which I now live in the flesh I live by the faith of the Son of God, who loved me, and gave himself for me.	**1 Pet 4:6** [6]For for this cause was the gospel preached also to them that are dead, that they might be judged according to men in the flesh, but live according to God in the spirit.

ROMANS 8:13—Living the Christian life (6:1–8:39), 56–58 CE

Theme	ROM	Mt	Paul
Alive in Spirit/ death to flesh	**8:13** [13]For if ye live after the flesh, ye shall die: but if ye through the Spirit do mortify the deeds of the body, ye shall live.	**5:29–30** [29]And if thy right eye offend thee, pluck it out, and cast it from thee: for it is profitable for thee that one of thy members should perish, and not that thy whole body should be cast into hell. [30]And if thy right hand offend thee, cut it off, and cast it from thee: for it is profitable for thee that one of thy members should perish, and not that thy whole body should be cast into hell.	**Gal 5:24** [24]And they that are Christ's have crucified the flesh with the affections and lusts. **Gal 6:8** [8]For he that soweth to his flesh shall of the flesh reap corruption; but he that soweth to the Spirit shall of the Spirit reap life everlasting. **Eph 4:22–24 (Pseudo)** [22]That ye put off concerning the former conversation the old man, which is corrupt according to the deceitful lusts; [23]And be renewed in the spirit of your mind; [24]And that ye put on the new man, which after God is created in righteousness and true holiness. **Col 3:5** [5]Mortify therefore your members which are upon the earth; fornication, uncleanness, inordinate affection, evil concupiscence, and covetousness, which is idolatry:

ROMANS 8:14—Living the Christian life (6:1–8:39), 56–58 CE

Theme	ROM	Paul
Led by the Spirit	**8:14** [14]For as many as are led by the Spirit of God, they are the sons of God.	**Gal 5:18** [18]But if ye be led of the Spirit, ye are not under the law.

ROMANS 8:15—Living the Christian life (6:1–8:39), 56–58 CE

Theme	ROM	Mt	Mk	Jn
God as Father	**8:15** [15]For ye have not received the spirit of bondage again to fear; but ye have received the Spirit of adoption, whereby we cry, Abba, Father.	**26:38** [38]Then saith he unto them, My soul is exceeding sorrowful, even unto death: tarry ye here, and watch with me. **26:41** [41]Watch and pray, that ye enter not into temptation: the spirit indeed is willing, but the flesh is weak.	**14:34** [34]And saith unto them, My soul is exceeding sorrowful unto death: tarry ye here, and watch. **14:36** [36]And he said, Abba, Father, all things are possible unto thee; take away this cup from me: nevertheless not what I will, but what thou wilt. **14:38** [38]Watch ye and pray, lest ye enter into temptation. The spirit truly is ready, but the flesh is weak.	**12:27** [27]Now is my soul troubled; and what shall I say? Father, save me from this hour: but for this cause came I unto this hour. **18:11** [11]Then said Jesus unto Peter, Put up thy sword into the sheath: the cup which my Father hath given me, shall I not drink it?

ROMANS 8:16—Living the Christian life (6:1–8:39), 56–58 CE

Theme	ROM	Jn	Paul
Spirit bears witness	**8:16** [16]The Spirit itself beareth witness with our spirit, that we are the children of God:	**1:12** [12]But as many as received him, to them gave he power to become the sons of God, even to them that believe on his name:	**Gal 3:26–29** [26]For ye are all the children of God by faith in Christ Jesus. [27]For as many of you as have been baptized into Christ have put on Christ. [28]There is neither Jew nor Greek, there is neither bond nor free, there is neither male nor female: for ye are all one in Christ Jesus. [29]And if ye be Christ's, then are ye Abraham's seed, and heirs according to the promise.

Paul	Jewish Writings
2 Cor 12:7–10 7 And lest I should be exalted above measure through the abundance of the revelations, there was given to me a thorn in the flesh, the messenger of Satan to buffet me, lest I should be exalted above measure. 8 For this thing I besought the Lord thrice, that it might depart from me. 9 And he said unto me, My grace is sufficient for thee: for my strength is made perfect in weakness. Most gladly therefore will I rather glory in my infirmities, that the power of Christ may rest upon me. 10 Therefore I take pleasure in infirmi- ties, in reproaches, in necessities, in persecutions, in distresses for Christ's sake: for when I am weak, then am I strong. **Gal 4:4–6** 4 But when the fulness of the time was come, God sent forth his Son, made of a woman, made under the law, 5 To redeem them that were under the law, that we might receive the adoption of sons. 6 And because ye are sons, God hath sent forth the Spirit of his Son into your hearts, crying, Abba, Father. **Phil 2:8** 8 And being found in fashion as a man, he humbled himself, and became obedient unto death, even the death of the cross. **Col 4:2** 2 Continue in prayer, and watch in the same with thanksgiving; **2 Tim 1:7 (Pseudo)** 7 For God hath not given us the spirit of fear; but of power, and of love, and of a sound mind.	**Is 31:3** 3 Now the Egyptians are men, and not God; and their horses flesh, and not spirit. When the LORD shall stretch out his hand, both he that helpeth shall fall, and he that is holpen shall fall down, and they all shall fail together.

ROMANS 8:17—Living the Christian life (6:1–8:39), 56–58 CE

Theme	ROM	Mt
Heirs of Christ	**8:17** [17]And if children, then heirs; heirs of God, and joint-heirs with Christ; if so be that we suffer with him, that we may be also glorified together. **5:3** [3]And not only so, but we glory in tribulations also: knowing that tribulation worketh patience;	**5:10–12** [10]Blessed are they which are persecuted for righteousness' sake: for theirs is the kingdom of heaven. [11]Blessed are ye, when men shall revile you, and persecute you, and shall say all manner of evil against you falsely, for my sake. [12]Rejoice, and be exceeding glad: for great is your reward in heaven: for so persecuted they the prophets which were before you. **24:6–22** [6]And ye shall hear of wars and rumours of wars: see that ye be not troubled: for all these things must come to pass, but the end is not yet. [7]For nation shall rise against nation, and kingdom against kingdom: and there shall be famines, and pestilences, and earthquakes, in divers places. [8]All these are the beginning of sorrows. [9]Then shall they deliver you up to be afflicted, and shall kill you: and ye shall be hated of all nations for my name's sake. [10]And then shall many be offended, and shall betray one another, and shall hate one another. [11]And many false prophets shall rise, and shall deceive many. [12]And because iniquity shall abound, the love of many shall wax cold. [13]But he that shall endure unto the end, the same shall be saved. [14]And this gospel of the kingdom shall be preached in all the world for a witness unto all nations; and then shall the end come. [15]When ye therefore shall see the abomination of desolation, spoken of by Daniel the prophet, stand in the holy place, (whoso readeth, let him understand:) [16]Then let them which be in Judaea flee into the mountains: [17]Let him which is on the housetop not come down to take any thing out of his house: [18]Neither let him which is in the field return back to take his clothes. [19]And woe unto them that are with child, and to them that give suck in those days! [20]But pray ye that your flight be not in the winter, neither on the sabbath day: [21]For then shall be great tribulation, such as was not since the beginning of the world to this time, no, nor ever shall be. [22]And except those days should be shortened, there should no flesh be saved: but for the elect's sake those days shall be shortened. **24:15–31** [15]When ye therefore shall see the abomination of desolation, spoken of by Daniel the prophet, stand in the holy place, (whoso readeth, let him understand:) [16]Then let them which be in Judaea flee into the mountains: [17]Let him which is on the housetop not come down to take any thing out of his house: [18]Neither let him which is in the field return back to take his clothes. [19]And woe unto them that are with child, and to them that give suck in those days! [20]But pray ye that your flight be not in the winter, neither on the sabbath day: **[21]For then shall be great tribulation, such as was not since the beginning of the world to this time, no, nor ever shall be.** [22]And except those days should be shortened, there should no flesh be saved: but for the elect's sake those days shall be shortened. [23]Then if any man shall say unto you, Lo, here is Christ, or there; believe it not. [24]For there shall arise false Christs, and false prophets, and shall show great signs and wonders; insomuch that, if it were possible, they shall deceive the very elect. [25]Behold, I have told you before. [26]Wherefore if they shall say unto you, Behold, he is in the desert; go not forth: behold, he is in the secret chambers; believe it not. [27]For as the lightning cometh out of the east, and shineth even unto the west; so shall also the coming of the Son of man be. [28]For wheresoever the carcase is, there will the eagles be gathered together. [29]Immediately after the tribulation of those days shall the sun be darkened, and the moon shall not give her light, and the stars shall fall from heaven, and the powers of the heavens shall be shaken: [30]And then shall appear the sign of the Son of man in heaven: and then shall all the tribes of the earth mourn, and they shall see the Son of man coming in the clouds of heaven with power and great glory. [31]And he shall send his angels with a great sound of a trumpet, and they shall gather together his elect from the four winds, from one end of heaven to the other

Mk
13:7–20
[7]And when ye shall hear of wars and rumours of wars, be ye not troubled: for such things must needs be; but the end shall not be yet. [8]For nation shall rise against nation, and kingdom against kingdom: and there shall be earthquakes in divers places, and there shall be famines and troubles: these are the beginnings of sorrows. **[9]But take heed to yourselves: for they shall deliver you up to councils; and in the synagogues ye shall be beaten: and ye shall be brought before rulers and kings for my sake, for a testimony against them.** [10]And the gospel must first be published among all nations. [11]But when they shall lead you, and deliver you up, take no thought beforehand what ye shall speak, neither do ye premeditate: but whatsoever shall be given you in that hour, that speak ye: for it is not ye that speak, but the Holy Ghost. [12]Now the brother shall betray the brother to death, and the father the son; and children shall rise up against their parents, and shall cause them to be put to death. [13]And ye shall be hated of all men for my name's sake: but he that shall endure unto the end, the same shall be saved. [14]But when ye shall see the abomination of desolation, spoken of by Daniel the prophet, standing where it ought not, (let him that readeth understand,) then let them that be in Judaea flee to the mountains: [15]And let him that is on the housetop not go down into the house, neither enter therein, to take any thing out of his house: [16]And let him that is in the field not turn back again for to take up his garment. [17]But woe to them that are with child, and to them that give suck in those days! [18]And pray ye that your flight be not in the winter. [19]For in those days shall be affliction, such as was not from the beginning of the creation which God created unto this time, neither shall be. [20]And except that the Lord had shortened those days, no flesh should be saved: but for the elect's sake, whom he hath chosen, he hath shortened the days.
13:21–27
[21]And then if any man shall say to you, Lo, here is Christ; or, lo, he is there; believe him not: [22]For false Christs and false prophets shall rise, and shall show signs and wonders, to seduce, if it were possible, even the elect. [23]But take ye heed: behold, I have foretold you all things.[24]But in those days, after that tribulation, the sun shall be darkened, and the moon shall not give her light, [25]And the stars of heaven shall fall, and the powers that are in heaven shall be shaken. [26]And then shall they see the Son of man coming in the clouds with great power and glory. [27]And then shall he send his angels, and shall gather together his elect from the four winds, from the uttermost part of the earth to the uttermost part of heaven

Romans 8:17 continued on next page

ROMANS 8:17—Living the Christian life (6:1–8:39), 56–58 CE (*continued*)

Theme	ROM	Lk
(*Cont.*) **Heirs of Christ**	**8:17 (above)** **5:3 (above)**	**6:22–23** [22]Blessed are ye, when men shall hate you, and when they shall separate you from their company, and shall reproach you, and cast out your name as evil, for the Son of man's sake. [23]Rejoice ye in that day, and leap for joy: for, behold, your reward is great in heaven: for in the like manner did their fathers unto the prophets. **21:9–14** [9]But when ye shall hear of wars and commotions, be not terrified: for these things must first come to pass; but the end is not by and by. [10]Then said he unto them, Nation shall rise against nation, and kingdom against kingdom: [11]And great earthquakes shall be in divers places, and famines, and pestilences; and fearful sights and great signs shall there be from heaven. [12]But before all these, they shall lay their hands on you, and persecute you, delivering you up to the synagogues, and into prisons, being brought before kings and rulers for my name's sake. [13]And it shall turn to you for a testimony. [14]Settle it therefore in your hearts, not to meditate before what ye shall answer: **21:20–27** [20]And when ye shall see Jerusalem compassed with armies, then know that the desolation thereof is nigh. [21]Then let them which are in Judaea flee to the mountains; and let them which are in the midst of it depart out; and let not them that are in the countries enter thereinto. [22]For these be the days of vengeance, that all things which are written may be fulfilled. **[23]But woe unto them that are with child, and to them that give suck, in those days! for there shall be great distress in the land, and wrath upon this people.** [24]And they shall fall by the edge of the sword, and shall be led away captive into all nations: and Jerusalem shall be trodden down of the Gentiles, until the times of the Gentiles be fulfilled. [25]And there shall be signs in the sun, and in the moon, and in the stars; and upon the earth distress of nations, with perplexity; the sea and the waves roaring; [26]Men's hearts failing them for fear, and for looking after those things which are coming on the earth: for the powers of heaven shall be shaken. [27]And then shall they see the Son of man coming in a cloud with power and great glory.

Paul	NT	Other
2 Cor 7:4 4Great is my boldness of speech toward you, great is my glorying of you: I am filled with comfort, I am exceeding joyful in all our tribulation. **2 Cor 12:10** 10Therefore I take pleasure in infirmities, in reproaches, in necessities, in persecutions, in distresses for Christ's sake: for when I am weak, then am I strong. **Gal 4:7** 7Wherefore thou art no more a servant, but a son; and if a son, then an heir of God through Christ. **Col 1:24** 24Who now rejoice in my sufferings for you, and fill up that which is behind of the afflictions of Christ in my flesh for his body's sake, which is the church: **1 Thes 2:4–13** 3For our exhortation was not of deceit, nor of uncleanness, nor in guile: 4But as we were allowed of God to be put in trust with the gospel, even so we speak; not as pleasing men, but God, which trieth our hearts. 5For neither at any time used we flattering words, as ye know, nor a cloak of covetousness; God is witness: 6Nor of men sought we glory, neither of you, nor yet of others, when we might have been burdensome, as the apostles of Christ. 7But we were gentle among you, even as a nurse cherisheth her children: 8So being affectionately desirous of you, we were willing to have imparted unto you, not the gospel of God only, but also our own souls, because ye were dear unto us. 9For ye remember, brethren, our labour and travail: for labouring night and day, because we would not be chargeable unto any of you, we preached unto you the gospel of God. 10Ye are witnesses, and God also, how holily and justly and unblameably we behaved ourselves among you that believe: 11As ye know how we exhorted and comforted and charged every one of you, as a father doth his children, 12That ye would walk worthy of God, who hath called you unto his kingdom and glory.13For this cause also thank we God without ceasing, because, when ye received the word of God which ye heard of us, ye received it not as the word of men, but as it is in truth, the word of God, which effectually worketh also in you that believe. **1 Thes 3:3–4** 3That no man should be moved by these afflictions: for yourselves know that we are appointed thereunto.4For verily, when we were with you, we told you before that we should suffer tribulation; even as it came to pass, and ye know. **2 Thes 2:8** 2That ye be not soon shaken in mind, or be troubled, neither by spirit, nor by word, nor by letter as from us, as that the day of Christ is at hand.	**1 Pet 4:13** 13But rejoice, inasmuch as ye are partakers of Christ's sufferings; that, when his glory shall be revealed, ye may be glad also with exceeding joy. **1 Pet 5:1** 1The elders which are among you I exhort, who am also an elder, and a witness of the sufferings of Christ, and also a partaker of the glory that shall be revealed:	**Q-Quelle** Beatitudes: Rom 8:17/Mt 5:3-12/Lk 6:20b-23 (QS 8); Day of SOM: Rom 8:17/[Mt 10:39], Mt 24:17-18, 23, 26-27, 28, [Mt 24:37-39, 24:40-41]/[Mk 13:14-16, 19-23]/[Lk 17:22-37 (QS 60 [Thom 3, 51, 61, 113])]

Romans 8:17 continued on next page

ROMANS 8:17—Living the Christian life (6:1–8:39), 56–58 CE (*continued*)

Theme	ROM	Mt	Mk	Lk
(*Cont.*) **Redemptive Suffering (variation supra)**	**8:17 (above)** **5:3 (above)**	**16:24–26** [24]Then said Jesus unto his disciples, If any man will come after me, let him deny himself, and take up his cross, and follow me. [25]For whosoever will save his life shall lose it: and whosoever will lose his life for my sake shall find it. **[26]For what is a man profited, if he shall gain the whole world, and lose his own soul? or what shall a man give in exchange for his soul?** **26:31** [31]Then saith Jesus unto them, All ye shall be offended because of me this night: for it is written, I will smite the shepherd, and the sheep of the flock shall be scattered abroad. **27:46** [46]And about the ninth hour Jesus cried with a loud voice, saying, Eli, Eli, lama sabachthani? that is to say, My God, my God, why hast thou forsaken me?	**8:34–37** [34]And when he had called the people unto him with his disciples also, he said unto them, Whosoever will come after me, let him deny himself, and take up his cross, and follow me. [35]For whosoever will save his life shall lose it; but whosoever shall lose his life for my sake and the gospel's, the same shall save it. [36]For what shall it profit a man, if he shall gain the whole world, and lose his own soul? [37]Or what shall a man give in exchange for his soul? **14:27** [27]And Jesus saith unto them, All ye shall be offended because of me this night: for it is written, I will smite the shepherd, and the sheep shall be scattered. **14:36** [36]And he said, Abba, Father, all things are possible unto thee; take away this cup from me: nevertheless not what I will, but what thou wilt. **15:34** [34]And at the ninth hour Jesus cried with a loud voice, saying, EloiEloi, EloiEloi, lamalama sabachthanisa-bachthani? which is, being interpreted, My God, my God, why hast thou forsaken me?	**9:23–26** [23]And he said to them all, If any man will come after me, let him deny himself, and take up his cross daily, and follow me. [24]For whosoever will save his life shall lose it: but whosoever will lose his life for my sake, the same shall save it. **[25]For what is a man advantaged, if he gain the whole world, and lose himself, or be cast away? [26]For whosoever shall be ashamed of me and of my words, of him shall the Son of man be ashamed, when he shall come in his own glory, and in his Father's, and of the holy angels.** **22:37** [37]For I say unto you, that this that is written must yet be accomplished in me, And he was reckoned among the transgressors: for the things concerning me have an end. **22:42** [42]Saying, Father, if thou be willing, remove this cup from me: nevertheless not my will, but thine, be done.

Jn	Paul	Jewish Writings
10:11 [11]I am the good shepherd: the good shepherd giveth his life for the sheep.	**1 Cor 10:16** [16]The cup of blessing which we bless, is it not the communion of the blood of Christ? The bread which we break, is it not the communion of the body of Christ? **Gal 2:19** [19]For I through the law am dead to the law, that I might live unto God. **Phil 3:10** [10]That I may know him, and the power of his resurrection, and the fellowship of his sufferings, being made conformable unto his death; **Phil 3:7–11** [7]But what things were gain to me, those I counted loss for Christ. [8]Yea doubtless, and I count all things but loss for the excellency of the knowledge of Christ Jesus my Lord: for whom I have suffered the loss of all things, and do count them but dung, that I may win Christ, [9]And be found in him, not having mine own righteousness, which is of the law, but that which is through the faith of Christ, the righteousness which is of God by faith: [10]That I may know him, and the power of his resurrection, and the fellowship of his sufferings, being made conformable unto his death; [11]If by any means I might attain unto the resurrection of the dead.	**Ps 22:1** [1]My God, my God, why hast thou forsaken me? why art thou so far from helping me, and from the words of my roaring? **Is 53:12** [12]Therefore will I divide him a portion with the great, and he shall divide the spoil with the strong; because he hath poured out his soul unto death: and he was numbered with the transgressors; and he bare the sin of many, and made intercession for the transgressors. **Zech 13:7** [7]Awake, O sword, against my shepherd, and against the man that is my fellow, saith the LORD of hosts: smite the shepherd, and the sheep shall be scattered: and I will turn mine hand upon the little ones.

Romans 8:17 continued on next page

ROMANS 8:17—Living the Christian life (6:1–8:39), 56–58 CE (*continued*)

Theme	ROM	Paul
(*Cont.*) **God's children glorified/ all creation redeemed (variation supra)**	(*Cont.*) **8:17** [17]And if children, then heirs; heirs of God, and joint-heirs with Christ; if so be that we suffer with him, that we may be also glorified together. **5:3** [3]And not only so, but we glory in tribulations also: knowing that tribulation worketh patience; **8:21** [21]Because the creature itself also shall be delivered from the bondage of corruption into the glorious liberty of the children of God. **8:23** [23]And not only they, but ourselves also, which have the firstfruits of the Spirit, even we ourselves groan within ourselves, waiting for the adoption, to wit, the redemption of our body. **11:26** [26]And so all Israel shall be saved: as it is written, There shall come out of Sion the Deliverer, and shall turn away ungodliness from Jacob:	**1 Cor 13:12** [12]For now we see through a glass, darkly; but then face to face: now I know in part; but then shall I know even as also I am known. **1 Cor 15:24–28** [24]Then cometh the end, when he shall have delivered up the kingdom to God, even the Father; when he shall have put down all rule and all authority and power. [25]For he must reign, till he hath put all enemies under his feet. [26]The last enemy that shall be destroyed is death. [27]For he hath put all things under his feet. But when he saith all things are put under him, it is manifest that he is excepted, which did put all things under him. [28]And when all things shall be subdued unto him, then shall the Son also himself be subject unto him that put all things under him, that God may be all in all. **1 Cor 15:52** [52]In a moment, in the twinkling of an eye, at the last trump: for the trumpet shall sound, and the dead shall be raised incorruptible, and we shall be changed. **Eph 1:10 (Pseudo)** [10]That in the dispensation of the fulness of times he might gather together in one all things in Christ, both which are in heaven, and which are on earth; even in him: **Col 1:16–20** [16]For by him were all things created, that are in heaven, and that are in earth, visible and invisible, whether they be thrones, or dominions, or principalities, or powers: all things were created by him, and for him: [17]And he is before all things, and by him all things consist. [18]And he is the head of the body, the church: who is the beginning, the firstborn from the dead; that in all things he might have the preeminence. [19]For it pleased the Father that in him should all fulness dwell; [20]And, having made peace through the blood of his cross, by him to reconcile all things unto himself; by him, I say, whether they be things in earth, or things in heaven. **1 Thes 1:10** [10]And to wait for his Son from heaven, whom he raised from the dead, even Jesus, which delivered us from the wrath to come. **1 Thes 4:17** [17]Then we which are alive and remain shall be caught up together with them in the clouds, to meet the Lord in the air: and so shall we ever be with the Lord. **2 Thes 1:10** [10]When he shall come to be glorified in his saints, and to be admired in all them that believe (because our testimony among you was believed) in that day.

Other
Q-Quelle
Lord's Prayer: Rom 8:17/1 Thes 1:10/[Mt 6:9-13]/[Lk 11:1-4 (QS 26)]; Parable of Mustard Seed: Rom 8:17/1 Thes 1:10/[Mt 13:31-32]/[Mk 4:30-32]/[Lk 13:18-19 (QS 46 [Thom 20, 96])]

ROMANS 8:18—Living the Christian life (6:1–8:39), 56–58 CE

Theme	ROM	Paul	Other
Reckoning suffering	**8:18** [18]For I reckon that the sufferings of this present time are not worthy to be compared with the glory which shall be revealed in us.	**2 Cor 4:17** [17]For our light affliction, which is but for a moment, worketh for us a far more exceeding and eternal weight of glory;	**Q-Quelle** Beatitudes: Rom 8:18/2 Cor 4:17/[Mt 5:3-12]/[Lk 6:20b-23 (QS 8 [Thom 54,68,69])]

ROMANS 8:20—Living the Christian life (6:1–8:39), 56–58 CE

Theme	ROM	Jewish Writings
Humanity subject to vanity	**8:20** [20]For the creature was made subject to vanity, not willingly, but by reason of him who hath subjected the same in hope,	**Gen 3:17–19** [17]And unto Adam he said, Because thou hast hearkened unto the voice of thy wife, and hast eaten of the tree, of which I commanded thee, saying, Thou shalt not eat of it: cursed is the ground for thy sake; in sorrow shalt thou eat of it all the days of thy life; [18]Thorns also and thistles shall it bring forth to thee; and thou shalt eat the herb of the field; [19]In the sweat of thy face shalt thou eat bread, till thou return unto the ground; for out of it wast thou taken: for dust thou art, and unto dust shalt thou return.

ROMANS 8:21—Living the Christian life (6:1–8:39), 56–58 CE

Theme	ROM	NT
Delivered from bondage to liberty	**8:21** [21]Because the creature itself also shall be delivered from the bondage of corruption into the glorious liberty of the children of God.	**2 Pet 3:12–13** [12]Looking for and hasting unto the coming of the day of God, wherein the heavens being on fire shall be dissolved, and the elements shall melt with fervent heat? [13]Nevertheless we, according to his promise, look for new heavens and a new earth, wherein dwelleth righteousness. **Rev 21:1** [1]And I saw a new heaven and a new earth: for the first heaven and the first earth were passed away; and there was no more sea.

ROMANS 8:22—Living the Christian life (6:1–8:39), 56–58 CE

Theme	ROM	Paul
Creation waits for redemption	**8:22** [22]For we know that the whole creation groaneth and travaileth in pain together until now.	**2 Cor 5:2–5** [2]For in this we groan, earnestly desiring to be clothed upon with our house which is from heaven: [3]If so be that being clothed we shall not be found naked. [4]For we that are in this tabernacle do groan, being burdened: not for that we would be unclothed, but clothed upon, that mortality might be swallowed up of life. [5]Now he that hath wrought us for the selfsame thing is God, who also hath given unto us the earnest of the Spirit.

ROMANS 8:23—Living the Christian life (6:1–8:39), 56–58 CE

Theme	ROM
Day of salvation, fruits of the Spirit (eschat)	**8:23** [23]And not only they, but ourselves also, which have the firstfruits of the Spirit, even we ourselves groan within ourselves, waiting for the adoption, to wit, the redemption of our body. **13:11–12** [11]And that, knowing the time, that now it is high time to awake out of sleep: for now is our salvation nearer than when we believed. [12]The night is far spent, the day is at hand: let us therefore cast off the works of darkness, and let us put on the armour of light.

Paul

1 Cor 3:16

[16]Know ye not that ye are the temple of God, and that the Spirit of God dwelleth in you?

1 Cor 12:1–13

[1]Now concerning spiritual gifts, brethren, I would not have you ignorant. [2]Ye know that ye were Gentiles, carried away unto these dumb idols, even as ye were led. [3]Wherefore I give you to understand, that no man speaking by the Spirit of God calleth Jesus accursed: and that no man can say that Jesus is the Lord, but by the Holy Ghost. [4]Now there are diversities of gifts, but the same Spirit. [5]And there are differences of administrations, but the same Lord. [6]And there are diversities of operations, but it is the same God which worketh all in all. [7]But the manifestation of the Spirit is given to every man to profit withal. [8]For to one is given by the Spirit the word of wisdom; to another the word of knowledge by the same Spirit; [9]To another faith by the same Spirit; to another the gifts of healing by the same Spirit; [10]To another the working of miracles; to another prophecy; to another discerning of spirits; to another divers kinds of tongues; to another the interpretation of tongues: [11]But all these worketh that one and the selfsame Spirit, dividing to every man severally as he will. [12]For as the body is one, and hath many members, and all the members of that one body, being many, are one body: so also is Christ. [13]For by one Spirit are we all baptized into one body, whether we be Jews or Gentiles, whether we be bond or free; and have been all made to drink into one Spirit.

1 Cor 15:20

[20]But now is Christ risen from the dead, and become the firstfruits of them that slept.

2 Cor 1:22

[22]Who hath also sealed us, and given the earnest of the Spirit in our hearts.

2 Cor 3:18

[18]But we all, with open face beholding as in a glass the glory of the Lord, are changed into the same image from glory to glory, even as by the Spirit of the Lord.

2 Cor 5:15

[15]And that he died for all, that they which live should not henceforth live unto themselves, but unto him which died for them, and rose again.

2 Cor 5:17

[17]Therefore if any man be in Christ, he is a new creature: old things are passed away; behold, all things are become new.

2 Cor 5:19

[19]To wit, that God was in Christ, reconciling the world unto himself, not imputing their trespasses unto them; and hath committed unto us the word of reconciliation.

2 Cor 6:2

[2](For he saith, I have heard thee in a time accepted, and in the day of salvation have I succoured thee: behold, now is the accepted time; behold, now is the day of salvation.)

Gal 4:4

[4]But when the fulness of the time was come, God sent forth his Son, made of a woman, made under the law,

Gal 5:5

[5]For we through the Spirit wait for the hope of righteousness by faith.

Gal 5:22

[22]But the fruit of the Spirit is love, joy, peace, longsuffering, gentleness, goodness, faith,

Gal 6:15

[15]For in Christ Jesus neither circumcision availeth any thing, nor uncircumcision, but a new creature.

Eph 1:10 (Pseudo)

[10]That in the dispensation of the fulness of times he might gather together in one all things in Christ, both which are in heaven, and which are on earth; even in him:

Eph 1:14 (Pseudo)

[14]As also ye have acknowledged us in part, that we are your rejoicing, even as ye also are ours in the day of the Lord Jesus.

1 Thes 1:5

[5]For our gospel came not unto you in word only, but also in power, and in the Holy Ghost, and in much assurance; as ye know what manner of men we were among you for your sake.

1 Thes 5:19–20

[19]Quench not the Spirit. [20]Despise not prophesyings.

Romans 8:23 continued on next page

ROMANS 8:23—Living the Christian life (6:1–8:39), 56–58 CE

Theme	ROM	Other
(*Cont.*) **Day of salvation, fruits of the Spirit (eschat)**	**8:23 (above)** **13:11–12 (above)**	**Q-Quelle** Leaven: Rom 8:23/1 Cor 3:16/[Mt 13:33]/[Lk 13:20-21(QS 46 [Thom 20, 96])],[Lk 12:11-12(QS 37 [Thom 44])]; Precedence: Rom 8:23/1 Cor 3:16/[Mt 19:28]/[Mk 10:41-45]/[Lk 22:28-30 (QS 62); Assistance of the HS: Rom 8:23/2 Cor 1:22/Eph 1:14/1 Thes 1:5/[Mt 10:19-20]/[Mk 13:11, 13:11]/ [Lk 12:11-12 (QS 37 [Thom 44])], [Lk 21:14-15]; Jesus' witness to John: Rom 8:23/Gal 4:4/[Mt 11:7-19, 21:31-32]/[Lk 7:24-35 (QS 17 [Thom 46, 74], QS 18)], [Lk 16:16 (QS 56)]

ROMANS 8:24—Living the Christian life (6:1–8:39), 56–58 CE

Theme	ROM	Paul	NT
Saved by hope not seen	**8:24** [24]For we are saved by hope: but hope that is seen is not hope: for what a man seeth, why doth he yet hope for?	**2 Cor 5:7** [7](For we walk by faith, not by sight:)	**Heb 11:1** [1]Now faith is the substance of things hoped for, the evidence of things not seen.

ROMANS 8:27—Living the Christian life (6:1–8:39), 56–58 CE

Theme	ROM	Paul	Jewish Writings
Spirit brings God's will	**8:27** [27]And he that searcheth the hearts knoweth what is the mind of the Spirit, because he maketh intercession for the saints according to the will of God.	**1 Cor 4:5** [5]Therefore judge nothing before the time, until the Lord come, who both will bring to light the hidden things of darkness, and will make manifest the counsels of the hearts: and then shall every man have praise of God.	**Ps 139:1** [1]O LORD, thou hast searched me, and known me.

ROMANS 8:28–29—Living the Christian life (6:1–8:39), 56–58 CE

Theme	ROM	Paul
All things work for good for God lovers	**8:28–29** [28]And we know that all things work together for good to them that love God, to them who are the called according to his purpose. [29]For whom he did foreknow, he also did predestinate to be conformed to the image of his Son, that he might be the firstborn among many brethren.	**Eph 1:4–14 (Pseudo)** [4]According as he hath chosen us in him before the foundation of the world, that we should be holy and without blame before him in love: [5]Having predestinated us unto the adoption of children by Jesus Christ to himself, according to the good pleasure of his will, [6]To the praise of the glory of his grace, wherein he hath made us accepted in the beloved. [7]In whom we have redemption through his blood, the forgiveness of sins, according to the riches of his grace; [8]Wherein he hath abounded toward us in all wisdom and prudence; [9]Having made known unto us the mystery of his will, according to his good pleasure which he hath purposed in himself: [10]That in the dispensation of the fulness of times he might gather together in one all things in Christ, both which are in heaven, and which are on earth; even in him: [11]In whom also we have obtained an inheritance, being predestinated according to the purpose of him who worketh all things after the counsel of his own will: [12]That we should be to the praise of his glory, who first trusted in Christ. [13]In whom ye also trusted, after that ye heard the word of truth, the gospel of your salvation: in whom also after that ye believed, ye were sealed with that holy Spirit of promise, [14]Which is the earnest of our inheritance until the redemption of the purchased possession, unto the praise of his glory. **Eph 3:11 (Pseudo)** [11]According to the eternal purpose which he purposed in Christ Jesus our Lord:

ROMANS 8:29—Living the Christian life (6:1–8:39), 56–58 CE

Theme	ROM	Paul	NT
Destiny in God's image	**8:29** [29]For whom he did foreknow, he also did predestinate to be conformed to the image of his Son, that he might be the firstborn among many brethren.	**Eph 1:5 (Pseudo)** [5]Having predestinated us unto the adoption of children by Jesus Christ to himself, according to the good pleasure of his will,	**1 Pet 1:2** [2]Elect according to the foreknowledge of God the Father, through sanctification of the Spirit, unto obedience and sprinkling of the blood of Jesus Christ: Grace unto you, and peace, be multiplied.

ROMANS 8:30—Living the Christian life (6:1–8:39), 56–58 CE

Theme	ROM	Paul	Jewish Writings
Called to God's service	**8:30** [30]Moreover whom he did predestinate, them he also called: and whom he called, them he also justified: and whom he justified, them he also glorified.	**2 Thes 2:13–14** [13]But we are bound to give thanks alway to God for you, brethren beloved of the Lord, because God hath from the beginning chosen you to salvation through sanctification of the Spirit and belief of the truth: [14]Whereunto he called you by our gospel, to the obtaining of the glory of our Lord Jesus Christ.	**Is 45:25** [25]In the LORD shall all the seed of Israel be justified, and shall glory.

ROMANS 8:31—Living the Christian life (6:1–8:39), 56–58 CE

Theme	ROM	NT	Jewish Writings
If God is for us	**8:31** [31]What shall we then say to these things? If God be for us, who can be against us?	**Heb 13:6** [6]So that we may boldly say, The Lord is my helper, and I will not fear what man shall do unto me.	**Ps 118:6** [6]The LORD is on my side; I will not fear: what can man do unto me?

ROMANS 8:32—Living the Christian life (6:1–8:39), 56–58 CE

Theme	ROM	Jn
God gives freely	**8:32** [32]He that spared not his own Son, but delivered him up for us all, how shall he not with him also freely give us all things?	**3:16** [16]For God so loved the world, that he gave his only begotten Son, that whosoever believeth in him should not perish, but have everlasting life.

ROMANS 8:33–34—Living the Christian life (6:1–8:39), 56–58 CE

Theme	ROM	Jewish Writings
God justifies elect	**8:33–34** [33]Who shall lay any thing to the charge of God's elect? It is God that justifieth. [34]Who is he that condemneth? It is Christ that died, yea rather, that is risen again, who is even at the right hand of God, who also maketh intercession for us.	**Is 50:8** [8]He is near that justifieth me; who will contend with me? let us stand together: who is mine adversary? let him come near to me.

ROMANS 8:34—Living the Christian life (6:1–8:39), 56–58 CE

Theme	ROM	Jn	NT	Jewish Writings
Christ renews world	**8:34** [34]Who is he that condemneth? It is Christ that died, yea rather, that is risen again, who is even at the right hand of God, who also maketh intercession for us.	**1 Jn 2:1** [1]My little children, these things write I unto you, that ye sin not. And if any man sin, we have an advocate with the Father, Jesus Christ the righteous:	**Heb 7:25** [25]Wherefore he is able also to save them to the uttermost that come unto God by him, seeing he ever liveth to make intercession for them.	**Ps 110:1** [1]The LORD said unto my Lord, Sit thou at my right hand, until I make thine enemies thy footstool.

ROMANS 8:36—Living the Christian life (6:1–8:39), 56–58 CE

Theme	ROM	Paul	Jewish Writings
Dying for Christ	**8:36** [36]As it is written, For thy sake we are killed all the day long; we are accounted as sheep for the slaughter.	**1 Cor 4:9** [9]For I think that God hath set forth us the apostles last, as it were appointed to death: for we are made a spectacle unto the world, and to angels, and to men. **1 Cor 15:30** [30]And why stand we in jeopardy every hour? **2 Cor 4:11** [11]For we which live are alway delivered unto death for Jesus' sake, that the life also of Jesus might be made manifest in our mortal flesh. **2 Tim 3:12 (Pseudo)** [12]Yea, and all that will live godly in Christ Jesus shall suffer persecution.	**Ps 44:23** [23]Awake, why sleepest thou, O Lord? arise, cast us not off for ever.

ROMANS 8:37—Living the Christian life (6:1–8:39), 56–58 CE

Theme	ROM	Jn
More than conquerors	**8:37** [37]Nay, in all these things we are more than conquerors through him that loved us.	**1 Jn 5:4** [4]For whatsoever is born of God overcometh the world: and this is the victory that overcometh the world, even our faith.

ROMANS 8:38–39—Living the Christian life (6:1–8:39), 56–58 CE

Theme	ROM	Paul	NT
Love of God invincible	**8:38–39** [38]For I am persuaded, that neither death, nor life, nor angels, nor principalities, nor powers, nor things present, nor things to come, [39]Nor height, nor depth, nor any other creature, shall be able to separate us from the love of God, which is in Christ Jesus our Lord.	**1 Cor 3:22** [22]Whether Paul, or Apollos, or Cephas, or the world, or life, or death, or things present, or things to come; all are yours; **Eph 1:21 (Pseudo)** [21]Far above all principality, and power, and might, and dominion, and every name that is named, not only in this world, but also in that which is to come:	**1 Pet 3:22** [22]Who is gone into heaven, and is on the right hand of God; angels and authorities and powers being made subject unto him.

GOD DESIRES JEWS AND GENTILES (9:1–11:36)

ROMANS 9:1—God desires Jews and Gentiles (9:1–11:36), 56–58 CE

Theme	ROM	Paul
Bearing witness in Holy Spirit	**9:1** [1]I say the truth in Christ, I lie not, my conscience also bearing me witness in the Holy Ghost,	**2 Cor 11:31** [31]The God and Father of our Lord Jesus Christ, which is blessed for evermore, knoweth that I lie not. **1 Tim 2:7 (Pseudo)** [7]Whereunto I am ordained a preacher, and an apostle, (I speak the truth in Christ, and lie not;) a teacher of the Gentiles in faith and verity.

ROMANS 9:3—God desires Jews and Gentiles (9:1–11:36), 56–58 CE

Theme	ROM	Jewish Writings
Israel lost heritage	**9:3** [3]For I could wish that myself were accursed from Christ for my brethren, my kinsmen according to the flesh:	**Ex 32:32** [32]Yet now, if thou wilt forgive their sin; and if not, blot me, I pray thee, out of thy book which thou hast written.

ROMANS 9:4–5—God desires Jews and Gentiles (9:1–11:36), 56–58 CE

Theme	ROM	Jewish Writings
Israel's fathers heirs	**9:4–5** [4]Who are Israelites; to whom pertaineth the adoption, and the glory, and the covenants, and the giving of the law, and the service of God, and the promises; [5]Whose are the fathers, and of whom as concerning the flesh Christ came, who is over all, God blessed for ever. Amen. **3:2** [2]Much every way: chiefly, because that unto them were committed the oracles of God.	**Ex 4:22** [22]And thou shalt say unto Pharaoh, Thus saith the LORD, Israel is my son, even my firstborn: **Dt 7:6** [6]For thou art an holy people unto the LORD thy God: the LORD thy God hath chosen thee to be a special people unto himself, above all people that are upon the face of the earth. **Dt 14:1–2** [1]Ye are the children of the LORD your God: ye shall not cut yourselves, nor make any baldness between your eyes for the dead. [2]For thou art an holy people unto the LORD thy God, and the LORD hath chosen thee to be a peculiar people unto himself, above all the nations that are upon the earth.

ROMANS 9:5—God desires Jews and Gentiles (9:1–11:36), 56–58 CE

Theme	ROM	Mt
Jewish Christ, over all	**9:5** [5]Whose are the fathers, and of whom as concerning the flesh Christ came who is over all, God blessed for ever. Amen. **10:9** [9]That if thou shalt confess with thy mouth the Lord Jesus, and shalt believe in thine heart that God hath raised him from the dead, thou shalt be saved. **10:13** [13]For whosoever shall call upon the name of the Lord shall be saved.	**1:1–16** [1]The book of the generation of Jesus Christ, the son of David, the son of Abraham. [2]Abraham begat Isaac; and Isaac begat Jacob; and Jacob begat Judas and his brethren; [3]And Judas begat Phares and Zara of Thamar; and Phares begat Esrom; and Esrom begat Aram; [4]And Aram begat Aminadab; and Aminadab begat Naasson; and Naasson begat Salmon; [5]And Salmon begat Booz of Rachab; and Booz begat Obed of Ruth; and Obed begat Jesse; [6]And Jesse begat David the king; and David the king begat Solomon of her that had been the wife of Urias; [7]And Solomon begat Roboam; and Roboam begat Abia; and Abia begat Asa; [8]And Asa begat Josaphat; and Josaphat begat Joram; and Joram begat Ozias; [9]And Ozias begat Joatham; and Joatham begat Achaz; and Achaz begat Ezekias; [10]And Ezekias begat Manasses; and Manasses begat Amon; and Amon begat Josias; [11]And Josias begat Jechonias and his brethren, about the time they were carried away to Babylon: [12]And after they were brought to Babylon, Jechonias begat Salathiel; and Salathiel begat Zorobabel; [13]And Zorobabel begat Abiud; and Abiud begat Eliakim; and Eliakim begat Azor; [14]And Azor begat Sadoc; and Sadoc begat Achim; and Achim begat Eliud; [15]And Eliud begat Eleazar; and Eleazar begat Matthan; and Matthan begat Jacob; **21:3** [3]And if any man say ought unto you, ye shall say, The Lord hath need of them; and straightway he will send them. **22:41–46** [41]While the Pharisees were gathered together, Jesus asked them, [42]Saying, What think ye of Christ? whose son is he? They say unto him, The Son of David. [43]He saith unto them, How then doth David in spirit call him Lord, saying, [44]The LORD said unto my Lord, Sit thou on my right hand, till I make thine enemies thy footstool? [45]If David then call him Lord, how is he his son? [46]And no man was able to answer him a word, neither durst any man from that day forth ask him any more questions **24:45–51** [45]Who then is a faithful and wise servant, whom his lord hath made ruler over his household, to give them meat in due season? [46]Blessed is that servant, whom his lord when he cometh shall find so doing. [47]Verily I say unto you, That he shall make him ruler over all his goods. [48]But if that evil servant shall say in his heart, My lord delayeth his coming; [49]And shall begin to smite his fellow servants, and to eat and drink with the drunken; [50]The lord of that servant shall come in a day when he looketh not for him, and in an hour that he is not aware of, [51]And shall cut him asunder, and appoint him his portion with the hypocrites: there shall be weeping and gnashing of teeth **25:14–30** [14]For the kingdom of heaven is as a man travelling into a far country, who called his own servants, and delivered unto them his goods. [15]And unto one he gave five talents, to another two, and to another one; to every man according to his several ability; and straightway took his journey. [16]Then he that had received the five talents went and traded with the same, and made them other five talents. [17]And likewise he that had received two, he also gained other two. [18]But he that had received one went and digged in the earth, and hid his lord's money. [19]After a long time the lord of those servants cometh, and reckoneth with them. [20]And so he that had received five talents came and brought other five talents, saying, Lord, thou deliveredst unto me five talents: behold, I have gained beside them five talents more. [21]His lord said unto him, Well done, thou good and faithful servant: thou hast been faithful over a few things, I will make thee ruler over many things: enter thou into the joy of thy lord. [22]He also that had received two talents came and said, Lord, thou deliveredst unto me two talents: behold, I have gained two other talents beside them. [23]His lord said unto him, Well done, good and faithful servant; thou hast been faithful over a few things, I will make thee ruler over many things: enter thou into the joy of thy lord. [24]Then he which had received the one talent came and said, Lord, I knew thee that thou art an hard man, reaping where thou hast not sown, and gathering where thou hast not strawed: [25]And I was afraid, and went and hid thy talent in the earth: lo, there thou hast that is thine. [26]His lord answered and said unto him, Thou wicked and slothful servant, thou knewest that I reap where I sowed not, and gather where I have not strawed: [27]Thou oughtest therefore to have put my money to the exchangers, and then at my coming I should have received mine own with usury. [28]Take therefore the talent from him, and give it unto him which hath ten talents. [29]For unto every one that hath shall be given, and he shall have abundance: but from him that hath not shall be taken away even that which he hath. [30]And cast ye the unprofitable servant into outer darkness: there shall be weeping and gnashing of teeth.

Mk	Lk
11:3 [3]And if any man say unto you, Why do ye this? say ye that the Lord hath need of him; and straightway he will send him hither. **12:35–37** [35]And Jesus answered and said, while he taught in the temple, How say the scribes that Christ is the Son of David? [36]For David himself said by the Holy Ghost, The LORD said to my Lord, Sit thou on my right hand, till I make thine enemies thy footstool. [37]David therefore himself calleth him Lord; and whence is he then his son? And the common people heard him gladly. **14:61** [61]But he held his peace, and answered nothing. Again the high priest asked him, and said unto him, Art thou the Christ, the Son of the Blessed?	**1:25** [25]Thus hath the Lord dealt with me in the days wherein he looked on me, to take away my reproach among men. **3:23–38** [23]And Jesus himself began to be about thirty years of age, being (as was supposed) the son of Joseph, which was the son of Heli, [24]Which was the son of Matthat, which was the son of Levi, which was the son of Melchi, which was the son of Janna, which was the son of Joseph, [25]Which was the son of Mattathias, which was the son of Amos, which was the son of Naum, which was the son of Esli, which was the son of Nagge, [26]Which was the son of Maath, which was the son of Mattathias, which was the son of Semei, which was the son of Joseph, which was the son of Juda, [27]Which was the son of Joanna, which was the son of Rhesa, which was the son of Zorobabel, which was the son of Salathiel, which was the son of Neri, [28]Which was the son of Melchi, which was the son of Addi, which was the son of Cosam, which was the son of Elmodam, which was the son of Er, [29]Which was the son of Jose, which was the son of Eliezer, which was the son of Jorim, which was the son of Matthat, which was the son of Levi, [30]Which was the son of Simeon, which was the son of Juda, which was the son of Joseph, which was the son of Jonan, which was the son of Eliakim, [31]Which was the son of Melea, which was the son of Menan, which was the son of Mattatha, which was the son of Nathan, which was the son of David, [32]Which was the son of Jesse, which was the son of Obed, which was the son of Booz, which was the son of Salmon, which was the son of Naasson, [33]Which was the son of Aminadab, which was the son of Aram, which was the son of Esrom, which was the son of Phares, which was the son of Juda, [34]Which was the son of Jacob, which was the son of Isaac, which was the son of Abraham, which was the son of Thara, which was the son of Nachor, [35]Which was the son of Saruch, which was the son of Ragau, which was the son of Phalec, which was the son of Heber, which was the son of Sala, [36]Which was the son of Cainan, which was the son of Arphaxad, which was the son of Sem, which was the son of Noe, which was the son of Lamech, [37]Which was the son of Mathusala, which was the son of Enoch, which was the son of Jared, which was the son of Maleleel, which was the son of Cainan, [38]Which was the son of Enos, which was the son of Seth, which was the son of Adam, which was the son of God. **12:41–46** [41]Then Peter said unto him, Lord, speakest thou this parable unto us, or even to all? [42]And the Lord said, Who then is that faithful and wise steward, whom his lord shall make ruler over his household, to give them their portion of meat in due season? [43]Blessed is that servant, whom his lord when he cometh shall find so doing. [44]Of a truth I say unto you, that he will make him ruler over all that he hath. [45]But and if that servant say in his heart, My lord delayeth his coming; and shall begin to beat the menservants and maidens, and to eat and drink, and to be drunken; [46]The lord of that servant will come in a day when he looketh not for him, and at an hour when he is not aware, and will cut him in sunder, and will appoint him his portion with the unbelievers. **19:11–27** [11]And as they heard these things, he added and spake a parable, because he was nigh to Jerusalem, and because they thought that the kingdom of God should immediately appear. [12]He said therefore, A certain nobleman went into a far country to receive for himself a kingdom, and to return. [13]And he called his ten servants, and delivered them ten pounds, and said unto them, Occupy till I come. [14]But his citizens hated him, and sent a message after him, saying, We will not have this man to reign over us. [15]And it came to pass, that when he was returned, having received the kingdom, then he commanded these servants to be called unto him, to whom he had given the money, that he might know how much every man had gained by trading. [16]Then came the first, saying, Lord, thy pound hath gained ten pounds. [17]And he said unto him, Well, thou good servant: because thou hast been faithful in a very little, have thou authority over ten cities. [18]And the second came, saying, Lord, thy pound hath gained five pounds. [19]And he said likewise to him, Be thou also over five cities. [20]And another came, saying, Lord, behold, here is thy pound, which I have kept laid up in a napkin: [21]For I feared thee, because thou art an austere man: thou takest up that thou layedst not down, and reapest that thou didst not sow. [22]And he saith unto him, Out of thine own mouth will I judge thee, thou wicked servant. Thou knewest that I was an austere man, taking up that I laid not down, and reaping that I did not sow: [23]Wherefore then gavest not thou my money into the bank, that at my coming I might have required mine own with usury? [24]And he said unto them that stood by, Take from him the pound, and give it to him that hath ten pounds. [25](And they said unto him, Lord, he hath ten pounds.) [26]For I say unto you, That unto every one which hath shall be given; and from him that hath not, even that he hath shall be taken away from him. [27]But those mine enemies, which would not that I should reign over them, bring hither, and slay them before me. **19:34** [34]And they said, The Lord hath need of him.

Romans 9:5 continued on next page

ROMANS 9:5—God desires Jews and Gentiles (9:1–11:36), 56–58 CE (*continued*)

Theme	ROM	Lk	Jn
(*Cont.*) **Jewish Christ, over all**	**9:5** (above) **10:9** (above) **10:13** (above)	***Continued*** **20:41–44** [41]And Jesus, moved with compassion, put forth his hand, and touched him, and saith unto him, I will; be thou clean. [42]And as soon as he had spoken, immediately the leprosy departed from him, and he was cleansed. [43]And he straitly charged him, and forthwith sent him away; [44]And saith unto him, See thou say nothing to any man: but go thy way, show thyself to the priest, and offer for thy cleansing those things which Moses commanded, for a testimony unto them. **21:3** [3]And if any man say ought unto you, ye shall say, The Lord hath need of them; and straightway he will send them. **22:41–46** [41]While the Pharisees were gathered together, Jesus asked them, [42]Saying, What think ye of Christ? whose son is he? They say unto him, The Son of David. [43]He saith unto them, How then doth David in spirit call him Lord, saying, [44]The LORD said unto my Lord, Sit thou on my right hand, till I make thine enemies thy footstool? [45]If David then call him Lord, how is he his son? [46]And no man was able to answer him a word, neither durst any man from that day forth ask him any more questions **24:45–51** [45]Who then is a faithful and wise servant, whom his lord hath made ruler over his household, to give them meat in due season? [46]Blessed is that servant, whom his lord when he cometh shall find so doing. [47]Verily I say unto you, That he shall make him ruler over all his goods. [48]But if that evil servant shall say in his heart, My lord delayeth his coming; [49]And shall begin to smite his fellow servants, and to eat and drink with the drunken; [50]The lord of that servant shall come in a day when he looketh not for him, and in an hour that he is not aware of, [51]And shall cut him asunder, and appoint him his portion with the hypocrites: there shall be weeping and gnashing of teeth.	**1:18** [18]No man hath seen God at any time; the only begotten Son, which is in the bosom of the Father, he hath declared him.

Paul	Jewish Writings	Other
1 Cor 12:3 [3]Wherefore I give you to understand, that no man speaking by the Spirit of God calleth Jesus accursed: and that no man can say that Jesus is the Lord, but by the Holy Ghost. **1 Cor 15:20–28** [20]But now is Christ risen from the dead, and become the firstfruits of them that slept. [21]For since by man came death, by man came also the resurrection of the dead. [22]For as in Adam all die, even so in Christ shall all be made alive. [23]But every man in his own order: Christ the firstfruits; afterward they that are Christ's at his coming. [24]Then cometh the end, when he shall have delivered up the kingdom to God, even the Father; when he shall have put down all rule and all authority and power. [25]For he must reign, till he hath put all enemies under his feet. [26]The last enemy that shall be destroyed is death. [27]For he hath put all things under his feet. But when he saith all things are put under him, it is manifest that he is excepted, which did put all things under him. [28]And when all things shall be subdued unto him, then shall the Son also himself be subject unto him that put all things under him, that God may be all in all. **Phil 2:5–11** [5]Let this mind be in you, which was also in Christ Jesus: [6]Who, being in the form of God, thought it not robbery to be equal with God: [7]But made himself of no reputation, and took upon him the form of a servant, and was made in the likeness of men: [8]And being found in fashion as a man, he humbled himself, and became obedient unto death, even the death of the cross. [9]Wherefore God also hath highly exalted him, and given him a name which is above every name: [10]That at the name of Jesus every knee should bow, of things in heaven, and things in earth, and things under the earth; [11]And that every tongue should confess that Jesus Christ is Lord, to the glory of God the Father. **2 Thes 1:1** [1]Paul, and Silvanus, and Timotheus, unto the church of the Thessalonians in God our Father and the Lord Jesus Christ: **Tit 2:13 (Pseudo)** [13]Looking for that blessed hope, and the glorious appearing of the great God and our Saviour Jesus Christ;	**Ps 110** [1]The LORD said unto my Lord, Sit thou at my right hand, until I make thine enemies thy footstool. [2]The LORD shall send the rod of thy strength out of Zion: rule thou in the midst of thine enemies. [3]Thy people shall be willing in the day of thy power, in the beauties of holiness from the womb of the morning: thou hast the dew of thy youth. [4]The LORD hath sworn, and will not repent, Thou art a priest for ever after the order of Melchizedek. [5]The Lord at thy right hand shall strike through kings in the day of his wrath. [6]He shall judge among the heathen, he shall fill the places with the dead bodies; he shall wound the heads over many countries. [7]He shall drink of the brook in the way: therefore shall he lift up the head. **Prov 8:22–31** [22]The LORD possessed me in the beginning of his way, before his works of old. [23]I was set up from everlasting, from the beginning, or ever the earth was. [24]When there were no depths, I was brought forth; when there were no fountains abounding with water. [25]Before the mountains were settled, before the hills was I brought forth: [26]While as yet he had not made the earth, nor the fields, nor the highest part of the dust of the world. [27]When he prepared the heavens, I was there: when he set a compass upon the face of the depth: [28]When he established the clouds above: when he strengthened the fountains of the deep: [29]When he gave to the sea his decree, that the waters should not pass his commandment: when he appointed the foundations of the earth: [30]Then I was by him, as one brought up with him: and I was daily his delight, rejoicing always before him; [31]Rejoicing in the habitable part of his earth; and my delights were with the sons of men. **Is 9:6,7** [6]For unto us a child is born, unto us a son is given: and the government shall be upon his shoulder: and his name shall be called Wonderful, Counsellor, The mighty God, The everlasting Father, The Prince of Peace. [7]Of the increase of his government and peace there shall be no end, upon the throne of David, and upon his kingdom, to order it, and to establish it with judgment and with justice from henceforth even for ever. The zeal of the LORD of hosts will perform this. **Is 11:1–2** [1]And there shall come forth a rod out of the stem of Jesse, and a Branch shall grow out of his roots: [2]And the spirit of the LORD shall rest upon him, the spirit of wisdom and understanding, the spirit of counsel and might, the spirit of knowledge and of the fear of the LORD;	**Q-Quelle** Watchful and Faithful: Rom 9:5/1 Cor 12:3/[Mt 24:42-51]/[Lk 12:35-48] (QS 41 [Thom 21:3, 103], QS 42); Parable of Pounds: Rom 9:5/1 Cor 12:3/[Mt 25:14-30]/[Lk 19:11-27] (QS 61 [Thom 41])

ROMANS 9:6—God desires Jews and Gentiles (9:1–11:36), 56–58 CE

Theme	ROM	Mt	Jewish Writings	Other
Not all Israelites	**9:6** [6]Not as though the word of God hath taken none effect. For they are not all Israel, which are of Israel:	**3:9** [9]And think not to say within yourselves, We have Abraham to our father: for I say unto you, that God is able of these stones to raise up children unto Abraham.	**Num 23:19** [19]God is not a man, that he should lie; neither the son of man, that he should repent: hath he said, and shall he not do it? or hath he spoken, and shall he not make it good?	**Q-Quelle** Preaching of John: Rom 9:6/Mt 3:7-10/[Lk 3:7-9(QS 4/)]

ROMANS 9:7—God desires Jews and Gentiles (9:1–11:36), 56–58 CE

Theme	ROM	Paul	Jewish Writings
Isaac's heirs called	**9:7** [7]Neither, because they are the seed of Abraham, are they all children: but, In Isaac shall thy seed be called.	**Gal 3:29** [29]But as then he that was born after the flesh persecuted him that was born after the Spirit, even so it is now.	**Gen 21:12** [12]And God said unto Abraham, Let it not be grievous in thy sight because of the lad, and because of thy bondwoman; in all that Sarah hath said unto thee, hearken unto her voice; for in Isaac shall thy seed be called.

ROMANS 9:8—God desires Jews and Gentiles (9:1–11:36), 56–58 CE

Theme	ROM	Paul
Children of flesh, not God's	**9:8** [8]That is, They which are the children of the flesh, these are not the children of God: but the children of the promise are counted for the seed.	**Gal 4:23** [23]But he who was of the bondwoman was born after the flesh; but he of the freewoman was by promise. **Gal 4:28** [28]Now we, brethren, as Isaac was, are the children of promise.

ROMANS 9:9—God desires Jews and Gentiles (9:1–11:36), 56–58 CE

Theme	ROM	Paul
Sarah to have a son	**9:9** [9]For this is the word of promise, At this time will I come, and Sarah shall have a son.	**Gen 18:10** [10]And he said, I will certainly return unto thee according to the time of life; and, lo, Sarah thy wife shall have a son. And Sarah heard it in the tent door, which was behind him. **Gen 18:14** [14]Is any thing too hard for the LORD? At the time appointed I will return unto thee, according to the time of life, and Sarah shall have a son.

ROMANS 9:10—God desires Jews and Gentiles (9:1–11:36), 56–58 CE

Theme	ROM	Jewish Writings
Rebecca conceived	**9:10** [10]And not only this; but when Rebecca also had conceived by one, even by our father Isaac;	**Gen 25:21** [21]And Isaac entreated the LORD for his wife, because she was barren: and the LORD was entreated of him, and Rebekah his wife conceived.

ROMANS 9:12—God desires Jews and Gentiles (9:1–11:36), 56–58 CE

Theme	ROM	Jewish Writings
Rebecca's oldest serves younger	**9:12** [12]It was said unto her, The elder shall serve the younger. **11:5–6** [5]Even so then at this present time also there is a remnant according to the election of grace. [6]And if by grace, then is it no more of works: otherwise grace is no more grace. But if it be of works, then is it no more grace: otherwise work is no more work.	**Gen 25:23–24** [23]And the LORD said unto her, Two nations are in thy womb, and two manner of people shall be separated from thy bowels; and the one people shall be stronger than the other people; and the elder shall serve the younger. [24]And when her days to be delivered were fulfilled, behold, there were twins in her womb

ROMANS 9:13—God desires Jews and Gentiles (9:1–11:36), 56–58 CE

Theme	ROM	Jewish Writings
Jacob and Esau	**9:13** [13]As it is written, Jacob have I loved, but Esau have I hated.	**Mal 1:3** [3]And I hated Esau, and laid his mountains and his heritage waste for the dragons of the wilderness.

ROMANS 9:14—God desires Jews and Gentiles (9:1–11:36), 56–58 CE

Theme	ROM	Jewish Writings
God's righteousness	**9:14** [14]What shall we say then? Is there unrighteousness with God? God forbid.	**Dt 32:4** [4]He is the Rock, his work is perfect: for all his ways are judgment: a God of truth and without iniquity, just and right is he.

ROMANS 9:15—God desires Jews and Gentiles (9:1–11:36), 56–58 CE

Theme	ROM	Jewish Writings
God and mercy	**9:15** [15]For he saith to Moses, I will have mercy on whom I will have mercy, and I will have compassion on whom I will have compassion.	**Ex 33:19** [19]And he said, I will make all my goodness pass before thee, and I will proclaim the name of the LORD before thee; and will be gracious to whom I will be gracious, and will show mercy on whom I will show mercy.

ROMANS 9:16—God desires Jews and Gentiles (9:1–11:36), 56–58 CE

Theme	ROM	Paul
God shows mercy	**9:16** [16]So then it is not of him that willeth, nor of him that runneth, but of God that showeth mercy.	**Eph 2:8 (Pseudo)** [8]For by grace are ye saved through faith; and that not of yourselves: it is the gift of God: **Tit 3:5 (Pseudo)** [5]Not by works of righteousness which we have done, but according to his mercy he saved us, by the washing of regeneration, and renewing of the Holy Ghost;

ROMANS 9:17—God desires Jews and Gentiles (9:1–11:36), 56–58 CE

Theme	ROM	Jewish Writings
Power in raising dead	**9:17** [17]For the scripture saith unto Pharaoh, Even for this same purpose have I raised thee up, that I might show my power in thee, and that my name might be declared throughout all the earth.	**Ex 9:16** [16]And in very deed for this cause have I raised thee up, for to show in thee my power; and that my name may be declared throughout all the earth.

ROMANS 9:18—God desires Jews and Gentiles (9:1–11:36), 56–58 CE

Theme	ROM	Jewish Writings
God's mercy and hardening of heart	**9:18** [18]Therefore hath he mercy on whom he will have mercy, and whom he will he hardeneth. **11:30–32** [30]For as ye in times past have not believed God, yet have now obtained mercy through their unbelief: [31]Even so have these also now not believed, that through your mercy they also may obtain mercy. [32]For God hath concluded them all in unbelief, that he might have mercy upon all.	**Ex 4:21** [21]And the LORD said unto Moses, When thou goest to return into Egypt, see that thou do all those wonders before Pharaoh, which I have put in thine hand: but I will harden his heart, that he shall not let the people go. **Ex 7:3** [3]And I will harden Pharaoh's heart, and multiply my signs and my wonders in the land of Egypt.

ROMANS 9:19—God desires Jews and Gentiles (9:1–11:36), 56–58 CE

Theme	ROM	Jewish Writings
Resisting God's will	**9:19** [19]Thou wilt say then unto me, Why doth he yet find fault? For who hath resisted his will? **3:7** [7]For if the truth of God hath more abounded through my lie unto his glory; why yet am I also judged as a sinner?	**Wis 2:12** [12]Therefore let us lie in wait for the righteous; because he is not for our turn, and he is clean contrary to our doings: he upbraideth us with our offending the law, and objecteth to our infamy the transgressings of our education.

ROMANS 9:20–21—God desires Jews and Gentiles (9:1–11:36), 56–58 CE

Theme	ROM	Jewish Writings
Replying against God	**9:20–21** [20]Nay but, O man, who art thou that repliest against God? Shall the thing formed say to him that formed it, Why hast thou made me thus? [21]Hath not the potter power over the clay, of the same lump to make one vessel unto honour, and another unto dishonour?	**Wis 15:7** [7]For the potter, tempering soft earth, fashioneth every vessel with much labour for our service: yea, of the same clay he maketh both the vessels that serve for clean uses, and likewise also all such as serve to the contrary: but what is the use of either sort, the potter himself is the judge. **Is 29:16** [16]Surely your turning of things upside down shall be esteemed as the potter's clay: for shall the work say of him that made it, He made me not? or shall the thing framed say of him that framed it, He had no understanding? **Is 45:9** [9]Woe unto him that striveth with his Maker! Let the potsherd strive with the potsherds of the earth. Shall the clay say to him that fashioneth it, What makest thou? or thy work, He hath no hands? **Jer 18:6** [6]O house of Israel, cannot I do with you as this potter? saith the LORD. Behold, as the clay is in the potter's hand, so are ye in mine hand, O house of Israel.

ROMANS 9:22—God desires Jews and Gentiles (9:1–11:36), 56–58 CE

Theme	ROM	Mt
God's wrath and Jesus' lament	**9:22** [22]What if God, willing to show his wrath, and to make his power known, endured with much longsuffering the vessels of wrath fitted to destruction: **2:4** [4]Or despisest thou the riches of his goodness and forbearance and longsuffering; not knowing that the goodness of God leadeth thee to repentance? **11:25** [25]For I would not, brethren, that ye should be ignorant of this mystery, lest ye should be wise in your own conceits; that blindness in part is happened to Israel, until the fulness of the Gentiles be come in.	**21:10** [10]And when he was come into Jerusalem, all the city was moved, saying, Who is this? **21:33–44** [33]Hear another parable: There was a certain householder, which planted a vineyard, and hedged it round about, and digged a winepress in it, and built a tower, and let it out to husbandmen, and went into a far country: [34]And when the time of the fruit drew near, he sent his servants to the husbandmen, that they might receive the fruits of it. [35]And the husbandmen took his servants, and beat one, and killed another, and stoned another. [36]Again, he sent other servants more than the first: and they did unto them likewise. [37]But last of all he sent unto them his son, saying, They will reverence my son. [38]But when the husbandmen saw the son, they said among themselves, This is the heir; come, let us kill him, and let us seize on his inheritance. [39]And they caught him, and cast him out of the vineyard, and slew him. [40]When the lord therefore of the vineyard cometh, what will he do unto those husbandmen? [41]They say unto him, He will miserably destroy those wicked men, and will let out his vineyard unto other husbandmen, which shall render him the fruits in their seasons. [42]Jesus saith unto them, Did ye never read in the scriptures, The stone which the builders rejected, the same is become the head of the corner: this is the Lord's doing, and it is marvellous in our eyes? [43]Therefore say I unto you, The kingdom of God shall be taken from you, and given to a nation bringing forth the fruits thereof. [44]And whosoever shall fall on this stone shall be broken: but on whomsoever it shall fall, it will grind him to powder. **22:1–10** [1]And Jesus answered and spake unto them again by parables, and said, [2]The kingdom of heaven is like unto a certain king, which made a marriage for his son, [3]And sent forth his servants to call them that were bidden to the wedding: and they would not come. [4]Again, he sent forth other servants, saying, Tell them which are bidden, Behold, I have prepared my dinner: my oxen and my fatlings are killed, and all things are ready: come unto the marriage. [5]But they made light of it, and went their ways, one to his farm, another to his merchandise: [6]And the remnant took his servants, and entreated them spitefully, and slew them. [7]But when the king heard thereof, he was wroth: and he sent forth his armies, and destroyed those murderers, and burned up their city. [8]Then saith he to his servants, The wedding is ready, but they which were bidden were not worthy. [9]Go ye therefore into the highways, and as many as ye shall find, bid to the marriage. [10]So those servants went out into the highways, and gathered together all as many as they found, both bad and good: and the wedding was furnished with guests. **23:29–39** [29]Woe unto you, scribes and Pharisees, hypocrites! because ye build the tombs of the prophets, and garnish the sepulchres of the righteous, [30]And say, If we had been in the days of our fathers, we would not have been partakers with them in the blood of the prophets. [31]Wherefore ye be witnesses unto yourselves, that ye are the children of them which killed the prophets. [32]Fill ye up then the measure of your fathers. [33]Ye serpents, ye generation of vipers, how can ye escape the damnation of hell? [34]Wherefore, behold, I send unto you prophets, and wise men, and scribes: and some of them ye shall kill and crucify; and some of them shall ye scourge in your synagogues, and persecute them from city to city: [35]That upon you may come all the righteous blood shed upon the earth, from the blood of righteous Abel unto the blood of Zacharias son of Barachias, whom ye slew between the temple and the altar. [36]Verily I say unto you, All these things shall come upon this generation. [37]O Jerusalem, Jerusalem, thou that killest the prophets, and stonest them which are sent unto thee, how often would I have gathered thy children together, even as a hen gathereth her chickens under her wings, and ye would not! [38]Behold, your house is left unto you desolate. [39]For I say unto you, Ye shall not see me henceforth, till ye shall say, Blessed is he that cometh in the name of the Lord.

Mk

11:11–26

11And Jesus entered into Jerusalem, and into the temple: and when he had looked round about upon all things, and now the eventide was come, he went out unto Bethany with the twelve. 12And on the morrow, when they were come from Bethany, he was hungry: 13And seeing a fig tree afar off having leaves, he came, if haply he might find any thing thereon: and when he came to it, he found nothing but leaves; for the time of figs was not yet. 14And Jesus answered and said unto it, No man eat fruit of thee hereafter for ever. And his disciples heard it. 15And they come to Jerusalem: and Jesus went into the temple, and began to cast out them that sold and bought in the temple, and overthrew the tables of the money changers, and the seats of them that sold doves; 16And would not suffer that any man should carry any vessel through the temple. 17And he taught, saying unto them, Is it not written, My house shall be called of all nations the house of prayer? but ye have made it a den of thieves. 18And the scribes and chief priests heard it, and sought how they might destroy him: for they feared him, because all the people was astonished at his doctrine. 19And when even was come, he went out of the city. 20And in the morning, as they passed by, they saw the fig tree dried up from the roots. 21And Peter calling to remembrance saith unto him, Master, behold, the fig tree which thou cursedst is withered away. 22And Jesus answering saith unto them, Have faith in God. 23For verily I say unto you, That whosoever shall say unto this mountain, Be thou removed, and be thou cast into the sea; and shall not doubt in his heart, but shall believe that those things which he saith shall come to pass; he shall have whatsoever he saith. 24Therefore I say unto you, What things soever ye desire, when ye pray, believe that ye receive them, and ye shall have them. 25And when ye stand praying, forgive, if ye have ought against any: that your Father also which is in heaven may forgive you your trespasses. 26But if ye do not forgive, neither will your Father which is in heaven forgive your trespasses.

12:1–12

1And he began to speak unto them by parables. A certain man planted a vineyard, and set an hedge about it, and digged a place for the winefat, and built a tower, and let it out to husbandmen, and went into a far country. 2And at the season he sent to the husbandmen a servant, that he might receive from the husbandmen of the fruit of the vineyard. 3And they caught him, and beat him, and sent him away empty. 4And again he sent unto them another servant; and at him they cast stones, and wounded him in the head, and sent him away shamefully handled. 5And again he sent another; and him they killed, and many others; beating some, and killing some. 6Having yet therefore one son, his wellbeloved, he sent him also last unto them, saying, They will reverence my son. 7But those husbandmen said among themselves, This is the heir; come, let us kill him, and the inheritance shall be ours. 8And they took him, and killed him, and cast him out of the vineyard. 9What shall therefore the lord of the vineyard do? he will come and destroy the husbandmen, and will give the vineyard unto others. 10And have ye not read this scripture; The stone which the builders rejected is become the head of the corner: 11This was the Lord's doing, and it is marvellous in our eyes? 12And they sought to lay hold on him, but feared the people: for they knew that he had spoken the parable against them: and they left him, and went their way.

Jn

11:47–51

47Then gathered the chief priests and the Pharisees a council, and said, What do we? for this man doeth many miracles. **48If we let him thus alone, all men will believe on him: and the Romans shall come and take away both our place and nation. 49And one of them, named Caiaphas, being the high priest that same year, said unto them, Ye know nothing at all, 50Nor consider that it is expedient for us, that one man should die for the people, and that the whole nation perish not. 51And this spake he not of himself: but being high priest that year, he prophesied that Jesus should die for that nation;**

13:34–35

34A new commandment I give unto you, That ye love one another; as I have loved you, that ye also love one another. 35By this shall all men know that ye are my disciples, if ye have love one to another.

20:9–19

9For as yet they knew not the scripture, that he must rise again from the dead. 10Then the disciples went away again unto their own home. 11But Mary stood without at the sepulchre weeping: and as she wept, she stooped down, and looked into the sepulchre, 12And seeth two angels in white sitting, the one at the head, and the other at the feet, where the body of Jesus had lain. 13And they say unto her, Woman, why weepest thou? She saith unto them, Because they have taken away my Lord, and I know not where they have laid him. 14And when she had thus said, she turned herself back, and saw Jesus standing, and knew not that it was Jesus. 15Jesus saith unto her, Woman, why weepest thou? whom seekest thou? She, supposing him to be the gardener, saith unto him, Sir, if thou have borne him hence, tell me where thou hast laid him, and I will take him away. 16Jesus saith unto her, Mary. She turned herself, and saith unto him, Rabboni; which is to say, Master. 17Jesus saith unto her, Touch me not; for I am not yet ascended to my Father: but go to my brethren, and say unto them, I ascend unto my Father, and your Father; and to my God, and your God. 18Mary Magdalene came and told the disciples that she had seen the Lord, and that he had spoken these things unto her. 19Then the same day at evening, being the first day of the week, when the doors were shut where the disciples were assembled for fear of the Jews, came Jesus and stood in the midst, and saith unto them, Peace be unto you.

21:23–24

23Then went this saying abroad among the brethren, that that disciple should not die: yet Jesus said not unto him, He shall not die; but, If I will that he tarry till I come, what is that to thee? 24This is the disciple which testifieth of these things, and wrote these things: and we know that his testimony is true.

Romans 9:22 continued on next page

ROMANS 9:22—God desires Jews and Gentiles (9:1–11:36), 56–58 CE

Theme	ROM	Paul	Jewish Writings	Other
(*Cont.*) **God's wrath and Jesus' lament**	**9:22 (above)** **2:4 (above)** **11:25 (above)**	**1 Thes 2:16** [16]Forbidding us to speak to the Gentiles that they might be saved, to fill up their sins alway: for the wrath is come upon them to the uttermost.	**Wis 12:20–21** [20] For if thou didst punish the enemies of thy children, and the condemned to death, with such deliberation, giving them time and place, whereby they might be delivered from their malice: [21] With how great circumspection didst thou judge thine own sons, unto whose fathers thou hast sworn, and made covenants of good promises? **Jer 50:25** [25]The LORD hath opened his armoury, and hath brought forth the weapons of his indignation: for this is the work of the Lord GOD of hosts in the land of the Chaldeans.	**Q-Quelle** Great Supper: Rom 9:22/ Mt 22:1-14/[Lk 14:15-24 (QS 51 [Thom 64])]; Lament over Jerusalem: Rom 9:22/Mt 23:37-39/ [Lk 13:34-35 (QS 49)]; Against Pharisees: Rom 9:22/1 Thes 2:16/Mt 23:4-36/[Mk 7:1-9]/[Lk11:37-54 (QS 34 [Thom 39:1, 89, 102])]

ROMANS 9:26—God desires Jews and Gentiles (9:1–11:36), 56–58 CE

Theme	ROM	Jewish Writings
God's people	**9:26** [26]And it shall come to pass, that in the place where it was said unto them, Ye are not my people; there shall they be called the children of the living God.	**Hos 2:1** [1]Say ye unto your brethren, Ammi; and to your sisters, Ruhamah.

ROMANS 9:27–28—God desires Jews and Gentiles (9:1–11:36), 56–58 CE

Theme	ROM	Jewish Writings
Remnant	**9:27–28** [27]Esaias also crieth concerning Israel, Though the number of the children of Israel be as the sand of the sea, a remnant shall be saved: [28]For he will finish the work, and cut it short in righteousness: because a short work will the Lord make upon the earth. **11:5** [5]Even so then at this present time also there is a remnant according to the election of grace.	**Is 10:22** [22]For though thy people Israel be as the sand of the sea, yet a remnant of them shall return: the consumption decreed shall overflow with righteousness. **Is 28:22** [22]Now therefore be ye not mockers, lest your bands be made strong: for I have heard from the Lord GOD of hosts a consumption, even determined upon the whole earth. **Hos 2:1** [1]Say ye unto your brethren, Ammi; and to your sisters, Ruhamah.

ROMANS 9:29—God desires Jews and Gentiles (9:1–11:36), 56–58 CE

Theme	ROM	Mt	Jewish Writings	Other
God's seed not of Sodom	**9:29** [29]And as Esaias said before, Except the Lord of Sabaoth had left us a seed, we had been as Sodoma, and been made like unto Gomorrha.	**10:15** [15]Verily I say unto you, It shall be more tolerable for the land of Sodom and Gomorrha in the day of judgment, than for that city.	**Is 1:9** [9]Except the LORD of hosts had left unto us a very small remnant, we should have been as Sodom, and we should have been like unto Gomorrah.	**Q-Quelle** Commissioning of 70: Rom 9:29/[Mt 9:37-38], Mt 10:7-16/[Lk 10:1-12 (QS 21)]

ROMANS 9:30—God desires Jews and Gentiles (9:1–11:36), 56–58 CE

Theme	ROM
Gentiles have righteousness	**9:30** [30]What shall we say then? That the Gentiles, which followed not after righteousness, have attained to righteousness, even the righteousness which is of faith. **10:4, 20** [4]For Christ is the end of the law for righteousness to every one that believeth. . . .[20]But Esaias is very bold, and saith, I was found of them that sought me not; I was made manifest unto them that asked not after me.

ROMANS 9:31—God desires Jews and Gentiles (9:1–11:36), 56–58 CE

Theme	ROM
Israel not righteous	**9:31** [31]But Israel, which followed after the law of righteousness, hath not attained to the law of righteousness. **10:3** [3]For they being ignorant of God's righteousness, and going about to establish their own righteousness, have not submitted themselves unto the righteousness of God.

ROMANS 9:32—God desires Jews and Gentiles (9:1–11:36), 56–58 CE

Theme	ROM	Jewish Writings
Faith above works	**9:32** [32]Wherefore? Because they sought it not by faith, but as it were by the works of the law. For they stumbled at that stumblingstone;	**Is 8:14** [14]And he shall be for a sanctuary; but for a stone of stumbling and for a rock of offence to both the houses of Israel, for a gin and for a snare to the inhabitants of Jerusalem.

ROMANS 9:33—God desires Jews and Gentiles (9:1–11:36), 56–58 CE

Theme	ROM	NT	Jewish Writings
Stumbling block in Zion	**9:33** [33]As it is written, Behold, I lay in Sion a stumblingstone and rock of offence: and whosoever believeth on him shall not be ashamed.	**1 Pet 2:6–8** [6]Wherefore also it is contained in the scripture, Behold, I lay in Sion a chief corner stone, elect, precious: and he that believeth on him shall not be confounded. [7]Unto you therefore which believe he is precious: but unto them which be disobedient, the stone which the builders disallowed, the same is made the head of the corner, [8]And a stone of stumbling, and a rock of offence, even to them which stumble at the word, being disobedient: whereunto also they were appointed.	**Is 28:16** [16]Therefore thus saith the Lord GOD, Behold, I lay in Zion for a foundation a stone, a tried stone, a precious corner stone, a sure foundation: he that believeth shall not make haste.

ROMANS 10:1—God desires Jews and Gentiles (9:1–11:36), 56–58 CE

Theme	ROM
Prayer for Israel's salvation	**10:1** [1]Brethren, my heart's desire and prayer to God for Israel is, that they might be saved. **9:13** [13]As it is written, Jacob have I loved, but Esau have I hated.

ROMANS 10:2—God desires Jews and Gentiles (9:1–11:36), 56–58 CE

Theme	ROM	Lk
Israel's zeal for God	**10:2** [2]For I bear them record that they have a zeal of God, but not according to knowledge.	**Acts 22:3** [3]I am verily a man which am a Jew, born in Tarsus, a city in Cilicia, yet brought up in this city at the feet of Gamaliel, and taught according to the perfect manner of the law of the fathers, and was zealous toward God, as ye all are this day.

ROMANS 10:3—God desires Jews and Gentiles (9:1–11:36), 56–58 CE

Theme	ROM	Paul
Ignorant of righteousness	**10:3** [3]For they being ignorant of God's righteousness, and going about to establish their own righteousness, have not submitted themselves unto the righteousness of God. **9:31–32** [31]But Israel, which followed after the law of righteousness, hath not attained to the law of righteousness. [32]Wherefore? Because they sought it not by faith, but as it were by the works of the law. For they stumbled at that stumblingstone;	**Phil 3:9** [9]And be found in him, not having mine own righteousness, which is of the law, but that which is through the faith of Christ, the righteousness which is of God by faith:

ROMANS 10:4—God desires Jews and Gentiles (9:1–11:36), 56–58 CE

Theme	ROM	Lk	Paul	NT
Christ is the end of the law for the faithful	**10:4** [4]For Christ is the end of the law for righteousness to every one that believeth.	**Acts 13:38–39** [38]Be it known unto you therefore, men and brethren, that through this man is preached unto you the forgiveness of sins: [39]And by him all that believe are justified from all things, from which ye could not be justified by the law of Moses.	**2 Cor 3:14** [14]But their minds were blinded: for until this day remaineth the same veil untaken away in the reading of the old testament; which veil is done away in Christ.	**Heb 8:13** [13]In that he saith, A new covenant, he hath made the first old. Now that which decayeth and waxeth old is ready to vanish away.

ROMANS 10:5—God desires Jews and Gentiles (9:1–11:36), 56–58 CE

Theme	ROM	Paul	Jewish Writings
Living by the law	**10:5** [5]For Moses describeth the righteousness which is of the law, That the man which doeth those things shall live by them.	**Gal 3:12** [12]And the law is not of faith: but, The man that doeth them shall live in them.	**Lev 18:5** [5]Ye shall therefore keep my statutes, and my judgments: which if a man do, he shall live in them: I am the LORD.

ROMANS 10:6—God desires Jews and Gentiles (9:1–11:36), 56–58 CE

Theme	ROM	Jewish Writings
Faith from heaven	**10:6** [6]But the righteousness which is of faith speaketh on this wise, Say not in thine heart, Who shall ascend into heaven? (that is, to bring Christ down from above:)	**Dt 9:4** [4]Speak not thou in thine heart, after that the LORD thy God hath cast them out from before thee, saying, For my righteousness the LORD hath brought me in to possess this land: but for the wickedness of these nations the LORD doth drive them out from before thee. **Dt 30:12** [12]It is not in heaven, that thou shouldest say, Who shall go up for us to heaven, and bring it unto us, that we may hear it, and do it?

ROMANS 10:7—God desires Jews and Gentiles (9:1–11:36), 56–58 CE

Theme	ROM	NT	Jewish Writings
Faith from depths	**10:7** [7]Or, Who shall descend into the deep? (that is, to bring up Christ again from the dead.)	**1 Pet 3:19** [19]By which also he went and preached unto the spirits in prison;	**Dt 30:13** [13]Neither is it beyond the sea, that thou shouldest say, Who shall go over the sea for us, and bring it unto us, that we may hear it, and do it?

ROMANS 10:8—God desires Jews and Gentiles (9:1–11:36), 56–58 CE

Theme	ROM	Jewish Writings
Faith in the mouth	**10:8** [8]But what saith it? The word is nigh thee, even in thy mouth, and in thy heart: that is, the word of faith, which we preach;	**Dt 30:14** [14]But the word is very nigh unto thee, in thy mouth, and in thy heart, that thou mayest do it.

ROMANS 10:9—God desires Jews and Gentiles (9:1–11:36), 56–58 CE

Theme	ROM	Paul	Other
Confess Jesus is Lord	**10:9** [9]That if thou shalt confess with thy mouth the Lord Jesus, and shalt believe in thine heart that God hath raised him from the dead, thou shalt be saved.	**1 Cor 12:3** [3]Wherefore I give you to understand, that no man speaking by the Spirit of God calleth Jesus accursed: and that no man can say that Jesus is the Lord, but by the Holy Ghost.	**Q-Quelle** Watchful and Faithful: Rom 10:9/1 Cor 12:3/[Phil 2:1-11]/[Tit 2:13]/[Mt 24:42-51]/[Lk 12:35-48 (QS 41 [Thom 21:3, 103], QS 42)]; Parable of Pounds: Rom 10:9/1 Cor 12:3/[Mt 25:14-30]/[Lk 19:11-27 (QS 61 [Thom 41])

ROMANS 10:11—God desires Jews and Gentiles (9:1–11:36), 56–58 CE

Theme	ROM	Jewish Writings
Confidence in Jesus	**10:11** [11]For the scripture saith, Whosoever believeth on him shall not be ashamed. **9:33** [33]As it is written, Behold, I lay in Sion a stumblingstone and rock of offence: and whosoever believeth on him shall not be ashamed.	**Is 28:16** [16]Therefore thus saith the Lord GOD, Behold, I lay in Zion for a foundation a stone, a tried stone, a precious corner stone, a sure foundation: he that believeth shall not make haste.

ROMANS 10:12—God desires Jews and Gentiles (9:1–11:36), 56–58 CE

Theme	ROM	Mt	Lk
Solidarity until the Son comes	**10:12** [12]For there is no difference between the Jew and the Greek: for the same Lord over all is rich unto all that call upon him. **1:16** [16]For I am not ashamed of the gospel of Christ: for it is the power of God unto salvation to every one that believeth; to the Jew first, and also to the Greek. **3:22–29** [22]Even the righteousness of God which is by faith of Jesus Christ unto all and upon all them that believe: for there is no difference: [23]For all have sinned, and come short of the glory of God; [24]Being justified freely by his grace through the redemption that is in Christ Jesus: [25]Whom God hath set forth to be a propitiation through faith in his blood, to declare his righteousness for the remission of sins that are past, through the forbearance of God; [26]To declare, I say, at this time his righteousness: that he might be just, and the justifier of him which believeth in Jesus. [27]Where is boasting then? It is excluded. By what law? of works? Nay: but by the law of faith. [28]Therefore we conclude that a man is justified by faith without the deeds of the law. [29]Is he the God of the Jews only? is he not also of the Gentiles? Yes, of the Gentiles also:	**10:23** [23]But when they persecute you in this city, flee ye into another: for verily I say unto you, Ye shall not have gone over the cities of Israel, till the Son of man be come. **28:19** [19]Go ye therefore, and teach all nations, baptizing them in the name of the Father, and of the Son, and of the Holy Ghost:	**Acts 10:34** [34]Then Peter opened his mouth, and said, Of a truth I perceive that God is no respecter of persons: **Acts 15:9** [9]And put no difference between us and them, purifying their hearts by faith. **Acts 15:11** [11]But we believe that through the grace of the Lord Jesus Christ we shall be saved, even as they.

ROMANS 10:13—God desires Jews and Gentiles (9:1–11:36), 56–58 CE

Theme	ROM	Lk	Jewish Writings
Saving name	**10:13** [13]For whosoever shall call upon the name of the Lord shall be saved.	**Acts 2:21** [21]And it shall come to pass, that whosoever shall call on the name of the Lord shall be saved.	**Joel 3:5** [5]Because ye have taken my silver and my gold, and have carried into your temples my goodly pleasant things:

ROMANS 10:14—God desires Jews and Gentiles (9:1–11:36), 56–58 CE

Theme	ROM	Lk
Belief	**10:14** [14]How then shall they call on him in whom they have not believed? and how shall they believe in him of whom they have not heard? and how shall they hear without a preacher?	**Acts 8:31** [31]And he said, How can I, except some man should guide me? And he desired Philip that he would come up and sit with him.

Paul
Gal 2:7–9 [7]But contrariwise, when they saw that the gospel of the uncircumcision was committed unto me, as the gospel of the circumcision was unto Peter; [8](For he that wrought effectually in Peter to the apostleship of the circumcision, the same was mighty in me toward the Gentiles:) [9]And when James, Cephas, and John, who seemed to be pil- lars, perceived the grace that was given unto me, they gave to me and Barnabas the right hands of fellowship; that we should go unto the heathen, and they unto the circumcision.
Gal 3:28 [28]There is neither Jew nor Greek, there is neither bond nor free, there is neither male nor female: for ye are all one in Christ Jesus.
Eph 2:14(Pseudo) [14]For he is our peace, who hath made both one, and hath broken down the middle wall of parti- tion between us;

ROMANS 10:15—God desires Jews and Gentiles (9:1–11:36), 56–58 CE

Theme	ROM	Paul	Jewish Writings
Sent to preach	**10:15** [15]And how shall they preach, except they be sent? as it is written, How beautiful are the feet of them that preach the gospel of peace, and bring glad tidings of good things!	**Eph 6:15 (Pseudo)** [15]And your feet shod with the preparation of the gospel of peace;	**Is 52:7** [7]How beautiful upon the mountains are the feet of him that bringeth good tidings, that publisheth peace; that bringeth good tidings of good, that publisheth salvation; that saith unto Zion, Thy God reigneth! **Nah 2:1** [1]He that dasheth in pieces is come up before thy face: keep the munition, watch the way, make thy loins strong, fortify thy power mightily.

ROMANS 10:16—God desires Jews and Gentiles (9:1–11:36), 56–58 CE

Theme	ROM	Jn	Jewish Writings
Obedience to gospel brings belief	**10:16** [16]But they have not all obeyed the gospel. For Esaias saith, Lord, who hath believed our report?	**12:38** [38]That the saying of Esaias the prophet might be fulfilled, which he spake, Lord, who hath believed our report? and to whom hath the arm of the Lord been revealed?	**Is 53:1** [1]Who hath believed our report? and to whom is the arm of the LORD revealed?

ROMANS 10:17—God desires Jews and Gentiles (9:1–11:36), 56–58 CE

Theme	ROM	Jn
Faith by hearing	**10:17** [17]So then faith cometh by hearing, and hearing by the word of God.	**17:20** [20]Neither pray I for these alone, but for them also which shall believe on me through their word;

ROMANS 10:18—God desires Jews and Gentiles (9:1–11:36), 56–58 CE

Theme	ROM	Mt	Jewish Writings
Hearing the gospel	**10:18** [18]But I say, Have they not heard? Yes verily, their sound went into all the earth, and their words unto the ends of the world.	**24:14** [14]And this gospel of the kingdom shall be preached in all the world for a witness unto all nations; and then shall the end come.	**Ps 19:5** [5]Which is as a bridegroom coming out of his chamber, and rejoiceth as a strong man to run a race.

ROMANS 10:19—God desires Jews and Gentiles (9:1–11:36), 56–58 CE

Theme	ROM	Jewish Writings
Salvation to others provokes Israel to jealousy	**10:19** [19]But I say, Did not Israel know? First Moses saith, I will provoke you to jealousy by them that are no people, and by a foolish nation I will anger you. **11:11** [11]I say then, Have they stumbled that they should fall? God forbid: but rather through their fall salvation is come unto the Gentiles, for to provoke them to jealousy. **11:14** [14]If by any means I may provoke to emulation them which are my flesh, and might save some of them.	**Dt 32:21** [21]They have moved me to jealousy with that which is not God; they have provoked me to anger with their vanities: and I will move them to jealousy with those which are not a people; I will provoke them to anger with a foolish nation.

ROMANS 10:20–21—God desires Jews and Gentiles (9:1–11:36), 56–58 CE

Theme	ROM	Jewish Writings
God's patience with Israel	**10:20–21** [20]But Esaias is very bold, and saith, I was found of them that sought me not; I was made manifest unto them that asked not after me. [21]But to Israel he saith, All day long I have stretched forth my hands unto a disobedient and gainsaying people. **9:30** [30]What shall we say then? That the Gentiles, which followed not after righteousness, have attained to righteousness, even the righteousness which is of faith.	**Is 65:1–2** [1]I am sought of them that asked not for me; I am found of them that sought me not: I said, Behold me, behold me, unto a nation that was not called by my name. [2]I have spread out my hands all the day unto a rebellious people, which walketh in a way that was not good, after their own thoughts;

ROMANS 11:1–2—God desires Jews and Gentiles (9:1–11:36), 56–58 CE

Theme	ROM	Jewish Writings
God will not forsake his own	**11:1–2** [1]I say then, Hath God cast away his people? God forbid. For I also am an Israelite, of the seed of Abraham, of the tribe of Benjamin. [2]God hath not cast away his people which he foreknew. Wot ye not what the scripture saith of Elias? how he maketh intercession to God against Israel, saying,	**1 Sam 12:22** [22]For the LORD will not forsake his people for his great name's sake: because it hath pleased the LORD to make you his people. **Ps 94:14** [14]For the LORD will not cast off his people, neither will he forsake his inheritance.

ROMANS 11:1—God desires Jews and Gentiles (9:1–11:36), 56–58 CE

Theme	ROM	Paul
Paul, son of Israel	**11:1** [1]I say then, Hath God cast away his people? God forbid. For I also am an Israelite, of the seed of Abraham, of the tribe of Benjamin.	**2 Cor 11:22** [22]Are they Hebrews? so am I. Are they Israelites? so am I. Are they the seed of Abraham? so am I. **Phil 3:5** [5]Circumcised the eighth day, of the stock of Israel, of the tribe of Benjamin, an Hebrew of the Hebrews; as touching the law, a Pharisee;

ROMANS 11:3—God desires Jews and Gentiles (9:1–11:36), 56–58 CE

Theme	ROM	Jewish Writings
Israel killed prophets	**11:3** [3]Lord, they have killed thy prophets, and digged down thine altars; and I am left alone, and they seek my life.	**1 Kgs 19:10** [10]And he said, I have been very jealous for the LORD God of hosts: for the children of Israel have forsaken thy covenant, thrown down thine altars, and slain thy prophets with the sword; and I, even I only, am left; and they seek my life, to take it away. **1 Kgs 19:14** [14]And he said, I have been very jealous for the LORD God of hosts: because the children of Israel have forsaken thy covenant, thrown down thine altars, and slain thy prophets with the sword; and I, even I only, am left; and they seek my life, to take it away.

ROMANS 11:4—God desires Jews and Gentiles (9:1–11:36), 56–58 CE

Theme	ROM	Jewish Writings
7,000 reserved	**11:4** [4]But what saith the answer of God unto him? I have reserved to myself seven thousand men, who have not bowed the knee to the image of Baal.	**1 Kgs 19:18** [18]Yet I have left me seven thousand in Israel, all the knees which have not bowed unto Baal, and every mouth which hath not kissed him.

ROMANS 11:5—God desires Jews and Gentiles (9:1–11:36), 56–58 CE

Theme	ROM
Remnant	**11:5** [5]Even so then at this present time also there is a remnant according to the election of grace. **9:27** [27]Esaias also crieth concerning Israel, Though the number of the children of Israel be as the sand of the sea, a remnant shall be saved:

ROMANS 11:6—God desires Jews and Gentiles (9:1–11:36), 56–58 CE

Theme	ROM	Paul
Grace before works	**11:6** [6]And if by grace, then is it no more of works: otherwise grace is no more grace. But if it be of works, then is it no more grace: otherwise work is no more work. **4:4** [4]Now to him that worketh is the reward not reckoned of grace, but of debt.	**Gal 3:18** [18]For if the inheritance be of the law, it is no more of promise: but God gave it to Abraham by promise.

ROMANS 11:7—God desires Jews and Gentiles (9:1–11:36), 56–58 CE

Theme	ROM
Israel did not attain righteousness	**11:7** [7]What then? Israel hath not obtained that which he seeketh for; but the election hath obtained it, and the rest were blinded **9:31** [31]But Israel, which followed after the law of righteousness, hath not attained to the law of righteousness.

ROMANS 11:8—God desires Jews and Gentiles (9:1–11:36), 56–58 CE

Theme	ROM	Mt	Lk
Blind eyes	**11:8** [8](According as it is written, God hath given them the spirit of slumber, eyes that they should not see, and ears that they should not hear;) unto this day.	**13:13–15** [13]Therefore speak I to them in parables: because they seeing see not; and hearing they hear not, neither do they understand. [14]And in them is fulfilled the prophecy of Esaias, which saith, By hearing ye shall hear, and shall not understand; and seeing ye shall see, and shall not perceive: [15]For this people's heart is waxed gross, and their ears are dull of hearing, and their eyes they have closed; lest at any time they should see with their eyes, and hear with their ears, and should understand with their heart, and should be converted, and I should heal them.	**Acts 28:26–27** [26]Saying, Go unto this people, and say, Hearing ye shall hear, and shall not understand; and seeing ye shall see, and not perceive: [27]For the heart of this people is waxed gross, and their ears are dull of hearing, and their eyes have they closed; lest they should see with their eyes, and hear with their ears, and understand with their heart, and should be converted, and I should heal them.

ROMANS 11:9–10—God desires Jews and Gentiles (9:1–11:36), 56–58 CE

Theme	ROM	Jewish Writings
Darkened eyes	**11:9–10** [9]And David saith, Let their table be made a snare, and a trap, and a stumblingblock, and a recompense unto them: [10]Let their eyes be darkened, that they may not see, and bow down their back alway.	**Ps 35:8** [8]Let destruction come upon him at unawares; and let his net that he hath hid catch himself: into that very destruction let him fall. **Ps 69:23–24** [23]Let their eyes be darkened, that they see not; and make their loins continually to shake. [24]Pour out thine indignation upon them, and let thy wrathful anger take hold of them

ROMANS 11:11—God desires Jews and Gentiles (9:1–11:36), 56–58 CE

Theme	ROM	Lk
Falling brings salvation	**11:11** [11]I say then, Have they stumbled that they should fall? God forbid: but rather through their fall salvation is come unto the Gentiles, for to provoke them to jealousy.	**Acts 10:19** [19]While Peter thought on the vision, the Spirit said unto him, Behold, three men seek thee. **Acts 13:46** [46]Then Paul and Barnabas waxed bold, and said, It was necessary that the word of God should first have been spoken to you: but seeing ye put it from you, and judge yourselves unworthy of everlasting life, lo, we turn to the Gentiles. **Acts 18:6** [6]And when they opposed themselves, and blasphemed, he shook his raiment, and said unto them, Your blood be upon your own heads; I am clean: from henceforth I will go unto the Gentiles. **Acts 28:28** [28]Be it known therefore unto you, that the salvation of God is sent unto the Gentiles, and that they will hear it.

ROMANS 11:13—God desires Jews and Gentiles (9:1–11:36), 56–58 CE

Theme	ROM
Apostle to the Gentiles	**11:13** [13]For I speak to you Gentiles, inasmuch as I am the apostle of the Gentiles, I magnify mine office: **1:5** [5]By whom we have received grace and apostleship, for obedience to the faith among all nations, for his name:

Jewish Writings	Other
Dt 29:3 [3]The great temptations which thine eyes have seen, the signs, and those great miracles: **Is 29:10** [10]For the LORD hath poured out upon you the spirit of deep sleep, and hath closed your eyes: the prophets and your rulers, the seers hath he covered.	**Q-Quelle** Thanks and blessings/Disciples: Acts 28:26/Rom 11:8/[Mt 11:25-27, 13:16-17]/[Lk 10:21-24 (QS 25)]

Jewish Writings
Dt 32:21 [21]They have moved me to jealousy with that which is not God; they have provoked me to anger with their vanities: and I will move them to jealousy with those which are not a people; I will provoke them to anger with a foolish nation.

ROMANS 11:16—God desires Jews and Gentiles (9:1–11:36), 56–58 CE

Theme	ROM	Jewish Writings
Holiness breeds holiness	**11:16** [16]For if the firstfruit be holy, the lump is also holy: and if the root be holy, so are the branches.	**Num 15:17–21** [17]And the LORD spake unto Moses, saying, [18]Speak unto the children of Israel, and say unto them, When ye come into the land whither I bring you, [19]Then it shall be, that, when ye eat of the bread of the land, ye shall offer up an heave offering unto the LORD. [20]Ye shall offer up a cake of the first of your dough for an heave offering: as ye do the heave offering of the threshingfloor, so shall ye heave it. [21]Of the first of your dough ye shall give unto the LORD an heave offering in your generations. **Neh 10:36–38** [36]Also the firstborn of our sons, and of our cattle, as it is written in the law, and the firstlings of our herds and of our flocks, to bring to the house of our God, unto the priests that minister in the house of our God: [37]And that we should bring the firstfruits of our dough, and our offerings, and the fruit of all manner of trees, of wine and of oil, unto the priests, to the chambers of the house of our God; and the tithes of our ground unto the Levites, that the same Levites might have the tithes in all the cities of our tillage. [38]And the priest the son of Aaron shall be with the Levites, when the Levites take tithes: and the Levites shall bring up the tithe of the tithes unto the house of our God, to the chambers, into the treasure house. **Ezek 44:30** [30]And the first of all the firstfruits of all things, and every oblation of all, of every sort of your oblations, shall be the priest's: ye shall also give unto the priest the first of your dough, that he may cause the blessing to rest in thine house.

ROMANS 11:17—God desires Jews and Gentiles (9:1–11:36), 56–58 CE

Theme	ROM	Paul
People grafted into the faith/ olive tree	**11:17** [17]And if some of the branches be broken off, and thou, being a wild olive tree, wert grafted in among them, and with them partakest of the root and fatness of the olive tree;	**Eph 2:11–19 (Pseudo)** [11]Wherefore remember, that ye being in time past Gentiles in the flesh, who are called Uncircumcision by that which is called the Circumcision in the flesh made by hands; [12]That at that time ye were without Christ, being aliens from the commonwealth of Israel, and strangers from the covenants of promise, having no hope, and without God in the world: [13]But now in Christ Jesus ye who sometimes were far off are made nigh by the blood of Christ. [14]For he is our peace, who hath made both one, and hath broken down the middle wall of partition between us; [15]Having abolished in his flesh the enmity, even the law of commandments contained in ordinances; for to make in himself of twain one new man, so making peace; [16]And that he might reconcile both unto God in one body by the cross, having slain the enmity thereby: [17]And came and preached peace to you which were afar off, and to them that were nigh. [18]For through him we both have access by one Spirit unto the Father. [19]Now therefore ye are no more strangers and foreigners, but fellowcitizens with the saints, and of the household of God;

ROMANS 11:18—God desires Jews and Gentiles (9:1–11:36), 56–58 CE

Theme	ROM	Paul
Honor new	**11:18** [18]Boast not against the branches. But if thou boast, thou bearest not the root, but the root thee.	**I Cor 1:31** [31]That, according as it is written, He that glorieth, let him glory in the Lord.

ROMANS 11:20—God desires Jews and Gentiles (9:1–11:36), 56–58 CE

Theme	ROM
Be not highminded	**11:20** [20]Well; because of unbelief they were broken off, and thou standest by faith. Be not highminded, but fear: **12:16** [16]Be of the same mind one toward another. Mind not high things, but condescend to men of low estate. Be not wise in your own conceits.

ROMANS 11:21—God desires Jews and Gentiles (9:1–11:36), 56–58 CE

Theme	ROM	Paul
Natural branches	**11:21** [21]For if God spared not the natural branches, take heed lest he also spare not thee.	**1 Cor 10:12** [12]Wherefore let him that thinketh he standeth take heed lest he fall.

ROMANS 11:22—God desires Jews and Gentiles (9:1–11:36), 56–58 CE

Theme	ROM	Jn	NT
God's goodness	**11:22** [22]Behold therefore the goodness and severity of God: on them which fell, severity; but toward thee, goodness, if thou continue in his goodness: otherwise thou also shalt be cut off.	**15:2** [2]Every branch in me that beareth not fruit he taketh away: and every branch that beareth fruit, he purgeth it, that it may bring forth more fruit. **15:4** [4]Abide in me, and I in you. As the branch cannot bear fruit of itself, except it abide in the vine; no more can ye, except ye abide in me.	**Heb 3:14** [14]For we are made partakers of Christ, if we hold the beginning of our confidence stedfast unto the end;

ROMANS 11:23—God desires Jews and Gentiles (9:1–11:36), 56–58 CE

Theme	ROM	Paul
God grafts and cuts	**11:23** [23]And they also, if they abide not still in unbelief, shall be grafted in: for God is able to graft them in again.	**2 Cor 3:16** [16]Nevertheless when it shall turn to the Lord, the veil shall be taken away.

ROMANS 11:25—God desires Jews and Gentiles (9:1–11:36), 56–58 CE

Theme	ROM	Mk	Lk	Jn
Israel blind until Gentile time complete	**11:25** [25]For I would not, brethren, that ye should be ignorant of this mystery, lest ye should be wise in your own conceits; that blindness in part is happened to Israel, until the fulness of the Gentiles be come in.	**13:10** [10]And the gospel must first be published among all nations.	**21:24** [24]And they shall fall by the edge of the sword, and shall be led away captive into all nations: and Jerusalem shall be trodden down of the Gentiles, until the times of the Gentiles be fulfilled.	**10:16** [16]And other sheep I have, which are not of this fold: them also I must bring, and they shall hear my voice; and there shall be one fold, and one shepherd.

ROMANS 11:26–27—God desires Jews and Gentiles (9:1–11:36), 56–58 CE

Theme	ROM
Deliverer will take sin away	**11:26–27** [26]And so all Israel shall be saved: as it is written, There shall come out of Sion the Deliverer, and shall turn away ungodliness from Jacob: [27]For this is my covenant unto them, when I shall take away their sins.

ROMANS 11:26—God desires Jews and Gentiles (9:1–11:36), 56–58 CE

Theme	ROM	Mt
Israel will be saved	**11:26** [26]And so all Israel shall be saved: as it is written, There shall come out of Sion the Deliverer, and shall turn away ungodliness from Jacob:	**23:39** [39]For I say unto you, Ye shall not see me henceforth, till ye shall say, Blessed is he that cometh in the name of the Lord.

ROMANS 11:27—God desires Jews and Gentiles (9:1–11:36), 56–58 CE

Theme	ROM
Covenant to take sins	**11:27** [27]For this is my covenant unto them, when I shall take away their sins.

Jewish Writings

Prov 3:7

[7]Be not wise in thine own eyes: fear the LORD, and depart from evil.

Prov 12:16

[16]A fool's wrath is presently known: but a prudent man covereth shame.

Jewish Writings

Ps 14:7

[7]Oh that the salvation of Israel were come out of Zion! when the LORD bringeth back the captivity of his people, Jacob shall rejoice, and Israel shall be glad.

Is 59:20–21

[20]And the Redeemer shall come to Zion, and unto them that turn from transgression in Jacob, saith the LORD. [21]As for me, this is my covenant with them, saith the LORD; My spirit that is upon thee, and my words which I have put in thy mouth, shall not depart out of thy mouth, nor out of the mouth of thy seed, nor out of the mouth of thy seed's seed, saith the LORD, from henceforth and for ever.

Jewish Writings

Is 27:9

[9]By this therefore shall the iniquity of Jacob be purged; and this is all the fruit to take away his sin; when he maketh all the stones of the altar as chalkstones that are beaten in sunder, the groves and images shall not stand up.

Jer 31:33–34

[33]But this shall be the covenant that I will make with the house of Israel; After those days, saith the LORD, I will put my law in their inward parts, and write it in their hearts; and will be their God, and they shall be my people. [34]And they shall teach no more every man his neighbour, and every man his brother, saying, Know the LORD: for they shall all know me, from the least of them unto the greatest of them, saith the LORD: for I will forgive their iniquity, and I will remember their sin no more.

ROMANS 11:28—God desires Jews and Gentiles (9:1–11:36), 56–58 CE

Theme	ROM	Paul
Jesus confirms truth of fathers	**11:28** [28]As concerning the gospel, they are enemies for your sakes: but as touching the election, they are beloved for the fathers' sakes. **15:8** [8]Now I say that Jesus Christ was a minister of the circumcision for the truth of God, to confirm the promises made unto the fathers:	**1 Thes 2:15–16** [15]Who both killed the Lord Jesus, and their own prophets, and have persecuted us; and they please not God, and are contrary to all men: [16]Forbidding us to speak to the Gentiles that they might be saved, to fill up their sins alway: for the wrath is come upon them to the uttermost.

ROMANS 11:29—God desires Jews and Gentiles (9:1–11:36), 56–58 CE

Theme	ROM	Jewish Writings
Gifts and calling	**11:29** [29]For the gifts and calling of God are without repentance. **9:6** [6]Not as though the word of God hath taken none effect. For they are not all Israel, which are of Israel:	**Num 23:19** [19]God is not a man, that he should lie; neither the son of man, that he should repent: hath he said, and shall he not do it? or hath he spoken, and shall he not make it good? **Is 54:10** [10]For the mountains shall depart, and the hills be removed; but my kindness shall not depart from thee, neither shall the covenant of my peace be removed, saith the LORD that hath mercy on thee.

ROMANS 11:32—God desires Jews and Gentiles (9:1–11:36), 56–58 CE

Theme	ROM	Paul
God has mercy	**11:32** [32]For God hath concluded them all in unbelief, that he might have mercy upon all.	**Gal 3:22** [22]But the scripture hath concluded all under sin, that the promise by faith of Jesus Christ might be given to them that believe. **1 Tim 2:4 (Pseudo)** [4]Who will have all men to be saved, and to come unto the knowledge of the truth.

ROMANS 11:33—God desires Jews and Gentiles (9:1–11:36), 56–58 CE

Theme	ROM	Jewish Writings
God is unsearchable	**11:33** [33]O the depth of the riches both of the wisdom and knowledge of God! how unsearchable are his judgments, and his ways past finding out!	**Job 11:7–8** [7]Canst thou by searching find out God? canst thou find out the Almighty unto perfection? [8]It is as high as heaven; what canst thou do? deeper than hell; what canst thou know? **Ps 139:6, 17–18** [6]Such knowledge is too wonderful for me; it is high, I cannot attain unto it. . . . [17]How precious also are thy thoughts unto me, O God! how great is the sum of them! [18]If I should count them, they are more in number than the sand: when I awake, I am still with thee. **Wis 17:1** [1]For great are thy judgments, and cannot be expressed: therefore unnurtured souls have erred. **Is 55:8–9** [8]For my thoughts are not your thoughts, neither are your ways my ways, saith the LORD. [9]For as the heavens are higher than the earth, so are my ways higher than your ways, and my thoughts than your thoughts.

ROMANS 11:34—God desires Jews and Gentiles (9:1–11:36), 56–58 CE

Theme	ROM	Paul	Jewish Writings
Mind of the Lord	**11:34** [34]For who hath known the mind of the Lord? or who hath been his counsellor?	**1 Cor 2:11–16** [11]For what man knoweth the things of a man, save the spirit of man which is in him? even so the things of God knoweth no man, but the Spirit of God. [12]Now we have received, not the spirit of the world, but the spirit which is of God; that we might know the things that are freely given to us of God. [13]Which things also we speak, not in the words which man's wisdom teacheth, but which the Holy Ghost teacheth; comparing spiritual things with spiritual. [14]But the natural man receiveth not the things of the Spirit of God: for they are foolishness unto him: neither can he know them, because they are spiritually discerned. [15]But he that is spiritual judgeth all things, yet he himself is judged of no man. [16]For who hath known the mind of the Lord, that he may instruct him? But we have the mind of Christ.	**Job 15:8** [8]Hast thou heard the secret of God? and dost thou restrain wisdom to thyself? **Wis 9:13** [13]For what man is he that can know the counsel of God? or who can think what the will of the Lord is? **Is 40:13** [13]Who hath directed the Spirit of the LORD, or being his counsellor hath taught him? **Jer 23:18** [18]For who hath stood in the counsel of the LORD, and hath perceived and heard his word? who hath marked his word, and heard it?

ROMANS 11:35—God desires Jews and Gentiles (9:1–11:36), 56–58 CE

Theme	ROM	Jewish Writings
No one counsels God	**11:35** [35]Or who hath first given to him, and it shall be recompensed unto him again?	**Job 41:3** [3]Will he make many supplications unto thee? will he speak soft words unto thee? **Is 40:14** [14]With whom took he counsel, and who instructed him, and taught him in the path of judgment, and taught him knowledge, and showed to him the way of understanding?

ROMANS 11:36—God desires Jews and Gentiles (9:1–11:36), 56–58 CE

Theme	ROM	Paul
All to God's glory	**11:36** [36]For of him, and through him, and to him, are all things: to whom be glory for ever. Amen.	**I Cor 8:6** [6]But to us there is but one God, the Father, of whom are all things, and we in him; and one Lord Jesus Christ, by whom are all things, and we by him. **Col 1:16–17** [16]For by him were all things created, that are in heaven, and that are in earth, visible and invisible, whether they be thrones, or dominions, or principalities, or powers: all things were created by him, and for him: [17]And he is before all things, and by him all things consist.

CHRISTIAN DUTY (12:1–15:13)

ROMANS 12:1—Christian duty (12:1–15:13), 56–58 CE

Theme	ROM	Mt	Mk	Jn
Glory of God/ transfor-mation	**12:1** [1]I beseech you therefore, brethren, by the mercies of God, that ye present your bodies a living sacrifice, holy, acceptable unto God, which is your reasonable service.	**17:4** [4]Then answered Peter, and said unto Jesus, Lord, it is good for us to be here: if thou wilt, let us make here three tabernacles; one for thee, and one for Moses, and one for Elias. **17:9** [9]And as they came down from the mountain, Jesus charged them, saying, Tell the vision to no man, until the Son of man be risen again from the dead.	**9:5** [5]And Peter answered and said to Jesus, Master, it is good for us to be here: and let us make three tabernacles; one for thee, and one for Moses, and one for Elias. **9:9** [9]And as they came down from the mountain, he charged them that they should tell no man what things they had seen, till the Son of man were risen from the dead.	**9:31–33** [31]Now we know that God heareth not sinners: but if any man be a worshipper of God, and doeth his will, him he heareth. [32]Since the world began was it not heard that any man opened the eyes of one that was born blind. [33]If this man were not of God, he could do nothing.

Paul	NT
1 Cor 2:8 [8]Which none of the princes of this world knew: for had they known it, they would not have crucified the Lord of glory. **2 Cor 1:3** [3]Blessed be God, even the Father of our Lord Jesus Christ, the Father of mercies, and the God of all comfort; **2 Cor 3:1–4** [1]Do we begin again to commend ourselves? or need we, as some others, epistles of commendation to you, or letters of commendation from you? [2]Ye are our epistle written in our hearts, known and read of all men: [3]Forasmuch as ye are manifestly declared to be the epistle of Christ ministered by us, written not with ink, but with the Spirit of the living God; not in tables of stone, but in fleshy tables of the heart. [4]And such trust have we through Christ to God-ward: [5]Not that we are sufficient of ourselves to think any thing as of ourselves; but our sufficiency is of God; **2 Cor 3:6** [6]Who also hath made us able ministers of the new testament; not of the letter, but of the spirit: for the letter killeth, but the spirit giveth life. **2 Cor 3:18** [18]But we all, with open face beholding as in a glass the glory of the Lord, are changed into the same image from glory to glory, even as by the Spirit of the Lord. **2 Cor 6:13** [13]Now for a recompence in the same, (I speak as unto my children,) be ye also enlarged. **Phil 3:21** [21]Who shall change our vile body, that it may be fashioned like unto his glorious body, according to the working whereby he is able even to subdue all things unto himself. **2 Thes 2:14** [14]Whereunto he called you by our gospel, to the obtaining of the glory of our Lord Jesus Christ. **2 Thes 3:1–4** [1]Finally, brethren, pray for us, that the word of the Lord may have free course, and be glorified, even as it is with you: [2]And that we may be delivered from unreasonable and wicked men: for all men have not faith. [3]But the Lord is faithful, who shall stablish you, and keep you from evil. [4]And we have confidence in the Lord touching you, that ye both do and will do the things which we command you. **2 Thes 3:6** [6]Now we command you, brethren, in the name of our Lord Jesus Christ, that ye withdraw yourselves from every brother that walketh disorderly, and not after the tradition which he received of us.	**1 Pet 2:5** [5]Ye also, as lively stones, are built up a spiritual house, an holy priesthood, to offer up spiritual sacrifices, acceptable to God by Jesus Christ.

ROMANS 12:2—Christian duty (12:1–15:13), 56–58 CE

Theme	ROM	Paul
Be not conformed to this world	**12:2** [2]And be not conformed to this world: but be ye transformed by the renewing of your mind, that ye may prove what is that good, and acceptable, and perfect, will of God.	**Eph 4:17–22 (Pseudo)** [17]This I say therefore, and testify in the Lord, that ye henceforth walk not as other Gentiles walk, in the vanity of their mind, [18]Having the understanding darkened, being alienated from the life of God through the ignorance that is in them, because of the blindness of their heart: [19]Who being past feeling have given themselves over unto lasciviousness, to work all uncleanness with greediness. [20]But ye have not so learned Christ; [21]If so be that ye have heard him, and have been taught by him, as the truth is in Jesus: [22]That ye put off concerning the former conversation the old man, which is corrupt according to the deceitful lusts; **Eph 5:10, 17 (Pseudo)** [10]Proving what is acceptable unto the Lord. [11]And have no fellowship with the unfruitful works of darkness, but rather reprove them. [12]For it is a shame even to speak of those things which are done of them in secret. [13]But all things that are reproved are made manifest by the light: for whatsoever doth make manifest is light. [14]Wherefore he saith, Awake thou that sleepest, and arise from the dead, and Christ shall give thee light. [15]See then that ye walk circumspectly, not as fools, but as wise, [16]Redeeming the time, because the days are evil. [17]Wherefore be ye not unwise, but understanding what the will of the Lord is. **Phil 1:10** [10]That ye may approve things that are excellent; that ye may be sincere and without offence till the day of Christ;

ROMANS 12:3—Christian duty (12:1–15:13), 56–58 CE

Theme	ROM	Paul
Salvation is by God's grace, not human endeavor	**12:3** [3]For I say, through the grace given unto me, to every man that is among you, not to think of himself more highly than he ought to think; but to think soberly, according as God hath dealt to every man the measure of faith. **15:15** [15]Nevertheless, brethren, I have written the more boldly unto you in some sort, as putting you in mind, because of the grace that is given to me of God,	**1 Cor 12:11** [11]But all these worketh that one and the selfsame Spirit, dividing to every man severally as he will. **Eph 4:7 (Pseudo)** [7]But unto every one of us is given grace according to the measure of the gift of Christ. **Phil 2:3** [3]Let nothing be done through strife or vainglory; but in lowliness of mind let each esteem other better than themselves.

ROMANS 12:4–5—Christian duty (12:1–15:13), 56–58 CE

Theme	ROM	Paul
Different offices	**12:4–5** [4]For as we have many members in one body, and all members have not the same office: [5]So we, being many, are one body in Christ, and every one members one of another.	**I Cor 12:12** [12]For as the body is one, and hath many members, and all the members of that one body, being many, are one body: so also is Christ. **I Cor 12:27** [27]Now ye are the body of Christ, and members in particular. **Eph 4:25 (Pseudo)** [24]And that ye put on the new man, which after God is created in righteousness and true holiness.

NT
1 Pet 1:14
[14]As obedient children, not fashioning yourselves according to the former lusts in your ignorance:

ROMANS 12:4—Christian duty (12:1–15:13), 56–58 CE

Theme	ROM	Mt	Mk	Jn
Jesus Christ and the corporate body	**12:4** [4]For as we have many members in one body, and all members have not the same office:	**12:46–50** [46]While he yet talked to the people, behold, his mother and his brethren stood without, desiring to speak with him. [47]Then one said unto him, Behold, thy mother and thy brethren stand without, desiring to speak with thee. [48]But he answered and said unto him that told him, Who is my mother? and who are my brethren? [49]And he stretched forth his hand toward his disciples, and said, Behold my mother and my brethren! [50]For whosoever shall do the will of my Father which is in heaven, the same is my brother, and sister, and mother.	**3:31–35** [31]There came then his brethren and his mother, and, standing without, sent unto him, calling him. [32]And the multitude sat about him, and they said unto him, Behold, thy mother and thy brethren without seek for thee. [33]And he answered them, saying, Who is my mother, or my brethren? [34]And he looked round about on them which sat about him, and said, Behold my mother and my brethren! [35]For whosoever shall do the will of God, the same is my brother, and my sister, and mother.	**8:19–21** [19]Then said they unto him, Where is thy Father? Jesus answered, Ye neither know me, nor my Father: if ye had known me, ye should have known my Father also. [20]These words spake Jesus in the treasury, as he taught in the temple: and no man laid hands on him; for his hour was not yet come. [21]Then said Jesus again unto them, I go my way, and ye shall seek me, and shall die in your sins: whither I go, ye cannot come.

ROMANS 12:6–8—Christian duty (12:1–15:13), 56–58 CE

Theme	ROM	Paul
Differing gifts	**12:6–8** [6]Having then gifts differing according to the grace that is given to us, whether prophecy, let us prophesy according to the proportion of faith; [7]Or ministry, let us wait on our ministering: or he that teacheth, on teaching; [8]Or he that exhorteth, on exhortation: he that giveth, let him do it with simplicity; he that ruleth, with diligence; he that showeth mercy, with cheerfulness.	**1 Cor 12:4–11, 28–31** [4]Now there are diversities of gifts, but the same Spirit. [5]And there are differences of administrations, but the same Lord. [6]And there are diversities of operations, but it is the same God which worketh all in all. [6]And there are diversities of operations, but it is the same God which worketh all in all. [7]But the manifestation of the Spirit is given to every man to profit withal. [8]For to one is given by the Spirit the word of wisdom; to another the word of knowledge by the same Spirit; [9]To another faith by the same Spirit; to another the gifts of healing by the same Spirit; [10]To another the working of miracles; to another prophecy; to another discerning of spirits; to another divers kinds of tongues; to another the interpretation of tongues: [11]But all these worketh that one and the selfsame Spirit, dividing to every man severally as he will. . . . [28]And God hath set some in the church, first apostles, secondarily prophets, thirdly teachers, after that miracles, then gifts of healings, helps, governments, diversities of tongues. [29]Are all apostles? are all prophets? are all teachers? are all workers of miracles? [30]Have all the gifts of healing? do all speak with tongues? do all interpret? [31]But covet earnestly the best gifts: and yet show I unto you a more excellent way. **2 Cor 9:7** [7]Every man according as he purposeth in his heart, so let him give; not grudgingly, or of necessity: for God loveth a cheerful giver. **Eph 4:7–12 (Pseudo)** [4]There is one body, and one Spirit, even as ye are called in one hope of your calling; [5]One Lord, one faith, one baptism, [6]One God and Father of all, who is above all, and through all, and in you all. [7]But unto every one of us is given grace according to the measure of the gift of Christ. [8]Wherefore he saith, When he ascended up on high, he led captivity captive, and gave gifts unto men. [9](Now that he ascended, what is it but that he also descended first into the lower parts of the earth? [10]He that descended is the same also that ascended up far above all heavens, that he might fill all things.) [11]And he gave some, apostles; and some, prophets; and some, evangelists; and some, pastors and teachers; [12]For the perfecting of the saints, for the work of the ministry, for the edifying of the body of Christ:

Paul

1 Cor 6:15

[15]Know ye not that your bodies are the members of Christ? shall I then take the members of Christ, and make them the members of an harlot? God forbid.

1 Cor 10:17

[17]For we being many are one bread, and one body: for we are all partakers of that one bread.

1 Cor 12:12–13

[12]For as the body is one, and hath many members, and all the members of that one body, being many, are one body: so also is Christ. [13]For by one Spirit are we all baptized into one body, whether we be Jews or Gentiles, whether we be bond or free; and have been all made to drink into one Spirit.

1 Cor 15:22

[22]For as in Adam all die, even so in Christ shall all be made alive.

Eph 1:22–23 (Pseudo)

[22]And hath put all things under his feet, and gave him to be the head over all things to the church, [23]Which is his body, the fulness of him that filleth all in all.

Eph 4:15 (Pseudo)

[15]But speaking the truth in love, may grow up into him in all things, which is the head, even Christ:

Eph 5:23 (Pseudo)

[23]For the husband is the head of the wife, even as Christ is the head of the church: and he is the saviour of the body.

Col 1:18

[18]For the preaching of the cross is to them that perish foolishness; but unto us which are saved it is the power of God.

NT

1 Pet 4:10–11

[10]As every man hath received the gift, even so minister the same one to another, as good stewards of the manifold grace of God. [11]If any man speak, let him speak as the oracles of God; if any man minister, let him do it as of the ability which God giveth: that God in all things may be glorified through Jesus Christ, to whom be praise and dominion for ever and ever. Amen.

ROMANS 12:9–21—Christian duty (12:1–15:13), 56–58 CE

Theme	ROM	Mt
Love and bless enemy	**12:9–21** [12]Rejoicing in hope; patient in tribulation; continuing instant in prayer; [13]Distributing to the necessity of saints; given to hospitality. [14]Bless them which persecute you: bless, and curse not. [15]Rejoice with them that do rejoice, and weep with them that weep. [16]Be of the same mind one toward another. Mind not high things, but condescend to men of low estate. Be not wise in your own conceits. [17]Recompense to no man evil for evil. Provide things honest in the sight of all men. [18]If it be possible, as much as lieth in you, live peaceably with all men. [19]Dearly beloved, avenge not yourselves, but rather give place unto wrath: for it is written, Vengeance is mine; I will repay, saith the Lord. [20]Therefore if thine enemy hunger, feed him; if he thirst, give him drink: for in so doing thou shalt heap coals of fire on his head. [21]Be not overcome of evil, but overcome evil with good. **5:2–3** [2]By whom also we have access by faith into this grace wherein we stand, and rejoice in hope of the glory of God. [3]And not only so, but we glory in tribulations also: knowing that tribulation worketh patience; **12:14** [14]Bless them which persecute you: bless, and curse not.	**5:38–48** [38]Ye have heard that it hath been said, An eye for an eye, and a tooth for a tooth: [39]But I say unto you, That ye resist not evil: but whosoever shall smite thee on thy right cheek, turn to him the other also. [40]And if any man will sue thee at the law, and take away thy coat, let him have thy cloak also. [41]And whosoever shall compel thee to go a mile, go with him twain. [42]Give to him that asketh thee, and from him that would borrow of thee turn not thou away. [43]Ye have heard that it hath been said, Thou shalt love thy neighbour, and hate thine enemy. [44]But I say unto you, Love your enemies, bless them that curse you, do good to them that hate you, and pray for them which despitefully use you, and persecute you; [45]That ye may be the children of your Father which is in heaven: for he maketh his sun to rise on the evil and on the good, and sendeth rain on the just and on the unjust. [46]For if ye love them which love you, what reward have ye? do not even the publicans the same? [47]And if ye salute your brethren only, what do ye more than others? do not even the publicans so? [48]Be ye therefore perfect, even as your Father which is in heaven is perfect. **20:20–28** [20]Then came to him the mother of Zebedee's children with her sons, worshipping him, and desiring a certain thing of him. [21]And he said unto her, What wilt thou? She saith unto him, Grant that these my two sons may sit, the one on thy right hand, and the other on the left, in thy kingdom. [22]But Jesus answered and said, Ye know not what ye ask. Are ye able to drink of the cup that I shall drink of, and to be baptized with the baptism that I am baptized with? They say unto him, We are able. [23]And he saith unto them, Ye shall drink indeed of my cup, and be baptized with the baptism that I am baptized with: but to sit on my right hand, and on my left, is not mine to give, but it shall be given to them for whom it is prepared of my Father. [24]And when the ten heard it, they were moved with indignation against the two brethren. [25]But Jesus called them unto him, and said, Ye know that the princes of the Gentiles exercise dominion over them, and they that are great exercise authority upon them. [26]But it shall not be so among you: but whosoever will be great among you, let him be your minister; [27]And whosoever will be chief among you, let him be your servant: [28]Even as the Son of man came not to be ministered unto, but to minister, and to give his life a ransom for many. **23:9–15** [9]And call no man your father upon the earth: for one is your Father, which is in heaven. [10]Neither be ye called masters: for one is your Master, even Christ. [11]But he that is greatest among you shall be your servant. [12]And whosoever shall exalt himself shall be abased; and he that shall humble himself shall be exalted. [13]But woe unto you, scribes and Pharisees, hypocrites! for ye shut up the kingdom of heaven against men: for ye neither go in yourselves, neither suffer ye them that are entering to go in. [14]Woe unto you, scribes and Pharisees, hypocrites! for ye devour widows' houses, and for a pretence make long prayer: therefore ye shall receive the greater damnation. [15]Woe unto you, scribes and Pharisees, hypocrites! for ye compass sea and land to make one proselyte, and when he is made, ye make him twofold more the child of hell than yourselves. **23:19** [19]Ye fools and blind: for whether is greater, the gift, or the altar that sanctifieth the gift?

Mk

9:33–42

[33]And he came to Capernaum: and being in the house he asked them, What was it that ye disputed among yourselves by the way? [34]But they held their peace: for by the way they had disputed among themselves, who should be the greatest. [35]And he sat down, and called the twelve, and saith unto them, If any man desire to be first, the same shall be last of all, and servant of all. [36]And he took a child, and set him in the midst of them: and when he had taken him in his arms, he said unto them, [37]Whosoever shall receive one of such children in my name, receiveth me: and whosoever shall receive me, receiveth not me, but him that sent me. [38]And John answered him, saying, Master, we saw one casting out devils in thy name, and he followeth not us: and we forbad him, because he followeth not us. [39]But Jesus said, Forbid him not: for there is no man which shall do a miracle in my name, that can lightly speak evil of me. [40]For he that is not against us is on our part. [41]For whosoever shall give you a cup of water to drink in my name, because ye belong to Christ, verily I say unto you, he shall not lose his reward. [42]And whosoever shall offend one of these little ones that believe in me, it is better for him that a millstone were hanged about his neck, and he were cast into the sea.

10:13–16

[13]And they brought young children to him, that he should touch them: and his disciples rebuked those that brought them. [14]But when Jesus saw it, he was much displeased, and said unto them, Suffer the little children to come unto me, and forbid them not: for of such is the kingdom of God. [15]Verily I say unto you, Whosoever shall not receive the kingdom of God as a little child, he shall not enter therein. [16]And he took them up in his arms, put his hands upon them, and blessed them.

10:35–45

[35]And James and John, the sons of Zebedee, come unto him, saying, Master, we would that thou shouldest do for us whatsoever we shall desire. [36]And he said unto them, What would ye that I should do for you? [37]They said unto him, Grant unto us that we may sit, one on thy right hand, and the other on thy left hand, in thy glory. [38]But Jesus said unto them, Ye know not what ye ask: can ye drink of the cup that I drink of? and be baptized with the baptism that I am baptized with? [39]And they said unto him, We can. And Jesus said unto them, Ye shall indeed drink of the cup that I drink of; and with the baptism that I am baptized withal shall ye be baptized: [40]But to sit on my right hand and on my left hand is not mine to give; but it shall be given to them for whom it is prepared. [41]And when the ten heard it, they began to be much displeased with James and John. [42]But Jesus called them to him, and saith unto them, Ye know that they which are accounted to rule over the Gentiles exercise lordship over them; and their great ones exercise authority upon them. [43]But so shall it not be among you: but whosoever will be great among you, shall be your minister: [44]And whosoever of you will be the chiefest, shall be servant of all. [45]For even the Son of man came not to be ministered unto, but to minister, and to give his life a ransom for many.

Romans 12:9–12 continued on next page

ROMANS 12:9–21—Christian duty (12:1–15:13), 56–58 CE

Theme	ROM	Lk	Jn	Paul
(*Cont.*) **Love children**	**12:9–21 (above)** **5:2–3 (above)** **12:14 (above)**	**Acts 18:25** [25]This man was instructed in the way of the Lord; and being fervent in the spirit, he spake and taught diligently the things of the Lord, knowing only the baptism of John.	**6:28** [28]Then said they unto him, What shall we do, that we might work the works of God? **13:34** [34]A new commandment I give unto you, That ye love one another; as I have loved you, that ye also love one another. **18:1–6** [1]When Jesus had spoken these words, he went forth with his disciples over the brook Cedron, where was a garden, into the which he entered, and his disciples. [2]And Judas also, which betrayed him, knew the place: for Jesus ofttimes resorted thither with his disciples. [3]Judas then, having received a band of men and officers from the chief priests and Pharisees, cometh thither with lanterns and torches and weapons. [4]Jesus therefore, knowing all things that should come upon him, went forth, and said unto them, Whom seek ye? [5]They answered him, Jesus of Nazareth. Jesus saith unto them, I am he. And Judas also, which betrayed him, stood with them. [6]As soon then as he had said unto them, I am he, they went backward, and fell to the ground. **18:15** [15]And Simon Peter followed Jesus, and so did another disciple: that disciple was known unto the high priest, and went in with Jesus into the palace of the high priest.	**1 Cor 4:12** [12]And labour, working with our own hands: being reviled, we bless; being persecuted, we suffer it: **2 Cor 6:6** [6]By pureness, by knowledge, by longsuffering, by kindness, by the Holy Ghost, by love unfeigned, **Gal 6:10** [10]As we have therefore opportunity, let us do good unto all men, especially unto them who are of the household of faith. **Gal 3:28** [28]There is neither Jew nor Greek, there is neither bond nor free, there is neither male nor female: for ye are all one in Christ Jesus. **Phil 2:3** [3]Let nothing be done through strife or vainglory; but in lowliness of mind let each esteem other better than themselves. **Col 4:2** [2]Continue in prayer, and watch in the same with thanksgiving; **1 Thes 4:9** [9]But as touching brotherly love ye need not that I write unto you: for ye yourselves are taught of God to love one another. **1 Thes 5:17** [17]Pray without ceasing. **1 Tim 1:5 (Pseudo)** [5]Now the end of the commandment is charity out of a pure heart, and of a good conscience, and of faith unfeigned:

NT	Jewish Writings	Other
Heb 13:2 [2]Be not forgetful to entertain strangers: for thereby some have entertained angels unawares. **1 Pet 1:22** [22]Seeing ye have purified your souls in obeying the truth through the Spirit unto unfeigned love of the brethren, see that ye love one another with a pure heart fervently: **1 Pet 2:17** [17]Honour all men. Love the brotherhood. Fear God. Honour the king. **1 Pet 3:9** [9]Not rendering evil for evil, or railing for railing: but contrariwise blessing; knowing that ye are thereunto called, that ye should inherit a blessing. **1 Pet 4:9** [9]Use hospitality one to another without grudging. **2 Pet 1:7** [7]And to godliness brotherly kindness; and to brotherly kindness charity.	**Amos 5:15** [15]Hate the evil, and love the good, and establish judgment in the gate: it may be that the LORD God of hosts will be gracious unto the remnant of Joseph.	**Q-Quelle** Love Enemies: Rom 12:9-21/Mt 5:38-48, [Mt 7:12]/[Lk 6:27-36 (QS 9 [Thom 95, 6:2]); Against Pharisees: Rom 12:9-21/ Mt 23:4-36/[Mk 7:1-9]/[Lk 11:37-54 (QS 34 [Thom 39:1,89, 102])]; Precedence: Rom 12:9-21/ [Mt 19:28]/Mk 10:41-45/ [Lk 22:28-30 (QS 62)]

ROMANS 12:9—Christian duty (12:1–15:13), 56–58 CE

Theme	ROM	Paul	NT	Jewish Writings
Love good	**12:9** [9]Let love be without dissimulation. Abhor that which is evil; cleave to that which is good.	**2 Cor 6:6** [6]By pureness, by knowledge, by longsuffering, by kindness, by the Holy Ghost, by love unfeigned, **1 Tim 1:5 (Pseudo)** [5]Now the end of the commandment is charity out of a pure heart, and of a good conscience, and of faith unfeigned:	**1 Pet 1:22** [22]Seeing ye have purified your souls in obeying the truth through the Spirit unto unfeigned love of the brethren, see that ye love one another with a pure heart fervently:	**Amos 5:15** [15]Hate the evil, and love the good, and establish judgment in the gate: it may be that the LORD God of hosts will be gracious unto the remnant of Joseph.

ROMANS 12:10—Christian duty (12:1–15:13), 56–58 CE

Theme	ROM	Mt	Jn	Paul
Greatest command—love Christians	**12:10** [10]Be kindly affectioned one to another with brotherly love; in honour preferring one another;	**9:50** [50]Salt is good: but if the salt have lost his saltness, wherewith will ye season it? Have salt in yourselves, and have peace one with another.	**13:34** [34]A new commandment I give unto you, That ye love one another; as I have loved you, that ye also love one another.	**Col 3:12–14** [12]Put on therefore, as the elect of God, holy and beloved, bowels of mercies, kindness, humbleness of mind, meekness, longsuffering; [13]Forbearing one another, and forgiving one another, if any man have a quarrel against any: even as Christ forgave you, so also do ye. [14]And above all these things put on charity, which is the bond of perfectness. [15]And let the peace of God rule in your hearts, to the which also ye are called in one body; and be ye thankful. **Eph 4:32 (Pseudo)** [32]And be ye kind one to another, tenderhearted, forgiving one another, even as God for Christ's sake hath forgiven you. **1 Thes 3:12** [12]And the Lord make you to increase and abound in love one toward another, and toward all men, even as we do toward you: **1 Thes 4:9** [9]But as touching brotherly love ye need not that I write unto you: for ye yourselves are taught of God to love one another. **1 Thes 5:12–13** [12]And we beseech you, brethren, to know them which labour among you, and are over you in the Lord, and admonish you; [13]And to esteem them very highly in love for their work's sake. And be at peace among yourselves **1 Thes 5:15** [15]See that none render evil for evil unto any man; but ever follow that which is good, both among yourselves, and to all men. **2 Thes 1:3** [3]Remembering without ceasing your work of faith, and labour of love, and patience of hope in our Lord Jesus Christ, in the sight of God and our Father **Phil 2:3** [3]Let nothing be done through strife or vainglory; but in lowliness of mind let each esteem other better than themselves.

NT	Other
1 Pet 2:17	**Q-Quelle**
[17]Honour all men. Love the brotherhood. Fear God. Honour the king. **2 Pet 1:7** [7]And to godliness brotherly kindness; and to brotherly kindness charity.	Against Pharisees: Rom 12:10/[1 Cor 9:19]/Phil 2:1-11/[Mt 23:4-36]/[Mk 7:1-9]/ [Lk 11:37-54 (QS 34 [Thom 39:1, 89, 102])]; Beatitudes: Rom 12:10/[2 Cor 7:4, 13:11]/[Gal 6:10]/Eph 4:32/1 Thes 3:12/[Mt 5:3-12]/[Lk 6:20b-23 (QS 8 [Thom 54,68,69])]; Love Enemies: Rom 12:10/Col 3:12-14/[Mt 5:38-48], [Mt 7:12]/[Lk 6:27-36 (QS 9 [Thom 95, 6:2])]

ROMANS 12:11—Christian duty (12:1–15:13), 56–58 CE

Theme	ROM	Lk
Fervent in Spirit, no sloth	**12:11** [11]Not slothful in business; fervent in spirit; serving the Lord;	**Acts 18:25** [25]This man was instructed in the way of the Lord; and being fervent in the spirit, he spake and taught diligently the things of the Lord, knowing only the baptism of John.

ROMANS 12:12—Christian duty (12:1–15:13), 56–58 CE

Theme	ROM	Paul
Rejoice in hope, patience, prayer	**12:12** [12]Rejoicing in hope; patient in tribulation; continuing instant in prayer; **5:2–3** [2]By whom also we have access by faith into this grace wherein we stand, and rejoice in hope of the glory of God. [3]And not only so, but we glory in tribulations also: knowing that tribulation worketh patience;	**Col 4:2** [2]Continue in prayer, and watch in the same with thanksgiving; **1 Thes 5:17** [17]Pray without ceasing.

ROMANS 12:13—Christian duty (12:1–15:13), 56–58 CE

Theme	ROM	NT
Giving to the saints' needs	**12:13** [13]Distributing to the necessity of saints; given to hospitality.	**Heb 13:2** [2]Be not forgetful to entertain strangers: for thereby some have entertained angels unawares. **1 Pet 4:9** [9]Use hospitality one to another without grudging.

ROMANS 12:14–21—Christian duty (12:1–15:13), 56–58 CE

Theme	ROM	Mt
Bless enemies, do not curse	**12:14–21** [14]Bless them which persecute you: bless, and curse not. [15]Rejoice with them that do rejoice, and weep with them that weep. [16]Be of the same mind one toward another. Mind not high things, but condescend to men of low estate. Be not wise in your own conceits. [17]Recompense to no man evil for evil. Provide things honest in the sight of all men. [18]If it be possible, as much as lieth in you, live peaceably with all men. [19]Dearly beloved, avenge not yourselves, but rather give place unto wrath: for it is written, Vengeance is mine; I will repay, saith the Lord. [20]Therefore if thine enemy hunger, feed him; if he thirst, give him drink: for in so doing thou shalt heap coals of fire on his head. [21]Be not overcome of evil, but overcome evil with good.	**5:38–48** [38]Ye have heard that it hath been said, An eye for an eye, and a tooth for a tooth: [39]But I say unto you, That ye resist not evil: but whosoever shall smite thee on thy right cheek, turn to him the other also. [40]And if any man will sue thee at the law, and take away thy coat, let him have thy cloak also. [41]And whosoever shall compel thee to go a mile, go with him twain. [42]Give to him that asketh thee, and from him that would borrow of thee turn not thou away. [43]Ye have heard that it hath been said, Thou shalt love thy neighbour, and hate thine enemy. [44]But I say unto you, Love your enemies, bless them that curse you, do good to them that hate you, and pray for them which despitefully use you, and persecute you; [45]That ye may be the children of your Father which is in heaven: for he maketh his sun to rise on the evil and on the good, and sendeth rain on the just and on the unjust. [46]For if ye love them which love you, what reward have ye? do not even the publicans the same? [47]And if ye salute your brethren only, what do ye more than others? do not even the publicans so? [48]Be ye therefore perfect, even as your Father which is in heaven is perfect.

Paul	NT	Other
1 Cor 4:12	**1 Pet 3:9**	**Q-Quelle**
[12]And labour, working with our own hands: being reviled, we bless; being persecuted, we suffer it:	[9]Not rendering evil for evil, or railing for railing: but contrariwise blessing; knowing that ye are thereunto called, that ye should inherit a blessing.	Love enemies: Rom 12:14-21/ Mt 5:38-48 [Mt 7:12]/[Lk 6:27-36 (QS 9,10)]

ROMANS 12:14—Christian duty (12:1–15:13), 56–58 CE

Theme	ROM	Lk	Other
Bless persecutors	**12:14** [14]Bless them which persecute you: bless, and curse not.	**6:27–28** [27]But I say unto you which hear, Love your enemies, do good to them which hate you, [28]Bless them that curse you, and pray for them which despitefully use you.	**Q-Quelle** Love enemies: Rom 12:14/ [Mt 5:38-48, 7:12]/Lk 6:27-36 (QS 9,10)

ROMANS 12:15—Christian duty (12:1–15:13), 56–58 CE

Theme	ROM	Paul	Jewish Writings
Weep with weeping, give joy for joy	**12:15** [15]Rejoice with them that do rejoice, and weep with them that weep.	**1 Cor 12:26** [26]And whether one member suffer, all the members suffer with it; or one member be honoured, all the members rejoice with it.	**Ps 35:13** [13]But as for me, when they were sick, my clothing was sackcloth: I humbled my soul with fasting; and my prayer returned into mine own bosom. **Sir 7:34** [34]Fail not to be with them that weep, and mourn with them that mourn.

ROMANS 12:16—Christian duty (12:1–15:13), 56–58 CE

Theme	ROM
Be of one mind, not conceited	**12:16** [16]Be of the same mind one toward another. Mind not high things, but condescend to men of low estate. Be not wise in your own conceits. **11:20** [20]Well; because of unbelief they were broken off, and thou standest by faith. Be not highminded, but fear: **15:5** [5]Now the God of patience and consolation grant you to be likeminded one toward another according to Christ Jesus:

ROMANS 12:17–20—Christian duty (12:1–15:13), 56–58 CE

Theme	ROM	Mt
Returning good for evil	**12:17–20** [17]Recompense to no man evil for evil. Provide things honest in the sight of all men. [18]If it be possible, as much as lieth in you, live peaceably with all men. [19]Dearly beloved, avenge not yourselves, but rather give place unto wrath: for it is written, Vengeance is mine; I will repay, saith the Lord. [20]Therefore if thine enemy hunger, feed him; if he thirst, give him drink: for in so doing thou shalt heap coals of fire on his head. **12:18–19** [18]If it be possible, as much as lieth in you, live peaceably with all men. [19]Dearly beloved, avenge not yourselves, but rather give place unto wrath: for it is written, Vengeance is mine; I will repay, saith the Lord. **12:20–21** [20]Therefore if thine enemy hunger, feed him; if he thirst, give him drink: for in so doing thou shalt heap coals of fire on his head. [21]Be not overcome of evil, but overcome evil with good.	**5:38** [38]Ye have heard that it hath been said, An eye for an eye, and a tooth for a tooth: **5:39–42** [39]But I say unto you, That ye resist not evil: but whosoever shall smite thee on thy right cheek, turn to him the other also. [40]And if any man will sue thee at the law, and take away thy coat, let him have thy cloak also. [41]And whosoever shall compel thee to go a mile, go with him twain. [42]Give to him that asketh thee, and from him that would borrow of thee turn not thou away.

Paul	Jewish Writings
Phil 2:2–3	**Prov 3:7**
[2]Fulfil ye my joy, that ye be likeminded, having the same love, being of one accord, of one mind. [3]Let nothing be done through strife or vainglory; but in lowliness of mind let each esteem other better than themselves.	[7]Be not wise in thine own eyes: fear the LORD, and depart from evil. **Is 5:21** [21]Woe unto them that are wise in their own eyes, and prudent in their own sight!

Jn	Paul	Other
6:27	**1 Cor 6:7**	**Q-Quelle**
[27]Labour not for the meat which perisheth, but for that meat which endureth unto everlasting life, which the Son of man shall give unto you: for him hath God the Father sealed. **6:29** [29]Jesus answered and said unto them, This is the work of God, that ye believe on him whom he hath sent. **6:30** [30]They said therefore unto him, What sign showest thou then, that we may see, and believe thee? what dost thou work?	[7]Now therefore there is utterly a fault among you, because ye go to law one with another. Why do ye not rather take wrong? why do ye not rather suffer yourselves to be defrauded?	Love Enemies: Rom 12:17-20/[1 Cor 4:12]/1 Cor 6:7/ [1 Thes 5:15]/Mt 5:38-48 [7:12]/ [Lk 6:27-36 (QS 9 [Thom 6:2, 95],QS10)]

ROMANS 12:17—Christian duty (12:1–15:13), 56–58 CE

Theme	ROM	Paul	NT
Do not do evil for evil	**12:17** [17]Recompense to no man evil for evil. Provide things honest in the sight of all men.	**1 Thes 5:15** [15]See that none render evil for evil unto any man; but ever follow that which is good, both among yourselves, and to all men.	**1 Pet 3:9** [9]Not rendering evil for evil, or railing for railing: but contrariwise blessing; knowing that ye are thereunto called, that ye should inherit a blessing.

ROMANS 12:18—Christian duty (12:1–15:13), 56–58 CE

Theme	ROM	NT
Live Peaceably	**12:18** [18]If it be possible, as much as lieth in you, live peaceably with all men.	**Heb 12:14** [14]Follow peace with all men, and holiness, without which no man shall see the Lord:

ROMANS 12:19—Christian duty (12:1–15:13), 56–58 CE

Theme	ROM	Mt	Paul	NT
Do no vengeance	**12:19** [19]Dearly beloved, avenge not yourselves, but rather give place unto wrath: for it is written, Vengeance is mine; I will repay, saith the Lord.	**5:39** [39]But I say unto you, That ye resist not evil: but whosoever shall smite thee on thy right cheek, turn to him the other also.	**1 Cor 6:6–7** [6]But brother goeth to law with brother, and that before the unbelievers. [7]Now therefore there is utterly a fault among you, because ye go to law one with another. Why do ye not rather take wrong? why do ye not rather suffer yourselves to be defrauded?	**Heb 10:30** [30]For we know him that hath said, Vengeance belongeth unto me, I will recompense, saith the Lord. And again, The Lord shall judge his people.

ROMANS 12:20—Christian duty (12:1–15:13), 56–58 CE

Theme	ROM	Mt
Feed, cloth enemy	**12:20** [20]Therefore if thine enemy hunger, feed him; if he thirst, give him drink: for in so doing thou shalt heap coals of fire on his head.	**5:44** [44]But I say unto you, Love your enemies, bless them that curse you, do good to them that hate you, and pray for them which despitefully use you, and persecute you;

Jewish Writings
Prov 3:4
[4]So shalt thou find favour and good understanding in the sight of God and man.

Jewish Writings	Other
Lev 19:18	**Q-Quelle**
[18]Thou shalt not avenge, nor bear any grudge against the children of thy people, but thou shalt love thy neighbour as thyself: I am the LORD. **Dt 32:35** [35]To me belongeth vengeance, and recompense; their foot shall slide in due time: for the day of their calamity is at hand, and the things that shall come upon them make haste.	Love enemies: Rom 12:19/Mt 5:38-48, [Mt 7:12]/[Lk 6:27-36 (QS 9,10)]

Jewish Writings	Other
Prov 25:21–22	**Q-Quelle**
[21]If thine enemy be hungry, give him bread to eat; and if he be thirsty, give him water to drink: [22]For thou shalt heap coals of fire upon his head, and the LORD shall reward thee.	Love enemies: Rom 12:20/ Mt 5:38-48, [Mt 7:12]/[Lk 6:27-36 (QS 9,10)]

ROMANS 13:1—Christian duty (12:1–15:13), 56–58 CE

Theme	ROM	Jn	Paul
All are subject to higher power	**13:1** [1]Let every soul be subject unto the higher powers. For there is no power but of God: the powers that be are ordained of God.	**19:11** [11]Jesus answered, Thou couldest have no power at all against me, except it were given thee from above: therefore he that delivered me unto thee hath the greater sin.	**Tit 3:1 (Pseudo)** [1]Put them in mind to be subject to principalities and powers, to obey magistrates, to be ready to every good work,

ROMANS 13:3—Christian duty (12:1–15:13), 56–58 CE

Theme	ROM	NT
Do good	**13:3** [3]For rulers are not a terror to good works, but to the evil. Wilt thou then not be afraid of the power? do that which is good, and thou shalt have praise of the same:	**1 Pet 2:13–14** [13]Submit yourselves to every ordinance of man for the Lord's sake: whether it be to the king, as supreme; [14]Or unto governors, as unto them that are sent by him for the punishment of evildoers, and for the praise of them that do well. **1 Pet 3:13** [13]And who is he that will harm you, if ye be followers of that which is good?

ROMANS 13:4–5—Christian duty (12:1–15:13), 56–58 CE

Theme	ROM	Paul	NT
Jews receive God's wrath	**13:4–5** [4]For he is the minister of God to thee for good. But if thou do that which is evil, be afraid; for he beareth not the sword in vain: for he is the minister of God, a revenger to execute wrath upon him that doeth evil. [5]Wherefore ye must needs be subject, not only for wrath, but also for conscience sake. **12:19** [19]Dearly beloved, avenge not yourselves, but rather give place unto wrath: for it is written, Vengeance is mine; I will repay, saith the Lord.	**1 Thes 2:16** [16]Forbidding us to speak to the Gentiles that they might be saved, to fill up their sins alway: for the wrath is come upon them to the uttermost.	**1 Pet 2:19** [19]For this is thankworthy, if a man for conscience toward God endure grief, suffering wrongfully.

NT	Jewish Writings
1 Pet 2:13–17	**Prov 8:15–16**
[13]Submit yourselves to every ordinance of man for the Lord's sake: whether it be to the king, as supreme; [14]Or unto governors, as unto them that are sent by him for the punishment of evildoers, and for the praise of them that do well. [15]For so is the will of God, that with well doing ye may put to silence the ignorance of foolish men: [16]As free, and not using your liberty for a cloak of maliciousness, but as the servants of God. [17]Honour all men. Love the brotherhood. Fear God. Honour the king.	[15]By me kings reign, and princes decree justice. [16]By me princes rule, and nobles, even all the judges of the earth. **Wis 6:3** [3]For power is given you of the Lord, and sovereignty from the Highest, who shall try your works, and search out your counsels.

ROMANS 13:7—Christian duty (12:1–15:13), 56–58 CE

Theme	ROM	Mt	Mk
Paying taxes: temple area	**13:7** [7]Render therefore to all their dues: tribute to whom tribute is due; custom to whom custom; fear to whom fear; honour to whom honour.	**22:15–22** [15]Then went the Pharisees, and took counsel how they might entangle him in his talk. [16]And they sent out unto him their disciples with the Herodians, saying, Master, we know that thou art true, and teachest the way of God in truth, neither carest thou for any man for thou regardest not the person of men. [17]Tell us therefore, What thinkest thou? Is it lawful to give tribute unto Caesar, or not? [18]But Jesus perceived their wickedness, and said, Why tempt ye me, ye hypocrites? [19]Show me the tribute money. And they brought unto him a penny. [20]And he saith unto them, Whose is this image and superscription? [21]They say unto him, Caesar's. Then saith he unto them, Render therefore unto Caesar the things which are Caesar's; and unto God the things that are God's. [22]When they had heard these words, they marvelled, and left him, and went their way **22:21** [21]They say unto him, Caesar's. Then saith he unto them, Render therefore unto Caesar the things which are Caesar's; and unto God the things that are God's.	**12:13–17** [13]And they send unto him certain of the Pharisees and of the Herodians, to catch him in his words. [14]And when they were come, they say unto him, Master, we know that thou art true, and carest for no man: for thou regardest not the person of men, but teachest the way of God in truth: Is it lawful to give tribute to Caesar, or not? [15]Shall we give, or shall we not give? But he, knowing their hypocrisy, said unto them, Why tempt ye me? bring me a penny, that I may see it. [16]And they brought it. And he saith unto them, Whose is this image and superscription? And they said unto him, Caesar's. [17]And Jesus answering said unto them, Render to Caesar the things that are Caesar's, and to God the things that are God's. And they marvelled at him.

Lk	Jn	Other
20:20–26	**3:2**	**PEger 2 3**
[20]And they watched him, and sent forth spies, which should feign themselves just men, that they might take hold of his words, that so they might deliver him unto the power and authority of the governor. [21]And they asked him, saying, Master, we know that thou sayest and teachest rightly, neither acceptest thou the person of any, but teachest the way of God truly: [22]Is it lawful for us to give tribute unto Caesar, or no? [23]But he perceived their craftiness, and said unto them, Why tempt ye me? [24]Show me a penny. Whose image and superscription hath it? They answered and said, Caesar's. [25]And he said unto them, Render therefore unto Caesar the things which be Caesar's, and unto God the things which be God's. [26]And they could not take hold of his words before the people: and they marvelled at his answer, and held their peace.	[2]The same came to Jesus by night, and said unto him, Rabbi, we know that thou art a teacher come from God: for no man can do these miracles that thou doest, except God be with him.	...[they came] to him and began rigorously testing him, saying "Teacher Jesus, we know that you have come from God. For the things you do give a testimony that is beyond all the prophets. And so, tell us; is it right to pay the kings the things that relate to their rule? Shall we pay them or not?" But when Jesus understood their thought he became incensed and said to them, "Why do you call me teacher with your mouth, when you do not listen to what I say? Well did Isaiah prophesy about you, "This people honors me with their lips, but their heart is far removed from me. In vain they do worship me, commandments...' "
20:25		**GThom 100**
[25]And he said unto them, Render therefore unto Caesar the things which be Caesar's, and unto God the things which be God's.		[100]They showed Jesus a gold coin and said to him, "Caesar's men demand taxes from us."

ROMANS 13:8–14—Christian duty (12:1–15:13), 56–58 CE

Theme	ROM	Mt	Mk
Holy commands	**13:8–14** [8]Owe no man any thing, but to love one another: for he that loveth another hath fulfilled the law. [9]For this, Thou shalt not commit adultery, Thou shalt not kill, Thou shalt not steal, Thou shalt not bear false witness, Thou shalt not covet; and if there be any other commandment, it is briefly comprehended in this saying, namely, Thou shalt love thy neighbour as thyself. [10]Love worketh no ill to his neighbour: therefore love is the fulfilling of the law. [11]And that, knowing the time, that now it is high time to awake out of sleep: for now is our salvation nearer than when we believed. [12]The night is far spent, the day is at hand: let us therefore cast off the works of darkness, and let us put on the armour of light. [13]Let us walk honestly, as in the day; not in rioting and drunkenness, not in chambering and wantonness, not in strife and envying. [14]But put ye on the Lord Jesus Christ, and make not provision for the flesh, to fulfil the lusts thereof.	**19:16–21** [16]And, behold, one came and said unto him, Good Master, what good thing shall I do, that I may have eternal life? [17]And he said unto him, Why callest thou me good? there is none good but one, that is, God: but if thou wilt enter into life, keep the commandments [18]He saith unto him, Which? Jesus said, Thou shalt do no murder, Thou shalt not commit adultery, Thou shalt not steal, Thou shalt not bear false witness, [19]Honour thy father and thy mother: and, Thou shalt love thy neighbour as thyself. [20]The young man saith unto him, All these things have I kept from my youth up: what lack I yet? [21]Jesus said unto him, If thou wilt be perfect, go and sell that thou hast, and give to the poor, and thou shalt have treasure in heaven: and come and follow me. **22:34–40** [34]But when the Pharisees had heard that he had put the Sadducees to silence, they were gathered together. [35]Then one of them, which was a lawyer, asked him a question, tempting him, and saying, [36]Master, which is the great commandment in the law? [37]Jesus said unto him, Thou shalt love the Lord thy God with all thy heart, and with all thy soul, and with all thy mind. [38]This is the first and great commandment. [39]And the second is like unto it, Thou shalt love thy neighbour as thyself. [40]On these two commandments hang all the law and the prophets.	**10:17–20** [17]And when he was gone forth into the way, there came one running, and kneeled to him, and asked him, Good Master, what shall I do that I may inherit eternal life? [18]And Jesus said unto him, Why callest thou me good? there is none good but one, that is, God. [19]Thou knowest the commandments, Do not commit adultery, Do not kill, Do not steal, Do not bear false witness, Defraud not, Honour thy father and mother. [20]And he answered and said unto him, Master, all these have I observed from my youth. **12:28–34** [28]And one of the scribes came, and having heard them reasoning together, and perceiving that he had answered them well, asked him, Which is the first commandment of all? [29]And Jesus answered him, The first of all the commandments is, Hear, O Israel; The Lord our God is one Lord: [30]And thou shalt love the Lord thy God with all thy heart, and with all thy soul, and with all thy mind, and with all thy strength: this is the first commandment. [31]And the second is like, namely this, Thou shalt love thy neighbour as thyself. There is none other commandment greater than these. [32]And the scribe said unto him, Well, Master, thou hast said the truth: for there is one God; and there is none other but he: [33]And to love him with all the heart, and with all the understanding, and with all the soul, and with all the strength, and to love his neighbour as himself, is more than all whole burnt offerings and sacrifices. [34]And when Jesus saw that he answered discreetly, he said unto him, Thou art not far from the kingdom of God. And no man after that durst ask him any question.

Jn	Paul	NT	Jewish Writings	Other
10:25–29 [25]Jesus answered them, I told you, and ye believed not: the works that I do in my Father's name, they bear witness of me. [26]But ye believe not, because ye are not of my sheep, as I said unto you. [27]My sheep hear my voice, and I know them, and they follow me: [28]And I give unto them eternal life; and they shall never perish, neither shall any man pluck them out of my hand. [29]My Father, which gave them me, is greater than all; and no man is able to pluck them out of my Father's hand. **18:18–21** [18]And the servants and officers stood there, who had made a fire of coals; for it was cold: and they warmed themselves: and Peter stood with them, and warmed himself. [19]The high priest then asked Jesus of his disciples, and of his doctrine. [20]Jesus answered him, I spake openly to the world; I ever taught in the synagogue, and in the temple, whither the Jews always resort; and in secret have I said nothing. [21]Why askest thou me? ask them which heard me, what I have said unto them: behold, they know what I said.	**Gal 5:14** [14]For all the law is fulfilled in one word, even in this; Thou shalt love thy neighbour as thyself.	**Jas 2:8** [8]If ye fulfil the royal law according to the scripture, Thou shalt love thy neighbour as thyself, ye do well:	**Lev 18:5** [5]Ye shall therefore keep my statutes, and my judgments: which if a man do, he shall live in them: I am the LORD. **Lev 19:18** [18]Thou shalt not avenge, nor bear any grudge against the children of thy people, but thou shalt love thy neighbour as thyself: I am the LORD. **Dt 6:5** [5]And thou shalt love the LORD thy God with all thine heart, and with all thy soul, and with all thy might.	**Barn 19:5** [5]Do not be of two minds whether this should happen or not. Do not take the Lord's name for a futile purpose. Love your neighbor more than yourself. Do not abort a fetus or kill a child that is already born. Do not remove your hand from your son or daughter, but from their youth teach them the reverential fear of God. **Did 1:2** [2]This then is the path of life. First, love the God who made you, and second, your neighbor as yourself. And whatever you do not want to happen to you, do not do to another. **GThom25** [25]Jesus said, "Love your bother like your soul, guard him like the pupil of your eye."

ROMANS 13:8–10—Christian duty (12:1–15:13), 56–58 CE

Theme	ROM	Mt	Mk	Lk
Greatest command—love	**13:8–10** [8]Owe no man any thing, but to love one another: for he that loveth another hath fulfilled the law. [9]For this, Thou shalt not commit adultery, Thou shalt not kill, Thou shalt not steal, Thou shalt not bear false witness, Thou shalt not covet; and if there be any other commandment, it is briefly comprehended in this saying, namely, Thou shalt love thy neighbour as thyself. [10]Love worketh no ill to his neighbour: therefore love is the fulfilling of the law.	**5:43–44** [43]Ye have heard that it hath been said, Thou shalt love thy neighbour, and hate thine enemy. [44]But I say unto you, Love your enemies, bless them that curse you, do good to them that hate you, and pray for them which despitefully use you, and persecute you; **19:18–19** [18]He saith unto him, Which? Jesus said, Thou shalt do no murder, Thou shalt not commit adultery, Thou shalt not steal, Thou shalt not bear false witness, [19]Honour thy father and thy mother: and, Thou shalt love thy neighbour as thyself. **22:34–40** [34]But when the Pharisees had heard that he had put the Sadducees to silence, they were gathered together. [35]Then one of them, which was a lawyer, asked him a question, tempting him, and saying, [36]Master, which is the great commandment in the law? [37]Jesus said unto him, Thou shalt love the Lord thy God with all thy heart, and with all thy soul, and with all thy mind. [38]This is the first and great commandment. [39]And the second is like unto it, Thou shalt love thy neighbour as thyself. [40]On these two commandments hang all the law and the prophets.[41]While the Pharisees were gathered together, Jesus asked them, [42]Saying, What think ye of Christ? whose son is he? They say unto him, The Son of David. [43]He saith unto them, How then doth David in spirit call him Lord, saying, [44]The LORD said unto my Lord, Sit thou on my right hand, till I make thine enemies thy footstool? [45]If David then call him Lord, how is he his son? [46]And no man was able to answer him a word, neither durst any man from that day forth ask him any more questions.	**12:28–34** [28]And one of the scribes came, and having heard them reasoning together, and perceiving that he had answered them well, asked him, Which is the first commandment of all? [29]And Jesus answered him, The first of all the commandments is, Hear, O Israel; The Lord our God is one Lord: [30]And thou shalt love the Lord thy God with all thy heart, and with all thy soul, and with all thy mind, and with all thy strength: this is the first commandment. [31]And the second is like, namely this, Thou shalt love thy neighbour as thyself. There is none other commandment greater than these. [32]And the scribe said unto him, Well, Master, thou hast said the truth: for there is one God; and there is none other but he: [33]And to love him with all the heart, and with all the understanding, and with all the soul, and with all the strength, and to love his neighbour as himself, is more than all whole burnt offerings and sacrifices. [34]And when Jesus saw that he answered discreetly, he said unto him, Thou art not far from the kingdom of God. And no man after that durst ask him any question.	**10:27** [27]And he answering said, Thou shalt love the Lord thy God with all thy heart, and with all thy soul, and with all thy strength, and with all thy mind; and thy neighbour as thyself.

Jn	Paul	NT	Jewish Writings	Other
10:25–29 [25]Jesus answered them, I told you, and ye believed not: the works that I do in my Father's name, they bear witness of me. [26]But ye believe not, because ye are not of my sheep, as I said unto you. [27]My sheep hear my voice, and I know them, and they follow me: [28]And I give unto them eternal life; and they shall never perish, neither shall any man pluck them out of my hand. [29]My Father, which gave them me, is greater than all; and no man is able to pluck them out of my Father's hand. **13:34** [34]A new commandment I give unto you, That ye love one another; as I have loved you, that ye also love one another.	**1 Cor 13:4–7** [4]Charity suffereth long, and is kind; charity envieth not; charity vaunteth not itself, is not puffed up, [5]Doth not behave itself unseemly, seeketh not her own, is not easily provoked, thinketh no evil; [6]Rejoiceth not in iniquity, but rejoiceth in the truth; [7]Beareth all things, believeth all things, hopeth all things, endureth all things. **Gal 5:13–15** [13]For, brethren, ye have been called unto liberty; only use not liberty for an occasion to the flesh, but by love serve one another. [14]For all the law is fulfilled in one word, even in this; Thou shalt love thy neighbour as thyself. [15]But if ye bite and devour one another, take heed that ye be not consumed one of another. **Gal 6:10** [10]As we have therefore opportunity, let us do good unto all men, especially unto them who are of the household of faith.	**Jas 2:8** [8]If ye fulfil the royal law according to the scripture, Thou shalt love thy neighbour as thyself, ye do well:	**Ex 20:13–17** [13]Thou shalt not kill. [14]Thou shalt not commit adultery. [15]Thou shalt not steal. [16]Thou shalt not bear false witness against thy neighbour. [17]Thou shalt not covet thy neighbour's house, thou shalt not covet thy neighbour's wife, nor his manservant, nor his maidservant, nor his ox, nor his ass, nor any thing that is thy neighbour's. **Lev 19:18** [18]Thou shalt not avenge, nor bear any grudge against the children of thy people, but thou shalt love thy neighbour as thyself: I am the LORD. **Dt 5:7–21** [7]Thou shalt have none other gods before me. [8]Thou shalt not make thee any graven image, or any likeness of any thing that is in heaven above, or that is in the earth beneath, or that is in the waters beneath the earth: [9]Thou shalt not bow down thyself unto them, nor serve them: for I the LORD thy God am a jealous God, visiting the iniquity of the fathers upon the children unto the third and fourth generation of them that hate me, [10]And showing mercy unto thousands of them that love me and keep my commandments. [11]Thou shalt not take the name of the LORD thy God in vain: for the LORD will not hold him guiltless that taketh his name in vain. [12]Keep the sabbath day to sanctify it, as the LORD thy God hath commanded thee. [13]Six days thou shalt labour, and do all thy work: [14]But the seventh day is the sabbath of the LORD thy God: in it thou shalt not do any work, thou, nor thy son, nor thy daughter, nor thy manservant, nor thy maidservant, nor thine ox, nor thine ass, nor any of thy cattle, nor thy stranger that is within thy gates; that thy manservant and thy maidservant may rest as well as thou. [15]And remember that thou wast a servant in the land of Egypt, and that the LORD thy God brought thee out thence through a mighty hand and by a stretched out arm: therefore the LORD thy God commanded thee to keep the sabbath day. [16]Honour thy father and thy mother, as the LORD thy God hath commanded thee; that thy days may be prolonged, and that it may go well with thee, in the land which the LORD thy God giveth thee. [17]Thou shalt not kill. [18]Neither shalt thou commit adultery. [19]Neither shalt thou steal. [20]Neither shalt thou bear false witness against thy neighbour. [21]Neither shalt thou desire thy neighbour's wife, neither shalt thou covet thy neighbour's house, his field, or his manservant, or his maidservant, his ox, or his ass, or any thing that is thy neighbour's. **Dt 6:5** [5]And thou shalt love the LORD thy God with all thine heart, and with all thy soul, and with all thy might.	**Barn 19:5** [5]Do not be of two minds whether this should happen or not. Do not take the Lord's name for a futile purpose. Love your neighbor more than yourself. Do not abort a fetus or kill a child that is already born. Do not remove your hand from your son or daughter, but from their youth teach them the reverential fear of God. **Did 1:2** [2]This then is the path of life. First, love the God who made you, and second, your neighbor as yourself. And whatever you do not want to happen to you, do not do to another. **GThom 25** [25]Jesus said, "Love your bother like your soul, guard him like the pupil of your eye." **Q-Quelle** Love enemies: Rom 13:8-10/Mt 5:38-48/[Mk 7:12]/[Lk 6:27-36 (QS 9 [Thom 6:2, 95], QS 10)]

ROMANS 13:11—Christian duty (12:1–15:13), 56–58 CE

Theme	ROM	Mt
Coming of the Lord: future harvest and salvation	**13:11** [11]And that, knowing the time, that now it is high time to awake out of sleep: for now is our salvation nearer than when we believed.	**6:10** [10]Thy kingdom come. Thy will be done in earth, as it is in heaven. **13:1–31** [1]The same day went Jesus out of the house, and sat by the sea side. [2]And great multitudes were gathered together unto him, so that he went into a ship, and sat; and the whole multitude stood on the shore. [3]And he spake many things unto them in parables, saying, Behold, a sower went forth to sow; [4]And when he sowed, some seeds fell by the way side, and the fowls came and devoured them up: [5]Some fell upon stony places, where they had not much earth: and forthwith they sprung up, because they had no deepness of earth: [6]And when the sun was up, they were scorched; and because they had no root, they withered away. [7]And some fell among thorns; and the thorns sprung up, and choked them: [8]But other fell into good ground, and brought forth fruit, some an hundredfold, some sixtyfold, some thirtyfold. [9]Who hath ears to hear, let him hear. [10]And the disciples came, and said unto him, Why speakest thou unto them in parables? [11]He answered and said unto them, Because it is given unto you to know the mysteries of the kingdom of heaven, but to them it is not given. [12]For whosoever hath, to him shall be given, and he shall have more abundance: but whosoever hath not, from him shall be taken away even that he hath. [13]Therefore speak I to them in parables: because they seeing see not; and hearing they hear not, neither do they understand. [14]And in them is fulfilled the prophecy of Esaias, which saith, By hearing ye shall hear, and shall not understand; and seeing ye shall see, and shall not perceive: [15]For this people's heart is waxed gross, and their ears are dull of hearing, and their eyes they have closed; lest at any time they should see with their eyes, and hear with their ears, and should understand with their heart, and should be converted, and I should heal them. [16]But blessed are your eyes, for they see: and your ears, for they hear. [17]For verily I say unto you, That many prophets and righteous men have desired to see those things which ye see, and have not seen them; and to hear those things which ye hear, and have not heard them. [18]Hear ye therefore the parable of the sower. [19]When any one heareth the word of the kingdom, and understandeth it not, then cometh the wicked one, and catcheth away that which was sown in his heart. This is he which received seed by the way side. [20]But he that received the seed into stony places, the same is he that heareth the word, and anon with joy receiveth it; [21]Yet hath he not root in himself, but dureth for a while: for when tribulation or persecution ariseth because of the word, by and by he is offended. [22]He also that received seed among the thorns is he that heareth the word; and the care of this world, and the deceitfulness of riches, choke the word, and he becometh unfruitful. [23]But he that received seed into the good ground is he that heareth the word, and understandeth it; which also beareth fruit, and bringeth forth, some an hundredfold, some sixty, some thirty. [24]Another parable put he forth unto them, saying, The kingdom of heaven is likened unto a man which sowed good seed in his field: [25]But while men slept, his enemy came and sowed tares among the wheat, and went his way. [26]But when the blade was sprung up, and brought forth fruit, then appeared the tares also. [27]So the servants of the householder came and said unto him, Sir, didst not thou sow good seed in thy field? from whence then hath it tares? [28]He said unto them, An enemy hath done this. The servants said unto him, Wilt thou then that we go and gather them up? [29]But he said, Nay; lest while ye gather up the tares, ye root up also the wheat with them. [30]Let both grow together until the harvest: and in the time of harvest I will say to the reapers, Gather ye together first the tares, and bind them in bundles to burn them: but gather the wheat into my barn. [31]Another parable put he forth unto them, saying, The kingdom of heaven is like to a grain of mustard seed, which a man took, and sowed in his field: **16:28** [28]Verily I say unto you, There be some standing here, which shall not taste of death, till they see the Son of man coming in his kingdom. **24:34** [34]Verily I say unto you, This generation shall not pass, till all these things be fulfilled. **24:37** [37]But as the days of Noe were, so shall also the coming of the Son of man be. **25:6–10** [6]And at midnight there was a cry made, Behold, the bridegroom cometh; go ye out to meet him. [7]Then all those virgins arose, and trimmed their lamps. [8]And the foolish said unto the wise, Give us of your oil; for our lamps are gone out. [9]But the wise answered, saying, Not so; lest there be not enough for us and you: but go ye rather to them that sell, and buy for yourselves. [10]And while they went to buy, the bridegroom came; and they that were ready went in with him to the marriage: and the door was shut.

Mk

1:14

[14]Now after that John was put in prison, Jesus came into Galilee, preaching the gospel of the kingdom of God,

4:1–32

[1]And he began again to teach by the sea side: and there was gathered unto him a great multitude, so that he entered into a ship, and sat in the sea; and the whole multitude was by the sea on the land. [2]And he taught them many things by parables, and said unto them in his doctrine, [3]Hearken; Behold, there went out a sower to sow: [4]And it came to pass, as he sowed, some fell by the way side, and the fowls of the air came and devoured it up. [5]And some fell on stony ground, where it had not much earth; and immediately it sprang up, because it had no depth of earth: [6]But when the sun was up, it was scorched; and because it had no root, it withered away. [7]And some fell among thorns, and the thorns grew up, and choked it, and it yielded no fruit. [8]And other fell on good ground, and did yield fruit that sprang up and increased; and brought forth, some thirty, and some sixty, and some an hundred. [9]And he said unto them, He that hath ears to hear, let him hear. [10]And when he was alone, they that were about him with the twelve asked of him the parable. [11]And he said unto them, Unto you it is given to know the mystery of the kingdom of God: but unto them that are without, all these things are done in parables: [12]That seeing they may see, and not perceive; and hearing they may hear, and not understand; lest at any time they should be converted, and their sins should be forgiven them. [13]And he said unto them, Know ye not this parable? and how then will ye know all parables? [14]The sower soweth the word. [15]And these are they by the way side, where the word is sown; but when they have heard, Satan cometh immediately, and taketh away the word that was sown in their hearts. [16]And these are they likewise which are sown on stony ground; who, when they have heard the word, immediately receive it with gladness; [17]And have no root in themselves, and so endure but for a time: afterward, when affliction or persecution ariseth for the word's sake, immediately they are offended. [18]And these are they which are sown among thorns; such as hear the word, [19]And the cares of this world, and the deceitfulness of riches, and the lusts of other things entering in, choke the word, and it becometh unfruitful. [20]And these are they which are sown on good ground; such as hear the word, and receive it, and bring forth fruit, some thirtyfold, some sixty, and some an hundred. [21]And he said unto them, Is a candle brought to be put under a bushel, or under a bed? and not to be set on a candlestick? [22]For there is nothing hid, which shall not be manifested; neither was any thing kept secret, but that it should come abroad. [23]If any man have ears to hear, let him hear. [24]And he said unto them, Take heed what ye hear: with what measure ye mete, it shall be measured to you: and unto you that hear shall more be given. [25]For he that hath, to him shall be given: and he that hath not, from him shall be taken even that which he hath. [26]And he said, So is the kingdom of God, as if a man should cast seed into the ground; [27]And should sleep, and rise night and day, and the seed should spring and grow up, he knoweth not how. [28]For the earth bringeth forth fruit of herself; first the blade, then the ear, after that the full corn in the ear. [29]But when the fruit is brought forth, immediately he putteth in the sickle, because the harvest is come. [30]And he said, Whereunto shall we liken the kingdom of God? or with what comparison shall we compare it? [31]It is like a grain of mustard seed, which, when it is sown in the earth, is less than all the seeds that be in the earth: [32]But when it is sown, it groweth up, and becometh greater than all herbs, and shooteth out great branches; so that the fowls of the air may lodge under the shadow of it.

9:1

[1]And he said unto them, Verily I say unto you, That there be some of them that stand here, which shall not taste of death, till they have seen the kingdom of God come with power.

13:30

[30]Verily I say unto you, that this generation shall not pass, till all these things be done.

13:33–36

[33]Take ye heed, watch and pray: for ye know not when the time is. [34]For the Son of man is as a man taking a far journey, who left his house, and gave authority to his servants, and to every man his work, and commanded the porter to watch. [35]Watch ye therefore: for ye know not when the master of the house cometh, at even, or at midnight, or at the cockcrowing, or in the morning: [36]Lest coming suddenly he find you sleeping.

Lk

Acts 1:6–7

[6]When they therefore were come together, they asked of him, saying, Lord, wilt thou at this time restore again the kingdom to Israel? [7]And he said unto them, It is not for you to know the times or the seasons, which the Father hath put in his own power.

Romans 13:11 continued on next page

ROMANS 13:11—Christian duty (12:1–15:13), 56–58 CE (*continued*)

Theme	ROM	Jn
(*Cont.*) **Coming of the Lord: future harvest and salvation**	**13:11 (above)**	**8:4–15** [4]They say unto him, Master, this woman was taken in adultery, in the very act. [5]Now Moses in the law commanded us, that such should be stoned: but what sayest thou? [6]This they said, tempting him, that they might have to accuse him. But Jesus stooped down, and with his finger wrote on the ground, as though he heard them not. [7]So when they continued asking him, he lifted up himself, and said unto them, He that is without sin among you, let him first cast a stone at her. [8]And again he stooped down, and wrote on the ground. [9]And they which heard it, being convicted by their own conscience, went out one by one, beginning at the eldest, even unto the last: and Jesus was left alone, and the woman standing in the midst. [10]When Jesus had lifted up himself, and saw none but the woman, he said unto her, Woman, where are those thine accusers? hath no man condemned thee? [11]She said, No man, Lord. And Jesus said unto her, Neither do I condemn thee: go, and sin no more. [12]Then spake Jesus again unto them, saying, I am the light of the world: he that followeth me shall not walk in darkness, but shall have the light of life. [13]The Pharisees therefore said unto him, Thou bearest record of thyself; thy record is not true. [14]Jesus answered and said unto them, Though I bear record of myself, yet my record is true: for I know whence I came, and whither I go; but ye cannot tell whence I come, and whither I go. [15]Ye judge after the flesh; I judge no man. **9:27** [27]He answered them, I have told you already, and ye did not hear: wherefore would ye hear it again? will ye also be his disciples? **11:12** [12]Then said his disciples, Lord, if he sleep, he shall do well. **12:36–40** [36]While ye have light, believe in the light, that ye may be the children of light. These things spake Jesus, and departed, and did hide himself from them. [37]But though he had done so many miracles before them, yet they believed not on him: [38]That the saying of Esaias the prophet might be fulfilled, which he spake, Lord, who hath believed our report? and to whom hath the arm of the Lord been revealed? [39]Therefore they could not believe, because that Esaias said again, [40]He hath blinded their eyes, and hardened their heart; that they should not see with their eyes, nor understand with their heart, and be converted, and I should heal them. **13:18–19** [18]I speak not of you all: I know whom I have chosen: but that the scripture may be fulfilled, He that eateth bread with me hath lifted up his heel against me. [19]Now I tell you before it come, that, when it is come to pass, ye may believe that I am he. **17:26** [26]And I have declared unto them thy name, and will declare it: that the love wherewith thou hast loved me may be in them, and I in them.

Paul	Jewish Writings	Other
1 Cor 7:29–31 [29]But this I say, brethren, the time is short: it remaineth, that both they that have wives be as though they had none; [30]And they that weep, as though they wept not; and they that rejoice, as though they rejoiced not; and they that buy, as though they possessed not; [31]And they that use this world, as not abusing it: for the fashion of this world passeth away. **1 Cor 10:11** [11]Now all these things happened unto them for ensamples: and they are written for our admonition, upon whom the ends of the world are come. **Eph 5:8–16 (pseudo)** [8]For ye were sometimes darkness, but now are ye light in the Lord: walk as children of light: [9](For the fruit of the Spirit is in all goodness and righteousness and truth;) [10]Proving what is acceptable unto the Lord. [11]And have no fellowship with the unfruitful works of darkness, but rather reprove them. [12]For it is a shame even to speak of those things which are done of them in secret. [13]But all things that are reproved are made manifest by the light: for whatsoever doth make manifest is light. [14]Wherefore he saith, Awake thou that sleepest, and arise from the dead, and Christ shall give thee light. [15]See then that ye walk circumspectly, not as fools, but as wise, [16]Redeeming the time, because the days are evil. **1 Thes 1:10** [10]And to wait for his Son from heaven, whom he raised from the dead, even Jesus, which delivered us from the wrath to come. **1 Thes 4:15** [15]For this we say unto you by the word of the Lord, that we which are alive and remain unto the coming of the Lord shall not prevent them which are asleep. **1 Thes 4:16–17** [16]For the Lord himself shall descend from heaven with a shout, with the voice of the archangel, and with the trump of God: and the dead in Christ shall rise first: [17]Then we which are alive and remain shall be caught up together with them in the clouds, to meet the Lord in the air: and so shall we ever be with the Lord. **1 Thes 5:6** [6]Therefore let us not sleep, as do others; but let us watch and be sober. **1 Thes 5:10** [10]Who died for us, that, whether we wake or sleep, we should live together with him. **1 Thes 5:1–3** [1]But of the times and the seasons, brethren, ye have no need that I write unto you. [2]For yourselves know perfectly that the day of the Lord so cometh as a thief in the night. [3]For when they shall say, Peace and safety; then sudden destruction cometh upon them, as travail upon a woman with child; and they shall not escape.	**Ps 117:1** [1]O praise the LORD, all ye nations: praise him, all ye people.	**Q-Quelle** Lord's Prayer: Rom 13:11/Mt 6:9-13/[Lk 11:1-4]; Thanks and blessing/Disciples: [Mt 11:25-27], Mt 13:16-17/[Lk 10:21-24]; Mustard seed: Rom 13:11/Mt 13:31-32/[Mk 4:30-32]/[Lk 13:18-19]; Judging: Rom 13:11/[Mt 7:1-5, 10:24-25, 12:36-37, 15:14]/Mk 4:24-25/[Lk 6:37-42 (QS 10, 11 [Thom 34], QS 12 [Thom 26])]

ROMANS 13:12—Christian duty (12:1–15:13), 56–58 CE

Theme	ROM	Jn	Paul	Other
Put on armour of light	**13:12** [12]The night is far spent, the day is at hand: let us therefore cast off the works of darkness, and let us put on the armour of light.	**2:8** [8]And he saith unto them, Draw out now, and bear unto the governor of the feast. And they bare it. **8:12** [12]Then spake Jesus again unto them, saying, I am the light of the world: he that followeth me shall not walk in darkness, but shall have the light of life.	**2 Cor 6:7** [7]By the word of truth, by the power of God, by the armour of righteousness on the right hand and on the left, **2 Cor 10:4** [4](For the weapons of our warfare are not carnal, but mighty through God to the pulling down of strong holds;) **Eph 5:11 (Pseudo)** [11]And have no fellowship with the unfruitful works of darkness, but rather reprove them. **Eph 6:13–17 (Pseudo)** [13]Wherefore take unto you the whole armour of God, that ye may be able to withstand in the evil day, and having done all, to stand. [14]Stand therefore, having your loins girt about with truth, and having on the breastplate of righteousness; [15]And your feet shod with the preparation of the gospel of peace; [16]Above all, taking the shield of faith, wherewith ye shall be able to quench all the fiery darts of the wicked. [17]And take the helmet of salvation, and the sword of the Spirit, which is the word of God: **1 Thes 5:4–8** [4]But ye, brethren, are not in darkness, that that day should overtake you as a thief. [5]Ye are all the children of light, and the children of the day: we are not of the night, nor of darkness. [6]Therefore let us not sleep, as do others; but let us watch and be sober. [7]For they that sleep sleep in the night; and they that be drunken are drunken in the night. [8]But let us, who are of the day, be sober, putting on the breastplate of faith and love; and for an helmet, the hope of salvation.	**Q-Quelle** Watchful and faithful: Rom 13:12-13/1 Thes 5:6/ [Mt 24:42-51]/[Lk 12:35-48 (QS 41 [Thom 21:3, 103], QS 42, 43])]

ROMANS 13:13—Christian duty (12:1–15:13), 56–58 CE

Theme	ROM	Lk	Paul
Walk honestly	**13:13** [13]Let us walk honestly, as in the day; not in rioting and drunkenness, not in chambering and wantonness, not in strife and envying.	**21:34** [34]And take heed to yourselves, lest at any time your hearts be overcharged with surfeiting, and drunkenness, and cares of this life, and so that day come upon you unawares.	**Eph 5:18 (Pseudo)** [18]And be not drunk with wine, wherein is excess; but be filled with the Spirit;

ROMANS 13:14—Christian duty (12:1–15:13), 56–58 CE

Theme	ROM	Paul
Jews receive God's wrath	**13:14** [14]But put ye on the Lord Jesus Christ, and make not provision for the flesh, to fulfil the lusts thereof.	**Gal 3:27** [27]For as many of you as have been baptized into Christ have put on Christ. **Gal 5:16** [16]This I say then, Walk in the Spirit, and ye shall not fulfil the lust of the flesh. **Eph 4:24 (Pseudo)** [24]And that ye put on the new man, which after God is created in righteousness and true holiness.

ROMANS 14:1–23—Christian duty (12:1–15:13), 56–58 CE

Theme	ROM	Paul
Do no offence to weak believer in eating, drinking, etc.	**14:1–23** [1]Him that is weak in the faith receive ye, but not to doubtful disputations. [2]For one believeth that he may eat all things: another, who is weak, eateth herbs. [3]Let not him that eateth despise him that eateth not; and let not him which eateth not judge him that eateth: for God hath received him. [4]Who art thou that judgest another man's servant? to his own master he standeth or falleth. Yea, he shall be holden up: for God is able to make him stand. [5]One man esteemeth one day above another: another esteemeth every day alike. Let every man be fully persuaded in his own mind. [6]He that regardeth the day, regardeth it unto the Lord; and he that regardeth not the day, to the Lord he doth not regard it. He that eateth, eateth to the Lord, for he giveth God thanks; and he that eateth not, to the Lord he eateth not, and giveth God thanks. [7]For none of us liveth to himself, and no man dieth to himself. [8]For whether we live, we live unto the Lord; and whether we die, we die unto the Lord: whether we live therefore, or die, we are the Lord's. [9]For to this end Christ both died, and rose, and revived, that he might be Lord both of the dead and living. [10]But why dost thou judge thy brother? or why dost thou set at nought thy brother? for we shall all stand before the judgment seat of Christ. [11]For it is written, As I live, saith the Lord, every knee shall bow to me, and every tongue shall confess to God. [12]So then every one of us shall give account of himself to God. [13]Let us not therefore judge one another any more: but judge this rather, that no man put a stumblingblock or an occasion to fall in his brother's way. [14]I know, and am persuaded by the Lord Jesus, that there is nothing unclean of itself: but to him that esteemeth any thing to be unclean, to him it is unclean. [15]But if thy brother be grieved with thy meat, now walkest thou not charitably. Destroy not him with thy meat, for whom Christ died. [16]Let not then your good be evil spoken of: [17]For the kingdom of God is not meat and drink; but righteousness, and peace, and joy in the Holy Ghost. [18]For he that in these things serveth Christ is acceptable to God, and approved of men. [19]Let us therefore follow after the things which make for peace, and things wherewith one may edify another. [20]For meat destroy not the work of God. All things indeed are pure; but it is evil for that man who eateth with offence. [21]It is good neither to eat flesh, nor to drink wine, nor any thing whereby thy brother stumbleth, or is offended, or is made weak. [22]Hast thou faith? have it to thyself before God. Happy is he that condemneth not himself in that thing which he alloweth. [23]And he that doubteth is damned if he eat, because he eateth not of faith: for whatsoever is not of faith is sin.	**1 Cor 8:1–3** [1]Now as touching things offered unto idols, we know that we all have knowledge. Knowledge puffeth up, but charity edifieth. [2]And if any man think that he knoweth any thing, he knoweth nothing yet as he ought to know. [3]But if any man love God, the same is known of him.

ROMANS 14:1–2—Christian duty (12:1–15:13), 56–58 CE

Theme	ROM	Mt	Mk	Lk	Jn
Ministry: care for weak	**14:1–2** [1]Him that is weak in the faith receive ye, but not to doubtful disputations. [2]For one believeth that he may eat all things: another, who is weak, eateth herbs. **14:21** [21]It is good neither to eat flesh, nor to drink wine, nor any thing whereby thy brother stumbleth, or is offended, or is made weak. **15:1** [1]We then that are strong ought to bear the infirmities of the weak, and not to please ourselves **15:7** [7]Wherefore receive ye one another, as Christ also received us to the glory of God.	**10:8** [8]Heal the sick, cleanse the lepers, raise the dead, cast out devils: freely ye have received, freely give.	**6:56** [56]And whithersoever he entered, into villages, or cities, or country, they laid the sick in the streets, and besought him that they might touch if it were but the border of his garment: and as many as touched him were made whole.	**Acts 20:35** [35]I have showed you all things, how that so labouring ye ought to support the weak, and to remember the words of the Lord Jesus, how he said, It is more blessed to give than to receive.	**5:15** [15]And they come to Jesus, and see him that was possessed with the devil, and had the legion, sitting, and clothed, and in his right mind: and they were afraid.

Paul	Jewish Writings	Other
1 Cor 8:1–13 [1]Now as touching things offered unto idols, we know that we all have knowledge. Knowledge puffeth up, but charity edifieth. [2]And if any man think that he knoweth any thing, he knoweth nothing yet as he ought to know. [3]But if any man love God, the same is known of him. [4]As concerning therefore the eating of those things that are offered in sacrifice unto idols, we know that an idol is nothing in the world, and that there is none other God but one. [5]For though there be that are called gods, whether in heaven or in earth, (as there be gods many, and lords many,) [6]But to us there is but one God, the Father, of whom are all things, and we in him; and one Lord Jesus Christ, by whom are all things, and we by him. [7]Howbeit there is not in every man that knowledge: for some with conscience of the idol unto this hour eat it as a thing offered unto an idol; and their conscience being weak is defiled. [8]But meat commendeth us not to God: for neither, if we eat, are we the better; neither, if we eat not, are we the worse. [9]But take heed lest by any means this liberty of yours become a stumblingblock to them that are weak. [10]For if any man see thee which hast knowledge sit at meat in the idol's temple, shall not the conscience of him which is weak be emboldened to eat those things which are offered to idols; [11]And through thy knowledge shall the weak brother perish, for whom Christ died? [12]But when ye sin so against the brethren, and wound their weak conscience, ye sin against Christ. [13]Wherefore, if meat make my brother to offend, I will eat no flesh while the world standeth, lest I make my brother to offend. **1 Cor 9:22** [22]To the weak became I as weak, that I might gain the weak: I am made all things to all men, that I might by all means save some. **1 Cor 10:14–33** [14]Wherefore, my dearly beloved, flee from idolatry. [15]I speak as to wise men; judge ye what I say. [16]The cup of blessing which we bless, is it not the communion of the blood of Christ? The bread which we break, is it not the communion of the body of Christ? [17]For we being many are one bread, and one body: for we are all partakers of that one bread. [18]Behold Israel after the flesh: are not they which eat of the sacrifices partakers of the altar? [19]What say I then? that the idol is any thing, or that which is offered in sacrifice to idols is any thing? [20]But I say, that the things which the Gentiles sacrifice, they sacrifice to devils, and not to God: and I would not that ye should have fellowship with devils. [21]Ye cannot drink the cup of the Lord, and the cup of devils: ye cannot be partakers of the Lord's table, and of the table of devils. [22]Do we provoke the Lord to jealousy? are we stronger than he? [23]All things are lawful for me, but all things are not expedient: all things are lawful for me, but all things edify not. [24]Let no man seek his own, but every man another's wealth. [25]Whatsoever is sold in the shambles, that eat, asking no question for conscience sake: [26]For the earth is the Lord's, and the fulness thereof. [27]If any of them that believe not bid you to a feast, and ye be disposed to go; whatsoever is set before you, eat, asking no question for conscience sake. [28]But if any man say unto you, This is offered in sacrifice unto idols, eat not for his sake that showed it, and for conscience sake: for the earth is the Lord's, and the fulness thereof: [29]Conscience, I say, not thine own, but of the other: for why is my liberty judged of another man's conscience? [30]For if I by grace be a partaker, why am I evil spoken of for that for which I give thanks? [31]Whether therefore ye eat, or drink, or whatsoever ye do, do all to the glory of God. [32]Give none offence, neither to the Jews, nor to the Gentiles, nor to the church of God: [33]Even as I please all men in all things, not seeking mine own profit, but the profit of many, that they may be saved. **1 Cor 11:30** [30]For this cause many are weak and sickly among you, and many sleep. **1 Thes 5:14** [14]Now we exhort you, brethren, warn them that are unruly, comfort the feebleminded, support the weak, be patient toward all men.	**Gen 1:29** [29]And God said, Behold, I have given you every herb bearing seed, which is upon the face of all the earth, and every tree, in the which is the fruit of a tree yielding seed; to you it shall be for meat.	**Q-Quelle** Commissioning of the 12: Rom 14:1-2/ [Mt 10:1], 7-11, [14]/ [Mk 6:6b-13]/[Lk 9:1-6]

ROMANS 14:3—Christian duty (12:1–15:13), 56–58 CE

Theme	ROM	Mt
Causing others to stumble	**14:3** [14]I know, and am persuaded by the Lord Jesus, that there is nothing unclean of itself: but to him that esteemeth any thing to be unclean, to him it is unclean. **14:10** [10]But why dost thou judge thy brother? or why dost thou set at nought thy brother? for we shall all stand before the judgment seat of Christ. **14:12–21** [12]So then every one of us shall give account of himself to God. [13]Let us not therefore judge one another any more: but judge this rather, that no man put a stumblingblock or an occasion to fall in his brother's way. [14]I know, and am persuaded by the Lord Jesus, that there is nothing unclean of itself: but to him that esteemeth any thing to be unclean, to him it is unclean. [15]But if thy brother be grieved with thy meat, now walkest thou not charitably. Destroy not him with thy meat, for whom Christ died. [16]Let not then your good be evil spoken of: [17]For the kingdom of God is not meat and drink; but righteousness, and peace, and joy in the Holy Ghost. [18]For he that in these things serveth Christ is acceptable to God, and approved of men. [19]Let us therefore follow after the things which make for peace, and things wherewith one may edify another. [20]For meat destroy not the work of God. All things indeed are pure; but it is evil for that man who eateth with offence. [21]It is good neither to eat flesh, nor to drink wine, nor any thing whereby thy brother stumbleth, or is offended, or is made weak. **14:15** [15]But if thy brother be grieved with thy meat, now walkest thou not charitably. Destroy not him with thy meat, for whom Christ died.	**18:6** [6]But whoso shall offend one of these little ones which believe in me, it were better for him that a millstone were hanged about his neck, and that he were drowned in the depth of the sea. **18:8** [8]Wherefore if thy hand or thy foot offend thee, cut them off, and cast them from thee: it is better for thee to enter into life halt or maimed, rather than having two hands or two feet to be cast into everlasting fire.

Mk	Jn	Paul	Other
9:42–47 [42]And whosoever shall offend one of these little ones that believe in me, it is better for him that a millstone were hanged about his neck, and he were cast into the sea. [43]And if thy hand offend thee, cut it off: it is better for thee to enter into life maimed, than having two hands to go into hell, into the fire that never shall be quenched: [44]Where their worm dieth not, and the fire is not quenched. [45]And if thy foot offend thee, cut it off: it is better for thee to enter halt into life, than having two feet to be cast into hell, into the fire that never shall be quenched: [46]Where their worm dieth not, and the fire is not quenched. [47]And if thine eye offend thee, pluck it out: it is better for thee to enter into the kingdom of God with one eye, than having two eyes to be cast into hell fire:	**6:37** [37]Judge not, and ye shall not be judged: condemn not, and ye shall not be condemned: forgive, and ye shall be forgiven: **17:2** [2]It were better for him that a millstone were hanged about his neck, and he cast into the sea, than that he should offend one of these little ones.	**1 Cor 8:11** [11]And through thy knowledge shall the weak brother perish, for whom Christ died? **1 Cor 8:13** [13]Wherefore, if meat make my brother to offend, I will eat no flesh while the world standeth, lest I make my brother to offend. **Col 2:16** [16]Let no man therefore judge you in meat, or in drink, or in respect of an holyday, or of the new moon, or of the sabbath days:	**Q-Quelle** Judging: Rom 14:3/1 Cor 8:13/[Mt 7:1-5, 10:24-25, 12:36-37, 15:14]/[Mk 4:24-25]/[Lk 37:37-42 (QS 10)]; Warning Against Offenses: Rom 14:3/1 Cor 8:13/Mt 18:6-7/Mk 9:42/[Lk 17:1-3a (QS 57, 58)]

ROMANS 14:4–12—Christian duty (12:1–15:13), 56–58 CE

Theme	ROM	Mt	Mk
Humble service/ ministry	**14:4–12** [4]Who art thou that judgest another man's servant? to his own master he standeth or falleth. Yea, he shall be holden up: for God is able to make him stand. [5]One man esteemeth one day above another: another esteemeth every day alike. Let every man be fully persuaded in his own mind. [6]He that regardeth the day, regardeth it unto the Lord; and he that regardeth not the day, to the Lord he doth not regard it. He that eateth, eateth to the Lord, for he giveth God thanks; and he that eateth not, to the Lord he eateth not, and giveth God thanks. [7]For none of us liveth to himself, and no man dieth to himself. [8]For whether we live, we live unto the Lord; and whether we die, we die unto the Lord: whether we live therefore, or die, we are the Lord's. [9]For to this end Christ both died, and rose, and revived, that he might be Lord both of the dead and living. [10]But why dost thou judge thy brother? or why dost thou set at nought thy brother? for we shall all stand before the judgment seat of Christ. [11]For it is written, As I live, saith the Lord, every knee shall bow to me, and every tongue shall confess to God. [12]So then every one of us shall give account of himself to God. **2:1** [1]Therefore thou art inexcusable, O man, whosoever thou art that judgest: for wherein thou judgest another, thou condemnest thyself; for thou that judgest doest the same things. **12:10** [10]Be kindly affectioned one to another with brotherly love; in honour preferring one another; **15:1–4** [1]We then that are strong ought to bear the infirmities of the weak, and not to please ourselves. [2]Let every one of us please his neighbour for his good to edification. [3]For even Christ pleased not himself; but, as it is written, The reproaches of them that reproached thee fell on me. [4]For whatsoever things were written aforetime were written for our learning, that we through patience and comfort of the scriptures might have hope. **15:7** [7]Wherefore receive ye one another, as Christ also received us to the glory of God.	**7:11** [11]If ye then, being evil, know how to give good gifts unto your children, how much more shall your Father which is in heaven give good things to them that ask him? **20:20** [20]Then came to him the mother of Zebedee's children with her sons, worshipping him, and desiring a certain thing of him. **23:12** [12]And whosoever shall exalt himself shall be abased; and he that shall humble himself shall be exalted.	**9:35** [35]And he sat down, and called the twelve, and saith unto them, If any man desire to be first, the same shall be last of all, and servant of all. **10:35–45** [35]And James and John, the sons of Zebedee, come unto him, saying, Master, we would that thou shouldest do for us whatsoever we shall desire. [36]And he said unto them, What would ye that I should do for you? [37]They said unto him, Grant unto us that we may sit, one on thy right hand, and the other on thy left hand, in thy glory. [38]But Jesus said unto them, Ye know not what ye ask: can ye drink of the cup that I drink of? and be baptized with the baptism that I am baptized with? [39]And they said unto him, We can. And Jesus said unto them, Ye shall indeed drink of the cup that I drink of; and with the baptism that I am baptized withal shall ye be baptized: [40]But to sit on my right hand and on my left hand is not mine to give; but it shall be given to them for whom it is prepared. [41]And when the ten heard it, they began to be much displeased with James and John. [42]But Jesus called them to him, and saith unto them, Ye know that they which are accounted to rule over the Gentiles exercise lordship over them; and their great ones exercise authority upon them. [43]But so shall it not be among you: but whosoever will be great among you, shall be your minister: [44]And whosoever of you will be the chiefest, shall be servant of all. [45]For even the Son of man came not to be ministered unto, but to minister, and to give his life a ransom for many.

Lk	Jn
9:48 48 And said unto them, Whosoever shall receive this child in my name receiveth me: and whosoever shall receive me receiveth him that sent me: for he that is least among you all, the same shall be great. **14:11** 11 For whosoever exalteth himself shall be abased; and he that humbleth himself shall be exalted. **18:14** 14 I tell you, this man went down to his house justified rather than the other: for every one that exalteth himself shall be abased; and he that humbleth himself shall be exalted. **22:24–27** 24 And there was also a strife among them, which of them should be accounted the greatest. 25 And he said unto them, The kings of the Gentiles exercise lordship over them; and they that exercise authority upon them are called benefactors. 26 But ye shall not be so: but he that is greatest among you, let him be as the younger; and he that is chief, as he that doth serve. 27 For whether is greater, he that sitteth at meat, or he that serveth? is not he that sitteth at meat? but I am among you as he that serveth.	**Ch 13** 1 Now before the feast of the passover, when Jesus knew that his hour was come that he should depart out of this world unto the Father, having loved his own which were in the world, he loved them unto the end. 2 And supper being ended, the devil having now put into the heart of Judas Iscariot, Simon's son, to betray him; 3 Jesus knowing that the Father had given all things into his hands, and that he was come from God, and went to God; 4 He riseth from supper, and laid aside his garments; and took a towel, and girded himself. 5 After that he poureth water into a basin, and began to wash the disciples' feet, and to wipe them with the towel wherewith he was girded. 6 Then cometh he to Simon Peter: and Peter saith unto him, Lord, dost thou wash my feet? 7 Jesus answered and said unto him, What I do thou knowest not now; but thou shalt know hereafter. 8 Peter saith unto him, Thou shalt never wash my feet. Jesus answered him, If I wash thee not, thou hast no part with me. 9 Simon Peter saith unto him, Lord, not my feet only, but also my hands and my head. 10 Jesus saith to him, He that is washed needeth not save to wash his feet, but is clean every whit: and ye are clean, but not all. 11 For he knew who should betray him; therefore said he, Ye are not all clean. 12 So after he had washed their feet, and had taken his garments, and was set down again, he said unto them, Know ye what I have done to you? 13 Ye call me Master and Lord: and ye say well; for so I am. 14 If I then, your Lord and Master, have washed your feet; ye also ought to wash one another's feet. 15 For I have given you an example, that ye should do as I have done to you. 16 Verily, verily, I say unto you, The servant is not greater than his lord; neither he that is sent greater than he that sent him. 17 If ye know these things, happy are ye if ye do them. 18 I speak not of you all: I know whom I have chosen: but that the scripture may be fulfilled, He that eateth bread with me hath lifted up his heel against me. 19 Now I tell you before it come, that, when it is come to pass, ye may believe that I am he. 20 Verily, verily, I say unto you, He that receiveth whomsoever I send receiveth me; and he that receiveth me receiveth him that sent me. 21 When Jesus had thus said, he was troubled in spirit, and testified, and said, Verily, verily, I say unto you, that one of you shall betray me. 22 Then the disciples looked one on another, doubting of whom he spake. 23 Now there was leaning on Jesus' bosom one of his disciples, whom Jesus loved. 24 Simon Peter therefore beckoned to him, that he should ask who it should be of whom he spake. 25 He then lying on Jesus' breast saith unto him, Lord, who is it? 26 Jesus answered, He it is, to whom I shall give a sop, when I have dipped it. And when he had dipped the sop, he gave it to Judas Iscariot, the son of Simon. 27 And after the sop Satan entered into him. Then said Jesus unto him, That thou doest, do quickly. 28 Now no man at the table knew for what intent he spake this unto him. 29 For some of them thought, because Judas had the bag, that Jesus had said unto him, Buy those things that we have need of against the feast; or, that he should give something to the poor. 30 He then having received the sop went immediately out: and it was night. 31 Therefore, when he was gone out, Jesus said, Now is the Son of man glorified, and God is glorified in him. 32 If God be glorified in him, God shall also glorify him in himself, and shall straightway glorify him. 33 Little children, yet a little while I am with you. Ye shall seek me: and as I said unto the Jews, Whither I go, ye cannot come; so now I say to you. 34 A new commandment I give unto you, That ye love one another; as I have loved you, that ye also love one another. 35 By this shall all men know that ye are my disciples, if ye have love one to another. 36 Simon Peter said unto him, Lord, whither goest thou? Jesus answered him, Whither I go, thou canst not follow me now; but thou shalt follow me afterwards. 37 Peter said unto him, Lord, why cannot I follow thee now? I will lay down my life for thy sake. 38 Jesus answered him, Wilt thou lay down thy life for my sake? Verily, verily, I say unto thee, The cock shall not crow, till thou hast denied me thrice.

Romans 14:4–12 continued on next page

ROMANS 14:4–12—Christian duty (12:1–15:13), 56–58 CE (*continued*)

Theme	ROM	Paul
(*Cont.*) Mix w/ humble (variation supra)	14:4–12 (above) 12:10 (above) 15:1–4 (above) 15:7 (above)	**1 Cor 9:19** [19]For though I be free from all men, yet have I made myself servant unto all, that I might gain the more. **1 Cor 9:22** [22]To the weak became I as weak, that I might gain the weak: I am made all things to all men, that I might by all means save some. **1 Cor 10:33–11:2** [33]Even as I please all men in all things, not seeking mine own profit, but the profit of many, that they may be saved. [1]Be ye followers of me, even as I also am of Christ. [2]Now I praise you, brethren, that ye remember me in all things, and keep the ordinances, as I delivered them to you. **2 Cor 4:5** [5]For we preach not ourselves, but Christ Jesus the Lord; and ourselves your servants for Jesus' sake. **2 Cor 11:7** [7]Have I committed an offence in abasing myself that ye might be exalted, because I have preached to you the gospel of God freely? **Gal 5:13c** [13]For, brethren, ye have been called unto liberty; **Phil 2:2–9** [2]Fulfil ye my joy, that ye be likeminded, having the same love, being of one accord, of one mind. [3]Let nothing be done through strife or vainglory; but in lowliness of mind let each esteem other better than themselves. [4]Look not every man on his own things, but every man also on the things of others. [5]Let this mind be in you, which was also in Christ Jesus: [6]Who, being in the form of God, thought it not robbery to be equal with God: [7]But made himself of no reputation, and took upon him the form of a servant, and was made in the likeness of men: [8]And being found in fashion as a man, he humbled himself, and became obedient unto death, even the death of the cross. [9]Wherefore God also hath highly exalted him, and given him a name which is above every name:

ROMANS 14:4—Christian duty (12:1–15:13), 56–58 CE

Theme	ROM	Mt
Do not judge	**14:4** [4]Who art thou that judgest another man's servant? to his own master he standeth or falleth. Yea, he shall be holden up: for God is able to make him stand. **2:1** [1]Therefore thou art inexcusable, O man, whosoever thou art that judgest: for wherein thou judgest another, thou condemnest thyself; for thou that judgest doest the same things.	**7:11** [11]If ye then, being evil, know how to give good gifts unto your children, how much more shall your Father which is in heaven give good things to them that ask him?

ROMANS 14:5—Christian duty (12:1–15:13), 56–58 CE

Theme	ROM	Paul
Observing special days	**14:5** [5]One man esteemeth one day above another: another esteemeth every day alike. Let every man be fully persuaded in his own mind.	**Gal 4:10** [10]Ye observe days, and months, and times, and years.

NT	Other
Jas 4:11–12	**Q-Quelle**
[11]Speak not evil one of another, brethren. He that speaketh evil of his brother, and judgeth his brother, speaketh evil of the law, and judgeth the law: but if thou judge the law, thou art not a doer of the law, but a judge. [12]There is one lawgiver, who is able to save and to destroy: who art thou that judgest another?	Encouragement to pray: Rom 14:4-12/ Mt 7:7-11/[Lk 11:9-13 (QS 27 [Thom 2, 92, 94])]; Against Pharisees: Rom 14:4-12/1 Cor 9:19/2 Cor 4:5/[Phil 2:1-11]/Mt 23:4-36/ [Mk 7:1-9]/ [Lk 11:37-54 (QS 34 [Thom 39:1, 89, 102])]; Precedence: Rom 14:4-12/1 Cor 9:19/[Mt 19:28]/Mk 10:41-45/Lk 22:28-30 (QS 62)

NT	Other
Jas 4:11–12	**Q-Quelle**
[11]Speak not evil one of another, brethren. He that speaketh evil of his brother, and judgeth his brother, speaketh evil of the law, and judgeth the law: but if thou judge the law, thou art not a doer of the law, but a judge. [12]There is one lawgiver, who is able to save and to destroy: who art thou that judgest another?	Encouragement to pray: Rom 14:4/Mt 7:7-11/[Lk 11:9-13 (QS 27 [Thom 2, 92, 94])]

ROMANS 14:8—Christian duty (12:1–15:13), 56–58 CE

Theme	ROM	Lk	Paul
Live to the Lord	**14:8** [8]For whether we live, we live unto the Lord; and whether we die, we die unto the Lord: whether we live therefore, or die, we are the Lord's.	**20:38** [38]For he is not a God of the dead, but of the living: for all live unto him.	**2 Cor 5:15** [15]And that he died for all, that they which live should not henceforth live unto themselves, but unto him which died for them, and rose again. **Gal 2:20** [20]I am crucified with Christ: nevertheless I live; yet not I, but Christ liveth in me: and the life which I now live in the flesh I live by the faith of the Son of God, who loved me, and gave himself for me. **1 Thes 5:10** [10]Who died for us, that, whether we wake or sleep, we should live together with him.

ROMANS 14:9—Christian duty (12:1–15:13), 56–58 CE

Theme	ROM	Lk
Christ died and rose	**14:9** [9]For to this end Christ both died, and rose, and revived, that he might be Lord both of the dead and living.	**Acts 10:42** [42]And he commanded us to preach unto the people, and to testify that it is he which was ordained of God to be the Judge of quick and dead.

ROMANS 14:10—Christian duty (12:1–15:13), 56–58 CE

Theme	ROM	Lk	Paul
Christ judges all	**14:10** [10]But why dost thou judge thy brother? or why dost thou set at nought thy brother? for we shall all stand before the judgment seat of Christ.	**Acts 17:31** [31]Because he hath appointed a day, in the which he will judge the world in righteousness by that man whom he hath ordained; whereof he hath given assurance unto all men, in that he hath raised him from the dead.	**2 Cor 5:10** [10]For we must all appear before the judgment seat of Christ; that every one may receive the things done in his body, according to that he hath done, whether it be good or bad.

ROMANS 14:11—Christian duty (12:1–15:13), 56–58 CE

Theme	ROM	Paul
Every knee bows	**14:11** [11]For it is written, As I live, saith the Lord, every knee shall bow to me, and every tongue shall confess to God.	**2 Cor 5:10** [10]For we must all appear before the judgment seat of Christ; that every one may receive the things done in his body, according to that he hath done, whether it be good or bad. **Phil 2:10–11** [10]That at the name of Jesus every knee should bow, of things in heaven, and things in earth, and things under the earth; [11]And that every tongue should confess that Jesus Christ is Lord, to the glory of God the Father. [12]Wherefore, my beloved, as ye have always obeyed, not as in my presence only, but now much more in my absence, work out your own salvation with fear and trembling.

ROMANS 14:12—Christian duty (12:1–15:13), 56–58 CE

Theme	ROM	Paul
Give account to God	**14:12** [12]So then every one of us shall give account of himself to God.	**Gal 6:5** [5]For every man shall bear his own burden.

ROMANS 14:13–23—Christian duty (12:1–15:13), 56–58 CE

Theme	ROM	Mt
Clean and unclean	**14:13–23** [13]Now I would not have you ignorant, brethren, that oftentimes I purposed to come unto you, (but was let hitherto,) that I might have some fruit among you also, even as among other Gentiles.[14]I know, and am persuaded by the Lord Jesus, that there is nothing unclean of itself: but to him that esteemeth any thing to be unclean, to him it is unclean. [15]But if thy brother be grieved with thy meat, now walkest thou not charitably. Destroy not him with thy meat, for whom Christ died. [16]Let not then your good be evil spoken of: [17]For the kingdom of God is not meat and drink; but righteousness, and peace, and joy in the Holy Ghost. [18]For he that in these things serveth Christ is acceptable to God, and approved of men. [19]Let us therefore follow after the things which make for peace, and things wherewith one may edify another. [20]For meat destroy not the work of God. All things indeed are pure; but it is evil for that man who eateth with offence. [21]It is good neither to eat flesh, nor to drink wine, nor any thing whereby thy brother stumbleth, or is offended, or is made weak. [22]Hast thou faith? Have it to thyself before God. Happy is he that condemneth not himself in that thing which he alloweth. [23]And he that doubteth is damned if he eat, because he eateth not of faith: for whatsoever is not of faith is sin.	**17:24–27** [24]And when they were come to Capernaum, they that received tribute money came to Peter, and said, Doth not your master pay tribute? [25]He saith, Yes. And when he was come into the house, Jesus prevented him, saying, What thinkest thou, Simon? of whom do the kings of the earth take custom or tribute? of their own children, or of strangers? [26]Peter saith unto him, Of strangers. Jesus saith unto him, Then are the children free. [27]Notwithstanding, lest we should offend them, go thou to the sea, and cast an hook, and take up the fish that first cometh up; and when thou hast opened his mouth, thou shalt find a piece of money: that take, and give unto them for me and thee

ROMANS 14:14—Christian duty (12:1–15:13), 56–58 CE

Theme	ROM	Mt	Mk
Righteousness above ritual observances **Clean and unclean**	**14:14** [14]I know, and am persuaded by the Lord Jesus, that there is nothing unclean of itself: but to him that esteemeth any thing to be unclean, to him it is unclean. **14:17** [17]For the kingdom of God is not meat and drink; but righteousness, and peace, and joy in the Holy Ghost. **14:20** [20]For meat destroy not the work of God. All things indeed are pure; but it is evil for that man who eateth with offence.	**5:20** [20]For I say unto you, That except your righteousness shall exceed the righteousness of the scribes and Pharisees, ye shall in no case enter into the kingdom of heaven. **15:15** [15]Then answered Peter and said unto him, Declare unto us this parable.	**7:5–20** [5]Then the Pharisees and scribes asked him, Why walk not thy disciples according to the tradition of the elders, but eat bread with unwashen hands? [6]He answered and said unto them, Well hath Esaias prophesied of you hypocrites, as it is written, This people honoureth me with their lips, but their heart is far from me. [7]Howbeit in vain do they worship me, teaching for doctrines the commandments of men. [8]For laying aside the commandment of God, ye hold the tradition of men, as the washing of pots and cups: and many other such like things ye do. [9]And he said unto them, Full well ye reject the commandment of God, that ye may keep your own tradition. [10]For Moses said, Honour thy father and thy mother; and, Whoso curseth father or mother, let him die the death: [11]But ye say, If a man shall say to his father or mother, It is Corban, that is to say, a gift, by whatsoever thou mightest be profited by me; he shall be free. [12]And ye suffer him no more to do ought for his father or his mother; [13]Making the word of God of none effect through your tradition, which ye have delivered: and many such like things do ye. [14]And when he had called all the people unto him, he said unto them, Hearken unto me every one of you, and understand: [15]There is nothing from without a man, that entering into him can defile him: but the things which come out of him, those are they that defile the man. [16]If any man have ears to hear, let him hear. [17]And when he was entered into the house from the people, his disciples asked him concerning the parable. [18]And he saith unto them, Are ye so without understanding also? Do ye not perceive, that whatsoever thing from without entereth into the man, it cannot defile him; [19]Because it entereth not into his heart, but into the belly, and goeth out into the draught, purging all meats? [20]And he said, That which cometh out of the man, that defileth the man. **7:8** [8]For laying aside the commandment of God, ye hold the tradition of men, as the washing of pots and cups: and many other such like things ye do. **7:19** [19]Because it entereth not into his heart, but into the belly, and goeth out into the draught, purging all meats?

Paul	Other
1 Cor 8	**Q-Quelle**
[1]Now as touching things offered unto idols, we know that we all have knowledge. Knowledge puffeth up, but charity edifieth. [2]And if any man think that he knoweth any thing, he knoweth nothing yet as he ought to know. [3]But if any man love God, the same is known of him. [4]As concerning therefore the eating of those things that are offered in sacrifice unto idols, we know that an idol is nothing in the world, and that there is none other God but one. [5]For though there be that are called gods, whether in heaven or in earth, (as there be gods many, and lords many,) [6]But to us there is but one God, the Father, of whom are all things, and we in him; and one Lord Jesus Christ, by whom are all things, and we by him. [7]Howbeit there is not in every man that knowledge: for some with conscience of the idol unto this hour eat it as a thing offered unto an idol; and their conscience being weak is defiled. [8]But meat commendeth us not to God: for neither, if we eat, are we the better; neither, if we eat not, are we the worse. [9]But take heed lest by any means this liberty of yours become a stumblingblock to them that are weak. [10]For if any man see thee which hast knowledge sit at meat in the idol's temple, shall not the conscience of him which is weak be emboldened to eat those things which are offered to idols; [11]And through thy knowledge shall the weak brother perish, for whom Christ died? [12]But when ye sin so against the brethren, and wound their weak conscience, ye sin against Christ. [13]Wherefore, if meat make my brother to offend, I will eat no flesh while the world standeth, lest I make my brother to offend.	Judging: Rom 14:13-23/1 Cor 8:13/[Mt 7:1-5, 10:24-25, 12:36-37, 15:14]/[Mk 4:24-25]/[Lk 37:37-42] (QS 10)]; Warning Against Offenses: Rom 14:12/1 Cor 8:13/[Mt 18:6-7]/[Mk 9:42]/[Lk 17:1-3a (QS 57, 58)]

Lk	Paul	Other
Acts 10:15	**1 Cor 6:9**	**Q-Quelle**
[1]There was a certain man in Caesarea called Cornelius, a centurion of the band called the Italian band,	[9]Know ye not that the unrighteous shall not inherit the kingdom of God? Be not deceived: neither fornicators, nor idolaters, nor adulterers, nor effeminate, nor abusers of themselves with mankind, **1 Cor 6:13** [13]Meats for the belly, and the belly for meats: but God shall destroy both it and them. Now the body is not for fornication, but for the Lord; and the Lord for the body. **1 Cor 10:25–27** [25]Whatsoever is sold in the shambles, that eat, asking no question for conscience sake: [26]For the earth is the Lord's, and the fulness thereof. [27]If any of them that believe not bid you to a feast, and ye be disposed to go; whatsoever is set before you, eat, asking no question for conscience sake. **Col 2:8** [8]Beware lest any man spoil you through philosophy and vain deceit, after the tradition of men, after the rudiments of the world, and not after Christ. **Col 2:21–22** [21](Touch not; taste not; handle not; [22]Which all are to perish with the using;) after the commandments and doctrines of men? **1 Tim 4:4 (Pseudo)** [4]For every creature of God is good, and nothing to be refused, if it be received with thanksgiving:	Anxiety: Rom 14:14/1 Cor 6:9-10/[Gal 5:19-21]/[Mt 6:25-34]/[Lk 12:22-32 (QS 9 [Thom 36])]; Against Pharisees: 14:14/1 Cor 6:9-10/[Mt 23:4-36]/Mk 7:1-9/[Lk 11:37-54 (QS 34 [Thom 39:1, 89, 102])]; Beezebul controversy: Rom 14:14/1 Cor 6:9-10/[Mt 9:32-34, 12:22-30]/[Mk 3:22-27]/[Lk 11:14-23] (QS 28 [Thom 35])

ROMANS 14:15—Christian duty (12:1–15:13), 56–58 CE

Theme	ROM	Paul
Do not frustrate weak	**14:15** [15]But if thy brother be grieved with thy meat, now walkest thou not charitably. Destroy not him with thy meat, for whom Christ died.	**1 Cor 8:11–15** [11]And through thy knowledge shall the weak brother perish, for whom Christ died? [12]But when ye sin so against the brethren, and wound their weak conscience, ye sin against Christ. [13]Wherefore, if meat make my brother to offend, I will eat no flesh while the world standeth, lest I make my brother to offend.

ROMANS 14:16—Christian duty (12:1–15:13), 56–58 CE

Theme	ROM	Paul
Uphold good over evil	**14:16** [16]Let not then your good be evil spoken of: **2:24** [24]For the name of God is blasphemed among the Gentiles through you, as it is written.	**Tit 2:5 (Pseudo)** [5]To be discreet, chaste, keepers at home, good, obedient to their own husbands, that the word of God be not blasphemed.

ROMANS 14:17—Christian duty (12:1–15:13), 56–58 CE

Theme	ROM	Mt	Jn
Coming of Holy Spirit/ Kingdom of God	**14:17** [17]For the kingdom of God is not meat and drink; but righteousness, and peace, and joy in the Holy Ghost.	**5:20** [20]For I say unto you, That except your righteousness shall exceed the righteousness of the scribes and Pharisees, ye shall in no case enter into the kingdom of heaven. **6:33** [33]But seek ye first the kingdom of God, and his righteousness; and all these things shall be added unto you. **12:28** [28]But if I cast out devils by the Spirit of God, then the kingdom of God is come unto you.	**11:20** [20]Then Martha, as soon as she heard that Jesus was coming, went and met him: but Mary sat still in the house. **12:31** [31]Now is the judgment of this world: now shall the prince of this world be cast out.

Paul	Other
1 Cor 4:20 [20]For the kingdom of God is not in word, but in power. **1 Cor 6:9** [9]Know ye not that the unrighteous shall not inherit the kingdom of God? Be not deceived: neither fornicators, nor idolaters, nor adulterers, nor effeminate, nor abusers of themselves with mankind, **1 Cor 6:10** [10]Nor thieves, nor covetous, nor drunkards, nor revilers, nor extortioners, shall inherit the kingdom of God. **1 Cor 8:8** [8] But meat commendeth us not to God: for neither, if we eat, are we the better; neither, if we eat not, are we the worse. **Gal 5:19–21** [19]Now the works of the flesh are manifest, which are these; Adultery, fornication, uncleanness, lasciviousness, [20]Idolatry, witchcraft, hatred, variance, emulations, wrath, strife, seditions, heresies, [21]Envyings, murders, drunkenness, revellings, and such like: of the which I tell you before, as I have also told you in time past, that they which do such things shall not inherit the kingdom of God. **Eph 5:5 (Pseudo)** [5]For this ye know, that no whoremonger, nor unclean person, nor covetous man, who is an idolater, hath any inheritance in the kingdom of Christ and of God.	**Q-Quelle** Assistance of the HS: Rom 14:17/Eph 5:5/[Mt 10:19-20]/[Mk 13:11/[Lk 12:11-12 (QS 37 [Thom 44])]

ROMANS 14:19—Christian duty (12:1–15:13), 56–58 CE

Theme	ROM	Mt	Lk	Jn
Living in peace	**14:19** [19]Let us therefore follow after the things which make for peace, and things wherewith one may edify another. **12:18** [18]If it be possible, as much as lieth in you, live peaceably with all men. **15:2** [2]Let every one of us please his neighbour for his good to edification.	**28:20** [20]Teaching them to observe all things whatsoever I have commanded you: and, lo, I am with you alway, even unto the end of the world. Amen.	**24:36** [36]And as they thus spake, Jesus himself stood in the midst of them, and saith unto them, Peace be unto you.	**20:19** [19]Then the same day at evening, being the first day of the week, when the doors were shut where the disciples were assembled for fear of the Jews, came Jesus and stood in the midst, and saith unto them, Peace be unto you. **20:21** [21]Then said Jesus to them again, Peace be unto you: as my Father hath sent me, even so send I you.

ROMANS 14:19–20—Christian duty (12:1–15:13), 56–58 CE

Theme	ROM	Paul
Clean and unclean	**14:19–20** [19]Let us therefore follow after the things which make for peace, and things wherewith one may edify another. [20]For meat destroy not the work of God. All things indeed are pure; but it is evil for that man who eateth with offence.	**2 Cor 13:10** [10]Therefore I write these things being absent, lest being present I should use sharpness, according to the power which the Lord hath given me to edification, and not to destruction. **Gal 2:18–19** [18]For if I build again the things which I destroyed, I make myself a transgressor. [19]For I through the law am dead to the law, that I might live unto God.

ROMANS 14:20–21—Christian duty (12:1–15:13), 56–58 CE

Theme	ROM	Paul
Do not cause weak believer to stumble	**14:20–21** [20]For meat destroy not the work of God. All things indeed are pure; but it is evil for that man who eateth with offence. [21]It is good neither to eat flesh, nor to drink wine, nor any thing whereby thy brother stumbleth, or is offended, or is made weak.	**1 Cor 8:11–13** [11]And through thy knowledge shall the weak brother perish, for whom Christ died? [12]But when ye sin so against the brethren, and wound their weak conscience, ye sin against Christ. [13]Wherefore, if meat make my brother to offend, I will eat no flesh while the world standeth, lest I make my brother to offend. **1 Cor 10:28–29** [28]But if any man say unto you, This is offered in sacrifice unto idols, eat not for his sake that showed it, and for conscience sake: for the earth is the Lord's, and the fulness thereof: [29]Conscience, I say, not thine own, but of the other: for why is my liberty judged of another man's conscience? **Tit 1:15 (Pseudo)** [15]Unto the pure all things are pure: but unto them that are defiled and unbelieving is nothing pure; but even their mind and conscience is defiled.

Paul

1 Cor 7:15

[15]But if the unbelieving depart, let him depart. A brother or a sister is not under bondage in such cases: but God hath called us to peace.

2 Cor 13:11

[11]Finally, brethren, farewell. Be perfect, be of good comfort, be of one mind, live in peace; and the God of love and peace shall be with you.

1 Thes 5:13

[13]And to esteem them very highly in love for their work's sake. And be at peace among yourselves.

Other

Q-Quelle

Divisions in Households: Rom 14:19-20/Gal 2:18-19/[Mt 10:34-36]/[Lk 12:49-53 (QS 43 [Thom 16])]

ROMANS 14:23—Christian duty (12:1–15:13), 56–58 CE

Theme	ROM	Paul	NT
Clean and unclean	**14:23** [23]And he that doubteth is damned if he eat, because he eateth not of faith: for whatsoever is not of faith is sin.	**Tit 1:15 (Pseudo)** [15]Unto the pure all things are pure: but unto them that are defiled and unbelieving is nothing pure; but even their mind and conscience is defiled.	**Jas 4:17** [17]Therefore to him that knoweth to do good, and doeth it not, to him it is sin.

ROMANS 15:1–8—Christian duty (12:1–15:13), 56–58 CE

Theme	ROM
Imitate me/ Christ	**15:1–8** [1]We then that are strong ought to bear the infirmities of the weak, and not to please ourselves. [2]Let every one of us please his neighbour for his good to edification. [3]For even Christ pleased not himself; but, as it is written, The reproaches of them that reproached thee fell on me. [4]For whatsoever things were written aforetime were written for our learning, that we through patience and comfort of the scriptures might have hope. [5]Now the God of patience and consolation grant you to be likeminded one toward another according to Christ Jesus: [6]That ye may with one mind and one mouth glorify God, even the Father of our Lord Jesus Christ. [7]Wherefore receive ye one another, as Christ also received us to the glory of God. [8]Now I say that Jesus Christ was a minister of the circumcision for the truth of God, to confirm the promises made unto the fathers:

ROMANS 15:1—Christian duty (12:1–15:13), 56–58 CE (54–58CE)

Theme	ROM	Mt
Bear others' burdens	**15:1** [1]We then that are strong ought to bear the infirmities of the weak, and not to please ourselves. **14:1–12** [1]Him that is weak in the faith receive ye, but not to doubtful disputations. [2]For one believeth that he may eat all things: another, who is weak, eateth herbs. [3]Let not him that eateth despise him that eateth not; and let not him which eateth not judge him that eateth: for God hath received him. [4]Who art thou that judgest another man's servant? to his own master he standeth or falleth. Yea, he shall be holden up: for God is able to make him stand. [5]One man esteemeth one day above another: another esteemeth every day alike. Let every man be fully persuaded in his own mind. [6]He that regardeth the day, regardeth it unto the Lord; and he that regardeth not the day, to the Lord he doth not regard it. He that eateth, eateth to the Lord, for he giveth God thanks; and he that eateth not, to the Lord he eateth not, and giveth God thanks. [7]For none of us liveth to himself, and no man dieth to himself. [8]For whether we live, we live unto the Lord; and whether we die, we die unto the Lord: whether we live therefore, or die, we are the Lord's. [9]For to this end Christ both died, and rose, and revived, that he might be Lord both of the dead and living. [10]But why dost thou judge thy brother? or why dost thou set at nought thy brother? for we shall all stand before the judgment seat of Christ. [11]For it is written, As I live, saith the Lord, every knee shall bow to me, and every tongue shall confess to God. [12]So then every one of us shall give account of himself to God.	**23:12** [12]And whosoever shall exalt himself shall be abased; and he that shall humble himself shall be exalted.

Paul
Phil 2:1–11
[1]If there be therefore any consolation in Christ, if any comfort of love, if any fellowship of the Spirit, if any bowels and mercies, [2]Fulfil ye my joy, that ye be likeminded, having the same love, being of one accord, of one mind. [3]Let nothing be done through strife or vainglory; but in lowliness of mind let each esteem other better than themselves. [4]Look not every man on his own things, but every man also on the things of others. [5]Let this mind be in you, which was also in Christ Jesus: [6]Who, being in the form of God, thought it not robbery to be equal with God: [7]But made himself of no reputation, and took upon him the form of a servant, and was made in the likeness of men: [8]And being found in fashion as a man, he humbled himself, and became obedient unto death, even the death of the cross. [9]Wherefore God also hath highly exalted him, and given him a name which is above every name: [10]That at the name of Jesus every knee should bow, of things in heaven, and things in earth, and things under the earth; [11]And that every tongue should confess that Jesus Christ is Lord, to the glory of God the Father.

Paul	Other
1 Cor 10:24	**Q-Quelle**
[24]Let no man seek his own, but every man another's wealth. **1 Cor 10:33** [33]Even as I please all men in all things, not seeking mine own profit, but the profit of many, that they may be saved. **1 Cor 13:5** [5]Doth not behave itself unseemly, seeketh not her own, is not easily provoked, thinketh no evil; **Phil 2:3** [3]Blessed be God, even the Father of our Lord Jesus Christ, the Father of mercies, and the God of all comfort; **Phil 2:7–9** [7]But made himself of no reputation, and took upon him the form of a servant, and was made in the likeness of men: [8]And being found in fashion as a man, he humbled himself, and became obedient unto death, even the death of the cross. [9]Wherefore God also hath highly exalted him, and given him a name which is above every name: **Phil 2:21** [21]For all seek their own, not the things which are Jesus Christ's.	Against Pharisees: Rom 15:1/ Mt 23:4-36/[Mk 37:1-9]/[Lk 11:37-54 (QS 34 [Thom 39:1; 89;102])]

ROMANS 15:2—Christian duty (12:1–15:13), 56–58 CE

Theme	ROM	Paul
Bear others' burdens	**15:2** [2]Let every one of us please his neighbour for his good to edification. **14:1** [1]Him that is weak in the faith receive ye, but not to doubtful disputations. **14:19** [19]Let us therefore follow after the things which make for peace, and things wherewith one may edify another.	**1 Cor 9:1** [1]Am I not an apostle? am I not free? have I not seen Jesus Christ our Lord? are not ye my work in the Lord? **1 Cor 10:24** [24]Let no man seek his own, but every man another's wealth. **1 Cor 10:33** [33]Even as I please all men in all things, not seeking mine own profit, but the profit of many, that they may be saved.

ROMANS 15:3—Christian duty (12:1–15:13), 56–58 CE

Theme	ROM	Jewish Writings
Bear others' burdens	**15:3** [3]For even Christ pleased not himself; but, as it is written, The reproaches of them that reproached thee fell on me.	**Ps 69:10** [10]When I wept, and chastened my soul with fasting, that was to my reproach.

ROMANS 15:4—Christian duty (12:1–15:13), 56–58 CE

Theme	ROM	Paul	Jewish Writings
Bear others' burdens	**15:4** [4]For whatsoever things were written aforetime were written for our learning, that we through patience and comfort of the scriptures might have hope. **4:23–24** [23]Now it was not written for his sake alone, that it was imputed to him; [24]But for us also, to whom it shall be imputed, if we believe on him that raised up Jesus our Lord from the dead;	**1 Cor 10:11** [11]Now all these things happened unto them for ensamples: and they are written for our admonition, upon whom the ends of the world are come. **2 Tim 3:16 (Pseudo)** [16]All scripture is given by inspiration of God, and is profitable for doctrine, for reproof, for correction, for instruction in righteousness:	**1 Mac 12:9** [9]Therefore we also, albeit we need none of these things, that we have the holy books of scripture in our hands to comfort us,

ROMANS 15:5—Christian duty (12:1–15:13), 56–58 CE

Theme	ROM	Paul
Bear others' burdens	**15:5** [5]Now the God of patience and consolation grant you to be likeminded one toward another according to Christ Jesus: **12:16** [16]Be of the same mind one toward another. Mind not high things, but condescend to men of low estate. Be not wise in your own conceits.	**Phil 2:2** [2]Fulfil ye my joy, that ye be likeminded, having the same love, being of one accord, of one mind. **Phil 4:2** [2]I beseech Euodias, and beseech Syntyche, that they be of the same mind in the Lord.

ROMANS 15:7—Christian duty (12:1–15:13), 56–58 CE

Theme	ROM	Mt	Mk
Welcoming/ receiving others, even children	**15:7** [7]Wherefore receive ye one another, as Christ also received us to the glory of God. **14:1** [1]Him that is weak in the faith receive ye, but not to doubtful disputations.	**10:14** [14]And whosoever shall not receive you, nor hear your words, when ye depart out of that house or city, shake off the dust of your feet. **10:40–42** [40]He that receiveth you receiveth me, and he that receiveth me receiveth him that sent me. [41]He that receiveth a prophet in the name of a prophet shall receive a prophet's reward; and he that receiveth a righteous man in the name of a righteous man shall receive a righteous man's reward. [42]And whosoever shall give to drink unto one of these little ones a cup of cold water only in the name of a disciple, verily I say unto you, he shall in no wise lose his reward. **18:5–6** [5]And whoso shall receive one such little child in my name receiveth me. [6]But whoso shall offend one of these little ones which believe in me, it were better for him that a millstone were hanged about his neck, and that he were drowned in the depth of the sea. **19:13–16** [13]Then were there brought unto him little children, that he should put his hands on them, and pray: and the disciples rebuked them. [14]But Jesus said, Suffer little children, and forbid them not, to come unto me: for of such is the kingdom of heaven. [15]And he laid his hands on them, and departed thence. [16]And, behold, one came and said unto him, Good Master, what good thing shall I do, that I may have eternal life?	**6:11** [11]And whosoever shall not receive you, nor hear you, when ye depart thence, shake off the dust under your feet for a testimony against them. Verily I say unto you, It shall be more tolerable for Sodom and Gomorrha in the day of judgment, than for that city. **9:36–37** [36]And he took a child, and set him in the midst of them: and when he had taken him in his arms, he said unto them, [37]Whosoever shall receive one of such children in my name, receiveth me: and whosoever shall receive me, receiveth not me, but him that sent me. **9:42** [42]And whosoever shall offend one of these little ones that believe in me, it is better for him that a millstone were hanged about his neck, and he were cast into the sea.

ROMANS 15:8—Christian duty (12:1–15:13), 56–58 CE

Theme	ROM	Mt	Mk	Lk
Jewish law and promise	**15:8** [8]Now I say that Jesus Christ was a minister of the circumcision for the truth of God, to confirm the promises made unto the fathers:	**10:5** [5]These twelve Jesus sent forth, and commanded them, saying, Go not into the way of the Gentiles, and into any city of the Samaritans enter ye not: **15:24** [24]But he answered and said, I am not sent but unto the lost sheep of the house of Israel.	**7:27** [27]But Jesus said unto her, Let the children first be filled: for it is not meet to take the children's bread, and to cast it unto the dogs.	**Acts 3:25** [25]Ye are the children of the prophets, and of the covenant which God made with our fathers, saying unto Abraham, And in thy seed shall all the kindreds of the earth be blessed.

Lk	Jn	Other
9:5 [5]And whosoever will not receive you, when ye go out of that city, shake off the very dust from your feet for a testimony against them. **9:8–10** [8]And of some, that Elias had appeared; and of others, that one of the old prophets was risen again. [9]And Herod said, John have I beheaded: but who is this, of whom I hear such things? And he desired to see him. [10]And the apostles, when they were returned, told him all that they had done. And he took them, and went aside privately into a desert place belonging to the city called Bethsaida. **9:47–48** [47]And Jesus, perceiving the thought of their heart, took a child, and set him by him, [48]And said unto them, Whosoever shall receive this child in my name receiveth me: and whosoever shall receive me receiveth him that sent me: for he that is least among you all, the same shall be great. **15:2** [2]And the Pharisees and scribes murmured, saying, This man receiveth sinners, and eateth with them. **18:15–17** [15]And they brought unto him also infants, that he would touch them: but when his disciples saw it, they rebuked them. [16]But Jesus called them unto him, and said, Suffer little children to come unto me, and forbid them not: for of such is the kingdom of God. [17]Verily I say unto you, Whosoever shall not receive the kingdom of God as a little child shall in no wise enter therein.	**13:20** [20]Verily, verily, I say unto you, He that receiveth whomsoever I send receiveth me; and he that receiveth me receiveth him that sent me.	**Q-Quelle** Commissioning of 12: Rom 15:7/[Mt 10:1, 7-11], Mt 10:14/Mk 6:6b-13/Lk 9:1-6; Commissioning of 70: Rom 15:7/[Mt 9:37-38], [Mt 10:7-16]/[Lk 10:1-12 (QS 20 [Thom 14:2, 73], QS 21)]; Warning against offences: Rom 15:7/ Mt 18:6-7/Mk 9:42/ [Lk 17:1-3a (QS 57, 58)]; Lost Sheep: Rom 15:7/ [Mt 18:12-14]/Lk 15:1-7 (QS 54 [Thom 1-7])

Paul	Jewish Writings
Gal 3:5 [5]He therefore that ministereth to you the Spirit, and worketh miracles among you, doeth he it by the works of the law, or by the hearing of faith? **Col 3:11** [11]Where there is neither Greek nor Jew, circumcision nor uncircumcision, Barbarian, Scythian, bond nor free: but Christ is all, and in all. **1 Thes 1:5** [5]For our gospel came not unto you in word only, but also in power, and in the Holy Ghost, and in much assurance; as ye know what manner of men we were among you for your sake.	**Mic 7:20** [20]Thou wilt perform the truth to Jacob, and the mercy to Abraham, which thou hast sworn unto our fathers from the days of old.

ROMANS 15:9—Christian duty (12:1–15:13), 56–58 CE

Theme	ROM	Jewish Writings
Gentiles glorify God in His mercy	**15:9** [9]And that the Gentiles might glorify God for his mercy; as it is written, For this cause I will confess to thee among the Gentiles, and sing unto thy name. **11:30** [30]For as ye in times past have not believed God, yet have now obtained mercy through their unbelief:	**2 Sam 22:50** [50]Therefore I will give thanks unto thee, O LORD, among the heathen, and I will sing praises unto thy name. **Ps 18:50** [50]Great deliverance giveth he to his king; and showeth mercy to his anointed, to David, and to his seed for evermore.

ROMANS 15:10—Christian duty (12:1–15:13), 56–58 CE

Theme	ROM	Jewish Writings
Gentiles rejoice	**15:10** [10]And again he saith, Rejoice, ye Gentiles, with his people.	**Dt 32:43** [43]Rejoice, O ye nations, with his people: for he will avenge the blood of his servants, and will render vengeance to his adversaries, and will be merciful unto his land, and to his people.

ROMANS 15:11—Christian duty (12:1–15:13), 56–58 CE

Theme	ROM	Jewish Writings
Praise the Lord	**15:11** [11]And again, Praise the Lord, all ye Gentiles; and laud him, all ye people.	**Ps 117:1** [1]O praise the LORD, all ye nations: praise him, all ye people.

ROMANS 15:12—Christian duty (12:1–15:13), 56–58 CE

Theme	ROM	NT	Jewish Writings
Root of Jesse	**15:12** [12]And again, Esaias saith, There shall be a root of Jesse, and he that shall rise to reign over the Gentiles; in him shall the Gentiles trust.	**Rev 5:5** [5]And one of the elders saith unto me, Weep not: behold, the Lion of the tribe of Juda, the Root of David, hath prevailed to open the book, and to loose the seven seals thereof. **Rev 22:16** [16]I Jesus have sent mine angel to testify unto you these things in the churches. I am the root and the offspring of David, and the bright and morning star.	**Is 11:10** [10]And in that day there shall be a root of Jesse, which shall stand for an ensign of the people; to it shall the Gentiles seek: and his rest shall be glorious.

ROMANS 15:13—Christian duty (12:1–15:13), 56–58 CE

Theme	ROM
Abound in hope	**15:13** [13]Now the God of hope fill you with all joy and peace in believing, that ye may abound in hope, through the power of the Holy Ghost. **5:1–2** [1]Therefore being justified by faith, we have peace with God through our Lord Jesus Christ: [2]By whom also we have access by faith into this grace wherein we stand, and rejoice in hope of the glory of God.

CONCLUDING REMARKS (15:15–16:27)

ROMANS 15:15—Concluding remarks, 56–58 CE

Theme	ROM
Grace of God for me	**15:15** [15]Nevertheless, brethren, I have written the more boldly unto you in some sort, as putting you in mind, because of the grace that is given to me of God, **1:5** [5]By whom we have received grace and apostleship, for obedience to the faith among all nations, for his name: **12:3** [3]For I say, through the grace given unto me, to every man that is among you, not to think of himself more highly than he ought to think; but to think soberly, according as God hath dealt to every man the measure of faith.

ROMANS 15:16—Concluding remarks, 56–58 CE

Theme	ROM	Paul
Minister of the Gentiles	**15:16** [16]That I should be the minister of Jesus Christ to the Gentiles, ministering the gospel of God, that the offering up of the Gentiles might be acceptable, being sanctified by the Holy Ghost. **11:13** [13]For I speak to you Gentiles, inasmuch as I am the apostle of the Gentiles, I magnify mine office:	**Phil 2:17** [17]Yea, and if I be offered upon the sacrifice and service of your faith, I joy, and rejoice with you all.

ROMANS 15:18–19—Concluding remarks, 56–58 CE

Theme	ROM	Paul
Christ's miracles in and through Paul	**15:18–19** [18]For I will not dare to speak of any of those things which Christ hath not wrought by me, to make the Gentiles obedient, by word and deed, [19]Through mighty signs and wonders, by the power of the Spirit of God; so that from Jerusalem, and round about unto Illyricum, I have fully preached the gospel of Christ.	**Gal 3:5** [5]He therefore that ministereth to you the Spirit, and worketh miracles among you, doeth he it by the works of the law, or by the hearing of faith? **1 Thes 1:5** [5]For our gospel came not unto you in word only, but also in power, and in the Holy Ghost, and in much assurance; as ye know what manner of men we were among you for your sake.

ROMANS 15:18—Concluding remarks, 56–58 CE

Theme	ROM	Lk	Paul
Gift to bring Gentiles to obedience	**15:18** [18]For I will not dare to speak of any of those things which Christ hath not wrought by me, to make the Gentiles obedient, by word and deed,	**Acts 15:12** [12]And by the hands of the apostles were many signs and wonders wrought among the people; (and they were all with one accord in Solomon's porch.	**2 Cor 12:12** [12]Truly the signs of an apostle were wrought among you in all patience, in signs, and wonders, and mighty deeds.

ROMANS 15:20—Concluding remarks, 56–58 CE

Theme	ROM	Paul
Preaching gospel	**15:20** [20]Yea, so have I strived to preach the gospel, not where Christ was named, lest I should build upon another man's foundation:	**2 Cor 10:13–18** [13]But we will not boast of things without our measure, but according to the measure of the rule which God hath distributed to us, a measure to reach even unto you. [14]For we stretch not ourselves beyond our measure, as though we reached not unto you: for we are come as far as to you also in preaching the gospel of Christ: [15]Not boasting of things without our measure, that is, of other men's labours; but having hope, when your faith is increased, that we shall be enlarged by you according to our rule abundantly, [16]To preach the gospel in the regions beyond you, and not to boast in another man's line of things made ready to our hand. [17]But he that glorieth, let him glory in the Lord. [18]For not he that commendeth himself is approved, but whom the Lord commendeth.

ROMANS 15:21—Concluding remarks, 56–58 CE

Theme	ROM	Jewish Writings
No understanding without hearing	**15:21** [21]But as it is written, To whom he was not spoken of, they shall see: and they that have not heard shall understand.	**Is 52:15** [15]So shall he sprinkle many nations; the kings shall shut their mouths at him: for that which had not been told them shall they see; and that which they had not heard shall they consider.

ROMANS 15:23—Concluding remarks, 56–58 CE

Theme	ROM	Lk
Purposed in Spirit	**15:23** [23]But now having no more place in these parts, and having a great desire these many years to come unto you; **1:10–13** [10]Making request, if by any means now at length I might have a prosperous journey by the will of God to come unto you. [11]For I long to see you, that I may impart unto you some spiritual gift, to the end ye may be established; [12]That is, that I may be comforted together with you by the mutual faith both of you and me. [13]Now I would not have you ignorant, brethren, that oftentimes I purposed to come unto you, (but was let hitherto,) that I might have some fruit among you also, even as among other Gentiles.	**Acts 19:21–22** [21]After these things were ended, Paul purposed in the spirit, when he had passed through Macedonia and Achaia, to go to Jerusalem, saying, After I have been there, I must also see Rome. [22]So he sent into Macedonia two of them that ministered unto him, Timotheus and Erastus; but he himself stayed in Asia for a season.

ROMANS 15:24—Concluding remarks, 56–58 CE

Theme	ROM	Paul
Journey to Spain	**15:24** [24]Whensoever I take my journey into Spain, I will come to you: for I trust to see you in my journey, and to be brought on my way thitherward by you, if first I be somewhat filled with your company.	**1 Cor 16:6** [6]And it may be that I will abide, yea, and winter with you, that ye may bring me on my journey whithersoever I go.

ROMANS 15:25—Concluding remarks, 56–58 CE

Theme	ROM	Lk
To Jerusalem	**15:25** [25]But now I go unto Jerusalem to minister unto the saints.	**Acts 19:21** [21]After these things were ended, Paul purposed in the spirit, when he had passed through Macedonia and Achaia, to go to Jerusalem, saying, After I have been there, I must also see Rome. **Acts 20:22** [22]And now, behold, I go bound in the spirit unto Jerusalem, not knowing the things that shall befall me there:

ROMANS 15:26–29—Concluding remarks, 56–58 CE

Theme	ROM	Paul
Give freely	**15:26–29**	**2 Cor 8**
	26 For it hath pleased them of Macedonia and Achaia to make a certain contribution for the poor saints which are at Jerusalem. 27 It hath pleased them verily; and their debtors they are. For if the Gentiles have been made partakers of their spiritual things, their duty is also to minister unto them in carnal things. 28 When therefore I have performed this, and have sealed to them this fruit, I will come by you into Spain. 29 And I am sure that, when I come unto you, I shall come in the fulness of the blessing of the gospel of Christ.	1 Moreover, brethren, we do you to wit of the grace of God bestowed on the churches of Macedonia; 2 How that in a great trial of affliction the abundance of their joy and their deep poverty abounded unto the riches of their liberality. 3 For to their power, I bear record, yea, and beyond their power they were willing of themselves; 4 Praying us with much entreaty that we would receive the gift, and take upon us the fellowship of the ministering to the saints. 5 And this they did, not as we hoped, but first gave their own selves to the Lord, and unto us by the will of God. 6 Insomuch that we desired Titus, that as he had begun, so he would also finish in you the same grace also. 7 Therefore, as ye abound in every thing, in faith, and utterance, and knowledge, and in all diligence, and in your love to us, see that ye abound in this grace also. 8 I speak not by commandment, but by occasion of the forwardness of others, and to prove the sincerity of your love. 9 For ye know the grace of our Lord Jesus Christ, that, though he was rich, yet for your sakes he became poor, that ye through his poverty might be rich. 10 And herein I give my advice: for this is expedient for you, who have begun before, not only to do, but also to be forward a year ago. 11 Now therefore perform the doing of it; that as there was a readiness to will, so there may be a performance also out of that which ye have. 12 For if there be first a willing mind, it is accepted according to that a man hath, and not according to that he hath not. 13 For I mean not that other men be eased, and ye burdened: 14 But by an equality, that now at this time your abundance may be a supply for their want, that their abundance also may be a supply for your want: that there may be equality: 15 As it is written, He that had gathered much had nothing over; and he that had gathered little had no lack. 16 But thanks be to God, which put the same earnest care into the heart of Titus for you. 17 For indeed he accepted the exhortation; but being more forward, of his own accord he went unto you. 18 And we have sent with him the brother, whose praise is in the gospel throughout all the churches; 19 And not that only, but who was also chosen of the churches to travel with us with this grace, which is administered by us to the glory of the same Lord, and declaration of your ready mind: 20 Avoiding this, that no man should blame us in this abundance which is administered by us: 21 Providing for honest things, not only in the sight of the Lord, but also in the sight of men. 22 And we have sent with them our brother, whom we have oftentimes proved diligent in many things, but now much more diligent, upon the great confidence which I have in you. 23 Whether any do inquire of Titus, he is my partner and fellowhelper concerning you: or our brethren be inquired of, they are the messengers of the churches, and the glory of Christ. 24 Wherefore show ye to them, and before the churches, the proof of your love, and of our boasting on your behalf. **2 Cor 9** 1 For as touching the ministering to the saints, it is superfluous for me to write to you: 2 For I know the forwardness of your mind, for which I boast of you to them of Macedonia, that Achaia was ready a year ago; and your zeal hath provoked very many. 3 Yet have I sent the brethren, lest our boasting of you should be in vain in this behalf; that, as I said, ye may be ready: 4 Lest haply if they of Macedonia come with me, and find you unprepared, we (that we say not, ye) should be ashamed in this same confident boasting. 5 Therefore I thought it necessary to exhort the brethren, that they would go before unto you, and make up beforehand your bounty, whereof ye had notice before, that the same might be ready, as a matter of bounty, and not as of covetousness. 6 But this I say, He which soweth sparingly shall reap also sparingly; and he which soweth bountifully shall reap also bountifully. 7 Every man according as he purposeth in his heart, so let him give; not grudgingly, or of necessity: for God loveth a cheerful giver. 8 And God is able to make all grace abound toward you; that ye, always having all sufficiency in all things, may abound to every good work: 9 (As it is written, He hath dispersed abroad; he hath given to the poor: his righteousness remaineth for ever. 10 Now he that ministereth seed to the sower both minister bread for your food, and multiply your seed sown, and increase the fruits of your righteousness;) 11 Being enriched in every thing to all bountifulness, which causeth through us thanksgiving to God. 12 For the administration of this service not only supplieth the want of the saints, but is abundant also by many thanksgivings unto God; 13 Whiles by the experiment of this ministration they glorify God for your professed subjection unto the gospel of Christ, and for your liberal distribution unto them, and unto all men; 14 And by their prayer for you, which long after you for the exceeding grace of God in you. 15 Thanks be unto God for his unspeakable gift.

ROMANS 15:26—Concluding remarks, 56–58 CE

Theme	ROM	Paul
Collection for the saints	**15:26** [26]For it hath pleased them of Macedonia and Achaia to make a certain contribution for the poor saints which are at Jerusalem.	**1 Cor 16:1–2** [1]Now concerning the collection for the saints, as I have given order to the churches of Galatia, even so do ye. [2]Upon the first day of the week let every one of you lay by him in store, as God hath prospered him, that there be no gatherings when I come. **2 Cor 8:1–4** [1]Moreover, brethren, we do you to wit of the grace of God bestowed on the churches of Macedonia; [2]How that in a great trial of affliction the abundance of their joy and their deep poverty abounded unto the riches of their liberality. [3]For to their power, I bear record, yea, and beyond their power they were willing of themselves; [4]Praying us with much entreaty that we would receive the gift, and take upon us the fellowship of the ministering to the saints. **2 Cor 9:2** [2]For I know the forwardness of your mind, for which I boast of you to them of Macedonia, that Achaia was ready a year ago; and your zeal hath provoked very many. **2 Cor 9:12** [12]For the administration of this service not only supplieth the want of the saints, but is abundant also by many thanksgivings unto God;

ROMANS 15:27—Concluding remarks, 56–58 CE

Theme	ROM	Paul
Gentiles partake in Spiritual blessings	**15:27** [27]It hath pleased them verily; and their debtors they are. For if the Gentiles have been made partakers of their spiritual things, their duty is also to minister unto them in carnal things. **9:4** [4]Who are Israelites; to whom pertaineth the adoption, and the glory, and the covenants, and the giving of the law, and the service of God, and the promises;	**1 Cor 9:11** [11]If we have sown unto you spiritual things, is it a great thing if we shall reap your carnal things?

ROMANS 15:30—Concluding remarks, 56–58 CE

Theme	ROM	Paul
Pray for Paul	**15:30** [30]Now I beseech you, brethren, for the Lord Jesus Christ's sake, and for the love of the Spirit, that ye strive together with me in your prayers to God for me;	**2 Cor 1:11** [11]Ye also helping together by prayer for us, that for the gift bestowed upon us by the means of many persons thanks may be given by many on our behalf. **Phil 1:27** [27]Only let your conversation be as it becometh the gospel of Christ: that whether I come and see you, or else be absent, I may hear of your affairs, that ye stand fast in one spirit, with one mind striving together for the faith of the gospel; **Col 4:3** [3]Withal praying also for us, that God would open unto us a door of utterance, to speak the mystery of Christ, for which I am also in bonds: **2 Thes 3:1** [1]Finally, brethren, pray for us, that the word of the Lord may have free course, and be glorified, even as it is with you:

ROMANS 15:33—Concluding remarks, 56–58 CE

Theme	ROM	Paul	NT
Live in peace	**15:33** [33]Now the God of peace be with you all. Amen. **16:20** [20]And the God of peace shall bruise Satan under your feet shortly. The grace of our Lord Jesus Christ be with you. Amen.	**2 Cor 13:11** [11]Finally, brethren, farewell. Be perfect, be of good comfort, be of one mind, live in peace; and the God of love and peace shall be with you. **Phil 4:9** [9]Those things, which ye have both learned, and received, and heard, and seen in me, do: and the God of peace shall be with you. **1 Thes 5:23** [23]And the very God of peace sanctify you wholly; and I pray God your whole spirit and soul and body be preserved blameless unto the coming of our Lord Jesus Christ. **2 Thes 3:16** [16]Now the Lord of peace himself give you peace always by all means. The Lord be with you all.	**Heb 13:20** [20]Now the God of peace, that brought again from the dead our Lord Jesus, that great shepherd of the sheep, through the blood of the everlasting covenant,

ROMANS 16:1—Concluding remarks, 56–58 CE

Theme	ROM	Lk
Phoebe in Cenchrea	**16:1** [1]I commend unto you Phebe our sister, which is a servant of the church which is at Cenchrea:	**Acts 18:18** [18]And Paul after this tarried there yet a good while, and then took his leave of the brethren, and sailed thence into Syria, and with him Priscilla and Aquila; having shorn his head in Cenchrea: for he had a vow.

ROMANS 16:3—Concluding remarks, 56–58 CE

Theme	ROM	Lk	Paul
Priscilla and Aquilla, helpers in Christ	**16:3** [3]Greet Priscilla and Aquila my helpers in Christ Jesus:	**Acts 18:2** [2]And found a certain Jew named Aquila, born in Pontus, lately come from Italy, with his wife Priscilla; (because that Claudius had commanded all Jews to depart from Rome:) and came unto them. **Acts 18:18–26** [18]And Paul after this tarried there yet a good while, and then took his leave of the brethren, and sailed thence into Syria, and with him Priscilla and Aquila; having shorn his head in Cenchrea: for he had a vow. [19]And he came to Ephesus, and left them there: but he himself entered into the synagogue, and reasoned with the Jews. [20]When they desired him to tarry longer time with them, he consented not; [21]But bade them farewell, saying, I must by all means keep this feast that cometh in Jerusalem: but I will return again unto you, if God will. And he sailed from Ephesus. [22]And when he had landed at Caesarea, and gone up, and saluted the church, he went down to Antioch. [23]And after he had spent some time there, he departed, and went over all the country of Galatia and Phrygia in order, strengthening all the disciples. [24]And a certain Jew named Apollos, born at Alexandria, an eloquent man, and mighty in the scriptures, came to Ephesus. [25]This man was instructed in the way of the Lord; and being fervent in the spirit, he spake and taught diligently the things of the Lord, knowing only the baptism of John. [26]And he began to speak boldly in the synagogue: whom when Aquila and Priscilla had heard, they took him unto them, and expounded unto him the way of God more perfectly.	**1 Cor 16:19** [19]The churches of Asia salute you. Aquila and Priscilla salute you much in the Lord, with the church that is in their house. **2 Tim 4:19 (Pseudo)** [19]Salute Prisca and Aquila, and the household of Onesiphorus.

ROMANS 16:5—Concluding remarks, 56–58 CE

Theme	ROM	Paul
Greetings to churches	**16:5** [5]Likewise greet the church that is in their house. Salute my wellbeloved Epaenetus, who is the firstfruits of Achaia unto Christ.	**1 Cor 16:15** [15]I beseech you, brethren, (ye know the house of Stephanas, that it is the firstfruits of Achaia, and that they have addicted themselves to the ministry of the saints,) **1 Cor 16:19** [19]The churches of Asia salute you. Aquila and Priscilla salute you much in the Lord, with the church that is in their house. **Col 4:15** [15]Salute the brethren which are in Laodicea, and Nymphas, and the church which is in his house. **Phlm 2** [2]And to our beloved Apphia, and Archippus our fellowsoldier, and to the church in thy house:

ROMANS 16:13—Concluding remarks, 56–58 CE

Theme	ROM	Mk
Chosen to serve the Lord	**16:13** [13]Salute Rufus chosen in the Lord, and his mother and mine.	**15:21** [21]And they compel one Simon a Cyrenian, who passed by, coming out of the country, the father of Alexander and Rufus, to bear his cross.

ROMANS 16:16—Concluding remarks, 56–58 CE

Theme	ROM	Paul	NT
Greet with holy kiss	**16:16** [16]Salute one another with an holy kiss. The churches of Christ salute you.	**1 Cor 16:20** [20]All the brethren greet you. Greet ye one another with an holy kiss. **2 Cor 13:12** [12]Greet one another with an holy kiss. **1 Thes 5:26** [26]Greet all the brethren with an holy kiss.	**1 Pet 5:14** [14]Greet ye one another with a kiss of charity. Peace be with you all that are in Christ Jesus. Amen.

ROMANS 16:17—Concluding remarks, 56–58 CE

Theme	ROM	Mt	Paul	Other
Avoid false doctrines	**16:17** [17]Now I beseech you, brethren, mark them which cause divisions and offences contrary to the doctrine which ye have learned; and avoid them.	**7:15** [15]Beware of false prophets, which come to you in sheep's clothing, but inwardly they are ravening wolves.	**Tit 3:10 (Pseudo)** [10]A man that is an heretic after the first and second admonition reject;	**Q-Quelle** Fruits: Rom 16:17/Mt 7:15-20, [Mt 12:33-35]/[Lk 6:43-45] (QS 13 [Thom 45]);Judging: Rom 16:17/Mt 7:15-20, [Mt 12:33-35]/[Lk 6:43-45 (QS 13 [Thom 45])]; On faith: Rom 16:17/Tit 3:10/[Mt 18:15, 21-22]/[Lk 17:3b-4 (QS 58)]

ROMANS 16:18—Concluding remarks, 56–58 CE

Theme	ROM	Paul	NT
Simple deceived by fair speech	**16:18** [18]For they that are such serve not our Lord Jesus Christ, but their own belly; and by good words and fair speeches deceive the hearts of the simple.	**Phil 3:18–19** [18](For many walk, of whom I have told you often, and now tell you even weeping, that they are the enemies of the cross of Christ: [19]Whose end is destruction, whose God is their belly, and whose glory is in their shame, who mind earthly things.) **Col 2:4** [4]And this I say, lest any man should beguile you with enticing words.	**2 Pet 2:3** [3]And through covetousness shall they with feigned words make merchandise of you: whose judgment now of a long time lingereth not, and their damnation slumbereth not.

ROMANS 16:19—Concluding remarks, 56–58 CE

Theme	ROM	Mt	Mk	Lk
Obedience **Wise, guileless**	**16:19** [19]For your obedience is come abroad unto all men. I am glad therefore on your behalf: but yet I would have you be wise unto that which is good, and simple concerning evil.	**10:16–23** **[16]Behold, I send you forth as sheep in the midst of wolves: be ye therefore wise as serpents, and harmless as doves.** [17]But beware of men: for they will deliver you up to the councils, and they will scourge you in their synagogues; [18]And ye shall be brought before governors and kings for my sake, for a testimony against them and the Gentiles. [19]But when they deliver you up, take no thought how or what ye shall speak: for it shall be given you in that same hour what ye shall speak. [20]For it is not ye that speak, but the Spirit of your Father which speaketh in you. [21]And the brother shall deliver up the brother to death, and the father the child: and the children shall rise up against their parents, and cause them to be put to death. [22]And ye shall be hated of all men for my name's sake: but he that endureth to the end shall be saved. [23]But when they persecute you in this city, flee ye into another: for verily I say unto you, Ye shall not have gone over the cities of Israel, till the Son of man be come. **24:9–14** [9]Then shall they deliver you up to be afflicted, and shall kill you: and ye shall be hated of all nations for my name's sake. [10]And then shall many be offended, and shall betray one another, and shall hate one another. [11]And many false prophets shall rise, and shall deceive many. [12]And because iniquity shall abound, the love of many shall wax cold. **[13]But he that shall endure unto the end, the same shall be saved. [14]And this gospel of the kingdom shall be preached in all the world for a witness unto all nations; and then shall the end come.**	**13:9–13** [9]But take heed to yourselves: for they shall deliver you up to councils; and in the synagogues ye shall be beaten: and ye shall be brought before rulers and kings for my sake, for a testimony against them. [10]And the gospel must first be published among all nations. [11]But when they shall lead you, and deliver you up, take no thought beforehand what ye shall speak, neither do ye premeditate: but whatsoever shall be given you in that hour, that speak ye: for it is not ye that speak, but the Holy Ghost. [12]Now the brother shall betray the brother to death, and the father the son; and children shall rise up against their parents, and shall cause them to be put to death. [13]And ye shall be hated of all men for my name's sake: but he that shall endure unto the end, the same shall be saved	**10:3** [3]Go your ways: behold, I send you forth as lambs among wolves. **12:11–12** [11]And when they bring you unto the synagogues, and unto magistrates, and powers, take ye no thought how or what thing ye shall answer, or what ye shall say: [12]For the Holy Ghost shall teach you in the same hour what ye ought to say. **12:19–21** [19]And I will say to my soul, Soul, thou hast much goods laid up for many years; take thine ease, eat, drink, and be merry. [20]But God said unto him, Thou fool, this night thy soul shall be required of thee: then whose shall those things be, which thou hast provided? [21]So is he that layeth up treasure for himself, and is not rich toward God.

Jn	Paul	Jewish	Other
14:26 [26]But the Comforter, which is the Holy Ghost, whom the Father will send in my name, he shall teach you all things, and bring all things to your remembrance, whatsoever I have said unto you. **15:18** [18]If the world hate you, ye know that it hated me before it hated you. **16:2** [2]They shall put you out of the synagogues: yea, the time cometh, that whosoever killeth you will think that he doeth God service.	**Phil 2:15** [15]That ye may be blameless and harmless, the sons of God, without rebuke, in the midst of a crooked and perverse nation, among whom ye shine as lights in the world;	**Mic 7:6** [6]For the son dishonoureth the father, the daughter riseth up against her mother, the daughter in law against her mother in law; a man's enemies are the men of his own house.	**2 Clem 5:2–4** [2]For the Lord says, "You will be like sheep in the midst of wolves." [3] But Peer replied to him, "What if the wolves rip apart the sheep?" [4] Jesus said to Peter, "After they are dead the sheep should fear the wolves no .longer. So too you: do not fear those who kill you and then do nothing more to you; but fear the one who, after you die, has the power to cast your body and sol into the hell of fire." **GNaz 7** [7]The name of that one (i.e., Barnabas) is interpreted to mean "son of their master" in the Gospel written according to the Hebrews. (Jerome, Commentary on Matthew 27,16) **GThom 39** [39]Jesus said, "The pharisees and the scribes have taken the keys of knowledge (gnosis) and hidden them. They themselves have not entered, nor have they allowed to enter those who wish to. You, however, be as wise as serpents and as innocent as doves." **Q-Quelle** Commissioning the 70: Rom 16:19/ [1 Cor 14:20]/Mt 10:7-16/Lk 10:1-12 (QS 20-23 [Thom 73;14:2])]; Assistance of the Holy Spirit: Rom 16:19/ Mt 10:19-20/[Mk 13:11]/ Lk 12:11-12 (QS 37 [Thom 44]) [Lk 21:14-15]

ROMANS 16:20—Concluding remarks, 56–58 CE

Theme	ROM	Lk	Paul	Jewish Writings
Satan bruised by peace	**16:20** [20]And the God of peace shall bruise Satan under your feet shortly. The grace of our Lord Jesus Christ be with you. Amen. **15:33** [33]Now the God of peace be with you all. Amen.	**10:19** [19]Behold, I give unto you power to tread on serpents and scorpions, and over all the power of the enemy: and nothing shall by any means hurt you.	**1 Cor 16:23** [23]The grace of our Lord Jesus Christ be with you. **1 Thes 5:28** [28]The grace of our Lord Jesus Christ be with you. Amen. **2 Thes 3:18** [18]The grace of our Lord Jesus Christ be with you all. Amen.	**Gen 3:15** [15]And I will put enmity between thee and the woman, and between thy seed and her seed; it shall bruise thy head, and thou shalt bruise his heel.

ROMANS 16:21—Concluding remarks, 56–58 CE

Theme	ROM	Lk	Paul	NT
Paul's fellow-workers	**16:21** [21]Timotheus my workfellow, and Lucius, and Jason, and Sosipater, my kinsmen, salute you.	**Acts 16:1–2** [1]Then came he to Derbe and Lystra: and, behold, a certain disciple was there, named Timotheus, the son of a certain woman, which was a Jewess, and believed; but his father was a Greek: [2]Which was well reported of by the brethren that were at Lystra and Iconium. **Acts 19:22** [22]So he sent into Macedonia two of them that ministered unto him, Timotheus and Erastus; but he himself stayed in Asia for a season. **Acts 20:4** [4]And there accompanied him into Asia Sopater of Berea; and of the Thessalonians, Aristarchus and Secundus; and Gaius of Derbe, and Timotheus; and of Asia, Tychicus and Trophimus.	**1 Cor 4:17** [17]For this cause have I sent unto you Timotheus, who is my beloved son, and faithful in the Lord, who shall bring you into remembrance of my ways which be in Christ, as I teach every where in every church. **1 Cor 16:10** [10]Now if Timotheus come, see that he may be with you without fear: for he worketh the work of the Lord, as I also do. **Phil 2:19–22** [19]But I trust in the Lord Jesus to send Timotheus shortly unto you, that I also may be of good comfort, when I know your state. [20]For I have no man likeminded, who will naturally care for your state. [21]For all seek their own, not the things which are Jesus Christ's. [22]But ye know the proof of him, that, as a son with the father, he hath served with me in the gospel.	**Heb 13:23** [23]Know ye that our brother Timothy is set at liberty; with whom, if he come shortly, I will see you.

ROMANS 16:23—Concluding remarks, 56–58 CE

Theme	ROM	Lk	Paul
Salute to Gaius	**16:23** [23]Gaius mine host, and of the whole church, saluteth you. Erastus the chamberlain of the city saluteth you, and Quartus a brother.	**Acts 19:29** [29]And the whole city was filled with confusion: and having caught Gaius and Aristarchus, men of Macedonia, Paul's companions in travel, they rushed with one accord into the theatre.	**1 Cor 1:14** [14]I thank God that I baptized none of you, but Crispus and Gaius; **2 Tim 4:20 (Pseudo)** [20]Erastus abode at Corinth: but Trophimus have I left at Miletum sick.

ROMANS 16:25—Concluding remarks, 56–58 CE

Theme	ROM	Paul
Gospel is God's message	**16:25** [25]Now to him that is of power to stablish you according to my gospel, and the preaching of Jesus Christ, according to the revelation of the mystery, which was kept secret since the world began,	**1 Cor 2:7** [7]But we speak the wisdom of God in a mystery, even the hidden wisdom, which God ordained before the world unto our glory: **Eph 1:9 (Pseudo)** [9]Having made known unto us the mystery of his will, according to his good pleasure which he hath purposed in himself: **Eph 3:3–9 (Pseudo)** [3]How that by revelation he made known unto me the mystery; (as I wrote afore in few words, [4]Whereby, when ye read, ye may understand my knowledge in the mystery of Christ) [5]Which in other ages was not made known unto the sons of men, as it is now revealed unto his holy apostles and prophets by the Spirit; [6]That the Gentiles should be fellowheirs, and of the same body, and partakers of his promise in Christ by the gospel: [7]Whereof I was made a minister, according to the gift of the grace of God given unto me by the effectual working of his power. [8]Unto me, who am less than the least of all saints, is this grace given, that I should preach among the Gentiles the unsearchable riches of Christ; [9]And to make all men see what is the fellowship of the mystery, which from the beginning of the world hath been hid in God, who created all things by Jesus Christ: **Col 1:26** [26]Even the mystery which hath been hid from ages and from generations, but now is made manifest to his saints:

ROMANS 16:26—Concluding remarks, 56–58 CE

Theme	ROM	Paul	NT
Obedience in the faith	**16:26** [26]But now is made manifest, and by the scriptures of the prophets, according to the commandment of the everlasting God, made known to all nations for the obedience of faith:	**Eph 3:4–5 (Pseudo)** [4]Since we heard of your faith in Christ Jesus, and of the love which ye have to all the saints, [5]For the hope which is laid up for you in heaven, whereof ye heard before in the word of the truth of the gospel; **Eph 3:9 (Pseudo)** [9]For this cause we also, since the day we heard it, do not cease to pray for you, and to desire that ye might be filled with the knowledge of his will in all wisdom and spiritual understanding; **2 Tim 1:5 (Pseudo)** [5]When I call to remembrance the unfeigned faith that is in thee, which dwelt first in thy grandmother Lois, and thy mother Eunice; and I am persuaded that in thee also. **2 Tim 1:10 (Pseudo)** [10]But is now made manifest by the appearing of our Saviour Jesus Christ, who hath abolished death, and hath brought life and immortality to light through the gospel:	**1 Pet 1:20** [20]Who verily was foreordained before the foundation of the world, but was manifest in these last times for you,

ROMANS 16:27—Concluding remarks, 56–58 CE

Theme	ROM	Paul	NT
Doxology	**16:27** [27]To God only wise, be glory through Jesus Christ for ever. Amen. **11:36** [36]For of him, and through him, and to him, are all things: to whom be glory for ever. Amen.	**Gal 1:5** [5]To whom be glory for ever and ever. Amen. **Eph 3:20–21 (Pseudo)** [20]Now unto him that is able to do exceedingly abundantly above all that we ask or think, according to the power that worketh in us, [21]Unto him be glory in the church by Christ Jesus throughout all ages, world without end. Amen. **Phil 4:20** [20]Now unto God and our Father be glory for ever and ever. Amen. **1 Tim 1:17 (Pseudo)** [17]Now unto the King eternal, immortal, invisible, the only wise God, be honour and glory for ever and ever. Amen. **2 Tim 4:18 (Pseudo)** [18]And the Lord shall deliver me from every evil work, and will preserve me unto his heavenly kingdom: to whom be glory for ever and ever. Amen.	**Heb 13:21** [21]Make you perfect in every good work to do his will, working in you that which is wellpleasing in his sight, through Jesus Christ; to whom be glory for ever and ever. Amen. **1 Pet 4:11** [11]If any man speak, let him speak as the oracles of God; if any man minister, let him do it as of the ability which God giveth: that God in all things may be glorified through Jesus Christ, to whom be praise and dominion for ever and ever. Amen. **2 Pet 3:18** [18]But grow in grace, and in the knowledge of our Lord and Saviour Jesus Christ. To him be glory both now and for ever. Amen. **Jude 25** [25]To the only wise God our Saviour, be glory and majesty, dominion and power, both now and for ever. Amen. **Rev 1:6** [6]And hath made us kings and priests unto God and his Father; to him be glory and dominion for ever and ever. Amen.

1 CORINTHIANS, 51 CE, SECOND MISSIONARY JOURNEY (ACTS 18)

1 CORINTHIANS Ch 1–4—Written from Ephesus (Acts 18:1–11), 51 CE

Theme	1 COR
Revealing the mysteries of Kingdom of God	**Ch 1–4** **1** [1]Paul, called to be an apostle of Jesus Christ through the will of God, and Sosthenes our brother, [2]Unto the church of God which is at Corinth, to them that are sanctified in Christ Jesus, called to be saints, with all that in every place call upon the name of Jesus Christ our Lord, both theirs and ours: [3]Grace be unto you, and peace, from God our Father, and from the Lord Jesus Christ. [4]I thank my God always on your behalf, for the grace of God which is given you by Jesus Christ; [5]That in every thing ye are enriched by him, in all utterance, and in all knowledge; [6]Even as the testimony of Christ was confirmed in you: [7]So that ye come behind in no gift; waiting for the coming of our Lord Jesus Christ [8]Who shall also confirm you unto the end, that ye may be blameless in the day of our Lord Jesus Christ. [9]God is faithful, by whom ye were called unto the fellowship of his Son Jesus Christ our Lord. [10]Now I beseech you, brethren, by the name of our Lord Jesus Christ, that ye all speak the same thing, and that there be no divisions among you; but that ye be perfectly joined together in the same mind and in the same judgment. [11]For it hath been declared unto me of you, my brethren, by them which are of the house of Chloe, that there are contentions among you. [12]Now this I say, that every one of you saith, I am of Paul; and I of Apollos; and I of Cephas; and I of Christ. [13]Is Christ divided? was Paul crucified for you? or were ye baptized in the name of Paul? [14]I thank God that I baptized none of you, but Crispus and Gaius; [15]Lest any should say that I had baptized in mine own name. [16]And I baptized also the household of Stephanas: besides, I know not whether I baptized any other. [17]For Christ sent me not to baptize, but to preach the gospel: not with wisdom of words, lest the cross of Christ should be made of none effect. [18]For the preaching of the cross is to them that perish foolishness; but unto us which are saved it is the power of God. [19]For it is written, I will destroy the wisdom of the wise, and will bring to nothing the understanding of the prudent. [20]Where is the wise? where is the scribe? where is the disputer of this world? hath not God made foolish the wisdom of this world? [21]For after that in the wisdom of God the world by wisdom knew not God, it pleased God by the foolishness of preaching to save them that believe. [22]For the Jews require a sign, and the Greeks seek after wisdom: [23]But we preach Christ crucified, unto the Jews a stumblingblock, and unto the Greeks foolishness; [24]But unto them which are called, both Jews and Greeks, Christ the power of God, and the wisdom of God. [25]Because the foolishness of God is wiser than men; and the weakness of God is stronger than men. [26]For ye see your calling, brethren, how that not many wise men after the flesh, not many mighty, not many noble, are called: [27]But God hath chosen the foolish things of the world to confound the wise; and God hath chosen the weak things of the world to confound the things which are mighty; [28]And base things of the world, and things which are despised, hath God chosen, yea, and things which are not, to bring to nought things that are: [29]That no flesh should glory in his presence. [30]But of him are ye in Christ Jesus, who of God is made unto us wisdom, and righteousness, and sanctification, and redemption: [31]That, according as it is written, He that glorieth, let him glory in the Lord. **2** [1]And I, brethren, when I came to you, came not with excellency of speech or of wisdom, declaring unto you the testimony of God. [2]For I determined not to know any thing among you, save Jesus Christ, and him crucified. [3]And I was with you in weakness, and in fear, and in much trembling. [4]And my speech and my preaching was not with enticing words of man's wisdom, but in demonstration of the Spirit and of power: [5]That your faith should not stand in the wisdom of men, but in the power of God. [6]Howbeit we speak wisdom among them that are perfect: yet not the wisdom of this world, nor of the princes of this world, that come to nought: [7]But we speak the wisdom of God in a mystery, even the hidden wisdom, which God ordained before the world unto our glory: [8]Which none of the princes of this world knew: for had they known it, they would not have crucified the Lord of glory. [9]But as it is written, Eye hath not seen, nor ear heard, neither have entered into the heart of man, the things which God hath prepared for them that love him. [10]But God hath revealed them unto us by his Spirit: for the Spirit searcheth all things, yea, the deep things of God. [11]For what man knoweth the things of a man, save the spirit of man which is in him? even so the things of God knoweth no man, but the Spirit of God. [12]Now we have received, not the spirit of the world, but the spirit which is of God; that we might know the things that are freely given to us of God. [13]Which things also we speak, not in the words which man's wisdom teacheth, but which the Holy Ghost teacheth; comparing spiritual things with spiritual. [14]But the natural man receiveth not the things of the Spirit of God: for they are foolishness unto him: neither can he know them, because they are spiritually discerned. [15]But he that is spiritual judgeth all things, yet he himself is judged of no man. [16]For who hath known the mind of the Lord, that he may instruct him? But we have the mind of Christ. (***Continued***)

Mt	Mk
11:25–27	**4:10-11**
[25]At that time Jesus answered and said, I thank thee, O Father, Lord of heaven and earth, because thou hast hid these things from the wise and prudent, and hast revealed them unto babes. [26]Even so, Father: for so it seemed good in thy sight. [27]All things are delivered unto me of my Father: and no man knoweth the Son, but the Father; neither knoweth any man the Father, save the Son, and he to whomsoever the Son will reveal him	[10]And when he was alone, they that were about him with the twelve asked of him the parable. [11]And he said unto them, Unto you it is given to know the mystery of the kingdom of God: but unto them that are without, all these things are done in parables:
13:11	
[11]He answered and said unto them, Because it is given unto you to know the mysteries of the kingdom of heaven, but to them it is not given.	
13:13	
[13]Therefore speak I to them in parables: because they seeing see not; and hearing they hear not, neither do they understand.	

1 CORINTHIANS Ch 1–4—Written from Ephesus (Acts 18:1–11), 51 CE (*continued*)

Theme	1 COR
(*Cont.*) **Reveal mysteries of Kingdom of God**	**(*continued*)** **Ch 1–4** **3** 1 And I, brethren, could not speak unto you as unto spiritual, but as unto carnal, even as unto babes in Christ. 2 I have fed you with milk, and not with meat: for hitherto ye were not able to bear it, neither yet now are ye able. 3 For ye are yet carnal: for whereas there is among you envying, and strife, and divisions, are ye not carnal, and walk as men? 4 For while one saith, I am of Paul; and another, I am of Apollos; are ye not carnal? 5 Who then is Paul, and who is Apollos, but ministers by whom ye believed, even as the Lord gave to every man? 6 I have planted, Apollos watered; but God gave the increase. 7 So then neither is he that planteth any thing, neither he that watereth; but God that giveth the increase. 8 Now he that planteth and he that watereth are one: and every man shall receive his own reward according to his own labour. 9 For we are labourers together with God: ye are God's husbandry, ye are God's building. 10 According to the grace of God which is given unto me, as a wise masterbuilder, I have laid the foundation, and another buildeth thereon. But let every man take heed how he buildeth thereupon. 11 For other foundation can no man lay than that is laid, which is Jesus Christ. 12 Now if any man build upon this foundation gold, silver, precious stones, wood, hay, stubble; 13 Every man's work shall be made manifest: for the day shall declare it, because it shall be revealed by fire; and the fire shall try every man's work of what sort it is. 14 If any man's work abide which he hath built thereupon, he shall receive a reward. 15 If any man's work shall be burned, he shall suffer loss: but he himself shall be saved; yet so as by fire. 16 Know ye not that ye are the temple of God, and that the Spirit of God dwelleth in you? 17 If any man defile the temple of God, him shall God destroy; for the temple of God is holy, which temple ye are. 18 Let no man deceive himself. If any man among you seemeth to be wise in this world, let him become a fool, that he may be wise. 19 For the wisdom of this world is foolishness with God. For it is written, He taketh the wise in their own craftiness. 20 And again, The Lord knoweth the thoughts of the wise, that they are vain. 21 Therefore let no man glory in men. For all things are yours; 22 Whether Paul, or Apollos, or Cephas, or the world, or life, or death, or things present, or things to come; all are yours; 23 And ye are Christ's; and Christ is God's. **4** 1 Let a man so account of us, as of the ministers of Christ, and stewards of the mysteries of God. 2 Moreover it is required in stewards, that a man be found faithful. 3 But with me it is a very small thing that I should be judged of you, or of man's judgment: yea, I judge not mine own self. 4 For I know nothing by myself; yet am I not hereby justified: but he that judgeth me is the Lord. 5 Therefore judge nothing before the time, until the Lord come, who both will bring to light the hidden things of darkness, and will make manifest the counsels of the hearts: and then shall every man have praise of God. 6 And these things, brethren, I have in a figure transferred to myself and to Apollos for your sakes; that ye might learn in us not to think of men above that which is written, that no one of you be puffed up for one against another. 7 For who maketh thee to differ from another? and what hast thou that thou didst not receive? now if thou didst receive it, why dost thou glory, as if thou hadst not received it? 8 Now ye are full, now ye are rich, ye have reigned as kings without us: and I would to God ye did reign, that we also might reign with you. 9 For I think that God hath set forth us the apostles last, as it were appointed to death: for we are made a spectacle unto the world, and to angels, and to men. 10 We are fools for Christ's sake, but ye are wise in Christ; we are weak, but ye are strong; ye are honourable, but we are despised. 11 Even unto this present hour we both hunger, and thirst, and are naked, and are buffeted, and have no certain dwellingplace; 12 And labour, working with our own hands: being reviled, we bless; being persecuted, we suffer it: 13 Being defamed, we entreat: we are made as the filth of the world, and are the offscouring of all things unto this day. 14 I write not these things to shame you, but as my beloved sons I warn you. 15 For though ye have ten thousand instructors in Christ, yet have ye not many fathers: for in Christ Jesus I have begotten you through the gospel. 16 Wherefore I beseech you, be ye followers of me. 17 For this cause have I sent unto you Timotheus, who is my beloved son, and faithful in the Lord, who shall bring you into remembrance of my ways which be in Christ, as I teach every where in every church. 18 Now some are puffed up, as though I would not come to you. 19 But I will come to you shortly, if the Lord will, and will know, not the speech of them which are puffed up, but the power. 20 For the kingdom of God is not in word, but in power. 21 What will ye? shall I come unto you with a rod, or in love, and in the spirit of meekness? **1:9** 9 God is faithful, by whom ye were called unto the fellowship of his Son Jesus Christ our Lord. **1:19** 19 For it is written, I will destroy the wisdom of the wise, and will bring to nothing the understanding of the prudent. **1:21** 21 For after that in the wisdom of God the world by wisdom knew not God, it pleased God by the foolishness of preaching to save them that believe.

Lk	Jewish	Other
8:10 [10]And he said, Unto you it is given to know the mysteries of the kingdom of God: but to others in parables; that seeing they might not see, and hearing they might not understand. **10:21–22** [21]In that hour Jesus rejoiced in spirit, and said, I thank thee, O Father, Lord of heaven and earth, that thou hast hid these things from the wise and prudent, and hast revealed them unto babes: even so, Father; for so it seemed good in thy sight. [22]All things are delivered to me of my Father: and no man knoweth who the Son is, but the Father; and who the Father is, but the Son, and he to whom the Son will reveal him.	**Is 29:14** [14]And Azor begat Sadoc; and Sadoc begat Achim; and Achim begat Eliud;	**Q-Quelle** Thanks and blessings/Disciples: 1 Cor Ch 1-4/Mt 11:25-27, [Mt 13:16-17]/Lk 10:21-24 (QS 24, 25)

ADDRESS 1:1–9

1 CORINTHIANS 1:1—Address (1:1–9), written from Ephesus (Acts 18:1–11), 51 CE

Theme	1 COR	Paul
Paul, an apostle and servant	**1:1** [1]Paul, called to be an apostle of Jesus Christ through the will of God, and Sosthenes our brother,	**Rom 1:1** [1]Paul, a servant of Jesus Christ, called to be an apostle, separated unto the gospel of God,

1 CORINTHIANS 1:2—Address (1:1–9), written from Ephesus (Acts 18:1–11), 51 CE

Theme	1 COR	Lk
Corinthian church	**1:2** [2]Unto the church of God which is at Corinth, to them that are sanctified in Christ Jesus, called to be saints, with all that in every place call upon the name of Jesus Christ our Lord, both theirs and ours:	**Acts 18:1–11** [1]After these things Paul departed from Athens, and came to Corinth; [2]And found a certain Jew named Aquila, born in Pontus, lately come from Italy, with his wife Priscilla; (because that Claudius had commanded all Jews to depart from Rome:) and came unto them. [3]And because he was of the same craft, he abode with them, and wrought: for by their occupation they were tentmakers. [4]And he reasoned in the synagogue every sabbath, and persuaded the Jews and the Greeks. [5]And when Silas and Timotheus were come from Macedonia, Paul was pressed in the spirit, and testified to the Jews that Jesus was Christ. [6]And when they opposed themselves, and blasphemed, he shook his raiment, and said unto them, Your blood be upon your own heads; I am clean: from henceforth I will go unto the Gentiles. [7]And he departed thence, and entered into a certain man's house, named Justus, one that worshipped God, whose house joined hard to the synagogue. [8]And Crispus, the chief ruler of the synagogue, believed on the Lord with all his house; and many of the Corinthians hearing believed, and were baptized. [9]Then spake the Lord to Paul in the night by a vision, Be not afraid, but speak, and hold not thy peace: [10]For I am with thee, and no man shall set on thee to hurt thee: for I have much people in this city. [11]And he continued there a year and six months, teaching the word of God among them.

1 CORINTHIANS 1:6—Address (1:1–9), written from Ephesus (Acts 18:1–11), 51 CE

Theme	1 COR	Mt
Living in Christ	**1:6** 6Even as the testimony of Christ was confirmed in you: **3:6** 6I have planted, Apollos watered; but God gave the increase. **3:9** 9For we are labourers together with God: ye are God's husbandry, ye are God's building. **9:7** 7Who goeth a warfare any time at his own charges? who planteth a vineyard, and eateth not of the fruit thereof? or who feedeth a flock, and eateth not of the milk of the flock? **9:11** 11If we have sown unto you spiritual things, is it a great thing if we shall reap your carnal things?	**13:1–30** 1The same day went Jesus out of the house, and sat by the sea side. 2And great multitudes were gathered together unto him, so that he went into a ship, and sat; and the whole multitude stood on the shore. 3And he spake many things unto them in parables, saying, Behold, a sower went forth to sow; 4And when he sowed, some seeds fell by the way side, and the fowls came and devoured them up: 5Some fell upon stony places, where they had not much earth: and forthwith they sprung up, because they had no deepness of earth: 6And when the sun was up, they were scorched; and because they had no root, they withered away. 7And some fell among thorns; and the thorns sprung up, and choked them: 8But other fell into good ground, and brought forth fruit, some an hundredfold, some sixtyfold, some thirtyfold. 9Who hath ears to hear, let him hear. 10And the disciples came, and said unto him, Why speakest thou unto them in parables? 11He answered and said unto them, Because it is given unto you to know the mysteries of the kingdom of heaven, but to them it is not given. 12For whosoever hath, to him shall be given, and he shall have more abundance: but whosoever hath not, from him shall be taken away even that he hath. 13Therefore speak I to them in parables: because they seeing see not; and hearing they hear not, neither do they understand. 14And in them is fulfilled the prophecy of Esaias, which saith, By hearing ye shall hear, and shall not understand; and seeing ye shall see, and shall not perceive: 15For this people's heart is waxed gross, and their ears are dull of hearing, and their eyes they have closed; lest at any time they should see with their eyes, and hear with their ears, and should understand with their heart, and should be converted, and I should heal them. 16But blessed are your eyes, for they see: and your ears, for they hear. 17For verily I say unto you, That many prophets and righteous men have desired to see those things which ye see, and have not seen them; and to hear those things which ye hear, and have not heard them. 18Hear ye therefore the parable of the sower. 19When any one heareth the word of the kingdom, and understandeth it not, then cometh the wicked one, and catcheth away that which was sown in his heart. This is he which received seed by the way side. 20But he that received the seed into stony places, the same is he that heareth the word, and anon with joy receiveth it; 21Yet hath he not root in himself, but dureth for a while: for when tribulation or persecution ariseth because of the word, by and by he is offended. 22He also that received seed among the thorns is he that heareth the word; and the care of this world, and the deceitfulness of riches, choke the word, and he becometh unfruitful. 23But he that received seed into the good ground is he that heareth the word, and understandeth it; which also beareth fruit, and bringeth forth, some an hundredfold, some sixty, some thirty. 24Another parable put he forth unto them, saying, The kingdom of heaven is likened unto a man which sowed good seed in his field: 25But while men slept, his enemy came and sowed tares among the wheat, and went his way. 26But when the blade was sprung up, and brought forth fruit, then appeared the tares also. 27So the servants of the householder came and said unto him, Sir, didst not thou sow good seed in thy field? from whence then hath it tares? 28He said unto them, An enemy hath done this. The servants said unto him, Wilt thou then that we go and gather them up? 29But he said, Nay; lest while ye gather up the tares, ye root up also the wheat with them. 30Let both grow together until the harvest: and in the time of harvest I will say to the reapers, Gather ye together first the tares, and bind them in undles to burn them: but gather the wheat into my barn.

Mk

4:1–20

[1]And he began again to teach by the sea side: and there was gathered unto him a great
multitude, so that he entered into a ship, and sat in the sea; and the whole multitude
was by the sea on the land. [2]And he taught them many things by parables, and said
unto them in his doctrine, [3]Hearken; Behold, there went out a sower to sow: [4]And it
came to pass, as he sowed, some fell by the way side, and the fowls of the air came and
devoured it up. [5]And some fell on stony ground, where it had not much earth; and
immediately it sprang up, because it had no depth of earth: [6]But when the sun was up,
it was scorched; and because it had no root, it withered away. [7]And some fell among
thorns, and the thorns grew up, and choked it, and it yielded no fruit. [8]And other fell
on good ground, and did yield fruit that sprang up and increased; and brought forth,
some thirty, and some sixty, and some an hundred. [9]And he said unto them, He that
hath ears to hear, let him hear. [10]And when he was alone, they that were about him
with the twelve asked of him the parable. [11]And he said unto them, Unto you it is
given to know the mystery of the kingdom of God: but unto them that are without, all
these things are done in parables: [12]That seeing they may see, and not perceive; and
hearing they may hear, and not understand; lest at any time they should be converted,
and their sins should be forgiven them. [13]And he said unto them, Know ye not this
parable? and how then will ye know all parables? [14]The sower soweth the word. [15]And
these are they by the way side, where the word is sown; but when they have heard,
Satan cometh immediately, and taketh away the word that was sown in their hearts.
[16]And these are they likewise which are sown on stony ground; who, when they have
heard the word, immediately receive it with gladness; [17]And have no root in themselves, and so endure but for a time: afterward, when affliction or persecution ariseth
for the word's sake, immediately they are offended. [18]And these are they which are
sown among thorns; such as hear the word, [19]And the cares of this world, and the
deceitfulness of riches, and the lusts of other things entering in, choke the word, and
it becometh unfruitful. [20]And these are they which are sown on good ground; such as
hear the word, and receive it, and bring forth fruit, some thirtyfold, some sixty, and
some an hundred.

4:26–29

[26]And he said, So is the kingdom of God, as if a man should cast seed into the ground;
[27]And should sleep, and rise night and day, and the seed should spring and grow up, he
knoweth not how. [28]For the earth bringeth forth fruit of herself; first the blade, then
the ear, after that the full corn in the ear. [29]But when the fruit is brought forth, immediately he putteth in the sickle, because the harvest is come.

1 Corinthians 1:6 continued on next page

1 CORINTHIANS 1:6—Address (1:1–9), written from Ephesus (Acts 18:1–11), 51 CE

Theme	1 COR	Lk
(*Cont.*) **Living in Christ**	**1:6** **(above)** **3:6** **(above)** **3:9** **(above)** **9:7** **(above)** **9:11** **(above)**	**8:4–15** [4]And when much people were gathered together, and were come to him out of every city, he spake by a parable: [5]A sower went out to sow his seed: and as he sowed, some fell by the way side; and it was trodden down, and the fowls of the air devoured it. [6]And some fell upon a rock; and as soon as it was sprung up, it withered away, because it lacked moisture. [7]And some fell among thorns; and the thorns sprang up with it, and choked it. [8]And other fell on good ground, and sprang up, and bare fruit an hundredfold. And when he had said these things, he cried, He that hath ears to hear, let him hear. [9]And his disciples asked him, saying, What might this parable be? [10]And he said, Unto you it is given to know the mysteries of the kingdom of God: but to others in parables; that seeing they might not see, and hearing they might not understand. [11]Now the parable is this: The seed is the word of God. [12]Those by the way side are they that hear; then cometh the devil, and taketh away the word out of their hearts, lest they should believe and be saved. [13]They on the rock are they, which, when they hear, receive the word with joy; and these have no root, which for a while believe, and in time of temptation fall away. [14]And that which fell among thorns are they, which, when they have heard, go forth, and are choked with cares and riches and pleasures of this life, and bring no fruit to perfection. [15]But that on the good ground are they, which in an honest and good heart, having heard the word, keep it, and bring forth fruit with patience.

Paul	**Other**
2 Cor 4:4	**Q-Quelle**
[4]In whom the god of this world hath blinded the minds of them which believe not, lest the light of the glorious gospel of Christ, who is the image of God, should shine unto them. **2 Cor 9:10** [10]Now he that ministereth seed to the sower both minister bread for your food, and multiply your seed sown, and increase the fruits of your righteousness;) **Gal 5** [1]Stand fast therefore in the liberty wherewith Christ hath made us free, and be not entangled again with the yoke of bondage. [2]Behold, I Paul say unto you, that if ye be circumcised, Christ shall profit you nothing. [3]For I testify again to every man that is circumcised, that he is a debtor to do the whole law. [4]Christ is become of no effect unto you, whosoever of you are justified by the law; ye are fallen from grace. [5]For we through the Spirit wait for the hope of righteousness by faith. [6]For in Jesus Christ neither circumcision availeth any thing, nor uncircumcision; but faith which worketh by love. [7]Ye did run well; who did hinder you that ye should not obey the truth? [8]This persuasion cometh not of him that calleth you. [9]A little leaven leaveneth the whole lump. [10]I have confidence in you through the Lord, that ye will be none otherwise minded: but he that troubleth you shall bear his judgment, whosoever he be. [11]And I, brethren, if I yet preach circumcision, why do I yet suffer persecution? then is the offence of the cross ceased. [12]I would they were even cut off which trouble you. [13]For, brethren, ye have been called unto liberty; only use not liberty for an occasion to the flesh, but by love serve one another. [14]For all the law is fulfilled in one word, even in this; Thou shalt love thy neighbour as thyself. [15]But if ye bite and devour one another, take heed that ye be not consumed one of another. [16]This I say then, Walk in the Spirit, and ye shall not fulfil the lust of the flesh. [17]For the flesh lusteth against the Spirit, and the Spirit against the flesh: and these are contrary the one to the other: so that ye cannot do the things that ye would. [18]But if ye be led of the Spirit, ye are not under the law. [19]Now the works of the flesh are manifest, which are these; Adultery, fornication, uncleanness, lasciviousness, [20]Idolatry, witchcraft, hatred, variance, emulations, wrath, strife, seditions, heresies, [21]Envyings, murders, drunkenness, revellings, and such like: of the which I tell you before, as I have also told you in time past, that they which do such things shall not inherit the kingdom of God. [22]But the fruit of the Spirit is love, joy, peace, longsuffering, gentleness, goodness, faith, [23]Meekness, temperance: against such there is no law. [24]And they that are Christ's have crucified the flesh with the affections and lusts. [25]If we live in the Spirit, let us also walk in the Spirit. [26]Let us not be desirous of vain glory, provoking one another, envying one another. **Gal 6:7–8** [7]Be not deceived; God is not mocked: for whatsoever a man soweth, that shall he also reap. [8]For he that soweth to his flesh shall of the flesh reap corruption; but he that soweth to the Spirit shall of the Spirit reap life everlasting. **Col 1:6** [6]Which is come unto you, as it is in all the world; and bringeth forth fruit, as it doth also in you, since the day ye heard of it, and knew the grace of God in truth: **Col 1:10** [10]That ye might walk worthy of the Lord unto all pleasing, being fruitful in every good work, and increasing in the knowledge of God; **1 Thes 1:6** [6]And ye became followers of us, and of the Lord, having received the word in much affliction, with joy of the Holy Ghost: **1 Thes 2:13** [13]For this cause also thank we God without ceasing, because, when ye received the word of God which ye heard of us, ye received it not as the word of men, but as it is in truth, the word of God, which effectually worketh also in you that believe.	Thanks and blessings/ disciples: 1 Cor 1:6/ [Mt 11:25-27], 13:16-17/[Lk 10:21–24] (QS 24, 25)

1 CORINTHIANS 1:7—Address (1:1–9), written from Ephesus (Acts 18:1–11), 51 CE

Theme	1 COR	Paul	Other
Sonship	**1:7** [7]So that ye come behind in no gift; waiting for the coming of our Lord Jesus Christ:	**Tit 2:13 (Pseudo)** [13]Looking for that blessed hope, and the glorious appearing of the great God and our Saviour Jesus Christ;	**Q-Quelle** Watchful and Faithful: 1 Cor 1:7/Tit 2:13/[Mt 24:42-51]/[Lk 12:35-48 (QS 41 [Thom 21:3, 103], QS 42)]

1 CORINTHIANS 1:8—Address (1:1–9), written from Ephesus (Acts 18:1–11), 51 CE

Theme	1 COR	Paul
Sonship	**1:8** [8]Who shall also confirm you unto the end, that ye may be blameless in the day of our Lord Jesus Christ.	**Phil 1:6** [6]Being confident of this very thing, that he which hath begun a good work in you will perform it until the day of Jesus Christ:

1 CORINTHIANS 1:9—Address (1:1–9), written from Ephesus (Acts 18:1–11), 51 CE

Theme	1 COR	Mt	Lk	Jn	Other
Sonship	**1:9** [9]God is faithful, by whom ye were called unto the fellowship of his Son Jesus Christ our Lord. **15:28** [28]And when all things shall be subdued unto him, then shall the Son also himself be subject unto him that put all things under him, that God may be all in all.	**11:25–27** [25]At that time Jesus answered and said, I thank thee, O Father, Lord of heaven and earth, because thou hast hid these things from the wise and prudent, and hast revealed them unto babes. [26]Even so, Father: for so it seemed good in thy sight. [27]All things are delivered unto me of my Father: and no man knoweth the Son, but the Father; neither knoweth any man the Father, save the Son, and he to whomsoever the Son will reveal him	**10:21–22** [21]In that hour Jesus rejoiced in spirit, and said, I thank thee, O Father, Lord of heaven and earth, that thou hast hid these things from the wise and prudent, and hast revealed them unto babes: even so, Father; for so it seemed good in thy sight. [22]All things are delivered to me of my Father: and no man knoweth who the Son is, but the Father; and who the Father is, but the Son, and he to whom the Son will reveal him.	**1 Jn 1:3** [3]That which we have seen and heard declare we unto you, that ye also may have fellowship with us: and truly our fellowship is with the Father, and with his Son Jesus Christ.	**Q-Quelle** Thanks and blessings/ Disciples: 1 Cor 1:9/Mt 11:25-27, [Mt 13:16-17]/Lk 10:21-24 (QS 24, 25)

DISORDER IN COMMUNITY (1:10–6:20)

UNITY AND DISUNITY (1:10–4:21)

1 CORINTHIANS 1:10—Unity and disunity (1:10-4:21), written from Ephesus, 51 CE

Theme	1 COR	Paul
Sonship	**1:10** [10]Now I beseech you, brethren, by the name of our Lord Jesus Christ, that ye all speak the same thing, and that there be no divisions among you; but that ye be perfectly joined together in the same mind and in the same judgment.	**Phil 2:2** [2]Fulfil ye my joy, that ye be like-minded, having the same love, being of one accord, of one mind.

1 CORINTHIANS 1:11–12—Unity and disunity (1:10-4:21), written from Ephesus, 51 CE

Theme	1 COR	Mt	Paul
Unity	**1:11–12** [11]For it hath been declared unto me of you, my brethren, by them which are of the house of Chloe, that there are contentions among you. [12]Now this I say, that every one of you saith, I am of Paul; and I of Apollos; and I of Cephas; and I of Christ. [13]Is Christ divided? was Paul crucified for you? or were ye baptized in the name of Paul?	**16:16–20** [16]And Simon Peter answered and said, Thou art the Christ, the Son of the living God. [17]And Jesus answered and said unto him, Blessed art thou, Simon Barjona: for flesh and blood hath not revealed it unto thee, but my Father which is in heaven. [18]And I say also unto thee, That thou art Peter, and upon this rock I will build my church; and the gates of hell shall not prevail against it. [19]And I will give unto thee the keys of the kingdom of heaven: and whatsoever thou shalt bind on earth shall be bound in heaven: and whatsoever thou shalt loose on earth shall be loosed in heaven. [20]Then charged he his disciples that they should tell no man that he was Jesus the Christ.	**2 Cor 12:19** [19]Again, think ye that we excuse ourselves unto you? we speak before God in Christ: but we do all things, dearly beloved, for your edifying. **2 Cor 13:10** [10]Therefore I write these things being absent, lest being present I should use sharpness, according to the power which the Lord hath given me to edification, and not to destruction.

1 CORINTHIANS 1:12—Unity and disunity (1:10-4:21), written from Ephesus, 51 CE

Theme	1 COR	Lk
Sonship	**1:12** [12]Now this I say, that every one of you saith, I am of Paul; and I of Apollos; and I of Cephas; and I of Christ. **3:4** [4]For while one saith, I am of Paul; and another, I am of Apollos; are ye not carnal?. **3:22** [22]Whether Paul, or Apollos, or Cephas, or the world, or life, or death, or things present, or things to come; all are yours; **16:22** [22]If any man love not the Lord Jesus Christ, let him be anathema. Maranatha.	**Acts 18:24–28** [24]And a certain Jew named Apollos, born at Alexandria, an eloquent man, and mighty in the scriptures, came to Ephesus. [25]This man was instructed in the way of the Lord; and being fervent in the spirit, he spake and taught diligently the things of the Lord, knowing only the baptism of John. [26]And he began to speak boldly in the synagogue: whom when Aquila and Priscilla had heard, they took him unto them, and expounded unto him the way of God more perfectly. [27]And when he was disposed to pass into Achaia, the brethren wrote, exhorting the disciples to receive him: who, when he was come, helped them much which had believed through grace: [28]For he mightily convinced the Jews, and that publicly, showing by the scriptures that Jesus was Christ.

1 CORINTHIANS 1:14—Unity and disunity (1:10-4:21), written from Ephesus, 51 CE

Theme	1 COR	Lk	Paul
Sonship	**1:14** [14]I thank God that I baptized none of you, but Crispus and Gaius;	**Acts 18:8** [8]And Crispus, the chief ruler of the synagogue, believed on the Lord with all his house; and many of the Corinthians hearing believed, and were baptized.	**Rom 16:23** [23]Gaius mine host, and of the whole church, saluteth you. Erastus the chamberlain of the city saluteth you, and Quartus a brother.

1 CORINTHIANS 1:16—Unity and disunity (1:10-4:21), written from Ephesus, 51 CE

Theme	1 COR
Sonship	**1:16** [16]And I baptized also the household of Stephanas: besides, I know not whether I baptized any other. **16:15–17** [15]I beseech you, brethren, (ye know the house of Stephanas, that it is the firstfruits of Achaia, and that they have addicted themselves to the ministry of the saints,) [16]That ye submit yourselves unto such, and to every one that helpeth with us, and laboureth. [17]I am glad of the coming of Stephanas and Fortunatus and Achaicus: for that which was lacking on your part they have supplied.

1 CORINTHIANS 1:17—Unity and disunity (1:10-4:21), written from Ephesus, 51 CE

Theme	1 COR
Sonship	**1:17** [17]For Christ sent me not to baptize, but to preach the gospel: not with wisdom of words, lest the cross of Christ should be made of none effect. **2:1, 4** [1]And I, brethren, when I came to you, came not with excellency of speech or of wisdom, declaring unto you the testimony of God. . . . [4]And my speech and my preaching was not with enticing words of man's wisdom, but in demonstration of the Spirit and of power:

1 CORINTHIANS 1:18—Unity and disunity (1:10-4:21), written from Ephesus, 51 CE

Theme	1 COR	Paul
Sonship	**1:18** [18]For the preaching of the cross is to them that perish foolishness; but unto us which are saved it is the power of God. **2:14** [14]But the natural man receiveth not the things of the Spirit of God: for they are foolishness unto him: neither can he know them, because they are spiritually discerned.	**Rom 1:16** [16]For I am not ashamed of the gospel of Christ: for it is the power of God unto salvation to every one that believeth; to the Jew first, and also to the Greek.

1 CORINTHIANS 1:19—Unity and disunity (1:10-4:21), written from Ephesus, 51 CE

Theme	1 COR	Paul
Sonship	**1:19** [19]For it is written, I will destroy the wisdom of the wise, and will bring to nothing the understanding of the prudent.	**Phil 1:6** [6]Being confident of this very thing, that he which hath begun a good work in you will perform it until the day of Jesus Christ:

1 CORINTHIANS 1:20—Unity and disunity (1:10-4:21), written from Ephesus, 51 CE

Theme	1 COR	Jewish Writings
Sonship	**1:20** [20]Where is the wise? where is the scribe? where is the disputer of this world? hath not God made foolish the wisdom of this world?	**Is 29:14** [14]Therefore, behold, I will proceed to do a marvellous work among this people, even a marvellous work and a wonder: for the wisdom of their wise men shall perish, and the understanding of their prudent men shall be hid.

1 CORINTHIANS 1:22—Unity and disunity (1:10-4:21), written from Ephesus, 51 CE

Theme	1 COR	Mt	Lk	Other
Sonship	**1:22** [22]For the Jews require a sign, and the Greeks seek after wisdom:	**12:38** [28]But if I cast out devils by the Spirit of God, then the kingdom of God is come unto you. **16:1** [1]The Pharisees also with the Sadducees came, and tempting desired him that he would show them a sign from heaven.	**Acts 17:18–21** [18]Then certain philosophers of the Epicureans, and of the Stoicks, encountered him. And some said, What will this babbler say? other some, He seemeth to be a setter forth of strange gods: because he preached unto them Jesus, and the resurrection. [19]And they took him, and brought him unto Areopagus, saying, May we know what this new doctrine, whereof thou speakest, is? [20]For thou bringest certain strange things to our ears: we would know therefore what these things mean. [21](For all the Athenians and strangers which were there spent their time in nothing else, but either to tell, or to hear some new thing.)	**Q-Quelle** Sign of Jonah: 1 Cor 1:22/ Mt 12:38-42, Mt 16:1-4/ [Mk 8:11-12]/ [Lk 11:16, 11:29-32 (QS 32)]

1 CORINTHIANS 1:23—Unity and disunity (1:10-4:21), written from Ephesus, 51 CE

Theme	1 COR	Mt	Mk	Lk
Crucifixion: Christ's death fulfills redemption	**1:23** [23]But we preach Christ crucified, unto the Jews a stumblingblock, and unto the Greeks foolishness; **2:2** [2]For I determined not to know any thing among you, save Jesus Christ, and him crucified. **13:2** [2]And though I have the gift of prophecy, and understand all mysteries, and all knowledge; and though I have all faith, so that I could remove mountains, and have not charity, I am nothing. **13:7** [7]Beareth all things, believeth all things, hopeth all things, endureth all things. **13:10** [10]But when that which is perfect is come, then that which is in part shall be done away. **15:3** [3]For I delivered unto you first of all that which I also received, how that Christ died for our sins according to the scriptures;	**Mt 16:21** [21]From that time forth began Jesus to show unto his disciples, how that he must go unto Jerusalem, and suffer many things of the elders and chief priests and scribes, and be killed, and be raised again the third day.	**8:31** [31]And he began to teach them, that the Son of man must suffer many things, and be rejected of the elders, and of the chief priests, and scribes, and be killed, and after three days rise again.	**9:22** [22]Saying, The Son of man must suffer many things, and be rejected of the elders and chief priests and scribes, and be slain, and be raised the third day.

1 CORINTHIANS 1:27—Unity and disunity (1:10-4:21), written from Ephesus, 51 CE

Theme	1 COR	NT
Sonship	**1:27** [27]But God hath chosen the foolish things of the world to confound the wise; and God hath chosen the weak things of the world to confound the things which are mighty;	**Jas 2:5** [5]Hearken, my beloved brethren, Hath not God chosen the poor of this world rich in faith, and heirs of the kingdom which he hath promised to them that love him?

1 CORINTHIANS 1:29—Unity and disunity (1:10-4:21), written from Ephesus, 51 CE

Theme	1 COR	Paul
Grace above human endeavor	**1:29** [29]That no flesh should glory in his presence.	**Eph 2:9 (Pseudo)** [9]Not of works, lest any man should boast.

Paul	Other
Rom 3:21–26 [21]But now the righteousness of God without the law is manifested, being witnessed by the law and the prophets; [22]Even the righteousness of God which is by faith of Jesus Christ unto all and upon all them that believe: for there is no difference: [23]For all have sinned, and come short of the glory of God; [24]Being justified freely by his grace through the redemption that is in Christ Jesus: [25]Whom God hath set forth to be a propitiation through faith in his blood, to declare his righteousness for the remission of sins that are past, through the forbearance of God; [26]To declare, I say, at this time his righteousness: that he might be just, and the justifier of him which believeth in Jesus. **Gal 3:1** [1]O foolish Galatians, who hath bewitched you, that ye should not obey the truth, before whose eyes Jesus Christ hath been evidently set forth, crucified among you? **Gal 5:11** [11]And I, brethren, if I yet preach circumcision, why do I yet suffer persecution? then is the offence of the cross ceased. **Gal 6:14** [14]But God forbid that I should glory, save in the cross of our Lord Jesus Christ, by whom the world is crucified unto me, and I unto the world.	**Q-Quelle** Lost Sheep: 1 Cor 1:23/ Rom 3:21-26/ [Mt 18:12-14]/ [Lk 15:1-7] (QS 54 [Thom 107]); Precedence: 1 Cor 1:23/Gal 6:14/[Mt 19:28]/ [Mk 10:41-45]/ [Lk 22:28-30 (QS 62)]

1 CORINTHIANS 1:30—Unity and disunity (1:10-4:21), written from Ephesus, 51 CE

Theme	1 COR	Paul
Sonship	**1:30** [30]But of him are ye in Christ Jesus, who of God is made unto us wisdom, and righteousness, and sanctification, and redemption:	**Rom 3:24–26** [24]Being justified freely by his grace through the redemption that is in Christ Jesus: [25]Whom God hath set forth to be a propitiation through faith in his blood, to declare his righteousness for the remission of sins that are past, through the forbearance of God; [26]To declare, I say, at this time his righteousness: that he might be just, and the justifier of him which believeth in Jesus. **Rom 4:17** [17](As it is written, I have made thee a father of many nations,) before him whom he believed, even God, who quickeneth the dead, and calleth those things which be not as though they were. **Rom 6:11** [11]Likewise reckon ye also yourselves to be dead indeed unto sin, but alive unto God through Jesus Christ our Lord. **2 Cor 5:21** [21]For he hath made him to be sin for us, who knew no sin; that we might be made the righteousness of God in him. **Eph 1:7 (Pseudo)** [7]In whom we have redemption through his blood, the forgiveness of sins, according to the riches of his grace; **Col 1:14** [14]In whom we have redemption through his blood, even the forgiveness of sins: **1 Thes 5:23** [23]And the very God of peace sanctify you wholly; and I pray God your whole spirit and soul and body be preserved blameless unto the coming of our Lord Jesus Christ.

1 CORINTHIANS 1:31—Unity and disunity (1:10-4:21), written from Ephesus, 51 CE

Theme	1 COR	Paul	Jewish Writings
Glory in the Lord	**1:31** [31]That, according as it is written, He that glorieth, let him glory in the Lord.	**2 Cor 10:17** [17]But he that glorieth, let him glory in the Lord.	**Jer 9:23** [23]Thus saith the LORD, Let not the wise man glory in his wisdom, neither let the mighty man glory in his might, let not the rich man glory in his riches:

1 CORINTHIANS 2:1—Unity and disunity (1:10-4:21), written from Ephesus, 51 CE

Theme	1 COR
Testimony of God	**2:1** [1]And I, brethren, when I came to you, came not with excellency of speech or of wisdom, declaring unto you the testimony of God. **1:17** [17] For Christ sent me not to baptize, but to preach the gospel: not with wisdom of words, lest the cross of Christ should be made of none effect.

1 CORINTHIANS 2:2—Unity and disunity (1:10-4:21), written from Ephesus, 51 CE

Theme	1 COR	Paul	Other
Preach Christ crucified	**2:2** [2]For I determined not to know any thing among you, save Jesus Christ, and him crucified. **1:23** [23]But we preach Christ crucified, unto the Jews a stumbling-block, and unto the Greeks foolishness;	**Gal 6:14** [14]But God forbid that I should glory, save in the cross of our Lord Jesus Christ, by whom the world is crucified unto me, and I unto the world.	**Q-Quelle** Precedence: 1 Cor 2:2/ Gal 6:14/[Mt 19:28]/ [Mk 10:41-45]/[Lk 22:28-30] (QS 62)

1 CORINTHIANS 2:4—Unity and disunity (1:10-4:21), written from Ephesus, 51 CE

Theme	1 COR	Paul
Sonship	**2:4** [4]And my speech and my preaching was not with enticing words of man's wisdom, but in demonstration of the Spirit and of power: **4:20** [20]For the kingdom of God is not in word, but in power.	**Rom 15:19** [19]Through mighty signs and wonders, by the power of the Spirit of God; so that from Jerusalem, and round about unto Illyricum, I have fully preached the gospel of Christ. **1 Thes 1:5** [5]For our gospel came not unto you in word only, but also in power, and in the Holy Ghost, and in much assurance; as ye know what manner of men we were among you for your sake.

1 CORINTHIANS 2:5—Unity and disunity (1:10-4:21), written from Ephesus, 51 CE

Theme	1 COR	Paul
Faith comes from God	**2:5** [5]That your faith should not stand in the wisdom of men, but in the power of God.	**2 Cor 4:7** [7]But we have this treasure in earthen vessels, that the excellency of the power may be of God, and not of us.

1 CORINTHIANS 2:6—Unity and disunity (1:10-4:21), written from Ephesus, 51 CE

Theme	1 COR
Revealing the mysteries of Kingdom of God	**2:6** [6]Howbeit we speak wisdom among them that are perfect: yet not the wisdom of this world, nor of the princes of this world, that come to nought: **2:7** [7]But we speak the wisdom of God in a mystery, even the hidden wisdom, which God ordained before the world unto our glory: **2:10-11** [10]But God hath revealed them unto us by his Spirit: for the Spirit searcheth all things, yea, the deep things of God. [11]For what man knoweth the things of a man, save the spirit of man which is in him? even so the things of God knoweth no man, but the Spirit of God. **3:1** [1]And I, brethren, could not speak unto you as unto spiritual, but as unto carnal, even as unto babes in Christ. **4:1** [1]Let a man so account of us, as of the ministers of Christ, and stewards of the mysteries of God. **4:8** [8]Now ye are full, now ye are rich, ye have reigned as kings without us: and I would to God ye did reign, that we also might reign with you. **13:1–2** [1]Though I speak with the tongues of men and of angels, and have not charity, I am become as sounding brass, or a tinkling cymbal. [2]And though I have the gift of prophecy, and understand all mysteries, and all knowledge; and though I have all faith, so that I could remove mountains, and have not charity, I am nothing. **13:7** [7]Beareth all things, believeth all things, hopeth all things, endureth all things. **15:28** [28]And when all things shall be subdued unto him, then shall the Son also himself be subject unto him that put all things under him, that God may be all in all.

1 CORINTHIANS 2:8–9—Unity and disunity (1:10-4:21), written from Ephesus, 51 CE

Theme	1 COR	Jewish Writings
God's Provision	**2:8–9** [8]Which none of the princes of this world knew: for had they known it, they would not have crucified the Lord of glory. [9]But as it is written, Eye hath not seen, nor ear heard, neither have entered into the heart of man, the things which God hath prepared for them that love him.	**Is 64:3** [3]When thou didst terrible things which we looked not for, thou camest down, the mountains flowed down at thy presence.

1 CORINTHIANS 2:10—Unity and disunity (1:10-4:21), written from Ephesus, 51 CE

Theme	1 COR	Mt	Other
Spirit reveals	**2:10** [10]But God hath revealed them unto us by his Spirit: for the Spirit searcheth all things, yea, the deep things of God.	**11:25** [25]At that time Jesus answered and said, I thank thee, O Father, Lord of heaven and earth, because thou hast hid these things from the wise and prudent, and hast revealed them unto babes. **13:11** [11]He answered and said unto them, Because it is given unto you to know the mysteries of the kingdom of heaven, but to them it is not given. **16:17** [17]And Jesus answered and said unto him, Blessed art thou, Simon Barjona: for flesh and blood hath not revealed it unto thee, but my Father which is in heaven.	**Q-Quelle** Thanks and blessings/ disciples: 1 Cor 2:10/ Mt 11:25-27, [Mt 13:16-17]/ [Lk 10:21-24 (QS 24, 25)]

1 CORINTHIANS 2:16—Unity and disunity (1:10-4:21), written from Ephesus, 51 CE

Theme	1 COR	Paul	Jewish Writings
Mind of Christ	**2:16** [16]For who hath known the mind of the Lord, that he may instruct him? But we have the mind of Christ.	**Rom 11:34** [34]For who hath known the mind of the Lord? or who hath been his counsellor?	**Wis 9:13** [13]For what man is he that can know the counsel of God? or who can think what the will of the Lord is? **Is 40:13** [13]Who hath directed the Spirit of the LORD, or being his counsellor hath taught him?

1 CORINTHIANS 3:2—Unity and disunity (1:10-4:21), written from Ephesus, 51 CE

Theme	1 COR	NT
Young take milk	**3:2** [2]I have fed you with milk, and not with meat: for hitherto ye were not able to bear it, neither yet now are ye able.	**Heb 5:12–14** [12]For when for the time ye ought to be teachers, ye have need that one teach you again which be the first principles of the oracles of God; and are become such as have need of milk, and not of strong meat. [13]For every one that useth milk is unskilful in the word of righteousness: for he is a babe. [14]But strong meat belongeth to them that are of full age, even those who by reason of use have their senses exercised to discern both good and evil.

1 CORINTHIANS 3:3—Unity and disunity (1:10-4:21), written from Ephesus, 51 CE

Theme	1 COR	NT
Admonish carnal patterns	**3:3** [3]For ye are yet carnal: for whereas there is among you envying, and strife, and divisions, are ye not carnal, and walk as men?	**Jas 3:13–16** [13]Who is a wise man and endued with knowledge among you? let him show out of a good conversation his works with meekness of wisdom. [14]But if ye have bitter envying and strife in your hearts, glory not, and lie not against the truth. [15]This wisdom descendeth not from above, but is earthly, sensual, devilish. [16]For where envying and strife is, there is confusion and every evil work.

1 CORINTHIANS 3:4—Unity and disunity (1:10-4:21), written from Ephesus, 51 CE

Theme	1 COR
Being of Christ, not Paul or Apollos	**3:4** [4]For while one saith, I am of Paul; and another, I am of Apollos; are ye not carnal? **1:12** [12]Now this I say, that every one of you saith, I am of Paul; and I of Apollos; and I of Cephas; and I of Christ.

1 CORINTHIANS 3:6—Unity and disunity (1:10-4:21), written from Ephesus, 51 CE

Theme	1 COR	Lk
Paul planted, Apollos watered	**3:6** [6]I have planted, Apollos watered; but God gave the increase.	**Acts 18:1–11** [1]After these things Paul departed from Athens, and came to Corinth; [2]And found a certain Jew named Aquila, born in Pontus, lately come from Italy, with his wife Priscilla; (because that Claudius had commanded all Jews to depart from Rome:) and came unto them. [3]And because he was of the same craft, he abode with them, and wrought: for by their occupation they were tentmakers. [4]And he reasoned in the synagogue every sabbath, and persuaded the Jews and the Greeks. [5]And when Silas and Timotheus were come from Macedonia, Paul was pressed in the spirit, and testified to the Jews that Jesus was Christ. [6]And when they opposed themselves, and blasphemed, he shook his raiment, and said unto them, Your blood be upon your own heads; I am clean: from henceforth I will go unto the Gentiles. [7]And he departed thence, and entered into a certain man's house, named Justus, one that worshipped God, whose house joined hard to the synagogue. [8]And Crispus, the chief ruler of the synagogue, believed on the Lord with all his house; and many of the Corinthians hearing believed, and were baptized. [9]Then spake the Lord to Paul in the night by a vision, Be not afraid, but speak, and hold not thy peace: [10]For I am with thee, and no man shall set on thee to hurt thee: for I have much people in this city. [11]And he continued there a year and six months, teaching the word of God among them. **Acts 18:24–28** [24]And a certain Jew named Apollos, born at Alexandria, an eloquent man, and mighty in the scriptures, came to Ephesus. [25]This man was instructed in the way of the Lord; and being fervent in the spirit, he spake and taught diligently the things of the Lord, knowing only the baptism of John. [26]And he began to speak boldly in the synagogue: whom when Aquila and Priscilla had heard, they took him unto them, and expounded unto him the way of God more perfectly. [27]And when he was disposed to pass into Achaia, the brethren wrote, exhorting the disciples to receive him: who, when he was come, helped them much which had believed through grace: [28]For he mightily convinced the Jews, and that publicly, showing by the scriptures that Jesus was Christ.

1 CORINTHIANS 3:9–15—Unity and disunity (1:10-4:21), written from Ephesus, 51 CE

Theme	1 COR	Mt
Building the church: wise & foolish builders	**3:9–15** [9]For we are labourers together with God: ye are God's husbandry, ye are God's building. [10]According to the grace of God which is given unto me, as a wise masterbuilder, I have laid the foundation, and another buildeth thereon. But let every man take heed how he buildeth thereupon. [11]For other foundation can no man lay than that is laid, which is Jesus Christ. [12]Now if any man build upon this foundation gold, silver, precious stones, wood, hay, stubble; [13]Every man's work shall be made manifest: for the day shall declare it, because it shall be revealed by fire; and the fire shall try every man's work of what sort it is. [14]If any man's work abide which he hath built thereupon, he shall receive a reward. [15]If any man's work shall be burned, he shall suffer loss: but he himself shall be saved; yet so as by fire.	**7:24–27** [24]Therefore whosoever heareth these sayings of mine, and doeth them, I will liken him unto a wise man, which built his house upon a rock: [25]And the rain descended, and the floods came, and the winds blew, and beat upon that house; and it fell not: for it was founded upon a rock.

1 CORINTHIANS 3:9—Unity and disunity (1:10-4:21), written from Ephesus, 51 CE

Theme	1 COR	Paul
God's laborers	**3:9** [9]For we are labourers together with God: ye are God's husbandry, ye are God's building.	**Eph 2:20-22 (Pseudo)** [20]And are built upon the foundation of the apostles and prophets, Jesus Christ himself being the chief corner stone; [21]In whom all the building fitly framed together groweth unto an holy temple in the Lord: [22]In whom ye also are builded together for an habitation of God through the Spirit.

Lk	Other
6:48–49	**Q-Quelle**
[48]He is like a man which built an house, and digged deep, and laid the foundation on a rock: and when the flood arose, the stream beat vehemently upon that house, and could not shake it: for it was founded upon a rock. [49]But he that heareth, and doeth not, is like a man that without a foundation built an house upon the earth; against which the stream did beat vehemently, and immediately it fell; and the ruin of that house was great.	House of Rock: 1 Cor 3:9-15/ [2 Cor 10:8]/ Mt 7:21-27/Lk 6:46-49 (QS 14)

NT
1 Pet 2:5
[5]Ye also, as lively stones, are built up a spiritual house, an holy priesthood, to offer up spiritual sacrifices, acceptable to God by Jesus Christ.

1 CORINTHIANS 3:11—Unity and disunity (1:10-4:21), written from Ephesus, 51 CE

Theme	1 COR
Building the temple of Christ	**3:11** [11]For other foundation can no man lay than that is laid, which is Jesus Christ. **1:11** [11]For it hath been declared unto me of you, my brethren, by them which are of the house of Chloe, that there are contentions among you. **1:12–13** [12]Now this I say, that every one of you saith, I am of Paul; and I of Apollos; and I of Cephas; and I of Christ. [13]Is Christ divided? was Paul crucified for you? or were ye baptized in the name of Paul? **3:9–15** [9]For we are labourers together with God: ye are God's husbandry, ye are God's building. [10]According to the grace of God which is given unto me, as a wise masterbuilder, I have laid the foundation, and another buildeth thereon. But let every man take heed how he buildeth thereupon. [11]For other foundation can no man lay than that is laid, which is Jesus Christ. [12]Now if any man build upon this foundation gold, silver, precious stones, wood, hay, stubble; [13]Every man's work shall be made manifest: for the day shall declare it, because it shall be revealed by fire; and the fire shall try every man's work of what sort it is. [14]If any man's work abide which he hath built thereupon, he shall receive a reward. [15]If any man's work shall be burned, he shall suffer loss: but he himself shall be saved; yet so as by fire.

1 CORINTHIANS 3:13—Unity and disunity (1:10-4:21), written from Ephesus, 51 CE

Theme	1 COR	Mt
God knows everyone's work	**3:13** [13]Every man's work shall be made manifest: for the day shall declare it, because it shall be revealed by fire; and the fire shall try every man's work of what sort it is.	**3:11–12** [11]I indeed baptize you with water unto repentance: but he that cometh after me is mightier than I, whose shoes I am not worthy to bear: he shall baptize you with the Holy Ghost, and with fire: [12]Whose fan is in his hand, and he will thoroughly purge his floor, and gather his wheat into the garner; but he will burn up the chaff with unquenchable fire.

1 CORINTHIANS 3:16–17—Unity and disunity (1:10-4:21), written from Ephesus, 51 CE

Theme	1 COR	Mt	Mk
Temple of God: human & corporeal (variation supra)	**3:16–17** [16]Know ye not that ye are the temple of God, and that the Spirit of God dwelleth in you? [17]If any man defile the temple of God, him shall God destroy; for the temple of God is holy, which temple ye are **6:19** [19]What? know ye not that your body is the temple of the Holy Ghost which is in you, which ye have of God, and ye are not your own? **15:22** [22]For as in Adam all die, even so in Christ shall all be made alive.	**16:16–20** [16]And Simon Peter answered and said, Thou art the Christ, the Son of the living God. [17]And Jesus answered and said unto him, Blessed art thou, Simon Barjona: for flesh and blood hath not revealed it unto thee, but my Father which is in heaven. [18]And I say also unto thee, That thou art Peter, and upon this rock I will build my church; and the gates of hell shall not prevail against it. [19]And I will give unto thee the keys of the kingdom of heaven: and whatsoever thou shalt bind on earth shall be bound in heaven: and whatsoever thou shalt loose on earth shall be loosed in heaven. [20]Then charged he his disciples that they should tell no man that he was Jesus the Christ. **21:42** [42]Jesus saith unto them, Did ye never read in the scriptures, The stone which the builders rejected, the same is become the head of the corner: this is the Lord's doing, and it is marvellous in our eyes? **26:61** [61]And said, This fellow said, I am able to destroy the temple of God, and to build it in three days.	**12:10-11** [10]And have ye not read this scripture; The stone which the builders rejected is become the head of the corner: [11]This was the Lord's doing, and it is marvellous in our eyes? [12]And they sought to lay hold on him, but feared the people: for they knew that he had spoken the parable against them: and they left him, and went their way. **14:58** [58]We heard him say, I will destroy this temple that is made with hands, and within three days I will build another made without hands.

Mt	Mk	Lk	Paul
21:42	**12:10-11**	**20:17**	**Eph 2:18–22 (Pseudo)**
[42]Jesus saith unto them, Did ye never read in the scriptures, The stone which the builders rejected, the same is become the head of the corner: this is the Lord's doing, and it is marvellous in our eyes?	[10]And have ye not read this scripture; The stone which the builders rejected is become the head of the corner: [11]This was the Lord's doing, and it is marvellous in our eyes?	[17]And he beheld them, and said, What is this then that is written, The stone which the builders rejected, the same is become the head of the corner?	[18]For through him we both have access by one Spirit unto the Father. [19]Now therefore ye are no more strangers and foreigners, but fellow citizens with the saints, and of the household of God; [20]And are built upon the foundation of the apostles and prophets, Jesus Christ himself being the chief corner stone; [21]In whom all the building fitly framed together groweth unto an holy temple in the Lord: [22]In whom ye also are builded together for an habitation of God through the Spirit.

Paul	Other
2 Thes 1:7–10	**Q-Quelle**
[7]And to you who are troubled rest with us, when the Lord Jesus shall be revealed from heaven with his mighty angels, [8]In flaming fire taking vengeance on them that know not God, and that obey not the gospel of our Lord Jesus Christ: [9]Who shall be punished with everlasting destruction from the presence of the Lord, and from the glory of his power; [10]When he shall come to be glorified in his saints, and to be admired in all them that believe (because our testimony among you was believed) in that day.	Preaching of John: 1 Cor 3:13/[Mt 3:7-10], Mt 3:11-12/ [Mk 1:7-8]/ [Lk 3:7-9, 15-18 (QS5)]

Lk	Jn	Paul
20:17	**2:19**	**2 Cor 5:1**
[17]And he beheld them, and said, What is this then that is written, The stone which the builders rejected, the same is become the head of the corner?	[19]And when he had gone a little further thence, he saw James the son of Zebedee, and John his brother, who also were in the ship mending their nets.	[1]For we know that if our earthly house of this tabernacle were dissolved, we have a building of God, an house not made with hands, eternal in the heavens. **2 Cor 6:14–17** [14]Be ye not unequally yoked together with unbelievers: for what fellowship hath righteousness with unrighteousness? and what communion hath light with darkness? [15]And what concord hath Christ with Belial? or what part hath he that believeth with an infidel? [16]And what agreement hath the temple of God with idols? for ye are the temple of the living God; as God hath said, I will dwell in them, and walk in them; and I will be their God, and they shall be my people. [17]Wherefore come out from among them, and be ye separate, saith the Lord, and touch not the unclean thing; and I will receive you, **Eph 2:18–22 (Pseudo)** [18]For through him we both have access by one Spirit unto the Father. [19]Now therefore ye are no more strangers and foreigners, but fellowcitizens with the saints, and of the household of God; [20]And are built upon the foundation of the apostles and prophets, Jesus Christ himself being the chief corner stone; [21]In whom all the building fitly framed together groweth unto an holy temple in the Lord: [22]In whom ye also are builded together for an habitation of God through the Spirit.

1 CORINTHIANS 3:16–17—Unity and disunity (1:10-4:21), written from Ephesus, 51 CE

Theme	1 COR	Jewish Writings
(*Cont.*) Temple: human body is for Holy Spirit (variation supra)	3:16–17 (above) 6:19 (above) 15:22 (above)	**2 Sam 7** [1]And it came to pass, when the king sat in his house, and the LORD had given him rest round about from all his enemies; [2]That the king said unto Nathan the prophet, See now, I dwell in an house of cedar, but the ark of God dwelleth within curtains. [3]And Nathan said to the king, Go, do all that is in thine heart; for the LORD is with thee. [4]And it came to pass that night, that the word of the LORD came unto Nathan, saying, [5]Go and tell my servant David, Thus saith the LORD, Shalt thou build me an house for me to dwell in? [6]Whereas I have not dwelt in any house since the time that I brought up the children of Israel out of Egypt, even to this day, but have walked in a tent and in a tabernacle. [7]In all the places wherein I have walked with all the children of Israel spake I a word with any of the tribes of Israel, whom I commanded to feed my people Israel, saying, Why build ye not me an house of cedar? [8]Now therefore so shalt thou say unto my servant David, Thus saith the LORD of hosts, I took thee from the sheepcote, from following the sheep, to be ruler over my people, over Israel: [9]And I was with thee whithersoever thou wentest, and have cut off all thine enemies out of thy sight, and have made thee a great name, like unto the name of the great men that are in the earth. [10]Moreover I will appoint a place for my people Israel, and will plant them, that they may dwell in a place of their own, and move no more; neither shall the children of wickedness afflict them any more, as beforetime, [11]And as since the time that I commanded judges to be over my people Israel, and have caused thee to rest from all thine enemies. Also the LORD telleth thee that he will make thee an house. [12]And when thy days be fulfilled, and thou shalt sleep with thy fathers, I will set up thy seed after thee, which shall proceed out of thy bowels, and I will establish his kingdom. [13]He shall build an house for my name, and I will stablish the throne of his kingdom for ever. [14]I will be his father, and he shall be my son. If he commit iniquity, I will chasten him with the rod of men, and with the stripes of the children of men: [15]But my mercy shall not depart away from him, as I took it from Saul, whom I put away before thee. [16]And thine house and thy kingdom shall be established for ever before thee: thy throne shall be established for ever. [17]According to all these words, and according to all this vision, so did Nathan speak unto David. [18]Then went king David in, and sat before the LORD, and he said, Who am I, O Lord GOD? and what is my house, that thou hast brought me hitherto? [19]And this was yet a small thing in thy sight, O Lord GOD; but thou hast spoken also of thy servant's house for a great while to come. And is this the manner of man, O Lord GOD? [20]And what can David say more unto thee? for thou, Lord GOD, knowest thy servant. [21]For thy word's sake, and according to thine own heart, hast thou done all these great things, to make thy servant know them. [22]Wherefore thou art great, O LORD God: for there is none like thee, neither is there any God beside thee, according to all that we have heard with our ears. [23]And what one nation in the earth is like thy people, even like Israel, whom God went to redeem for a people to himself, and to make him a name, and to do for you great things and terrible, for thy land, before thy people, which thou redeemedst to thee from Egypt, from the nations and their gods? [24]For thou hast confirmed to thyself thy people Israel to be a people unto thee for ever: and thou, LORD, art become their God. [25]And now, O LORD God, the word that thou hast spoken concerning thy servant, and concerning his house, establish it for ever, and do as thou hast said. [26]And let thy name be magnified for ever, saying, The LORD of hosts is the God over Israel: and let the house of thy servant David be established before thee. [27]For thou, O LORD of hosts, God of Israel, hast revealed to thy servant, saying, I will build thee an house: therefore hath thy servant found in his heart to pray this prayer unto thee. [28]And now, O Lord GOD, thou art that God, and thy words be true, and thou hast promised this goodness unto thy servant: [29]Therefore now let it please thee to bless the house of thy servant, that it may continue for ever before thee: for thou, O Lord GOD, hast spoken it: and with thy blessing let the house of thy servant be blessed for ever.

1 CORINTHIANS 3:16—Unity and disunity (1:10-4:21), written from Ephesus, 51 CE

Theme	1 COR	Mt	Mk
Inheriting God's Kingdom	**3:16** [16]Know ye not that ye are the temple of God, and that the Spirit of God dwelleth in you? **5:6** [6]Your glorying is not good. Know ye not that a little leaven leaveneth the whole lump? **6:9** [9]Know ye not that the unrighteous shall not inherit the kingdom of God? Be not deceived: neither fornicators, nor idolaters, nor adulterers, nor effeminate, nor abusers of themselves with mankind. **6:15–16** [15]Know ye not that your bodies are the members of Christ? shall I then take the members of Christ, and make them the members of an harlot? God forbid. [16]What? know ye not that he which is joined to an harlot is one body? for two, saith he, shall be one flesh. **6:19** [19]What? know ye not that your body is the temple of the Holy Ghost which is in you, which ye have of God, and ye are not your own? **12:1–13** [1]Now concerning spiritual gifts, brethren, I would not have you ignorant. [2]Ye know that ye were Gentiles, carried away unto these dumb idols, even as ye were led. [3]Wherefore I give you to understand, that no man speaking by the Spirit of God calleth Jesus accursed: and that no man can say that Jesus is the Lord, but by the Holy Ghost. [4]Now there are diversities of gifts, but the same Spirit. [5]And there are differences of administrations, but the same Lord. [6]And there are diversities of operations, but it is the same God which worketh all in all. [7]But the manifestation of the Spirit is given to every man to profit withal. [8]For to one is given by the Spirit the word of wisdom; to another the word of knowledge by the same Spirit; [9]To another faith by the same Spirit; to another the gifts of healing by the same Spirit; [10]To another the working of miracles; to another prophecy; to another discerning of spirits; to another divers kinds of tongues; to another the interpretation of tongues: [11]But all these worketh that one and the selfsame Spirit, dividing to every man severally as he will. [12]For as the body is one, and hath many members, and all the members of that one body, being many, are one body: so also is Christ. [13]For by one Spirit are we all baptized into one body, whether we be Jews or Gentiles, whether we be bond or free; and have been all made to drink into one Spirit.	**5:29** [29]And if thy right eye offend thee, pluck it out, and cast it from thee: for it is profitable for thee that one of thy members should perish, and not that thy whole body should be cast into hell. **10:20** [20]For it is not ye that speak, but the Spirit of your Father which speaketh in you. **13:33** [33]Another parable spake he unto them; The kingdom of heaven is like unto leaven, which a woman took, and hid in three measures of meal, till the whole was leavened. **16:6–12** [6]Then Jesus said unto them, Take heed and beware of the leaven of the Pharisees and of the Sadducees. [7]And they reasoned among themselves, saying, It is because we have taken no bread. [8]Which when Jesus perceived, he said unto them, O ye of little faith, why reason ye among yourselves, because ye have brought no bread? [9]Do ye not yet understand, neither remember the five loaves of the five thousand, and how many baskets ye took up? [10]Neither the seven loaves of the four thousand, and how many baskets ye took up? [11]How is it that ye do not understand that I spake it not to you concerning bread, that ye should beware of the leaven of the Pharisees and of the Sadducees? [12]Then understood they how that he bade them not beware of the leaven of bread, but of the doctrine of the Pharisees and of the Sadducees. **19:5** [5]And said, For this cause shall a man leave father and mother, and shall cleave to his wife: and they twain shall be one flesh? **19:28** [28]And Jesus said unto them, Verily I say unto you, That ye which have followed me, in the regeneration when the Son of man shall sit in the throne of his glory, ye also shall sit upon twelve thrones, judging the twelve tribes of Israel. **24:43–44** [43]But know this, that if the goodman of the house had known in what watch the thief would come, he would have watched, and would not have suffered his house to be broken up. [44]Therefore be ye also ready: for in such an hour as ye think not the Son of man cometh.	**7:21–22** [21]For from within, out of the heart of men, proceed evil thoughts, adulteries, fornications, murders, [22]Thefts, covetousness, wickedness, deceit, lasciviousness, an evil eye, blasphemy, pride, foolishness: **8:15** [15]And he charged them, saying, Take heed, beware of the leaven of the Pharisees, and of the leaven of Herod. **13:9–13** [9]But take heed to yourselves: for they shall deliver you up to councils; and in the synagogues ye shall be beaten: and ye shall be brought before rulers and kings for my sake, for a testimony against them. **[10]And the gospel must first be published among all nations. [11]But when they shall lead you, and deliver you up, take no thought beforehand what ye shall speak, neither do ye premeditate: but whatsoever shall be given you in that hour, that speak ye: for it is not ye that speak, but the Holy Ghost.** [12]Now the brother shall betray the brother to death, and the father the son; and children shall rise up against their parents, and shall cause them to be put to death. [13]And ye shall be hated of all men for my name's sake: but he that shall endure unto the end, the same shall be saved. **14:58** [58]We heard him say, I will destroy this temple that is made with hands, and within three days I will build another made without hands.

1 CORINTHIANS 3:16—Unity and disunity (1:10-4:21), written from Ephesus, 51 CE

Theme	1 COR	Lk	Paul
(*Cont.*) **Inheriting God's Kingdom**	**3:16 (above)** **5:6 (above)** **6:9 (above)** **6:15–16 (above)** **6:19 (above)** **12:1–13 (above)**	**12:1** [1]In the mean time, when there were gathered together an innumerable multitude of people, insomuch that they trode one upon another, he began to say unto his disciples first of all, Beware ye of the leaven of the Pharisees, which is hypocrisy. **12:12** [12]For the Holy Ghost shall teach you in the same hour what ye ought to say. **13:21** [21]It is like leaven, which a woman took and hid in three measures of meal, till the whole was leavened.	**Rom 8:23** [23]And not only they, but ourselves also, which have the firstfruits of the Spirit, even we ourselves groan within ourselves, waiting for the adoption, to wit, the redemption of our body. **2 Cor 1:22** [22]Who hath also sealed us, and given the earnest of the Spirit in our hearts. **2 Cor 3:18** [18]But we all, with open face beholding as in a glass the glory of the Lord, are changed into the same image from glory to glory, even as by the Spirit of the Lord. **2 Cor 5:15** [15]And that he died for all, that they which live should not henceforth live unto themselves, but unto him which died for them, and rose again. **2 Cor 6:16** [16]And what agreement hath the temple of God with idols? for ye are the temple of the living God; as God hath said, I will dwell in them, and walk in them; and I will be their God, and they shall be my people. **Gal 5:22** [22]But the fruit of the Spirit is love, joy, peace, longsuffering, gentleness, goodness, faith, **Eph 1:14 (Pseudo)** [15]And that he died for all, that they which live should not henceforth live unto themselves, but unto him which died for them, and rose again. **Eph 2:20-22 (Pseudo)** [20]And are built upon the foundation of the apostles and prophets, Jesus Christ himself being the chief corner stone; [21]In whom all the building fitly framed together groweth unto an holy temple in the Lord: [22]In whom ye also are builded together for an habitation of God through the Spirit. **1 Thes 1:5** [5]For our gospel came not unto you in word only, but also in power, and in the Holy Ghost, and in much assurance; as ye know what manner of men we were among you for your sake. **1 Thes 3:3–4** [3]That no man should be moved by these afflictions: for yourselves know that we are appointed thereunto. [4]For verily, when we were with you, we told you before that we should suffer tribulation; even as it came to pass, and ye know. **1 Thes 4:2** [2]For ye know what commandments we gave you by the Lord Jesus. **1 Thes 5:2** [2]For yourselves know perfectly that the day of the Lord so cometh as a thief in the night. **1 Thes 5:19** [19]Quench not the Spirit. **2 Thes 2:6** [6]And now ye know what withholdeth that he might be revealed in his time.

Jewish Writings	Other
Jer 31:31–34	**Q-Quelle**
[31]Behold, the days come, saith the LORD, that I will make a new covenant with the house of Israel, and with the house of Judah: [32]Not according to the covenant that I made with their fathers in the day that I took them by the hand to bring them out of the land of Egypt; which my covenant they brake, although I was an husband unto them, saith the LORD: [33]But this shall be the covenant that I will make with the house of Israel; After those days, saith the LORD, I will put my law in their inward parts, and write it in their hearts; and will be their God, and they shall be my people. [34]And they shall teach no more every man his neighbour, and every man his brother, saying, Know the LORD: for they shall all know me, from the least of them unto the greatest of them, saith the LORD: for I will forgive their iniquity, and I will remember their sin no more.	Leaven: 1 Cor 3:16/[Mt 13:33]/Lk 13:20-21(QS 46 [Thom 20, 96]), Lk 12:11-12(QS 37 [Thom 44]); Precedence: 1 Cor 3:16/Mt 19:28/[Mk 10:41-45]/[Lk 22:28-30 (QS 62); Assistance of the HS: 1 Cor 3:16/2 Cor 1:22/Eph 1:14/1 Thes 1:5/[Mt 10:19-20]/ [Mk 13:11]/Lk 12:11-12 (QS 37 [Thom 44]), [Lk 21:14-15]

1 CORINTHIANS 3:18—Unity and disunity (1:10-4:21), written from Ephesus, 51 CE

Theme	1 COR	Paul	Jewish Writings
Be not wise to world	**3:18** [18]Let no man deceive himself. If any man among you seemeth to be wise in this world, let him become a fool, that he may be wise. **8:2** [2]And if any man think that he knoweth any thing, he knoweth nothing yet as he ought to know.	**Gal 6:3** [3]For if a man think himself to be something, when he is nothing, he deceiveth himself.	**Is 5:21** [21]Woe unto them that are wise in their own eyes, and prudent in their own sight!

1 CORINTHIANS 3:19—Unity and disunity (1:10-4:21), written from Ephesus, 51 CE

Theme	1 COR	Jewish Writings
Worldly foolishness	**3:19** [19]For the wisdom of this world is foolishness with God. For it is written, He taketh the wise in their own craftiness. **1:20** [20]Where is the wise? where is the scribe? where is the disputer of this world? hath not God made foolish the wisdom of this world?	**Job 5:13** [13]He taketh the wise in their own craftiness: and the counsel of the froward is carried headlong.

1 CORINTHIANS 3:20—Unity and disunity (1:10-4:21), written from Ephesus, 51 CE

Theme	1 COR	Jewish Writings
God knows thoughts	**3:20** [20]And again, The Lord knoweth the thoughts of the wise, that they are vain.	**Ps 94:11** [11]The LORD knoweth the thoughts of man, that they are vanity.

1 CORINTHIANS 3:21—Unity and disunity (1:10-4:21), written from Ephesus, 51 CE

Theme	1 COR	Paul
Avoid self praise	**3:21** [21]Therefore let no man glory in men. For all things are yours; **4:6** [6]And these things, brethren, I have in a figure transferred to myself and to Apollos for your sakes; that ye might learn in us not to think of men above that which is written, that no one of you be puffed up for one against another.	**Rom 8:32** [32]He that spared not his own Son, but delivered him up for us all, how shall he not with him also freely give us all things?

1 CORINTHIANS 4:1–5—Unity and disunity (1:10-4:21), written from Ephesus, 51 CE

Theme	1 COR
Ministers judged by God	**4:1–5** [1]Let a man so account of us, as of the ministers of Christ, and stewards of the mysteries of God. [2]Moreover it is required in stewards, that a man be found faithful. [3]But with me it is a very small thing that I should be judged of you, or of man's judgment: yea, I judge not mine own self. [4]For I know nothing by myself; yet am I not hereby justified: but he that judgeth me is the Lord. [5]Therefore judge nothing before the time, until the Lord come, who both will bring to light the hidden things of darkness, and will make manifest the counsels of the hearts: and then shall every man have praise of God. **3:12–15** [12]Now if any man build upon this foundation gold, silver, precious stones, wood, hay, stubble; [13]Every man's work shall be made manifest: for the day shall declare it, because it shall be revealed by fire; and the fire shall try every man's work of what sort it is. [14]If any man's work abide which he hath built thereupon, he shall receive a reward. [15]If any man's work shall be burned, he shall suffer loss: but he himself shall be saved; yet so as by fire. **15:24–28** [24]Then cometh the end, when he shall have delivered up the kingdom to God, even the Father; when he shall have put down all rule and all authority and power. **[25]For he must reign, till he hath put all enemies under his feet. [26]The last enemy that shall be destroyed is death. [27]For he hath put all things under his feet. But when he saith all things are put under him, it is manifest that he is excepted, which did put all things under him. [28]And when all things shall be subdued unto him, then shall the Son also himself be subject unto him that put all things under him, that God may be all in all.**

Mt

7:21–27

21 Not every one that saith unto me, Lord, Lord, shall enter into the kingdom of heaven; but he that doeth the will of my Father which is in heaven. 22 Many will say to me in that day, Lord, Lord, have we not prophesied in thy name? and in thy name have cast out devils? and in thy name done many wonderful works? 23 And then will I profess unto them, I never knew you: depart from me, ye that work iniquity. 24 Therefore whosoever heareth these sayings of mine, and doeth them, I will liken him unto a wise man, which built his house upon a rock: 25 And the rain descended, and the floods came, and the winds blew, and beat upon that house; and it fell not: for it was founded upon a rock. 26 And every one that heareth these sayings of mine, and doeth them not, shall be likened unto a foolish man, which built his house upon the sand: 27 And the rain descended, and the floods came, and the winds blew, and beat upon that house; and it fell: and great was the fall of it.

13:24–30

24 Another parable put he forth unto them, saying, The kingdom of heaven is likened unto a man which sowed good seed in his field: 25 But while men slept, his enemy came and sowed tares among the wheat, and went his way. 26 But when the blade was sprung up, and brought forth fruit, then appeared the tares also. 27 So the servants of the householder came and said unto him, Sir, didst not thou sow good seed in thy field? from whence then hath it tares? 28 He said unto them, An enemy hath done this. The servants said unto him, Wilt thou then that we go and gather them up? 29 But he said, Nay; lest while ye gather up the tares, ye root up also the wheat with them. 30 Let both grow together until the harvest: and in the time of harvest I will say to the reapers, Gather ye together first the tares, and bind them in bundles to burn them: but gather the wheat into my barn.

13:47–50

47 Again, the kingdom of heaven is like unto a net, that was cast into the sea, and gathered of every kind: 48 Which, when it was full, they drew to shore, and sat down, and gathered the good into vessels, but cast the bad away. 49 So shall it be at the end of the world: the angels shall come forth, and sever the wicked from among the just, 50 And shall cast them into the furnace of fire: there shall be wailing and gnashing of teeth.

24:37–39

37 But as the days of Noe were, so shall also the coming of the Son of man be. 38 For as in the days that were before the flood they were eating and drinking, marrying and giving in marriage, until the day that Noe entered into the ark, 39 And knew not until the flood came, and took them all away; so shall also the coming of the Son of man be.

25:31–46

31 When the Son of man shall come in his glory, and all the holy angels with him, then shall he sit upon the throne of his glory: 32 And before him shall be gathered all nations: and he shall separate them one from another, as a shepherd divideth his sheep from the goats: 33 And he shall set the sheep on his right hand, but the goats on the left. 34 Then shall the King say unto them on his right hand, Come, ye blessed of my Father, inherit the kingdom prepared for you from the foundation of the world: 35 For I was an hungered, and ye gave me meat: I was thirsty, and ye gave me drink: I was a stranger, and ye took me in: 36 Naked, and ye clothed me: I was sick, and ye visited me: I was in prison, and ye came unto me. 37 Then shall the righteous answer him, saying, Lord, when saw we thee an hungered, and fed thee? or thirsty, and gave thee drink? 38 When saw we thee a stranger, and took thee in? or naked, and clothed thee? 39 Or when saw we thee sick, or in prison, and came unto thee? 40 And the King shall answer and say unto them, Verily I say unto you, Inasmuch as ye have done it unto one of the least of these my brethren, ye have done it unto me. 41 Then shall he say also unto them on the left hand, Depart from me, ye cursed, into everlasting fire, prepared for the devil and his angels: 42 For I was an hungered, and ye gave me no meat: I was thirsty, and ye gave me no drink: 43 I was a stranger, and ye took me not in: naked, and ye clothed me not: sick, and in prison, and ye visited me not. 44 Then shall they also answer him, saying, Lord, when saw we thee an hungered, or athirst, or a stranger, or naked, or sick, or in prison, and did not minister unto thee? 45 Then shall he answer them, saying, Verily I say unto you, Inasmuch as ye did it not to one of the least of these, ye did it not to me. 46 And these shall go away into everlasting punishment: but the righteous into life eternal.

1 CORINTHIANS 4:1–5—Unity and disunity (1:10–4:21), written from Ephesus, 51 CE

Theme	1 COR	Mark	Lk
(*Cont.*) **Ministers judged by God**	**4:1–5 (above)** **3:12–15 (above)** **15:24–28 (above)**	**9:42–48** [42]And whosoever shall offend one of these little ones that believe in me, it is better for him that a millstone were hanged about his neck, and he were cast into the sea. [43]And if thy hand offend thee, cut it off: it is better for thee to enter into life maimed, than having two hands to go into hell, into the fire that never shall be quenched: [44]Where their worm dieth not, and the fire is not quenched. [45]And if thy foot offend thee, cut it off: it is better for thee to enter halt into life, than having two feet to be cast into hell, into the fire that never shall be quenched: [46]Where their worm dieth not, and the fire is not quenched. [47]And if thine eye offend thee, pluck it out: it is better for thee to enter into the kingdom of God with one eye, than having two eyes to be cast into hell fire: [48]Where their worm dieth not, and the fire is not quenched.	**6:46–49** [46]And why call ye me, Lord, Lord, and do not the things which I say? **[47]Whosoever cometh to me, and heareth my sayings, and doeth them, I will show you to whom he is like: [48]He is like a man which built an house, and digged deep, and laid the foundation on a rock: and when the flood arose, the stream beat vehemently upon that house, and could not shake it: for it was founded upon a rock. [49]But he that heareth, and doeth not, is like a man that without a foundation built an house upon the earth; against which the stream did beat vehemently, and immediately it fell; and the ruin of that house was great** **13:25–27** [25]When once the master of the house is risen up, and hath shut to the door, and ye begin to stand without, and to knock at the door, saying, Lord, Lord, open unto us; and he shall answer and say unto you, I know you not whence ye are: [26]Then shall ye begin to say, We have eaten and drunk in thy presence, and thou hast taught in our streets. [27]But he shall say, I tell you, I know you not whence ye are; depart from me, all ye workers of iniquity. **16:19–31** [19]There was a certain rich man, which was clothed in purple and fine linen, and fared sumptuously every day: [20]And there was a certain beggar named Lazarus, which was laid at his gate, full of sores, [21]And desiring to be fed with the crumbs which fell from the rich man's table: moreover the dogs came and licked his sores. [22]And it came to pass, that the beggar died, and was carried by the angels into Abraham's bosom: the rich man also died, and was buried; [23]And in hell he lift up his eyes, being in torments, and seeth Abraham afar off, and Lazarus in his bosom. [24]And he cried and said, Father Abraham, have mercy on me, and send Lazarus, that he may dip the tip of his finger in water, and cool my tongue; for I am tormented in this flame. [25]But Abraham said, Son, remember that thou in thy lifetime receivedst thy good things, and likewise Lazarus evil things: but now he is comforted, and thou art tormented. [26]And beside all this, between us and you there is a great gulf fixed: so that they which would pass from hence to you cannot; neither can they pass to us, that would come from thence. [27]Then he said, I pray thee therefore, father, that thou wouldest send him to my father's house: [28]For I have five brethren; that he may testify unto them, lest they also come into this place of torment. [29]Abraham saith unto him, They have Moses and the prophets; let them hear them. [30]And he said, Nay, father Abraham: but if one went unto them from the dead, they will repent. [31]And he said unto him, If they hear not Moses and the prophets, neither will they be persuaded, though one rose from the dead. **17:22–37** [22]And he said unto the disciples, The days will come, when ye shall desire to see one of the days of the Son of man, and ye shall not see it. [23]And they shall say to you, See here; or, see there: go not after them, nor follow them. [24]For as the lightning, that lighteneth out of the one part under heaven, shineth unto the other part under heaven; so shall also the Son of man be in his day. [25]But first must he suffer many things, and be rejected of this generation. [26]And as it was in the days of Noe, so shall it be also in the days of the Son of man. [27]They did eat, they drank, they married wives, they were given in marriage, until the day that Noe entered into the ark, and the flood came, and destroyed them all. [28]Likewise also as it was in the days of Lot; they did eat, they drank, they bought, they sold, they planted, they builded; [29]But the same day that Lot went out of Sodom it rained fire and brimstone from heaven, and destroyed them all. [30]Even thus shall it be in the day when the Son of man is revealed. [31]In that day, he which shall be upon the housetop, and his stuff in the house, let him not come down to take it away: and he that is in the field, let him likewise not return back. [32]Remember Lot's wife. [33]Whosoever shall seek to save his life shall lose it; and whosoever shall lose his life shall preserve it. [34]I tell you, in that night there shall be two men in one bed; the one shall be taken, and the other shall be left. [35]Two women shall be grinding together; the one shall be taken, and the other left. [36]Two men shall be in the field; the one shall be taken, and the other left. [37]And they answered and said unto him, Where, Lord? And he said unto them, Wheresoever the body is, thither will the eagles be gathered together.

Paul	Other
Rom 2:6 [6]Who will render to every man according to his deeds: **Rom 8:21** [21]Because the creature itself also shall be delivered from the bondage of corruption into the glorious liberty of the children of God. **2 Cor 5 :10** [10]For we must all appear before the judgment seat of Christ; that every one may receive the things done in his body, according to that he hath done, whether it be good or bad. **Eph 1:10 (Pseudo)** [10]That in the dispensation of the fulness of times he might gather together in one all things in Christ, both which are in heaven, and which are on earth; even in him: **Col 1:16–20** [16]For by him were all things created, that are in heaven, and that are in earth, visible and invisible, whether they be thrones, or dominions, or principalities, or powers: all things were created by him, and for him: [17]And he is before all things, and by him all things consist. [18]And he is the head of the body, the church: who is the beginning, the firstborn from the dead; that in all things he might have the preeminence. [19]For it pleased the Father that in him should all fulness dwell; [20]And, having made peace through the blood of his cross, by him to reconcile all things unto himself; by him, I say, whether they be things in earth, or things in heaven. **1 Thes 5:1–11** [1]But of the times and the seasons, brethren, ye have no need that I write unto you. [2]For yourselves know perfectly that the day of the Lord so cometh as a thief in the night. [3]For when they shall say, Peace and safety; then sudden destruction cometh upon them, as travail upon a woman with child; and they shall not escape. [4]But ye, brethren, are not in darkness, that that day should overtake you as a thief. [5]Ye are all the children of light, and the children of the day: we are not of the night, nor of darkness. [6]Therefore let us not sleep, as do others; but let us watch and be sober. [7]For they that sleep sleep in the night; and they that be drunken are drunken in the night. [8]But let us, who are of the day, be sober, putting on the breastplate of faith and love; and for an helmet, the hope of salvation. [9]For God hath not appointed us to wrath, but to obtain salvation by our Lord Jesus Christ, [10]Who died for us, that, whether we wake or sleep, we should live together with him. [11]Wherefore comfort yourselves together, and edify one another, even as also ye do.	**Q-Quelle** Exclusion from Kingdom of God: 1 Cor 4:1-5/[Mt 7:13-14], Mt 7:22-23, [Mt 8:11-12, 19:30]/Lk 13:22-30 (QS 47, 48); House on rock: 1 Cor 4:1-5/1 Thes 5:1-11/ Mt 7:21-27/Lk 6:46-49(QS 14); Day of SOM: 1 Cor 4:1-5/[Mt 10:39, 24:17-18, 24:23, 24:26-27], Mt 24:37-39, [Mt 24:40-41, 24:28]/[Mk 13:19-23, 13:14-16]/ Lk 17:22-37 (QS 60 [Thom 3, 51, 61, 113])

1 CORINTHIANS 4:1—Unity and disunity (1:10-4:21), written from Ephesus, 51 CE

Theme	1 COR	Paul	NT	Other
Ministers of Christ	**4:1** [1]Let a man so account of us, as of the ministers of Christ, and stewards of the mysteries of God.	**Tit 1:7 (Pseudo)** [7]For a bishop must be blameless, as the steward of God; not self-willed, not soon angry, not given to wine, no striker, not given to filthy lucre;	**1 Pet 4:10** [10]As every man hath received the gift, even so minister the same one to another, as good stewards of the manifold grace of God.	**Q-Quelle** House on Rock: 1 Cor 4:1-5/[1 Thes 5:1-11]/[Mt 7:21-27]/[Lk 6:46-49 (QS 14)]

1 CORINTHIANS 4:4—Unity and disunity (1:10-4:21), written from Ephesus, 51 CE

Theme	1 COR	Paul
Not self-justified	**4:4** [4]For I know nothing by myself; yet am I not hereby justified: but he that judgeth me is the Lord.	**Rom 2:16** [16]In the day when God shall judge the secrets of men by Jesus Christ according to my gospel. **2 Cor 1:12** [12]Now this I say, that every one of you saith, I am of Paul; and I of Apollos; and I of Cephas; and I of Christ. **2 Cor 5:10** [10]For we must all appear before the judgment seat of Christ; that every one may receive the things done in his body, according to that he hath done, whether it be good or bad.

1 CORINTHIANS 4:5—Unity and disunity (1:10-4:21), written from Ephesus, 51 CE

Theme	1 COR	Mk	Lk	Paul
Piety in private	**4:5** [5]Therefore judge nothing before the time, until the Lord come, who both will bring to light the hidden things of darkness, and will make manifest the counsels of the hearts: and then shall every man have praise of God. **14:25** [25]And thus are the secrets of his heart made manifest; and so falling down on his face he will worship God, and report that God is in you of a truth.	**4:22** [22]For there is nothing hid, which shall not be manifested; neither was any thing kept secret, but that it should come abroad.	**8:17** [17]For nothing is secret, that shall not be made manifest; neither any thing hid, that shall not be known and come abroad.	**Rom 2:16** [16]In the day when God shall judge the secrets of men by Jesus Christ according to my gospel. **Rom 2:28–29** [28]For he is not a Jew, which is one outwardly; neither is that circumcision, which is outward in the flesh: [29]But he is a Jew, which is one inwardly; and circumcision is that of the heart, in the spirit, and not in the letter; whose praise is not of men, but of God.

1 CORINTHIANS 4:9—Unity and disunity (1:10-4:21), written from Ephesus, 51 CE

Theme	1 COR	Paul	NT
Apostles are last in line	**4:9** [9]For I think that God hath set forth us the apostles last, as it were appointed to death: for we are made a spectacle unto the world, and to angels, and to men. **15:31** [31]I protest by your rejoicing which I have in Christ Jesus our Lord, I die daily.	**Rom 8:36** [36]As it is written, For thy sake we are killed all the day long; we are accounted as sheep for the slaughter. **2 Cor 4:8–12** [8]We are troubled on every side, yet not distressed; we are perplexed, but not in despair; [9]Persecuted, but not forsaken; cast down, but not destroyed; [10]Always bearing about in the body the dying of the Lord Jesus, that the life also of Jesus might be made manifest in our body. [11]For we which live are alway delivered unto death for Jesus' sake, that the life also of Jesus might be made manifest in our mortal flesh. [12]So then death worketh in us, but life in you. **2 Cor 11:23** [23]Are they ministers of Christ? (I speak as a fool) I am more; in labours more abundant, in stripes above measure, in prisons more frequent, in deaths oft.	**Heb 10:33** [33]Partly, whilst ye were made a gazingstock both by reproaches and afflictions; and partly, whilst ye became companions of them that were so used.

1 CORINTHIANS 4:10—Unity and disunity (1:10-4:21), written from Ephesus, 51 CE

Theme	1 COR	Paul
Fools for Christ	**4:10** [10]We are fools for Christ's sake, but ye are wise in Christ; we are weak, but ye are strong; ye are honourable, but we are despised. **1:18** [18]For the preaching of the cross is to them that perish foolishness; but unto us which are saved it is the power of God. **3:16** [16]Know ye not that ye are the temple of God, and that the Spirit of God dwelleth in you?	**2 Cor 2:3** [3]And I wrote this same unto you, lest, when I came, I should have sorrow from them of whom I ought to rejoice; having confidence in you all, that my joy is the joy of you all. **2 Cor 11:19** [19]For ye suffer fools gladly, seeing ye yourselves are wise. **2 Cor 13:9** [9]For we are glad, when we are weak, and ye are strong: and this also we wish, even your perfection.

1 CORINTHIANS 4:11—Unity and disunity (1:10-4:21), written from Ephesus, 51 CE

Theme	1 COR	Paul
Willingness to suffer for the Gospel	**4:11** [11]Even unto this present hour we both hunger, and thirst, and are naked, and are buffeted, and have no certain dwelling-place;	**Rom 8:35** [35]Who shall separate us from the love of Christ? shall tribulation, or distress, or persecution, or famine, or nakedness, or peril, or sword? **2 Cor 11:23–27** [23]Are they ministers of Christ? (I speak as a fool) I am more; in labours more abundant, in stripes above measure, in prisons more frequent, in deaths oft. [24]Of the Jews five times received I forty stripes save one. [25]Thrice was I beaten with rods, once was I stoned, thrice I suffered shipwreck, a night and a day I have been in the deep; [26]In journeyings often, in perils of waters, in perils of robbers, in perils by mine own countrymen, in perils by the heathen, in perils in the city, in perils in the wilderness, in perils in the sea, in perils among false brethren; [27]In weariness and painfulness, in watchings often, in hunger and thirst, in fastings often, in cold and nakedness.

1 CORINTHIANS 4:12b—Unity and disunity (1:10-4:21), written from Ephesus, 51 CE

Theme	1 COR	Mt	Mk	Lk
Bless in adversity	**4:12** [12]And labour, working with our own hands: being reviled, we bless; being persecuted, we suffer it: **6:7** [7]Now therefore there is utterly a fault among you, because ye go to law one with another. Why do ye not rather take wrong? why do ye not rather suffer yourselves to be defrauded?	**5:38** [38]Ye have heard that it hath been said, An eye for an eye, and a tooth for a tooth: **5:39–42** [39]But I say unto you, That ye resist not evil: but whosoever shall smite thee on thy right cheek, turn to him the other also. [40]And if any man will sue thee at the law, and take away thy coat, let him have thy cloak also. [41]And whosoever shall compel thee to go a mile, go with him twain. [42]Give to him that asketh thee, and from him that would borrow of thee turn not thou away. **5:44** [44]But I say unto you, Love your enemies, bless them that curse you, do good to them that hate you, and pray for them which despitefully use you, and persecute you;	**6:28** [28]And brought his head in a charger, and gave it to the damsel: and the damsel gave it to her mother.	**6:27** [27]But I say unto you which hear, Love your enemies, do good to them which hate you, **6:29–30** [29]And unto him that smiteth thee on the one cheek offer also the other; and him that taketh away thy cloak forbid not to take thy coat also. [30]Give to every man that asketh of thee; and of him that taketh away thy goods ask them not again **6:33** [33]And if ye do good to them which do good to you, what thank have ye? for sinners also do even the same. **12:14** [14]And he said unto him, Man, who made me a judge or a divider over you? **Acts 9:6–14** [6]And he trembling and astonished said, Lord, what wilt thou have me to do? And the Lord said unto him, Arise, and go into the city, and it shall be told thee what thou must do. [7]And the men which journeyed with him stood speechless, hearing a voice, but seeing no man. [8]And Saul arose from the earth; and when his eyes were opened, he saw no man: but they led him by the hand, and brought him into Damascus. [9]And he was three days without sight, and neither did eat nor drink. [10]And there was a certain disciple at Damascus, named Ananias; and to him said the Lord in a vision, Ananias. And he said, Behold, I am here, Lord. [11]And the Lord said unto him, Arise, and go into the street which is called Straight, and inquire in the house of Judas for one called Saul, of Tarsus: for, behold, he prayeth, [12]And hath seen in a vision a man named Ananias coming in, and putting his hand on him, that he might receive his sight. [13]Then Ananias answered, Lord, I have heard by many of this man, how much evil he hath done to thy saints at Jerusalem: [14]And here he hath authority from the chief priests to bind all that call on thy name. **Acts 18:3** [3]And because he was of the same craft, he abode with them, and wrought: for by their occupation they were tentmakers. **Acts 20:34** [34]Yea, ye yourselves know, that these hands have ministered unto my necessities, and to them that were with me.

1 CORINTHIANS 4:15—Unity and disunity (1:10-4:21), written from Ephesus, 51 CE

Theme	1 COR
Instructors in Christ	**4:15** [15]For though ye have ten thousand instructors in Christ, yet have ye not many fathers: for in Christ Jesus I have begotten you through the gospel.

Paul	NT	Other
Rom 12:17–20	**1 Pet 3:9**	**Q-Quelle**
[17]Recompense to no man evil for evil. Provide things honest in the sight of all men. **[18]If it be possible, as much as lieth in you, live peaceably with all men. [19]Dearly beloved, avenge not yourselves, but rather give place unto wrath: for it is written, Vengeance is mine; I will repay, saith the Lord.** [20]Therefore if thine enemy hunger, feed him; if he thirst, give him drink: for in so doing thou shalt heap coals of fire on his head. **1 Thes 2:9** [9]For ye remember, brethren, our labour and travail: for labouring night and day, because we would not be chargeable unto any of you, we preached unto you the gospel of God.	[9]Not rendering evil for evil, or railing for railing: but contrariwise blessing; knowing that ye are thereunto called, that ye should inherit a blessing.	Love enemies: 1 Cor 4:12/ Rom 12:9-21, 12:14-21/Mt 5:38-48/ [7:12]/Lk 6:27-36 (QS 9 [Thom 95, 6:2])

Paul
Gal 4:19
[19]My little children, of whom I travail in birth again until Christ be formed in you,
Phlm 10
[10]I beseech thee for my son Onesimus, whom I have begotten in my bonds:

1 CORINTHIANS 4:16—Unity and disunity (1:10-4:21), written from Ephesus, 51 CE

Theme	1 COR	Paul
Followers of Paul as he is of Christ	**4:16** [16]Wherefore I beseech you, be ye followers of me. **11:1** [1]Be ye followers of me, even as I also am of Christ.	**Phil 3:17** [17]Brethren, be followers together of me, and mark them which walk so as ye have us for an ensample. **Phil 4:9** [9]Those things, which ye have both learned, and received, and heard, and seen in me, do: and the God of peace shall be with you. **1 Thes 1:6** [6]And ye became followers of us, and of the Lord, having received the word in much affliction, with joy of the Holy Ghost: **2 Thes 3:7, 9** [7]For yourselves know how ye ought to follow us: for we behaved not ourselves disorderly among you; . . . [9]Not because we have not power, but to make ourselves an ensample unto you to follow us.

1 CORINTHIANS 4:17—Unity and disunity (1:10-4:21), written from Ephesus, 51 CE

Theme	1 COR	Lk
Timotheus, son of Paul in Christ	**4:17** [17]For this cause have I sent unto you Timotheus, who is my beloved son, and faithful in the Lord, who shall bring you into remembrance of my ways which be in Christ, as I teach every where in every church. **16:10** [10]Now if Timotheus come, see that he may be with you without fear: for he worketh the work of the Lord, as I also do.	**Acts 19:22** [22]So he sent into Macedonia two of them that ministered unto him, Timotheus and Erastus; but he himself stayed in Asia for a season.

1 CORINTHIANS 4:20—Unity and disunity (1:10-4:21), written from Ephesus, 51 CE

Theme	1 COR	Mt	Paul	Other
Power in the Kingdom of God	**4:20** [20]For the kingdom of God is not in word, but in power. **2:4** [4]And my speech and my preaching was not with enticing words of man's wisdom, but in demonstration of the Spirit and of power:	**12:28** [28]But if I cast out devils by the Spirit of God, then the kingdom of God is come unto you.	**Gal 5:19–21** [19]Now the works of the flesh are manifest, which are these; Adultery, fornication, uncleanness, lasciviousness, [20]Idolatry, witchcraft, hatred, variance, emulations, wrath, strife, seditions, heresies, [21]Envyings, murders, drunkenness, revellings, and such like: of the which I tell you before, as I have also told you in time past, that they which do such things shall not inherit the kingdom of God. **Eph 5:5 (Pseudo)** [5]To whom be glory for ever and ever. Amen. **1 Thes 1:5** [5]For our gospel came not unto you in word only, but also in power, and in the Holy Ghost, and in much assurance; as ye know what manner of men we were among you for your sake.	**Q-Quelle** Anxiety: 1 Cor 4:20/ [Rom 14:17]/Gal 5:19-21/[Mt 6:25-34]/[Lk 12:22-32 (QS 39 [Thom 36])]; Beezebul controversy: 1 Cor 4:20/[Mt 9:32-34], Mt 12:22-30/ [Mk 3:22-27]/[Lk 11:14-23]/[Rom 14:17] (QS 28 [Thom 35]); Assistance of the HS: 1 Cor 4:20/ Eph 5:5/[Mt 10:19-20]/ [Mk 13:11]/[Lk 12:11-12] (QS 37 [Thom 44])

1 CORINTHIANS 4:21—Unity and disunity (1:10-4:21), written from Ephesus, 51 CE

Theme	1 COR	Paul
Come with rod or in love	**4:21** [21]What will ye? shall I come unto you with a rod, or in love, and in the spirit of meekness?	**2 Cor 1:23** [23]Moreover I call God for a record upon my soul, that to spare you I came not as yet unto Corinth. **2 Cor 10:2** [2]But I beseech you, that I may not be bold when I am present with that confidence, wherewith I think to be bold against some, which think of us as if we walked according to the flesh.

IMMORALITY IN THE COMMUNITY (5:1–6:20)

1 CORINTHIANS 5:1—Morality and immorality (5:1–6:20), written from Ephesus, 51 CE

Theme	1 COR	Jewish Writings
Fornication	**5:1** [1]It is reported commonly that there is fornication among you, and such fornication as is not so much as named among the Gentiles, that one should have his father's wife.	**Lev 18:7–8** [7]The nakedness of thy father, or the nakedness of thy mother, shalt thou not uncover: she is thy mother; thou shalt not uncover her nakedness. [8]The nakedness of thy father's wife shalt thou not uncover: it is thy father's nakedness. **Lev 20:11** [11]And the man that lieth with his father's wife hath uncovered his father's nakedness: both of them shall surely be put to death; their blood shall be upon them. **Dt 27:20** [20]Cursed be he that lieth with his father's wife; because he uncovereth his father's skirt. And all the people shall say, Amen.

1 CORINTHIANS 5:3–5—Morality and immorality (5:1–6:20), written from Ephesus, 51 CE

Theme	1 COR	Mt	Paul	Other
Instructions for discipleship	**5:3–5** [3]For I verily, as absent in body, but present in spirit, have judged already, as though I were present, concerning him that hath so done this deed, [4]In the name of our Lord Jesus Christ, when ye are gathered together, and my spirit, with the power of our Lord Jesus Christ, [5]To deliver such an one unto Satan for the destruction of the flesh, that the spirit may be saved in the day of the Lord Jesus.	**18:15–20** [15]Moreover if thy brother shall trespass against thee, go and tell him his fault between thee and him alone: if he shall hear thee, thou hast gained thy brother. [16]But if he will not hear thee, then take with thee one or two more, that in the mouth of two or three witnesses every word may be established. [17]And if he shall neglect to hear them, tell it unto the church: but if he neglect to hear the church, let him be unto thee as an heathen man and a publican. [18]Verily I say unto you, Whatsoever ye shall bind on earth shall be bound in heaven: and whatsoever ye shall loose on earth shall be loosed in heaven. [19]Again I say unto you, That if two of you shall agree on earth as touching any thing that they shall ask, it shall be done for them of my Father which is in heaven. [20]For where two or three are gathered together in my name, there am I in the midst of them	**Col 2:5** [5]For though I be absent in the flesh, yet am I with you in the spirit, joying and beholding your order, and the stedfastness of your faith in Christ. **1 Tim 1:20 (Pseudo)** [20]Of whom is Hymenaeus and Alexander; whom I have delivered unto Satan, that they may learn not to blaspheme.	**Q-Quelle** On Forgiveness: 1 Cor 5:3-5/Mt 18:15, [Mt 18:21-22]/ [Lk 17:3b-4 (QS 58)

1 CORINTHIANS 5:6—Morality and immorality (5:1–6:20), written from Ephesus, 51 CE

Theme	1 COR	Paul
Pride is sin	**5:6** [6]Your glorying is not good. Know ye not that a little leaven leaveneth the whole lump?	**Gal 5:9** [9]A little leaven leaveneth the whole lump.

1 CORINTHIANS 5:7—Morality and immorality (5:1–6:20), written from Ephesus, 51 CE

Theme	1 COR	NT
Purge old leaven	**5:7** [7]Purge out therefore the old leaven, that ye may be a new lump, as ye are unleavened. For even Christ our passover is sacrificed for us:	**1 Pet 1:19** [19]But with the precious blood of Christ, as of a lamb without blemish and without spot:

1 CORINTHIANS 5:8—Morality and immorality (5:1–6:20), written from Ephesus, 51 CE

Theme	1 COR
Do not feast with sinners	**5:8** [8]Therefore let us keep the feast, not with old leaven, neither with the leaven of malice and wickedness; but with the unleavened bread of sincerity and truth.

Jewish Writings

Ex 12:1–13

1 And the LORD spake unto Moses and Aaron in the land of Egypt, saying, 2 This month shall be unto you the beginning of
months: it shall be the first month of the year to you. 3 Speak ye unto all the congregation of Israel, saying, In the tenth day
of this month they shall take to them every man a lamb, according to the house of their fathers, a lamb for an house: 4 And if
the household be too little for the lamb, let him and his neighbour next unto his house take it according to the number of the
souls; every man according to his eating shall make your count for the lamb. 5 Your lamb shall be without blemish, a male of
the first year: ye shall take it out from the sheep, or from the goats: 6 And ye shall keep it up until the fourteenth day of the same
month: and the whole assembly of the congregation of Israel shall kill it in the evening. 7 And they shall take of the blood, and
strike it on the two side posts and on the upper door post of the houses, wherein they shall eat it. 8 And they shall eat the flesh
in that night, roast with fire, and unleavened bread; and with bitter herbs they shall eat it. 9 Eat not of it raw, nor sodden at all
with water, but roast with fire; his head with his legs, and with the purtenance thereof. 10 And ye shall let nothing of it remain
until the morning; and that which remaineth of it until the morning ye shall burn with fire. 11 And thus shall ye eat it; with
your loins girded, your shoes on your feet, and your staff in your hand; and ye shall eat it in haste: it is the LORD'S passover.
12 For I will pass through the land of Egypt this night, and will smite all the firstborn in the land of Egypt, both man and beast;
and against all the gods of Egypt I will execute judgment: I am the LORD. 13 And the blood shall be to you for a token upon the
houses where ye are: and when I see the blood, I will pass over you, and the plague shall not be upon you to destroy you, when
I smite the land of Egypt.

Dt 16:1–2

1 Observe the month of Abib, and keep the passover unto the LORD thy God: for in the month of Abib the LORD thy God
brought thee forth out of Egypt by night. 2 Thou shalt therefore sacrifice the passover unto the LORD thy God, of the flock and
the herd, in the place which the LORD shall choose to place his name there.

Jewish Writings

Ex 12:15–20

15 Seven days shall ye eat unleavened bread; even the first day ye shall put away leaven out of your houses: for whosoever eateth
leavened bread from the first day until the seventh day, that soul shall be cut off from Israel. 16 And in the first day there shall
be an holy convocation, and in the seventh day there shall be an holy convocation to you; no manner of work shall be done in
them, save that which every man must eat, that only may be done of you. 17 And ye shall observe the feast of unleavened bread;
for in this selfsame day have I brought your armies out of the land of Egypt: therefore shall ye observe this day in your generations by an ordinance for ever. 18 In the first month, on the fourteenth day of the month at even, ye shall eat unleavened bread,
until the one and twentieth day of the month at even. 19 Seven days shall there be no leaven found in your houses: for whosoever eateth that which is leavened, even that soul shall be cut off from the congregation of Israel, whether he be a stranger, or
born in the land. 20 Ye shall eat nothing leavened; in all your habitations shall ye eat unleavened bread.

Ex 13:7

7 Unleavened bread shall be eaten seven days; and there shall no leavened bread be seen with thee, neither shall there be leaven seen with thee in all thy quarters.

Dt 16:3

3 Thou shalt eat no leavened bread with it; seven days shalt thou eat unleavened bread therewith, even the bread of affliction; for thou camest forth out of the land of Egypt in haste: that thou mayest remember the day when thou camest forth out of the land of Egypt all the days of thy life.

1 CORINTHIANS 5:10—Morality and immorality (5:1–6:20), written from Ephesus, 51 CE

Theme	1 COR	Jn
Do not feast with sinners	**5:10** [10]Yet not altogether with the fornicators of this world, or with the covetous, or extortioners, or with idolaters; for then must ye needs go out of the world. **10:27** [27]If any of them that believe not bid you to a feast, and ye be disposed to go; whatsoever is set before you, eat, asking no question for conscience sake.	**17:15** [15]I pray not that thou shouldest take them out of the world, but that thou shouldest keep them from the evil.

1 CORINTHIANS 5:11—Morality and immorality (5:1–6:20), written from Ephesus, 51 CE

Theme	1 COR	Mt
Do not eat with sinful brother	**5:11** [11]But now I have written unto you not to keep company, if any man that is called a brother be a fornicator, or covetous, or an idolater, or a railer, or a drunkard, or an extortioner; with such an one no not to eat.	**18:17** [17]And if he shall neglect to hear them, tell it unto the church: but if he neglect to hear the church, let him be unto thee as an heathen man and a publican.

1 CORINTHIANS 5:13—Morality and immorality (5:1–6:20), written from Ephesus, 51 CE

Theme	1 COR	Jewish Writings
Sinners are judgmental	**5:13** [13]But them that are without God judgeth. Therefore put away from among yourselves that wicked person.	**Dt 13:6** [6]If thy brother, the son of thy mother, or thy son, or thy daughter, or the wife of thy bosom, or thy friend, which is as thine own soul, entice thee secretly, saying, Let us go and serve other gods, which thou hast not known, thou, nor thy fathers; **Dt 17:7** [7]The hands of the witnesses shall be first upon him to put him to death, and afterward the hands of all the people. So thou shalt put the evil away from among you. **Dt 22:24** [24]Then ye shall bring them both out unto the gate of that city, and ye shall stone them with stones that they die; the damsel, because she cried not, being in the city; and the man, because he hath humbled his neighbour's wife: so thou shalt put away evil from among you.

1 CORINTHIANS 6:2—Morality and immorality (5:1–6:20), written from Ephesus, 51 CE

Theme	1 COR	Mt
Judge righteously	**6:2** [2]Do ye not know that the saints shall judge the world? and if the world shall be judged by you, are ye unworthy to judge the smallest matters?	**19:28** [28]And Jesus said unto them, Verily I say unto you, That ye which have followed me, in the regeneration when the Son of man shall sit in the throne of his glory, ye also shall sit upon twelve thrones, judging the twelve tribes of Israel.

Jn	Paul
2 Jn 10	**2 Thes 3:6**
[10]If there come any unto you, and bring not this doctrine, receive him not into your house, neither bid him God speed:	[6]Now we command you, brethren, in the name of our Lord Jesus Christ, that ye withdraw yourselves from every brother that walketh disorderly, and not after the tradition which he received of us. **2 Thes 3:14** [14]And if any man obey not our word by this epistle, note that man, and have no company with him, that he may be ashamed.

NT	Jewish Writings	Other
Rev 20:4	**Wis 3:8**	**Q-Quelle**
[4]And I saw thrones, and they sat upon them, and judgment was given unto them: and I saw the souls of them that were beheaded for the witness of Jesus, and for the word of God, and which had not worshipped the beast, neither his image, neither had received his mark upon their foreheads, or in their hands; and they lived and reigned with Christ a thousand years.	[8]They shall judge the nations, and have dominion over the people, and their Lord shall reign for ever.	Precedence: 1 Cor 6:2/Mt 19:28/ [Mk 10:41-45]/[Lk 22:28-30 (QS 62)

1 CORINTHIANS 6:7—Morality and immorality (5:1–6:20), written from Ephesus, 51 CE

Theme	1 COR	Mt
Suffer rather than sue	**6:7** [7]Now therefore there is utterly a fault among you, because ye go to law one with another. Why do ye not rather take wrong? why do ye not rather suffer yourselves to be defrauded?	**5:38–42** [38]Ye have heard that it hath been said, An eye for an eye, and a tooth for a tooth: [39]But I say unto you, That ye resist not evil: but whosoever shall smite thee on thy right cheek, turn to him the other also. [40]And if any man will sue thee at the law, and take away thy coat, let him have thy cloak also. [41]And whosoever shall compel thee to go a mile, go with him twain. [42]Give to him that asketh thee, and from him that would borrow of thee turn not thou away.

1 CORINTHIANS 6:9–10—Morality and immorality (5:1–6:20), written from Ephesus, 51 CE

Theme	1 COR	Mt	Mk
Right values for God's Kingdom	**6:9–10** [9]Know ye not that the unrighteous shall not inherit the kingdom of God? Be not deceived: neither fornicators, nor idolaters, nor adulterers, nor effeminate, nor abusers of themselves with mankind, [10]Nor thieves, nor covetous, nor drunkards, nor revilers, nor extortioners, shall inherit the kingdom of God. **4:20** For the kingdom of God is not in word, but in power. **6:12–13** [12]All things are lawful unto me, but all things are not expedient: all things are lawful for me, but I will not be brought under the power of any. [13]Meats for the belly, and the belly for meats: but God shall destroy both it and them. Now the body is not for fornication, but for the Lord; and the Lord for the body. **15:50** [50]Now this I say, brethren, that flesh and blood cannot inherit the kingdom of God; neither doth corruption inherit incorruption.	**5:20** [20]For I say unto you, That except your righteousness shall exceed the righteousness of the scribes and Pharisees, ye shall in no case enter into the kingdom of heaven. **6:33** [33]But seek ye first the kingdom of God, and his righteousness; and all these things shall be added unto you. **15:15** [15]Then answered Peter and said unto him, Declare unto us this parable. **15:17** [17]Do not ye yet understand, that whatsoever entereth in at the mouth goeth into the belly, and is cast out into the draught? **18:3** [3]And said, Verily I say unto you, Except ye be converted, and become as little children, ye shall not enter into the kingdom of heaven.	**7:19** [19]Because it entereth not into his heart, but into the belly, and goeth out into the draught, purging all meats? **10:15** [15]Verily I say unto you, Whosoever shall not receive the kingdom of God as a little child, he shall not enter therein.

1 CORINTHIANS 6:11—Morality and immorality (5:1–6:20), written from Ephesus, 51 CE

Theme	1 COR
Washed, sanctified, justified	**6:11** [11]And such were some of you: but ye are washed, but ye are sanctified, but ye are justified in the name of the Lord Jesus, and by the Spirit of our God.

Paul	Other
Rom 12:17–21	**Q-Quelle**
[17]Recompense to no man evil for evil. Provide things honest in the sight of all men. [18]If it be possible, as much as lieth in you, live peaceably with all men. [19]Dearly beloved, avenge not yourselves, but rather give place unto wrath: for it is written, Vengeance is mine; I will repay, saith the Lord. [20]Therefore if thine enemy hunger, feed him; if he thirst, give him drink: for in so doing thou shalt heap coals of fire on his head. [21]Be not overcome of evil, but overcome evil with good.	Love enemies: 1 Cor 6:7/Rom 12:17-20/ Mt 5:38-48, [Mt 7:12]/[Lk 6:27-36 (QS 9 [Thom 95, 6:2], QS 10)]
1 Thes 5:15	
[15]See that none render evil for evil unto any man; but ever follow that which is good, both among yourselves, and to all men.	

Luke	John	Paul	Other
11:20	**3:5**	**Rom 14:14**	**Q-Quelle**
[20]But if I with the finger of God cast out devils, no doubt the kingdom of God is come upon you. **12:31** [31]But rather seek ye the kingdom of God; and all these things shall be added unto you.	[5]Jesus answered, Verily, verily, I say unto thee, Except a man be born of water and of the Spirit, he cannot enter into the kingdom of God.	[14]I know, and am persuaded by the Lord Jesus, that there is nothing unclean of itself: but to him that esteemeth any thing to be unclean, to him it is unclean. **Rom 14:17** [17]For the kingdom of God is not meat and drink; but righteousness, and peace, and joy in the Holy Ghost. **Rom 14:20** [20]For meat destroy not the work of God. All things indeed are pure; but it is evil for that man who eateth with offence. **Gal 5:19–21** [19]Now the works of the flesh are manifest, which are these; Adultery, fornication, uncleanness, lasciviousness, [20]Idolatry, witchcraft, hatred, variance, emulations, wrath, strife, seditions, heresies, [21]Envyings, murders, drunkenness, revellings, and such like: of the which I tell you before, as I have also told you in time past, that they which do such things shall not inherit the kingdom of God. **Eph 5:5** [5]For this ye know, that no whoremonger, nor unclean person, nor covetous man, who is an idolater, hath any inheritance in the kingdom of Christ and of God.	Anxiety: 1 Cor 6:9-10/Rom 14:17/Gal 5:19-21/Mt 6:25-34/Lk 12:22-32 (QS 9 [Thom 36])/[Mt 23:4-36]/[Mk 7:1-9]/[Lk 11:37-54 (QS); Beezebul Controversy: 1 Cor 6:9-10/Rom 14:17/[Mt 9:32-34, 12:22-30]/[Mk 3:22-27]/ Lk 11:14-23 (QS 28 [Thom 35]); Against Pharisees: 1 Cor 6:9-10/Rom 14:14/[Mt 23:4-36]/[Mk 7:1-9]/[Lk 11:37-54 (QS 34 [Thom 39:1, 89, 102])]; Assistance of the HS: 1 Cor 6:9-10/Eph 5:5/ [Mt 10:19-20]/[Mk 13:11] / [Lk 12:11-12 (QS 37 [Thom 44])]

Paul
Tit 3:3–7 (Pseudo)
[3]For we ourselves also were sometimes foolish, disobedient, deceived, serving divers lusts and pleasures, living in malice and envy, hateful, and hating one another. [4]But after that the kindness and love of God our Saviour toward man appeared, [5]Not by works of righteousness which we have done, but according to his mercy he saved us, by the washing of regeneration, and renewing of the Holy Ghost; [6]Which he shed on us abundantly through Jesus Christ our Saviour; [7]That being justified by his grace, we should be made heirs according to the hope of eternal life.

1 CORINTHIANS 6:12—Morality and immorality (5:1–6:20), written from Ephesus, 51 CE

Theme	1 COR
Anti-nomianism	**6:12** [12]All things are lawful unto me, but all things are not expedient: all things are lawful for me, but I will not be brought under the power of any. **7:19** [19]Circumcision is nothing, and uncircumcision is nothing, but the keeping of the commandments of God. **10:23** [23]All things are lawful for me, but all things are not expedient: all things are lawful for me, but all things edify not.

1 CORINTHIANS 6:14—Morality and immorality (5:1–6:20), written from Ephesus, 51 CE

Theme	1 COR
God raises dead	**6:14** [14]And God hath both raised up the Lord, and will also raise up us by his own power.

1 CORINTHIANS 6:15—Morality and immorality (5:1–6:20), written from Ephesus, 51 CE

Theme	1 COR	Mt	Mk	Lk
Corporate body of Christ	**6:15** [15]Know ye not that your bodies are the members of Christ? shall I then take the members of Christ, and make them the members of an harlot? God forbid. **10:17** [17]For we being many are one bread, and one body: for we are all partakers of that one bread. **12:27** [27]Now ye are the body of Christ, and members in particular.	**12:46–50** [46]While he yet talked to the people, behold, his mother and his brethren stood without, desiring to speak with him. [47]Then one said unto him, Behold, thy mother and thy brethren stand without, desiring to speak with thee. [48]But he answered and said unto him that told him, Who is my mother? and who are my brethren? [49]And he stretched forth his hand toward his disciples, and said, Behold my mother and my brethren! [50]For whosoever shall do the will of my Father which is in heaven, the same is my brother, and sister, and mother.	**3:31–35** [31]There came then his brethren and his mother, and, standing without, sent unto him, calling him. [32]And the multitude sat about him, and they said unto him, Behold, thy mother and thy brethren without seek for thee. [33]And he answered them, saying, Who is my mother, or my brethren? [34]And he looked round about on them which sat about him, and said, Behold my mother and my brethren! [35]For whosoever shall do the will of God, the same is my brother, and my sister, and mother.	**8:19–21** [19]Then came to him his mother and his brethren, and could not come at him for the press. [20]And it was told him by certain which said, Thy mother and thy brethren stand without, desiring to see thee. [21]And he answered and said unto them, My mother and my brethren are these which hear the word of God, and do it.

Paul
Rom 3:8
[8]And not rather, (as we be slanderously reported, and as some affirm that we say,) Let us do evil, that good may come? whose damnation is just.
Rom 6:1
[1]What shall we say then? Shall we continue in sin, that grace may abound?

Paul
2 Cor 4:14
[14]Knowing that he which raised up the Lord Jesus shall raise up us also by Jesus, and shall present us with you.

Paul
Rom 12:4
[4]For as we have many members in one body, and all members have not the same office:
Rom 12:5
[5]So we, being many, are one body in Christ, and every one members one of another.
Rom 12:12–13
[12]Rejoicing in hope; patient in tribulation; continuing instant in prayer; [13]Distributing to the necessity of saints; given to hospitality.
Rom 15:22
[22]For which cause also I have been much hindered from coming to you.
Eph 1:22–23 (Pseudo)
[22]And hath put all things under his feet, and gave him to be the head over all things to the church, [23]Which is his body, the fulness of him that filleth all in all.
Eph 4:15 (Pseudo)
[15]But speaking the truth in love, may grow up into him in all things, which is the head, even Christ:
Eph 5:23 (Pseudo)
[23]For the husband is the head of the wife, even as Christ is the head of the church: and he is the saviour of the body.
Eph 5:30 (Pseudo)
[30]For we are members of his body, of his flesh, and of his bones.
Col 1:18
[18]And he is the head of the body, the church: who is the beginning, the firstborn from the dead; that in all things he might have the preeminence.

1 CORINTHIANS 6:16—Morality and immorality (5:1–6:20), written from Ephesus, 51 CE

Theme	1 COR	Mt	Mk
Do not join body with harlot	**6:16** [16]What? know ye not that he which is joined to an harlot is one body? for two, saith he, shall be one flesh.	**19:5** [5]And said, For this cause shall a man leave father and mother, and shall cleave to his wife: and they twain shall be one flesh?	**10:8** [8]And they twain shall be one flesh: so then they are no more twain, but one flesh.

1 CORINTHIANS 6:17—Morality and immorality (5:1–6:20), written from Ephesus, 51 CE

Theme	1 COR	Paul
Of one spirit with Lord	**6:17** [17]But he that is joined unto the Lord is one spirit.	**Rom 8:9–10** [9]But ye are not in the flesh, but in the Spirit, if so be that the Spirit of God dwell in you. Now if any man have not the Spirit of Christ, he is none of his. [10]And if Christ be in you, the body is dead because of sin; but the Spirit is life because of righteousness. **2 Cor 3:17** [17]Now the Lord is that Spirit: and where the Spirit of the Lord is, there is liberty.

1 CORINTHIANS 6:19—Morality and immorality (5:1–6:20), written from Ephesus, 51 CE

Theme	1 COR
Body is temple of Christ	**6:19** [19]What? know ye not that your body is the temple of the Holy Ghost which is in you, which ye have of God, and ye are not your own? **3:16–17** [16]Know ye not that ye are the temple of God, and that the Spirit of God dwelleth in you? [17]If any man defile the temple of God, him shall God destroy; for the temple of God is holy, which temple ye are.

Paul	Jewish Writings
Eph 5:31 (Pseudo)	**Gen 2:24**
[31]For this cause shall a man leave his father and mother, and shall be joined unto his wife, and they two shall be one flesh.	[24]Therefore shall a man leave his father and his mother, and shall cleave unto his wife: and they shall be one flesh.

Paul
Rom 5:5
[5]And hope maketh not ashamed; because the love of God is shed abroad in our hearts by the Holy Ghost which is given unto us.

QUESTIONS OF THE FAITH (7:1–11:1)

ABOUT CALLING AND ABSTINENCE FROM SEXUAL RELATIONS (7:1–40)

1 CORINTHIANS Ch 7—Calling, sexual conduct, and abstinence (7:1–40), written from Ephesus, 51 CE

Theme	1 COR
Marital relations	**Ch 7** 1 Now concerning the things whereof ye wrote unto me: It is good for a man not to touch a woman. 2 Nevertheless, to avoid fornication, let every man have his own wife, and let every woman have her own husband. 3 Let the husband render unto the wife due benevolence: and likewise also the wife unto the husband. 4 The wife hath not power of her own body, but the husband: and likewise also the husband hath not power of his own body, but the wife. 5 Defraud ye not one the other, except it be with consent for a time, that ye may give yourselves to fasting and prayer; and come together again, that Satan tempt you not for your incontinency. 6 But I speak this by permission, and not of commandment. 7 For I would that all men were even as I myself. But every man hath his proper gift of God, one after this manner, and another after that. 8 I say therefore to the unmarried and widows, It is good for them if they abide even as I. 9 But if they cannot contain, let them marry: for it is better to marry than to burn. 10 And unto the married I command, yet not I, but the Lord, Let not the wife depart from her husband: 11 But and if she depart, let her remain unmarried, or be reconciled to her husband: and let not the husband put away his wife. 12 But to the rest speak I, not the Lord: If any brother hath a wife that believeth not, and she be pleased to dwell with him, let him not put her away. 13 And the woman which hath an husband that believeth not, and if he be pleased to dwell with her, let her not leave him. 14 For the unbelieving husband is sanctified by the wife, and the unbelieving wife is sanctified by the husband: else were your children unclean; but now are they holy. 15 But if the unbelieving depart, let him depart. A brother or a sister is not under bondage in such cases: but God hath called us to peace. 16 For what knowest thou, O wife, whether thou shalt save thy husband? or how knowest thou, O man, whether thou shalt save thy wife? 17 But as God hath distributed to every man, as the Lord hath called every one, so let him walk. And so ordain I in all churches. 18 Is any man called being circumcised? let him not become uncircumcised. Is any called in uncircumcision? let him not be circumcised. 19 Circumcision is nothing, and uncircumcision is nothing, but the keeping of the commandments of God. 20 Let every man abide in the same calling wherein he was called. 21 Art thou called being a servant? care not for it: but if thou mayest be made free, use it rather. 22 For he that is called in the Lord, being a servant, is the Lord's freeman: likewise also he that is called, being free, is Christ's servant. 23 Ye are bought with a price; be not ye the servants of men. 24 Brethren, let every man, wherein he is called, therein abide with God. 25 Now concerning virgins I have no commandment of the Lord: yet I give my judgment, as one that hath obtained mercy of the Lord to be faithful. 26 I suppose therefore that this is good for the present distress, I say, that it is good for a man so to be. 27 Art thou bound unto a wife? seek not to be loosed. Art thou loosed from a wife? seek not a wife. 28 But and if thou marry, thou hast not sinned; and if a virgin marry, she hath not sinned. Nevertheless such shall have trouble in the flesh: but I spare you. 29 But this I say, brethren, the time is short: it remaineth, that both they that have wives be as though they had none; 30 And they that weep, as though they wept not; and they that rejoice, as though they rejoiced not; and they that buy, as though they possessed not; 31 And they that use this world, as not abusing it: for the fashion of this world passeth away. 32 But I would have you without carefulness. He that is unmarried careth for the things that belong to the Lord, how he may please the Lord: 33 But he that is married careth for the things that are of the world, how he may please his wife. 34 There is difference also between a wife and a virgin. The unmarried woman careth for the things of the Lord, that she may be holy both in body and in spirit: but she that is married careth for the things of the world, how she may please her husband. 35 And this I speak for your own profit; not that I may cast a snare upon you, but for that which is comely, and that ye may attend upon the Lord without distraction. 36 But if any man think that he behaveth himself uncomely toward his virgin, if she pass the flower of her age, and need so require, let him do what he will, he sinneth not: let them marry. 37 Nevertheless he that standeth stedfast in his heart, having no necessity, but hath power over his own will, and hath so decreed in his heart that he will keep his virgin, doeth well. 38 So then he that giveth her in marriage doeth well; but he that giveth her not in marriage doeth better. 39 The wife is bound by the law as long as her husband liveth; but if her husband be dead, she is at liberty to be married to whom she will; only in the Lord. 40 But she is happier if she so abide, after my judgment: and I think also that I have the Spirit of God.

Mt	Mk	Lk
5:32 [32]But I say unto you, That whosoever shall put away his wife, saving for the cause of fornication, causeth her to commit adultery: and whosoever shall marry her that is divorced committeth adultery. **19:6** [6]Wherefore they are no more twain, but one flesh. What therefore God hath joined together, let not man put asunder. **19:9** [19]Honour thy father and thy mother: and, Thou shalt love thy neighbour as thyself.	**10:9** [9]What therefore God hath joined together, let not man put asunder. **10:11–12** [11]And he saith unto them, Whosoever shall put away his wife, and marry another, committeth adultery against her. [12]And if a woman shall put away her husband, and be married to another, she committeth adultery.	**16:18** [18]Whosoever putteth away his wife, and marrieth another, committeth adultery: and whosoever marrieth her that is put away from her husband committeth adultery.

1 CORINTHIANS Ch 7 and 9—Calling, sexual conduct, and abstinence, written from Ephesus, 51 CE

Theme	1 COR—Ch 7
Bodily holiness	**Ch 7** 1Now concerning the things whereof ye wrote unto me: It is good for a man not to touch a woman. 2Nevertheless, to avoid fornication, let every man have his own wife, and let every woman have her own husband. 3Let the husband render unto the wife due benevolence: and likewise also the wife unto the husband. 4The wife hath not power of her own body, but the husband: and likewise also the husband hath not power of his own body, but the wife. 5Defraud ye not one the other, except it be with consent for a time, that ye may give yourselves to fasting and prayer; and come together again, that Satan tempt you not for your incontinency. 6But I speak this by permission, and not of commandment. 7For I would that all men were even as I myself. But every man hath his proper gift of God, one after this manner, and another after that. 8I say therefore to the unmarried and widows, It is good for them if they abide even as I. 9But if they cannot contain, let them marry: for it is better to marry than to burn. 10And unto the married I command, yet not I, but the Lord, Let not the wife depart from her husband: 11But and if she depart, let her remain unmarried, or be reconciled to her husband: and let not the husband put away his wife. 12But to the rest speak I, not the Lord: If any brother hath a wife that believeth not, and she be pleased to dwell with him, let him not put her away. 13And the woman which hath an husband that believeth not, and if he be pleased to dwell with her, let her not leave him. 14For the unbelieving husband is sanctified by the wife, and the unbelieving wife is sanctified by the husband: else were your children unclean; but now are they holy. 15But if the unbelieving depart, let him depart. A brother or a sister is not under bondage in such cases: but God hath called us to peace. 16For what knowest thou, O wife, whether thou shalt save thy husband? or how knowest thou, O man, whether thou shalt save thy wife? 17But as God hath distributed to every man, as the Lord hath called every one, so let him walk. And so ordain I in all churches. 18Is any man called being circumcised? let him not become uncircumcised. Is any called in uncircumcision? let him not be circumcised. 19Circumcision is nothing, and uncircumcision is nothing, but the keeping of the commandments of God. 20Let every man abide in the same calling wherein he was called. 21Art thou called being a servant? care not for it: but if thou mayest be made free, use it rather. 22For he that is called in the Lord, being a servant, is the Lord's freeman: likewise also he that is called, being free, is Christ's servant. 23Ye are bought with a price; be not ye the servants of men. 24Brethren, let every man, wherein he is called, therein abide with God. 25Now concerning virgins I have no commandment of the Lord: yet I give my judgment, as one that hath obtained mercy of the Lord to be faithful. 26I suppose therefore that this is good for the present distress, I say, that it is good for a man so to be. 27Art thou bound unto a wife? seek not to be loosed. Art thou loosed from a wife? seek not a wife. 28But and if thou marry, thou hast not sinned; and if a virgin marry, she hath not sinned. Nevertheless such shall have trouble in the flesh: but I spare you. 29But this I say, brethren, the time is short: it remaineth, that both they that have wives be as though they had none; 30And they that weep, as though they wept not; and they that rejoice, as though they rejoiced not; and they that buy, as though they possessed not; 31And they that use this world, as not abusing it: for the fashion of this world passeth away. 32But I would have you without carefulness. He that is unmarried careth for the things that belong to the Lord, how he may please the Lord: 33But he that is married careth for the things that are of the world, how he may please his wife. 34There is difference also between a wife and a virgin. The unmarried woman careth for the things of the Lord, that she may be holy both in body and in spirit: but she that is married careth for the things of the world, how she may please her husband. 35And this I speak for your own profit; not that I may cast a snare upon you, but for that which is comely, and that ye may attend upon the Lord without distraction. 36But if any man think that he behaveth himself uncomely toward his virgin, if she pass the flower of her age, and need so require, let him do what he will, he sinneth not: let them marry. 37Nevertheless he that standeth stedfast in his heart, having no necessity, but hath power over his own will, and hath so decreed in his heart that he will keep his virgin, doeth well. 38So then he that giveth her in marriage doeth well; but he that giveth her not in marriage doeth better. 39The wife is bound by the law as long as her husband liveth; but if her husband be dead, she is at liberty to be married to whom she will; only in the Lord. 40But she is happier if she so abide, after my judgment: and I think also that I have the Spirit of God.

1 COR—Ch 9	Mt	Mk
Ch 9	**19:1–2**	**10:9**
[1]Am I not an apostle? am I not free? have I not seen Jesus Christ our Lord? are not ye my work in the Lord? [2]If I be not an apostle unto others, yet doubtless I am to you: for the seal of mine apostleship are ye in the Lord. [3]Mine answer to them that do examine me is this, [4]Have we not power to eat and to drink? [5]Have we not power to lead about a sister, a wife, as well as other apostles, and as the brethren of the Lord, and Cephas? [6]Or I only and Barnabas, have not we power to forbear working? [7]Who goeth a warfare any time at his own charges? who planteth a vineyard, and eateth not of the fruit thereof? or who feedeth a flock, and eateth not of the milk of the flock? [8]Say I these things as a man? or saith not the law the same also? [9]For it is written in the law of Moses, Thou shalt not muzzle the mouth of the ox that treadeth out the corn. Doth God take care for oxen? [10]Or saith he it altogether for our sakes? For our sakes, no doubt, this is written: that he that ploweth should plow in hope; and that he that thresheth in hope should be partaker of his hope. [11]If we have sown unto you spiritual things, is it a great thing if we shall reap your carnal things? [12]If others be partakers of this power over you, are not we rather? Nevertheless we have not used this power; but suffer all things, lest we should hinder the gospel of Christ. [13]Do ye not know that they which minister about holy things live of the things of the temple? and they which wait at the altar are partakers with the altar? [14]Even so hath the Lord ordained that they which preach the gospel should live of the gospel. [15]But I have used none of these things: neither have I written these things, that it should be so done unto me: for it were better for me to die, than that any man should make my glorying void. [16]For though I preach the gospel, I have nothing to glory of: for necessity is laid upon me; yea, woe is unto me, if I preach not the gospel! [17]For if I do this thing willingly, I have a reward: but if against my will, a dispensation of the gospel is committed unto me. [18]What is my reward then? Verily that, when I preach the gospel, I may make the gospel of Christ without charge, that I abuse not my power in the gospel. [19]For though I be free from all men, yet have I made myself servant unto all, that I might gain the more. [20]And unto the Jews I became as a Jew, that I might gain the Jews; to them that are under the law, as under the law, that I might gain them that are under the law; [21]To them that are without law, as without law, (being not without law to God, but under the law to Christ,) that I might gain them that are without law. [22]To the weak became I as weak, that I might gain the weak: I am made all things to all men, that I might by all means save some. [23]And this I do for the gospel's sake, that I might be partaker thereof with you. [24]Know ye not that they which run in a race run all, but one receiveth the prize? So run, that ye may obtain. [25]And every man that striveth for the mastery is temperate in all things. Now they do it to obtain a corruptible crown; but we an incorruptible. [26]I therefore so run, not as uncertainly; so fight I, not as one that beateth the air: [27]But I keep under my body, and bring it into subjection: lest that by any means, when I have preached to others, I myself should be a castaway.	[1]And it came to pass, that when Jesus had finished these sayings, he departed from Galilee, and came into the coasts of Judaea beyond Jordan; [2]And great multitudes followed him; and he healed them there. **19:6** [6]Wherefore they are no more twain, but one flesh. What therefore God hath joined together, let not man put asunder. **19:9** [9]And I say unto you, Whosoever shall put away his wife, except it be for fornication, and shall marry another, committeth adultery: and whoso marrieth her which is put away doth commit adultery.	[9]What therefore God hath joined together, let not man put asunder. **10:11** [11]And he saith unto them, Whosoever shall put away his wife, and marry another, committeth adultery against her.

1 CORINTHIANS 7:3–4—Calling, sexual conduct, and abstinence (7:1–40), written from Ephesus, 51 CE

Theme	1 COR	Jewish Writings
Mutuality & respect	**7:3–4** [3]Let the husband render unto the wife due benevolence: and likewise also the wife unto the husband. [4]The wife hath not power of her own body, but the husband: and likewise also the husband hath not power of his own body, but the wife. **11:11–12** [11]Nevertheless neither is the man without the woman, neither the woman without the man, in the Lord. [12]For as the woman is of the man, even so is the man also by the woman; but all things of God.	**Gen 1:27** [27]So God created man in his own image, in the image of God created he him; male and female created he them.

1 CORINTHIANS 7:7–8—Calling, sexual conduct, and abstinence (7:1–40), written from Ephesus, 51 CE

Theme	1 COR	Mt
Celibacy	**7:7–8** [7]For I would that all men were even as I myself. But every man hath his proper gift of God, one after this manner, and another after that. [8]I say therefore to the unmarried and widows, It is good for them if they abide even as I. **4:8–9** [8]Now ye are full, now ye are rich, ye have reigned as kings without us: and I would to God ye did reign, that we also might reign with you. [9]For I think that God hath set forth us the apostles last, as it were appointed to death: for we are made a spectacle unto the world, and to angels, and to men. **7:12–14** [12]But to the rest speak I, not the Lord: If any brother hath a wife that believeth not, and she be pleased to dwell with him, let him not put her away. [13]And the woman which hath an husband that believeth not, and if he be pleased to dwell with her, let her not leave him. [14]For the unbelieving husband is sanctified by the wife, and the unbelieving wife is sanctified by the husband: else were your children unclean; but now are they holy. **7:26** [26]I suppose therefore that this is good for the present distress, I say, that it is good for a man so to be. **7:29** [29]But this I say, brethren, the time is short: it remaineth, that both they that have wives be as though they had none; **9:5** [5]Have we not power to lead about a sister, a wife, as well as other apostles, and as the brethren of the Lord, and Cephas?	**19:11–12** [11]But he said unto them, All men cannot receive this saying, save they to whom it is given. [12]For there are some eunuchs, which were so born from their mother's womb: and there are some eunuchs, which were made eunuchs of men: and there be eunuchs, which have made themselves eunuchs for the kingdom of heaven's sake. He that is able to receive it, let him receive it. **22:30** [30]For in the resurrection they neither marry, nor are given in marriage, but are as the angels of God in heaven.

Mk	Lk	Paul
12:25	**20:35–36**	**Gal 3:27–28**
[25]For when they shall rise from the dead, they neither marry, nor are given in marriage; but are as the angels which are in heaven.	[35]But they which shall be accounted worthy to obtain that world, and the resurrection from the dead, neither marry, nor are given in marriage: [36]Neither can they die any more: for they are equal unto the angels; and are the children of God, being the children of the resurrection.	[27]For as many of you as have been baptized into Christ have put on Christ. [28]There is neither Jew nor Greek, there is neither bond nor free, there is neither male nor female: for ye are all one in Christ Jesus. **1 Tim 5:11–16 (Pseudo)** [11]But the younger widows refuse: for when they have begun to wax wanton against Christ, they will marry; [12]Having damnation, because they have cast off their first faith. [13]And withal they learn to be idle, wandering about from house to house; and not only idle, but tattlers also and busybodies, speaking things which they ought not. [14]I will therefore that the younger women marry, bear children, guide the house, give none occasion to the adversary to speak reproachfully. [15]For some are already turned aside after Satan. [16]If any man or woman that believeth have widows, let them relieve them, and let not the church be charged; that it may relieve them that are widows indeed.

1 CORINTHIANS 7:10-11—Calling, sexual conduct, and abstinence (7:1–40), written from Ephesus, 51 CE

Theme	1 COR	Mt
Divorce	**7:10-11** [10]And unto the married I command, yet not I, but the Lord, Let not the wife depart from her husband:[11]But and if she depart, let her remain unmarried, or be reconciled to her husband: and let not the husband put away his wife. **7:12–16** [12]But to the rest speak I, not the Lord: If any brother hath a wife that believeth not, and she be pleased to dwell with him, let him not put her away. [13]And the woman which hath an husband that believeth not, and if he be pleased to dwell with her, let her not leave him. [14]For the unbelieving husband is sanctified by the wife, and the unbelieving wife is sanctified by the husband: else were your children unclean; but now are they holy. [15]But if the unbelieving depart, let him depart. A brother or a sister is not under bondage in such cases: but God hath called us to peace. [16]For what knowest thou, O wife, whether thou shalt save thy husband? or how knowest thou, O man, whether thou shalt save thy wife?	**5:31–32** [31]It hath been said, Whosoever shall put away his wife, let him give her a writing of divorcement: [32]But I say unto you, That whosoever shall put away his wife, saving for the cause of fornication, causeth her to commit adultery: and whosoever shall marry her that is divorced committeth adultery. **14:1–12** [1]At that time Herod the tetrarch heard of the fame of Jesus, [2]And said unto his servants, This is John the Baptist; he is risen from the dead; and therefore mighty works do show forth themselves in him. [3]For Herod had laid hold on John, and bound him, and put him in prison for Herodias' sake, his brother Philip's wife. [4]For John said unto him, It is not lawful for thee to have her. [5]And when he would have put him to death, he feared the multitude, because they counted him as a prophet. [6]But when Herod's birthday was kept, the daughter of Herodias danced before them, and pleased Herod. [7]Whereupon he promised with an oath to give her whatsoever she would ask. [8]And she, being before instructed of her mother, said, Give me here John Baptist's head in a charger. [9]And the king was sorry: nevertheless for the oath's sake, and them which sat with him at meat, he commanded it to be given her. [10]And he sent, and beheaded John in the prison. [11]And his head was brought in a charger, and given to the damsel: and she brought it to her mother. [12]And his disciples came, and took up the body, and buried it, and went and told Jesus. **19:6** [6]But that ye may know that the Son of man hath power on earth to forgive sins, (then saith he to the sick of the palsy,) Arise, take up thy bed, and go unto thine house. **19:9** [9]And I say unto you, Whosoever shall put away his wife, except it be for fornication, and shall marry another, committeth adultery: and whoso marrieth her which is put away doth commit adultery.

1 CORINTHIANS 7:14—Calling, sexual conduct, and abstinence (7:1–40), written from Ephesus, 51 CE

Theme	1 COR	Paul
Spouse sanctified	**7:14** [14]For the unbelieving husband is sanctified by the wife, and the unbelieving wife is sanctified by the husband: else were your children unclean; but now are they holy.	**Rom 11:16** [16]For if the firstfruit be holy, the lump is also holy: and if the root be holy, so are the branches.

Mk	Luke
6:14–29	**16:18**
[14]And king Herod heard of him; (for his name was spread abroad:) and he said, That John the Baptist was risen from the dead, and therefore mighty works do show forth them-selves in him. [15]Others said, That it is Elias. And others said, That it is a prophet, or as one of the prophets. [16]But when Herod heard thereof, he said, It is John, whom I beheaded: he is risen from the dead. [17]For Herod himself had sent forth and laid hold upon John, and bound him in prison for Herodias' sake, his brother Philip's wife: for he had married her. [18]For John had said unto Herod, It is not lawful for thee to have thy brother's wife. [19]Therefore Herodias had a quarrel against him, and would have killed him; but she could not: [20]For Herod feared John, knowing that he was a just man and an holy, and observed him; and when he heard him, he did many things, and heard him gladly. [21]And when a convenient day was come, that Herod on his birthday made a supper to his lords, high captains, and chief estates of Galilee; [22]And when the daughter of the said Herodias came in, and danced, and pleased Herod and them that sat with him, the king said unto the damsel, Ask of me whatsoever thou wilt, and I will give it thee. [23]And he sware unto her, Whatsoever thou shalt ask of me, I will give it thee, unto the half of my kingdom. [24]And she went forth, and said unto her mother, What shall I ask? And she said, The head of John the Baptist. [25]And she came in straightway with haste unto the king, and asked, saying, I will that thou give me by and by in a charger the head of John the Baptist. [26]And the king was exceeding sorry; yet for his oath's sake, and for their sakes which sat with him, he would not reject her. [27]And immediately the king sent an executioner, and commanded his head to be brought: and he went and beheaded him in the prison, [28]And brought his head in a charger, and gave it to the damsel: and the damsel gave it to her mother. [29]And when his disciples heard of it, they came and took up his corpse, and laid it in a tomb.	[18]Whosoever putteth away his wife, and marrieth another, committeth adultery: and whosoever marrieth her that is put away from her husband committeth adultery.
10:9	
[9]What therefore God hath joined together, let not man put asunder.	

1 CORINTHIANS 7:15—Calling, sexual conduct, and abstinence (7:1–40), written from Ephesus, 51 CE

Theme	1 COR	Mk	Jn
Marital separation	**7:15** [15]But if the unbelieving depart, let him depart. A brother or a sister is not under bondage in such cases: but God hath called us to peace.	**9:50** [50]Salt is good: but if the salt have lost his saltness, wherewith will ye season it? Have salt in yourselves, and have peace one with another.	**13:34** [34]A new commandment I give unto you, That ye love one another; as I have loved you, that ye also love one another. **15:12** [12]This is my commandment, That ye love one another, as I have loved you. **15:17** [17]These things I command you, that ye love one another. **1 Jn 4:11** [11]Beloved, if God so loved us, we ought also to love one another.

Paul	Other
Rom 8:3 [3]For what the law could not do, in that it was weak through the flesh, God sending his own Son in the likeness of sinful flesh, and for sin, condemned sin in the flesh:	**Q-Quelle** Beatitudes: 1 Cor 7:15/2 Cor 13:11/Gal 6:10/ Eph 4:32/1 Thes 3:12/[Mt 5:3-12]/ [Lk 6:20b-23 (QS 8 [Thom 54,68,69])]: Love enemies: 1 Cor 7:15/Col 3:12-14/ [Mt 5:38-48, 7:12]/[Lk 6:27-36 (QS 9 [Thom 95, 6:2]); Parable of salt: 1 Cor 7:15/ [Mt 5:13]/Mk 9:49-53/[Lk 14:34-35 (QS 53)]
Rom 12:10 [10]Be kindly affectioned one to another with brotherly love; in honour preferring one another;	
Rom 12:18 [18]If it be possible, as much as lieth in you, live peaceably with all men.	
Rom 13:8 [8]Owe no man any thing, but to love one another: for he that loveth another hath fulfilled the law.	
2 Cor 13:11 [11]Finally, brethren, farewell. Be perfect, be of good comfort, be of one mind, live in peace; and the God of love and peace shall be with you.	
Gal 5:13 [13]For, brethren, ye have been called unto liberty; only use not liberty for an occasion to the flesh, but by love serve one another.	
Gal 6:2 [2]Bear ye one another's burdens, and so fulfil the law of Christ.	
Gal 6:10 [10]As we have therefore opportunity, let us do good unto all men, especially unto them who are of the household of faith.	
Eph 4:32 (Pseudo) [32]And be ye kind one to another, tenderhearted, forgiving one another, even as God for Christ's sake hath forgiven you.	
Col 3:12–14 [12]Put on therefore, as the elect of God, holy and beloved, bowels of mercies, kindness, humbleness of mind, meekness, longsuffering; [13]Forbearing one another, and forgiving one another, if any man have a quarrel against any: even as Christ forgave you, so also do ye. [14]And above all these things put on charity, which is the bond of perfectness.	
1 Thes 3:12 [12]And the Lord make you to increase and abound in love one toward another, and toward all men, even as we do toward you:	
1 Thes 4:9 [9]But as touching brotherly love ye need not that I write unto you: for ye yourselves are taught of God to love one another.	
1 Thes 5:5 [5]Ye are all the children of light, and the children of the day: we are not of the night, nor of darkness.	
1 Thes 5:12–13 [12]And we beseech you, brethren, to know them which labour among you, and are over you in the Lord, and admonish you; [13]And to esteem them very highly in love for their work's sake. And be at peace among yourselves.	
2 Thes 1:3 [3]We are bound to thank God always for you, brethren, as it is meet, because that your faith groweth exceedingly, and the charity of every one of you all toward each other aboundeth;	

1 CORINTHIANS 7:18—Calling, sexual conduct, and abstinence (7:1–40), written from Ephesus, 51 CE

Theme	1 COR	Lk	Jewish Writings
Call of uncircum-cised	**7:18** [18]Is any man called being circumcised? let him not become uncircumcised. Is any called in uncircumci-sion? let him not be circumcised.	**Acts 15:1–2** [1] And certain men which came down from Judaea taught the brethren, and said, Except ye be circumcised after the manner of Moses, ye cannot be saved. [2] When therefore Paul and Barnabas had no small dissension and disputation with them, they determined that Paul and Barnabas, and certain other of them, should go up to Jerusalem unto the apostles and elders about this question.	**Mic 1:15** [15]Yet will I bring an heir unto thee, O inhabitant of Mare-shah: he shall come unto Adullam the glory of Israel

1 CORINTHIANS 7:19—Calling, sexual conduct, and abstinence (7:1–40), written from Ephesus, 51 CE

Theme	1 COR	Paul
Keeping the law	**7:19** [19]Circumcision is nothing, and uncircumcision is nothing, but the keeping of the command-ments of God.	**Rom 2:25–29** [25]For circumcision verily profiteth, if thou keep the law: but if thou be a breaker of the law, thy cir-cumcision is made uncircumcision. [26]Therefore if the uncircumcision keep the righteousness of the law, shall not his uncircumcision be counted for circumcision? [27]And shall not uncircumcision which is by nature, if it fulfil the law, judge thee, who by the letter and circumcision dost transgress the law? [28]For he is not a Jew, which is one outwardly; neither is that circumcision, which is outward in the flesh: [29]But he is a Jew, which is one inwardly; and circumcision is that of the heart, in the spirit, and not in the letter; whose praise is not of men, but of God. **Gal 5:6** [6]For in Jesus Christ neither circumcision availeth any thing, nor uncircumcision; but faith which worketh by love. **Gal 6:15** [15]For in Christ Jesus neither circumcision availeth any thing, nor uncircumcision, but a new creature.

1 CORINTHIANS 7:22—Calling, sexual conduct, and abstinence (7:1–40), written from Ephesus, 51 CE

Theme	1 COR	Paul
Freedom in serving Christ	**7:22** [22]For he that is called in the Lord, being a servant, is the Lord's freeman: likewise also he that is called, being free, is Christ's servant.	**Eph 6:5–9 (Pseudo)** [5]Servants, be obedient to them that are your masters according to the flesh, with fear and trembling, in singleness of your heart, as unto Christ; [6]Not with eyeservice, as menpleasers; but as the servants of Christ, doing the will of God from the heart; [7]With good will doing service, as to the Lord, and not to men: [8]Knowing that whatsoever good thing any man doeth, the same shall he receive of the Lord, whether he be bond or free. [9]And, ye masters, do the same things unto them, forbearing threatening: knowing that your Master also is in heaven; neither is there respect of persons with him. **Col 3:11** [11]Where there is neither Greek nor Jew, circumcision nor uncircumcision, Barbarian, Scythian, bond nor free: but Christ is all, and in all. **Phlm 16** [16]Not now as a servant, but above a servant, a brother beloved, specially to me, but how much more unto thee, both in the flesh, and in the Lord?

1 CORINTHIANS 7:23—Calling, sexual conduct, and abstinence (7:1–40), written from Ephesus, 51 CE

Theme	1 COR
Bought with a price	**7:23** [23]Ye are bought with a price; be not ye the servants of men. **6:20** [20]For ye are bought with a price: therefore glorify God in your body, and in your spirit, which are God's.

1 CORINTHIANS 7:26—Calling, sexual conduct, and abstinence (7:1–40), written from Ephesus, 51 CE

Theme	1 COR
Unmarried and widows	**7:26** [26]I suppose therefore that this is good for the present distress, I say, that it is good for a man so to be. **7:8** [8]I say therefore to the unmarried and widows, It is good for them if they abide even as I.

1 CORINTHIANS 7:29–31—Calling, sexual conduct, and abstinence (7:1–40), written from Ephesus, 51 CE

Theme	1 COR	Mt	Mk	Lk	Paul	Other
Salvation is near	**7:29–31** [29]But this I say, brethren, the time is short: it remaineth, that both they that have wives be as though they had none; [30]And they that weep, as though they wept not; and they that rejoice, as though they rejoiced not; and they that buy, as though they possessed not; [31]And they that use this world, as not abusing it: for the fashion of this world passeth away. **10:11** [11]Now all these things happened unto them for ensamples: and they are written for our admonition, upon whom the ends of the world are come.	**16:28** [28]Verily I say unto you, There be some standing here, which shall not taste of death, till they see the Son of man coming in his kingdom.	**9:1** [1]And he said unto them, Verily I say unto you, That there be some of them that stand here, which shall not taste of death, till they have seen the kingdom of God come with power.	**9:27** [27]But I tell you of a truth, there be some standing here, which shall not taste of death, till they see the kingdom of God.	**Rom 13:11–12** [11]And that, knowing the time, that now it is high time to awake out of sleep: for now is our salvation nearer than when we believed. [12]The night is far spent, the day is at hand: let us therefore cast off the works of darkness, and let us put on the armour of light. **1 Thes 1:10** [10]And to wait for his Son from heaven, whom he raised from the dead, even Jesus, which delivered us from the wrath to come. **1 Thes 4:15** [15]For this we say unto you by the word of the Lord, that we which are alive and remain unto the coming of the Lord shall not prevent them which are asleep. **1 Thes 5:13** [13]And to esteem them very highly in love for their work's sake. And be at peace among yourselves.	**Q-Quelle** Lord's Prayer: 1 Cor 7:29-31/Rom 13:11/[Mt 6:9-13]/[Lk 11:1-4]

1 CORINTHIANS 7:33—Calling, sexual conduct, and abstinence (7:1–40), written from Ephesus, 51 CE

Theme	1 COR	Lk	Other
Marriage distracts	**7:33** [33]But he that is married careth for the things that are of the world, how he may please his wife.	**14:20** [20]And another said, I have married a wife, and therefore I cannot come.	**Q-Quelle** Great Supper: 1 Cor 7:33/[Mt 22:1-14]/Lk 14:15-20 (QS 51 [Thom 64])

1 CORINTHIANS 7:34—Calling, sexual conduct, and abstinence (7:1–40), written from Ephesus, 51 CE

Theme	1 COR	Paul
Unmarried cares for Lord	**7:34** [34]There is difference also between a wife and a virgin. The unmarried woman careth for the things of the Lord, that she may be holy both in body and in spirit: but she that is married careth for the things of the world, how she may please her husband.	**1 Tim 5:5 (Pseudo)** [5]Now she that is a widow indeed, and desolate, trusteth in God, and continueth in supplications and prayers night and day.

1 CORINTHIANS 7:35—Calling, sexual conduct, and abstinence (7:1–40), written from Ephesus, 51 CE

Theme	1 COR	Lk
Attend to the Lord	**7:35** [35]And this I speak for your own profit; not that I may cast a snare upon you, but for that which is comely, and that ye may attend upon the Lord without distraction.	**10:39–42** [39]And she had a sister called Mary, which also sat at Jesus' feet, and heard his word. [40]But Martha was cumbered about much serving, and came to him, and said, Lord, dost thou not care that my sister hath left me to serve alone? bid her therefore that she help me. [41]And Jesus answered and said unto her, Martha, Martha, thou art careful and troubled about many things: [42]But one thing is needful: and Mary hath chosen that good part, which shall not be taken away from her.

1 CORINTHIANS 7:39—Calling, sexual conduct, and abstinence (7:1–40), written from Ephesus, 51 CE

Theme	1 COR	Paul	Other
Widow, marry in the Lord	**7:39** [39]The wife is bound by the law as long as her husband liveth; but if her husband be dead, she is at liberty to be married to whom she will; only in the Lord.	**Rom 7:2** [2]For the woman which hath an husband is bound by the law to her husband so long as he liveth; but if the husband be dead, she is loosed from the law of her husband.	**Q-Quelle** Watchful & Faithful: 1 Cor 7:39/Rom 7:1-4/ [Mt 24:42-51]/[Lk 12:35-48 (QS 40)]

1 CORINTHIANS 7:40—Calling, sexual conduct, and abstinence (7:1–40), written from Ephesus, 51 CE

Theme	1 COR
Paul has spirit of God	**7:40** [40]But she is happier if she so abide, after my judgment: and I think also that I have the Spirit of God. **7:25** [25]Now concerning virgins I have no commandment of the Lord: yet I give my judgment, as one that hath obtained mercy of the Lord to be faithful.

OFFERINGS TO IDOLS (8:1–11:1)

1 CORINTHIANS 8:1—Offerings to God vis-à-vis idols (8:1–11:1), written from Ephesus, 51 CE

Theme	1 COR	Paul
Knowledge puffs up, charity edifies	**8:1** [1]Now as touching things offered unto idols, we know that we all have knowledge. Knowledge puffeth up, but charity edifieth.	**Rom 13:1–13** [1]Let every soul be subject unto the higher powers. For there is no power but of God: the powers that be are ordained of God. [2]Whosoever therefore resisteth the power, resisteth the ordinance of God: and they that resist shall receive to themselves damnation. [3]For rulers are not a terror to good works, but to the evil. Wilt thou then not be afraid of the power? do that which is good, and thou shalt have praise of the same: [4]For he is the minister of God to thee for good. But if thou do that which is evil, be afraid; for he beareth not the sword in vain: for he is the minister of God, a revenger to execute wrath upon him that doeth evil. [5]Wherefore ye must needs be subject, not only for wrath, but also for conscience sake. [6]For for this cause pay ye tribute also: for they are God's ministers, attending continually upon this very thing. [7]Render therefore to all their dues: tribute to whom tribute is due; custom to whom custom; fear to whom fear; honour to whom honour. [8]Owe no man any thing, but to love one another: for he that loveth another hath fulfilled the law. [9]For this, Thou shalt not commit adultery, Thou shalt not kill, Thou shalt not steal, Thou shalt not bear false witness, Thou shalt not covet; and if there be any other commandment, it is briefly comprehended in this saying, namely, Thou shalt love thy neighbour as thyself. [10]Love worketh no ill to his neighbour: therefore love is the fulfilling of the law. [11]And that, knowing the time, that now it is high time to awake out of sleep: for now is our salvation nearer than when we believed. [12]The night is far spent, the day is at hand: let us therefore cast off the works of darkness, and let us put on the armour of light. [13]Let us walk honestly, as in the day; not in rioting and drunkenness, not in chambering and wantonness, not in strife and envying. **Rom 14:15** [15]But if thy brother be grieved with thy meat, now walkest thou not charitably. Destroy not him with thy meat, for whom Christ died. **Rom 14:19** [19]Let us therefore follow after the things which make for peace, and things wherewith one may edify another. **Rom 15:14** [14]And I myself also am persuaded of you, my brethren, that ye also are full of goodness, filled with all knowledge, able also to admonish one another.

1 CORINTHIANS 8:3—Offerings to God vis-à-vis idols (8:1–11:1), written from Ephesus, 51 CE

Theme	1 COR	Paul
Loving God is knowing God	**8:3** [3]But if any man love God, the same is known of him.	**Rom 8:29** [29]For whom he did foreknow, he also did predestinate to be conformed to the image of his Son, that he might be the firstborn among many brethren. **Gal 4:9** [9]But now, after that ye have known God, or rather are known of God, how turn ye again to the weak and beggarly elements, whereunto ye desire again to be in bondage?

1 CORINTHIANS 8:4—Offerings to God vis-à-vis idols (8:1–11:1), written from Ephesus, 51 CE

Theme	1 COR	Jewish Writings
Idols are nothing	**8:4** [4]As concerning therefore the eating of those things that are offered in sacrifice unto idols, we know that an idol is nothing in the world, and that there is none other God but one. **10:19** [19]What say I then? that the idol is any thing, or that which is offered in sacrifice to idols is any thing?	**Dt 6:4** [6]And these words, which I command thee this day, shall be in thine heart:

1 CORINTHIANS 8:6—Offerings to God vis-à-vis idols (8:1–11:1), written from Ephesus, 51 CE

Theme	1 COR	Jn	Paul	Jewish Writings
One God, one Lord	**8:6** [6]But to us there is but one God, the Father, of whom are all things, and we in him; and one Lord Jesus Christ, by whom are all things, and we by him. **1:2–3** [2]Unto the church of God which is at Corinth, to them that are sanctified in Christ Jesus, called to be saints, with all that in every place call upon the name of Jesus Christ our Lord, both theirs and ours: [3]Grace be unto you, and peace, from God our Father, and from the Lord Jesus Christ.	**1:3** [3]All things were made by him; and without him was not any thing made that was made.	**Rom 11:36** [36]For of him, and through him, and to him, are all things: to whom be glory for ever. Amen. **Eph 4:5–6 (Pseudo)** [5]One Lord, one faith, one baptism, [6]One God and Father of all, who is above all, and through all, and in you all. **Col 1:16** [16]For by him were all things created, that are in heaven, and that are in earth, visible and invisible, whether they be thrones, or dominions, or principalities, or powers: all things were created by him, and for him:	**Mal 2:10** [10]Have we not all one father? hath not one God created us? why do we deal treacherously every man against his brother, by profaning the covenant of our fathers?

1 CORINTHIANS 8:7—Offerings to God vis-à-vis idols (8:1–11:1), written from Ephesus, 51 CE

Theme	1 COR	Paul
Do not defile the weak conscience	**8:7** [7]Howbeit there is not in every man that knowledge: for some with conscience of the idol unto this hour eat it as a thing offered unto an idol; and their conscience being weak is defiled. **10:28** [28]But if any man say unto you, This is offered in sacrifice unto idols, eat not for his sake that showed it, and for conscience sake: for the earth is the Lord's, and the fulness thereof:	**Rom 14:1** [1]Him that is weak in the faith receive ye, but not to doubtful disputations. **Rom 14:23** [23]And he that doubteth is damned if he eat, because he eateth not of faith: for whatsoever is not of faith is sin. **Rom 15:1** [1]We then that are strong ought to bear the infirmities of the weak, and not to please ourselves.

1 CORINTHIANS 8:9—Offerings to God vis-à-vis idols (8:1–11:1), written from Ephesus, 51 CE

Theme	1 COR	Paul
Do not cause weak to stumble	**8:9** [9]But take heed lest by any means this liberty of yours become a stumblingblock to them that are weak.	**Rom 14:13** [13]Let us not therefore judge one another any more: but judge this rather, that no man put a stumblingblock or an occasion to fall in his brother's way. **Rom 14:20-21** [20]For meat destroy not the work of God. All things indeed are pure; but it is evil for that man who eateth with offence. [21]It is good neither to eat flesh, nor to drink wine, nor any thing whereby thy brother stumbleth, or is offended, or is made weak.

1 CORINTHIANS 8:11—Offerings to God vis-à-vis idols (8:1–11:1), written from Ephesus, 51 CE

Theme	1 COR	Paul
Do not cause weak to stumble	**8:11** [11]And through thy knowledge shall the weak brother perish, for whom Christ died?	**Rom 14:15** [15]But if thy brother be grieved with thy meat, now walkest thou not charitably. Destroy not him with thy meat, for whom Christ died. **Rom 14:20** [20]For meat destroy not the work of God. All things indeed are pure; but it is evil for that man who eateth with offence.

1 CORINTHIANS 8:13—Offerings to God vis-à-vis idols (8:1–11:1), written from Ephesus, 51 CE

Theme	1 COR	Mt	Mk
Prevent stumbling	**8:13** [13]Wherefore, if meat make my brother to offend, I will eat no flesh while the world standeth, lest I make my brother to offend. **8:11** [11]And through thy knowledge shall the weak brother perish, for whom Christ died?	**7:1** [1]Judge not, that ye be not judged. **7:24–27** [24]Therefore whosoever heareth these sayings of mine, and doeth them, I will liken him unto a wise man, which built his house upon a rock: [25]And the rain descended, and the floods came, and the winds blew, and beat upon that house; and it fell not: for it was founded upon a rock. [26]And every one that heareth these sayings of mine, and doeth them not, shall be likened unto a foolish man, which built his house upon the sand: [27]And the rain descended, and the floods came, and the winds blew, and beat upon that house; and it fell: and great was the fall of it. **18:6–9** [6]But whoso shall offend one of these little ones which believe in me, it were better for him that a millstone were hanged about his neck, and that he were drowned in the depth of the sea. [7]Woe unto the world because of offences! for it must needs be that offences come; but woe to that man by whom the offence cometh! [8]Wherefore if thy hand or thy foot offend thee, cut them off, and cast them from thee: it is better for thee to enter into life halt or maimed, rather than having two hands or two feet to be cast into everlasting fire. [9]And if thine eye offend thee, pluck it out, and cast it from thee: it is better for thee to enter into life with one eye, rather than having two eyes to be cast into hell fire. **18:18** [18]Verily I say unto you, Whatsoever ye shall bind on earth shall be bound in heaven: and whatsoever ye shall loose on earth shall be loosed in heaven.	**9:42–47** [42]And whosoever shall offend one of these little ones that believe in me, it is better for him that a millstone were hanged about his neck, and he were cast into the sea. [43]And if thy hand offend thee, cut it off: it is better for thee to enter into life maimed, than having two hands to go into hell, into the fire that never shall be quenched: [44]Where their worm dieth not, and the fire is not quenched. [45]And if thy foot offend thee, cut it off: it is better for thee to enter halt into life, than having two feet to be cast into hell, into the fire that never shall be quenched: [46]Where their worm dieth not, and the fire is not quenched. [47]And if thine eye offend thee, pluck it out: it is better for thee to enter into the kingdom of God with one eye, than having two eyes to be cast into hell fire:

Lk	Paul	Other
6:37 [37]Judge not, and ye shall not be judged: condemn not, and ye shall not be condemned: forgive, and ye shall be forgiven: **17:2** [2]It were better for him that a millstone were hanged about his neck, and he cast into the sea, than that he should offend one of these little ones.	**Rom 14:3** [3]Let not him that eateth despise him that eateth not; and let not him which eateth not judge him that eateth: for God hath received him. **Rom 14:10** [10]But why dost thou judge thy brother? or why dost thou set at nought thy brother? for we shall all stand before the judgment seat of Christ. **Rom 14:12** [12]So then every one of us shall give account of himself to God. **Rom 14:13–23** [13]Let us not therefore judge one another any more: but judge this rather, that no man put a stumblingblock or an occasion to fall in his brother's way. [14]I know, and am persuaded by the Lord Jesus, that there is nothing unclean of itself: but to him that esteemeth any thing to be unclean, to him it is unclean. [15]**But if thy brother be grieved with thy meat, now walkest thou not charitably. Destroy not him with thy meat, for whom Christ died.** [16]Let not then your good be evil spoken of: [17]For the kingdom of God is not meat and drink; but righteousness, and peace, and joy in the Holy Ghost. [18]For he that in these things serveth Christ is acceptable to God, and approved of men. [19]Let us therefore follow after the things which make for peace, and things wherewith one may edify another. [20]For meat destroy not the work of God. All things indeed are pure; but it is evil for that man who eateth with offence. [21]It is good neither to eat flesh, nor to drink wine, nor any thing whereby thy brother stumbleth, or is offended, or is made weak. [22]Hast thou faith? have it to thyself before God. Happy is he that condemneth not himself in that thing which he alloweth. [23]And he that doubteth is damned if he eat, because he eateth not of faith: for whatsoever is not of faith is sin.	**Q-Quelle** Judging: 1 Cor 8:13/Mt 7:1-5, [Mt 10:24-25,12:36-37, 15:14]/[Mk 4:24-25]/Lk 6:37-42 (QS 10); Warning against offenses: 1 Cor 8:13/ [Mt 18:6-7]/Mk 9:42/Lk 17:1-3a (QS 57)

1 CORINTHIANS 9:1–6—Offerings to God vis-à-vis idols (8:1–11:1), written from Ephesus, 51 CE

Theme	1 COR	Mt	Mk
Authority & apostleship	**9:1–6** [1]Am I not an apostle? am I not free? have I not seen Jesus Christ our Lord? are not ye my work in the Lord? [2]If I be not an apostle unto others, yet doubtless I am to you: for the seal of mine apostleship are ye in the Lord. [3]Mine answer to them that do examine me is this, [4]Have we not power to eat and to drink? [5]Have we not power to lead about a sister, a wife, as well as other apostles, and as the brethren of the Lord, and Cephas? [6]Or I only and Barnabas, have not we power to forbear working? **9:12** [12]If others be partakers of this power over you, are not we rather? Nevertheless we have not used this power; but suffer all things, lest we should hinder the gospel of Christ. **9:18** [18]What is my reward then? Verily that, when I preach the gospel, I may make the gospel of Christ without charge, that I abuse not my power in the gospel. **9:27** [27]But I keep under my body, and bring it into subjection: lest that by any means, when I have preached to others, I myself should be a castaway.	**10:1** [1]And when he had called unto him his twelve disciples, he gave them power against unclean spirits, to cast them out, and to heal all manner of sickness and all manner of disease. **10:7–8** [7]And as ye go, preach, saying, The kingdom of heaven is at hand. [8]Heal the sick, cleanse the lepers, raise the dead, cast out devils: freely ye have received, freely give. **10:40** [40]He that receiveth you receiveth me, and he that receiveth me receiveth him that sent me.	**6:7** [7]And he called unto him the twelve, and began to send them forth by two and two; and gave them power over unclean spirits;

1 CORINTHIANS 9:1—Offerings to God vis-à-vis idols (8:1–11:1), written from Ephesus, 51 CE

Theme	1 COR
Authority & apostleship	**9:1** [1]Am I not an apostle? am I not free? have I not seen Jesus Christ our Lord? are not ye my work in the Lord? **9:19** [19]For though I be free from all men, yet have I made myself servant unto all, that I might gain the more. **15:8–9** [8]And last of all he was seen of me also, as of one born out of due time. [9]For I am the least of the apostles, that am not meet to be called an apostle, because I persecuted the church of God.

Lk	Jn	Paul	Other
9:2 [2]And he sent them to preach the kingdom of God, and to heal the sick. **10:9** [9]And heal the sick that are therein, and say unto them, The kingdom of God is come nigh unto you. **10:16** [16]He that heareth you heareth me; and he that despiseth you despiseth me; and he that despiseth me despiseth him that sent me.	**13:20** [20]Verily, verily, I say unto you, He that receiveth whomsoever I send receiveth me; and he that receiveth me receiveth him that sent me.	**1 Thes 4:8** [8]He therefore that despiseth, despiseth not man, but God, who hath also given unto us his holy Spirit.	**Q-Quelle** Commissioning of 12: 1 Cor 9:1-6/ Mt 10:1, 10:7-11, [10:14]/Mk 6:6b-13/ Lk 9:1-6; Commissioning of 70: 1 Cor 9:1-6/[Mt 9:37-38], Mt 10:7-16/ Lk 10:1-12 (QS 20 [Thom 73, 14:2]); Whoever hears you hears me: 1 Cor 9:1-6/[Mt 10:40]/Lk 10:16 (QS 23)

Lk	Paul
Acts 9:17 [17]And Ananias went his way, and entered into the house; and putting his hands on him said, Brother Saul, the Lord, even Jesus, that appeared unto thee in the way as thou camest, hath sent me, that thou mightest receive thy sight, and be filled with the Holy Ghost. **Acts 26:16** [16]But rise, and stand upon thy feet: for I have appeared unto thee for this purpose, to make thee a minister and a witness both of these things which thou hast seen, and of those things in the which I will appear unto thee;	**2 Cor 12:12** [12]Truly the signs of an apostle were wrought among you in all patience, in signs, and wonders, and mighty deeds.

1 CORINTHIANS 9:6—Offerings to God vis-à-vis idols (8:1–11:1), written from Ephesus, 51 CE

Theme	1 COR	Lk
Barnabas	**9:6** 6Or I only and Barnabas, have not we power to forbear working?	**Acts 4:36–37** 36And Joses, who by the apostles was surnamed Barnabas, (which is, being interpreted, The son of consolation,) a Levite, and of the country of Cyprus, 37Having land, sold it, and brought the money, and laid it at the apostles' feet. **Acts 13:1–12** 1Now there were in the church that was at Antioch certain prophets and teachers; as Barnabas, and Simeon that was called Niger, and Lucius of Cyrene, and Manaen, which had been brought up with Herod the tetrarch, and Saul. 2As they ministered to the Lord, and fasted, the Holy Ghost said, Separate me Barnabas and Saul for the work whereunto I have called them. 3And when they had fasted and prayed, and laid their hands on them, they sent them away. 4So they, being sent forth by the Holy Ghost, departed unto Seleucia; and from thence they sailed to Cyprus. 5And when they were at Salamis, they preached the word of God in the synagogues of the Jews: and they had also John to their minister. 6And when they had gone through the isle unto Paphos, they found a certain sorcerer, a false prophet, a Jew, whose name was Barjesus: 7Which was with the deputy of the country, Sergius Paulus, a prudent man; who called for Barnabas and Saul, and desired to hear the word of God. 8But Elymas the sorcerer (for so is his name by interpretation) withstood them, seeking to turn away the deputy from the faith. 9Then Saul, (who also is called Paul,) filled with the Holy Ghost, set his eyes on him, 10And said, O full of all subtlety and all mischief, thou child of the devil, thou enemy of all righteousness, wilt thou not cease to pervert the right ways of the Lord? 11And now, behold, the hand of the Lord is upon thee, and thou shalt be blind, not seeing the sun for a season. And immediately there fell on him a mist and a darkness; and he went about seeking some to lead him by the hand. 12Then the deputy, when he saw what was done, believed, being astonished at the doctrine of the Lord.

1 CORINTHIANS 9:7—Offerings to God vis-à-vis idols (8:1–11:1), written from Ephesus, 51 CE

Theme	1 COR	Paul
Partaking in work	**9:7** 7Who goeth a warfare any time at his own charges? who planteth a vineyard, and eateth not of the fruit thereof? or who feedeth a flock, and eateth not of the milk of the flock?	**2 Tim 2:3–4 (Pseudo)** 3Thou therefore endure hardness, as a good soldier of Jesus Christ. 4No man that warreth entangleth himself with the affairs of this life; that he may please him who hath chosen him to be a soldier

1 CORINTHIANS 9:9—Offerings to God vis-à-vis idols (8:1–11:1), written from Ephesus, 51 CE

Theme	1 COR	Paul
God takes care	**9:9** 9For it is written in the law of Moses, Thou shalt not muzzle the mouth of the ox that treadeth out the corn. Doth God take care for oxen?	**1 Tim 5:18 (Pseudo)** 18For the scripture saith, Thou shalt not muzzle the ox that treadeth out the corn. And, The labourer is worthy of his reward.

1 CORINTHIANS 9:10—Offerings to God vis-à-vis idols (8:1–11:1), written from Ephesus, 51 CE

Theme	1 COR	Paul
Plow in hope	**9:10** 10Or saith he it altogether for our sakes? For our sakes, no doubt, this is written: that he that ploweth should plow in hope; and that he that thresheth in hope should be partaker of his hope.	**2 Tim 2:6 (Pseudo)** 6The husbandman that laboureth must be first partaker of the fruits.

Paul

Gal 2:1

[1]Then fourteen years after I went up again to Jerusalem with Barnabas, and took Titus with me also.

Gal 2:9

[9]And when James, Cephas, and John, who seemed to be pillars, perceived the grace that was given unto me, they gave to me and Barnabas the right hands of fellowship; that we should go unto the heathen, and they unto the circumcision.

Gal 2:13

[13]And the other Jews dissembled likewise with him; insomuch that Barnabas also was carried away with their dissimulation.

Col 4:10

[10]Aristarchus my fellowprisoner saluteth you, and Marcus, sister's son to Barnabas, (touching whom ye received commandments: if he come unto you, receive him;)

Jewish Writings

Dt 25:4

[4]Thou shalt not muzzle the ox when he treadeth out the corn.

1 CORINTHIANS 9:11—Offerings to God vis-à-vis idols (8:1–11:1), written from Ephesus, 51 CE

Theme	1 COR	Paul
Workers sharing in benefits	**9:11** [11]If we have sown unto you spiritual things, is it a great thing if we shall reap your carnal things?	**Rom 15:27** [27]It hath pleased them verily; and their debtors they are. For if the Gentiles have been made partakers of their spiritual things, their duty is also to minister unto them in carnal things.

1 CORINTHIANS 9:12—Offerings to God vis-à-vis idols (8:1–11:1), written from Ephesus, 51 CE

Theme	1 COR
Suffer all things for gospel	**9:12** [12]If others be partakers of this power over you, are not we rather? Nevertheless we have not used this power; but suffer all things, lest we should hinder the gospel of Christ.

1 CORINTHIANS 9:13—Offerings to God vis-à-vis idols (8:1–11:1), written from Ephesus, 51 CE

Theme	1 COR
Holy lifestyle	**9:13** [13]Do ye not know that they which minister about holy things live of the things of the temple? and they which wait at the altar are partakers with the altar?

Paul

2 Cor 11:7–12

[7]Have I committed an offence in abasing myself that ye might be exalted, because I have preached to you the gospel
of God freely? [8]I robbed other churches, taking wages of them, to do you service. [9]And when I was present with you,
and wanted, I was chargeable to no man: for that which was lacking to me the brethren which came from Macedonia
supplied: and in all things I have kept myself from being burdensome unto you, and so will I keep myself. [10]As the truth
of Christ is in me, no man shall stop me of this boasting in the regions of Achaia. [11]Wherefore? because I love you not?
God knoweth. [12]But what I do, that I will do, that I may cut off occasion from them which desire occasion; that wherein
they glory, they may be found even as we.

2 Cor 12: 13–18

[13]For what is it wherein ye were inferior to other churches, except it be that I myself was not burdensome to you? forgive
me this wrong. [14]Behold, the third time I am ready to come to you; and I will not be burdensome to you: for I seek not
yours, but you: for the children ought not to lay up for the parents, but the parents for the children. [15]And I will very
gladly spend and be spent for you; though the more abundantly I love you, the less I be loved. [16]But be it so, I did not
burden you: nevertheless, being crafty, I caught you with guile. [17]Did I make a gain of you by any of them whom I sent
unto you? [18]I desired Titus, and with him I sent a brother. Did Titus make a gain of you? walked we not in the same
spirit? walked we not in the same steps?

2 Thes 3:6–12

[6]Now we command you, brethren, in the name of our Lord Jesus Christ, that ye withdraw yourselves from every
brother that walketh disorderly, and not after the tradition which he received of us. [7]For yourselves know how ye ought
to follow us: for we behaved not ourselves disorderly among you; [8]Neither did we eat any man's bread for nought; but
wrought with labour and travail night and day, that we might not be chargeable to any of you: [9]Not because we have
not power, but to make ourselves an ensample unto you to follow us. [10]For even when we were with you, this we commanded you, that if any would not work, neither should he eat. [11]For we hear that there are some which walk among you
disorderly, working not at all, but are busybodies. [12]Now them that are such we command and exhort by our Lord Jesus
Christ, that with quietness they work, and eat their own bread.

Jewish Writings

Num 18:8

[8]And the LORD spake unto Aaron, Behold, I also have given thee the charge of mine heave offerings of all the hallowed things
of the children of Israel; unto thee have I given them by reason of the anointing, and to thy sons, by an ordinance for eve.

Num 18:31

[31]And ye shall eat it in every place, ye and your households: for it is your reward for your service in the tabernacle of the congregation.

Dt 18:1–5

[1]The priests the Levites, and all the tribe of Levi, shall have no part nor inheritance with Israel: they shall eat the offerings of
the LORD made by fire, and his inheritance. [2]Therefore shall they have no inheritance among their brethren: the LORD is
their inheritance, as he hath said unto them. [3]And this shall be the priest's due from the people, from them that offer a sacrifice, whether it be ox or sheep; and they shall give unto the priest the shoulder, and the two cheeks, and the maw. [4]The firstfruit
also of thy corn, of thy wine, and of thine oil, and the first of the fleece of thy sheep, shalt thou give him. [5]For the LORD thy
God hath chosen him out of all thy tribes, to stand to minister in the name of the LORD, him and his sons for ever.

1 CORINTHIANS 9:14—Offerings to God vis-à-vis idols (8:1–11:1), written from Ephesus, 51 CE

Theme	1 COR	Mt	Mk
Instructing the charge	**9:14** [14]Even so hath the Lord ordained that they which preach the gospel should live of the gospel.	**4:17** [17]From that time Jesus began to preach, and to say, Repent: for the kingdom of heaven is at hand. **10:5–15** [5]These twelve Jesus sent forth, and commanded them, saying, Go not into the way of the Gentiles, and into any city of the Samaritans enter ye not: [6]But go rather to the lost sheep of the house of Israel. [7]And as ye go, preach, saying, The kingdom of heaven is at hand. [8]Heal the sick, cleanse the lepers, raise the dead, cast out devils: freely ye have received, freely give. [9]Provide neither gold, nor silver, nor brass in your purses, [10]Nor scrip for your journey, neither two coats, neither shoes, nor yet staves: for the workman is worthy of his meat. [11]And into whatsoever city or town ye shall enter, inquire who in it is worthy; and there abide till ye go thence. [12]And when ye come into an house, salute it. [13]And if the house be worthy, let your peace come upon it: but if it be not worthy, let your peace return to you. [14]And whosoever shall not receive you, nor hear your words, when ye depart out of that house or city, shake off the dust of your feet. [15]Verily I say unto you, It shall be more tolerable for the land of Sodom and Gomorrha in the day of judgment, than for that city. **15:24** [24]But he answered and said, I am not sent but unto the lost sheep of the house of Israel.	**1:15** [15]And saying, The time is fulfilled, and the kingdom of God is at hand: repent ye, and believe the gospel. **6:7–13** [7]And he called unto him the twelve, and began to send them forth by two and two; and gave them power over unclean spirits; [8]And commanded them that they should take nothing for their journey, save a staff only; no scrip, no bread, no money in their purse: [9]But be shod with sandals; and not put on two coats. [10]And he said unto them, In what place soever ye enter into an house, there abide till ye depart from that place. [11]And whosoever shall not receive you, nor hear you, when ye depart thence, shake off the dust under your feet for a testimony against them. Verily I say unto you, It shall be more tolerable for Sodom and Gomorrha in the day of judgment, than for that city. [12]And they went out, and preached that men should repent. [13]And they cast out many devils, and anointed with oil many that were sick, and healed them.

1 CORINTHIANS 9:15—Offerings to God vis-à-vis idols (8:1–11:1), written from Ephesus, 51 CE

Theme	1 COR	Paul	Jewish	Other
Lacking no good thing	**9:15** [15]But I have used none of these things: neither have I written these things, that it should be so done unto me: for it were better for me to die, than that any man should make my glorying void.	**2 Cor 11:9–10** [9]And when I was present with you, and wanted, I was chargeable to no man: for that which was lacking to me the brethren which came from Macedonia supplied: and in all things I have kept myself from being burdensome unto you, and so will I keep myself. [10]As the truth of Christ is in me, no man shall stop me of this boasting in the regions of Achaia.	**Ps 23:1** [1]The LORD is my shepherd; I shall not want.	**Q-Quelle** 1 Cor 9:13-15 (9:14)

Lk	Paul	Other
9:1–6 [1]Then he called his twelve disciples together, and gave them power and authority over all devils, and to cure diseases. [2]And he sent them to preach the kingdom of God, and to heal the sick. [3]And he said unto them, Take nothing for your journey, neither staves, nor scrip, neither bread, neither money; neither have two coats apiece. [4]And whatsoever house ye enter into, there abide, and thence depart. [5]And whosoever will not receive you, when ye go out of that city, shake off the very dust from your feet for a testimony against them. [6]And they departed, and went through the towns, preaching the gospel, and healing every where. **10:1–16** [1]After these things the Lord appointed other seventy also, and sent them two and two before his face into every city and place, whither he himself would come. [2]Therefore said he unto them, The harvest truly is great, but the labourers are few: pray ye therefore the Lord of the harvest, that he would send forth labourers into his harvest. [3]Go your ways: behold, I send you forth as lambs among wolves. [4]Carry neither purse, nor scrip, nor shoes: and salute no man by the way. [5]And into whatsoever house ye enter, first say, Peace be to this house. [6]And if the son of peace be there, your peace shall rest upon it: if not, it shall turn to you again. [7]And in the same house remain, eating and drinking such things as they give: for the labourer is worthy of his hire. Go not from house to house. [8]And into whatsoever city ye enter, and they receive you, eat such things as are set before you: [9]And heal the sick that are therein, and say unto them, The kingdom of God is come nigh unto you. [10]But into whatsoever city ye enter, and they receive you not, go your ways out into the streets of the same, and say, [11]Even the very dust of your city, which cleaveth on us, we do wipe off against you: notwithstanding be ye sure of this, that the kingdom of God is come nigh unto you. [12]But I say unto you, that it shall be more tolerable in that day for Sodom, than for that city. [13]Woe unto thee, Chorazin! woe unto thee, Bethsaida! for if the mighty works had been done in Tyre and Sidon, which have been done in you, they had a great while ago repented, sitting in sackcloth and ashes. [14]But it shall be more tolerable for Tyre and Sidon at the judgment, than for you. [15]And thou, Capernaum, which art exalted to heaven, shalt be thrust down to hell. [16]He that heareth you heareth me; and he that despiseth you despiseth me; and he that despiseth me despiseth him that sent me. **22:35–36** [35]And he said unto them, When I sent you without purse, and scrip, and shoes, lacked ye any thing? And they said, Nothing. [36]Then said he unto them, But now, he that hath a purse, let him take it, and likewise his scrip: and he that hath no sword, let him sell his garment, and buy one.	**1 Tim 5:18 (Pseudo)** [18]For the scripture saith, Thou shalt not muzzle the ox that treadeth out the corn. And, The labourer is worthy of his reward.	**Did 13:1** [13]Every true prophet who wants to settle down with you deserves his food. **Q-Quelle** Commissioning of 12: 1 Cor 9:14/ [2 Cor 11:7][Gal 2:7-9]/1 Tim 5:18/[Mt 10:1], Mt 10:7-11, 14/ Mk 6:6b-13/Lk 9:1-6; Commissioning of 70: 1 Cor 9:14/ [Mt 9:37-38], Mt 10:7-16/Lk 10:1-12 (QS 20 [Thom 14:2, 73]); Whoever hears you hears me: 1 Cor 9:14/ [Mt 10:40]/Lk 10:16 (QS 23)

1 CORINTHIANS 9:16—Offerings to God vis-à-vis idols (8:1–11:1), written from Ephesus, 51 CE

Theme	1 COR	Lk
Commitment to gospel message	**9:16** [16]For though I preach the gospel, I have nothing to glory of: for necessity is laid upon me; yea, woe is unto me, if I preach not the gospel!	**Acts 26:14–18** [14]And when we were all fallen to the earth, I heard a voice speaking unto me, and saying in the Hebrew tongue, Saul, Saul, why persecutest thou me? it is hard for thee to kick against the pricks. [15]And I said, Who art thou, Lord? And he said, I am Jesus whom thou persecutest. [16]But rise, and stand upon thy feet: for I have appeared unto thee for this purpose, to make thee a minister and a witness both of these things which thou hast seen, and of those things in the which I will appear unto thee; [17]Delivering thee from the people, and from the Gentiles, unto whom now I send thee, [18]To open their eyes, and to turn them from darkness to light, and from the power of Satan unto God, that they may receive forgiveness of sins, and inheritance among them which are sanctified by faith that is in me.

1 CORINTHIANS 9:17—Offerings to God vis-à-vis idols (8:1–11:1), written from Ephesus, 51 CE

Theme	1 COR	Paul
Paul's committed service	**9:17** [17]For if I do this thing willingly, I have a reward: but if against my will, a dispensation of the gospel is committed unto me. **4:1** [1]Let a man so account of us, as of the ministers of Christ, and stewards of the mysteries of God.	**Gal 2:7** [7]But contrariwise, when they saw that the gospel of the uncircumcision was committed unto me, as the gospel of the circumcision was unto Peter;

1 CORINTHIANS 9:18—Offerings to God vis-à-vis idols (8:1–11:1), written from Ephesus, 51 CE

Theme	1 COR	Mt	Lk
Christian teaching is free	**9:18** [18]What is my reward then? Verily that, when I preach the gospel, I may make the gospel of Christ without charge, that I abuse not my power in the gospel. **9:4** [4]Have we not power to eat and to drink?	**10:5–6** [5]These twelve Jesus sent forth, and commanded them, saying, Go not into the way of the Gentiles, and into any city of the Samaritans enter ye not: [6]But go rather to the lost sheep of the house of Israel. **10:8** [8]Heal the sick, cleanse the lepers, raise the dead, cast out devils: freely ye have received, freely give. **11:18** [18]For John came neither eating nor drinking, and they say, He hath a devil.	**10:7–8** [7]And in the same house remain, eating and drinking such things as they give: for the labourer is worthy of his hire. Go not from house to house. [8]And into whatsoever city ye enter, and they receive you, eat such things as are set before you:

Paul	**Other**
2 Cor 11:7–12	**Q-Quelle**
[7]Have I committed an offence in abasing myself that ye might be exalted, because I have preached to you the gospel of God freely? [8]I robbed other churches, taking wages of them, to do you service. [9]And when I was present with you, and wanted, I was chargeable to no man: for that which was lacking to me the brethren which came from Macedonia supplied: and in all things I have kept myself from being burdensome unto you, and so will I keep myself. [10]As the truth of Christ is in me, no man shall stop me of this boasting in the regions of Achaia. [11]Wherefore? because I love you not? God knoweth. [12]But what I do, that I will do, that I may cut off occasion from them which desire occasion; that wherein they glory, they may be found even as we.	Commissioning of 12: 1 Cor 9:18/2 Cor 11:7/ Gal 2:7-9/[2 Thes 3:8-9]/ [Mt 10:1, 7-11, 14]/[Mk 6:6b-13]/[Lk 9:1-6]; Commissioning of 70: [Mt 9:37-38], Mt 10:7-16/Lk 10:1-12 (QS 20 [Thom73, 14:2], QS 21)
Gal 2:8–9	
[8](For he that wrought effectually in Peter to the apostleship of the circumcision, the same was mighty in me toward the Gentiles:) [9]And when James, Cephas, and John, who seemed to be pillars, perceived the grace that was given unto me, they gave to me and Barnabas the right hands of fellowship; that we should go unto the heathen, and they unto the circumcision.	

1 CORINTHIANS 9:19—Offerings to God vis-à-vis idols (8:1–11:1), written from Ephesus, 51 CE

Theme	1 COR	Mt	Mk	Lk
Humble service to God	**9:19** [19]For though I be free from all men, yet have I made myself servant unto all, that I might gain the more. **9:22** [22]To the weak became I as weak, that I might gain the weak: I am made all things to all men, that I might by all means save some. **10:3** [3]And did all eat the same spiritual meat; **10:33–11:1** [33]Even as I please all men in all things, not seeking mine own profit, but the profit of many, that they may be saved. [1]Be ye followers of me, even as I also am of Christ.	**20:20** [20]Then came to him the mother of Zebedee's children with her sons, worshipping him, and desiring a certain thing of him. **20:26** [26]But it shall not be so among you: but whosoever will be great among you, let him be your minister; **20:27–28** [27]And whosoever will be chief among you, let him be your servant: [28]Even as the Son of man came not to be ministered unto, but to minister, and to give his life a ransom for many. **23:12** [12]And whosoever shall exalt himself shall be abased; and he that shall humble himself shall be exalted.	**9:35** [35]And he sat down, and called the twelve, and saith unto them, If any man desire to be first, the same shall be last of all, and servant of all. **10:35–45** [35]And James and John, the sons of Zebedee, come unto him, saying, Master, we would that thou shouldest do for us whatsoever we shall desire. [36]And he said unto them, What would ye that I should do for you? [37]They said unto him, Grant unto us that we may sit, one on thy right hand, and the other on thy left hand, in thy glory. [38]But Jesus said unto them, Ye know not what ye ask: can ye drink of the cup that I drink of? and be baptized with the baptism that I am baptized with? [39]And they said unto him, We can. And Jesus said unto them, Ye shall indeed drink of the cup that I drink of; and with the baptism that I am baptized withal shall ye be baptized: [40]But to sit on my right hand and on my left hand is not mine to give; but it shall be given to them for whom it is prepared. [41]And when the ten heard it, they began to be much displeased with James and John. [42]But Jesus called them to him, and saith unto them, Ye know that they which are accounted to rule over the Gentiles exercise lordship over them; and their great ones exercise authority upon them. [43]But so shall it not be among you: but whosoever will be great among you, shall be your minister: [44]And whosoever of you will be the chiefest, shall be servant of all. [45]For even the Son of man came not to be ministered unto, but to minister, and to give his life a ransom for many.	**14:11** [11]For whosoever exalteth himself shall be abased; and he that humbleth himself shall be exalted. **18:9** [9]And he spake this parable unto certain which trusted in themselves that they were righteous, and despised others: **18:14** [14]I tell you, this man went down to his house justified rather than the other: for every one that exalteth himself shall be abased; and he that humbleth himself shall be exalted. **22:24–27** [24]And there was also a strife among them, which of them should be accounted the greatest. [25]And he said unto them, The kings of the Gentiles exercise lordship over them; and they that exercise authority upon them are called benefactors. [26]But ye shall not be so: but he that is greatest among you, let him be as the younger; and he that is chief, as he that doth serve. [27]For whether is greater, he that sitteth at meat, or he that serveth? is not he that sitteth at meat? but I am among you as he that serveth.

Jn
Ch 13
[1]Now before the feast of the passover, when Jesus knew that his hour was come that he should depart out of this world unto the Father, having loved his own which were in the world, he loved them unto the end. [2]And supper being ended, the devil having now put into the heart of Judas Iscariot, Simon's son, to betray him; [3]Jesus knowing that the Father had given all things into his hands, and that he was come from God, and went to God; [4]He riseth from supper, and laid aside his garments; and took a towel, and girded himself. [5]After that he poureth water into a basin, and began to wash the disciples' feet, and to wipe them with the towel wherewith he was girded. [6]Then cometh he to Simon Peter: and Peter saith unto him, Lord, dost thou wash my feet? [7]Jesus answered and said unto him, What I do thou knowest not now; but thou shalt know hereafter. [8]Peter saith unto him, Thou shalt never wash my feet. Jesus answered him, If I wash thee not, thou hast no part with me. [9]Simon Peter saith unto him, Lord, not my feet only, but also my hands and my head. [10]Jesus saith to him, He that is washed needeth not save to wash his feet, but is clean every whit: and ye are clean, but not all. [11]For he knew who should betray him; therefore said he, Ye are not all clean. [12]So after he had washed their feet, and had taken his garments, and was set down again, he said unto them, Know ye what I have done to you? [13]Ye call me Master and Lord: and ye say well; for so I am. [14]If I then, your Lord and Master, have washed your feet; ye also ought to wash one another's feet. [15]For I have given you an example, that ye should do as I have done to you. [16]Verily, verily, I say unto you, The servant is not greater than his lord; neither he that is sent greater than he that sent him. [17]If ye know these things, happy are ye if ye do them. [18]I speak not of you all: I know whom I have chosen: but that the scripture may be fulfilled, He that eateth bread with me hath lifted up his heel against me. [19]Now I tell you before it come, that, when it is come to pass, ye may believe that I am he. [20]Verily, verily, I say unto you, He that receiveth whomsoever I send receiveth me; and he that receiveth me receiveth him that sent me. [21]When Jesus had thus said, he was troubled in spirit, and testified, and said, Verily, verily, I say unto you, that one of you shall betray me. [22]Then the disciples looked one on another, doubting of whom he spake. [23]Now there was leaning on Jesus' bosom one of his disciples, whom Jesus loved. [24]Simon Peter therefore beckoned to him, that he should ask who it should be of whom he spake. [25]He then lying on Jesus' breast saith unto him, Lord, who is it? [26]Jesus answered, He it is, to whom I shall give a sop, when I have dipped it. And when he had dipped the sop, he gave it to Judas Iscariot, the son of Simon. [27]And after the sop Satan entered into him. Then said Jesus unto him, That thou doest, do quickly. [28]Now no man at the table knew for what intent he spake this unto him. [29]For some of them thought, because Judas had the bag, that Jesus had said unto him, Buy those things that we have need of against the feast; or, that he should give something to the poor. [30]He then having received the sop went immedi- ately out: and it was night. [31]Therefore, when he was gone out, Jesus said, Now is the Son of man glori- fied, and God is glorified in him. [32]If God be glorified in him, God shall also glorify him in himself, and shall straightway glorify him. [33]Little children, yet a little while I am with you. Ye shall seek me: and as I said unto the Jews, Whither I go, ye cannot come; so now I say to you. [34]A new commandment I give unto you, That ye love one another; as I have loved you, that ye also love one another. [35]By this shall all men know that ye are my disciples, if ye have love one to another. [36]Simon Peter said unto him, Lord, whither goest thou? Jesus answered him, Whither I go, thou canst not follow me now; but thou shalt follow me afterwards. [37]Peter said unto him, Lord, why cannot I follow thee now? I will lay down my life for thy sake. [38]Jesus answered him, Wilt thou lay down thy life for my sake? Verily, verily, I say unto thee, The cock shall not crow, till thou hast denied me thrice.

1 Corinthians 9:19 continued on next page

1 CORINTHIANS 9:19—Offerings to God vis-à-vis idols (8:1–11:1), written from Ephesus, 51 CE

Theme	1 COR	Paul
(*Cont.*) **Humble service to God**	**9:19 (above)** **9:22 (above)** **10:3 (above)** **10:33–11:1 (above)**	**Rom 12:10** [10]Be kindly affectioned one to another with brotherly love; in honour preferring one another; **Rom 14:4–12** [4]Who art thou that judgest another man's servant? to his own master he standeth or falleth. Yea, he shall be holden up: for God is able to make him stand. [5]One man esteemeth one day above another: another esteemeth every day alike. Let every man be fully persuaded in his own mind. [6]He that regardeth the day, regardeth it unto the Lord; and he that regardeth not the day, to the Lord he doth not regard it. He that eateth, eateth to the Lord, for he giveth God thanks; and he that eateth not, to the Lord he eateth not, and giveth God thanks. [7]For none of us liveth to himself, and no man dieth to himself. [8]For whether we live, we live unto the Lord; and whether we die, we die unto the Lord: whether we live therefore, or die, we are the Lord's. [9]For to this end Christ both died, and rose, and revived, that he might be Lord both of the dead and living. [10]But why dost thou judge thy brother? or why dost thou set at nought thy brother? for we shall all stand before the judgment seat of Christ. [11]For it is written, As I live, saith the Lord, every knee shall bow to me, and every tongue shall confess to God. [12]So then every one of us shall give account of himself to God. **Rom 15:1–4** [1]We then that are strong ought to bear the infirmities of the weak, and not to please ourselves. [2]Let every one of us please his neighbour for his good to edification. [3]For even Christ pleased not himself; but, as it is written, The reproaches of them that reproached thee fell on me. [4]For whatsoever things were written aforetime were written for our learning, that we through patience and comfort of the scriptures might have hope. **Rom 15:7** [7]Wherefore receive ye one another, as Christ also received us to the glory of God. **2 Cor 4:5** [5]For we preach not ourselves, but Christ Jesus the Lord; and ourselves your servants for Jesus' sake. **2 Cor 11:7** [7]Have I committed an offence in abasing myself that ye might be exalted, because I have preached to you the gospel of God freely? **Gal 5:13c** [13]For, brethren, ye have been called unto liberty; only use not liberty for an occasion to the flesh, but by love serve one another. **Phil 2:2–9** [2]Fulfil ye my joy, that ye be likeminded, having the same love, being of one accord, of one mind. [3]Let nothing be done through strife or vainglory; but in lowliness of mind let each esteem other better than themselves. [4]Look not every man on his own things, but every man also on the things of others. [5]Let this mind be in you, which was also in Christ Jesus: [6]Who, being in the form of God, thought it not robbery to be equal with God: [7]But made himself of no reputation, and took upon him the form of a servant, and was made in the likeness of men: [8]And being found in fashion as a man, he humbled himself, and became obedient unto death, even the death of the cross. [9]Wherefore God also hath highly exalted him, and given him a name which is above every name: **Phil 2:21** [21]For all seek their own, not the things which are Jesus Christ's.

Other
Q-Quelle
Precedence: 1 Cor 9:19/[Mt 19:28]/Mk 10:41-45/[Lk 22:28-30 (QS 62)]]/Mt 23:4-36/[Mk 7:1-9] /[Lk 11:37-54 (QS 34 [Thom 39:1, 89, 102]); Encourage Prayer: 1 Cor 9:19/Rom 14:4-12/[Mt 7:7-11]/[Lk 11:9-13 (QS 27 [Thom 2, 92, 94])]; Against Pharisees: 1 Cor 9:19/Phil 2:1-11/Mt 23:4-36/[Mk 7:1-9]/[Lk 11:37-54 (QS 34 [Thom 39:1, 89, 102])]

1 CORINTHIANS 9:21—Offerings to God vis-à-vis idols (8:1–11:1), written from Ephesus, 51 CE

Theme	1 COR	Mt
Bear burdens of others	**9:21** [21]To them that are without law, as without law, (being not without law to God, but under the law to Christ,) that I might gain them that are without law.	**5:3–6** [3]Blessed are the poor in spirit: for theirs is the kingdom of heaven. [4]Blessed are they that mourn: for they shall be comforted. [5]Blessed are the meek: for they shall inherit the earth. [6]Blessed are they which do hunger and thirst after righteousness: for they shall be filled. **11:12–13** [12]And from the days of John the Baptist until now the kingdom of heaven suffereth violence, and the violent take it by force. [13]For all the prophets and the law prophesied until John. **11:28–30** [28]Come unto me, all ye that labour and are heavy laden, and I will give you rest. [29]Take my yoke upon you, and learn of me; for I am meek and lowly in heart: and ye shall find rest unto your souls. [30]For my yoke is easy, and my burden is light. **23:4** [4]For they bind heavy burdens and grievous to be borne, and lay them on men's shoulders; but they themselves will not move them with one of their fingers.

1 CORINTHIANS 9:22—Offerings to God vis-à-vis idols (8:1–11:1), written from Ephesus, 51 CE

Theme	1 COR	Paul
Becoming all things to all people	**9:22** [22]To the weak became I as weak, that I might gain the weak: I am made all things to all men, that I might by all means save some. **10:33** [33]Even as I please all men in all things, not seeking mine own profit, but the profit of many, that they may be saved.	**Rom 15:1** [1]We then that are strong ought to bear the infirmities of the weak, and not to please ourselves. **2 Cor 11:29** [29]Who is weak, and I am not weak? who is offended, and I burn not?

1 CORINTHIANS 9:24—Offerings to God vis-à-vis idols (8:1–11:1), written from Ephesus, 51 CE

Theme	1 COR	NT
Seek prize	**9:24** [24]Know ye not that they which run in a race run all, but one receiveth the prize? So run, that ye may obtain.	**Heb 12:1** [1]Wherefore seeing we also are compassed about with so great a cloud of witnesses, let us lay aside every weight, and the sin which doth so easily beset us, and let us run with patience the race that is set before us,

1 CORINTHIANS 9:25—Offerings to God vis-à-vis idols (8:1–11:1), written from Ephesus, 51 CE

Theme	1 COR	Paul
Strive for mastery	**9:25** [25]And every man that striveth for the mastery is temperate in all things. Now they do it to obtain a corruptible crown; but we an incorruptible.	**2 Tim 2:5 (Pseudo)** [5]And if a man also strive for masteries, yet is he not crowned, except he strive lawfully. **2 Tim 4:7–8 (Pseudo)** [7]I have fought a good fight, I have finished my course, I have kept the faith: [8]Henceforth there is laid up for me a crown of righteousness, which the Lord, the righteous judge, shall give me at that day: and not to me only, but unto all them also that love his appearing.

Lk	Paul	Jewish Writings	Other
6:20-21 [20]And he lifted up his eyes on his disciples, and said, Blessed be ye poor: for yours is the kingdom of God. [21]Blessed are ye that hunger now: for ye shall be filled. Blessed are ye that weep now: for ye shall laugh. **16:16** [16]The law and the prophets were until John: since that time the kingdom of God is preached, and every man presseth into it.	**Gal 6:2** [2]Bear ye one another's burdens, and so fulfil the law of Christ. **Col 3:17** [17]And whatsoever ye do in word or deed, do all in the name of the Lord Jesus, giving thanks to God and the Father by him.	**Is 53:4** [4]Surely he hath borne our griefs, and carried our sorrows: yet we did esteem him stricken, smitten of God, and afflicted. **Jer 31:32** [32]Not according to the covenant that I made with their fathers in the day that I took them by the hand to bring them out of the land of Egypt; which my covenant they brake, although I was an husband unto them, saith the LORD:	**Q-Quelle** Beatitudes: 1 Cor 9:21/Gal 6:2/Mt 5:3-12/Lk 6:20b-23; Against Pharisees: 1 Cor 9:21/Gal 6:2/Mt 23:4-36/[Mk 7:1-9]/[Lk 11:37-54(QS 34 [Thom 39:1, 89, 102])]; Concerning the Law: 1 Cor 9:21/[Mt 5:18], Mt 11:12-13/Lk 16:16-17 (QS 56)

NT
Jas 1:12 [12]Blessed is the man that endureth temptation: for when he is tried, he shall receive the crown of life, which the Lord hath promised to them that love him. **1 Pet 5:4** [4]And when the chief Shepherd shall appear, ye shall receive a crown of glory that fadeth not away.

1 CORINTHIANS Ch 10 (Acts 18:1–11, writing from Ephesus)

Theme	1 COR	Mt	Mk
Redemption	**Ch 10** [1]Moreover, brethren, I would not that ye should be ignorant, how that all our fathers were under the cloud, and all passed through the sea; [2]And were all baptized unto Moses in the cloud and in the sea; [3]And did all eat the same spiritual meat; [4]And did all drink the same spiritual drink: for they drank of that spiritual Rock that followed them: and that Rock was Christ. [5]But with many of them God was not well pleased: for they were overthrown in the wilderness. [6]Now these things were our examples, to the intent we should not lust after evil things, as they also lusted. [7]Neither be ye idolaters, as were some of them; as it is written, The people sat down to eat and drink, and rose up to play. [8]Neither let us commit fornication, as some of them committed, and fell in one day three and twenty thousand. [9]Neither let us tempt Christ, as some of them also tempted, and were destroyed of serpents. [10]Neither murmur ye, as some of them also murmured, and were destroyed of the destroyer. [11]Now all these things happened unto them for ensamples: and they are written for our admonition, upon whom the ends of the world are come. [12]Wherefore let him that thinketh he standeth take heed lest he fall. [13]There hath no temptation taken you but such as is common to man: but God is faithful, who will not suffer you to be tempted above that ye are able; but will with the temptation also make a way to escape, that ye may be able to bear it. [14]Wherefore, my dearly beloved, flee from idolatry. [15]I speak as to wise men; judge ye what I say. [16]The cup of blessing which we bless, is it not the communion of the blood of Christ? The bread which we break, is it not the communion of the body of Christ? [17]For we being many are one bread, and one body: for we are all partakers of that one bread. [18]Behold Israel after the flesh: are not they which eat of the sacrifices partakers of the altar? [19]What say I then? that the idol is any thing, or that which is offered in sacrifice to idols is any thing? [20]But I say, that the things which the Gentiles sacrifice, they sacrifice to devils, and not to God: and I would not that ye should have fellowship with devils. [21]Ye cannot drink the cup of the Lord, and the cup of devils: ye cannot be partakers of the Lord's table, and of the table of devils. [22]Do we provoke the Lord to jealousy? are we stronger than he? [23]All things are lawful for me, but all things are not expedient: all things are lawful for me, but all things edify not. [24]Let no man seek his own, but every man another's wealth. [25]Whatsoever is sold in the shambles, that eat, asking no question for conscience sake: [26]For the earth is the Lord's, and the fulness thereof. [27]If any of them that believe not bid you to a feast, and ye be disposed to go; whatsoever is set before you, eat, asking no question for conscience sake. [28]But if any man say unto you, This is offered in sacrifice unto idols, eat not for his sake that showed it, and for conscience sake: for the earth is the Lord's, and the fulness thereof: [29]Conscience, I say, not thine own, but of the other: for why is my liberty judged of another man's conscience? [30]For if I by grace be a partaker, why am I evil spoken of for that for which I give thanks? [31]Whether therefore ye eat, or drink, or whatsoever ye do, do all to the glory of God. [32]Give none offence, neither to the Jews, nor to the Gentiles, nor to the church of God: [33]Even as I please all men in all things, not seeking mine own profit, but the profit of many, that they may be saved.	**20:28** [28]Even as the Son of man came not to be ministered unto, but to minister, and to give his life a ransom for many.	**10:45** [45]For even the Son of man came not to be ministered unto, but to minister, and to give his life a ransom for many.

Paul	NT
Rom 3:24 24 Being justified freely by his grace through the redemption that is in Christ Jesus: **Rom 3:25** 25 Whom God hath set forth to be a propitiation through faith in his blood, to declare his righteousness for the remission of sins that are past, through the forbearance of God; **Rom 6:14** 14 For sin shall not have dominion over you: for ye are not under the law, but under grace. **Rom 8:3** 3 For what the law could not do, in that it was weak through the flesh, God sending his own Son in the likeness of sinful flesh, and for sin, condemned sin in the flesh: **2 Cor 5:21** 21 For he hath made him to be sin for us, who knew no sin; that we might be made the righteousness of God in him. **Gal 3:13** 13 Christ hath redeemed us from the curse of the law, being made a curse for us: for it is written, Cursed is every one that hangeth on a tree: **Gal 3:23–5:1** **3** 23 But before faith came, we were kept under the law, shut up unto the faith which should afterwards be revealed. 24 Wherefore the law was our schoolmaster to bring us unto Christ, that we might be justified by faith. 25 But after that faith is come, we are no longer under a schoolmaster. 26 For ye are all the children of God by faith in Christ Jesus. 27 For as many of you as have been baptized into Christ have put on Christ. 28 There is neither Jew nor Greek, there is neither bond nor free, there is neither male nor female: for ye are all one in Christ Jesus. 29 And if ye be Christ's, then are ye Abraham's seed, and heirs according to the promise. **4** 1 Now I say, That the heir, as long as he is a child, differeth nothing from a servant, though he be lord of all; 2 But is under tutors and governors until the time appointed of the father. 3 Even so we, when we were children, were in bondage under the elements of the world: 4 But when the fulness of the time was come, God sent forth his Son, made of a woman, made under the law, 5 To redeem them that were under the law, that we might receive the adoption of sons. 6 And because ye are sons, God hath sent forth the Spirit of his Son into your hearts, crying, Abba, Father. 7 Wherefore thou art no more a servant, but a son; and if a son, then an heir of God through Christ. 8 Howbeit then, when ye knew not God, ye did service unto them which by nature are no gods. 9 But now, after that ye have known God, or rather are known of God, how turn ye again to the weak and beggarly elements, whereunto ye desire again to be in bondage? 10 Ye observe days, and months, and times, and years. 11 I am afraid of you, lest I have bestowed upon you labour in vain. 12 Brethren, I beseech you, be as I am; for I am as ye are: ye have not injured me at all. 13 Ye know how through infirmity of the flesh I preached the gospel unto you at the first. 14 And my temptation which was in my flesh ye despised not, nor rejected; but received me as an angel of God, even as Christ Jesus. 15 Where is then the blessedness ye spake of? for I bear you record, that, if it had been possible, ye would have plucked out your own eyes, and have given them to me. 16 Am I therefore become your enemy, because I tell you the truth? 17 They zealously affect you, but not well; yea, they would exclude you, that ye might affect them. 18 But it is good to be zealously affected always in a good thing, and not only when I am present with you. 19 My little children, of whom I travail in birth again until Christ be formed in you, 20 I desire to be present with you now, and to change my voice; for I stand in doubt of you. 21 Tell me, ye that desire to be under the law, do ye not hear the law? 22 For it is written, that Abraham had two sons, the one by a bondmaid, the other by a freewoman. 23 But he who was of the bondwoman was born after the flesh; but he of the freewoman was by promise. 24 Which things are an allegory: for these are the two covenants; the one from the mount Sinai, which gendereth to bondage, which is Agar. 25 For this Agar is mount Sinai in Arabia, and answereth to Jerusalem which now is, and is in bondage with her children. 26 But Jerusalem which is above is free, which is the mother of us all. 27 For it is written, Rejoice, thou barren that bearest not; break forth and cry, thou that travailest not: for the desolate hath many more children than she which hath an husband. 28 Now we, brethren, as Isaac was, are the children of promise. 29 But as then he that was born after the flesh persecuted him that was born after the Spirit, even so it is now. 30 Nevertheless what saith the scripture? Cast out the bondwoman and her son: for the son of the bondwoman shall not be heir with the son of the freewoman. 31 So then, brethren, we are not children of the bondwoman, but of the free. **5** 1 Stand fast therefore in the liberty wherewith Christ hath made us free, and be not entangled again with the yoke of bondage.	**Heb 9:5** 5 And over it the cherubims of glory shadowing the mercyseat; of which we cannot now speak particularly.

1 Corinthians Ch. 10 continued on next page

1 CORINTHIANS Ch 10—Offerings to God vis-à-vis idols (8:1–11:1), written from Ephesus, 51 CE (*continued*)

Theme	1 COR	Jewish Writings
(*Cont.*) Redemption	**Ch 10 (above)**	**Ex 15:13** [13]Thou in thy mercy hast led forth the people which thou hast redeemed: thou hast guided them in thy strength unto thy holy habitation. **Ex 25:16–21** [16]And thou shalt put into the ark the testimony which I shall give thee. [17]And thou shalt make a mercy seat of pure gold: two cubits and a half shall be the length thereof, and a cubit and a half the breadth thereof. [18]And thou shalt make two cherubims of gold, of beaten work shalt thou make them, in the two ends of the mercy seat. [19]And make one cherub on the one end, and the other cherub on the other end: even of the mercy seat shall ye make the cherubims on the two ends thereof. [20]And the cherubims shall stretch forth their wings on high, covering the mercy seat with their wings, and their faces shall look one to another; toward the mercy seat shall the faces of the cherubims be. [21]And thou shalt put the mercy seat above upon the ark; and in the ark thou shalt put the testimony that I shall give thee. **Lev 1:4** [4]And he shall put his hand upon the head of the burnt offering; and it shall be accepted for him to make atonement for him. **Lev 4–5** **4**[1]And the LORD spake unto Moses, saying, [2]Speak unto the children of Israel, saying, If a soul shall sin through ignorance against any of the commandments of the LORD concerning things which ought not to be done, and shall do against any of them: [3]If the priest that is anointed do sin according to the sin of the people; then let him bring for his sin, which he hath sinned, a young bullock without blemish unto the LORD for a sin offering. [4]And he shall bring the bullock unto the door of the tabernacle of the congregation before the LORD; and shall lay his hand upon the bullock's head, and kill the bullock before the LORD. [5]And the priest that is anointed shall take of the bullock's blood, and bring it to the tabernacle of the congregation: [6]And the priest shall dip his finger in the blood, and sprinkle of the blood seven times before the LORD, before the veil of the sanctuary. [7]And the priest shall put some of the blood upon the horns of the altar of sweet incense before the LORD, which is in the tabernacle of the congregation; and shall pour all the blood of the bullock at the bottom of the altar of the burnt offering, which is at the door of the tabernacle of the congregation. [8]And he shall take off from it all the fat of the bullock for the sin offering; the fat that covereth the inwards, and all the fat that is upon the inwards, [9]And the two kidneys, and the fat that is upon them, which is by the flanks, and the caul above the liver, with the kidneys, it shall he take away, [10]As it was taken off from the bullock of the sacrifice of peace offerings: and the priest shall burn them upon the altar of the burnt offering. [11]And the skin of the bullock, and all his flesh, with his head, and with his legs, and his inwards, and his dung, [12]Even the whole bullock shall he carry forth without the camp unto a clean place, where the ashes are poured out, and burn him on the wood with fire: where the ashes are poured out shall he be burnt. [13]And if the whole congregation of Israel sin through ignorance, and the thing be hid from the eyes of the assembly, and they have done somewhat against any of the commandments of the LORD concerning things which should not be done, and are guilty; [14]When the sin, which they have sinned against it, is known, then the congregation shall offer a young bullock for the sin, and bring him before the tabernacle of the congregation. [15]And the elders of the congregation shall lay their hands upon the head of the bullock before the LORD: and the bullock shall be killed before the LORD. [16]And the priest that is anointed shall bring of the bullock's blood to the tabernacle of the congregation: [17]And the priest shall dip his finger in some of the blood, and sprinkle it seven times before the LORD, even before the veil. [18]And he shall put some of the blood upon the horns of the altar which is before the LORD, that is in the tabernacle of the congregation, and shall pour out all the blood at the bottom of the altar of the burnt offering, which is at the door of the tabernacle of the congregation. [19]And he shall take all his fat from him, and burn it upon the altar. [20]And he shall do with the bullock as he did with the bullock for a sin offering, so shall he do with this: and the priest shall make an atonement for them, and it shall be forgiven them. [21]And he shall carry forth the bullock without the camp, and burn him as he burned the first bullock: it is a sin offering for the congregation. [22]When a ruler hath sinned, and done somewhat through ignorance against any of the commandments of the LORD his God concerning things which should not be done, and is guilty; [23]Or if his sin, wherein he hath sinned, come to his knowledge; he shall bring his offering, a kid of the goats, a male without blemish: [24]And he shall lay his hand upon the head of the goat, and kill it in the place where they kill the burnt offering before the LORD: it is a sin offering. [25]And the priest shall take of the blood of the sin offering with his finger, and put it upon the horns of the altar of burnt offering, and shall pour out his blood at the bottom of the altar of burnt offering. [26]And he shall burn all his fat upon the altar, as the fat of the sacrifice of peace offerings: and the priest shall make an atonement for him as concerning his sin, and it shall be forgiven him. [27]And if any one of the common people sin through ignorance, while he doeth somewhat against any of the commandments of the LORD concerning things which ought not to be done, and be guilty; [28]Or if his sin, which he hath sinned, come to his knowledge: then he shall bring his offering, a kid of the goats, a female without blemish, for his sin which he hath sinned.

1 CORINTHIANS Ch 10—Offerings to God vis-à-vis idols (8:1–11:1), written from Ephesus, 51 CE (*continued*)

Theme	1 COR	Jewish Writings	Other
(*Cont.*) **Redemption**	**Ch 10 (above)**	**Lev 4–5 (*continued*)** 29 And he shall lay his hand upon the head of the sin offering, and slay the sin offering in the place of the burnt offering. 30 And the priest shall take of the blood thereof with his finger, and put it upon the horns of the altar of burnt offering, and shall pour out all the blood thereof at the bottom of the altar. 31 And he shall take away all the fat thereof, as the fat is taken away from off the sacrifice of peace offerings; and the priest shall burn it upon the altar for a sweet savour unto the LORD; and the priest shall make an atonement for him, and it shall be forgiven him. 32 And if he bring a lamb for a sin offering, he shall bring it a female without blemish. 33 And he shall lay his hand upon the head of the sin offering, and slay it for a sin offering in the place where they kill the burnt offering. 34 And the priest shall take of the blood of the sin offering with his finger, and put it upon the horns of the altar of burnt offering, and shall pour out all the blood thereof at the bottom of the altar: 35 And he shall take away all the fat thereof, as the fat of the lamb is taken away from the sacrifice of the peace offerings; and the priest shall burn them upon the altar, according to the offerings made by fire unto the LORD: and the priest shall make an atonement for his sin that he hath committed, and it shall be forgiven him. **LEV 5:1–19** **5** 1 And if a soul sin, and hear the voice of swearing, and is a witness, whether he hath seen or known of it; if he do not utter it, then he shall bear his iniquity. 2 Or if a soul touch any unclean thing, whether it be a carcase of an unclean beast, or a carcase of unclean cattle, or the carcase of unclean creeping things, and if it be hidden from him; he also shall be unclean, and guilty. 3 Or if he touch the uncleanness of man, whatsoever uncleanness it be that a man shall be defiled withal, and it be hid from him; when he knoweth of it, then he shall be guilty. 4 Or if a soul swear, pronouncing with his lips to do evil, or to do good, whatsoever it be that a man shall pronounce with an oath, and it be hid from him; when he knoweth of it, then he shall be guilty in one of these. 5 And it shall be, when he shall be guilty in one of these things, that he shall confess that he hath sinned in that thing: 6 And he shall bring his trespass offering unto the LORD for his sin which he hath sinned, a female from the flock, a lamb or a kid of the goats, for a sin offering; and the priest shall make an atonement for him concerning his sin. 7 And if he be not able to bring a lamb, then he shall bring for his trespass, which he hath committed, two turtledoves, or two young pigeons, unto the LORD; one for a sin offering, and the other for a burnt offering. 8 And he shall bring them unto the priest, who shall offer that which is for the sin offering first, and wring off his head from his neck, but shall not divide it asunder: 9 And he shall sprinkle of the blood of the sin offering upon the side of the altar; and the rest of the blood shall be wrung out at the bottom of the altar: it is a sin offering. 10 And he shall offer the second for a burnt offering, according to the manner: and the priest shall make an atonement for him for his sin which he hath sinned, and it shall be forgiven him. 11 But if he be not able to bring two turtledoves, or two young pigeons, then he that sinned shall bring for his offering the tenth part of an ephah of fine flour for a sin offering; he shall put no oil upon it, neither shall he put any frankincense thereon: for it is a sin offering. 12 Then shall he bring it to the priest, and the priest shall take his handful of it, even a memorial thereof, and burn it on the altar, according to the offerings made by fire unto the LORD: it is a sin offering. 13 And the priest shall make an atonement for him as touching his sin that he hath sinned in one of these, and it shall be forgiven him: and the remnant shall be the priest's, as a meat offering. 14 And the LORD spake unto Moses, saying, 15 If a soul commit a trespass, and sin through ignorance, in the holy things of the LORD; then he shall bring for his trespass unto the LORD a ram without blemish out of the flocks, with thy estimation by shekels of silver, after the shekel of the sanctuary, for a trespass offering: 16 And he shall make amends for the harm that he hath done in the holy thing, and shall add the fifth part thereto, and give it unto the priest: and the priest shall make an atonement for him with the ram of the trespass offering, and it shall be forgiven him. 17 And if a soul sin, and commit any of these things which are forbidden to be done by the commandments of the LORD; though he wist it not, yet is he guilty, and shall bear his iniquity. 18 And he shall bring a ram without blemish out of the flock, with thy estimation, for a trespass offering, unto the priest: and the priest shall make an atonement for him concerning his ignorance wherein he erred and wist it not, and it shall be forgiven him. 19 It is a trespass offering: he hath certainly trespassed against the LORD. **Is 41:14** 14 Fear not, thou worm Jacob, and ye men of Israel; I will help thee, saith the LORD, and thy redeemer, the Holy One of Israel.	**Q-Quelle** Precedence: 1 Cor Ch 10/[Gal 6:14]/[Mt 19:28]/Mk 10:41-45/ [Lk 22:28-30 (QS 62)

1 CORINTHIANS 10:1—Offerings to God vis-à-vis idols (8:1–11:1), written from Ephesus, 51 CE

Theme	1 COR
All fathers passed through the sea	**10:1** [1]Moreover, brethren, I would not that ye should be ignorant, how that all our fathers were under the cloud, and all passed through the sea;

Jewish Writings

Ex 13:21–22

21 And the LORD went before them by day in a pillar of a cloud, to lead them the way; and by night in a pillar of fire, to give them light; to go by day and night: 22 He took not away the pillar of the cloud by day, nor the pillar of fire by night, from before the people.

Ex 14:19–20

19 And the angel of God, which went before the camp of Israel, removed and went behind them; and the pillar of the cloud went from before their face, and stood behind them: 20 And it came between the camp of the Egyptians and the camp of Israel; and it was a cloud and darkness to them, but it gave light by night to these: so that the one came not near the other all the night.

Ex 14:21–22

21 And Moses stretched out his hand over the sea; and the LORD caused the sea to go back by a strong east wind all that night, and made the sea dry land, and the waters were divided. 22 And the children of Israel went into the midst of the sea upon the dry ground: and the waters were a wall unto them on their right hand, and on their left.

Ex 14:26–30

26 And the LORD said unto Moses, Stretch out thine hand over the sea, that the waters may come again upon the Egyptians, upon their chariots, and upon their horsemen. 27 And Moses stretched forth his hand over the sea, and the sea returned to his strength when the morning appeared; and the Egyptians fled against it; and the LORD overthrew the Egyptians in the midst of the sea. 28 And the waters returned, and covered the chariots, and the horsemen, and all the host of Pharaoh that came into the sea after them; there remained not so much as one of them. 29 But the children of Israel walked upon dry land in the midst of the sea; and the waters were a wall unto them on their right hand, and on their left. 30 Thus the LORD saved Israel that day out of the hand of the Egyptians; and Israel saw the Egyptians dead upon the sea shore.

1 CORINTHIANS 10:2—Offerings to God vis-à-vis idols (8:1–11:1), written from Ephesus, 51 CE

Theme	1 COR	Paul
Baptized into sea of Moses	**10:2** [2]And were all baptized unto Moses in the cloud and in the sea;	**Rom 6:3** [3]Know ye not, that so many of us as were baptized into Jesus Christ were baptized into his death? **Gal 3:27** [27]For as many of you as have been baptized into Christ have put on Christ.

Jewish Writings

Ex 16:4–35

[4]Then said the LORD unto Moses, Behold, I will rain bread from heaven for you; and the people shall go out and gather a certain rate every day, that I may prove them, whether they will walk in my law, or no. [5]And it shall come to pass, that on the sixth day they shall prepare that which they bring in; and it shall be twice as much as they gather daily. [6]And Moses and Aaron said unto all the children of Israel, At even, then ye shall know that the LORD hath brought you out from the land of Egypt: [7]And in the morning, then ye shall see the glory of the LORD; for that he heareth your murmurings against the LORD: and what are we, that ye murmur against us? [8]And Moses said, This shall be, when the LORD shall give you in the evening flesh to eat, and in the morning bread to the full; for that the LORD heareth your murmurings which ye murmur against him: and what are we? your murmurings are not against us, but against the LORD. [9]And Moses spake unto Aaron, Say unto all the congregation of the children of Israel, Come near before the LORD: for he hath heard your murmurings. [10]And it came to pass, as Aaron spake unto the whole congregation of the children of Israel, that they looked toward the wilderness, and, behold, the glory of the LORD appeared in the cloud. [11]And the LORD spake unto Moses, saying, [12]I have heard the murmurings of the children of Israel: speak unto them, saying, At even ye shall eat flesh, and in the morning ye shall be filled with bread; and ye shall know that I am the LORD your God. [13]And it came to pass, that at even the quails came up, and covered the camp: and in the morning the dew lay round about the host. [14]And when the dew that lay was gone up, behold, upon the face of the wilderness there lay a small round thing, as small as the hoar frost on the ground. [15]And when the children of Israel saw it, they said one to another, It is manna: for they wist not what it was. And Moses said unto them, This is the bread which the LORD hath given you to eat. [16]This is the thing which the LORD hath commanded, Gather of it every man according to his eating, an omer for every man, according to the number of your persons; take ye every man for them which are in his tents. [17]And the children of Israel did so, and gathered, some more, some less. [18]And when they did mete it with an omer, he that gathered much had nothing over, and he that gathered little had no lack; they gathered every man according to his eating. [19]And Moses said, Let no man leave of it till the morning. [20]Notwithstanding they hearkened not unto Moses; but some of them left of it until the morning, and it bred worms, and stank: and Moses was wroth with them. [21]And they gathered it every morning, every man according to his eating: and when the sun waxed hot, it melted. [22]And it came to pass, that on the sixth day they gathered twice as much bread, two omers for one man: and all the rulers of the congregation came and told Moses. [23]And he said unto them, This is that which the LORD hath said, To morrow is the rest of the holy sabbath unto the LORD: bake that which ye will bake to day, and seethe that ye will seethe; and that which remaineth over lay up for you to be kept until the morning. [24]And they laid it up till the morning, as Moses bade: and it did not stink, neither was there any worm therein. [25]And Moses said, Eat that to day; for to day is a sabbath unto the LORD: to day ye shall not find it in the field. [26]Six days ye shall gather it; but on the seventh day, which is the sabbath, in it there shall be none. [27]And it came to pass, that there went out some of the people on the seventh day for to gather, and they found none. [28]And the LORD said unto Moses, How long refuse ye to keep my commandments and my laws? [29]See, for that the LORD hath given you the sabbath, therefore he giveth you on the sixth day the bread of two days; abide ye every man in his place, let no man go out of his place on the seventh day. [30]So the people rested on the seventh day. [31]And the house of Israel called the name thereof Manna: and it was like coriander seed, white; and the taste of it was like wafers made with honey. [32]And Moses said, This is the thing which the LORD commandeth, Fill an omer of it to be kept for your generations; that they may see the bread wherewith I have fed you in the wilderness, when I brought you forth from the land of Egypt. [33]And Moses said unto Aaron, Take a pot, and put an omer full of manna therein, and lay it up before the LORD, to be kept for your generations. [34]As the LORD commanded Moses, so Aaron laid it up before the Testimony, to be kept. [35]And the children of Israel did eat manna forty years, until they came to a land inhabited; they did eat manna, until they came unto the borders of the land of Canaan.

1 CORINTHIANS 10:4—Offerings to God vis-à-vis idols (8:1–11:1), written from Ephesus, 51 CE

Theme	1 COR	Jewish Writings
Drink from spiritual rock	**10:4** [4]And did all drink the same spiritual drink: for they drank of that spiritual Rock that followed them: and that Rock was Christ.	**Ex 17:1–7** [1]And all the congregation of the children of Israel journeyed from the wilderness of Sin, after their journeys, according to the commandment of the LORD, and pitched in Rephidim: and there was no water for the people to drink. [2]Wherefore the people did chide with Moses, and said, Give us water that we may drink. And Moses said unto them, Why chide ye with me? wherefore do ye tempt the LORD? [3]And the people thirsted there for water; and the people murmured against Moses, and said, Wherefore is this that thou hast brought us up out of Egypt, to kill us and our children and our cattle with thirst? [4]And Moses cried unto the LORD, saying, What shall I do unto this people? they be almost ready to stone me. [5]And the LORD said unto Moses, Go on before the people, and take with thee of the elders of Israel; and thy rod, wherewith thou smotest the river, take in thine hand, and go. [6]Behold, I will stand before thee there upon the rock in Horeb; and thou shalt smite the rock, and there shall come water out of it, that the people may drink. And Moses did so in the sight of the elders of Israel. [7]And he called the name of the place Massah, and Meribah, because of the chiding of the children of Israel, and because they tempted the LORD, saying, Is the LORD among us, or not? **Num 20:7–11** [7]And the LORD spake unto Moses, saying, [8]Take the rod, and gather thou the assembly together, thou, and Aaron thy brother, and speak ye unto the rock before their eyes; and it shall give forth his water, and thou shalt bring forth to them water out of the rock: so thou shalt give the congregation and their beasts drink. [9]And Moses took the rod from before the LORD, as he commanded him. [10]And Moses and Aaron gathered the congregation together before the rock, and he said unto them, Hear now, ye rebels; must we fetch you water out of this rock? [11]And Moses lifted up his hand, and with his rod he smote the rock twice: and the water came out abundantly, and the congregation drank, and their beasts also. **Dt 8:15** [15]Who led thee through that great and terrible wilderness, wherein were fiery serpents, and scorpions, and drought, where there was no water; who brought thee forth water out of the rock of flint;

1 CORINTHIANS 10:5—Offerings to God vis-à-vis idols (8:1–11:1), written from Ephesus, 51 CE

Theme	1 COR	Jewish Writings	NT
God displeased in the wilderness	**10:5** [5]But with many of them God was not well pleased: for they were overthrown in the wilderness.	**Num 14:28–38** [28]Say unto them, As truly as I live, saith the LORD, as ye have spoken in mine ears, so will I do to you: [29]Your carcases shall fall in this wilderness; and all that were numbered of you, according to your whole number, from twenty years old and upward, which have murmured against me, [30]Doubtless ye shall not come into the land, concerning which I sware to make you dwell therein, save Caleb the son of Jephunneh, and Joshua the son of Nun. [31]But your little ones, which ye said should be a prey, them will I bring in, and they shall know the land which ye have despised. [32]But as for you, your carcases, they shall fall in this wilderness. [33]And your children shall wander in the wilderness forty years, and bear your whoredoms, until your carcases be wasted in the wilderness. [34]After the number of the days in which ye searched the land, even forty days, each day for a year, shall ye bear your iniquities, even forty years, and ye shall know my breach of promise. [35]I the LORD have said, I will surely do it unto all this evil congregation, that are gathered together against me: in this wilderness they shall be consumed, and there they shall die. [6]And the men, which Moses sent to search the land, who returned, and made all the congregation to murmur against him, by bringing up a slander upon the land, [37]Even those men that did bring up the evil report upon the land, died by the plague before the LORD. [38]But Joshua the son of Nun, and Caleb the son of Jephunneh, which were of the men that went to search the land, lived still.	**Jude 5** [5]I will therefore put you in remembrance, though ye once knew this, how that the Lord, having saved the people out of the land of Egypt, afterward destroyed them that believed not.

1 CORINTHIANS 10:6—Offerings to God vis-à-vis idols (8:1–11:1), written from Ephesus, 51 CE

Theme	1 COR	Jewish Writings
Do not lust after evil	**10:6** [6]Now these things were our examples, to the intent we should not lust after evil things, as they also lusted.	**Num 11:04** [4]And the mixed multitude that was among them fell a lusting: and the children of Israel also wept again, and said, Who shall give us flesh to eat? **Num 11:34** [34]And he called the name of that place Kibrothhattaavah: because there they buried the people that lusted.

1 CORINTHIANS 10:7—Offerings to God vis-à-vis idols (8:1–11:1), written from Ephesus, 51 CE

Theme	1 COR	Jewish Writings
Do not be idolater	**10:7** [7]Neither be ye idolaters, as were some of them; as it is written, The people sat down to eat and drink, and rose up to play.	**Ex 32:6** [6]And they rose up early on the morrow, and offered burnt offerings, and brought peace offerings; and the people sat down to eat and to drink, and rose up to play.

1 CORINTHIANS 10:8—Offerings to God vis-à-vis idols (8:1–11:1), written from Ephesus, 51 CE

Theme	1 COR	Jewish Writings
Do not fornicate	**10:8** [8]Neither let us commit fornication, as some of them committed, and fell in one day three and twenty thousand.	**Num 25:1–9** [1]And Israel abode in Shittim, and the people began to commit whoredom with the daughters of Moab. [2]And they called the people unto the sacrifices of their gods: and the people did eat, and bowed down to their gods. [3]And Israel joined himself unto Baalpeor: and the anger of the LORD was kindled against Israel. [4]And the LORD said unto Moses, Take all the heads of the people, and hang them up before the LORD against the sun, that the fierce anger of the LORD may be turned away from Israel. [5]And Moses said unto the judges of Israel, Slay ye every one his men that were joined unto Baalpeor. [6]And, behold, one of the children of Israel came and brought unto his brethren a Midianitish woman in the sight of Moses, and in the sight of all the congregation of the children of Israel, who were weeping before the door of the tabernacle of the congregation. [7]And when Phinehas, the son of Eleazar, the son of Aaron the priest, saw it, he rose up from among the congregation, and took a javelin in his hand; [8]And he went after the man of Israel into the tent, and thrust both of them through, the man of Israel, and the woman through her belly. So the plague was stayed from the children of Israel. [9]And those that died in the plague were twenty and four thousand.

1 CORINTHIANS 10:9—Offerings to God vis-à-vis idols (8:1–11:1), written from Ephesus, 51 CE

Theme	1 COR	Jewish Writings
Let us not test God	**10:9** [9]Neither let us tempt Christ, as some of them also tempted, and were destroyed of serpents.	**Num 21:5–9** [5]And the people spake against God, and against Moses, Wherefore have ye brought us up out of Egypt to die in the wilderness? for there is no bread, neither is there any water; and our soul loatheth this light bread. [6]And the LORD sent fiery serpents among the people, and they bit the people; and much people of Israel died. [7]Therefore the people came to Moses, and said, We have sinned, for we have spoken against the LORD, and against thee; pray unto the LORD, that he take away the serpents from us. And Moses prayed for the people. [8]And the LORD said unto Moses, Make thee a fiery serpent, and set it upon a pole: and it shall come to pass, that every one that is bitten, when he looketh upon it, shall live. [9]And Moses made a serpent of brass, and put it upon a pole, and it came to pass, that if a serpent had bitten any man, when he beheld the serpent of brass, he lived.

1 CORINTHIANS 10:10—Offerings to God vis-à-vis idols (8:1–11:1), written from Ephesus, 51 CE

Theme	1 COR	Jewish Writings
Do not murmur against God	**10:10** [10]Neither murmur ye, as some of them also murmured, and were destroyed of the destroyer.	**Num 14:2–37** [2]And all the children of Israel murmured against Moses and against Aaron: and the whole congregation said unto them, Would God that we had died in the land of Egypt! or would God we had died in this wilderness! [3]And wherefore hath the LORD brought us unto this land, to fall by the sword, that our wives and our children should be a prey? were it not better for us to return into Egypt? [4]And they said one to another, Let us make a captain, and let us return into Egypt. [5]Then Moses and Aaron fell on their faces before all the assembly of the congregation of the children of Israel. [6]And Joshua the son of Nun, and Caleb the son of Jephunneh, which were of them that searched the land, rent their clothes: [7]And they spake unto all the company of the children of Israel, saying, The land, which we passed through to search it, is an exceeding good land. [8]If the LORD delight in us, then he will bring us into this land, and give it us; a land which floweth with milk and honey. [9]Only rebel not ye against the LORD, neither fear ye the people of the land; for they are bread for us: their defence is departed from them, and the LORD is with us: fear them not. [10]But all the congregation bade stone them with stones. And the glory of the LORD appeared in the tabernacle of the congregation before all the children of Israel. [11]And the LORD said unto Moses, How long will this people provoke me? and how long will it be ere they believe me, for all the signs which I have showed among them? [12]I will smite them with the pestilence, and disinherit them, and will make of thee a greater nation and mightier than they. [13]And Moses said unto the LORD, Then the Egyptians shall hear it, (for thou broughtest up this people in thy might from among them;) [14]And they will tell it to the inhabitants of this land: for they have heard that thou LORD art among this people, that thou LORD art seen face to face, and that thy cloud standeth over them, and that thou goest before them, by day time in a pillar of a cloud, and in a pillar of fire by night. [15]Now if thou shalt kill all this people as one man, then the nations which have heard the fame of thee will speak, saying, [16]Because the LORD was not able to bring this people into the land which he sware unto them, therefore he hath slain them in the wilderness. [17]And now, I beseech thee, let the power of my Lord be great, according as thou hast spoken, saying, [18]The LORD is longsuffering, and of great mercy, forgiving iniquity and transgression, and by no means clearing the guilty, visiting the iniquity of the fathers upon the children unto the third and fourth generation. [19]Pardon, I beseech thee, the iniquity of this people according unto the greatness of thy mercy, and as thou hast forgiven this people, from Egypt even until now. [20]And the LORD said, I have pardoned according to thy word: [21]But as truly as I live, all the earth shall be filled with the glory of the LORD. [22]Because all those men which have seen my glory, and my miracles, which I did in Egypt and in the wilderness, and have tempted me now these ten times, and have not hearkened to my voice; [23]Surely they shall not see the land which I sware unto their fathers, neither shall any of them that provoked me see it: [24]But my servant Caleb, because he had another spirit with him, and hath followed me fully, him will I bring into the land whereinto he went; and his seed shall possess it. [25](Now the Amalekites and the Canaanites dwelt in the valley.) To morrow turn you, and get you into the wilderness by the way of the Red sea. [26]And the LORD spake unto Moses and unto Aaron, saying, [27]How long shall I bear with this evil congregation, which murmur against me? I have heard the murmurings of the children of Israel, which they murmur against me. [28]Say unto them, As truly as I live, saith the LORD, as ye have spoken in mine ears, so will I do to you: [29]Your carcases shall fall in this wilderness; and all that were numbered of you, according to your whole number, from twenty years old and upward, which have murmured against me, [30]Doubtless ye shall not come into the land, concerning which I sware to make you dwell therein, save Caleb the son of Jephunneh, and Joshua the son of Nun. [31]But your little ones, which ye said should be a prey, them will I bring in, and they shall know the land which ye have despised. [32]But as for you, your carcases, they shall fall in this wilderness. [33]And your children shall wander in the wilderness forty years, and bear your whoredoms, until your carcases be wasted in the wilderness. [34]After the number of the days in which ye searched the land, even forty days, each day for a year, shall ye bear your iniquities, even forty years, and ye shall know my breach of promise. [35]I the LORD have said, I will surely do it unto all this evil congregation, that are gathered together against me: in this wilderness they shall be consumed, and there they shall die. [36]And the men, which Moses sent to search the land, who returned, and made all the congregation to murmur against him, by bringing up a slander upon the land, [37]Even those men that did bring up the evil report upon the land, died by the plague before the LORD.

1 CORINTHIANS 10:10—Offerings to God vis-à-vis idols (8:1–11:1), written from Ephesus, 51 CE (*continued*)

Theme	1 COR	Jewish Writings
(*Cont.*) **Do not murmur against God**	**10:10** **(above)**	**Num 16:1–35** [1]Now Korah, the son of Izhar, the son of Kohath, the son of Levi, and Dathan and Abiram, the sons of Eliab, and On, the son of Peleth, sons of Reuben, took men: [2]And they rose up before Moses, with certain of the children of Israel, two hundred and fifty princes of the assembly, famous in the congregation, men of renown: [3]And they gathered themselves together against Moses and against Aaron, and said unto them, Ye take too much upon you, seeing all the congregation are holy, every one of them, and the LORD is among them: wherefore then lift ye up yourselves above the congregation of the LORD? [4]And when Moses heard it, he fell upon his face: [5]And he spake unto Korah and unto all his company, saying, Even to morrow the LORD will show who are his, and who is holy; and will cause him to come near unto him: even him whom he hath chosen will he cause to come near unto him. [6]This do; Take you censers, Korah, and all his company; [7]And put fire therein, and put incense in them before the LORD to morrow: and it shall be that the man whom the LORD doth choose, he shall be holy: ye take too much upon you, ye sons of Levi. [8]And Moses said unto Korah, Hear, I pray you, ye sons of Levi: [9]Seemeth it but a small thing unto you, that the God of Israel hath separated you from the congregation of Israel, to bring you near to himself to do the service of the tabernacle of the LORD, and to stand before the congregation to minister unto them? [10]And he hath brought thee near to him, and all thy brethren the sons of Levi with thee: and seek ye the priesthood also? [11]For which cause both thou and all thy company are gathered together against the LORD: and what is Aaron, that ye murmur against him? [12]And Moses sent to call Dathan and Abiram, the sons of Eliab: which said, We will not come up: [13]Is it a small thing that thou hast brought us up out of a land that floweth with milk and honey, to kill us in the wilderness, except thou make thyself altogether a prince over us? [14]Moreover thou hast not brought us into a land that floweth with milk and honey, or given us inheritance of fields and vineyards: wilt thou put out the eyes of these men? we will not come up. [15]And Moses was very wroth, and said unto the LORD, Respect not thou their offering: I have not taken one ass from them, neither have I hurt one of them. [16]And Moses said unto Korah, Be thou and all thy company before the LORD, thou, and they, and Aaron, to morrow: [17]And take every man his censer, and put incense in them, and bring ye before the LORD every man his censer, two hundred and fifty censers; thou also, and Aaron, each of you his censer. [18]And they took every man his censer, and put fire in them, and laid incense thereon, and stood in the door of the tabernacle of the congregation with Moses and Aaron. [19]And Korah gathered all the congregation against them unto the door of the tabernacle of the congregation: and the glory of the LORD appeared unto all the congregation. [20]And the LORD spake unto Moses and unto Aaron, saying, [21]Separate yourselves from among this congregation, that I may consume them in a moment. [22]And they fell upon their faces, and said, O God, the God of the spirits of all flesh, shall one man sin, and wilt thou be wroth with all the congregation? [23]And the LORD spake unto Moses, saying, [24]Speak unto the congregation, saying, Get you up from about the tabernacle of Korah, Dathan, and Abiram. [25]And Moses rose up and went unto Dathan and Abiram; and the elders of Israel followed him. [26]And he spake unto the congregation, saying, Depart, I pray you, from the tents of these wicked men, and touch nothing of theirs, lest ye be consumed in all their sins. [27]So they gat up from the tabernacle of Korah, Dathan, and Abiram, on every side: and Dathan and Abiram came out, and stood in the door of their tents, and their wives, and their sons, and their little children. [28]And Moses said, Hereby ye shall know that the LORD hath sent me to do all these works; for I have not done them of mine own mind. [29]If these men die the common death of all men, or if they be visited after the visitation of all men; then the LORD hath not sent me. [30]But if the LORD make a new thing, and the earth open her mouth, and swallow them up, with all that appertain unto them, and they go down quick into the pit; then ye shall understand that these men have provoked the LORD. [31]And it came to pass, as he had made an end of speaking all these words, that the ground clave asunder that was under them: [32]And the earth opened her mouth, and swallowed them up, and their houses, and all the men that appertained unto Korah, and all their goods. [33]They, and all that appertained to them, went down alive into the pit, and the earth closed upon them: and they perished from among the congregation. [34]And all Israel that were round about them fled at the cry of them: for they said, Lest the earth swallow us up also. [35]And there came out a fire from the LORD, and consumed the two hundred and fifty men that offered incense.

1 CORINTHIANS 10:13—Offerings to God vis-à-vis idols (8:1–11:1), written from Ephesus, 51 CE

Theme	1 COR	Mt
Do not be tempted	**10:13** [13]There hath no temptation taken you but such as is common to man: but God is faithful, who will not suffer you to be tempted above that ye are able; but will with the temptation also make a way to escape, that ye may be able to bear it.	**6:13** [13]And lead us not into temptation, but deliver us from evil: For thine is the kingdom, and the power, and the glory, for ever. Amen.

1 CORINTHIANS 10:14—Offerings to God vis-à-vis idols (8:1–11:1), written from Ephesus, 51 CE

Theme	1 COR	Jn
Flee from idolatry	**10:14** [14]Wherefore, my dearly beloved, flee from idolatry.	**1 Jn 5:21** [21]Little children, keep yourselves from idols. Amen.

1 CORINTHIANS 10:16—Offerings to God vis-à-vis idols (8:1–11:1), written from Ephesus, 51 CE

Them	1 COR	Mt
Sacraments	**10:16** [16]The cup of blessing which we bless, is it not the communion of the blood of Christ? The bread which we break, is it not the communion of the body of Christ? **1:16** [16]And I baptized also the household of Stephanas: besides, I know not whether I baptized any other.	**16:24–26** [24]Then said Jesus unto his disciples, If any man will come after me, let him deny himself, and take up his cross, and follow me. [25]For whosoever will save his life shall lose it: and whosoever will lose his life for my sake shall find it. [26]For what is a man profited, if he shall gain the whole world, and lose his own soul? or what shall a man give in exchange for his soul? **20:22–23** [22]But Jesus answered and said, Ye know not what ye ask. Are ye able to drink of the cup that I shall drink of, and to be baptized with the baptism that I am baptized with? They say unto him, We are able. [23]And he saith unto them, Ye shall drink indeed of my cup, and be baptized with the baptism that I am baptized with: but to sit on my right hand, and on my left, is not mine to give, but it shall be given to them for whom it is prepared of my Father. **26:26–29** [26]And as they were eating, Jesus took bread, and blessed it, and brake it, and gave it to the disciples, and said, Take, eat; this is my body. [27]And he took the cup, and gave thanks, and gave it to them, saying, Drink ye all of it; [28]For this is my blood of the new testament, which is shed for many for the remission of sins. [29]But I say unto you, I will not drink henceforth of this fruit of the vine, until that day when I drink it new with you in my Father's kingdom. **26:31** [31]Then saith Jesus unto them, All ye shall be offended because of me this night: for it is written, I will smite the shepherd, and the sheep of the flock shall be scattered abroad. **27:46** [46]And about the ninth hour Jesus cried with a loud voice, saying, EliEli, EliEli, lamalama sabachthanisabachthani? that is to say, My God, my God, why hast thou forsaken me?

NT
Jas 1:9
[9]Let the brother of low degree rejoice in that he is exalted:
Jas 1:13–14
[13]Let no man say when he is tempted, I am tempted of God: for God cannot be tempted with evil, neither tempteth he any man: [14]But every man is tempted, when he is drawn away of his own lust, and enticed.

Mk	Lk	Jn
8:34–37 [34]And when he had called the people unto him with his disciples also, he said unto them, Whosoever will come after me, let him deny himself, and take up his cross, and follow me. [35]For whosoever will save his life shall lose it; but whosoever shall lose his life for my sake and the gospel's, the same shall save it. [36]For what shall it profit a man, if he shall gain the whole world, and lose his own soul? [37]Or what shall a man give in exchange for his soul? **8:36** [36]For what shall it profit a man, if he shall gain the whole world, and lose his own soul? **8:38** [38]Whosoever therefore shall be ashamed of me and of my words in this adulterous and sinful generation; of him also shall the Son of man be ashamed, when he cometh in the glory of his Father with the holy angels. **10:38** [38]But Jesus said unto them, Ye know not what ye ask: can ye drink of the cup that I drink of? and be baptized with the baptism that I am baptized with? **14:27** [27]And Jesus saith unto them, All ye shall be offended because of me this night: for it is written, I will smite the shepherd, and the sheep shall be scattered. **15:34** [34]And at the ninth hour Jesus cried with a loud voice, saying, EloiEloi, EloiEloi, lamalama sabachthanisabachthani? which is, being interpreted, My God, my God, why hast thou forsaken me?	**9:23–26** [23]And he said to them all, If any man will come after me, let him deny himself, and take up his cross daily, and follow me. [24]For whosoever will save his life shall lose it: but whosoever will lose his life for my sake, the same shall save it. [25]For what is a man advantaged, if he gain the whole world, and lose himself, or be cast away? [26]For whosoever shall be ashamed of me and of my words, of him shall the Son of man be ashamed, when he shall come in his own glory, and in his Father's, and of the holy angels. **12:50** [50]But I have a baptism to be baptized with; & how am I straitened till it be accomplished! **22:37** [37]For I say unto you, that this that is written must yet be accomplished in me, And he was reckoned among the transgressors: for the things concerning me have an end. **22:42** [42]Saying, Father, if thou be willing, remove this cup from me: nevertheless not my will, but thine, be done. **Acts 2:42** [42]And they continued stedfastly in the apostles' doctrine and fellowship, and in breaking of bread, and in prayers.	**10:11** [11]I am the good shepherd: the good shepherd giveth his life for the sheep.

1 Corinthians 10:16 continued on next page

1 Corinthians 10:16—Offerings to God vis-à-vis idols (8:1–11:1), written from Ephesus, 51 CE

Theme	1 COR	Paul
(*Cont.*) Sacraments	10:16 (above)	**Rom 6:3–4** [3]Know ye not, that so many of us as were baptized into Jesus Christ were baptized into his death? [4]Therefore we are buried with him by baptism into death: that like as Christ was raised up from the dead by the glory of the Father, even so we also should walk in newness of life. **Rom 8:17** [17]And if children, then heirs; heirs of God, and joint-heirs with Christ; if so be that we suffer with him, that we may be also glorified together. **Gal 2:19** [19]For I through the law am dead to the law, that I might live unto God. **Phil 1:20** [20]According to my earnest expectation and my hope, that in nothing I shall be ashamed, but that with all boldness, as always, so now also Christ shall be magnified in my body, whether it be by life, or by death. **Phil 3:7–11** [7]But what things were gain to me, those I counted loss for Christ. [8]Yea doubtless, and I count all things but loss for the excellency of the knowledge of Christ Jesus my Lord: for whom I have suffered the loss of all things, and do count them but dung, that I may win Christ, [9]And be found in him, not having mine own righteousness, which is of the law, but that which is through the faith of Christ, the righteousness which is of God by faith: [10]That I may know him, and the power of his resurrection, and the fellowship of his sufferings, being made conformable unto his death; [11]If by any means I might attain unto the resurrection of the dead. **Col 2:8–12** [8]Beware lest any man spoil you through philosophy and vain deceit, after the tradition of men, after the rudiments of the world, and not after Christ. [9]For in him dwelleth all the fulness of the Godhead bodily. [10]And ye are complete in him, which is the head of all principality and power: [11]In whom also ye are circumcised with the circumcision made without hands, in putting off the body of the sins of the flesh by the circumcision of Christ: [12]Buried with him in baptism, wherein also ye are risen with him through the faith of the operation of God, who hath raised him from the dead.

1 CORINTHIANS 10:17—Offerings to God vis-à-vis idols (8:1–11:1), written from Ephesus, 51 CE

Theme	1 COR	Paul
One bread, one body	**10:17** [17]For we being many are one bread, and one body: for we are all partakers of that one bread.	**Rom 12:5** [5]So we, being many, are one body in Christ, and every one members one of another. **Eph 4:4 (Pseudo)** [4]There is one body, and one Spirit, even as ye are called in one hope of your calling;

1 CORINTHIANS 10:18—Offerings to God vis-à-vis idols (8:1–11:1), written from Ephesus, 51 CE

Theme	1 COR	Jewish Writings
Israel, after the flesh	**10:18** [18]Behold Israel after the flesh: are not they which eat of the sacrifices partakers of the altar?	**Lev 7:6** [6]Every male among the priests shall eat thereof: it shall be eaten in the holy place: it is most holy.

Jewish Writings	Other
Ps 22:1 [1]My God, my God, why hast thou forsaken me? why art thou so far from helping me, and from the words of my roaring? **Is 53:12** [12]Therefore will I divide him a portion with the great, and he shall divide the spoil with the strong; because he hath poured out his soul unto death: and he was numbered with the transgressors; and he bare the sin of many, and made intercession for the transgressors. **Zech 13:7** [7]Awake, O sword, against my shepherd, and against the man that is my fellow, saith the LORD of hosts: smite the shepherd, and the sheep shall be scattered: and I will turn mine hand upon the little ones.	**Q-Quelle** Divisions in Households: 1 Cor 10:16/Gal 2:18-19/Phil3:7-11/[Mt 10:34-36]/[Lk 12:49-53] (QS 43 [Thom 16])

1 CORINTHIANS 10:20—Offerings to God vis-à-vis idols (8:1–11:1), written from Ephesus, 51 CE

Theme	1 COR	Jewish Writings
Sacrifices to devils	**10:20** [20]But I say, that the things which the Gentiles sacrifice, they sacrifice to devils, and not to God: and I would not that ye should have fellowship with devils.	**Dt 32:17** [17]They sacrificed unto devils, not to God; to gods whom they knew not, to new gods that came newly up, whom your fathers feared not.

1 CORINTHIANS 10:21—Offerings to God vis-à-vis idols (8:1–11:1), written from Ephesus, 51 CE

Theme	1 COR	Paul
Cannot drink cup of Lord and devils	**10:21** [21]Ye cannot drink the cup of the Lord, and the cup of devils: ye cannot be partakers of the Lord's table, and of the table of devils.	**2 Cor 6:14–18** [14]Be ye not unequally yoked together with unbelievers: for what fellowship hath righteousness with unrighteousness? and what communion hath light with darkness? [15]And what concord hath Christ with Belial? or what part hath he that believeth with an infidel? [16]And what agreement hath the temple of God with idols? for ye are the temple of the living God; as God hath said, I will dwell in them, and walk in them; and I will be their God, and they shall be my people. [17]Wherefore come out from among them, and be ye separate, saith the Lord, and touch not the unclean thing; and I will receive you, [18]And will be a Father unto you, and ye shall be my sons and daughters, saith the Lord Almighty.

1 CORINTHIANS 10:22—Offerings to God vis-à-vis idols (8:1–11:1), written from Ephesus, 51 CE

Theme	1 COR
Do not provoke the Lord	**10:22** [22]Do we provoke the Lord to jealousy? are we stronger than he? **6:12** [12]All things are lawful unto me, but all things are not expedient: all things are lawful for me, but I will not be brought under the power of any.

1 CORINTHIANS 10:23—Offerings to God vis-à-vis idols (8:1–11:1), written from Ephesus, 51 CE

Theme	1 COR
Things lawful may not edify	**10:23** [23]All things are lawful for me, but all things are not expedient: all things are lawful for me, but all things edify not. **6:12** [12]All things are lawful unto me, but all things are not expedient: all things are lawful for me, but I will not be brought under the power of any.

1 CORINTHIANS 10:24—Offerings to God vis-à-vis idols (8:1–11:1), written from Ephesus, 51 CE

Theme	1 COR	Paul	Other
Do good unto others	**10:24** [24]Let no man seek his own, but every man another's wealth. **13:5** [5]Doth not behave itself unseemly, seeketh not her own, is not easily provoked, thinketh no evil;	**Rom 15:2** [2]Let every one of us please his neighbour for his good to edification. **Phil 2:4** [4]Look not every man on his own things, but every man also on the things of others. **Phil 2:21** [21]For all seek their own, not the things which are Jesus Christ's.	**Q-Quelle** Against Pharisees: 1 Cor 10:24/Rom 15:1/[Mt 23:4-36]/[Mk 37:1-9]/[Lk 11:37-54] (QS 34 [Thom 39:1; 89;102])

1 CORINTHIANS 10:26—Offerings to God vis-à-vis idols (8:1–11:1), written from Ephesus, 51 CE

Theme	1 COR	Jewish Writings
Earth is the Lord's	**10:26** [26]For the earth is the Lord's, and the fulness thereof.	**Ps 24:1** [1]The earth is the LORD'S, and the fulness thereof; the world, and they that dwell therein. **Ps 50:12** [12]If I were hungry, I would not tell thee: for the world is mine, and the fulness thereof.

1 CORINTHIANS 10:27—Offerings to God vis-à-vis idols (8:1–11:1), written from Ephesus, 51 CE

Theme	1 COR	Mt	Lk	Other
Provision during mission	**10:27** [27]If any of them that believe not bid you to a feast, and ye be disposed to go; whatsoever is set before you, eat, asking no question for conscience sake. **9:14** [14]Even so hath the Lord ordained that they which preach the gospel should live of the gospel.	**10:10** [10]Nor scrip for your journey, neither two coats, neither shoes, nor yet staves: for the workman is worthy of his meat.	**10:7** [7]And in the same house remain, eating and drinking such things as they give: for the labourer is worthy of his hire. Go not from house to house.	**Q-Quelle** Commissioning of 12: 1 Cor 10:27/[2 Cor 11:7]/[Gal 2:7,9]/[Mt 10:1], Mt 10:7-11, [Mt 10:14]/[Mk 6:6b-13]/[Lk 9:1-6]; Commissioning of 70: 1 Cor 10:27/[2 Cor 11:7]/[Gal 2:7,9]/[Mt 9:37-38], Mt 10:7-16/Lk 10:1-12 (QS 20 [Thom73, 14:2], QS 21)

1 CORINTHIANS 10:30—Offerings to God vis-à-vis idols (8:1–11:1), written from Ephesus, 51 CE

Theme	1 COR	Paul
Partaker by grace	**10:30** [30]For if I by grace be a partaker, why am I evil spoken of for that for which I give thanks?	**Rom 14:6** [6]He that regardeth the day, regardeth it unto the Lord; and he that regardeth not the day, to the Lord he doth not regard it. He that eateth, eateth to the Lord, for he giveth God thanks; and he that eateth not, to the Lord he eateth not, and giveth God thanks. **1 Tim 4:3–4 (Pseudo)** [3]Forbidding to marry, and commanding to abstain from meats, which God hath created to be received with thanksgiving of them which believe and know the truth. [4]For every creature of God is good, and nothing to be refused, if it be received with thanksgiving:

1 CORINTHIANS 10:33—Offerings to God vis-à-vis idols (8:1–11:1), written from Ephesus, 51 CE

Theme	1 COR	Paul	Other
Seeking salvation of others	**10:33** [33]Even as I please all men in all things, not seeking mine own profit, but the profit of many, that they may be saved. **9:22** [22]To the weak became I as weak, that I might gain the weak: I am made all things to all men, that I might by all means save some.	**Rom 15:2** [2]Let every one of us please his neighbour for his good to edification.	**Q-Quelle** Against Pharisees: [Rom 15:1]/[Mt 23:4-36]/[Mk 7:1-9]/[Lk 11:37-54 (QS 34 [Thom 39:1, 89, 102])]

1 CORINTHIANS 11:1—Offerings to God vis-à-vis idols (8:1–11:1), written from Ephesus, 51 CE

Theme	1 COR	Paul
Follow Paul, follow Christ	**11:1** [1]Be ye followers of me, even as I also am of Christ. **4:16** [16]Wherefore I beseech you, be ye followers of me.	**Phil 3:17** [17]Brethren, be followers together of me, and mark them which walk so as ye have us for an ensample.

BEHAVIOR ISSUES DURING LITURGY (11:2–14:40)

ORDINANCES (11:3–16)

1 CORINTHIANS 11:2—Ordinances (11:3–16), written from Ephesus, 51 CE

Theme	1 COR	Paul
Remember Paul & keep ordinances	**11:2** [2]Now I praise you, brethren, that ye remember me in all things, and keep the ordinances, as I delivered them to you. **15:3** [3]For I delivered unto you first of all that which I also received, how that Christ died for our sins according to the scriptures;	**1 Thes 2:15** [15]Who both killed the Lord Jesus, and their own prophets, and have persecuted us; and they please not God, and are contrary to all men:

1 CORINTHIANS 11:3—Ordinances (11:3–16), written from Ephesus, 51 CE

Theme	1 COR	Paul
Christ, head of every man	**11:3** [3]But I would have you know, that the head of every man is Christ; and the head of the woman is the man; and the head of Christ is God.	**Eph 5:23 (Pseudo)** [23]For the husband is the head of the wife, even as Christ is the head of the church: and he is the saviour of the body.

1 CORINTHIANS 11:7—Ordinances (11:3–16), written from Ephesus, 51 CE

Theme	1 COR	Jewish Writings
Covering head	**11:7** [7]For a man indeed ought not to cover his head, forasmuch as he is the image and glory of God: but the woman is the glory of the man.	**Gen 1:26–27** [26]And God said, Let us make man in our image, after our likeness: and let them have dominion over the fish of the sea, and over the fowl of the air, and over the cattle, and over all the earth, and over every creeping thing that creepeth upon the earth. [27]So God created man in his own image, in the image of God created he him; male and female created he them. **Gen 5:1** [1]This is the book of the generations of Adam. In the day that God created man, in the likeness of God made he him;

1 CORINTHIANS 11:8—Ordinances (11:3–16), written from Ephesus, 51 CE

Theme	1 COR	Jewish Writings
Men and women	**11:8** [8]For the man is not of the woman; but the woman of the man.	**Gen 2:21–23** [21]And the LORD God caused a deep sleep to fall upon Adam, and he slept: and he took one of his ribs, and closed up the flesh instead thereof; [22]And the rib, which the LORD God had taken from man, made he a woman, and brought her unto the man. [23]And Adam said, This is now bone of my bones, and flesh of my flesh: she shall be called Woman, because she was taken out of Man.

1 CORINTHIANS 11:9—Ordinances (11:3–16), written from Ephesus, 51 CE

Theme	1 COR	Jewish Writings
Men and women	**11:9** [9]Neither was the man created for the woman; but the woman for the man.	**Gen 2:18** [18]And the LORD God said, It is not good that the man should be alone; I will make him an help meet for him.

1 CORINTHIANS 11:11—Ordinances (11:3–16), written from Ephesus, 51 CE

Theme	1 COR	Paul
Men & women, in the Lord	**11:11** [11]Nevertheless neither is the man without the woman, neither the woman without the man, in the Lord.	**Gal 3:27–28** [27]For as many of you as have been baptized into Christ have put on Christ. [28]There is neither Jew nor Greek, there is neither bond nor free, there is neither male nor female: for ye are all one in Christ Jesus.

1 CORINTHIANS 11:12—Ordinances (11:3–16), written from Ephesus, 51 CE

Theme	1 COR	Paul
All of God	**11:12** [12]For as the woman is of the man, even so is the man also by the woman; but all things of God. **8:6** [6]But to us there is but one God, the Father, of whom are all things, and we in him; and one Lord Jesus Christ, by whom are all things, and we by him.	**Rom 11:36** [36]For of him, and through him, and to him, are all things: to whom be glory for ever. Amen.

BEHAVIOR DURING THE EUCHARIST (11:17–34)

1 CORINTHIANS 11:18—Behavior during the Eucharist (11:17–34), 51 CE

Theme	1 COR	Paul
Divisions among believers	**11:18** [18]For first of all, when ye come together in the church, I hear that there be divisions among you; and I partly believe it. **1:10-12** [10]Now I beseech you, brethren, by the name of our Lord Jesus Christ, that ye all speak the same thing, and that there be no divisions among you; but that ye be perfectly joined together in the same mind and in the same judgment. [11]For it hath been declared unto me of you, my brethren, by them which are of the house of Chloe, that there are contentions among you. [12]Now this I say, that every one of you saith, I am of Paul; and I of Apollos; and I of Cephas; and I of Christ.	**Gal 5:20** [20]Idolatry, witchcraft, hatred, variance, emulations, wrath, strife, seditions, heresies,

1 CORINTHIANS 11:22—Behavior during the Eucharist (11:17–34), 51 CE

Theme	1 COR	NT
Poor behavior for Lord's Communion	**11:22** [22]What? have ye not houses to eat and to drink in? or despise ye the church of God, and shame them that have not? What shall I say to you? shall I praise you in this? I praise you not.	**Jas 2:1–7** [1]My brethren, have not the faith of our Lord Jesus Christ, the Lord of glory, with respect of persons. [2]For if there come unto your assembly a man with a gold ring, in goodly apparel, and there come in also a poor man in vile raiment; [3]And ye have respect to him that weareth the gay clothing, and say unto him, Sit thou here in a good place; and say to the poor, Stand thou there, or sit here under my footstool: [4]Are ye not then partial in yourselves, and are become judges of evil thoughts? [5]Hearken, my beloved brethren, Hath not God chosen the poor of this world rich in faith, and heirs of the kingdom which he hath promised to them that love him? [6]But ye have despised the poor. Do not rich men oppress you, and draw you before the judgment seats? [7]Do not they blaspheme that worthy name by the which ye are called?

1 CORINTHIANS 11:23–25—Behavior during the Eucharist (11:17–34), 51 CE

Them	1 COR	Mt	Mk
Bread and cup	**11:23–25** 23For I have received of the Lord that which also I delivered unto you, That the Lord Jesus the same night in which he was betrayed took bread: 24And when he had given thanks, he brake it, and said, Take, eat: this is my body, which is broken for you: this do in remembrance of me. 25After the same manner also he took the cup, when he had supped, saying, This cup is the new testament in my blood: this do ye, as oft as ye drink it, in remembrance of me.	**26:17–19** 17Now the first day of the feast of unleavened bread the disciples came to Jesus, saying unto him, Where wilt thou that we prepare for thee to eat the passover? 18And he said, Go into the city to such a man, and say unto him, The Master saith, My time is at hand; I will keep the passover at thy house with my disciples. 19And the disciples did as Jesus had appointed them; and they made ready the passover. **26:20-25** 20Now when the even was come, he sat down with the twelve. 21And as they did eat, he said, Verily I say unto you, that one of you shall betray me. 22And they were exceeding sorrowful, and began every one of them to say unto him, Lord, is it I? 23And he answered and said, He that dippeth his hand with me in the dish, the same shall betray me. 24The Son of man goeth as it is written of him: but woe unto that man by whom the Son of man is betrayed! it had been good for that man if he had not been born. 25Then Judas, which betrayed him, answered and said, Master, is it I? He said unto him, Thou hast said. **26:26–29** 26And as they were eating, Jesus took bread, and blessed it, and brake it, and gave it to the disciples, and said, Take, eat; this is my body. 27And he took the cup, and gave thanks, and gave it to them, saying, Drink ye all of it; 28For this is my blood of the new testament, which is shed for many for the remission of sins. 29But I say unto you, I will not drink henceforth of this fruit of the vine, until that day when I drink it new with you in my Father's kingdom.	**14:12–16** 13And the first day of unleavened bread, when they killed the passover, his disciples said unto him, Where wilt thou that we go and prepare that thou mayest eat the passover? 14And he sendeth forth two of his disciples, and saith unto them, Go ye into the city, and there shall meet you a man bearing a pitcher of water: follow him. 14And wheresoever he shall go in, say ye to the goodman of the house, The Master saith, Where is the guestchamber, where I shall eat the passover with my disciples? 15And he will show you a large upper room furnished and prepared: there make ready for us. 16And his disciples went forth, and came into the city, and found as he had said unto them: and they made ready the passover. **14:17–21** 17And in the evening he cometh with the twelve. 18And as they sat and did eat, Jesus said, Verily I say unto you, One of you which eateth with me shall betray me. 19And they began to be sorrowful, and to say unto him one by one, Is it I? and another said, Is it I? 20And he answered and said unto them, It is one of the twelve, that dippeth with me in the dish. 21The Son of man indeed goeth, as it is written of him: but woe to that man by whom the Son of man is betrayed! good were it for that man if he had never been born. **14:22–25** 22And as they did eat, Jesus took bread, and blessed, and brake it, and gave to them, and said, Take, eat: this is my body. 23And he took the cup, and when he had given thanks, he gave it to them: and they all drank of it. 24And he said unto them, This is my blood of the new testament, which is shed for many. 25Verily I say unto you, I will drink no more of the fruit of the vine, until that day that I drink it new in the kingdom of God.

Lk

9:16

[16]Then he took the five loaves and the two fishes, and looking up to heaven, he blessed them, and brake, and gave to the disciples to set before the multitude.

9:22

[22]Saying, The Son of man must suffer many things, and be rejected of the elders and chief priests and scribes, and be slain, and be raised the third day.

9:44

[44]Let these sayings sink down into your ears: for the Son of man shall be delivered into the hands of men.

17:25

[25]But first must he suffer many things, and be rejected of this generation.

18:31–33

[31]Then he took unto him the twelve, and said unto them, Behold, we go up to Jerusalem, and all things that are written by the prophets concerning the Son of man shall be accomplished. [32]For he shall be delivered unto the Gentiles, and shall be mocked, and spitefully entreated, and spitted on: [33]And they shall scourge him, and put him to death: and the third day he shall rise again.

22:7–13

[7]Then came the day of unleavened bread, when the passover must be killed. [8]And he sent Peter and John, saying, Go and prepare us the passover, that we may eat. [9]And they said unto him, Where wilt thou that we prepare? [10]And he said unto them, Behold, when ye are entered into the city, there shall a man meet you, bearing a pitcher of water; follow him into the house where he entereth in. [11]And ye shall say unto the goodman of the house, The Master saith unto thee, Where is the guestchamber, where I shall eat the passover with my disciples? [12]And he shall show you a large upper room furnished: there make ready. [13]And they went, and found as he had said unto them: and they made ready the passover.

22:14–23

[14]And when the hour was come, he sat down, and the twelve apostles with him. [15]And he said unto them, With desire I have desired to eat this passover with you before I suffer: [16]For I say unto you, I will not any more eat thereof, until it be fulfilled in the kingdom of God. [17]And he took the cup, and gave thanks, and said, Take this, and divide it among yourselves: [18]For I say unto you, I will not drink of the fruit of the vine, until the kingdom of God shall come. [19]And he took bread, and gave thanks, and brake it, and gave unto them, saying, This is my body which is given for you: this do in remembrance of me. [20]Likewise also the cup after supper, saying, This cup is the new testament in my blood, which is shed for you. [21]But, behold, the hand of him that betrayeth me is with me on the table. [22]And truly the Son of man goeth, as it was determined: but woe unto that man by whom he is betrayed! [23]And they began to inquire among themselves, which of them it was that should do this thing.

24:6–8

[6]He is not here, but is risen: remember how he spake unto you when he was yet in Galilee, [7]Saying, The Son of man must be delivered into the hands of sinful men, and be crucified, and the third day rise again. [8]And they remembered his words,

24:26

[26]Ought not Christ to have suffered these things, and to enter into his glory?

24:30

[30]And it came to pass, as he sat at meat with them, he took bread, and blessed it, and brake, and gave to them.

24:46

[46]And said unto them, Thus it is written, and thus it behoved Christ to suffer, and to rise from the dead the third day:

1 Corinthians 11:23-25 continued on next page

1 CORINTHIANS 11:23–25—Behavior during the Eucharist (11:17–34), 51 CE (*continued*)

Theme	1 COR	Jn	Jewish
(*Cont.*) **Bread and cup**	**11:23–25 (above)**	**6:48–58** [48]I am that bread of life. [49]Your fathers did eat manna in the wilderness, and are dead. [50]This is the bread which cometh down from heaven, that a man may eat thereof, and not die. [51]I am the living bread which came down from heaven: if any man eat of this bread, he shall live for ever: and the bread that I will give is my flesh, which I will give for the life of the world. [52]The Jews therefore strove among them-selves, saying, How can this man give us his flesh to eat? [53]Then Jesus said unto them, Verily, verily, I say unto you, Except ye eat the flesh of the Son of man, and drink his blood, ye have no life in you. [54]Whoso eateth my flesh, and drinketh my blood, hath eternal life; and I will raise him up at the last day. [55]For my flesh is meat indeed, and my blood is drink indeed. [56]He that eateth my flesh, and drinketh my blood, dwelleth in me, and I in him. [57]As the living Father hath sent me, and I live by the Father: so he that eateth me, even he shall live by me. [58]This is that bread which came down from heaven: not as your fathers did eat manna, and are dead: he that eateth of this bread shall live for ever. **13:21–30** [21]When Jesus had thus said, he was troubled in spirit, and testified, and said, Verily, verily, I say unto you, that one of you shall betray me. [22]Then the disciples looked one on another, doubting of whom he spake. [23]Now there was leaning on Jesus' bosom one of his disciples, whom Jesus loved. [24]Simon Peter therefore beckoned to him, that he should ask who it should be of whom he spake. [25]He then lying on Jesus' breast saith unto him, Lord, who is it? [26]Jesus answered, He it is, to whom I shall give a sop, when I have dipped it. And when he had dipped the sop, he gave it to Judas Iscariot, the son of Simon. [27]And after the sop Satan entered into him. Then said Jesus unto him, That thou doest, do quickly. [28]Now no man at the table knew for what intent he spake this unto him. [29]For some of them thought, because Judas had the bag, that Jesus had said unto him, Buy those things that we have need of against the feast; or, that he should give something to the poor. [30]He then having received the sop went immediately out: and it was night.	**Ex 24:8** [8]And Moses took the blood, and sprinkled it on the people, and said, Behold the blood of the covenant, which the LORD hath made with you concerning all these words. **Ps 41:9** [9]Yea, mine own familiar friend, in whom I trusted, which did eat of my bread, hath lifted up his heel against me. **Jer 31:31** [31]Behold, the days come, saith the LORD, that I will make a new covenant with the house of Israel, and with the house of Judah: **Zech 9:11** [11]As for thee also, by the blood of thy covenant I have sent forth thy prisoners out of the pit wherein is no water.

Other

Did 9:1–5

[1]And with respect to the thanksgiving meal, you shall give thanks as follows: [2]First with respect to the cup: "We give you thanks, our Father, for the holy vine of David, your child, which you made known to us through Jesus your child. To you be the glory forever." [3]And with respect to the fragment of bread: "We give you thanks to you, our Father, for the life and knowledge that you made known to us through Jesus your child. To you be the glory forever. [4]As this fragment of bread was scattered upon the mountains and was gathered to be come one, so may your church be gathered together from the ends of the earth into your kingdom. For the glory and the power are yours forever through Jesus Christ forever. [5]But let no one eat or drink from your thanksgiving meal unless they have been baptized in the name of the Lord. For also the Lord has said about this, "Do not give what is holy to the dogs."

GEbi 7

[7]They do not allege that he was born from God the Father, but that he was created from one of the archangels, yet was made greater than they, since he rules over the angels and all things made by the Almighty. And as found in their gospel, they say that when he came he taught, "I have come to destroy the sacrifices. And if you do not stop making sacrifice, God's wrath will not stop afflicting you. (Epiphanius, Panarion, 30, 16, 4-5)

Justin, Apol, 1.66

And this food is called among us Eukaristia [the Eucharist], of which no one is allowed to partake but the man who believes that the things which we teach are true, and who has been washed with the washing that is for the remission of sins, and unto regeneration, and who is so living as Christ has enjoined. For not as common bread and common drink do we receive these; but in like manner as Jesus Christ our Saviour, having been made flesh by the Word of God, had both flesh and blood for our salvation, so likewise have we been taught that the food which is blessed by the prayer of His word, and from which our blood and flesh by transmutation are nourished, is the flesh and blood of that Jesus who was made flesh. For the apostles, in the memoirs composed by them, which are called Gospels, have thus delivered unto us what was enjoined upon them; that Jesus took bread, and when He had given thanks, said, "This do ye in remembrance of Me, this is My body;" and that, after the same manner, having taken the cup and given thanks, He said, "This is My blood;" and gave it to them alone. Which the wicked devils have imitated in the mysteries of Mithras, commanding the same thing to be done. For, that bread and a cup of water are placed with certain incantations in the mystic rites of one who is being initiated, you either know or can learn. so the Lord has said about this, "Do not give what is holy to the dogs."

Q-Quelle

Day of SOM: 1 Cor 11:23-25/[Mt 10:39, 24:17-18,24:23, 24:26-27, 24:28, 24:37-39, 24:40-41]/[Mk 13:14-16, 13:19-23]/Lk 17:22-37 (Qs 60 [Thom 3, 51,61, 113])

1 CORINTHIANS 11:23—Behavior during the Eucharist (11:17–34), 51 CE

Theme	1 COR
Lord took bread...	**11:23** [23]For I have received of the Lord that which also I delivered unto you, That the Lord Jesus the same night in which he was betrayed took bread: **1 Cor 2** [1]And I, brethren, when I came to you, came not with excellency of speech or of wisdom, declaring unto you the testimony of God. [2]For I determined not to know any thing among you, save Jesus Christ, and him crucified. [3]And I was with you in weakness, and in fear, and in much trembling. [4]And my speech and my preaching was not with enticing words of man's wisdom, but in demonstration of the Spirit and of power: [5]That your faith should not stand in the wisdom of men, but in the power of God. [6]Howbeit we speak wisdom among them that are perfect: yet not the wisdom of this world, nor of the princes of this world, that come to nought: [7]But we speak the wisdom of God in a mystery, even the hidden wisdom, which God ordained before the world unto our glory: [8]Which none of the princes of this world knew: for had they known it, they would not have crucified the Lord of glory. [9]But as it is written, Eye hath not seen, nor ear heard, neither have entered into the heart of man, the things which God hath prepared for them that love him. [10]But God hath revealed them unto us by his Spirit: for the Spirit searcheth all things, yea, the deep things of God. [11]For what man knoweth the things of a man, save the spirit of man which is in him? even so the things of God knoweth no man, but the Spirit of God. [12]Now we have received, not the spirit of the world, but the spirit which is of God; that we might know the things that are freely given to us of God. [13]Which things also we speak, not in the words which man's wisdom teacheth, but which the Holy Ghost teacheth; comparing spiritual things with spiritual. [14]But the natural man receiveth not the things of the Spirit of God: for they are foolishness unto him: neither can he know them, because they are spiritually discerned. [15]But he that is spiritual judgeth all things, yet he himself is judged of no man. [16]For who hath known the mind of the Lord, that he may instruct him? But we have the mind of Christ. **10:16–17** [16]The cup of blessing which we bless, is it not the communion of the blood of Christ? The bread which we break, is it not the communion of the body of Christ? [17]For we being many are one bread, and one body: for we are all partakers of that one bread. **15:3** [3]For I delivered unto you first of all that which I also received, how that Christ died for our sins according to the scriptures;

1 CORINTHIANS 11:25—Behavior during the Eucharist (11:17–34), 51 CE

Theme	1 COR	Paul
Lord took the cup...	**11:25** [25]After the same manner also he took the cup, when he had supped, saying, This cup is the new testament in my blood: this do ye, as oft as ye drink it, in remembrance of me.	**2 Cor 3:6** [6]Who also hath made us able ministers of the new testament; not of the letter, but of the spirit: for the letter killeth, but the spirit giveth life.

Mt	Mk	Lk
26:26–29	**14:22–25**	**22:14–20**
[26]And as they were eating, Jesus took bread, and blessed it, and brake it, and gave it to the disciples, and said, Take, eat; this is my body. [27]And he took the cup, and gave thanks, and gave it to them, saying, Drink ye all of it; [28]For this is my blood of the new testament, which is shed for many for the remission of sins. [29]But I say unto you, I will not drink henceforth of this fruit of the vine, until that day when I drink it new with you in my Father's kingdom.	[22]And as they did eat, Jesus took bread, and blessed, and brake it, and gave to them, and said, Take, eat: this is my body. [23]And he took the cup, and when he had given thanks, he gave it to them: and they all drank of it. [24]And he said unto them, This is my blood of the new testament, which is shed for many. [25]Verily I say unto you, I will drink no more of the fruit of the vine, until that day that I drink it new in the kingdom of God.	[14]And when the hour was come, he sat down, and the twelve apostles with him. [15]And he said unto them, With desire I have desired to eat this passover with you before I suffer: [16]For I say unto you, I will not any more eat thereof, until it be fulfilled in the kingdom of God. [17]And he took the cup, and gave thanks, and said, Take this, and divide it among yourselves: [18]For I say unto you, I will not drink of the fruit of the vine, until the kingdom of God shall come. [19]And he took bread, and gave thanks, and brake it, and gave unto them, saying, This is my body which is given for you: this do in remembrance of me. [20]Likewise also the cup after supper, saying, This cup is the new testament in my blood, which is shed for you.

NT	Jewish Writings
Heb 8:6–13	**Ex 24:8**
[6]But now hath he obtained a more excellent ministry, by how much also he is the mediator of a better covenant, which was established upon better promises. [7]For if that first covenant had been faultless, then should no place have been sought for the second. [8]For finding fault with them, he saith, Behold, the days come, saith the Lord, when I will make a new covenant with the house of Israel and with the house of Judah: [9]Not according to the covenant that I made with their fathers in the day when I took them by the hand to lead them out of the land of Egypt; because they continued not in my covenant, and I regarded them not, saith the Lord. [10]For this is the covenant that I will make with the house of Israel after those days, saith the Lord; I will put my laws into their mind, and write them in their hearts: and I will be to them a God, and they shall be to me a people: [11]And they shall not teach every man his neighbour, and every man his brother, saying, Know the Lord: for all shall know me, from the least to the greatest. [12]For I will be merciful to their unrighteousness, and their sins and their iniquities will I remember no more. [13]In that he saith, A new covenant, he hath made the first old. Now that which decayeth and waxeth old is ready to vanish away.	[8]And Moses took the blood, and sprinkled it on the people, and said, Behold the blood of the covenant, which the LORD hath made with you concerning all these words.

1 CORINTHIANS 11:32—Behavior during the Eucharist (11:17–34), 51 CE

Theme	1 COR
Admonished in the Lord	**11:32** [32]But when we are judged, we are chastened of the Lord, that we should not be condemned with the world.

GIFTS OF THE HOLY SPIRIT (12:1–14, 13:4–34)

1 CORINTHIANS 12:2—Gifts of the Holy Spirit (12:1–14), 51 CE

Theme	1 COR
Idols of the Gentiles	**12:2** [2]Ye know that ye were Gentiles, carried away unto these dumb idols, even as ye were led.

NT	Jewish Writings
Heb 12:5–11	**Dt 8:5**
[5]And ye have forgotten the exhortation which speaketh unto you as unto children, My son, despise not thou the chas- tening of the Lord, nor faint when thou art rebuked of him: [6]For whom the Lord loveth he chasteneth, and scourgeth every son whom he receiveth. [7]If ye endure chastening, God dealeth with you as with sons; for what son is he whom the father chasteneth not? [8]But if ye be without chastisement, whereof all are partakers, then are ye bastards, and not sons. [9]Furthermore we have had fathers of our flesh which corrected us, and we gave them reverence: shall we not much rather be in subjection unto the Father of spirits, and live? [10]For they verily for a few days chastened us after their own pleasure; but he for our profit, that we might be partakers of his holiness. [11]Now no chastening for the pres- ent seemeth to be joyous, but grievous: nevertheless afterward it yieldeth the peaceable fruit of righteousness unto them which are exercised thereby.	[5]Thou shalt also consider in thine heart, that, as a man chasteneth his son, so the LORD thy God chasteneth thee.

Paul
Eph 2:11–18 (Pseudo)
[11]Wherefore remember, that ye being in time past Gentiles in the flesh, who are called Uncircumcision by that which is called the Circumcision in the flesh made by hands; [12]That at that time ye were without Christ, being aliens from the commonwealth of Israel, and strangers from the covenants of promise, having no hope, and without God in the world: [13]But now in Christ Jesus ye who sometimes were far off are made nigh by the blood of Christ. [14]For he is our peace, who hath made both one, and hath broken down the middle wall of partition between us; [15]Having abolished in his flesh the enmity, even the law of commandments contained in ordinances; for to make in himself of twain one new man, so making peace; [16]And that he might reconcile both unto God in one body by the cross, having slain the enmity thereby: [17]And came and preached peace to you which were afar off, and to them that were nigh. [18]For through him we both have access by one Spirit unto the Father.

1 CORINTHIANS 12:3—Gifts of the Holy Spirit (12:1–14), 51 CE

Theme	1 COR
Holy Spirit confesses Jesus	**12:3** [3]Wherefore I give you to understand, that no man speaking by the Spirit of God calleth Jesus accursed: and that no man can say that Jesus is the Lord, but by the Holy Ghost. **15:20-28** [15]Yea, and we are found false witnesses of God; because we have testified of God that he raised up Christ: whom he raised not up, if so be that the dead rise not. [16]For if the dead rise not, then is not Christ raised: [17]And if Christ be not raised, your faith is vain; ye are yet in your sins. [18]Then they also which are fallen asleep in Christ are perished. [9]If in this life only we have hope in Christ, we are of all men most miserable. [20]But now is Christ risen from the dead, and become the firstfruits of them that slept. [21]For since by man came death, by man came also the resurrection of the dead. [22]For as in Adam all die, even so in Christ shall all be made alive. [23]But every man in his own order: Christ the firstfruits; afterward they that are Christ's at his coming. [24]Then cometh the end, when he shall have delivered up the kingdom to God, even the Father; when he shall have put down all rule and all authority and power. [25]For he must reign, till he hath put all enemies under his feet. [26]The last enemy that shall be destroyed is death.[27]For he hath put all things under his feet. But when he saith all things are put under him, it is manifest that he is excepted, which did put all things under him. [28]And when all things shall be subdued unto him, then shall the Son also himself be subject unto him that put all things under him, that God may be all in all.

Mt	Mk
21:3 3And if any man say ought unto you, ye shall say, The Lord hath need of them; and straightway he will send them. **22:41–46** 41While the Pharisees were gathered together, Jesus asked them, 42Saying, What think ye of Christ? whose son is he? They say unto him, The Son of David. 43He saith unto them, How then doth David in spirit call him Lord, saying, 44The LORD said unto my Lord, Sit thou on my right hand, till I make thine enemies thy footstool? 45If David then call him Lord, how is he his son? 46And no man was able to answer him a word, neither durst any man from that day forth ask him any more questions. **24:45–51** 45Who then is a faithful and wise servant, whom his lord hath made ruler over his household, to give them meat in due season? 46Blessed is that servant, whom his lord when he cometh shall find so doing. 47Verily I say unto you, That he shall make him ruler over all his goods. 48But and if that evil servant shall say in his heart, My lord delayeth his coming; 49And shall begin to smite his fellowservants, and to eat and drink with the drunken; 50The lord of that servant shall come in a day when he looketh not for him, and in an hour that he is not aware of, 51And shall cut him asunder, and appoint him his portion with the hypocrites: there shall be weeping and gnashing of teeth. **25:14–30** 14For the kingdom of heaven is as a man travelling into a far country, who called his own servants, and delivered unto them his goods. 15And unto one he gave five talents, to another two, and to another one; to every man according to his several ability; and straightway took his journey. 16Then he that had received the five talents went and traded with the same, and made them other five talents. 17And likewise he that had received two, he also gained other two. 18But he that had received one went and digged in the earth, and hid his lord's money. 19After a long time the lord of those servants cometh, and reckoneth with them. 20And so he that had received five talents came and brought other five talents, saying, Lord, thou deliveredst unto me five talents: behold, I have gained beside them five talents more. 21His lord said unto him, Well done, thou good and faithful servant: thou hast been faithful over a few things, I will make thee ruler over many things: enter thou into the joy of thy lord. 22He also that had received two talents came and said, Lord, thou deliveredst unto me two talents: behold, I have gained two other talents beside them. 23His lord said unto him, Well done, good and faithful servant; thou hast been faithful over a few things, I will make thee ruler over many things: enter thou into the joy of thy lord. 24Then he which had received the one talent came and said, Lord, I knew thee that thou art an hard man, reaping where thou hast not sown, and gathering where thou hast not strawed: 25And I was afraid, and went and hid thy talent in the earth: lo, there thou hast that is thine. 26His lord answered and said unto him, Thou wicked and slothful servant, thou knewest that I reap where I sowed not, and gather where I have not strawed: 27Thou oughtest therefore to have put my money to the exchangers, and then at my coming I should have received mine own with usury. 28Take therefore the talent from him, and give it unto him which hath ten talents. 29For unto every one that hath shall be given, and he shall have abundance: but from him that hath not shall be taken away even that which he hath. 30And cast ye the unprofitable servant into outer darkness: there shall be weeping and gnashing of teeth.	**11:3** 3And if any man say unto you, Why do ye this? say ye that the Lord hath need of him; and straightway he will send him hither. **12:35–37a** 35And Jesus answered and said, while he taught in the temple, How say the scribes that Christ is the Son of David? 36For David himself said by the Holy Ghost, The LORD said to my Lord, Sit thou on my right hand, till I make thine enemies thy footstool. 37David therefore himself calleth him Lord; and whence is he then his son? And the common people heard him gladly.

1 Corinthians 12:3 continued on next page

1 CORINTHIANS 12:3—Gifts of the Holy Spirit (12:1–14), 51 CE (*continued*)

Theme	1 COR	Lk	Jn
(*Cont.*) **Holy Spirit confesses Jesus**	**12:3** **(above)** **15:20-28** **(above)**	**12:41–46** [41]Then Peter said unto him, Lord, speakest thou this parable unto us, or even to all? [42]And the Lord said, Who then is that faithful and wise steward, whom his lord shall make ruler over his household, to give them their portion of meat in due season? [43]Blessed is that servant, whom his lord when he cometh shall find so doing. [44]Of a truth I say unto you, that he will make him ruler over all that he hath. [45]But and if that servant say in his heart, My lord delayeth his coming; and shall begin to beat the menservants and maidens, and to eat and drink, and to be drunken; [46]The lord of that servant will come in a day when he looketh not for him, and at an hour when he is not aware, and will cut him in sunder, and will appoint him his portion with the unbelievers. **19:11–27** [11]And as they heard these things, he added and spake a parable, because he was nigh to Jerusalem, and because they thought that the kingdom of God should immediately appear. [12]He said therefore, A certain nobleman went into a far country to receive for himself a kingdom, and to return. [13]And he called his ten servants, and delivered them ten pounds, and said unto them, Occupy till I come. [14]But his citizens hated him, and sent a message after him, saying, We will not have this man to reign over us. [15]And it came to pass, that when he was returned, having received the kingdom, then he commanded these servants to be called unto him, to whom he had given the money, that he might know how much every man had gained by trading. [16]Then came the first, saying, Lord, thy pound hath gained ten pounds. [17]And he said unto him, Well, thou good servant: because thou hast been faithful in a very little, have thou authority over ten cities. [18]And the second came, saying, Lord, thy pound hath gained five pounds. [19]And he said likewise to him, Be thou also over five cities. [20]And another came, saying, Lord, behold, here is thy pound, which I have kept laid up in a napkin: [21]For I feared thee, because thou art an austere man: thou takest up that thou layedst not down, and reapest that thou didst not sow. [22]And he saith unto him, Out of thine own mouth will I judge thee, thou wicked servant. Thou knewest that I was an austere man, taking up that I laid not down, and reaping that I did not sow: [23]Wherefore then gavest not thou my money into the bank, that at my coming I might have required mine own with usury? [24]And he said unto them that stood by, Take from him the pound, and give it to him that hath ten pounds. [25](And they said unto him, Lord, he hath ten pounds.) [26]For I say unto you, That unto every one which hath shall be given; and from him that hath not, even that he hath shall be taken away from him. [27]But those mine enemies, which would not that I should reign over them, bring hither, and slay them before me. **19:34** [34]And they said, The Lord hath need of him. **20:41–44** [41]And he said unto them, How say they that Christ is David's son? [42]And David himself saith in the book of Psalms, The LORD said unto my Lord, Sit thou on my right hand, [43]Till I make thine enemies thy footstool. [44]David therefore calleth him Lord, how is he then his son?	**1 Jn 4:2–3** [2]Hereby know ye the Spirit of God: Every spirit that confesseth that Jesus Christ is come in the flesh is of God: [3]And every spirit that confesseth not that Jesus Christ is come in the flesh is not of God: and this is that spirit of antichrist, whereof ye have heard that it should come; and even now already is it in the world.

Paul

Rom 1:3

[3]Concerning his Son Jesus Christ our Lord, which was made of the seed of David according to the flesh;

Rom 5

[1]Therefore being justified by faith, we have peace with God through our Lord Jesus Christ: [2]By whom also we have
access by faith into this grace wherein we stand, and rejoice in hope of the glory of God. [3]And not only so, but we glory
in tribulations also: knowing that tribulation worketh patience; [4]And patience, experience; and experience, hope: [5]And
hope maketh not ashamed; because the love of God is shed abroad in our hearts by the Holy Ghost which is given unto
us. [6]For when we were yet without strength, in due time Christ died for the ungodly. [7]For scarcely for a righteous man
will one die: yet peradventure for a good man some would even dare to die. [8]But God commendeth his love toward
us, in that, while we were yet sinners, Christ died for us. [9]Much more then, being now justified by his blood, we shall
be saved from wrath through him. [10]For if, when we were enemies, we were reconciled to God by the death of his Son,
much more, being reconciled, we shall be saved by his life. [11]And not only so, but we also joy in God through our Lord
Jesus Christ, by whom we have now received the atonement. [12]Wherefore, as by one man sin entered into the world,
and death by sin; and so death passed upon all men, for that all have sinned: [13](For until the law sin was in the world:
but sin is not imputed when there is no law. [14]Nevertheless death reigned from Adam to Moses, even over them that
had not sinned after the similitude of Adam's transgression, who is the figure of him that was to come. [15]But not as the
offence, so also is the free gift. For if through the offence of one many be dead, much more the grace of God, and the
gift by grace, which is by one man, Jesus Christ, hath abounded unto many. [16]And not as it was by one that sinned, so is
the gift: for the judgment was by one to condemnation, but the free gift is of many offences unto justification. [17]For if by
one man's offence death reigned by one; much more they which receive abundance of grace and of the gift of righteousness shall reign in life by one, Jesus Christ.) [18]Therefore as by the offence of one judgment came upon all men to condemnation; even so by the righteousness of one the free gift came upon all men unto justification of life. [19]For as by one
man's disobedience many were made sinners, so by the obedience of one shall many be made righteous. [20]Moreover the
law entered, that the offence might abound. But where sin abounded, grace did much more abound: [21]That as sin hath
reigned unto death, even so might grace reign through righteousness unto eternal life by Jesus Christ our Lord.

Rom 9:5

[5]Whose are the fathers, and of whom as concerning the flesh Christ came, who is over all, God blessed for ever. Amen.

Rom 10:9

[9]That if thou shalt confess with thy mouth the Lord Jesus, and shalt believe in thine heart that God hath raised him from the dead, thou shalt be saved.

2 Cor 3:18

[18]But we all, with open face beholding as in a glass the glory of the Lord, are changed into the same image from glory to glory, even as by the Spirit of the Lord.

Gal 4:4

[4]But when the fulness of the time was come, God sent forth his Son, made of a woman, made under the law,

1 Corinthians 12:3 continued on next page

1 CORINTHIANS 12:3—Gifts of the Holy Spirit (12:1–14), 51 CE (*continued*)

Theme	1 COR	Paul
(*Cont.*) **Holy Spirit confesses Jesus**	**12:3** (above) **15:20-28** (above)	(*Continued*) **Phil 2** 1If there be therefore any consolation in Christ, if any comfort of love, if any fellowship of the Spirit, if any bowels and mercies, 2Fulfil ye my joy, that ye be likeminded, having the same love, being of one accord, of one mind. 3Let nothing be done through strife or vainglory; but in lowliness of mind let each esteem other better than themselves. 4Look not every man on his own things, but every man also on the things of others. **5Let this mind be in you, which was also in Christ Jesus: 6Who, being in the form of God, thought it not robbery to be equal with God: 7But made himself of no reputation, and took upon him the form of a servant, and was made in the likeness of men: 8And being found in fashion as a man, he humbled himself, and became obedient unto death, even the death of the cross. 9Wherefore God also hath highly exalted him, and given him a name which is above every name: 10That at the name of Jesus every knee should bow, of things in heaven, and things in earth, and things under the earth; 11And that every tongue should confess that Jesus Christ is Lord, to the glory of God the Father.** 12Wherefore, my beloved, as ye have always obeyed, not as in my presence only, but now much more in my absence, work out your own salvation with fear and trembling. 13For it is God which worketh in you both to will and to do of his good pleasure. 14Do all things without murmurings and disputings: 15That ye may be blameless and harmless, the sons of God, without rebuke, in the midst of a crooked and perverse nation, among whom ye shine as lights in the world; 16Holding forth the word of life; that I may rejoice in the day of Christ, that I have not run in vain, neither laboured in vain. 17Yea, and if I be offered upon the sacrifice and service of your faith, I joy, and rejoice with you all. 18For the same cause also do ye joy, and rejoice with me. 19But I trust in the Lord Jesus to send Timotheus shortly unto you, that I also may be of good comfort, when I know your state. 20For I have no man likeminded, who will naturally care for your state. 21For all seek their own, not the things which are Jesus Christ's. 22But ye know the proof of him, that, as a son with the father, he hath served with me in the gospel. 23Him therefore I hope to send presently, so soon as I shall see how it will go with me. 24But I trust in the Lord that I also myself shall come shortly. 25Yet I supposed it necessary to send to you Epaphroditus, my brother, and companion in labour, and fellowsoldier, but your messenger, and he that ministered to my wants. 26For he longed after you all, and was full of heaviness, because that ye had heard that he had been sick. 27For indeed he was sick nigh unto death: but God had mercy on him; and not on him only, but on me also, lest I should have sorrow upon sorrow. 28I sent him therefore the more carefully, that, when ye see him again, ye may rejoice, and that I may be the less sorrowful. 29Receive him therefore in the Lord with all gladness; and hold such in reputation: 30Because for the work of Christ he was nigh unto death, not regarding his life, to supply your lack of service toward me. **Phil 3:21** 21Who shall change our vile body, that it may be fashioned like unto his glorious body, according to the working whereby he is able even to subdue all things unto himself. **Col 3:10** 10And have put on the new man, which is renewed in knowledge after the image of him that created him:

1 CORINTHIANS 12:4—Gifts of the Holy Spirit (12:1–14), 51 CE

Theme	1 COR	Paul
Diversity of gifts	**12:4** 4Now there are diversities of gifts, but the same Spirit.	**Rom 12:6** 6Having then gifts differing according to the grace that is given to us, whether prophecy, let us prophesy according to the proportion of faith; **Eph 4:7 (Pseudo)** 7But unto every one of us is given grace according to the measure of the gift of Christ. **Eph 4:11 (Pseudo)** 11And he gave some, apostles; and some, prophets; and some, evangelists; and some, pastors and teachers;

Jewish Writings	Other
Ps 110 [1]The LORD said unto my Lord, Sit thou at my right hand, until I make thine enemies thy footstool. [2]The LORD shall send the rod of thy strength out of Zion: rule thou in the midst of thine enemies. [3]Thy people shall be willing in the day of thy power, in the beauties of holiness from the womb of the morning: thou hast the dew of thy youth. [4]The LORD hath sworn, and will not repent, Thou art a priest for ever after the order of Melchizedek. [5]The Lord at thy right hand shall strike through kings in the day of his wrath. [6]He shall judge among the heathen, he shall fill the places with the dead bodies; he shall wound the heads over many countries. [7]He shall drink of the brook in the way: therefore shall he lift up the head.	**Q-Quelle** Watchful and faithful: 1 Cor 12:3/Rom 9:5/[Tit 2:13]/Mt 24:42-51/Lk 12:35-48 (QS 41 [Thom 21:3, 103], QS 42); Parable of Pounds: 1 Cor 12:3/Mt 25:14-30/Lk 19:11-27 (QS 61 [Thom 41])

1 CORINTHIANS 12:8—Gifts of the Holy Spirit (12:1–14), 51 CE

Theme	1 COR
Gifts of wisdom & knowledge	**12:8** [8]For to one is given by the Spirit the word of wisdom; to another the word of knowledge by the same Spirit; **2:6–13** [6]Howbeit we speak wisdom among them that are perfect: yet not the wisdom of this world, nor of the princes of this world, that come to nought: [7]But we speak the wisdom of God in a mystery, even the hidden wisdom, which God ordained before the world unto our glory: [8]Which none of the princes of this world knew: for had they known it, they would not have crucified the Lord of glory. [9]But as it is written, Eye hath not seen, nor ear heard, neither have entered into the heart of man, the things which God hath prepared for them that love him. [10]But God hath revealed them unto us by his Spirit: for the Spirit searcheth all things, yea, the deep things of God. [11]For what man knoweth the things of a man, save the spirit of man which is in him? even so the things of God knoweth no man, but the Spirit of God. [12]Now we have received, not the spirit of the world, but the spirit which is of God; that we might know the things that are freely given to us of God. [13]Which things also we speak, not in the words which man's wisdom teacheth, but which the Holy Ghost teacheth; comparing spiritual things with spiritual.

1 CORINTHIANS 12:10—Gifts of the Holy Spirit (12:1–14), 51 CE

Theme	1 COR
Gifts of miracles, prophesy, discernment, tongues, interpretation	**12:10** [10]To another the working of miracles; to another prophecy; to another discerning of spirits; to another divers kinds of tongues; to another the interpretation of tongues: **14:5** [5]I would that ye all spake with tongues, but rather that ye prophesied: for greater is he that prophesieth than he that speaketh with tongues, except he interpret, that the church may receive edifying. **14:26** [26]How is it then, brethren? when ye come together, every one of you hath a psalm, hath a doctrine, hath a tongue, hath a revelation, hath an interpretation. Let all things be done unto edifying. **14:39** [39]Wherefore, brethren, covet to prophesy, and forbid not to speak with tongues.

1 CORINTHIANS 12:11—Gifts of the Holy Spirit (12:1–14), 51 CE

Theme	1 COR
Many gifts, one spirit	**12:11** [11]But all these worketh that one and the selfsame Spirit, dividing to every man severally as he will. **7:7** [7]For I would that all men were even as I myself. But every man hath his proper gift of God, one after this manner, and another after that.

Lk
Acts 2:4
[4]And they were all filled with the Holy Ghost, and began to speak with other tongues, as the Spirit gave them utterance.

Paul
Eph 4:7 (Pseudo)
[7]But unto every one of us is given grace according to the measure of the gift of Christ.

1 CORINTHIANS 12:12–13—Gifts of the Holy Spirit (12:1–14), 51 CE

Theme	1 COR	Mt	Mk	Lk
Body of Christ	**12:12–13** [12]For as the body is one, and hath many members, and all the members of that one body, being many, are one body: so also is Christ. [13]For by one Spirit are we all baptized into one body, whether we be Jews or Gentiles, whether we be bond or free; and have been all made to drink into one Spirit.	**12:28** [28]But if I cast out devils by the Spirit of God, then the kingdom of God is come unto you.	**1:1** [1]The beginning of the gospel of Jesus Christ, the Son of God;	**3:22** [22]And the Holy Ghost descended in a bodily shape like a dove upon him, and a voice came from heaven, which said, Thou art my beloved Son; in thee I am well pleased. **4:18–21** [18]The Spirit of the Lord is upon me, because he hath anointed me to preach the gospel to the poor; he hath sent me to heal the brokenhearted, to preach deliverance to the captives, and recovering of sight to the blind, to set at liberty them that are bruised, [19]To preach the acceptable year of the Lord. [20]And he closed the book, and he gave it again to the minister, and sat down. And the eyes of all them that were in the synagogue were fastened on him. [21]And he began to say unto them, This day is this scripture fulfilled in your ears.

1 CORINTHIANS 12:12—Gifts of the Holy Spirit (12:1–14), 51 CE

Theme	1 COR	Paul
One body, many members	**12:12** [12]For as the body is one, and hath many members, and all the members of that one body, being many, are one body: so also is Christ. **10:17** [17]For we being many are one bread, and one body: for we are all partakers of that one bread.	**Rom 12:4–5** [4]For as we have many members in one body, and all members have not the same office: [5]So we, being many, are one body in Christ, and every one members one of another. **Eph 2:16 (Pseudo)** [16]And that he might reconcile both unto God in one body by the cross, having slain the enmity thereby: **Col 3:15** [15]And let the peace of God rule in your hearts, to the which also ye are called in one body; and be ye thankful.

1 CORINTHIANS 12:13—Gifts of the Holy Spirit (12:1–14), 51 CE

Theme	1 COR	Jn
Same one spirit for all baptized	**12:13** [13]For by one Spirit are we all baptized into one body, whether we be Jews or Gentiles, whether we be bond or free; and have been all made to drink into one Spirit.	**7:37–39** [37]In the last day, that great day of the feast, Jesus stood and cried, saying, If any man thirst, let him come unto me, and drink. [38]He that believeth on me, as the scripture hath said, out of his belly shall flow rivers of living water. [39](But this spake he of the Spirit, which they that believe on him should receive: for the Holy Ghost was not yet given; because that Jesus was not yet glorified.)

Paul	Jewish Writings	Other
Rom 10:13 [13]For whosoever shall call upon the name of the Lord shall be saved. **Gal 3:28** [28]There is neither Jew nor Greek, there is neither bond nor free, there is neither male nor female: for ye are all one in Christ Jesus. **Col 3:11** [11]Where there is neither Greek nor Jew, circumcision nor uncircumcision, Barbarian, Scythian, bond nor free: but Christ is all, and in all.	**Joel 3:1–5** [28]And it shall come to pass afterward, that I will pour out my spirit upon all flesh; and your sons and your daughters shall prophesy, your old men shall dream dreams, your young men shall see visions: [29]And also upon the servants and upon the handmaids in those days will I pour out my spirit. [30]And I will show wonders in the heavens and in the earth, blood, and fire, and pillars of smoke. [31]The sun shall be turned into darkness, and the moon into blood, before the great and the terrible day of the LORD come. [32]And it shall come to pass, that whosoever shall call on the name of the LORD shall be delivered: for in mount Zion and in Jerusalem shall be deliverance, as the LORD hath said, and in the remnant whom the LORD shall call.	**Q-Quelle** Beezebul Controversy: 1 Cor 12:12-13/Mt 12:22-30, [Mt 9:32-34]/[Mk 3:22-27]/[Lk 11:14-23 (QS 28 [Thom 35])

Paul
Gal 3:28 [28]There is neither Jew nor Greek, there is neither bond nor free, there is neither male nor female: for ye are all one in Christ Jesus. **Eph 2:13–18 (Pseudo)** [13]But now in Christ Jesus ye who sometimes were far off are made nigh by the blood of Christ. [14]For he is our peace, who hath made both one, and hath broken down the middle wall of partition between us; [15]Having abolished in his flesh the enmity, even the law of commandments contained in ordinances; for to make in himself of twain one new man, so making peace; [16]And that he might reconcile both unto God in one body by the cross, having slain the enmity thereby: [17]And came and preached peace to you which were afar off, and to them that were nigh. [18]For through him we both have access by one Spirit unto the Father. **Col 3:11** [11]Where there is neither Greek nor Jew, circumcision nor uncircumcision, Barbarian, Scythian, bond nor free: but Christ is all, and in all.

1 CORINTHIANS 12:27—Body of Christ (12:27–13:3), 51 CE

Theme	1 COR	Paul
Body and members of Christ	**12:27** [27]Now ye are the body of Christ, and members in particular.	**Rom 12:5–8** [5]So we, being many, are one body in Christ, and every one members one of another. [6]Having then gifts differing according to the grace that is given to us, whether prophecy, let us prophesy according to the proportion of faith; [7]Or ministry, let us wait on our ministering: or he that teacheth, on teaching; [8]Or he that exhorteth, on exhortation: he that giveth, let him do it with simplicity; he that ruleth, with diligence; he that showeth mercy, with cheerfulness. **Eph 1:23 (Pseudo)** [23]Which is his body, the fulness of him that filleth all in all. **Eph 4:12 (Pseudo)** [12]For the perfecting of the saints, for the work of the ministry, for the edifying of the body of Christ: **Eph 5:30 (Pseudo)** [30]For we are members of his body, of his flesh, and of his bones. **Col 1:18–24** [18]And he is the head of the body, the church: who is the beginning, the firstborn from the dead; that in all things he might have the preeminence. [19]For it pleased the Father that in him should all fulness dwell; [20]And, having made peace through the blood of his cross, by him to reconcile all things unto himself; by him, I say, whether they be things in earth, or things in heaven. [21]And you, that were sometime alienated and enemies in your mind by wicked works, yet now hath he reconciled [22]In the body of his flesh through death, to present you holy and unblameable and unreproveable in his sight: [23]If ye continue in the faith grounded and settled, and be not moved away from the hope of the gospel, which ye have heard, and which was preached to every creature which is under heaven; whereof I Paul am made a minister; [24]Who now rejoice in my sufferings for you, and fill up that which is behind of the afflictions of Christ in my flesh for his body's sake, which is the church:

1 CORINTHIANS 12:28—Body of Christ (12:27–13:3), 51 CE

Theme	1 COR	Paul
Church positions: apostles, prophets	**12:28** [28]And God hath set some in the church, first apostles, secondarily prophets, thirdly teachers, after that miracles, then gifts of healings, helps, governments, diversities of tongues.	**Eph 2:20 (Pseudo)** [20]And are built upon the foundation of the apostles and prophets, Jesus Christ himself being the chief corner stone; **Eph 3:5 (Pseudo)** [5]Which in other ages was not made known unto the sons of men, as it is now revealed unto his holy apostles and prophets by the Spirit; **Eph 4:11 (Pseudo)** [11]And he gave some, apostles; and some, prophets; and some, evangelists; and some, pastors and teachers;

1 CORINTHIANS 13:1—Body of Christ (12:27–13:3), 51 CE

Theme	1 COR	Paul
Charity more dear than tongues	**13:1** [1]Though I speak with the tongues of men and of angels, and have not charity, I am become as sounding brass, or a tinkling cymbal. **8:1** [1]Now as touching things offered unto idols, we know that we all have knowledge. Knowledge puffeth up, but charity edifieth. **16:14** [14]Let all your things be done with charity.	**Rom 12:9–10** [9]Let love be without dissimulation. Abhor that w[illegible] is evil; cleave to that which is good. [10]Be kindly affectioned one to another with brotherly love; in honour preferring one another; **Rom 13:8–10** [8]Owe no man any thing, but to love one another: for he that loveth another hath fulfilled the law. [9]For this, Thou shalt not commit adultery, Thou shalt not kill, Thou shalt not steal, Thou shalt not bear false witness, Thou shalt not covet; and if there be any other commandment, it is briefly comprehended in this saying, namely, Thou shalt love thy neighbour as thyself. [10]Love worketh no ill to his neighbour: therefore love is the fulfilling of the law.

1 CORINTHIANS 13:2—Body of Christ (12:27–13:3), 51 CE

Theme	1 COR	Mt	Mk	Lk	Paul	Other
Faith & love	**13:2** [2]And though I have the gift of prophecy, and understand all mysteries, and all knowledge; and though I have all faith, so that I could remove mountains, and have not charity, I am nothing. **4:1** [1]Let a man so account of us, as of the ministers of Christ, and stewards of the mysteries of God. **16:14** [14]Let all your things be done with charity.	**17:20** [20]And Jesus said unto them, Because of your unbelief: for verily I say unto you, If ye have faith as a grain of mustard seed, ye shall say unto this mountain, Remove hence to yonder place; and it shall remove; and nothing shall be impossible unto you. **21:21** [21]Jesus answered and said unto them, Verily I say unto you, If ye have faith, and doubt not, ye shall not only do this which is done to the fig tree, but also if ye shall say unto this mountain, Be thou removed, and be thou cast into the sea; it shall be done.	**11:22–23** [22]And Jesus answering saith unto them, Have faith in God. [23]For verily I say unto you, That whosoever shall say unto this mountain, Be thou removed, and be thou cast into the sea; and shall not doubt in his heart, but shall believe that those things which he saith shall come to pass; he shall have whatsoever he saith.	**17:6** [6]And the Lord said, If ye had faith as a grain of mustard seed, ye might say unto this sycamine tree, Be thou plucked up by the root, and be thou planted in the sea; and it should obey you.	**Col 2:3** [3]In whom are hid all the treasures of wisdom and knowledge.	**Q-Quelle** On faith: 1 Cor 13:2/ Mt 17:19-20/[Mk 9:28-29]/Lk 17:5-6 (QS 59)

1 CORINTHIANS 13:3—Body of Christ (12:27–13:3), 51 CE

Theme	1 Cor	Mt	Mk
Love is greatest gift	**13:3** [3]And though I bestow all my goods to feed the poor, and though I give my body to be burned, and have not charity, it profiteth me nothing.	**6:2** [2]Therefore when thou doest thine alms, do not sound a trumpet before thee, as the hypocrites do in the synagogues and in the streets, that they may have glory of men. Verily I say unto you, They have their reward. **9:21** [21]For she said within herself, If I may but touch his garment, I shall be whole.	**12:33** [33]And to love him with all the heart, and with all the understanding, and with all the soul, and with all the strength, and to love his neighbour as himself, is more than all whole burnt offerings and sacrifices.

Lk

Acts 4–5 (Barnabas)

4 [1]And as they spake unto the people, the priests, and the captain of the temple, and the Sadducees, came upon them, [2]Being
grieved that they taught the people, and preached through Jesus the resurrection from the dead. [3]And they laid hands on
them, and put them in hold unto the next day: for it was now eventide. [4]Howbeit many of them which heard the word believed;
and the number of the men was about five thousand. [5]And it came to pass on the morrow, that their rulers, and elders, and
scribes, [6]And Annas the high priest, and Caiaphas, and John, and Alexander, and as many as were of the kindred of the high
priest, were gathered together at Jerusalem. [7]And when they had set them in the midst, they asked, By what power, or by what
name, have ye done this? [8]Then Peter, filled with the Holy Ghost, said unto them, Ye rulers of the people, and elders of Israel,
[9]If we this day be examined of the good deed done to the impotent man, by what means he is made whole; [10]Be it known unto
you all, and to all the people of Israel, that by the name of Jesus Christ of Nazareth, whom ye crucified, whom God raised
from the dead, even by him doth this man stand here before you whole. [11]This is the stone which was set at nought of you
builders, which is become the head of the corner. [12]Neither is there salvation in any other: for there is none other name under
heaven given among men, whereby we must be saved. [13]Now when they saw the boldness of Peter and John, and perceived
that they were unlearned and ignorant men, they marvelled; and they took knowledge of them, that they had been with Jesus.
[14]And beholding the man which was healed standing with them, they could say nothing against it. [15]But when they had commanded them to go aside out of the council, they conferred among themselves, [16]Saying, What shall we do to these men? for
that indeed a notable miracle hath been done by them is manifest to all them that dwell in Jerusalem; and we cannot deny it.
[17]But that it spread no further among the people, let us straitly threaten them, that they speak henceforth to no man in this
name. [18]And they called them, and commanded them not to speak at all nor teach in the name of Jesus. [19]But Peter and John
answered and said unto them, Whether it be right in the sight of God to hearken unto you more than unto God, judge ye.
[20]For we cannot but speak the things which we have seen and heard. [21]So when they had further threatened them, they let
them go, finding nothing how they might punish them, because of the people: for all men glorified God for that which was
done. [22]For the man was above forty years old, on whom this miracle of healing was showed. [23]And being let go, they went to
their own company, and reported all that the chief priests and elders had said unto them. [24]And when they heard that, they
lifted up their voice to God with one accord, and said, Lord, thou art God, which hast made heaven, and earth, and the sea,
and all that in them is: [25]Who by the mouth of thy servant David hast said, Why did the heathen rage, and the people imagine
vain things? [26]The kings of the earth stood up, and the rulers were gathered together against the Lord, and against his Christ.
[27]For of a truth against thy holy child Jesus, whom thou hast anointed, both Herod, and Pontius Pilate, with the Gentiles, and
the people of Israel, were gathered together, [28]For to do whatsoever thy hand and thy counsel determined before to be done.
[29]And now, Lord, behold their threatenings: and grant unto thy servants, that with all boldness they may speak thy word, [30]By
stretching forth thine hand to heal; and that signs and wonders may be done by the name of thy holy child Jesus. [31]And when
they had prayed, the place was shaken where they were assembled together; and they were all filled with the Holy Ghost,
and they spake the word of God with boldness. [32]And the multitude of them that believed were of one heart and of one soul:
neither said any of them that ought of the things which he possessed was his own; but they had all things common. [33]And with
great power gave the apostles witness of the resurrection of the Lord Jesus: and great grace was upon them all. [34]Neither was
there any among them that lacked: for as many as were possessors of lands or houses sold them, and brought the prices of the
things that were sold, [35]And laid them down at the apostles' feet: and distribution was made unto every man according as he
had need. [36]And Joses, who by the apostles was surnamed Barnabas, (which is, being interpreted, The son of consolation,) a
Levite, and of the country of Cyprus, [37]Having land, sold it, and brought the money, and laid it at the apostles' feet.
5 [1]But a certain man named Ananias, with Sapphira his wife, sold a possession, [2]And kept back part of the price, his wife also
being privy to it, and brought a certain part, and laid it at the apostles' feet. [3]But Peter said, Ananias, why hath Satan filled
thine heart to lie to the Holy Ghost, and to keep back part of the price of the land? [4]Whiles it remained, was it not thine own?
and after it was sold, was it not in thine own power? why hast thou conceived this thing in thine heart? thou hast not lied unto
men, but unto God. [5]And Ananias hearing these words fell down, and gave up the ghost: and great fear came on all them that
heard these things. [6]And the young men arose, wound him up, and carried him out, and buried him. [7]And it was about the
space of three hours after, when his wife, not knowing what was done, came in. [8]And Peter answered unto her, Tell me whether
ye sold the land for so much? And she said, Yea, for so much. [9]Then Peter said unto her, How is it that ye have agreed together
to tempt the Spirit of the Lord? behold, the feet of them which have buried thy husband are at the door, and shall carry thee
out. [10]Then fell she down straightway at his feet, and yielded up the ghost: and the young men came in, and found her dead,
and, carrying her forth, buried her by her husband. [11]And great fear came upon all the church, and upon as many as heard
these things. [12]And by the hands of the apostles were many signs and wonders wrought among the people; (and they were
all with one accord in Solomon's porch. [13]And of the rest durst no man join himself to them: but the people magnified them.
[14]And believers were the more added to the Lord, multitudes both of men and women.) [15]Insomuch that they brought forth
the sick into the streets, and laid them on beds and couches, that at the least the shadow of Peter passing by might overshadow
some of them. [16]There came also a multitude out of the cities round about unto Jerusalem, bringing sick folks, and them which
were vexed with unclean spirits: and they were healed every one. [17]Then the high priest rose up, and all they that were with him,

1 Corinthians 13:3 continued on next page

1 CORINTHIANS 13:3—Body of Christ (12:27–13:3), 51 CE (*continued*)

Theme	1 COR	Lk
(*Cont.*) **Love is greatest gift**	**13:3** **(above)**	**(*Continued*)** (which is the sect of the Sadducees,) and were filled with indignation, [18]And laid their hands on the apostles, and put them in the common prison. [19]But the angel of the Lord by night opened the prison doors, and brought them forth, and said, [20]Go, stand and speak in the temple to the people all the words of this life. [21]And when they heard that, they entered into the temple early in the morning, and taught. But the high priest came, and they that were with him, and called the council together, and all the senate of the children of Israel, and sent to the prison to have them brought. [22]But when the officers came, and found them not in the prison, they returned, and told, [23]Saying, The prison truly found we shut with all safety, and the keepers standing without before the doors: but when we had opened, we found no man within. [24]Now when the high priest and the captain of the temple and the chief priests heard these things, they doubted of them whereunto this would grow. [25]Then came one and told them, saying, Behold, the men whom ye put in prison are standing in the temple, and teaching the people. [26]Then went the captain with the officers, and brought them without violence: for they feared the people, lest they should have been stoned. [27]And when they had brought them, they set them before the council: and the high priest asked them, [28]Saying, Did not we straitly command you that ye should not teach in this name? and, behold, ye have filled Jerusalem with your doctrine, and intend to bring this man's blood upon us. [29]Then Peter and the other apostles answered and said, We ought to obey God rather than men. [30]The God of our fathers raised up Jesus, whom ye slew and hanged on a tree. [31]Him hath God exalted with his right hand to be a Prince and a Saviour, for to give repentance to Israel, and forgiveness of sins. [32]And we are his witnesses of these things; and so is also the Holy Ghost, whom God hath given to them that obey him. [33]When they heard that, they were cut to the heart, and took counsel to slay them. [34]Then stood there up one in the council, a Pharisee, named Gamaliel, a doctor of the law, had in reputation among all the people, and commanded to put the apostles forth a little space; [35]And said unto them, Ye men of Israel, take heed to yourselves what ye intend to do as touching these men. [36]For before these days rose up Theudas, boasting himself to be somebody; to whom a number of men, about four hundred, joined themselves: who was slain; and all, as many as obeyed him, were scattered, and brought to nought. [37]After this man rose up Judas of Galilee in the days of the taxing, and drew away much people after him: he also perished; and all, even as many as obeyed him, were dispersed. [38]And now I say unto you, Refrain from these men, and let them alone: for if this counsel or this work be of men, it will come to nought: [39]But if it be of God, ye cannot overthrow it; lest haply ye be found even to fight against God. [40]And to him they agreed: and when they had called the apostles, and beaten them, they commanded that they should not speak in the name of Jesus, and let them go. [41]And they departed from the presence of the council, rejoicing that they were counted worthy to suffer shame for his name. [42]And daily in the temple, and in every house, they ceased not to teach and preach Jesus Christ.

Paul

Rom 15:26–29

[26]For it hath pleased them of Macedonia and Achaia to make a certain contribution for the poor saints which are at
Jerusalem. [27]It hath pleased them verily; and their debtors they are. For if the Gentiles have been made partakers of
their spiritual things, their duty is also to minister unto them in carnal things. [28]When therefore I have performed this,
and have sealed to them this fruit, I will come by you into Spain. [29]And I am sure that, when I come unto you, I shall
come in the fulness of the blessing of the gospel of Christ.

2 Cor 8–9

8 [1]Moreover, brethren, we do you to wit of the grace of God bestowed on the churches of Macedonia; [2]How that in a
great trial of affliction the abundance of their joy and their deep poverty abounded unto the riches of their liberality.
[3]For to their power, I bear record, yea, and beyond their power they were willing of themselves; [4]Praying us with much
entreaty that we would receive the gift, and take upon us the fellowship of the ministering to the saints. [5]And this they
did, not as we hoped, but first gave their own selves to the Lord, and unto us by the will of God. [6]Insomuch that we
desired Titus, that as he had begun, so he would also finish in you the same grace also. [7]Therefore, as ye abound in every
thing, in faith, and utterance, and knowledge, and in all diligence, and in your love to us, see that ye abound in this
grace also. [8]I speak not by commandment, but by occasion of the forwardness of others, and to prove the sincerity of
your love. [9]For ye know the grace of our Lord Jesus Christ, that, though he was rich, yet for your sakes he became poor,
that ye through his poverty might be rich. [10]And herein I give my advice: for this is expedient for you, who have begun
before, not only to do, but also to be forward a year ago. [11]Now therefore perform the doing of it; that as there was a
readiness to will, so there may be a performance also out of that which ye have. [12]For if there be first a willing mind, it is
accepted according to that a man hath, and not according to that he hath not. [13]For I mean not that other men be eased,
and ye burdened: [14]But by an equality, that now at this time your abundance may be a supply for their want, that their
abundance also may be a supply for your want: that there may be equality: [15]As it is written, He that had gathered much
had nothing over; and he that had gathered little had no lack. [16]But thanks be to God, which put the same earnest care
into the heart of Titus for you. [17]For indeed he accepted the exhortation; but being more forward, of his own accord
he went unto you. [18]And we have sent with him the brother, whose praise is in the gospel throughout all the churches;
[19]And not that only, but who was also chosen of the churches to travel with us with this grace, which is administered by
us to the glory of the same Lord, and declaration of your ready mind: [20]Avoiding this, that no man should blame us in
this abundance which is administered by us: [21]Providing for honest things, not only in the sight of the Lord, but also in
the sight of men. [22]And we have sent with them our brother, whom we have oftentimes proved diligent in many things,
but now much more diligent, upon the great confidence which I have in you. [23]Whether any do inquire of Titus, he is
my partner and fellowhelper concerning you: or our brethren be inquired of, they are the messengers of the churches,
and the glory of Christ. [24]Wherefore show ye to them, and before the churches, the proof of your love, and of our boasting on your behalf.
9 [1]For as touching the ministering to the saints, it is superfluous for me to write to you: [2]For I know the forwardness
of your mind, for which I boast of you to them of Macedonia, that Achaia was ready a year ago; and your zeal hath
provoked very many. [3]Yet have I sent the brethren, lest our boasting of you should be in vain in this behalf; that, as I
said, ye may be ready: [4]Lest haply if they of Macedonia come with me, and find you unprepared, we (that we say not,
ye) should be ashamed in this same confident boasting. [5]Therefore I thought it necessary to exhort the brethren, that
they would go before unto you, and make up beforehand your bounty, whereof ye had notice before, that the same
might be ready, as a matter of bounty, and not as of covetousness. [6]But this I say, He which soweth sparingly shall reap
also sparingly; and he which soweth bountifully shall reap also bountifully. [7]Every man according as he purposeth in
his heart, so let him give; not grudgingly, or of necessity: for God loveth a cheerful giver. [8]And God is able to make all
grace abound toward you; that ye, always having all sufficiency in all things, may abound to every good work: [9](As it
is written, He hath dispersed abroad; he hath given to the poor: his righteousness remaineth for ever. [10]Now he that
ministereth seed to the sower both minister bread for your food, and multiply your seed sown, and increase the fruits
of your righteousness;) [11]Being enriched in every thing to all bountifulness, which causeth through us thanksgiving
to God. [12]For the administration of this service not only supplieth the want of the saints, but is abundant also by many
thanksgivings unto God; [13]Whiles by the experiment of this ministration they glorify God for your professed subjection unto the gospel of Christ, and for your liberal distribution unto them, and unto all men; [14]And by their prayer for
you, which long after you for the exceeding grace of God in you. [15]Thanks be unto God for his unspeakable gift.

1 CORINTHIANS 13:4—Gifts of the Holy Spirit (13:4—14:34), 51 CE

Theme	1 COR	Paul
Faith & love	**13:4** [4]Charity suffereth long, and is kind; charity envieth not; charity vaunteth not itself, is not puffed up, **8:1** [1]Now as touching things offered unto idols, we know that we all have knowledge. Knowledge puf-feth up, but charity edifieth.	**Eph 4:2 (Pseudo)** [4]There is one body, and one Spirit, even as ye are called in one hope of your calling; **Eph 4:6 (Pseudo)** [6]One God and Father of all, who is above all, and through all, and in you all. **Eph 4:18 (Pseudo)** [18]Having the understanding darkened, being alienated from the life of God through the ignorance that is in them, because of the blindness of their heart: **Eph 5:2 (Pseudo)** [2]And walk in love, as Christ also hath loved us, and hath given himself for us an offering and a sacrifice to God for a sweetsmelling savour.

1 CORINTHIANS 13:5—Gifts of the Holy Spirit (13:4–14:34), 51 CE

Theme	1 COR	Paul
Attributes of charity	**13:5** [5]Doth not behave itself unseemly, seeketh not her own, is not easily provoked, thinketh no evil; **10:24, 33** [24]Let no man seek his own, but every man another's wealth. [33]Even as I please all men in all things, not seeking mine own profit, but the profit of many, that they may be saved.	**Phil 2:4** [4]Look not every man on his own things, but every man also on the things of others. **Phil 2:21** [21]For all seek their own, not the things which are Jesus Christ's. **1 Thes 5:15** [15]See that none render evil for evil unto any man; but ever follow that which is good, both among yourselves, and to all men.

1 CORINTHIANS 13:7—Gifts of the Holy Spirit (13:4–14:34), 51 CE

Theme	1 COR	NT	Jewish Writings
Attributes of charity	**13:7** [7]Beareth all things, believeth all things, hopeth all things, endureth all things.	**1 Pet 4:8** [8]And above all things have fervent charity among your-selves: for charity shall cover the multitude of sins	**Prov 10:12** [12]Hatred stirreth up strifes: but love covereth all sins.

1 CORINTHIANS 13:12—Gifts of the Holy Spirit (13:4–14:34), 51 CE

Theme	1 COR	Jn	Paul	NT
Seeing darkly, knowing in part; then seeing God face to face, knowing...	**13:12** [12]For now we see through a glass, darkly; but then face to face: now I know in part; but then shall I know even as also I am known.	**1 Jn 3:2** [2]Beloved, now are we the sons of God, and it doth not yet appear what we shall be: but we know that, when he shall appear, we shall be like him; for we shall see him as he is.	**2 Cor 5:7** [7](For we walk by faith, not by sight:) **2 Tim 2:19 (Pseudo)** [19]Nevertheless the foundation of God standeth sure, having this seal, The Lord knoweth them that are his. And, Let every one that nameth the name of Christ depart from iniquity.	**Heb 11:1** [1]Now faith is the substance of things hoped for, the evidence of things not seen.

1 CORINTHIANS 13:13—Gifts of the Holy Spirit (13:4–14:34), 51 CE

Theme	1 COR	Paul
Abide in faith, hope, and love	**13:13** [13]And now abideth faith, hope, charity, these three; but the greatest of these is charity.	**Col 1:4** [4]Since we heard of your faith in Christ Jesus, and of the love which ye have to all the saints, **1 Thes 1:3** [3]Remembering without ceasing your work of faith, and labour of love, and patience of hope in our Lord Jesus Christ, in the sight of God and our Father; **1 Thes 5:8** [8]But let us, who are of the day, be sober, putting on the breastplate of faith and love; and for an helmet, the hope of salvation.

1 CORINTHIANS 14:1—Gifts of the Holy Spirit (13:4–14:34), 51 CE

Theme	1 COR
Be charitable and desire gifts	**14:1** [1]Follow after charity, and desire spiritual gifts, but rather that ye may prophesy. **5:12** [12]For what have I to do to judge them also that are without? do not ye judge them that are within? **14:39** [39]Wherefore, brethren, covet to prophesy, and forbid not to speak with tongues.

1 CORINTHIANS 14:3—Gifts of the Holy Spirit (13:4–14:34), 51 CE

Theme	1 COR	Paul	Other
Tongues	**14:3** [13]Wherefore let him that speaketh in an unknown tongue pray that he may interpret. **3:9** [9]For we are labourers together with God: ye are God's husbandry, ye are God's building. **10:23** [23]All things are lawful for me, but all things are not expedient: all things are lawful for me, but all things edify not. **14:5** [5]I would that ye all spake with tongues, but rather that ye prophesied: for greater is he that prophesieth than he that speaketh with tongues, except he interpret, that the church may receive edifying. **14:12** [12]Even so ye, forasmuch as ye are zealous of spiritual gifts, seek that ye may excel to the edifying of the church. **14:17** [17]For thou verily givest thanks well, but the other is not edified. **14:26** [26]How is it then, brethren? when ye come together, every one of you hath a psalm, hath a doctrine, hath a tongue, hath a revelation, hath an interpretation. Let all things be done unto edifying.	**2 Cor 10:8** [8]For though I should boast somewhat more of our authority, which the Lord hath given us for edification, and not for your destruction, I should not be ashamed:	**Q-Quelle** House of Rock: 1 Cor 14:3/2 Cor 10:8/[Mt 7:21-27]/[Lk 6:46-49 (QS 14)]

1 CORINTHIANS 14:15—Gifts of the Holy Spirit (13:4–14:34), 51 CE

Theme	1 COR	Paul
Pray/Sing in spirit and with mind	**14:15** [15]What is it then? I will pray with the spirit, and I will pray with the understanding also: I will sing with the spirit, and I will sing with the understanding also.	**Eph 5:19 (Pseudo)** [19]Speaking to yourselves in psalms and hymns and spiritual songs, singing and making melody in your heart to the Lord; **Col 3:16** [16]Let the word of Christ dwell in you richly in all wisdom; teaching and admonishing one another in psalms and hymns and spiritual songs, singing with grace in your hearts to the Lord.

1 CORINTHIANS 14:20—Gifts of the Holy Spirit (13:4–14:34), 51 CE

Theme	1 COR	Mt	Paul	Other
Be mature in understand-ing, be a child in malice	**14:20** [20]Brethren, be not children in under-standing: howbeit in malice be ye children, but in understanding be men.	**10:16** [16]Behold, I send you forth as sheep in the midst of wolves: be ye therefore wise as serpents, and harmless as doves.	**Rom 16:19** [19]For your obedience is come abroad unto all men. I am glad therefore on your behalf: but yet I would have you wise unto that which is good, and simple concerning evil. **Eph 4:14 (Pseudo)** [14]That we henceforth be no more children, tossed to and fro, and carried about with every wind of doctrine, by the sleight of men, and cunning craftiness, whereby they lie in wait to deceive;	**Q-Quelle** Commis-sioning the 70: 1 Cor 14:20/[Mt 9:37-38], Mt 10:7-16/[Lk 10:1-12 (2QS 23)]

1 CORINTHIANS 14:21—Gifts of the Holy Spirit (13:4–14:34), 51 CE

Theme	1 COR	Jewish Writings
Some will not hear	**14:21** [21]In the law it is writ-ten, With men of other tongues and other lips will I speak unto this people; and yet for all that will they not hear me, saith the Lord.	**Dt 28:49** [49]The LORD shall bring a nation against thee from far, from the end of the earth, as swift as the eagle flieth; a nation whose tongue thou shalt not understand; **Is 28:11–12** [11]For with stammering lips and another tongue will he speak to this people. [12]To whom he said, This is the rest wherewith ye may cause the weary to rest; and this is the refreshing: yet they would not hear.

1 CORINTHIANS 14:23—Gifts of the Holy Spirit (13:4–14:34), 51 CE

Theme	1 COR	Lk
Speak in language people understand	**14:23** [23]If therefore the whole church be come together into one place, and all speak with tongues, and there come in those that are unlearned, or unbe-lievers, will they not say that ye are mad?	**Acts 2:6–13** [6]Now when this was noised abroad, the multitude came together, and were confounded, because that every man heard them speak in his own language. [7]And they were all amazed and marvelled, saying one to another, Behold, are not all these which speak Galilaeans? [8]And how hear we every man in our own tongue, wherein we were born? [9]Parthians, and Medes, and Elamites, and the dwellers in Mesopotamia, and in Judaea, and Cappadocia, in Pontus, and Asia, [10]Phrygia, and Pamphylia, in Egypt, and in the parts of Libya about Cyrene, and strangers of Rome, Jews and proselytes, [11]Cretes and Arabians, we do hear them speak in our tongues the wonderful works of God. [12]And they were all amazed, and were in doubt, saying one to another, What meaneth this? [13]Others mocking said, These men are full of new wine.

1 CORINTHIANS 14:25—Gifts of the Holy Spirit (13:4–14:34), 51 CE

Theme	1 COR	Jewish Writings
Express secrets of heart	**14:25** [25]And thus are the secrets of his heart made manifest; and so falling down on his face he will worship God, and report that God is in you of a truth. **4:5** [5]Therefore judge nothing before the time, until the Lord come, who both will bring to light the hidden things of darkness, and will make manifest the counsels of the hearts: and then shall every man have praise of God.	**Is 45:14** [14]Thus saith the LORD, The labour of Egypt, and merchandise of Ethiopia and of the Sabeans, men of stature, shall come over unto thee, and they shall be thine: they shall come after thee; in chains they shall come over, and they shall fall down unto thee, they shall make supplication unto thee, saying, Surely God is in thee; and there is none else, there is no God. **Zech 8:23** [23]Thus saith the LORD of hosts; In those days it shall come to pass, that ten men shall take hold out of all languages of the nations, even shall take hold of the skirt of him that is a Jew, saying, We will go with you: for we have heard that God is with you.

1 CORINTHIANS 14:26—Gifts of the Holy Spirit (13:4–14:34), 51 CE

Theme	1 COR	Paul
Do all to edify	**14:26** [26]How is it then, brethren? when ye come together, every one of you hath a psalm, hath a doctrine, hath a tongue, hath a revelation, hath an interpretation. Let all things be done unto edifying.	**Eph 4:12 (Pseudo)** [12]For the perfecting of the saints, for the work of the ministry, for the edifying of the body of Christ:

1 CORINTHIANS 14:34—Gifts of the Holy Spirit (13:4–14:34), 51 CE

Theme	1 COR	Paul	NT
Silence in the church	**14:34** [34]Let your women keep silence in the churches: for it is not permitted unto them to speak; but they are commanded to be under obedience, as also saith the law.	**1 Tim 2:11–15 (Pseudo)** [11]Let the woman learn in silence with all subjection. [12]But I suffer not a woman to teach, nor to usurp authority over the man, but to be in silence. [13]For Adam was first formed, then Eve. [14]And Adam was not deceived, but the woman being deceived was in the transgression. [15]Notwithstanding she shall be saved in childbearing, if they continue in faith and charity and holiness with sobriety.	**1 Pet 3:1** [1]Likewise, ye wives, be in subjection to your own husbands; that, if any obey not the word, they also may without the word be won by the conversation of the wives;

RESURRECTION (15:1–58)

JESUS' RESURRECTION (15:1–11)

1 CORINTHIANS 15:3–9—Jesus' Resurrection (15:1–11), 51 CE

Theme	1 COR	Lk	Jn
Apostleship	**15:3–9** [3]For I delivered unto you first of all that which I also received, how that Christ died for our sins according to the scriptures; [4]And that he was buried, and that he rose again the third day according to the scriptures: [5]And that he was seen of Cephas, then of the twelve: [6]After that, he was seen of above five hundred brethren at once; of whom the greater part remain unto this present, but some are fallen asleep. [7]After that, he was seen of James; then of all the apostles. [8]And last of all he was seen of me also, as of one born out of due time. [9]For I am the least of the apostles, that am not meet to be called an apostle, because I persecuted the church of God.	**24:33–34** [33]And they rose up the same hour, and returned to Jerusalem, and found the eleven gathered together, and them that were with them, [34]Saying, The Lord is risen indeed, and hath appeared to Simon. [35]And they told what things were done in the way, and how he was known of them in breaking of bread. [36]And as they thus spake, Jesus himself stood in the midst of them, and saith unto them, Peace be unto you. [37]But they were terrified and affrighted, and supposed that they had seen a spirit. [38]And he said unto them, Why are ye troubled? and why do thoughts arise in your hearts? [39]Behold my hands and my feet, that it is I myself: handle me, and see; for a spirit hath not flesh and bones, as ye see me have. [40]And when he had thus spoken, he showed them his hands and his feet. [41]And while they yet believed not for joy, and wondered, he said unto them, Have ye here any meat? [42]And they gave him a piece of a broiled fish, and of an honeycomb. [43]And he took it, and did eat before them. [44]And he said unto them, These are the words which I spake unto you, while I was yet with you, that all things must be fulfilled, which were written in the law of Moses, and in the prophets, and in the psalms, concerning me. **24:36** [36]And as they thus spake, Jesus himself stood in the midst of them, and saith unto them, Peace be unto you.	**20:19–23** [19]Then the same day at evening, being the first day of the week, when the doors were shut where the disciples were assembled for fear of the Jews, came Jesus and stood in the midst, and saith unto them, Peace be unto you. [20]And when he had so said, he showed unto them his hands and his side. Then were the disciples glad, when they saw the Lord. [21]Then said Jesus to them again, Peace be unto you: as my Father hath sent me, even so send I you. [22]And when he had said this, he breathed on them, and saith unto them, Receive ye the Holy Ghost: [23]Whose soever sins ye remit, they are remitted unto them; and whose soever sins ye retain, they are retained.

1 CORINTHIANS 15:3—Jesus' Resurrection (15:1–11), 51 CE

Theme	1 COR	NT	Jewish Writings
Paul delivered what he received	**15:3** [3]For I delivered unto you first of all that which I also received, how that Christ died for our sins according to the scriptures; **11:23** [23]For I have received of the Lord that which also I delivered unto you, That the Lord Jesus the same night in which he was betrayed took bread:	**1 Pet 2:24** [24]Who his own self bare our sins in his own body on the tree, that we, being dead to sins, should live unto righteousness: by whose stripes ye were healed. **1 Pet 3:18** [18]For Christ also hath once suffered for sins, the just for the unjust, that he might bring us to God, being put to death in the flesh, but quickened by the Spirit:	**Is 53:4–12** [4]Surely he hath borne our griefs, and carried our sorrows: yet we did esteem him stricken, smitten of God, and afflicted. [5]But he was wounded for our transgressions, he was bruised for our iniquities: the chastisement of our peace was upon him; and with his stripes we are healed. [6]All we like sheep have gone astray; we have turned every one to his own way; and the LORD hath laid on him the iniquity of us all. [7]He was oppressed, and he was afflicted, yet he opened not his mouth: he is brought as a lamb to the slaughter, and as a sheep before her shearers is dumb, so he openeth not his mouth. [8]He was taken from prison and from judgment: and who shall declare his generation? for he was cut off out of the land of the living: for the transgression of my people was he stricken. [9]And he made his grave with the wicked, and with the rich in his death; because he had done no violence, neither was any deceit in his mouth. [10]Yet it pleased the LORD to bruise him; he hath put him to grief: when thou shalt make his soul an offering for sin, he shall see his seed, he shall prolong his days, and the pleasure of the LORD shall prosper in his hand. [11]He shall see of the travail of his soul, and shall be satisfied: by his knowledge shall my righteous servant justify many; for he shall bear their iniquities. [12]Therefore will I divide him a portion with the great, and he shall divide the spoil with the strong; because he hath poured out his soul unto death: and he was numbered with the transgressors; and he bare the sin of many, and made intercession for the transgressors.

1 CORINTHIANS 15:4—Jesus' Resurrection (15:1–11), 51 CE

Theme	1 COR	Lk	Jewish Writings
Scriptures say, Christ died, was buried, and rose	**15:4** [4]And that he was buried, and that he rose again the third day according to the scriptures:	**Acts 2:23–24** [23]Him, being delivered by the determinate counsel and foreknowledge of God, ye have taken, and by wicked hands have crucified and slain: [24]Whom God hath raised up, having loosed the pains of death: because it was not possible that he should be holden of it.	**Ps 16:8–11** [8]I have set the LORD always before me: because he is at my right hand, I shall not be moved. [9]Therefore my heart is glad, and my glory rejoiceth: my flesh also shall rest in hope. [10]For thou wilt not leave my soul in hell; neither wilt thou suffer thine Holy One to see corruption. [11]Thou wilt show me the path of life: in thy presence is fulness of joy; at thy right hand there are pleasures for evermore. **Hos 6:1–2** [1]Come, and let us return unto the LORD: for he hath torn, and he will heal us; he hath smitten, and he will bind us up. [2]After two days will he revive us: in the third day he will raise us up, and we shall live in his sight. **Jonah 2:1** [1]Then Jonah prayed unto the LORD his God out of the fish's belly,

1 CORINTHIANS 15:5—Jesus' Resurrection (15:1–11), 51 CE

Theme	1 COR	Mt	Mk
Christ seen by Cephas (Peter, then by the 12)	**15:5** [5]And that he was seen of Cephas, then of the twelve:	**28:16–17** [16]Then the eleven disciples went away into Galilee, into a mountain where Jesus had appointed them. [17]And when they saw him, they worshipped him: but some doubted.	**16:14** [14]Afterward he appeared unto the eleven as they sat at meat, and upbraided them with their unbelief and hardness of heart, because they believed not them which had seen him after he was risen.

1 CORINTHIANS 15:8—Jesus' Resurrection (15:1–11), 51 CE

Theme	1 COR
Paul saw Christ last	**15:8** [8]And last of all he was seen of me also, as of one born out of due time. **9:1** [1]Am I not an apostle? am I not free? have I not seen Jesus Christ our Lord? are not ye my work in the Lord?

1 CORINTHIANS 15:9—Jesus' Resurrection (15:1–11), 51 CE

Theme	1 COR	Lk
Paul, least of the Apostles	**15:9** [9]For I am the least of the apostles, that am not meet to be called an apostle, because I persecuted the church of God.	**Acts 8:3** [3]As for Saul, he made havock of the church, entering into every house, and haling men and women committed them to prison. **Acts 9:1–2** [1]And Saul, yet breathing out threatenings and slaughter against the disciples of the Lord, went unto the high priest, [2]And desired of him letters to Damascus to the synagogues, that if he found any of this way, whether they were men or women, he might bring them bound unto Jerusalem.

Lk	Jn
24:36	**20:19**
[36]And as they thus spake, Jesus himself stood in the midst of them, and saith unto them, Peace be unto you.	[19]Then the same day at evening, being the first day of the week, when the doors were shut where the disciples were assembled for fear of the Jews, came Jesus and stood in the midst, and saith unto them, Peace be unto you.

Lk	Paul
Acts 9:3–6	**Gal 1:16**
[3]And as he journeyed, he came near Damascus: and suddenly there shined round about him a light from heaven: [4]And he fell to the earth, and heard a voice saying unto him, Saul, Saul, why persecutest thou me? [5]And he said, Who art thou, Lord? And the Lord said, I am Jesus whom thou persecutest: it is hard for thee to kick against the pricks. [6]And he trembling and astonished said, Lord, what wilt thou have me to do? And the Lord said unto him, Arise, and go into the city, and it shall be told thee what thou must do.	[16]To reveal his Son in me, that I might preach him among the heathen; immediately I conferred not with flesh and blood:

Paul
Gal 1:23
[23]But they had heard only, That he which persecuted us in times past now preacheth the faith which once he destroyed.
Eph 3:8 (Pseudo)
[8]Unto me, who am less than the least of all saints, is this grace given, that I should preach among the Gentiles the unsearchable riches of Christ;
1 Tim 1:15 (Pseudo)
[15]This is a faithful saying, and worthy of all acceptation, that Christ Jesus came into the world to save sinners; of whom I am chief.

RESURRECTION OF THE DEAD (15:12–34)

1 CORINTHIANS 15:12—Resurrection of the dead (15:12–57), 51 CE

Theme	1 COR	Mt	Mk
Questions on Resurrection	**15:12** [12]Now if Christ be preached that he rose from the dead, how say some among you that there is no resurrection of the dead?	**7:28–29** [28]And it came to pass, when Jesus had ended these sayings, the people were astonished at his doctrine: [29]For he taught them as one having authority, and not as the scribes **13:54** [54]And when he was come into his own country, he taught them in their synagogue, insomuch that they were astonished, and said, Whence hath this man this wisdom, and these mighty works? **22:23–33** [23]The same day came to him the Sadducees, which say that there is no resurrection, and asked him, [24]Saying, Master, Moses said, If a man die, having no children, his brother shall marry his wife, and raise up seed unto his brother. [25]Now there were with us seven brethren: and the first, when he had married a wife, deceased, and, having no issue, left his wife unto his brother: [26]Likewise the second also, and the third, unto the seventh. [27]And last of all the woman died also. [28]Therefore in the resurrection whose wife shall she be of the seven? for they all had her. [29]Jesus answered and said unto them, Ye do err, not knowing the scriptures, nor the power of God. [30]For in the resurrection they neither marry, nor are given in marriage, but are as the angels of God in heaven. [31]But as touching the resurrection of the dead, have ye not read that which was spoken unto you by God, saying, [32]I am the God of Abraham, and the God of Isaac, and the God of Jacob? God is not the God of the dead, but of the living. [33]And when the multitude heard this, they were astonished at his doctrine. **22:46** [46]And no man was able to answer him a word, neither durst any man from that day forth ask him any more questions.	**12:18–27** [18]Then come unto him the Sadducees, which say there is no resurrection; and they asked him, saying, [19]Master, Moses wrote unto us, If a man's brother die, and leave his wife behind him, and leave no children, that his brother should take his wife, and raise up seed unto his brother. [20]Now there were seven brethren: and the first took a wife, and dying left no seed. [21]And the second took her, and died, neither left he any seed: and the third likewise. [22]And the seven had her, and left no seed: last of all the woman died also. [23]In the resurrection therefore, when they shall rise, whose wife shall she be of them? for the seven had her to wife. [24]And Jesus answering said unto them, Do ye not therefore err, because ye know not the scriptures, neither the power of God? [25]For when they shall rise from the dead, they neither marry, nor are given in marriage; but are as the angels which are in heaven. [26]And as touching the dead, that they rise: have ye not read in the book of Moses, how in the bush God spake unto him, saying, I am the God of Abraham, and the God of Isaac, and the God of Jacob? [27]He is not the God of the dead, but the God of the living: ye therefore do greatly err. **12:32** [32]And the scribe said unto him, Well, Master, thou hast said the truth: for there is one God; and there is none other but he: **12:34** [34]And when Jesus saw that he answered discreetly, he said unto him, Thou art not far from the kingdom of God. And no man after that durst ask him any question.

1 CORINTHIANS 15:13—Resurrection of the dead (15:12–57), 51 CE

Theme	1 COR	Paul
Resurrection of the dead	**15:13** [13]But if there be no resurrection of the dead, then is Christ not risen:	**1 Thes 4:14** [14]For if we believe that Jesus died and rose again, even so them also which sleep in Jesus will God bring with him.

Lk	Jewish
20:27–40	**Gen 38:8**
27Then came to him certain of the Sadducees, which deny that there is any resurrection; and they asked him, 28Saying, Master, Moses wrote unto us, If any man's brother die, having a wife, and he die without children, that his brother should take his wife, and raise up seed unto his brother. 29There were therefore seven brethren: and the first took a wife, and died without children. 30And the second took her to wife, and he died childless. 31And the third took her; and in like manner the seven also: and they left no children, and died. 32Last of all the woman died also. 33Therefore in the resurrection whose wife of them is she? for seven had her to wife. 34And Jesus answering said unto them, The children of this world marry, and are given in marriage: 35But they which shall be accounted worthy to obtain that world, and the resurrection from the dead, neither marry, nor are given in marriage: 36Neither can they die any more: for they are equal unto the angels; and are the children of God, being the children of the resurrection. 37Now that the dead are raised, even Moses showed at the bush, when he calleth the Lord the God of Abraham, and the God of Isaac, and the God of Jacob. 38For he is not a God of the dead, but of the living: for all live unto him. 39Then certain of the scribes answering said, Master, thou hast well said. 40And after that they durst not ask him any question at all.	8And Judah said unto Onan, Go in unto thy brother's wife, and marry her, and raise up seed to thy brother. **Ex 3:6** 6Moreover he said, I am the God of thy father, the God of Abraham, the God of Isaac, and the God of Jacob. And Moses hid his face; for he was afraid to look upon God. **Dt 25:5–6** 5If brethren dwell together, and one of them die, and have no child, the wife of the dead shall not marry without unto a stranger: her husband's brother shall go in unto her, and take her to him to wife, and perform the duty of an husband's brother unto her. 6And it shall be, that the firstborn which she beareth shall succeed in the name of his brother which is dead, that his name be not put out of Israel.

1 CORINTHIANS 15:20-28—Resurrection of the dead (15:12–57), 51 CE

Theme	1 COR	Mt	Mk	Lk
Christ's first fruits	**15:20-28** [20]But now is Christ risen from the dead, and become the firstfruits of them that slept. [21]For since by man came death, by man came also the resurrection of the dead. [22]For as in Adam all die, even so in Christ shall all be made alive. [23]But every man in his own order: Christ the firstfruits; afterward they that are Christ's at his coming. [4]Then cometh the end, when he shall have delivered up the kingdom to God, even the Father; when he shall have put down all rule and all authority and power. [25]For he must reign, till he hath put all enemies under his feet. [6]The last enemy that shall be destroyed is death. [27]For he hath put all things under his feet. But when he saith all things are put under him, it is manifest that he is excepted, which did put all things under him. [28]And when all things shall be subdued unto him, then shall the Son also himself be subject unto him that put all things under him, that God may be all in all. **15:49** [49]And as we have borne the image of the earthy, we shall also bear the image of the heavenly.	**19:8** [8]He saith unto them, Moses because of the hardness of your hearts suffered you to put away your wives: but from the beginning it was not so. **22:41–46** [41]While the Pharisees were gathered together, Jesus asked them, [42]Saying, What think ye of Christ? whose son is he? They say unto him, The Son of David. [43]He saith unto them, How then doth David in spirit call him Lord, saying, [44]The LORD said unto my Lord, Sit thou on my right hand, till I make thine enemies thy footstool? [45]If David then call him Lord, how is he his son? [46]And no man was able to answer him a word, neither durst any man from that day forth ask him any more questions.	**10:6** [6]But from the beginning of the creation God made them male and female. **12:34** [34]And when Jesus saw that he answered discreetly, he said unto him, Thou art not far from the kingdom of God. And no man after that durst ask him any question. **12:35–37** [35]And Jesus answered and said, while he taught in the temple, How say the scribes that Christ is the Son of David? [36]For David himself said by the Holy Ghost, The LORD said to my Lord, Sit thou on my right hand, till I make thine enemies thy footstool. [37]David therefore himself calleth him Lord; and whence is he then his son? And the common people heard him gladly.	**20:40** [40]And after that they durst not ask him any question at all. **20:41–44** [41]And he said unto them, How say they that Christ is David's son? [42]And David himself saith in the book of Psalms, The LORD said unto my Lord, Sit thou on my right hand, [43]Till I make thine enemies thy footstool. [44]David therefore calleth him Lord, how is he then his son? **22:69** [69]Hereafter shall the Son of man sit on the right hand of the power of God. **Acts 2:34–35** [34]For David is not ascended into the heavens: but he saith himself, The LORD said unto my Lord, Sit thou on my right hand, [35]Until I make thy foes thy footstool. **Acts 7:55–56** [55]But he, being full of the Holy Ghost, looked up stedfastly into heaven, and saw the glory of God, and Jesus standing on the right hand of God, [56]And said, Behold, I see the heavens opened, and the Son of man standing on the right hand of God.

Jn	Jewish Writings
7:40-44	**Gen 1:28**
[40]Many of the people therefore, when they heard this saying, said, Of a truth this is the Prophet. [41]Others said, This is the Christ. But some said, Shall Christ come out of Galilee? [42]Hath not the scripture said, That Christ cometh of the seed of David, and out of the town of Bethlehem, where David was? [43]So there was a division among the people because of him. [44]And some of them would have taken him; but no man laid hands on him	[28]And God blessed them, and God said unto them, Be fruitful, and multiply, and replenish the earth, and subdue it: and have dominion over the fish of the sea, and over the fowl of the air, and over every living thing that moveth upon the earth. **2 Sam 7:12–16** [12]And when thy days be fulfilled, and thou shalt sleep with thy fathers, I will set up thy seed after thee, which shall proceed out of thy bowels, and I will establish his kingdom. [13]He shall build an house for my name, and I will stablish the throne of his kingdom for ever. [14]I will be his father, and he shall be my son. If he commit iniquity, I will chasten him with the rod of men, and with the stripes of the children of men: [15]But my mercy shall not depart away from him, as I took it from Saul, whom I put away before thee. [16]And thine house and thy kingdom shall be established for ever before thee: thy throne shall be established for ever. **Ps 89:3–4** [3]I have made a covenant with my chosen, I have sworn unto David my servant, [4]Thy seed will I establish for ever, and build up thy throne to all generations. Selah **Ps 110:1** [1]The LORD said unto my Lord, Sit thou at my right hand, until I make thine enemies thy footstool. **Mic 5:2** [2]But thou, Bethlehem Ephratah, though thou be little among the thousands of Judah, yet out of thee shall he come forth unto me that is to be ruler in Israel; whose goings forth have been from of old, from everlasting.

1 CORINTHIANS 15:20—Resurrection of the dead (15:12–57), 51 CE

Theme	1 COR	Mk	Lk	Paul
Risen Lord/ eschatology	**15:20** [20]But now is Christ risen from the dead, and become the firstfruits of them that slept.	**1:15** [15]And saying, The time is fulfilled, and the kingdom of God is at hand: repent ye, and believe the gospel.	**4:19** [19]To preach the accept-able year of the Lord.	**Rom 8:11** [11]But if the Spirit of him that raised up Jesus from the dead dwell in you, he that raised up Christ from the dead shall also quicken your mortal bodies by his Spirit that dwelleth in you. **Rom 8:23** [23]And not only they, but ourselves also, which have the firstfruits of the Spirit, even we ourselves groan within ourselves, waiting for the adoption, to wit, the redemption of our body. **Rom 13:11–12** [11]And that, knowing the time, that now it is high time to awake out of sleep: for now is our salvation nearer than when we believed. [12]The night is far spent, the day is at hand: let us therefore cast off the works of darkness, and let us put on the armour of light. **2 Cor 5:17** [17]Therefore if any man be in Christ, he is a new creature: old things are passed away; behold, all things are become new. **2 Cor 5:19** [19]To wit, that God was in Christ, reconciling the world unto himself, not imputing their trespasses unto them; and hath committed unto us the word of reconciliation. **2 Cor 6:2** [2](For he saith, I have heard thee in a time accepted, and in the day of salvation have I succoured thee: behold, now is the accepted time; behold, now is the day of salvation.) **Gal 4:4** [4]But when the fulness of the time was come, God sent forth his Son, made of a woman, made under the law, **Gal 6:15** [15]For in Christ Jesus neither circumcision availeth any thing, nor uncircumcision, but a new creature. **Eph 1:10 (Pseudo)** [10]That in the dispensation of the fulness of times he might gather together in one all things in Christ, both which are in heaven, and which are on earth; even in him: **Col 1:18** [18]And he is the head of the body, the church: who is the beginning, the firstborn from the dead; that in all things he might have the preeminence. **1 Thes 4:14** [14]For if we believe that Jesus died and rose again, even so them also which sleep in Jesus will God bring with him.

Jewish Writings

Is 49

1Listen, O isles, unto me; and hearken, ye people, from far; The LORD hath called me from the womb;
from the bowels of my mother hath he made mention of my name. 2And he hath made my mouth like a
sharp sword; in the shadow of his hand hath he hid me, and made me a polished shaft; in his quiver hath
he hid me; 3And said unto me, Thou art my servant, O Israel, in whom I will be glorified. 4Then I said, I
have laboured in vain, I have spent my strength for nought, and in vain: yet surely my judgment is with
the LORD, and my work with my God. 5And now, saith the LORD that formed me from the womb to be
his servant, to bring Jacob again to him, Though Israel be not gathered, yet shall I be glorious in the eyes
of the LORD, and my God shall be my strength. 6And he said, It is a light thing that thou shouldest be my
servant to raise up the tribes of Jacob, and to restore the preserved of Israel: I will also give thee for a light
to the Gentiles, that thou mayest be my salvation unto the end of the earth. 7Thus saith the LORD, the
Redeemer of Israel, and his Holy One, to him whom man despiseth, to him whom the nation abhorreth,
to a servant of rulers, Kings shall see and arise, princes also shall worship, because of the LORD that is
faithful, and the Holy One of Israel, and he shall choose thee. 8Thus saith the LORD, In an acceptable time
have I heard thee, and in a day of salvation have I helped thee: and I will preserve thee, and give thee for a
covenant of the people, to establish the earth, to cause to inherit the desolate heritages; 9That thou mayest
say to the prisoners, Go forth; to them that are in darkness, Show yourselves. They shall feed in the ways,
and their pastures shall be in all high places. 10They shall not hunger nor thirst; neither shall the heat nor
sun smite them: for he that hath mercy on them shall lead them, even by the springs of water shall he guide
them. 11And I will make all my mountains a way, and my highways shall be exalted. 12Behold, these shall
come from far: and, lo, these from the north and from the west; and these from the land of Sinim. 13Sing, O
heavens; and be joyful, O earth; and break forth into singing, O mountains: for the LORD hath comforted
his people, and will have mercy upon his afflicted. 14But Zion said, The LORD hath forsaken me, and my
Lord hath forgotten me. 15Can a woman forget her sucking child, that she should not have compassion on
the son of her womb? yea, they may forget, yet will I not forget thee. 16Behold, I have graven thee upon the
palms of my hands; thy walls are continually before me. 17Thy children shall make haste; thy destroyers
and they that made thee waste shall go forth of thee. 18Lift up thine eyes round about, and behold: all these
gather themselves together, and come to thee. As I live, saith the LORD, thou shalt surely clothe thee with
them all, as with an ornament, and bind them on thee, as a bride doeth. 19For thy waste and thy desolate
places, and the land of thy destruction, shall even now be too narrow by reason of the inhabitants, and
they that swallowed thee up shall be far away. 20The children which thou shalt have, after thou hast lost the
other, shall say again in thine ears, The place is too strait for me: give place to me that I may dwell. 21Then
shalt thou say in thine heart, Who hath begotten me these, seeing I have lost my children, and am desolate,
a captive, and removing to and fro? and who hath brought up these? Behold, I was left alone; these, where
had they been? 22Thus saith the Lord GOD, Behold, I will lift up mine hand to the Gentiles, and set up my
standard to the people: and they shall bring thy sons in their arms, and thy daughters shall be carried upon
their shoulders. 23And kings shall be thy nursing fathers, and their queens thy nursing mothers: they shall
bow down to thee with their face toward the earth, and lick up the dust of thy feet; and thou shalt know
that I am the LORD: for they shall not be ashamed that wait for me. 24Shall the prey be taken from the
mighty, or the lawful captive delivered? 25But thus saith the LORD, Even the captives of the mighty shall
be taken away, and the prey of the terrible shall be delivered: for I will contend with him that contendeth
with thee, and I will save thy children. 26And I will feed them that oppress thee with their own flesh; and
they shall be drunken with their own blood, as with sweet wine: and all flesh shall know that I the LORD
am thy Saviour and thy Redeemer, the mighty One of Jacob.

1 CORINTHIANS 15:22—Resurrection of the dead (15:12–57), 51 CE

Theme	1 COR	Paul	Jewish Writings
All die in Adam, all live in Christ	**15:22** [22]For as in Adam all die, even so in Christ shall all be made alive.	**Rom 5:12–19** [12]Wherefore, as by one man sin entered into the world, and death by sin; and so death passed upon all men, for that all have sinned: [13](For until the law sin was in the world: but sin is not imputed when there is no law. [14]Nevertheless death reigned from Adam to Moses, even over them that had not sinned after the similitude of Adam's transgression, who is the figure of him that was to come. [15]But not as the offence, so also is the free gift. For if through the offence of one many be dead, much more the grace of God, and the gift by grace, which is by one man, Jesus Christ, hath abounded unto many. [16]And not as it was by one that sinned, so is the gift: for the judgment was by one to condemnation, but the free gift is of many offences unto justification. [17]For if by one man's offence death reigned by one; much more they which receive abundance of grace and of the gift of righteousness shall reign in life by one, Jesus Christ.) [18]Therefore as by the offence of one judgment came upon all men to condemnation; even so by the righteousness of one the free gift came upon all men unto justification of life. [19]For as by one man's disobedience many were made sinners, so by the obedience of one shall many be made righteous.	**Gen 3:17–19** [17]And unto Adam he said, Because thou hast hearkened unto the voice of thy wife, and hast eaten of the tree, of which I commanded thee, saying, Thou shalt not eat of it: cursed is the ground for thy sake; in sorrow shalt thou eat of it all the days of thy life; [18]Thorns also and thistles shall it bring forth to thee; and thou shalt eat the herb of the field; [19]In the sweat of thy face shalt thou eat bread, till thou return unto the ground; for out of it wast thou taken: for dust thou art, and unto dust shalt thou return.

1 CORINTHIANS 15:23—Resurrection of the dead (15:12–57), 51 CE

Theme	1 COR	Paul
Christ, first fruits	**15:23** [23]But every man in his own order: Christ the firstfruits; afterward they that are Christ's at his coming.	**1 Thes 4:15–17** [15]For this we say unto you by the word of the Lord, that we which are alive and remain unto the coming of the Lord shall not prevent them which are asleep. [16]For the Lord himself shall descend from heaven with a shout, with the voice of the archangel, and with the trump of God: and the dead in Christ shall rise first: [17]Then we which are alive and remain shall be caught up together with them in the clouds, to meet the Lord in the air: and so shall we ever be with the Lord.

1 CORINTHIANS 15:24—Resurrection of the dead (15:12–57), 51 CE

Theme	1 COR	Paul
In end, Christ delivers to God	**15:24** [24]Then cometh the end, when he shall have delivered up the kingdom to God, even the Father; when he shall have put down all rule and all authority and power.	**Eph 1:22 (Pseudo)** [22]And hath put all things under his feet, and gave him to be the head over all things to the church,

1 CORINTHIANS 15:25—Resurrection of the dead (15:12–57), 51 CE

Theme	1 COR	Jewish Writings
All put under Christ	**15:25** [25]For he must reign, till he hath put all enemies under his feet.	**Ps 110:1** [1]The LORD said unto my Lord, Sit thou at my right hand, until I make thine enemies thy footstool.

1 CORINTHIANS 15:26—Resurrection of the dead (15:12–57), 51 CE

Theme	1 COR	Paul	NT
Death destroyed	**15:26** [26]The last enemy that shall be destroyed is death.	**Rom 6:9** [9]Knowing that Christ being raised from the dead dieth no more; death hath no more dominion over him. **2 Tim 1:10 (Pseudo)** [10]But is now made manifest by the appearing of our Saviour Jesus Christ, who hath abolished death, and hath brought life and immortality to light through the gospel:	**Rev 20:14** [14]And death and hell were cast into the lake of fire. This is the second death.

1 CORINTHIANS 15:27—Resurrection of the dead (15:12–57), 51 CE

Theme	1 COR	Paul	Jewish Writings
All under Christ	**15:27** [27]For he hath put all things under his feet. But when he saith all things are put under him, it is manifest that he is excepted, which did put all things under him.	**Eph 1:22 (Pseudo)** [22]And hath put all things under his feet, and gave him to be the head over all things to the church, **Phil 3:21** [21]Who shall change our vile body, that it may be fashioned like unto his glorious body, according to the working whereby he is able even to subdue all things unto himself.	**Ps 8:7** [7]All sheep and oxen, yea, and the beasts of the field;

1 CORINTHIANS 15:28—Resurrection of the dead (15:12–57), 51 CE

Theme	1 COR	Paul
All subject to Christ so God is all	**15:28** [28]And when all things shall be subdued unto him, then shall the Son also himself be subject unto him that put all things under him, that God may be all in all.	**Eph 4:6 (Pseudo)** [6]One God and Father of all, who is above all, and through all, and in you all. **Col 3:11** [11]Where there is neither Greek nor Jew, circumcision nor uncircumcision, Barbarian, Scythian, bond nor free: but Christ is all, and in all.

1 CORINTHIANS 15:30—Resurrection of the dead (15:12–57), 51 CE

Theme	1 COR	Paul
In jeopardy every hour	**15:30** [30]And why stand we in jeopardy every hour?	**2 Cor 4:8–12** [8]We are troubled on every side, yet not distressed; we are perplexed, but not in despair; [9]Persecuted, but not forsaken; cast down, but not destroyed; [10]Always bearing about in the body the dying of the Lord Jesus, that the life also of Jesus might be made manifest in our body. [11]For we which live are alway delivered unto death for Jesus' sake, that the life also of Jesus might be made manifest in our mortal flesh. [12]So then death worketh in us, but life in you. **2 Cor 11:23–27** [23]Are they ministers of Christ? (I speak as a fool) I am more; in labours more abundant, in stripes above measure, in prisons more frequent, in deaths oft. [24]Of the Jews five times received I forty stripes save one. [25]Thrice was I beaten with rods, once was I stoned, thrice I suffered shipwreck, a night and a day I have been in the deep; [26]In journeyings often, in perils of waters, in perils of robbers, in perils by mine own countrymen, in perils by the heathen, in perils in the city, in perils in the wilderness, in perils in the sea, in perils among false brethren; [27]In weariness and painfulness, in watchings often, in hunger and thirst, in fastings often, in cold and nakedness.

1 CORINTHIANS 15:31—Resurrection of the dead (15:12–57), 51 CE

Theme	1 COR	Paul	Jewish Writings
Die daily	**15:31** [31]I protest by your rejoicing which I have in Christ Jesus our Lord, I die daily.	**Rom 8:36** [36]As it is written, For thy sake we are killed all the day long; we are accounted as sheep for the slaughter.	**Ps 44:23** [23]Awake, why sleepest thou, O Lord? arise, cast us not off for ever.

1 CORINTHIANS 15:32—Resurrection of the dead (15:12–57), 51 CE

Theme	1 COR	Lk	Paul	Jewish Writings	Other
Striving for heaven	**15:32** [32]If after the manner of men I have fought with beasts at Ephesus, what advantageth it me, if the dead rise not? let us eat and drink; for tomorrow we die. **4:9** [9]For I think that God hath set forth us the apostles last, as it were appointed to death: for we are made a spectacle unto the world, and to angels, and to men.	**12:13–21** [13]And one of the company said unto him, Master, speak to my brother, that he divide the inheritance with me. [14]And he said unto him, Man, who made me a judge or a divider over you? [15]And he said unto them, Take heed, and beware of covetousness: for a man's life consisteth not in the abundance of the things which he possesseth. [16]And he spake a parable unto them, saying, The ground of a certain rich man brought forth plentifully: [17]And he thought within himself, saying, What shall I do, because I have no room where to bestow my fruits? [18]And he said, This will I do: I will pull down my barns, and build greater; and there will I bestow all my fruits and my goods. [19]And I will say to my soul, Soul, thou hast much goods laid up for many years; take thine ease, eat, drink, and be merry. [20]But God said unto him, Thou fool, this night thy soul shall be required of thee: then whose shall those things be, which thou hast provided? [21]So is he that layeth up treasure for himself, and is not rich toward God. **12:33–34** [33]Sell that ye have, and give alms; provide yourselves bags which wax not old, a treasure in the heavens that faileth not, where no thief approacheth, neither moth corrupteth. [34]For where your treasure is, there will your heart be also. **18:22** [22]Now when Jesus heard these things, he said unto him, Yet lackest thou one thing: sell all that thou hast, and distribute unto the poor, and thou shalt have treasure in heaven: and come, follow me.	**2 Cor 4:10-11** [10]Always bearing about in the body the dying of the Lord Jesus, that the life also of Jesus might be made manifest in our body. [11]For we which live are alway delivered unto death for Jesus' sake, that the life also of Jesus might be made manifest in our mortal flesh.	**Wis 2:5–7** [5]For our time is a very shadow that passeth away; and after our end there is no returning: for it is fast sealed, so that no man cometh again. [6]Come on therefore, let us enjoy the good things that are present: and let us speedily use the creatures like as in youth. [7]Let us fill ourselves with costly wine and ointments: and let no flower of the spring pass by us: **Is 22:13** [13]And behold joy and gladness, slaying oxen, and killing sheep, eating flesh, and drinking wine: let us eat and drink; for tomorrow we shall die.	**GThom 63** [63]Jesus said, "There was a rich man who had much money. He said, 'I shall put my money to use so that I may sow, reap, plant, and fill my storehouse with produce, with the result that I shall lack nothing.' Such were his intentions, but that same night he died. Let him who has ears hear." **GThom 72** [72][A man said] to him, "Tell my brothers to divide my father's possessions with me." He said to him, "O man, who has made me a divider?" He turned to his disciples and said to them, "I am not a divider, am I?" **Q-Quelle** Treasures in heaven: 1 Cor 15:32[Mt 6:19-21]/ Lk 12:33-34 (Qs 40 [Thom 76:2])

1 CORINTHIANS 15:34—Resurrection of the dead (15:12–57), 51 CE

Theme	1 COR	Mt	Mk
Awake and be righteous	**15:34** [34]Awake to righteousness, and sin not; for some have not the knowledge of God: I speak this to your shame.	**22:29** [29]Jesus answered and said unto them, Ye do err, not knowing the scriptures, nor the power of God.	**12:24** [24]And Jesus answering said unto them, Do ye not therefore err, because ye know not the scriptures, neither the power of God?

1 CORINTHIANS 15:36—Resurrection of the dead (15:12–57), 51 CE

Theme	1 COR	Jn
Must die to live	**15:36** [36]Thou fool, that which thou sowest is not quickened, except it die:	**12:24** [24]Verily, verily, I say unto you, Except a corn of wheat fall into the ground and die, it abideth alone: but if it die, it bringeth forth much fruit.

1 CORINTHIANS 15:38—Resurrection of the dead (15:12–57), 51 CE

Theme	1 COR	Jewish Writings
God giveth a body	**15:38** [38]But God giveth it a body as it hath pleased him, and to every seed his own body.	**Gen 1:11** [11]And God said, Let the earth bring forth grass, the herb yielding seed, and the fruit tree yielding fruit after his kind, whose seed is in itself, upon the earth: and it was so.

1 CORINTHIANS 15:43—Resurrection of the dead (15:12–57), 51 CE

Theme	1 COR	Paul
Sown in dishonor raised in glory	**15:43** [43]It is sown in dishonour; it is raised in glory: it is sown in weakness; it is raised in power:	**Phil 3:20-21** [20]For our conversation is in heaven; from whence also we look for the Saviour, the Lord Jesus Christ: [21]Who shall change our vile body, that it may be fashioned like unto his glorious body, according to the working whereby he is able even to subdue all things unto himself. **Col 3:4** [4]When Christ, who is our life, shall appear, then shall ye also appear with him in glory.

1 CORINTHIANS 15:45—Resurrection of the dead (15:12–57), 51 CE

Theme	1 COR	Jn	Paul	Jewish Writings
First Adam has living soul; last Adam quickens spirit	**15:45** [45]And so it is written, The first man Adam was made a living soul; the last Adam was made a quickening spirit.	**5:21–29** [21]For as the Father raiseth up the dead, and quickeneth them; even so the Son quickeneth whom he will. [22]For the Father judgeth no man, but hath committed all judgment unto the Son: [23]That all men should honour the Son, even as they honour the Father. He that honoureth not the Son honoureth not the Father which hath sent him. [24]Verily, verily, I say unto you, He that heareth my word, and believeth on him that sent me, hath everlasting life, and shall not come into condemnation; but is passed from death unto life. [25]Verily, verily, I say unto you, The hour is coming, and now is, when the dead shall hear the voice of the Son of God: and they that hear shall live. [26]For as the Father hath life in himself; so hath he given to the Son to have life in himself; [27]And hath given him authority to execute judgment also, because he is the Son of man. [28]Marvel not at this: for the hour is coming, in the which all that are in the graves shall hear his voice, [29]And shall come forth; they that have done good, unto the resurrection of life; and they that have done evil, unto the resurrection of damnation.	**2 Cor 3:6, 17** [6]Who also hath made us able ministers of the new testament; not of the letter, but of the spirit: for the letter killeth, but the spirit giveth life. [17]Now the Lord is that Spirit: and where the Spirit of the Lord is, there is liberty.	**Gen 2:7** [7]And the LORD God formed man of the dust of the ground, and breathed into his nostrils the breath of life; and man became a living soul.

1 CORINTHIANS 15:49—Resurrection of the dead (15:12–57), 51 CE

Theme	1 COR	Paul	Jewish Writings
Image of the heavenly	**15:49** [49]And as we have borne the image of the earthy, we shall also bear the image of the heavenly.	**Rom 8:29** [29]For whom he did foreknow, he also did predestinate to be conformed to the image of his Son, that he might be the firstborn among many brethren. **Phil 3:21** [21]Who shall change our vile body, that it may be fashioned like unto his glorious body, according to the working whereby he is able even to subdue all things unto himself.	**Gen 5:3** [3]And Adam lived an hundred and thirty years, and begat a son in his own likeness, after his image; and called his name Seth:

1 CORINTHIANS 15:50—Resurrection of the dead (15:12–57), 51 CE

Theme	1 COR	Jn
Flesh does not inherit kingdom	**15:50** [50]Now this I say, brethren, that flesh and blood cannot inherit the kingdom of God; neither doth corruption inherit incorruption.	**3:3–6** [3]Jesus answered and said unto him, Verily, verily, I say unto thee, Except a man be born again, he cannot see the kingdom of God. [4]Nicodemus saith unto him, How can a man be born when he is old? can he enter the second time into his mother's womb, and be born? [5]Jesus answered, Verily, verily, I say unto thee, Except a man be born of water and of the Spirit, he cannot enter into the kingdom of God. [6]That which is born of the flesh is flesh; and that which is born of the Spirit is spirit.

1 CORINTHIANS 15:51—Resurrection of the dead (15:12–57), 51 CE

Theme	1 COR	Paul
Mystery of Godly change	**15:51** [51]Behold, I show you a mystery; We shall not all sleep, but we shall all be changed,	**1 Thes 4:14–17** [14]For if we believe that Jesus died and rose again, even so them also which sleep in Jesus will God bring with him. [15]For this we say unto you by the word of the Lord, that we which are alive and remain unto the coming of the Lord shall not prevent them which are asleep. [16]For the Lord himself shall descend from heaven with a shout, with the voice of the archangel, and with the trump of God: and the dead in Christ shall rise first: [17]Then we which are alive and remain shall be caught up together with them in the clouds, to meet the Lord in the air: and so shall we ever be with the Lord.

1 CORINTHIANS 15:52—Resurrection of the dead (15:12–57), 51 CE

Theme	1 COR	Mt	NT	Jewish Writings
Change in twinkling of an eye	**15:52** [52]In a moment, in the twinkling of an eye, at the last trump: for the trumpet shall sound, and the dead shall be raised incorruptible, and we shall be changed.	**24:31** [31]And he shall send his angels with a great sound of a trumpet, and they shall gather together his elect from the four winds, from one end of heaven to the other.	**Rev 11:15–18** [15]And the seventh angel sounded; and there were great voices in heaven, saying, The kingdoms of this world are become the kingdoms of our Lord, and of his Christ; and he shall reign for ever and ever. [16]And the four and twenty elders, which sat before God on their seats, fell upon their faces, and worshipped God, [17]Saying, We give thee thanks, O Lord God Almighty, which art, and wast, and art to come; because thou hast taken to thee thy great power, and hast reigned. [18]And the nations were angry, and thy wrath is come, and the time of the dead, that they should be judged, and that thou shouldest give reward unto thy servants the prophets, and to the saints, and them that fear thy name, small and great; and shouldest destroy them which destroy the earth.	**Joel 2:1** [1]Blow ye the trumpet in Zion, and sound an alarm in my holy mountain: let all the inhabitants of the land tremble: for the day of the LORD cometh, for it is nigh at hand; **Zech 9:14** [14]And the LORD shall be seen over them, and his arrow shall go forth as the lightning: and the Lord GOD shall blow the trumpet, and shall go with whirlwinds of the south.

1 CORINTHIANS 15:53—Resurrection of the dead (15:12–57), 51 CE

Theme	1 COR	Paul
Corruptible becomes incorruptible	**15:53** [53]For this corruptible must put on incorruption, and this mortal must put on immortality.	**2 Cor 5:2–4** [2]For in this we groan, earnestly desiring to be clothed upon with our house which is from heaven: [3]If so be that being clothed we shall not be found naked. [4]For we that are in this tabernacle do groan, being burdened: not for that we would be unclothed, but clothed upon, that mortality might be swallowed up of life.

1 CORINTHIANS 15:54—Resurrection of the dead (15:12–57), 51 CE

Theme	1 COR	Paul	NT	Jewish Writings
Death swallowed in victory	**15:54** [54]So when this corruptible shall have put on incorruption, and this mortal shall have put on immortality, then shall be brought to pass the saying that is written, Death is swallowed up in victory.	**2 Cor 5:4** [4]For we that are in this tabernacle do groan, being burdened: not for that we would be unclothed, but clothed upon, that mortality might be swallowed up of life. **2 Tim 1:10 (Pseudo)** [10]When he shall come to be glorified in his saints, and to be admired in all them that believe (because our testimony among you was believed) in that day.	**Heb 2:14–15** [14]Forasmuch then as the children are partakers of flesh and blood, he also himself likewise took part of the same; that through death he might destroy him that had the power of death, that is, the devil; [15]And deliver them who through fear of death were all their lifetime subject to bondage.	**Is 25:8** [8]He will swallow up death in victory; and the Lord GOD will wipe away tears from off all faces; and the rebuke of his people shall he take away from off all the earth: for the LORD hath spoken it.

1 CORINTHIANS 15:55—Resurrection of the dead (15:12–57), 51 CE

Theme	1 COR	Jewish Writings
Death, where is victory	**15:55** [55]O death, where is thy sting? O grave, where is thy victory?	**Hos 13:14** [14]I will ransom them from the power of the grave; I will redeem them from death: O death, I will be thy plagues; O grave, I will be thy destruction: repentance shall be hid from mine eyes.

1 CORINTHIANS 15:56—Resurrection of the dead (15:12–57), 51 CE

Theme	1 COR	Paul
Sting of death is sin	**15:56** [56]The sting of death is sin; and the strength of sin is the law.	**Rom 4:15** [15]Because the law worketh wrath: for where no law is, there is no transgression. **Rom 7:7** [7]What shall we say then? Is the law sin? God forbid. Nay, I had not known sin, but by the law: for I had not known lust, except the law had said, Thou shalt not covet. **Rom 7:13** [13]Was then that which is good made death unto me? God forbid. But sin, that it might appear sin, working death in me by that which is good; that sin by the commandment might become exceeding sinful.

1 CORINTHIANS 15:57—Resurrection of the dead (15:12–57), 51 CE

Theme	1 COR	Jn
Victory in Christ	**15:57** [57]But thanks be to God, which giveth us the victory through our Lord Jesus Christ.	**16:33** [33]These things I have spoken unto you, that in me ye might have peace. In the world ye shall have tribulation: but be of good cheer; I have overcome the world. **1 Jn 5:4** [4]For whatsoever is born of God overcometh the world: and this is the victory that overcometh the world, even our faith.

CONCLUSIONS

1 CORINTHIANS 16:1—Conclusion, 51 CE

Theme	1 COR	Lk
Collection for churches	**16:1** [1]Now concerning the collection for the saints, as I have given order to the churches of Galatia, even so do ye.	**Acts 24:17** [17]Now after many years I came to bring alms to my nation, and offerings.

Paul

Rom 15:25–32

25But now I go unto Jerusalem to minister unto the saints. 26For it hath pleased them of Macedonia and Achaia to make a certain contribution for the poor saints which are at Jerusalem. 27It hath pleased them verily; and their debtors they are. For if the Gentiles have been made partakers of their spiritual things, their duty is also to minister unto them in carnal things. 28When therefore I have performed this, and have sealed to them this fruit, I will come by you into Spain. 29And I am sure that, when I come unto you, I shall come in the fulness of the blessing of the gospel of Christ. 30Now I beseech you, brethren, for the Lord Jesus Christ's sake, and for the love of the Spirit, that ye strive together with me in your prayers to God for me; 31That I may be delivered from them that do not believe in Judaea; and that my service which I have for Jerusalem may be accepted of the saints; 32That I may come unto you with joy by the will of God, and may with you be refreshed.

2 Cor 8–9

8 1Moreover, brethren, we do you to wit of the grace of God bestowed on the churches of Macedonia; 2How that in a great trial of affliction the abundance of their joy and their deep poverty abounded unto the riches of their liberality. 3For to their power, I bear record, yea, and beyond their power they were willing of themselves; 4Praying us with much entreaty that we would receive the gift, and take upon us the fellowship of the ministering to the saints. 5And this they did, not as we hoped, but first gave their own selves to the Lord, and unto us by the will of God. 6Insomuch that we desired Titus, that as he had begun, so he would also finish in you the same grace also. 7Therefore, as ye abound in every thing, in faith, and utterance, and knowledge, and in all diligence, and in your love to us, see that ye abound in this grace also. 8I speak not by commandment, but by occasion of the forwardness of others, and to prove the sincerity of your love. 9For ye know the grace of our Lord Jesus Christ, that, though he was rich, yet for your sakes he became poor, that ye through his poverty might be rich. 10And herein I give my advice: for this is expedient for you, who have begun before, not only to do, but also to be forward a year ago. 11Now therefore perform the doing of it; that as there was a readiness to will, so there may be a performance also out of that which ye have. 12For if there be first a willing mind, it is accepted according to that a man hath, and not according to that he hath not. 13For I mean not that other men be eased, and ye burdened: 14But by an equality, that now at this time your abundance may be a supply for their want, that their abundance also may be a supply for your want: that there may be equality: 15As it is written, He that had gathered much had nothing over; and he that had gathered little had no lack. 16But thanks be to God, which put the same earnest care into the heart of Titus for you. 17For indeed he accepted the exhortation; but being more forward, of his own accord he went unto you. 18And we have sent with him the brother, whose praise is in the gospel throughout all the churches; 19And not that only, but who was also chosen of the churches to travel with us with this grace, which is administered by us to the glory of the same Lord, and declaration of your ready mind: 20Avoiding this, that no man should blame us in this abundance which is administered by us: 21Providing for honest things, not only in the sight of the Lord, but also in the sight of men. 22And we have sent with them our brother, whom we have oftentimes proved diligent in many things, but now much more diligent, upon the great confidence which I have in you. 23Whether any do inquire of Titus, he is my partner and fellowhelper concerning you: or our brethren be inquired of, they are the messengers of the churches, and the glory of Christ. 24Wherefore show ye to them, and before the churches, the proof of your love, and of our boasting on your behalf.

9 1For as touching the ministering to the saints, it is superfluous for me to write to you: 2For I know the forwardness of your mind, for which I boast of you to them of Macedonia, that Achaia was ready a year ago; and your zeal hath provoked very many. 3Yet have I sent the brethren, lest our boasting of you should be in vain in this behalf; that, as I said, ye may be ready: 4Lest haply if they of Macedonia come with me, and find you unprepared, we (that we say not, ye) should be ashamed in this same confident boasting. 5Therefore I thought it necessary to exhort the brethren, that they would go before unto you, and make up beforehand your bounty, whereof ye had notice before, that the same might be ready, as a matter of bounty, and not as of covetousness. 6But this I say, He which soweth sparingly shall reap also sparingly; and he which soweth bountifully shall reap also bountifully. 7Every man according as he purposeth in his heart, so let him give; not grudgingly, or of necessity: for God loveth a cheerful giver. 8And God is able to make all grace abound toward you; that ye, always having all sufficiency in all things, may abound to every good work: 9(As it is written, He hath dispersed abroad; he hath given to the poor: his righteousness remaineth for ever. 10Now he that ministereth seed to the sower both minister bread for your food, and multiply your seed sown, and increase the fruits of your righteousness;) 11Being enriched in every thing to all bountifulness, which causeth through us thanksgiving to God. 12For the administration of this service not only supplieth the want of the saints, but is abundant also by many thanksgivings unto God; 13Whiles by the experiment of this ministration they glorify God for your professed subjection unto the gospel of Christ, and for your liberal distribution unto them, and unto all men; 14And by their prayer for you, which long after you for the exceeding grace of God in you. 15Thanks be unto God for his unspeakable gift.

Gal 2:10

10Only they would that we should remember the poor; the same which I also was forward to do.

1 CORINTHIANS 16:5—Conclusion, 51 CE

Theme	1 COR	Lk	Paul
Pass through Macedonia	**16:5** [5]Now I will come unto you, when I shall pass through Macedonia: for I do pass through Macedonia.	**Acts 19:21** [21]After these things were ended, Paul purposed in the spirit, when he had passed through Macedonia and Achaia, to go to Jerusalem, saying, After I have been there, I must also see Rome.	**Rom 15:26** [26]For it hath pleased them of Macedonia and Achaia to make a certain contribution for the poor saints which are at Jerusalem. **2 Cor 1:15–16** [15]Lest any should say that I had baptized in mine own name. [16]And I baptized also the household of Stephanas: besides, I know not whether I baptized any other.

1 CORINTHIANS 16:7—Conclusion, 51 CE

Theme	1 COR	Lk
Stay in Ephesus	**16:7** [7]For I will not see you now by the way; but I trust to tarry a while with you, if the Lord permit.	**Acts 18:21** [21]But bade them farewell, saying, I must by all means keep this feast that cometh in Jerusalem: but I will return again unto you, if God will. And he sailed from Ephesus.

1 CORINTHIANS 16:8—Conclusion, 51 CE

Theme	1 COR	Lk
Stay in Ephesus	**16:8** [8]But I will tarry at Ephesus until Pentecost. **15:32** [32]If after the manner of men I have fought with beasts at Ephesus, what advantageth it me, if the dead rise not? let us eat and drink; for to morrow we die.	**Acts 18:19** [19]And he came to Ephesus, and left them there: but he himself entered into the synagogue, and reasoned with the Jews. **Acts 19:1–10** [1]And it came to pass, that, while Apollos was at Corinth, Paul having passed through the upper coasts came to Ephesus: and finding certain disciples, [2]He said unto them, Have ye received the Holy Ghost since ye believed? And they said unto him, We have not so much as heard whether there be any Holy Ghost. [3]And he said unto them, Unto what then were ye baptized? And they said, Unto John's baptism. [4]Then said Paul, John verily baptized with the baptism of repentance, saying unto the people, that they should believe on him which should come after him, that is, on Christ Jesus. [5]When they heard this, they were baptized in the name of the Lord Jesus. [6]And when Paul had laid his hands upon them, the Holy Ghost came on them; and they spake with tongues, and prophesied. [7]And all the men were about twelve. [8]And he went into the synagogue, and spake boldly for the space of three months, disputing and persuading the things concerning the kingdom of God. [9]But when divers were hardened, and believed not, but spake evil of that way before the multitude, he departed from them, and separated the disciples, disputing daily in the school of one Tyrannus. [10]And this continued by the space of two years; so that all they which dwelt in Asia heard the word of the Lord Jesus, both Jews and Greeks.

1 CORINTHIANS 16:9—Conclusion, 51 CE

Theme	1 COR	Lk	Paul
Many adversities	**16:9** [9]For a great door and effectual is opened unto me, and there are many adversaries.	**Acts 14:27** [27]And when they were come, and had gathered the church together, they rehearsed all that God had done with them, and how he had opened the door of faith unto the Gentiles.	**2 Cor 2:12** [12]Furthermore, when I came to Troas to preach Christ's gospel, and a door was opened unto me of the Lord,

1 CORINTHIANS 16:10—Conclusion, 51 CE

Theme	1 COR	Lk	Paul
Timotheus does Lord's work	**16:10** [10]Now if Timotheus come, see that he may be with you without fear: for he worketh the work of the Lord, as I also do. **4:17** [17]For this cause have I sent unto you Timotheus, who is my beloved son, and faithful in the Lord, who shall bring you into remembrance of my ways which be in Christ, as I teach every where in every church.	**Acts 16:1** [1]Then came he to Derbe and Lystra: and, behold, a certain disciple was there, named Timotheus, the son of a certain woman, which was a Jewess, and believed; but his father was a Greek: **Acts 19:22** [22]So he sent into Macedonia two of them that ministered unto him, Timotheus and Erastus; but he himself stayed in Asia for a season.	**Phil 2:19–23** [19]But I trust in the Lord Jesus to send Timotheus shortly unto you, that I also may be of good comfort, when I know your state. [20]For I have no man likeminded, who will naturally care for your state. [21]For all seek their own, not the things which are Jesus Christ's. [22]But ye know the proof of him, that, as a son with the father, he hath served with me in the gospel. [23]Him therefore I hope to send presently, so soon as I shall see how it will go with me.

1 CORINTHIANS 16:12—Conclusion, 51 CE

Theme	1 COR	Lk
Apollos will come	**16:12** [12]As touching our brother Apollos, I greatly desired him to come unto you with the brethren: but his will was not at all to come at this time; but he will come when he shall have convenient time. **1:12** [12]Now this I say, that every one of you saith, I am of Paul; and I of Apollos; and I of Cephas; and I of Christ. **3:4–6** [4]For while one saith, I am of Paul; and another, I am of Apollos; are ye not carnal? [5]Who then is Paul, and who is Apollos, but ministers by whom ye believed, even as the Lord gave to every man? [6]I have planted, Apollos watered; but God gave the increase. **3:22** [22]Whether Paul, or Apollos, or Cephas, or the world, or life, or death, or things present, or things to come; all are yours;	**Acts 18:24–28** [24]And a certain Jew named Apollos, born at Alexandria, an eloquent man, and mighty in the scriptures, came to Ephesus. [25]This man was instructed in the way of the Lord; and being fervent in the spirit, he spake and taught diligently the things of the Lord, knowing only the baptism of John. [26]And he began to speak boldly in the synagogue: whom when Aquila and Priscilla had heard, they took him unto them, and expounded unto him the way of God more perfectly. [27]And when he was disposed to pass into Achaia, the brethren wrote, exhorting the disciples to receive him: who, when he was come, helped them much which had believed through grace: [28]For he mightily convinced the Jews, and that publicly, showing by the scriptures that Jesus was Christ.

1 CORINTHIANS 16:15—Conclusion, 51 CE

Theme	1 COR
Stephanas & ministry	**16:15** [15]I beseech you, brethren, (ye know the house of Stephanas, that it is the firstfruits of Achaia, and that they have addicted themselves to the ministry of the saints,) **1:16** [16]And I baptized also the household of Stephanas: besides, I know not whether I baptized any other.

1 CORINTHIANS 16:18—Conclusion, 51 CE

Theme	1 COR	Paul
Honor workers	**16:18** [18]For they have refreshed my spirit and yours: therefore acknowledge ye them that are such.	**1 Thes 5:12–13** [12]And we beseech you, brethren, to know them which labour among you, and are over you in the Lord, and admonish you; [13]And to esteem them very highly in love for their work's sake. And be at peace among yourselves.

1 CORINTHIANS 16:19—Conclusion, 51 CE

Theme	1 COR	Lk	Paul
Aquila & Priscilla send greetings	**16:19** [19]The churches of Asia salute you. Aquila and Priscilla salute you much in the Lord, with the church that is in their house.	**Acts 18:2** [2]And found a certain Jew named Aquila, born in Pontus, lately come from Italy, with his wife Priscilla; (because that Claudius had commanded all Jews to depart from Rome:) and came unto them. **Acts 18:18** [18]And Paul after this tarried there yet a good while, and then took his leave of the brethren, and sailed thence into Syria, and with him Priscilla and Aquila; having shorn his head in Cenchrea: for he had a vow. **Acts 18:26** [26]And he began to speak boldly in the synagogue: whom when Aquila and Priscilla had heard, they took him unto them, and expounded unto him the way of God more perfectly.	**Rom 16:3–5** [3]Him would Paul have to go forth with him; and took and circumcised him because of the Jews which were in those quarters: for they knew all that his father was a Greek. [4]And as they went through the cities, they delivered them the decrees for to keep, that were ordained of the apostles and elders which were at Jerusalem. [5]And so were the churches established in the faith, and increased in number daily.

1 CORINTHIANS 16:20—Conclusion, 51 CE

Theme	1 COR	Paul	NT
Greet with a holy kiss	**16:20** [20]All the brethren greet you. Greet ye one another with an holy kiss.	**Rom 16:16** [16]Salute one another with an holy kiss. The churches of Christ salute you. **2 Cor 13:12** [12]Greet one another with an holy kiss. **1 Thes 5:26** [26]Greet all the brethren with an holy kiss.	**1 Pet 5:14** [14]Greet ye one another with a kiss of charity. Peace be with you all that are in Christ Jesus. Amen.

1 CORINTHIANS 16:21—Conclusion, 51 CE

Theme	1 COR	Paul
Paul's own writing	**16:21** [21]The salutation of me Paul with mine own hand.	**Gal 6:11** [11]Ye see how large a letter I have written unto you with mine own hand. **Col 4:18** [18]The salutation by the hand of me Paul. Remember my bonds. Grace be with you. Amen. **2 Thes 3:17** [17]The salutation of Paul with mine own hand, which is the token in every epistle: so I write.

1 CORINTHIANS 16:22—Conclusion, 51 CE

Theme	1 COR	Paul	NT
Not loving the Lord	**16:22** [22]If any man love not the Lord Jesus Christ, let him be anathema. Maranatha. **12:3** [3]Wherefore I give you to understand, that no man speaking by the Spirit of God calleth Jesus accursed: and that no man can say that Jesus is the Lord, but by the Holy Ghost.	**Rom 9:3** [3]For I could wish that myself were accursed from Christ for my brethren, my kinsmen according to the flesh: **Gal 1:8–9** [8]But though we, or an angel from heaven, preach any other gospel unto you than that which we have preached unto you, let him be accursed. [9]As we said before, so say I now again, If any man preach any other gospel unto you than that ye have received, let him be accursed.	**Rev 22:20** [20]He which testifieth these things saith, Surely I come quickly. Amen. Even so, come, Lord Jesus.

1 CORINTHIANS 16:23—Conclusion, 51 CE

Theme	1 COR	Paul
Grace to listeners	**16:23** [23]The grace of our Lord Jesus Christ be with you.	**Rom 16:20** [20]And the God of peace shall bruise Satan under your feet shortly. The grace of our Lord Jesus Christ be with you. Amen.

2 CORINTHIANS

Written from Macedonia, 57 CE (possibly a compilation of epistles)

ADDRESS (1:1–11)

2 CORINTHIANS 1:1—Address (1:1–11), 57 CE

Theme	2 COR
Paul, an Apostle	**1:1** [1]Paul, an apostle of Jesus Christ by the will of God, and Timothy our brother, unto the church of God which is at Corinth, with all the saints which are in all Achaia:

Lk	Paul
Acts 16 [1]Then came he to Derbe and Lystra: and, behold, a certain disciple was there, named Timotheus, the son of a certain woman, which was a Jewess, and believed; but his father was a Greek: [2]Which was well reported of by the brethren that were at Lystra and Iconium. [3]Him would Paul have to go forth with him; and took and circumcised him because of the Jews which were in those quarters: for they knew all that his father was a Greek. [4]And as they went through the cities, they delivered them the decrees for to keep, that were ordained of the apostles and elders which were at Jerusalem. [5]And so were the churches established in the faith, and increased in number daily. [6]Now when they had gone throughout Phrygia and the region of Galatia, and were forbidden of the Holy Ghost to preach the word in Asia, [7]After they were come to Mysia, they assayed to go into Bithynia: but the Spirit suffered them not. [8]And they passing by Mysia came down to Troas. [9]And a vision appeared to Paul in the night; There stood a man of Macedonia, and prayed him, saying, Come over into Macedonia, and help us. [10]And after he had seen the vision, immediately we endeavoured to go into Macedonia, assuredly gathering that the Lord had called us for to preach the gospel unto them. [11]Therefore loosing from Troas, we came with a straight course to Samothracia, and the next day to Neapolis; [12]And from thence to Philippi, which is the chief city of that part of Macedonia, and a colony: and we were in that city abiding certain days. [13]And on the sabbath we went out of the city by a river side, where prayer was wont to be made; and we sat down, and spake unto the women which resorted thither. [14]And a certain woman named Lydia, a seller of purple, of the city of Thyatira, which worshipped God, heard us: whose heart the Lord opened, that she attended unto the things which were spoken of Paul. [15]And when she was baptized, and her household, she besought us, saying, If ye have judged me to be faithful to the Lord, come into my house, and abide there. And she constrained us. [16]And it came to pass, as we went to prayer, a certain damsel possessed with a spirit of divination met us, which brought her masters much gain by soothsaying: [17]The same followed Paul and us, and cried, saying, These men are the servants of the most high God, which show unto us the way of salvation. [18]And this did she many days. But Paul, being grieved, turned and said to the spirit, I command thee in the name of Jesus Christ to come out of her. And he came out the same hour. [19]And when her masters saw that the hope of their gains was gone, they caught Paul and Silas, and drew them into the marketplace unto the rulers, [20]And brought them to the magistrates, saying, These men, being Jews, do exceedingly trouble our city, [21]And teach customs, which are not lawful for us to receive, neither to observe, being Romans. [22]And the multitude rose up together against them: and the magistrates rent off their clothes, and commanded to beat them. [23]And when they had laid many stripes upon them, they cast them into prison, charging the jailor to keep them safely: [24]Who, having received such a charge, thrust them into the inner prison, and made their feet fast in the stocks. [25]And at midnight Paul and Silas prayed, and sang praises unto God: and the prisoners heard them. [26]And suddenly there was a great earthquake, so that the foundations of the prison were shaken: and immediately all the doors were opened, and every one's bands were loosed. [27]And the keeper of the prison awaking out of his sleep, and seeing the prison doors open, he drew out his sword, and would have killed himself, supposing that the prisoners had been fled. [28]But Paul cried with a loud voice, saying, Do thyself no harm: for we are all here. [29]Then he called for a light, and sprang in, and came trembling, and fell down before Paul and Silas, [30]And brought them out, and said, Sirs, what must I do to be saved? [31]And they said, Believe on the Lord Jesus Christ, and thou shalt be saved, and thy house. [32]And they spake unto him the word of the Lord, and to all that were in his house. [33]And he took them the same hour of the night, and washed their stripes; and was baptized, he and all his, straightway. [34]And when he had brought them into his house, he set meat before them, and rejoiced, believing in God with all his house. [35]And when it was day, the magistrates sent the serjeants, saying, Let those men go. [36]And the keeper of the prison told this saying to Paul, The magistrates have sent to let you go: now therefore depart, and go in peace. [37]But Paul said unto them, They have beaten us openly uncondemned, being Romans, and have cast us into prison; and now do they thrust us out privily? nay verily; but let them come themselves and fetch us out. [38]And the serjeants told these words unto the magistrates: and they feared, when they heard that they were Romans. [39]And they came and besought them, and brought them out, and desired them to depart out of the city. [40]And they went out of the prison, and entered into the house of Lydia: and when they had seen the brethren, they comforted them, and departed.	**Rom 1:7** [7]To all that be in Rome, beloved of God, called to be saints: Grace to you and peace from God our Father, and the Lord Jesus Christ. **1 Cor 1:2** [2]Unto the church of God which is at Corinth, to them that are sanctified in Christ Jesus, called to be saints, with all that in every place call upon the name of Jesus Christ our Lord, both theirs and ours: **Eph 1:1 (Pseudo)** [1]Paul, an apostle of Jesus Christ by the will of God, to the saints which are at Ephesus, and to the faithful in Christ Jesus: **Col 1:1** [1]Paul, an apostle of Jesus Christ by the will of God, and Timotheus our brother, **Col 1:19** [19]For it pleased the Father that in him should all fulness dwell;

2 CORINTHIANS 1:3—Address (1:1–11), 57 CE

Theme	2 COR	Paul	NT
Doxology	**1:3** [3]Blessed be God, even the Father of our Lord Jesus Christ, the Father of mercies, and the God of all comfort;	**Rom 15:5** [5]Now the God of patience and consolation grant you to be likeminded one toward another according to Christ Jesus: **1 Cor 15:24** [24]Then cometh the end, when he shall have delivered up the kingdom to God, even the Father; when he shall have put down all rule and all authority and power. **Eph 1:3 (Pseudo)** [3]Blessed be the God and Father of our Lord Jesus Christ, who hath blessed us with all spiritual blessings in heavenly places in Christ:	**1 Pet 1:3** [3]Blessed be the God and Father of our Lord Jesus Christ, which according to his abundant mercy hath begotten us again unto a lively hope by the resurrection of Jesus Christ from the dead,

2 CORINTHIANS 1:4—Address (1:1–11), 57 CE

Theme	2 COR	Paul
Comfort and console	**1:4** [4]Who comforteth us in all our tribulation, that we may be able to comfort them which are in any trouble, by the comfort wherewith we ourselves are comforted of God. **7:6–7, 13** [6]Nevertheless God, that comforteth those that are cast down, comforted us by the coming of Titus; [7]And not by his coming only, but by the consolation wherewith he was comforted in you, when he told us your earnest desire, your mourning, your fervent mind toward me; so that I rejoiced the more. . . .[13]Therefore we were comforted in your comfort: yea, and exceedingly the more joyed we for the joy of Titus, because his spirit was refreshed by you all.	**1 Thes 1:6–8** [6]And ye became followers of us, and of the Lord, having received the word in much affliction, with joy of the Holy Ghost: [7]So that ye were ensamples to all that believe in Macedonia and Achaia. [8]For from you sounded out the word of the Lord not only in Macedonia and Achaia, but also in every place your faith to God-ward is spread abroad; so that we need not to speak any thing. **2 Thes 2:16** [16]Now our Lord Jesus Christ himself, and God, even our Father, which hath loved us, and hath given us everlasting consolation and good hope through grace,

2 CORINTHIANS 1:8—Address (1:1–11), 57 CE

Theme	2 COR	Lk	Paul
Trouble in Asia	**1:8** [8]For we would not, brethren, have you ignorant of our trouble which came to us in Asia, that we were pressed out of measure, above strength, insomuch that we despaired even of life:	**Acts 20:18–19** [18]And when they were come to him, he said unto them, Ye know, from the first day that I came into Asia, after what manner I have been with you at all seasons, [19]Serving the Lord with all humility of mind, and with many tears, and temptations, which befell me by the lying in wait of the Jews:	**1 Cor 15:32** [32]If after the manner of men I have fought with beasts at Ephesus, what advantageth it me, if the dead rise not? let us eat and drink; for to morrow we die.

2 CORINTHIANS 1:9—Address (1:1–11), 57 CE

Theme	2 COR	Paul
Trusted not in ourselves	**1:9** [9]But we had the sentence of death in ourselves, that we should not trust in ourselves, but in God which raiseth the dead: **4:7–11** [7]But we have this treasure in earthen vessels, that the excellency of the power may be of God, and not of us. [8]We are troubled on every side, yet not distressed; we are perplexed, but not in despair; [9]Persecuted, but not forsaken; cast down, but not destroyed; [10]Always bearing about in the body the dying of the Lord Jesus, that the life also of Jesus might be made manifest in our body. [11]For we which live are alway delivered unto death for Jesus' sake, that the life also of Jesus might be made manifest in our mortal flesh.	**Rom 4:17** [17](As it is written, I have made thee a father of many nations,) before him whom he believed, even God, who quickeneth the dead, and calleth those things which be not as though they were.

2 CORINTHIANS 1:10—Address (1:1–11), 57 CE

Theme	2 COR	Paul
Delivered from death	**1:10** [10]Who delivered us from so great a death, and doth deliver: in whom we trust that he will yet deliver us;	**2 Tim 4:18 (Pseudo)** [18]And the Lord shall deliver me from every evil work, and will preserve me unto his heavenly kingdom: to whom be glory for ever and ever. Amen.

2 CORINTHIANS 1:11—Address (1:1–11), 57 CE

Theme	2 COR
Prayer, thanks, & grace	**1:11** [11]Ye also helping together by prayer for us, that for the gift bestowed upon us by the means of many persons thanks may be given by many on our behalf. **4:15** [15]For all things are for your sakes, that the abundant grace might through the thanksgiving of many redound to the glory of God. **9:12** [12]For the administration of this service not only supplieth the want of the saints, but is abundant also by many thanksgivings unto God;

CRISIS AT CORINTH (1:12–7:16)

RELATIONSHIPS IN CHRIST (1:12–2:13)

2 CORINTHIANS 1:14—Relationships in Christ (1:12–2:13), 57 CE

Theme	2 COR	Paul
Rejoice in "Day of the Lord"	**1:14** [14]As also ye have acknowledged us in part, that we are your rejoicing, even as ye also are ours in the day of the Lord Jesus.	**Phil 2:16** [16]Holding forth the word of life; that I may rejoice in the day of Christ, that I have not run in vain, neither laboured in vain. **1 Thes 2:19–20** [19]For what is our hope, or joy, or crown of rejoicing? Are not even ye in the presence of our Lord Jesus Christ at his coming? [20]For ye are our glory and joy.

2 CORINTHIANS 1:16—Relationships in Christ (1:12–2:13), 57 CE

Theme	2 COR	Mt	Lk	Paul	NT
Passing Macedonia	**1:16** [16]And to pass by you into Macedonia, and to come again out of Macedonia unto you, and of you to be brought on my way toward Judaea.	**5:37** [37]But let your communication be, Yea, yea; Nay, nay: for whatsoever is more than these cometh of evil.	**Acts 19:21** [21]After these things were ended, Paul purposed in the spirit, when he had passed through Macedonia and Achaia, to go to Jerusalem, saying, After I have been there, I must also see Rome.	**1 Cor 16:5–9** [5]Now I will come unto you, when I shall pass through Macedonia: for I do pass through Macedonia. [6]And it may be that I will abide, yea, and winter with you, that ye may bring me on my journey whithersoever I go. [7]For I will not see you now by the way; but I trust to tarry a while with you, if the Lord permit. [8]But I will tarry at Ephesus until Pentecost. [9]For a great door and effectual is opened unto me, and there are many adversaries.	**Jas 5:12** [12]But above all things, my brethren, swear not, neither by heaven, neither by the earth, neither by any other oath: but let your yea be yea; and your nay, nay; lest ye fall into condemnation.

2 CORINTHIANS 1:17–21—Relationships in Christ (1:12–2:13), 57 CE

Theme	2 COR	Mt
Gospel foolishness	**1:17–21** [17]For Christ sent me not to baptize, but to preach the gospel: not with wisdom of words, lest the cross of Christ should be made of none effect. [18]For the preaching of the cross is to them that perish foolishness; but unto us which are saved it is the power of God. [19]For it is written, I will destroy the wisdom of the wise, and will bring to nothing the understanding of the prudent. [20]Where is the wise? where is the scribe? where is the disputer of this world? hath not God made foolish the wisdom of this world? [21]For after that in the wisdom of God the world by wisdom knew not God, it pleased God by the foolishness of preaching to save them that believe.	**5:33–37** [33]Again, ye have heard that it hath been said by them of old time, Thou shalt not forswear thyself, but shalt perform unto the Lord thine oaths: [34]But I say unto you, Swear not at all; neither by heaven; for it is God's throne: [35]Nor by the earth; for it is his footstool: neither by Jerusalem; for it is the city of the great King. [36]Neither shalt thou swear by thy head, because thou canst not make one hair white or black. [37]But let your communication be, Yea, yea; Nay, nay: for whatsoever is more than these cometh of evil.

2 CORINTHIANS 1:17—Relationships in Christ (1:12–2:13), 57 CE

Theme	2 COR	Mt	NT
Purpose according to flesh	**1:17** [17]When I therefore was thus minded, did I use lightness? or the things that I purpose, do I purpose according to the flesh, that with me there should be yea yea, and nay nay?	**5:37** [37]But let your communication be, Yea, yea; Nay, nay: for whatsoever is more than these cometh of evil.	**Jas 5:12** [12]But above all things, my brethren, swear not, neither by heaven, neither by the earth, neither by any other oath: but let your yea be yea; and your nay, nay; lest ye fall into condemnation.

2 CORINTHIANS 1:19—Relationships in Christ (1:12–2:13), 57 CE

Theme	2 COR	Lk	Paul
Preaching "yes" in Christ	**1:19** [19]For the Son of God, Jesus Christ, who was preached among you by us, even by me and Silvanus and Timotheus, was not yea and nay, but in him was yea.	**Acts 16:1–3** [1]Then came he to Derbe and Lystra: and, behold, a certain disciple was there, named Timotheus, the son of a certain woman, which was a Jewess, and believed; but his father was a Greek: [2]Which was well reported of by the brethren that were at Lystra and Iconium. [3]Him would Paul have to go forth with him; and took and circumcised him because of the Jews which were in those quarters: for they knew all that his father was a Greek.	**1 Thes 1:1** [1]Paul, and Silvanus, and Timotheus, unto the church of the Thessalonians which is in God the Father and in the Lord Jesus Christ: Grace be unto you, and peace, from God our Father, and the Lord Jesus Christ. **2 Thes 1:1** [1]Paul, and Silvanus, and Timotheus, unto the church of the Thessalonians in God our Father and the Lord Jesus Christ:

2 CORINTHIANS 1:20—Relationships in Christ (1:12–2:13), 57 CE

Theme	2 COR	Paul	NT
Promises of God to his glory	**1:20** [20]For all the promises of God in him are yea, and in him Amen, unto the glory of God by us.	**1 Cor 14:16** [16]Else when thou shalt bless with the spirit, how shall he that occupieth the room of the unlearned say Amen at thy giving of thanks, seeing he understandeth not what thou sayest?	**Rev 3:14** [14]And unto the angel of the church of the Laodiceans write; These things saith the Amen, the faithful and true witness, the beginning of the creation of God;

2 CORINTHIANS 1:21—Relationships in Christ (1:12–2:13), 57 CE

Theme	2 COR	Jn
God anoints preachers	**1:21** [21]Now he which stablisheth us with you in Christ, and hath anointed us, is God;	**1 Jn 2:20** [20]But ye have an unction from the Holy One, and ye know all things. **1 Jn 2:27** [27]But the anointing which ye have received of him abideth in you, and ye need not that any man teach you: but as the same anointing teacheth you of all things, and is truth, and is no lie, and even as it hath taught you, ye shall abide in him.

2 CORINTHIANS 1:22—Relationships in Christ (1:12–2:13), 57 CE

Theme	2 COR	Mt	Mk	Lk
Seal of the Spirit	**1:22** [22]Who hath also sealed us, and given the earnest of the Spirit in our hearts. **1:3** [3]Blessed be God, even the Father of our Lord Jesus Christ, the Father of mercies, and the God of all comfort; **1:18** [18]But as God is true, our word toward you was not yea and nay. **5:15** [15]And that he died for all, that they which live should not henceforth live unto themselves, but unto him which died for them, and rose again.	**10:20** [20]For it is not ye that speak, but the Spirit of your Father which speaketh in you.	**13:11** [11]But when they shall lead you, and deliver you up, take no thought beforehand what ye shall speak, neither do ye premeditate: but whatsoever shall be given you in that hour, that speak ye: for it is not ye that speak, but the Holy Ghost.	**12:12** [12]For the Holy Ghost shall teach you in the same hour what ye ought to say.

Paul

Rom 5:5

[5]And hope maketh not ashamed; because the love of God is shed abroad in our hearts by the Holy Ghost which is given unto us.

Rom 8:16–23

[16]The Spirit itself beareth witness with our spirit, that we are the children of God: [17]And if children, then heirs; heirs of God, and joint-heirs with Christ; if so be that we suffer with him, that we may be also glorified together. [18]For I reckon that the sufferings of this present time are not worthy to be compared with the glory which shall be revealed in us. [19]For the earnest expectation of the creature waiteth for the manifestation of the sons of God. [20]For the creature was made subject to vanity, not willingly, but by reason of him who hath subjected the same in hope, [21]Because the creature itself also shall be delivered from the bondage of corruption into the glorious liberty of the children of God. [22]For we know that the whole creation groaneth and travaileth in pain together until now. [23]And not only they, but ourselves also, which have the firstfruits of the Spirit, even we ourselves groan within ourselves, waiting for the adoption, to wit, the redemption of our body.

1 Cor 3:16

[16]Know ye not that ye are the temple of God, and that the Spirit of God dwelleth in you?

1 Cor 12:1–13

[1]Now concerning spiritual gifts, brethren, I would not have you ignorant. [2]Ye know that ye were Gentiles, carried away unto these dumb idols, even as ye were led. [3]Wherefore I give you to understand, that no man speaking by the Spirit of God calleth Jesus accursed: and that no man can say that Jesus is the Lord, but by the Holy Ghost. [4]Now there are diversities of gifts, but the same Spirit. [5]And there are differences of administrations, but the same Lord. [6]And there are diversities of operations, but it is the same God which worketh all in all. [7]But the manifestation of the Spirit is given to every man to profit withal. [8]For to one is given by the Spirit the word of wisdom; to another the word of knowledge by the same Spirit; [9]To another faith by the same Spirit; to another the gifts of healing by the same Spirit; [10]To another the working of miracles; to another prophecy; to another discerning of spirits; to another divers kinds of tongues; to another the interpretation of tongues: [11]But all these worketh that one and the selfsame Spirit, dividing to every man severally as he will. [12]For as the body is one, and hath many members, and all the members of that one body, being many, are one body: so also is Christ. [13]For by one Spirit are we all baptized into one body, whether we be Jews or Gentiles, whether we be bond or free; and have been all made to drink into one Spirit.

Gal 5:22

[22]But the fruit of the Spirit is love, joy, peace, longsuffering, gentleness, goodness, faith,

Eph 1:13–14 (Pseudo)

[13]In whom ye also trusted, after that ye heard the word of truth, the gospel of your salvation: in whom also after that ye believed, ye were sealed with that holy Spirit of promise,[14]Which is the earnest of our inheritance until the redemption of the purchased possession, unto the praise of his glory.

Eph 4:30 (Pseudo)

[30]And grieve not the holy Spirit of God, whereby ye are sealed unto the day of redemption.

Eph 5:5 (Pseudo)

[5]For this ye know, that no whoremonger, nor unclean person, nor covetous man, who is an idolater, hath any inheritance in the kingdom of Christ and of God.

1 Thes 1:5

[5]For our gospel came not unto you in word only, but also in power, and in the Holy Ghost, and in much assurance; as ye know what manner of men we were among you for your sake.

1 Thes 5:19–20

[19]Quench not the Spirit. [20]Despise not prophesyings.

2 CORINTHIANS 1:22—Relationships in Christ (1:12–2:13), 57 CE

Theme	2 COR	Jewish Writings	Other
(*Cont.*) **Seal of the Spirit**	**1:22 (above)** **1:3 (above)** **1:18 (above)** **5:15 (above)**	**Jer 31:31–34** [31]Behold, the days come, saith the LORD, that I will make a new covenant with the house of Israel, and with the house of Judah: [32]Not according to the covenant that I made with their fathers in the day that I took them by the hand to bring them out of the land of Egypt; which my covenant they brake, although I was an husband unto them, saith the LORD: [33]But this shall be the covenant that I will make with the house of Israel; After those days, saith the LORD, I will put my law in their inward parts, and write it in their hearts; and will be their God, and they shall be my people. [34]And they shall teach no more every man his neighbour, and every man his brother, saying, Know the LORD: for they shall all know me, from the least of them unto the greatest of them, saith the LORD: for I will forgive their iniquity, and I will remember their sin no more.	**Q-Quelle** Assistance of the HS: 2 Cor 1:21-22/Eph 1:14/1 Thes 1:5/Mt 10:19-20/Mk 13:11/Lk 12:11-12 (QS 37 [Thom 44]), [Lk 21:14-15]; Leaven: 1 Cor 3:16/2 Cor 1:21-22/[Mt 13:33]/Lk 12:11-12 (QS 37 [Thom 44]), [Lk 13:20-21(QS 46 [Thom 20, 96])]

2 CORINTHIANS 1:23—Relationships in Christ (1:12–2:13), 57 CE

Theme	2 COR
Waiting to return to Corinth	**1:23** [23]Moreover I call God for a record upon my soul, that to spare you I came not as yet unto Corinth. **13:2** [2]I told you before, and foretell you, as if I were present, the second time; and being absent now I write to them which heretofore have sinned, and to all other, that, if I come again, I will not spare:

2 CORINTHIANS 2:7—Relationships in Christ (1:12–2:13), 57 CE

Theme	2 COR	Paul
Forgive & comfort	**2:7** [7]So that contrariwise ye ought rather to forgive him, and comfort him, lest perhaps such a one should be swallowed up with overmuch sorrow.	**Col 3:13** [13]Forbearing one another, and forgiving one another, if any man have a quarrel against any: even as Christ forgave you, so also do ye.

2 CORINTHIANS 2:9—Relationships in Christ (1:12–2:13), 57 CE

Theme	2 COR
Obedient in all	**2:9** [9]For to this end also did I write, that I might know the proof of you, whether ye be obedient in all things. **7:15** [15]And his inward affection is more abundant toward you, whilst he remembereth the obedience of you all, how with fear and trembling ye received him.

2 CORINTHIANS 2:11—Relationships in Christ (1:12–2:13), 57 CE

Theme	2 COR	Paul
Do not be ignorant	**2:11** [11]Lest Satan should get an advantage of us: for we are not ignorant of his devices.	**Eph 4:27 (Pseudo)** [27]Neither give place to the devil.

2 CORINTHIANS 2:12—Relationships in Christ (1:12–2:13), 57 CE

Theme	2 COR	Lk
Door open in Troas	**2:12** [12]Furthermore, when I came to Troas to preach Christ's gospel, and a door was opened unto me of the Lord,	**Acts 16:8** [8]And they passing by Mysia came down to Troas.

2 CORINTHIANS 2:13—Relationships in Christ (1:12–2:13), 57 CE

Theme	2 COR	Paul
Titus not found	**2:13** [13]I had no rest in my spirit, because I found not Titus my brother: but taking my leave of them, I went from thence into Macedonia. **7:6** [6]Nevertheless God, that comforteth those that are cast down, comforted us by the coming of Titus;	**1 Tim 1:3 (Pseudo)** [3]As I besought thee to abide still at Ephesus, when I went into Macedonia, that thou mightest charge some that they teach no other doctrine,

PAUL'S MINISTRY (2:14–7:4)

2 CORINTHIANS 2:15—Paul's ministry (2:14–7:4), 57 CE

Theme	2 COR	Paul
Saved aroma Christ	**2:15** [15]For we are unto God a sweet savour of Christ, in them that are saved, and in them that perish: **4:3** [3]But if our gospel be hid, it is hid to them that are lost:	**1 Cor 1:18** [18]For the preaching of the cross is to them that perish foolishness; but unto us which are saved it is the power of God.

2 CORINTHIANS 2:17—Paul's ministry (2:14–7:4), 57 CE

Theme	2 COR	Paul
Speaking in Christ	**2:17** [17]For we are not as many, which corrupt the word of God: but as of sincerity, but as of God, in the sight of God speak we in Christ. **4:2** [2]But have renounced the hidden things of dishonesty, not walking in craftiness, nor handling the word of God deceitfully; but by manifestation of the truth commending ourselves to every man's conscience in the sight of God.	**1 Cor 5:8** [8]Therefore let us keep the feast, not with old leaven, neither with the leaven of malice and wickedness; but with the unleavened bread of sincerity and truth.

2 CORINTHIANS Ch 3—Paul's ministry (2:14–7:4), 57 CE

Theme	2 COR	Mt	Lk	Paul
Jesus' law written on human hearts	**Ch 3** [1]Do we begin again to commend ourselves? or need we, as some others, epistles of commendation to you, or letters of commendation from you? [2]Ye are our epistle written in our hearts, known and read of all men: [3]Forasmuch as ye are manifestly declared to be the epistle of Christ ministered by us, written not with ink, but with the Spirit of the living God; not in tables of stone, but in fleshy tables of the heart. [4]And such trust have we through Christ to God-ward: [5]Not that we are sufficient of ourselves to think any thing as of ourselves; but our sufficiency is of God; [6]Who also hath made us able ministers of the new testament; not of the letter, but of the spirit: for the letter killeth, but the spirit giveth life. [7]But if the ministration of death, written and engraven in stones, was glorious, so that the children of Israel could not stedfastly behold the face of Moses for the glory of his countenance; which glory was to be done away: [8]How shall not the ministration of the spirit be rather glorious? [9]For if the ministration of condemnation be glory, much more doth the ministration of righteousness exceed in glory. [10]For even that which was made glorious had no glory in this respect, by reason of the glory that excelleth. [11]For if that which is done away was glorious, much more that which remaineth is glorious. [12]Seeing then that we have such hope, we use great plainness of speech: [13]And not as Moses, which put a veil over his face, that the children of Israel could not stedfastly look to the end of that which is abolished: [14]But their minds were blinded: for until this day remaineth the same veil untaken away in the reading of the old testament; which veil is done away in Christ. [15]But even unto this day, when Moses is read, the veil is upon their heart. [16]Nevertheless when it shall turn to the Lord, the veil shall be taken away. [17]Now the Lord is that Spirit: and where the Spirit of the Lord is, there is liberty. [18]But we all, with open face beholding as in a glass the glory of the Lord, are changed into the same image from glory to glory, even as by the Spirit of the Lord.	**5:17–20** [17]Think not that I am come to destroy the law, or the prophets: I am not come to destroy, but to fulfil. [18]For verily I say unto you, Till heaven and earth pass, one jot or one tittle shall in no wise pass from the law, till all be fulfilled. [19]Whosoever therefore shall break one of these least commandments, and shall teach men so, he shall be called the least in the kingdom of heaven: but whosoever shall do and teach them, the same shall be called great in the kingdom of heaven. [20]For I say unto you, That except your righteousness shall exceed the righteousness of the scribes and Pharisees, ye shall in no case enter into the kingdom of heaven.	**24:44** [44]And he said unto them, These are the words which I spake unto you, while I was yet with you, that all things must be fulfilled, which were written in the law of Moses, and in the prophets, and in the psalms, concerning me.	**Rom 7:12** [12]Wherefore the law is holy, and the commandment holy, and just, and good. **Rom 8:4** [4]That the righteousness of the law might be fulfilled in us, who walk not after the flesh, but after the Spirit. **Rom 12:8–10** [8]Or he that exhorteth, on exhortation: he that giveth, let him do it with simplicity; he that ruleth, with diligence; he that showeth mercy, with cheerfulness. [9]Let love be without dissimulation. Abhor that which is evil; cleave to that which is good. [10]Be kindly affectioned one to another with brotherly love; in honour preferring one another; **Gal 5:14** [14]For all the law is fulfilled in one word, even in this; Thou shalt love thy neighbour as thyself.

Jewish Writings	Other
Jer 31	**Q-Quelle**
[1]At the same time, saith the LORD, will I be the God of all the families of Israel, and they shall be my people. [2]Thus saith the LORD, The people which were left of the sword found grace in the wilderness; even Israel, when I went to cause him to rest. [3]The LORD hath appeared of old unto me, saying, Yea, I have loved thee with an everlasting love: therefore with lovingkindness have I drawn thee. [4]Again I will build thee, and thou shalt be built, O virgin of Israel: thou shalt again be adorned with thy tabrets, and shalt go forth in the dances of them that make merry. [5]Thou shalt yet plant vines upon the mountains of Samaria: the planters shall plant, and shall eat them as common things. [6]For there shall be a day, that the watchmen upon the mount Ephraim shall cry, Arise ye, and let us go up to Zion unto the LORD our God. [7]For thus saith the LORD; Sing with gladness for Jacob, and shout among the chief of the nations: publish ye, praise ye, and say, O LORD, save thy people, the remnant of Israel. [8]Behold, I will bring them from the north country, and gather them from the coasts of the earth, and with them the blind and the lame, the woman with child and her that travaileth with child together: a great company shall return thither. [9]They shall come with weeping, and with supplications will I lead them: I will cause them to walk by the rivers of waters in a straight way, wherein they shall not stumble: for I am a father to Israel, and Ephraim is my firstborn. [10]Hear the word of the LORD, O ye nations, and declare it in the isles afar off, and say, He that scattered Israel will gather him, and keep him, as a shepherd doth his flock. [11]For the LORD hath redeemed Jacob, and ransomed him from the hand of him that was stronger than he. [12]Therefore they shall come and sing in the height of Zion, and shall flow together to the goodness of the LORD, for wheat, and for wine, and for oil, and for the young of the flock and of the herd: and their soul shall be as a watered garden; and they shall not sorrow any more at all. [13]Then shall the virgin rejoice in the dance, both young men and old together: for I will turn their mourning into joy, and will comfort them, and make them rejoice from their sorrow. [14]And I will satiate the soul of the priests with fatness, and my people shall be satisfied with my goodness, saith the LORD. [15]Thus saith the LORD; A voice was heard in Ramah, lamentation, and bitter weeping; Rahel weeping for her children refused to be comforted for her children, because they were not. [16]Thus saith the LORD; Refrain thy voice from weeping, and thine eyes from tears: for thy work shall be rewarded, saith the LORD; and they shall come again from the land of the enemy. [17]And there is hope in thine end, saith the LORD, that thy children shall come again to their own border. [18]I have surely heard Ephraim bemoaning himself thus; Thou hast chastised me, and I was chastised, as a bullock unaccustomed to the yoke: turn thou me, and I shall be turned; for thou art the LORD my God. [19]Surely after that I was turned, I repented; and after that I was instructed, I smote upon my thigh: I was ashamed, yea, even confounded, because I did bear the reproach of my youth. [20]Is Ephraim my dear son? is he a pleasant child? for since I spake against him, I do earnestly remember him still: therefore my bowels are troubled for him; I will surely have mercy upon him, saith the LORD. [21]Set thee up waymarks, make thee high heaps: set thine heart toward the highway, even the way which thou wentest: turn again, O virgin of Israel, turn again to these thy cities. [22]How long wilt thou go about, O thou backsliding daughter? for the LORD hath created a new thing in the earth, A woman shall compass a man. [23]Thus saith the LORD of hosts, the God of Israel; As yet they shall use this speech in the land of Judah and in the cities thereof, when I shall bring again their captivity; The LORD bless thee, O habitation of justice, and mountain of holiness. [24]And there shall dwell in Judah itself, and in all the cities thereof together, husbandmen, and they that go forth with flocks. [25]For I have satiated the weary soul, and I have replenished every sorrowful soul. [26]Upon this I awaked, and beheld; and my sleep was sweet unto me. [27]Behold, the days come, saith the LORD, that I will sow the house of Israel and the house of Judah with the seed of man, and with the seed of beast. [28]And it shall come to pass, that like as I have watched over them, to pluck up, and to break down, and to throw down, and to destroy, and to afflict; so will I watch over them, to build, and to plant, saith the LORD. [29]In those days they shall say no more, The fathers have eaten a sour grape, and the children's teeth are set on edge. [30]But every one shall die for his own iniquity: every man that eateth the sour grape, his teeth shall be set on edge. [31]Behold, the days come, saith the LORD, that I will make a new covenant with the house of Israel, and with the house of Judah: [32]Not according to the covenant that I made with their fathers in the day that I took them by the hand to bring them out of the land of Egypt; which my covenant they brake, although I was an husband unto them, saith the LORD: [33]But this shall be the covenant that I will make with the house of Israel; After those days, saith the LORD, I will put my law in their inward parts, and write it in their hearts; and will be their God, and they shall be my people. [34]And they shall teach no more every man his neighbour, and every man his brother, saying, Know the LORD: for they shall all know me, from the least of them unto the greatest of them, saith the LORD: for I will forgive their iniquity, and I will remember their sin no more. [35]Thus saith the LORD, which giveth the sun for a light by day, and the ordinances of the moon and of the stars for a light by night, which divideth the sea when the waves thereof roar; The LORD of hosts is his name: [36]If those ordinances depart from before me, saith the LORD, then the seed of Israel also shall cease from being a nation before me for ever. [37]Thus saith the LORD; If heaven above can be measured, and the foundations of the earth searched out beneath, I will also cast off all the seed of Israel for all that they have done, saith the LORD. [38]Behold, the days come, saith the LORD, that the city shall be built to the LORD from the tower of Hananeel unto the gate of the corner. [39]And the measuring line shall yet go forth over against it upon the hill Gareb, and shall compass about to Goath. [40]And the whole valley of the dead bodies, and of the ashes, and all the fields unto the brook of Kidron, unto the corner of the horse gate toward the east, shall be holy unto the LORD; it shall not be plucked up, nor thrown down any more for ever.	Concerning Law: 2 Cor Ch 3/Rom 7:12/Mt 5:18, [Mt 11:12-13]/ [Lk 16:16-17 (QS 56)]

2 CORINTHIANS 3:1—Paul's ministry (2:14–7:4), 57 CE

Theme	2 COR	Lk	Paul
Re: letters of commen-dation	**3:1** [1]Do we begin again to commend ourselves? or need we, as some others, epistles of commendation to you, or letters of commendation from you?	**Acts 18:27** [27]And when he was disposed to pass into Achaia, the brethren wrote, exhorting the disciples to receive him: who, when he was come, helped them much which had believed through grace:	**Rom 16:1** [1]I commend unto you Phebe our sister, which is a servant of the church which is at Cenchrea: **1 Cor 16:3** [3]And when I come, whomsoever ye shall approve by your letters, them will I send to bring your liberality unto Jerusalem.

2 CORINTHIANS 3:3—Paul's ministry (2:14–7:4), 57 CE

Theme	2 COR	Jewish Writings
Gospel is spiritual message	**3:3** [3]Forasmuch as ye are manifestly declared to be the epistle of Christ ministered by us, written not with ink, but with the Spirit of the living God; not in tables of stone, but in fleshy tables of the heart.	**Ex 24:12** [12]And the LORD said unto Moses, Come up to me into the mount, and be there: and I will give thee tables of stone, and a law, and commandments which I have written; that thou mayest teach them. **Ex 31:18** [18]And he gave unto Moses, when he had made an end of communing with him upon mount Sinai, two tables of testimony, tables of stone, written with the finger of God. **Ex 32:15–19** [15]And Moses turned, and went down from the mount, and the two tables of the testimony were in his hand: the tables were written on both their sides; on the one side and on the other were they written. [16]And the tables were the work of God, and the writing was the writing of God, graven upon the tables. [17]And when Joshua heard the noise of the people as they shouted, he said unto Moses, There is a noise of war in the camp. [18]And he said, It is not the voice of them that shout for mastery, neither is it the voice of them that cry for being overcome: but the noise of them that sing do I hear. [19]And it came to pass, as soon as he came nigh unto the camp, that he saw the calf, and the dancing: and Moses' anger waxed hot, and he cast the tables out of his hands, and brake them beneath the mount. **Jer 31:33** [33]But this shall be the covenant that I will make with the house of Israel; After those days, saith the LORD, I will put my law in their inward parts, and write it in their hearts; and will be their God, and they shall be my people. **Ezek 11:19** [19]And I will give them one heart, and I will put a new spirit within you; and I will take the stony heart out of their flesh, and will give them an heart of flesh: **Ezek 36:26–27** [26]A new heart also will I give you, and a new spirit will I put within you: and I will take away the stony heart out of your flesh, and I will give you an heart of flesh. [27]And I will put my spirit within you, and cause you to walk in my statutes, and ye shall keep my judgments, and do them.

2 CORINTHIANS 3:5—Paul's ministry (2:14–7:4), 57 CE

Theme	2 COR	Jn
Sufficiency in God	**3:5** [5]Not that we are sufficient of ourselves to think any thing as of ourselves; but our sufficiency is of God;	**3:27** [27]John answered and said, A man can receive nothing, except it be given him from heaven.

2 CORINTHIANS 3:6—Paul's ministry (2:14–7:4), 57 CE

Theme	2 COR	Paul	Jewish Writings
Spirit gives life & makes able ministers	**3:6** [6]Who also hath made us able ministers of the new testament; not of the letter, but of the spirit: for the letter killeth, but the spirit giveth life.	**Eph 3:7 (Pseudo)** [7]Whereof I was made a minister, according to the gift of the grace of God given unto me by the effectual working of his power.	**Jer 31:31–34** [31]Behold, the days come, saith the LORD, that I will make a new covenant with the house of Israel, and with the house of Judah: [32]Not according to the covenant that I made with their fathers in the day that I took them by the hand to bring them out of the land of Egypt; which my covenant they brake, although I was an husband unto them, saith the LORD: [33]But this shall be the covenant that I will make with the house of Israel; After those days, saith the LORD, I will put my law in their inward parts, and write it in their hearts; and will be their God, and they shall be my people. [34]And they shall teach no more every man his neighbour, and every man his brother, saying, Know the LORD: for they shall all know me, from the least of them unto the greatest of them, saith the LORD: for I will forgive their iniquity, and I will remember their sin no more.

2 CORINTHIANS 3:7—Paul's ministry (2:14–7:4), 57 CE

Theme	2 COR	Jewish Writings
Israel's children could not see God's face	**3:7** [7]But if the ministration of death, written and engraven in stones, was glorious, so that the children of Israel could not stedfastly behold the face of Moses for the glory of his countenance; which glory was to be done away:	**Ex 34:29–35** [29]And it came to pass, when Moses came down from mount Sinai with the two tables of testimony in Moses' hand, when he came down from the mount, that Moses wist not that the skin of his face shone while he talked with him. [30]And when Aaron and all the children of Israel saw Moses, behold, the skin of his face shone; and they were afraid to come nigh him. [31]And Moses called unto them; and Aaron and all the rulers of the congregation returned unto him: and Moses talked with them. [32]And afterward all the children of Israel came nigh: and he gave them in commandment all that the LORD had spoken with him in mount Sinai. [33]And till Moses had done speaking with them, he put a veil on his face. [34]But when Moses went in before the LORD to speak with him, he took the veil off, until he came out. And he came out, and spake unto the children of Israel that which he was commanded. [35]And the children of Israel saw the face of Moses, that the skin of Moses' face shone: and Moses put the veil upon his face again, until he went in to speak with him.

2 CORINTHIANS 3:15—Paul's ministry (2:14–7:4), 57 CE

Theme	2 COR	Paul
Moses wore veil before Israel	**3:15** [15]But even unto this day, when Moses is read, the veil is upon their heart.	**Rom 11:7–10** [7]What then? Israel hath not obtained that which he seeketh for; but the election hath obtained it, and the rest were blinded [8](According as it is written, God hath given them the spirit of slumber, eyes that they should not see, and ears that they should not hear;) unto this day. [9]And David saith, Let their table be made a snare, and a trap, and a stumblingblock, and a recompense unto them: [10]Let their eyes be darkened, that they may not see, and bow down their back alway.

2 CORINTHIANS 3:16—Paul's ministry (2:14–7:4), 57 CE

Theme	2 COR	Jewish Writings
With Christ veil is removed	**3:16** [16]Nevertheless when it shall turn to the Lord, the veil shall be taken away.	**Ex 34:34** [34]But when Moses went in before the LORD to speak with him, he took the veil off, until he came out. And he came out, and spake unto the children of Israel that which he was commanded.

2 CORINTHIANS 3:18—Paul's ministry (2:14–7:4), 57 CE

Theme	2 COR	Mt	Mk	Jn
Glory of the Lord	**3:18** [18]But we all, with open face beholding as in a glass the glory of the Lord, are changed into the same image from glory to glory, even as by the Spirit of the Lord.	**19:8** [8]He saith unto them, Moses because of the hardness of your hearts suffered you to put away your wives: but from the beginning it was not so.	**10:6** [6]But from the beginning of the creation God made them male and female.	**1 Jn 3:2** [2]Beloved, now are we the sons of God, and it doth not yet appear what we shall be: but we know that, when he shall appear, we shall be like him; for we shall see him as he is.

Paul

Rom 1:3

[3]Concerning his Son Jesus Christ our Lord, which was made of the seed of David according to the flesh;

Rom 5

[1]Therefore being justified by faith, we have peace with God through our Lord Jesus Christ: [2]By whom also we have access by faith into this grace wherein we stand, and rejoice in hope of the glory of God. [3]And not only so, but we glory in tribulations also: knowing that tribulation worketh patience; [4]And patience, experience; and experience, hope: [5]And hope maketh not ashamed; because the love of God is shed abroad in our hearts by the Holy Ghost which is given unto us. [6]For when we were yet without strength, in due time Christ died for the ungodly. [7]For scarcely for a righteous man will one die: yet peradventure for a good man some would even dare to die. [8]But God commendeth his love toward us, in that, while we were yet sinners, Christ died for us. [9]Much more then, being now justified by his blood, we shall be saved from wrath through him. [10]For if, when we were enemies, we were reconciled to God by the death of his Son, much more, being reconciled, we shall be saved by his life. [11]And not only so, but we also joy in God through our Lord Jesus Christ, by whom we have now received the atonement. [12]Wherefore, as by one man sin entered into the world, and death by sin; and so death passed upon all men, for that all have sinned: [13](For until the law sin was in the world: but sin is not imputed when there is no law. [14]Nevertheless death reigned from Adam to Moses, even over them that had not sinned after the similitude of Adam's transgression, who is the figure of him that was to come. [15]But not as the offence, so also is the free gift. For if through the offence of one many be dead, much more the grace of God, and the gift by grace, which is by one man, Jesus Christ, hath abounded unto many. [16]And not as it was by one that sinned, so is the gift: for the judgment was by one to condemnation, but the free gift is of many offences unto justification. [17]For if by one man's offence death reigned by one; much more they which receive abundance of grace and of the gift of righteousness shall reign in life by one, Jesus Christ.) [18]Therefore as by the offence of one judgment came upon all men to condemnation; even so by the righteousness of one the free gift came upon all men unto justification of life. [19]For as by one man's disobedience many were made sinners, so by the obedience of one shall many be made righteous. [20]Moreover the law entered, that the offence might abound. But where sin abounded, grace did much more abound: [21]That as sin hath reigned unto death, even so might grace reign through righteousness unto eternal life by Jesus Christ our Lord.

Rom 8:29–30

[29]For whom he did foreknow, he also did predestinate to be conformed to the image of his Son, that he might be the firstborn among many brethren. [30]Moreover whom he did predestinate, them he also called: and whom he called, them he also justified: and whom he justified, them he also glorified.

Rom 12:2

[2]And be not conformed to this world: but be ye transformed by the renewing of your mind, that ye may prove what is that good, and acceptable, and perfect, will of God.

1 Cor 15:27

[27]For he hath put all things under his feet. But when he saith all things are put under him, it is manifest that he is excepted, which did put all things under him.

1 Cor 15:49

[49]And as we have borne the image of the earthy, we shall also bear the image of the heavenly.

Gal 4:4

[4]But when the fulness of the time was come, God sent forth his Son, made of a woman, made under the law,

Gal 4:19

[19]My little children, of whom I travail in birth again until Christ be formed in you,

(*Continued*)

2 CORINTHIANS 3:18—Paul's ministry (2:14–7:4), 57 CE

Theme	2 COR	Paul
(Cont.) **Glory of the Lord**	**3:18 (above)**	***(Continued)*** **Phil 2** 1If there be therefore any consolation in Christ, if any comfort of love, if any fellowship of the Spirit, if any bowels and mercies, 2Fulfil ye my joy, that ye be likeminded, having the same love, being of one accord, of one mind. 3Let nothing be done through strife or vainglory; but in lowliness of mind let each esteem other better than themselves. 4Look not every man on his own things, but every man also on the things of others. 5Let this mind be in you, which was also in Christ Jesus: 6Who, being in the form of God, thought it not robbery to be equal with God: 7But made himself of no reputation, and took upon him the form of a servant, and was made in the likeness of men: 8And being found in fashion as a man, he humbled himself, and became obedient unto death, even the death of the cross. 9Wherefore God also hath highly exalted him, and given him a name which is above every name: 10That at the name of Jesus every knee should bow, of things in heaven, and things in earth, and things under the earth; 11And that every tongue should confess that Jesus Christ is Lord, to the glory of God the Father. 12Wherefore, my beloved, as ye have always obeyed, not as in my presence only, but now much more in my absence, work out your own salvation with fear and trembling. 13For it is God which worketh in you both to will and to do of his good pleasure. 14Do all things without murmurings and disputings: 15That ye may be blameless and harmless, the sons of God, without rebuke, in the midst of a crooked and perverse nation, among whom ye shine as lights in the world; 16Holding forth the word of life; that I may rejoice in the day of Christ, that I have not run in vain, neither laboured in vain. 17Yea, and if I be offered upon the sacrifice and service of your faith, I joy, and rejoice with you all. 18For the same cause also do ye joy, and rejoice with me. 19But I trust in the Lord Jesus to send Timotheus shortly unto you, that I also may be of good comfort, when I know your state. 20For I have no man likeminded, who will naturally care for your state. 21For all seek their own, not the things which are Jesus Christ's. 22But ye know the proof of him, that, as a son with the father, he hath served with me in the gospel. 23Him therefore I hope to send presently, so soon as I shall see how it will go with me. 24But I trust in the Lord that I also myself shall come shortly. 25Yet I supposed it necessary to send to you Epaphroditus, my brother, and companion in labour, and fellowsoldier, but your messenger, and he that ministered to my wants. 26For he longed after you all, and was full of heaviness, because that ye had heard that he had been sick. 27For indeed he was sick nigh unto death: but God had mercy on him; and not on him only, but on me also, lest I should have sorrow upon sorrow. 28I sent him therefore the more carefully, that, when ye see him again, ye may rejoice, and that I may be the less sorrowful. 29Receive him therefore in the Lord with all gladness; and hold such in reputation: 30Because for the work of Christ he was nigh unto death, not regarding his life, to supply your lack of service toward me. **Phil 3:10** 10That I may know him, and the power of his resurrection, and the fellowship of his sufferings, being made conformable unto his death; **Phil 3:20-21** 20For our conversation is in heaven; from whence also we look for the Saviour, the Lord Jesus Christ: 21Who shall change our vile body, that it may be fashioned like unto his glorious body, according to the working whereby he is able even to subdue all things unto himself. **Phil 4:4–6** 4Rejoice in the Lord alway: and again I say, Rejoice. 5Let your moderation be known unto all men. The Lord is at hand. 6Be careful for nothing; but in every thing by prayer and supplication with thanksgiving let your requests be made known unto God. **Col 1:15** 15Who is the image of the invisible God, the firstborn of every creature: **Col 3:9–11** 9Lie not one to another, seeing that ye have put off the old man with his deeds; 10And have put on the new man, which is renewed in knowledge after the image of him that created him: 11Where there is neither Greek nor Jew, circumcision nor uncircumcision, Barbarian, Scythian, bond nor free: but Christ is all, and in all. **Col 3:10** 10And have put on the new man, which is renewed in knowledge after the image of him that created him:

Jewish Writings	Other
Gen 1:28	**Q-Quelle**
[28]And God blessed them, and God said unto them, Be fruitful, and multiply, and replenish the earth, and subdue it: and have dominion over the fish of the sea, and over the fowl of the air, and over every living thing that moveth upon the earth.	Jesus' witness to John: 2 Cor 3:18/Gal 4:4/[Mt 11:7-19, 21:31-32]/[Lk 7:24-35 (QS 17 [Thom 46, 74], QS 18)], [Lk 16:16 (QS 56)]; Against Pharisees: 2 Cor 3:18/Gal 4:4/ [Mt 23:4-36]/[Mk 7:1-9]/[Lk 11:37-54 (QS 34 [Thom 39:1, 89, 102])]

2 CORINTHIANS 4:2—Paul's ministry (2:14–7:4), 57 CE

Theme	2 COR	Paul
Renounce evil, walk in truth	**4:2** [2]But have renounced the hidden things of dishonesty, not walking in craftiness, nor handling the word of God deceitfully; but by manifestation of the truth commending ourselves to every man's conscience in the sight of God. **2:17** [17]For we are not as many, which corrupt the word of God: but as of sincerity, but as of God, in the sight of God speak we in Christ.	**1 Thes 2:4–7** [4]But as we were allowed of God to be put in trust with the gospel, even so we speak; not as pleasing men, but God, which trieth our hearts. [5]For neither at any time used we flattering words, as ye know, nor a cloak of covetousness; God is witness: [6]Nor of men sought we glory, neither of you, nor yet of others, when we might have been burdensome, as the apostles of Christ. [7]But we were gentle among you, even as a nurse cherisheth her children:

2 CORINTHIANS 4:3—Paul's ministry (2:14–7:4), 57 CE

Theme	2 COR	Paul
Gospel hidden to lost	**4:3** [3]But if our gospel be hid, it is hid to them that are lost: **2:15–16** [15]For we are unto God a sweet savour of Christ, in them that are saved, and in them that perish: [16]To the one we are the savour of death unto death; and to the other the savour of life unto life. And who is sufficient for these things?	**2 Thes 2:10** [10]And with all deceivableness of unrighteousness in them that perish; because they received not the love of the truth, that they might be saved.

2 CORINTHIANS 4:4—Paul's ministry (2:14–7:4), 57 CE

Theme	2 COR	Mt
Sowing and reaping	**4:4** [4]In whom the god of this world hath blinded the minds of them which believe not, lest the light of the glorious gospel of Christ, who is the image of God, should shine unto them. **9:10** [10]Now he that ministereth seed to the sower both minister bread for your food, and multiply your seed sown, and increase the fruits of your righteousness;)	**13:1–30** [1]The same day went Jesus out of the house, and sat by the sea side. [2]And great multitudes were gathered together unto him, so that he went into a ship, and sat; and the whole multitude stood on the shore. [3]And he spake many things unto them in parables, saying, Behold, a sower went forth to sow; [4]And when he sowed, some seeds fell by the way side, and the fowls came and devoured them up: [5]Some fell upon stony places, where they had not much earth: and forthwith they sprung up, because they had no deepness of earth: [6]And when the sun was up, they were scorched; and because they had no root, they withered away. [7]And some fell among thorns; and the thorns sprung up, and choked them: [8]But other fell into good ground, and brought forth fruit, some an hundredfold, some sixtyfold, some thirtyfold. [9]Who hath ears to hear, let him hear. [10]And the disciples came, and said unto him, Why speakest thou unto them in parables? [11]He answered and said unto them, Because it is given unto you to know the mysteries of the kingdom of heaven, but to them it is not given. [12]For whosoever hath, to him shall be given, and he shall have more abundance: but whosoever hath not, from him shall be taken away even that he hath. [13]Therefore speak I to them in parables: because they seeing see not; and hearing they hear not, neither do they understand. [14]And in them is fulfilled the prophecy of Esaias, which saith, By hearing ye shall hear, and shall not understand; and seeing ye shall see, and shall not perceive: [15]For this people's heart is waxed gross, and their ears are dull of hearing, and their eyes they have closed; lest at any time they should see with their eyes, and hear with their ears, and should understand with their heart, and should be converted, and I should heal them. [16]But blessed are your eyes, for they see: and your ears, for they hear. [17]For verily I say unto you, That many prophets and righteous men have desired to see those things which ye see, and have not seen them; and to hear those things which ye hear, and have not heard them. [18]Hear ye therefore the parable of the sower. [19]When any one heareth the word of the kingdom, and understandeth it not, then cometh the wicked one, and catcheth away that which was sown in his heart. This is he which received seed by the way side. [20]But he that received the seed into stony places, the same is he that heareth the word, and anon with joy receiveth it; [21]Yet hath he not root in himself, but dureth for a while: for when tribulation or persecution ariseth because of the word, by and by he is offended. [22]He also that received seed among the thorns is he that heareth the word; and the care of this world, and the deceitfulness of riches, choke the word, and he becometh unfruitful. [23]But he that received seed into the good ground is he that heareth the word, and understandeth it; which also beareth fruit, and bringeth forth, some an hundredfold, some sixty, some thirty. [24]Another parable put he forth unto them, saying, The kingdom of heaven is likened unto a man which sowed good seed in his field: [25]But while men slept, his enemy came and sowed tares among the wheat, and went his way. [26]But when the blade was sprung up, and brought forth fruit, then appeared the tares also. [27]So the servants of the householder came and said unto him, Sir, didst not thou sow good seed in thy field? from whence then hath it tares? [28]He said unto them, An enemy hath done this. The servants said unto him, Wilt thou then that we go and gather them up? [29]But he said, Nay; lest while ye gather up the tares, ye root up also the wheat with them. [30]Let both grow together until the harvest: and in the time of harvest I will say to the reapers, Gather ye together first the tares, and bind them in bundles to burn them: but gather the wheat into my barn.

Mk	Lk	Jn
4:1–20 1And he began again to teach by the sea side: and there was gathered unto him a great multitude, so that he entered into a ship, and sat in the sea; and the whole multitude was by the sea on the land. 2And he taught them many things by parables, and said unto them in his doctrine, 3Hearken; Behold, there went out a sower to sow: 4And it came to pass, as he sowed, some fell by the way side, and the fowls of the air came and devoured it up. 5And some fell on stony ground, where it had not much earth; and immediately it sprang up, because it had no depth of earth: 6But when the sun was up, it was scorched; and because it had no root, it withered away. 7And some fell among thorns, and the thorns grew up, and choked it, and it yielded no fruit. 8And other fell on good ground, and did yield fruit that sprang up and increased; and brought forth, some thirty, and some sixty, and some an hundred. 9And he said unto them, He that hath ears to hear, let him hear. 10And when he was alone, they that were about him with the twelve asked of him the parable. 11And he said unto them, Unto you it is given to know the mystery of the kingdom of God: but unto them that are without, all these things are done in parables: 12That seeing they may see, and not perceive; and hearing they may hear, and not understand; lest at any time they should be converted, and their sins should be forgiven them. 13And he said unto them, Know ye not this parable? and how then will ye know all parables? 14The sower soweth the word. **15And these are they by the way side, where the word is sown; but when they have heard, Satan cometh immediately, and taketh away the word that was sown in their hearts.** 16And these are they likewise which are sown on stony ground; who, when they have heard the word, immediately receive it with gladness; 17And have no root in themselves, and so endure but for a time: afterward, when affliction or persecution ariseth for the word's sake, immediately they are offended. 18And these are they which are sown among thorns; such as hear the word, 19And the cares of this world, and the deceitfulness of riches, and the lusts of other things entering in, choke the word, and it becometh unfruitful. 20And these are they which are sown on good ground; such as hear the word, and receive it, and bring forth fruit, some thirtyfold, some sixty, and some an hundred. **4:26–29** 26And he said, So is the kingdom of God, as if a man should cast seed into the ground; 27And should sleep, and rise night and day, and the seed should spring and grow up, he knoweth not how. 28For the earth bringeth forth fruit of herself; first the blade, then the ear, after that the full corn in the ear. 29But when the fruit is brought forth, immediately he putteth in the sickle, because the harvest is come.	**8:4–15** 4And when much people were gathered together, and were come to him out of every city, he spake by a parable: 5A sower went out to sow his seed: and as he sowed, some fell by the way side; and it was trodden down, and the fowls of the air devoured it. 6And some fell upon a rock; and as soon as it was sprung up, it withered away, because it lacked moisture. 7And some fell among thorns; and the thorns sprang up with it, and choked it. 8And other fell on good ground, and sprang up, and bare fruit an hundredfold. And when he had said these things, he cried, He that hath ears to hear, let him hear. 9And his disciples asked him, saying, What might this parable be? 10And he said, Unto you it is given to know the mysteries of the kingdom of God: but to others in parables; that seeing they might not see, and hearing they might not understand. 11Now the parable is this: The seed is the word of God. 12Those by the way side are they that hear; then cometh the devil, and taketh away the word out of their hearts, lest they should believe and be saved. 13They on the rock are they, which, when they hear, receive the word with joy; and these have no root, which for a while believe, and in time of temptation fall away. 14And that which fell among thorns are they, which, when they have heard, go forth, and are choked with cares and riches and pleasures of this life, and bring no fruit to perfection. 15But that on the good ground are they, which in an honest and good heart, having heard the word, keep it, and bring forth fruit with patience.	**12:31–36** 31Now is the judgment of this world: now shall the prince of this world be cast out. 32And I, if I be lifted up from the earth, will draw all men unto me. 33This he said, signifying what death he should die. 34The people answered him, We have heard out of the law that Christ abideth for ever: and how sayest thou, The Son of man must be lifted up? who is this Son of man? 35Then Jesus said unto them, Yet a little while is the light with you. Walk while ye have the light, lest darkness come upon you: for he that walketh in darkness knoweth not whither he goeth. 36While ye have light, believe in the light, that ye may be the children of light. These things spake Jesus, and departed, and did hide himself from them.

2 Corinthians 4:4 continued on next page

2 CORINTHIANS 4:4—Paul's ministry (2:14–7:4), 57 CE

Theme	2 COR	Paul
(*Cont.*) **Sowing and reaping**	**4:4** **(above)** **9:10** **(above)**	**1 Cor 3:6** [6]I have planted, Apollos watered; but God gave the increase. **1 Cor 9** [1]Am I not an apostle? am I not free? have I not seen Jesus Christ our Lord? are not ye my work in the Lord? [2]If I be not an apostle unto others, yet doubtless I am to you: for the seal of mine apostleship are ye in the Lord. [3]Mine answer to them that do examine me is this, [4]Have we not power to eat and to drink? [5]Have we not power to lead about a sister, a wife, as well as other apostles, and as the brethren of the Lord, and Cephas? [6]Or I only and Barnabas, have not we power to forbear working? [7]Who goeth a warfare any time at his own charges? who planteth a vineyard, and eateth not of the fruit thereof? or who feedeth a flock, and eateth not of the milk of the flock? [8]Say I these things as a man? or saith not the law the same also? [9]For it is written in the law of Moses, Thou shalt not muzzle the mouth of the ox that treadeth out the corn. Doth God take care for oxen? [10]Or saith he it altogether for our sakes? For our sakes, no doubt, this is written: that he that ploweth should plow in hope; and that he that thresheth in hope should be partaker of his hope. [11]If we have sown unto you spiritual things, is it a great thing if we shall reap your carnal things? [12]If others be partakers of this power over you, are not we rather? Nevertheless we have not used this power; but suffer all things, lest we should hinder the gospel of Christ. [13]Do ye not know that they which minister about holy things live of the things of the temple? and they which wait at the altar are partakers with the altar? [14]Even so hath the Lord ordained that they which preach the gospel should live of the gospel. [15]But I have used none of these things: neither have I written these things, that it should be so done unto me: for it were better for me to die, than that any man should make my glorying void. [16]For though I preach the gospel, I have nothing to glory of: for necessity is laid upon me; yea, woe is unto me, if I preach not the gospel! [17]For if I do this thing willingly, I have a reward: but if against my will, a dispensation of the gospel is committed unto me. [18]What is my reward then? Verily that, when I preach the gospel, I may make the gospel of Christ without charge, that I abuse not my power in the gospel. [19]For though I be free from all men, yet have I made myself servant unto all, that I might gain the more. [20]And unto the Jews I became as a Jew, that I might gain the Jews; to them that are under the law, as under the law, that I might gain them that are under the law; [21]To them that are without law, as without law, (being not without law to God, but under the law to Christ,) that I might gain them that are without law. [22]To the weak became I as weak, that I might gain the weak: I am made all things to all men, that I might by all means save some. [23]And this I do for the gospel's sake, that I might be partaker thereof with you. [24]Know ye not that they which run in a race run all, but one receiveth the prize? So run, that ye may obtain. [25]And every man that striveth for the mastery is temperate in all things. Now they do it to obtain a corruptible crown; but we an incorruptible. [26]I therefore so run, not as uncertainly; so fight I, not as one that beateth the air: [27]But I keep under my body, and bring it into subjection: lest that by any means, when I have preached to others, I myself should be a castaway. **1 Cor 9:7** [7]Who goeth a warfare any time at his own charges? who planteth a vineyard, and eateth not of the fruit thereof? or who feedeth a flock, and eateth not of the milk of the flock? **1 Cor, 9:11** [11]If we have sown unto you spiritual things, is it a great thing if we shall reap your carnal things?

Paul (*Continued*)	Other
Continued **Gal 5** [1]Stand fast therefore in the liberty wherewith Christ hath made us free, and be not entangled again with the yoke of bondage. [2]Behold, I Paul say unto you, that if ye be circumcised, Christ shall profit you nothing. [3]For I testify again to every man that is circumcised, that he is a debtor to do the whole law. [4]Christ is become of no effect unto you, whosoever of you are justified by the law; ye are fallen from grace. [5]For we through the Spirit wait for the hope of righteousness by faith. [6]For in Jesus Christ neither circumcision availeth any thing, nor uncircumcision; but faith which worketh by love. [7]Ye did run well; who did hinder you that ye should not obey the truth? [8]This persuasion cometh not of him that calleth you. [9]A little leaven leaveneth the whole lump. [10]I have confidence in you through the Lord, that ye will be none otherwise minded: but he that troubleth you shall bear his judgment, whosoever he be. [11]And I, brethren, if I yet preach circumcision, why do I yet suffer persecution? then is the offence of the cross ceased. [12]I would they were even cut off which trouble you. [13]For, brethren, ye have been called unto liberty; only use not liberty for an occasion to the flesh, but by love serve one another. [14]For all the law is fulfilled in one word, even in this; Thou shalt love thy neighbour as thyself. [15]But if ye bite and devour one another, take heed that ye be not consumed one of another. [16]This I say then, Walk in the Spirit, and ye shall not fulfil the lust of the flesh. [17]For the flesh lusteth against the Spirit, and the Spirit against the flesh: and these are contrary the one to the other: so that ye cannot do the things that ye would. [18]But if ye be led of the Spirit, ye are not under the law. [19]Now the works of the flesh are manifest, which are these; Adultery, fornication, uncleanness, lasciviousness, [20]Idolatry, witchcraft, hatred, variance, emulations, wrath, strife, seditions, heresies, [21]Envyings, murders, drunkenness, revellings, and such like: of the which I tell you before, as I have also told you in time past, that they which do such things shall not inherit the kingdom of God. [22]But the fruit of the Spirit is love, joy, peace, longsuffering, gentleness, goodness, faith, [23]Meekness, temperance: against such there is no law. [24]And they that are Christ's have crucified the flesh with the affections and lusts. [25]If we live in the Spirit, let us also walk in the Spirit. [26]Let us not be desirous of vain glory, provoking one another, envying one another. **Gal 6:7–8** [7]Be not deceived; God is not mocked: for whatsoever a man soweth, that shall he also reap. [8]For he that soweth to his flesh shall of the flesh reap corruption; but he that soweth to the Spirit shall of the Spirit reap life everlasting. **Col 1:6** [6]Which is come unto you, as it is in all the world; and bringeth forth fruit, as it doth also in you, since the day ye heard of it, and knew the grace of God in truth: **Col 1:10** [10]That ye might walk worthy of the Lord unto all pleasing, being fruitful in every good work, and increasing in the knowledge of God; **1 Thes 1:6** [6]And ye became followers of us, and of the Lord, having received the word in much affliction, with joy of the Holy Ghost: **1 Thes 2:13** [13]For this cause also thank we God without ceasing, because, when ye received the word of God which ye heard of us, ye received it not as the word of men, but as it is in truth, the word of God, which effectually worketh also in you that believe. **1 Tim 1:11 (Pseudo)** [11]According to the glorious gospel of the blessed God, which was committed to my trust.	**Q-Quelle** Thanks and Blessings for Disciples: 2 Cor 4:4/[1 Cor 1:6]/Col 1:6/[Mt 11:25-27], Mt 13:16-17/[Lk 10:21-24 (QS 24, 25)]

2 CORINTHIANS 4:5—Paul's ministry (2:14–7:4), 57 CE

Theme	2 COR	Mt	Mk	Lk
Humble service/ ministry	**4:5** [5]For we preach not ourselves, but Christ Jesus the Lord; and ourselves your servants for Jesus' sake. **9:14** [14]And by their prayer for you, which long after you for the exceeding grace of God in you. **11:7** [7]Have I committed an offence in abasing myself that ye might be exalted, because I have preached to you the gospel of God freely?	**20:20** [20]Then came to him the mother of Zebedee's children with her sons, wor-ship-ping him, and desiring a certain thing of him. **23:12** [12]And who-soever shall exalt himself shall be abased; and he that shall humble himself shall be exalted.	**9:35** [35]And he sat down, and called the twelve, and saith unto them, If any man desire to be first, the same shall be last of all, and servant of all. **10:35–45** [35]And James and John, the sons of Zebedee, come unto him, saying, Master, we would that thou shouldest do for us whatsoever we shall desire. [36]And he took a child, and set him in the midst of them: and when he had taken him in his arms, he said unto them, [37]Who-soever shall receive one of such children in my name, receiveth me: and whosoever shall receive me, receiveth not me, but him that sent me. [38]And John answered him, saying, Master, we saw one casting out devils in thy name, and he followeth not us: and we forbad him, because he followeth not us. [39]But Jesus said, Forbid him not: for there is no man which shall do a miracle in my name, that can lightly speak evil of me. [40]For he that is not against us is on our part. [41]For whosoever shall give you a cup of water to drink in my name, because ye belong to Christ, verily I say unto you, he shall not lose his reward. [42]And whosoever shall offend one of these little ones that believe in me, it is better for him that a millstone were hanged about his neck, and he were cast into the sea. [43]And if thy hand offend thee, cut it off: it is better for thee to enter into life maimed, than having two hands to go into hell, into the fire that never shall be quenched: [44]Where their worm dieth not, and the fire is not quenched. [45]And if thy foot offend thee, cut it off: it is better for thee to enter halt into life, than having two feet to be cast into hell, into the fire that never shall be quenched:	**9:48** [48]And said unto them, Whosoever shall receive this child in my name receiv-eth me:& whosoever shall receive me receiveth him that sent me: for he that is least among you all, the same shall be great. **14:11** [11]For whosoever exalteth himself shall be abased; and he that humbleth him-self shall be exalted. **18:14** [14]I tell you, this man went down to his house justified rather than the other: for every one that exalteth himself shall be abased; and he that humbleth himself shall be exalted. **22:24–27** [24]And there was also a strife among them, which of them should be accounted the greatest. [25]And he said unto them, The kings of the Gentiles exercise lordship over them; and they that exercise authority upon them are called benefactors. [26]But ye shall not be so: but he that is greatest among you, let him be as the younger; and he that is chief, as he that doth serve. [27]For whether is greater, he that sitteth at meat, or he that serveth? is not he that sitteth at meat? but I am among you as he that serveth.

Jn	Paul
Ch 13	**Rom 14:4–12**
1Now before the feast of the passover, when Jesus knew that his hour was come that he should depart out of this world unto the Father, having loved his own which were in the world, he loved them unto the end. 2And supper being ended, the devil having now put into the heart of Judas Iscariot, Simon's son, to betray him; 3Jesus knowing that the Father had given all things into his hands, and that he was come from God, and went to God; 4He riseth from supper, and laid aside his garments; and took a towel, and girded himself. 5After that he poureth water into a basin, and began to wash the disciples' feet, and to wipe them with the towel wherewith he was girded. 6Then cometh he to Simon Peter: and Peter saith unto him, Lord, dost thou wash my feet? 7Jesus answered and said unto him, What I do thou knowest not now; but thou shalt know hereafter. 8Peter saith unto him, Thou shalt never wash my feet. Jesus answered him, If I wash thee not, thou hast no part with me. 9Simon Peter saith unto him, Lord, not my feet only, but also my hands and my head. 10Jesus saith to him, He that is washed needeth not save to wash his feet, but is clean every whit: and ye are clean, but not all. 11For he knew who should betray him; therefore said he, Ye are not all clean. 12So after he had washed their feet, and had taken his garments, and was set down again, he said unto them, Know ye what I have done to you? 13Ye call me Master and Lord: and ye say well; for so I am. 14If I then, your Lord and Master, have washed your feet; ye also ought to wash one another's feet. 15For I have given you an example, that ye should do as I have done to you. 16Verily, verily, I say unto you, The servant is not greater than his lord; neither he that is sent greater than he that sent him. 17If ye know these things, happy are ye if ye do them. 18I speak not of you all: I know whom I have chosen: but that the scripture may be fulfilled, He that eateth bread with me hath lifted up his heel against me. 19Now I tell you before it come, that, when it is come to pass, ye may believe that I am he. 20Verily, verily, I say unto you, He that receiveth whomsoever I send receiveth me; and he that receiveth me receiveth him that sent me. 21When Jesus had thus said, he was troubled in spirit, and testified, and said, Verily, verily, I say unto you, that one of you shall betray me. 22Then the disciples looked one on another, doubting of whom he spake. 23Now there was leaning on Jesus' bosom one of his disciples, whom Jesus loved. 24Simon Peter therefore beckoned to him, that he should ask who it should be of whom he spake. 25He then lying on Jesus' breast saith unto him, Lord, who is it? 26Jesus answered, He it is, to whom I shall give a sop, when I have dipped it. And when he had dipped the sop, he gave it to Judas Iscariot, the son of Simon. 27And after the sop Satan entered into him. Then said Jesus unto him, That thou doest, do quickly. 28Now no man at the table knew for what intent he spake this unto him. 29For some of them thought, because Judas had the bag, that Jesus had said unto him, Buy those things that we have need of against the feast; or, that he should give something to the poor. 30He then having received the sop went immediately out: and it was night. 31Therefore, when he was gone out, Jesus said, Now is the Son of man glorified, and God is glorified in him. 32If God be glorified in him, God shall also glorify him in himself, and shall straightway glorify him. 33Little children, yet a little while I am with you. Ye shall seek me: and as I said unto the Jews, Whither I go, ye cannot come; so now I say to you. 34A new commandment I give unto you, That ye love one another; as I have loved you, that ye also love one another. 35By this shall all men know that ye are my disciples, if ye have love one to another. 36Simon Peter said unto him, Lord, whither goest thou? Jesus answered him, Whither I go, thou canst not follow me now; but thou shalt follow me afterwards. 37Peter said unto him, Lord, why cannot I follow thee now? I will lay down my life for thy sake. 38Jesus answered him, Wilt thou lay down thy life for my sake? Verily, verily, I say unto thee, The cock shall not crow, till thou hast denied me thrice.	4Who art thou that judgest another man's servant? to his own master he standeth or falleth. Yea, he shall be holden up: for God is able to make him stand. 5One man esteemeth one day above another: another esteemeth every day alike. Let every man be fully persuaded in his own mind. 6He that regardeth the day, regardeth it unto the Lord; and he that regardeth not the day, to the Lord he doth not regard it. He that eateth, eateth to the Lord, for he giveth God thanks; and he that eateth not, to the Lord he eateth not, and giveth God thanks. 7For none of us liveth to himself, and no man dieth to himself. 8For whether we live, we live unto the Lord; and whether we die, we die unto the Lord: whether we live therefore, or die, we are the Lord's. 9For to this end Christ both died, and rose, and revived, that he might be Lord both of the dead and living. 10But why dost thou judge thy brother? or why dost thou set at nought thy brother? for we shall all stand before the judgment seat of Christ. 11For it is written, As I live, saith the Lord, every knee shall bow to me, and every tongue shall confess to God. 12So then every one of us shall give account of himself to God. **Rom 15:7** 7Wherefore receive ye one another, as Christ also received us to the glory of God.

2 CORINTHIANS 4:5—Paul's ministry (2:14–7:4), 57 CE (*continued*)

Theme	2 Cor	Paul
(*Cont.*) Mix w/ humble (variation of above)	4:5 (above) 11:7 (above)	**Rom 12:10** [10]Be kindly affectioned one to another with brotherly love; in honour preferring one another; **Rom 12:12** [12]Rejoicing in hope; patient in tribulation; continuing instant in prayer; **Rom 15:1–4** [1]We then that are strong ought to bear the infirmities of the weak, and not to please ourselves. [2]Let every one of us please his neighbour for his good to edification. [3]For even Christ pleased not himself; but, as it is written, The reproaches of them that reproached thee fell on me. [4]For whatsoever things were written aforetime were written for our learning, that we through patience and comfort of the scriptures might have hope. **1 Cor 9:19** [19]For though I be free from all men, yet have I made myself servant unto all, that I might gain the more. **1 Cor 9:22** [22]To the weak became I as weak, that I might gain the weak: I am made all things to all men, that I might by all means save some. **1 Cor 10:33–11:2** **10**[33]Even as I please all men in all things, not seeking mine own profit, but the profit of many, that they may be saved. **11**[1]Be ye followers of me, even as I also am of Christ. [2]Now I praise you, brethren, that ye remember me in all things, and keep the ordinances, as I delivered them to you. **Gal 5:13c** [13]but by love serve one another. **Phil 2:2–9** [2]Fulfil ye my joy, that ye be likeminded, having the same love, being of one accord, of one mind. [3]Let nothing be done through strife or vainglory; but in lowliness of mind let each esteem other better than themselves. [4]Look not every man on his own things, but every man also on the things of others. [5]Let this mind be in you, which was also in Christ Jesus: [6]Who, being in the form of God, thought it not robbery to be equal with God: [7]But made himself of no reputation, and took upon him the form of a servant, and was made in the likeness of men: [8]And being found in fashion as a man, he humbled himself, and became obedient unto death, even the death of the cross. [9]Wherefore God also hath highly exalted him, and given him a name which is above every name

2 CORINTHIANS 4:6—Christian Ministry (2:14–7:4), 57 CE

Theme	2 COR	Lk	Jn
God shines in human hearts	**4:6** [6]For God, who commanded the light to shine out of darkness, hath shined in our hearts, to give the light of the knowledge of the glory of God in the face of Jesus Christ.	**Acts 26:13** [13]At midday, O king, I saw in the way a light from heaven, above the brightness of the sun, shining round about me and them which journeyed with me.	**8:12** [12]Then spake Jesus again unto them, saying, I am the light of the world: he that followeth me shall not walk in darkness, but shall have the light of life.

Paul	NT	Jewish Writings
Gal 1:15–16	**Heb 1:3**	**Gen 1:3**
[15]But when it pleased God, who separated me from my mother's womb, and called me by his grace, [16]To reveal his Son in me, that I might preach him among the heathen; immediately I conferred not with flesh and blood:	[3]Who being the brightness of his glory, and the express image of his person, and upholding all things by the word of his power, when he had by himself purged our sins, sat down on the right hand of the Majesty on high;	[3]And God said, Let there be light: and there was light. **Is 9:1** [1]Nevertheless the dimness shall not be such as was in her vexation, when at the first he lightly afflicted the land of Zebulun and the land of Naphtali, and afterward did more grievously afflict her by the way of the sea, beyond Jordan, in Galilee of the nations.

2 CORINTHIANS 4:8—Christian Ministry (2:14–7:4), 57 CE

Theme	2 COR	Paul
Troubled, but not distressed	**4:8** [8]We are troubled on every side, yet not distressed; we are perplexed, but not in despair; **6:4–10** [4]But in all things approving ourselves as the ministers of God, in much patience, in afflictions, in necessities, in distresses, [5]In stripes, in imprisonments, in tumults, in labours, in watchings, in fastings; [6]By pureness, by knowledge, by longsuffering, by kindness, by the Holy Ghost, by love unfeigned, [7]By the word of truth, by the power of God, by the armour of righteousness on the right hand and on the left, [8]By honour and dishonour, by evil report and good report: as deceivers, and yet true; [9]As unknown, and yet well known; as dying, and, behold, we live; as chastened, and not killed; [10]As sorrowful, yet alway rejoicing; as poor, yet making many rich; as having nothing, and yet possessing all things.	**1 Cor 4:9–13** [9]For I think that God hath set forth us the apostles last, as it were appointed to death: for we are made a spectacle unto the world, and to angels, and to men. [10]We are fools for Christ's sake, but ye are wise in Christ; we are weak, but ye are strong; ye are honourable, but we are despised. [11]Even unto this present hour we both hunger, and thirst, and are naked, and are buffeted, and have no certain dwellingplace; [12]And labour, working with our own hands: being reviled, we bless; being persecuted, we suffer it: [13]Being defamed, we entreat: we are made as the filth of the world, and are the offscouring of all things unto this day.

2 CORINTHIANS 4:10—Christian Ministry (2:14–7:4), 57 CE

Theme	2 COR	Paul
Death of Jesus in our body	**4:10** [10]Always bearing about in the body the dying of the Lord Jesus, that the life also of Jesus might be made manifest in our body.	**Col 1:24** [24]Who now rejoice in my sufferings for you, and fill up that which is behind of the afflictions of Christ in my flesh for his body's sake, which is the church:

2 CORINTHIANS 4:11—Christian Ministry (2:14–7:4), 57 CE

Theme	2 COR	Paul
Death so life can be made manifest	**4:11** [11]For we which live are alway delivered unto death for Jesus' sake, that the life also of Jesus might be made manifest in our mortal flesh.	**Rom 8:36** [36]As it is written, For thy sake we are killed all the day long; we are accounted as sheep for the slaughter. **1 Cor 15:31** [31]I protest by your rejoicing which I have in Christ Jesus our Lord, I die daily.

2 CORINTHIANS 4:13—Christian Ministry (2:14–7:4), 57 CE

Theme	2 COR	Jewish Writings
Believe & speak	**4:13** [13]We having the same spirit of faith, according as it is written, I believed, and therefore have I spoken; we also believe, and therefore speak;	**Ps 116:10** [10]Now I beseech you, brethren, by the name of our Lord Jesus Christ, that ye all speak the same thing, and that there be no divisions among you; but that ye be perfectly joined together in the same mind and in the same judgment.

2 CORINTHIANS 4:14—Christian Ministry (2:14–7:4), 57 CE

Theme	2 COR	Paul
God who raised Jesus will raise us	**4:14** [14]Knowing that he which raised up the Lord Jesus shall raise up us also by Jesus, and shall present us with you.	**Rom 4:24–25** [24]But for us also, to whom it shall be imputed, if we believe on him that raised up Jesus our Lord from the dead; [25]Who was delivered for our offences, and was raised again for our justification. **Rom 8:11** [11]But if the Spirit of him that raised up Jesus from the dead dwell in you, he that raised up Christ from the dead shall also quicken your mortal bodies by his Spirit that dwelleth in you. **1 Cor 6:14** [14]And God hath both raised up the Lord, and will also raise up us by his own power. **1 Thes 4:14** [14]For if we believe that Jesus died and rose again, even so them also which sleep in Jesus will God bring with him.

2 CORINTHIANS 4:15—Christian Ministry (2:14–7:4), 57 CE

Theme	2 COR
Grace to God's glory	**4:15** [15]For all things are for your sakes, that the abundant grace might through the thanksgiving of many redound to the glory of God. **1:11** [11]Ye also helping together by prayer for us, that for the gift bestowed upon us by the means of many persons thanks may be given by many on our behalf.

2 CORINTHIANS 4:16—Christian Ministry (2:14–7:4), 57 CE

Theme	2 COR
Inwardly renewed every day	**4:16** [16]For which cause we faint not; but though our outward man perish, yet the inward man is renewed day by day. **4:1a** [1]Therefore seeing we have this ministry...

2 CORINTHIANS 4:17—Christian Ministry (2:14–7:4), 57 CE

Theme	2 COR	Mt	Paul
Affliction is only a moment, glory is eternal	**4:17** [17]For our light affliction, which is but for a moment, worketh for us a far more exceeding and eternal weight of glory;	**5:11–12** [11]Blessed are ye, when men shall revile you, and persecute you, and shall say all manner of evil against you falsely, for my sake. [12]Rejoice, and be exceeding glad: for great is your reward in heaven: for so persecuted they the prophets which were before you.	**Rom 8:18** [18]For I reckon that the sufferings of this present time are not worthy to be compared with the glory which shall be revealed in us.

2 CORINTHIANS 5:1—Christian Ministry (2:14–7:4), 57 CE

Theme	2 COR	Mt	Mk	Lk	Jn
Temple of the Holy Spirit	**5:1** [1]For we know that if our earthly house of this tabernacle were dissolved, we have a building of God, an house not made with hands, eternal in the heavens. **6:14–17** [14]Be ye not unequally yoked together with unbelievers: for what fellowship hath righteousness with unrighteousness? and what communion hath light with darkness? [15]And what concord hath Christ with Belial? or what part hath he that believeth with an infidel? [16]And what agreement hath the temple of God with idols? for ye are the temple of the living God; as God hath said, I will dwell in them, and walk in them; and I will be their God, and they shall be my people. [17]Wherefore come out from among them, and be ye separate, saith the Lord, and touch not the unclean thing; and I will receive you,	**16:16–20** [16]And Simon Peter answered and said, Thou art the Christ, the Son of the living God. [17]And Jesus answered and said unto him, Blessed art thou, Simon Barjona: for flesh and blood hath not revealed it unto thee, but my Father which is in heaven. [18]And I say also unto thee, That thou art Peter, and upon this rock I will build my church; and the gates of hell shall not prevail against it. [19]And I will give unto thee the keys of the kingdom of heaven: and whatsoever thou shalt bind on earth shall be bound in heaven: and whatsoever thou shalt loose on earth shall be loosed in heaven. [20]Then charged he his disciples that they should tell no man that he was Jesus the Christ. **21:42** [42]Jesus saith unto them, Did ye never read in the scriptures, The stone which the builders rejected, the same is become the head of the corner: this is the Lord's doing, and it is marvellous in our eyes? **26:61** [61]And said, This fellow said, I am able to destroy the temple of God, and to build it in three days.	**12:10-11** [10]And have ye not read this scripture; The stone which the builders rejected is become the head of the corner: [11]This was the Lord's doing, and it is marvellous in our eyes? **14:58** [58]We heard him say, I will destroy this temple that is made with hands, and within three days I will build another made without hands.	**20:17** [17]And he beheld them, and said, What is this then that is written, The stone which the builders rejected, the same is become the head of the corner?	**2:19** [19]Jesus answered and said unto them, Destroy this temple, and in three days I will raise it up.

Paul	NT	Jewish Writings
Rom 3:16–17 [16]Destruction and misery are in their ways: [17]And the way of peace have they not known: **Rom 6:19** [19]I speak after the manner of men because of the infirmity of your flesh: for as ye have yielded your members servants to uncleanness and to iniquity unto iniquity; even so now yield your members servants to righteousness unto holiness. **Eph 2:18–22 (Pseudo)** [18]For through him we both have access by one Spirit unto the Father. [19]Now therefore ye are no more strangers and foreigners, but fellowcitizens with the saints, and of the household of God; [20]And are built upon the foundation of the apostles and prophets, Jesus Christ himself being the chief corner stone; [21]In whom all the building fitly framed together groweth unto an holy temple in the Lord: [22]In whom ye also are builded together for an habitation of God through the Spirit. **Col 2:11** [11]In whom also ye are circumcised with the circumcision made without hands, in putting off the body of the sins of the flesh by the circumcision of Christ: **Col 3:1–4** [1]If ye then be risen with Christ, seek those things which are above, where Christ sitteth on the right hand of God. [2]Set your affection on things above, not on things on the earth. [3]For ye are dead, and your life is hid with Christ in God. [4]When Christ, who is our life, shall appear, then shall ye also appear with him in glory.	**Heb 9:11, 24** [11]But Christ being come an high priest of good things to come, by a greater and more perfect tabernacle, not made with hands, that is to say, not of this building; . . . [24]For Christ is not entered into the holy places made with hands, which are the figures of the true; but into heaven itself, now to appear in the presence of God for us:	**Is 38:12** [12]Mine age is departed, and is removed from me as a shepherd's tent: I have cut off like a weaver my life: he will cut me off with pining sickness: from day even to night wilt thou make an end of me. **2 Sam 7** [1]And it came to pass, when the king sat in his house, and the LORD had given him rest round about from all his enemies; [2]That the king said unto Nathan the prophet, See now, I dwell in an house of cedar, but the ark of God dwelleth within curtains. [3]And Nathan said to the king, Go, do all that is in thine heart; for the LORD is with thee. [4]And it came to pass that night, that the word of the LORD came unto Nathan, saying, [5]Go and tell my servant David, Thus saith the LORD, Shalt thou build me an house for me to dwell in? [6]Whereas I have not dwelt in any house since the time that I brought up the children of Israel out of Egypt, even to this day, but have walked in a tent and in a tabernacle. [7]In all the places wherein I have walked with all the children of Israel spake I a word with any of the tribes of Israel, whom I commanded to feed my people Israel, saying, Why build ye not me an house of cedar? [8]Now therefore so shalt thou say unto my servant David, Thus saith the LORD of hosts, I took thee from the sheepcote, from following the sheep, to be ruler over my people, over Israel: [9]And I was with thee whithersoever thou wentest, and have cut off all thine enemies out of thy sight, and have made thee a great name, like unto the name of the great men that are in the earth. [10]Moreover I will appoint a place for my people Israel, and will plant them, that they may dwell in a place of their own, and move no more; neither shall the children of wickedness afflict them any more, as beforetime, [11]And as since the time that I commanded judges to be over my people Israel, and have caused thee to rest from all thine enemies. Also the LORD telleth thee that he will make thee an house. [12]And when thy days be fulfilled, and thou shalt sleep with thy fathers, I will set up thy seed after thee, which shall proceed out of thy bowels, and I will establish his kingdom. [13]He shall build an house for my name, and I will stablish the throne of his kingdom for ever. [14]I will be his father, and he shall be my son. If he commit iniquity, I will chasten him with the rod of men, and with the stripes of the children of men: [15]But my mercy shall not depart away from him, as I took it from Saul, whom I put away before thee. [16]And thine house and thy kingdom shall be established for ever before thee: thy throne shall be established for ever. [17]According to all these words, and according to all this vision, so did Nathan speak unto David. [18]Then went king David in, and sat before the LORD, and he said, Who am I, O Lord GOD? and what is my house, that thou hast brought me hitherto? [19]And this was yet a small thing in thy sight, O Lord GOD; but thou hast spoken also of thy servant's house for a great while to come. And is this the manner of man, O Lord GOD? [20]And what can David say more unto thee? for thou, Lord GOD, knowest thy servant. [21]For thy word's sake, and according to thine own heart, hast thou done all these great things, to make thy servant know them. [22]Wherefore thou art great, O LORD God: for there is none like thee, neither is there any God beside thee, according to all that we have heard with our ears. [23]And what one nation in the earth is like thy people, even like Israel, whom God went to redeem for a people to himself, and to make him a name, and to do for you great things and terrible, for thy land, before thy people, which thou redeemedst to thee from Egypt, from the nations and their gods? [24]For thou hast confirmed to thyself thy people Israel to be a people unto thee for ever: and thou, LORD, art become their God. [25]And now, O LORD God, the word that thou hast spoken concerning thy servant, and concerning his house, establish it for ever, and do as thou hast said. [26]And let thy name be magnified for ever, saying, The LORD of hosts is the God over Israel: and let the house of thy servant David be established before thee. [27]For thou, O LORD of hosts, God of Israel, hast revealed to thy servant, saying, I will build thee an house: therefore hath thy servant found in his heart to pray this prayer unto thee. [28]And now, O Lord GOD, thou art that God, and thy words be true, and thou hast promised this goodness unto thy servant: [29]Therefore now let it please thee to bless the house of thy servant, that it may continue for ever before thee: for thou, O Lord GOD, hast spoken it: and with thy blessing let the house of thy servant be blessed for ever.

2 CORINTHIANS 5:2—Christian Ministry (2:14–7:4), 57 CE

Theme	2 COR	Paul
Groaning, desiring heavenly home	**5:2** [2]For in this we groan, earnestly desiring to be clothed upon with our house which is from heaven:	**Rom 8:23** [23]And not only they, but ourselves also, which have the firstfruits of the Spirit, even we ourselves groan within ourselves, waiting for the adoption, to wit, the redemption of our body. **1 Cor 15:51–54** [51]Behold, I show you a mystery; We shall not all sleep, but we shall all be changed, [52]In a moment, in the twinkling of an eye, at the last trump: for the trumpet shall sound, and the dead shall be raised incorruptible, and we shall be changed. [53]For this corruptible must put on incorruption, and this mortal must put on immortality. [54]So when this corruptible shall have put on incorruption, and this mortal shall have put on immortality, then shall be brought to pass the saying that is written, Death is swallowed up in victory.

2 CORINTHIANS 5:4—Christian Ministry (2:14–7:4), 57 CE

Theme	2 COR	Paul	Jewish Writings
Clothed in mortality, awaiting heaven	**5:4** [4]For we that are in this tabernacle do groan, being burdened: not for that we would be unclothed, but clothed upon, that mortality might be swallowed up of life.	**1 Cor 15:54** [54]So when this corruptible shall have put on incorruption, and this mortal shall have put on immortality, then shall be brought to pass the saying that is written, Death is swallowed up in victory.	**Is 25:8** [8]He will swallow up death in victory; and the Lord GOD will wipe away tears from off all faces; and the rebuke of his people shall he take away from off all the earth: for the LORD hath spoken it.

2 CORINTHIANS 5:8—Christian Ministry (2:14–7:4), 57 CE

Theme	2 COR
Absent from body, present with the Lord	**5:8** [8]We are confident, I say, and willing rather to be absent from the body, and to be present with the Lord. **1:22** [22]Who hath also sealed us, and given the earnest of the Spirit in our hearts.

2 CORINTHIANS 5:10—Christian Ministry (2:14–7:4), 57 CE

Theme	2 COR	Mt	Paul	Other
Judged by actions	**5:10** [10]For we must all appear before the judgment seat of Christ; that every one may receive the things done in his body, according to that he hath done, whether it be good or bad.	**16:27** [27]For the Son of man shall come in the glory of his Father with his angels; and then he shall reward every man according to his works. **25:31–46** [31]When the Son of man shall come in his glory, and all the holy angels with him, then shall he sit upon the throne of his glory: [32]And before him shall be gathered all nations: and he shall separate them one from another, as a shepherd divideth his sheep from the goats: [33]And he shall set the sheep on his right hand, but the goats on the left. [34]Then shall the King say unto them on his right hand, Come, ye blessed of my Father, inherit the kingdom prepared for you from the foundation of the world: [35]For I was an hungered, and ye gave me meat: I was thirsty, and ye gave me drink: I was a stranger, and ye took me in: [36]Naked, and ye clothed me: I was sick, and ye visited me: I was in prison, and ye came unto me. [37]Then shall the righteous answer him, saying, Lord, when saw we thee an hungered, and fed thee? or thirsty, and gave thee drink? [38]When saw we thee a stranger, and took thee in? or naked, and clothed thee? [39]Or when saw we thee sick, or in prison, and came unto thee? [40]And the King shall answer and say unto them, Verily I say unto you, Inasmuch as ye have done it unto one of the least of these my brethren, ye have done it unto me. [41]Then shall he say also unto them on the left hand, Depart from me, ye cursed, into everlasting fire, prepared for the devil and his angels: [42]For I was an hungered, and ye gave me no meat: I was thirsty, and ye gave me no drink: [43]I was a stranger, and ye took me not in: naked, and ye clothed me not: sick, and in prison, and ye visited me not. [44]Then shall they also answer him, saying, Lord, when saw we thee an hungered, or athirst, or a stranger, or naked, or sick, or in prison, and did not minister unto thee? [45]Then shall he answer them, saying, Verily I say unto you, Inasmuch as ye did it not to one of the least of these, ye did it not to me. [46]And these shall go away into everlasting punishment: but the righteous into life eternal.	**Rom 2:6** [6]Who will render to every man according to his deeds: **Rom 2:16** [16]In the day when God shall judge the secrets of men by Jesus Christ according to my gospel. **Rom 14:10-11** [10]But why dost thou judge thy brother? or why dost thou set at nought thy brother? for we shall all stand before the judgment seat of Christ. [11]For it is written, As I live, saith the Lord, every knee shall bow to me, and every tongue shall confess to God. **1 Cor 3:12–15** [12]Now if any man build upon this foundation gold, silver, precious stones, wood, hay, stubble; [13]Every man's work shall be made manifest: for the day shall declare it, because it shall be revealed by fire; and the fire shall try every man's work of what sort it is. [14]If any man's work abide which he hath built thereupon, he shall receive a reward. [15]If any man's work shall be burned, he shall suffer loss: but he himself shall be saved; yet so as by fire. **1 Cor 4:4** [4]For I know nothing by myself; yet am I not hereby justified: but he that judgeth me is the Lord. **1 Cor 5:2** [2]And ye are puffed up, and have not rather mourned, that he that hath done this deed might be taken away from among you.	**Q-Quelle** Exclusion from Kingdom of God: 2 Cor 5:10/Rom 2:6/1 Cor 4:1-5/[Mt 7:13-14, 22-23, 8:11-12, 19:30]/[Lk 13:22-30 (QS47, 48)]; House on Rock: 2 Cor 5:10/Rom 2:6/1 Cor 4:1-5/[Mt 7:21-27]/[Lk 6:46-49(QS 14)]; Day of SOM: 2 Cor 5:10/Rom 2:6/[Mt 10:39, 24:17-18, 23, 24:26-27, 28, 37-39, 40-41]/[Mk 13:14-16, 19-23]/[Lk 17:22-37]; Warning of Offenses: Rom 2:6/2 Cor 5:10/[Mt 18:6-7]/[Mk 9:42]/[Lk 17:1-3a (QS 57, 58)]

2 CORINTHIANS 5:11—Christian Ministry (2:14–7:4), 57 CE

Theme	2 COR
Fear of God, clear conscience	**5:11** [11]Knowing therefore the terror of the Lord, we persuade men; but we are made manifest unto God; and I trust also are made manifest in your consciences. **1:12–14** [12]For our rejoicing is this, the testimony of our conscience, that in simplicity and godly sincerity, not with fleshly wisdom, but by the grace of God, we have had our conversation in the world, and more abundantly to you-ward. [13]For we write none other things unto you, than what ye read or acknowledge; and I trust ye shall acknowledge even to the end; [14]As also ye have acknowledged us in part, that we are your rejoicing, even as ye also are ours in the day of the Lord Jesus.

2 CORINTHIANS 5:12—Christian Ministry (2:14–7:4), 57 CE

Theme	2 COR	Paul
Commended to God's work	**5:12** [12]For we commend not ourselves again unto you, but give you occasion to glory on our behalf, that ye may have somewhat to answer them which glory in appearance, and not in heart. **1:14** [14]As also ye have acknowledged us in part, that we are your rejoicing, even as ye also are ours in the day of the Lord Jesus. **3:1** [1]Do we begin again to commend ourselves? or need we, as some others, epistles of commendation to you, or letters of commendation from you?	**Phil 1:26** [26]That your rejoicing may be more abundant in Jesus Christ for me by my coming to you again.

2 CORINTHIANS 5:17—Christian Ministry (2:14–7:4), 57 CE

Theme	2 COR	Paul	NT	Jewish Writings
New creation in Christ	**5:17** [17]Therefore if any man be in Christ, he is a new creature: old things are passed away; behold, all things are become new.	**Gal 6:16** [16]And as many as walk according to this rule, peace be on them, and mercy, and upon the Israel of God. **Eph 2:15 (Pseudo)** [15]Having abolished in his flesh the enmity, even the law of commandments contained in ordinances; for to make in himself of twain one new man, so making peace;	**Rev 21:5** [5]And he that sat upon the throne said, Behold, I make all things new. And he said unto me, Write: for these words are true and faithful.	**Is 43:18–21** [18]Remember ye not the former things, neither consider the things of old. [19]Behold, I will do a new thing; now it shall spring forth; shall ye not know it? I will even make a way in the wilderness, and rivers in the desert. [20]The beast of the field shall honour me, the dragons and the owls: because I give waters in the wilderness, and rivers in the desert, to give drink to my people, my chosen. [21]This people have I formed for myself; they shall show forth my praise.

2 CORINTHIANS 5:19—Christian Ministry (2:14–7:4), 57 CE

Theme	2 COR	Paul
Reconciliation with God through Christ	**5:19** [19]To wit, that God was in Christ, reconciling the world unto himself, not imputing their trespasses unto them; and hath committed unto us the word of reconciliation.	**Rom 5:10-11** [10]For if, when we were enemies, we were reconciled to God by the death of his Son, much more, being reconciled, we shall be saved by his life. [11]And not only so, but we also joy in God through our Lord Jesus Christ, by whom we have now received the atonement. **Col 1:20** [20]And, having made peace through the blood of his cross, by him to reconcile all things unto himself; by him, I say, whether they be things in earth, or things in heaven.

2 CORINTHIANS 5:20—Christian Ministry (2:14–7:4), 57 CE

Theme	2 COR	Paul
Ambassadors in Christ	**5:20** [20]Now then we are ambassadors for Christ, as though God did beseech you by us: we pray you in Christ's stead, be ye reconciled to God.	**Eph 6:20 (Pseudo)** [20]For which I am an ambassador in bonds: that therein I may speak boldly, as I ought to speak. **Phlm 9** [9]Yet for love's sake I rather beseech thee, being such an one as Paul the aged, and now also a prisoner of Jesus Christ.

2 CORINTHIANS 5:21—Christian Ministry (2:14–7:4), 57 CE

Theme	2 COR	Mt	Mk	Jn
Redemption	**5:21** [21]For he hath made him to be sin for us, who knew no sin; that we might be made the righteousness of God in him.	**20:28** [28]Even as the Son of man came not to be ministered unto, but to minister, and to give his life a ransom for many.	**10:45** [45]For even the Son of man came not to be ministered unto, but to minister, and to give his life a ransom for many.	**1 Jn 3:5–8** [5]And ye know that he was manifested to take away our sins; and in him is no sin. [6]Whosoever abideth in him sinneth not: whosoever sinneth hath not seen him, neither known him. [7]Little children, let no man deceive you: he that doeth righteousness is righteous, even as he is righteous. [8]He that committeth sin is of the devil; for the devil sinneth from the beginning. For this purpose the Son of God was manifested, that he might destroy the

Paul

Rom 3:24–26

[24]Being justified freely by his grace through the redemption that is in Christ Jesus: [25]Whom God hath set forth to be
a propitiation through faith in his blood, to declare his righteousness for the remission of sins that are past, through
the forbearance of God; [26]To declare, I say, at this time his righteousness: that he might be just, and the justifier of him
which believeth in Jesus.

Rom 3:25

[25]Whom God hath set forth to be a propitiation through faith in his blood, to declare his righteousness for the remission of sins that are past, through the forbearance of God;

Rom 6:14

[14]For sin shall not have dominion over you: for ye are not under the law, but under grace.

Rom 8:3

[3]For what the law could not do, in that it was weak through the flesh, God sending his own Son in the likeness of sinful flesh, and for sin, condemned sin in the flesh:

I Cor 1:30

[30]But of him are ye in Christ Jesus, who of God is made unto us wisdom, and righteousness, and sanctification, and redemption:

1 Cor 10

[1]Moreover, brethren, I would not that ye should be ignorant, how that all our fathers were under the cloud, and all
passed through the sea; [2]And were all baptized unto Moses in the cloud and in the sea; [3]And did all eat the same spiritual meat; [4]And did all drink the same spiritual drink: for they drank of that spiritual Rock that followed them: and
that Rock was Christ. [5]But with many of them God was not well pleased: for they were overthrown in the wilderness.
[6]Now these things were our examples, to the intent we should not lust after evil things, as they also lusted. [7]Neither be
ye idolaters, as were some of them; as it is written, The people sat down to eat and drink, and rose up to play. [8]Neither
let us commit fornication, as some of them committed, and fell in one day three and twenty thousand. [9]Neither let us
tempt Christ, as some of them also tempted, and were destroyed of serpents. [10]Neither murmur ye, as some of them
also murmured, and were destroyed of the destroyer. [11]Now all these things happened unto them for ensamples: and
they are written for our admonition, upon whom the ends of the world are come. [12]Wherefore let him that thinketh he
standeth take heed lest he fall. [13]There hath no temptation taken you but such as is common to man: but God is faithful,
who will not suffer you to be tempted above that ye are able; but will with the temptation also make a way to escape,
that ye may be able to bear it. [14]Wherefore, my dearly beloved, flee from idolatry. [15]I speak as to wise men; judge ye what
I say. [16]The cup of blessing which we bless, is it not the communion of the blood of Christ? The bread which we break, is
it not the communion of the body of Christ? [17]For we being many are one bread, and one body: for we are all partakers
of that one bread. [18]Behold Israel after the flesh: are not they which eat of the sacrifices partakers of the altar? [19]What
say I then? that the idol is any thing, or that which is offered in sacrifice to idols is any thing? [20]But I say, that the things
which the Gentiles sacrifice, they sacrifice to devils, and not to God: and I would not that ye should have fellowship
with devils. [21]Ye cannot drink the cup of the Lord, and the cup of devils: ye cannot be partakers of the Lord's table, and
of the table of devils. [22]Do we provoke the Lord to jealousy? are we stronger than he? [23]All things are lawful for me, but
all things are not expedient: all things are lawful for me, but all things edify not. [24]Let no man seek his own, but every
man another's wealth. [25]Whatsoever is sold in the shambles, that eat, asking no question for conscience sake: [26]For
the earth is the Lord's, and the fulness thereof. [27]If any of them that believe not bid you to a feast, and ye be disposed
to go; whatsoever is set before you, eat, asking no question for conscience sake. [28]But if any man say unto you, This is
offered in sacrifice unto idols, eat not for his sake that showed it, and for conscience sake: for the earth is the Lord's,
and the fulness thereof: [29]Conscience, I say, not thine own, but of the other: for why is my liberty judged of another
man's conscience? [30]For if I by grace be a partaker, why am I evil spoken of for that for which I give thanks? [31]Whether
therefore ye eat, or drink, or whatsoever ye do, do all to the glory of God. [32]Give none offence, neither to the Jews, nor
to the Gentiles, nor to the church of God: [33]Even as I please all men in all things, not seeking mine own profit, but the
profit of many, that they may be saved.

Continued

2 Corinthians 5:21 continued on next page

2 CORINTHIANS 5:21—Christian Ministry (2:14–7:4), 57 CE (*continued*)

Theme	2 COR	Paul
(*Cont.*) Redemption	**5:21 (above)**	**(*Continued*)** **Gal 3:13** [13]Christ hath redeemed us from the curse of the law, being made a curse for us: for it is written, Cursed is every one that hangeth on a tree: **Gal 3:23–5:1** **3** [23]But before faith came, we were kept under the law, shut up unto the faith which should afterwards be revealed. [24]Wherefore the law was our schoolmaster to bring us unto Christ, that we might be justified by faith. [25]But after that faith is come, we are no longer under a schoolmaster. [26]For ye are all the children of God by faith in Christ Jesus. [27]For as many of you as have been baptized into Christ have put on Christ. [28]There is neither Jew nor Greek, there is neither bond nor free, there is neither male nor female: for ye are all one in Christ Jesus. [29]And if ye be Christ's, then are ye Abraham's seed, and heirs according to the promise. **4** [1]Now I say, That the heir, as long as he is a child, differeth nothing from a servant, though he be lord of all; [2]But is under tutors and governors until the time appointed of the father. [3]Even so we, when we were children, were in bondage under the elements of the world: [4]But when the fulness of the time was come, God sent forth his Son, made of a woman, made under the law, [5]To redeem them that were under the law, that we might receive the adoption of sons. [6]And because ye are sons, God hath sent forth the Spirit of his Son into your hearts, crying, Abba, Father. [7]Wherefore thou art no more a servant, but a son; and if a son, then an heir of God through Christ. [8]Howbeit then, when ye knew not God, ye did service unto them which by nature are no gods. [9]But now, after that ye have known God, or rather are known of God, how turn ye again to the weak and beggarly elements, whereunto ye desire again to be in bondage? [10]Ye observe days, and months, and times, and years. [11]I am afraid of you, lest I have bestowed upon you labour in vain. [12]Brethren, I beseech you, be as I am; for I am as ye are: ye have not injured me at all. [13]Ye know how through infirmity of the flesh I preached the gospel unto you at the first. [14]And my temptation which was in my flesh ye despised not, nor rejected; but received me as an angel of God, even as Christ Jesus. [15]Where is then the blessedness ye spake of? for I bear you record, that, if it had been possible, ye would have plucked out your own eyes, and have given them to me. [16]Am I therefore become your enemy, because I tell you the truth? [17]They zealously affect you, but not well; yea, they would exclude you, that ye might affect them. [18]But it is good to be zealously affected always in a good thing, and not only when I am present with you. [19]My little children, of whom I travail in birth again until Christ be formed in you, [20]I desire to be present with you now, and to change my voice; for I stand in doubt of you. [21]Tell me, ye that desire to be under the law, do ye not hear the law? [22]For it is written, that Abraham had two sons, the one by a bondmaid, the other by a freewoman. [23]But he who was of the bondwoman was born after the flesh; but he of the freewoman was by promise. [24]Which things are an allegory: for these are the two covenants; the one from the mount Sinai, which gendereth to bondage, which is Agar. [25]For this Agar is mount Sinai in Arabia, and answereth to Jerusalem which now is, and is in bondage with her children. [26]But Jerusalem which is above is free, which is the mother of us all. [27]For it is written, Rejoice, thou barren that bearest not; break forth and cry, thou that travailest not: for the desolate hath many more children than she which hath an husband. [28]Now we, brethren, as Isaac was, are the children of promise. [29]But as then he that was born after the flesh persecuted him that was born after the Spirit, even so it is now. [30]Nevertheless what saith the scripture? Cast out the bondwoman and her son: for the son of the bondwoman shall not be heir with the son of the freewoman. [31]So then, brethren, we are not children of the bondwoman, but of the free. **5** [1]Stand fast therefore in the liberty wherewith Christ hath made us free, and be not entangled again with the yoke of bondage.

2 CORINTHIANS 6:1—Christian Ministry (2:14–7:4), 57 CE

Theme	2 COR	Paul
Workers, receive grace	**6:1** [1]We then, as workers together with him, beseech you also that ye receive not the grace of God in vain.	**1 Cor 3:9** [9]For we are labourers together with God: ye are God's husbandry, ye are God's building. **1 Thes 3:2** [2]And sent Timotheus, our brother, and minister of God, and our fellowlabourer in the gospel of Christ, to establish you, and to comfort you concerning your faith:

NT	Jewish Writings	Other
1 Pet 2:24 [24]Who his own self bare our sins in his own body on the tree, that we, being dead to sins, should live unto righteousness: by whose stripes ye were healed. **Heb 9:5** [5]And over it the cherubims of glory shadowing the mercyseat; of which we cannot now speak particularly.	**Ex 15:13** [13]Thou in thy mercy hast led forth the people which thou hast redeemed: thou hast guided them in thy strength unto thy holy habitation. **Ex 25:16–21** [16]And thou shalt put into the ark the testimony which I shall give thee. [17]And thou shalt make a mercy seat of pure gold: two cubits and a half shall be the length thereof, and a cubit and a half the breadth thereof. [18]And thou shalt make two cherubims of gold, of beaten work shalt thou make them, in the two ends of the mercy seat. [19]And make one cherub on the one end, and the other cherub on the other end: even of the mercy seat shall ye make the cherubims on the two ends thereof. [20]And the cherubims shall stretch forth their wings on high, covering the mercy seat with their wings, and their faces shall look one to another; toward the mercy seat shall the faces of the cherubims be. [21]And thou shalt put the mercy seat above upon the ark; and in the ark thou shalt put the testimony that I shall give thee. **Lev 1:4–5** [4]And he shall put his hand upon the head of the burnt offering; and it shall be accepted for him to make atonement for him. [5]And he shall kill the bullock before the LORD: and the priests, Aaron's sons, shall bring the blood, and sprinkle the blood round about upon the altar that is by the door of the tabernacle of the congregation. **Is 41:14** [14]Fear not, thou worm Jacob, and ye men of Israel; I will help thee, saith the LORD, and thy redeemer, the Holy One of Israel. **Is 53:6–9** [6]All we like sheep have gone astray; we have turned every one to his own way; and the LORD hath laid on him the iniquity of us all. [7]He was oppressed, and he was afflicted, yet he opened not his mouth: he is brought as a lamb to the slaughter, and as a sheep before her shearers is dumb, so he openeth not his mouth. [8]He was taken from prison and from judgment: and who shall declare his generation? for he was cut off out of the land of the living: for the transgression of my people was he stricken. [9]And he made his grave with the wicked, and with the rich in his death; because he had done no violence, neither was any deceit in his mouth.	**Q-Quelle** Precedence: 2 Cor 5:21/1 Cor 10/[Mt 19:28]/Mk 10:41-45/[Lk 22:28-30 (QS 62)]

2 CORINTHIANS 6:2—Christian Ministry (2:14–7:4), 57 CE

Theme	2 COR	Mk	Lk	Paul
Day of the Lord/ eschatology	**6:2** [2](For he saith, I have heard thee in a time accepted, and in the day of salvation have I succoured thee: behold, now is the accepted time; behold, now is the day of salvation.)	**1:15** [15]And saying, The time is fulfilled, and the kingdom of God is at hand: repent ye, and believe the gospel.	**4:19** [19]To preach the acceptable year of the Lord.	**Rom 8:23** [23]And not only they, but ourselves also, which have the firstfruits of the Spirit, even we ourselves groan within ourselves, waiting for the adoption, to wit, the redemption of our body. **Rom 13:11–12** [11]And that, knowing the time, that now it is high time to awake out of sleep: for now is our salvation nearer than when we believed. [12]The night is far spent, the day is at hand: let us therefore cast off the works of darkness, and let us put on the armour of light. **Rom 15:20** [20]Yea, so have I strived to preach the gospel, not where Christ was named, lest I should build upon another man's foundation: **Gal 4:4** [4]But when the fulness of the time was come, God sent forth his Son, made of a woman, made under the law, **Gal 6:15** [15]For in Christ Jesus neither circumcision availeth any thing, nor uncircumcision, but a new creature. **Eph 1:10** [10]That in the dispensation of the fulness of times he might gather together in one all things in Christ, both which are in heaven, and which are on earth; even in him:

2 CORINTHIANS 6:3—Christian Ministry (2:14–7:4), 57 CE

Theme	2 COR	Paul
Ministers must not offend others	**6:3** [3]Giving no offence in any thing, that the ministry be not blamed: **8:20-21** [20]Avoiding this, that no man should blame us in this abundance which is administered by us: [21]Providing for honest things, not only in the sight of the Lord, but also in the sight of men.	**1 Cor 9:12** [12]If others be partakers of this power over you, are not we rather? Nevertheless we have not used this power; but suffer all things, lest we should hinder the gospel of Christ. **1 Cor 10:32** [32]Give none offence, neither to the Jews, nor to the Gentiles, nor to the church of God:

Jewish Writings

Is 49

1 Listen, O isles, unto me; and hearken, ye people, from far; The LORD hath called me from the womb; from the bowels
of my mother hath he made mention of my name. 2 And he hath made my mouth like a sharp sword; in the shadow of
his hand hath he hid me, and made me a polished shaft; in his quiver hath he hid me; 3 And said unto me, Thou art my
servant, O Israel, in whom I will be glorified. 4 Then I said, I have laboured in vain, I have spent my strength for nought,
and in vain: yet surely my judgment is with the LORD, and my work with my God. 5 And now, saith the LORD that
formed me from the womb to be his servant, to bring Jacob again to him, Though Israel be not gathered, yet shall I be
glorious in the eyes of the LORD, and my God shall be my strength. 6 And he said, It is a light thing that thou shouldest be my servant to raise up the tribes of Jacob, and to restore the preserved of Israel: I will also give thee for a light
to the Gentiles, that thou mayest be my salvation unto the end of the earth. 7 Thus saith the LORD, the Redeemer of
Israel, and his Holy One, to him whom man despiseth, to him whom the nation abhorreth, to a servant of rulers, Kings
shall see and arise, princes also shall worship, because of the LORD that is faithful, and the Holy One of Israel, and he
shall choose thee. **8 Thus saith the LORD, In an acceptable time have I heard thee, and in a day of salvation have I
helped thee: and I will preserve thee, and give thee for a covenant of the people, to establish the earth, to cause
to inherit the desolate heritages**; 9 That thou mayest say to the prisoners, Go forth; to them that are in darkness, Show
yourselves. They shall feed in the ways, and their pastures shall be in all high places. 10 They shall not hunger nor thirst;
neither shall the heat nor sun smite them: for he that hath mercy on them shall lead them, even by the springs of water
shall he guide them. 11 And I will make all my mountains a way, and my highways shall be exalted. 12 Behold, these shall
come from far: and, lo, these from the north and from the west; and these from the land of Sinim. 13 Sing, O heavens;
and be joyful, O earth; and break forth into singing, O mountains: for the LORD hath comforted his people, and will
have mercy upon his afflicted. 14 But Zion said, The LORD hath forsaken me, and my Lord hath forgotten me. 15 Can a
woman forget her sucking child, that she should not have compassion on the son of her womb? yea, they may forget,
yet will I not forget thee. 16 Behold, I have graven thee upon the palms of my hands; thy walls are continually before me.
17 Thy children shall make haste; thy destroyers and they that made thee waste shall go forth of thee. 18 Lift up thine eyes
round about, and behold: all these gather themselves together, and come to thee. As I live, saith the LORD, thou shalt
surely clothe thee with them all, as with an ornament, and bind them on thee, as a bride doeth. 19 For thy waste and thy
desolate places, and the land of thy destruction, shall even now be too narrow by reason of the inhabitants, and they
that swallowed thee up shall be far away. 20 The children which thou shalt have, after thou hast lost the other, shall say
again in thine ears, The place is too strait for me: give place to me that I may dwell. 21 Then shalt thou say in thine heart,
Who hath begotten me these, seeing I have lost my children, and am desolate, a captive, and removing to and fro? and
who hath brought up these? Behold, I was left alone; these, where had they been? 22 Thus saith the Lord GOD, Behold, I
will lift up mine hand to the Gentiles, and set up my standard to the people: and they shall bring thy sons in their arms,
and thy daughters shall be carried upon their shoulders. 23 And kings shall be thy nursing fathers, and their queens thy
nursing mothers: they shall bow down to thee with their face toward the earth, and lick up the dust of thy feet; and
thou shalt know that I am the LORD: for they shall not be ashamed that wait for me. 24 Shall the prey be taken from
the mighty, or the lawful captive delivered? 25 But thus saith the LORD, Even the captives of the mighty shall be taken
away, and the prey of the terrible shall be delivered: for I will contend with him that contendeth with thee, and I will
save thy children. 26 And I will feed them that oppress thee with their own flesh; and they shall be drunken with their
own blood, as with sweet wine: and all flesh shall know that I the LORD am thy Saviour and thy Redeemer, the mighty
One of Jacob.

2 CORINTHIANS 6:4—Christian Ministry (2:14–7:4), 57 CE

Theme	2 COR	Paul
Ministers be patient in affliction & distresses	**6:4** [4]But in all things approving ourselves as the ministers of God, in much patience, in afflictions, in necessities, in distresses, **4:8–11** [8]We are troubled on every side, yet not distressed; we are perplexed, but not in despair; [9]Persecuted, but not forsaken; cast down, but not destroyed; [10]Always bearing about in the body the dying of the Lord Jesus, that the life also of Jesus might be made manifest in our body. [11]For we which live are alway delivered unto death for Jesus' sake, that the life also of Jesus might be made manifest in our mortal flesh. **11:23–27** [23]Are they ministers of Christ? (I speak as a fool) I am more; in labours more abundant, in stripes above measure, in prisons more frequent, in deaths oft. [24]Of the Jews five times received I forty stripes save one. [25]Thrice was I beaten with rods, once was I stoned, thrice I suffered shipwreck, a night and a day I have been in the deep; [26]In journeyings often, in perils of waters, in perils of robbers, in perils by mine own countrymen, in perils by the heathen, in perils in the city, in perils in the wilderness, in perils in the sea, in perils among false brethren; [27]In weariness and painfulness, in watchings often, in hunger and thirst, in fastings often, in cold and nakedness.	**1 Cor 4:9–13** [9]For I think that God hath set forth us the apostles last, as it were appointed to death: for we are made a spectacle unto the world, and to angels, and to men. [10]We are fools for Christ's sake, but ye are wise in Christ; we are weak, but ye are strong; ye are honourable, but we are despised. [11]Even unto this present hour we both hunger, and thirst, and are naked, and are buffeted, and have no certain dwellingplace; [12]And labour, working with our own hands: being reviled, we bless; being persecuted, we suffer it: [13]Being defamed, we entreat: we are made as the filth of the world, and are the offscouring of all things unto this day.

2 CORINTHIANS 6:5—Christian Ministry (2:14–7:4), 57 CE

Theme	2 COR	Lk
Patience in challenges	**6:5** [5]In stripes, in imprisonments, in tumults, in labours, in watchings, in fastings;	**Acts 16:23** [23]And when they had laid many stripes upon them, they cast them into prison, charging the jailor to keep them safely:

2 CORINTHIANS 6:6—Christian Ministry (2:14–7:4), 57 CE

Theme	2 COR	Paul	Other
Purity in loyalty	**6:6** [6]By pureness, by knowledge, by longsuffering, by kindness, by the Holy Ghost, by love unfeigned,	**Gal 5:22–23** [22]But the fruit of the Spirit is love, joy, peace, longsuffering, gentleness, goodness, faith, [23]Meekness, temperance: against such there is no law.	**Q-Quelle** Love enemies: [Rom 12:9-21]/2 Cor 6:6/[Mt 5:38-48, 7:12]/[Lk 6:27-36 (QS 9 [Thom 95, 6:2])]; Against Pharisees: [Rom 12:9-21]/2 Cor 6:6/ [Mt 23:4-36]/[Mk 7:1-9]/ [Lk 11:37-54 (QS 34 [Thom 39:1,89, 102])]; Precedence: [Rom 12:9-21]/2 Cor 6:6/ [Mt 19:28]/[Mk 10:41-45]/[Lk 22:28-30 (QS 62)]

2 CORINTHIANS 6:7—Christian Ministry (2:14–7:4), 57 CE

Theme	2 COR	Paul
Armour of righteousness	**6:7** [7]By the word of truth, by the power of God, by the armour of righteousness on the right hand and on the left, **10:4** [4](For the weapons of our warfare are not carnal, but mighty through God to the pulling down of strong holds;)	**Rom 13:12** [12]The night is far spent, the day is at hand: let us therefore cast off the works of darkness, and let us put on the armour of light. **Eph 6:11–17(Pseudo)** [11]Put on the whole armour of God, that ye may be able to stand against the wiles of the devil. [12]For we wrestle not against flesh and blood, but against principalities, against powers, against the rulers of the darkness of this world, against spiritual wickedness in high places. [13]Wherefore take unto you the whole armour of God, that ye may be able to withstand in the evil day, and having done all, to stand. [14]Stand therefore, having your loins girt about with truth, and having on the breastplate of righteousness; [15]And your feet shod with the preparation of the gospel of peace; [16]Above all, taking the shield of faith, wherewith ye shall be able to quench all the fiery darts of the wicked. [17]And take the helmet of salvation, and the sword of the Spirit, which is the word of God:

2 CORINTHIANS 6:9—Christian Ministry (2:14–7:4), 57 CE

Theme	2 COR	Paul
Chastised, not killed	**6:9** [9]As unknown, and yet well known; as dying, and, behold, we live; as chastened, and not killed; **4:10-11** [10]Always bearing about in the body the dying of the Lord Jesus, that the life also of Jesus might be made manifest in our body. [11]For we which live are alway delivered unto death for Jesus' sake, that the life also of Jesus might be made manifest in our mortal flesh.	**Rom 8:36** [36]As it is written, For thy sake we are killed all the day long; we are accounted as sheep for the slaughter.

2 CORINTHIANS 6:10—Christian Ministry (2:14–7:4), 57 CE

Theme	2 COR	Paul
Rejoice even in sorrow	**6:10** [10]As sorrowful, yet alway rejoicing; as poor, yet making many rich; as having nothing, and yet possessing all things.	**Rom 8:32** [32]He that spared not his own Son, but delivered him up for us all, how shall he not with him also freely give us all things? **1 Cor 3:21** [21]Therefore let no man glory in men. For all things are yours;

2 CORINTHIANS 6:12—Christian Ministry (2:14–7:4), 57 CE

Theme	2 COR
Stay on straight path	**6:12** [12]Ye are not straitened in us, but ye are straitened in your own bowels. **7:3** [3]I speak not this to condemn you: for I have said before, that ye are in our hearts to die and live with you.

2 CORINTHIANS 6:13—Christian Ministry (2:14–7:4), 57 CE

Theme	2 COR	Paul
Grow in Christ	**6:13** [13]Now for a recompense in the same, (I speak as unto my children,) be ye also enlarged.	**Gal 4:19** [19]My little children, of whom I travail in birth again until Christ be formed in you,

2 CORINTHIANS 6:16—Christian Ministry (2:14–7:4), 57 CE

Theme	2 COR	Paul	Jewish Writings	Other
Believers are temple of God	**6:16** [16]And what agreement hath the temple of God with idols? for ye are the temple of the living God; as God hath said, I will dwell in them, and walk in them; and I will be their God, and they shall be my people.	**1 Cor 3:16–17** [16]Know ye not that ye are the temple of God, and that the Spirit of God dwelleth in you? [17]If any man defile the temple of God, him shall God destroy; for the temple of God is holy, which temple ye are. **1 Cor 6:19** [19]What? know ye not that your body is the temple of the Holy Ghost which is in you, which ye have of God, and ye are not your own? **1 Cor 10:20-21** [20]But I say, that the things which the Gentiles sacrifice, they sacrifice to devils, and not to God: and I would not that ye should have fellowship with devils. [21]Ye cannot drink the cup of the Lord, and the cup of devils: ye cannot be partakers of the Lord's table, and of the table of devils.	**Ex 25:8** [8]And let them make me a sanctuary; that I may dwell among them. **Lev 26:12** [12]And I will walk among you, and will be your God, and ye shall be my people. **Jer 31:1** [1]At the same time, saith the LORD, will I be the God of all the families of Israel, and they shall be my people. **Ezek 37:27** [27]My tabernacle also shall be with them: yea, I will be their God, and they shall be my people.	**Q-Quelle** Leaven: 2 Cor 6:16/1 Cor 3:16/[Mt 13:33]/[Lk 12:11-12(QS 37 [Thom 44]), [Lk 13:20-21(QS 46 [Thom 20, 96])]; Precedence: 2 Cor 6:16/1 Cor 3:16/[Mt 19:28]/[Mk 10:41-45]/[Lk 22:28-30 (QS 62)]

2 CORINTHIANS 6:17—Christian Ministry (2:14–7:4), 57 CE

Theme	2 COR	NT	Jewish Writings
Separate from misbelievers	**6:17** [17]Wherefore come out from among them, and be ye separate, saith the Lord, and touch not the unclean thing; and I will receive you,	**Rev 18:4** [4]And I heard another voice from heaven, saying, Come out of her, my people, that ye be not partakers of her sins, and that ye receive not of her plagues. **Rev 21:27** [27]And there shall in no wise enter into it any thing that defileth, neither whatsoever worketh abomination, or maketh a lie: but they which are written in the Lamb's book of life.	**Is 52:11** [11]Depart ye, depart ye, go ye out from thence, touch no unclean thing; go ye out of the midst of her; be ye clean, that bear the vessels of the LORD. **Ezek 20:34, 41** [34]And I will bring you out from the people, and will gather you out of the countries wherein ye are scattered, with a mighty hand, and with a stretched out arm, and with fury poured out. . . . [41]I will accept you with your sweet savour, when I bring you out from the people, and gather you out of the countries wherein ye have been scattered; and I will be sanctified in you before the heathen.

2 CORINTHIANS 6:18—Christian Ministry (2:14–7:4), 57 CE

Theme	2 COR	NT	Jewish Writings
Paul, a father to converts	**6:18** [18]And will be a Father unto you, and ye shall be my sons and daughters, saith the Lord Almighty.	**Rev 4:8** [8]And the four beasts had each of them six wings about him; and they were full of eyes within: and they rest not day and night, saying, Holy, holy, holy, Lord God Almighty, which was, and is, and is to come. **Rev 11:17** [17]Saying, We give thee thanks, O Lord God Almighty, which art, and wast, and art to come; because thou hast taken to thee thy great power, and hast reigned. **Rev 21:7** [7]He that overcometh shall inherit all things; and I will be his God, and he shall be my son.	**2 Sam 7:14** [14]I will be his father, and he shall be my son. If he commit iniquity, I will chasten him with the rod of men, and with the stripes of the children of men: **Ps 2:7** [7]I will declare the decree: the LORD hath said unto me, Thou art my Son; this day have I begotten thee. **Is 43:6** [6]I will say to the north, Give up; and to the south, Keep not back: bring my sons from far, and my daughters from the ends of the earth; **Jer 31:9** [9]They shall come with weeping, and with supplications will I lead them: I will cause them to walk by the rivers of waters in a straight way, wherein they shall not stumble: for I am a father to Israel, and Ephraim is my firstborn.

2 CORINTHIANS 7:3—Christian Ministry (2:14–7:4), 57 CE

Theme	2 COR
Be faithful	**7:3** [3]I speak not this to condemn you: for I have said before, that ye are in our hearts to die and live with you. **6:11–13** [11]O ye Corinthians, our mouth is open unto you, our heart is enlarged. [12]Ye are not straitened in us, but ye are straitened in your own bowels. [13]Now for a recompense in the same, (I speak as unto my children,) be ye also enlarged.

2 CORINTHIANS 7:4—Christian Ministry (2:14–7:4), 57 CE

Theme	2 COR	Mt
Christians called to suffer	**7:4** [4]Great is my boldness of speech toward you, great is my glorying of you: I am filled with comfort, I am exceeding joyful in all our tribulation. **5:3** [3]If so be that being clothed we shall not be found naked. **12:10** [10]Therefore I take pleasure in infirmities, in reproaches, in necessities, in persecutions, in distresses for Christ's sake: for when I am weak, then am I strong.	**5:10-12** [10]Blessed are they which are persecuted for righteousness' sake: for theirs is the kingdom of heaven. [11]Blessed are ye, when men shall revile you, and persecute you, and shall say all manner of evil against you falsely, for my sake. [12]Rejoice, and be exceeding glad: for great is your reward in heaven: for so persecuted they the prophets which were before you. **24:6–22** [6]And ye shall hear of wars and rumours of wars: see that ye be not troubled: for all these things must come to pass, but the end is not yet. [7]For nation shall rise against nation, and kingdom against kingdom: and there shall be famines, and pestilences, and earthquakes, in divers places. [8]All these are the beginning of sorrows. [9]Then shall they deliver you up to be afflicted, and shall kill you: and ye shall be hated of all nations for my name's sake. [10]And then shall many be offended, and shall betray one another, and shall hate one another. [11]And many false prophets shall rise, and shall deceive many. [12]And because iniquity shall abound, the love of many shall wax cold. [13]But he that shall endure unto the end, the same shall be saved. [14]And this gospel of the kingdom shall be preached in all the world for a witness unto all nations; and then shall the end come. [15]When ye therefore shall see the abomination of desolation, spoken of by Daniel the prophet, stand in the holy place, (whoso readeth, let him understand:) [16]Then let them which be in Judaea flee into the mountains: [17]Let him which is on the housetop not come down to take any thing out of his house: [18]Neither let him which is in the field return back to take his clothes. [19]And woe unto them that are with child, and to them that give suck in those days! [20]But pray ye that your flight be not in the winter, neither on the sabbath day: **[21]For then shall be great tribulation, such as was not since the beginning of the world to this time, no, nor ever shall be.** [22]And except those days should be shortened, there should no flesh be saved: but for the elect's sake those days shall be shortened. **24:15–31** [15]When ye therefore shall see the abomination of desolation, spoken of by Daniel the prophet, stand in the holy place, (whoso readeth, let him understand:) [16]Then let them which be in Judaea flee into the mountains: [17]Let him which is on the housetop not come down to take any thing out of his house: [18]Neither let him which is in the field return back to take his clothes. [19]And woe unto them that are with child, and to them that give suck in those days! [20]But pray ye that your flight be not in the winter, neither on the sabbath day: [21]For then shall be great tribulation, such as was not since the beginning of the world to this time, no, nor ever shall be. [22]And except those days should be shortened, there should no flesh be saved: but for the elect's sake those days shall be shortened. [23]Then if any man shall say unto you, Lo, here is Christ, or there; believe it not. [24]For there shall arise false Christs, and false prophets, and shall show great signs and wonders; insomuch that, if it were possible, they shall deceive the very elect. [25]Behold, I have told you before. [26]Wherefore if they shall say unto you, Behold, he is in the desert; go not forth: behold, he is in the secret chambers; believe it not. [27]For as the lightning cometh out of the east, and shineth even unto the west; so shall also the coming of the Son of man be. [28]For wheresoever the carcase is, there will the eagles be gathered together. [29]Immediately after the tribulation of those days shall the sun be darkened, and the moon shall not give her light, and the stars shall fall from heaven, and the powers of the heavens shall be shaken: [30]And then shall appear the sign of the Son of man in heaven: and then shall all the tribes of the earth mourn, and they shall see the Son of man coming in the clouds of heaven with power and great glory. [31]And he shall send his angels with a great sound of a trumpet, and they shall gather together his elect from the four winds, from one end of heaven to the other.

Mk	Lk
13:7–20 [7]And when ye shall hear of wars and rumours of wars, be ye not troubled: for such things must needs be; but the end shall not be yet. [8]For nation shall rise against nation, and kingdom against kingdom: and there shall be earthquakes in divers places, and there shall be famines and troubles: these are the beginnings of sorrows. [9]But take heed to yourselves: for they shall deliver you up to councils; and in the synagogues ye shall be beaten: and ye shall be brought before rulers and kings for my sake, for a testimony against them. [10]And the gospel must first be published among all nations. [11]But when they shall lead you, and deliver you up, take no thought beforehand what ye shall speak, neither do ye premeditate: but whatsoever shall be given you in that hour, that speak ye: for it is not ye that speak, but the Holy Ghost. [12]Now the brother shall betray the brother to death, and the father the son; and children shall rise up against their parents, and shall cause them to be put to death. [13]And ye shall be hated of all men for my name's sake: but he that shall endure unto the end, the same shall be saved. [14]But when ye shall see the abomination of desolation, spoken of by Daniel the prophet, standing where it ought not, (let him that readeth understand,) then let them that be in Judaea flee to the mountains: [15]And let him that is on the housetop not go down into the house, neither enter therein, to take any thing out of his house: [16]And let him that is in the field not turn back again for to take up his garment. [17]But woe to them that are with child, and to them that give suck in those days! [18]And pray ye that your flight be not in the winter. [19]For in those days shall be affliction, such as was not from the beginning of the creation which God created unto this time, neither shall be. [20]And except that the Lord had shortened those days, no flesh should be saved: but for the elect's sake, whom he hath chosen, he hath shortened the days. **13:14–27** [14]But when ye shall see the abomination of desolation, spoken of by Daniel the prophet, standing where it ought not, (let him that readeth understand,) then let them that be in Judaea flee to the mountains: [15]And let him that is on the housetop not go down into the house, neither enter therein, to take any thing out of his house: [16]And let him that is in the field not turn back again for to take up his garment. [17]But woe to them that are with child, and to them that give suck in those days! [18]And pray ye that your flight be not in the winter. [19]For in those days shall be affliction, such as was not from the beginning of the creation which God created unto this time, neither shall be. [20]And except that the Lord had shortened those days, no flesh should be saved: but for the elect's sake, whom he hath chosen, he hath shortened the days. [21]And then if any man shall say to you, Lo, here is Christ; or, lo, he is there; believe him not: [22]For false Christs and false prophets shall rise, and shall show signs and wonders, to seduce, if it were possible, even the elect. [23]But take ye heed: behold, I have foretold you all things. [24]But in those days, after that tribulation, the sun shall be darkened, and the moon shall not give her light, [25]And the stars of heaven shall fall, and the powers that are in heaven shall be shaken. [26]And then shall they see the Son of man coming in the clouds with great power and glory. [27]And then shall he send his angels, and shall gather together his elect from the four winds, from the uttermost part of the earth to the uttermost part of heaven.	**6:22–23** [22]Blessed are ye, when men shall hate you, and when they shall separate you from their company, and shall reproach you, and cast out your name as evil, for the Son of man's sake. [23]Rejoice ye in that day, and leap for joy: for, behold, your reward is great in heaven: for in the like manner did their fathers unto the prophets. **21:9–14** [9]But when ye shall hear of wars and commotions, be not terrified: for these things must first come to pass; but the end is not by and by. [10]Then said he unto them, Nation shall rise against nation, and kingdom against kingdom: [11]And great earthquakes shall be in divers places, and famines, and pestilences; and fearful sights and great signs shall there be from heaven. [12]But before all these, they shall lay their hands on you, and persecute you, delivering you up to the synagogues, and into prisons, being brought before kings and rulers for my name's sake. [13]And it shall turn to you for a testimony. [14]Settle it therefore in your hearts, not to meditate before what ye shall answer: **21:20-27** [20]And when ye shall see Jerusalem compassed with armies, then know that the desolation thereof is nigh. [21]Then let them which are in Judaea flee to the mountains; and let them which are in the midst of it depart out; and let not them that are in the countries enter thereinto. [22]For these be the days of vengeance, that all things which are written may be fulfilled. **[23]But woe unto them that are with child, and to them that give suck, in those days! for there shall be great distress in the land, and wrath upon this people.** [24]And they shall fall by the edge of the sword, and shall be led away captive into all nations: and Jerusalem shall be trodden down of the Gentiles, until the times of the Gentiles be fulfilled. [25]And there shall be signs in the sun, and in the moon, and in the stars; and upon the earth distress of nations, with perplexity; the sea and the waves roaring; [26]Men's hearts failing them for fear, and for looking after those things which are coming on the earth: for the powers of heaven shall be shaken. [27]And then shall they see the Son of man coming in a cloud with power and great glory.

2 Corinthians 7:4 continued on next page

2 CORINTHIANS 7:4—Christian Ministry (2:14–7:4), 57 CE

Theme	2 COR	Paul	Other
(*Cont.*) **Christians called to suffer**	**7:4 (above)** **5:3 (above)** **12:10 (above)**	**Rom 5:3** [3]And not only so, but we glory in tribulations also: knowing that tribulation worketh patience; **Rom 8:17** [17]And if children, then heirs; heirs of God, and joint-heirs with Christ; if so be that we suffer with him, that we may be also glorified together. **Rom 12:10** [10]Be kindly affectioned one to another with brotherly love; in honour preferring one another; **Col 1:24** [24]Who now rejoice in my sufferings for you, and fill up that which is behind of the afflictions of Christ in my flesh for his body's sake, which is the church: **1 Thes 2:14–16** [14]For ye, brethren, became followers of the churches of God which in Judaea are in Christ Jesus: for ye also have suffered like things of your own countrymen, even as they have of the Jews: [15]Who both killed the Lord Jesus, and their own prophets, and have persecuted us; and they please not God, and are contrary to all men: [16]Forbidding us to speak to the Gentiles that they might be saved, to fill up their sins alway: for the wrath is come upon them to the uttermost **1 Thes 3:3–4** [3]That no man should be moved by these afflictions: for yourselves know that we are appointed thereunto. [4]For verily, when we were with you, we told you before that we should suffer tribulation; even as it came to pass, and ye know. **2 Thes 2:8** [8]And then shall that Wicked be revealed, whom the Lord shall consume with the spirit of his mouth, and shall destroy with the brightness of his coming:	**Q-Quelle** Beatitudes: 2 Cor 7:4/Col 1:24/Mt 5:3-12/Lk 6:20b-23 (QS 8 [Thom 54, 68, 69]) Day of SOM: 2 Cor 7:4/ Rom 8:17/[Mt 10:39], Mt 24:17-18, 23, 26-27, 28, [Mt 24:37-39, 24:40-41]/Mk 13:14-16, 13:19-23/[Lk 17:22-37 (QS 60 [Thom 3, 51, 61, 113])]; Assistance of the Holy Spirit: 2 Cor 7:4/[Mt 10:19-20]/Mk 13:11/[Lk 12:11-12 (QS 37 [Thom 44])], [Lk 21:14-15]

RESOLUTION OF THE CRISIS (7:5–16)

2 CORINTHIANS 7:5—Resolution in God's compassion (7:5–16), 57 CE

Theme	2 COR
Trouble in Macedonia	**7:5** [5]For, when we were come into Macedonia, our flesh had no rest, but we were troubled on every side; without were fightings, within were fears. **2:13** [13]I had no rest in my spirit, because I found not Titus my brother: but taking my leave of them, I went from thence into Macedonia.

2 CORINTHIANS 7:6—Resolution in God's compassion (7:5–16), 57 CE

Theme	2 COR
God comforts down-trodden	**7:6** [6]Nevertheless God, that comforteth those that are cast down, comforted us by the coming of Titus; **2:13** [13]I had no rest in my spirit, because I found not Titus my brother: but taking my leave of them, I went from thence into Macedonia. **7:6–7** [6]Nevertheless God, that comforteth those that are cast down, comforted us by the coming of Titus; [7]And not by his coming only, but by the consolation wherewith he was comforted in you, when he told us your earnest desire, your mourning, your fervent mind toward me; so that I rejoiced the more. **7:13–14** [13]Therefore we were comforted in your comfort: yea, and exceedingly the more joyed we for the joy of Titus, because his spirit was refreshed by you all. [14]For if I have boasted any thing to him of you, I am not ashamed; but as we spake all things to you in truth, even so our boasting, which I made before Titus, is found a truth. **8:16** [16]But thanks be to God, which put the same earnest care into the heart of Titus for you. **8:23** [23]Whether any do inquire of Titus, he is my partner and fellowhelper concerning you: or our brethren be inquired of, they are the messengers of the churches, and the glory of Christ. **12:18** [18]I desired Titus, and with him I sent a brother. Did Titus make a gain of you? walked we not in the same spirit? walked we not in the same steps?

2 CORINTHIANS 7:8—Resolution in God's compassion (7:5–16), 57 CE

Theme	2 COR	Paul
Sorry for a season	**7:8** [8]For though I made you sorry with a letter, I do not repent, though I did repent: for I perceive that the same epistle hath made you sorry, though it were but for a season. **6:10** [10]To whom ye forgive any thing, I forgive also: for if I forgave any thing, to whom I forgave it, for your sakes forgave I it in the person of Christ;	**Phil 2:6–8** [6]Who, being in the form of God, thought it not robbery to be equal with God: [7]But made himself of no reputation, and took upon him the form of a servant, and was made in the likeness of men: [8]And being found in fashion as a man, he humbled himself, and became obedient unto death, even the death of the cross.

2 CORINTHIANS 7:10—Resolution in God's compassion (7:5–16), 57 CE

Theme	2 COR
Caring for those who are learning faith	**7:12** [12]Wherefore, though I wrote unto you, I did it not for his cause that had done the wrong, nor for his cause that suffered wrong, but that our care for you in the sight of God might appear unto you. **2:3** [3]And I wrote this same unto you, lest, when I came, I should have sorrow from them of whom I ought to rejoice; having confidence in you all, that my joy is the joy of you all. **2:9** [9]For to this end also did I write, that I might know the proof of you, whether ye be obedient in all things. **7:8** [8]For though I made you sorry with a letter, I do not repent, though I did repent: for I perceive that the same epistle hath made you sorry, though it were but for a season.

2 CORINTHIANS 7:15—Resolution in God's compassion (7:5–16), 57 CE

Theme	2 COR
Inward affection for students	**7:15** [15]And his inward affection is more abundant toward you, whilst he remembereth the obedience of you all, how with fear and trembling ye received him. **2:9** [9]For to this end also did I write, that I might know the proof of you, whether ye be obedient in all things.

COLLECTION FOR JERUSALEM (8:1–9:15)

2 CORINTHIANS Chapters 8–9—Collection for Jerusalem (8:1–9:15), 57 CE

Theme	2 COR	Paul
Abound in love and grace while ministering to the saints	**Ch 8–9** **8** 1Moreover, brethren, we do you to wit of the grace of God bestowed on the churches of Macedonia; 2How that in a great trial of affliction the abundance of their joy and their deep poverty abounded unto the riches of their liberality. 3For to their power, I bear record, yea, and beyond their power they were willing of themselves; 4Praying us with much entreaty that we would receive the gift, and take upon us the fellowship of the ministering to the saints. 5And this they did, not as we hoped, but first gave their own selves to the Lord, and unto us by the will of God. 6Insomuch that we desired Titus, that as he had begun, so he would also finish in you the same grace also. 7Therefore, as ye abound in every thing, in faith, and utterance, and knowledge, and in all diligence, and in your love to us, see that ye abound in this grace also. 8I speak not by commandment, but by occasion of the forwardness of others, and to prove the sincerity of your love. 9For ye know the grace of our Lord Jesus Christ, that, though he was rich, yet for your sakes he became poor, that ye through his poverty might be rich. 10And herein I give my advice: for this is expedient for you, who have begun before, not only to do, but also to be forward a year ago. 11Now therefore perform the doing of it; that as there was a readiness to will, so there may be a performance also out of that which ye have. 12For if there be first a willing mind, it is accepted according to that a man hath, and not according to that he hath not. 13For I mean not that other men be eased, and ye burdened: 14But by an equality, that now at this time your abundance may be a supply for their want, that their abundance also may be a supply for your want: that there may be equality: 15As it is written, He that had gathered much had nothing over; and he that had gathered little had no lack. 16But thanks be to God, which put the same earnest care into the heart of Titus for you. 17For indeed he accepted the exhortation; but being more forward, of his own accord he went unto you. 18And we have sent with him the brother, whose praise is in the gospel throughout all the churches; 19And not that only, but who was also chosen of the churches to travel with us with this grace, which is administered by us to the glory of the same Lord, and declaration of your ready mind: 20Avoiding this, that no man should blame us in this abundance which is administered by us: 21Providing for honest things, not only in the sight of the Lord, but also in the sight of men. 22And we have sent with them our brother, whom we have oftentimes proved diligent in many things, but now much more diligent, upon the great confidence which I have in you. 23Whether any do inquire of Titus, he is my partner and fellowhelper concerning you: or our brethren be inquired of, they are the messengers of the churches, and the glory of Christ. 24Wherefore show ye to them, and before the churches, the proof of your love, and of our boasting on your behalf. **9** 1For as touching the ministering to the saints, it is superfluous for me to write to you: 2For I know the forwardness of your mind, for which I boast of you to them of Macedonia, that Achaia was ready a year ago; and your zeal hath provoked very many. 3Yet have I sent the brethren, lest our boasting of you should be in vain in this behalf; that, as I said, ye may be ready: 4Lest haply if they of Macedonia come with me, and find you unprepared, we (that we say not, ye) should be ashamed in this same confident boasting. 5Therefore I thought it necessary to exhort the brethren, that they would go before unto you, and make up beforehand your bounty, whereof ye had notice before, that the same might be ready, as a matter of bounty, and not as of covetousness. 6But this I say, He which soweth sparingly shall reap also sparingly; and he which soweth bountifully shall reap also bountifully. 7Every man according as he purposeth in his heart, so let him give; not grudgingly, or of necessity: for God loveth a cheerful giver. 8And God is able to make all grace abound toward you; that ye, always having all sufficiency in all things, may abound to every good work: 9(As it is written, He hath dispersed abroad; he hath given to the poor: his righteousness remaineth for ever. 10Now he that ministereth seed to the sower both minister bread for your food, and multiply your seed sown, and increase the fruits of your righteousness;) 11Being enriched in every thing to all bountifulness, which causeth through us thanksgiving to God. 12For the administration of this service not only supplieth the want of the saints, but is abundant also by many thanksgivings unto God; 13Whiles by the experiment of this ministration they glorify God for your professed subjection unto the gospel of Christ, and for your liberal distribution unto them, and unto all men; 14And by their prayer for you, which long after you for the exceeding grace of God in you. 15Thanks be unto God for his unspeakable gift.	**Rom 15:26–29** 26For it hath pleased them of Macedonia and Achaia to make a certain contribution for the poor saints which are at Jerusalem. 27It hath pleased them verily; and their debtors they are. For if the Gentiles have been made partakers of their spiritual things, their duty is also to minister unto them in carnal things. 28When therefore I have performed this, and have sealed to them this fruit, I will come by you into Spain. 29And I am sure that, when I come unto you, I shall come in the fulness of the blessing of the gospel of Christ.

2 CORINTHIANS 8:1—Collection for Jerusalem (8:1–9:15), 57 CE

Theme	2 COR	Paul
Grace on churches of Macedonia	**8:1** [1]Moreover, brethren, we do you to wit of the grace of God bestowed on the churches of Macedonia; **11:9** [9]And when I was present with you, and wanted, I was chargeable to no man: for that which was lacking to me the brethren which came from Macedonia supplied: and in all things I have kept myself from being burdensome unto you, and so will I keep myself.	**Rom 15:26** [26]For it hath pleased them of Macedonia and Achaia to make a certain contribution for the poor saints which are at Jerusalem.

2 CORINTHIANS 8:4—Collection for Jerusalem (8:1–9:15), 57 CE

Theme	2 COR	Lk	Paul
Pray for gift of ministering	**8:4** [4]Praying us with much entreaty that we would receive the gift, and take upon us the fellowship of the ministering to the saints.	**Acts 24:17** [17]Now after many years I came to bring alms to my nation, and offerings.	**Rom 15:31** [31]That I may be delivered from them that do not believe in Judaea; and that my service which I have for Jerusalem may be accepted of the saints;

2 CORINTHIANS 8:6—Collection for Jerusalem (8:1–9:15), 57 CE

Theme	2 COR
Titus to minister to Corinthians	**8:6** [6]Insomuch that we desired Titus, that as he had begun, so he would also finish in you the same grace also. **2:13** [13]I had no rest in my spirit, because I found not Titus my brother: but taking my leave of them, I went from thence into Macedonia. **7:6–7** [6]Nevertheless God, that comforteth those that are cast down, comforted us by the coming of Titus; [7]And not by his coming only, but by the consolation wherewith he was comforted in you, when he told us your earnest desire, your mourning, your fervent mind toward me; so that I rejoiced the more. **7:13–14** [13]Therefore we were comforted in your comfort: yea, and exceedingly the more joyed we for the joy of Titus, because his spirit was refreshed by you all. [14]For if I have boasted any thing to him of you, I am not ashamed; but as we spake all things to you in truth, even so our boasting, which I made before Titus, is found a truth. **8:16** [16]But thanks be to God, which put the same earnest care into the heart of Titus for you. **8:23** [23]Whether any do inquire of Titus, he is my partner and fellowhelper concerning you: or our brethren be inquired of, they are the messengers of the churches, and the glory of Christ. **12:18** [18]I desired Titus, and with him I sent a brother. Did Titus make a gain of you? walked we not in the same spirit? walked we not in the same steps?

2 CORINTHIANS 8:7—Collection for Jerusalem (8:1–9:15), 57 CE

Theme	2 COR	Paul
Abound in God's ways	**8:7** [7]Therefore, as ye abound in every thing, in faith, and utterance, and knowledge, and in all diligence, and in your love to us, see that ye abound in this grace also.	**1 Cor 1:5** [5]That in every thing ye are enriched by him, in all utterance, and in all knowledge;

2 CORINTHIANS 8:9—Collection for Jerusalem (8:1–9:15), 57 CE

Theme	2 COR	Paul
Though rich, Jesus became poor to teach	**8:9** [9]For ye know the grace of our Lord Jesus Christ, that, though he was rich, yet for your sakes he became poor, that ye through his poverty might be rich. **6:10** [10]As sorrowful, yet alway rejoicing; as poor, yet making many rich; as having nothing, and yet possessing all things.	**Phil 2:6–8** [6]Who, being in the form of God, thought it not robbery to be equal with God: [7]But made himself of no reputation, and took upon him the form of a servant, and was made in the likeness of men: [8]And being found in fashion as a man, he humbled himself, and became obedient unto death, even the death of the cross.

2 CORINTHIANS 8:10—Collection for Jerusalem (8:1–9:15), 57 CE

Theme	2 COR	Paul
Advice	**8:10** [10]And herein I give my advice: for this is expedient for you, who have begun before, not only to do, but also to be forward a year ago. **9:2** [2]For I know the forwardness of your mind, for which I boast of you to them of Macedonia, that Achaia was ready a year ago; and your zeal hath provoked very many.	**1 Cor 16:4** [4]And if it be meet that I go also, they shall go with me.

2 CORINTHIANS 8:15—Collection for Jerusalem (8:1–9:15), 57 CE

Theme	2 COR	Jewish Writings
Adequate provisions	**8:15** [15]As it is written, He that had gathered much had nothing over; and he that had gathered little had no lack.	**Ex 16:18** [18]And when they did mete it with an omer, he that gathered much had nothing over, and he that gathered little had no lack; they gathered every man according to his eating.

2 CORINTHIANS 8:18—Collection for Jerusalem (8:1–9:15), 57 CE

Theme	2 COR
Brother who is favored	**8:18** [18]And we have sent with him the brother, whose praise is in the gospel throughout all the churches; **12:18** [18]I desired Titus, and with him I sent a brother. Did Titus make a gain of you? walked we not in the same spirit? walked we not in the same steps?

2 CORINTHIANS 8:19—Collection for Jerusalem (8:1–9:15), 57 CE

Theme	2 COR	Paul
Traveling companion	**8:19** [19]And not that only, but who was also chosen of the churches to travel with us with this grace, which is administered by us to the glory of the same Lord, and declaration of your ready mind:	**1 Cor 16:3–4** [3]And when I come, whomsoever ye shall approve by your letters, them will I send to bring your liberality unto Jerusalem. [4]And if it be meet that I go also, they shall go with me.

2 CORINTHIANS 8:21—Collection for Jerusalem (8:1–9:15), 57 CE

Theme	2 COR	Paul
Honesty for God & humanity	**8:21** [21]Providing for honest things, not only in the sight of the Lord, but also in the sight of men.	**Rom 12:17** [17]Recompense to no man evil for evil. Provide things honest in the sight of all men.

2 CORINTHIANS 9:2—Collection for Jerusalem (8:1–9:15), 57 CE

Theme	2 COR	Paul
Achaia ready a year ago, zealous	**9:2** [2]For I know the forwardness of your mind, for which I boast of you to them of Macedonia, that Achaia was ready a year ago; and your zeal hath provoked very many. **8:10** [10]And herein I give my advice: for this is expedient for you, who have begun before, not only to do, but also to be forward a year ago.	**Rom 15:26** [26]For it hath pleased them of Macedonia and Achaia to make a certain contribution for the poor saints which are at Jerusalem.

2 CORINTHIANS 9:6—Collection for Jerusalem (8:1–9:15), 57 CE

Theme	2 COR	Jewish Writings
Sow abundantly	**9:6** [6]But this I say, He which soweth sparingly shall reap also sparingly; and he which soweth bountifully shall reap also bountifully.	**Prov 11:24–25** [24]There is that scattereth, and yet increaseth; and there is that withholdeth more than is meet, but it tendeth to poverty. [25]The liberal soul shall be made fat: and he that watereth shall be watered also himself.

2 CORINTHIANS 9:7—Collection for Jerusalem (8:1–9:15), 57 CE

Theme	2 COR	Jewish Writings
Give with a good heart	**9:7** [7]Every man according as he purposeth in his heart, so let him give; not grudgingly, or of necessity: for God loveth a cheerful giver.	**Prov 22:8 (See LXX)** [8]He that soweth iniquity shall reap vanity: and the rod of his anger shall fail.

2 CORINTHIANS 9:9—Collection for Jerusalem (8:1–9:15), 57 CE

Theme	2 COR	Jewish Writings
Give to the poor	**9:9** [9](As it is written, He hath dispersed abroad; he hath given to the poor: his righteousness remaineth for ever.	**Ps 112:9** [9]He hath dispersed, he hath given to the poor; his righteousness endureth for ever; his horn shall be exalted with honour.

2 CORINTHIANS 9:10—Collection for Jerusalem (8:1–9:15), 57 CE

Theme	2 COR	Jewish Writings	Other
God provides bread & seed	**9:10** [10]Now he that ministereth seed to the sower both minister bread for your food, and multiply your seed sown, and increase the fruits of your righteousness;)	**Is 55:10** [10]For as the rain cometh down, and the snow from heaven, and returneth not thither, but watereth the earth, and maketh it bring forth and bud, that it may give seed to the sower, and bread to the eater:	**Q-Quelle** Thanks and Blessings for Disciples: 2 Cor 9:10/[Col 1:6]/ [Mt 11:25-27, Mt 13:16-17]/ [Lk 10:21-24 (QS 24, 25)]

2 CORINTHIANS 9:13—Collection for Jerusalem (8:1–9:15), 57 CE

Theme	2 COR	Paul
Ministers see progress	**9:13** [13]Whiles by the experiment of this ministration they glorify God for your professed subjection unto the gospel of Christ, and for your liberal distribution unto them, and unto all men; **8:4** [4]Praying us with much entreaty that we would receive the gift, and take upon us the fellowship of the ministering to the saints.	**Rom 15:31** [31]That I may be delivered from them that do not believe in Judaea; and that my service which I have for Jerusalem may be accepted of the saints;

2 CORINTHIANS 9:14—Collection for Jerusalem (8:1–9:15), 57 CE

Theme	2 COR	Mt	Paul
God's grace	**9:14** [14]And by their prayer for you, which long after you for the exceeding grace of God in you.	**23:12** [12]And whosoever shall exalt himself shall be abased; and he that shall humble himself shall be exalted.	**Phil 2:7–9** [7]But made himself of no reputation, and took upon him the form of a servant, and was made in the likeness of men: [8]And being found in fashion as a man, he humbled himself, and became obedient unto death, even the death of the cross. [9]Wherefore God also hath highly exalted him, and given him a name which is above every name:

2 CORINTHIANS 9:15—Collection for Jerusalem (8:1–9:15), 57 CE

Theme	2 COR	Paul
Thank God for abundance	**9:15** [15]Thanks be unto God for his unspeakable gift.	**Rom 5:15–16** [15]But not as the offence, so also is the free gift. For if through the offence of one many be dead, much more the grace of God, and the gift by grace, which is by one man, Jesus Christ, hath abounded unto many. [16]And not as it was by one that sinned, so is the gift: for the judgment was by one to condemnation, but the free gift is of many offences unto justification.

PAUL'S EXPLANATION OF HIS MINISTRY (10:1–13:10)

2 CORINTHIANS 10:2—Paul's explanation of his ministry (10:1–13:10), 57 CE

Theme	2 COR	Paul
Paul's boldness	**10:2** [2]But I beseech you, that I may not be bold when I am present with that confidence, wherewith I think to be bold against some, which think of us as if we walked according to the flesh. **13:2** [2]I told you before, and foretell you, as if I were present, the second time; and being absent now I write to them which heretofore have sinned, and to all other, that, if I come again, I will not spare. **13:10** [10]Therefore I write these things being absent, lest being present I should use sharpness, according to the power which the Lord hath given me to edification, and not to destruction.	**1 Cor 4:21** [21]What will ye? shall I come unto you with a rod, or in love, and in the spirit of meekness?

2 CORINTHIANS 10:4—Paul's explanation of his ministry (10:1–13:10), 57 CE

Theme	2 COR	Paul
Weapons are not carnal	**10:4** [4](For the weapons of our warfare are not carnal, but mighty through God to the pulling down of strong holds;) **6:7** [7]By the word of truth, by the power of God, by the armour of righteousness on the right hand and on the left, **13:2–3** [2]I told you before, and foretell you, as if I were present, the second time; and being absent now I write to them which heretofore have sinned, and to all other, that, if I come again, I will not spare: [3]Since ye seek a proof of Christ speaking in me, which to you-ward is not weak, but is mighty in you.	**1 Cor 1:25** [25]Because the foolishness of God is wiser than men; and the weakness of God is stronger than men. **Eph 6:10-14 (Pseudo)** [10]Finally, my brethren, be strong in the Lord, and in the power of his might. [11]Put on the whole armour of God, that ye may be able to stand against the wiles of the devil. [12]For we wrestle not against flesh and blood, but against principalities, against powers, against the rulers of the darkness of this world, against spiritual wickedness in high places. [13]Wherefore take unto you the whole armour of God, that ye may be able to withstand in the evil day, and having done all, to stand. [14]Stand therefore, having your loins girt about with truth, and having on the breastplate of righteousness

2 CORINTHIANS 10:6—Paul's explanation of his ministry (10:1–13:10), 57 CE

Theme	2 COR
Readiness to avenge dis-obedience	**10:6** [6]And having in a readiness to revenge all disobedience, when your obedience is fulfilled. **2:9** [9](As it is written, He hath dispersed abroad; he hath given to the poor: his righteousness remaineth for ever.

2 CORINTHIANS 10:7—Paul's explanation of his ministry (10:1–13:10), 57 CE

Theme	2 COR	Paul
Being in Christ	**10:7** [7]Do ye look on things after the outward appearance? If any man trust to himself that he is Christ's, let him of himself think this again, that, as he is Christ's, even so are we Christ's.	**1 Cor 1:12** [12]Now this I say, that every one of you saith, I am of Paul; and I of Apollos; and I of Cephas; and I of Christ.

2 CORINTHIANS 10:8—Paul's explanation of his ministry (10:1–13:10), 57 CE

Theme	2 COR	Mt	Lk
Authority in Christ	**10:8** [8]For though I should boast somewhat more of our authority, which the Lord hath given us for edification, and not for your destruction, I should not be ashamed: **12:19** [19]Again, think ye that we excuse ourselves unto you? we speak before God in Christ: but we do all things, dearly beloved, for your edifying. **13:10** [10]Therefore I write these things being absent, lest being present I should use sharpness, according to the power which the Lord hath given me to edification, and not to destruction.	**7:24–27** [24]Therefore whosoever heareth these sayings of mine, and doeth them, I will liken him unto a wise man, which built his house upon a rock: [25]And the rain descended, and the floods came, and the winds blew, and beat upon that house; and it fell not: for it was founded upon a rock. [26]And every one that heareth these sayings of mine, and doeth them not, shall be likened unto a foolish man, which built his house upon the sand: [27]And the rain descended, and the floods came, and the winds blew, and beat upon that house; and it fell: and great was the fall of it. **16:16–20** [16]And Simon Peter answered and said, Thou art the Christ, the Son of the living God. [17]And Jesus answered and said unto him, Blessed art thou, Simon Barjona: for flesh and blood hath not revealed it unto thee, but my Father which is in heaven. [18]And I say also unto thee, That thou art Peter, and upon this rock I will build my church; and the gates of hell shall not prevail against it. [19]And I will give unto thee the keys of the kingdom of heaven: and whatsoever thou shalt bind on earth shall be bound in heaven: and whatsoever thou shalt loose on earth shall be loosed in heaven. [20]Then charged he his disciples that they should tell no man that he was Jesus the Christ.	**6:48–49** [48]He is like a man which built an house, and digged deep, and laid the foundation on a rock: and when the flood arose, the stream beat vehemently upon that house, and could not shake it: for it was founded upon a rock. [49]But he that heareth, and doeth not, is like a man that without a foundation built an house upon the earth; against which the stream did beat vehemently, and immediately it fell; and the ruin of that house was great.

2 CORINTHIANS 10:10—Paul's explanation of his ministry (10:1–13:10), 57 CE

Theme	2 COR	Paul
Letters weighty, weak bodily presence	**10:10** [10]For his letters, say they, are weighty and powerful; but his bodily presence is weak, and his speech contemptible.	**1 Cor 2:3** [3]And I was with you in weakness, and in fear, and in much trembling.

2 CORINTHIANS 10:11—Paul's explanation of his ministry (10:1–13:10), 57 CE

Theme	2 COR
Matching word and deed	**10:11** [11]Let such an one think this, that, such as we are in word by letters when we are absent, such will we be also in deed when we are present. **13:1–2** [1]This is the third time I am coming to you. In the mouth of two or three witnesses shall every word be established. [2]I told you before, and foretell you, as if I were present, the second time; and being absent now I write to them which heretofore have sinned, and to all other, that, if I come again, I will not spare:

Paul	Other
1 Cor 1:11–12	**Q-Quelle**
[11]For it hath been declared unto me of you, my brethren, by them which are of the house of Chloe, that there are contentions among you. [12]Now this I say, that every one of you saith, I am of Paul; and I of Apollos; and I of Cephas; and I of Christ.	House on Rock: 2 Cor 10:8/Mt 7:21-27/Lk 6:46-49 (QS 14)
1 Cor 3:9–15	
[9]For we are labourers together with God: ye are God's husbandry, ye are God's building. [10]According to the grace of God which is given unto me, as a wise masterbuilder, I have laid the foundation, and another buildeth thereon. But let every man take heed how he buildeth thereupon. [11]For other foundation can no man lay than that is laid, which is Jesus Christ. [12]Now if any man build upon this foundation gold, silver, precious stones, wood, hay, stubble; [13]Every man's work shall be made manifest: for the day shall declare it, because it shall be revealed by fire; and the fire shall try every man's work of what sort it is. [14]If any man's work abide which he hath built thereupon, he shall receive a reward. [15]If any man's work shall be burned, he shall suffer loss: but he himself shall be saved; yet so as by fire.	
1 Cor 13:10	
[10]But when that which is perfect is come, then that which is in part shall be done away.	
1 Cor 14:3	
[3]But he that prophesieth speaketh unto men to edification, and exhortation, and comfort.	
1 Cor 14:5	
[5]I would that ye all spake with tongues, but rather that ye prophesied: for greater is he that prophesieth than he that speaketh with tongues, except he interpret, that the church may receive edifying.	
1 Cor 14:12	
[12]Even so ye, forasmuch as ye are zealous of spiritual gifts, seek that ye may excel to the edifying of the church.	
1 Cor 14:26	
[26]How is it then, brethren? when ye come together, every one of you hath a psalm, hath a doctrine, hath a tongue, hath a revelation, hath an interpretation. Let all things be done unto edifying.	

2 CORINTHIANS 10:12—Paul's explanation of his ministry (10:1–13:10), 57 CE

Theme	2 COR
Not wise to compare	**10:12** [12]For we dare not make ourselves of the number, or compare ourselves with some that commend themselves: but they measuring themselves by themselves, and comparing themselves among themselves, are not wise. **3:1–2** [1]Do we begin again to commend ourselves? or need we, as some others, epistles of commendation to you, or letters of commendation from you? [2]Ye are our epistle written in our hearts, known and read of all men: **4:2** [2]But have renounced the hidden things of dishonesty, not walking in craftiness, nor handling the word of God deceitfully; but by manifestation of the truth commending ourselves to every man's conscience in the sight of God. **5:12** [12]For we commend not ourselves again unto you, but give you occasion to glory on our behalf, that ye may have somewhat to answer them which glory in appearance, and not in heart. **6:4** [4]But in all things approving ourselves as the ministers of God, in much patience, in afflictions, in necessities, in distresses, **10:18** [18]For not he that commendeth himself is approved, but whom the Lord commendeth. **12:11** [11]I am become a fool in glorying; ye have compelled me: for I ought to have been commended of you: for in nothing am I behind the very chiefest apostles, though I be nothing.

2 CORINTHIANS 10:16—Paul's explanation of his ministry (10:1–13:10), 57 CE

Theme	2 COR	Paul
Not to boast in other's doings	**10:16** [16]To preach the gospel in the regions beyond you, and not to boast in another man's line of things made ready to our hand.	**Rom 15:20-21** [20]Yea, so have I strived to preach the gospel, not where Christ was named, lest I should build upon another man's foundation: [21]But as it is written, To whom he was not spoken of, they shall see: and they that have not heard shall understand.

2 CORINTHIANS 10:17—Paul's explanation of his ministry (10:1–13:10), 57 CE

Theme	2 COR	Paul	Jewish Writings
Glory in the Lord	**10:17** [17]But he that glorieth, let him glory in the Lord.	**1 Cor 1:31** [31]That, according as it is written, He that glorieth, let him glory in the Lord.	**Jer 9:22–23** [22]Speak, Thus saith the LORD, Even the carcases of men shall fall as dung upon the open field, and as the handful after the harvestman, and none shall gather them. [23]Thus saith the LORD, Let not the wise man glory in his wisdom, neither let the mighty man glory in his might, let not the rich man glory in his riches:

2 CORINTHIANS 10:18—Paul's explanation of his ministry (10:1–13:10), 57 CE

Theme	2 COR
Lord commandeth	**10:18** [18]For not he that commendeth himself is approved, but whom the Lord commendeth. **13:3–9** [3]Since ye seek a proof of Christ speaking in me, which to you-ward is not weak, but is mighty in you. [4]For though he was crucified through weakness, yet he liveth by the power of God. For we also are weak in him, but we shall live with him by the power of God toward you. [5]Examine yourselves, whether ye be in the faith; prove your own selves. Know ye not your own selves, how that Jesus Christ is in you, except ye be reprobates? [6]But I trust that ye shall know that we are not reprobates. [7]Now I pray to God that ye do no evil; not that we should appear approved, but that ye should do that which is honest, though we be as reprobates. [8]For we can do nothing against the truth, but for the truth. [9]For we are glad, when we are weak, and ye are strong: and this also we wish, even your perfection.

2 CORINTHIANS 11:1—Paul's explanation of his ministry (10:1–13:10), 57 CE

Theme	2 COR
Bear with Paul	**11:1** [1]Would to God ye could bear with me a little in my folly: and indeed bear with me. **11:21** [21]I speak as concerning reproach, as though we had been weak. Howbeit whereinsoever any is bold, (I speak foolishly,) I am bold also. **12:11** [11]I am become a fool in glorying; ye have compelled me: for I ought to have been commended of you: for in nothing am I behind the very chiefest apostles, though I be nothing.

2 CORINTHIANS 11:2—Paul's explanation of his ministry (10:1–13:10), 57 CE

Theme	2 COR	Paul	Jewish Writings
Jealous over followers	**11:2** [2]For I am jealous over you with godly jealousy: for I have espoused you to one husband, that I may present you as a chaste virgin to Christ.	**Eph 5:26–27 (Pseudo)** [26]That he might sanctify and cleanse it with the washing of water by the word, [27]That he might present it to himself a glorious church, not having spot, or wrinkle, or any such thing; but that it should be holy and without blemish.	**Hos 2:21–22** [21]And it shall come to pass in that day, I will hear, saith the LORD, I will hear the heavens, and they shall hear the earth; [22]And the earth shall hear the corn, and the wine, and the oil; and they shall hear Jezreel.

2 CORINTHIANS 11:3—Paul's explanation of his ministry (10:1–13:10), 57 CE

Theme	2 COR	Jewish Writings
Christ's simplicity is beguiling	**11:3** [3]But I fear, lest by any means, as the serpent beguiled Eve through his subtlety, so your minds should be corrupted from the simplicity that is in Christ.	**Gen 3:1–6** [1]Now the serpent was more subtle than any beast of the field which the LORD God had made. And he said unto the woman, Yea, hath God said, Ye shall not eat of every tree of the garden? [2]And the woman said unto the serpent, We may eat of the fruit of the trees of the garden: [3]But of the fruit of the tree which is in the midst of the garden, God hath said, Ye shall not eat of it, neither shall ye touch it, lest ye die. [4]And the serpent said unto the woman, Ye shall not surely die: [5]For God doth know that in the day ye eat thereof, then your eyes shall be opened, and ye shall be as gods, knowing good and evil. [6]And when the woman saw that the tree was good for food, and that it was pleasant to the eyes, and a tree to be desired to make one wise, she took of the fruit thereof, and did eat, and gave also unto her husband with her; and he did eat.

2 CORINTHIANS 11:4—Paul's explanation of his ministry (10:1–13:10), 57 CE

Theme	2 COR	Paul
Only one Jesus, that of Paul	**11:4** [4]For if he that cometh preacheth another Jesus, whom we have not preached, or if ye receive another spirit, which ye have not received, or another gospel, which ye have not accepted, ye might well bear with him.	**Gal 1:6–9** [6]I marvel that ye are so soon removed from him that called you into the grace of Christ unto another gospel: [7]Which is not another; but there be some that trouble you, and would pervert the gospel of Christ. [8]But though we, or an angel from heaven, preach any other gospel unto you than that which we have preached unto you, let him be accursed. [9]As we said before, so say I now again, If any man preach any other gospel unto you than that ye have received, let him be accursed.

2 CORINTHIANS 11:5—Paul's explanation of his ministry (10:1–13:10), 57 CE

Theme	2 COR
Least of the apostles	**11:5** [5]For I suppose I was not a whit behind the very chiefest apostles. **12:11** [11]I am become a fool in glorying; ye have compelled me: for I ought to have been commended of you: for in nothing am I behind the very chiefest apostles, though I be nothing.

2 CORINTHIANS 11:6—Paul's explanation of his ministry (10:1–13:10), 57 CE

Theme	2 COR	Paul
Rude in speech, but manifesting all things	**11:6** [6]But though I be rude in speech, yet not in knowledge; but we have been thoroughly made manifest among you in all things.	**1 Cor 1:5** [5]That in every thing ye are enriched by him, in all utterance, and in all knowledge; **1 Cor 1:17** [17]For Christ sent me not to baptize, but to preach the gospel: not with wisdom of words, lest the cross of Christ should be made of none effect. **1 Cor 2:1–5** [1]And I, brethren, when I came to you, came not with excellency of speech or of wisdom, declaring unto you the testimony of God. [2]For I determined not to know any thing among you, save Jesus Christ, and him crucified. [3]And I was with you in weakness, and in fear, and in much trembling. [4]And my speech and my preaching was not with enticing words of man's wisdom, but in demonstration of the Spirit and of power: [5]That your faith should not stand in the wisdom of men, but in the power of God.

2 CORINTHIANS 11:7—Paul's explanation of his ministry (10:1–13:10), 57 CE

Theme	2 COR	Mt	Lk
Gospel message is free	**11:7** [7]Have I committed an offence in abasing myself that ye might be exalted, because I have preached to you the gospel of God freely? **12:13–18** [13]For what is it wherein ye were inferior to other churches, except it be that I myself was not burden-some to you? forgive me this wrong. [14]Behold, the third time I am ready to come to you; and I will not be burdensome to you: for I seek not yours, but you: for the children ought not to lay up for the parents, but the parents for the children. [15]And I will very gladly spend and be spent for you; though the more abundantly I love you, the less I be loved. [16]But be it so, I did not burden you: nevertheless, being crafty, I caught you with guile. [17]Did I make a gain of you by any of them whom I sent unto you? [18]I desired Titus, and with him I sent a brother. Did Titus make a gain of you? walked we not in the same spirit? walked we not in the same steps?	**10:8** [8]Heal the sick, cleanse the lepers, raise the dead, cast out devils: freely ye have received, freely give. **10:10** [10]Nor scrip for your journey, neither two coats, neither shoes, nor yet staves: for the workman is worthy of his meat. **11:18** [18]For John came neither eating nor drinking, and they say, He hath a devil.	**10:7–8** [7]And in the same house remain, eating and drinking such things as they give: for the labourer is worthy of his hire. Go not from house to house. [8]And into whatsoever city ye enter, and they receive you, eat such things as are set before you: **Acts 18:3** [3]And because he was of the same craft, he abode with them, and wrought: for by their occupation they were tentmakers.

2 CORINTHIANS 11:9—Paul's explanation of his ministry (10:1–13:10), 57 CE

Theme	2 COR
Paul, not a burden to others	**11:9** [9]And when I was present with you, and wanted, I was chargeable to no man: for that which was lacking to me the brethren which came from Macedonia supplied: and in all things I have kept myself from being burdensome unto you, and so will I keep myself.

2 CORINTHIANS 11:10—Paul's explanation of his ministry (10:1–13:10), 57 CE

Theme	2 COR	Paul
Truth of Christ in Paul	**11:10** [10]As the truth of Christ is in me, no man shall stop me of this boasting in the regions of Achaia.	**1 Cor 9:15** [15]But I have used none of these things: neither have I written these things, that it should be so done unto me: for it were better for me to die, than that any man should make my glorying void.

<table>
<tr><th>Paul</th><th>Other</th></tr>
<tr><td>

1 Cor 9:4

[4]Have we not power to eat and to drink?

1 Cor 9:6–18

[6]Or I only and Barnabas, have not we power to forbear working? [7]Who goeth a warfare any time at his own charges? who planteth a vineyard, and eateth not of the fruit thereof? or who feedeth a flock, and eateth not of the milk of the flock? [8]Say I these things as a man? or saith not the law the same also? [9]For it is written in the law of Moses, Thou shalt not muzzle the mouth of the ox that treadeth out the corn. Doth God take care for oxen? [10]Or saith he it altogether for our sakes? For our sakes, no doubt, this is written: that he that ploweth should plow in hope; and that he that thresheth in hope should be partaker of his hope. [11]If we have sown unto you spiritual things, is it a great thing if we shall reap your carnal things? [12]If others be partakers of this power over you, are not we rather? Nevertheless we have not used this power; but suffer all things, lest we should hinder the gospel of Christ. [13]Do ye not know that they which minister about holy things live of the things of the temple? and they which wait at the altar are partakers with the altar? [14]Even so hath the Lord ordained that they which preach the gospel should live of the gospel. [15]But I have used none of these things: neither have I written these things, that it should be so done unto me: for it were better for me to die, than that any man should make my glorying void. [16]For though I preach the gospel, I have nothing to glory of: for necessity is laid upon me; yea, woe is unto me, if I preach not the gospel! [17]For if I do this thing willingly, I have a reward: but if against my will, a dispensation of the gospel is committed unto me. [18]What is my reward then? Verily that, when I preach the gospel, I may make the gospel of Christ without charge, that I abuse not my power in the gospel.

1 Cor 9:14

[14]Even so hath the Lord ordained that they which preach the gospel should live of the gospel.

1 Cor 10:27

[27]If any of them that believe not bid you to a feast, and ye be disposed to go; whatsoever is set before you, eat, asking no question for conscience sake.

2 Thes 3:8–9

[8]Neither did we eat any man's bread for nought; but wrought with labour and travail night and day, that we might not be chargeable to any of you: [9]Not because we have not power, but to make ourselves an ensample unto you to follow us.

</td><td>

Q-Quelle

Commissioning the 12: 2 Cor 11:7/[Gal 2:7-9]/2 Thes 3:8-9/[Mt 10:1]/Mt 10:7-11, [Mt 10:14]/[Mk 6:6b-13]/[Lk 9:1-6]/ Commissioning the 70: 2 Cor 11:7/[Gal 2:7-9]/[Mt 9:37-38], Mt 10:7-16/Lk 10:1-12 (QS 20 [Thom73, 14:2], QS 21)

</td></tr>
</table>

Paul
Phil 4:15–18
[15]Now ye Philippians know also, that in the beginning of the gospel, when I departed from Macedonia, no church communicated with me as concerning giving and receiving, but ye only. [16]For even in Thessalonica ye sent once and again unto my necessity. [17]Not because I desire a gift: but I desire fruit that may abound to your account. [18]But I have all, and abound: I am full, having received of Epaphroditus the things which were sent from you, an odour of a sweet smell, a sacrifice acceptable, wellpleasing to God.

2 CORINTHIANS 11:11—Paul's explanation of his ministry (10:1–13:10), 57 CE

Theme	2 COR
God knows Paul loves followers	**11:11** [11]Wherefore? because I love you not? God knoweth. **12:15** [15]And I will very gladly spend and be spent for you; though the more abundantly I love you, the less I be loved.

2 CORINTHIANS 11:22—Paul's explanation of his ministry (10:1–13:10), 57 CE

Theme	2 COR	Lk	Paul
Paul a Hebrew of Hebrews	**11:22** [22]Are they Hebrews? so am I. Are they Israelites? so am I. Are they the seed of Abraham? so am I.	**Acts 22:3** [3]I am verily a man which am a Jew, born in Tarsus, a city in Cilicia, yet brought up in this city at the feet of Gamaliel, and taught according to the perfect manner of the law of the fathers, and was zealous toward God, as ye all are this day.	**Rom 11:1** [1]I say then, Hath God cast away his people? God forbid. For I also am an Israelite, of the seed of Abraham, of the tribe of Benjamin. **Phil 3:5–6** [5]Circumcised the eighth day, of the stock of Israel, of the tribe of Benjamin, an Hebrew of the Hebrews; as touching the law, a Pharisee; [6]Concerning zeal, persecuting the church; touching the righteousness which is in the law, blameless.

2 CORINTHIANS 11:23—Paul's explanation of his ministry (10:1–13:10), 57 CE

Theme	2 COR	Lk	Paul
Brags about enduring trials	**11:23** [23]Are they ministers of Christ? (I speak as a fool) I am more; in labours more abundant, in stripes above measure, in prisons more frequent, in deaths oft. **6:5** [5]In stripes, in imprisonments, in tumults, in labours, in watchings, in fastings;	**Acts 16:22–24** [22]And the multitude rose up together against them: and the magistrates rent off their clothes, and commanded to beat them. [23]And when they had laid many stripes upon them, they cast them into prison, charging the jailor to keep them safely: [24]Who, having received such a charge, thrust them into the inner prison, and made their feet fast in the stocks.	**1 Cor 15:31–32** [31]I protest by your rejoicing which I have in Christ Jesus our Lord, I die daily. [32]If after the manner of men I have fought with beasts at Ephesus, what advantageth it me, if the dead rise not? let us eat and drink; for to morrow we die.

2 CORINTHIANS 11:24—Paul's explanation of his ministry (10:1–13:10), 57 CE

Theme	2 COR	Jewish Writings
39 lashes	**11:24** [24]Of the Jews five times received I forty stripes save one.	**Dt 25:2–3** [2]And it shall be, if the wicked man be worthy to be beaten, that the judge shall cause him to lie down, and to be beaten before his face, according to his fault, by a certain number. [3]Forty stripes he may give him, and not exceed: lest, if he should exceed, and beat him above these with many stripes, then thy brother should seem vile unto thee.

2 CORINTHIANS 11:25—Paul's explanation of his ministry (10:1–13:10), 57 CE

Theme	2 COR	Lk
Beaten, stoned, shipwrecked & faithful	**11:25** [25]Thrice was I beaten with rods, once was I stoned, thrice I suffered shipwreck, a night and a day I have been in the deep;	**Acts 14:19** [19]And there came thither certain Jews from Antioch and Iconium, who persuaded the people, and, having stoned Paul, drew him out of the city, supposing he had been dead. **Acts 27:43–44** [43]But the centurion, willing to save Paul, kept them from their purpose; and commanded that they which could swim should cast themselves first into the sea, and get to land: [44]And the rest, some on boards, and some on broken pieces of the ship. And so it came to pass, that they escaped all safe to land.

2 CORINTHIANS 11:27—Paul's explanation of his ministry (10:1–13:10), 57 CE

Theme	2 COR	Paul
Serving in fasting, hunger, thirst, cold	**11:27** [27]In weariness and painfulness, in watchings often, in hunger and thirst, in fastings often, in cold and nakedness.	**1 Cor 4:11** [11]Even unto this present hour we both hunger, and thirst, and are naked, and are buffeted, and have no certain dwelling-place;

2 CORINTHIANS 11:29—Paul's explanation of his ministry (10:1–13:10), 57 CE

Theme	2 COR	Paul
Weakness and offense	**11:29** [29]Who is weak, and I am not weak? who is offended, and I burn not?	**1 Cor 9:22** [22]To the weak became I as weak, that I might gain the weak: I am made all things to all men, that I might by all means save some.

2 CORINTHIANS 11:33—Paul's explanation of his ministry (10:1–13:10), 57 CE

Theme	2 COR	Lk
Escaped in a basket let down through a window	**11:33** [33]And through a window in a basket was I let down by the wall, and escaped his hands.	**Acts 9:23–25** [23]And after that many days were fulfilled, the Jews took counsel to kill him: [24]But their laying await was known of Saul. And they watched the gates day and night to kill him. [25]Then the disciples took him by night, and let him down by the wall in a basket.

2 CORINTHIANS 12:4—Paul's explanation of his ministry (10:1–13:10), 57 CE

Theme	2 COR	Lk	NT
Caught into paradise	**12:4** [4]How that he was caught up into paradise, and heard unspeakable words, which it is not lawful for a man to utter.	**23:43** [43]And Jesus said unto him, Verily I say unto thee, To day shalt thou be with me in paradise.	**Rev 2:7** [7]He that hath an ear, let him hear what the Spirit saith unto the churches; To him that overcometh will I give to eat of the tree of life, which is in the midst of the paradise of God.

2 CORINTHIANS 12:7–10—Paul's explanation of his ministry (10:1–13:10), 57 CE

Theme	2 COR	Mt	Mk	Jn	Paul
Perfected through weakness	**12:7–10** [7]And lest I should be exalted above measure through the abundance of the revelations, there was given to me a thorn in the flesh, the messenger of Satan to buffet me, lest I should be exalted above measure. [8]For this thing I besought the Lord thrice, that it might depart from me. [9]And he said unto me, My grace is sufficient for thee: for my strength is made perfect in weakness. Most gladly therefore will I rather glory in my infirmities, that the power of Christ may rest upon me. [10]Therefore I take pleasure in infirmities, in reproaches, in necessities, in persecutions, in distresses for Christ's sake: for when I am weak, then am I strong.	**26:38** [38]Then saith he unto them, My soul is exceeding sorrowful, even unto death: tarry ye here, and watch with me. **26:41** [41]Watch and pray, that ye enter not into temptation: the spirit indeed is willing, but the flesh is weak.	**14:34** [34]And saith unto them, My soul is exceeding sorrowful unto death: tarry ye here, and watch. **14:36** [36]And he said, Abba, Father, all things are possible unto thee; take away this cup from me: nevertheless not what I will, but what thou wilt. **14:38** [38]Watch ye and pray, lest ye enter into temptation. The spirit truly is ready, but the flesh is weak.	**12:27** [27]Now is my soul troubled; and what shall I say? Father, save me from this hour: but for this cause came I unto this hour. **18:11** [11]Then said Jesus unto Peter, Put up thy sword into the sheath: the cup which my Father hath given me, shall I not drink it?	**Rom 8:15** [15]John bare witness of him, and cried, saying, This was he of whom I spake, He that cometh after me is preferred before me: for he was before me. **Gal 4:4–6** [4]But when the fulness of the time was come, God sent forth his Son, made of a woman, made under the law, [5]To redeem them that were under the law, that we might receive the adoption of sons. [6]And because ye are sons, God hath sent forth the Spirit of his Son into your hearts, crying, Abba, Father. **Phil 2:8** [8]And being found in fashion as a man, he humbled himself, and became obedient unto death, even the death of the cross. **Col 4:2** [2]Continue in prayer, and watch in the same with thanksgiving;

2 CORINTHIANS 12:7—Paul's explanation of his ministry (10:1–13:10), 57 CE

Theme	2 COR
Abundance of revelations	**12:7** [7]And lest I should be exalted above measure through the abundance of the revelations, there was given to me a thorn in the flesh, the messenger of Satan to buffet me, lest I should be exalted above measure.

2 CORINTHIANS 12:8—Paul's explanation of his ministry (10:1–13:10), 57 CE

Theme	2 COR
Pleading for mercy	**12:8** [8]For this thing I besought the Lord thrice, that it might depart from me.

Jewish Writings

Num 33:55

55 But if ye will not drive out the inhabitants of the land from before you; then it shall come to pass, that those which ye let remain of them shall be pricks in your eyes, and thorns in your sides, and shall vex you in the land wherein ye dwell.

Jos 23:13

13 Know for a certainty that the LORD your God will no more drive out any of these nations from before you; but they shall be snares and traps unto you, and scourges in your sides, and thorns in your eyes, until ye perish from off this good land which the LORD your God hath given you.

Is 31:3

3 Now the Egyptians are men, and not God; and their horses flesh, and not spirit. When the LORD shall stretch out his hand, both he that helpeth shall fall, and he that is holpen shall fall down, and they all shall fail together.

Ezek 28:24

24 And there shall be no more a pricking brier unto the house of Israel, nor any grieving thorn of all that are round about them, that despised them; and they shall know that I am the Lord GOD.

Jewish Writings

Num 33:55

55 But if ye will not drive out the inhabitants of the land from before you; then it shall come to pass, that those which ye let remain of them shall be pricks in your eyes, and thorns in your sides, and shall vex you in the land wherein ye dwell.

Jos 23:13

13 Know for a certainty that the LORD your God will no more drive out any of these nations from before you; but they shall be snares and traps unto you, and scourges in your sides, and thorns in your eyes, until ye perish from off this good land which the LORD your God hath given you.

Ezek 28:24

24 And there shall be no more a pricking brier unto the house of Israel, nor any grieving thorn of all that are round about them, that despised them; and they shall know that I am the Lord GOD.

Mt

26:39–44

39 And he went a little further, and fell on his face, and prayed, saying, O my Father, if it be possible, let this cup pass from me: nevertheless not as I will, but as thou wilt. 40 And he cometh unto the disciples, and findeth them asleep, and saith unto Peter, What, could ye not watch with me one hour? 41 Watch and pray, that ye enter not into temptation: the spirit indeed is willing, but the flesh is weak. 42 He went away again the second time, and prayed, saying, O my Father, if this cup may not pass away from me, except I drink it, thy will be done. 43 And he came and found them asleep again: for their eyes were heavy. 44 And he left them, and went away again, and prayed the third time, saying the same words.

2 CORINTHIANS 12:9—Paul's explanation of his ministry (10:1–13:10), 57 CE

Theme	2 COR
Grace is sufficient for Paul	**12:9** [9]And he said unto me, My grace is sufficient for thee: for my strength is made perfect in weakness. Most gladly therefore will I rather glory in my infirmities, that the power of Christ may rest upon me. **4:7** [7]But we have this treasure in earthen vessels, that the excellency of the power may be of God, and not of us.

2 CORINTHIANS 12:10—Paul's explanation of his ministry (10:1–13:10), 57 CE

Theme	2 COR	Paul
Willing to suffer for gospel	**12:10** [10]Therefore I take pleasure in infirmities, in reproaches, in necessities, in persecutions, in distresses for Christ's sake: for when I am weak, then am I strong. **6:4–5** [4]But in all things approving ourselves as the ministers of God, in much patience, in afflictions, in necessities, in distresses, [5]In stripes, in imprisonments, in tumults, in labours, in watchings, in fastings;	**Rom 5:3** [3]And not only so, but we glory in tribulations also: knowing that tribulation worketh patience; **Phil 4:13** [13]I can do all things through Christ which strengtheneth me.

2 CORINTHIANS 12:11—Paul's explanation of his ministry (10:1–13:10), 57 CE

Theme	2 COR
Equal with apostles, though nothing	**12:11** [11]I am become a fool in glorying; ye have compelled me: for I ought to have been commended of you: for in nothing am I behind the very chiefest apostles, though I be nothing. **11:5** [5]For I suppose I was not a whit behind the very chiefest apostles.

2 CORINTHIANS 12:12—Paul's explanation of his ministry (10:1–13:10), 57 CE

Theme	2 COR	Mt	Mk	Lk	Paul	Other
Signs of wonder and healing	**12:12** [12]Truly the signs of an apostle were wrought among you in all patience, in signs, and wonders, and mighty deeds.	**10:1** [1]And when he had called unto him his twelve disciples, he gave them power against unclean spirits, to cast them out, and to heal all manner of sickness and all manner of disease.	**6:7** [7]And he called unto him the twelve, and began to send them forth by two and two; and gave them power over unclean spirits;	**9:1** [1]Then he called his twelve disciples together, and gave them power and authority over all devils, and to cure diseases. **10:9** [9]And heal the sick that are therein, and say unto them, The kingdom of God is come nigh unto you.	**Rom 15:19** [19]Through mighty signs and wonders, by the power of the Spirit of God; so that from Jerusalem, and round about unto Illyricum, I have fully preached the gospel of Christ. **1 Thes 1:5** [5]For our gospel came not unto you in word only, but also in power, and in the Holy Ghost, and in much assurance; as ye know what manner of men we were among you for your sake.	**Q-Quelle** Commissioning of 12: 2 Cor 12:12/Mt 10:1, [10:7-11, 10:14]/ Mk 6:6b-13/Lk 9:1-6

2 CORINTHIANS 12:13—Paul's explanation of his ministry (10:1–13:10), 57 CE

Theme	2 COR
Inferior to other churches	**12:13** [13]For what is it wherein ye were inferior to other churches, except it be that I myself was not burdensome to you? forgive me this wrong. **11:9–10** [9]And when I was present with you, and wanted, I was chargeable to no man: for that which was lacking to me the brethren which came from Macedonia supplied: and in all things I have kept myself from being burdensome unto you, and so will I keep myself. [10]As the truth of Christ is in me, no man shall stop me of this boasting in the regions of Achaia.

2 CORINTHIANS 12:16—Paul's explanation of his ministry (10:1–13:10), 57 CE

Theme	2 COR
Caught in guile	**12:16** [16]But be it so, I did not burden you: nevertheless, being crafty, I caught you with guile. **11:3, 13** [3]But I fear, lest by any means, as the serpent beguiled Eve through his subtlety, so your minds should be corrupted from the simplicity that is in Christ. . . . [13]For such are false apostles, deceitful workers, transforming themselves into the apostles of Christ.

2 CORINTHIANS 12:18—Paul's explanation of his ministry (10:1–13:10), 57 CE

Theme	2 COR
Titus in same spirit	**12:18** [18]I desired Titus, and with him I sent a brother. Did Titus make a gain of you? walked we not in the same spirit? walked we not in the same steps? **2:13** [13]I had no rest in my spirit, because I found not Titus my brother: but taking my leave of them, I went from thence into Macedonia. **8:16, 23** [16]But thanks be to God, which put the same earnest care into the heart of Titus for you. . . . [23]Whether any do inquire of Titus, he is my partner and fellowhelper concerning you: or our brethren be inquired of, they are the messengers of the churches, and the glory of Christ.

2 CORINTHIANS 12:20—Paul's explanation of his ministry (10:1–13:10), 57 CE

Theme	2 COR	Paul
Conten-tious believers	**12:20** [20]For I fear, lest, when I come, I shall not find you such as I would, and that I shall be found unto you such as ye would not: lest there be debates, envyings, wraths, strifes, backbitings, whisperings, swellings, tumults:	**1 Cor 1:11** [11]For it hath been declared unto me of you, my brethren, by them which are of the house of Chloe, that there are contentions among you. **1 Cor 3:3** [3]For ye are yet carnal: for whereas there is among you envying, and strife, and divisions, are ye not carnal, and walk as men?

2 CORINTHIANS 13:1—Paul's explanation of his ministry (10:1–13:10), 57 CE

Theme	2 COR	Mt	Jn
Witnesses to contentious behavior	**13:1** [1]This is the third time I am coming to you. In the mouth of two or three witnesses shall every word be established.	**18:16** [16]But if he will not hear thee, then take with thee one or two more, that in the mouth of two or three witnesses every word may be established.	**8:17** [17]It is also written in your law, that the testimony of two men is true.

2 CORINTHIANS 13:10—Paul's explanation of his ministry (10:1–13:10), 57 CE

Theme	2 COR	Mt	Mk	Lk
Christian correction	**13:10** [10]Therefore I write these things being absent, lest being present I should use sharpness, according to the power which the Lord hath given me to edification, and not to destruction. **10:8** [8]For though I should boast somewhat more of our authority, which the Lord hath given us for edification, and not for your destruction, I should not be ashamed:	**12:46–50** [46]While he yet talked to the people, behold, his mother and his brethren stood without, desiring to speak with him. [47]Then one said unto him, Behold, thy mother and thy brethren stand without, desiring to speak with thee. [48]But he answered and said unto him that told him, Who is my mother? and who are my brethren? [49]And he stretched forth his hand toward his disciples, and said, Behold my mother and my brethren! [50]For whosoever shall do the will of my Father which is in heaven, the same is my brother, and sister, and mother.	**3:31–35** [31]There came then his brethren and his mother, and, standing without, sent unto him, calling him. [32]And the multitude sat about him, and they said unto him, Behold, thy mother and thy brethren without seek for thee. [33]And he answered them, saying, Who is my mother, or my brethren? [34]And he looked round about on them which sat about him, and said, Behold my mother and my brethren! [35]For whosoever shall do the will of God, the same is my brother, and my sister, and mother.	**8:19–21** [19]Then came to him his mother and his brethren, and could not come at him for the press. [20]And it was told him by certain which said, Thy mother and thy brethren stand without, desiring to see thee. [21]And he answered and said unto them, My mother and my brethren are these which hear the word of God, and do it.

NT	Jewish Writings
Heb 10:28	**Dt 19:15**
[28]He that despised Moses' law died without mercy under two or three witnesses	[15]One witness shall not rise up against a man for any iniquity, or for any sin, in any sin that he sinneth: at the mouth of two witnesses, or at the mouth of three witnesses, shall the matter be established.

Paul	Other
Rom 12:4 [4]For as we have many members in one body, and all members have not the same office: **Rom 14:19–20** [19]Let us therefore follow after the things which make for peace, and things wherewith one may edify another. [20]For meat destroy not the work of God. All things indeed are pure; but it is evil for that man who eateth with offence. **1 Cor 6:15** [15]Know ye not that your bodies are the members of Christ? shall I then take the members of Christ, and make them the members of an harlot? God forbid. **1 Cor 10:17** [17]For we being many are one bread, and one body: for we are all partakers of that one bread. **1 Cor 12:12–13** [12]For as the body is one, and hath many members, and all the members of that one body, being many, are one body: so also is Christ. [13]For by one Spirit are we all baptized into one body, whether we be Jews or Gentiles, whether we be bond or free; and have been all made to drink into one Spirit. **1 Cor 15:22** [22]For as in Adam all die, even so in Christ shall all be made alive. **Gal 2:18–19** [18]For if I build again the things which I destroyed, I make myself a transgressor. [19]For I through the law am dead to the law, that I might live unto God. **Eph 1:22–23** [22]And hath put all things under his feet, and gave him to be the head over all things to the church, [23]Which is his body, the fulness of him that filleth all in all. **Eph 4:15 (Pseudo)** [15]But speaking the truth in love, may grow up into him in all things, which is the head, even Christ: **Eph 5:23 (Pseudo)** [23]For the husband is the head of the wife, even as Christ is the head of the church: and he is the saviour of the body.	**Q-Quelle** Divisions in Households: 2 Cor 13:10/Gal 2:18-19/[Mt 10:34-36]/[Lk 12:49-53 (QS 43 [Thom 16])]

CONCLUDING REMARKS (13:11–13)

2 CORINTHIANS 13:11—Conclusion (13:11–13), 57 CE

Theme	2 COR	Mk	Paul
Love one another	**13:11** [11]Finally, brethren, farewell. Be perfect, be of good comfort, be of one mind, live in peace; and the God of love and peace shall be with you.	**9:50** [50]And he, casting away his garment, rose, and came to Jesus.	**Rom 12:10** [10]Be kindly affectioned one to another with brotherly love; in honour preferring one another; **Rom 12:18** [18]If it be possible, as much as lieth in you, live peaceably with all men. **Rom 14:19** [19]Let us therefore follow after the things which make for peace, and things wherewith one may edify another. **1 Cor 7:15** [15]But if the unbelieving depart, let him depart. A brother or a sister is not under bondage in such cases: but God hath called us to peace. **Gal 6:10** [10]As we have therefore opportunity, let us do good unto all men, especially unto them who are of the household of faith. **Eph 4:32 (Pseudo)** [32]And be ye kind one to another, tenderhearted, forgiving one another, even as God for Christ's sake hath forgiven you. **Col 3:12–14** [12]Put on therefore, as the elect of God, holy and beloved, bowels of mercies, kindness, humbleness of mind, meekness, longsuffering; [13]Forbearing one another, and forgiving one another, if any man have a quarrel against any: even as Christ forgave you, so also do ye. [14]And above all these things put on charity, which is the bond of perfectness. **1 Thes 3:12** [12]And the Lord make you to increase and abound in love one toward another, and toward all men, even as we do toward you: **1 Thes 4:9** [9]But as touching brotherly love ye need not that I write unto you: for ye yourselves are taught of God to love one another. **1 Thes 5:12–13** [12]And we beseech you, brethren, to know them which labour among you, and are over you in the Lord, and admonish you; [13]And to esteem them very highly in love for their work's sake. And be at peace among yourselves. **1 Thes 5:15** [15]See that none render evil for evil unto any man; but ever follow that which is good, both among yourselves, and to all men. **2 Thes 1:3** [3]We are bound to thank God always for you, brethren, as it is meet, because that your faith groweth exceedingly, and the charity of every one of you all toward each other aboundeth;

2 CORINTHIANS 13:12—Conclusion (13:11–13), 57 CE

Theme	2 COR	Paul	NT
Greet with holy kiss	**13:12** [12]Greet one another with an holy kiss.	**Rom 16:16** [16]Salute one another with an holy kiss. The churches of Christ salute you. **1 Cor 16:20** [20]All the brethren greet you. Greet ye one another with an holy kiss. **Phil 4:22** [22]All the saints salute you, chiefly they that are of Caesar's household. **1 Thes 5:26** [26]Greet all the brethren with an holy kiss.	**1 Pet 5:14** [14]Greet ye one another with a kiss of charity. Peace be with you all that are in Christ Jesus. Amen.

2 CORINTHIANS 13:13—Conclusion (13:11–13), 57 CE

Theme	2 COR	Paul
Saints salute church at Corinth	**13:13** [13]All the saints salute you.	**Rom 16:20** [20]And the God of peace shall bruise Satan under your feet shortly. The grace of our Lord Jesus Christ be with you. Amen. **1 Cor 16:23** [23]The grace of our Lord Jesus Christ be with you.

GALATIANS

Paul wrote from Ephesus to converted pagans visited during second and third missionary journeys. Time Range: 48–50, 54, or 55 CE

ADDRESS (1:1–5)

GALATIANS 1:1–3—Address (1:1–5). Time range: 48–50, 54, or 55 CE

Theme	GAL
Paul, an apostle by Christ	**1:1–3** [1]Paul, an apostle, (not of men, neither by man, but by Jesus Christ, and God the Father, who raised him from the dead;) [2]And all the brethren which are with me, unto the churches of Galatia: [3]Grace be to you and peace from God the Father, and from our Lord Jesus Christ,

GALATIANS 1:1—Address (1:1–5). Time range: 48–50, 54, or 55 CE

Theme	GAL
Paul, an Apostle	**1:1** [1]Paul, an apostle, (not of men, neither by man, but by Jesus Christ, and God the Father, who raised him from the dead;) **1:11–12** [11]But I certify you, brethren, that the gospel which was preached of me is not after man. [12]For I neither received it of man, neither was I taught it, but by the revelation of Jesus Christ.

Paul
Rom 1:1–7
[1]Paul, a servant of Jesus Christ, called to be an apostle, separated unto the gospel of God, [2](Which he had promised afore by his prophets in the holy scriptures,) [3]Concerning his Son Jesus Christ our Lord, which was made of the seed of David according to the flesh; [4]And declared to be the Son of God with power, according to the spirit of holiness, by the resurrection from the dead: [5]By whom we have received grace and apostleship, for obedience to the faith among all nations, for his name: [6]Among whom are ye also the called of Jesus Christ: [7]To all that be in Rome, beloved of God, called to be saints: Grace to you and peace from God our Father, and the Lord Jesus Christ.
1 Cor 1:1–3
[1]Paul, called to be an apostle of Jesus Christ through the will of God, and Sosthenes our brother, [2]Unto the church of God which is at Corinth, to them that are sanctified in Christ Jesus, called to be saints, with all that in every place call upon the name of Jesus Christ our Lord, both theirs and ours: [3]Grace be unto you, and peace, from God our Father, and from the Lord Jesus Christ.

GALATIANS 1:3–4—Address (1:1–5), Christian liberty. Time range: 48–50, 54, or 55 CE

Theme	GAL	Mt	Mk	Lk	Jn	Paul
Being doers of God's will	**1:3–4** [3]Grace be to you and peace from God the Father, and from our Lord Jesus Christ, [4]Who gave himself for our sins, that he might deliver us from this present evil world, according to the will of God and our Father: **1:7** [7]Which is not another; but there be some that trouble you, and would pervert the gospel of Christ. **1:15** [15]But when it pleased God, who separated me from my mother's womb, and called me by his grace, **2:20** [20]I am crucified with Christ: nevertheless I live; yet not I, but Christ liveth in me: and the life which I now live in the flesh I live by the faith of the Son of God, who loved me, and gave himself for me.	**11:19** [19]The Son of man came eating and drinking, and they say, Behold a man gluttonous, and a winebibber, a friend of publicans and sinners. But wisdom is justified of her children. **23:34** [34]Wherefore, behold, I send unto you prophets, and wise men, and scribes: and some of them ye shall kill and crucify; and some of them shall ye scourge in your synagogues, and persecute them from city to city:	**14:36** [36]And he said, Abba, Father, all things are possible unto thee; take away this cup from me: nevertheless not what I will, but what thou wilt.	**7:35** [35]But wisdom is justified of all her children. **11:49** [49]Therefore also said the wisdom of God, I will send them prophets and apostles, and some of them they shall slay and persecute:	**1 Jn 5:19** [19]And we know that we are of God, and the whole world lieth in wickedness.	**Rom 12:2** [2]And be not conformed to this world: but be ye transformed by the renewing of your mind, that ye may prove what is that good, and acceptable, and perfect, will of God. **Gal 4:4** [4]But when the fulness of the time was come, God sent forth his Son, made of a woman, made under the law, **Gal 4:6** [6]And because ye are sons, God hath sent forth the Spirit of his Son into your hearts, crying, Abba, Father. **Eph 5:2 (Pseudo)** [2]And walk in love, as Christ also hath loved us, and hath given himself for us an offering and a sacrifice to God for a sweetsmelling savour. **Eph 5:16 (Pseudo)** [16]Redeeming the time, because the days are evil. **Col 1:16** [16]For by him were all things created, that are in heaven, and that are in earth, visible and invisible, whether they be thrones, or dominions, or principalities, or powers: all things were created by him, and for him: **1 Tim 2:6 (Pseudo)** [6]Who gave himself a ransom for all, to be testified in due time.

NT	Jewish Writings	Other
Heb 10:10 [10]By the which will we are sanctified through the offering of the body of Jesus Christ once for all.	**Ps 110** [1]The LORD said unto my Lord, Sit thou at my right hand, until I make thine enemies thy footstool. [2]The LORD shall send the rod of thy strength out of Zion: rule thou in the midst of thine enemies. [3]Thy people shall be willing in the day of thy power, in the beauties of holiness from the womb of the morning: thou hast the dew of thy youth. [4]The LORD hath sworn, and will not repent, Thou art a priest for ever after the order of Melchizedek. [5]The Lord at thy right hand shall strike through kings in the day of his wrath. [6]He shall judge among the heathen, he shall fill the places with the dead bodies; he shall wound the heads over many countries. [7]He shall drink of the brook in the way: therefore shall he lift up the head. **Dan 7** [1]In the first year of Belshazzar king of Babylon Daniel had a dream and visions of his head upon his bed: then he wrote the dream, and told the sum of the matters. [2]Daniel spake and said, I saw in my vision by night, and, behold, the four winds of the heaven strove upon the great sea. [3]And four great beasts came up from the sea, diverse one from another. [4]The first was like a lion, and had eagle's wings: I beheld till the wings thereof were plucked, and it was lifted up from the earth, and made stand upon the feet as a man, and a man's heart was given to it. [5]And behold another beast, a second, like to a bear, and it raised up itself on one side, and it had three ribs in the mouth of it between the teeth of it: and they said thus unto it, Arise, devour much flesh. [6]After this I beheld, and lo another, like a leopard, which had upon the back of it four wings of a fowl; the beast had also four heads; and dominion was given to it. [7]After this I saw in the night visions, and behold a fourth beast, dreadful and terrible, and strong exceedingly; and it had great iron teeth: it devoured and brake in pieces, and stamped the residue with the feet of it: and it was diverse from all the beasts that were before it; and it had ten horns. [8]I considered the horns, and, behold, there came up among them another little horn, before whom there were three of the first horns plucked up by the roots: and, behold, in this horn were eyes like the eyes of man, and a mouth speaking great things. [9]I beheld till the thrones were cast down, and the Ancient of days did sit, whose garment was white as snow, and the hair of his head like the pure wool: his throne was like the fiery flame, and his wheels as burning fire. [10]A fiery stream issued and came forth from before him: thousand thousands ministered unto him, and ten thousand times ten thousand stood before him: the judgment was set, and the books were opened. [11]I beheld then because of the voice of the great words which the horn spake: I beheld even till the beast was slain, and his body destroyed, and given to the burning flame. [12]As concerning the rest of the beasts, they had their dominion taken away: yet their lives were prolonged for a season and time. [13]I saw in the night visions, and, behold, one like the Son of man came with the clouds of heaven, and came to the Ancient of days, and they brought him near before him. [14]And there was given him dominion, and glory, and a kingdom, that all people, nations, and languages, should serve him: his dominion is an everlasting dominion, which shall not pass away, and his kingdom that which shall not be destroyed. [15]I Daniel was grieved in my spirit in the midst of my body, and the visions of my head troubled me. [16]I came near unto one of them that stood by, and asked him the truth of all this. So he told me, and made me know the interpretation of the things. [17]These great beasts, which are four, are four kings, which shall arise out of the earth. [18]But the saints of the most High shall take the kingdom, and possess the kingdom for ever, even for ever and ever. [19]Then I would know the truth of the fourth beast, which was diverse from all the others, exceeding dreadful, whose teeth were of iron, and his nails of brass; which devoured, brake in pieces, and stamped the residue with his feet; [20]And of the ten horns that were in his head, and of the other which came up, and before whom three fell; even of that horn that had eyes, and a mouth that spake very great things, whose look was more stout than his fellows. [21]I beheld, and the same horn made war with the saints, and prevailed against them; [22]Until the Ancient of days came, and judgment was given to the saints of the most High; and the time came that the saints possessed the kingdom. [23]Thus he said, The fourth beast shall be the fourth kingdom upon earth, which shall be diverse from all kingdoms, and shall devour the whole earth, and shall tread it down, and break it in pieces. [24]And the ten horns out of this kingdom are ten kings that shall arise: and another shall rise after them; and he shall be diverse from the first, and he shall subdue three kings. [25]And he shall speak great words against the most High, and shall wear out the saints of the most High, and think to change times and laws: and they shall be given into his hand until a time and times and the dividing of time. [26]But the judgment shall sit, and they shall take away his dominion, to consume and to destroy it unto the end. [27]And the kingdom and dominion, and the greatness of the kingdom under the whole heaven, shall be given to the people of the saints of the most High, whose kingdom is an everlasting kingdom, and all dominions shall serve and obey him. [28]Hitherto is the end of the matter. As for me Daniel, my cogitations much troubled me, and my countenance changed in me: but I kept the matter in my heart.	**Q-Quelle** Jesus' witness to John: Gal 1:3-4/ [Mt 11:7-19, 21:31-32]/ Lk 7:24-35 (QS 18), [Lk 16:16 (QS 56)]; Against Pharisees: Gal 1:3-4/ Mt 23:4-36/ [Mk 7:1-9]/ Lk 11:37-54 (QS 34 [Thom 39:1, 89, 102])

GALATIANS 1:4—Address (1:1–5), Christian liberty. Time range: 48–50, 54, or 55 CE

Theme	GAL	Jn	Paul	NT
Christ delivered believers	**1:4** [4]Who gave himself for our sins, that he might deliver us from this present evil world, according to the will of God and our Father: **2:20** [20]I am crucified with Christ: nevertheless I live; yet not I, but Christ liveth in me: and the life which I now live in the flesh I live by the faith of the Son of God, who loved me, and gave himself for me.	**1 Jn 5:19** [19]Then answered Jesus and said unto them, Verily, verily, I say unto you, The Son can do nothing of himself, but what he seeth the Father do: for what things soever he doeth, these also doeth the Son likewise.	**Rom 12:2** [2]And be not conformed to this world: but be ye transformed by the renewing of your mind, that ye may prove what is that good, and acceptable, and perfect, will of God. **Eph 5:2 (Pseudo)** [2]And walk in love, as Christ also hath loved us, and hath given himself for us an offering and a sacrifice to God for a sweetsmelling savour. **Eph 5:16 (Pseudo)** [16]Redeeming the time, because the days are evil. **1 Tim 2:6 (Pseudo)** [6]Who gave himself a ransom for all, to be testified in due time.	**Heb 10:10** [10]By the which will we are sanctified through the offering of the body of Jesus Christ once for all.

GALATIANS 1:5—Address (1:1–5), Christian liberty. Time range: 48–50, 54, or 55 CE

Theme	GAL	Paul
Doxology	**1:5** [5]To whom be glory for ever and ever. Amen.	**Rom 16:27** [27]To God only wise, be glory through Jesus Christ for ever. Amen. **2 Tim 4:18 (Pseudo)** [18]And the Lord shall deliver me from every evil work, and will preserve me unto his heavenly kingdom: to whom be glory for ever and ever. Amen.

LOYALTY TO PAUL'S TEACHING

GALATIANS 1:6–7—Loyalty to Paul's teaching. Time range: 48–50, 54, or 55 CE

Theme	GAL	Lk	Paul
Careful to avoid false teachings	**1:6–7** [6]I marvel that ye are so soon removed from him that called you into the grace of Christ unto another gospel: [7]Which is not another; but there be some that trouble you, and would pervert the gospel of Christ. **5:8, 10** [8]This persuasion cometh not of him that calleth you. . . . [10]I have confidence in you through the Lord, that ye will be none otherwise minded: but he that troubleth you shall bear his judgment, whosoever he be.	**Acts 15:1, 24** [1]And certain men which came down from Judaea taught the brethren, and said, Except ye be circumcised after the manner of Moses, ye cannot be saved. . . . [24]Forasmuch as we have heard, that certain which went out from us have troubled you with words, subverting your souls, saying, Ye must be circumcised, and keep the law: to whom we gave no such commandment:	**2 Cor 11:4** [4]For if he that cometh preacheth another Jesus, whom we have not preached, or if ye receive another spirit, which ye have not received, or another gospel, which ye have not accepted, ye might well bear with him.

GALATIANS 1:8–9—Loyalty to Paul's teaching. Time range: 48–50, 54, or 55 CE

Theme	GAL	Paul
Only one gospel	**1:8–9** [8]But though we, or an angel from heaven, preach any other gospel unto you than that which we have preached unto you, let him be accursed. [9]As we said before, so say I now again, If any man preach any other gospel unto you than that ye have received, let him be accursed. **5:3, 21** [3]For I testify again to every man that is circumcised, that he is a debtor to do the whole law. . . . [21]Envyings, murders, drunkenness, revellings, and such like: of the which I tell you before, as I have also told you in time past, that they which do such things shall not inherit the kingdom of God.	**1 Cor 5:3** [3]For I verily, as absent in body, but present in spirit, have judged already, as though I were present, concerning him that hath so done this deed, **1 Cor 16:22** [22]If any man love not the Lord Jesus Christ, let him be anathema. Maranatha. **2 Cor 13:2** [2]I told you before, and foretell you, as if I were present, the second time; and being absent now I write to them which heretofore have sinned, and to all other, that, if I come again, I will not spare:

GALATIANS 1:10—Loyalty to Paul's teaching. Time range: 48–50, 54, or 55 CE

Theme	GAL	Paul
Please God, not human beings	**1:10** [10]For do I now persuade men, or God? or do I seek to please men? for if I yet pleased men, I should not be the servant of Christ.	**2 Cor 5:11** [11]Knowing therefore the terror of the Lord, we persuade men; but we are made manifest unto God; and I trust also are made manifest in your consciences. **1 Thes 2:4** [4]But as we were allowed of God to be put in trust with the gospel, even so we speak; not as pleasing men, but God, which trieth our hearts.

PAUL EXPLAINS GOSPEL AND HIS AUTHORITY (1:11–2:21)

GALATIANS 1:11–12—Paul explains Gospel and his authority (1:11–2:21). Time range: 48–50, 54, or 55 CE

Theme	GAL	Paul
Gospel received is from Christ	**1:11–12** [11]But I certify you, brethren, that the gospel which was preached of me is not after man. [12]For I neither received it of man, neither was I taught it, but by the revelation of Jesus Christ.	**1 Cor 1:1** [1]Paul, called to be an apostle of Jesus Christ through the will of God, and Sosthenes our brother, **1 Cor 15:1** [1]Moreover, brethren, I declare unto you the gospel which I preached unto you, which also ye have received, and wherein ye stand; **Eph 3:3 (Pseudo)** [3]How that by revelation he made known unto me the mystery; (as I wrote afore in few words,

GALATIANS 1:13—Paul explains Gospel and his authority (1:11–2:21). Time range: 48–50, 54, or 55 CE

Theme	GAL	Lk	Paul
Paul persecuted church before his conversion	**1:13** [13]For ye have heard of my conversation in time past in the Jews' religion, how that beyond measure I persecuted the church of God, and wasted it:	**Acts 8:1–3** [1]And Saul was consenting unto his death. And at that time there was a great persecution against the church which was at Jerusalem; and they were all scattered abroad throughout the regions of Judaea and Samaria, except the apostles. [2]And devout men carried Stephen to his burial, and made great lamentation over him. [3]As for Saul, he made havock of the church, entering into every house, and haling men and women committed them to prison. **Acts 9:1–2** [1]And Saul, yet breathing out threatenings and slaughter against the disciples of the Lord, went unto the high priest, [2]And desired of him letters to Damascus to the synagogues, that if he found any of this way, whether they were men or women, he might bring them bound unto Jerusalem.	**1 Cor 15:9** [9]For I am the least of the apostles, that am not meet to be called an apostle, because I persecuted the church of God.

GALATIANS 1:14—Paul explains Gospel and his authority (1:11–2:21). Time range: 48–50, 54, or 55 CE

Theme	GAL	Lk
Zealous for God	**1:14** [14]And profited in the Jews' religion above many my equals in mine own nation, being more exceedingly zealous of the traditions of my fathers.	**Acts 26:4–5** [4]My manner of life from my youth, which was at the first among mine own nation at Jerusalem, know all the Jews; [5]Which knew me from the beginning, if they would testify, that after the most straitest sect of our religion I lived a Pharisee.

GALATIANS 1:15–16—Paul explains Gospel and his authority (1:11–2:21). Time range: 48–50, 54, or 55 CE

Theme	GAL	Mt
God's calling	**1:15–16** [15]But when it pleased God, who separated me from my mother's womb, and called me by his grace, [16]To reveal his Son in me, that I might preach him among the heathen; immediately I conferred not with flesh and blood **1:11–12** [11]But I certify you, brethren, that the gospel which was preached of me is not after man. [12]For I neither received it of man, neither was I taught it, but by the revelation of Jesus Christ. **2:7** [7]But contrariwise, when they saw that the gospel of the uncircumcision was committed unto me, as the gospel of the circumcision was unto Peter; **2:9** [9]And when James, Cephas, and John, who seemed to be pillars, perceived the grace that was given unto me, they gave to me and Barnabas the right hands of fellowship; that we should go unto the heathen, and they unto the circumcision.	**16:16–20** [16]And Simon Peter answered and said, Thou art the Christ, the Son of the living God. **[17]And Jesus answered and said unto him, Blessed art thou, Simon Barjona: for flesh and blood hath not revealed it unto thee, but my Father which is in heaven.** [18]And I say also unto thee, That thou art Peter, and upon this rock I will build my church; and the gates of hell shall not prevail against it. [19]And I will give unto thee the keys of the kingdom of heaven: and whatsoever thou shalt bind on earth shall be bound in heaven: and whatsoever thou shalt loose on earth shall be loosed in heaven. [20]Then charged he his disciples that they should tell no man that he was Jesus the Christ

Lk	Paul	Jewish Writings
Acts 2:2, 7 [2]And suddenly there came a sound from heaven as of a rushing mighty wind, and it filled all the house where they were sitting. . . . [7]And they were all amazed and marvelled, saying one to another, Behold, are not all these which speak Galilaeans? **Acts 9:3–9** [3]And as he journeyed, he came near Damascus: and suddenly there shined round about him a light from heaven: [4]And he fell to the earth, and heard a voice saying unto him, Saul, Saul, why persecutest thou me? [5]And he said, Who art thou, Lord? And the Lord said, I am Jesus whom thou persecutest: it is hard for thee to kick against the pricks. [6]And he trembling and astonished said, Lord, what wilt thou have me to do? And the Lord said unto him, Arise, and go into the city, and it shall be told thee what thou must do. [7]And the men which journeyed with him stood speechless, hearing a voice, but seeing no man. [8]And Saul arose from the earth; and when his eyes were opened, he saw no man: but they led him by the hand, and brought him into Damascus. [9]And he was three days without sight, and neither did eat nor drink.	**Rom 1:5** [5]By whom we have received grace and apostleship, for obedience to the faith among all nations, for his name: **1 Cor 15:10** [10]But by the grace of God I am what I am: and his grace which was bestowed upon me was not in vain; but I laboured more abundantly than they all: yet not I, but the grace of God which was with me.	**Is 49:1** [1]Listen, O isles, unto me; and hearken, ye people, from far; The LORD hath called me from the womb; from the bowels of my mother hath he made mention of my name. **Jer 1:4** [4]Then the word of the LORD came unto me, saying,

GALATIANS 1:15—Paul explains Gospel and his authority (1:11–2:21). Time range: 48–50, 54, or 55 CE

Theme	GAL	Jewish Writings
God's calling	**1:15** [15]But when it pleased God, who separated me from my mother's womb, and called me by his grace,	**Is 49:1** [1]Listen, O isles, unto me; and hearken, ye people, from far; The LORD hath called me from the womb; from the bowels of my mother hath he made mention of my name. **Jer 1:4** [4]Then the word of the LORD came unto me, saying,

GALATIANS 1:18—Paul explains Gospel and his authority (1:11–2:21). Time range: 48–50, 54, or 55 CE

Theme	GAL	Lk	Jn
Paul & Peter meet in Jerusalem	**1:18** [18]Then after three years I went up to Jerusalem to see Peter, and abode with him fifteen days.	**Acts 9:26–30** [26]And when Saul was come to Jerusalem, he assayed to join himself to the disciples: but they were all afraid of him, and believed not that he was a disciple. [27]But Barnabas took him, and brought him to the apostles, and declared unto them how he had seen the Lord in the way, and that he had spoken to him, and how he had preached boldly at Damascus in the name of Jesus. [28]And he was with them coming in and going out at Jerusalem. [29]And he spake boldly in the name of the Lord Jesus, and disputed against the Grecians: but they went about to slay him. [30]Which when the brethren knew, they brought him down to Caesarea, and sent him forth to Tarsus.	**1:42** [42]And he brought him to Jesus. And when Jesus beheld him, he said, Thou art Simon the son of Jona: thou shalt be called Cephas, which is by interpretation, A stone.

GALATIANS 1:19—Paul explains Gospel and his authority (1:11–2:21). Time range: 48–50, 54, or 55 CE

Theme	GAL	Mt	Lk
Paul met James, Lord's brother	**1:19** [19]But other of the apostles saw I none, save James the Lord's brother. **2:9** [9]And when James, Cephas, and John, who seemed to be pillars, perceived the grace that was given unto me, they gave to me and Barnabas the right hands of fellowship; that we should go unto the heathen, and they unto the circumcision.	**13:55** [55]Is not this the carpenter's son? is not his mother called Mary? and his brethren, James, and Joses, and Simon, and Judas?	**Acts 12:17** [17]But he, beckoning unto them with the hand to hold their peace, declared unto them how the Lord had brought him out of the prison. And he said, Go show these things unto James, and to the brethren. And he departed, and went into another place.

GALATIANS 1:20—Paul explains Gospel and his authority (1:11–2:21). Time range: 48–50, 54, or 55 CE

Theme	GAL	Paul
Paul telling truth	**1:20** [20]Now the things which I write unto you, behold, before God, I lie not.	**Rom 9:1** [1]I say the truth in Christ, I lie not, my conscience also bearing me witness in the Holy Ghost, **2 Cor 11:31** [31]The God and Father of our Lord Jesus Christ, which is blessed for evermore, knoweth that I lie not.

GALATIANS 1:21—Paul explains Gospel and his authority (1:11–2:21). Time range: 48–50, 54, or 55 CE

Theme	GAL	Lk
Mission, Syria & Cilicia	**1:21** [21]Afterwards I came into the regions of Syria and Cilicia;	**Acts 9:30** [30]Which when the brethren knew, they brought him down to Caesarea, and sent him forth to Tarsus.

GALATIANS 1:23—Paul explains Gospel and his authority (1:11–2:21). Time range: 48–50, 54, or 55 CE

Theme	GAL
Conversion	**1:23** [23]But they had heard only, That he which persecuted us in times past now preacheth the faith which once he destroyed. **1:13** [13]For ye have heard of my conversation in time past in the Jews' religion, how that beyond measure I persecuted the church of God, and wasted it:

GALATIANS 2:1—Paul explains Gospel and his authority (1:11–2:21). Time range: 48–50, 54, or 55 CE

Theme	GAL	Lk
To Jerusalem with Barnabas & Titus	**2:1** [1]Then fourteen years after I went up again to Jerusalem with Barnabas, and took Titus with me also.	**Acts 15:2** [2]When therefore Paul and Barnabas had no small dissension and disputation with them, they determined that Paul and Barnabas, and certain other of them, should go up to Jerusalem unto the apostles and elders about this question.

GALATIANS 2:2—Paul explains Gospel and his authority (1:11–2:21). Time range: 48–50, 54, or 55 CE

Theme	GAL	Paul
Explained revelation and gospel teachings	**2:2** [2]And I went up by revelation, and communicated unto them that gospel which I preach among the Gentiles, but privately to them which were of reputation, lest by any means I should run, or had run, in vain. **1:11–12** [11]But I certify you, brethren, that the gospel which was preached of me is not after man. [12]For I neither received it of man, neither was I taught it, but by the revelation of Jesus Christ. **1:16** [16]To reveal his Son in me, that I might preach him among the heathen; immediately I conferred not with flesh and blood:	**Phil 2:16** [16]Holding forth the word of life; that I may rejoice in the day of Christ, that I have not run in vain, neither laboured in vain.

GALATIANS 2:3—Paul explains Gospel (1:11–2:21). Time range: 48–50, 54, or 55 CE

Theme	GAL	Paul
Titus compelled to circumcision	**2:3** [3]But neither Titus, who was with me, being a Greek, was compelled to be circumcised: **2:14** [14]But when I saw that they walked not uprightly according to the truth of the gospel, I said unto Peter before them all, If thou, being a Jew, livest after the manner of Gentiles, and not as do the Jews, why compellest thou the Gentiles to live as do the Jews? **6:12** [12]As many as desire to make a fair show in the flesh, they constrain you to be circumcised; only lest they should suffer persecution for the cross of Christ.	**2 Cor 2:13** [13]I had no rest in my spirit, because I found not Titus my brother: but taking my leave of them, I went from thence into Macedonia. **2 Cor 7:6–7** [6]Nevertheless God, that comforteth those that are cast down, comforted us by the coming of Titus; [7]And not by his coming only, but by the consolation wherewith he was comforted in you, when he told us your earnest desire, your mourning, your fervent mind toward me; so that I rejoiced the more. **2 Cor 8:16–17** [16]But thanks be to God, which put the same earnest care into the heart of Titus for you. [17]For indeed he accepted the exhortation; but being more forward, of his own accord he went unto you. **2 Cor 12:18** [18]I desired Titus, and with him I sent a brother. Did Titus make a gain of you? walked we not in the same spirit? walked we not in the same steps? **Tit 1:4 (Pseudo)** [4]To Titus, mine own son after the common faith: Grace, mercy, and peace, from God the Father and the Lord Jesus Christ our Saviour.

GALATIANS 2:4—Paul explains Gospel (1:11–2:21). Time range: 48–50, 54, or 55 CE

Theme	GAL	Lk
Stand for Christ	**2:4** [4]And that because of false brethren unawares brought in, who came in privily to spy out our liberty which we have in Christ Jesus, that they might bring us into bondage: **5:1** [1]Stand fast therefore in the liberty wherewith Christ hath made us free, and be not entangled again with the yoke of bondage.	**Acts 15:1, 24** [1]And certain men which came down from Judaea taught the brethren, and said, Except ye be circumcised after the manner of Moses, ye cannot be saved. . . . [24]Forasmuch as we have heard, that certain which went out from us have troubled you with words, subverting your souls, saying, Ye must be circumcised, and keep the law: to whom we gave no such commandment:

GALATIANS 2:5—Paul explains Gospel and Christian liberty (1:11–2:21). Time range: 48–50, 54, or 55 CE

Theme	GAL
Truth continues in Galatia	**2:5** [5]To whom we gave place by subjection, no, not for an hour; that the truth of the gospel might continue with you. **2:14** [14]But when I saw that they walked not uprightly according to the truth of the gospel, I said unto Peter before them all, If thou, being a Jew, livest after the manner of Gentiles, and not as do the Jews, why compellest thou the Gentiles to live as do the Jews? **4:16** [16]Am I therefore become your enemy, because I tell you the truth?

GALATIANS 2:6—Paul explains Gospel and Christian liberty (1:11–2:21). Time range: 48–50, 54, or 55 CE

Theme	GAL	Paul	Jewish Writings
Equal before God	**2:6** [6]But of these who seemed to be somewhat, (whatsoever they were, it maketh no matter to me: God accepteth no man's person:) for they who seemed to be somewhat in conference added nothing to me:	**Rom 2:11** [11]For there is no respect of persons with God.	**Dt 10:17** [17]For the LORD your God is God of gods, and Lord of lords, a great God, a mighty, and a terrible, which regardeth not persons, nor taketh reward:

GALATIANS 2:7–9—Paul explains Gospel and Christian liberty (1:11–2:21). Time range: 48–50, 54, or 55 CE

Theme	Gal	Mt	Mk	Luke
Revealed grace	**2:7–9** [7]But contrariwise, when they saw that the gospel of the uncircumcision was committed unto me, as the gospel of the circumcision was unto Peter; [8](For he that wrought effectually in Peter to the apostleship of the circumcision, the same was mighty in me toward the Gentiles:) [9]And when James, Cephas, and John, who seemed to be pillars, perceived the grace that was given unto me, they gave to me and Barnabas the right hands of fellowship; that we should go unto the heathen, and they unto the circumcision. **1:15–16** [15]But when it pleased God, who separated me from my mother's womb, and called me by his grace, [16]To reveal his Son in me, that I might preach him among the heathen; immediately I conferred not with flesh and blood:	**10:5–6** [5]These twelve Jesus sent forth, and commanded them, saying, Go not into the way of the Gentiles, and into any city of the Samaritans enter ye not: [6]But go rather to the lost sheep of the house of Israel. **10:8** [8]Heal the sick, cleanse the lepers, raise the dead, cast out devils: freely ye have received, freely give. **10:10** [10]Nor scrip for your journey, neither two coats, neither shoes, nor yet staves: for the workman is worthy of his meat. **11:18** [18]For John came neither eating nor drinking, and they say, He hath a devil. **28:19** [19]Go ye therefore, and teach all nations, baptizing them in the name of the Father, and of the Son, and of the Holy Ghost:	**7:27** [27]But Jesus said unto her, Let the children first be filled: for it is not meet to take the children's bread, and to cast it unto the dogs.	**10:7–8** [7]And in the same house remain, eating and drinking such things as they give: for the labourer is worthy of his hire. Go not from house to house. [8]And into whatsoever city ye enter, and they receive you, eat such things as are set before you: **Acts 2:1** [1]And when the day of Pentecost was fully come, they were all with one accord in one place. **Acts 9:15** [15]But the Lord said unto him, Go thy way: for he is a chosen vessel unto me, to bear my name before the Gentiles, and kings, and the children of Israel: **Acts 12:17** [17]But he, beckoning unto them with the hand to hold their peace, declared unto them how the Lord had brought him out of the prison. And he said, Go show these things unto James, and to the brethren. And he departed, and went into another place. **Acts 15:12** [12]Then all the multitude kept silence, and gave audience to Barnabas and Paul, declaring what miracles and wonders God had wrought among the Gentiles by them. **Acts 22:21** [21]And he said unto me, Depart: for I will send thee far hence unto the Gentiles.

GALATIANS 2:10—Paul explains Gospel and Christian liberty (1:11–2:21). Time range: 48–50, 54, or 55 CE

Theme	GAL	Lk
Give to poor	**2:10** [10]Only they would that we should remember the poor; the same which I also was forward to do.	**Acts 11:29–30** [29]Then the disciples, every man according to his ability, determined to send relief unto the brethren which dwelt in Judaea: [30]Which also they did, and sent it to the elders by the hands of Barnabas and Saul.

Jn	Paul	Other
1:42 [42]And he brought him to Jesus. And when Jesus beheld him, he said, Thou art Simon the son of Jona: thou shalt be called Cephas, which is by interpretation, A stone.	**Rom 1:5** [5]By whom we have received grace and apostleship, for obedience to the faith among all nations, for his name: **Rom 1:18–19** [18]For the wrath of God is revealed from heaven against all ungodliness and unrighteousness of men, who hold the truth in unrighteousness; [19]Because that which may be known of God is manifest in them; for God hath showed it unto them. **Rom 15:8** [8]Now I say that Jesus Christ was a minister of the circumcision for the truth of God, to confirm the promises made unto the fathers: **Rom 15:15** [15]Nevertheless, brethren, I have written the more boldly unto you in some sort, as putting you in mind, because of the grace that is given to me of God, **1 Cor 9:4** [4]Have we not power to eat and to drink? **1 Cor 9:14** [14]Even so hath the Lord ordained that they which preach the gospel should live of the gospel. **1 Cor 9:18** [18]What is my reward then? Verily that, when I preach the gospel, I may make the gospel of Christ without charge, that I abuse not my power in the gospel. **1 Cor 10:27** [27]If any of them that believe not bid you to a feast, and ye be disposed to go; whatsoever is set before you, eat, asking no question for conscience sake. **2 Cor 11:7** [7]Have I committed an offence in abasing myself that ye might be exalted, because I have preached to you the gospel of God freely?	**Q-Quelle** Commissioning of 70: Gal 2:7-9/ [Mt 9:37-38], Mt 10:7-16/ [Lk 10:1-12 (QS 20 [Thom 73, 14:2])]; Commissioning the 12: Gal 2:7-9/[Mt 10:1], 10:7-11, [Mt 10:14]/[Mk 6:6b-13]/[Lk 9:1-6]

Paul
Rom 15:25–28 [25]But now I go unto Jerusalem to minister unto the saints. [26]For it hath pleased them of Macedonia and Achaia to make a certain contribution for the poor saints which are at Jerusalem. [27]It hath pleased them verily; and their debtors they are. For if the Gentiles have been made partakers of their spiritual things, their duty is also to minister unto them in carnal things. [28]When therefore I have performed this, and have sealed to them this fruit, I will come by you into Spain. **1 Cor 16:1–4** [1]Now concerning the collection for the saints, as I have given order to the churches of Galatia, even so do ye. [2]Upon the first day of the week let every one of you lay by him in store, as God hath prospered him, that there be no gatherings when I come. [3]And when I come, whomsoever ye shall approve by your letters, them will I send to bring your liberality unto Jerusalem. [4]And if it be meet that I go also, they shall go with me. **2 Cor 8:9** [9]For ye know the grace of our Lord Jesus Christ, that, though he was rich, yet for your sakes he became poor, that ye through his poverty might be rich.

GALATIANS 2:11—Paul explains Gospel and Christian liberty (1:11–2:21). Time range: 48–50, 54, or 55 CE

Theme	GAL	Lk
Paul challenges Peter	**2:11** [11]But when Peter was come to Antioch, I withstood him to the face, because he was to be blamed. **1:18** [18]Then after three years I went up to Jerusalem to see Peter, and abode with him fifteen days.	**Acts 11:19–30** [11]And, behold, immediately there were three men already come unto the house where I was, sent from Caesarea unto me. [12]And the Spirit bade me go with them, nothing doubting. Moreover these six brethren accompanied me, and we entered into the man's house: [13]And he showed us how he had seen an angel in his house, which stood and said unto him, Send men to Joppa, and call for Simon, whose surname is Peter; [14]Who shall tell thee words, whereby thou and all thy house shall be saved. [15]And as I began to speak, the Holy Ghost fell on them, as on us at the beginning. [16]Then remembered I the word of the Lord, how that he said, John indeed baptized with water; but ye shall be baptized with the Holy Ghost. [17]Forasmuch then as God gave them the like gift as he did unto us, who believed on the Lord Jesus Christ; what was I, that I could withstand God? [18]When they heard these things, they held their peace, and glorified God, saying, Then hath God also to the Gentiles granted repentance unto life. [19]Now they which were scattered abroad upon the persecution that arose about Stephen travelled as far as Phenice, and Cyprus, and Antioch, preaching the word to none but unto the Jews only. [20]And some of them were men of Cyprus and Cyrene, which, when they were come to Antioch, spake unto the Grecians, preaching the Lord Jesus. [21]And the hand of the Lord was with them: and a great number believed, and turned unto the Lord. [22]Then tidings of these things came unto the ears of the church which was in Jerusalem: and they sent forth Barnabas, that he should go as far as Antioch. [23]Who, when he came, and had seen the grace of God, was glad, and exhorted them all, that with purpose of heart they would cleave unto the Lord. [24]For he was a good man, and full of the Holy Ghost and of faith: and much people was added unto the Lord. [25]Then departed Barnabas to Tarsus, for to seek Saul: [26]And when he had found him, he brought him unto Antioch. And it came to pass, that a whole year they assembled themselves with the church, and taught much people. And the disciples were called Christians first in Antioch. [27]And in these days came prophets from Jerusalem unto Antioch. [28]And there stood up one of them named Agabus, and signified by the Spirit that there should be great dearth throughout all the world: which came to pass in the days of Claudius Caesar. [29]Then the disciples, every man according to his ability, determined to send relief unto the brethren which dwelt in Judaea: [30]Which also they did, and sent it to the elders by the hands of Barnabas and Saul. **Acts 15:1–2** [1]And certain men which came down from Judaea taught the brethren, and said, Except ye be circumcised after the manner of Moses, ye cannot be saved. [2]When therefore Paul and Barnabas had no small dissension and disputation with them, they determined that Paul and Barnabas, and certain other of them, should go up to Jerusalem unto the apostles and elders about this question.

GALATIANS 2:12—Paul explains Gospel and Christian liberty (1:11–2:21). Time range: 48–50, 54, or 55 CE

Theme	GAL	Lk
Peter eats separate from Gentiles	**2:12** [12]For before that certain came from James, he did eat with the Gentiles: but when they were come, he withdrew and separated himself, fearing them which were of the circumcision.	**Acts 10:15–28** [15]And the voice spake unto him again the second time, What God hath cleansed, that call not thou common. [16]This was done thrice: and the vessel was received up again into heaven. [17]Now while Peter doubted in himself what this vision which he had seen should mean, behold, the men which were sent from Cornelius had made inquiry for Simon's house, and stood before the gate, [18]And called, and asked whether Simon, which was surnamed Peter, were lodged there. [19]While Peter thought on the vision, the Spirit said unto him, Behold, three men seek thee. [20]Arise therefore, and get thee down, and go with them, doubting nothing: for I have sent them. [21]Then Peter went down to the men which were sent unto him from Cornelius; and said, Behold, I am he whom ye seek: what is the cause wherefore ye are come? [22]And they said, Cornelius the centurion, a just man, and one that feareth God, and of good report among all the nation of the Jews, was warned from God by an holy angel to send for thee into his house, and to hear words of thee. [23]Then called he them in, and lodged them. And on the morrow Peter went away with them, and certain brethren from Joppa accompanied him. [24]And the morrow after they entered into Caesarea. And Cornelius waited for them, and had called together his kinsmen and near friends. [25]And as Peter was coming in, Cornelius met him, and fell down at his feet, and worshipped him. [26]But Peter took him up, saying, Stand up; I myself also am a man. [27]And as he talked with him, he went in, and found many that were come together. [28]And he said unto them, Ye know how that it is an unlawful thing for a man that is a Jew to keep company, or come unto one of another nation; but God hath showed me that I should not call any man common or unclean. **Acts 11:3** [3]Saying, Thou wentest in to men uncircumcised, and didst eat with them.

GALATIANS 2:13—Paul explains Gospel and Christian liberty (1:11–2:21). Time range: 48–50, 54, or 55 CE

Theme	GAL
Barnabas joins Paul's debate	**2:13** [13]And the other Jews dissembled likewise with him; insomuch that Barnabas also was carried away with their dissimulation. **2:1** [1]Then fourteen years after I went up again to Jerusalem with Barnabas, and took Titus with me also. **2:9** [9]And when James, Cephas, and John, who seemed to be pillars, perceived the grace that was given unto me, they gave to me and Barnabas the right hands of fellowship; that we should go unto the heathen, and they unto the circumcision.

GALATIANS 2:14—Paul explains Gospel and Christian liberty (1:11–2:21). Time range: 48–50, 54, or 55 CE

Theme	GAL
Compelling Gentiles to live as Jews	**2:14** [14]But when I saw that they walked not uprightly according to the truth of the gospel, I said unto Peter before them all, If thou, being a Jew, livest after the manner of Gentiles, and not as do the Jews, why compellest thou the Gentiles to live as do the Jews? **1:18** [18]Then after three years I went up to Jerusalem to see Peter, and abode with him fifteen days. **2:3** [3]But neither Titus, who was with me, being a Greek, was compelled to be circumcised: **2:5** [5]To whom we gave place by subjection, no, not for an hour; that the truth of the gospel might continue with you. **2:9** [9]And when James, Cephas, and John, who seemed to be pillars, perceived the grace that was given unto me, they gave to me and Barnabas the right hands of fellowship; that we should go unto the heathen, and they unto the circumcision.

GALATIANS 2:16—Paul explains Gospel and Christian liberty (1:11–2:21). Time range: 48–50, 54, or 55 CE

Theme	GAL	Paul	Jewish Writings
Justified by faith	**2:16** [16]Knowing that a man is not justified by the works of the law, but by the faith of Jesus Christ, even we have believed in Jesus Christ, that we might be justified by the faith of Christ, and not by the works of the law: for by the works of the law shall no flesh be justified. **3:2, 11** [2]This only would I learn of you, Received ye the Spirit by the works of the law, or by the hearing of faith? . . . [11]But that no man is justified by the law in the sight of God, it is evident: for, The just shall live by faith.	**Rom 3:20, 28** [20]Therefore by the deeds of the law there shall no flesh be justified in his sight: for by the law is the knowledge of sin. . . . [28]Therefore we conclude that a man is justified by faith without the deeds of the law. **Rom 4:5** [5]But to him that worketh not, but believeth on him that justifieth the ungodly, his faith is counted for righteousness. **Rom 11:6** [6]And if by grace, then is it no more of works: otherwise grace is no more grace. But if it be of works, then is it no more grace: otherwise work is no more work. **Eph 2:8–9 (Pseudo)** [8]For by grace are ye saved through faith; and that not of yourselves: it is the gift of God: [9]Not of works, lest any man should boast. **Phil 3:9** [9]And be found in him, not having mine own righteousness, which is of the law, but that which is through the faith of Christ, the righteousness which is of God by faith:	**Ps 143:1–2** [1]Hear my prayer, O LORD, give ear to my supplications: in thy faithfulness answer me, and in thy righteousness. [2]And enter not into judgment with thy servant: for in thy sight shall no man living be justified.

GALATIANS 2:17—Paul explains Gospel and Christian liberty (1:11–2:21). Time range: 48–50, 54, or 55 CE

Theme	GAL	Mt
Justified by Christ	**2:17** [17]But if, while we seek to be justified by Christ, we ourselves also are found sinners, is therefore Christ the minister of sin? God forbid.	**5** [1]And seeing the multitudes, he went up into a mountain: and when he was set, his disciples came unto him: [2]And he opened his mouth, and taught them, saying, [3]Blessed are the poor in spirit: for theirs is the kingdom of heaven. [4]Blessed are they that mourn: for they shall be comforted. [5]Blessed are the meek: for they shall inherit the earth. [6]Blessed are they which do hunger and thirst after righteousness: for they shall be filled. [7]Blessed are the merciful: for they shall obtain mercy. [8]Blessed are the pure in heart: for they shall see God. [9]Blessed are the peacemakers: for they shall be called the children of God. [10]Blessed are they which are persecuted for righteousness' sake: for theirs is the kingdom of heaven. [11]Blessed are ye, when men shall revile you, and persecute you, and shall say all manner of evil against you falsely, for my sake. [12]Rejoice, and be exceeding glad: for great is your reward in heaven: for so persecuted they the prophets which were before you. [13]Ye are the salt of the earth: but if the salt have lost his savour, wherewith shall it be salted? it is thenceforth good for nothing, but to be cast out, and to be trodden under foot of men. [14]Ye are the light of the world. A city that is set on an hill cannot be hid. [15]Neither do men light a candle, and put it under a bushel, but on a candlestick; and it giveth light unto all that are in the house. [16]Let your light so shine before men, that they may see your good works, and glorify your Father which is in heaven. [17]Think not that I am come to destroy the law, or the prophets: I am not come to destroy, but to fulfil. [18]For verily I say unto you, Till heaven and earth pass, one jot or one tittle shall in no wise pass from the law, till all be fulfilled. [19]Whosoever therefore shall break one of these least commandments, and shall teach men so, he shall be called the least in the kingdom of heaven: but whosoever shall do and teach them, the same shall be called great in the kingdom of heaven. [20]For I say unto you, That except your righteousness shall exceed the righteousness of the scribes and Pharisees, ye shall in no case enter into the kingdom of heaven. [21]Ye have heard that it was said by them of old time, Thou shalt not kill; and whosoever shall kill shall be in danger of the judgment: [22]But I say unto you, That whosoever is angry with his brother without a cause shall be in danger of the judgment: and whosoever shall say to his brother, RacaRaca, shall be in danger of the council: but whosoever shall say, Thou fool, shall be in danger of hell fire. [23]Therefore if thou bring thy gift to the altar, and there rememberest that thy brother hath ought against thee; [24]Leave there thy gift before the altar, and go thy way; first be reconciled to thy brother, and then come and offer thy gift. [25]Agree with thine adversary quickly, whiles thou art in the way with him; lest at any time the adversary deliver thee to the judge, and the judge deliver thee to the officer, and thou be cast into prison. [26]Verily I say unto thee, Thou shalt by no means come out thence, till thou hast paid the uttermost farthing. [27]Ye have heard that it was said by them of old time, Thou shalt not commit adultery: [28]But I say unto you, That whosoever looketh on a woman to lust after her hath committed adultery with her already in his heart. [29]And if thy right eye offend thee, pluck it out, and cast it from thee: for it is profitable for thee that one of thy members should perish, and not that thy whole body should be cast into hell. [30]And if thy right hand offend thee, cut it off, and cast it from thee: for it is profitable for thee that one of thy members should perish, and not that thy whole body should be cast into hell. [31]It hath been said, Whosoever shall put away his wife, let him give her a writing of divorcement: [32]But I say unto you, That whosoever shall put away his wife, saving for the cause of fornication, causeth her to commit adultery: and whosoever shall marry her that is divorced committeth adultery. [33]Again, ye have heard that it hath been said by them of old time, Thou shalt not forswear thyself, but shalt perform unto the Lord thine oaths: [34]But I say unto you, Swear not at all; neither by heaven; for it is God's throne: [35]Nor by the earth; for it is his footstool: neither by Jerusalem; for it is the city of the great King. [36]Neither shalt thou swear by thy head, because thou canst not make one hair white or black. [37]But let your communication be, Yea, yea; Nay, nay: for whatsoever is more than these cometh of evil. [38]Ye have heard that it hath been said, An eye for an eye, and a tooth for a tooth: [39]But I say unto you, That ye resist not evil: but whosoever shall smite thee on thy right cheek, turn to him the other also. [40]And if any man will sue thee at the law, and take away thy coat, let him have thy cloak also. [41]And whosoever shall compel thee to go a mile, go with him twain. [42]Give to him that asketh thee, and from him that would borrow of thee turn not thou away. [43]Ye have heard that it hath been said, Thou shalt love thy neighbour, and hate thine enemy. [44]But I say unto you, Love your enemies, bless them that curse you, do good to them that hate you, and pray for them which despitefully use you, and persecute you; [45]That ye may be the children of your Father which is in heaven: for he maketh his sun to rise on the evil and on the good, and sendeth rain on the just and on the unjust. [46]For if ye love them which love you, what reward have ye? do not even the publicans the same? [47]And if ye salute your brethren only, what do ye more than others? do not even the publicans so? [48]Be ye therefore perfect, even as your Father which is in heaven is perfect.

Galatians 2:17 continued on next page

GALATIANS 2:17—Paul explains Gospel and Christian liberty (1:11–2:21). Time range: 48–50, 54, or 55 CE

Theme	GAL	Mt
(*Cont.*) **Justified by Christ**	**2:17** **(above)**	**6** [1]Take heed that ye do not your alms before men, to be seen of them: otherwise ye have no reward of your Father which is in heaven. [2]Therefore when thou doest thine alms, do not sound a trumpet before thee, as the hypocrites do in the synagogues and in the streets, that they may have glory of men. Verily I say unto you, They have their reward. [3]But when thou doest alms, let not thy left hand know what thy right hand doeth: [4]That thine alms may be in secret: and thy Father which seeth in secret himself shall reward thee openly. [5]And when thou prayest, thou shalt not be as the hypocrites are: for they love to pray standing in the synagogues and in the corners of the streets, that they may be seen of men. Verily I say unto you, They have their reward. [6]But thou, when thou prayest, enter into thy closet, and when thou hast shut thy door, pray to thy Father which is in secret; and thy Father which seeth in secret shall reward thee openly. [7]But when ye pray, use not vain repetitions, as the heathen do: for they think that they shall be heard for their much speaking. [8]Be not ye therefore like unto them: for your Father knoweth what things ye have need of, before ye ask him. [9]After this manner therefore pray ye: Our Father which art in heaven, Hallowed be thy name. [10]Thy kingdom come. Thy will be done in earth, as it is in heaven. [11]Give us this day our daily bread. [12]And forgive us our debts, as we forgive our debtors. [13]And lead us not into temptation, but deliver us from evil: For thine is the kingdom, and the power, and the glory, for ever. Amen. [14]For if ye forgive men their trespasses, your heavenly Father will also forgive you: [15]But if ye forgive not men their trespasses, neither will your Father forgive your trespasses. [16]Moreover when ye fast, be not, as the hypocrites, of a sad countenance: for they disfigure their faces, that they may appear unto men to fast. Verily I say unto you, They have their reward. [17]But thou, when thou fastest, anoint thine head, and wash thy face; [18]That thou appear not unto men to fast, but unto thy Father which is in secret: and thy Father, which seeth in secret, shall reward thee openly. [19]Lay not up for yourselves treasures upon earth, where moth and rust doth corrupt, and where thieves break through and steal: [20]But lay up for yourselves treasures in heaven, where neither moth nor rust doth corrupt, and where thieves do not break through nor steal: [21]For where your treasure is, there will your heart be also. [22]The light of the body is the eye: if therefore thine eye be single, thy whole body shall be full of light. [23]But if thine eye be evil, thy whole body shall be full of darkness. If therefore the light that is in thee be darkness, how great is that darkness! [24]No man can serve two masters: for either he will hate the one, and love the other; or else he will hold to the one, and despise the other. Ye cannot serve God and mammon. [25]Therefore I say unto you, Take no thought for your life, what ye shall eat, or what ye shall drink; nor yet for your body, what ye shall put on. Is not the life more than meat, and the body than raiment? [26]Behold the fowls of the air: for they sow not, neither do they reap, nor gather into barns; yet your heavenly Father feedeth them. Are ye not much better than they? [27]Which of you by taking thought can add one cubit unto his stature? [28]And why take ye thought for raiment? Consider the lilies of the field, how they grow; they toil not, neither do they spin: [29]And yet I say unto you, That even Solomon in all his glory was not arrayed like one of these. [30]Wherefore, if God so clothe the grass of the field, which to day is, and to morrow is cast into the oven, shall he not much more clothe you, O ye of little faith? [31]Therefore take no thought, saying, What shall we eat? or, What shall we drink? or, Wherewithal shall we be clothed? [32](For after all these things do the Gentiles seek:) for your heavenly Father knoweth that ye have need of all these things. [33]But seek ye first the kingdom of God, and his righteousness; and all these things shall be added unto you. [34]Take therefore no thought for the morrow: for the morrow shall take thought for the things of itself. Sufficient unto the day is the evil thereof.

Mt (*Continued*)
15
[1]Then came to Jesus scribes and Pharisees, which were of Jerusalem, saying, [2]Why do thy disciples transgress the tradition of the elders? for they wash not their hands when they eat bread. [3]But he answered and said unto them, Why do ye also transgress the commandment of God by your tradition? [4]For God commanded, saying, Honour thy father and mother: and, He that curseth father or mother, let him die the death. [5]But ye say, Whosoever shall say to his father or his mother, It is a gift, by whatsoever thou mightest be profited by me; [6]And honour not his father or his mother, he shall be free. Thus have ye made the commandment of God of none effect by your tradition. [7]Ye hypocrites, well did Esaias prophesy of you, saying, [8]This people draweth nigh unto me with their mouth, and honoureth me with their lips; but their heart is far from me. [9]But in vain they do worship me, teaching for doctrines the commandments of men. [10]And he called the multitude, and said unto them, Hear, and understand: [11]Not that which goeth into the mouth defileth a man; but that which cometh out of the mouth, this defileth a man. [12]Then came his disciples, and said unto him, Knowest thou that the Pharisees were offended, after they heard this saying? [13]But he answered and said, Every plant, which my heavenly Father hath not planted, shall be rooted up. **[14]Let them alone: they be blind leaders of the blind. And if the blind lead the blind, both shall fall into the ditch.** [15]Then answered Peter and said unto him, Declare unto us this parable. [16]And Jesus said, Are ye also yet without understanding? [17]Do not ye yet understand, that whatsoever entereth in at the mouth goeth into the belly, and is cast out into the draught? [18]But those things which proceed out of the mouth come forth from the heart; and they defile the man. [19]For out of the heart proceed evil thoughts, murders, adulteries, fornications, thefts, false witness, blasphemies: [20]These are the things which defile a man: but to eat with unwashen hands defileth not a man. [21]Then Jesus went thence, and departed into the coasts of Tyre and Sidon. [22]And, behold, a woman of Canaan came out of the same coasts, and cried unto him, saying, Have mercy on me, O Lord, thou Son of David; my daughter is grievously vexed with a devil. [23]But he answered her not a word. And his disciples came and besought him, saying, Send her away; for she crieth after us. [24]But he answered and said, I am not sent but unto the lost sheep of the house of Israel. [25]Then came she and worshipped him, saying, Lord, help me. [26]But he answered and said, It is not meet to take the children's bread, and to cast it to dogs. [27]And she said, Truth, Lord: yet the dogs eat of the crumbs which fall from their masters' table. [28]Then Jesus answered and said unto her, O woman, great is thy faith: be it unto thee even as thou wilt. And her daughter was made whole from that very hour. [29]And Jesus departed from thence, and came nigh unto the sea of Galilee; and went up into a mountain, and sat down there. [30]And great multitudes came unto him, having with them those that were lame, blind, dumb, maimed, and many others, and cast them down at Jesus' feet; and he healed them: [31]Insomuch that the multitude wondered, when they saw the dumb to speak, the maimed to be whole, the lame to walk, and the blind to see: and they glorified the God of Israel. [32]Then Jesus called his disciples unto him, and said, I have compassion on the multitude, because they continue with me now three days, and have nothing to eat: and I will not send them away fasting, lest they faint in the way. [33]And his disciples say unto him, Whence should we have so much bread in the wilderness, as to fill so great a multitude? [34]And Jesus saith unto them, How many loaves have ye? And they said, Seven, and a few little fishes. [35]And he commanded the multitude to sit down on the ground. [36]And he took the seven loaves and the fishes, and gave thanks, and brake them, and gave to his disciples, and the disciples to the multitude. [37]And they did all eat, and were filled: and they took up of the broken meat that was left seven baskets full. [38]And they that did eat were four thousand men, beside women and children. [39]And he sent away the multitude, and took ship, and came into the coasts of Magdala.
19:26
[26]But Jesus beheld them, and said unto them, With men this is impossible; but with God all things are possible.

Galatians 2:17 continued on next page

GALATIANS 2:17—Paul explains Gospel and Christian liberty (1:11–2:21). Time range: 48–50, 54, or 55 CE (*continued*)

Theme	GAL	Mt
(*Cont.*) **Justified by Christ**	**2:17 (above)**	**23** 1Then spake Jesus to the multitude, and to his disciples, 2Saying, The scribes and the Pharisees sit in Moses' seat: 3All therefore whatsoever they bid you observe, that observe and do; but do not ye after their works: for they say, and do not. 4For they bind heavy burdens and grievous to be borne, and lay them on men's shoulders; but they themselves will not move them with one of their fingers. 5But all their works they do for to be seen of men: they make broad their phylacteries, and enlarge the borders of their garments, 6And love the uppermost rooms at feasts, and the chief seats in the synagogues, 7And greetings in the markets, and to be called of men, Rabbi, Rabbi. 8But be not ye called Rabbi: for one is your Master, even Christ; and all ye are brethren. 9And call no man your father upon the earth: for one is your Father, which is in heaven. 10Neither be ye called masters: for one is your Master, even Christ. 11But he that is greatest among you shall be your servant. 12And whosoever shall exalt himself shall be abased; and he that shall humble himself shall be exalted. 13But woe unto you, scribes and Pharisees, hypocrites! for ye shut up the kingdom of heaven against men: for ye neither go in yourselves, neither suffer ye them that are entering to go in. 14Woe unto you, scribes and Pharisees, hypocrites! for ye devour widows' houses, and for a pretence make long prayer: therefore ye shall receive the greater damnation. 15Woe unto you, scribes and Pharisees, hypocrites! for ye compass sea and land to make one proselyte, and when he is made, ye make him twofold more the child of hell than yourselves. **16Woe unto you, ye blind guides, which say, Whosoever shall swear by the temple, it is nothing; but whosoever shall swear by the gold of the temple, he is a debtor!** 17Ye fools and blind: for whether is greater, the gold, or the temple that sanctifieth the gold? 18And, Whosoever shall swear by the altar, it is nothing; but whosoever sweareth by the gift that is upon it, he is guilty. 19Ye fools and blind: for whether is greater, the gift, or the altar that sanctifieth the gift? 20Whoso therefore shall swear by the altar, sweareth by it, and by all things thereon. 21And whoso shall swear by the temple, sweareth by it, and by him that dwelleth therein. 22And he that shall swear by heaven, sweareth by the throne of God, and by him that sitteth thereon. 23Woe unto you, scribes and Pharisees, hypocrites! for ye pay tithe of mint and anise and cummin, and have omitted the weightier matters of the law, judgment, mercy, and faith: these ought ye to have done, and not to leave the other undone. 24Ye blind guides, which strain at a gnat, and swallow a camel. 25Woe unto you, scribes and Pharisees, hypocrites! for ye make clean the outside of the cup and of the platter, but within they are full of extortion and excess. 26Thou blind Pharisee, cleanse first that which is within the cup and platter, that the outside of them may be clean also. 27Woe unto you, scribes and Pharisees, hypocrites! for ye are like unto whited sepulchres, which indeed appear beautiful outward, but are within full of dead men's bones, and of all uncleanness. 28Even so ye also outwardly appear righteous unto men, but within ye are full of hypocrisy and iniquity. 29Woe unto you, scribes and Pharisees, hypocrites! because ye build the tombs of the prophets, and garnish the sepulchres of the righteous, 30And say, If we had been in the days of our fathers, we would not have been partakers with them in the blood of the prophets. 31Wherefore ye be witnesses unto yourselves, that ye are the children of them which killed the prophets. 32Fill ye up then the measure of your fathers. 33Ye serpents, ye generation of vipers, how can ye escape the damnation of hell? 34Wherefore, behold, I send unto you prophets, and wise men, and scribes: and some of them ye shall kill and crucify; and some of them shall ye scourge in your synagogues, and persecute them from city to city: 35That upon you may come all the righteous blood shed upon the earth, from the blood of righteous Abel unto the blood of Zacharias son of Barachias, whom ye slew between the temple and the altar. 36Verily I say unto you, All these things shall come upon this generation. 37O Jerusalem, Jerusalem, thou that killest the prophets, and stonest them which are sent unto thee, how often would I have gathered thy children together, even as a hen gathereth her chickens under her wings, and ye would not! 38Behold, your house is left unto you desolate. 39For I say unto you, Ye shall not see me henceforth, till ye shall say, Blessed is he that cometh in the name of the Lord.

Mk

7

[1]Then came together unto him the Pharisees, and certain of the scribes, which came from Jerusalem. [2]And
when they saw some of his disciples eat bread with defiled, that is to say, with unwashen, hands, they found
fault. [3]For the Pharisees, and all the Jews, except they wash their hands oft, eat not, holding the tradition of
the elders. [4]And when they come from the market, except they wash, they eat not. And many other things
there be, which they have received to hold, as the washing of cups, and pots, brazen vessels, and of tables.
[5]Then the Pharisees and scribes asked him, Why walk not thy disciples according to the tradition of the
elders, but eat bread with unwashen hands? [6]He answered and said unto them, Well hath Esaias prophesied
of you hypocrites, as it is written, This people honoureth me with their lips, but their heart is far from me.
[7]Howbeit in vain do they worship me, teaching for doctrines the commandments of men. [8]For laying aside
the commandment of God, ye hold the tradition of men, as the washing of pots and cups: and many other
such like things ye do. [9]And he said unto them, Full well ye reject the commandment of God, that ye may
keep your own tradition. [10]For Moses said, Honour thy father and thy mother; and, Whoso curseth father or
mother, let him die the death: [11]But ye say, If a man shall say to his father or mother, It is Corban, that is to
say, a gift, by whatsoever thou mightest be profited by me; he shall be free. [12]And ye suffer him no more to do
ought for his father or his mother; [13]Making the word of God of none effect through your tradition, which
ye have delivered: and many such like things do ye. [14]And when he had called all the people unto him, he
said unto them, Hearken unto me every one of you, and understand: [15]There is nothing from without a man,
that entering into him can defile him: but the things which come out of him, those are they that defile the
man. [16]If any man have ears to hear, let him hear. [17]And when he was entered into the house from the people,
his disciples asked him concerning the parable. [18]And he saith unto them, Are ye so without understanding
also? Do ye not perceive, that whatsoever thing from without entereth into the man, it cannot defile him;
[19]Because it entereth not into his heart, but into the belly, and goeth out into the draught, purging all meats?
[20]And he said, That which cometh out of the man, that defileth the man. [21]For from within, out of the heart
of men, proceed evil thoughts, adulteries, fornications, murders, [22]Thefts, covetousness, wickedness, deceit,
lasciviousness, an evil eye, blasphemy, pride, foolishness: [23]All these evil things come from within, and defile
the man. [24]And from thence he arose, and went into the borders of Tyre and Sidon, and entered into an house,
and would have no man know it: but he could not be hid. [25]For a certain woman, whose young daughter had
an unclean spirit, heard of him, and came and fell at his feet: [26]The woman was a Greek, a Syrophenician by
nation; and she besought him that he would cast forth the devil out of her daughter. [27]But Jesus said unto her,
Let the children first be filled: for it is not meet to take the children's bread, and to cast it unto the dogs. [28]And
she answered and said unto him, Yes, Lord: yet the dogs under the table eat of the children's crumbs. [29]And
he said unto her, For this saying go thy way; the devil is gone out of thy daughter. [30]And when she was come
to her house, she found the devil gone out, and her daughter laid upon the bed. [31]And again, departing from
the coasts of Tyre and Sidon, he came unto the sea of Galilee, through the midst of the coasts of Decapolis.
[32]And they bring unto him one that was deaf, and had an impediment in his speech; and they beseech him
to put his hand upon him. [33]And he took him aside from the multitude, and put his fingers into his ears, and
he spit, and touched his tongue; [34]And looking up to heaven, he sighed, and saith unto him, Ephphatha, that
is, Be opened. [35]And straightway his ears were opened, and the string of his tongue was loosed, and he spake
plain. [36]And he charged them that they should tell no man: but the more he charged them, so much the more
a great deal they published it; [37]And were beyond measure astonished, saying, He hath done all things well:
he maketh both the deaf to hear, and the dumb to speak.

Galatians 2:17 continued on next page

GALATIANS 2:17—Paul explains Gospel and Christian liberty (1:11–2:21). Time range: 48–50, 54, or 55 CE (*continued*)

Theme	GAL	Mk
(*Cont.*) **Justified by Christ**	**2:17 (above)**	**10:27** [27]And Jesus looking upon them saith, With men it is impossible, but not with God: for with God all things are possible. **12** [1]And he began to speak unto them by parables. A certain man planted a vineyard, and set an hedge about it, and digged a place for the winefat, and built a tower, and let it out to husbandmen, and went into a far country. [2]And at the season he sent to the husbandmen a servant, that he might receive from the husbandmen of the fruit of the vineyard. [3]And they caught him, and beat him, and sent him away empty. [4]And again he sent unto them another servant; and at him they cast stones, and wounded him in the head, and sent him away shamefully handled. [5]And again he sent another; and him they killed, and many others; beating some, and killing some. [6]Having yet therefore one son, his wellbeloved, he sent him also last unto them, saying, They will reverence my son. [7]But those husbandmen said among themselves, This is the heir; come, let us kill him, and the inheritance shall be ours. [8]And they took him, and killed him, and cast him out of the vineyard. [9]What shall therefore the lord of the vineyard do? he will come and destroy the husbandmen, and will give the vineyard unto others. [10]And have ye not read this scripture; The stone which the builders rejected is become the head of the corner: [11]This was the Lord's doing, and it is marvellous in our eyes? [12]And they sought to lay hold on him, but feared the people: for they knew that he had spoken the parable against them: and they left him, and went their way. [13]And they send unto him certain of the Pharisees and of the Herodians, to catch him in his words. [14]And when they were come, they say unto him, Master, we know that thou art true, and carest for no man: for thou regardest not the person of men, but teachest the way of God in truth: Is it lawful to give tribute to Caesar, or not? [15]Shall we give, or shall we not give? But he, knowing their hypocrisy, said unto them, Why tempt ye me? bring me a penny, that I may see it. [16]And they brought it. And he saith unto them, Whose is this image and superscription? And they said unto him, Caesar's. [17]And Jesus answering said unto them, Render to Caesar the things that are Caesar's, and to God the things that are God's. And they marvelled at him. [18]Then come unto him the Sadducees, which say there is no resurrection; and they asked him, saying, [19]Master, Moses wrote unto us, If a man's brother die, and leave his wife behind him, and leave no children, that his brother should take his wife, and raise up seed unto his brother. [20]Now there were seven brethren: and the first took a wife, and dying left no seed. [21]And the second took her, and died, neither left he any seed: and the third likewise. [22]And the seven had her, and left no seed: last of all the woman died also. [23]In the resurrection therefore, when they shall rise, whose wife shall she be of them? for the seven had her to wife. [24]And Jesus answering said unto them, Do ye not therefore err, because ye know not the scriptures, neither the power of God? [25]For when they shall rise from the dead, they neither marry, nor are given in marriage; but are as the angels which are in heaven. [26]And as touching the dead, that they rise: have ye not read in the book of Moses, how in the bush God spake unto him, saying, I am the God of Abraham, and the God of Isaac, and the God of Jacob? [27]He is not the God of the dead, but the God of the living: ye therefore do greatly err. [28]And one of the scribes came, and having heard them reasoning together, and perceiving that he had answered them well, asked him, Which is the first commandment of all? [29]And Jesus answered him, The first of all the commandments is, Hear, O Israel; The Lord our God is one Lord: [30]And thou shalt love the Lord thy God with all thy heart, and with all thy soul, and with all thy mind, and with all thy strength: this is the first commandment. [31]And the second is like, namely this, Thou shalt love thy neighbour as thyself. There is none other commandment greater than these. [32]And the scribe said unto him, Well, Master, thou hast said the truth: for there is one God; and there is none other but he: [33]And to love him with all the heart, and with all the understanding, and with all the soul, and with all the strength, and to love his neighbour as himself, is more than all whole burnt offerings and sacrifices. [34]And when Jesus saw that he answered discreetly, he said unto him, Thou art not far from the kingdom of God. And no man after that durst ask him any question. [35]And Jesus answered and said, while he taught in the temple, How say the scribes that Christ is the Son of David? [36]For David himself said by the Holy Ghost, The LORD said to my Lord, Sit thou on my right hand, till I make thine enemies thy footstool. [37]David therefore himself calleth him Lord; and whence is he then his son? And the common people heard him gladly. [38]And he said unto them in his doctrine, Beware of the scribes, which love to go in long clothing, and love salutations in the marketplaces, [39]And the chief seats in the synagogues, and the uppermost rooms at feasts: [40]Which devour widows' houses, and for a pretence make long prayers: these shall receive greater damnation. [41]And Jesus sat over against the treasury, and beheld how the people cast money into the treasury: and many that were rich cast in much. [42]And there came a certain poor widow, and she threw in two mites, which make a farthing. [43]And he called unto him his disciples, and saith unto them, Verily I say unto you, That this poor widow hath cast more in, than all they which have cast into the treasury: [44]For all they did cast in of their abundance; but she of her want did cast in all that she had, even all her living.

Lk	Paul	Other
11:37–54	**Rom 2:19**	**Q-Quelle**
[37]And as he spake, a certain Pharisee besought him to dine with him: and he went in, and sat down to meat. [38]And when the Pharisee saw it, he marvelled that he had not first washed before dinner. [39]And the Lord said unto him, Now do ye Pharisees make clean the outside of the cup and the platter; but your inward part is full of ravening and wickedness. [40]Ye fools, did not he that made that which is without make that which is within also? [41]But rather give alms of such things as ye have; and, behold, all things are clean unto you. [42]But woe unto you, Pharisees! for ye tithe mint and rue and all manner of herbs, and pass over judgment and the love of God: these ought ye to have done, and not to leave the other undone. [43]Woe unto you, Pharisees! for ye love the uppermost seats in the synagogues, and greetings in the markets. [44]Woe unto you, scribes and Pharisees, hypocrites! for ye are as graves which appear not, and the men that walk over them are not aware of them. [45]Then answered one of the lawyers, and said unto him, Master, thus saying thou reproachest us also. [46]And he said, Woe unto you also, ye lawyers! for ye lade men with burdens grievous to be borne, and ye yourselves touch not the burdens with one of your fingers. [47]Woe unto you! for ye build the sepulchres of the prophets, and your fathers killed them. [48]Truly ye bear witness that ye allow the deeds of your fathers: for they indeed killed them, and ye build their sepulchres. [49]Therefore also said the wisdom of God, I will send them prophets and apostles, and some of them they shall slay and persecute: [50]That the blood of all the prophets, which was shed from the foundation of the world, may be required of this generation; [51]From the blood of Abel unto the blood of Zacharias, which perished between the altar and the temple: verily I say unto you, It shall be required of this generation. [52]Woe unto you, lawyers! for ye have taken away the key of knowledge: ye entered not in yourselves, and them that were entering in ye hindered. [53]And as he said these things unto them, the scribes and the Pharisees began to urge him vehemently, and to provoke him to speak of many things: [54]Laying wait for him, and seeking to catch something out of his mouth, that they might accuse him.	[19]And art confident that thou thyself art a guide of the blind, a light of them which are in darkness,	Beatitudes: Gal 2:17/Mt 5:3-12/[Lk 6:20b-23 (QS 8 [Thom 54,68,69])]; Agreement w/Accuser: Gal 2:17/Mt 5:25-26/[Lk 12:57-59]; Sound eye: Gal 2:17/Mt 6:22-23/[Lk 11:34-36 (QS 33 [Thom 33:2])]; Anxiety: Gal 2:17/Mt 6:25-34/[Lk 12:22-32 (QS 39 [Thom 36])]; Against Pharisees: Gal 2:17/[Mt 23:4-36]/[Mk 7:1-9]/Lk 11:37-54 (QS 34 [Thom 39:1, 89, 102])
18:27		
[27]And he said, The things which are impossible with men are possible with God.		

GALATIANS 2:18–19—Paul explains Gospel and Christian liberty (1:11–2:21). Time range: 48–50, 54, or 55 CE

Theme	GAL	Mt	Mk	Lk	Jn
Living law of Christ	**2:18–19** [18]For if I build again the things which I destroyed, I make myself a transgressor. [19]For I through the law am dead to the law, that I might live unto God. **6:14** [14]But God forbid that I should glory, save in the cross of our Lord Jesus Christ, by whom the world is crucified unto me, and I unto the world.	**16:24–26** [24]Then said Jesus unto his disciples, If any man will come after me, let him deny himself, and take up his cross, and follow me. [25]For whosoever will save his life shall lose it: and whosoever will lose his life for my sake shall find it. [26]For what is a man profited, if he shall gain the whole world, and lose his own soul? or what shall a man give in exchange for his soul? **20:22–23** [22]But Jesus answered and said, Ye know not what ye ask. Are ye able to drink of the cup that I shall drink of, and to be baptized with the baptism that I am baptized with? They say unto him, We are able. [23]And he saith unto them, Ye shall drink indeed of my cup, and be baptized with the baptism that I am baptized with: but to sit on my right hand, and on my left, is not mine to give, but it shall be given to them for whom it is prepared of my Father. [24]And when the ten heard it, they were moved with indignation against the two brethren. **26:31** [31]Then saith Jesus unto them, All ye shall be offended because of me this night: for it is written, I will smite the shepherd, and the sheep of the flock shall be scattered abroad. **27:46** [46]And about the ninth hour Jesus cried with a loud voice, saying, EliEli, EliEli, lamalama sabachthanisabachthani? that is to say, My God, my God, why hast thou forsaken me?	**8:34–37** [34]And when he had called the people unto him with his disciples also, he said unto them, Whosoever will come after me, let him deny himself, and take up his cross, and follow me. [35]For whosoever will save his life shall lose it; but whosoever shall lose his life for my sake and the gospel's, the same shall save it. [36]For what shall it profit a man, if he shall gain the whole world, and lose his own soul? [37]Or what shall a man give in exchange for his soul? **8:38** [38]Whosoever therefore shall be ashamed of me and of my words in this adulterous and sinful generation; of him also shall the Son of man be ashamed, when he cometh in the glory of his Father with the holy angels. **10:38** [38]But Jesus said unto them, Ye know not what ye ask: can ye drink of the cup that I drink of? and be baptized with the baptism that I am baptized with? **14:27** [27]And Jesus saith unto them, All ye shall be offended because of me this night: for it is written, I will smite the shepherd, and the sheep shall be scattered. **14:36** [36]And he said, Abba, Father, all things are possible unto thee; take away this cup from me: nevertheless not what I will, but what thou wilt. **15:34** [34]And at the ninth hour Jesus cried with a loud voice, saying, EloiEloi, EloiEloi, lamalama sabachthanisabachthani? which is, being interpreted, My God, my God, why hast thou forsaken me?	**9:23–26** [23]And he said to them all, If any man will come after me, let him deny himself, and take up his cross daily, and follow me. [24]For whosoever will save his life shall lose it: but whosoever will lose his life for my sake, the same shall save it. [25]For what is a man advantaged, if he gain the whole world, and lose himself, or be cast away? [26]For whosoever shall be ashamed of me and of my words, of him shall the Son of man be ashamed, when he shall come in his own glory, and in his Father's, and of the holy angels. **12:50** [50]But I have a baptism to be baptized with; and how am I straitened till it be accomplished! **22:37** [37]For I say unto you, that this that is written must yet be accomplished in me, And he was reckoned among the transgressors: for the things concerning me have an end. **22:42** [42]Saying, Father, if thou be willing, remove this cup from me: nevertheless not my will, but thine, be done.	**10:11** [11]I am the good shepherd: the good shepherd giveth his life for the sheep.

Paul	Jewish Writings
Rom 6:3–4 [3]Know ye not, that so many of us as were baptized into Jesus Christ were baptized into his death? [4]Therefore we are buried with him by baptism into death: that like as Christ was raised up from the dead by the glory of the Father, even so we also should walk in newness of life. **Rom 6:6** [6]Knowing this, that our old man is crucified with him, that the body of sin might be destroyed, that henceforth we should not serve sin. **Rom 6:8** [8]Now if we be dead with Christ, we believe that we shall also live with him: **Rom 6:10** [10]For in that he died, he died unto sin once: but in that he liveth, he liveth unto God. **Rom 7:6** [6]But now we are delivered from the law, that being dead wherein we were held; that we should serve in newness of spirit, and not in the oldness of the letter. **Rom 8:17** [17]And if children, then heirs; heirs of God, and joint-heirs with Christ; if so be that we suffer with him, that we may be also glorified together. **Rom 14:19–20** [19]Let us therefore follow after the things which make for peace, and things wherewith one may edify another. [20]For meat destroy not the work of God. All things indeed are pure; but it is evil for that man who eateth with offence. **1 Cor 1:16** [16]And I baptized also the household of Stephanas: besides, I know not whether I baptized any other. **1 Cor 10:16** [16]The cup of blessing which we bless, is it not the communion of the blood of Christ? The bread which we break, is it not the communion of the body of Christ? **2 Cor 13:10** [10]Therefore I write these things being absent, lest being present I should use sharpness, according to the power which the Lord hath given me to edification, and not to destruction. **Phil 1:20** [20]According to my earnest expectation and my hope, that in nothing I shall be ashamed, but that with all boldness, as always, so now also Christ shall be magnified in my body, whether it be by life, or by death. **Phil 3:7–11** [7]But what things were gain to me, those I counted loss for Christ. [8]Yea doubtless, and I count all things but loss for the excellency of the knowledge of Christ Jesus my Lord: for whom I have suffered the loss of all things, and do count them but dung, that I may win Christ, [9]And be found in him, not having mine own righteousness, which is of the law, but that which is through the faith of Christ, the righteousness which is of God by faith: **[10]That I may know him, and the power of his resurrection, and the fellowship of his sufferings, being made conformable unto his death**; [11]If by any means I might attain unto the resurrection of the dead. **Col 2:8–12** [8]Beware lest any man spoil you through philosophy and vain deceit, after the tradition of men, after the rudiments of the world, and not after Christ. [9]For in him dwelleth all the fulness of the Godhead bodily. [10]And ye are complete in him, which is the head of all principality and power: [11]In whom also ye are circumcised with the circumcision made without hands, in putting off the body of the sins of the flesh by the circumcision of Christ: [12]Buried with him in baptism, wherein also ye are risen with him through the faith of the operation of God, who hath raised him from the dead.	**Ps 22:1** [1]My God, my God, why hast thou forsaken me? why art thou so far from helping me, and from the words of my roaring? **Is 53:12** [12]Therefore will I divide him a portion with the great, and he shall divide the spoil with the strong; because he hath poured out his soul unto death: and he was numbered with the transgressors; and he bare the sin of many, and made intercession for the transgressors. **Zech 13:7** [7]Awake, O sword, against my shepherd, and against the man that is my fellow, saith the LORD of hosts: smite the shepherd, and the sheep shall be scattered: and I will turn mine hand upon the little ones.

GALATIANS 2:19—Paul explains Gospel and Christian liberty (1:11–2:21). Time range: 48–50, 54, or 55 CE

Theme	GAL	Paul
Living law of Christ	**2:19** [19]For I through the law am dead to the law, that I might live unto God. **6:14** [14]But God forbid that I should glory, save in the cross of our Lord Jesus Christ, by whom the world is crucified unto me, and I unto the world.	**Rom 6:6** [6]Knowing this, that our old man is crucified with him, that the body of sin might be destroyed, that henceforth we should not serve sin. **Rom 6:8** [8]Now if we be dead with Christ, we believe that we shall also live with him: **Rom 6:10** [10]For in that he died, he died unto sin once: but in that he liveth, he liveth unto God. **Rom 7:6** [6]But now we are delivered from the law, that being dead wherein we were held; that we should serve in newness of spirit, and not in the oldness of the letter.

GALATIANS 2:20—Paul explains Gospel and Christian liberty (1:11–2:21). Time range: 48–50, 54, or 55 CE

Theme	GAL	Paul
Crucified with Christ, to let Christ live	**2:20** [20]I am crucified with Christ: nevertheless I live; yet not I, but Christ liveth in me: and the life which I now live in the flesh I live by the faith of the Son of God, who loved me, and gave himself for me. **1:4** [4]Who gave himself for our sins, that he might deliver us from this present evil world, according to the will of God and our Father:	**Rom 8:10-12** [10]And if Christ be in you, the body is dead because of sin; but the Spirit is life because of righteousness. [11]But if the Spirit of him that raised up Jesus from the dead dwell in you, he that raised up Christ from the dead shall also quicken your mortal bodies by his Spirit that dwelleth in you. [12]Therefore, brethren, we are debtors, not to the flesh, to live after the flesh. **Col 3:3–4** [3]For ye are dead, and your life is hid with Christ in God. [4]When Christ, who is our life, shall appear, then shall ye also appear with him in glory.

GALATIANS 2:21—Paul explains Gospel and Christian liberty (1:11–2:21). Time range: 48–50, 54, or 55 CE

Theme	GAL
Right by grace	**2:21** [21]I do not frustrate the grace of God: for if righteousness come by the law, then Christ is dead in vain. **5:2** [2]Behold, I Paul say unto you, that if ye be circumcised, Christ shall profit you nothing.

FAITH AND FREEDOM (3:1–4:31)

GALATIANS 3:1—Faith and freedom (3:1–4:31). Time range: 48–50, 54, or 55 CE

Theme	GAL	Paul
Obey the truth	**3:1** [1]O foolish Galatians, who hath bewitched you, that ye should not obey the truth, before whose eyes Jesus Christ hath been evidently set forth, crucified among you? **5:7** [7]Ye did run well; who did hinder you that ye should not obey the truth?	**1 Cor 1:23** [23]But we preach Christ crucified, unto the Jews a stumblingblock, and unto the Greeks foolishness;

GALATIANS 3:2—Faith and freedom (3:1–4:31). Time range: 48–50, 54, or 55 CE

Theme	GAL	Paul
Spirit by faith, not law	**3:2** [2]This only would I learn of you, Received ye the Spirit by the works of the law, or by the hearing of faith? **2:16** [16]Knowing that a man is not justified by the works of the law, but by the faith of Jesus Christ, even we have believed in Jesus Christ, that we might be justified by the faith of Christ, and not by the works of the law: for by the works of the law shall no flesh be justified. **3:14** [14]That the blessing of Abraham might come on the Gentiles through Jesus Christ; that we might receive the promise of the Spirit through faith.	**Rom 10:17** [17]So then faith cometh by hearing, and hearing by the word of God.

GALATIANS 3:3—Faith and freedom (3:1–4:31). Time range: 48–50, 54, or 55 CE

Theme	GAL
Spirit, not flesh	**3:3** [3]Are ye so foolish? having begun in the Spirit, are ye now made perfect by the flesh? **5:16–18** [16]This I say then, Walk in the Spirit, and ye shall not fulfil the lust of the flesh. [17]For the flesh lusteth against the Spirit, and the Spirit against the flesh: and these are contrary the one to the other: so that ye cannot do the things that ye would. [18]But if ye be led of the Spirit, ye are not under the law.

GALATIANS 3:5—Faith and freedom (3:1–4:31). Time range: 48–50, 54, or 55 CE

Theme	GAL
By spirit, not law	**3:5** [5]He therefore that ministereth to you the Spirit, and worketh miracles among you, doeth he it by the works of the law, or by the hearing of faith? **2:16** [16]Knowing that a man is not justified by the works of the law, but by the faith of Jesus Christ, even we have believed in Jesus Christ, that we might be justified by the faith of Christ, and not by the works of the law: for by the works of the law shall no flesh be justified.

GALATIANS 3:6—Faith and freedom (3:1–4:31). Time range: 48–50, 54, or 55 CE

Theme	GAL	Paul	NT	Jewish Writings
Abraham believed God	**3:6** [6]Even as Abraham believed God, and it was accounted to him for righteousness.	**Rom 4:3** [3]For what saith the scripture? Abraham believed God, and it was counted unto him for righteousness.	**Jas 2:23** [23]And the scripture was fulfilled which saith, Abraham believed God, and it was imputed unto him for righteousness: and he was called the Friend of God.	**Gen 15:6** [6]And he believed in the LORD; and he counted it to him for righteousness.

GALATIANS 3:7—Faith and freedom (3:1–4:31). Time range: 48–50, 54, or 55 CE

Theme	GAL	Paul	Jewish Writings
Faith children of Abraham	**3:7** [7]Know ye therefore that they which are of faith, the same are the children of Abraham. **3:29** [29]And if ye be Christ's, then are ye Abraham's seed, and heirs according to the promise.	**Rom 4:11–12** [11]And he received the sign of circumcision, a seal of the righteousness of the faith which he had yet being uncircumcised: that he might be the father of all them that believe, though they be not circumcised; that righteousness might be imputed unto them also: [12]And the father of circumcision to them who are not of the circumcision only, but who also walk in the steps of that faith of our father Abraham, which he had being yet uncircumcised.	**Sir 44:19–21** [19]Abraham was a great father of many people: in glory was there none like unto him; [20]Who kept the law of the most High, and was in covenant with him: he established the covenant in his flesh; and when he was proved, he was found faithful. [21]Therefore he assured him by an oath, that he would bless the nations in his seed, and that he would multiply him as the dust of the earth, and exalt his seed as the stars, and cause them to inherit from sea to sea, and from the river unto the utmost part of the land.

GALATIANS 3:8—Faith and freedom (3:1–4:31). Time range: 48–50, 54, or 55 CE

Theme	GAL	Lk	Jewish Writings
All nations blessed in Abraham	**3:8** [8]And the scripture, foreseeing that God would justify the heathen through faith, preached before the gospel unto Abraham, saying, In thee shall all nations be blessed.	**Acts 3:25** [25]Ye are the children of the prophets, and of the covenant which God made with our fathers, saying unto Abraham, And in thy seed shall all the kindreds of the earth be blessed.	**Gen 12:3** [3]And I will bless them that bless thee, and curse him that curseth thee: and in thee shall all families of the earth be blessed. **Gen 18:17–19** [17]And the LORD said, Shall I hide from Abraham that thing which I do; [18]Seeing that Abraham shall surely become a great and mighty nation, and all the nations of the earth shall be blessed in him? [19]For I know him, that he will command his children and his household after him, and they shall keep the way of the LORD, to do justice and judgment; that the LORD may bring upon Abraham that which he hath spoken of him.

GALATIANS 3:9—Faith and freedom (3:1–4:31). Time range: 48–50, 54, or 55 CE

Theme	GAL	Paul
Blessed with faith	**3:9** [9]So then they which be of faith are blessed with faithful Abraham.	**Rom 4:16** [16]Therefore it is of faith, that it might be by grace; to the end the promise might be sure to all the seed; not to that only which is of the law, but to that also which is of the faith of Abraham; who is the father of us all,

GALATIANS 3:10—Faith and freedom (3:1–4:31). Time range: 48–50, 54, or 55 CE

Theme	GAL	Jewish Writings	NT
Abide in law, too	**3:10** [10]For as many as are of the works of the law are under the curse: for it is written, Cursed is every one that continueth not in all things which are written in the book of the law to do them.	**Dt 27:26** [26]Cursed be he that confirmeth not all the words of this law to do them. And all the people shall say, Amen.	**Jas 2:10** [10]For whosoever shall keep the whole law, and yet offend in one point, he is guilty of all.

GALATIANS 3:11—Faith and freedom (3:1–4:31). Time range: 48–50, 54, or 55 CE

Theme	GAL	Paul	NT
Not justified by law	**3:11** [11]But that no man is justified by the law in the sight of God, it is evident: for, The just shall live by faith. **2:16** [16]Knowing that a man is not justified by the works of the law, but by the faith of Jesus Christ, even we have believed in Jesus Christ, that we might be justified by the faith of Christ, and not by the works of the law: for by the works of the law shall no flesh be justified.	**Rom 1:17** [17]For therein is the righteousness of God revealed from faith to faith: as it is written, The just shall live by faith.	**Heb 2:4** [4]God also bearing them witness, both with signs and wonders, and with divers miracles, and gifts of the Holy Ghost, according to his own will?

GALATIANS 3:12—Faith and freedom (3:1–4:31). Time range: 48–50, 54, or 55 CE

Theme	GAL	Paul	Jewish Writings
Law is not of faith	**3:12** [12]And the law is not of faith: but, The man that doeth them shall live in them.	**Rom 10:5** [5]For Moses describeth the righteousness which is of the law, That the man which doeth those things shall live by them.	**Lev 18:5** [5]Ye shall therefore keep my statutes, and my judgments: which if a man do, he shall live in them: I am the LORD.

GALATIANS 3:13—Faith and freedom (3:1–4:31). Time range: 48–50, 54, or 55 CE

Theme	GAL	Paul	NT
Christ's atonement	**3:13** [13]Christ hath redeemed us from the curse of the law, being made a curse for us: for it is written, Cursed is every one that hangeth on a tree:	**Rom 3:25** [25]Whom God hath set forth to be a propitiation through faith in his blood, to declare his righteousness for the remission of sins that are past, through the forbearance of God; **Rom 8:3** [3]For what the law could not do, in that it was weak through the flesh, God sending his own Son in the likeness of sinful flesh, and for sin, condemned sin in the flesh: **2 Cor 5:21** [21]For he hath made him to be sin for us, who knew no sin; that we might be made the righteousness of God in him.	**Heb 9:5** [5]And over it the cherubims of glory shadowing the mercyseat; of which we cannot now speak particularly.

Jewish Writings

Ex 25:16–21

[16]And thou shalt put into the ark the testimony which I shall give thee. [17]And thou shalt make a mercy seat of pure gold: two cubits and a half shall be the length thereof, and a cubit and a half the breadth thereof. [18]And thou shalt make two cherubims of gold, of beaten work shalt thou make them, in the two ends of the mercy seat. [19]And make one cherub on the one end, and the other cherub on the other end: even of the mercy seat shall ye make the cherubims on the two ends thereof. [20]And the cherubims shall stretch forth their wings on high, covering the mercy seat with their wings, and their faces shall look one to another; toward the mercy seat shall the faces of the cherubims be. [21]And thou shalt put the mercy seat above upon the ark; and in the ark thou shalt put the testimony that I shall give thee.

Lev 1:4

[4]And he shall put his hand upon the head of the burnt offering; and it shall be accepted for him to make atonement for him.

Lev 4–5

4[1]And the LORD spake unto Moses, saying, [2]Speak unto the children of Israel, saying, If a soul shall sin through ignorance against any of the commandments of the LORD concerning things which ought not to be done, and shall do against any of them: [3]If the priest that is anointed do sin according to the sin of the people; then let him bring for his sin, which he hath sinned, a young bullock without blemish unto the LORD for a sin offering. [4]And he shall bring the bullock unto the door of the tabernacle of the congregation before the LORD; and shall lay his hand upon the bullock's head, and kill the bullock before the LORD. [5]And the priest that is anointed shall take of the bullock's blood, and bring it to the tabernacle of the congregation: [6]And the priest shall dip his finger in the blood, and sprinkle of the blood seven times before the LORD, before the veil of the sanctuary. [7]And the priest shall put some of the blood upon the horns of the altar of sweet incense before the LORD, which is in the tabernacle of the congregation; and shall pour all the blood of the bullock at the bottom of the altar of the burnt offering, which is at the door of the tabernacle of the congregation. [8]And he shall take off from it all the fat of the bullock for the sin offering; the fat that covereth the inwards, and all the fat that is upon the inwards, [9]And the two kidneys, and the fat that is upon them, which is by the flanks, and the caul above the liver, with the kidneys, it shall he take away, [10]As it was taken off from the bullock of the sacrifice of peace offerings: and the priest shall burn them upon the altar of the burnt offering. [11]And the skin of the bullock, and all his flesh, with his head, and with his legs, and his inwards, and his dung, [12]Even the whole bullock shall he carry forth without the camp unto a clean place, where the ashes are poured out, and burn him on the wood with fire: where the ashes are poured out shall he be burnt. [13]And if the whole congregation of Israel sin through ignorance, and the thing be hid from the eyes of the assembly, and they have done somewhat against any of the commandments of the LORD concerning things which should not be done, and are guilty; [14]When the sin, which they have sinned against it, is known, then the congregation shall offer a young bullock for the sin, and bring him before the tabernacle of the congregation. [15]And the elders of the congregation shall lay their hands upon the head of the bullock before the LORD: and the bullock shall be killed before the LORD. [16]And the priest that is anointed shall bring of the bullock's blood to the tabernacle of the congregation: [17]And the priest shall dip his finger in some of the blood, and sprinkle it seven times before the LORD, even before the veil. [18]And he shall put some of the blood upon the horns of the altar which is before the LORD, that is in the tabernacle of the congregation, and shall pour out all the blood at the bottom of the altar of the burnt offering, which is at the door of the tabernacle of the congregation. [19]And he shall take all his fat from him, and burn it upon the altar. [20]And he shall do with the bullock as he did with the bullock for a sin offering, so shall he do with this: and the priest shall make an atonement for them, and it shall be forgiven them. [21]And he shall carry forth the bullock without the camp, and burn him as he burned the first bullock: it is a sin offering for the congregation. [22]When a ruler hath sinned, and done somewhat through ignorance against any of the commandments of the LORD his God concerning things which should not be done, and is guilty; [23]Or if his sin, wherein he hath sinned, come to his knowledge; he shall bring his offering, a kid of the goats, a male without blemish: [24]And he shall lay his hand upon the head of the goat, and kill it in the place where they kill the burnt offering before the LORD: it is a sin offering. [25]And the priest shall take of the blood of the sin offering with his finger, and put it upon the horns of the altar of burnt offering, and shall pour out his blood at the bottom of the altar of burnt offering. [26]And he shall burn all his fat upon the altar, as the fat of the sacrifice of peace offerings: and the priest shall make an atonement for him as concerning his sin, and it shall be forgiven him. [27]And if any one of the common people sin through ignorance, while he doeth somewhat against any of the commandments of the LORD concerning things which ought not to be done, and be guilty; [28]Or if his sin, which he hath sinned, come to his knowledge: then he shall bring his offering, a kid of the goats, a female without blemish, for his sin which he hath sinned. [29]And he shall lay his hand upon the head of the sin offering, and slay the sin offering in the place of the burnt

(*Continued*)

GALATIANS 3:13—Faith and freedom (3:1–4:31). Time range: 48–50, 54, or 55 CE

Theme	GAL	Jewish Writings
(*Cont.*) Christ's atonement for sin	**3:13 (above)**	**(*Continued*)** **Lev 4–5** **4** offering. [30]And the priest shall take of the blood thereof with his finger, and put it upon the horns of the altar of burnt offering, and shall pour out all the blood thereof at the bottom of the altar. [31]And he shall take away all the fat thereof, as the fat is taken away from off the sacrifice of peace offerings; and the priest shall burn it upon the altar for a sweet savour unto the LORD; and the priest shall make an atonement for him, and it shall be forgiven him. [32]And if he bring a lamb for a sin offering, he shall bring it a female without blemish. [33]And he shall lay his hand upon the head of the sin offering, and slay it for a sin offering in the place where they kill the burnt offering. [34]And the priest shall take of the blood of the sin offering with his finger, and put it upon the horns of the altar of burnt offering, and shall pour out all the blood thereof at the bottom of the altar: [35]And he shall take away all the fat thereof, as the fat of the lamb is taken away from the sacrifice of the peace offerings; and the priest shall burn them upon the altar, according to the offerings made by fire unto the LORD: and the priest shall make an atonement for his sin that he hath committed, and it shall be forgiven him. **5** [1]And if a soul sin, and hear the voice of swearing, and is a witness, whether he hath seen or known of it; if he do not utter it, then he shall bear his iniquity. [2]Or if a soul touch any unclean thing, whether it be a carcase of an unclean beast, or a carcase of unclean cattle, or the carcase of unclean creeping things, and if it be hidden from him; he also shall be unclean, and guilty. [3]Or if he touch the uncleanness of man, whatsoever uncleanness it be that a man shall be defiled withal, and it be hid from him; when he knoweth of it, then he shall be guilty. [4]Or if a soul swear, pronouncing with his lips to do evil, or to do good, whatsoever it be that a man shall pronounce with an oath, and it be hid from him; when he knoweth of it, then he shall be guilty in one of these. [5]And it shall be, when he shall be guilty in one of these things, that he shall confess that he hath sinned in that thing: [6]And he shall bring his trespass offering unto the LORD for his sin which he hath sinned, a female from the flock, a lamb or a kid of the goats, for a sin offering; and the priest shall make an atonement for him concerning his sin. [7]And if he be not able to bring a lamb, then he shall bring for his trespass, which he hath committed, two turtledoves, or two young pigeons, unto the LORD; one for a sin offering, and the other for a burnt offering. [8]And he shall bring them unto the priest, who shall offer that which is for the sin offering first, and wring off his head from his neck, but shall not divide it asunder: [9]And he shall sprinkle of the blood of the sin offering upon the side of the altar; and the rest of the blood shall be wrung out at the bottom of the altar: it is a sin offering. [10]And he shall offer the second for a burnt offering, according to the manner: and the priest shall make an atonement for him for his sin which he hath sinned, and it shall be forgiven him. [11]But if he be not able to bring two turtledoves, or two young pigeons, then he that sinned shall bring for his offering the tenth part of an ephah of fine flour for a sin offering; he shall put no oil upon it, neither shall he put any frankincense thereon: for it is a sin offering. [12]Then shall he bring it to the priest, and the priest shall take his handful of it, even a memorial thereof, and burn it on the altar, according to the offerings made by fire unto the LORD: it is a sin offering. [13]And the priest shall make an atonement for him as touching his sin that he hath sinned in one of these, and it shall be forgiven him: and the remnant shall be the priest's, as a meat offering. [14]And the LORD spake unto Moses, saying, [15]If a soul commit a trespass, and sin through ignorance, in the holy things of the LORD; then he shall bring for his trespass unto the LORD a ram without blemish out of the flocks, with thy estimation by shekels of silver, after the shekel of the sanctuary, for a trespass offering: [16]And he shall make amends for the harm that he hath done in the holy thing, and shall add the fifth part thereto, and give it unto the priest: and the priest shall make an atonement for him with the ram of the trespass offering, and it shall be forgiven him. [17]And if a soul sin, and commit any of these things which are forbidden to be done by the commandments of the LORD; though he wist it not, yet is he guilty, and shall bear his iniquity. [18]And he shall bring a ram without blemish out of the flock, with thy estimation, for a trespass offering, unto the priest: and the priest shall make an atonement for him concerning his ignorance wherein he erred and wist it not, and it shall be forgiven him. [19]It is a trespass offering: he hath certainly trespassed against the LORD.

Jewish Writings (*Continued*)
Dt 21:23
[23]His body shall not remain all night upon the tree, but thou shalt in any wise bury him that day; (for he that is hanged is accursed of God;) that thy land be not defiled, which the LORD thy God giveth thee for an inheritance.

GALATIANS 3:14—Faith and freedom (3:1–4:31). Time range: 48–50, 54, or 55 CE

Theme	GAL	Lk	Jewish Writings
Abraham's blessing comes through Jesus	**3:14** [14]That the blessing of Abraham might come on the Gentiles through Jesus Christ; that we might receive the promise of the Spirit through faith. **3:2–3, 5** [2]This only would I learn of you, Received ye the Spirit by the works of the law, or by the hearing of faith? [3]Are ye so foolish? having begun in the Spirit, are ye now made perfect by the flesh? . . . [5]He therefore that ministereth to you the Spirit, and worketh miracles among you, doeth he it by the works of the law, or by the hearing of faith?	**Acts 2:33** [33]Therefore being by the right hand of God exalted, and having received of the Father the promise of the Holy Ghost, he hath shed forth this, which ye now see and hear.	**Is 44:3** [3]For I will pour water upon him that is thirsty, and floods upon the dry ground: I will pour my spirit upon thy seed, and my blessing upon thine offspring: **Joel 3:1–2** [1]For, behold, in those days, and in that time, when I shall bring again the captivity of Judah and Jerusalem, [2]I will also gather all nations, and will bring them down into the valley of Jehoshaphat, and will plead with them there for my people and for my heritage Israel, whom they have scattered among the nations, and parted my land.

GALATIANS 3:15—Faith and freedom (3:1–4:31). Time range: 48–50, 54, or 55 CE

Theme	GAL	Paul	NT
Confirmed covenant	**3:15** [15]Brethren, I speak after the manner of men; Though it be but a man's covenant, yet if it be confirmed, no man disannulleth, or addeth thereto.	**Rom 3:5** [5]But if our unrighteousness commend the righteousness of God, what shall we say? Is God unrighteous who taketh vengeance? (I speak as a man)	**Heb 9:16–17** [16]For where a testament is, there must also of necessity be the death of the testator. [17]For a testament is of force after men are dead: otherwise it is of no strength at all while the testator liveth.

GALATIANS 3:17—Faith and freedom (3:1–4:31). Time range: 48–50, 54, or 55 CE

Theme	GAL	Jewish Writings
Confirmed covenant	**3:17** [17]And this I say, that the covenant, that was confirmed before of God in Christ, the law, which was four hundred and thirty years after, cannot disannul, that it should make the promise of none effect.	**Ex 12:40** [40]Now the sojourning of the children of Israel, who dwelt in Egypt, was four hundred and thirty years.

GALATIANS 3:18—Faith and freedom (3:1–4:31). Time range: 48–50, 54, or 55 CE

Theme	GAL	Paul
God's promise to Abraham	**3:18** [18]For if the inheritance be of the law, it is no more of promise: but God gave it to Abraham by promise.	**Rom 4:16** [16]Therefore it is of faith, that it might be by grace; to the end the promise might be sure to all the seed; not to that only which is of the law, but to that also which is of the faith of Abraham; who is the father of us all, **Rom 11:6** [6]And if by grace, then is it no more of works: otherwise grace is no more grace. But if it be of works, then is it no more grace: otherwise work is no more work.

GALATIANS 3:19—Faith and freedom (3:1–4:31). Time range: 48–50, 54, or 55 CE

Theme	GAL	Lk	Paul
Ordained by angels, law added sin until Promise came	**3:19** [19]Wherefore then serveth the law? It was added because of transgressions, till the seed should come to whom the promise was made; and it was ordained by angels in the hand of a mediator.	**Acts 7:38** [38]This is he, that was in the church in the wilderness with the angel which spake to him in the mount Sina, and with our fathers: who received the lively oracles to give unto us: **Acts 7:53** [53]Who have received the law by the disposition of angels, and have not kept it.	**Rom 4:15** [15]Because the law worketh wrath: for where no law is, there is no transgression. **Rom 5:20** [20]Moreover the law entered, that the offence might abound. But where sin abounded, grace did much more abound: **Rom 7:7** [7]What shall we say then? Is the law sin? God forbid. Nay, I had not known sin, but by the law: for I had not known lust, except the law had said, Thou shalt not covet. **Rom 7:13** [13]Was then that which is good made death unto me? God forbid. But sin, that it might appear sin, working death in me by that which is good; that sin by the commandment might become exceeding sinful.

GALATIANS 3:20—Faith and freedom (3:1–4:31). Time range: 48–50, 54, or 55 CE

Theme	GAL	Jewish Writings
God is one	**3:20** [20]Now a mediator is not a mediator of one, but God is one.	**Dt 6:4** [4]Hear, O Israel: The LORD our God is one LORD:

GALATIANS 3:21–26—Faith and freedom (3:1–4:31). Time range: 48–50, 54, or 55 CE

Theme	GAL	Paul	Jn
Faith is freedom	**3:21–26** [21]Is the law then against the promises of God? God forbid: for if there had been a law given which could have given life, verily righteousness should have been by the law. [22]But the scripture hath concluded all under sin, that the promise by faith of Jesus Christ might be given to them that believe. [23]But before faith came, we were kept under the law, shut up unto the faith which should afterwards be revealed. [24]Wherefore the law was our schoolmaster to bring us unto Christ, that we might be justified by faith. [25]But after that faith is come, we are no longer under a schoolmaster. [26] For ye are all the children of God by faith in Christ Jesus. **2:16** [16]Knowing that a man is not justified by the works of the law, but by the faith of Jesus Christ, even we have believed in Jesus Christ, that we might be justified by the faith of Christ, and not by the works of the law: for by the works of the law shall no flesh be justified. **4:3–7** [3]Even so we, when we were children, were in bondage under the elements of the world: [4]But when the fulness of the time was come, God sent forth his Son, made of a woman, made under the law, [5]To redeem them that were under the law, that we might receive the adoption of sons. [6]And because ye are sons, God hath sent forth the Spirit of his Son into your hearts, crying, Abba, Father. [7]Wherefore thou art no more a servant, but a son; and if a son, then an heir of God through Christ. **5:18** [18]But it is good to be zealously affected always in a good thing, and not only when I am present with you.	**Rom 3:9–20, 23** [9]What then? are we better than they? No, in no wise: for we have before proved both Jews and Gentiles, that they are all under sin; [10]As it is written, There is none righteous, no, not one: [11]There is none that understandeth, there is none that seeketh after God. [12]They are all gone out of the way, they are together become unprofitable; there is none that doeth good, no, not one. [13]Their throat is an open sepulchre; with their tongues they have used deceit; the poison of asps is under their lips: [14]Whose mouth is full of cursing and bitterness: [15]Their feet are swift to shed blood: [16]Destruction and misery are in their ways: [17]And the way of peace have they not known: [18]There is no fear of God before their eyes. [19]Now we know that what things soever the law saith, it saith to them who are under the law: that every mouth may be stopped, and all the world may become guilty before God. [20]Therefore by the deeds of the law there shall no flesh be justified in his sight: for by the law is the knowledge of sin. . . . [23]For all have sinned, and come short of the glory of God; **Rom 7:7,10** [7]What shall we say then? Is the law sin? God forbid. Nay, I had not known sin, but by the law: for I had not known lust, except the law had said, Thou shalt not covet. . . . [10]And the commandment, which was ordained to life, I found to be unto death. **Rom 8:2–4** [2]For the law of the Spirit of life in Christ Jesus hath made me free from the law of sin and death. [3]For what the law could not do, in that it was weak through the flesh, God sending his own Son in the likeness of sinful flesh, and for sin, condemned sin in the flesh: [4]That the righteousness of the law might be fulfilled in us, who walk not after the flesh, but after the Spirit. **Rom 8:14–17** [14]For as many as are led by the Spirit of God, they are the sons of God. [15]For ye have not received the spirit of bondage again to fear; but ye have received the Spirit of adoption, whereby we cry, Abba, Father. [16]The Spirit itself beareth witness with our spirit, that we are the children of God: [17]And if children, then heirs; heirs of God, and joint-heirs with Christ; if so be that we suffer with him, that we may be also glorified together. **Rom 10:4** [4]For Christ is the end of the law for righteousness to every one that believeth. **Rom 11:32** [32]For God hath concluded them all in unbelief, that he might have mercy upon all.	**1:12** [12]But as many as received him, to them gave he power to become the sons of God, [even] to them that believe on his name:

GALATIANS 3:21—Faith and freedom (3:1–4:31). Time range: 48–50, 54, or 55 CE

Theme	GAL	Paul
Faith is freedom	**3:21** [21]Is the law then against the promises of God? God forbid: for if there had been a law given which could have given life, verily righteousness should have been by the law.	**Rom 7:7,10** [7]What shall we say then? Is the law sin? God forbid. Nay, I had not known sin, but by the law: for I had not known lust, except the law had said, Thou shalt not covet. . . . [10]And the commandment, which was ordained to life, I found to be unto death. **Rom 8:2–4** [2]For the law of the Spirit of life in Christ Jesus hath made me free from the law of sin and death. [3]For what the law could not do, in that it was weak through the flesh, God sending his own Son in the likeness of sinful flesh, and for sin, condemned sin in the flesh: [4]That the righteousness of the law might be fulfilled in us, who walk not after the flesh, but after the Spirit.

GALATIANS 3:22—Faith and freedom (3:1–4:31). Time range: 48–50, 54, or 55 CE

Theme	GAL	Paul
Faith is freedom	**3:22** [22]But the scripture hath concluded all under sin, that the promise by faith of Jesus Christ might be given to them that believe.	**Rom 3:9–20, 23** [9]What then? are we better than they? No, in no wise: for we have before proved both Jews and Gentiles, that they are all under sin; [10]As it is written, There is none righteous, no, not one: [11]There is none that understandeth, there is none that seeketh after God. [12]They are all gone out of the way, they are together become unprofitable; there is none that doeth good, no, not one. [13]Their throat is an open sepulchre; with their tongues they have used deceit; the poison of asps is under their lips: [14]Whose mouth is full of cursing and bitterness: [15]Their feet are swift to shed blood: [16]Destruction and misery are in their ways: [17]And the way of peace have they not known: [18]There is no fear of God before their eyes. [19]Now we know that what things soever the law saith, it saith to them who are under the law: that every mouth may be stopped, and all the world may become guilty before God. [20]Therefore by the deeds of the law there shall no flesh be justified in his sight: for by the law is the knowledge of sin. . . .[23]For all have sinned, and come short of the glory of God; **Rom 11:32** [32]For God hath concluded them all in unbelief, that he might have mercy upon all.

GALATIANS 3:23–5:1—Faith and freedom (3:1–4:31). Time range: 48–50, 54, or 55 CE

Theme	GAL	Mt	Mk
Redemption	**3:23–5:1**	**20:28**	**10:45**
	3 [23]But before faith came, we were kept under the law, shut up unto the faith which should afterwards be revealed. [24]Wherefore the law was our schoolmaster to bring us unto Christ, that we might be justified by faith. [25]But after that faith is come, we are no longer under a schoolmaster [26]For ye are all the children of God by faith in Christ Jesus. [27]For as many of you as have been baptized into Christ have put on Christ. [28]There is neither Jew nor Greek, there is neither bond nor free, there is neither male nor female: for ye are all one in Christ Jesus. [29]And if ye be Christ's, then are ye Abraham's seed, and heirs according to the promise. **4** [1]Now I say, That the heir, as long as he is a child, differeth nothing from a servant, though he be lord of all; [2]But is under tutors and governors until the time appointed of the father. [3]Even so we, when we were children, were in bondage under the elements of the world: [4]But when the fulness of the time was come, God sent forth his Son, made of a woman, made under the law, [5]To redeem them that were under the law, that we might receive the adoption of sons. [6]And because ye are sons, God hath sent forth the Spirit of his Son into your hearts, crying, Abba, Father. [7]Wherefore thou art no more a servant, but a son; and if a son, then an heir of God through Christ. [8]Howbeit then, when ye knew not God, ye did service unto them which by nature are no gods. [9]But now, after that ye have known God, or rather are known of God, how turn ye again to the weak and beggarly elements, whereunto ye desire again to be in bondage? [10]Ye observe days, and months, and times, and years. [11]I am afraid of you, lest I have bestowed upon you labour in vain. [12]Brethren, I beseech you, be as I am; for I am as ye are: ye have not injured me at all. [13]Ye know how through infirmity of the flesh I preached the gospel unto you at the first. [14]And my temptation which was in my flesh ye despised not, nor rejected; but received me as an angel of God, even as Christ Jesus. [15]Where is then the blessedness ye spake of? for I bear you record, that, if it had been possible, ye would have plucked out your own eyes, and have given them to me. [16]Am I therefore become your enemy, because I tell you the truth? [17]They zealously affect you, but not well; yea, they would exclude you, that ye might affect them. [18]But it is good to be zealously affected always in a good thing, and not only when I am present with you. [19]My little children, of whom I travail in birth again until Christ be formed in you, [20]I desire to be present with you now, and to change my voice; for I stand in doubt of you. [21]Tell me, ye that desire to be under the law, do ye not hear the law? [22]For it is written, that Abraham had two sons, the one by a bondmaid, the other by a freewoman. [23]But he who was of the bondwoman was born after the flesh; but he of the freewoman was by promise. [24]Which things are an allegory: for these are the two covenants; the one from the mount Sinai, which gendereth to bondage, which is Agar. [25]For this Agar is mount Sinai in Arabia, and answereth to Jerusalem which now is, and is in bondage with her children. [26]But Jerusalem which is above is free, which is the mother of us all. [27]For it is written, Rejoice, thou barren that bearest not; break forth and cry, thou that travailest not: for the desolate hath many more children than she which hath an husband. [28]Now we, brethren, as Isaac was, are the children of promise. [29]But as then he that was born after the flesh persecuted him that was born after the Spirit, even so it is now. [30]Nevertheless what saith the scripture? Cast out the bondwoman and her son: for the son of the bondwoman shall not be heir with the son of the freewoman. [31]So then, brethren, we are not children of the bondwoman, but of the free. **5** [1]Stand fast therefore in the liberty wherewith Christ hath made us free, and be not entangled again with the yoke of bondage.	[28]Even as the Son of man came not to be ministered unto, but to minister, and to give his life a ransom for many.	[45]For even the Son of man came not to be ministered unto, but to minister, and to give his life a ransom for many.
	2:16		
	[16]Knowing that a man is not justified by the works of the law, but by the faith of Jesus Christ, even we have believed in Jesus Christ, that we might be justified by the faith of Christ, and not by the works of the law: for by the works of the law shall no flesh be justified.		

Paul	NT	Jewish	Other
Rom 3:24 24Being justified freely by his grace through the redemption that is in Christ Jesus: **Rom 6:14** 14For sin shall not have dominion over you: for ye are not under the law, but under grace. **1 Cor 10** 1Moreover, brethren, I would not that ye should be ignorant, how that all our fathers were under the cloud, and all passed through the sea; 2And were all baptized unto Moses in the cloud and in the sea; 3And did all eat the same spiritual meat; 4And did all drink the same spiritual drink: for they drank of that spiritual Rock that followed them: and that Rock was Christ. 5But with many of them God was not well pleased: for they were overthrown in the wilderness. 6Now these things were our examples, to the intent we should not lust after evil things, as they also lusted. 7Neither be ye idolaters, as were some of them; as it is written, The people sat down to eat and drink, and rose up to play. 8Neither let us commit fornication, as some of them committed, and fell in one day three and twenty thousand. 9Neither let us tempt Christ, as some of them also tempted, and were destroyed of serpents. 10Neither murmur ye, as some of them also murmured, and were destroyed of the destroyer. 11Now all these things happened unto them for ensamples: and they are written for our admonition, upon whom the ends of the world are come. 12Wherefore let him that thinketh he standeth take heed lest he fall. 13There hath no temptation taken you but such as is common to man: but God is faithful, who will not suffer you to be tempted above that ye are able; but will with the temptation also make a way to escape, that ye may be able to bear it. 14Wherefore, my dearly beloved, flee from idolatry. 15I speak as to wise men; judge ye what I say. 16The cup of blessing which we bless, is it not the communion of the blood of Christ? The bread which we break, is it not the communion of the body of Christ? 17For we being many are one bread, and one body: for we are all partakers of that one bread. 18Behold Israel after the flesh: are not they which eat of the sacrifices partakers of the altar? 19What say I then? that the idol is any thing, or that which is offered in sacrifice to idols is any thing? 20But I say, that the things which the Gentiles sacrifice, they sacrifice to devils, and not to God: and I would not that ye should have fellowship with devils. 21Ye cannot drink the cup of the Lord, and the cup of devils: ye cannot be partakers of the Lord's table, and of the table of devils. 22Do we provoke the Lord to jealousy? are we stronger than he? 23All things are lawful for me, but all things are not expedient: all things are lawful for me, but all things edify not. 24Let no man seek his own, but every man another's wealth. 25Whatsoever is sold in the shambles, that eat, asking no question for conscience sake: 26For the earth is the Lord's, and the fulness thereof. 27If any of them that believe not bid you to a feast, and ye be disposed to go; whatsoever is set before you, eat, asking no question for conscience sake. 28But if any man say unto you, This is offered in sacrifice unto idols, eat not for his sake that showed it, and for conscience sake: for the earth is the Lord's, and the fulness thereof: 29Conscience, I say, not thine own, but of the other: for why is my liberty judged of another man's conscience? 30For if I by grace be a partaker, why am I evil spoken of for that for which I give thanks? 31Whether therefore ye eat, or drink, or whatsoever ye do, do all to the glory of God. 32Give none offence, neither to the Jews, nor to the Gentiles, nor to the church of God: 33Even as I please all men in all things, not seeking mine own profit, but the profit of many, that they may be saved.	**Heb 9:5** 5And over it the cherubims of glory shadowing the mercyseat; of which we cannot now speak particularly.	**Ex 15:13** 13Thou in thy mercy hast led forth the people which thou hast redeemed: thou hast guided them in thy strength unto thy holy habitation. **Is 41:14** 14Fear not, thou worm Jacob, and ye men of Israel; I will help thee, saith the LORD, and thy redeemer, the Holy One of Israel.	**Q-Quelle** Precedence: Gal 3:23-5:1/1 Cor 10/[Mt 19:28]/[Mk 10:41-45]/[Lk 22:28-30 (QS 62)]

GALATIANS 3:23—Faith and freedom (3:1–4:31). Time range: 48–50, 54, or 55 CE

Theme	GAL
Faith is freedom	**3:23** [23]But before faith came, we were kept under the law, shut up unto the faith which should afterwards be revealed. **4:3–5** [3]Even so we, when we were children, were in bondage under the elements of the world: [4]But when the fulness of the time was come, God sent forth his Son, made of a woman, made under the law, [5]To redeem them that were under the law, that we might receive the adoption of sons. **5:18** [18]But if ye be led of the Spirit, ye are not under the law.

GALATIANS 3:24—Faith and freedom (3:1–4:31). Time range: 48–50, 54, or 55 CE

Theme	GAL
Faith is freedom	**3:24** [24]Wherefore the law was our schoolmaster to bring us unto Christ, that we might be justified by faith. **2:16** [16]Knowing that a man is not justified by the works of the law, but by the faith of Jesus Christ, even we have believed in Jesus Christ, that we might be justified by the faith of Christ, and not by the works of the law: for by the works of the law shall no flesh be justified.

GALATIANS 3:25—Faith and freedom (3:1–4:31). Time range: 48–50, 54, or 55 CE

Theme	GAL	Paul
Faith is freedom	**3:25** [25]But after that faith is come, we are no longer under a schoolmaster.	**Rom 10:4** [4]For Christ is the end of the law for righteousness to every one that believeth.

GALATIANS 3:26—Faith and freedom (3:1–4:31). Time range: 48–50, 54, or 55 CE

Theme	GAL	Paul	Jn
Faith is freedom	**3:26** [26]For ye are all the children of God by faith in Christ Jesus. **4:5–7** [5]To redeem them that were under the law, that we might receive the adoption of sons.	**Rom 8:14–17** [14]For as many as are led by the Spirit of God, they are the sons of God. [15]For ye have not received the spirit of bondage again to fear; but ye have received the Spirit of adoption, whereby we cry, Abba, Father. [16]The Spirit itself beareth witness with our spirit, that we are the children of God: [17]And if children, then heirs; heirs of God, and joint-heirs with Christ; if so be that we suffer with him, that we may be also glorified together.	**1:12** [12]But as many as received him, to them gave he power to become the sons of God, even to them that believe on his name:

GALATIANS 3:27—Faith and freedom (3:1–4:31). Time range: 48–50, 54, or 55 CE

Theme	GAL	Paul	Other
Baptized put on Christ	**3:27** [27]For as many of you as have been baptized into Christ have put on Christ.	**Rom 6:3** [3]Know ye not, that so many of us as were baptized into Jesus Christ were baptized into his death? **Rom 13:14** [14]But put ye on the Lord Jesus Christ, and make not provision for the flesh, to fulfil the lusts thereof. **Eph 4:24 (Pseudo)** [24]And that ye put on the new man, which after God is created in righteousness and true holiness.	**Q-Quelle** Divisions in Households: Gal 3:27/Rom 6:3-4/[Mt 10:34-36]/[Lk 12:49-53 (QS 43 [Thom 16])]

GALATIANS 3:28—Faith and freedom (3:1–4:31). Time range: 48–50, 54, or 55 CE

Theme	GAL	Mt	Paul	Jewish Writings	Other
Equality in Christ	**3:28** [28]There is neither Jew nor Greek, there is neither bond nor free, there is neither male nor female: for ye are all one in Christ Jesus.	**10:5** [5]These twelve Jesus sent forth, and commanded them, saying, Go not into the way of the Gentiles, and into any city of the Samaritans enter ye not: **10:23** [23]But when they persecute you in this city, flee ye into another: for verily I say unto you, Ye shall not have gone over the cities of Israel, till the Son of man be come. **15:24** [24]But he answered and said, I am not sent but unto the lost sheep of the house of Israel. **28:19** [19]Go ye therefore, and teach all nations, baptizing them in the name of the Father, and of the Son, and of the Holy Ghost:	**Rom 10:12** [12]For there is no difference between the Jew and the Greek: for the same Lord over all is rich unto all that call upon him. **1 Cor 7:3–4** [3]Let the husband render unto the wife due benevolence: and likewise also the wife unto the husband. [4]The wife hath not power of her own body, but the husband: and likewise also the husband hath not power of his own body, but the wife. **1 Cor 11:11–12** [11]Nevertheless neither is the man without the woman, neither the woman without the man, in the Lord. [12]For as the woman is of the man, even so is the man also by the woman; but all things of God. **1 Cor 12:13** [13]For by one Spirit are we all baptized into one body, whether we be Jews or Gentiles, whether we be bond or free; and have been all made to drink into one Spirit. **Col 3:11** [11]Where there is neither Greek nor Jew, circumcision nor uncircumcision, Barbarian, Scythian, bond nor free: but Christ is all, and in all.	**Gen 1:27** [27]So God created man in his own image, in the image of God created he him; male and female created he them.	**Q-Quelle** Beezebul Controversy: Gal 3:28/1 Cor 12:12-13/[Mt 9:32-34, 12:22-30]/[Mk 3:22-27]/[Lk 11:14-23 (QS 28 [Thom 35])]

GALATIANS 3:29—Faith and freedom (3:1–4:31). Time range: 48–50, 54, or 55 CE

Theme	GAL	Paul	NT
In Christ, Abraham's seed	**3:29** [29]And if ye be Christ's, then are ye Abraham's seed, and heirs according to the promise. **3:7, 14, 16, 18** [7]Know ye therefore that they which are of faith, the same are the children of Abraham. . . .[14]That the blessing of Abraham might come on the Gentiles through Jesus Christ; that we might receive the promise of the Spirit through faith. . . .[16]Now to Abraham and his seed were the promises made. He saith not, And to seeds, as of many; but as of one, And to thy seed, which is Christ. . . .[8]For if the inheritance be of the law, it is no more of promise: but God gave it to Abraham by promise.	**Rom 4:1, 7** [1]What shall we say then that Abraham our father, as pertaining to the flesh, hath found? . . .[7]Saying, Blessed are they whose iniquities are forgiven, and whose sins are covered. **Rom 4:13–14** [13]For the promise, that he should be the heir of the world, was not to Abraham, or to his seed, through the law, but through the righteousness of faith. [14]For if they which are of the law be heirs, faith is made void, and the promise made of none effect: **Rom 4:16–17** [16]Therefore it is of faith, that it might be by grace; to the end the promise might be sure to all the seed; not to that only which is of the law, but to that also which is of the faith of Abraham; who is the father of us all, [17](As it is written, I have made thee a father of many nations,) before him whom he believed, even God, who quickeneth the dead, and calleth those things which be not as though they were. **Rom 8:17** [17]And if children, then heirs; heirs of God, and joint-heirs with Christ; if so be that we suffer with him, that we may be also glorified together. **Rom 9:7** [7]Neither, because they are the seed of Abraham, are they all children: but, In Isaac shall thy seed be called.	**Heb 6:12** [12]That ye be not slothful, but followers of them who through faith and patience inherit the promises. **Jas 2:5** [5]Hearken, my beloved brethren, Hath not God chosen the poor of this world rich in faith, and heirs of the kingdom which he hath promised to them that love him?

GALATIANS 4:3—Faith and freedom (3:1–4:31). Time range: 48–50, 54, or 55 CE

Theme	GAL	Paul
Children in bondage	**4:3** [3]Even so we, when we were children, were in bondage under the elements of the world: **3:23** [23]But before faith came, we were kept under the law, shut up unto the faith which should afterwards be revealed. **4:9** [9]But now, after that ye have known God, or rather are known of God, how turn ye again to the weak and beggarly elements, whereunto ye desire again to be in bondage?	**Col 2:20** [20]Wherefore if ye be dead with Christ from the rudiments of the world, why, as though living in the world, are ye subject to ordinances,

GALATIANS 4:4—Faith and freedom (3:1–4:31). Time range: 48–50, 54, or 55 CE

Theme	GAL	Mt	Mk
Jesus' humanness and eschatology	**4:4** [4]But when the fulness of the time was come, God sent forth his Son, made of a woman, made under the law,	**11:19** [19]The Son of man came eating and drinking, and they say, Behold a man gluttonous, and a winebibber, a friend of publicans and sinners. But wisdom is justified of her children. **19:8** [8]He saith unto them, Moses because of the hardness of your hearts suffered you to put away your wives: but from the beginning it was not so. **21:33–44** [33]Hear another parable: There was a certain householder, which planted a vineyard, and hedged it round about, and digged a winepress in it, and built a tower, and let it out to husbandmen, and went into a far country: [34]And when the time of the fruit drew near, he sent his servants to the husbandmen, that they might receive the fruits of it. [35]And the husbandmen took his servants, and beat one, and killed another, and stoned another. [36]Again, he sent other servants more than the first: and they did unto them likewise. [37]But last of all he sent unto them his son, saying, They will reverence my son. [38]But when the husbandmen saw the son, they said among themselves, This is the heir; come, let us kill him, and let us seize on his inheritance. [39]And they caught him, and cast him out of the vineyard, and slew him. [40]When the lord therefore of the vineyard cometh, what will he do unto those husbandmen? [41]They say unto him, He will miserably destroy those wicked men, and will let out his vineyard unto other husbandmen, which shall render him the fruits in their seasons. [42]Jesus saith unto them, Did ye never read in the scriptures, The stone which the builders rejected, the same is become the head of the corner: this is the Lord's doing, and it is marvellous in our eyes? [43]Therefore say I unto you, The kingdom of God shall be taken from you, and given to a nation bringing forth the fruits thereof. [44]And whosoever shall fall on this stone shall be broken: but on whomsoever it shall fall, it will grind him to powder. **23:34** [34]Wherefore, behold, I send unto you prophets, and wise men, and scribes: and some of them ye shall kill and crucify; and some of them shall ye scourge in your synagogues, and persecute them from city to city:	**1:15** [15]And saying, The time is fulfilled, and the kingdom of God is at hand: repent ye, and believe the gospel. **10:6** [6]But from the beginning of the creation God made them male and female. **12:1–22** [1]And he began to speak unto them by parables. A certain man planted a vineyard, and set an hedge about it, and digged a place for the winefat, and built a tower, and let it out to husbandmen, and went into a far country. [2]And at the season he sent to the husbandmen a servant, that he might receive from the husbandmen of the fruit of the vineyard. [3]And they caught him, and beat him, and sent him away empty. [4]And again he sent unto them another servant; and at him they cast stones, and wounded him in the head, and sent him away shamefully handled. [5]And again he sent another; and him they killed, and many others; beating some, and killing some. [6]Having yet therefore one son, his wellbeloved, he sent him also last unto them, saying, They will reverence my son. [7]But those husbandmen said among themselves, This is the heir; come, let us kill him, and the inheritance shall be ours. [8]And they took him, and killed him, and cast him out of the vineyard. [9]What shall therefore the lord of the vineyard do? he will come and destroy the husbandmen, and will give the vineyard unto others. [10]And have ye not read this scripture; The stone which the builders rejected is become the head of the corner: [11]This was the Lord's doing, and it is marvellous in our eyes? [12]And they sought to lay hold on him, but feared the people: for they knew that he had spoken the parable against them: and they left him, and went their way. [13]And they send unto him certain of the Pharisees and of the Herodians, to catch him in his words. [14]And when they were come, they say unto him, Master, we know that thou art true, and carest for no man: for thou regardest not the person of men, but teachest the way of God in truth: Is it lawful to give tribute to Caesar, or not? [15]Shall we give, or shall we not give? But he, knowing their hypocrisy, said unto them, Why tempt ye me? bring me a penny, that I may see it. [16]And they brought it. And he saith unto them, Whose is this image and superscription? And they said unto him, Caesar's. [17]And Jesus answering said unto them, Render to Caesar the things that are Caesar's, and to God the things that are God's. And they marvelled at him. [18]Then come unto him the Sadducees, which say there is no resurrection; and they asked him, saying, [19]Master, Moses wrote unto us, If a man's brother die, and leave his wife behind him, and leave no children, that his brother should take his wife, and raise up seed unto his brother. [20]Now there were seven brethren: and the first took a wife, and dying left no seed. [21]And the second took her, and died, neither left he any seed: and the third likewise. [22]And the seven had her, and left no seed: last of all the woman died also.

Galatians 4:4 continued on next page

GALATIANS 4:4—Faith and freedom (3:1–4:31). Time range: 48–50, 54, or 55 CE

Theme	GAL	Luke
(*Cont.*) **Jesus' humanness and eschatology**	**4:4 (above)**	**4:19** [19]To preach the acceptable year of the Lord. **7:35** [35]But wisdom is justified of all her children. **11:49** [49]Therefore also said the wisdom of God, I will send them prophets and apostles, and some of them they shall slay and persecute: **20:9–19** [9]Then began he to speak to the people this parable; A certain man planted a vineyard, and let it forth to husbandmen, and went into a far country for a long time. [10]And at the season he sent a servant to the husbandmen, that they should give him of the fruit of the vineyard: but the husbandmen beat him, and sent him away empty. [11]And again he sent another servant: and they beat him also, and entreated him shamefully, and sent him away empty. [12]And again he sent a third: and they wounded him also, and cast him out. [13]Then said the lord of the vineyard, What shall I do? I will send my beloved son: it may be they will reverence him when they see him. [14]But when the husbandmen saw him, they reasoned among themselves, saying, This is the heir: come, let us kill him, that the inheritance may be ours. [15]So they cast him out of the vineyard, and killed him. What therefore shall the lord of the vineyard do unto them? [16]He shall come and destroy these husbandmen, and shall give the vineyard to others. And when they heard it, they said, God forbid. [17]And he beheld them, and said, What is this then that is written, The stone which the builders rejected, the same is become the head of the corner? [18]Whosoever shall fall upon that stone shall be broken; but on whomsoever it shall fall, it will grind him to powder. [19]And the chief priests and the scribes the same hour sought to lay hands on him; and they feared the people: for they perceived that he had spoken this parable against them.

Paul

Rom 1:3

[3]Concerning his Son Jesus Christ our Lord, which was made of the seed of David according to the flesh;

Rom 5

[1]Therefore being justified by faith, we have peace with God through our Lord Jesus Christ: [2]By whom also we have access by faith into this grace wherein we stand, and rejoice in hope of the glory of God. [3]And not only so, but we glory in tribulations also: knowing that tribulation worketh patience; [4]And patience, experience; and experience, hope: [5]And hope maketh not ashamed; because the love of God is shed abroad in our hearts by the Holy Ghost which is given unto us. [6]For when we were yet without strength, in due time Christ died for the ungodly. [7]For scarcely for a righteous man will one die: yet peradventure for a good man some would even dare to die. [8]But God commendeth his love toward us, in that, while we were yet sinners, Christ died for us. [9]Much more then, being now justified by his blood, we shall be saved from wrath through him. [10]For if, when we were enemies, we were reconciled to God by the death of his Son, much more, being reconciled, we shall be saved by his life. [11]And not only so, but we also joy in God through our Lord Jesus Christ, by whom we have now received the atonement. [12]Wherefore, as by one man sin entered into the world, and death by sin; and so death passed upon all men, for that all have sinned: [13](For until the law sin was in the world: but sin is not imputed when there is no law. [14]Nevertheless death reigned from Adam to Moses, even over them that had not sinned after the similitude of Adam's transgression, who is the figure of him that was to come. [15]But not as the offence, so also is the free gift. For if through the offence of one many be dead, much more the grace of God, and the gift by grace, which is by one man, Jesus Christ, hath abounded unto many. [16]And not as it was by one that sinned, so is the gift: for the judgment was by one to condemnation, but the free gift is of many offences unto justification. [17]For if by one man's offence death reigned by one; much more they which receive abundance of grace and of the gift of righteousness shall reign in life by one, Jesus Christ.) [18]Therefore as by the offence of one judgment came upon all men to condemnation; even so by the righteousness of one the free gift came upon all men unto justification of life. [19]For as by one man's disobedience many were made sinners, so by the obedience of one shall many be made righteous. [20]Moreover the law entered, that the offence might abound. But where sin abounded, grace did much more abound: [21]That as sin hath reigned unto death, even so might grace reign through righteousness unto eternal life by Jesus Christ our Lord.

Rom 8:3

[3]For what the law could not do, in that it was weak through the flesh, God sending his own Son in the likeness of sinful flesh, and for sin, condemned sin in the flesh:

Rom 8:23

[23]And not only they, but ourselves also, which have the firstfruits of the Spirit, even we ourselves groan within ourselves, waiting for the adoption, to wit, the redemption of our body.

Rom 13:11–12

[11]And that, knowing the time, that now it is high time to awake out of sleep: for now is our salvation nearer than when we believed. [12]The night is far spent, the day is at hand: let us therefore cast off the works of darkness, and let us put on the armour of light.

Rom 15:20

[20]Yea, so have I strived to preach the gospel, not where Christ was named, lest I should build upon another man's foundation:

1 Cor 15:27

[27]For he hath put all things under his feet. But when he saith all things are put under him, it is manifest that he is excepted, which did put all things under him.

1 Cor 15:49

[49]And as we have borne the image of the earthy, we shall also bear the image of the heavenly.

Galatians 4:4 continued on next page

GALATIANS 4:4—Christian liberty (Church founded by Paul in Acts 16:6, approx 55CE)

Theme	GAL	Paul
(*Cont.*) Jesus' humanness and eschatology	**4:4 (above)**	***Continued*** **2 Cor 3:18** [18]But we all, with open face beholding as in a glass the glory of the Lord, are changed into the same image from glory to glory, even as by the Spirit of the Lord. **2 Cor 5:17** [17]Therefore if any man be in Christ, he is a new creature: old things are passed away; behold, all things are become new. **2 Cor 5:19** [19]To wit, that God was in Christ, reconciling the world unto himself, not imputing their trespasses unto them; and hath committed unto us the word of reconciliation. **2 Cor 6:2** [2](For he saith, I have heard thee in a time accepted, and in the day of salvation have I succoured thee: behold, now is the accepted time; behold, now is the day of salvation.) **Eph 1:10 (Pseudo)** [10]That in the dispensation of the fulness of times he might gather together in one all things in Christ, both which are in heaven, and which are on earth; even in him: **Phil 2** [1]If there be therefore any consolation in Christ, if any comfort of love, if any fellowship of the Spirit, if any bowels and mercies, [2]Fulfil ye my joy, that ye be likeminded, having the same love, being of one accord, of one mind. [3]Let nothing be done through strife or vainglory; but in lowliness of mind let each esteem other better than themselves. [4]Look not every man on his own things, but every man also on the things of others. [5]Let this mind be in you, which was also in Christ Jesus: [6]Who, being in the form of God, thought it not robbery to be equal with God: [7]But made himself of no reputation, and took upon him the form of a servant, and was made in the likeness of men: [8]And being found in fashion as a man, he humbled himself, and became obedient unto death, even the death of the cross. [9]Wherefore God also hath highly exalted him, and given him a name which is above every name: [10]That at the name of Jesus every knee should bow, of things in heaven, and things in earth, and things under the earth; [11]And that every tongue should confess that Jesus Christ is Lord, to the glory of God the Father. [12]Wherefore, my beloved, as ye have always obeyed, not as in my presence only, but now much more in my absence, work out your own salvation with fear and trembling. [13]For it is God which worketh in you both to will and to do of his good pleasure. [14]Do all things without murmurings and disputings: [15]That ye may be blameless and harmless, the sons of God, without rebuke, in the midst of a crooked and perverse nation, among whom ye shine as lights in the world; [16]Holding forth the word of life; that I may rejoice in the day of Christ, that I have not run in vain, neither laboured in vain. [17]Yea, and if I be offered upon the sacrifice and service of your faith, I joy, and rejoice with you all. [18]For the same cause also do ye joy, and rejoice with me. [19]But I trust in the Lord Jesus to send Timotheus shortly unto you, that I also may be of good comfort, when I know your state. [20]For I have no man likeminded, who will naturally care for your state. [21]For all seek their own, not the things which are Jesus Christ's. [22]But ye know the proof of him, that, as a son with the father, he hath served with me in the gospel. [23]Him therefore I hope to send presently, so soon as I shall see how it will go with me. [24]But I trust in the Lord that I also myself shall come shortly. [25]Yet I supposed it necessary to send to you Epaphroditus, my brother, and companion in labour, and fellowsoldier, but your messenger, and he that ministered to my wants. [26]For he longed after you all, and was full of heaviness, because that ye had heard that he had been sick. [27]For indeed he was sick nigh unto death: but God had mercy on him; and not on him only, but on me also, lest I should have sorrow upon sorrow. [28]I sent him therefore the more carefully, that, when ye see him again, ye may rejoice, and that I may be the less sorrowful. [29]Receive him therefore in the Lord with all glad- ness; and hold such in reputation: [30]Because for the work of Christ he was nigh unto death, not regarding his life, to supply your lack of service toward me. **Col 3:10** [10]And have put on the new man, which is renewed in knowledge after the image of him that created him:

Jewish Writings

Gen 1:28

[28]And God blessed them, and God said unto them, Be fruitful, and multiply, and replenish the earth, and subdue it: and have dominion over the fish of the sea, and over the fowl of the air, and over every living thing that moveth upon the earth.

Is 49

[1]Listen, O isles, unto me; and hearken, ye people, from far; The LORD hath called me from the womb; from the bowels of my mother hath he made mention of my name. [2]And he hath made my mouth like a sharp sword; in the shadow of his hand hath he hid me, and made me a polished shaft; in his quiver hath he hid me; [3]And said unto me, Thou art my servant, O Israel, in whom I will be glorified. [4]Then I said, I have laboured in vain, I have spent my strength for nought, and in vain: yet surely my judgment is with the LORD, and my work with my God. [5]And now, saith the LORD that formed me from the womb to be his servant, to bring Jacob again to him, Though Israel be not gathered, yet shall I be glorious in the eyes of the LORD, and my God shall be my strength. [6]And he said, It is a light thing that thou shouldest be my servant to raise up the tribes of Jacob, and to restore the preserved of Israel: I will also give thee for a light to the Gentiles, that thou mayest be my salvation unto the end of the earth. [7]Thus saith the LORD, the Redeemer of Israel, and his Holy One, to him whom man despiseth, to him whom the nation abhorreth, to a servant of rulers, Kings shall see and arise, princes also shall worship, because of the LORD that is faithful, and the Holy One of Israel, and he shall choose thee. [8]Thus saith the LORD, In an acceptable time have I heard thee, and in a day of salvation have I helped thee: and I will preserve thee, and give thee for a covenant of the people, to establish the earth, to cause to inherit the desolate heritages; [9]That thou mayest say to the prisoners, Go forth; to them that are in darkness, Show yourselves. They shall feed in the ways, and their pastures shall be in all high places. [10]They shall not hunger nor thirst; neither shall the heat nor sun smite them: for he that hath mercy on them shall lead them, even by the springs of water shall he guide them. [11]And I will make all my mountains a way, and my highways shall be exalted. [12]Behold, these shall come from far: and, lo, these from the north and from the west; and these from the land of Sinim. [13]Sing, O heavens; and be joyful, O earth; and break forth into singing, O mountains: for the LORD hath comforted his people, and will have mercy upon his afflicted. [14]But Zion said, The LORD hath forsaken me, and my Lord hath forgotten me. [15]Can a woman forget her sucking child, that she should not have compassion on the son of her womb? yea, they may forget, yet will I not forget thee. [16]Behold, I have graven thee upon the palms of my hands; thy walls are continually before me. [17]Thy children shall make haste; thy destroyers and they that made thee waste shall go forth of thee. [18]Lift up thine eyes round about, and behold: all these gather themselves together, and come to thee. As I live, saith the LORD, thou shalt surely clothe thee with them all, as with an ornament, and bind them on thee, as a bride doeth. [19]For thy waste and thy desolate places, and the land of thy destruction, shall even now be too narrow by reason of the inhabitants, and they that swallowed thee up shall be far away. [20]The children which thou shalt have, after thou hast lost the other, shall say again in thine ears, The place is too strait for me: give place to me that I may dwell. [21]Then shalt thou say in thine heart, Who hath begotten me these, seeing I have lost my children, and am desolate, a captive, and removing to and fro? and who hath brought up these? Behold, I was left alone; these, where had they been? [22]Thus saith the Lord GOD, Behold, I will lift up mine hand to the Gentiles, and set up my standard to the people: and they shall bring thy sons in their arms, and thy daughters shall be carried upon their shoulders. [23]And kings shall be thy nursing fathers, and their queens thy nursing mothers: they shall bow down to thee with their face toward the earth, and lick up the dust of thy feet; and thou shalt know that I am the LORD: for they shall not be ashamed that wait for me. [24]Shall the prey be taken from the mighty, or the lawful captive delivered? [25]But thus saith the LORD, Even the captives of the mighty shall be taken away, and the prey of the terrible shall be delivered: for I will contend with him that contendeth with thee, and I will save thy children. [26]And I will feed them that oppress thee with their own flesh; and they shall be drunken with their own blood, as with sweet wine: and all flesh shall know that I the LORD am thy Saviour and thy Redeemer, the mighty One of Jacob.

Other

Q-Quelle

Jesus' witness to John: Gal 4:4/[Col 1:15-16]/Mt 11:7-19, [Mt 21:31-32]/Lk 7:24-35 (QS 17 [Thom 46, 74], QS 18), [Lk 16:16 (QS 56)]; Against Pharisees: Gal 4:4/[Col 1:15-16]Mt 23:4-36/[Mk 7:1-9]/Lk 11:37-54 (QS 34 [Thom 39:1, 89, 102])

Galatians 4:4 continued on next page

GALATIANS 4:5—Faith and freedom (3:1–4:31). Time range: 48–50, 54, or 55 CE

Theme	GAL	Paul
Adoption as sons of God	**4:5** [5]To redeem them that were under the law, that we might receive the adoption of sons. **3:13, 26** [13]Christ hath redeemed us from the curse of the law, being made a curse for us: for it is written, Cursed is every one that hangeth on a tree:. . .[26]For ye are all the children of God by faith in Christ Jesus.	**Rom 8:2** [2]For the law of the Spirit of life in Christ Jesus hath made me free from the law of sin and death.

GALATIANS 4:6—Faith and freedom (3:1–4:31). Time range: 48–50, 54, or 55 CE

Theme	GAL	Mk	Paul
Lord/ ABBA	**4:6** [6]And because ye are sons, God hath sent forth the Spirit of his Son into your hearts, crying, Abba, Father. **3:26** [26]For ye are all the children of God by faith in Christ Jesus.	**14:36** [36]And he said, Abba, Father, all things are possible unto thee; take away this cup from me: nevertheless not what I will, but what thou wilt.	**Rom 8:15** [15]For ye have not received the spirit of bondage again to fear; but ye have received the Spirit of adoption, whereby we cry, Abba, Father.

GALATIANS 4:7—Faith and freedom (3:1–4:31). Time range: 48–50, 54, or 55 CE

Theme	GAL	Paul	Other
Not a servant, but a son	**4:7** [7]Wherefore thou art no more a servant, but a son; and if a son, then an heir of God through Christ. **3:29** [29]And if ye be Christ's, then are ye Abraham's seed, and heirs according to the promise.	**Rom 8:16–17** [16]The Spirit itself beareth witness with our spirit, that we are the children of God: [17]And if children, then heirs; heirs of God, and joint-heirs with Christ; if so be that we suffer with him, that we may be also glorified together.	**Q-Quelle** Beatitudes: Gal 4:7/Rom 8:17/[Mt 5:3-12]/[Lk 6:20b-23 (QS 8 [Thom 54, 68, 69])[; Day of SOM: Gal 4:7/Rom 8:17/[Mt 10:39, 24:17-18, 23, 26-27, 28, 37-39, 40-41]/[Mk 13:14-16, 19-23]/[Lk 17:22-37 (QS 60 [Thom 3, 51, 61, 113])]

GALATIANS 4:8—Faith and freedom (3:1–4:31). Time range: 48–50, 54, or 55 CE

Theme	GAL	Paul
Served idols	**4:8** [8]Howbeit then, when ye knew not God, ye did service unto them which by nature are no gods.	**1 Cor 12:2** [2]Ye know that ye were Gentiles, carried away unto these dumb idols, even as ye were led.

GALATIANS 4:9—Faith and freedom (3:1–4:31). Time range: 48–50, 54, or 55 CE

Theme	GAL	Paul
Turning after being known to God	**4:9** [9]But now, after that ye have known God, or rather are known of God, how turn ye again to the weak and beggarly elements, whereunto ye desire again to be in bondage? **4:3** [3]Even so we, when we were children, were in bondage under the elements of the world:	**Col 2:20** [20]Wherefore if ye be dead with Christ from the rudiments of the world, why, as though living in the world, are ye subject to ordinances,

GALATIANS 4:10—Faith and freedom (3:1–4:31). Time range: 48–50, 54, or 55 CE

Theme	GAL	Paul
Observing special days	**4:10** [10]Ye observe days, and months, and times, and years.	**Col 2:16–20** [16]Let no man therefore judge you in meat, or in drink, or in respect of an holyday, or of the new moon, or of the sabbath days: [17]Which are a shadow of things to come; but the body is of Christ. [18]Let no man beguile you of your reward in a voluntary humility and worshipping of angels, intruding into those things which he hath not seen, vainly puffed up by his fleshly mind, [19]And not holding the Head, from which all the body by joints and bands having nourishment ministered, and knit together, increaseth with the increase of God. [20]Wherefore if ye be dead with Christ from the rudiments of the world, why, as though living in the world, are ye subject to ordinances,

GALATIANS 4:12—Faith and freedom (3:1–4:31). Time range: 48–50, 54, or 55 CE

Theme	GAL	Paul
Be as Paul	**4:12** [12]Brethren, I beseech you, be as I am; for I am as ye are: ye have not injured me at all.	**1 Cor 11:1** [1]Be ye followers of me, even as I also am of Christ.

GALATIANS 4:17—Faith and freedom (3:1–4:31). Time range: 48–50, 54, or 55 CE

Theme	GAL	Lk
Turned away because of the gospel	**4:17** [17]They zealously affect you, but not well; yea, they would exclude you, that ye might affect them. **1:7** [7]Which is not another; but there be some that trouble you, and would pervert the gospel of Christ. **6:12** [12]As many as desire to make a fair show in the flesh, they constrain you to be circumcised; only lest they should suffer persecution for the cross of Christ.	**Acts 20:30** [30]Also of your own selves shall men arise, speaking perverse things, to draw away disciples after them.

GALATIANS 4:19—Christian liberty (Church founded by Paul in Acts 16:6, approx 55CE)

Theme	GAL	Paul
Awaiting Christ's formation in followers	**4:19** [19]My little children, of whom I travail in birth again until Christ be formed in you,	**1 Cor 4:14–15** [14]I write not these things to shame you, but as my beloved sons I warn you. [15]For though ye have ten thousand instructors in Christ, yet have ye not many fathers: for in Christ Jesus I have begotten you through the gospel. **2 Cor 6:13** [13]Now for a recompense in the same, (I speak as unto my children,) be ye also enlarged. **1 Thes 2:7–8** [7]But we were gentle among you, even as a nurse cherisheth her children: [8]So being affectionately desirous of you, we were willing to have imparted unto you, not the gospel of God only, but also our own souls, because ye were dear unto us.

GALATIANS 4:22—Christian liberty (Church founded by Paul in Acts 16:6, approx 55CE)

Theme	GAL	Jewish Writings
Abraham had 2 sons	**4:22** [22]For it is written, that Abraham had two sons, the one by a bondmaid, the other by a freewoman.	**Gen 16:15** [15]And Hagar bare Abram a son: and Abram called his son's name, which Hagar bare, Ishmael. **Gen 21:2–3** [2]For Sarah conceived, and bare Abraham a son in his old age, at the set time of which God had spoken to him. [3]And Abraham called the name of his son that was born unto him, whom Sarah bare to him, Isaac

GALATIANS 4:23—Faith and freedom (3:1–4:31). Time range: 48–50, 54, or 55 CE

Theme	GAL	Paul	Jewish Writings
Abraham's son by slave & a son by a free woman	**4:23** [23]But he who was of the bondwoman was born after the flesh; but he of the freewoman was by promise.	**Rom 4:19–20** [19]And being not weak in faith, he considered not his own body now dead, when he was about an hundred years old, neither yet the deadness of Sarah's womb: [20]He staggered not at the promise of God through unbelief; but was strong in faith, giving glory to God; **Rom 9:7–9** [7]Neither, because they are the seed of Abraham, are they all children: but, In Isaac shall thy seed be called. [8]That is, They which are the children of the flesh, these are not the children of God: but the children of the promise are counted for the seed. [9]For this is the word of promise, At this time will I come, and Sarah shall have a son.	**Gen 17:16** [16]And I will bless her, and give thee a son also of her: yea, I will bless her, and she shall be a mother of nations; kings of people shall be of her.

GALATIANS 4:24—Faith and freedom (3:1–4:31). Time range: 48–50, 54, or 55 CE

Theme	GAL	Jewish Writings
2 Covenants	**4:24** [24]Which things are an allegory: for these are the two covenants; the one from the mount Sinai, which gendereth to bondage, which is Agar. **3:17** [17]And this I say, that the covenant, that was confirmed before of God in Christ, the law, which was four hundred and thirty years after, cannot disannul, that it should make the promise of none effect.	**Gen 16:1** [1]Now Sarai Abram's wife bare him no children: and she had an handmaid, an Egyptian, whose name was Hagar. **Ex 19:20** [20]And the LORD came down upon mount Sinai, on the top of the mount: and the LORD called Moses up to the top of the mount; and Moses went up.

GALATIANS 4:26—Faith and freedom (3:1–4:31). Time range: 48–50, 54, or 55 CE

Theme	GAL	NT
Jerusalem is mother of all	**4:26** [26]But Jerusalem which is above is free, which is the mother of us all.	**Heb 12:22** [22]But ye are come unto mount Sion, and unto the city of the living God, the heavenly Jerusalem, and to an innumerable company of angels, **Rev 21:2** [2]And I John saw the holy city, new Jerusalem, coming down from God out of heaven, prepared as a bride adorned for her husband.

GALATIANS 4:27—Faith and freedom (3:1–4:31). Time range: 48–50, 54, or 55 CE

Theme	GAL	Jewish Writings
Barren woman will sing	**4:27** [27]For it is written, Rejoice, thou barren that bearest not; break forth and cry, thou that travailest not: for the desolate hath many more children than she which hath an husband.	**Is 54:1** [1]Sing, O barren, thou that didst not bear; break forth into singing, and cry aloud, thou that didst not travail with child: for more are the children of the desolate than the children of the married wife, saith the LORD.

GALATIANS 4:28—Faith and freedom (3:1–4:31). Time range: 48–50, 54, or 55 CE

Theme	GAL	Paul
Isaac is example of promise	**4:28** [28]Now we, brethren, as Isaac was, are the children of promise.	**Rom 9:8** [8]That is, They which are the children of the flesh, these are not the children of God: but the children of the promise are counted for the seed.

GALATIANS 4:30—Faith and freedom (3:1–4:31). Time range: 48–50, 54, or 55 CE

Theme	GAL	Jewish Writings
Son of slave is cast out	**4:30** [30]Nevertheless what saith the scripture? Cast out the bondwoman and her son: for the son of the bondwoman shall not be heir with the son of the freewoman.	**Gen 21:10** [10]Wherefore she said unto Abraham, Cast out this bondwoman and her son: for the son of this bondwoman shall not be heir with my son, even with Isaac.

GALATIANS 4:31—Faith and freedom (3:1–4:31). Time range: 48–50, 54, or 55 CE

Theme	GAL	Jn
Jesus' followers are free children	**4:31** [31]So then, brethren, we are not children of the bondwoman, but of the free. **3:29** [29]And if ye be Christ's, then are ye Abraham's seed, and heirs according to the promise.	**8:35** [35]And the servant abideth not in the house for ever: but the Son abideth ever.

EXHORTATION TO LIVING AS CHRISTIANS (5:1–6:10)

GALATIANS 5—Living as Christians (5:1–6:10). Time range: 48–50, 54, or 55 CE

Theme	GAL
Right behavior **Sowing & reaping a harvest**	**5** 1Stand fast therefore in the liberty wherewith Christ hath made us free, and be not entangled again with the yoke of bondage. 2Behold, I Paul say unto you, that if ye be circumcised, Christ shall profit you nothing. 3For I testify again to every man that is circumcised, that he is a debtor to do the whole law. 4Christ is become of no effect unto you, whosoever of you are justified by the law; ye are fallen from grace. 5For we through the Spirit wait for the hope of righteousness by faith. 6For in Jesus Christ neither circumcision availeth any thing, nor uncircumcision; but faith which worketh by love. 7Ye did run well; who did hinder you that ye should not obey the truth? 8This persuasion cometh not of him that calleth you. 9A little leaven leaveneth the whole lump. 10I have confidence in you through the Lord, that ye will be none otherwise minded: but he that troubleth you shall bear his judgment, whosoever he be. 11And I, brethren, if I yet preach circumcision, why do I yet suffer persecution? then is the offence of the cross ceased. 12I would they were even cut off which trouble you. 13For, brethren, ye have been called unto liberty; only use not liberty for an occasion to the flesh, but by love serve one another. 14For all the law is fulfilled in one word, even in this; Thou shalt love thy neighbour as thyself. 15But if ye bite and devour one another, take heed that ye be not consumed one of another. 16This I say then, Walk in the Spirit, and ye shall not fulfil the lust of the flesh. 17For the flesh lusteth against the Spirit, and the Spirit against the flesh: and these are contrary the one to the other: so that ye cannot do the things that ye would. 18But if ye be led of the Spirit, ye are not under the law. 19Now the works of the flesh are manifest, which are these; Adultery, fornication, uncleanness, lasciviousness, 20Idolatry, witchcraft, hatred, variance, emulations, wrath, strife, seditions, heresies, 21Envyings, murders, drunkenness, revellings, and such like: of the which I tell you before, as I have also told you in time past, that they which do such things shall not inherit the kingdom of God. 22But the fruit of the Spirit is love, joy, peace, longsuffering, gentleness, goodness, faith, 23Meekness, temperance: against such there is no law. 24And they that are Christ's have crucified the flesh with the affections and lusts. 25If we live in the Spirit, let us also walk in the Spirit. 26Let us not be desirous of vain glory, provoking one another, envying one another. **Gal 6:7–8** 7Be not deceived; God is not mocked: for whatsoever a man soweth, that shall he also reap. 8For he that soweth to his flesh shall of the flesh reap corruption; but he that soweth to the Spirit shall of the Spirit reap life everlasting.

Mt

13:1–23

1The same day went Jesus out of the house, and sat by the sea side. 2And great multitudes were gathered together unto
him, so that he went into a ship, and sat; and the whole multitude stood on the shore. 3And he spake many things unto
them in parables, saying, Behold, a sower went forth to sow; 4And when he sowed, some seeds fell by the way side, and
the fowls came and devoured them up: 5Some fell upon stony places, where they had not much earth: and forthwith
they sprung up, because they had no deepness of earth: 6And when the sun was up, they were scorched; and because
they had no root, they withered away. 7And some fell among thorns; and the thorns sprung up, and choked them: 8But
other fell into good ground, and brought forth fruit, some an hundredfold, some sixtyfold, some thirtyfold. 9Who hath
ears to hear, let him hear. 10And the disciples came, and said unto him, Why speakest thou unto them in parables? 11He
answered and said unto them, Because it is given unto you to know the mysteries of the kingdom of heaven, but to them
it is not given. 12For whosoever hath, to him shall be given, and he shall have more abundance: but whosoever hath not,
from him shall be taken away even that he hath. 13Therefore speak I to them in parables: because they seeing see not;
and hearing they hear not, neither do they understand. 14And in them is fulfilled the prophecy of Esaias, which saith,
By hearing ye shall hear, and shall not understand; and seeing ye shall see, and shall not perceive: 15For this people's
heart is waxed gross, and their ears are dull of hearing, and their eyes they have closed; lest at any time they should
see with their eyes, and hear with their ears, and should understand with their heart, and should be converted, and I
should heal them. 16But blessed are your eyes, for they see: and your ears, for they hear. 17For verily I say unto you, That
many prophets and righteous men have desired to see those things which ye see, and have not seen them; and to hear
those things which ye hear, and have not heard them. 18Hear ye therefore the parable of the sower. 19When any one
heareth the word of the kingdom, and understandeth it not, then cometh the wicked one, and catcheth away that which
was sown in his heart. This is he which received seed by the way side. 20But he that received the seed into stony places,
the same is he that heareth the word, and anon with joy receiveth it; 21Yet hath he not root in himself, but dureth for a
while: for when tribulation or persecution ariseth because of the word, by and by he is offended. 22He also that received
seed among the thorns is he that heareth the word; and the care of this world, and the deceitfulness of riches, choke the
word, and he becometh unfruitful. 23But he that received seed into the good ground is he that heareth the word, and
understandeth it; which also beareth fruit, and bringeth forth, some an hundredfold, some sixty, some thirty.

13:24–30

24Another parable put he forth unto them, saying, The kingdom of heaven is likened unto a man which sowed good seed
in his field: 25But while men slept, his enemy came and sowed tares among the wheat, and went his way. 26But when the
blade was sprung up, and brought forth fruit, then appeared the tares also. 27So the servants of the householder came
and said unto him, Sir, didst not thou sow good seed in thy field? from whence then hath it tares? 28He said unto them,
An enemy hath done this. The servants said unto him, Wilt thou then that we go and gather them up? 29But he said,
Nay; lest while ye gather up the tares, ye root up also the wheat with them. 30Let both grow together until the harvest:
and in the time of harvest I will say to the reapers, Gather ye together first the tares, and bind them in bundles to burn
them: but gather the wheat into my barn.

GALATIANS 5—Living as Christians (5:1–6:10). Time range: 48–50, 54, or 55 CE

Theme	GAL	Mk	Lk
(*Cont.*) **Right behavior** **Sowing & reaping a harvest**	**Ch 5 (above)** **Gal 6:7–8 (above)**	**4:1–20** 1And he began again to teach by the sea side: and there was gathered unto him a great multitude, so that he entered into a ship, and sat in the sea; and the whole multitude was by the sea on the land. 2And he taught them many things by parables, and said unto them in his doctrine, 3Hearken; Behold, there went out a sower to sow: 4And it came to pass, as he sowed, some fell by the way side, and the fowls of the air came and devoured it up. 5And some fell on stony ground, where it had not much earth; and immediately it sprang up, because it had no depth of earth: 6But when the sun was up, it was scorched; and because it had no root, it withered away. 7And some fell among thorns, and the thorns grew up, and choked it, and it yielded no fruit. 8And other fell on good ground, and did yield fruit that sprang up and increased; and brought forth, some thirty, and some sixty, and some an hundred. 9And he said unto them, He that hath ears to hear, let him hear. 10And when he was alone, they that were about him with the twelve asked of him the parable. 11And he said unto them, Unto you it is given to know the mystery of the kingdom of God: but unto them that are without, all these things are done in parables: 12That seeing they may see, and not perceive; and hearing they may hear, and not understand; lest at any time they should be converted, and their sins should be forgiven them. 13And he said unto them, Know ye not this parable? and how then will ye know all parables? 14The sower soweth the word. 15And these are they by the way side, where the word is sown; but when they have heard, Satan cometh immediately, and taketh away the word that was sown in their hearts. 16And these are they likewise which are sown on stony ground; who, when they have heard the word, immediately receive it with gladness; 17And have no root in themselves, and so endure but for a time: afterward, when affliction or persecution ariseth for the word's sake, immediately they are offended. 18And these are they which are sown among thorns; such as hear the word, 19And the cares of this world, and the deceitfulness of riches, and the lusts of other things entering in, choke the word, and it becometh unfruitful. 20And these are they which are sown on good ground; such as hear the word, and receive it, and bring forth fruit, some thirty-fold, some sixty, and some an hundred. **4:26–29** 26And he said, So is the kingdom of God, as if a man should cast seed into the ground; 27And should sleep, and rise night and day, and the seed should spring and grow up, he knoweth not how. 28For the earth bringeth forth fruit of herself; first the blade, then the ear, after that the full corn in the ear. 29But when the fruit is brought forth, immediately he putteth in the sickle, because the harvest is come.	**8:4–15** 4And when much people were gathered together, and were come to him out of every city, he spake by a parable: 5A sower went out to sow his seed: and as he sowed, some fell by the way side; and it was trodden down, and the fowls of the air devoured it. 6And some fell upon a rock; and as soon as it was sprung up, it withered away, because it lacked moisture. 7And some fell among thorns; and the thorns sprang up with it, and choked it. 8And other fell on good ground, and sprang up, and bare fruit an hundredfold. And when he had said these things, he cried, He that hath ears to hear, let him hear. 9And his disciples asked him, saying, What might this parable be? 10And he said, Unto you it is given to know the mysteries of the kingdom of God: but to others in parables; that seeing they might not see, and hearing they might not understand. 11Now the parable is this: The seed is the word of God. 12Those by the way side are they that hear; then cometh the devil, and taketh away the word out of their hearts, lest they should believe and be saved. 13They on the rock are they, which, when they hear, receive the word with joy; and these have no root, which for a while believe, and in time of temptation fall away. 14And that which fell among thorns are they, which, when they have heard, go forth, and are choked with cares and riches and pleasures of this life, and bring no fruit to perfection. 15But that on the good ground are they, which in an honest and good heart, having heard the word, keep it, and bring forth fruit with patience.

Paul	Other
Rom 1:6 [6]Among whom are ye also the called of Jesus Christ: **1 Cor 3:6** [6]I have planted, Apollos watered; but God gave the increase. **1 Cor 3:9** [9]For we are labourers together with God: ye are God's husbandry, ye are God's building. **1 Cor 9:7** [7]Who goeth a warfare any time at his own charges? who planteth a vineyard, and eateth not of the fruit thereof? or who feedeth a flock, and eateth not of the milk of the flock? **1 Cor 9:11** [11]If we have sown unto you spiritual things, is it a great thing if we shall reap your carnal things? **2 Cor 4:4** [4]In whom the god of this world hath blinded the minds of them which believe not, lest the light of the glorious gospel of Christ, who is the image of God, should shine unto them. **2 Cor 9:10** [10]Now he that ministereth seed to the sower both minister bread for your food, and multiply your seed sown, and increase the fruits of your righteousness;) **Col 1:6** [6]Which is come unto you, as it is in all the world; and bringeth forth fruit, as it doth also in you, since the day ye heard of it, and knew the grace of God in truth: **Col 1:10** [10]That ye might walk worthy of the Lord unto all pleasing, being fruitful in every good work, and increasing in the knowledge of God; **1 Thes 1:6** [6]And ye became followers of us, and of the Lord, having received the word in much affliction, with joy of the Holy Ghost: **1 Thes 2:13** [13]For this cause also thank we God without ceasing, because, when ye received the word of God which ye heard of us, ye received it not as the word of men, but as it is in truth, the word of God, which effectually worketh also in you that believe.	**Q-Quelle** Thanks and Blessings for Disciples: Gal Ch 5/[1 Cor 1:6]/2 Cor 4:4/[Mt 11:25-27], Mt 13:16-17/[Lk 10:21-24 (QS 24, 25)]

GALATIANS 5:1—Living as Christians (5:1–6:10). Time range: 48–50, 54, or 55 CE

Theme	GAL	Jn
Stay in Christ	**5:1** [1]Stand fast therefore in the liberty wherewith Christ hath made us free, and be not entangled again with the yoke of bondage. **2:4** [4]And that because of false brethren unawares brought in, who came in privily to spy out our liberty which we have in Christ Jesus, that they might bring us into bondage: **4:5, 9** [5]To redeem them that were under the law, that we might receive the adoption of sons. . . . [9]But now, after that ye have known God, or rather are known of God, how turn ye again to the weak and beggarly elements, whereunto ye desire again to be in bondage?	**8:32, 36** [32]And ye shall know the truth, and the truth shall make you free. . . . [36]If the Son therefore shall make you free, ye shall be free indeed.

GALATIANS 5:2—Living as Christians (5:1–6:10). Time range: 48–50, 54, or 55 CE

Theme	GAL	Lk
Circumcision counts for nothing	**5:2** [2]Behold, I Paul say unto you, that if ye be circumcised, Christ shall profit you nothing. **2:21** [21]I do not frustrate the grace of God: for if righteousness come by the law, then Christ is dead in vain.	**Acts 15:1–29** [1]And certain men which came down from Judaea taught the brethren, and said, Except ye be circumcised after the manner of Moses, ye cannot be saved. [2]When therefore Paul and Barnabas had no small dissension and disputation with them, they determined that Paul and Barnabas, and certain other of them, should go up to Jerusalem unto the apostles and elders about this question. [3]And being brought on their way by the church, they passed through Phenice and Samaria, declaring the conversion of the Gentiles: and they caused great joy unto all the brethren. [4]And when they were come to Jerusalem, they were received of the church, and of the apostles and elders, and they declared all things that God had done with them. [5]But there rose up certain of the sect of the Pharisees which believed, saying, That it was needful to circumcise them, and to command them to keep the law of Moses. [6]And the apostles and elders came together for to consider of this matter. [7]And when there had been much disputing, Peter rose up, and said unto them, Men and brethren, ye know how that a good while ago God made choice among us, that the Gentiles by my mouth should hear the word of the gospel, and believe. [8]And God, which knoweth the hearts, bare them witness, giving them the Holy Ghost, even as he did unto us; [9]And put no difference between us and them, purifying their hearts by faith. [10]Now therefore why tempt ye God, to put a yoke upon the neck of the disciples, which neither our fathers nor we were able to bear? [11]But we believe that through the grace of the Lord Jesus Christ we shall be saved, even as they. [12]Then all the multitude kept silence, and gave audience to Barnabas and Paul, declaring what miracles and wonders God had wrought among the Gentiles by them. [13]And after they had held their peace, James answered, saying, Men and brethren, hearken unto me: [14]Simeon hath declared how God at the first did visit the Gentiles, to take out of them a people for his name. [15]And to this agree the words of the prophets; as it is written, [16]After this I will return, and will build again the tabernacle of David, which is fallen down; and I will build again the ruins thereof, and I will set it up: [17]That the residue of men might seek after the Lord, and all the Gentiles, upon whom my name is called, saith the Lord, who doeth all these things. [18]Known unto God are all his works from the beginning of the world. [19]Wherefore my sentence is, that we trouble not them, which from among the Gentiles are turned to God: [20]But that we write unto them, that they abstain from pollutions of idols, and from fornication, and from things strangled, and from blood. [21]For Moses of old time hath in every city them that preach him, being read in the synagogues every sabbath day. [22]Then pleased it the apostles and elders, with the whole church, to send chosen men of their own company to Antioch with Paul and Barnabas; namely, Judas surnamed Barsabas, and Silas, chief men among the brethren: [23]And they wrote letters by them after this manner; The apostles and elders and brethren send greeting unto the brethren which are of the Gentiles in Antioch and Syria and Cilicia: [24]Forasmuch as we have heard, that certain which went out from us have troubled you with words, subverting your souls, saying, Ye must be circumcised, and keep the law: to whom we gave no such commandment: [25]It seemed good unto us, being assembled with one accord, to send chosen men unto you with our beloved Barnabas and Paul, [26]Men that have hazarded their lives for the name of our Lord Jesus Christ. [27]We have sent therefore Judas and Silas, who shall also tell you the same things by mouth. [28]For it seemed good to the Holy Ghost, and to us, to lay upon you no greater burden than these necessary things; [29]That ye abstain from meats offered to idols, and from blood, and from things strangled, and from fornication: from which if ye keep yourselves, ye shall do well. Fare ye well.

GALATIANS 5:3—Living as Christians (5:1–6:10). Time range: 48–50, 54, or 55 CE

Theme	GAL	Paul	NT
Circumcised must obey whole law	**5:3** [3]For I testify again to every man that is circumcised, that he is a debtor to do the whole law. **3:10** [10]For as many as are of the works of the law are under the curse: for it is written, Cursed is every one that continueth not in all things which are written in the book of the law to do them.	**Rom 2:25** [25]For circumcision verily profiteth, if thou keep the law: but if thou be a breaker of the law, thy circumcision is made uncircumcision.	**Jas 2:10** [10]For whosoever shall keep the whole law, and yet offend in one point, he is guilty of all.

GALATIANS 5:5—Living as Christians (5:1–6:10). Time range: 48–50, 54, or 55 CE

Theme	GAL	Paul
Righteousness by faith	**5:5** [5]For we through the Spirit wait for the hope of righteousness by faith.	**Rom 8:23** [23]And not only they, but ourselves also, which have the firstfruits of the Spirit, even we ourselves groan within ourselves, waiting for the adoption, to wit, the redemption of our body. **Rom 8:25** [25]But if we hope for that we see not, then do we with patience wait for it.

GALATIANS 5:6—Living as Christians (5:1–6:10). Time range: 48–50, 54, or 55 CE

Theme	GAL	Paul
Faith in Christ, not circumcision	**5:6** [6]For in Jesus Christ neither circumcision availeth any thing, nor uncircumcision; but faith which worketh by love. **3:28** [28]There is neither Jew nor Greek, there is neither bond nor free, there is neither male nor female: for ye are all one in Christ Jesus. **6:15** [15]For in Christ Jesus neither circumcision availeth any thing, nor uncircumcision, but a new creature.	**1 Cor 7:19** [19]Circumcision is nothing, and uncircumcision is nothing, but the keeping of the commandments of God.

GALATIANS 5:8—Living as Christians (5:1–6:10). Time range: 48–50, 54, or 55 CE

Theme	GAL
Do not be persuaded in another	**5:8** [8]This persuasion cometh not of him that calleth you. **1:6** [6]I marvel that ye are so soon removed from him that called you into the grace of Christ unto another gospel:

GALATIANS 5:9—Living as Christians (5:1–6:10). Time range: 48–50, 54, or 55 CE

Theme	GAL	Paul
Leaven affects much	**5:9** [9]A little leaven leaveneth the whole lump.	**1 Cor 5:6** [6]Your glorying is not good. Know ye not that a little leaven leaveneth the whole lump?

GALATIANS 5:10—Living as Christians (5:1–6:10). Time range: 48–50, 54, or 55 CE

Theme	GAL
Confidence through the Lord	**5:10** [10]I have confidence in you through the Lord, that ye will be none otherwise minded: but he that troubleth you shall bear his judgment, whosoever he be. **1:7** [7]Which is not another; but there be some that trouble you, and would pervert the gospel of Christ.

GALATIANS 5:11—Living as Christians (5:1–6:10). Time range: 48–50, 54, or 55 CE

Theme	GAL	Paul
Offense of cross	**5:11** [11]And I, brethren, if I yet preach circumcision, why do I yet suffer persecution? then is the offence of the cross ceased. **6:12** [12]As many as desire to make a fair show in the flesh, they constrain you to be circumcised; only lest they should suffer persecution for the cross of Christ. **6:14** [14]But God forbid that I should glory, save in the cross of our Lord Jesus Christ, by whom the world is crucified unto me, and I unto the world.	**1 Cor 1:23** [23]But we preach Christ crucified, unto the Jews a stumbling-block, and unto the Greeks foolishness;

GALATIANS 5:13–15—Living as Christians (5:1–6:10). Time range: 48–50, 54, or 55 CE

Theme	GAL	Mt
Greatest commands: love God and neighbor	**5:13–15** [13]For, brethren, ye have been called unto liberty; only use not liberty for an occasion to the flesh, but by love serve one another. [14]For all the law is fulfilled in one word, even in this; Thou shalt love thy neighbour as thyself. [15]But if ye bite and devour one another, take heed that ye be not consumed one of another.	**5:17** [17]Think not that I am come to destroy the law, or the prophets: I am not come to destroy, but to fulfil. **5:21–26** [21]Ye have heard that it was said by them of old time, Thou shalt not kill; and whosoever shall kill shall be in danger of the judgment: [22]But I say unto you, That whosoever is angry with his brother without a cause shall be in danger of the judgment: and whosoever shall say to his brother, RacaRaca, shall be in danger of the council: but whosoever shall say, Thou fool, shall be in danger of hell fire. [23]Therefore if thou bring thy gift to the altar, and there rememberest that thy brother hath ought against thee; [24]Leave there thy gift before the altar, and go thy way; first be reconciled to thy brother, and then come and offer thy gift. [25]Agree with thine adversary quickly, whiles thou art in the way with him; lest at any time the adversary deliver thee to the judge, and the judge deliver thee to the officer, and thou be cast into prison. [26]Verily I say unto thee, Thou shalt by no means come out thence, till thou hast paid the uttermost farthing. **5:43–48** [43]Ye have heard that it hath been said, Thou shalt love thy neighbour, and hate thine enemy. [44]But I say unto you, Love your enemies, bless them that curse you, do good to them that hate you, and pray for them which despitefully use you, and persecute you; [45]That ye may be the children of your Father which is in heaven: for he maketh his sun to rise on the evil and on the good, and sendeth rain on the just and on the unjust. [46]For if ye love them which love you, what reward have ye? do not even the publicans the same? [47]And if ye salute your brethren only, what do ye more than others? Do not even the publicans so? [48]Be ye therefore perfect, even as your Father which is in heaven is perfect. **7:12** [12]Therefore all things whatsoever ye would that men should do to you, do ye even so to them: for this is the law and the prophets. **19:16–21** [16]And, behold, one came and said unto him, Good Master, what good thing shall I do, that I may have eternal life? [17]And he said unto him, Why callest thou me good? there is none good but one, that is, God: but if thou wilt enter into life, keep the commandments. [18]He saith unto him, Which? Jesus said, Thou shalt do no murder, Thou shalt not commit adultery, Thou shalt not steal, Thou shalt not bear false witness, [19]Honour thy father and thy mother: and, Thou shalt love thy neighbour as thyself. [20]The young man saith unto him, All these things have I kept from my youth up: what lack I yet? [21]Jesus said unto him, If thou wilt be perfect, go and sell that thou hast, and give to the poor, and thou shalt have treasure in heaven: and come and follow me. **22:34–40** [34]But when the Pharisees had heard that he had put the Sadducees to silence, they were gathered together. [35]Then one of them, which was a lawyer, asked him a question, tempting him, and saying, [36]Master, which is the great commandment in the law? [37]Jesus said unto him, Thou shalt love the Lord thy God with all thy heart, and with all thy soul, and with all thy mind. [38]This is the first and great commandment. [39]And the second is like unto it, Thou shalt love thy neighbour as thyself. [40]On these two commandments hang all the law and the prophets.

Mk	Lk	Jn
10:17–20 [17]And Jesus answering said unto them, Render to Caesar the things that are Caesar's, and to God the things that are God's. And they marvelled at him. [18]Then come unto him the Sadducees, which say there is no resurrection; and they asked him, saying, [19]Master, Moses wrote unto us, If a man's brother die, and leave his wife behind him, and leave no children, that his brother should take his wife, and raise up seed unto his brother. [20]Now there were seven brethren: and the first took a wife, and dying left no seed. **12:28–34** [28]And one of the scribes came, and having heard them reasoning together, and perceiving that he had answered them well, asked him, Which is the first commandment of all? [29]And Jesus answered him, The first of all the commandments is, Hear, O Israel; The Lord our God is one Lord: [30]And thou shalt love the Lord thy God with all thy heart, and with all thy soul, and with all thy mind, and with all thy strength: this is the first commandment. [31]And the second is like, namely this, Thou shalt love thy neighbour as thyself. There is none other commandment greater than these. [32]And the scribe said unto him, Well, Master, thou hast said the truth: for there is one God; and there is none other but he: [33]And to love him with all the heart, and with all the understanding, and with all the soul, and with all the strength, and to love his neighbour as himself, is more than all whole burnt offerings and sacrifices. [34]And when Jesus saw that he answered discreetly, he said unto him, Thou art not far from the kingdom of God. And no man after that durst ask him any question.	**6:31** [31]And as ye would that men should do to you, do ye also to them likewise. **10:25–29** [25]And, behold, a certain lawyer stood up, and tempted him, saying, Master, what shall I do to inherit eternal life? [26]He said unto him, What is written in the law? how readest thou? [27]And he answering said, Thou shalt love the Lord thy God with all thy heart, and with all thy soul, and with all thy strength, and with all thy mind; and thy neighbour as thyself. [28]And he said unto him, Thou hast answered right: this do, and thou shalt live. [29]But he, willing to justify himself, said unto Jesus, And who is my neighbour? **18:18–21** [18]And a certain ruler asked him, saying, Good Master, what shall I do to inherit eternal life? [19]And Jesus said unto him, Why callest thou me good? none is good, save one, that is, God. [20]Thou knowest the commandments, Do not commit adultery, Do not kill, Do not steal, Do not bear false witness, Honour thy father and thy mother. [21]And he said, All these have I kept from my youth up.	**13:34** [34]A new commandment I give unto you, That ye love one another; as I have loved you, that ye also love one another. **15:12** [12]This is my commandment, That ye love one another, as I have loved you. **15:17** [17]These things I command you, that ye love one another. **1 Jn 4:11** [11]Beloved, if God so loved us, we ought also to love one another.

GALATIANS 5:13–15—Living as Christians (5:1–6:10). Time range: 48–50, 54, or 55 CE

Theme	GAL	Paul	NT
Greatest commands: love God and neighbor	**5:13–15 (above)**	**Rom 3:31** [31]Do we then make void the law through faith? God forbid: yea, we establish the law. **Rom 8:3** [3]For what the law could not do, in that it was weak through the flesh, God sending his own Son in the likeness of sinful flesh, and for sin, condemned sin in the flesh: **Rom 8:4** [4]That the righteousness of the law might be fulfilled in us, who walk not after the flesh, but after the Spirit. **Rom 12:8–10** [8]Or he that exhorteth, on exhortation: he that giveth, let him do it with simplicity; he that ruleth, with diligence; he that showeth mercy, with cheerfulness. [9]Let love be without dissimulation. Abhor that which is evil; cleave to that which is good. [10]Be kindly affectioned one to another with brotherly love; in honour preferring one another; **Rom 13:8–10** [8]Owe no man any thing, but to love one another: for he that loveth another hath fulfilled the law. [9]For this, Thou shalt not commit adultery, Thou shalt not kill, Thou shalt not steal, Thou shalt not bear false witness, Thou shalt not covet; and if there be any other commandment, it is briefly comprehended in this saying, namely, Thou shalt love thy neighbour as thyself. [10]Love worketh no ill to his neighbour: therefore love is the fulfilling of the law. **Rom 15:9–12** [9]And that the Gentiles might glorify God for his mercy; as it is written, For this cause I will confess to thee among the Gentiles, and sing unto thy name. [10]And again he saith, Rejoice, ye Gentiles, with his people. [11]And again, Praise the Lord, all ye Gentiles; and laud him, all ye people. [12]And again, Esaias saith, There shall be a root of Jesse, and he that shall rise to reign over the Gentiles; in him shall the Gentiles trust. **2 Cor 3** [1]Do we begin again to commend ourselves? or need we, as some others, epistles of commendation to you, or letters of commendation from you? [2]Ye are our epistle written in our hearts, known and read of all men: [3]Forasmuch as ye are manifestly declared to be the epistle of Christ ministered by us, written not with ink, but with the Spirit of the living God; not in tables of stone, but in fleshy tables of the heart. [4]And such trust have we through Christ to God-ward: [5]Not that we are sufficient of ourselves to think any thing as of ourselves; but our sufficiency is of God; [6]Who also hath made us able ministers of the new testament; not of the letter, but of the spirit: for the letter killeth, but the spirit giveth life. [7]But if the ministration of death, written and engraven in stones, was glorious, so that the children of Israel could not stedfastly behold the face of Moses for the glory of his countenance; which glory was to be done away: [8]How shall not the ministration of the spirit be rather glorious? [9]For if the ministration of condemnation be glory, much more doth the ministration of righteousness exceed in glory. [10]For even that which was made glorious had no glory in this respect, by reason of the glory that excelleth. [11]For if that which is done away was glorious, much more that which remaineth is glorious. [12]Seeing then that we have such hope, we use great plainness of speech: [13]And not as Moses, which put a veil over his face, that the children of Israel could not stedfastly look to the end of that which is abolished: [14]But their minds were blinded: for until this day remaineth the same veil untaken away in the reading of the old testament; which veil is done away in Christ. [15]But even unto this day, when Moses is read, the veil is upon their heart. [16]Nevertheless when it shall turn to the Lord, the veil shall be taken away. [17]Now the Lord is that Spirit: and where the Spirit of the Lord is, there is liberty. [18]But we all, with open face beholding as in a glass the glory of the Lord, are changed into the same image from glory to glory, even as by the Spirit of the Lord.	**Jas 2:8** [8]If ye fulfil the royal law according to the scripture, Thou shalt love thy neighbour as thyself, ye do well:

Jewish Writings

Jer 31

[1]At the same time, saith the LORD, will I be the God of all the families of Israel, and they shall be my people. [2]Thus saith the
LORD, The people which were left of the sword found grace in the wilderness; even Israel, when I went to cause him to rest.
[3]The LORD hath appeared of old unto me, saying, Yea, I have loved thee with an everlasting love: therefore with lovingkind-
ness have I drawn thee. [4]Again I will build thee, and thou shalt be built, O virgin of Israel: thou shalt again be adorned with
thy tabrets, and shalt go forth in the dances of them that make merry. [5]Thou shalt yet plant vines upon the mountains of
Samaria: the planters shall plant, and shall eat them as common things. [6]For there shall be a day, that the watchmen upon the
mount Ephraim shall cry, Arise ye, and let us go up to Zion unto the LORD our God. [7]For thus saith the LORD; Sing with
gladness for Jacob, and shout among the chief of the nations: publish ye, praise ye, and say, O LORD, save thy people, the remnant of Israel. [8]Behold, I will bring them from the north country, and gather them from the coasts of the earth, and with them
the blind and the lame, the woman with child and her that travaileth with child together: a great company shall return thither.
[9]They shall come with weeping, and with supplications will I lead them: I will cause them to walk by the rivers of waters in a
straight way, wherein they shall not stumble: for I am a father to Israel, and Ephraim is my firstborn. [10]Hear the word of the
LORD, O ye nations, and declare it in the isles afar off, and say, He that scattered Israel will gather him, and keep him, as a
shepherd doth his flock. [11]For the LORD hath redeemed Jacob, and ransomed him from the hand of him that was stronger
than he. [12]Therefore they shall come and sing in the height of Zion, and shall flow together to the goodness of the LORD, for
wheat, and for wine, and for oil, and for the young of the flock and of the herd: and their soul shall be as a watered garden;
and they shall not sorrow any more at all. [13]Then shall the virgin rejoice in the dance, both young men and old together: for
I will turn their mourning into joy, and will comfort them, and make them rejoice from their sorrow. [14]And I will satiate the
soul of the priests with fatness, and my people shall be satisfied with my goodness, saith the LORD. [15]Thus saith the LORD;
A voice was heard in Ramah, lamentation, and bitter weeping; Rahel weeping for her children refused to be comforted for
her children, because they were not. [16]Thus saith the LORD; Refrain thy voice from weeping, and thine eyes from tears: for
thy work shall be rewarded, saith the LORD; and they shall come again from the land of the enemy. [17]And there is hope in
thine end, saith the LORD, that thy children shall come again to their own border. [18]I have surely heard Ephraim bemoaning
himself thus; Thou hast chastised me, and I was chastised, as a bullock unaccustomed to the yoke: turn thou me, and I shall
be turned; for thou art the LORD my God. [19]Surely after that I was turned, I repented; and after that I was instructed, I smote
upon my thigh: I was ashamed, yea, even confounded, because I did bear the reproach of my youth. [20]Is Ephraim my dear
son? is he a pleasant child? for since I spake against him, I do earnestly remember him still: therefore my bowels are troubled
for him; I will surely have mercy upon him, saith the LORD. [21]Set thee up waymarks, make thee high heaps: set thine heart
toward the highway, even the way which thou wentest: turn again, O virgin of Israel, turn again to these thy cities. [22]How
long wilt thou go about, O thou backsliding daughter? for the LORD hath created a new thing in the earth, A woman shall
compass a man. [23]Thus saith the LORD of hosts, the God of Israel; As yet they shall use this speech in the land of Judah and
in the cities thereof, when I shall bring again their captivity; The LORD bless thee, O habitation of justice, and mountain of
holiness. [24]And there shall dwell in Judah itself, and in all the cities thereof together, husbandmen, and they that go forth with
flocks. [25]For I have satiated the weary soul, and I have replenished every sorrowful soul. [26]Upon this I awaked, and beheld;
and my sleep was sweet unto me. [27]Behold, the days come, saith the LORD, that I will sow the house of Israel and the house
of Judah with the seed of man, and with the seed of beast. [28]And it shall come to pass, that like as I have watched over them,
to pluck up, and to break down, and to throw down, and to destroy, and to afflict; so will I watch over them, to build, and to
plant, saith the LORD. [29]In those days they shall say no more, The fathers have eaten a sour grape, and the children's teeth
are set on edge. [30]But every one shall die for his own iniquity: every man that eateth the sour grape, his teeth shall be set on
edge. [31]Behold, the days come, saith the LORD, that I will make a new covenant with the house of Israel, and with the house
of Judah: [32]Not according to the covenant that I made with their fathers in the day that I took them by the hand to bring them
out of the land of Egypt; which my covenant they brake, although I was an husband unto them, saith the LORD: [33]But this
shall be the covenant that I will make with the house of Israel; After those days, saith the LORD, I will put my law in their
inward parts, and write it in their hearts; and will be their God, and they shall be my people. [34]And they shall teach no more
every man his neighbour, and every man his brother, saying, Know the LORD: for they shall all know me, from the least of
them unto the greatest of them, saith the LORD: for I will forgive their iniquity, and I will remember their sin no more. [35]Thus
saith the LORD, which giveth the sun for a light by day, and the ordinances of the moon and of the stars for a light by night,
which divideth the sea when the waves thereof roar; The LORD of hosts is his name: [36]If those ordinances depart from before
me, saith the LORD, then the seed of Israel also shall cease from being a nation before me for ever. [37]Thus saith the LORD; If
heaven above can be measured, and the foundations of the earth searched out beneath, I will also cast off all the seed of Israel
for all that they have done, saith the LORD. [38]Behold, the days come, saith the LORD, that the city shall be built to the LORD
from the tower of Hananeel unto the gate of the corner. [39]And the measuring line shall yet go forth over against it upon the hill
Gareb, and shall compass about to Goath. [40]And the whole valley of the dead bodies, and of the ashes, and all the fields unto
the brook of Kidron, unto the corner of the horse gate toward the east, shall be holy unto the LORD; it shall not be plucked
up, nor thrown down any more for ever.

GALATIANS 5:13–15—Living as Christians (5:1–6:10). Time range: 48–50, 54, or 55 CE

Theme	GAL	Jewish Writings
(Cont.) **Greatest commands: love God and neighbor**	**5:13–15 (above)**	**Lev 18:15** [15]Thou shalt not uncover the nakedness of thy daughter in law: she is thy son's wife; thou shalt not uncover her nakedness. **Lev 19:18** [18]Thou shalt not avenge, nor bear any grudge against the children of thy people, but thou shalt love thy neighbour as thyself: I am the LORD. **Dt 6:5** [5]And thou shalt love the LORD thy God with all thine heart, and with all thy soul, and with all thy might.

GALATIANS 5:13—Living as Christians (5:1–6:10). Time range: 48–50, 54, or 55 CE

Theme	GAL	Paul
Christian liberty	**5:13** [13]For, brethren, ye have been called unto liberty; only use not liberty for an occasion to the flesh, but by love serve one another. **5:1** [1]Stand fast therefore in the liberty wherewith Christ hath made us free, and be not entangled again with the yoke of bondage.	**Rom 6:18** [18]Being then made free from sin, ye became the servants of righteousness. **Rom 12:10** [10]Be kindly affectioned one to another with brotherly love; in honour preferring one another; **Rom 12:16** [16]Be of the same mind one toward another. Mind not high things, but condescend to men of low estate. Be not wise in your own conceits. **Rom 15:1–4** [1]We then that are strong ought to bear the infirmities of the weak, and not to please ourselves. [2]Let every one of us please his neighbour for his good to edification. [3]For even Christ pleased not himself; but, as it is written, The reproaches of them that reproached thee fell on me. [4]For whatsoever things were written aforetime were written for our learning, that we through patience and comfort of the scriptures might have hope. **1 Cor 8:9** [9]But ye are not in the flesh, but in the Spirit, if so be that the Spirit of God dwell in you. Now if any man have not the Spirit of Christ, he is none of his. **1 Cor 9:19** [19]For though I be free from all men, yet have I made myself servant unto all, that I might gain the more. **1 Cor 10:33–11:1** [33]Even as I please all men in all things, not seeking mine own profit, but the profit of many, that they may be saved. [1]Be ye followers of me, even as I also am of Christ. **2 Cor 4:5** [5]For we preach not ourselves, but Christ Jesus the Lord; and ourselves your servants for Jesus' sake. **2 Cor 11:7** [7]Have I committed an offence in abasing myself that ye might be exalted, because I have preached to you the gospel of God freely? **Phil 2:29** [29]Receive him therefore in the Lord with all gladness; and hold such in reputation:

Other
Barn 19:5
[5] Do not be of two minds whether this should happen or not. Do not take the Lord's name for a futile purpose. Love your neighbor more than yourself. Do not abort a fetus or kill a child that is already born. Do not remove your hand from your son or daughter, but from their youth teach them the reverential fear of God.
Did 1:2
[2] This then is the path of life. First, love the God who made you, and second, your neighbor as yourself. And whatever you do not want to happen to you, do not do to another.
GThom 25
[25] Jesus said, "Love your bother like your soul, guard him like the pupil of your eye."
Q-Quelle
Love enemies: Gal 5:13-15/Rom 13:8-10/Mt 5:38-48/[Mk 7:12]/Lk 6:27-36 (QS 9 [Thom 6:2, 95], QS 10)

NT	Other
1 Pet 2:16	**Q-Quelle**
[16]As free, and not using your liberty for a cloak of maliciousness, but as the servants of God.	Against Pharisees: Gal 5:13/[Rom 14:4-12]/1 Cor 9:19/[Mt 23:4-36]/[Mk 7:1-9]/[Lk 11:37-54 (QS 34 [Thom 39:1, 89, 102])]; Precedence: [Rom 14:4-12]/1 Cor 9:19/Gal 5:13/ [Mt 19:28]/[Mk 10:41-45]/[Lk 22:28-30 (QS 62)]

GALATIANS 5:14—Living as Christians (5:1–6:10). Time range: 48–50, 54, or 55 CE

Theme	GAL	Mt	Paul	Jewish Writings
Love fulfills the law	**5:14** [14]For all the law is fulfilled in one word, even in this; Thou shalt love thy neighbour as thyself.	**22:39** [39]And the second is like unto it, Thou shalt love thy neighbour as thyself.	**Rom 13:8–10** [8]Owe no man any thing, but to love one another: for he that loveth another hath fulfilled the law. [9]For this, Thou shalt not commit adultery, Thou shalt not kill, Thou shalt not steal, Thou shalt not bear false witness, Thou shalt not covet; and if there be any other commandment, it is briefly comprehended in this saying, namely, Thou shalt love thy neighbour as thyself. [10]Love worketh no ill to his neighbour: therefore love is the fulfilling of the law.	**Lev 19:18** [18]Thou shalt not avenge, nor bear any grudge against the children of thy people, but thou shalt love thy neighbour as thyself: I am the LORD.

GALATIANS 5:16—Living as Christians (5:1–6:10). Time range: 48–50, 54, or 55 CE

Theme	GAL	Paul
Walk in spirit	**5:16** [16]This I say then, Walk in the Spirit, and ye shall not fulfil the lust of the flesh. **5:24–25** [24]And they that are Christ's have crucified the flesh with the affections and lusts. [25]If we live in the Spirit, let us also walk in the Spirit.	**Rom 8:5** [5]For they that are after the flesh do mind the things of the flesh; but they that are after the Spirit the things of the Spirit.

GALATIANS 5:17—Living as Christians (5:1–6:10). Time range: 48–50, 54, or 55 CE

Theme	GAL	Paul
Spirit & flesh are contrary	**5:17** [17]For the flesh lusteth against the Spirit, and the Spirit against the flesh: and these are contrary the one to the other: so that ye cannot do the things that ye would.	**Rom 7:15** [15]For that which I do I allow not: for what I would, that do I not; but what I hate, that do I. **Rom 7:23** [23]But I see another law in my members, warring against the law of my mind, and bringing me into captivity to the law of sin which is in my members. **Rom 8:6** [6]For to be carnally minded is death; but to be spiritually minded is life and peace.

GALATIANS 5:18—Living as Christians (5:1–6:10). Time range: 48–50, 54, or 55 CE

Theme	GAL	Paul
Led by Spirit, not law	**5:18** [18]But if ye be led of the Spirit, ye are not under the law.	**Rom 6:14** [14]For sin shall not have dominion over you: for ye are not under the law, but under grace. **Rom 8:14** [14]For as many as are led by the Spirit of God, they are the sons of God.

GALATIANS 5:19–21—Living as Christians (5:1–6:10). Time range: 48–50, 54, or 55 CE

Theme	GAL	Mt	Mk	Lk	Jn
Behavior unfitting for the kingdom of God	**5:19–21** [19]Now the works of the flesh are manifest, which are these; Adultery, fornication, uncleanness, lasciviousness, [20]Idolatry, witchcraft, hatred, variance, emulations, wrath, strife, seditions, heresies, [21]Envyings, murders, drunkenness, revellings, and such like: of the which I tell you before, as I have also told you in time past, that they which do such things shall not inherit the kingdom of God.	**5:20** [20]For I say unto you, That except your righteousness shall exceed the righteousness of the scribes and Pharisees, ye shall in no case enter into the kingdom of heaven. **6:33** [33]But seek ye first the kingdom of God, and his righteousness; and all these things shall be added unto you. **12:28** [28]But if I cast out devils by the Spirit of God, then the kingdom of God is come unto you. **18:3** [3]And said, Verily I say unto you, Except ye be converted, and become as little children, ye shall not enter into the kingdom of heaven.	**10:15** [15]Verily I say unto you, Whosoever shall not receive the kingdom of God as a little child, he shall not enter therein.	**11:20** [20]But if I with the finger of God cast out devils, no doubt the kingdom of God is come upon you. **12:31** [31]But rather seek ye the kingdom of God; and all these things shall be added unto you.	**3:5** [5]Jesus answered, Verily, verily, I say unto thee, Except a man be born of water and of the Spirit, he cannot enter into the kingdom of God.

GALATIANS 5:20—Living as Christians (5:1–6:10). Time range: 48–50, 54, or 55 CE

Theme	GAL
Contentious behavior	**5:20** [20]Idolatry, witchcraft, hatred, variance, emulations, wrath, strife, seditions, heresies,

GALATIANS 5:22—Living as Christians (5:1–6:10). Time range: 48–50, 54, or 55 CE

Theme	GAL	Paul
Fruit of the Spirit	**5:22** [22]But the fruit of the Spirit is love, joy, peace, longsuffering, gentleness, goodness, faith,	**1 Cor 13:4–7** [4]Charity suffereth long, and is kind; charity envieth not; charity vaunteth not itself, is not puffed up, [5]Doth not behave itself unseemly, seeketh not her own, is not easily provoked, thinketh no evil; [6]Rejoiceth not in iniquity, but rejoiceth in the truth; [7]Beareth all things, believeth all things, hopeth all things, endureth all things. **2 Cor 6:6** [6]By pureness, by knowledge, by longsuffering, by kindness, by the Holy Ghost, by love unfeigned, **Eph 5:9** [9](For the fruit of the Spirit is in all goodness and righteousness and truth;) **1 Tim 4:12 (Pseudo)** [12]Let no man despise thy youth; but be thou an example of the believers, in word, in conversation, in charity, in spirit, in faith, in purity.

Paul	Other
Rom 1:29–31 29 Being filled with all unrighteousness, fornication, wickedness, covetousness, maliciousness; full of envy, murder, debate, deceit, malignity; whisperers, 30 Backbiters, haters of God, despiteful, proud, boasters, inventors of evil things, disobedient to parents, 31 Without understanding, covenantbreakers, without natural affection, implacable, unmerciful: **Rom 6:9–10** 9 Knowing that Christ being raised from the dead dieth no more; death hath no more dominion over him. 10 For in that he died, he died unto sin once: but in that he liveth, he liveth unto God. **Rom 14:17** 17 For the kingdom of God is not meat and drink; but righteousness, and peace, and joy in the Holy Ghost. **1 Cor 4:20** 20 For the kingdom of God is not in word, but in power. **1 Cor 6:9** 9 Know ye not that the unrighteous shall not inherit the kingdom of God? Be not deceived: neither fornicators, nor idolaters, nor adulterers, nor effeminate, nor abusers of themselves with mankind, **1 Cor 6:10** 10 Nor thieves, nor covetous, nor drunkards, nor revilers, nor extortioners, shall inherit the kingdom of God. **Eph 5:5 (Pseudo)** 5 For this ye know, that no whoremonger, nor unclean person, nor covetous man, who is an idolater, hath any inheri- tance in the kingdom of Christ and of God. **Col 3:5–8** 5 Mortify therefore your members which are upon the earth; fornication, uncleanness, inordinate affection, evil con- cupiscence, and covetousness, which is idolatry: 6 For which things' sake the wrath of God cometh on the children of disobedience: 7 In the which ye also walked some time, when ye lived in them. 8 But now ye also put off all these; anger, wrath, malice, blasphemy, filthy communication out of your mouth.	**Q-Quelle** Anxiety: Gal 5:19-21/Rom 14:17/1 Cor 6:9-10/Mt 6:25-34/Lk 12:22-32 (QS 39 [Thom 36]); Against Pharisees: Gal 5:19-21/1 Cor 6:9-10/[Mt 24:4-36]/[Mk 7:1-9]/Lk 11:37-54 (QS 34 [Thom 39:1, 89, 102]); Beezebul Controversy: Gal 5:19-21/Rom 14:17/1 Cor 6:9-10/Mt 9:32-34]/Mt 12:22-30/[Mk 3:22-27]/Lk 11:14-23 (QS 28 [Thom 35]); Assistance of the HS: Gal 5:19-21/Eph 5:5/[Mt 10:19-20]/[Mk 13:11]/[Lk 12:11-12 (QS 37 [Thom 44])]

NT
Rev 22:15 15 For without are dogs, and sorcerers, and whoremongers, and murderers, and idolaters, and whosoever loveth and maketh a lie.

NT
2 Pet 1:6 6 And to knowledge temperance; and to temperance patience; and to patience godliness;

GALATIANS 5:23—Living as Christians (5:1–6:10). Time range: 48–50, 54, or 55 CE

Theme	GAL	Paul
Meekness & temperance	**5:23** [23]Meekness, temperance: against such there is no law.	**1 Tim 1:9 (Pseudo)** [9]Knowing this, that the law is not made for a righteous man, but for the lawless and disobedient, for the ungodly and for sinners, for unholy and profane, for murderers of fathers and murderers of mothers, for manslayers,

GALATIANS 5:24—Living as Christians (5:1–6:10). Time range: 48–50, 54, or 55 CE

Theme	GAL	Paul
Lust crucified with Christ	**5:24** [24]And they that are Christ's have crucified the flesh with the affections and lusts.	**Rom 6:6** [6]Knowing this, that our old man is crucified with him, that the body of sin might be destroyed, that henceforth we should not serve sin.
	2:19 [19]For I through the law am dead to the law, that I might live unto God.	**Rom 8:13** [13]For if ye live after the flesh, ye shall die: but if ye through the Spirit do mortify the deeds of the body, ye shall live.

GALATIANS 5:25—Living as Christians (5:1–6:10). Time range: 48–50, 54, or 55 CE

Theme	GAL
Live in Spirit	**5:25** [25]If we live in the Spirit, let us also walk in the Spirit.
	5:16 [16]This I say then, Walk in the Spirit, and ye shall not fulfil the lust of the flesh.

GALATIANS 6:1—Living as Christians (5:1–6:10). Time range: 48–50, 54, or 55 CE

Theme	GAL	Mt	Paul	NT	Other
Restore fallen friends in faith in meekness	**6:1** [1]Brethren, if a man be overtaken in a fault, ye which are spiritual, restore such an one in the spirit of meekness; considering thyself, lest thou also be tempted.	**18:15** [15]And he touched her hand, and the fever left her: and she arose, and ministered unto them.	**1 Cor 10:12–13** [12]Wherefore let him that thinketh he standeth take heed lest he fall. [13]There hath no temptation taken you but such as is common to man: but God is faithful, who will not suffer you to be tempted above that ye are able; but will with the temptation also make a way to escape, that ye may be able to bear it.	**Jas 5:9** [9]Grudge not one against another, brethren, lest ye be condemned: behold, the judge standeth before the door	**Q-Quelle** On forgiveness: Gal 6:1/Mt 18:15, [Mt 18:21-22]/ [Lk 17:3b-4 (QS 58)]

GALATIANS 6:2—Living as Christians (5:1–6:10). Time range: 48–50, 54, or 55 CE

Theme	GAL	Mt	Lk	Paul	Jewish	Other
Bear burdens for others	**6:2** [2]Bear ye one another's burdens, and so fulfil the law of Christ.	**5:3–6** [3]Blessed are the poor in spirit: for theirs is the kingdom of heaven. [4]Blessed are they that mourn: for they shall be comforted. [5]Blessed are the meek: for they shall inherit the earth. [6]Blessed are they which do hunger and thirst after righteousness: for they shall be filled. **11:28–30** [28]Come unto me, all ye that labour and are heavy laden, and I will give you rest. [29]Take my yoke upon you, and learn of me; for I am meek and lowly in heart: and ye shall find rest unto your souls. [30]For my yoke is easy, and my burden is light. **23:4** [4]For they bind heavy burdens and grievous to be borne, and lay them on men's shoulders; but they themselves will not move them with one of their fingers.	**6:20** [20]And he lifted up his eyes on his disciples, and said, Blessed be ye poor: for yours is the kingdom of God.	**1 Cor 9:21** [21]To them that are without law, as without law, (being not without law to God, but under the law to Christ,) that I might gain them that are without law. **Col 3:13** [13]Forbearing one another, and forgiving one another, if any man have a quarrel against any: even as Christ forgave you, so also do ye. **Col 3:17** [17]And whatsoever ye do in word or deed, do all in the name of the Lord Jesus, giving thanks to God and the Father by him.	**Is 53:4** [4]Surely he hath borne our griefs, and carried our sorrows: yet we did esteem him stricken, smitten of God, and afflicted.	**Q-Quelle** Beatitudes: Gal 6:2/1 Cor 9:21/Col 3:17/Mt 5:3-12/Lk 6:20b-23 (QS 8 [Thom 54,68,69); Concerning the Law: Gal 6:2/1 Cor 9:21/ [Mt 5:18, 11:12-13]/ [Lk 16:16-17 (QS 56)]

GALATIANS 6:3–4—Living as Christians (5:1–6:10). Time range: 48–50, 54, or 55 CE

Theme	GAL	Paul
Person's work proves favor	**6:3–4** [3]For if a man think himself to be something, when he is nothing, he deceiveth himself. [4]But let every man prove his own work, and then shall he have rejoicing in himself alone, and not in another.	**1 Cor 3:18** [18]Let no man deceive himself. If any man among you seemeth to be wise in this world, let him become a fool, that he may be wise. **1 Cor 8:2** [2]And if any man think that he knoweth any thing, he knoweth nothing yet as he ought to know. **2 Cor 12:11** [11]But all these worketh that one and the selfsame Spirit, dividing to every man severally as he will.

GALATIANS 6:5—Living as Christians (5:1–6:10). Time range: 48–50, 54, or 55 CE

Theme	GAL	Paul
Bear own burden	**6:5** [5]For every man shall bear his own burden.	**Rom 14:12** [12]So then every one of us shall give account of himself to God.

GALATIANS 6:6—Living as Christians (5:1–6:10). Time range: 48–50, 54, or 55 CE

Theme	GAL	Paul
Teach all good things	**6:6** [6]Let him that is taught in the word communicate unto him that teacheth in all good things.	**1 Cor 9:14** [14]Even so hath the Lord ordained that they which preach the gospel should live of the gospel.

GALATIANS 6:8—Living as Christians (5:1–6:10). Time range: 48–50, 54, or 55 CE

Theme	GAL	Paul	Jewish Writings	Other
Flesh sows corruption	**6:8** [8]For he that soweth to his flesh shall of the flesh reap corruption; but he that soweth to the Spirit shall of the Spirit reap life everlasting.	**Rom 8:6** [6]For to be carnally minded is death; but to be spiritually minded is life and peace. **Rom 8:13** [13]For if ye live after the flesh, ye shall die: but if ye through the Spirit do mortify the deeds of the body, ye shall live.	**Prov 11:18** [18]The wicked worketh a deceitful work: but to him that soweth righteousness shall be a sure reward.	**Q-Quelle** Preaching of John: Gal 6:8/Rom 8:6/[Mt 3:7-10, 11-12]/[Mk 1:7-8]/[Lk 3:15-18 (QS 5)]; Thanks and blessings/Disciples: [1 Cor 1:6]/[2 Cor 4:4]/Gal 6:7-8/[Mt 11:25-27, 13:16-17]/[Lk 10:21-24 (QS 24, 25)]

GALATIANS 6:9—Living as Christians (5:1–6:10). Time range: 48–50, 54, or 55 CE

Theme	GAL	Paul	NT
Will reap in due season	**6:9** [9]And let us not be weary in well doing: for in due season we shall reap, if we faint not.	**2 Thes 3:13** [13]But ye, brethren, be not weary in well doing.	**Heb 12:13** [13]And make straight paths for your feet, lest that which is lame be turned out of the way; but let it rather be healed.

GALATIANS 6:10—Living as Christians (5:1–6:10). Time range: 48–50, 54, or 55 CE

Theme	GAL	Mk	Paul	Other
Love all	**6:10** [10]As we have therefore opportunity, let us do good unto all men, especially unto them who are of the household of faith.	**9:50** [50]Salt is good: but if the salt have lost his saltness, wherewith will ye season it? Have salt in yourselves, and have peace one with another.	**Rom 4:9** [9]Cometh this blessedness then upon the circumcision only, or upon the uncircumcision also? for we say that faith was reckoned to Abraham for righteousness. **Rom 5:15** [15]But not as the offence, so also is the free gift. For if through the offence of one many be dead, much more the grace of God, and the gift by grace, which is by one man, Jesus Christ, hath abounded unto many. **Rom 12:10** [10]Be kindly affectioned one to another with brotherly love; in honour preferring one another; **Rom 12:18** [18]If it be possible, as much as lieth in you, live peaceably with all men. **Rom 13:12** [12]The night is far spent, the day is at hand: let us therefore cast off the works of darkness, and let us put on the armour of light. **Rom 14:19** [19]Let us therefore follow after the things which make for peace, and things wherewith one may edify another. **1 Cor 7:15** [15]But if the unbelieving depart, let him depart. A brother or a sister is not under bondage in such cases: but God hath called us to peace. **2 Cor 13:11** [11]Finally, brethren, farewell. Be perfect, be of good comfort, be of one mind, live in peace; and the God of love and peace shall be with you. **Eph 4:32 (Pseudo)** [32]And be ye kind one to another, tenderhearted, forgiving one another, even as God for Christ's sake hath forgiven you. **Col 3:12–14** [12]Put on therefore, as the elect of God, holy and beloved, bowels of mercies, kindness, humbleness of mind, meekness, longsuffering; [13]Forbearing one another, and forgiving one another, if any man have a quarrel against any: even as Christ forgave you, so also do ye. [14]And above all these things put on charity, which is the bond of perfectness. **1 Thes 5:12–13** [12]And we beseech you, brethren, to know them which labour among you, and are over you in the Lord, and admonish you; [13]And to esteem them very highly in love for their work's sake. And be at peace among yourselves. **1 Thes 5:15** [15]See that none render evil for evil unto any man; but ever follow that which is good, both among yourselves, and to all men. **2 Thes 1:3** [3]We are bound to thank God always for you, brethren, as it is meet, because that your faith groweth exceedingly, and the charity of every one of you all toward each other aboundeth;	**Q-Quelle** Parable of the salt: Gal 6:10/1 Cor 7:15/[Mt 5:13]/Mk 9:49-50/[Lk 14:34-35 (QS 53)]; Love enemies: Gal 6:10/Rom 12:9-21, [13:8-10]/[Mt 5:38-48], [Mt 7:12]/[Lk 6:27-36 (QS 9 [Thom 95, 6:2])] Beatitudes: Gal 6:10/2 Cor 13:11/Eph 4:32/Col 3:12-14/[1 Thes 3:12]/[Mt 5:3-12]/[Lk 6:20b-23 (QS 8 [Thom 54,68,69])]

CONCLUDING REMARKS (6:11–18)

GALATIANS 6:11—Conclusions (6:11–18). Time range: 48–50, 54, or 55 CE

Theme	GAL	Paul
Writing is Paul's	**6:11** [11]Ye see how large a letter I have written unto you with mine own hand.	**1 Cor 16:21** [21]The salutation of me Paul with mine own hand.

GALATIANS 6:12—Conclusions (6:11–18). Time range: 48–50, 54, or 55 CE

Theme	GAL
Circum-cision & persecution	**6:12** [12]As many as desire to make a fair show in the flesh, they constrain you to be circumcised; only lest they should suffer persecution for the cross of Christ. **5:2** [2]Behold, I Paul say unto you, that if ye be circumcised, Christ shall profit you nothing. **5:11** [11]And I, brethren, if I yet preach circumcision, why do I yet suffer persecution? then is the offence of the cross ceased.

GALATIANS 6:14—Conclusions (6:11–18). Time range: 48–50, 54, or 55 CE

Theme	GAL	Mt	Mk
Proclamation of the cross	**6:14** [14]But God forbid that I should glory, save in the cross of our Lord Jesus Christ, by whom the world is crucified unto me, and I unto the world. **2:20** [20]I am crucified with Christ: nevertheless I live; yet not I, but Christ liveth in me: and the life which I now live in the flesh I live by the faith of the Son of God, who loved me, and gave himself for me. **3:23–5:1** **3** [23]But before faith came, we were kept under the law, shut up unto the faith which should afterwards be revealed. [24]Wherefore the law was our schoolmaster to bring us unto Christ, that we might be justified by faith. [25]But after that faith is come, we are no longer under a schoolmaster [26]For ye are all the children of God by faith in Christ Jesus. [27]For as many of you as have been baptized into Christ have put on Christ. [28]There is neither Jew nor Greek, there is neither bond nor free, there is neither male nor female: for ye are all one in Christ Jesus. [29]And if ye be Christ's, then are ye Abraham's seed, and heirs according to the prom- ise. **4** [1]Now I say, That the heir, as long as he is a child, differeth nothing from a servant, though he be lord of all; [2]But is under tutors and governors until the time appointed of the father. [3]Even so we, when we were children, were in bondage under the elements of the world: [4]But when the fulness of the time was come, God sent forth his Son, made of a woman, made under the law, [5]To redeem them that were under the law, that we might receive the adoption of sons. [6]And because ye are sons, God hath sent forth the Spirit of his Son into your hearts, crying, Abba, Father. [7]Wherefore thou art no more a servant, but a son; and if a son, then an heir of God through Christ. [8]Howbeit then, when ye knew not God, ye did service unto them which by nature are no gods. [9]But now, after that ye have known God, or rather are known of God, how turn ye again to the weak and beggarly elements, whereunto ye desire again to be in bondage? [10]Ye observe days, and months, and times, and years. [11]I am afraid of you, lest I have bestowed upon you labour in vain. [12]Brethren, I beseech you, be as I am; for I am as ye are: ye have not injured me at all. [13]Ye know how through infirmity of the flesh I preached the gospel unto you at the first. [14]And my temptation which was in my flesh ye despised not, nor rejected; but received me as an angel of God, even as Christ Jesus. [15]Where is then the blessedness ye spake of? for I bear you record, that, if it had been possible, ye would have plucked out your own eyes, and have given them to me. [16]Am I therefore become your enemy, because I tell you the truth? [17]They zealously affect you, but not well; yea, they would exclude you, that ye might affect them. [18]But it is good to be zealously affected always in a good thing, and not only when I am present with you. [19]My little children, of whom I travail in birth again until Christ be formed in you, [20]I desire to be present with you now, and to change my voice; for I stand in doubt of you. [21]Tell me, ye that desire to be under the law, do ye not hear the law? [22]For it is written, that Abraham had two sons, the one by a bondmaid, the other by a freewoman. [23]But he who was of the bondwoman was born after the flesh; but he of the freewoman was by promise. [24]Which things are an allegory: for these are the two covenants; the one from the mount Sinai, which gendereth to bondage, which is Agar. [25]For this Agar is mount Sinai in Arabia, and answereth to Jerusalem which now is, and is in bondage with her children. [26]But Jerusalem which is above is free, which is the mother of us all. [27]For it is written, Rejoice, thou barren that bearest not; break forth and cry, thou that travailest not: for the desolate hath many more children than she which hath an husband. [28]Now we, brethren, as Isaac was, are the children of promise. [29]But as then he that was born after the flesh persecuted him that was born after the Spirit, even so it is now. [30]Nevertheless what saith the scripture? Cast out the bondwoman and her son: for the son of the bondwoman shall not be heir with the son of the freewoman. [31]So then, brethren, we are not children of the bondwoman, but of the free. **5** [1]Stand fast therefore in the liberty wherewith Christ hath made us free, and be not entangled again with the yoke of bondage.	**16:21** [21]For where your treasure is, there will your heart be also. **20:28** [28]Even as the Son of man came not to be ministered unto, but to minister, and to give his life a ransom for many.	**8:31** [31]And he began to teach them, that the Son of man must suffer many things, and be rejected of the elders, and of the chief priests, and scribes, and be killed, and after three days rise again. **10:4** [4]And they said, Moses suffered to write a bill of divorcement, and to put her away. **10:45** [45]For even the Son of man came not to be ministered unto, but to minister, and to give his life a ransom for many.

Lk	Paul	Jewish	Other
9:22 [22]Saying, The Son of man must suffer many things, and be rejected of the elders and chief priests and scribes, and be slain, and be raised the third day.	**Rom 3:21–26** [21]But now the righteousness of God without the law is manifested, being witnessed by the law and the prophets; [22]Even the righteousness of God which is by faith of Jesus Christ unto all and upon all them that believe: for there is no difference: [23]For all have sinned, and come short of the glory of God; [24]Being justified freely by his grace through the redemption that is in Christ Jesus: [25]Whom God hath set forth to be a propitiation through faith in his blood, to declare his righteousness for the remission of sins that are past, through the forbearance of God; [26]To declare, I say, at this time his righteousness: that he might be just, and the justifier of him which believeth in Jesus. **Rom 6:14** [14]For sin shall not have dominion over you: for ye are not under the law, but under grace. **1 Cor 1:23** [23]But we preach Christ crucified, unto the Jews a stumblingblock, and unto the Greeks foolishness; **1 Cor 2:2** [2] For I determined not to know any thing among you, save Jesus Christ, and him crucified. **1 Cor 10** [1]Moreover, brethren, I would not that ye should be ignorant, how that all our fathers were under the cloud, and all passed through the sea; [2]And were all baptized unto Moses in the cloud and in the sea; [3]And did all eat the same spiritual meat; [4]And did all drink the same spiritual drink: for they drank of that spiritual Rock that followed them: and that Rock was Christ. [5]But with many of them God was not well pleased: for they were overthrown in the wilderness. [6]Now these things were our examples, to the intent we should not lust after evil things, as they also lusted. [7]Neither be ye idolaters, as were some of them; as it is written, The people sat down to eat and drink, and rose up to play. [8]Neither let us commit fornication, as some of them committed, and fell in one day three and twenty thousand. [9]Neither let us tempt Christ, as some of them also tempted, and were destroyed of serpents. [10]Neither murmur ye, as some of them also murmured, and were destroyed of the destroyer. [11]Now all these things happened unto them for ensamples: and they are written for our admonition, upon whom the ends of the world are come. [12]Wherefore let him that thinketh he standeth take heed lest he fall. [13]There hath no temptation taken you but such as is common to man: but God is faithful, who will not suffer you to be tempted above that ye are able; but will with the temptation also make a way to escape, that ye may be able to bear it. [14]Wherefore, my dearly beloved, flee from idolatry. [15]I speak as to wise men; judge ye what I say. [16]The cup of blessing which we bless, is it not the communion of the blood of Christ? The bread which we break, is it not the communion of the body of Christ? [17]For we being many are one bread, and one body: for we are all partakers of that one bread. [18]Behold Israel after the flesh: are not they which eat of the sacrifices partakers of the altar? [19]What say I then? that the idol is any thing, or that which is offered in sacrifice to idols is any thing? [20]But I say, that the things which the Gentiles sacrifice, they sacrifice to devils, and not to God: and I would not that ye should have fellowship with devils. [21]Ye cannot drink the cup of the Lord, and the cup of devils: ye cannot be partakers of the Lord's table, and of the table of devils. [22]Do we provoke the Lord to jealousy? are we stronger than he? [23]All things are lawful for me, but all things are not expedient: all things are lawful for me, but all things edify not. [24]Let no man seek his own, but every man another's wealth. [25]Whatsoever is sold in the shambles, that eat, asking no question for conscience sake: [26]For the earth is the Lord's, and the fulness thereof. [27]If any of them that believe not bid you to a feast, and ye be disposed to go; whatsoever is set before you, eat, asking no question for conscience sake. [28]But if any man say unto you, This is offered in sacrifice unto idols, eat not for his sake that showed it, and for conscience sake: for the earth is the Lord's, and the fulness thereof: [29]Conscience, I say, not thine own, but of the other: for why is my liberty judged of another man's conscience? [30]For if I by grace be a partaker, why am I evil spoken of for that for which I give thanks? [31]Whether therefore ye eat, or drink, or whatsoever ye do, do all to the glory of God. [32]Give none offence, neither to the Jews, nor to the Gentiles, nor to the church of God: [33]Even as I please all men in all things, not seeking mine own profit, but the profit of many, that they may be saved. **1 Cor 15:3** [10]But by the grace of God I am what I am: and his grace which was bestowed upon me was not in vain; but I laboured more abundantly than they all: yet not I, but the grace of God which was with me.	**Ex 15:13** [13]Thou in thy mercy hast led forth the people which thou hast redeemed: thou hast guided them in thy strength unto thy holy habitation. **Is 41:14** [14]Fear not, thou worm Jacob, and ye men of Israel; I will help thee, saith the LORD, and thy redeemer, the Holy One of Israel.	**Q-Quelle** Precedence: Gal 6:14/ [Mt 19:28]/ Mk 10:41-45/[Lk 22:28-30 (QS 62)]; Lost Sheep: Gal 6:14/ Rom 3:21-26/[Mt 18:12-14]/ [Lk 15:1-7 (QS 54 [Thom 107])]

GALATIANS 6:15—Conclusions (6:11–18). Time range: 48–50, 54, or 55 CE

Theme	GAL	Paul
New creature in Christ	**6:15** [15]For in Christ Jesus neither circumcision availeth any thing, nor uncircumcision, but a new creature. **5:6** [6]For in Jesus Christ neither circumcision availeth any thing, nor uncircumcision; but faith which worketh by love.	**1 Cor 7:19** [19]Circumcision is nothing, and uncircumcision is nothing, but the keeping of the commandments of God. **2 Cor 5:17** [17]Therefore if any man be in Christ, he is a new creature: old things are passed away; behold, all things are become new.

GALATIANS 6:16—Conclusions (6:11–18). Time range: 48–50, 54, or 55 CE

Theme	GAL	Jewish Writings
Peace & mercy for faithful	**6:16** [16]And as many as walk according to this rule, peace be on them, and mercy, and upon the Israel of God.	**Ps 125:5** [5]As for such as turn aside unto their crooked ways, the LORD shall lead them forth with the workers of iniquity: but peace shall be upon Israel. **Ps 128:6** [6] Yea, thou shalt see thy children's children, and peace upon Israel.

GALATIANS 6:17—Conclusions (6:11–18). Time range: 48–50, 54, or 55 CE

Theme	GAL	Paul
Marks of the Lord on the body	**6:17** [17]From henceforth let no man trouble me: for I bear in my body the marks of the Lord Jesus.	**2 Cor 4:10** [10]Always bearing about in the body the dying of the Lord Jesus, that the life also of Jesus might be made manifest in our body.

GALATIANS 6:18—Conclusions (6:11–18). Time range: 48–50, 54, or 55 CE

Theme	GAL	Paul
Grace be with your Spirit	**6:18** [18]Brethren, the grace of our Lord Jesus Christ be with your spirit. Amen. **5:2, 11** [2]Behold, I Paul say unto you, that if ye be circumcised, Christ shall profit you nothing. . . . [11]And I, brethren, if I yet preach circumcision, why do I yet suffer persecution? then is the offence of the cross ceased.	**Phil 4:23** [23]The grace of our Lord Jesus Christ be with you all. Amen. **2 Tim 4:22 (Pseudo)** [22]The Lord Jesus Christ be with thy spirit. Grace be with you. Amen.

EPHESIANS

Pseudo-Pauline

ADDRESS (1:1–14)

EPHESIANS (PSEUDO) 1:1—Address (1:1–14)

Theme	EPH	Paul
Paul, an Apostle	**1:1** [1]Paul, an apostle of Jesus Christ by the will of God, to the saints which are at Ephesus, and to the faithful in Christ Jesus:	**Rom 1:7** [7]To all that be in Rome, beloved of God, called to be saints: Grace to you and peace from God our Father, and the Lord Jesus Christ. **1 Cor 1:1–2** [1]Paul, called to be an apostle of Jesus Christ through the will of God, and Sosthenes our brother, [2]Unto the church of God which is at Corinth, to them that are sanctified in Christ Jesus, called to be saints, with all that in every place call upon the name of Jesus Christ our Lord, both theirs and ours **Col 1:1** [1]Paul, an apostle of Jesus Christ by the will of God, and Timotheus our brother,

EPHESIANS (PSEUDO) 1:2—Address (1:1–14)

Theme	EPH	Paul
Grace & peace	**1:2** [2]Grace be to you, and peace, from God our Father, and from the Lord Jesus Christ.	**Col 1:2** [2]To the saints and faithful brethren in Christ which are at Colosse: Grace be unto you, and peace, from God our Father and the Lord Jesus Christ.

EPHESIANS (PSEUDO) 1:3—Address (1:1–14)

Theme	EPH	Paul
Doxology	**1:3** [3]Blessed be the God and Father of our Lord Jesus Christ, who hath blessed us with all spiritual blessings in heavenly places in Christ: **2:6** [6]And hath raised us up together, and made us sit together in heavenly places in Christ Jesus:	**2 Cor 1:3** [3]Blessed be God, even the Father of our Lord Jesus Christ, the Father of mercies, and the God of all comfort;

EPHESIANS (PSEUDO) 1:4—Address (1:1–14)

Theme	EPH	Jn	Paul
Chosen from the foundation of the earth	**1:4** [4]According as he hath chosen us in him before the foundation of the world, that we should be holy and without blame before him in love: **5:27** [27]That he might present it to himself a glorious church, not having spot, or wrinkle, or any such thing; but that it should be holy and without blemish.	**15:16** [16]Ye have not chosen me, but I have chosen you, and ordained you, that ye should go and bring forth fruit, and that your fruit should remain: that whatsoever ye shall ask of the Father in my name, he may give it you. **17:24** [24]Father, I will that they also, whom thou hast given me, be with me where I am; that they may behold my glory, which thou hast given me: for thou lovedst me before the foundation of the world.	**Rom 8:29** [29]For whom he did foreknow, he also did predestinate to be conformed to the image of his Son, that he might be the firstborn among many brethren. **2 Thes 2:13** [13]But we are bound to give thanks alway to God for you, brethren beloved of the Lord, because God hath from the beginning chosen you to salvation through sanctification of the Spirit and belief of the truth:

EPHESIANS (PSEUDO) 1:5—Address (1:1–14)

Theme	EPH	Jn
Predestined	**1:5** [5]Having predestinated us unto the adoption of children by Jesus Christ to himself, according to the good pleasure of his will,	**1:12** [12]But as many as received him, to them gave he power to become the sons of God, even to them that believe on his name: **1 Jn 3:1** [1]Behold, what manner of love the Father hath bestowed upon us, that we should be called the sons of God: therefore the world knoweth us not, because it knew him not.

EPHESIANS (PSEUDO) 1:6—Address (1:1–14)

Theme	EPH	Mt	Paul
Doxology for acceptance	**1:6** [6]To the praise of the glory of his grace, wherein he hath made us accepted in the beloved.	**3:17** [17]And lo a voice from heaven, saying, This is my beloved Son, in whom I am well pleased.	**Col 1:13** [13]Who hath delivered us from the power of darkness, and hath translated us into the kingdom of his dear Son:

EPHESIANS (PSEUDO) 1:7—Address (1:1–14)

Theme	EPH	Paul	Other
Redeemed and forgiven	**1:7** [7]In whom we have redemption through his blood, the forgiveness of sins, according to the riches of his grace; **2:7–13** [7]That in the ages to come he might show the exceeding riches of his grace in his kindness toward us through Christ Jesus. [8]For by grace are ye saved through faith; and that not of yourselves: it is the gift of God: [9]Not of works, lest any man should boast. [10]For we are his workmanship, created in Christ Jesus unto good works, which God hath before ordained that we should walk in them. [11]Wherefore remember, that ye being in time past Gentiles in the flesh, who are called Uncircumcision by that which is called the Circumcision in the flesh made by hands; [12]That at that time ye were without Christ, being aliens from the commonwealth of Israel, and strangers from the covenants of promise, having no hope, and without God in the world: [13]But now in Christ Jesus ye who sometimes were far off are made nigh by the blood of Christ.	**Rom 3:24** [24]Being justified freely by his grace through the redemption that is in Christ Jesus: **Col 1:14** [14]In whom we have redemption through his blood, even the forgiveness of sins: **Col 1:20** [20]And, having made peace through the blood of his cross, by him to reconcile all things unto himself; by him, I say, whether they be things in earth, or things in heaven.	**Q-Quelle** Precedence: Eph 1:7/Rom 3:24/[Mt 19:28]/[Mk 10:41-45]/[Lk 22:28-30 (QS 62)]

EPHESIANS (PSEUDO) 1:8—Address (1:1–14)

Theme	EPH	Paul
Wisdom & prudence	**1:8** [8]Wherein he hath abounded toward us in all wisdom and prudence;	**Col 1:9** [9]For this cause we also, since the day we heard it, do not cease to pray for you, and to desire that ye might be filled with the knowledge of his will in all wisdom and spiritual understanding;

EPHESIANS (PSEUDO) 1:9—Address (1:1–14)

Theme	EPH	Paul
God's good pleasure revealed	**1:9** [9]Having made known unto us the mystery of his will, according to his good pleasure which he hath purposed in himself: **3:3** [3]How that by revelation he made known unto me the mystery; (as I wrote afore in few words, **3:9** [9]And to make all men see what is the fellowship of the mystery, which from the beginning of the world hath been hid in God, who created all things by Jesus Christ:	**Rom 16:25** [25]Now to him that is of power to stablish you according to my gospel, and the preaching of Jesus Christ, according to the revelation of the mystery, which was kept secret since the world began,

EPHESIANS (PSEUDO) 1:10—Address (1:1–14)

Theme	EPH	Mk	Lk
Day of the Lord/eschatology: **All creation redeemed**	**1:10** [10]That in the dispensation of the fulness of times he might gather together in one all things in Christ, both which are in heaven, and which are on earth; even in him:	**1:15** [15]And saying, The time is fulfilled, and the kingdom of God is at hand: repent ye, and believe the gospel.	**4:19** [19]To preach the acceptable year of the Lord.

Paul

Rom 8:21

[21]Because the creature itself also shall be delivered from the bondage of corruption into the glorious liberty of the children of God.

Rom 8:23

[23]And not only they, but ourselves also, which have the firstfruits of the Spirit, even we ourselves groan within ourselves, waiting for the adoption, to wit, the redemption of our body.

Rom 13:11–12

[11]And that, knowing the time, that now it is high time to awake out of sleep: for now is our salvation nearer than when we believed. [12]The night is far spent, the day is at hand: let us therefore cast off the works of darkness, and let us put on the armour of light.

Rom 15:20

[20]Yea, so have I strived to preach the gospel, not where Christ was named, lest I should build upon another man's foundation:

1 Cor 15:20

[20]But now is Christ risen from the dead, and become the firstfruits of them that slept.

1 Cor 15:24–28

[24]Then cometh the end, when he shall have delivered up the kingdom to God, even the Father; when he shall have put down all rule and all authority and power. [25]For he must reign, till he hath put all enemies under his feet. [26]The last enemy that shall be destroyed is death. [27]For he hath put all things under his feet. But when he saith all things are put under him, it is manifest that he is excepted, which did put all things under him. [28]And when all things shall be subdued unto him, then shall the Son also himself be subject unto him that put all things under him, that God may be all in all.

2 Cor 5:17

[17]Therefore if any man be in Christ, he is a new creature: old things are passed away; behold, all things are become new.

2 Cor 5:19

[19]To wit, that God was in Christ, reconciling the world unto himself, not imputing their trespasses unto them; and hath committed unto us the word of reconciliation.

2 Cor 6:2

[2](For he saith, I have heard thee in a time accepted, and in the day of salvation have I succoured thee: behold, now is the accepted time; behold, now is the day of salvation.)

Gal 4:4

[4]But when the fulness of the time was come, God sent forth his Son, made of a woman, made under the law,

Gal 4:14

[14]And my temptation which was in my flesh ye despised not, nor rejected; but received me as an angel of God, even as Christ Jesus.

Gal 6:15

[15]For in Christ Jesus neither circumcision availeth any thing, nor uncircumcision, but a new creature.

Col 1:16–20

[16]For by him were all things created, that are in heaven, and that are in earth, visible and invisible, whether they be thrones, or dominions, or principalities, or powers: all things were created by him, and for him: [17]And he is before all things, and by him all things consist. [18]And he is the head of the body, the church: who is the beginning, the firstborn from the dead; that in all things he might have the preeminence. [19]For it pleased the Father that in him should all fulness dwell; [20]And, having made peace through the blood of his cross, by him to reconcile all things unto himself; by him, I say, whether they be things in earth, or things in heaven.

Ephesians (Pseudo) 1:10 continued on next page

EPHESIANS (PSEUDO) 1:10—Address (1:1–14) (*continued*)

Theme	EPH	Jewish Writings
(*Cont.*) **Day of the Lord/eschatology:** **All creation redeemed**	**1:10 (above)**	**Is 49** [1]Listen, O isles, unto me; and hearken, ye people, from far; The LORD hath called me from the womb; from the bowels of my mother hath he made mention of my name. [2]And he hath made my mouth like a sharp sword; in the shadow of his hand hath he hid me, and made me a polished shaft; in his quiver hath he hid me; [3]And said unto me, Thou art my servant, O Israel, in whom I will be glorified. [4]Then I said, I have laboured in vain, I have spent my strength for nought, and in vain: yet surely my judgment is with the LORD, and my work with my God. [5]And now, saith the LORD that formed me from the womb to be his servant, to bring Jacob again to him, Though Israel be not gathered, yet shall I be glorious in the eyes of the LORD, and my God shall be my strength. [6]And he said, It is a light thing that thou shouldest be my servant to raise up the tribes of Jacob, and to restore the preserved of Israel: I will also give thee for a light to the Gentiles, that thou mayest be my salvation unto the end of the earth. [7]Thus saith the LORD, the Redeemer of Israel, and his Holy One, to him whom man despiseth, to him whom the nation abhorreth, to a servant of rulers, Kings shall see and arise, princes also shall worship, because of the LORD that is faithful, and the Holy One of Israel, and he shall choose thee. [8]Thus saith the LORD, In an acceptable time have I heard thee, and in a day of salvation have I helped thee: and I will preserve thee, and give thee for a covenant of the people, to establish the earth, to cause to inherit the desolate heritages; [9]That thou mayest say to the prisoners, Go forth; to them that are in darkness, Show yourselves. They shall feed in the ways, and their pastures shall be in all high places. [10]They shall not hunger nor thirst; neither shall the heat nor sun smite them: for he that hath mercy on them shall lead them, even by the springs of water shall he guide them. [11]And I will make all my mountains a way, and my highways shall be exalted. [12]Behold, these shall come from far: and, lo, these from the north and from the west; and these from the land of Sinim. [13]Sing, O heavens; and be joyful, O earth; and break forth into singing, O mountains: for the LORD hath comforted his people, and will have mercy upon his afflicted. [14]But Zion said, The LORD hath forsaken me, and my Lord hath forgotten me. [15]Can a woman forget her sucking child, that she should not have compassion on the son of her womb? yea, they may forget, yet will I not forget thee. [16]Behold, I have graven thee upon the palms of my hands; thy walls are continually before me. [17]Thy children shall make haste; thy destroyers and they that made thee waste shall go forth of thee. [18]Lift up thine eyes round about, and behold: all these gather themselves together, and come to thee. As I live, saith the LORD, thou shalt surely clothe thee with them all, as with an ornament, and bind them on thee, as a bride doeth. [19]For thy waste and thy desolate places, and the land of thy destruction, shall even now be too narrow by reason of the inhabitants, and they that swallowed thee up shall be far away. [20]The children which thou shalt have, after thou hast lost the other, shall say again in thine ears, The place is too strait for me: give place to me that I may dwell. [21]Then shalt thou say in thine heart, Who hath begotten me these, seeing I have lost my children, and am desolate, a captive, and removing to and fro? and who hath brought up these? Behold, I was left alone; these, where had they been? [22]Thus saith the Lord GOD, Behold, I will lift up mine hand to the Gentiles, and set up my standard to the people: and they shall bring thy sons in their arms, and thy daughters shall be carried upon their shoulders. [23]And kings shall be thy nursing fathers, and their queens thy nursing mothers: they shall bow down to thee with their face toward the earth, and lick up the dust of thy feet; and thou shalt know that I am the LORD: for they shall not be ashamed that wait for me. [24]Shall the prey be taken from the mighty, or the lawful captive delivered? [25]But thus saith the LORD, Even the captives of the mighty shall be taken away, and the prey of the terrible shall be delivered: for I will contend with him that contendeth with thee, and I will save thy children. [26]And I will feed them that oppress thee with their own flesh; and they shall be drunken with their own blood, as with sweet wine: and all flesh shall know that I the LORD am thy Saviour and thy Redeemer, the mighty One of Jacob.

EPHESIANS (PSEUDO) 1:11—Address (1:1–14)

Theme	EPH	Paul	NT	Jewish Writings
Pre-destined by God	**1:11** [11]In whom also we have obtained an inheritance, being predestinated according to the purpose of him who worketh all things after the counsel of his own will:	**Rom 8:28** [28]And we know that all things work together for good to them that love God, to them who are the called according to his purpose. **Col 1:12** [12]Giving thanks unto the Father, which hath made us meet to be partakers of the inheritance of the saints in light:	**Rev 4:11** [11]Thou art worthy, O Lord, to receive glory and honour and power: for thou hast created all things, and for thy pleasure they are and were created.	**Is 46:10** [10]Declaring the end from the beginning, and from ancient times the things that are not yet done, saying, My counsel shall stand, and I will do all my pleasure:

EPHESIANS (PSEUDO) 1:13—Address (1:1–14)

Theme	EPH	Lk	Paul	Other
Sealed with the Holy Spirit	**1:13** [13]In whom ye also trusted, after that ye heard the word of truth, the gospel of your salvation: in whom also after that ye believed, ye were sealed with that holy Spirit of promise, **4:30** [30]And grieve not the holy Spirit of God, whereby ye are sealed unto the day of redemption.	**Acts 2:33** [33]Therefore being by the right hand of God exalted, and having received of the Father the promise of the Holy Ghost, he hath shed forth this, which ye now see and hear.	**Col 1:5–6** [5]For the hope which is laid up for you in heaven, whereof ye heard before in the word of the truth of the gospel; [6]Which is come unto you, as it is in all the world; and bringeth forth fruit, as it doth also in you, since the day ye heard of it, and knew the grace of God in truth:	**Q-Quelle** Preaching of John: Eph 1:13/ Acts 1:4-8/Col 1:5/[Mt 3:7-10, 11-12]/[Mk 1:7-8]/[Lk 3:7-9 (QS4)], Lk 3:15-18 (QS5)]

EPHESIANS (PSEUDO) 1:14—Address (1:1–14)

Theme	EPH	Mt	Mk	Lk
Gift of the Spirit/ promise of sonship	**1:14** [14]Which is the earnest of our inheritance until the redemption of the purchased possession, unto the praise of his glory.	**10:20** [20]For it is not ye that speak, but the Spirit of your Father which speaketh in you. **12:28** [28]But if I cast out devils by the Spirit of God, then the kingdom of God is come unto you.	**1:11** [11]And there came a voice from heaven, saying, Thou art my beloved Son, in whom I am well pleased. **13:11** [11]But when they shall lead you, and deliver you up, take no thought beforehand what ye shall speak, neither do ye premeditate: but whatsoever shall be given you in that hour, that speak ye: for it is not ye that speak, but the Holy Ghost.	**3:22** [22]And the Holy Ghost descended in a bodily shape like a dove upon him, and a voice came from heaven, which said, Thou art my beloved Son; in thee I am well pleased. **4:18** [18]The Spirit of the Lord is upon me, because he hath anointed me to preach the gospel to the poor; he hath sent me to heal the brokenhearted, to preach deliverance to the captives, and recovering of sight to the blind, to set at liberty them that are bruised, **12:12** [12]For the Holy Ghost shall teach you in the same hour what ye ought to say.

Paul	Jewish Writings	Other
Rom 8:23 [23]And not only they, but ourselves also, which have the firstfruits of the Spirit, even we ourselves groan within ourselves, waiting for the adoption, to wit, the redemption of our body. **1 Cor 3:16** [16]Know ye not that ye are the temple of God, and that the Spirit of God dwelleth in you? **1 Cor 12:1–13** [1]Now concerning spiritual gifts, brethren, I would not have you ignorant. [2]Ye know that ye were Gentiles, carried away unto these dumb idols, even as ye were led. [3]Wherefore I give you to understand, that no man speaking by the Spirit of God calleth Jesus accursed: and that no man can say that Jesus is the Lord, but by the Holy Ghost. [4]Now there are diversities of gifts, but the same Spirit. [5]And there are differences of administrations, but the same Lord. [6]And there are diversities of operations, but it is the same God which worketh all in all. [7]But the manifestation of the Spirit is given to every man to profit withal. [8]For to one is given by the Spirit the word of wisdom; to another the word of knowledge by the same Spirit; [9]To another faith by the same Spirit; to another the gifts of healing by the same Spirit; [10]To another the working of miracles; to another prophecy; to another discerning of spirits; to another divers kinds of tongues; to another the interpretation of tongues: [11]But all these worketh that one and the selfsame Spirit, dividing to every man severally as he will. [12]For as the body is one, and hath many members, and all the members of that one body, being many, are one body: so also is Christ. **[13]For by one Spirit are we all baptized into one body, whether we be Jews or Gentiles, whether we be bond or free; and have been all made to drink into one Spirit.** **2 Cor 1:22** [22]Who hath also sealed us, and given the earnest of the Spirit in our hearts. **2 Cor 3:18** [18]But we all, with open face beholding as in a glass the glory of the Lord, are changed into the same image from glory to glory, even as by the Spirit of the Lord. **2 Cor 5:5** [5]Now he that hath wrought us for the selfsame thing is God, who also hath given unto us the earnest of the Spirit. **2 Cor 5:15** [15]And that he died for all, that they which live should not henceforth live unto themselves, but unto him which died for them, and rose again. **Gal 5:22** [22]But the fruit of the Spirit is love, joy, peace, longsuffering, gentleness, goodness, faith, **1 Thes 1:5** [5]For our gospel came not unto you in word only, but also in power, and in the Holy Ghost, and in much assurance; as ye know what manner of men we were among you for your sake. **1 Thes 5:19–20** [19]Quench not the Spirit. [20]Despise not prophesyings.	**Jer 31:31–34** [31]Behold, the days come, saith the LORD, that I will make a new covenant with the house of Israel, and with the house of Judah: [32]Not according to the covenant that I made with their fathers in the day that I took them by the hand to bring them out of the land of Egypt; which my covenant they brake, although I was an husband unto them, saith the LORD: [33]But this shall be the covenant that I will make with the house of Israel; After those days, saith the LORD, I will put my law in their inward parts, and write it in their hearts; and will be their God, and they shall be my people. [34]And they shall teach no more every man his neighbour, and every man his brother, saying, Know the LORD: for they shall all know me, from the least of them unto the greatest of them, saith the LORD: for I will forgive their iniquity, and I will remember their sin no more. **Joel 2:28–32** [28]And it shall come to pass afterward, that I will pour out my spirit upon all flesh; and your sons and your daughters shall prophesy, your old men shall dream dreams, your young men shall see visions: [29]And also upon the servants and upon the handmaids in those days will I pour out my spirit. [30]And I will show wonders in the heavens and in the earth, blood, and fire, and pillars of smoke. [31]The sun shall be turned into darkness, and the moon into blood, before the great and the terrible day of the LORD come. [32]And it shall come to pass, that whosoever shall call on the name of the LORD shall be delivered: for in mount Zion and in Jerusalem shall be deliverance, as the LORD hath said, and in the remnant whom the LORD shall call.	**Q-Quelle** Assistance of the HS: Eph 1:14/2 Cor 1:22/1 Thes 1:5/Mt 10:19-20/Mk 13:11/Lk 12:11-12 (QS 37 [Thom 44]), [21:14-15]; Leaven: Eph 1:14/1 Cor 3:16/[Mt 13:33]/[Lk 13:20-21(QS 46 [Thom 20, 96])], Lk 12:11-12(QS 37 [Thom 44]); Precedence: Eph 1:14/1 Cor 3:16/[Mt 19:28]/[Mk 10:41-45]/ [Lk 22:28-30 (QS 62)

THANKS, PRAYERS, AND LORDSHIP OF JESUS CHRIST (1:15–23)

EPHESIANS (PSEUDO) 1:15—Thanks, prayers, and Lordship (1:15–23)

Theme	EPH	Paul
Prayers for faithful	**1:15** [15]Wherefore I also, after I heard of your faith in the Lord Jesus, and love unto all the saints,	**Col 1:3–4** [3]We give thanks to God and the Father of our Lord Jesus Christ, praying always for you, [4]Since we heard of your faith in Christ Jesus, and of the love which ye have to all the saints, **Phlm 4–5** [4]I thank my God, making mention of thee always in my prayers, [5]Hearing of thy love and faith, which thou hast toward the Lord Jesus, and toward all saints;

EPHESIANS (PSEUDO) 1:16—Thanks, prayers, and Lordship (1:15–23)

Theme	EPH	Paul
Thanks for the faithful	**1:16** [16]Cease not to give thanks for you, making mention of you in my prayers;	**Col 1:3–9** [3]We give thanks to God and the Father of our Lord Jesus Christ, praying always for you, [4]Since we heard of your faith in Christ Jesus, and of the love which ye have to all the saints, [5]For the hope which is laid up for you in heaven, whereof ye heard before in the word of the truth of the gospel; [6]Which is come unto you, as it is in all the world; and bringeth forth fruit, as it doth also in you, since the day ye heard of it, and knew the grace of God in truth: [7]As ye also learned of Epaphras our dear fellowservant, who is for you a faithful minister of Christ; [8]Who also declared unto us your love in the Spirit. [9]For this cause we also, since the day we heard it, do not cease to pray for you, and to desire that ye might be filled with the knowledge of his will in all wisdom and spiritual understanding;

EPHESIANS (PSEUDO) 1:17—Thanks, prayers, and Lordship (1:15–23)

Theme	EPH	Jn	Paul
Gift of wisdom & revelation	**1:17** [17]That the God of our Lord Jesus Christ, the Father of glory, may give unto you the spirit of wisdom and revelation in the knowledge of him: **3:14, 16** [14]For this cause I bow my knees unto the Father of our Lord Jesus Christ, . . . [16]That he would grant you, according to the riches of his glory, to be strengthened with might by his Spirit in the inner man;	**1 Jn 5:20** [20]And we know that the Son of God is come, and hath given us an understanding, that we may know him that is true, and we are in him that is true, even in his Son Jesus Christ. This is the true God, and eternal life.	**Col 1:9–10** [9]For this cause we also, since the day we heard it, do not cease to pray for you, and to desire that ye might be filled with the knowledge of his will in all wisdom and spiritual understanding; [10]That ye might walk worthy of the Lord unto all pleasing, being fruitful in every good work, and increasing in the knowledge of God;

EPHESIANS (PSEUDO) 1:18—Thanks, prayers, and Lordship (1:15–23)

Theme	EPH	Paul	Other
Enlightened eyes, hope for his calling	**1:18** [18]The eyes of your understanding being enlightened; that ye may know what is the hope of his calling, and what the riches of the glory of his inheritance in the saints, **4:4** [4]There is one body, and one Spirit, even as ye are called in one hope of your calling;	**Col 1:12, 27** [12]Giving thanks unto the Father, which hath made us meet to be partakers of the inheritance of the saints in light: . . . [27]To whom God would make known what is the riches of the glory of this mystery among the Gentiles; which is Christ in you, the hope of glory:	**Q-Quelle** Preaching of John: Col 1:5/Eph 1:18/ [Mt 3:7-10, 11-12]/ [Mk 1:7-8]/[Lk 3:7-9 (QS4)], Lk 3:15-18 (QS5)]

EPHESIANS (PSEUDO) 1:19—Thanks, prayers, and Lordship (1:15–23)

Theme	EPH	Paul
God's working for us	**1:19** [19]And what is the exceeding greatness of his power to us-ward who believe, according to the working of his mighty power,	**2 Cor 13:4** [4]For though he was crucified through weakness, yet he liveth by the power of God. For we also are weak in him, but we shall live with him by the power of God toward you. **Col 1:11** [11]Strengthened with all might, according to his glorious power, unto all patience and longsuffering with joyfulness; **Col 2:12** [12]Buried with him in baptism, wherein also ye are risen with him through the faith of the operation of God, who hath raised him from the dead.

EPHESIANS (PSEUDO) 1:20—Thanks, prayers, and Lordship (1:15–23)

Theme	EPH	NT	Jewish Writings
Raising Christ to right hand	**1:20** [20]Which he wrought in Christ, when he raised him from the dead, and set him at his own right hand in the heavenly places,	**Heb 1:3** [3]Who being the brightness of his glory, and the express image of his person, and upholding all things by the word of his power, when he had by himself purged our sins, sat down on the right hand of the Majesty on high;	**Ps 110:1** [1]The LORD said unto my Lord, Sit thou at my right hand, until I make thine enemies thy footstool.

EPHESIANS (PSEUDO) 1:21—Thanks, prayers, and Lordship (1:15–23)

Theme	EPH	Paul	NT
God above all	**1:21** [21]Far above all principality, and power, and might, and dominion, and every name that is named, not only in this world, but also in that which is to come:	**Phil 2:9** [9]Wherefore God also hath highly exalted him, and given him a name which is above every name: **Col 1:16** [16]For by him were all things created, that are in heaven, and that are in earth, visible and invisible, whether they be thrones, or dominions, or principalities, or powers: all things were created by him, and for him:	**1 Pet 3:22** [22]Who is gone into heaven, and is on the right hand of God; angels and authorities and powers being made subject unto him.

EPHESIANS (PSEUDO) 1:22–23—Thanks, prayers, and Lordship (1:15–23)

Theme	EPH	Mt	Mk	Lk
Jesus Christ/ corporate image: **Disciples, Jews, forming Church**	**1:22–23** [22]And hath put all things under his feet, and gave him to be the head over all things to the church, [23]Which is his body, the fulness of him that filleth all in all. **4:15** [15]But speaking the truth in love, may grow up into him in all things, which is the head, even Christ: **5:23** [23]For the husband is the head of the wife, even as Christ is the head of the church: and he is the saviour of the body.	**12:46–50** [46]While he yet talked to the people, behold, his mother and his brethren stood without, desiring to speak with him. [47]Then one said unto him, Behold, thy mother and thy brethren stand with-out, desiring to speak with thee. [48]But he answered and said unto him that told him, Who is my mother? and who are my brethren? [49]And he stretched forth his hand toward his disciples, and said, Behold my mother and my brethren! [50]For whosoever shall do the will of my Father which is in heaven, the same is my brother, and sister, and mother. **28:18** [18]And Jesus came and spake unto them, saying, All power is given unto me in heaven and in earth.	**3:31–35** [31]There came then his brethren and his mother, and, standing without, sent unto him, calling him. [32]And the multitude sat about him, and they said unto him, Behold, thy mother and thy brethren without seek for thee. [33]And he answered them, saying, Who is my mother, or my brethren? [34]And he looked round about on them which sat about him, and said, Behold my mother and my brethren! [35]For whosoever shall do the will of God, the same is my brother, and my sister, and mother.	**8:19–21** [19]Then came to him his mother and his brethren, and could not come at him for the press. [20]And it was told him by certain which said, Thy mother and thy brethren stand without, desiring to see thee. [21]And he answered and said unto them, My mother and my brethren are these which hear the word of God, and do it.

EPHESIANS (PSEUDO) 1:23—Thanks, prayers, and Lordship (1:15–23)

Theme	EPH	Paul
God fills all in all	**1:23** [23]Which is his body, the fulness of him that filleth all in all. **4:10, 12** [10]He that descended is the same also that ascended up far above all heavens, that he might fill all things.) ... [12]For the perfecting of the saints, for the work of the ministry, for the edifying of the body of Christ:	**Rom 12:5** [5]So we, being many, are one body in Christ, and every one members one of another. **1 Cor 12:27** [27]Now ye are the body of Christ, and members in particular. **Col 1:19** [19]For it pleased the Father that in him should all fulness dwell;

MERCY OF GOD (2:1–17)

EPHESIANS (PSEUDO) 2:1—Mercy of God (2:1–17)

Theme	EPH	Paul
Once dead, alive in Christ	**2:1** [1]And you hath he quickened, who were dead in trespasses and sins;	**Col 1:21** [21]And you, that were sometime alienated and enemies in your mind by wicked works, yet now hath he reconciled **Col 2:13** [13]And you, being dead in your sins and the uncircumcision of your flesh, hath he quickened together with him, having forgiven you all trespasses;

Paul	Jewish
1 Cor 6:15 [15]Know ye not that your bodies are the members of Christ? shall I then take the members of Christ, and make them the members of an harlot? God forbid. **1 Cor 10:17** [17]For we being many are one bread, and one body: for we are all partakers of that one bread. **1 Cor 12:12–13** [12]For as the body is one, and hath many members, and all the members of that one body, being many, are one body: so also is Christ. [13]For by one Spirit are we all baptized into one body, whether we be Jews or Gentiles, whether we be bond or free; and have been all made to drink into one Spirit. **1 Cor 15:22** [22]For as in Adam all die, even so in Christ shall all be made alive. **Col 1:18** [18]And he is the head of the body, the church: who is the beginning, the firstborn from the dead; that in all things he might have the preeminence.	**Ps 8:7** [7]All sheep and oxen, yea, and the beasts of the field;

EPHESIANS (PSEUDO) 2:2—Mercy of God (2:1–17)

Theme	EPH	Jn	Paul
Children of disobe-dience	**2:2** [2]Wherein in time past ye walked according to the course of this world, according to the prince of the power of the air, the spirit that now worketh in the children of disobedience: **6:12** [12]For we wrestle not against flesh and blood, but against principalities, against powers, against the rulers of the darkness of this world, against spiritual wickedness in high places.	**12:31** [31]Now is the judgment of this world: now shall the prince of this world be cast out.	**Col 1:13** [13]Who hath delivered us from the power of darkness, and hath translated us into the kingdom of his dear Son:

EPHESIANS (PSEUDO) 2:3—Mercy of God (2:1–17)

Theme	EPH	Paul
Children of desire/ wrath	**2:3** [3]Among whom also we all had our conversation in times past in the lusts of our flesh, fulfilling the desires of the flesh and of the mind; and were by nature the children of wrath, even as others.	**Col 3:6–7** [6]For which things' sake the wrath of God cometh on the children of disobedience: [7]In the which ye also walked some time, when ye lived in them.

EPHESIANS (PSEUDO) 2:5—Mercy of God (2:1–17)

Theme	EPH	Paul
Grace saves even the lowest	**2:5** [5]Even when we were dead in sins, hath quickened us together with Christ, (by grace ye are saved;)	**Rom 5:8** [8]But God commendeth his love toward us, in that, while we were yet sinners, Christ died for us. **Rom 6:13** [13]Neither yield ye your members as instruments of unrighteousness unto sin: but yield yourselves unto God, as those that are alive from the dead, and your members as instruments of righteousness unto God. **Col 2:13** [13]And you, being dead in your sins and the uncircumcision of your flesh, hath he quickened together with him, having forgiven you all trespasses;

EPHESIANS (PSEUDO) 2:6—Mercy of God (2:1–17)

Theme	EPH	Paul
Raised us to heavenly places	**2:6** [6]And hath raised us up together, and made us sit together in heavenly places in Christ Jesus:	**Rom 8:10-11** [10]And if Christ be in you, the body is dead because of sin; but the Spirit is life because of righteousness. [11]But if the Spirit of him that raised up Jesus from the dead dwell in you, he that raised up Christ from the dead shall also quicken your mortal bodies by his Spirit that dwelleth in you. **Phil 3:20** [20]For our conversation is in heaven; from whence also we look for the Saviour, the Lord Jesus Christ: **Col 2:12** [12]Buried with him in baptism, wherein also ye are risen with him through the faith of the operation of God, who hath raised him from the dead.

EPHESIANS (PSEUDO) 2:7—Mercy of God (2:1–17)

Theme	EPH
Exceeding riches of grace	**2:7** [7]That in the ages to come he might show the exceeding riches of his grace in his kindness toward us through Christ Jesus. **1:7** [7]In whom we have redemption through his blood, the forgiveness of sins, according to the riches of his grace;

EPHESIANS (PSEUDO) 2:8—Mercy of God (2:1–17)

Theme	EPH	Paul	Other
Saved by grace through faith	**2:8** [8]For by grace are ye saved through faith; and that not of yourselves: it is the gift of God:	**Rom 3:24** [24]Being justified freely by his grace through the redemption that is in Christ Jesus: **Gal 2:16** [16]Knowing that a man is not justified by the works of the law, but by the faith of Jesus Christ, even we have believed in Jesus Christ, that we might be justified by the faith of Christ, and not by the works of the law: for by the works of the law shall no flesh be justified.	**Q-Quelle** Precedence: Eph 2:8/Rom 3:24/[Mt 19:28]/[Mk 10:41-45]/[Lk 22:28-30 (QS 62)]

EPHESIANS (PSEUDO) 2:9—Mercy of God (2:1–17)

Theme	EPH	Paul
God's work, not ours for boasting	**2:9** [9]Not of works, lest any man should boast.	**1 Cor 1:29** [29]That no flesh should glory in his presence.

EPHESIANS (PSEUDO) 2:10—Mercy of God (2:1–17)

Theme	EPH	Paul
Created for God's good works	**2:10** [10]For we are his workmanship, created in Christ Jesus unto good works, which God hath before ordained that we should walk in them. **4:24** [24]And that ye put on the new man, which after God is created in righteousness and true holiness.	**Tit 2:14 (Pseudo)** [14]Who gave himself for us, that he might redeem us from all iniquity, and purify unto himself a peculiar people, zealous of good works.

EPHESIANS (PSEUDO) 2:12—Mercy of God (2:1–17)

Theme	EPH	Paul
Strangers of promise	**2:12** [12]That at that time ye were without Christ, being aliens from the commonwealth of Israel, and strangers from the covenants of promise, having no hope, and without God in the world:	**Rom 9:14** [14]What shall we say then? Is there unrighteousness with God? God forbid. **Col 1:21, 27** [21]And you, that were sometime alienated and enemies in your mind by wicked works, yet now hath he reconciled . . . [27]To whom God would make known what is the riches of the glory of this mystery among the Gentiles; which is Christ in you, the hope of glory:

EPHESIANS (PSEUDO) 2:13—Mercy of God (2:1–17)

Theme	EPH	Paul	Jewish Writings
Those far off made whole Christ's blood	**2:13** [13]But now in Christ Jesus ye who sometimes were far off are made nigh by the blood of Christ. **2:17** [17]And came and preached peace to you which were afar off, and to them that were nigh.	**Col 1:20** [20]And, having made peace through the blood of his cross, by him to reconcile all things unto himself; by him, I say, whether they be things in earth, or things in heaven.	**Is 57:19** [19]I create the fruit of the lips; Peace, peace to him that is far off, and to him that is near, saith the LORD; and I will heal him.

EPHESIANS (PSEUDO) 2:14—Mercy of God (2:1–17)

Theme	EPH	Paul
Jesus is our peace	**2:14** [14]For he is our peace, who hath made both one, and hath broken down the middle wall of partition between us;	**Gal 3:28** [28]There is neither Jew nor Greek, there is neither bond nor free, there is neither male nor female: for ye are all one in Christ Jesus.

EPHESIANS (PSEUDO) 2:15—Mercy of God (2:1–17)

Theme	EPH	Lk	Paul
New humanity	**2:15** [15]Having abolished in his flesh the enmity, even the law of commandments contained in ordinances; for to make in himself of twain one new man, so making peace;	**15:24** [24]For this my son was dead, and is alive again; he was lost, and is found. And they began to be merry.	**2 Cor 5:17** [17]Therefore if any man be in Christ, he is a new creature: old things are passed away; behold, all things are become new. **Col 2:14** [14]Blotting out the handwriting of ordinances that was against us, which was contrary to us, and took it out of the way, nailing it to his cross;

EPHESIANS (PSEUDO) 2:16—Mercy of God (2:1–17)

Theme	EPH	Paul
Cross reconciles body to God	**2:16** [16]And that he might reconcile both unto God in one body by the cross, having slain the enmity thereby:	**Col 1:20** [20]And, having made peace through the blood of his cross, by him to reconcile all things unto himself; by him, I say, whether they be things in earth, or things in heaven. **Col 1:22** [22]In the body of his flesh through death, to present you holy and unblameable and unreproveable in his sight:

EPHESIANS (PSEUDO) 2:17—Mercy of God (2:1–17)

Theme	EPH	Jewish Writings
Preaching peace to those far off	**2:17** [17]And came and preached peace to you which were afar off, and to them that were nigh.	**Is 57:19** [19]I create the fruit of the lips; Peace, peace to him that is far off, and to him that is near, saith the LORD; and I will heal him. **Zech 9:10** [10]And I will cut off the chariot from Ephraim, and the horse from Jerusalem, and the battle bow shall be cut off: and he shall speak peace unto the heathen: and his dominion shall be from sea even to sea, and from the river even to the ends of the earth.

BODY OF CHRIST (2:18–22)

EPHESIANS (PSEUDO) 2:18–22—Body of Christ (2:18–22)

Theme	EPH	Mt	Mk	Lk
One Spirit	**2:18–22** [18]For through him we both have access by one Spirit unto the Father. [19]Now therefore ye are no more strangers and foreigners, but fellowcitizens with the saints, and of the household of God; [20]And are built upon the foundation of the apostles and prophets, Jesus Christ himself being the chief corner stone; [21]In whom all the building fitly framed together groweth unto an holy temple in the Lord: [22]In whom ye also are builded together for an habitation of God through the Spirit. **3:12** [12]In whom we have boldness and access with confidence by the faith of him.	**16:16–20** [16]And Simon Peter answered and said, Thou art the Christ, the Son of the living God. [17]And Jesus answered and said unto him, Blessed art thou, Simon Barjona: for flesh and blood hath not revealed it unto thee, but my Father which is in heaven. [18]And I say also unto thee, That thou art Peter, and upon this rock I will build my church; and the gates of hell shall not prevail against it. [19]And I will give unto thee the keys of the kingdom of heaven: and whatsoever thou shalt bind on earth shall be bound in heaven: and whatsoever thou shalt loose on earth shall be loosed in heaven. [20]Then charged he his disciples that they should tell no man that he was Jesus the Christ. **21:42** [42]Jesus saith unto them, Did ye never read in the scriptures, The stone which the builders rejected, the same is become the head of the corner: this is the Lord's doing, and it is marvellous in our eyes?	**12:10-11** [10]And have ye not read this scripture; The stone which the builders rejected is become the head of the corner: [11]This was the Lord's doing, and it is marvellous in our eyes? [12]And they sought to lay hold on him, but feared the people: for they knew that he had spoken the parable against them: and they left him, and went their way.	**20:17** [17]And he beheld them, and said, What is this then that is written, The stone which the builders rejected, the same is become the head of the corner?

Ephesians (Pseudo) 2:18-22 continued on next page

EPHESIANS (PSEUDO) 2:18–22—Body of Christ (2:18–22) (*continued*)

Theme	EPH	Paul
(*Cont.*) **One Spirit**	**2:18–22 (above)**	**Rom 3:16–17** [16]Destruction and misery are in their ways: [17]And the way of peace have they not known: **Rom 6:19** [19]I speak after the manner of men because of the infirmity of your flesh: for as ye have yielded your members servants to uncleanness and to iniquity unto iniquity; even so now yield your members servants to righteousness unto holiness. **1 Cor 1:11–13** [11]For it hath been declared unto me of you, my brethren, by them which are of the house of Chloe, that there are contentions among you. [12]Now this I say, that every one of you saith, I am of Paul; and I of Apollos; and I of Cephas; and I of Christ. [13]Is Christ divided? was Paul crucified for you? or were ye baptized in the name of Paul? **1 Cor 3** [1]And I, brethren, could not speak unto you as unto spiritual, but as unto carnal, even as unto babes in Christ. [2]I have fed you with milk, and not with meat: for hitherto ye were not able to bear it, neither yet now are ye able. [3]For ye are yet carnal: for whereas there is among you envying, and strife, and divisions, are ye not carnal, and walk as men? [4]For while one saith, I am of Paul; and another, I am of Apollos; are ye not carnal? [5]Who then is Paul, and who is Apollos, but ministers by whom ye believed, even as the Lord gave to every man? [6]I have planted, Apollos watered; but God gave the increase. [7]So then neither is he that planteth any thing, neither he that watereth; but God that giveth the increase. [8]Now he that planteth and he that watereth are one: and every man shall receive his own reward according to his own labour. [9]For we are labourers together with God: ye are God's husbandry, ye are God's building. [10]According to the grace of God which is given unto me, as a wise masterbuilder, I have laid the foundation, and another buildeth thereon. But let every man take heed how he buildeth thereupon. [11]For other foundation can no man lay than that is laid, which is Jesus Christ. [12]Now if any man build upon this foundation gold, silver, precious stones, wood, hay, stubble; [13]Every man's work shall be made manifest: for the day shall declare it, because it shall be revealed by fire; and the fire shall try every man's work of what sort it is. [14]If any man's work abide which he hath built thereupon, he shall receive a reward. [15]If any man's work shall be burned, he shall suffer loss: but he himself shall be saved; yet so as by fire. **[16]Know ye not that ye are the temple of God, and that the Spirit of God dwelleth in you?** [17]If any man defile the temple of God, him shall God destroy; for the temple of God is holy, which temple ye are. [18]Let no man deceive himself. If any man among you seemeth to be wise in this world, let him become a fool, that he may be wise. [19]For the wisdom of this world is foolishness with God. For it is written, He taketh the wise in their own craftiness. [20]And again, The Lord knoweth the thoughts of the wise, that they are vain. [21]Therefore let no man glory in men. For all things are yours; [22]Whether Paul, or Apollos, or Cephas, or the world, or life, or death, or things present, or things to come; all are yours; [23]And ye are Christ's; and Christ is God's. **1 Cor 6:19** [19]What? know ye not that your body is the temple of the Holy Ghost which is in you, which ye have of God, and ye are not your own? **2 Cor 5:1** [1]For we know that if our earthly house of this tabernacle were dissolved, we have a building of God, an house not made with hands, eternal in the heavens. **2 Cor 6:14–7:1** **6** [14]Be ye not unequally yoked together with unbelievers: for what fellowship hath righteousness with unrighteousness? and what communion hath light with darkness? [15]And what concord hath Christ with Belial? or what part hath he that believeth with an infidel? [16]And what agreement hath the temple of God with idols? for ye are the temple of the living God; as God hath said, I will dwell in them, and walk in them; and I will be their God, and they shall be my people. [17]Wherefore come out from among them, and be ye separate, saith the Lord, and touch not the unclean thing; and I will receive you, [18]And will be a Father unto you, and ye shall be my sons and daughters, saith the Lord Almighty. **7** [1]Having therefore these promises, dearly beloved, let us cleanse ourselves from all filthiness of the flesh and spirit, perfecting holiness in the fear of God. **Col 2:19** [19]And not holding the Head, from which all the body by joints and bands having nourishment ministered, and knit together, increaseth with the increase of God.

NT	Jewish Writings
Heb 12:22–23 22But ye are come unto mount Sion, and unto the city of the living God, the heavenly Jerusalem, and to an innumerable company of angels, 23To the general assembly and church of the firstborn, which are written in heaven, and to God the Judge of all, and to the spirits of just men made perfect, **Rev 21:14** 14And the wall of the city had twelve foundations, and in them the names of the twelve apostles of the Lamb.	**2 Sam 7** 1And it came to pass, when the king sat in his house, and the LORD had given him rest round about from all his enemies; 2That the king said unto Nathan the prophet, See now, I dwell in an house of cedar, but the ark of God dwelleth within curtains. 3And Nathan said to the king, Go, do all that is in thine heart; for the LORD is with thee. 4And it came to pass that night, that the word of the LORD came unto Nathan, saying, 5Go and tell my servant David, Thus saith the LORD, Shalt thou build me an house for me to dwell in? 6Whereas I have not dwelt in any house since the time that I brought up the children of Israel out of Egypt, even to this day, but have walked in a tent and in a tabernacle. 7In all the places wherein I have walked with all the children of Israel spake I a word with any of the tribes of Israel, whom I commanded to feed my people Israel, saying, Why build ye not me an house of cedar? 8Now therefore so shalt thou say unto my servant David, Thus saith the LORD of hosts, I took thee from the sheepcote, from following the sheep, to be ruler over my people, over Israel: 9And I was with thee whithersoever thou wentest, and have cut off all thine enemies out of thy sight, and have made thee a great name, like unto the name of the great men that are in the earth. 10Moreover I will appoint a place for my people Israel, and will plant them, that they may dwell in a place of their own, and move no more; neither shall the children of wickedness afflict them any more, as beforetime, 11And as since the time that I commanded judges to be over my people Israel, and have caused thee to rest from all thine enemies. Also the LORD telleth thee that he will make thee an house. 12And when thy days be fulfilled, and thou shalt sleep with thy fathers, I will set up thy seed after thee, which shall proceed out of thy bowels, and I will establish his kingdom. 13He shall build an house for my name, and I will stablish the throne of his kingdom for ever. 14I will be his father, and he shall be my son. If he commit iniquity, I will chasten him with the rod of men, and with the stripes of the children of men: 15But my mercy shall not depart away from him, as I took it from Saul, whom I put away before thee. 16And thine house and thy kingdom shall be established for ever before thee: thy throne shall be established for ever. 17According to all these words, and according to all this vision, so did Nathan speak unto David. 18Then went king David in, and sat before the LORD, and he said, Who am I, O Lord GOD? and what is my house, that thou hast brought me hitherto? 19And this was yet a small thing in thy sight, O Lord GOD; but thou hast spoken also of thy servant's house for a great while to come. And is this the manner of man, O Lord GOD? 20And what can David say more unto thee? for thou, Lord GOD, knowest thy servant. 21For thy word's sake, and according to thine own heart, hast thou done all these great things, to make thy servant know them. 22Wherefore thou art great, O LORD God: for there is none like thee, neither is there any God beside thee, according to all that we have heard with our ears. 23And what one nation in the earth is like thy people, even like Israel, whom God went to redeem for a people to himself, and to make him a name, and to do for you great things and terrible, for thy land, before thy people, which thou redeemedst to thee from Egypt, from the nations and their gods? 24For thou hast confirmed to thyself thy people Israel to be a people unto thee for ever: and thou, LORD, art become their God. 25And now, O LORD God, the word that thou hast spoken concerning thy servant, and concerning his house, establish it for ever, and do as thou hast said. 26And let thy name be magnified for ever, saying, The LORD of hosts is the God over Israel: and let the house of thy servant David be established before thee. 27For thou, O LORD of hosts, God of Israel, hast revealed to thy servant, saying, I will build thee an house: therefore hath thy servant found in his heart to pray this prayer unto thee. 28And now, O Lord GOD, thou art that God, and thy words be true, and thou hast promised this goodness unto thy servant: 29Therefore now let it please thee to bless the house of thy servant, that it may continue for ever before thee: for thou, O Lord GOD, hast spoken it: and with thy blessing let the house of thy servant be blessed for ever. **Is 28:16** 16Therefore thus saith the Lord GOD, Behold, I lay in Zion for a foundation a stone, a tried stone, a precious corner stone, a sure foundation: he that believeth shall not make haste.

EPHESIANS (PSEUDO) 2:18—Body of Christ (2:18–22)

Theme	EPH
Access to one Spirit	**2:18** [18]For through him we both have access by one Spirit unto the Father. **3:12** [12]In whom we have boldness and access with confidence by the faith of him.

EPHESIANS (PSEUDO) 2:19—Body of Christ (2:18–22)

Theme	EPH	NT
Fellow citizens with saints	**2:19** [19]Now therefore ye are no more strangers and foreigners, but fellowcitizens with the saints, and of the household of God;	**Heb 12:22–23** [22]But ye are come unto mount Sion, and unto the city of the living God, the heavenly Jerusalem, and to an innumerable company of angels, [23]To the general assembly and church of the firstborn, which are written in heaven, and to God the Judge of all, and to the spirits of just men made perfect,

EPHESIANS (PSEUDO) 2:20—Body of Christ (2:18–22)

Theme	EPH	NT	Jewish Writings
Built into foundation of prophets	**2:20** [20]And are built upon the foundation of the apostles and prophets, Jesus Christ himself being the chief corner stone;	**Rev 21:14** [14]And the wall of the city had twelve foundations, and in them the names of the twelve apostles of the Lamb.	**Is 28:16** [16]Therefore thus saith the Lord GOD, Behold, I lay in Zion for a foundation a stone, a tried stone, a precious corner stone, a sure foundation: he that believeth shall not make haste.

EPHESIANS (PSEUDO) 2:21—Body of Christ (2:18–22)

Theme	EPH	Paul
Growing into holy temple	**2:21** [21]In whom all the building fitly framed together groweth unto an holy temple in the Lord:	**1 Cor 3:16** [16]Know ye not that ye are the temple of God, and that the Spirit of God dwelleth in you? **Col 2:19** [19]And not holding the Head, from which all the body by joints and bands having nourishment ministered, and knit together, increaseth with the increase of God.

EPHESIANS (PSEUDO) 2:22—Body of Christ (2:18–22)

Theme	EPH	NT
Habitation of God through Spirit	**2:22** [22]In whom ye also are builded together for an habitation of God through the Spirit.	**1 Pet 2:5** [5]Ye also, as lively stones, are built up a spiritual house, an holy priesthood, to offer up spiritual sacrifices, acceptable to God by Jesus Christ.

CHURCH'S WORLD MISSION (3:1–4:24)

EPHESIANS (PSEUDO) 3:1—Church's world mission (3:1–4:24)

Theme	EPH	Paul
Paul, prisoner of Christ, for Gentiles	**3:1** [1]For this cause I Paul, the prisoner of Jesus Christ for you Gentiles,	**Phil 1:7, 13** [7]Even as it is meet for me to think this of you all, because I have you in my heart; inasmuch as both in my bonds, and in the defence and confirmation of the gospel, ye all are partakers of my grace. . . . [13]So that my bonds in Christ are manifest in all the palace, and in all other places; **Col 1:24–29** [24]Who now rejoice in my sufferings for you, and fill up that which is behind of the afflictions of Christ in my flesh for his body's sake, which is the church: [25]Whereof I am made a minister, according to the dispensation of God which is given to me for you, to fulfil the word of God; [26]Even the mystery which hath been hid from ages and from generations, but now is made manifest to his saints: [27]To whom God would make known what is the riches of the glory of this mystery among the Gentiles; which is Christ in you, the hope of glory: [28]Whom we preach, warning every man, and teaching every man in all wisdom; that we may present every man perfect in Christ Jesus: [29]Whereunto I also labour, striving according to his working, which worketh in me mightily. **Col 4:18** [18]The salutation by the hand of me Paul. Remember my bonds. Grace be with you. Amen. **2 Tim 2:9 (Pseudo)** [9]Wherein I suffer trouble, as an evil doer, even unto bonds; but the word of God is not bound. **Phlm 1:9** [9]Yet for love's sake I rather beseech thee, being such an one as Paul the aged, and now also a prisoner of Jesus Christ.

EPHESIANS (PSEUDO) 3:2—Church's world mission (3:1–4:24)

Theme	EPH	Paul
Grace for faithful	**3:2** [2]If ye have heard of the dispensation of the grace of God which is given me to you-ward:	**Col 1:25** [25]Whereof I am made a minister, according to the dispensation of God which is given to me for you, to fulfil the word of God;

EPHESIANS (PSEUDO) 3:3—Church's world mission (3:1–4:24)

Theme	EPH	Paul
Revelation of mystery	**3:3** [3]How that by revelation he made known unto me the mystery; (as I wrote afore in few words, **1:9–10** [9]Having made known unto us the mystery of his will, according to his good pleasure which he hath purposed in himself: [10]That in the dispensation of the fulness of times he might gather together in one all things in Christ, both which are in heaven, and which are on earth; even in him:	**Col 1:26** [26]Even the mystery which hath been hid from ages and from generations, but now is made manifest to his saints:

EPHESIANS (PSEUDO) 3:5—Church's world mission (3:1–4:24)

Theme	EPH	Paul
Mystery for apostles & prophets	**3:5** [5]Which in other ages was not made known unto the sons of men, as it is now revealed unto his holy apostles and prophets by the Spirit;	**Col 1:26** [26]Even the mystery which hath been hid from ages and from generations, but now is made manifest to his saints:

EPHESIANS (PSEUDO) 3:6—Church's world mission (3:1–4:24)

Theme	EPH
Gentiles are fellow heirs	**3:6** [6]That the Gentiles should be fellowheirs, and of the same body, and partakers of his promise in Christ by the gospel: **2:13, 18–19** [13]But now in Christ Jesus ye who sometimes were far off are made nigh by the blood of Christ. . . . [18]For through him we both have access by one Spirit unto the Father. [19]Now therefore ye are no more strangers and foreigners, but fellowcitizens with the saints, and of the household of God;

EPHESIANS (PSEUDO) 3:7—Church's world mission (3:1–4:24)

Theme	EPH	Paul
Minister by grace	**3:7** [7]Whereof I was made a minister, according to the gift of the grace of God given unto me by the effectual working of his power.	**Rom 15:15** [15]Nevertheless, brethren, I have written the more boldly unto you in some sort, as putting you in mind, because of the grace that is given to me of God, **Col 1:25** [25]Whereof I am made a minister, according to the dispensation of God which is given to me for you, to fulfil the word of God; **Col 1:29** [29]Whereunto I also labour, striving according to his working, which worketh in me mightily.

EPHESIANS (PSEUDO) 3:8—Church's world mission (3:1–4:24)

Theme	EPH	Paul
Least of the saints	**3:8** [8]Unto me, who am less than the least of all saints, is this grace given, that I should preach among the Gentiles the unsearchable riches of Christ;	**1 Cor 15:8–10** [8]And last of all he was seen of me also, as of one born out of due time. [9]For I am the least of the apostles, that am not meet to be called an apostle, because I persecuted the church of God. [10]But by the grace of God I am what I am: and his grace which was bestowed upon me was not in vain; but I laboured more abundantly than they all: yet not I, but the grace of God which was with me. **Gal 1:16** [16]To reveal his Son in me, that I might preach him among the heathen; immediately I conferred not with flesh and blood: **Gal 2:7–9** [7]But contrariwise, when they saw that the gospel of the uncircumcision was committed unto me, as the gospel of the circumcision was unto Peter; [8](For he that wrought effectually in Peter to the apostleship of the circumcision, the same was mighty in me toward the Gentiles:) [9]And when James, Cephas, and John, who seemed to be pillars, perceived the grace that was given unto me, they gave to me and Barnabas the right hands of fellowship; that we should go unto the heathen, and they unto the circumcision.

EPHESIANS (PSEUDO) 3:9—Church's world mission (3:1–4:24)

Theme	EPH	Paul
Mystery of all things created in Jesus	**3:9** [9]And to make all men see what is the fellowship of the mystery, which from the beginning of the world hath been hid in God, who created all things by Jesus Christ:	**Rom 16:25** [25]Now to him that is of power to stablish you according to my gospel, and the preaching of Jesus Christ, according to the revelation of the mystery, which was kept secret since the world began, **Col 1:26–27** [26]Even the mystery which hath been hid from ages and from generations, but now is made manifest to his saints: [27]To whom God would make known what is the riches of the glory of this mystery among the Gentiles; which is Christ in you, the hope of glory:

EPHESIANS (PSEUDO) 3:10—Church's world mission (3:1–4:24)

Theme	EPH	NT
Mystery revealed in church	**3:10** [10]To the intent that now unto the principalities and powers in heavenly places might be known by the church the manifold wisdom of God,	**1 Pet 1:12** [12]Unto whom it was revealed, that not unto themselves, but unto us they did minister the things, which are now reported unto you by them that have preached the gospel unto you with the Holy Ghost sent down from heaven; which things the angels desire to look into.

EPHESIANS (PSEUDO) 3:12—Church's world mission (3:1–4:24)

Theme	EPH	Paul	NT
Boldness for access by faith	**3:12** [12]In whom we have boldness and access with confidence by the faith of him.	**Rom 5:1–2** [1]Therefore being justified by faith, we have peace with God through our Lord Jesus Christ: [2]By whom also we have access by faith into this grace wherein we stand, and rejoice in hope of the glory of God.	**Heb 4:16** [16]Let us therefore come boldly unto the throne of grace, that we may obtain mercy, and find grace to help in time of need.

EPHESIANS (PSEUDO) 3:13—Church's world mission (3:1–4:24)

Theme	EPH	Paul
Tribulations are your glory	**3:13** [13]Wherefore I desire that ye faint not at my tribulations for you, which is your glory.	**Col 1:22, 24** [22]In the body of his flesh through death, to present you holy and unblameable and unreproveable in his sight: . . . [24]Who now rejoice in my sufferings for you, and fill up that which is behind of the afflictions of Christ in my flesh for his body's sake, which is the church: **2 Tim 2:10 (Pseudo)** [10]Therefore I endure all things for the elect's sakes, that they may also obtain the salvation which is in Christ Jesus with eternal glory.

EPHESIANS (PSEUDO) 3:16—Church's world mission (3:1–4:24)

Theme	EPH	Paul
Strengthened by inner Spirit	**3:16** [16]That he would grant you, according to the riches of his glory, to be strengthened with might by his Spirit in the inner man; **6:10** [10]Finally, my brethren, be strong in the Lord, and in the power of his might.	**Rom 7:22** [22]For I delight in the law of God after the inward man: **2 Cor 4:16** [16]For which cause we faint not; but though our outward man perish, yet the inward man is renewed day by day. **Col 1:11** [11]Strengthened with all might, according to his glorious power, unto all patience and longsuffering with joyfulness;

EPHESIANS (PSEUDO) 3:17—Church's world mission (3:1–4:24)

Theme	EPH	Jn	Paul
Christ dwelling in heart, by love	**3:17** [17]That Christ may dwell in your hearts by faith; that ye, being rooted and grounded in love,	**14:23** [23]Jesus answered and said unto him, If a man love me, he will keep my words: and my Father will love him, and we will come unto him, and make our abode with him.	**Col 1:23** [23]If ye continue in the faith grounded and settled, and be not moved away from the hope of the gospel, which ye have heard, and which was preached to every creature which is under heaven; whereof I Paul am made a minister; **Col 2:7** [7]Rooted and built up in him, and stablished in the faith, as ye have been taught, abounding therein with thanksgiving.

EPHESIANS (PSEUDO) 3:18—Church's world mission (3:1–4:24)

Theme	EPH	Paul
Depth, breadth of God's love	**3:18** [18]May be able to comprehend with all saints what is the breadth, and length, and depth, and height;	**Col 2:2** [2]That their hearts might be comforted, being knit together in love, and unto all riches of the full assurance of understanding, to the acknowledgement of the mystery of God, and of the Father, and of Christ;

EPHESIANS (PSEUDO) 3:19—Church's world mission (3:1–4:24)

Theme	EPH	Paul
Love passes all knowledge	**3:19** [19]And to know the love of Christ, which passeth knowledge, that ye might be filled with all the fulness of God.	**Col 2:3, 9** [3]In whom are hid all the treasures of wisdom and knowledge. . . .[9]For in him dwelleth all the fulness of the Godhead bodily.

EPHESIANS (PSEUDO) 3:20—Church's world mission (3:1–4:24)

Theme	EPH	Paul
Abundant power, working in us	**3:20** [20]Now unto him that is able to do exceeding abundantly above all that we ask or think, according to the power that worketh in us,	**Rom 16:25–27** [25]Now to him that is of power to stablish you according to my gospel, and the preaching of Jesus Christ, according to the revelation of the mystery, which was kept secret since the world began, [26]But now is made manifest, and by the scriptures of the prophets, according to the commandment of the everlasting God, made known to all nations for the obedience of faith: [27]To God only wise, be glory through Jesus Christ for ever. Amen. **Col 1:29** [29]Whereunto I also labour, striving according to his working, which worketh in me mightily.

EPHESIANS (PSEUDO) 4:1—Church's world mission (3:1–4:24)

Theme	EPH	Paul
Prisoner of Lord, urge worthiness of vocation	**4:1** [1]I therefore, the prisoner of the Lord, beseech you that ye walk worthy of the vocation wherewith ye are called, **3:1** [1]For this cause I Paul, the prisoner of Jesus Christ for you Gentiles,	**Col 1:10** [10]That ye might walk worthy of the Lord unto all pleasing, being fruitful in every good work, and increasing in the knowledge of God;

EPHESIANS (PSEUDO) 4:2—Church's world mission (3:1–4:24)

Theme	EPH	Paul
Bear with other in love	**4:2** [2]With all lowliness and meekness, with longsuffering, forbearing one another in love;	**Col 3:12–13** [12]Put on therefore, as the elect of God, holy and beloved, bowels of mercies, kindness, humbleness of mind, meekness, longsuffering; [13]Forbearing one another, and forgiving one another, if any man have a quarrel against any: even as Christ forgave you, so also do ye.

EPHESIANS (PSEUDO) 4:3—Church's world mission (3:1–4:24)

Theme	EPH	Paul
Unity of Spirit, bond of peace	**4:3** [3]Endeavouring to keep the unity of the Spirit in the bond of peace.	**Col 3:14–15** [14]And above all these things put on charity, which is the bond of perfectness. [15]And let the peace of God rule in your hearts, to the which also ye are called in one body; and be ye thankful.

EPHESIANS (PSEUDO) 4:4—Church's world mission (3:1–4:24)

Theme	EPH	Paul
One body, one Spirit	**4:4** [4]There is one body, and one Spirit, even as ye are called in one hope of your calling;	**Rom 12:5** [5]So we, being many, are one body in Christ, and every one members one of another. **1 Cor 10:17** [17]For we being many are one bread, and one body: for we are all partakers of that one bread. **1 Cor 12:12–13** [12]For as the body is one, and hath many members, and all the members of that one body, being many, are one body: so also is Christ. [13]For by one Spirit are we all baptized into one body, whether we be Jews or Gentiles, whether we be bond or free; and have been all made to drink into one Spirit.

EPHESIANS (PSEUDO) 4:5—Church's world mission (3:1–4:24)

Theme	EPH	Paul
One Lord, one faith, one baptism	**4:5** [5]One Lord, one faith, one baptism,	**1 Cor 8:6** [6]But to us there is but one God, the Father, of whom are all things, and we in him; and one Lord Jesus Christ, by whom are all things, and we by him.

EPHESIANS (PSEUDO) 4:6—Church's world mission (3:1–4:24)

Theme	EPH	Paul
One God	**4:6** [6]One God and Father of all, who is above all, and through all, and in you all.	**1 Cor 12:6** [6]And there are diversities of operations, but it is the same God which worketh all in all.

EPHESIANS (PSEUDO) 4:7—Church's world mission (3:1–4:24)

Theme	EPH	Paul
Grace by measure of Christ	**4:7** [7]But unto every one of us is given grace according to the measure of the gift of Christ.	**Rom 12:3, 6** [3]For I say, through the grace given unto me, to every man that is among you, not to think of himself more highly than he ought to think; but to think soberly, according as God hath dealt to every man the measure of faith. . . . [6]Having then gifts differing according to the grace that is given to us, whether prophecy, let us prophesy according to the proportion of faith; **1 Cor 12:28** [28]And God hath set some in the church, first apostles, secondarily prophets, thirdly teachers, after that miracles, then gifts of healings, helps, governments, diversities of tongues.

EPHESIANS (PSEUDO) 4:8—Church's world mission (3:1–4:24)

Theme	EPH	Paul	Jewish Writings
Ascended to give gifts to humanity	**4:8** [8]Wherefore he saith, When he ascended up on high, he led captivity captive, and gave gifts unto men.	**Col 2:15** [15]And having spoiled principalities and powers, he made a show of them openly, triumphing over them in it.	**Ps 68:19** [19]Blessed be the Lord, who daily loadeth us with benefits, even the God of our salvation. Selah

EPHESIANS (PSEUDO) 4:11—Church's world mission (3:1–4:24)

Theme	EPH	Paul
Apostles, prophets, evangelists, pastors, teachers	**4:11** [11]And he gave some, apostles; and some, prophets; & some, evangelists; and some, pastors and teachers;	**1 Cor 12:28** [28]And God hath set some in the church, first apostles, secondarily prophets, thirdly teachers, after that miracles, then gifts of healings, helps, governments, diversities of tongues.

EPHESIANS (PSEUDO) 4:13—Church's world mission (3:1–4:24)

Theme	EPH	Paul
Unity of faith	**4:13** [13]Till we all come in the unity of the faith, and of the knowledge of the Son of God, unto a perfect man, unto the measure of the stature of the fulness of Christ:	**Col 1:28** [28]Whom we preach, warning every man, and teaching every man in all wisdom; that we may present every man perfect in Christ Jesus:

EPHESIANS (PSEUDO) 4:14—Church's world mission (3:1–4:24)

Theme	EPH	Paul	NT	Other
Doctrinal shifts	**4:14** [14]That we henceforth be no more children, tossed to and fro, and carried about with every wind of doctrine, by the sleight of men, and cunning craftiness, whereby they lie in wait to deceive;	**1 Cor 14:20** [20]Brethren, be not children in understanding: howbeit in malice be ye children, but in understanding be men. **Col 2:4, 8** [4]And this I say, lest any man should beguile you with enticing words. . . . [8]Beware lest any man spoil you through philosophy and vain deceit, after the tradition of men, after the rudiments of the world, and not after Christ.	**Heb 13:9** [6]So that we may boldly say, The Lord is my helper, and I will not fear what man shall do unto me. **Jas 1:6** [6]But let him ask in faith, nothing wavering. For he that wavereth is like a wave of the sea driven with the wind and tossed.	**Q-Quelle** Commissioning the 70: Eph 4:14/1 Cor 14:20/[Mt 10:7-16]/[Lk 10:1-12 (QS 20-23 [Thom 73;14:2])]

EPHESIANS (PSEUDO) 4:15—Church's world mission (3:1–4:24)

Theme	EPH	Paul
Speaking truth in love	**4:15** [15]But speaking the truth in love, may grow up into him in all things, which is the head, even Christ:	**1 Cor 11:3** [3]But I would have you know, that the head of every man is Christ; and the head of the woman is the man; and the head of Christ is God. **Col 1:18** [18]And he is the head of the body, the church: who is the beginning, the firstborn from the dead; that in all things he might have the preeminence. **Col 2:19** [19]And not holding the Head, from which all the body by joints and bands having nourishment ministered, and knit together, increaseth with the increase of God.

EPHESIANS (PSEUDO) 4:16—Church's world mission (3:1–4:24)

Theme	EPH	Paul
Effective workings of body	**4:16** [16]From whom the whole body fitly joined together and compacted by that which every joint supplieth, according to the effectual working in the measure of every part, maketh increase of the body unto the edifying of itself in love.	**Col 2:19** [19]And not holding the Head, from which all the body by joints and bands having nourishment ministered, and knit together, increaseth with the increase of God.

EPHESIANS (PSEUDO) 4:17—Church's world mission (3:1–4:24)

Theme	EPH	Paul
Vanity of Gentiles	**4:17** [17]This I say therefore, and testify in the Lord, that ye henceforth walk not as other Gentiles walk, in the vanity of their mind,	**Rom 1:21** [21]Because that, when they knew God, they glorified him not as God, neither were thankful; but became vain in their imaginations, and their foolish heart was darkened.

EPHESIANS (PSEUDO) 4:18—Church's world mission (3:1–4:24)

Theme	EPH	Paul	NT
Alienation	**4:18** [18]Having the understanding darkened, being alienated from the life of God through the ignorance that is in them, because of the blindness of their heart:	**Col 1:21** [21]And you, that were sometime alienated and enemies in your mind by wicked works, yet now hath he reconciled	**1 Pet 1:14** [14]As obedient children, not fashioning yourselves according to the former lusts in your ignorance:

EPHESIANS (PSEUDO) 4:19—Church's world mission (3:1–4:24)

Theme	EPH	Paul
Uncleanliness	**4:19** [19]Who being past feeling have given themselves over unto lasciviousness, to work all uncleanness with greediness.	**Col 3:5** [5]Mortify therefore your members which are upon the earth; fornication, uncleanness, inordinate affection, evil concupiscence, and covetousness, which is idolatry:

EPHESIANS (PSEUDO) 4:22—Church's world mission (3:1–4:24)

Theme	EPH	Paul
Old man is corrupt	**4:22** [22]That ye put off concerning the former conversation the old man, which is corrupt according to the deceitful lusts;	**Rom 8:13** [13]For if ye live after the flesh, ye shall die: but if ye through the Spirit do mortify the deeds of the body, ye shall live. **Gal 6:8** [8]For he that soweth to his flesh shall of the flesh reap corruption; but he that soweth to the Spirit shall of the Spirit reap life everlasting. **Col 3:9** [9]Lie not one to another, seeing that ye have put off the old man with his deeds;

EPHESIANS (PSEUDO) 4:23—Church's world mission (3:1–4:24)

Theme	EPH	Paul
Renewed in spirit of mind	**4:23** [23]And be renewed in the spirit of your mind;	**Rom 12:2** [2]And be not conformed to this world: but be ye transformed by the renewing of your mind, that ye may prove what is that good, and acceptable, and perfect, will of God.

EPHESIANS (PSEUDO) 4:24—Church's world mission (3:1–4:24)

Theme	EPH	Paul	Jewish Writings
New person is holy	**4:24** [24]And that ye put on the new man, which after God is created in righteousness and true holiness.	**Col 3:10** [10]And have put on the new man, which is renewed in knowledge after the image of him that created him:	**Gen 1:26–27** [26]And God said, Let us make man in our image, after our likeness: and let them have dominion over the fish of the sea, and over the fowl of the air, and over the cattle, and over all the earth, and over every creeping thing that creepeth upon the earth. [27]So God created man in his own image, in the image of God created he him; male and female created he them.

UNIFYING BEHAVIOR (4:25–6:20)

EPHESIANS (PSEUDO) 4:25—Unifying Behavior (4:25–6:20)

Theme	EPH	Jewish Writings
Put away lying, speak truth	**4:25** [25]Wherefore putting away lying, speak every man truth with his neighbour: for we are members one of another.	**Zech 8:16** [16]These are the things that ye shall do; Speak ye every man the truth to his neighbour; execute the judgment of truth and peace in your gates:

EPHESIANS (PSEUDO) 4:26—Unifying Behavior (4:25–6:20)

Theme	EPH	Mt	Jewish Writings
Be angry, sin not	**4:26** [26]Be ye angry, and sin not: let not the sun go down upon your wrath:	**Mt 5:22** [22]But I say unto you, That whosoever is angry with his brother without a cause shall be in danger of the judgment: and whosoever shall say to his brother, RacaRaca, shall be in danger of the council: but whosoever shall say, Thou fool, shall be in danger of hell fire.	**Ps 4:5 (See LXX)** [5]Offer the sacrifices of righteousness, and put your trust in the LORD.

EPHESIANS (PSEUDO) 4:27—Unifying Behavior (4:25–6:20)

Theme	EPH	Paul
Turn from devil	**4:27** [27]Neither give place to the devil.	**2 Cor 2:11** [11]Lest Satan should get an advantage of us: for we are not ignorant of his devices.

EPHESIANS (PSEUDO) 4:28—Unifying Behavior (4:25–6:20)

Theme	EPH	Paul
Labor in good	**4:28** [28]Let him that stole steal no more: but rather let him labour, working with his hands the thing which is good, that he may have to give to him that needeth.	**1 Thes 4:11** [11]And that ye study to be quiet, and to do your own business, and to work with your own hands, as we commanded you;

EPHESIANS (PSEUDO) 4:29—Unifying Behavior (4:25–6:20)

Theme	EPH	Paul
Edify others	**4:29** [29]Let no corrupt communication proceed out of your mouth, but that which is good to the use of edifying, that it may minister grace unto the hearers. **5:4** [4]Neither filthiness, nor foolish talking, nor jesting, which are not convenient: but rather giving of thanks.	**Col 3:16** [16]Let the word of Christ dwell in you richly in all wisdom; teaching and admonishing one another in psalms and hymns and spiritual songs, singing with grace in your hearts to the Lord. **Col 4:6** [6]Let your speech be alway with grace, seasoned with salt, that ye may know how ye ought to answer every man.

EPHESIANS (PSEUDO) 4:31—Unifying Behavior (4:25–6:20)

Theme	EPH	Paul
Do not be angry	**4:31** [31]Let all bitterness, and wrath, and anger, and clamour, and evil speaking, be put away from you, with all malice:	**Col 3:8** [8]But now ye also put off all these; anger, wrath, malice, blasphemy, filthy communication out of your mouth.

EPHESIANS (PSEUDO) 4:32—Unifying Behavior (4:25–6:20)

Theme	EPH	Mt	Mk	Paul	Other
Love one another	**4:32** [32]And be ye kind one to another, tender-hearted, forgiving one another, even as God for Christ's sake hath forgiven you.	**6:14** [14]For if ye forgive men their trespasses, your heavenly Father will also forgive you:	**9:50** [50]Salt is good: but if the salt have lost his saltness, wherewith will ye season it? Have salt in yourselves, and have peace one with another.	**Rom 12:10** [10]Be kindly affectioned one to another with brotherly love; in honour preferring one another; **Rom 12:18** [18]If it be possible, as much as lieth in you, live peaceably with all men. **Rom 14:19** [19]Let us therefore follow after the things which make for peace, and things wherewith one may edify another. **1 Cor 7:15** [15]But if the unbelieving depart, let him depart. A brother or a sister is not under bondage in such cases: but God hath called us to peace. **2 Cor 13:11** [11]Finally, brethren, farewell. Be perfect, be of good comfort, be of one mind, live in peace; and the God of love and peace shall be with you. **Gal 6:10** [10]As we have therefore opportunity, let us do good unto all men, especially unto them who are of the household of faith. **Col 3:12–14** [12]Put on therefore, as the elect of God, holy and beloved, bowels of mercies, kindness, humbleness of mind, meekness, longsuffering; [13]Forbearing one another, and forgiving one another, if any man have a quarrel against any: even as Christ forgave you, so also do ye. [14]And above all these things put on charity, which is the bond of perfectness. **1 Thes 3:12** [12]And the Lord make you to increase and abound in love one toward another, and toward all men, even as we do toward you: **1 Thes 4:9** [9]But as touching brotherly love ye need not that I write unto you: for ye yourselves are taught of God to love one another. **1 Thes 5:12–13** [12]And we beseech you, brethren, to know them which labour among you, and are over you in the Lord, and admonish you; [13]And to esteem them very highly in love for their work's sake. And be at peace among yourselves. **1 Thes 5:15** [15]See that none render evil for evil unto any man; but ever follow that which is good, both among yourselves, and to all men. **2 Thes 1:3** [3]We are bound to thank God always for you, brethren, as it is meet, because that your faith groweth exceedingly, and the charity of every one of you all toward each other aboundeth;	**Q-Quelle** Beatitudes: Eph 4:32/2 Cor 13:11/Gal 6:10/1 Thes 3:12/[Mt 5:3-12]/[Lk 6:20b-23 (QS 8 [Thom 54,68,69])]; Parable of Salt: Eph 4:32/1 Cor 7:15/[Mt 5:13]/Mk 9:49-50/[Lk 14:34-35 (QS 53)

EPHESIANS (PSEUDO) 5:1—Unifying Behavior (4:25–6:20)

Theme	EPH	Mt	Other
Follow God	**5:1** [1]Be ye therefore followers of God, as dear children;	**5:45** [45]That ye may be the children of your Father which is in heaven: for he maketh his sun to rise on the evil and on the good, and sendeth rain on the just and on the unjust. **5:48** [48]Be ye therefore perfect, even as your Father which is in heaven is perfect.	**Q-Quelle** Love of enemies: Eph 5:1/Mt 5:38-48, [Mt 7:12]/[Lk 6:27-36 (QS 9 [Thom 95, 6:2])]

EPHESIANS (PSEUDO) 5:2—Unifying Behavior (4:25–6:20)

Theme	EPH	Jn	Paul	Jewish Writings
Walk in love	**5:2** [2]And walk in love, as Christ also hath loved us, and hath given himself for us an offering and a sacrifice to God for a sweetsmelling savour.	**1 Jn 3:16** [16]Hereby perceive we the love of God, because he laid down his life for us: and we ought to lay down our lives for the brethren.	**Gal 2:20** [20]I am crucified with Christ: nevertheless I live; yet not I, but Christ liveth in me: and the life which I now live in the flesh I live by the faith of the Son of God, who loved me, and gave himself for me.	**Ex 29:18** [18]And thou shalt burn the whole ram upon the altar: it is a burnt offering unto the LORD: it is a sweet savour, an offering made by fire unto the LORD. **Ps 40:7** [7]Then said I, Lo, I come: in the volume of the book it is written of me,

EPHESIANS (PSEUDO) 5:3—Unifying Behavior (4:25–6:20)

Theme	EPH	Paul
Become saints	**5:3** [3]But fornication, and all uncleanness, or covetousness, let it not be once named among you, as becometh saints;	**Gal 5:19** [19]Now the works of the flesh are manifest, which are these; Adultery, fornication, uncleanness, lasciviousness, **Col 3:5** [5]Mortify therefore your members which are upon the earth; fornication, uncleanness, inordinate affection, evil concupiscence, and covetousness, which is idolatry:

EPHESIANS (PSEUDO) 5:4—Unifying Behavior (4:25–6:20)

Theme	EPH	Paul
Do not sin, but give thanks in all things	**5:4** [4]Neither filthiness, nor foolish talking, nor jesting, which are not convenient: but rather giving of thanks. **4:29** [29]Let no corrupt communication proceed out of your mouth, but that which is good to the use of edifying, that it may minister grace unto the hearers.	**Col 3:8** [8]But now ye also put off all these; anger, wrath, malice, blasphemy, filthy communication out of your mouth.

EPHESIANS (PSEUDO) 5:5—Unifying Behavior (4:25–6:20)

Theme	EPH	Mt	Mk	Lk	Jn
Behavior unbefitting God's Kingdom	**5:5** [5]For this ye know, that no whore-monger, nor unclean person, nor covetous man, who is an idolater, hath any inheritance in the kingdom of Christ and of God.	**5:20** [20]For I say unto you, That except your righteousness shall exceed the righteousness of the scribes and Pharisees, ye shall in no case enter into the kingdom of heaven. **6:33** [33]But seek ye first the kingdom of God, and his righteousness; and all these things shall be added unto you. **12:28** [28]But if I cast out devils by the Spirit of God, then the kingdom of God is come unto you. **18:3** [3]And said, Verily I say unto you, Except ye be converted, and become as little children, ye shall not enter into the kingdom of heaven.	**10:15** [15]Verily I say unto you, Whosoever shall not receive the kingdom of God as a little child, he shall not enter therein.	**11:20** [20]But if I with the finger of God cast out devils, no doubt the kingdom of God is come upon you. **12:31** [31]But rather seek ye the kingdom of God; and all these things shall be added unto you.	**3:5** [5]Jesus answered, Verily, verily, I say unto thee, Except a man be born of water and of the Spirit, he cannot enter into the kingdom of God.

EPHESIANS (PSEUDO) 5:6—Unifying Behavior (4:25–6:20)

Theme	EPH	Paul
Do not be deceived	**5:6** [6]Let no man deceive you with vain words: for because of these things cometh the wrath of God upon the children of disobedience.	**Rom 1:18** [18]For the wrath of God is revealed from heaven against all ungodliness and unrighteousness of men, who hold the truth in unrighteousness; **Col 2:4** [4]And this I say, lest any man should beguile you with enticing words. **Col 2:8** [8]Beware lest any man spoil you through philosophy and vain deceit, after the tradition of men, after the rudiments of the world, and not after Christ.

EPHESIANS (PSEUDO) 5:8—Unifying Behavior (4:25–6:20)

Theme	EPH
Walk as children of light	**5:8** [8]For ye were sometimes darkness, but now are ye light in the Lord: walk as children of light: **2:11–13** [11]Wherefore remember, that ye being in time past Gentiles in the flesh, who are called Uncircumcision by that which is called the Circumcision in the flesh made by hands; [12]That at that time ye were without Christ, being aliens from the commonwealth of Israel, and strangers from the covenants of promise, having no hope, and without God in the world: [13]But now in Christ Jesus ye who sometimes were far off are made nigh by the blood of Christ.

Paul	Other
Rom 14:17 [17](As it is written, I have made thee a father of many nations,) before him whom he believed, even God, who quickeneth the dead, and calleth those things which be not as though they were. **1 Cor 4:20** [20]For the kingdom of God is not in word, but in power. **1 Cor 6:9–10** [9]Know ye not that the unrighteous shall not inherit the kingdom of God? Be not deceived: neither fornicators, nor idolaters, nor adulterers, nor effeminate, nor abusers of themselves with mankind, [10]Nor thieves, nor covetous, nor drunkards, nor revilers, nor extortioners, shall inherit the kingdom of God. **Gal 5:19–21** [19]Because that which may be known of God is manifest in them; for God hath showed it unto them. [20]For the invisible things of him from the creation of the world are clearly seen, being understood by the things that are made, even his eternal power and Godhead; so that they are without excuse: [21]Because that, when they knew God, they glorified him not as God, neither were thankful; but became vain in their imaginations, and their foolish heart was darkened. **Col 3:5** [5]Mortify therefore your members which are upon the earth; fornication, uncleanness, inordinate affection, evil concupiscence, and covetousness, which is idolatry:	**Q-Quelle** Anxiety: Eph 5:5/ Rom 14:17/1 Cor 6:9-10/Gal 5:19-21/Mt 6:25-34/Lk 12:22-32 (QS 39 [Thom 36]); Beezebul controversy: Eph 5:5/Rom 14:17/[Mt 9:32-34, 22-30]/[Mk 3:22-27]/Lk 11:14-23(QS 28 [Thom 35])

Jn	Paul
12:36 [36]While ye have light, believe in the light, that ye may be the children of light. These things spake Jesus, and departed, and did hide himself from them.	**Col 1:12–13** [12]Giving thanks unto the Father, which hath made us meet to be partakers of the inheritance of the saints in light: [13]Who hath delivered us from the power of darkness, and hath translated us into the kingdom of his dear Son:

EPHESIANS (PSEUDO) 5:9—Unifying Behavior (4:25–6:20)

Theme	EPH	Paul
Fruit of Spirit	**5:9** [9](For the fruit of the Spirit is in all goodness and righteousness and truth;)	**Gal 5:22** [22]But the fruit of the Spirit is love, joy, peace, longsuffering, gentleness, goodness, faith,

EPHESIANS (PSEUDO) 5:10—Unifying Behavior (4:25–6:20)

Theme	EPH	Paul
Acceptable behavior	**5:10** [10]Proving what is acceptable unto the Lord.	**Rom 12:12** [12]Rejoicing in hope; patient in tribulation; continuing instant in prayer;

EPHESIANS (PSEUDO) 5:11—Unifying Behavior (4:25–6:20)

Theme	EPH	Paul
Reprove darkness	**5:11** [11]And have no fellowship with the unfruitful works of darkness, but rather reprove them.	**Rom 13:12** [12]The night is far spent, the day is at hand: let us therefore cast off the works of darkness, and let us put on the armour of light.

EPHESIANS (PSEUDO) 5:13—Unifying Behavior (4:25–6:20)

Theme	EPH	Jn
Manifest light	**5:13** [13]But all things that are reproved are made manifest by the light: for whatsoever doth make manifest is light.	**3:20-21** [20]For every one that doeth evil hateth the light, neither cometh to the light, lest his deeds should be reproved. [21]But he that doeth truth cometh to the light, that his deeds may be made manifest, that they are wrought in God.

EPHESIANS (PSEUDO) 5:14—Unifying Behavior (4:25–6:20)

Theme	EPH	Jewish Writings
Awake from sleep to Christ's light	**5:14** [14]Wherefore he saith, Awake thou that sleepest, and arise from the dead, and Christ shall give thee light.	**Is 26:19** [19]Thy dead men shall live, together with my dead body shall they arise. Awake and sing, ye that dwell in dust: for thy dew is as the dew of herbs, and the earth shall cast out the dead. **Is 60:1** [1]Arise, shine; for thy light is come, and the glory of the LORD is risen upon thee.

EPHESIANS (PSEUDO) 5:15–16—Unifying Behavior (4:25–6:20)

Theme	EPH	Paul
Walk wisely	**5:15–16** [15]See then that ye walk circumspectly, not as fools, but as wise, [16]Redeeming the time, because the days are evil.	**Col 4:5** [5]Walk in wisdom toward them that are without, redeeming the time.

EPHESIANS (PSEUDO) 5:18—Unifying Behavior (4:25–6:20)

Theme	EPH	Lk	Jewish Writings
Be filled with Spirit	**5:18** [18]And be not drunk with wine, wherein is excess; but be filled with the Spirit;	**21:34** [34]And take heed to yourselves, lest at any time your hearts be overcharged with surfeiting, and drunkenness, and cares of this life, and so that day come upon you unawares.	**Prov 23:31 (See LXX)** [31]Look not thou upon the wine when it is red, when it giveth his colour in the cup, when it moveth itself aright.

EPHESIANS (PSEUDO) 5:19—Unifying Behavior (4:25–6:20)

Theme	EPH	Paul
Use psalms, hymns, songs	**5:19** [19]Speaking to yourselves in psalms and hymns and spiritual songs, singing and making melody in your heart to the Lord;	**Col 3:16** [16]Let the word of Christ dwell in you richly in all wisdom; teaching and admonishing one another in psalms and hymns and spiritual songs, singing with grace in your hearts to the Lord.

EPHESIANS (PSEUDO) 5:20—Unifying Behavior (4:25–6:20)

Theme	EPH	Paul
Thanks to God	**5:20** [20]Giving thanks always for all things unto God and the Father in the name of our Lord Jesus Christ;	**Col 3:17** [17]And whatsoever ye do in word or deed, do all in the name of the Lord Jesus, giving thanks to God and the Father by him.

EPHESIANS (PSEUDO) 5:21—Unifying Behavior (4:25–6:20)

Theme	EPH	NT
Submit to one another	**5:21** [21]Submitting yourselves one to another in the fear of God.	**1 Pet 5:5** [5]Likewise, ye younger, submit yourselves unto the elder. Yea, all of you be subject one to another, and be clothed with humility: for God resisteth the proud, and giveth grace to the humble.

EPHESIANS (PSEUDO) 5:22—Unifying Behavior (4:25–6:20)

Theme	EPH	Paul	NT
Submit in marriage, as lesson in Christ	**5:22** [22]Wives, submit yourselves unto your own husbands, as unto the Lord.	**Col 3:18—4:1** [18]Wives, submit yourselves unto your own husbands, as it is fit in the Lord. [19]Husbands, love your wives, and be not bitter against them. [20]Children, obey your parents in all things: for this is well pleasing unto the Lord. [21]Fathers, provoke not your children to anger, lest they be discouraged. [22]Servants, obey in all things your masters according to the flesh; not with eyeservice, as menpleasers; but in singleness of heart, fearing God: [23]And whatsoever ye do, do it heartily, as to the Lord, and not unto men; [24]Knowing that of the Lord ye shall receive the reward of the inheritance: for ye serve the Lord Christ. [25]But he that doeth wrong shall receive for the wrong which he hath done: and there is no respect of persons. [1]Masters, give unto your servants that which is just and equal; knowing that ye also have a Master in heaven.	**1 Pet 3:1–7** [1]Likewise, ye wives, be in subjection to your own husbands; that, if any obey not the word, they also may without the word be won by the conversation of the wives; [2]While they behold your chaste conversation coupled with fear. [3]Whose adorning let it not be that outward adorning of plaiting the hair, and of wearing of gold, or of putting on of apparel; [4]But let it be the hidden man of the heart, in that which is not corruptible, even the ornament of a meek and quiet spirit, which is in the sight of God of great price. [5]For after this manner in the old time the holy women also, who trusted in God, adorned themselves, being in subjection unto their own husbands: [6]Even as Sarah obeyed Abraham, calling him lord: whose daughters ye are, as long as ye do well, and are not afraid with any amazement. [7]Likewise, ye husbands, dwell with them according to knowledge, giving honour unto the wife, as unto the weaker vessel, and as being heirs together of the grace of life; that your prayers be not hindered.

EPHESIANS (PSEUDO) 5:23—Unifying Behavior (4:25–6:20)

Theme	EPH	Paul
Christ head of church, husband head of wife	**5:23** [23]For the husband is the head of the wife, even as Christ is the head of the church: and he is the saviour of the body.	**1 Cor 11:3** [3]But I would have you know, that the head of every man is Christ; and the head of the woman is the man; and the head of Christ is God. **Col 1:18** [18]And he is the head of the body, the church: who is the beginning, the firstborn from the dead; that in all things he might have the preeminence.

EPHESIANS (PSEUDO) 5:24–33—Unifying Behavior (4:25–6:20)

Theme	EPH	Mt	Mk	Lk
Example of marital union: church & Christ	**5:24–33** [24]Therefore as the church is subject unto Christ, so let the wives be to their own husbands in every thing. [25]Husbands, love your wives, even as Christ also loved the church, and gave himself for it; [26]That he might sanctify and cleanse it with the washing of water by the word, [27]That he might present it to himself a glorious church, not having spot, or wrinkle, or any such thing; but that it should be holy and without blemish. [28]So ought men to love their wives as their own bodies. He that loveth his wife loveth himself. [29]For no man ever yet hated his own flesh; but nourisheth and cherisheth it, even as the Lord the church: [30]For we are members of his body, of his flesh, and of his bones. [31]For this cause shall a man leave his father and mother, and shall be joined unto his wife, and they two shall be one flesh. [32]This is a great mystery: but I speak concerning Christ and the church. [33]Nevertheless let every one of you in particular so love his wife even as himself; and the wife see that she reverence her husband.	**2:1–4** [1]Now when Jesus was born in Bethlehem of Judaea in the days of Herod the king, behold, there came wise men from the east to Jerusalem, [2]Saying, Where is he that is born King of the Jews? for we have seen his star in the east, and are come to worship him. [3]When Herod the king had heard these things, he was troubled, and all Jerusalem with him. [4]And when he had gathered all the chief priests and scribes of the people together, he demanded of them where Christ should be born. **9:15** [15]And Jesus said unto them, Can the children of the bridechamber mourn, as long as the bridegroom is with them? but the days will come, when the bridegroom shall be taken from them, and then shall they fast. **25:1–13** [1]Then shall the kingdom of heaven be likened unto ten virgins, which took their lamps, and went forth to meet the bridegroom. [2]And five of them were wise, and five were foolish. [3]They that were foolish took their lamps, and took no oil with them: [4]But the wise took oil in their vessels with their lamps. [5]While the bridegroom tarried, they all slumbered and slept. [6]And at midnight there was a cry made, Behold, the bridegroom cometh; go ye out to meet him. [7]Then all those virgins arose, and trimmed their lamps. [8]And the foolish said unto the wise, Give us of your oil; for our lamps are gone out. [9]But the wise answered, saying, Not so; lest there be not enough for us and you: but go ye rather to them that sell, and buy for yourselves. [10]And while they went to buy, the bridegroom came; and they that were ready went in with him to the marriage: and the door was shut. [11]Afterward came also the other virgins, saying, Lord, Lord, open to us. [12]But he answered and said, Verily I say unto you, I know you not. [13]Watch therefore, for ye know neither the day nor the hour wherein the Son of man cometh.	**2:1** [1]And again he entered into Capernaum after some days; and it was noised that he was in the house.	**5:34** [34]And he said unto them, Can ye make the children of the bridechamber fast, while the bridegroom is with them? **12:36** [36]And ye yourselves like unto men that wait for their lord, when he will return from the wedding; that when he cometh and knocketh, they may open unto him immediately.

Paul	Jewish Writings	Other
Rom 7:1–4	**Gen 2**	**Q-Quelle**
[1]Know ye not, brethren, (for I speak to them that know the law,) how that the law hath dominion over a man as long as he liveth? [2]For the woman which hath an husband is bound by the law to her husband so long as he liveth; but if the husband be dead, she is loosed from the law of her husband. [3]So then if, while her husband liveth, she be married to another man, she shall be called an adulteress: but if her husband be dead, she is free from that law; so that she is no adulteress, though she be married to another man. [4]Wherefore, my brethren, ye also are become dead to the law by the body of Christ; that ye should be married to another, even to him who is raised from the dead, that we should bring forth fruit unto God.	[1]Thus the heavens and the earth were finished, and all the host of them. [2]And on the seventh day God ended his work which he had made; and he rested on the seventh day from all his work which he had made. [3]And God blessed the seventh day, and sanctified it: because that in it he had rested from all his work which God created and made. [4]These are the generations of the heavens and of the earth when they were created, in the day that the LORD God made the earth and the heavens, [5]And every plant of the field before it was in the earth, and every herb of the field before it grew: for the LORD God had not caused it to rain upon the earth, and there was not a man to till the ground. [6]But there went up a mist from the earth, and watered the whole face of the ground. [7]And the LORD God formed man of the dust of the ground, and breathed into his nostrils the breath of life; and man became a living soul. [8]And the LORD God planted a garden eastward in Eden; and there he put the man whom he had formed. [9]And out of the ground made the LORD God to grow every tree that is pleasant to the sight, and good for food; the tree of life also in the midst of the garden, and the tree of knowledge of good and evil. [10]And a river went out of Eden to water the garden; and from thence it was parted, and became into four heads. [11]The name of the first is Pison: that is it which compasseth the whole land of Havilah, where there is gold; [12]And the gold of that land is good: there is bdellium and the onyx stone. [13]And the name of the second river is Gihon: the same is it that compasseth the whole land of Ethiopia. [14]And the name of the third river is Hiddekel: that is it which goeth toward the east of Assyria. And the fourth river is Euphrates. [15]And the LORD God took the man, and put him into the garden of Eden to dress it and to keep it. [16]And the LORD God commanded the man, saying, Of every tree of the garden thou mayest freely eat: [17]But of the tree of the knowledge of good and evil, thou shalt not eat of it: for in the day that thou eatest thereof thou shalt surely die. [18]And the LORD God said, It is not good that the man should be alone; I will make him an help meet for him. [19]And out of the ground the LORD God formed every beast of the field, and every fowl of the air; and brought them unto Adam to see what he would call them: and whatsoever Adam called every living creature, that was the name thereof. [20]And Adam gave names to all cattle, and to the fowl of the air, and to every beast of the field; but for Adam there was not found an help meet for him. [21]And the LORD God caused a deep sleep to fall upon Adam, and he slept: and he took one of his ribs, and closed up the flesh instead thereof; [22]And the rib, which the LORD God had taken from man, made he a woman, and brought her unto the man. [23]And Adam said, This is now bone of my bones, and flesh of my flesh: she shall be called Woman, because she was taken out of Man. [24]Therefore shall a man leave his father and his mother, and shall cleave unto his wife: and they shall be one flesh. [25]And they were both naked, the man and his wife, and were not ashamed.	Watchful & Faithful: Eph 5:24-33/ Rom 7:1-4/[Mt 24:42-51]/ Lk 12:35-48 (QS 40)

EPHESIANS (PSEUDO) 5:25—Unifying Behavior (4:25–6:20)

Theme	EPH	Paul
Love wife as Christ loves church	**5:25** [25]Husbands, love your wives, even as Christ also loved the church, and gave himself for it;	**Col 3:19** [19]Husbands, love your wives, and be not bitter against them. **1 Tim 2:6 (Pseudo)** [6]Who gave himself a ransom for all, to be testified in due time.

EPHESIANS (PSEUDO) 5:26—Unifying Behavior (4:25–6:20)

Theme	EPH	Paul
Be cleansed in the word	**5:26** [26]That he might sanctify and cleanse it with the washing of water by the word,	**Rom 6:4** [4]Therefore we are buried with him by baptism into death: that like as Christ was raised up from the dead by the glory of the Father, even so we also should walk in newness of life. **Tit 3:5–7 (Pseudo)** [5]Not by works of righteousness which we have done, but according to his mercy he saved us, by the washing of regeneration, and renewing of the Holy Ghost; [6]Which he shed on us abundantly through Jesus Christ our Saviour; [7]That being justified by his grace, we should be made heirs according to the hope of eternal life.

EPHESIANS (PSEUDO) 5:27—Unifying Behavior (4:25–6:20)

Theme	EPH	Paul
Present self as holy	**5:27** [27]That he might present it to himself a glorious church, not having spot, or wrinkle, or any such thing; but that it should be holy and without blemish.	**2 Cor 11:2** [2]For I am jealous over you with godly jealousy: for I have espoused you to one husband, that I may present you as a chaste virgin to Christ. **Col 1:22** [22]In the body of his flesh through death, to present you holy and unblameable and unreproveable in his sight:

EPHESIANS (PSEUDO) 5:30—Unifying Behavior (4:25–6:20)

Theme	EPH	Paul
Members of Christ's body	**5:30** [30]For we are members of his body, of his flesh, and of his bones.	**Rom 12:5** [5]So we, being many, are one body in Christ, and every one members one of another. **1 Cor 6:15** [15]Know ye not that your bodies are the members of Christ? shall I then take the members of Christ, and make them the members of an harlot? God forbid.

EPHESIANS (PSEUDO) 5:31—Unifying Behavior (4:25–6:20)

Theme	EPH	Mt	Mk	Jewish Writings
Leave parents to be joined with wife	**5:31** [31]For this cause shall a man leave his father and mother, and shall be joined unto his wife, and they two shall be one flesh.	**19:5** [5]And said, For this cause shall a man leave father and mother, and shall cleave to his wife: and they twain shall be one flesh?	**10:7–8** [7]For this cause shall a man leave his father and mother, and cleave to his wife; [8]And they twain shall be one flesh: so then they are no more twain, but one flesh.	**Gen 2:24** [24]Therefore shall a man leave his father and his mother, and shall cleave unto his wife: and they shall be one flesh.

EPHESIANS (PSEUDO) 5:32—Unifying Behavior (4:25–6:20)

Theme	EPH	NT
Marriage, mystery concerning Christ & church	**5:32** [32]This is a great mystery: but I speak concerning Christ and the church.	**Rev 19:7** [7]Let us be glad and rejoice, and give honour to him: for the marriage of the Lamb is come, and his wife hath made herself ready.

EPHESIANS (PSEUDO) 6:1—Unifying Behavior (4:25–6:20)

Theme	EPH	Paul	Jewish Writings
Children obey parents	**6:1** [1]Children, obey your parents in the Lord: for this is right.	**Col 3:20** [20]Children, obey your parents in all things: for this is well pleasing unto the Lord.	**Prov 6:20** [20]My son, keep thy father's commandment, and forsake not the law of thy mother: **Sir 3:1–6** [1]Hear me your father, O children, and do thereafter, that ye may be safe. [2]For the Lord hath given the father honour over the children, and hath confirmed the authority of the mother over the sons. [3]Whoso honoureth his father maketh an atonement for his sins: [4]And he that honoureth his mother is as one that layeth up treasure. [5]Whoso honoureth his father shall have joy of his own children; and when he maketh his prayer, he shall be heard. [6]He that honoureth his father shall have a long life; and he that is obedient unto the Lord shall be a comfort to his mother.

EPHESIANS (PSEUDO) 6:2–3—Unifying Behavior (4:25–6:20)

Theme	EPH	Jewish Writings
Honor parents	**6:2–3** [2]Honour thy father and mother; (which is the first commandment with promise;) [3]That it may be well with thee, and thou mayest live long on the earth.	**Ex 20:12** [12]Honour thy father and thy mother: that thy days may be long upon the land which the LORD thy God giveth thee. **Dt 5:16** [16]Honour thy father and thy mother, as the LORD thy God hath commanded thee; that thy days may be prolonged, and that it may go well with thee, in the land which the LORD thy God giveth thee.

EPHESIANS (PSEUDO) 6:4—Unifying Behavior (4:25–6:20)

Theme	EPH	Paul
Nurture & admonish children	**6:4** [4]And, ye fathers, provoke not your children to wrath: but bring them up in the nurture and admonition of the Lord.	**Col 3:21–22** [21]Fathers, provoke not your children to anger, lest they be discouraged. [22]Servants, obey in all things your masters according to the flesh; not with eyeservice, as menpleasers; but in singleness of heart, fearing God:

EPHESIANS (PSEUDO) 6:5—Unifying Behavior (4:25–6:20)

Theme	EPH	Paul
Servants obey masters	**6:5** [5]Servants, be obedient to them that are your masters according to the flesh, with fear and trembling, in singleness of your heart, as unto Christ;	**Col 3:22–25** [22]Servants, obey in all things your masters according to the flesh; not with eyeservice, as menpleasers; but in singleness of heart, fearing God: [23]And whatsoever ye do, do it heartily, as to the Lord, and not unto men; [24]Knowing that of the Lord ye shall receive the reward of the inheritance: for ye serve the Lord Christ. [25]But he that doeth wrong shall receive for the wrong which he hath done: and there is no respect of persons. **1 Tim 6:1–2 (Pseudo)** [1]Let as many servants as are under the yoke count their own masters worthy of all honour, that the name of God and his doctrine be not blasphemed. [2]And they that have believing masters, let them not despise them, because they are brethren; but rather do them service, because they are faithful and beloved, partakers of the benefit. These things teach and exhort. **Tit 2:9–10 (Pseudo)** [9]Exhort servants to be obedient unto their own masters, and to please them well in all things; not answering again; [10]Not purloining, but showing all good fidelity; that they may adorn the doctrine of God our Saviour in all things

EPHESIANS (PSEUDO) 6:6—Unifying Behavior (4:25–6:20)

Theme	EPH	NT
Serve God by serving humanity	**6:6** [6]Not with eyeservice, as menpleasers; but as the servants of Christ, doing the will of God from the heart;	**1 Pet 2:18** [18]Servants, be subject to your masters with all fear; not only to the good and gentle, but also to the froward.

EPHESIANS (PSEUDO) 6:9—Unifying Behavior (4:25–6:20)

Theme	EPH	Paul
Treat all equally	**6:9** [9]And, ye masters, do the same things unto them, forbearing threatening: knowing that your Master also is in heaven; neither is there respect of persons with him.	**Col 4:1** [1]Masters, give unto your servants that which is just and equal; knowing that ye also have a Master in heaven.

EPHESIANS (PSEUDO) 6:11—Unifying Behavior (4:25–6:20)

Theme	EPH	Paul
Wear armor of God to protect from evil	**6:11** [11]Put on the whole armour of God, that ye may be able to stand against the wiles of the devil.	**Rom 13:12** [12]The night is far spent, the day is at hand: let us therefore cast off the works of darkness, and let us put on the armour of light. **2 Cor 6:7** [7]By the word of truth, by the power of God, by the armour of righteousness on the right hand and on the left, **2 Cor 10:4** [4](For the weapons of our warfare are not carnal, but mighty through God to the pulling down of strong holds;)

EPHESIANS (PSEUDO) 6:12—Unifying Behavior (4:25–6:20)

Theme	EPH	Paul
Problem is not flesh & blood, but dark powers	**6:12** [12]For we wrestle not against flesh and blood, but against principalities, against powers, against the rulers of the darkness of this world, against spiritual wickedness in high places. **1:21** [21]Far above all principality, and power, and might, and dominion, and every name that is named, not only in this world, but also in that which is to come: **2:2** [2]Wherein in time past ye walked according to the course of this world, according to the prince of the power of the air, the spirit that now worketh in the children of disobedience:	**Col 1:13** [13]Who hath delivered us from the power of darkness, and hath translated us into the kingdom of his dear Son:

EPHESIANS (PSEUDO) 6:13—Unifying Behavior (4:25–6:20)

Theme	EPH	Paul
Armor of God withstands evil	**6:13** [13]Wherefore take unto you the whole armour of God, that ye may be able to withstand in the evil day, and having done all, to stand.	**Rom 13:12** [12]The night is far spent, the day is at hand: let us therefore cast off the works of darkness, and let us put on the armour of light.

EPHESIANS (PSEUDO) 6:14—Unifying Behavior (4:25–6:20)

Theme	EPH	Lk	Paul	Jewish Writings	Other
Belt of truth & breastplate of righteousness	**6:14** [14]Stand therefore, having your loins girt about with truth, and having on the breastplate of righteousness;	**12:35** [35]Let your loins be girded about, and your lights burning;	**1 Thes 5:8** [8]But let us, who are of the day, be sober, putting on the breastplate of faith and love; and for an helmet, the hope of salvation.	**Wis 5:17–20** [17]He shall take to him his jealousy for complete armour, and make the creature his weapon for the revenge of his enemies. [18]He shall put on righteousness as a breastplate, and true judgment instead of an helmet. [19]He shall take holiness for an invincible shield. [20]His severe wrath shall he sharpen for a sword, and the world shall fight with him against the unwise. **Is 11:5** [5]And righteousness shall be the girdle of his loins, and faithfulness the girdle of his reins.	**Q-Quelle** Watchful and faithful: Eph 6:14/[Mt 24:42-51]/ Lk 12:35-48 (QS 41 [Thom 21:3, 103], QS 42)

EPHESIANS (PSEUDO) 6:15—Unifying Behavior (4:25–6:20)

Theme	EPH	Jewish Writings
Feet shod with gospel	**6:15** [15]And your feet shod with the preparation of the gospel of peace;	**Is 52:7** [7]How beautiful upon the mountains are the feet of him that bringeth good tidings, that publisheth peace; that bringeth good tidings of good, that publisheth salvation; that saith unto Zion, Thy God reigneth!

EPHESIANS (PSEUDO) 6:16—Unifying Behavior (4:25–6:20)

Theme	EPH	NT
Shield of faith	**6:16** [16]Above all, taking the shield of faith, wherewith ye shall be able to quench all the fiery darts of the wicked.	**1 Pet 5:9** [9]Whom resist stedfast in the faith, knowing that the same afflictions are accomplished in your brethren that are in the world.

EPHESIANS (PSEUDO) 6:17—Unifying Behavior (4:25–6:20)

Theme	EPH	Paul	Jewish Writings
Helmet of salvation, sword (Word) of Spirit	**6:17** [17]And take the helmet of salvation, and the sword of the Spirit, which is the word of God:	**1 Thes 5:8** [8]But let us, who are of the day, be sober, putting on the breastplate of faith and love; and for an helmet, the hope of salvation.	**Is 59:17** [17]For he put on righteousness as a breastplate, and an helmet of salvation upon his head; and he put on the garments of vengeance for clothing, and was clad with zeal as a cloak.

EPHESIANS (PSEUDO) 6:18—Unifying Behavior (4:25–6:20)

Theme	EPH	Mt	Paul
Pray always	**6:18** [18]Praying always with all prayer and supplication in the Spirit, and watching thereunto with all perseverance and supplication for all saints;	**26:41** [41]Watch and pray, that ye enter not into temptation: the spirit indeed is willing, but the flesh is weak.	**Col 4:2–3** [2]Continue in prayer, and watch in the same with thanksgiving; [3]Withal praying also for us, that God would open unto us a door of utterance, to speak the mystery of Christ, for which I am also in bonds:

EPHESIANS (PSEUDO) 6:19—Unifying Behavior (4:25–6:20)

Theme	EPH	Lk	Paul
Boldness in proclamation	**6:19** [19]And for me, that utterance may be given unto me, that I may open my mouth boldly, to make known the mystery of the gospel,	**Acts 4:29** [29]And now, Lord, behold their threatenings: and grant unto thy servants, that with all boldness they may speak thy word,	**Col 4:3** [3]Withal praying also for us, that God would open unto us a door of utterance, to speak the mystery of Christ, for which I am also in bonds: **2 Thes 3:1** [1]Finally, brethren, pray for us, that the word of the Lord may have free course, and be glorified, even as it is with you:

EPHESIANS (PSEUDO) 6:20—Unifying Behavior (4:25–6:20)

Theme	EPH	Paul
Ambassador of gospel	**6:20** [20]For which I am an ambassador in bonds: that therein I may speak boldly, as I ought to speak.	**2 Cor 5:20** [20]Now then we are ambassadors for Christ, as though God did beseech you by us: we pray you in Christ's stead, be ye reconciled to God. **Col 4:4** [4]That I may make it manifest, as I ought to speak.

CONCLUDING REMARKS (6:21–24)

EPHESIANS (PSEUDO) 6:21—Ministry to Churches (6:21–24)

Theme	EPH	Lk	Paul
Tychicus will bring you knowledge	**6:21** [21]But that ye also may know my affairs, and how I do, Tychicus, a beloved brother and faithful minister in the Lord, shall make known to you all things:	**Acts 20:4** [4]And there accompanied him into Asia Sopater of Berea; and of the Thessalonians, Aristarchus and Secundus; and Gaius of Derbe, and Timotheus; and of Asia, Tychicus and Trophimus.	**Col 4:7** [7]All my state shall Tychicus declare unto you, who is a beloved brother, and a faithful minister and fellowservant in the Lord: **2 Tim 4:12 (Pseudo)** [12]And Tychicus have I sent to Ephesus.

EPHESIANS (PSEUDO) 6:22—Ministry to Churches (6:21–24)

Theme	EPH	Paul
Comfort for hearts	**6:22** [22]Whom I have sent unto you for the same purpose, that ye might know our affairs, and that he might comfort your hearts.	**Col 4:8** [8]Whom I have sent unto you for the same purpose, that he might know your estate, and comfort your hearts;

EPHESIANS (PSEUDO) 6:24—Ministry to Churches (6:21–24)

Theme	EPH	NT
Grace to faithful	**6:24** [24]Grace be with all them that love our Lord Jesus Christ in sincerity. Amen.	**1 Pet 1:8** [8]Whom having not seen, ye love; in whom, though now ye see him not, yet believing, ye rejoice with joy unspeakable and full of glory:

PHILIPPIANS

As early as 57 to 58 CE written from prison in Caesarea or 57 to 63 CE from confinement in Rome, perhaps has segments from three letters.

ADDRESS (1:1–11)

PHILIPPIANS 1:1—Address (1:1–11), written while in confinement Caesarea 57–58 CE or Rome 57–63 CE

Theme	PHIL	Paul
Greetings from Paul & Timotheus	**1:1** [1]Paul and Timotheus, the servants of Jesus Christ, to all the saints in Christ Jesus which are at Philippi, with the bishops and deacons:	**Rom 1:1** [1]Paul, a servant of Jesus Christ, called to be an apostle, separated unto the gospel of God, **2 Cor 1:1** [1]Paul, an apostle of Jesus Christ by the will of God, and Timothy our brother, unto the church of God which is at Corinth, with all the saints which are in all Achaia: **1 Thes 1:1** [1]Paul, and Silvanus, and Timotheus, unto the church of the Thessalonians which is in God the Father and in the Lord Jesus Christ: Grace be unto you, and peace, from God our Father, and the Lord Jesus Christ. **1 Tim 3:1–13 (Pseudo)** [1]This is a true saying, If a man desire the office of a bishop, he desireth a good work. [2]A bishop then must be blameless, the husband of one wife, vigilant, sober, of good behaviour, given to hospitality, apt to teach; [3]Not given to wine, no striker, not greedy of filthy lucre; but patient, not a brawler, not covetous; [4]One that ruleth well his own house, having his children in subjection with all gravity; [5](For if a man know not how to rule his own house, how shall he take care of the church of God?) [6]Not a novice, lest being lifted up with pride he fall into the condemnation of the devil. [7]Moreover he must have a good report of them which are without; lest he fall into reproach and the snare of the devil. [8]Likewise must the deacons be grave, not doubletongued, not given to much wine, not greedy of filthy lucre; [9]Holding the mystery of the faith in a pure conscience. [10]And let these also first be proved; then let them use the office of a deacon, being found blameless. [11]Even so must their wives be grave, not slanderers, sober, faithful in all things. [12]Let the deacons be the husbands of one wife, ruling their children and their own houses well. [13]For they that have used the office of a deacon well purchase to themselves a good degree, and great boldness in the faith which is in Christ Jesus. **Phlm 1** [1]Paul, a prisoner of Jesus Christ, and Timothy our brother, unto Philemon our dearly beloved, and fellowlabourer,

PHILIPPIANS 1:2—Address (1:1–11), written while in confinement Caesarea 57–58 CE or Rome 57–63 CE

Theme	PHIL	Paul
Grace & peace	**1:2** [2]Grace be unto you, and peace, from God our Father, and from the Lord Jesus Christ.	**Rom 1:7** [7]To all that be in Rome, beloved of God, called to be saints: Grace to you and peace from God our Father, and the Lord Jesus Christ. **Gal 1:3** [3]Grace be to you and peace from God the Father, and from our Lord Jesus Christ, **Phlm 3** [3]Grace to you, and peace, from God our Father and the Lord Jesus Christ.

PHILIPPIANS 1:3—Address (1:1–11), written while in confinement Caesarea 57–58 CE or Rome 57–63 CE

Theme	PHIL	Paul
Thank God for the church	**1:3** [3]I thank my God upon every remembrance of you,	**Rom 1:8** [8]First, I thank my God through Jesus Christ for you all, that your faith is spoken of throughout the whole world. **1 Cor 1:4** [4]I thank my God always on your behalf, for the grace of God which is given you by Jesus Christ; **1 Thes 1:2** [2]We give thanks to God always for you all, making mention of you in our prayers;

PHILIPPIANS 1:6—Address (1:1–11), written while in confinement Caesarea 57–58 CE or Rome 57–63 CE

Theme	PHIL	Paul
Good work begun	**1:6** [6]Being confident of this very thing, that he which hath begun a good work in you will perform it until the day of Jesus Christ: **1:10** [10]That ye may approve things that are excellent; that ye may be sincere and without offence till the day of Christ; **2:13** [13]For it is God which worketh in you both to will and to do of his good pleasure. **2:16** [16]Holding forth the word of life; that I may rejoice in the day of Christ, that I have not run in vain, neither laboured in vain.	**1 Cor 1:8** [8]Who shall also confirm you unto the end, that ye may be blameless in the day of our Lord Jesus Christ.

PHILIPPIANS 1:8—Address (1:1–11), written while in confinement Caesarea 57–58 CE or Rome 57–63 CE

Theme	PHIL	Mt	Mk
Devoted ministry	**1:8** [8]For God is my record, how greatly I long after you all in the bowels of Jesus Christ. **2:1** [1]If there be therefore any consolation in Christ, if any comfort of love, if any fellowship of the Spirit, if any bowels and mercies,	**14:14** [14]And Jesus went forth, and saw a great multitude, and was moved with compassion toward them, and he healed their sick. **15:32** [32]Then Jesus called his disciples unto him, and said, I have compassion on the multitude, because they continue with me now three days, and have nothing to eat: and I will not send them away fasting, lest they faint in the way. **18:27** [27]Then the lord of that servant was moved with compassion, and loosed him, and forgave him the debt. **20:34** [34]So Jesus had compassion on them, and touched their eyes: and immediately their eyes received sight, and they followed him.	**6:34** [34]And Jesus, when he came out, saw much people, and was moved with compassion toward them, because they were as sheep not having a shepherd: and he began to teach them many things. **8:2** [2]I have compassion on the multitude, because they have now been with me three days, and have nothing to eat:

PHILIPPIANS 1:9—Address (1:1–11), written while in confinement Caesarea 57–58 CE or Rome 57–63 CE

Theme	PHIL	Paul
Pray love will abound	**1:9** [9]And this I pray, that your love may abound yet more and more in knowledge and in all judgment;	**Eph 3:14–19 (Pseudo)** [14]For this cause I bow my knees unto the Father of our Lord Jesus Christ, [15]Of whom the whole family in heaven and earth is named, [16]That he would grant you, according to the riches of his glory, to be strengthened with might by his Spirit in the inner man; [17]That Christ may dwell in your hearts by faith; that ye, being rooted and grounded in love, [18]May be able to comprehend with all saints what is the breadth, and length, and depth, and height; [19]And to know the love of Christ, which passeth knowledge, that ye might be filled with all the fulness of God. **Col 1:9–10** [9]For this cause we also, since the day we heard it, do not cease to pray for you, and to desire that ye might be filled with the knowledge of his will in all wisdom and spiritual understanding; [10]That ye might walk worthy of the Lord unto all pleasing, being fruitful in every good work, and increasing in the knowledge of God; **Phlm 6** [6]That the communication of thy faith may become effectual by the acknowledging of every good thing which is in you in Christ Jesus.

Lk	Paul
10:33 [33]But a certain Samaritan, as he journeyed, came where he was: and when he saw him, he had compassion on him, **15:20** [20]And he arose, and came to his father. But when he was yet a great way off, his father saw him, and had compassion, and ran, and fell on his neck, and kissed him.	**Rom 1:9** [9]For God is my witness, whom I serve with my spirit in the gospel of his Son, that without ceasing I make mention of you always in my prayers; **2 Cor 1:23** [23]Moreover I call God for a record upon my soul, that to spare you I came not as yet unto Corinth. **Col 3:12** [12]Put on therefore, as the elect of God, holy and beloved, bowels of mercies, kindness, humbleness of mind, meekness, longsuffering; **1 Thes 2:5** [5]For neither at any time used we flattering words, as ye know, nor a cloak of covetousness; God is witness:

PHILIPPIANS 1:10—Address (1:1–11), written while in confinement Caesarea 57–58 CE and/or Rome 57–63 CE

Theme	PHIL	Paul
Approve of excellence	**1:10** [10]That ye may approve things that are excellent; that ye may be sincere and without offence till the day of Christ;	**Rom 1:6** [6]Among whom are ye also the called of Jesus Christ: **Rom 2:18** [18]And knowest his will, and approvest the things that are more excellent, being instructed out of the law; **Rom 12:2** [2]And be not conformed to this world: but be ye transformed by the renewing of your mind, that ye may prove what is that good, and acceptable, and perfect, will of God.

PHILIPPIANS 1:11—Address (1:1–11), written while in confinement Caesarea 57–58 CE and/or Rome 57–63 CE

Theme	PHIL	Jn
Be filled with righteousness	**1:11** [11]Being filled with the fruits of righteousness, which are by Jesus Christ, unto the glory and praise of God.	**15:8** [8]Herein is my Father glorified, that ye bear much fruit; so shall ye be my disciples.

SPREADING THE GOSPEL (1:12–26)

PHILIPPIANS 1:12–13—Spreading the Gospel (1:12–26), written while in confinement Caesarea 57–58 CE and/or Rome 57–63 CE

Theme	PHIL	Paul
Furtherance of gospel	**1:12–13** [12]But I would ye should understand, brethren, that the things which happened unto me have fallen out rather unto the furtherance of the gospel; [13]So that my bonds in Christ are manifest in all the palace, and in all other places;	**Eph 3:1 (Pseudo)** [1]For this cause I Paul, the prisoner of Jesus Christ for you Gentiles, **Eph 6:20 (Pseudo)** [20]For which I am an ambassador in bonds: that therein I may speak boldly, as I ought to speak. **2 Tim 2:9 (Pseudo)** [9]Wherein I suffer trouble, as an evil doer, even unto bonds; but the word of God is not bound. **Phlm 9** [9]Yet for love's sake I rather beseech thee, being such an one as Paul the aged, and now also a prisoner of Jesus Christ.

PHILIPPIANS 1:18—Spreading the Gospel (1:12–26), written while in confinement Caesarea 57–58 CE and/or Rome 57–63 CE

Theme	PHIL
Christ will be preached	**1:18** [18]What then? notwithstanding, every way, whether in pretence, or in truth, Christ is preached; and I therein do rejoice, yea, and will rejoice. **4:10** [10]But I rejoiced in the Lord greatly, that now at the last your care of me hath flourished again; wherein ye were also careful, but ye lacked opportunity.

PHILIPPIANS 1:19—Spreading the Gospel (1:12–26), written while in confinement Caesarea 57–58 CE and/or Rome 57–63 CE

Theme	PHIL	Paul	Jewish Writings
Credit to Salvation and Spirit	**1:19** [19]For I know that this shall turn to my salvation through your prayer, and the supply of the Spirit of Jesus Christ,	**2 Cor 1:11** [11]Ye also helping together by prayer for us, that for the gift bestowed upon us by the means of many persons thanks may be given by many on our behalf.	**Job 13:16** [16]He also shall be my salvation: for an hypocrite shall not come before him.

PHILIPPIANS 1:20—Spreading the Gospel (1:12–26), written while in confinement Caesarea 57–58 CE and/or Rome 57–63 CE

Theme	PHIL	Paul	NT
Christ magnified in body	**1:20** [20]According to my earnest expectation and my hope, that in nothing I shall be ashamed, but that with all boldness, as always, so now also Christ shall be magnified in my body, whether it be by life, or by death.	**1 Cor 6:20** [20]For ye are bought with a price: therefore glorify God in your body, and in your spirit, which are God's.	**1 Pet 4:16** [20]For ye are bought with a price: therefore glorify God in your body, and in your spirit, which are God's.

PHILIPPIANS 1:21—Spreading the Gospel (1:12–26), written while in confinement Caesarea 57–58 CE and/or Rome 57–63 CE

Theme	PHIL	Paul
To live is Christ & to die is gain	**1:21** [21]For to me to live is Christ, and to die is gain.	**Gal 2:20** [20]I am crucified with Christ: nevertheless I live; yet not I, but Christ liveth in me: and the life which I now live in the flesh I live by the faith of the Son of God, who loved me, and gave himself for me.

PHILIPPIANS 1:22—Spreading the Gospel (1:12–26), written while in confinement Caesarea 57–58 CE and/or Rome 57–63 CE

Theme	PHIL	Paul
Live in flesh & desire to be w/Christ	**1:22** [22]But if I live in the flesh, this is the fruit of my labour: yet what I shall choose I wot not.	**Rom 1:13** [13]Now I would not have you ignorant, brethren, that oftentimes I purposed to come unto you, (but was let hitherto,) that I might have some fruit among you also, even as among other Gentiles.

PHILIPPIANS 1:23—Spreading the Gospel (1:12–26), written while in confinement Caesarea 57–58 CE and/or Rome 57–63 CE

Theme	PHIL	Paul
To be with Christ is better	**1:23** [23]For I am in a strait betwixt two, having a desire to depart, and to be with Christ; which is far better:	**2 Cor 5:8** [8]We are confident, I say, and willing rather to be absent from the body, and to be present with the Lord.

STRIVING IN CHRIST (1:27–30)

PHILIPPIANS 1:27—Striving in Christ (1:27–30), written while in confinement Caesarea 57–58 CE and/or Rome 57–63 CE

Theme	PHIL	Paul
Conversation and mind becoming to gospel	**1:27** [27]Only let your conversation be as it becometh the gospel of Christ: that whether I come and see you, or else be absent, I may hear of your affairs, that ye stand fast in one spirit, with one mind striving together for the faith of the gospel;	**Eph 4:1 (Pseudo)** [1]I therefore, the prisoner of the Lord, beseech you that ye walk worthy of the vocation wherewith ye are called, **Col 1:10** [10]That ye might walk worthy of the Lord unto all pleasing, being fruitful in every good work, and increasing in the knowledge of God; **1 Thes 2:12** [12]That ye would walk worthy of God, who hath called you unto his kingdom and glory. **1 Thes 4:3** [3]For this is the will of God, even your sanctification, that ye should abstain from fornication:

PHILIPPIANS 1:29—Striving in Christ (1:27–30), written while in confinement Caesarea 57–58 CE and/or Rome 57–63 CE

Theme	PHIL	Mt	Mk	Lk	Other
Believe and suffering in Christ	**1:29** [29]For unto you it is given in the behalf of Christ, not only to believe on him, but also to suffer for his sake;	**5:10** [10]Blessed are they which are persecuted for righteousness' sake: for theirs is the kingdom of heaven.	**8:34** [34]And when he had called the people unto him with his disciples also, he said unto them, Whosoever will come after me, let him deny himself, and take up his cross, and follow me.	**Acts 5:41** [41]And they departed from the presence of the council, rejoicing that they were counted worthy to suffer shame for his name.	**Q-Quelle** Beatitudes: Phil 1:29/Mt 5:3-12/ [Lk 6:20b-23 (QS 8 [Thom 54, 68,69])]

PHILIPPIANS 1:30—Striving in Christ (1:27–30), written while in confinement Caesarea 57–58 CE and/or Rome 57–63 CE

Theme	PHIL	Lk
Paul's conflict	**1:30** [30]Having the same conflict which ye saw in me, and now hear to be in me. **1:13** [13]So that my bonds in Christ are manifest in all the palace, and in all other places;	**Acts 16:22–24** [22]And the multitude rose up together against them: and the magistrates rent off their clothes, and commanded to beat them. [23]And when they had laid many stripes upon them, they cast them into prison, charging the jailor to keep them safely: [24]Who, having received such a charge, thrust them into the inner prison, and made their feet fast in the stocks.

HUMANITY OF CHRIST (2:1–8)

PHILIPPIANS 2—Humanity of Christ (2:1–8), written while in confinement Caesarea 57–58 CE and/or Rome 57–63 CE

Theme	PHIL	Mt	Mk
Jesus' humanness	**Ch 2** [1]If there be therefore any consolation in Christ, if any comfort of love, if any fellowship of the Spirit, if any bowels and mercies, [2]Fulfil ye my joy, that ye be likeminded, having the same love, being of one accord, of one mind. [3]Let nothing be done through strife or vainglory; but in lowliness of mind let each esteem other better than themselves. [4]Look not every man on his own things, but every man also on the things of others. [5]Let this mind be in you, which was also in Christ Jesus: [6]Who, being in the form of God, thought it not robbery to be equal with God: [7]But made himself of no reputation, and took upon him the form of a servant, and was made in the likeness of men: [8]And being found in fashion as a man, he humbled himself, and became obedient unto death, even the death of the cross. [9]Wherefore God also hath highly exalted him, and given him a name which is above every name: [10]That at the name of Jesus every knee should bow, of things in heaven, and things in earth, and things under the earth; [11]And that every tongue should confess that Jesus Christ is Lord, to the glory of God the Father. [12]Wherefore, my beloved, as ye have always obeyed, not as in my presence only, but now much more in my absence, work out your own salvation with fear and trembling. [13]For it is God which worketh in you both to will and to do of his good pleasure. [14]Do all things without murmurings and disputings: [15]That ye may be blameless and harmless, the sons of God, without rebuke, in the midst of a crooked and perverse nation, among whom ye shine as lights in the world; [16]Holding forth the word of life; that I may rejoice in the day of Christ, that I have not run in vain, neither laboured in vain. [17]Yea, and if I be offered upon the sacrifice and service of your faith, I joy, and rejoice with you all. [18]For the same cause also do ye joy, and rejoice with me. [19]But I trust in the Lord Jesus to send Timotheus shortly unto you, that I also may be of good comfort, when I know your state. [20]For I have no man likeminded, who will naturally care for your state. [21]For all seek their own, not the things which are Jesus Christ's. [22]But ye know the proof of him, that, as a son with the father, he hath served with me in the gospel. [23]Him therefore I hope to send presently, so soon as I shall see how it will go with me. [24]But I trust in the Lord that I also myself shall come shortly. [25]Yet I supposed it necessary to send to you Epaphroditus, my brother, and companion in labour, and fellowsoldier, but your messenger, and he that ministered to my wants. [26]For he longed after you all, and was full of heaviness, because that ye had heard that he had been sick. [27]For indeed he was sick nigh unto death: but God had mercy on him; and not on him only, but on me also, lest I should have sorrow upon sorrow. [28]I sent him therefore the more carefully, that, when ye see him again, ye may rejoice, and that I may be the less sorrowful. [29]Receive him therefore in the Lord with all gladness; and hold such in reputation: [30]Because for the work of Christ he was nigh unto death, not regarding his life, to supply your lack of service toward me.	**19:8** [8]He saith unto them, Moses because of the hardness of your hearts suffered you to put away your wives: but from the beginning it was not so.	**10:6** [6]But from the beginning of the creation God made them male and female.

Paul	Jewish Writings
Rom 1:3 [3]Concerning his Son Jesus Christ our Lord, which was made of the seed of David according to the flesh; **Rom 1:5** [5]By whom we have received grace and apostleship, for obedience to the faith among all nations, for his name: **1 Cor 15:27** [27]For he hath put all things under his feet. But when he saith all things are put under him, it is manifest that he is excepted, which did put all things under him. **1 Cor 15:49** [49]And as we have borne the image of the earthy, we shall also bear the image of the heavenly. **2 Cor 3:18** [18]But we all, with open face beholding as in a glass the glory of the Lord, are changed into the same image from glory to glory, even as by the Spirit of the Lord. **Gal 4:4** [4]But when the fulness of the time was come, God sent forth his Son, made of a woman, made under the law, **Col 3:10** [10]And have put on the new man, which is renewed in knowledge after the image of him that created him:	**Gen 1:28** [28]And God blessed them, and God said unto them, Be fruitful, and multiply, and replenish the earth, and subdue it: and have dominion over the fish of the sea, and over the fowl of the air, and over every living thing that moveth upon the earth.

PHILIPPIANS 2:1–11—Humanity of Christ (2:1–8), written while in confinement Caesarea 57–58 CE and/or Rome 57–63 CE

Theme	PHIL	Mt
Humble service: God came in human form	**2:1–11** [1]If there be therefore any consolation in Christ, if any comfort of love, if any fellowship of the Spirit, if any bowels and mercies, [2]Fulfil ye my joy, that ye be likeminded, having the same love, being of one accord, of one mind. [3]Let nothing be done through strife or vainglory; but in lowliness of mind let each esteem other better than themselves. [4]Look not every man on his own things, but every man also on the things of others. [5]Let this mind be in you, which was also in Christ Jesus: [6]Who, being in the form of God, thought it not robbery to be equal with God: [7]But made himself of no reputation, and took upon him the form of a servant, and was made in the likeness of men: [8]And being found in fashion as a man, he humbled himself, and became obedient unto death, even the death of the cross. [9]Wherefore God also hath highly exalted him, and given him a name which is above every name: [10]That at the name of Jesus every knee should bow, of things in heaven, and things in earth, and things under the earth; [11]And that every tongue should confess that Jesus Christ is Lord, to the glory of God the Father. **2:21** [21]For all seek their own, not the things which are Jesus Christ's.	**20:20** [20]Then came to him the mother of Zebedee's children with her sons, worshipping him, and desiring a certain thing of him. **20:27–28** [27]And whosoever will be chief among you, let him be your servant: [28]Even as the Son of man came not to be ministered unto, but to minister, and to give his life a ransom for many. **21:3** [3]And if any man say ought unto you, ye shall say, The Lord hath need of them; and straightway he will send them. **22:41–46** [41]While the Pharisees were gathered together, Jesus asked them, [42]Saying, What think ye of Christ? whose son is he? They say unto him, The Son of David. [43]He saith unto them, How then doth David in spirit call him Lord, saying, [44]The LORD said unto my Lord, Sit thou on my right hand, till I make thine enemies thy footstool? [45]If David then call him Lord, how is he his son? [46]And no man was able to answer him a word, neither durst any man from that day forth ask him any more questions. **23:12** [12]And whosoever shall exalt himself shall be abased; and he that shall humble himself shall be exalted. **24:45–51** [45]Who then is a faithful and wise servant, whom his lord hath made ruler over his household, to give them meat in due season? [46]Blessed is that servant, whom his lord when he cometh shall find so doing. [47]Verily I say unto you, That he shall make him ruler over all his goods. [48]But and if that evil servant shall say in his heart, My lord delayeth his coming; [49]And shall begin to smite his fellowservants, and to eat and drink with the drunken; [50]The lord of that servant shall come in a day when he looketh not for him, and in an hour that he is not aware of, [51]And shall cut him asunder, and appoint him his portion with the hypocrites: there shall be weeping and gnashing of teeth. **25:14–30** [14]For the kingdom of heaven is as a man travelling into a far country, who called his own servants, and delivered unto them his goods. [15]And unto one he gave five talents, to another two, and to another one; to every man according to his several ability; and straightway took his journey. [16]Then he that had received the five talents went and traded with the same, and made them other five talents. [17]And likewise he that had received two, he also gained other two. [18]But he that had received one went and digged in the earth, and hid his lord's money. [19]After a long time the lord of those servants cometh, and reckoneth with them. [20]And so he that had received five talents came and brought other five talents, saying, Lord, thou deliveredst unto me five talents: behold, I have gained beside them five talents more. [21]His lord said unto him, Well done, thou good and faithful servant: thou hast been faithful over a few things, I will make thee ruler over many things: enter thou into the joy of thy lord. [22]He also that had received two talents came and said, Lord, thou deliveredst unto me two talents: behold, I have gained two other talents beside them. [23]His lord said unto him, Well done, good and faithful servant; thou hast been faithful over a few things, I will make thee ruler over many things: enter thou into the joy of thy lord. [24]Then he which had received the one talent came and said, Lord, I knew thee that thou art an hard man, reaping where thou hast not sown, and gathering where thou hast not strawed: [25]And I was afraid, and went and hid thy talent in the earth: lo, there thou hast that is thine. [26]His lord answered and said unto him, Thou wicked and slothful servant, thou knewest that I reap where I sowed not, and gather where I have not strawed: [27]Thou oughtest therefore to have put my money to the exchangers, and then at my coming I should have received mine own with usury. [28]Take therefore the talent from him, and give it unto him which hath ten talents. [29]For unto every one that hath shall be given, and he shall have abundance: but from him that hath not shall be taken away even that which he hath. [30]And cast ye the unprofitable servant into outer darkness: there shall be weeping and gnashing of teeth.

Mk	Lk
9:35 35 And he sat down, and called the twelve, and saith unto them, If any man desire to be first, the same shall be last of all, and servant of all. **10:35–45** 35 And James and John, the sons of Zebedee, come unto him, saying, Master, we would that thou shouldest do for us whatsoever we shall desire. 36 And he said unto them, What would ye that I should do for you? 37 They said unto him, Grant unto us that we may sit, one on thy right hand, and the other on thy left hand, in thy glory. 38 But Jesus said unto them, Ye know not what ye ask: can ye drink of the cup that I drink of? and be baptized with the baptism that I am baptized with? 39 And they said unto him, We can. And Jesus said unto them, Ye shall indeed drink of the cup that I drink of; and with the baptism that I am baptized withal shall ye be baptized: 40 But to sit on my right hand and on my left hand is not mine to give; but it shall be given to them for whom it is prepared. 41 And when the ten heard it, they began to be much displeased with James and John. 42 But Jesus called them to him, and saith unto them, Ye know that they which are accounted to rule over the Gentiles exercise lordship over them; and their great ones exercise authority upon them. 43 But so shall it not be among you: but whosoever will be great among you, shall be your minister: 44 And whosoever of you will be the chiefest, shall be servant of all. 45 For even the Son of man came not to be ministered unto, but to minister, and to give his life a ransom for many. **11:3** 3 And if any man say unto you, Why do ye this? say ye that the Lord hath need of him; and straightway he will send him hither. **12:35–37a** 35 And Jesus answered and said, while he taught in the temple, How say the scribes that Christ is the Son of David? 36 For David himself said by the Holy Ghost, The LORD said to my Lord, Sit thou on my right hand, till I make thine enemies thy footstool. 37 David therefore himself calleth him Lord;	**9:48** 48 And said unto them, Whosoever shall receive this child in my name receiveth me: and whosoever shall receive me receiveth him that sent me: for he that is least among you all, the same shall be great. **12:41–46** 41 Then Peter said unto him, Lord, speakest thou this parable unto us, or even to all? 42 And the Lord said, Who then is that faithful and wise steward, whom his lord shall make ruler over his household, to give them their portion of meat in due season? 43 Blessed is that servant, whom his lord when he cometh shall find so doing. 44 Of a truth I say unto you, that he will make him ruler over all that he hath. 45 But and if that servant say in his heart, My lord delayeth his coming; and shall begin to beat the menservants and maidens, and to eat and drink, and to be drunken; 46 The lord of that servant will come in a day when he looketh not for him, and at an hour when he is not aware, and will cut him in sunder, and will appoint him his portion with the unbelievers. **14:11** 11 For whosoever exalteth himself shall be abased; and he that humbleth himself shall be exalted. **18:14** 14 I tell you, this man went down to his house justified rather than the other: for every one that exalteth himself shall be abased; and he that humbleth himself shall be exalted. **19:11–27** 11 And as they heard these things, he added and spake a parable, because he was nigh to Jerusalem, and because they thought that the kingdom of God should immediately appear. 12 He said therefore, A certain nobleman went into a far country to receive for himself a kingdom, and to return. 13 And he called his ten servants, and delivered them ten pounds, and said unto them, Occupy till I come. 14 But his citizens hated him, and sent a message after him, saying, We will not have this man to reign over us. 15 And it came to pass, that when he was returned, having received the kingdom, then he commanded these servants to be called unto him, to whom he had given the money, that he might know how much every man had gained by trading. 16 Then came the first, saying, Lord, thy pound hath gained ten pounds. 17 And he said unto him, Well, thou good servant: because thou hast been faithful in a very little, have thou authority over ten cities. 18 And the second came, saying, Lord, thy pound hath gained five pounds. 19 And he said likewise to him, Be thou also over five cities. 20 And another came, saying, Lord, behold, here is thy pound, which I have kept laid up in a napkin: 21 For I feared thee, because thou art an austere man: thou takest up that thou layedst not down, and reapest that thou didst not sow. 22 And he saith unto him, Out of thine own mouth will I judge thee, thou wicked servant. Thou knewest that I was an austere man, taking up that I laid not down, and reaping that I did not sow: 23 Wherefore then gavest not thou my money into the bank, that at my coming I might have required mine own with usury? 24 And there was also a strife among them, which of them should be accounted the greatest. 25 And he said unto them, The kings of the Gentiles exercise lordship over them; and they that exercise authority upon them are called benefactors. 26 But ye shall not be so: but he that is greatest among you, let him be as the younger; and he that is chief, as he that doth serve. 27 For whether is greater, he that sitteth at meat, or he that serveth? is not he that sitteth at meat? but I am among you as he that serveth. **19:34** 34 And they said, The Lord hath need of him. **20:41–44** 41 And he said unto them, How say they that Christ is David's son? 42 And David himself saith in the book of Psalms, The LORD said unto my Lord, Sit thou on my right hand, 43 Till I make thine enemies thy footstool. 44 David therefore calleth him Lord, how is he then his son?

PHILIPPIANS 2:1–11—Humanity of Christ (2:1–8), written while in confinement Caesarea 57–58 CE and/or Rome 57–63 CE

Theme	PHIL	Jn
(*Cont.*) **Humble service: God came in human form**	**2:1–11 (above)** **2:21 (above)**	**Ch 13** [1]Now before the feast of the passover, when Jesus knew that his hour was come that he should depart out of this world unto the Father, having loved his own which were in the world, he loved them unto the end. [2]And supper being ended, the devil having now put into the heart of Judas Iscariot, Simon's son, to betray him; [3]Jesus knowing that the Father had given all things into his hands, and that he was come from God, and went to God; [4]He riseth from supper, and laid aside his garments; and took a towel, and girded himself. [5]After that he poureth water into a basin, and began to wash the disciples' feet, and to wipe them with the towel wherewith he was girded. [6]Then cometh he to Simon Peter: and Peter saith unto him, Lord, dost thou wash my feet? [7]Jesus answered and said unto him, What I do thou knowest not now; but thou shalt know hereafter. [8]Peter saith unto him, Thou shalt never wash my feet. Jesus answered him, If I wash thee not, thou hast no part with me. [9]Simon Peter saith unto him, Lord, not my feet only, but also my hands and my head. [10]Jesus saith to him, He that is washed needeth not save to wash his feet, but is clean every whit: and ye are clean, but not all. [11]For he knew who should betray him; therefore said he, Ye are not all clean. [12]So after he had washed their feet, and had taken his garments, and was set down again, he said unto them, Know ye what I have done to you? [13]Ye call me Master and Lord: and ye say well; for so I am. [14]If I then, your Lord and Master, have washed your feet; ye also ought to wash one another's feet. [15]For I have given you an example, that ye should do as I have done to you. [16]Verily, verily, I say unto you, The servant is not greater than his lord; neither he that is sent greater than he that sent him. [17]If ye know these things, happy are ye if ye do them. [18]I speak not of you all: I know whom I have chosen: but that the scripture may be fulfilled, He that eateth bread with me hath lifted up his heel against me. [19]Now I tell you before it come, that, when it is come to pass, ye may believe that I am he. [20]Verily, verily, I say unto you, He that receiveth whomsoever I send receiveth me; and he that receiveth me receiveth him that sent me. [21]When Jesus had thus said, he was troubled in spirit, and testified, and said, Verily, verily, I say unto you, that one of you shall betray me. [22]Then the disciples looked one on another, doubting of whom he spake. [23]Now there was leaning on Jesus' bosom one of his disciples, whom Jesus loved. [24]Simon Peter therefore beckoned to him, that he should ask who it should be of whom he spake. [25]He then lying on Jesus' breast saith unto him, Lord, who is it? [26]Jesus answered, He it is, to whom I shall give a sop, when I have dipped it. And when he had dipped the sop, he gave it to Judas Iscariot, the son of Simon. [27]And after the sop Satan entered into him. Then said Jesus unto him, That thou doest, do quickly. [28]Now no man at the table knew for what intent he spake this unto him. [29]For some of them thought, because Judas had the bag, that Jesus had said unto him, Buy those things that we have need of against the feast; or, that he should give something to the poor. [30]He then having received the sop went immediately out: and it was night. [31]Therefore, when he was gone out, Jesus said, Now is the Son of man glorified, and God is glorified in him. [32]If God be glorified in him, God shall also glorify him in himself, and shall straightway glorify him. [33]Little children, yet a little while I am with you. Ye shall seek me: and as I said unto the Jews, Whither I go, ye cannot come; so now I say to you. [34]A new commandment I give unto you, That ye love one another; as I have loved you, that ye also love one another. [35]By this shall all men know that ye are my disciples, if ye have love one to another. [36]Simon Peter said unto him, Lord, whither goest thou? Jesus answered him, Whither I go, thou canst not follow me now; but thou shalt follow me afterwards. [37]Peter said unto him, Lord, why cannot I follow thee now? I will lay down my life for thy sake. [38]Jesus answered him, Wilt thou lay down thy life for my sake? Verily, verily, I say unto thee, The cock shall not crow, till thou hast denied me thrice. **1 Jn 2:18–23** [18]Little children, it is the last time: and as ye have heard that antichrist shall come, even now are there many antichrists; whereby we know that it is the last time. [19]They went out from us, but they were not of us; for if they had been of us, they would no doubt have continued with us: but they went out, that they might be made manifest that they were not all of us. [20]But ye have an unction from the Holy One, and ye know all things. [21]I have not written unto you because ye know not the truth, but because ye know it, and that no lie is of the truth. [22]Who is a liar but he that denieth that Jesus is the Christ? He is antichrist, that denieth the Father and the Son. [23]Whosoever denieth the Son, the same hath not the Father: (but) he that acknowledgeth the Son hath the Father also.

Paul

Rom 1:1–4

[1]Paul, a servant of Jesus Christ, called to be an apostle, separated unto the gospel of God, [2](Which he had promised afore by his prophets in the holy scriptures,) [3]Concerning his Son Jesus Christ our Lord, which was made of the seed of David according to the flesh; [4]And declared to be the Son of God with power, according to the spirit of holiness, by the resurrection from the dead:

Rom 10:9

[9]That if thou shalt confess with thy mouth the Lord Jesus, and shalt believe in thine heart that God hath raised him from the dead, thou shalt be saved.

Rom 12:10

[10]Be kindly affectioned one to another with brotherly love; in honour preferring one another;

Rom 13

[1]Let every soul be subject unto the higher powers. For there is no power but of God: the powers that be are ordained of God. [2]Whosoever therefore resisteth the power, resisteth the ordinance of God: and they that resist shall receive to themselves damnation. [3]For rulers are not a terror to good works, but to the evil. Wilt thou then not be afraid of the power? do that which is good, and thou shalt have praise of the same: [4]For he is the minister of God to thee for good. But if thou do that which is evil, be afraid; for he beareth not the sword in vain: for he is the minister of God, a revenger to execute wrath upon him that doeth evil. [5]Wherefore ye must needs be subject, not only for wrath, but also for conscience sake. [6]For for this cause pay ye tribute also: for they are God's ministers, attending continually upon this very thing. [7]Render therefore to all their dues: tribute to whom tribute is due; custom to whom custom; fear to whom fear; honour to whom honour. [8]Owe no man any thing, but to love one another: for he that loveth another hath fulfilled the law. [9]For this, Thou shalt not commit adultery, Thou shalt not kill, Thou shalt not steal, Thou shalt not bear false witness, Thou shalt not covet; and if there be any other commandment, it is briefly comprehended in this saying, namely, Thou shalt love thy neighbour as thyself. [10]Love worketh no ill to his neighbour: therefore love is the fulfilling of the law. [11]And that, knowing the time, that now it is high time to awake out of sleep: for now is our salvation nearer than when we believed. [12]The night is far spent, the day is at hand: let us therefore cast off the works of darkness, and let us put on the armour of light. [13]Let us walk honestly, as in the day; not in rioting and drunkenness, not in chambering and wantonness, not in strife and envying. [14]But put ye on the Lord Jesus Christ, and make not provision for the flesh, to fulfil the lusts thereof.

Rom 14:4–12

[4]Who art thou that judgest another man's servant? to his own master he standeth or falleth. Yea, he shall be holden up: for God is able to make him stand. [5]One man esteemeth one day above another: another esteemeth every day alike. Let every man be fully persuaded in his own mind. [6]He that regardeth the day, regardeth it unto the Lord; and he that regardeth not the day, to the Lord he doth not regard it. He that eateth, eateth to the Lord, for he giveth God thanks; and he that eateth not, to the Lord he eateth not, and giveth God thanks. [7]For none of us liveth to himself, and no man dieth to himself. [8]For whether we live, we live unto the Lord; and whether we die, we die unto the Lord: whether we live therefore, or die, we are the Lord's. [9]For to this end Christ both died, and rose, and revived, that he might be Lord both of the dead and living. [10]But why dost thou judge thy brother? or why dost thou set at nought thy brother? for we shall all stand before the judgment seat of Christ. [11]For it is written, As I live, saith the Lord, every knee shall bow to me, and every tongue shall confess to God. [12]So then every one of us shall give account of himself to God.

Rom 15:1–8

[1]We then that are strong ought to bear the infirmities of the weak, and not to please ourselves. [2]Let every one of us please his neighbour for his good to edification. [3]For even Christ pleased not himself; but, as it is written, The reproaches of them that reproached thee fell on me. [4]For whatsoever things were written aforetime were written for our learning, that we through patience and comfort of the scriptures might have hope. [5]Now the God of patience and consolation grant you to be likeminded one toward another according to Christ Jesus: [6]That ye may with one mind and one mouth glorify God, even the Father of our Lord Jesus Christ. [7]Wherefore receive ye one another, as Christ also received us to the glory of God. [8]Now I say that Jesus Christ was a minister of the circumcision for the truth of God, to confirm the promises made unto the fathers:

1 Cor 9:19

[19]For though I be free from all men, yet have I made myself servant unto all, that I might gain the more.

1 Cor 9:22

[22]To the weak became I as weak, that I might gain the weak: I am made all things to all men, that I might by all means save some.

1 Cor 10:3

[3]And did all eat the same spiritual meat;

PHILIPPIANS 2:1–11—Humanity of Christ (2:1–8), written while in confinement Caesarea 57–58 CE and/or Rome 57–63 CE

Theme	PHIL	Other
(*Cont.*) **Humble service: God came in human form**	**2:1–11 (above)** **2:21 (above)**	**Q-Quelle** Against Pharisees: Phil 2:1-11/Mt 23:4-36/[Mk 7:1-9]/[Lk 11:37-54 (QS 34 [Thom 39:1, 89, 102])]/ Parable of pounds: Phil 2:1-11/Mt 25:14-30/Lk 19:11-27 (QS 61 [Thom 41]); Watchful and faithful: Phil 2:1-11/ [Mt 24:42-51]/Lk 12:35-48 (QS 42)

PHILIPPIANS 2:2—Humanity of Christ (2:1–8), written while in confinement Caesarea 57–58 CE and/or Rome 57–63 CE

Theme	PHIL	Paul
Be of the same mind	**2:2** [2]Fulfil ye my joy, that ye be likeminded, having the same love, being of one accord, of one mind.	**Rom 15:5** [5]Now the God of patience and consolation grant you to be likeminded one toward another according to Christ Jesus: **1 Cor 1:10** [10]Now I beseech you, brethren, by the name of our Lord Jesus Christ, that ye all speak the same thing, and that there be no divisions among you; but that ye be perfectly joined together in the same mind and in the same judgment.

PHILIPPIANS 2:3—Humanity of Christ (2:1–8), written while in confinement Caesarea 57–58 CE and/or Rome 57–63 CE

Theme	PHIL	Paul	Other
Esteem others above self	**2:3** [3]Let nothing be done through strife or vainglory; but in lowliness of mind let each esteem other better than themselves.	**Rom 12:3, 10** [3]For I say, through the grace given unto me, to every man that is among you, not to think of himself more highly than he ought to think; but to think soberly, according as God hath dealt to every man the measure of faith. . . . [10]Be kindly affectioned one to another with brotherly love; in honour preferring one another; **Gal 5:26** [26]Let us not be desirous of vain glory, provoking one another, envying one another.	**Q-Quelle** Love enemies: Phil 2:3/Rom 12:9-21/ [Mt 5:38-48], [Mt 7:12]/[Lk 6:27-36 (QS 9 [Thom 95, 6:2])]; Against Pharisees: Phil 2:3/Rom 12:9-21/[Rom 15:1]/[Mt 23:4-36]/[Mk 7:1-9][/Lk 11:37-54 (QS 34 [Thom 39:1,89, 102])]; Precedence: Phil 2:3/Rom 12:9-21/[Mt 19:28]/[Mk 10:41-45]/[Lk 22:28-30 (QS 62)]

PHILIPPIANS 2:4—Humanity of Christ (2:1–8), written while in confinement Caesarea 57–58 CE and/or Rome 57–63 CE

Theme	PHIL	Paul
Look after others	**2:4** [4]Look not every man on his own things, but every man also on the things of others.	**1 Cor 10:24, 33** [24]Let no man seek his own, but every man another's wealth. . . . [33]Even as I please all men in all things, not seeking mine own profit, but the profit of many, that they may be saved. **1 Cor 13:5** [5]Doth not behave itself unseemly, seeketh not her own, is not easily provoked, thinketh no evil;

PHILIPPIANS 2:5–11—Humanity of Christ (2:1–8), written while in confinement Caesarea 57–58 CE and/or Rome 57–63 CE

Theme	PHIL	Paul	Other
Humble service: God came in human form	**2:5–11** [5]Let this mind be in you, which was also in Christ Jesus: [6]Who, being in the form of God, thought it not robbery to be equal with God: [7]But made himself of no reputation, and took upon him the form of a servant, and was made in the likeness of men: [8]And being found in fashion as a man, he humbled himself, and became obedient unto death, even the death of the cross. [9]Wherefore God also hath highly exalted him, and given him a name which is above every name: [10]That at the name of Jesus every knee should bow, of things in heaven, and things in earth, and things under the earth; [11]And that every tongue should confess that Jesus Christ is Lord, to the glory of God the Father.	**1 Cor 10:24** [24]Let no man seek his own, but every man another's wealth. **1 Cor 10:33–11:2** [33]Even as I please all men in all things, not seeking mine own profit, but the profit of many, that they may be saved. **11** [1]Be ye followers of me, even as I also am of Christ. [2]Now I praise you, brethren, that ye remember me in all things, and keep the ordinances, as I delivered them to you. **1 Cor 12:3** [3]Wherefore I give you to understand, that no man speaking by the Spirit of God calleth Jesus accursed: and that no man can say that Jesus is the Lord, but by the Holy Ghost. **1 Cor 13:5** [5]Doth not behave itself unseemly, seeketh not her own, is not easily provoked, thinketh no evil; **1 Cor 15:20–28** [20]But now is Christ risen from the dead, and become the firstfruits of them that slept. [21]For since by man came death, by man came also the resurrection of the dead. [22]For as in Adam all die, even so in Christ shall all be made alive. [23]But every man in his own order: Christ the firstfruits; afterward they that are Christ's at his coming. [24]Then cometh the end, when he shall have delivered up the kingdom to God, even the Father; when he shall have put down all rule and all authority and power. [25]For he must reign, till he hath put all enemies under his feet. [26]The last enemy that shall be destroyed is death. [27]For he hath put all things under his feet. But when he saith all things are put under him, it is manifest that he is excepted, which did put all things under him. [28]And when all things shall be subdued unto him, then shall the Son also himself be subject unto him that put all things under him, that God may be all in all. **2 Cor 4:5** [5]For we preach not ourselves, but Christ Jesus the Lord; and ourselves your servants for Jesus' sake. **2 Cor 11:7** [7]Have I committed an offence in abasing myself that ye might be exalted, because I have preached to you the gospel of God freely? **Gal 5:13c** [13] . . . but by love serve one another. **2 Thes 1:1** [1]Paul, and Silvanus, and Timotheus, unto the church of the Thessalonians in God our Father and the Lord Jesus Christ: **Tit 2:13 (Pseudo)** [13]Looking for that blessed hope, and the glorious appearing of the great God and our Saviour Jesus Christ;	**Q-Quelle** Watchful and faithful: Phil 2:5-11/[Rom 9:5]/ Tit 2:13/[Mt 24:42-51]/[Lk 12:35-48 (QS 41 [Thom 21:3, 103], QS 42)]

PHILIPPIANS 2:6—Humanity of Christ (2:1–8), written while in confinement Caesarea 57–58 CE and/or Rome 57–63 CE

Theme	PHIL	Jn	Paul
Equality with God	**2:6** [6]Who, being in the form of God, thought it not robbery to be equal with God:	**1:1–2** [1]In the beginning was the Word, and the Word was with God, and the Word was God. [2]The same was in the beginning with God.	**Col 2:9** [9]For in him dwelleth all the fulness of the Godhead bodily.

PHILIPPIANS 2:7—Humanity of Christ (2:1–8), written while in confinement Caesarea 57–58 CE and/or Rome 57–63 CE

Theme	PHIL	Jn	Paul
Jesus, in the form of a servant	**2:7** [7]But made himself of no reputation, and took upon him the form of a servant, & was made in the likeness of men:	**1:14** [14]And the Word was made flesh, and dwelt among us, (and we beheld his glory, the glory as of the only begotten of the Father,) full of grace and truth.	**Rom 8:3** [3]For what the law could not do, in that it was weak through the flesh, God sending his own Son in the likeness of sinful flesh, and for sin, condemned sin in the flesh: **2 Cor 8:9** [9]For ye know the grace of our Lord Jesus Christ, that, though he was rich, yet for your sakes he became poor, that ye through his poverty might be rich. **Gal 4:4** [4]But when the fulness of the time was come, God sent forth his Son, made of a woman, made under the law,

PHILIPPIANS 2:8—Humanity of Christ (2:1–8), written while in confinement Caesarea 57–58 CE and/or Rome 57–63 CE

Theme	PHIL	Mt	Jn
As a human, Jesus was humbled	**2:8** [8]And being found in fashion as a man, he humbled himself, and became obedient unto death, even the death of the cross.	**26:39** [39]And he went a little further, and fell on his face, and prayed, saying, O my Father, if it be possible, let this cup pass from me: nevertheless not as I will, but as thou wilt.	**10:17** [17]Therefore doth my Father love me, because I lay down my life, that I might take it again.

LORDSHIP OF CHRIST (2:9–16)

PHILIPPIANS 2:9—Lordship of Christ (2:9–16), written while in confinement Caesarea 57–58 CE and/or Rome 57–63 CE

Theme	PHIL	Mt	Lk
God exalted Jesus	**2:9** [9]Wherefore God also hath highly exalted him, and given him a name which is above every name:	**23:12** [12]And whosoever shall exalt himself shall be abased; and he that shall humble himself shall be exalted.	**Acts 2:33** [33]Therefore being by the right hand of God exalted, and having received of the Father the promise of the Holy Ghost, he hath shed forth this, which ye now see and hear.

NT	Jewish Writings
Heb 1:3	**Gen 1:1, 27**
[3]Who being the brightness of his glory, and the express image of his person, and upholding all things by the word of his power, when he had by himself purged our sins, sat down on the right hand of the Majesty on high;	[1]In the beginning God created the heaven and the earth. . . . [27]So God created man in his own image, in the image of God created he him; male and female created he them.

NT	Jewish Writings
Heb 2:14, 17	**Is 53:3**
[14]Forasmuch then as the children are partakers of flesh and blood, he also himself likewise took part of the same; that through death he might destroy him that had the power of death, that is, the devil; . . . [7]Wherefore in all things it behoved him to be made like unto his brethren, that he might be a merciful and faithful high priest in things pertaining to God, to make reconciliation for the sins of the people.	[3]He is despised and rejected of men; a man of sorrows, and acquainted with grief: and we hid as it were our faces from him; he was despised, and we esteemed him not. **Is 53:11** [11]He shall see of the travail of his soul, and shall be satisfied: by his knowledge shall my righteous servant justify many; for he shall bear their iniquities.

NT
Heb 1:3–4
[3]Who being the brightness of his glory, and the express image of his person, and upholding all things by the word of his power, when he had by himself purged our sins, sat down on the right hand of the Majesty on high; [4]Being made so much better than the angels, as he hath by inheritance obtained a more excellent name than they.
Heb 5:8
[8]Though he were a Son, yet learned he obedience by the things which he suffered;

Paul	Jewish Writings
Eph 1:20–21 (Pseudo)	**Heb 1:3–4**
[20]Which he wrought in Christ, when he raised him from the dead, and set him at his own right hand in the heavenly places, [21]Far above all principality, and power, and might, and dominion, and every name that is named, not only in this world, but also in that which is to come:	[3]Who being the brightness of his glory, and the express image of his person, and upholding all things by the word of his power, when he had by himself purged our sins, sat down on the right hand of the Majesty on high; [4]Being made so much better than the angels, as he hath by inheritance obtained a more excellent name than they.

PHILIPPIANS 2:10—Lordship of Christ (2:9–16), written while in confinement Caesarea 57–58 CE and/or Rome 57–63 CE

Theme	PHIL	Jn	Paul	NT	Jewish Writings
Every knee will bow to Jesus' name	**2:10** [10]That at the name of Jesus every knee should bow, of things in heaven, and things in earth, and things under the earth;	**5:23** [23]That all men should honour the Son, even as they honour the Father. He that honoureth not the Son honoureth not the Father which hath sent him.	**Rom 14:11** [11]For it is written, As I live, saith the Lord, every knee shall bow to me, and every tongue shall confess to God.	**Rev 5:13** [13]And every creature which is in heaven, and on the earth, and under the earth, and such as are in the sea, and all that are in them, heard I saying, Blessing, and honour, and glory, and power, be unto him that sitteth upon the throne, and unto the Lamb for ever and ever.	**Is 45:23** [23]I have sworn by myself, the word is gone out of my mouth in righteousness, and shall not return, That unto me every knee shall bow, every tongue shall swear.

PHILIPPIANS 2:11—Lordship of Christ (2:9–16), written while in confinement Caesarea 57–58 CE and/or Rome 57–63 CE

Theme	PHIL	Lk	Paul
Ever tongue will confess Jesus as Lord	**2:11** [11]And that every tongue should confess that Jesus Christ is Lord, to the glory of God the Father.	**Acts 2:36** [36]Therefore let all the house of Israel know assuredly, that God hath made that same Jesus, whom ye have crucified, both Lord and Christ.	**Rom 10:9** [9]That if thou shalt confess with thy mouth the Lord Jesus, and shalt believe in thine heart that God hath raised him from the dead, thou shalt be saved. **1 Cor 12:3** [3]Wherefore I give you to understand, that no man speaking by the Spirit of God calleth Jesus accursed: and that no man can say that Jesus is the Lord, but by the Holy Ghost.

PHILIPPIANS 2:12—Lordship of Christ (2:9–16), written while in confinement Caesarea 57–58 CE and/or Rome 57–63 CE

Theme	PHIL	Paul	Jewish Writings
Salvation through fear and trembling	**2:12** [12]Wherefore, my beloved, as ye have always obeyed, not as in my presence only, but now much more in my absence, work out your own salvation with fear and trembling.	**1 Cor 2:3** [3]And I was with you in weakness, and in fear, and in much trembling. **2 Cor 7:15** [15]And his inward affection is more abundant toward you, whilst he remembereth the obedience of you all, how with fear and trembling ye received him.	**Ps 2:11** [11]Serve the LORD with fear, and rejoice with trembling.

PHILIPPIANS 2:13—Lordship of Christ (2:9–16), written while in confinement Caesarea 57–58 CE and/or Rome 57–63 CE

Theme	PHIL	Paul
God works our will & pleasure	**2:13** [13]For it is God which worketh in you both to will and to do of his good pleasure. **1:6** [6]Being confident of this very thing, that he which hath begun a good work in you will perform it until the day of Jesus Christ:	**1 Cor 12:6** [6]And there are diversities of operations, but it is the same God which worketh all in all. **1 Cor 15:10** [10]But by the grace of God I am what I am: and his grace which was bestowed upon me was not in vain; but I laboured more abundantly than they all: yet not I, but the grace of God which was with me. **2 Cor 3:6** [6]Who also hath made us able ministers of the new testament; not of the letter, but of the spirit: for the letter killeth, but the spirit giveth life.

PHILIPPIANS 2:14—Lordship of Christ (2:9–16), written while in confinement Caesarea 57–58 CE and/or Rome 57–63 CE

Theme	PHIL	Paul	NT
Do not murmur	**2:14** [14]Do all things without murmurings and disputings:	**1 Cor 10:10** [10]Neither murmur ye, as some of them also murmured, and were destroyed of the destroyer.	**1 Pet 4:9** [9]Use hospitality one to another without grudging.

PHILIPPIANS 2:15—Lordship of Christ (2:9–16), written while in confinement Caesarea 57–58 CE and/or Rome 57–63 CE

Theme	PHIL	Mt	Lk
Be a light (*phos/ phoster*) & do not blame	**2:15** [15]That ye may be blameless and harmless, the sons of God, without rebuke, in the midst of a crooked and perverse nation, among whom ye shine as lights in the world;	**5:13–14** [13]Ye are the salt of the earth: but if the salt have lost his savour, wherewith shall it be salted? it is thenceforth good for nothing, but to be cast out, and to be trodden under foot of men. [14]Ye are the light of the world. A city that is set on an hill cannot be hid **5:16** [16]Let your light so shine before men, that they may see your good works, and glorify your Father which is in heaven. **10:16** [16]Behold, I send you forth as sheep in the midst of wolves: be ye therefore wise as serpents, and harmless as doves.	**Acts 2:40** [40]And with many other words did he testify and exhort, saying, Save yourselves from this untoward generation.

PHILIPPIANS 2:16—Lordship of Christ (2:9–16), written while in confinement Caesarea 57–58 CE and/or Rome 57–63 CE

Theme	PHIL	Paul	Jewish Writings
Word of life is not empty	**2:16** [16]Holding forth the word of life; that I may rejoice in the day of Christ, that I have not run in vain, neither laboured in vain.	**Gal 2:2** [2]And I went up by revelation, and communicated unto them that gospel which I preach among the Gentiles, but privately to them which were of reputation, lest by any means I should run, or had run, in vain. **1 Thes 2:19** [19]For what is our hope, or joy, or crown of rejoicing? Are not even ye in the presence of our Lord Jesus Christ at his coming?	**Is 49:4** [4]Then I said, I have laboured in vain, I have spent my strength for nought, and in vain: yet surely my judgment is with the LORD, and my work with my God. **Is 65:23** [23]They shall not labour in vain, nor bring forth for trouble; for they are the seed of the blessed of the LORD, and their offspring with them.

FAITHFUL IN MINISTRY (2:17–3:6)

PHILIPPIANS 2:17—Faithful in ministry (2:17–3:6), written while in confinement Caesarea 57–58 CE and/or Rome 57–63 CE

Theme	PHIL	Paul
Paul rejoices to be a sacrifice for faithful	**2:17** [17]Yea, and if I be offered upon the sacrifice and service of your faith, I joy, and rejoice with you all.	**Rom 5:16** [16]And not as it was by one that sinned, so is the gift: for the judgment was by one to condemnation, but the free gift is of many offences unto justification. **2 Tim 4:6 (Pseudo)** [6]For I am now ready to be offered, and the time of my departure is at hand.

Paul	Jewish Writings	Other
Rom 16:19 [19]For your obedience is come abroad unto all men. I am glad therefore on your behalf: but yet I would have you wise unto that which is good, and simple concerning evil. **Eph 5:8 (Pseudo)** [8]For ye were sometimes darkness, but now are ye light in the Lord: walk as children of light: **1 Thes 3:13** [13]To the end he may stablish your hearts unblameable in holiness before God, even our Father, at the coming of our Lord Jesus Christ with all his saints.	**Dt 32:5** [5]They have corrupted themselves, their spot is not the spot of his children: they are a perverse and crooked generation. **Dan 2:3** [3]And the king said unto them, I have dreamed a dream, and my spirit was troubled to know the dream.	**Q-Quelle** Commissioning the 70: Phil 2:15/Rom 16:19/ Mt 10:7-16/[Lk 10:1-12 (QS 20-23 [Thom 73;14:2])]; Assistance of the HS: Phil 2:15/Rom 16:19/[Mt 10:19-20]/ [Mk 13:11]/[Lk 12:11-12 (QS 37 [Thom 44]), Lk 21:14-15]]

PHILIPPIANS 2:18—Faithful in ministry (2:17–3:6), written while in confinement Caesarea 57–58 CE and/or Rome 57–63 CE

Theme	PHIL
Rejoice in the Lord	**2:18** [18]For the same cause also do ye joy, and rejoice with me. **3:1** [1]Finally, my brethren, rejoice in the Lord. To write the same things to you, to me indeed is not grievous, but for you it is safe. **4:4** [4]Rejoice in the Lord alway: and again I say, Rejoice.

PHILIPPIANS 2:19—Faithful in ministry (2:17–3:6), written while in confinement Caesarea 57–58 CE and/or Rome 57–63 CE

Theme	PHIL	Lk	Paul
Timotheus is coming	**2:19** [19]But I trust in the Lord Jesus to send Timotheus shortly unto you, that I also may be of good comfort, when I know your state.	**Acts 16:1–3** [1]Then came he to Derbe and Lystra: and, behold, a certain disciple was there, named Timotheus, the son of a certain woman, which was a Jewess, and believed; but his father was a Greek: [2]Which was well reported of by the brethren that were at Lystra and Iconium. [3]Him would Paul have to go forth with him; and took and circumcised him because of the Jews which were in those quarters: for they knew all that his father was a Greek. **Acts 17:14–15** [14]And then immediately the brethren sent away Paul to go as it were to the sea: but Silas and Timotheus abode there still. [15]And they that conducted Paul brought him unto Athens: and receiving a commandment unto Silas and Timotheus for to come to him with all speed, they departed.	**1 Cor 4:17** [17]For this cause have I sent unto you Timotheus, who is my beloved son, and faithful in the Lord, who shall bring you into remembrance of my ways which be in Christ, as I teach every where in every church. **I Cor 16:10** [10]Now if Timotheus come, see that he may be with you without fear: for he worketh the work of the Lord, as I also do.

PHILIPPIANS 2:21—Faithful in ministry (2:17–3:6), written while in confinement Caesarea 57–58 CE and/or Rome 57–63 CE

Theme	PHIL	Paul
Seeking own, not Christ	**2:21** [21]For all seek their own, not the things which are Jesus Christ's.	**1 Cor 13:5** [5]Doth not behave itself unseemly, seeketh not her own, is not easily provoked, thinketh no evil; **2 Tim 4:10 (Pseudo)** [10]For Demas hath forsaken me, having loved this present world, and is departed unto Thessalonica; Crescens to Galatia, Titus unto Dalmatia.

PHILIPPIANS 2:25—Faithful in ministry (2:17–3:6), written while in confinement Caesarea 57–58 CE and/or Rome 57–63 CE

Theme	PHIL
Sending of Epaphroditus to care for Paul	**2:25** [25]Yet I supposed it necessary to send to you Epaphroditus, my brother, and companion in labour, and fellowsoldier, but your messenger, and he that ministered to my wants. **4:10–11, 15–16, 18** [10]But I rejoiced in the Lord greatly, that now at the last your care of me hath flourished again; wherein ye were also careful, but ye lacked opportunity. [11]Not that I speak in respect of want: for I have learned, in whatsoever state I am, therewith to be content. . . . [15]Now ye Philippians know also, that in the beginning of the gospel, when I departed from Macedonia, no church communicated with me as concerning giving and receiving, but ye only. [16]For even in Thessalonica ye sent once and again unto my necessity. . . . [18]But I have all, and abound: I am full, having received of Epaphroditus the things which were sent from you, an odour of a sweet smell, a sacrifice acceptable, wellpleasing to God.

PHILIPPIANS 2:29—Faithful in ministry (2:17–3:6), written while in confinement Caesarea 57–58 CE and/or Rome 57–63 CE

Theme	PHIL	Paul
Receive brother in the Lord	**2:29** [29]Receive him therefore in the Lord with all gladness; and hold such in reputation:	**1 Cor 16:18** [18]For they have refreshed my spirit and yours: therefore acknowledge ye them that are such.

PHILIPPIANS 3:1—Faithful in ministry (2:17–3:6), written while in confinement Caesarea 57–58 CE and/or Rome 57–63 CE

Theme	PHIL
Writing for believers' safety is not a burden	**3:1** [1]Finally, my brethren, rejoice in the Lord. To write the same things to you, to me indeed is not grievous, but for you it is safe. **2:18** [18]For the same cause also do ye joy, and rejoice with me. **4:4** [4]Rejoice in the Lord alway: and again I say, Rejoice.

PHILIPPIANS 3:2—Faithful in ministry (2:17–3:6), written while in confinement Caesarea 57–58 CE and/or Rome 57–63 CE

Theme	PHIL	Paul	NT	Jewish Writings
Beware of evil	**3:2** [2]Beware of dogs, beware of evil workers, beware of the concision.	**2 Cor 11:13** [13]For such are false apostles, deceitful workers, transforming themselves into the apostles of Christ. **Gal 5:6, 12** [6]For in Jesus Christ neither circumcision availeth any thing, nor uncircumcision; but faith which worketh by love. . . . [12]I would they were even cut off which trouble you.	**Rev 22:15** [15]For without are dogs, and sorcerers, and whore-mongers, and murderers, and idolaters, and whosoever loveth and maketh a lie.	**Ps 22:17, 21** [17]I may tell all my bones: they look and stare upon me. . . . [21]Save me from the lion's mouth: for thou hast heard me from the horns of the unicorns.

PHILIPPIANS 3:3—Faithful in ministry (2:17–3:6), written while in confinement Caesarea 57–58 CE and/or Rome 57–63 CE

Theme	PHIL	Paul
Rejoice in Christ, not flesh	**3:3** [3]For we are the circumcision, which worship God in the spirit, and rejoice in Christ Jesus, and have no confidence in the flesh.	**Rom 2:28–29** [28]For he is not a Jew, which is one outwardly; neither is that circumcision, which is outward in the flesh: [29]But he is a Jew, which is one inwardly; and circumcision is that of the heart, in the spirit, and not in the letter; whose praise is not of men, but of God.

PHILIPPIANS 3:4—Faithful in ministry (2:17–3:6), written while in confinement Caesarea 57–58 CE and/or Rome 57–63 CE

Theme	PHIL	Paul
Some rejoice in the flesh	**3:4** [4]Though I might also have confidence in the flesh. If any other man thinketh that he hath whereof he might trust in the flesh, I more:	**2 Cor 11:18, 21–23** [18]Seeing that many glory after the flesh, I will glory also. . . . [21]I speak as concerning reproach, as though we had been weak. Howbeit whereinsoever any is bold, (I speak foolishly,) I am bold also. . . . [22]Are they Hebrews? so am I. Are they Israelites? so am I. Are they the seed of Abraham? so am I. [23]Are they ministers of Christ? (I speak as a fool) I am more; in labours more abundant, in stripes above measure, in prisons more frequent, in deaths oft.

PHILIPPIANS 3:5—Faithful in ministry (2:17–3:6), written while in confinement Caesarea 57–58 CE and/or Rome 57–63 CE

Theme	PHIL	Lk
Circumcised and Jewish	**3:5** [5]Circumcised the eighth day, of the stock of Israel, of the tribe of Benjamin, an Hebrew of the Hebrews; as touching the law, a Pharisee;	**1:59** [59]And it came to pass, that on the eighth day they came to circumcise the child; and they called him Zacharias, after the name of his father. **2:21** [21]And when eight days were accomplished for the circumcising of the child, his name was called JESUS, which was so named of the angel before he was conceived in the womb. **Acts 22:3** [3]I am verily a man which am a Jew, born in Tarsus, a city in Cilicia, yet brought up in this city at the feet of Gamaliel, and taught according to the perfect manner of the law of the fathers, and was zealous toward God, as ye all are this day. **Acts 23:6** [6]But when Paul perceived that the one part were Sadducees, and the other Pharisees, he cried out in the council, Men and brethren, I am a Pharisee, the son of a Pharisee: of the hope and resurrection of the dead I am called in question. **Acts 26:5** [5]Which knew me from the beginning, if they would testify, that after the most straitest sect of our religion I lived a Pharisee.

PHILIPPIANS 3:6—Faithful in ministry (2:17–3:6), written while in confinement Caesarea 57–58 CE and/or Rome 57–63 CE

Theme	PHIL	Lk
Zeal for faith, persecuted church	**3:6** [6]Concerning zeal, persecuting the church; touching the righteousness which is in the law, blameless.	**Acts 8:3** [3]As for Saul, he made havock of the church, entering into every house, and haling men and women committed them to prison. **Acts 22:4** [4]And I persecuted this way unto the death, binding and delivering into prisons both men and women. **Acts 26:9–11** [9]I verily thought with myself, that I ought to do many things contrary to the name of Jesus of Nazareth. [10]Which thing I also did in Jerusalem: and many of the saints did I shut up in prison, having received authority from the chief priests; and when they were put to death, I gave my voice against them. [11]And I punished them oft in every synagogue, and compelled them to blaspheme; and being exceedingly mad against them, I persecuted them even unto strange cities.

CHARACTER OF CHRIST (3:7–21)

PHILIPPIANS 3:7–11—Character of Christ (3:7–21), written while in confinement Caesarea 57–58 CE and/or Rome 57–63 CE

Theme	PHIL	Mt	Mk
Faith in Christ's resurrection	**3:7–11** [7]But what things were gain to me, those I counted loss for Christ. [8]Yea doubtless, and I count all things but loss for the excellency of the knowledge of Christ Jesus my Lord: for whom I have suffered the loss of all things, and do count them but dung, that I may win Christ, [9]And be found in him, not having mine own righteousness, which is of the law, but that which is through the faith of Christ, the righteousness which is of God by faith: [10]That I may know him, and the power of his resurrection, and the fellowship of his sufferings, being made conformable unto his death; [11]If by any means I might attain unto the resurrection of the dead. **1:20** [20]According to my earnest expectation and my hope, that in nothing I shall be ashamed, but that with all boldness, as always, so now also Christ shall be magnified in my body, whether it be by life, or by death.	**16:24** [24]Then said Jesus unto his disciples, If any man will come after me, let him deny himself, and take up his cross, and follow me. **16:26** [26]For what is a man profited, if he shall gain the whole world, and lose his own soul? or what shall a man give in exchange for his soul? **20:22–23** [22]But Jesus answered and said, Ye know not what ye ask. Are ye able to drink of the cup that I shall drink of, and to be baptized with the baptism that I am baptized with? They say unto him, We are able. [23]And he saith unto them, Ye shall drink indeed of my cup, and be baptized with the baptism that I am baptized with: but to sit on my right hand, and on my left, is not mine to give, but it shall be given to them for whom it is prepared of my Father. **26:31** [31]Then saith Jesus unto them, All ye shall be offended because of me this night: for it is written, I will smite the shepherd, and the sheep of the flock shall be scattered abroad. **27:46** [46]And about the ninth hour Jesus cried with a loud voice, saying, EliEli, EliEli, lamalama sabachthanisabachthani? that is to say, My God, my God, why hast thou forsaken me?	**8:34** [34]And when he had called the people unto him with his disciples also, he said unto them, Whosoever will come after me, let him deny himself, and take up his cross, and follow me. **8:36** [36]For what shall it profit a man, if he shall gain the whole world, and lose his own soul? **8:38** [38]Whosoever therefore shall be ashamed of me and of my words in this adulterous and sinful generation; of him also shall the Son of man be ashamed, when he cometh in the glory of his Father with the holy angels. **10:38** [38]But Jesus said unto them, Ye know not what ye ask: can ye drink of the cup that I drink of? and be baptized with the baptism that I am baptized with? **14:27** [27]And Jesus saith unto them, All ye shall be offended because of me this night: for it is written, I will smite the shepherd, and the sheep shall be scattered. **15:34** [34]And at the ninth hour Jesus cried with a loud voice, saying, EloiEloi, EloiEloi, lamalama sabachthanisabachthani? which is, being interpreted, My God, my God, why hast thou forsaken me?

PHILIPPIANS 3:7—Character of Christ (3:7–21), written while in confinement Caesarea 57–58 CE and/or Rome 57–63 CE

Theme	PHIL*	Mt
World gain is loss in Christ	3:7 [7]But what things were gain to me, those I counted loss for Christ.	**13:44–46** [44]Again, the kingdom of heaven is like unto treasure hid in a field; the which when a man hath found, he hideth, and for joy thereof goeth and selleth all that he hath, and buyeth that field. [45]Again, the kingdom of heaven is like unto a merchant man, seeking goodly pearls: [46]Who, when he had found one pearl of great price, went and sold all that he had, and bought it.

Lk	Paul	Jewish Writings
9:23–26	**Rom 6:3–4**	**Ps 22:1**
[23]And he said to them all, If any man will come after me, let him deny himself, and take up his cross daily, and follow me. [24]For whosoever will save his life shall lose it: but whosoever will lose his life for my sake, the same shall save it. [25]For what is a man advantaged, if he gain the whole world, and lose himself, or be cast away? [26]For whosoever shall be ashamed of me and of my words, of him shall the Son of man be ashamed, when he shall come in his own glory, and in his Father's, and of the holy angels.	[3]Know ye not, that so many of us as were baptized into Jesus Christ were baptized into his death? [4]Therefore we are buried with him by baptism into death: that like as Christ was raised up from the dead by the glory of the Father, even so we also should walk in newness of life.	[1]My God, my God, why hast thou forsaken me? why art thou so far from helping me, and from the words of my roaring?
12:50	**Rom 8:17**	**Is 53:12**
[50]But I have a baptism to be baptized with; and how am I straitened till it be accomplished!	[17]And if children, then heirs; heirs of God, and joint-heirs with Christ; if so be that we suffer with him, that we may be also glorified together.	[12]Therefore will I divide him a portion with the great, and he shall divide the spoil with the strong; because he hath poured out his soul unto death: and he was numbered with the transgressors; and he bare the sin of many, and made intercession for the transgressors.
22:37	**1 Cor 10:16**	**Zech 13:7**
[37]For I say unto you, that this that is written must yet be accomplished in me, And he was reckoned among the transgressors: for the things concerning me have an end.	[16]The cup of blessing which we bless, is it not the communion of the blood of Christ? The bread which we break, is it not the communion of the body of Christ?	[7]Awake, O sword, against my shepherd, and against the man that is my fellow, saith the LORD of hosts: smite the shepherd, and the sheep shall be scattered: and I will turn mine hand upon the little ones.
	Gal 2:19	
	[19]For I through the law am dead to the law, that I might live unto God.	
	Col 2:8–12	
	[8]Beware lest any man spoil you through philosophy and vain deceit, after the tradition of men, after the rudiments of the world, and not after Christ. [9]For in him dwelleth all the fulness of the Godhead bodily. [10]And ye are complete in him, which is the head of all principality and power: [11]In whom also ye are circumcised with the circumcision made without hands, in putting off the body of the sins of the flesh by the circumcision of Christ: [12]Buried with him in baptism, wherein also ye are risen with him through the faith of the operation of God, who hath raised him from the dead.	

Lk	Other
14:33	**Q-Quelle**
[33]So likewise, whosoever he be of you that forsaketh not all that he hath, he cannot be my disciple.	Conditions/Discipleship: Phil 3:7/[Mt 10:37-38]/Lk 14:25-33 (QS 52 [Thom 55, 101

PHILIPPIANS 3:9—Character of Christ (3:7–21), written while in confinement Caesarea 57–58 CE and/or Rome 57–63 CE

Theme	PHIL	Paul
Righteousness by faith	**3:9** [9]And be found in him, not having mine own righteousness, which is of the law, but that which is through the faith of Christ, the righteousness which is of God by faith:	**Rom 3:21–22** [21]But now the righteousness of God without the law is manifested, being witnessed by the law and the prophets; [22]Even the righteousness of God which is by faith of Jesus Christ unto all and upon all them that believe: for there is no difference:

PHILIPPIANS 3:10—Character of Christ (3:7–21), written while in confinement Caesarea 57–58 CE and/or Rome 57–63 CE

Theme	PHIL	Mt	Mk	Lk	Jn
Following way of the cross	**3:10** [10]That I may know him, and the power of his resurrection, and the fellowship of his sufferings, being made conformable unto his death;	**16:24–26** [24]Then said Jesus unto his disciples, If any man will come after me, let him deny himself, and take up his cross, and follow me. [25]For whosoever will save his life shall lose it: & whosoever will lose his life for my sake shall find it. [26]For what is a man profited, if he shall gain the whole world, and lose his own soul? or what shall a man give in exchange for his soul?	**8:34–37** [34]And when he had called the people unto him with his disciples also, he said unto them, Whosoever will come after me, let him deny himself, and take up his cross, and follow me. [35]For whosoever will save his life shall lose it; but whosoever shall lose his life for my sake and the gospel's, the same shall save it. [36]For what shall it profit a man, if he shall gain the whole world, and lose his own soul? [37]Or what shall a man give in exchange for his soul? **14:36** [36]And he said, Abba, Father, all things are possible unto thee; take away this cup from me: nevertheless not what I will, but what thou wilt.	**22:42** [42]Saying, Father, if thou be willing, remove this cup from me: nevertheless not my will, but thine, be done.	**10:11** [11]I am the good shepherd: the good shepherd giveth his life for the sheep.

PHILIPPIANS 3:11—Character of Christ (3:7–21), written while in confinement Caesarea 57–58 CE and/or Rome 57–63 CE

Theme	PHIL	Lk	Jn
Attain to resurrection of dead	**3:11** [11]If by any means I might attain unto the resurrection of the dead.	**Acts 4:2** [2]Being grieved that they taught the people, and preached through Jesus the resurrection from the dead.	**11:23–26** [23]Jesus saith unto her, Thy brother shall rise again. [24]Martha saith unto him, I know that he shall rise again in the resurrection at the last day. [25]Jesus said unto her, I am the resurrection, and the life: he that believeth in me, though he were dead, yet shall he live: [26]And whosoever liveth and believeth in me shall never die. Believest thou this?

PHILIPPIANS 3:12—Character of Christ (3:7–21), written while in confinement Caesarea 57–58 CE and/or Rome 57–63 CE

Theme	PHIL
Apprehending Christ	**3:12** [12]Not as though I had already attained, either were already perfect: but I follow after, if that I may apprehend that for which also I am apprehended of Christ Jesus.

Paul	Other
Rom 6:3–5 [3]Know ye not, that so many of us as were baptized into Jesus Christ were baptized into his death? [4]Therefore we are buried with him by baptism into death: that like as Christ was raised up from the dead by the glory of the Father, even so we also should walk in newness of life. [5]For if we have been planted together in the likeness of his death, we shall be also in the likeness of his resurrection: **Rom 8:17** [17]And if children, then heirs; heirs of God, and joint-heirs with Christ; if so be that we suffer with him, that we may be also glorified together. **Gal 2:19** [19]For I through the law am dead to the law, that I might live unto God. **Gal 6:17** [17]From henceforth let no man trouble me: for I bear in my body the marks of the Lord Jesus.	**Q-Quelle** Against Pharisees: Phil 3:10/Rom 1:3-4/ Mt 23:4-36/[Mk 7:1-9]/[Lk 11:37-54 (QS 34 [Thom 39:1, 89, 102])]

NT
Rev 20:5–6 [5]But the rest of the dead lived not again until the thousand years were finished. This is the first resurrection. [6]Blessed and holy is he that hath part in the first resurrection: on such the second death hath no power, but they shall be priests of God and of Christ, and shall reign with him a thousand years.

Paul
1 Tim 6:12, 19 (Pseudo) [12]Fight the good fight of faith, lay hold on eternal life, whereunto thou art also called, and hast professed a good profession before many witnesses. . . . [19]Laying up in store for themselves a good foundation against the time to come, that they may lay hold on eternal life.

PHILIPPIANS 3:14—Character of Christ (3:7–21), written while in confinement Caesarea 57–58 CE and/or Rome 57–63 CE

Theme	PHIL	Paul
Paul follows God's call	**3:14** [14]I press toward the mark for the prize of the high calling of God in Christ Jesus.	**1 Cor 9:24–25** [24]Know ye not that they which run in a race run all, but one receiveth the prize? So run, that ye may obtain. [25]And every man that striveth for the mastery is temperate in all things. Now they do it to obtain a corruptible crown; but we an incorruptible. **2 Tim 4:7 (Pseudo)** [7]I have fought a good fight, I have finished my course, I have kept the faith:

PHILIPPIANS 3:17—Character of Christ (3:7–21), written while in confinement Caesarea 57–58 CE and/or Rome 57–63 CE

Theme	PHIL	Paul	NT
Be followers with Paul	**3:17** [17]Brethren, be followers together of me, and mark them which walk so as ye have us for an ensample.	**1 Cor 4:16** [16]Wherefore I beseech you, be ye followers of me. **1 Cor 11:1** [1]Be ye followers of me, even as I also am of Christ. **1 Thes 1:7** [7]So that ye were ensamples to all that believe in Macedonia and Achaia.	**1 Pet 5:3** [3]Neither as being lords over God's heritage, but being ensamples to the flock.

PHILIPPIANS 3:18—Character of Christ (3:7–21), written while in confinement Caesarea 57–58 CE and/or Rome 57–63 CE

Theme	PHIL	Paul
Enemies of the cross	**3:18** [18](For many walk, of whom I have told you often, and now tell you even weeping, that they are the enemies of the cross of Christ:	**1 Cor 1:17** [17]For Christ sent me not to baptize, but to preach the gospel: not with wisdom of words, lest the cross of Christ should be made of none effect. **1 Cor 1:23** [23]But we preach Christ crucified, unto the Jews a stumblingblock, and unto the Greeks foolishness; **Gal 6:12** [12]As many as desire to make a fair show in the flesh, they constrain you to be circumcised; only lest they should suffer persecution for the cross of Christ.

PHILIPPIANS 3:19—Character of Christ (3:7–21), written while in confinement Caesarea 57–58 CE and/or Rome 57–63 CE

Theme	PHIL	Paul
Those whose god is the belly and shame	**3:19** [19]Whose end is destruction, whose God is their belly, and whose glory is in their shame, who mind earthly things.)	**Rom 8:5–6** [5]For they that are after the flesh do mind the things of the flesh; but they that are after the Spirit the things of the Spirit. [6]For to be carnally minded is death; but to be spiritually minded is life and peace. **Rom 16:18** [16]Salute one another with an holy kiss. The churches of Christ salute you. [17]Now I beseech you, brethren, mark them which cause divisions and offences contrary to the doctrine which ye have learned; and avoid them. [18]For they that are such serve not our Lord Jesus Christ, but their own belly; and by good words and fair speeches deceive the hearts of the simple.

PHILIPPIANS 3:20—Character of Christ (3:7–21), written while in confinement Caesarea 57–58 CE and/or Rome 57–63 CE

Theme	PHIL	Paul	NT
Look for Jesus in heaven	**3:20** [20]For our conversation is in heaven; from whence also we look for the Saviour, the Lord Jesus Christ:	**Eph 2:6 (Pseudo)** [6]And hath raised us up together, and made us sit together in heavenly places in Christ Jesus: **Eph 2:19 (Pseudo)** [19]Now therefore ye are no more strangers and foreigners, but fellowcitizens with the saints, and of the household of God; **Col 3:1–3** [1]If ye then be risen with Christ, seek those things which are above, where Christ sitteth on the right hand of God. [2]Set your affection on things above, not on things on the earth. [3]For ye are dead, and your life is hid with Christ in God.	**Heb 12:22** [22]But ye are come unto mount Sion, and unto the city of the living God, the heavenly Jerusalem, and to an innumerable company of angels,

PHILIPPIANS 3:21—Character of Christ (3:7–21), written while in confinement Caesarea 57–58 CE and/or Rome 57–63 CE

Theme	PHIL	Mt	Mk	Lk
Transformation in Christ	**3:21** [21]Who shall change our vile body, that it may be fashioned like unto his glorious body, according to the working whereby he is able even to subdue all things unto himself.	**22:41–46** [41]While the Pharisees were gathered together, Jesus asked them, [42]Saying, What think ye of Christ? whose son is he? They say unto him, The Son of David. [43]He saith unto them, How then doth David in spirit call him Lord, saying, [44]The LORD said unto my Lord, Sit thou on my right hand, till I make thine enemies thy footstool? [45]If David then call him Lord, how is he his son? [46]And no man was able to answer him a word, neither durst any man from that day forth ask him any more questions.	**12:35–37** [35]And Jesus answered and said, while he taught in the temple, How say the scribes that Christ is the Son of David? [36]For David himself said by the Holy Ghost, The LORD said to my Lord, Sit thou on my right hand, till I make thine enemies thy footstool. [37]David therefore himself calleth him Lord; and whence is he then his son? And the common people heard him gladly. **14:61** [61]But he held his peace, and answered nothing. Again the high priest asked him, and said unto him, Art thou the Christ, the Son of the Blessed?	**20:41–44** [41]And he said unto them, How say they that Christ is David's son? [42]And David himself saith in the book of Psalms, The LORD said unto my Lord, Sit thou on my right hand, [43]Till I make thine enemies thy footstool. [44]David therefore calleth him Lord, how is he then his son?

Paul

Rom 8:23–29

23And not only they, but ourselves also, which have the firstfruits of the Spirit, even we ourselves groan within ourselves, waiting for the adoption, to wit, the redemption of our body. 24For we are saved by hope: but hope that is seen is not hope: for what a man seeth, why doth he yet hope for? 25But if we hope for that we see not, then do we with patience wait for it. 26Likewise the Spirit also helpeth our infirmities: for we know not what we should pray for as we ought: but the Spirit itself maketh inter-cession for us with groanings which cannot be uttered. 27And he that searcheth the hearts knoweth what is the mind of the Spirit, because he maketh intercession for the saints according to the will of God. 28And we know that all things work together for good to them that love God, to them who are the called according to his purpose. 29For whom he did foreknow, he also did predestinate to be conformed to the image of his Son, that he might be the firstborn among many brethren. 30Moreover whom he did predestinate, them he also called: and whom he called, them he also justified: and whom he justified

Rom 9:5

5Whose are the fathers, and of whom as concerning the flesh Christ came, who is over all, God blessed for ever. Amen.

1 Cor 15:27–28

27For he hath put all things under his feet. But when he saith all things are put under him, it is manifest that he is excepted, which did put all things under him. 28And when all things shall be subdued unto him, then shall the Son also himself be subject unto him that put all things under him, that God may be all in all.

1 Cor 15:42–57

42So also is the resurrection of the dead. It is sown in corruption; it is raised in incorruption: 43It is sown in dishonour; it is raised in glory: it is sown in weakness; it is raised in power: 44It is sown a natural body; it is raised a spiritual body. There is a natural body, and there is a spiritual body. 45And so it is written, The first man Adam was made a living soul; the last Adam was made a quickening spirit. 46Howbeit that was not first which is spiritual, but that which is natural; and afterward that which is spiritual. 47The first man is of the earth, earthy: the second man is the Lord from heaven. 48As is the earthy, such are they also that are earthy: and as is the heavenly, such are they also that are heavenly. 49And as we have borne the image of the earthy, we shall also bear the image of the heavenly. 50Now this I say, brethren, that flesh and blood cannot inherit the kingdom of God; neither doth corruption inherit incorruption. 51Behold, I show you a mystery; We shall not all sleep, but we shall all be changed, 52In a moment, in the twinkling of an eye, at the last trump: for the trumpet shall sound, and the dead shall be raised incorruptible, and we shall be changed. 53For this corruptible must put on incorruption, and this mortal must put on immortality. 54So when this corruptible shall have put on incorruption, and this mortal shall have put on immortality, then shall be brought to pass the saying that is written, Death is swallowed up in victory. 55O death, where is thy sting? O grave, where is thy victory? 56The sting of death is sin; and the strength of sin is the law. 57But thanks be to God, which giveth us the victory through our Lord Jesus Christ.

2 Cor 3:18

18But we all, with open face beholding as in a glass the glory of the Lord, are changed into the same image from glory to glory, even as by the Spirit of the Lord.

2 Cor 5:1–5

1For we know that if our earthly house of this tabernacle were dissolved, we have a building of God, an house not made with hands, eternal in the heavens. 2For in this we groan, earnestly desiring to be clothed upon with our house which is from heaven: 3If so be that being clothed we shall not be found naked. 4For we that are in this tabernacle do groan, being burdened: not for that we would be unclothed, but clothed upon, that mortality might be swallowed up of life. 5Now he that hath wrought us for the selfsame thing is God, who also hath given unto us the earnest of the Spirit.

Jewish Writings

Gen 1:28

28And God blessed them, and God said unto them, Be fruitful, and multiply, and replenish the earth, and subdue it: and have dominion over the fish of the sea, and over the fowl of the air, and over every living thing that moveth upon the earth.

Is 1:1–2

1The vision of Isaiah the son of Amoz, which he saw concerning Judah and Jerusalem in the days of Uzziah, Jotham, Ahaz, and Hezekiah, kings of Judah. 2Hear, O heavens, and give ear, O earth: for the LORD hath spoken, I have nourished and brought up children, and they have rebelled against me.

Is 9:6–7

6For unto us a child is born, unto us a son is given: and the government shall be upon his shoulder: and his name shall be called Wonderful, Counsellor, The mighty God, The everlasting Father, The Prince of Peace. 7Of the increase of his government and peace there shall be no end, upon the throne of David, and upon his kingdom, to order it, and to establish it with judgment and with justice from henceforth even for ever. The zeal of the LORD of hosts will perform this.

INSTRUCTIONS FOR CHRISTIANS (4:1–9)

PHILIPPIANS 4:1—Instructions for Christians (4:1–9), written while in confinement Caesarea 57–58 CE and/or Rome 57–63 CE

Theme	PHIL	Paul
Stand fast in Jesus	**4:1** [1]Therefore, my brethren dearly beloved and longed for, my joy and crown, so stand fast in the Lord, my dearly beloved.	**1 Thes 2:19–20** [19]For what is our hope, or joy, or crown of rejoicing? Are not even ye in the presence of our Lord Jesus Christ at his coming? [20]For ye are our glory and joy.

PHILIPPIANS 4:3—Instructions for Christians (4:1–9), written while in confinement Caesarea 57–58 CE and/or Rome 57–63 CE

Theme	PHIL	Lk	NT
Fellow laborers, women, and Clement	**4:3** [3]And I entreat thee also, true yokefellow, help those women which laboured with me in the gospel, with Clement also, and with other my fellow-labourers, whose names are in the book of life.	**10:20** [20]Notwithstanding in this rejoice not, that the spirits are subject unto you; but rather rejoice, because your names are written in heaven.	**Rev 3:5** [5]He that overcometh, the same shall be clothed in white raiment; and I will not blot out his name out of the book of life, but I will confess his name before my Father, and before his angels. **Rev 13:8** [8]And all that dwell upon the earth shall worship him, whose names are not written in the book of life of the Lamb slain from the foundation of the world. **Rev 17:8** [8]The beast that thou sawest was, and is not; and shall ascend out of the bottomless pit, and go into perdition: and they that dwell on the earth shall wonder, whose names were not written in the book of life from the foundation of the world, when they behold the beast that was, and is not, and yet is. **Rev 20:12** [12]And I saw the dead, small and great, stand before God; and the books were opened: and another book was opened, which is the book of life: and the dead were judged out of those things which were written in the books, according to their works. **Rev 20:15** [15]And whosoever was not found written in the book of life was cast into the lake of fire. **Rev 21:27** [27]And there shall in no wise enter into it any thing that defileth, neither whatsoever worketh abomination, or maketh a lie: but they which are written in the Lamb's book of life.

PHILIPPIANS 4:4—Instructions for Christians (4:1–9), written while in confinement Caesarea 57–58 CE and/or Rome 57–63 CE

Theme	PHIL
Rejoice in the Lord always	**4:4** [4]Rejoice in the Lord alway: and again I say, Rejoice. **2:18** [18]For the same cause also do ye joy, and rejoice with me. **3:1** [1]Finally, my brethren, rejoice in the Lord. To write the same things to you, to me indeed is not grievous, but for you it is safe.

Jewish Writings

Ex 32:32–33

[32]Yet now, if thou wilt forgive their
sin—; and if not, blot me, I pray thee,
out of thy book which thou hast written. [33]And the LORD said unto Moses,
Whosoever hath sinned against me,
him will I blot out of my book.

Ps 69:29

[29]But I am poor and sorrowful: let thy salvation, O God, set me up on high.

Dan 12:1

[1]And at that time shall Michael stand up, the great prince which standeth for the children of thy people: and there shall be a time of trouble, such as never was since there was a nation even to that same time: and at that time thy people shall be delivered, every one that shall be found written in the book.

PHILIPPIANS 4:5—Instructions for Christians (4:1–9), written while in confinement Caesarea 57–58 CE and/or Rome 57–63 CE

Theme	PHIL	Paul
Be moderate for Lord's sake	**4:5** [5]Let your moderation be known unto all men. The Lord is at hand.	**Tit 3:2 (Pseudo)** [2]To speak evil of no man, to be no brawlers, but gentle, showing all meekness unto all men.

PHILIPPIANS 4:6—Instructions for Christians (4:1–9), written while in confinement Caesarea 57–58 CE and/or Rome 57–63 CE

Theme	PHIL	Mt	Lk
Prayer and thanks-giving	**4:6** [6]Be careful for nothing; but in every thing by prayer and supplication with thanks-giving let your requests be made known unto God.	**6:19–21** [19]Lay not up for yourselves treasures upon earth, where moth and rust doth corrupt, and where thieves break through and steal: [20]But lay up for yourselves treasures in heaven, where neither moth nor rust doth corrupt, and where thieves do not break through nor steal: [21]For where your treasure is, there will your heart be also. **6:25–34** [25]Therefore I say unto you, Take no thought for your life, what ye shall eat, or what ye shall drink; nor yet for your body, what ye shall put on. Is not the life more than meat, and the body than raiment? [26]Behold the fowls of the air: for they sow not, neither do they reap, nor gather into barns; yet your heavenly Father feedeth them. Are ye not much better than they? [27]Which of you by taking thought can add one cubit unto his stature? [28]And why take ye thought for raiment? Consider the lilies of the field, how they grow; they toil not, neither do they spin: [29]And yet I say unto you, That even Solomon in all his glory was not arrayed like one of these. [30]Wherefore, if God so clothe the grass of the field, which to day is, and to morrow is cast into the oven, shall he not much more clothe you, O ye of little faith? [31]Therefore take no thought, saying, What shall we eat? or, What shall we drink? or, Wherewithal shall we be clothed? [32](For after all these things do the Gentiles seek:) for your heavenly Father knoweth that ye have need of all these things. [33]But seek ye first the kingdom of God, and his righteousness; and all these things shall be added unto you. [34]Take therefore no thought for the morrow: for the morrow shall take thought for the things of itself. Sufficient unto the day is the evil thereof.	**12:7** [7]But even the very hairs of your head are all numbered. Fear not therefore: ye are of more value than many sparrows. **12:21** [21]So is he that layeth up treasure for himself, and is not rich toward God. **12:22–34** [22]And he said unto his disciples, Therefore I say unto you, Take no thought for your life, what ye shall eat; neither for the body, what ye shall put on. [23]The life is more than meat, and the body is more than raiment. [24]Consider the ravens: for they neither sow nor reap; which neither have storehouse nor barn; and God feedeth them: how much more are ye better than the fowls? [25]And which of you with taking thought can add to his stature one cubit? [26]If ye then be not able to do that thing which is least, why take ye thought for the rest? [27]Consider the lilies how they grow: they toil not, they spin not; and yet I say unto you, that Solomon in all his glory was not arrayed like one of these. [28]If then God so clothe the grass, which is to day in the field, and to morrow is cast into the oven; how much more will he clothe you, O ye of little faith? [29]And seek not ye what ye shall eat, or what ye shall drink, neither be ye of doubtful mind. [30]For all these things do the nations of the world seek after: and your Father knoweth that ye have need of these things. [31]But rather seek ye the kingdom of God; and all these things shall be added unto you. [32]Fear not, little flock; for it is your Father's good pleasure to give you the kingdom. [33]Sell that ye have, and give alms; provide yourselves bags which wax not old, a treasure in the heavens that faileth not, where no thief approacheth, neither moth corrupteth. [34]For where your treasure is, there will your heart be also. **18:22** [22]Now when Jesus heard these things, he said unto him, Yet lackest thou one thing: sell all that thou hast, and distribute unto the poor, and thou shalt have treasure in heaven:& come, follow me.

NT	Jewish Writings
Heb 10:37 [37]For yet a little while, and he that shall come will come, and will not tarry. **Jas 5:8–9** [8]Be ye also patient; stablish your hearts: for the coming of the Lord draweth nigh. [9]Grudge not one against another, brethren, lest ye be condemned: behold, the judge standeth before the door.	**Ps 145:18** [18]The LORD is nigh unto all them that call upon him, to all that call upon him in truth.

Paul	NT	Other
Col 4:2 [2]Continue in prayer, and watch in the same with thanksgiving;	**1 Pet 5:7** [7]Casting all your care upon him; for he careth for you.	**Clem, Strom 1.24.158** Apollo, interpreted mystically by "privation of many," means the one God. Well, then, that fire like a pillar, and the fire in the desert, is the symbol of the holy light which passed through from earth and returned again to heaven, by the wood [of the cross], by which also the gift of intellectual vision was bestowed on us. **GThom 36** [36]Jesus said, "Do not be concerned from morning until evening and from evening until morning about what you will wear." **GThom 76** [76]Jesus said, "The kingdom of the father is like a merchant who had consignment on merchandise and who discovered a pearl. That merchant was shrewd. He sold the merchandise and bought the pearl alone for himself. You too, seek his unfailing and enduring treasure where no moth comes near to devour and no worm destroys." **Q-Quelle** Treasures in Heaven: Phil 4:6/Mt 6:19-21/[Lk 12:33-34 (QS 40 [Thom 76:2)]; Anxiety: Mt 6:25-34/Lk 12:22-32 (QS 39 [Thom 36]); Fearless Confession: Phil 4:6/[Mt 10:26-33]/[Lk 12:2-9/ (QS 36)]

PHILIPPIANS 4:7—Instructions for Christians (4:1–9), written while in confinement Caesarea 57–58 CE and/or Rome 57–63 CE

Theme	PHIL	Jn	Paul
Peace that passes all understanding	**4:7** [7]And the peace of God, which passeth all understanding, shall keep your hearts and minds through Christ Jesus.	**14:27** [27]Peace I leave with you, my peace I give unto you: not as the world giveth, give I unto you. Let not your heart be troubled, neither let it be afraid.	**Col 3:15** [15]And let the peace of God rule in your hearts, to the which also ye are called in one body; and be ye thankful.

PHILIPPIANS 4:8—Instructions for Christians (4:1–9), written while in confinement Caesarea 57–58 CE and/or Rome 57–63 CE

Theme	PHIL	Paul
Think on things that are honest and pure	**4:8** [8]Finally, brethren, whatsoever things are true, whatsoever things are honest, whatsoever things are just, whatsoever things are pure, whatsoever things are lovely, whatsoever things are of good report; if there be any virtue, and if there be any praise, think on these things.	**Rom 12:17** [17]Recompense to no man evil for evil. Provide things honest in the sight of all men.

PHILIPPIANS 4:9—Instructions for Christians (4:1–9), written while in confinement Caesarea 57–58 CE and/or Rome 57–63 CE

Theme	PHIL	Paul
Do as Paul teaches & does	**4:9** [9]Those things, which ye have both learned, and received, and heard, and seen in me, do: and the God of peace shall be with you.	**Rom 15:33** [33]Now the God of peace be with you all. Amen. **Rom 16:20** [20]And the God of peace shall bruise Satan under your feet shortly. The grace of our Lord Jesus Christ be with you. Amen. **1 Cor 14:33** [33]For God is not the author of confusion, but of peace, as in all churches of the saints. **1 Thes 4:1** [1]Furthermore then we beseech you, brethren, and exhort you by the Lord Jesus, that as ye have received of us how ye ought to walk and to please God, so ye would abound more and more. **1 Thes 5:23** [23]And the very God of peace sanctify you wholly; and I pray God your whole spirit and soul and body be preserved blameless unto the coming of our Lord Jesus Christ.

THANKSGIVING FOR GENEROSITY (4:10–20)

PHILIPPIANS 4:10—Thanksgiving for generosity (4:10–20), written while in confinement Caesarea 57–58 CE and/or Rome 57–63 CE

Theme	PHIL	Paul
Paul flourished due to church's care	**4:10** [10]But I rejoiced in the Lord greatly, that now at the last your care of me hath flourished again; wherein ye were also careful, but ye lacked opportunity. **1:18** [18]What then? notwithstanding, every way, whether in pretence, or in truth, Christ is preached; and I therein do rejoice, yea, and will rejoice. **2:25** [25]Yet I supposed it necessary to send to you Epaphroditus, my brother, and companion in labour, and fellowsoldier, but your messenger, and he that ministered to my wants.	**1 Cor 9:11** [11]If we have sown unto you spiritual things, is it a great thing if we shall reap your carnal things? **2 Cor 11:9** [9]But as it is written, Eye hath not seen, nor ear heard, neither have entered into the heart of man, the things which God hath prepared for them that love him.

PHILIPPIANS 4:11–12—Thanksgiving for generosity (4:10–20), written while in confinement Caesarea 57–58 CE and/or Rome 57–63 CE

Theme	PHIL	Paul
Being content	**4:11–12** [11]Not that I speak in respect of want: for I have learned, in whatsoever state I am, therewith to be content. [12]I know both how to be abased, and I know how to abound: every where and in all things I am instructed both to be full and to be hungry, both to abound and to suffer need.	**1 Cor 4:11** [11]Even unto this present hour we both hunger, and thirst, and are naked, and are buffeted, and have no certain dwellingplace; **2 Cor 6:10** [10]As sorrowful, yet alway rejoicing; as poor, yet making many rich; as having nothing, and yet possessing all things. **2 Cor 11:27** [27]In weariness and painfulness, in watchings often, in hunger and thirst, in fastings often, in cold and nakedness. **2 Cor 12:9–10** [9]And he said unto me, My grace is sufficient for thee: for my strength is made perfect in weakness. Most gladly therefore will I rather glory in my infirmities, that the power of Christ may rest upon me. [10]Therefore I take pleasure in infirmities, in reproaches, in necessities, in persecutions, in distresses for Christ's sake: for when I am weak, then am I strong.

PHILIPPIANS 4:13—Thanksgiving for generosity (4:10–20), written while in confinement Caesarea 57–58 CE and/or Rome 57–63 CE

Theme	PHIL	Paul
Christ empowers all things	**4:13** [13]I can do all things through Christ which strengtheneth me.	**Col 1:29** [29]Whereunto I also labour, striving according to his working, which worketh in me mightily. **2 Tim 4:17 (Pseudo)** [17]Notwithstanding the Lord stood with me, and strengthened me; that by me the preaching might be fully known, and that all the Gentiles might hear: and I was delivered out of the mouth of the lion.

PHILIPPIANS 4:18—Thanksgiving for generosity (4:10–20), written while in confinement Caesarea 57–58 CE and/or Rome 57–63 CE

Theme	PHIL	Paul	NT	Jewish Writings
Epaphroditus brought Philippians' gifts	**4:18** [18]But I have all, and abound: I am full, having received of Epaphroditus the things which were sent from you, an odour of a sweet smell, a sacrifice acceptable, wellpleasing to God.	**Eph 5:2 (Pseudo)** [2]And walk in love, as Christ also hath loved us, and hath given himself for us an offering and a sacrifice to God for a sweetsmelling savour.	**Heb 13:16** [16]But to do good and to communicate forget not: for with such sacrifices God is well pleased.	**Gen 8:21** [21]And the LORD smelled a sweet savour; and the LORD said in his heart, I will not again curse the ground any more for man's sake; for the imagination of man's heart is evil from his youth; neither will I again smite any more every thing living, as I have done. **Ex 29:18** [18]And thou shalt burn the whole ram upon the altar: it is a burnt offering unto the LORD: it is a sweet savour, an offering made by fire unto the LORD.

PHILIPPIANS 4:19—Thanksgiving for generosity (4:10–20), written while in confinement Caesarea 57–58 CE and/or Rome 57–63 CE

Theme	PHIL	Paul
God will supply churches	**4:19** [19]But my God shall supply all your need according to his riches in glory by Christ Jesus.	**1 Thes 3:11, 13** [11]Now God himself and our Father, and our Lord Jesus Christ, direct our way unto you.... [13]To the end he may stablish your hearts unblameable in holiness before God, even our Father, at the coming of our Lord Jesus Christ with all his saints.

PHILIPPIANS 4:20—Thanksgiving for generosity (4:10–20), written while in confinement Caesarea 57–58 CE and/or Rome 57–63 CE

Theme	PHIL	Paul
Give glory to God	**4:20** [20]Now unto God and our Father be glory for ever and ever. Amen.	**Rom 16:27** [27]To God only wise, be glory through Jesus Christ for ever. Amen. **Eph 5:20 (Pseudo)** [20]Giving thanks always for all things unto God and the Father in the name of our Lord Jesus Christ;

CONCLUDING REMARKS (4:21–22)

PHILIPPIANS 4:22—Concluding remarks (4:21–22), written while in confinement Caesarea 57–58 CE and/or Rome 57–63 CE

Theme	PHIL
Greetings from church and Caesar's house	**4:22** [22]All the saints salute you, chiefly they that are of Caesar's household. **1:13** [13]So that my bonds in Christ are manifest in all the palace, and in all other places;

COLOSSIANS

Written from prison (geographic location of prison is not known, which makes the date uncertain)

ADDRESS (1:1–14)

COLOSSIANS 1:1—Address (1:1–14), written from prison (undetermined location and date)

Theme	COL	Paul
Greeting	**1:1** [1]Paul, an apostle of Jesus Christ by the will of God, and Timotheus our brother,	**Eph 1:1 (Pseudo)** [1]Paul, an apostle of Jesus Christ by the will of God, to the saints which are at Ephesus, and to the faithful in Christ Jesus:

COLOSSIANS 1:3—Address (1:1–14), written from prison (undetermined location and date)

Theme	COL	Paul
Thanks to God	**1:3** [3]We give thanks to God and the Father of our Lord Jesus Christ, praying always for you,	**Eph 1:15–16 (Pseudo)** [15]Wherefore I also, after I heard of your faith in the Lord Jesus, and love unto all the saints, [16]Cease not to give thanks for you, making mention of you in my prayers; **Phlm 4–5** [4]I thank my God, making mention of thee always in my prayers, [5]Hearing of thy love and faith, which thou hast toward the Lord Jesus, and toward all saints;

COLOSSIANS 1:5—Address (1:1–14), written from prison (undetermined location and date)

Theme	COL	Paul	NT
Hope laid up in heaven	**1:5** [5]For the hope which is laid up for you in heaven, whereof ye heard before in the word of the truth of the gospel;	**Eph 1:13 (Pseudo)** [13]In whom ye also trusted, after that ye heard the word of truth, the gospel of your salvation: in whom also after that ye believed, ye were sealed with that holy Spirit of promise, **Eph 1:18 (Pseudo)** [18]The eyes of your understanding being enlightened; that ye may know what is the hope of his calling, and what the riches of the glory of his inheritance in the saints,	**1 Pet 1:4** [4]To an inheritance incorruptible, and undefiled, and that fadeth not away, reserved in heaven for you,

COLOSSIANS 1:6—Address (1:1–14), written from prison (undetermined location and date)

Theme	COL	Mt
Fruit: sowing and reaping	**1:6** [6]Which is come unto you, as it is in all the world; and bringeth forth fruit, as it doth also in you, since the day ye heard of it, and knew the grace of God in truth:	**13:1–23** [1]The same day went Jesus out of the house, and sat by the sea side. [2]And great multitudes were gathered together unto him, so that he went into a ship, and sat; and the whole multitude stood on the shore. [3]And he spake many things unto them in parables, saying, Behold, a sower went forth to sow; [4]And when he sowed, some seeds fell by the way side, and the fowls came and devoured them up: [5]Some fell upon stony places, where they had not much earth: and forthwith they sprung up, because they had no deepness of earth: [6]And when the sun was up, they were scorched; and because they had no root, they withered away. [7]And some fell among thorns; and the thorns sprung up, and choked them: [8]But other fell into good ground, and brought forth fruit, some an hundredfold, some sixtyfold, some thirtyfold. [9]Who hath ears to hear, let him hear. [10]And the disciples came, and said unto him, Why speakest thou unto them in parables? [11]He answered and said unto them, Because it is given unto you to know the mysteries of the kingdom of heaven, but to them it is not given. [12]For whosoever hath, to him shall be given, and he shall have more abundance: but whosoever hath not, from him shall be taken away even that he hath. [13]Therefore speak I to them in parables: because they seeing see not; and hearing they hear not, neither do they understand. [14]And in them is fulfilled the prophecy of Esaias, which saith, By hearing ye shall hear, and shall not understand; and seeing ye shall see, and shall not perceive: [15]For this people's heart is waxed gross, and their ears are dull of hearing, and their eyes they have closed; lest at any time they should see with their eyes, and hear with their ears, and should understand with their heart, and should be converted, and I should heal them. [16]But blessed are your eyes, for they see: and your ears, for they hear. [17]For verily I say unto you, That many prophets and righteous men have desired to see those things which ye see, and have not seen them; and to hear those things which ye hear, and have not heard them. [18]Hear ye therefore the parable of the sower. [19]When any one heareth the word of the kingdom, and understandeth it not, then cometh the wicked one, and catcheth away that which was sown in his heart. This is he which received seed by the way side. [20]But he that received the seed into stony places, the same is he that heareth the word, and anon with joy receiveth it; [21]Yet hath he not root in himself, but dureth for a while: for when tribulation or persecution ariseth because of the word, by and by he is offended. [22]He also that received seed among the thorns is he that heareth the word; and the care of this world, and the deceitfulness of riches, choke the word, and he becometh unfruitful. [23]But he that received seed into the good ground is he that heareth the word, and understandeth it; which also beareth fruit, and bringeth forth, some an hundredfold, some sixty, some thirty. **13:24–30** [24]Another parable put he forth unto them, saying, The kingdom of heaven is likened unto a man which sowed good seed in his field: [25]But while men slept, his enemy came and sowed tares among the wheat, and went his way. [26]But when the blade was sprung up, and brought forth fruit, then appeared the tares also. [27]So the servants of the householder came and said unto him, Sir, didst not thou sow good seed in thy field? from whence then hath it tares? [28]He said unto them, An enemy hath done this. The servants said unto him, Wilt thou then that we go and gather them up? [29]But he said, Nay; lest while ye gather up the tares, ye root up also the wheat with them. [30]Let both grow together until the harvest: and in the time of harvest I will say to the reapers, Gather ye together first the tares, and bind them in bundles to burn them: but gather the wheat into my barn.

Mk	Lk	Paul	Other
4:1–20 [1]And he began again to teach by the sea side: and there was gathered unto him a great multitude, so that he entered into a ship, and sat in the sea; and the whole multitude was by the sea on the land. [2]And he taught them many things by parables, and said unto them in his doctrine, [3]Hearken; Behold, there went out a sower to sow: [4]And it came to pass, as he sowed, some fell by the way side, and the fowls of the air came and devoured it up. [5]And some fell on stony ground, where it had not much earth; and immediately it sprang up, because it had no depth of earth: [6]But when the sun was up, it was scorched; and because it had no root, it withered away. [7]And some fell among thorns, and the thorns grew up, and choked it, and it yielded no fruit. [8]And other fell on good ground, and did yield fruit that sprang up and increased; and brought forth, some thirty, and some sixty, and some an hundred. [9]And he said unto them, He that hath ears to hear, let him hear. [10]And when he was alone, they that were about him with the twelve asked of him the parable. [11]And he said unto them, Unto you it is given to know the mystery of the kingdom of God: but unto them that are without, all these things are done in parables: [12]That seeing they may see, and not perceive; and hearing they may hear, and not understand; lest at any time they should be converted, and their sins should be forgiven them. [13]And he said unto them, Know ye not this parable? and how then will ye know all parables? [14]The sower soweth the word. **[15]And these are they by the way side, where the word is sown; but when they have heard, Satan cometh immediately, and taketh away the word that was sown in their hearts.** [16]And these are they likewise which are sown on stony ground; who, when they have heard the word, immediately receive it with gladness; [17]And have no root in themselves, and so endure but for a time: afterward, when affliction or persecution ariseth for the word's sake, immediately they are offended. [18]And these are they which are sown among thorns; such as hear the word, [19]And the cares of this world, and the deceitfulness of riches, and the lusts of other things entering in, choke the word, and it becometh unfruitful. [20]And these are they which are sown on good ground; such as hear the word, and receive it, and bring forth fruit, some thirtyfold, some sixty, and some an hundred. **4:26–29** [26]And he said, So is the kingdom of God, as if a man should cast seed into the ground; [27]And should sleep, and rise night and day, and the seed should spring and grow up, he knoweth not how. [28]For the earth bringeth forth fruit of herself; first the blade, then the ear, after that the full corn in the ear. [29]But when the fruit is brought forth, immediately he putteth in the sickle, because the harvest is come.	**8:4–15** [4]And when much people were gathered together, and were come to him out of every city, he spake by a parable: [5]A sower went out to sow his seed: and as he sowed, some fell by the way side; and it was trodden down, and the fowls of the air devoured it. [6]And some fell upon a rock; and as soon as it was sprung up, it withered away, because it lacked moisture. [7]And some fell among thorns; and the thorns sprang up with it, and choked it. [8]And other fell on good ground, and sprang up, and bare fruit an hundredfold. And when he had said these things, he cried, He that hath ears to hear, let him hear. [9]And his disciples asked him, saying, What might this parable be? [10]And he said, Unto you it is given to know the mysteries of the kingdom of God: but to others in parables; that seeing they might not see, and hearing they might not understand. [11]Now the parable is this: The seed is the word of God. [12]Those by the way side are they that hear; then cometh the devil, and taketh away the word out of their hearts, lest they should believe and be saved. [13]They on the rock are they, which, when they hear, receive the word with joy; and these have no root, which for a while believe, and in time of temptation fall away. [14]And that which fell among thorns are they, which, when they have heard, go forth, and are choked with cares and riches and pleasures of this life, and bring no fruit to perfection. [15]But that on the good ground are they, which in an honest and good heart, having heard the word, keep it, and bring forth fruit with patience.	**1 Cor 3:6** [6]I have planted, Apollos watered; but God gave the increase. **1 Cor 3:9** [9]For we are labourers together with God: ye are God's husbandry, ye are God's building. **1 Cor 9:7** [7]Who goeth a warfare any time at his own charges? who planteth a vineyard, and eateth not of the fruit thereof? or who feedeth a flock, and eateth not of the milk of the flock? **1 Cor 9:11** [11]If we have sown unto you spiritual things, is it a great thing if we shall reap your carnal things? **2 Cor 4:4** [4]In whom the god of this world hath blinded the minds of them which believe not, lest the light of the glorious gospel of Christ, who is the image of God, should shine unto them. **2 Cor 9:10** [10]Now he that ministereth seed to the sower both minister bread for your food, and multiply your seed sown, and increase the fruits of your righteousness;) **1 Thes 1:6** [6]And ye became followers of us, and of the Lord, having received the word in much affliction, with joy of the Holy Ghost: **1 Thes 2:13** [13]For this cause also thank we God without ceasing, because, when ye received the word of God which ye heard of us, ye received it not as the word of men, but as it is in truth, the word of God, which effectually worketh also in you that believe.	**Q-Quelle** Thanks and Blessings for disciples: Col 1:6/2 Cor 4:4/1 Thes 2:13/[Mt 11:25-27]/Mt 13:16-17/ [Lk 10:21-24 (QS 24, 25)]

COLOSSIANS 1:7—Address (1:1–14), written from prison (undetermined location and date)

Theme	COL	Paul
Learned from Epaphras	**1:7** [7]As ye also learned of Epaphras our dear fellowservant, who is for you a faithful minister of Christ;	**Phlm 23** [23]There salute thee Epaphras, my fellowprisoner in Christ Jesus;

COLOSSIANS 1:9—Address (1:1–14), written from prison (undetermined location and date)

Theme	COL	Paul
Keep praying	**1:9** [9]For this cause we also, since the day we heard it, do not cease to pray for you, and to desire that ye might be filled with the knowledge of his will in all wisdom and spiritual understanding;	**Eph 1:15–17 (Pseudo)** [15]Wherefore I also, after I heard of your faith in the Lord Jesus, and love unto all the saints, [16]Cease not to give thanks for you, making mention of you in my prayers; [17]That the God of our Lord Jesus Christ, the Father of glory, may give unto you the spirit of wisdom and revelation in the knowledge of him: **Eph 5:17 (Pseudo)** [17]Wherefore be ye not unwise, but understanding what the will of the Lord is. **Phil 1:9** [9]And this I pray, that your love may abound yet more and more in knowledge and in all judgment;

COLOSSIANS 1:12—Address (1:1–14), written from prison (undetermined location and date)

Theme	COL	Lk	Jn	Paul	NT
Thanks as partakers	**1:12** [12]Giving thanks unto the Father, which hath made us meet to be partakers of the inheritance of the saints in light: **3:17** [17]And whatsoever ye do in word or deed, do all in the name of the Lord Jesus, giving thanks to God and the Father by him.	**Acts 26:18** [18]To open their eyes, and to turn them from darkness to light, and from the power of Satan unto God, that they may receive forgiveness of sins, and inheritance among them which are sanctified by faith that is in me.	**8:12** [12]Then spake Jesus again unto them, saying, I am the light of the world: he that followeth me shall not walk in darkness, but shall have the light of life.	**1 Tim 6:16 (Pseudo)** [16]Who only hath immortality, dwelling in the light which no man can approach unto; whom no man hath seen, nor can see: to whom be honour and power everlasting. Amen.	**1 Pet 2:9** [9]But ye are a chosen generation, a royal priesthood, an holy nation, a peculiar people; that ye should show forth the praises of him who hath called you out of darkness into his marvellous light:

COLOSSIANS 1:14—Address (1:1–14), written from prison (undetermined location and date)

Theme	COL	Paul
Redeemed & forgiven	**1:14** [14]In whom we have redemption through his blood, even the forgiveness of sins:	**Eph 1:7 (Pseudo)** [7]In whom we have redemption through his blood, the forgiveness of sins, according to the riches of his grace;

PREVENIENT CHRIST (1:15–2:3)

COLOSSIANS 1:15-16—Prevenient Christ (1:15–2:3), written from prison (undetermined location and date)

Theme	COL	Mt
Christ in God's grand design	**1:15–16** [15]Who is the image of the invisible God, the firstborn of every creature: [16]For by him were all things created, that are in heaven, and that are in earth, visible and invisible, whether they be thrones, or dominions, or principalities, or powers: all things were created by him, and for him: **2:8–19** [8]Beware lest any man spoil you through philosophy and vain deceit, after the tradition of men, after the rudiments of the world, and not after Christ. [9]For in him dwelleth all the fulness of the Godhead bodily. [10]And ye are complete in him, which is the head of all principality and power: [11]In whom also ye are circumcised with the circumcision made without hands, in putting off the body of the sins of the flesh by the circumcision of Christ: [12]Buried with him in baptism, wherein also ye are risen with him through the faith of the operation of God, who hath raised him from the dead. [13]And you, being dead in your sins and the uncircumcision of your flesh, hath he quickened together with him, having forgiven you all trespasses; [14]Blotting out the handwriting of ordinances that was against us, which was contrary to us, and took it out of the way, nailing it to his cross; [15]And having spoiled principalities and powers, he made a show of them openly, triumphing over them in it. [16]Let no man therefore judge you in meat, or in drink, or in respect of an holyday, or of the new moon, or of the Sabbath days: [17]Which are a shadow of things to come; but the body is of Christ. [18]Let no man beguile you of your reward in a voluntary humility and worshipping of angels, intruding into those things which he hath not seen, vainly puffed up by his fleshly mind, [19]And not holding the Head, from which all the body by joints and bands having nourishment ministered, and knit together, increaseth with the increase of God.	**11:19** [19]The Son of man came eating and drinking, and they say, Behold a man gluttonous, and a winebibber, a friend of publicans and sinners. But wisdom is justified of her children. **21:33–44** [33]Hear another parable: There was a certain householder, which planted a vineyard, and hedged it round about, and digged a winepress in it, and built a tower, and let it out to husbandmen, and went into a far country: [34]And when the time of the fruit drew near, he sent his servants to the husbandmen, that they might receive the fruits of it. [35]And the husbandmen took his servants, and beat one, and killed another, and stoned another. [36]Again, he sent other servants more than the first: and they did unto them likewise. [37]But last of all he sent unto them his son, saying, They will reverence my son. [38]But when the husbandmen saw the son, they said among themselves, This is the heir; come, let us kill him, and let us seize on his inheritance. [39]And they caught him, and cast him out of the vineyard, and slew him. [40]When the lord therefore of the vineyard cometh, what will he do unto those husbandmen? [41]They say unto him, He will miserably destroy those wicked men, and will let out his vineyard unto other husbandmen, which shall render him the fruits in their seasons. [42]Jesus saith unto them, Did ye never read in the scriptures, The stone which the builders rejected, the same is become the head of the corner: this is the Lord's doing, and it is marvellous in our eyes? [43]Therefore say I unto you, The kingdom of God shall be taken from you, and given to a nation bringing forth the fruits thereof. [44]And whosoever shall fall on this stone shall be broken: but on whomsoever it shall fall, it will grind him to powder. **22:41–46** [41]While the Pharisees were gathered together, Jesus asked them, [42]Saying, What think ye of Christ? whose son is he? They say unto him, The Son of David. [43]He saith unto them, How then doth David in spirit call him Lord, saying, [44]The LORD said unto my Lord, Sit thou on my right hand, till I make thine enemies thy footstool? [45]If David then call him Lord, how is he his son? [46]And no man was able to answer him a word, neither durst any man from that day forth ask him any more questions. **23:34** [34]Wherefore, behold, I send unto you prophets, and wise men, and scribes: and some of them ye shall kill and crucify; and some of them shall ye scourge in your synagogues, and persecute them from city to city:

Colossians 1:15-16 continued on next page

COLOSSIANS 1:15–16—Prevenient Christ (1:15–2:3), written from prison (undetermined location and date) (*continued*)

Theme	COL	Mk
(*Cont.*) **Christ in God's grand design**	**1:15–16 (above)** **2:8–19 (above)**	**12:1–22** [1]And he began to speak unto them by parables. A certain man planted a vineyard, and set an hedge about it, and digged a place for the winefat, and built a tower, and let it out to husbandmen, and went into a far country. [2]And at the season he sent to the husbandmen a servant, that he might receive from the husbandmen of the fruit of the vineyard. [3]And they caught him, and beat him, and sent him away empty. [4]And again he sent unto them another servant; and at him they cast stones, and wounded him in the head, and sent him away shamefully handled. [5]And again he sent another; and him they killed, and many others; beating some, and killing some. [6]Having yet therefore one son, his wellbeloved, he sent him also last unto them, saying, They will reverence my son. [7]But those husbandmen said among themselves, This is the heir; come, let us kill him, and the inheritance shall be ours. [8]And they took him, and killed him, and cast him out of the vineyard. [9]What shall therefore the lord of the vineyard do? he will come and destroy the husbandmen, and will give the vineyard unto others. [10]And have ye not read this scripture; The stone which the builders rejected is become the head of the corner: [11]This was the Lord's doing, and it is marvellous in our eyes? [12]And they sought to lay hold on him, but feared the people: for they knew that he had spoken the parable against them: and they left him, and went their way. [13]And they send unto him certain of the Pharisees and of the Herodians, to catch him in his words. [14]And when they were come, they say unto him, Master, we know that thou art true, and carest for no man: for thou regardest not the person of men, but teachest the way of God in truth: Is it lawful to give tribute to Caesar, or not? [15]Shall we give, or shall we not give? But he, knowing their hypocrisy, said unto them, Why tempt ye me? bring me a penny, that I may see it. [16]And they brought it. And he saith unto them, Whose is this image and superscription? And they said unto him, Caesar's. [17]And Jesus answering said unto them, Render to Caesar the things that are Caesar's, and to God the things that are God's. And they marvelled at him. [18]Then come unto him the Sadducees, which say there is no resurrection; and they asked him, saying, [19]Master, Moses wrote unto us, If a man's brother die, and leave his wife behind him, and leave no children, that his brother should take his wife, and raise up seed unto his brother. [20]Now there were seven brethren: and the first took a wife, and dying left no seed. [21]And the second took her, and died, neither left he any seed: and the third likewise. [22]And the seven had her, and left no seed: last of all the woman died also. **12:35–37** [35]And Jesus answered and said, while he taught in the temple, How say the scribes that Christ is the Son of David? [36]For David himself said by the Holy Ghost, The LORD said to my Lord, Sit thou on my right hand, till I make thine enemies thy footstool. [37]David therefore himself calleth him Lord; and whence is he then his son? And the common people heard him gladly. **14:36** [36]And he said, Abba, Father, all things are possible unto thee; take away this cup from me: nevertheless not what I will, but what thou wilt. **14:61** [61]But he held his peace, and answered nothing. Again the high priest asked him, and said unto him, Art thou the Christ, the Son of the Blessed?

Lk	Jn	Paul	Jewish Writings
7:35 35But wisdom is justified of all her children. **11:49** 49Therefore also said the wisdom of God, I will send them prophets and apostles, and some of them they shall slay and persecute: **20:9–19** 9Then began he to speak to the people this parable; A certain man planted a vineyard, and let it forth to husbandmen, and went into a far country for a long time. 10And at the season he sent a servant to the husbandmen, that they should give him of the fruit of the vineyard: but the husbandmen beat him, and sent him away empty. 11And again he sent another servant: and they beat him also, and entreated him shamefully, and sent him away empty. 12And again he sent a third: and they wounded him also, and cast him out. 13Then said the lord of the vineyard, What shall I do? I will send my beloved son: it may be they will reverence him when they see him. 14But when the husbandmen saw him, they reasoned among themselves, saying, This is the heir: come, let us kill him, that the inheritance may be ours. 15So they cast him out of the vineyard, and killed him. What therefore shall the lord of the vineyard do unto them? 16He shall come and destroy these husbandmen, and shall give the vineyard to others. And when they heard it, they said, God forbid. 17And he beheld them, and said, What is this then that is written, The stone which the builders rejected, the same is become the head of the corner? 18Whosoever shall fall upon that stone shall be broken; but on whomsoever it shall fall, it will grind him to powder. 19And the chief priests and the scribes the same hour sought to lay hands on him; and they feared the people: for they perceived that he had spoken this parable against them. **20:41–44** 41And he said unto them, How say they that Christ is David's son? 42And David himself saith in the book of Psalms, The LORD said unto my Lord, Sit thou on my right hand, 43Till I make thine enemies thy footstool. 44David therefore calleth him Lord, how is he then his son?	**1:18** 18No man hath seen God at any time; the only begotten Son, which is in the bosom of the Father, he hath declared him. **1 Jn 2:18–23** 18Little children, it is the last time: and as ye have heard that antichrist shall come, even now are there many antichrists; whereby we know that it is the last time. 19They went out from us, but they were not of us; for if they had been of us, they would no doubt have continued with us: but they went out, that they might be made manifest that they were not all of us. 20But ye have an unction from the Holy One, and ye know all things. 21I have not written unto you because ye know not the truth, but because ye know it, and that no lie is of the truth. 22Who is a liar but he that denieth that Jesus is the Christ? He is antichrist, that denieth the Father and the Son. 23Whosoever denieth the Son, the same hath not the Father: (but) he that acknowledgeth the Son hath the Father also.	**Rom 1:3–4** 3Concerning his Son Jesus Christ our Lord, which was made of the seed of David according to the flesh; 4And declared to be the Son of God with power, according to the spirit of holiness, by the resurrection from the dead: **Rom 1:7** 7To all that be in Rome, beloved of God, called to be saints: Grace to you and peace from God our Father, and the Lord Jesus Christ. **Rom 8:3** 3For what the law could not do, in that it was weak through the flesh, God sending his own Son in the likeness of sinful flesh, and for sin, condemned sin in the flesh: **Rom 8:15** 15For ye have not received the spirit of bondage again to fear; but ye have received the Spirit of adoption, whereby we cry, Abba, Father. **Rom 9:5** 5Whose are the fathers, and of whom as concerning the flesh Christ came, who is over all, God blessed for ever. Amen. **Gal 4:4** 4But when the fulness of the time was come, God sent forth his Son, made of a woman, made under the law, **Gal 4:6** 6And because ye are sons, God hath sent forth the Spirit of his Son into your hearts, crying, Abba, Father	**Prov 8:22–31** 22The LORD possessed me in the beginning of his way, before his works of old. 23I was set up from everlasting, from the beginning, or ever the earth was. 24When there were no depths, I was brought forth; when there were no fountains abounding with water. 25Before the mountains were settled, before the hills was I brought forth: 26While as yet he had not made the earth, nor the fields, nor the highest part of the dust of the world. 27When he prepared the heavens, I was there: when he set a compass upon the face of the depth: 28When he established the clouds above: when he strengthened the fountains of the deep: 29When he gave to the sea his decree, that the waters should not pass his commandment: when he appointed the foundations of the earth: 30Then I was by him, as one brought up with him: and I was daily his delight, rejoicing always before him; 31Rejoicing in the habitable part of his earth; and my delights were with the sons of men. **Is 9:6–7** 6For unto us a child is born, unto us a son is given: and the government shall be upon his shoulder: and his name shall be called Wonderful, Counsellor, The mighty God, The everlasting Father, The Prince of Peace. 7Of the increase of his government and peace there shall be no end, upon the throne of David, and upon his kingdom, to order it, and to establish it with judgment and with justice from henceforth even for ever. The zeal of the LORD of hosts will perform this. **Is 11:1–2** 1And there shall come forth a rod out of the stem of Jesse, and a Branch shall grow out of his roots: 2And the spirit of the LORD shall rest upon him, the spirit of wisdom and understanding, the spirit of counsel and might, the spirit of knowledge and of the fear of the LORD;

Colossians 1:15-16 continued on next page

COLOSSIANS 1:15–16—Prevenient Christ (1:15–2:3), written from prison (undetermined location and date) (*continued*)

Theme	COL	Jewish Writings
(*Cont.*) **Christ in God's grand design**	**1:15–16 (above)** **2:8–19 (above)**	(***Continued***) **Dan 7** [1]In the first year of Belshazzar king of Babylon Daniel had a dream and visions of his head upon his bed: then he wrote the dream, and told the sum of the matters. [2]Daniel spake and said, I saw in my vision by night, and, behold, the four winds of the heaven strove upon the great sea. [3]And four great beasts came up from the sea, diverse one from another. [4]The first was like a lion, and had eagle's wings: I beheld till the wings thereof were plucked, and it was lifted up from the earth, and made stand upon the feet as a man, and a man's heart was given to it. [5]And behold another beast, a second, like to a bear, and it raised up itself on one side, and it had three ribs in the mouth of it between the teeth of it: and they said thus unto it, Arise, devour much flesh. [6]After this I beheld, and lo another, like a leopard, which had upon the back of it four wings of a fowl; the beast had also four heads; and dominion was given to it. [7]After this I saw in the night visions, and behold a fourth beast, dreadful and terrible, and strong exceedingly; and it had great iron teeth: it devoured and brake in pieces, and stamped the residue with the feet of it: and it was diverse from all the beasts that were before it; and it had ten horns. [8]I considered the horns, and, behold, there came up among them another little horn, before whom there were three of the first horns plucked up by the roots: and, behold, in this horn were eyes like the eyes of man, and a mouth speaking great things. [9]I beheld till the thrones were cast down, and the Ancient of days did sit, whose garment was white as snow, and the hair of his head like the pure wool: his throne was like the fiery flame, and his wheels as burning fire. [10]A fiery stream issued and came forth from before him: thousand thousands ministered unto him, and ten thousand times ten thousand stood before him: the judgment was set, and the books were opened. [11]I beheld then because of the voice of the great words which the horn spake: I beheld even till the beast was slain, and his body destroyed, and given to the burning flame. [12]As concerning the rest of the beasts, they had their dominion taken away: yet their lives were prolonged for a season and time. [13]I saw in the night visions, and, behold, one like the Son of man came with the clouds of heaven, and came to the Ancient of days, and they brought him near before him. [14]And there was given him dominion, and glory, and a kingdom, that all people, nations, and languages, should serve him: his dominion is an everlasting dominion, which shall not pass away, and his kingdom that which shall not be destroyed. [15]I Daniel was grieved in my spirit in the midst of my body, and the visions of my head troubled me. [16]I came near unto one of them that stood by, and asked him the truth of all this. So he told me, and made me know the interpretation of the things. [17]These great beasts, which are four, are four kings, which shall arise out of the earth. [18]But the saints of the most High shall take the kingdom, and possess the kingdom for ever, even for ever and ever. [19]Then I would know the truth of the fourth beast, which was diverse from all the others, exceeding dreadful, whose teeth were of iron, and his nails of brass; which devoured, brake in pieces, and stamped the residue with his feet; [20]And of the ten horns that were in his head, and of the other which came up, and before whom three fell; even of that horn that had eyes, and a mouth that spake very great things, whose look was more stout than his fellows. [21]I beheld, and the same horn made war with the saints, and prevailed against them; [22]Until the Ancient of days came, and judgment was given to the saints of the most High; and the time came that the saints possessed the kingdom. [23]Thus he said, The fourth beast shall be the fourth kingdom upon earth, which shall be diverse from all kingdoms, and shall devour the whole earth, and shall tread it down, and break it in pieces. [24]And the ten horns out of this kingdom are ten kings that shall arise: and another shall rise after them; and he shall be diverse from the first, and he shall subdue three kings. [25]And he shall speak great words against the most High, and shall wear out the saints of the most High, and think to change times and laws: and they shall be given into his hand until a time and times and the dividing of time. [26]But the judgment shall sit, and they shall take away his dominion, to consume and to destroy it unto the end. [27]And the kingdom and dominion, and the greatness of the kingdom under the whole heaven, shall be given to the people of the saints of the most High, whose kingdom is an everlasting kingdom, and all dominions shall serve and obey him. [28]Hitherto is the end of the matter. As for me Daniel, my cogitations much troubled me, and my countenance changed in me: but I kept the matter in my heart.

COLOSSIANS 1:15—Prevenient Christ (1:15–2:3), written from prison (undetermined location and date)

Theme	COL	Jn	Paul	Jewish Writings
Image of God, firstborn	**1:15** [15]Who is the image of the invisible God, the firstborn of every creature:	**1:3, 18** [3]All things were made by him; and without him was not any thing made that was made. . . . [18]No man hath seen God at any time; the only begotten Son, which is in the bosom of the Father, he hath declared him.	**2 Cor 4:4** [4]In whom the god of this world hath blinded the minds of them which believe not, lest the light of the glorious gospel of Christ, who is the image of God, should shine unto them.	**Ps 89:28** [28]My mercy will I keep for him for evermore, and my covenant shall stand fast with him.

COLOSSIANS 1:16–20—Prevenient Christ (1:15–2:3), written from prison (undetermined location and date)

Theme	COL	Paul
Christ redeems all things	**1:16–20** [16]For by him were all things created, that are in heaven, and that are in earth, visible and invisible, whether they be thrones, or dominions, or principalities, or powers: all things were created by him, and for him: [17]And he is before all things, and by him all things consist. [18]And he is the head of the body, the church: who is the beginning, the firstborn from the dead; that in all things he might have the preeminence. [19]For it pleased the Father that in him should all fulness dwell; [20]And, having made peace through the blood of his cross, by him to reconcile all things unto himself; by him, I say, whether they be things in earth, or things in heaven.	**Rom 8:21** [21]Because the creature itself also shall be delivered from the bondage of corruption into the glorious liberty of the children of God. **1 Cor 15:24–28** [24]Then cometh the end, when he shall have delivered up the kingdom to God, even the Father; when he shall have put down all rule and all authority and power. [25]For he must reign, till he hath put all enemies under his feet. [26]The last enemy that shall be destroyed is death. [27]For he hath put all things under his feet. But when he saith all things are put under him, it is manifest that he is excepted, which did put all things under him. [28]And when all things shall be subdued unto him, then shall the Son also himself be subject unto him that put all things under him, that God may be all in all. **Eph 1:10 (Pseudo)** [10]That in the dispensation of the fulness of times he might gather together in one all things in Christ, both which are in heaven, and which are on earth; even in him:

COLOSSIANS 1:16—Prevenient Christ (1:15–2:3), written from prison (undetermined location and date)

Theme	COL	Paul
God created all things	**1:16** [16]For by him were all things created, that are in heaven, and that are in earth, visible and invisible, whether they be thrones, or dominions, or principalities, or powers: all things were created by him, and for him:	**1 Cor 8:6** [6]But to us there is but one God, the Father, of whom are all things, and we in him; and one Lord Jesus Christ, by whom are all things, and we by him. **Eph 1:10–21 (Pseudo)** [10]That in the dispensation of the fulness of times he might gather together in one all things in Christ, both which are in heaven, and which are on earth; even in him: [11]In whom also we have obtained an inheritance, being predestinated according to the purpose of him who worketh all things after the counsel of his own will: [12]That we should be to the praise of his glory, who first trusted in Christ. [13]In whom ye also trusted, after that ye heard the word of truth, the gospel of your salvation: in whom also after that ye believed, ye were sealed with that holy Spirit of promise, [14]Which is the earnest of our inheritance until the redemption of the purchased possession, unto the praise of his glory. [15]Wherefore I also, after I heard of your faith in the Lord Jesus, and love unto all the saints, [16]Cease not to give thanks for you, making mention of you in my prayers; [17]That the God of our Lord Jesus Christ, the Father of glory, may give unto you the spirit of wisdom and revelation in the knowledge of him: [18]The eyes of your understanding being enlightened; that ye may know what is the hope of his calling, and what the riches of the glory of his inheritance in the saints, [19]And what is the exceeding greatness of his power to us-ward who believe, according to the working of his mighty power, [20]Which he wrought in Christ, when he raised him from the dead, and set him at his own right hand in the heavenly places, [21]Far above all principality, and power, and might, and dominion, and every name that is named, not only in this world, but also in that which is to come:

COLOSSIANS 1:18—Prevenient Christ (1:15–2:3), written from prison (undetermined location and date)

Theme	COL	Paul	NT
Jesus, head over all	**1:18** [18]And he is the head of the body, the church: who is the beginning, the firstborn from the dead; that in all things he might have the preeminence.	**Rom 14:19–20** [19]Let us therefore follow after the things which make for peace, and things wherewith one may edify another. [20]For meat destroy not the work of God. All things indeed are pure; but it is evil for that man who eateth with offence. **1 Cor 11:3** [3]But I would have you know, that the head of every man is Christ; and the head of the woman is the man; and the head of Christ is God. **1 Cor 12:12, 27** [12]For as the body is one, and hath many members, and all the members of that one body, being many, are one body: so also is Christ. . . . [27]Now ye are the body of Christ, and members in particular. **1 Cor 15:20** [20]But now is Christ risen from the dead, and become the firstfruits of them that slept. **2 Cor 13:10** [10]Therefore I write these things being absent, lest being present I should use sharpness, according to the power which the Lord hath given me to edification, and not to destruction. **Gal 2:18–19** [18]For if I build again the things which I destroyed, I make myself a transgressor. [19]For I through the law am dead to the law, that I might live unto God. **Eph 1:22–23 (Pseudo)** [22]And hath put all things under his feet, and gave him to be the head over all things to the church, [23]Which is his body, the fulness of him that filleth all in all.	**Rev 1:5** [5]And from Jesus Christ, who is the faithful witness, and the first begotten of the dead, and the prince of the kings of the earth. Unto him that loved us, and washed us from our sins in his own blood,

COLOSSIANS 1:20—Prevenient Christ (1:15–2:3), written from prison (undetermined location and date)

Theme	COL	Paul
Peace through Christ's blood	**1:20** [20]And, having made peace through the blood of his cross, by him to reconcile all things unto himself; by him, I say, whether they be things in earth, or things in heaven.	**2 Cor 5:18–19** [18]And all things are of God, who hath reconciled us to himself by Jesus Christ, and hath given to us the ministry of reconciliation; [19]To wit, that God was in Christ, reconciling the world unto himself, not imputing their trespasses unto them; and hath committed unto us the word of reconciliation. **Eph 1:10 (Pseudo)** [10]That in the dispensation of the fulness of times he might gather together in one all things in Christ, both which are in heaven, and which are on earth; even in him:

COLOSSIANS 1:21—Prevenient Christ (1:15–2:3), written from prison (undetermined location and date)

Theme	COL	Paul
Alienation	**1:21** [21]And you, that were sometime alienated and enemies in your mind by wicked works, yet now hath he reconciled	**Eph 2:14–16 (Pseudo)** [14]Which is the earnest of our inheritance until the redemption of the purchased possession, unto the praise of his glory. [15]Wherefore I also, after I heard of your faith in the Lord Jesus, and love unto all the saints, [16]Cease not to give thanks for you, making mention of you in my prayers;

COLOSSIANS 1:24—Prevenient Christ (1:15–2:3), written from prison (undetermined location and date)

Theme	COL	Mt	Mk	Lk
Suffering for the faithful	**1:24** [24]Who now rejoice in my sufferings for you, and fill up that which is behind of the afflictions of Christ in my flesh for his body's sake, which is the church:	**5:10–12** [10]Blessed are they which are persecuted for righteousness' sake: for theirs is the kingdom of heaven. [11]Blessed are ye, when men shall revile you, and persecute you, and shall say all manner of evil against you falsely, for my sake. [12]Rejoice, and be exceeding glad: for great is your reward in heaven: for so persecuted they the prophets which were before you. **12:46–50** [46]While he yet talked to the people, behold, his mother and his brethren stood without, desiring to speak with him. [47]Then one said unto him, Behold, thy mother and thy brethren stand without, desiring to speak with thee. [48]But he answered and said unto him that told him, Who is my mother? and who are my brethren? [49]And he stretched forth his hand toward his disciples, and said, Behold my mother and my brethren! [50]For whosoever shall do the will of my Father which is in heaven, the same is my brother, and sister, and mother.	**3:31–35** [31]There came then his brethren and his mother, and, standing without, sent unto him, calling him. [32]And the multitude sat about him, and they said unto him, Behold, thy mother and thy brethren without seek for thee. [33]And he answered them, saying, Who is my mother, or my brethren? [34]And he looked round about on them which sat about him, and said, Behold my mother and my brethren! [35]For whosoever shall do the will of God, the same is my brother, and my sister, and mother.	**6:22–23** [22]Blessed are ye, when men shall hate you, and when they shall separate you from their company, and shall reproach you, and cast out your name as evil, for the Son of man's sake. [23]Rejoice ye in that day, and leap for joy: for, behold, your reward is great in heaven: for in the like manner did their fathers unto the prophets. **8:19–21** [19]Then came to him his mother and his brethren, and could not come at him for the press. [20]And it was told him by certain which said, Thy mother and thy brethren stand without, desiring to see thee. [21]And he answered and said unto them, My mother and my brethren are these which hear the word of God, and do it.

Paul	Other
Rom 5:3 [3]And not only so, but we glory in tribulations also: knowing that tribulation worketh patience; **Rom 8:17** [17]And if children, then heirs; heirs of God, and joint-heirs with Christ; if so be that we suffer with him, that we may be also glorified together. **Rom 12:4** [4]For as we have many members in one body, and all members have not the same office: **1 Cor 6:15** [15]Know ye not that your bodies are the members of Christ? shall I then take the members of Christ, and make them the members of an harlot? God forbid. **1 Cor 10:17** [17]For we being many are one bread, and one body: for we are all partakers of that one bread. **1 Cor 12:12–13** [12]For as the body is one, and hath many members, and all the members of that one body, being many, are one body: so also is Christ. [13]For by one Spirit are we all baptized into one body, whether we be Jews or Gentiles, whether we be bond or free; and have been all made to drink into one Spirit. **1 Cor 15:22** [22]For as in Adam all die, even so in Christ shall all be made alive. **2 Cor 7:4** [4]Great is my boldness of speech toward you, great is my glorying of you: I am filled with comfort, I am exceeding joyful in all our tribulation. **2 Cor 12:10** [10]Therefore I take pleasure in infirmities, in reproaches, in necessities, in persecutions, in distresses for Christ's sake: for when I am weak, then am I strong. **Eph 1:22–23 (Pseudo)** [22]And hath put all things under his feet, and gave him to be the head over all things to the church, [23]Which is his body, the fulness of him that filleth all in all. **Eph 4:15 (Pseudo)** [15]But speaking the truth in love, may grow up into him in all things, which is the head, even Christ: **Eph 5:23 (Pseudo)** [23]For the husband is the head of the wife, even as Christ is the head of the church: and he is the saviour of the body. **1 Thes 3:4** [4]For verily, when we were with you, we told you before that we should suffer tribulation; even as it came to pass, and ye know.	**Q-Quelle** Beatitudes: Col 1:24/Rom 8:17/2 Cor 7:4/ Mt 5:3-12/Lk 6:20b-23 (QS 8 [Thom 54, 68, 69])

COLOSSIANS 1:26—Prevenient Christ (1:15–2:3), written from prison (undetermined location and date)

Theme	COL	Paul
Mystery was hidden for ages	**1:26** [26]Even the mystery which hath been hid from ages and from generations, but now is made manifest to his saints:	**Rom 16:25–26** [25]Now to him that is of power to stablish you according to my gospel, and the preaching of Jesus Christ, according to the revelation of the mystery, which was kept secret since the world began, [26]But now is made manifest, and by the scriptures of the prophets, according to the commandment of the everlasting God, made known to all nations for the obedience of faith: **1 Cor 2:7** [7]But we speak the wisdom of God in a mystery, even the hidden wisdom, which God ordained before the world unto our glory: **Eph 3:3, 9 (Pseudo)** [3]How that by revelation he made known unto me the mystery; (as I wrote afore in few words, . . . [9]And to make all men see what is the fellowship of the mystery, which from the beginning of the world hath been hid in God, who created all things by Jesus Christ:

COLOSSIANS 1:27—Prevenient Christ (1:15–2:3), written from prison (undetermined location and date)

Theme	COL	Paul
God made riches known	**1:27** [27]To whom God would make known what is the riches of the glory of this mystery among the Gentiles; which is Christ in you, the hope of glory: **3:4** [4]When Christ, who is our life, shall appear, then shall ye also appear with him in glory.	**Rom 8:10** [10]And if Christ be in you, the body is dead because of sin; but the Spirit is life because of righteousness.

COLOSSIANS 1:28—Prevenient Christ (1:15–2:3), written from prison (undetermined location and date)

Theme	COL	Paul
Teach and warn using wisdom	**1:28** [28]Whom we preach, warning every man, and teaching every man in all wisdom; that we may present every man perfect in Christ Jesus:	**Eph 4:13 (Pseudo)** [13]Till we all come in the unity of the faith, and of the knowledge of the Son of God, unto a perfect man, unto the measure of the stature of the fulness of Christ:

COLOSSIANS 1:29—Prevenient Christ (1:15–2:3), written from prison (undetermined location and date)

Theme	COL	Paul
Striving to do God's work	**1:29** [29]Whereunto I also labour, striving according to his working, which worketh in me mightily. **2:1** [1]For I would that ye knew what great conflict I have for you, and for them at Laodicea, and for as many as have not seen my face in the flesh; **4:12** [12]Epaphras, who is one of you, a servant of Christ, saluteth you, always labouring fervently for you in prayers, that ye may stand perfect and complete in all the will of God.	**Phil 4:13** [13]I can do all things through Christ which strengtheneth me.

COLOSSIANS 2:2—Prevenient Christ (1:15–2:3), written from prison (undetermined location and date)

Theme	COL	Paul
Assured of God's under-standing & comfort	**2:2** [2]That their hearts might be comforted, being knit together in love, and unto all riches of the full assurance of understanding, to the acknowledgement of the mystery of God, and of the Father, and of Christ; **1:26–27** [26]Even the mystery which hath been hid from ages and from generations, but now is made manifest to his saints: [27]To whom God would make known what is the riches of the glory of this mystery among the Gentiles; which is Christ in you, the hope of glory:	**Eph 3:18–19 (Pseudo)** [18]May be able to comprehend with all saints what is the breadth, and length, and depth, and height; [19]And to know the love of Christ, which passeth knowledge, that ye might be filled with all the fulness of God.

COLOSSIANS 2:3—Prevenient Christ (1:15–2:3), written from prison (undetermined location and date)

Theme	COL	Paul	Jewish Writings
Wisdom and knowledge hidden in God	**2:3** [3]In whom are hid all the treasures of wisdom and knowledge.	**Rom 11:33** [33]O the depth of the riches both of the wisdom and knowledge of God! how unsearchable are his judgments, and his ways past finding out! **1 Cor 1:30** [30]But of him are ye in Christ Jesus, who of God is made unto us wisdom, and righteousness, and sanctification, and redemption:	**Prov 2:4–5** [4]If thou seekest her as silver, and searchest for her as for hid treasures; [5]Then shalt thou understand the fear of the LORD, and find the knowledge of God. **Is 45:3** [3]And I will give thee the treasures of darkness, and hidden riches of secret places, that thou mayest know that I, the LORD, which call thee by thy name, am the God of Israel.

DO NOT FOLLOW FALSE TEACHERS (2:4–23)

COLOSSIANS 2:4—Do not follow false teachers (2:4–23), written from prison (undetermined location and date)

Theme	COL	Paul
Do not be beguiled	**2:4** [4]And this I say, lest any man should beguile you with enticing words.	**Eph 4:14 (Pseudo)** [14]That we henceforth be no more children, tossed to and fro, and carried about with every wind of doctrine, by the sleight of men, and cunning craftiness, whereby they lie in wait to deceive;

COLOSSIANS 2:5—Do not follow false teachers (2:4–23), written from prison (undetermined location and date)

Theme	COL	Paul	Other
Absent in person, but there in spirit	**2:5** [5]For though I be absent in the flesh, yet am I with you in the spirit, joying and beholding your order, and the stedfastness of your faith in Christ.	**1 Cor 5:3** [3]For I verily, as absent in body, but present in spirit, have judged already, as though I were present, concerning him that hath so done this deed, **Phil 1:27** [27]Only let your conversation be as it becometh the gospel of Christ: that whether I come and see you, or else be absent, I may hear of your affairs, that ye stand fast in one spirit, with one mind striving together for the faith of the gospel;	**Q-Quelle** Forgiveness: Col 2:5/1 Cor 5:3-5/[Mt 18:15, 21-22]/ [Lk 17:3b-4 (QS 58)

COLOSSIANS 2:8–12—Do not follow false teachers (2:4–23), written from prison (undetermined location and date)

Theme	COL	Mt	Mk	Lk
Christ over culture	**2:8–12** [8]Beware lest any man spoil you through philosophy and vain deceit, after the tradition of men, after the rudiments of the world, and not after Christ. [9]For in him dwelleth all the fulness of the Godhead bodily. [10]And ye are complete in him, which is the head of all principality and power: [11]In whom also ye are circumcised with the circumcision made without hands, in putting off the body of the sins of the flesh by the circumcision of Christ: [12]Buried with him in baptism, wherein also ye are risen with him through the faith of the operation of God, who hath raised him from the dead. **2:21–22** [21](Touch not; taste not; handle not; [22]Which all are to perish with the using;) after the commandments and doctrines of men	**15:9** [9]But in vain they do worship me, teaching for doctrines the commandments of men. **15:15** [15]Then answered Peter and said unto him, Declare unto us this parable. **16:24–26** [24]Then said Jesus unto his disciples, If any man will come after me, let him deny himself, and take up his cross, and follow me. [25]For whosoever will save his life shall lose it: and whosoever will lose his life for my sake shall find it. [26]For what is a man profited, if he shall gain the whole world, and lose his own soul? or what shall a man give in exchange for his soul? **20:22–23** [22]But Jesus answered and said, Ye know not what ye ask. Are ye able to drink of the cup that I shall drink of, and to be baptized with the baptism that I am baptized with? They say unto him, We are able. [23]And he saith unto them, Ye shall drink indeed of my cup, and be baptized with the baptism that I am baptized with: but to sit on my right hand, and on my left, is not mine to give, but it shall be given to them for whom it is prepared of my Father. **26:31** [31]Then saith Jesus unto them, All ye shall be offended because of me this night: for it is written, I will smite the shepherd, and the sheep of the flock shall be scattered abroad. **27:46** [46]And about the ninth hour Jesus cried with a loud voice, saying, EliEli, EliEli, lamalama sabachthanisabachthani? that is to say, My God, my God, why hast thou forsaken me?	**7:8** [8]For laying aside the commandment of God, ye hold the tradition of men, as the washing of pots and cups: and many other such like things ye do. **7:13** [13]Making the word of God of none effect through your tradition, which ye have delivered: and many such like things do ye. **7:19** [19]Because it entereth not into his heart, but into the belly, and goeth out into the draught, purging all meats? **8:34–37** **[34]And when he had called the people unto him with his disciples also, he said unto them, Whosoever will come after me, let him deny himself, and take up his cross, and follow me.** [35]For whosoever will save his life shall lose it; but whosoever shall lose his life for my sake and the gospel's, the same shall save it. **[36]For what shall it profit a man, if he shall gain the whole world, and lose his own soul?** [37]Or what shall a man give in exchange for his soul? **10:38** [38]But Jesus said unto them, Ye know not what ye ask: can ye drink of the cup that I drink of? and be baptized with the baptism that I am baptized with? **14:27** [27]And Jesus saith unto them, All ye shall be offended because of me this night: for it is written, I will smite the shepherd, and the sheep shall be scattered. **14:36** [36]And he said, Abba, Father, all things are possible unto thee; take away this cup from me: nevertheless not what I will, but what thou wilt. **15:34** [34]And at the ninth hour Jesus cried with a loud voice, saying, EloiEloi, EloiEloi, lamalama sabachthanisabachthani? which is, being interpreted, My God, my God, why hast thou forsaken me?	**9:23–26** [23]And he said to them all, If any man will come after me, let him deny himself, and take up his cross daily, and follow me. [24]For whosoever will save his life shall lose it: but whosoever will lose his life for my sake, the same shall save it. [25]For what is a man advantaged, if he gain the whole world, and lose himself, or be cast away? [26]For whosoever shall be ashamed of me and of my words, of him shall the Son of man be ashamed, when he shall come in his own glory, and in his Father's, and of the holy angels. **12:50** [50]But I have a baptism to be baptized with; and how am I straitened till it be accomplished! **22:37** [37]For I say unto you, that this that is written must yet be accomplished in me, And he was reckoned among the transgressors: for the things concerning me have an end. **22:42** [42]Saying, Father, if thou be willing, remove this cup from me: nevertheless not my will, but thine, be done.

Jn	Paul	Jewish Writings	Other
10:11 [11]I am the good shepherd: the good shepherd giveth his life for the sheep.	**Rom 6:3–4** [3]Know ye not, that so many of us as were baptized into Jesus Christ were baptized into his death? [4]Therefore we are buried with him by baptism into death: that like as Christ was raised up from the dead by the glory of the Father, even so we also should walk in newness of life **Rom 8:17** [17]And if children, then heirs; heirs of God, and joint-heirs with Christ; if so be that we suffer with him, that we may be also glorified together. **Rom 14:14** [14]I know, and am persuaded by the Lord Jesus, that there is nothing unclean of itself: but to him that esteemeth any thing to be unclean, to him it is unclean. **Rom 14:20** [20]For meat destroy not the work of God. All things indeed are pure; but it is evil for that man who eateth with offence. **1 Cor 1:16** [16]And I baptized also the household of Stephanas: besides, I know not whether I baptized any other. **1 Cor 10:16** [16]The cup of blessing which we bless, is it not the communion of the blood of Christ? The bread which we break, is it not the communion of the body of Christ? **Gal 2:19** [19]For I through the law am dead to the law, that I might live unto God. **Phil 1:20** [20]According to my earnest expectation and my hope, that in nothing I shall be ashamed, but that with all boldness, as always, so now also Christ shall be magnified in my body, whether it be by life, or by death. **Phil 3:7–11** [7]But what things were gain to me, those I counted loss for Christ. [8]Yea doubtless, and I count all things but loss for the excellency of the knowledge of Christ Jesus my Lord: for whom I have suffered the loss of all things, and do count them but dung, that I may win Christ, [9]And be found in him, not having mine own righteousness, which is of the law, but that which is through the faith of Christ, the righteousness which is of God by faith: [10]That I may know him, and the power of his resurrection, and the fellowship of his sufferings, being made conformable unto his death; [11]If by any means I might attain unto the resurrection of the dead.	**Ps 22:1** [1]My God, my God, why hast thou forsaken me? why art thou so far from helping me, and from the words of my roaring? **Is 53:12** [12]Therefore will I divide him a portion with the great, and he shall divide the spoil with the strong; because he hath poured out his soul unto death: and he was numbered with the transgressors; and he bare the sin of many, and made intercession for the transgressors. **Zech 13:7** [7]Awake, O sword, against my shepherd, and against the man that is my fellow, saith the LORD of hosts: smite the shepherd, and the sheep shall be scattered: and I will turn mine hand upon the little ones.	**Q-Quelle** Divisions in Households: Col 2:8-12/ Rom 6:3-4/1 Cor 10:16/Gal 2:18-19/ Phil 3:7-11/[Mt 10:34-36]/Lk 12:49-53 (QS 43 [Thom 16])

COLOSSIANS 2:8—Do not follow false teachers (2:4–23), written from prison (undetermined location and date)

Theme	COL	Paul
Do not be deceived	**2:8** [8]Beware lest any man spoil you through philosophy and vain deceit, after the tradition of men, after the rudiments of the world, and not after Christ.	**Gal 4:3** [3]Even so we, when we were children, were in bondage under the elements of the world: **Eph 5:6 (Pseudo)** [6]Let no man deceive you with vain words: for because of these things cometh the wrath of God upon the children of disobedience.

COLOSSIANS 2:9—Do not follow false teachers (2:4–23), written from prison (undetermined location and date)

Theme	COL	Paul
God is fully in Jesus	**2:9** [9]For in him dwelleth all the fulness of the Godhead bodily. **1:19** [19]For it pleased the Father that in him should all fulness dwell;	**Eph 3:19 (Pseudo)** [19]And to know the love of Christ, which passeth knowledge, that ye might be filled with all the fulness of God.

COLOSSIANS 2:11—Do not follow false teachers (2:4–23), written from prison (undetermined location and date)

Theme	COL	Paul	Jewish Writings
Christ circumcised without hands	**2:11** [11]In whom also ye are circumcised with the circumcision made without hands, in putting off the body of the sins of the flesh by the circumcision of Christ: **1:22** [22]In the body of his flesh through death, to present you holy and unblameable and unreproveable in his sight:	**Rom 2:25–29** [25]For circumcision verily profiteth, if thou keep the law: but if thou be a breaker of the law, thy circumcision is made uncircumcision. [26]Therefore if the uncircumcision keep the righteousness of the law, shall not his uncircumcision be counted for circumcision? [27]And shall not uncircumcision which is by nature, if it fulfil the law, judge thee, who by the letter and circumcision dost transgress the law? [28]For he is not a Jew, which is one outwardly; neither is that circumcision, which is outward in the flesh: [29]But he is a Jew, which is one inwardly; and circumcision is that of the heart, in the spirit, and not in the letter; whose praise is not of men, but of God. **Phil 3:3** [3]For we are the circumcision, which worship God in the spirit, and rejoice in Christ Jesus, and have no confidence in the flesh.	**Jer 4:4** [4]Circumcise yourselves to the LORD, and take away the foreskins of your heart, ye men of Judah and inhabitants of Jerusalem: lest my fury come forth like fire, and burn that none can quench it, because of the evil of your doings.

COLOSSIANS 2:12—Do not follow false teachers (2:4–23), written from prison (undetermined location and date)

Theme	COL	Paul
Buried with Christ in baptism	**2:12** [12]Buried with him in baptism, wherein also ye are risen with him through the faith of the operation of God, who hath raised him from the dead.	**Rom 6:3–4** [3]Know ye not, that so many of us as were baptized into Jesus Christ were baptized into his death? [4]Therefore we are buried with him by baptism into death: that like as Christ was raised up from the dead by the glory of the Father, even so we also should walk in newness of life.

COLOSSIANS 2:13—Do not follow false teachers (2:4–23), written from prison (undetermined location and date)

Theme	COL	Paul
Sins forgiven	**2:13** [13]And you, being dead in your sins and the uncircumcision of your flesh, hath he quickened together with him, having forgiven you all trespasses;	**Eph 2:1 (Pseudo)** [1]And you hath he quickened, who were dead in trespasses and sins; **Eph 2:5 (Pseudo)** [5]Even when we were dead in sins, hath quickened us together with Christ, (by grace ye are saved;)

COLOSSIANS 2:14—Do not follow false teachers (2:4–23), written from prison (undetermined location and date)

Theme	COL	Paul
Sins on cross	**2:14** [14]Blotting out the handwriting of ordinances that was against us, which was contrary to us, and took it out of the way, nailing it to his cross;	**Eph 2:14–15 (Pseudo)** [14]For he is our peace, who hath made both one, and hath broken down the middle wall of partition between us; [15]Having abolished in his flesh the enmity, even the law of commandments contained in ordinances; for to make in himself of twain one new man, so making peace;

COLOSSIANS 2:15—Do not follow false teachers (2:4–23), written from prison (undetermined location and date)

Theme	COL	Paul
Jesus overtook powers & principalities	**2:15** [15]And having spoiled principalities and powers, he made a show of them openly, triumphing over them in it. **1:16, 20** [16]For by him were all things created, that are in heaven, and that are in earth, visible and invisible, whether they be thrones, or dominions, or principalities, or powers: all things were created by him, and for him: . . . [20]And, having made peace through the blood of his cross, by him to reconcile all things unto himself; by him, I say, whether they be things in earth, or things in heaven.	**2 Cor 2:14** [14]Now thanks be unto God, which always causeth us to triumph in Christ, and maketh manifest the savour of his knowledge by us in every place. **Eph 1:21 (Pseudo)** [21]Far above all principality, and power, and might, and dominion, and every name that is named, not only in this world, but also in that which is to come:

COLOSSIANS 2:16—Do not follow false teachers (2:4–23), written from prison (undetermined location and date)

Theme	COL	Paul
Let no one judge by food or day	**2:16** [16]Let no man therefore judge you in meat, or in drink, or in respect of an holyday, or of the new moon, or of the sab-bath days:	**Rom 14:3–4** [3]Let not him that eateth despise him that eateth not; and let not him which eateth not judge him that eateth: for God hath received him. [4]Who art thou that judgest another man's servant? to his own master he standeth or falleth. Yea, he shall be holden up: for God is able to make him stand. **1 Tim 4:3 (Pseudo)** [3]Forbidding to marry, and commanding to abstain from meats, which God hath created to be received with thanksgiving of them which believe and know the truth.

COLOSSIANS 2:17—Do not follow false teachers (2:4–23), written from prison (undetermined location and date)

Theme	COL	NT
Shadow of things to come	**2:17** [17]Which are a shadow of things to come; but the body is of Christ.	**Heb 8:5** [5]Who serve unto the example and shadow of heavenly things, as Moses was admonished of God when he was about to make the tabernacle: for, See, saith he, that thou make all things according to the pattern showed to thee in the mount. **Heb 10:1** [1]For the law having a shadow of good things to come, and not the very image of the things, can never with those sacrifices which they offered year by year continually make the comers thereunto perfect.

COLOSSIANS 2:18—Do not follow false teachers (2:4–23), written from prison (undetermined location and date)

Theme	COL	Mt
Do not be beguiled	**2:18** [18]Let no man beguile you of your reward in a voluntary humility and worshipping of angels, intruding into those things which he hath not seen, vainly puffed up by his fleshly mind, **2:23** [23]Which things have indeed a show of wisdom in will worship, and humility, and neglecting of the body; not in any honour to the satisfying of the flesh.	**24:4** [4]And Jesus answered and said unto them, Take heed that no man deceive you.

COLOSSIANS 2:19—Do not follow false teachers (2:4–23), written from prison (undetermined location and date)

Theme	COL	Paul
Not holding Head	**2:19** [19]And not holding the Head, from which all the body by joints and bands having nourishment ministered, and knit together, increaseth with the increase of God.	**Eph 2:21–22 (Pseudo)** [21]In whom all the building fitly framed together groweth unto an holy temple in the Lord: [22]In whom ye also are builded together for an habitation of God through the Spirit.

COLOSSIANS 2:22—Do not follow false teachers (2:4–23), written from prison (undetermined location and date)

Theme	COL	Jewish Writings
All perish	**2:22** [22]Which all are to perish with the using;) after the commandments and doctrines of men?	**Is 29:13** [13]Wherefore the Lord said, Forasmuch as this people draw near me with their mouth, and with their lips do honour me, but have removed their heart far from me, and their fear toward me is taught by the precept of men:

IDEAL CHRISTIANITY IN THIS WORLD (3:1–4:6)

COLOSSIANS 3:1—Ideal Christianity in this world (3:1–4:6), written from prison (undetermined location and date)

Theme	COL	Paul	Jewish Writings
Seek things above	**3:1** [1]If ye then be risen with Christ, seek those things which are above, where Christ sitteth on the right hand of God. **2:12** [12]Buried with him in baptism, wherein also ye are risen with him through the faith of the operation of God, who hath raised him from the dead.	**Eph 2:6 (Pseudo)** [6]And hath raised us up together, and made us sit together in heavenly places in Christ Jesus: **Phil 3:20** [20]For our conversation is in heaven; from whence also we look for the Saviour, the Lord Jesus Christ:	**Ps 110:1** [1]The LORD said unto my Lord, Sit thou at my right hand, until I make thine enemies thy footstool.

COLOSSIANS 3:3—Ideal Christianity in this world (3:1–4:6), written from prison (undetermined location and date)

Theme	COL	Paul
Life hid with Christ in God	**3:3** [3]For ye are dead, and your life is hid with Christ in God.	**Rom 6:2–5** [2]God forbid. How shall we, that are dead to sin, live any longer therein? [3]Know ye not, that so many of us as were baptized into Jesus Christ were baptized into his death? [4]Therefore we are buried with him by baptism into death: that like as Christ was raised up from the dead by the glory of the Father, even so we also should walk in newness of life. [5]For if we have been planted together in the likeness of his death, we shall be also in the likeness of his resurrection:

COLOSSIANS 3:5—Ideal Christianity in this world (3:1–4:6), written from prison (undetermined location and date)

Theme	COL	Mt	Paul	Other
Flesh & Spirit: death to earthly ways	**3:5** [5]Mortify therefore your members which are upon the earth; fornication, uncleanness, inordinate affection, evil concupiscence, and covetousness, which is idolatry:	**5:19** [19]Whosoever therefore shall break one of these least commandments, and shall teach men so, he shall be called the least in the kingdom of heaven: but whosoever shall do and teach them, the same shall be called great in the kingdom of heaven. **5:29–30** [29]And if thy right eye offend thee, pluck it out, and cast it from thee: for it is profitable for thee that one of thy members should perish, and not that thy whole body should be cast into hell. [30]And if thy right hand offend thee, cut it off, and cast it from thee: for it is profitable for thee that one of thy members should perish, and not that thy whole body should be cast into hell.	**Rom 1:29–30** [29]Being filled with all unrighteousness, fornication, wickedness, covetousness, maliciousness; full of envy, murder, debate, deceit, malignity; whisperers, [30]Backbiters, haters of God, despiteful, proud, boasters, inventors of evil things, disobedient to parents, **Rom 8:13** [13]For if ye live after the flesh, ye shall die: but if ye through the Spirit do mortify the deeds of the body, ye shall live. **Gal 5:19–21** [19]Now the works of the flesh are manifest, which are these; Adultery, fornication, uncleanness, lasciviousness, [20]Idolatry, witchcraft, hatred, variance, emulations, wrath, strife, seditions, heresies, [21]Envyings, murders, drunkenness, revellings, and such like: of the which I tell you before, as I have also told you in time past, that they which do such things shall not inherit the kingdom of God. **Gal 5:24** [24]And they that are Christ's have crucified the flesh with the affections and lusts. **Eph 5:3–5 (Pseudo)** [3]But fornication, and all uncleanness, or covetousness, let it not be once named among you, as becometh saints; [4]Neither filthiness, nor foolish talking, nor jesting, which are not convenient: but rather giving of thanks. [5]For this ye know, that no whoremonger, nor unclean person, nor covetous man, who is an idolater, hath any inheritance in the kingdom of Christ and of God.	**Q-Quelle** Anxiety: Col 3:5/Gal 5:19-21/[Mt 6:25-34]/ [Lk 12:22-32 (QS 39 [Thom 36])]; Assistance of the HS: Col 3:5/ Eph 5:5/[Mt 10:19-20]/ [Mk 13:11]/ [Lk 12:11-12 (QS 37 [Thom 44])]

COLOSSIANS 3:6—Ideal Christianity in this world (3:1–4:6), written from prison (undetermined location and date)

Theme	COL	Paul
Wrath & disobedience	**3:6** [6]For which things' sake the wrath of God cometh on the children of disobedience:	**Rom 1:18** [18]For the wrath of God is revealed from heaven against all ungodliness and unrighteousness of men, who hold the truth in unrighteousness;

COLOSSIANS 3:8—Ideal Christianity in this world (3:1–4:6), written from prison (undetermined location and date)

Theme	COL	Paul
Put off bad behavior	**3:8** [8]But now ye also put off all these; anger, wrath, malice, blasphemy, filthy communication out of your mouth.	**Eph 4:22 (Pseudo)** [22]That ye put off concerning the former conversation the old man, which is corrupt according to the deceitful lusts; **Eph 4:25 (Pseudo)** [25]Wherefore putting away lying, speak every man truth with his neighbour: for we are members one of another. **Eph 4:31 (Pseudo)** [31]Let all bitterness, and wrath, and anger, and clamour, and evil speaking, be put away from you, with all malice:

COLOSSIANS 3:9—Ideal Christianity in this world (3:1–4:6), written from prison (undetermined location and date)

Theme	COL	Paul	NT
Do not lie	**3:9** [9]Lie not one to another, seeing that ye have put off the old man with his deeds;	**Rom 6:4, 6** [4]Therefore we are buried with him by baptism into death: that like as Christ was raised up from the dead by the glory of the Father, even so we also should walk in newness of life. . . . [6]Knowing this, that our old man is crucified with him, that the body of sin might be destroyed, that henceforth we should not serve sin. **Eph 4:22–25** [22]That ye put off concerning the former conversation the old man, which is corrupt according to the deceitful lusts; [23]And be renewed in the spirit of your mind; [24]And that ye put on the new man, which after God is created in righteousness and true holiness. [25]Wherefore putting away lying, speak every man truth with his neighbour: for we are members one of another.	**Heb 12:1** [1]Wherefore seeing we also are compassed about with so great a cloud of witnesses, let us lay aside every weight, and the sin which doth so easily beset us, and let us run with patience the race that is set before us, **1 Pet 2:1** [1]Wherefore laying aside all malice, and all guile, and hypocrisies, and envies, and all evil speakings, **1 Pet 4:2** [2]That he no longer should live the rest of his time in the flesh to the lusts of men, but to the will of God.

COLOSSIANS 3:10—Ideal Christianity in this world (3:1–4:6), written from prison (undetermined location and date)

Theme	COL	Mt	Mk	Paul
Image of God	**3:10** [10]And have put on the new man, which is renewed in knowledge after the image of him that created him:	**19:8** [8]He saith unto them, Moses because of the hardness of your hearts suffered you to put away your wives: but from the beginning it was not so.	**10:6** [6]But from the beginning of the creation God made them male and female.	**Rom 1:3** [3]Concerning his Son Jesus Christ our Lord, which was made of the seed of David according to the flesh; **Rom 5** [1]Therefore being justified by faith, we have peace with God through our Lord Jesus Christ: [2]By whom also we have access by faith into this grace wherein we stand, and rejoice in hope of the glory of God. [3]And not only so, but we glory in tribulations also: knowing that tribulation worketh patience; [4]And patience, experience; and experience, hope: [5]And hope maketh not ashamed; because the love of God is shed abroad in our hearts by the Holy Ghost which is given unto us. [6]For when we were yet without strength, in due time Christ died for the ungodly. [7]For scarcely for a righteous man will one die: yet peradventure for a good man some would even dare to die. [8]But God commendeth his love toward us, in that, while we were yet sinners, Christ died for us. [9]Much more then, being now justified by his blood, we shall be saved from wrath through him. [10]For if, when we were enemies, we were reconciled to God by the death of his Son, much more, being reconciled, we shall be saved by his life. [11]And not only so, but we also joy in God through our Lord Jesus Christ, by whom we have now received the atonement. [12]Wherefore, as by one man sin entered into the world, and death by sin; and so death passed upon all men, for that all have sinned: [13](For until the law sin was in the world: but sin is not imputed when there is no law. [14]Nevertheless death reigned from Adam to Moses, even over them that had not sinned after the similitude of Adam's transgression, who is the figure of him that was to come. [15]But not as the offence, so also is the free gift. For if through the offence of one many be dead, much more the grace of God, and the gift by grace, which is by one man, Jesus Christ, hath abounded unto many. [16]And not as it was by one that sinned, so is the gift: for the judgment was by one to condemnation, but the free gift is of many offences unto justification. [17]For if by one man's offence death reigned by one; much more they which receive abundance of grace and of the gift of righteousness shall reign in life by one, Jesus Christ.) [18]Therefore as by the offence of one judgment came upon all men to condemnation; even so by the righteousness of one the free gift came upon all men unto justification of life. [19]For as by one man's disobedience many were made sinners, so by the obedience of one shall many be made righteous. [20]Moreover the law entered, that the offence might abound. But where sin abounded, grace did much more abound: [21]That as sin hath reigned unto death, even so might grace reign through righteousness unto eternal life by Jesus Christ our Lord. **1 Cor 15:27** [27]For he hath put all things under his feet. But when he saith all things are put under him, it is manifest that he is excepted, which did put all things under him. **1 Cor 15:49** [49]And as we have borne the image of the earthy, we shall also bear the image of the heavenly. **2 Cor 3:18** [18]But we all, with open face beholding as in a glass the glory of the Lord, are changed into the same image from glory to glory, even as by the Spirit of the Lord.

Paul (*Continued*)

(*Continued*)

Gal 4:4

[4]But when the fulness of the time was come, God sent forth his Son, made of a woman, made under the law,

Phil 2

[1]If there be therefore any consolation in Christ, if any comfort of love, if any fellowship of the Spirit, if any bowels and mercies, [2]Fulfil ye my joy, that ye be likeminded, having the same love, being of one accord, of one mind. [3]Let nothing be done through strife or vainglory; but in lowliness of mind let each esteem other better than themselves. [4]Look not every man on his own things, but every man also on the things of others. [5]Let this mind be in you, which was also in Christ Jesus: [6]Who, being in the form of God, thought it not robbery to be equal with God: [7]But made himself of no reputation, and took upon him the form of a servant, and was made in the likeness of men: [8]And being found in fashion as a man, he humbled himself, and became obedient unto death, even the death of the cross. [9]Wherefore God also hath highly exalted him, and given him a name which is above every name: [10]That at the name of Jesus every knee should bow, of things in heaven, and things in earth, and things under the earth; [11]And that every tongue should confess that Jesus Christ is Lord, to the glory of God the Father. [12]Wherefore, my beloved, as ye have always obeyed, not as in my presence only, but now much more in my absence, work out your own salvation with fear and trembling. [13]For it is God which worketh in you both to will and to do of his good pleasure. [14]Do all things without murmurings and disputings: [15]That ye may be blameless and harmless, the sons of God, without rebuke, in the midst of a crooked and perverse nation, among whom ye shine as lights in the world; [16]Holding forth the word of life; that I may rejoice in the day of Christ, that I have not run in vain, neither laboured in vain. [17]Yea, and if I be offered upon the sacrifice and service of your faith, I joy, and rejoice with you all. [18]For the same cause also do ye joy, and rejoice with me. [19]But I trust in the Lord Jesus to send Timotheus shortly unto you, that I also may be of good comfort, when I know your state. [20]For I have no man likeminded, who will naturally care for your state. [21]For all seek their own, not the things which are Jesus Christ's. [22]But ye know the proof of him, that, as a son with the father, he hath served with me in the gospel. [23]Him therefore I hope to send presently, so soon as I shall see how it will go with me. [24]But I trust in the Lord that I also myself shall come shortly. [25]Yet I supposed it necessary to send to you Epaphroditus, my brother, and companion in labour, and fellowsoldier, but your messenger, and he that ministered to my wants. [26]For he longed after you all, and was full of heaviness, because that ye had heard that he had been sick. [27]For indeed he was sick nigh unto death: but God had mercy on him; and not on him only, but on me also, lest I should have sorrow upon sorrow. [28]I sent him therefore the more carefully, that, when ye see him again, ye may rejoice, and that I may be the less sorrowful. [29]Receive him therefore in the Lord with all gladness; and hold such in reputation: [30]Because for the work of Christ he was nigh unto death, not regarding his life, to supply your lack of service toward me.

Jewish Writings

Gen 1:26–27

[26]And God said, Let us make man in our image, after our likeness: and let them have dominion over the fish of the sea, and over the fowl of the air, and over the cattle, and over all the earth, and over every creeping thing that creepeth upon the earth. [27]So God created man in his own image, in the image of God created he him; male and female created he them.

Gen 1:28

[28]And God blessed them, and God said unto them, Be fruitful, and multiply, and replenish the earth, and subdue it: and have dominion over the fish of the sea, and over the fowl of the air, and over every living thing that moveth upon the earth.

COLOSSIANS 3:11—Ideal Christianity in this world (3:1–4:6), written from prison (undetermined location and date)

Theme	COL	Mt	Mk
No discrimination	**3:11** [11]Where there is neither Greek nor Jew, circumcision nor uncircumcision, Barbarian, Scythian, bond nor free: but Christ is all, and in all.	**10:5** [5]These twelve Jesus sent forth, and commanded them, saying, Go not into the way of the Gentiles, and into any city of the Samaritans enter ye not: **10:23** [23]But when they persecute you in this city, flee ye into another: for verily I say unto you, Ye shall not have gone over the cities of Israel, till the Son of man be come. **28:19** [19]Go ye therefore, and teach all nations, baptizing them in the name of the Father, and of the Son, and of the Holy Ghost:	**7:27** [27]But Jesus said unto her, Let the children first be filled: for it is not meet to take the children's bread, and to cast it unto the dogs.

COLOSSIANS 3:12–14—Ideal Christianity in this world (3:1–4:6), written from prison (undetermined location and date)

Theme	COL	Mt	Mk
Holy behavior	**3:12–14** [12]Put on therefore, as the elect of God, holy and beloved, bowels of mercies, kindness, humbleness of mind, meekness, long suffering; [13]Forbearing one another, and forgiving one another, if any man have a quarrel against any: even as Christ forgave you, so also do ye. [14]And above all these things put on charity, which is the bond of perfectness. **3:16** [16]Let the word of Christ dwell in you richly in all wisdom; teaching and admonishing one another in psalms and hymns and spiritual songs, singing with grace in your hearts to the Lord.	**5:48** [48]Be ye therefore perfect, even as your Father which is in heaven is perfect. **14:14** [14]And Jesus went forth, and saw a great multitude, and was moved with compassion toward them, and he healed their sick. **15:32** [32]Then Jesus called his disciples unto him, and said, I have compassion on the multitude, because they continue with me now three days, and have nothing to eat: and I will not send them away fasting, lest they faint in the way. **18:27** [27]Then the lord of that servant was moved with compassion, and loosed him, and forgave him the debt. **20:34** [34]So Jesus had compassion on them, and touched their eyes: and immediately their eyes received sight, and they followed him.	**6:34** [34]And Jesus, when he came out, saw much people, and was moved with compassion toward them, because they were as sheep not having a shepherd: and he began to teach them many things. **8:2** [2]I have compassion on the multitude, because they have now been with me three days, and have nothing to eat: **9:50** [50]Salt is good: but if the salt have lost his saltness, wherewith will ye season it? Have salt in yourselves, and have peace one with another.

Paul	Other
Rom 10:12 [12]For there is no difference between the Jew and the Greek: for the same Lord over all is rich unto all that call upon him. **Rom 15:8** [8]Now I say that Jesus Christ was a minister of the circumcision for the truth of God, to confirm the promises made unto the fathers: **1 Cor 12:13** [13]For by one Spirit are we all baptized into one body, whether we be Jews or Gentiles, whether we be bond or free; and have been all made to drink into one Spirit. **Gal 2:7–9** [7]But contrariwise, when they saw that the gospel of the uncircumcision was committed unto me, as the gospel of the circumcision was unto Peter; [8](For he that wrought effectually in Peter to the apostleship of the circumcision, the same was mighty in me toward the Gentiles:) [9]And when James, Cephas, and John, who seemed to be pillars, perceived the grace that was given unto me, they gave to me and Barnabas the right hands of fellowship; that we should go unto the heathen, and they unto the circumcision. **Gal 3:27–28** [27]For as many of you as have been baptized into Christ have put on Christ.[28]There is neither Jew nor Greek, there is neither bond nor free, there is neither male nor female: for ye are all one in Christ Jesus.	**Q-Quelle** Commissioning of 12: Col 3:11/ Rom 15:8/[Mt 10:1, 7-11, 14]/ [Mk 6:6b-13/[Lk 9:1-6]

Lk	Paul
6:35–36 [35]But love ye your enemies, and do good, and lend, hoping for nothing again; and your reward shall be great, and ye shall be the children of the Highest: for he is kind unto the unthankful and to the evil. [36]Be ye therefore merciful, as your Father also is merciful. **10:33** [33]But a certain Samaritan, as he journeyed, came where he was: and when he saw him, he had compassion on him, **15:20** [20]And he arose, and came to his father. But when he was yet a great way off, his father saw him, and had compassion, and ran, and fell on his neck, and kissed him.	**Phil 1:8** [8]For God is my record, how greatly I long after you all in the bowels of Jesus Christ. **Phil 2:1** [1]If there be therefore any consolation in Christ, if any comfort of love, if any fellowship of the Spirit, if any bowels and mercies,

Colossians 3:12-14 continued on next page

COLOSSIANS 3:12–14—Ideal Christianity in this world (3:1–4:6), written from prison (undetermined location and date) (*continued*)

Theme	COL	Paul	Other
(*Cont.*) **Holy behavior**	**3:12–14 (above)** **3:16 (above)**	**Rom 12:10** [10]Be kindly affectioned one to another with brotherly love; in honour preferring one another; **Rom 12:18** [18]If it be possible, as much as lieth in you, live peaceably with all men. **Rom 14:19** [19]Let us therefore follow after the things which make for peace, and things wherewith one may edify another. **1 Cor 7:15** [15]But if the unbelieving depart, let him depart. A brother or a sister is not under bondage in such cases: but God hath called us to peace. **2 Cor 13:11** [11]Finally, brethren, farewell. Be perfect, be of good comfort, be of one mind, live in peace; and the God of love and peace shall be with you. **Gal 6:10** [10]As we have therefore opportunity, let us do good unto all men, especially unto them who are of the household of faith. **Eph 4:32 (Pseudo)** [32]And be ye kind one to another, tenderhearted, forgiving one another, even as God for Christ's sake hath forgiven you. **1 Thes 3:12** [12]And the Lord make you to increase and abound in love one toward another, and toward all men, even as we do toward you: **1 Thes 4:9** [9]But as touching brotherly love ye need not that I write unto you: for ye yourselves are taught of God to love one another. **1 Thes 5:12–13** [12]And we beseech you, brethren, to know them which labour among you, and are over you in the Lord, and admonish you; [13]And to esteem them very highly in love for their work's sake. And be at peace among yourselves. **1 Thes 5:15** [15]See that none render evil for evil unto any man; but ever follow that which is good, both among yourselves, and to all men. **2 Thes 1:3** [3]We are bound to thank God always for you, brethren, as it is meet, because that your faith groweth exceedingly, and the charity of every one of you all toward each other aboundeth;	**Q-Quelle** Love enemies: Col 3:12-14/ Mt 5:38-48, [Mt 7:12]/Lk 6:27-36 (QS 9 [Thom 95, 6:2]); Parable of salt: Col 3:12-14/1 Cor 7:15/Gal 6:10/Eph 4:32/1 Thes 3:12/[Mt 5:13]/Mk 9:49-53/[Lk 14:34-35 (QS 53)]

COLOSSIANS 3:12—Ideal Christianity in this world (3:1–4:6), written from prison (undetermined location and date)

Theme	COL	Paul
Holy behavior	**3:12** [12]Put on therefore, as the elect of God, holy and beloved, bowels of mercies, kindness, humbleness of mind, meekness, longsuffering;	**Eph 4:1–2, 32 (Pseudo)** [1]I therefore, the prisoner of the Lord, beseech you that ye walk worthy of the vocation wherewith ye are called, [2]With all lowliness and meekness, with longsuffering, forbearing one another in love; . . . [32]And be ye kind one to another, tenderhearted, forgiving one another, even as God for Christ's sake hath forgiven you. **1 Thes 5:15** [15]See that none render evil for evil unto any man; but ever follow that which is good, both among yourselves, and to all men.

COLOSSIANS 3:13—Ideal Christianity in this world (3:1–4:6), written from prison (undetermined location and date)

Theme	COL	Mt	Paul	Other
Forgive and bear with others	**3:13** [13]Forbearing one another, and forgiving one another, if any man have a quarrel against any: even as Christ forgave you, so also do ye.	**6:14** [14]For if ye forgive men their trespasses, your heavenly Father will also forgive you: **18:21–35** [21]Then came Peter to him, and said, Lord, how oft shall my brother sin against me, and I forgive him? till seven times? [22]Jesus saith unto him, I say not unto thee, Until seven times: but, Until seventy times seven. [23]Therefore is the kingdom of heaven likened unto a certain king, which would take account of his servants. [24]And when he had begun to reckon, one was brought unto him, which owed him ten thousand talents. [25]But forasmuch as he had not to pay, his lord commanded him to be sold, and his wife, and children, and all that he had, and payment to be made. [26]The servant therefore fell down, and worshipped him, saying, Lord, have patience with me, and I will pay thee all. [27]Then the lord of that servant was moved with compassion, and loosed him, and forgave him the debt. [8]But the same servant went out, and found one of his fellowservants, which owed him an hundred pence: and he laid hands on him, and took him by the throat, saying, Pay me that thou owest. [29]And his fellowservant fell down at his feet, and besought him, saying, Have patience with me, and I will pay thee all. [30]And he would not: but went and cast him into prison, till he should pay the debt. [31]So when his fellowservants saw what was done, they were very sorry, and came and told unto their lord all that was done. [32]Then his lord, after that he had called him, said unto him, O thou wicked servant, I forgave thee all that debt, because thou desiredst me: [33]Shouldest not thou also have had compassion on thy fellowservant, even as I had pity on thee? [34]And his lord was wroth, and delivered him to the tormentors, till he should pay all that was due unto him. [35]So likewise shall my heavenly Father do also unto you, if ye from your hearts forgive not every one his brother their trespasses.	**Eph 4:32 (Pseudo)** [32]And be ye kind one to another, tenderhearted, forgiving one another, even as God for Christ's sake hath forgiven you.	**Q-Quelle** On forgiveness: Col 3:13/Mt 18:21-22/[Lk 17:3b-4 (QS 58)]

COLOSSIANS 3:14—Ideal Christianity in this world (3:1–4:6), written from prison (undetermined location and date)

Theme	COL	Paul
Be charitable	**3:14** [14]And above all these things put on charity, which is the bond of perfectness.	**Rom 13:8–10** [8]Owe no man any thing, but to love one another: for he that loveth another hath fulfilled the law. [9]For this, Thou shalt not commit adultery, Thou shalt not kill, Thou shalt not steal, Thou shalt not bear false witness, Thou shalt not covet; and if there be any other commandment, it is briefly comprehended in this saying, namely, Thou shalt love thy neighbour as thyself. [10]Love worketh no ill to his neighbour: therefore love is the fulfilling of the law.

COLOSSIANS 3:15—Ideal Christianity in this world (3:1–4:6), written from prison (undetermined location and date)

Theme	COL	Paul
Let God's peace rule your heart	**3:15** [15]And let the peace of God rule in your hearts, to the which also ye are called in one body; and be ye thankful.	**Rom 12:5** [5]So we, being many, are one body in Christ, and every one members one of another. **1 Cor 12:12** [12]For as the body is one, and hath many members, and all the members of that one body, being many, are one body: so also is Christ. **Eph 2:16 (Pseudo)** [16]And that he might reconcile both unto God in one body by the cross, having slain the enmity thereby: **Eph 4:3–4 (Pseudo)** [3]Endeavouring to keep the unity of the Spirit in the bond of peace. [4]There is one body, and one Spirit, even as ye are called in one hope of your calling; **Phil 4:7** [7]And the peace of God, which passeth all understanding, shall keep your hearts and minds through Christ Jesus.

COLOSSIANS 3:16—Ideal Christianity in this world (3:1–4:6), written from prison (undetermined location and date)

Theme	COL	Paul
Let Word of dwell in heart	**3:16** [16]Let the word of Christ dwell in you richly in all wisdom; teaching and admonishing one another in psalms and hymns and spiritual songs, singing with grace in your hearts to the Lord.	**Eph 5:19–20 (Pseudo)** [19]Speaking to yourselves in psalms and hymns and spiritual songs, singing and making melody in your heart to the Lord; [20]Giving thanks always for all things unto God and the Father in the name of our Lord Jesus Christ;

COLOSSIANS 3:17—Ideal Christianity in this world (3:1–4:6), written from prison (undetermined location and date)

Theme	COL	Mt	Lk	Paul	Other
Imitate Jesus	**3:17** [17]And whatsoever ye do in word or deed, do all in the name of the Lord Jesus, giving thanks to God and the Father by him.	**5:3–6** [3]Blessed are the poor in spirit: for theirs is the kingdom of heaven. [4]Blessed are they that mourn: for they shall be comforted. [5]Blessed are the meek: for they shall inherit the earth. [6]Blessed are they which do hunger and thirst after righteousness: for they shall be filled. **11:28–30** [28]Come unto me, all ye that labour and are heavy laden, and I will give you rest. [29]Take my yoke upon you, and learn of me; for I am meek and lowly in heart: and ye shall find rest unto your souls. [30]For my yoke is easy, and my burden is light.	**6:20–21** [20]And he lifted up his eyes on his disciples, and said, Blessed be ye poor: for yours is the kingdom of God. [21]Blessed are ye that hunger now: for ye shall be filled. Blessed are ye that weep now: for ye shall laugh.	**1 Cor 10:31** [31]Whether therefore ye eat, or drink, or whatsoever ye do, do all to the glory of God. **Gal 6:2** [2]Bear ye one another's burdens, and so fulfil the law of Christ.	**Q-Quelle** Beatitudes: Col 3:17/[1 Cor 9:21]/Gal 6:2/Mt 5:3-12/Lk 6:20b-23 (QS 8 [Thom 95, 6:2]); Against Pharisees: Col 3:17/Gal 6:2/[Mt 23:4-36]/[Mk 7:1-9]/[Lk 11:37-54(QS 34 [Thom 39:1, 89, 102])]

COLOSSIANS 3:18—Ideal Christianity in this world (3:1–4:6), written from prison (undetermined location and date)

Theme	COL	Paul	NT
Learn to obey God by submitting to spouse	**3:18** [18]Wives, submit yourselves unto your own husbands, as it is fit in the Lord.	**Eph 5:22 (Pseudo)** [22]Wives, submit yourselves unto your own husbands, as unto the Lord. **Tit 2:5 (Pseudo)** [5]To be discreet, chaste, keepers at home, good, obedient to their own husbands, that the word of God be not blasphemed.	**1 Pet 3:1** [1]Likewise, ye wives, be in subjection to your own husbands; that, if any obey not the word, they also may without the word be won by the conversation of the wives;

COLOSSIANS 3:20—Ideal Christianity in this world (3:1–4:6), written from prison (undetermined location and date)

Theme	COL	Paul
Children obey parents	**3:20** [20]Children, obey your parents in all things: for this is well pleasing unto the Lord.	**Eph 6:1 (Pseudo)** [1]Children, obey your parents in the Lord: for this is right.

COLOSSIANS 3:21—Ideal Christianity in this world (3:1–4:6), written from prison (undetermined location and date)

Theme	COL	Paul
Do not anger children	**3:21** [21]Fathers, provoke not your children to anger, lest they be discouraged.	**Eph 6:4 (Pseudo)** [4]And, ye fathers, provoke not your children to wrath: but bring them up in the nurture and admonition of the Lord.

COLOSSIANS 3:22—Ideal Christianity in this world (3:1–4:6), written from prison (undetermined location and date)

Theme	COL	Paul	NT
Servants obey Masters as God	**3:22** [22]Servants, obey in all things your masters according to the flesh; not with eyeservice, as menpleasers; but in singleness of heart, fearing God:	**Eph 6:5 (Pseudo)** [5]Servants, be obedient to them that are your masters according to the flesh, with fear and trembling, in singleness of your heart, as unto Christ; **1 Tim 6:1 (Pseudo)** [1]Let as many servants as are under the yoke count their own masters worthy of all honour, that the name of God and his doctrine be not blasphemed. **Tit 2:9–10 (Pseudo)** [9]Exhort servants to be obedient unto their own masters, and to please them well in all things; not answering again; [10]Not purloining, but showing all good fidelity; that they may adorn the doctrine of God our Saviour in all things.	**1 Pet 2:18** [18]Servants, be subject to your masters with all fear; not only to the good and gentle, but also to the froward.

COLOSSIANS 3:25—Ideal Christianity in this world (3:1–4:6), written from prison (undetermined location and date)

Theme	COL	Paul
No prejudice	**3:25** [25]But he that doeth wrong shall receive for the wrong which he hath done: and there is no respect of persons.	**Rom 2:11** [11]For there is no respect of persons with God.

COLOSSIANS 4:2—Ideal Christianity in this world (3:1–4:6), written from prison (undetermined location and date)

Theme	COL	Lk	Paul	Other
Prayer with thanks	**4:2** [2]Continue in prayer, and watch in the same with thanksgiving;	**18:1** [1]And he spake a parable unto them to this end, that men ought always to pray, and not to faint;	**Rom 12:12** [12]Rejoicing in hope; patient in tribulation; continuing instant in prayer; **Eph 6:18–20 (Pseudo)** [18]Being then made free from sin, ye became the servants of righteousness. [19]I speak after the manner of men because of the infirmity of your flesh: for as ye have yielded your members servants to uncleanness and to iniquity unto iniquity; even so now yield your members servants to righteousness unto holiness. [20]For when ye were the servants of sin, ye were free from righteousness. **1 Thes 5:17** [17]Pray without ceasing.	**Q-Quelle** Love enemies: Col 4:2/ Rom 12:9-21/[Mt 5:38-48, 7:12]/[Lk 6:27-36 (QS 9 [Thom 95, 6:2])]; Against Pharisees: Col 4:2/Rom 12:9-21/[Mt 23:4-36]/[Mk 7:1-9]/[Lk 11:37-54 (QS 34 [Thom 39:1,89, 102])]; Precedence: Col 4:2/Rom 12:9-21/[Mt 19:28]/[Mk 10:41-45]/[[Lk 22:28-30 (QS 62)]

COLOSSIANS 4:3—Ideal Christianity in this world (3:1–4:6), written from prison (undetermined location and date)

Theme	COL	Paul
Pray that God will reveal mystery in Christ	**4:3** [3]Withal praying also for us, that God would open unto us a door of utterance, to speak the mystery of Christ, for which I am also in bonds:	**Rom 15:30** [30]Now I beseech you, brethren, for the Lord Jesus Christ's sake, and for the love of the Spirit, that ye strive together with me in your prayers to God for me; **1 Cor 16:9** [9]For a great door and effectual is opened unto me, and there are many adversaries. **Eph 6:19 (Pseudo)** [19]And for me, that utterance may be given unto me, that I may open my mouth boldly, to make known the mystery of the gospel, **2 Thes 3:1** [1]Finally, brethren, pray for us, that the word of the Lord may have free course, and be glorified, even as it is with you:

COLOSSIANS 4:5–6—Ideal Christianity in this world (3:1–4:6), written from prison (undetermined location and date)

Theme	COL	Mt	Mk	Lk
Be as Christ	**4:5–6** [5]Walk in wisdom toward them that are without, redeeming the time. [6]Let your speech be alway with grace, seasoned with salt, that ye may know how ye ought to answer every man.	**5:13–14** [13]Ye are the salt of the earth: but if the salt have lost his savour, wherewith shall it be salted? it is thenceforth good for nothing, but to be cast out, and to be trodden under foot of men. [14]Ye are the light of the world. A city that is set on an hill cannot be hid. **5:17** [17]Think not that I am come to destroy the law, or the prophets: I am not come to destroy, but to fulfil.	**4:21** [21]And he said unto them, Is a candle brought to be put under a bushel, or under a bed? and not to be set on a candlestick? **9:49–50** [49]For every one shall be salted with fire, and every sacrifice shall be salted with salt. [50]Salt is good: but if the salt have lost his saltness, wherewith will ye season it? Have salt in yourselves, and have peace one with another. **14:34–35** [34]And saith unto them, My soul is exceeding sorrowful unto death: tarry ye here, and watch. [35]And he went forward a little, and fell on the ground, and prayed that, if it were possible, the hour might pass from him.	**8:16** [16]No man, when he hath lighted a candle, covereth it with a vessel, or putteth it under a bed; but setteth it on a candle stick, that they which enter in may see the light. **11:33** [33]No man, when he hath lighted a candle, putteth it in a secret place, neither under a bushel, but on a candlestick, that they which come in may see the light.

COLOSSIANS 4:5—Ideal Christianity in this world (3:1–4:6), written from prison (undetermined location and date)

Theme	COL	Paul
Be wise to those without	**4:5** [5]Walk in wisdom toward them that are without, redeeming the time.	**Eph 5:15–16 (Pseudo)** [15]See then that ye walk circumspectly, not as fools, but as wise, [16]Redeeming the time, because the days are evil.

CO-WORKERS IN CHRIST (4:7–18), written from prison (undetermined location and date)

COLOSSIANS 4:7—Co-workers in Christ (4:7–18), written from prison (undetermined location and date)

Theme	COL	Lk
Introduce Tychicus who will tell of Paul's state	**4:7** [7]All my state shall Tychicus declare unto you, who is a beloved brother, and a faithful minister and fellowservant in the Lord:	**Acts 20:4** [4]And there accompanied him into Asia Sopater of Berea; and of the Thessalonians, Aristarchus and Secundus; and Gaius of Derbe, and Timotheus; and of Asia, Tychicus and Trophimus.

Jn	Paul	NT
8:12	**1 Tim 5:23 (Pseudo)**	**1 Pet 2:9**
[12]Then spake Jesus again unto them, saying, I am the light of the world: he that followeth me shall not walk in darkness, but shall have the light of life.	[23]Drink no longer water, but use a little wine for thy stomach's sake and thine often infirmities.	[9]But ye are a chosen generation, a royal priesthood, an holy nation, a peculiar people; that ye should show forth the praises of him who hath called you out of darkness into his marvellous light: **1 Pet 2:12** [12]Having your conversation honest among the Gentiles: that, whereas they speak against you as evildoers, they may by your good works, which they shall behold, glorify God in the day of visitation.

Paul
Eph 6:21–22 (Pseudo)
[21]But that ye also may know my affairs, and how I do, Tychicus, a beloved brother and faithful minister in the Lord, shall make known to you all things: [22]Whom I have sent unto you for the same purpose, that ye might know our affairs, and that he might comfort your hearts.
Phil 1:12
[12]But I would ye should understand, brethren, that the things which happened unto me have fallen out rather unto the furtherance of the gospel;

COLOSSIANS 4:9—Co-workers in Christ (4:7–18), written from prison (undetermined location and date)

Theme	COL	Paul
Onesimus	**4:9** [9]With Onesimus, a faithful and beloved brother, who is one of you. They shall make known unto you all things which are done here.	**Phlm 11** [11]Which in time past was to thee unprofitable, but now profitable to thee and to me:

COLOSSIANS 4:10—Co-workers in Christ (4:7–18), written from prison (undetermined location and date)

Theme	COL	Lk
Aristarcus, Marcus, and coworkers	**4:10** [10]Aristarchus my fellowprisoner saluteth you, and Marcus, sister's son to Barnabas, (touching whom ye received commandments: if he come unto you, receive him;)	**Acts 12:12** [12]And when he had considered the thing, he came to the house of Mary the mother of John, whose surname was Mark; where many were gathered together praying. **Acts 12:25** [25]And Barnabas and Saul returned from Jerusalem, when they had fulfilled their ministry, and took with them John, whose surname was Mark. **Acts 13:13** [13]And as Peter knocked at the door of the gate, a damsel came to hearken, named Rhoda. **Acts 15:37, 40** [37]And Barnabas determined to take with them John, whose surname was Mark.... [40]And Paul chose Silas, and departed, being recommended by the brethren unto the grace of God. **Acts 19:29** [29]And the whole city was filled with confusion: and having caught Gaius and Aristarchus, men of Macedonia, Paul's companions in travel, they rushed with one accord into the theatre. **Acts 20:4** [4]And there accompanied him into Asia Sopater of Berea; and of the Thessalonians, Aristarchus and Secundus; and Gaius of Derbe, and Timotheus; and of Asia, Tychicus and Trophimus. **Acts 27:2** [2]And entering into a ship of Adramyttium, we launched, meaning to sail by the coasts of Asia; one Aristarchus, a Macedonian of Thessalonica, being with us.

Paul	NT
Phlm 24 [24]Marcus, Aristarchus, Demas, Lucas, my fellow-labourers. **2 Tim 4:11 (Pseudo)** [11]Only Luke is with me. Take Mark, and bring him with thee: for he is profitable to me for the ministry.	**1 Pet 5:13** [13]The church that is at Babylon, elected together with you, saluteth you; and so doth Marcus my son.

COLOSSIANS 4:11—Co-workers in Christ (4:7–18), written from prison (undetermined location and date)

Theme	COL	Mt	Mk	Lk
Steadfastness	**4:11** [11]And Jesus, which is called Justus, who are of the circumcision. These only are my fellowworkers unto the kingdom of God, which have been a comfort unto me.	**4:18–22** [18]And Jesus, walking by the sea of Galilee, saw two brethren, Simon called Peter, and Andrew his brother, casting a net into the sea: for they were fishers. [19]And he saith unto them, Follow me, and I will make you fishers of men. [20]And they straightway left their nets, and followed him. [21]And going on from thence, he saw other two brethren, James the son of Zebedee, and John his brother, in a ship with Zebedee their father, mending their nets; and he called them. [22]And they immediately left the ship and their father, and followed him. **5:10–11** [10]Blessed are they which are persecuted for righteousness' sake: for theirs is the kingdom of heaven. [11]Blessed are ye, when men shall revile you, and persecute you, and shall say all manner of evil against you falsely, for my sake. **9:13** [13]But go ye and learn what that meaneth, I will have mercy, and not sacrifice: for I am not come to call the righteous, but sinners to repentance. **18:3** [3]And said, Verily I say unto you, Except ye be converted, and become as little children, ye shall not enter into the kingdom of heaven.	**1:16–20** [16]Now as he walked by the sea of Galilee, he saw Simon and Andrew his brother casting a net into the sea: for they were fishers. [17]And Jesus said unto them, Come ye after me, and I will make you to become fishers of men. [18]And straightway they forsook their nets, and followed him. [19]And when he had gone a little further thence, he saw James the son of Zebedee, and John his brother, who also were in the ship mending their nets. [20]And straightway he called them: and they left their father Zebedee in the ship with the hired servants, and went after him. **2:17** [17]When Jesus heard it, he saith unto them, They that are whole have no need of the physician, but they that are sick: I came not to call the righteous, but sinners to repentance. **10:15** [15]Verily I say unto you, Whosoever shall not receive the kingdom of God as a little child, he shall not enter therein.	**5:32** [32]I came not to call the righteous, but sinners to repentance. **6:22** [22]Blessed are ye, when men shall hate you, and when they shall separate you from their company, and shall reproach you, and cast out your name as evil, for the Son of man's sake.

COLOSSIANS 4:12—Co-workers in Christ (4:7–18), written from prison (undetermined location and date)

Theme	COL	Paul
Epaphrasus labors for Christ	**4:12** [12]Epaphras, who is one of you, a servant of Christ, saluteth you, always labouring fervently for you in prayers, that ye may stand perfect and complete in all the will of God. **1:7** [7]As ye also learned of Epaphras our dear fellowservant, who is for you a faithful minister of Christ;	**Rom 15:30** [30]Now I beseech you, brethren, for the Lord Jesus Christ's sake, and for the love of the Spirit, that ye strive together with me in your prayers to God for me;

Jn	Paul	Other
3:5	**1 Cor 6:9–10**	**Q-Quelle**
[5]Jesus answered, Verily, verily, I say unto thee, Except a man be born of water and of the Spirit, he cannot enter into the kingdom of God.	[9]Know ye not that the unrighteous shall not inherit the kingdom of God? Be not deceived: neither fornicators, nor idolaters, nor adulterers, nor effeminate, nor abusers of themselves with mankind, [10]Nor thieves, nor covetous, nor drunkards, nor revilers, nor extortioners, shall inherit the kingdom of God. **Gal 5:19–21** [19]Now the works of the flesh are manifest, which are these; Adultery, fornication, uncleanness, lasciviousness, [20]Idolatry, witchcraft, hatred, variance, emulations, wrath, strife, seditions, heresies, [21]Envyings, murders, drunkenness, revellings, and such like: of the which I tell you before, as I have also told you in time past, that they which do such things shall not inherit the kingdom of God. **Eph 5:5 (Pseudo)** [5]For this ye know, that no whoremonger, nor unclean person, nor covetous man, who is an idolater, hath any inheritance in the kingdom of Christ and of God. **1 Thes 2:12** [12]That ye would walk worthy of God, who hath called you unto his kingdom and glory. **2 Thes 1:4** [4]So that we ourselves glory in you in the churches of God for your patience and faith in all your persecutions and tribulations that ye endure:	Beatitudes: Col 4:11/1 Thes 2:12/2 Thes 1:4/ Mt 5:3-12/Lk 6:20b-23 (QS 8 [Thom 95, 6:2])

COLOSSIANS 4:14—Co-workers in Christ (4:7–18), written from prison (undetermined location and date)

Theme	COL	Paul
Luke & Demas greeting	**4:14** [14]Luke, the beloved physician, and Demas, greet you.	**Phlm 24** [24]Marcus, Aristarchus, Demas, Lucas, my fellowlabourers. **2 Tim 4:10–11 (Pseudo)** [10]For Demas hath forsaken me, having loved this present world, and is departed unto Thessalonica; Crescens to Galatia, Titus unto Dalmatia. [11]Only Luke is with me. Take Mark, and bring him with thee: for he is profitable to me for the ministry.

CONCLUDING REMARKS (4:17–18)

COLOSSIANS 4:17—Co-workers in Christ (4:7–18), written from prison (undetermined location and date)

Theme	COL	Paul
Encourage Archippus' ministry	**4:17** [17]And say to Archippus, Take heed to the ministry which thou hast received in the Lord, that thou fulfil it.	**Phlm 2** [2]And to our beloved Apphia, and Archippus our fellowsoldier, and to the church in thy house:

COLOSSIANS 4:18—Co-workers in Christ (4:7–18), written from prison (undetermined location and date)

Theme	COL	Paul
Peace sent by Paul's hand-writing	**4:18** [18]The salutation by the hand of me Paul. Remember my bonds. Grace be with you. Amen.	**1 Cor 16:21** [21]The salutation of me Paul with mine own hand. **Gal 6:11** [11]Ye see how large a letter I have written unto you with mine own hand. **Eph 3:1 (Pseudo)** [1]For this cause I Paul, the prisoner of Jesus Christ for you Gentiles, **2 Thes 3:17** [17]The salutation of Paul with mine own hand, which is the token in every epistle: so I write.

1 THESSALONIANS, 50 or 51 CE

ADDRESS (1:1–10)

1 THESSALONIANS 1:1—Address (1:1–10), written from Corinth, 50 or 51 CE

Theme	1 THES	Lk	Paul
Greeting	**1:1** [1]Paul, and Silvanus, and Timotheus, unto the church of the Thessalonians which is in God the Father and in the Lord Jesus Christ: Grace be unto you, and peace, from God our Father, and the Lord Jesus Christ.	**Acts 15:40** [40]And Paul chose Silas, and departed, being recommended by the brethren unto the grace of God. **Acts 16:1–3, 19** [1]Then came he to Derbe and Lystra: and, behold, a certain disciple was there, named Timotheus, the son of a certain woman, which was a Jewess, and believed; but his father was a Greek: [2]Which was well reported of by the brethren that were at Lystra and Iconium. [3]Him would Paul have to go forth with him; and took and circumcised him because of the Jews which were in those quarters: for they knew all that his father was a Greek.... [19]And when her masters saw that the hope of their gains was gone, they caught Paul and Silas, and drew them into the marketplace unto the rulers, **Acts 17:14–15** [14]And then immediately the brethren sent away Paul to go as it were to the sea: but Silas and Timotheus abode there still. [15]And they that conducted Paul brought him unto Athens: and receiving a commandment unto Silas and Timotheus for to come to him with all speed, they departed.	**2 Thes 1:1–2** [1]Paul, and Silvanus, and Timotheus, unto the church of the Thessalonians in God our Father and the Lord Jesus Christ: [2]Grace unto you, and peace, from God our Father and the Lord Jesus Christ.

1 THESSALONIANS 1:2—Address (1:1–10), written from Corinth, 50 or 51 CE

Theme	1 THES	Paul
Thanks	**1:2** [2]We give thanks to God always for you all, making mention of you in our prayers;	**2 Thes 1:3** [3]We are bound to thank God always for you, brethren, as it is meet, because that your faith groweth exceedingly, and the charity of every one of you all toward each other aboundeth; [3]We are bound to thank God always for you, brethren, as it is meet, because that your faith groweth exceedingly, and the charity of every one of you all toward each other aboundeth;

1 THESSALONIANS 1:4—Address (1:1–10), written from Corinth, 50 or 51 CE

Theme	1 THES	Paul
Election by God	**1:4** [4]Knowing, brethren beloved, your election of God.	**2 Thes 2:13** [13]But we are bound to give thanks alway to God for you, brethren beloved of the Lord, because God hath from the beginning chosen you to salvation through sanctification of the Spirit and belief of the truth:

1 THESSALONIANS 1:5—Address (1:1–10), written from Corinth, 50 or 51 CE

Theme	1 THES	Mt	Mk	Lk
Gospel in word & surety	**1:5** [5]For our gospel came not unto you in word only, but also in power, and in the Holy Ghost, and in much assurance; as ye know what manner of men we were among you for your sake. **5:19–20** [19]Quench not the Spirit. [20]Despise not prophesyings.	**10:20** [20]For it is not ye that speak, but the Spirit of your Father which speaketh in you.	**13:11** [11]But when they shall lead you, and deliver you up, take no thought beforehand what ye shall speak, neither do ye pre-meditate: but whatsoever shall be given you in that hour, that speak ye: for it is not ye that speak, but the Holy Ghost.	**12:12** [12]For the Holy Ghost shall teach you in the same hour what ye ought to say. **Acts 13:52** [52]And the disciples were filled with joy, and with the Holy Ghost. **Acts 17:1–9** [1]Now when they had passed through Amphipolis and Apollonia, they came to Thessalonica, where was a synagogue of the Jews: [2]And Paul, as his manner was, went in unto them, and three sabbath days reasoned with them out of the scriptures, [3]Opening and alleging, that Christ must needs have suffered, and risen again from the dead; and that this Jesus, whom I preach unto you, is Christ. [4]And some of them believed, and consorted with Paul and Silas; and of the devout Greeks a great multitude, and of the chief women not a few. [5]But the Jews which believed not, moved with envy, took unto them certain lewd fellows of the baser sort, and gathered a company, and set all the city on an uproar, and assaulted the house of Jason, and sought to bring them out to the people. [6]And when they found them not, they drew Jason and certain brethren unto the rulers of the city, crying, These that have turned the world upside down are come hither also; [7]Whom Jason hath received: and these all do contrary to the decrees of Caesar, saying that there is another king, one Jesus. [8]And they troubled the people and the rulers of the city, when they heard these things. [9]And when they had taken security of Jason, and of the other, they let them go.

Paul	Jewish Writings	Other
Rom 8:23 [23]And not only they, but ourselves also, which have the firstfruits of the Spirit, even we ourselves groan within ourselves, waiting for the adoption, to wit, the redemption of our body. **1 Cor 3:16** [16]Know ye not that ye are the temple of God, and that the Spirit of God dwelleth in you? **1 Cor 12:1–13** [1]Now concerning spiritual gifts, brethren, I would not have you ignorant. [2]Ye know that ye were Gentiles, carried away unto these dumb idols, even as ye were led. [3]Wherefore I give you to understand, that no man speaking by the Spirit of God calleth Jesus accursed: and that no man can say that Jesus is the Lord, but by the Holy Ghost. [4]Now there are diversities of gifts, but the same Spirit. [5]And there are differences of administrations, but the same Lord. [6]And there are diversities of operations, but it is the same God which worketh all in all. [7]But the manifestation of the Spirit is given to every man to profit withal. [8]For to one is given by the Spirit the word of wisdom; to another the word of knowledge by the same Spirit; [9]To another faith by the same Spirit; to another the gifts of healing by the same Spirit; [10]To another the working of miracles; to another prophecy; to another discerning of spirits; to another divers kinds of tongues; to another the interpretation of tongues: [11]But all these worketh that one and the selfsame Spirit, dividing to every man severally as he will. [12]For as the body is one, and hath many members, and all the members of that one body, being many, are one body: so also is Christ. [13]For by one Spirit are we all baptized into one body, whether we be Jews or Gentiles, whether we be bond or free; and have been all made to drink into one Spirit. **2 Cor 1:22** [22]Who hath also sealed us, and given the earnest of the Spirit in our hearts. **2 Cor 3:18** [18]But we all, with open face beholding as in a glass the glory of the Lord, are changed into the same image from glory to glory, even as by the Spirit of the Lord. **2 Cor 5:15** [15]And that he died for all, that they which live should not henceforth live unto themselves, but unto him which died for them, and rose again. **Gal 5:22** [22]But the fruit of the Spirit is love, joy, peace, longsuffering, gentleness, goodness, faith, **Eph 1:14 (Pseudo)** [14]Which is the earnest of our inheritance until the redemption of the purchased possession, unto the praise of his glory.	**Jer 31:31–34** [31]Behold, the days come, saith the LORD, that I will make a new covenant with the house of Israel, and with the house of Judah: [32]Not according to the covenant that I made with their fathers in the day that I took them by the hand to bring them out of the land of Egypt; which my covenant they brake, although I was an husband unto them, saith the LORD: [33]But this shall be the covenant that I will make with the house of Israel; After those days, saith the LORD, I will put my law in their inward parts, and write it in their hearts; and will be their God, and they shall be my people. [34]And they shall teach no more every man his neighbour, and every man his brother, saying, Know the LORD: for they shall all know me, from the least of them unto the greatest of them, saith the LORD: for I will forgive their iniquity, and I will remember their sin no more.	**Q-Quelle** Assistance of HS: 1 Thes 1:5/2 Cor 1:22/ Eph 1:14/Col 1:5/Mt 10:19-20/Mk 13:11/ Lk 12:11-12 (QS 37 [Thom 44]), [21:14-15]; Commissioning of 12: 1 Thes 1:5/[Rom 15:8]/1 Cor 12:12/[Col 1:5]/[Mt 10:1, 7-11, 14]/[Mk 6:6b-13/[Lk 9:1-6]; Leaven: 1 Cor 3:16/1 Thes 1:5/Mt 13:33/[Lk 13:20-21(QS 46 [Thom 20, 96])], Lk 12:11-12(QS 37 [Thom 44]); Precedence: 1 Thes 1:5/1 Cor 3:16/ [Mt 19:28]/[Mk 10:41-45]/[Lk 22:28-30 (QS 62)]

1 THESSALONIANS 1:6—Address (1:1–10), written from Corinth, 50 or 51 CE

Theme	1 THES	Mt	Mk
Receiving the Word	**1:6** [6]And ye became followers of us, and of the Lord, having received the word in much affliction, with joy of the Holy Ghost:	**13:24–30** [24]Another parable put he forth unto them, saying, The kingdom of heaven is likened unto a man which sowed good seed in his field: [25]But while men slept, his enemy came and sowed tares among the wheat, and went his way. [26]But when the blade was sprung up, and brought forth fruit, then appeared the tares also. [27]So the servants of the householder came and said unto him, Sir, didst not thou sow good seed in thy field? from whence then hath it tares? [28]He said unto them, An enemy hath done this. The servants said unto him, Wilt thou then that we go and gather them up? [29]But he said, Nay; lest while ye gather up the tares, ye root up also the wheat with them. [30]Let both grow together until the harvest: and in the time of harvest I will say to the reapers, Gather ye together first the tares, and bind them in bundles to burn them: but gather the wheat into my barn.	**4:26–29** [26]And he said, So is the kingdom of God, as if a man should cast seed into the ground; [27]And should sleep, and rise night and day, and the seed should spring and grow up, he knoweth not how. [28]For the earth bringeth forth fruit of herself; first the blade, then the ear, after that the full corn in the ear. [29]But when the fruit is brought forth, immediately he putteth in the sickle, because the harvest is come.

Paul

1 Cor 3:6

6I have planted, Apollos watered; but God gave the increase.

1 Cor 9:7

7Who goeth a warfare any time at his own charges? who planteth a vineyard, and eateth not of the fruit thereof? or who feedeth a flock, and eateth not of the milk of the flock?

1 Cor 9:11

11If we have sown unto you spiritual things, is it a great thing if we shall reap your carnal things?

2 Cor 9:10

10Now he that ministereth seed to the sower both minister bread for your food, and multiply your seed sown, and increase the fruits of your righteousness;)

Gal 5

1Stand fast therefore in the liberty wherewith Christ hath made us free, and be not entangled again with the yoke of bondage. 2Behold, I Paul say unto you, that if ye be circumcised, Christ shall profit you nothing. 3For I testify again to every man that is circumcised, that he is a debtor to do the whole law. 4Christ is become of no effect unto you, whosoever of you are justified by the law; ye are fallen from grace. 5For we through the Spirit wait for the hope of righteousness by faith. 6For in Jesus Christ neither circumcision availeth any thing, nor uncircumcision; but faith which worketh by love. 7Ye did run well; who did hinder you that ye should not obey the truth? 8This persuasion cometh not of him that calleth you. 9A little leaven leaveneth the whole lump. 10I have confidence in you through the Lord, that ye will be none otherwise minded: but he that troubleth you shall bear his judgment, whosoever he be. 11And I, brethren, if I yet preach circumcision, why do I yet suffer persecution? then is the offence of the cross ceased. 12I would they were even cut off which trouble you. 13For, brethren, ye have been called unto liberty; only use not liberty for an occasion to the flesh, but by love serve one another. 14For all the law is fulfilled in one word, even in this; Thou shalt love thy neighbour as thyself. 15But if ye bite and devour one another, take heed that ye be not consumed one of another. 16This I say then, Walk in the Spirit, and ye shall not fulfil the lust of the flesh. 17For the flesh lusteth against the Spirit, and the Spirit against the flesh: and these are contrary the one to the other: so that ye cannot do the things that ye would. 18But if ye be led of the Spirit, ye are not under the law. 19Now the works of the flesh are manifest, which are these; Adultery, fornication, uncleanness, lasciviousness, 20Idolatry, witchcraft, hatred, variance, emulations, wrath, strife, seditions, heresies, 21Envyings, murders, drunkenness, revellings, and such like: of the which I tell you before, as I have also told you in time past, that they which do such things shall not inherit the kingdom of God. 22But the fruit of the Spirit is love, joy, peace, longsuffering, gentleness, goodness, faith, 23Meekness, temperance: against such there is no law. 24And they that are Christ's have crucified the flesh with the affections and lusts. 25If we live in the Spirit, let us also walk in the Spirit. 26Let us not be desirous of vain glory, provoking one another, envying one another.

Gal 6:7–8

7Be not deceived; God is not mocked: for whatsoever a man soweth, that shall he also reap. 8For he that soweth to his flesh shall of the flesh reap corruption; but he that soweth to the Spirit shall of the Spirit reap life everlasting.

Col 1:10

10That ye might walk worthy of the Lord unto all pleasing, being fruitful in every good work, and increasing in the knowledge of God;

1 THESSALONIANS 1:7—Address (1:1–10), written from Corinth, 50 or 51 CE

Theme	1 THES	Paul
Exemplars for Macedonia & Achaia	**1:7** [7]So that ye were ensamples to all that believe in Macedonia and Achaia.	**1 Cor 2:14** [14]But the natural man receiveth not the things of the Spirit of God: for they are foolishness unto him: neither can he know them, because they are spiritually discerned. **1 Cor 4:16** [16]Wherefore I beseech you, be ye followers of me. **1 Cor 11:1** [1]Be ye followers of me, even as I also am of Christ. **Phil 3:17** [17]Brethren, be followers together of me, and mark them which walk so as ye have us for an ensample. **2 Thes 1:4** [4]So that we ourselves glory in you in the churches of God for your patience and faith in all your persecutions and tribulations that ye endure:

1 THESSALONIANS 1:8—Address (1:1–10), written from Corinth, 50 or 51 CE

Theme	1 THES	Paul
Faith spreads	**1:8** [8]For from you sounded out the word of the Lord not only in Macedonia and Achaia, but also in every place your faith to God-ward is spread abroad; so that we need not to speak any thing.	**Rom 1:8** [8]First, I thank my God through Jesus Christ for you all, that your faith is spoken of throughout the whole world.

1 THESSALONIANS 1:9—Address (1:1–10), written from Corinth, 50 or 51 CE

Theme	1 THES	Lk	Paul
Turned from idols to God	**1:9** [9]For they themselves show of us what manner of entering in we had unto you, and how ye turned to God from idols to serve the living and true God;	**Acts 14:15** [15]And saying, Sirs, why do ye these things? We also are men of like passions with you, and preach unto you that ye should turn from these vanities unto the living God, which made heaven, and earth, and the sea, and all things that are therein:	**Gal 4:5** [5]To redeem them that were under the law, that we might receive the adoption of sons. **Gal 4:8** [8]Howbeit then, when ye knew not God, ye did service unto them which by nature are no gods.

1 THESSALONIANS 1:10—Address (1:1–10), written from Corinth, 50 or 51 CE

Theme	1 THES	Mt
Deliverance	**1:10** [10]And to wait for his Son from heaven, whom he raised from the dead, even Jesus, which delivered us from the wrath to come.	**6:10** [10]Thy kingdom come. Thy will be done in earth, as it is in heaven. **13:1–31** [1]The same day went Jesus out of the house, and sat by the sea side. [2]And great multitudes were gathered together unto him, so that he went into a ship, and sat; and the whole multitude stood on the shore. [3]And he spake many things unto them in parables, saying, Behold, a sower went forth to sow; [4]And when he sowed, some seeds fell by the way side, and the fowls came and devoured them up: [5]Some fell upon stony places, where they had not much earth: and forthwith they sprung up, because they had no deepness of earth: [6]And when the sun was up, they were scorched; and because they had no root, they withered away. [7]And some fell among thorns; and the thorns sprung up, and choked them: [8]But other fell into good ground, and brought forth fruit, some an hundredfold, some sixtyfold, some thirtyfold. [9]Who hath ears to hear, let him hear. [10]And the disciples came, and said unto him, Why speakest thou unto them in parables? [11]He answered and said unto them, Because it is given unto you to know the mysteries of the kingdom of heaven, but to them it is not given. [12]For whosoever hath, to him shall be given, and he shall have more abundance: but whosoever hath not, from him shall be taken away even that he hath. [13]Therefore speak I to them in parables: because they seeing see not; and hearing they hear not, neither do they under-stand. [14]And in them is fulfilled the prophecy of Esaias, which saith, By hearing ye shall hear, and shall not understand; and seeing ye shall see, and shall not perceive: [15]For this people's heart is waxed gross, and their ears are dull of hearing, and their eyes they have closed; lest at any time they should see with their eyes, and hear with their ears, and should understand with their heart, and should be converted, and I should heal them. [16]But blessed are your eyes, for they see: and your ears, for they hear. [17]For verily I say unto you, That many prophets and righteous men have desired to see those things which ye see, and have not seen them; and to hear those things which ye hear, and have not heard them. [18]Hear ye therefore the parable of the sower. [19]When any one heareth the word of the kingdom, and understandeth it not, then cometh the wicked one, and catcheth away that which was sown in his heart. This is he which received seed by the way side. [20]But he that received the seed into stony places, the same is he that heareth the word, and anon with joy receiveth it; [21]Yet hath he not root in himself, but dureth for a while: for when tribulation or persecution ariseth because of the word, by and by he is offended. [22]He also that received seed among the thorns is he that heareth the word; and the care of this world, and the deceitfulness of riches, choke the word, and he becometh unfruitful. [23]But he that received seed into the good ground is he that heareth the word, and understandeth it; which also beareth fruit, and bringeth forth, some an hundredfold, some sixty, some thirty. [24]Another parable put he forth unto them, saying, The kingdom of heaven is likened unto a man which sowed good seed in his field: [25]But while men slept, his enemy came and sowed tares among the wheat, and went his way. [26]But when the blade was sprung up, and brought forth fruit, then appeared the tares also. [27]So the servants of the householder came and said unto him, Sir, didst not thou sow good seed in thy field? from whence then hath it tares? [28]He said unto them, An enemy hath done this. The servants said unto him, Wilt thou then that we go and gather them up? [29]But he said, Nay; lest while ye gather up the tares, ye root up also the wheat with them. [30]Let both grow together until the harvest: and in the time of harvest I will say to the reapers, Gather ye together first the tares, and bind them in bundles to burn them: but gather the wheat into my barn. [31]Another parable put he forth unto them, saying, The kingdom of heaven is like to a grain of mustard seed, which a man took, and sowed in his field:

1 Thessalonians 1:10 continued on next page

1 THESSALONIANS 1:10—Address (1:1–10), written from Corinth, 50 or 51 CE

Theme	1 THES	Mk	Lk
(Cont.) **Deliverance**	**1:10 (above)**	**4:1–32** 1And he began again to teach by the sea side: and there was gathered unto him a great multitude, so that he entered into a ship, and sat in the sea; and the whole multitude was by the sea on the land. 2And he taught them many things by parables, and said unto them in his doctrine, 3Hearken; Behold, there went out a sower to sow: 4And it came to pass, as he sowed, some fell by the way side, and the fowls of the air came and devoured it up. 5And some fell on stony ground, where it had not much earth; and immediately it sprang up, because it had no depth of earth: 6But when the sun was up, it was scorched; and because it had no root, it withered away. 7And some fell among thorns, and the thorns grew up, and choked it, and it yielded no fruit. 8And other fell on good ground, and did yield fruit that sprang up and increased; and brought forth, some thirty, and some sixty, and some an hundred. 9And he said unto them, He that hath ears to hear, let him hear. 10And when he was alone, they that were about him with the twelve asked of him the parable. 11And he said unto them, Unto you it is given to know the mystery of the kingdom of God: but unto them that are without, all these things are done in parables: 12That seeing they may see, and not perceive; and hearing they may hear, and not understand; lest at any time they should be converted, and their sins should be forgiven them. 13And he said unto them, Know ye not this parable? and how then will ye know all parables? 14The sower soweth the word. 15And these are they by the way side, where the word is sown; but when they have heard, Satan cometh immediately, and taketh away the word that was sown in their hearts. 16And these are they likewise which are sown on stony ground; who, when they have heard the word, immediately receive it with gladness; 17And have no root in themselves, and so endure but for a time: afterward, when affliction or persecution ariseth for the word's sake, immediately they are offended. 18And these are they which are sown among thorns; such as hear the word, 19And the cares of this world, and the deceitfulness of riches, and the lusts of other things entering in, choke the word, and it becometh unfruitful. 20And these are they which are sown on good ground; such as hear the word, and receive it, and bring forth fruit, some thirtyfold, some sixty, and some an hundred. 21And he said unto them, Is a candle brought to be put under a bushel, or under a bed? and not to be set on a candlestick? 22For there is nothing hid, which shall not be manifested; neither was any thing kept secret, but that it should come abroad. 23If any man have ears to hear, let him hear. 24And he said unto them, Take heed what ye hear: with what measure ye mete, it shall be measured to you: and unto you that hear shall more be given. 25For he that hath, to him shall be given: and he that hath not, from him shall be taken even that which he hath. 26And he said, So is the kingdom of God, as if a man should cast seed into the ground; 27And should sleep, and rise night and day, and the seed should spring and grow up, he knoweth not how. 28For the earth bringeth forth fruit of herself; first the blade, then the ear, after that the full corn in the ear. 29But when the fruit is brought forth, immediately he putteth in the sickle, because the harvest is come. 30And he said, Whereunto shall we liken the kingdom of God? or with what comparison shall we compare it? 31It is like a grain of mustard seed, which, when it is sown in the earth, is less than all the seeds that be in the earth: 32But when it is sown, it groweth up, and becometh greater than all herbs, and shooteth out great branches; so that the fowls of the air may lodge under the shadow of it.	**8:4–15** 4And when much people were gathered together, and were come to him out of every city, he spake by a parable: 5A sower went out to sow his seed: and as he sowed, some fell by the way side; and it was trodden down, and the fowls of the air devoured it. 6And some fell upon a rock; and as soon as it was sprung up, it withered away, because it lacked moisture. 7And some fell among thorns; and the thorns sprang up with it, and choked it. 8And other fell on good ground, and sprang up, and bare fruit an hundredfold. And when he had said these things, he cried, He that hath ears to hear, let him hear. 9And his disciples asked him, saying, What might this parable be? 10And he said, Unto you it is given to know the mysteries of the kingdom of God: but to others in parables; that seeing they might not see, and hearing they might not understand. 11Now the parable is this: The seed is the word of God. 12Those by the way side are they that hear; then cometh the devil, and taketh away the word out of their hearts, lest they should believe and be saved. 13They on the rock are they, which, when they hear, receive the word with joy; and these have no root, which for a while believe, and in time of temptation fall away. 14And that which fell among thorns are they, which, when they have heard, go forth, and are choked with cares and riches and pleasures of this life, and bring no fruit to perfection. 15But that on the good ground are they, which in an honest and good heart, having heard the word, keep it, and bring forth fruit with patience. **11:2** 2And he said unto them, When ye pray, say, Our Father which art in heaven, Hallowed be thy name. Thy kingdom come. Thy will be done, as in heaven, so in earth. **13:18–19** 18Then said he, Unto what is the kingdom of God like? and whereunto shall I resemble it? 19It is like a grain of mustard seed, which a man took, and cast into his garden; and it grew, and waxed a great tree; and the fowls of the air lodged in the branches of it.

Paul

Rom 2:1–16

[1]Therefore thou art inexcusable, O man, whosoever thou art that judgest: for wherein thou judgest another, thou condemnest thyself; for thou that judgest doest the same things. [2]But we are sure that the judgment of God is according to truth against them which commit such things. [3]And thinkest thou this, O man, that judgest them which do such things, and doest the same, that thou shalt escape the judgment of God? [4]Or despisest thou the riches of his goodness and forbearance and longsuffering; not knowing that the goodness of God leadeth thee to repentance? [5]But after thy hardness and impenitent heart treasurest up unto thyself wrath against the day of wrath and revelation of the righteous judgment of God; [6]Who will render to every man according to his deeds: [7]To them who by patient continuance in well doing seek for glory and honour and immortality, eternal life: [8]But unto them that are contentious, and do not obey the truth, but obey unrighteousness, indignation and wrath, [9]Tribulation and anguish, upon every soul of man that doeth evil, of the Jew first, and also of the Gentile; [10]But glory, honour, and peace, to every man that worketh good, to the Jew first, and also to the Gentile: [11]For there is no respect of persons with God. [12]For as many as have sinned without law shall also perish without law: and as many as have sinned in the law shall be judged by the law; [13](For not the hearers of the law are just before God, but the doers of the law shall be justified. [14]For when the Gentiles, which have not the law, do by nature the things contained in the law, these, having not the law, are a law unto themselves: [15]Which show the work of the law written in their hearts, their conscience also bearing witness, and their thoughts the mean while accusing or else excusing one another;) [16]In the day when God shall judge the secrets of men by Jesus Christ according to my gospel.

Rom 5:9

[9]Much more then, being now justified by his blood, we shall be saved from wrath through him.

Rom 8:17

[17]And if children, then heirs; heirs of God, and joint-heirs with Christ; if so be that we suffer with him, that we may be also glorified together.

Rom 8:23

[23]And not only they, but ourselves also, which have the firstfruits of the Spirit, even we ourselves groan within ourselves, waiting for the adoption, to wit, the redemption of our body.

Rom 11:26

[26]And so all Israel shall be saved: as it is written, There shall come out of Sion the Deliverer, and shall turn away ungodliness from Jacob:

Rom 13:4

[4]For he is the minister of God to thee for good. But if thou do that which is evil, be afraid; for he beareth not the sword in vain: for he is the minister of God, a revenger to execute wrath upon him that doeth evil.

1 Cor 13:12

[12]For now we see through a glass, darkly; but then face to face: now I know in part; but then shall I know even as also I am known.

1 Cor 15:52

[52]In a moment, in the twinkling of an eye, at the last trump: for the trumpet shall sound, and the dead shall be raised incorruptible, and we shall be changed.

1 Thes 4:17

[17]Then we which are alive and remain shall be caught up together with them in the clouds, to meet the Lord in the air: and so shall we ever be with the Lord.

2 Thes 1:10

[10]When he shall come to be glorified in his saints, and to be admired in all them that believe (because our testimony among you was believed) in that day.

RELATIONS WITH THE COMMUNITY (2:1–3:13)

1 THESSALONIANS 2:2—Relations with the community (2:1–3:13), written from Corinth, 50 or 51 CE

Theme	1 THES	Lk
Bold to speak gospel to contentious	**2:2** [2]But even after that we had suffered before, and were shamefully entreated, as ye know, at Philippi, we were bold in our God to speak unto you the gospel of God with much contention.	**Acts 16:19–17:10** **16**[19]And when her masters saw that the hope of their gains was gone, they caught Paul and Silas, and drew them into the marketplace unto the rulers, [20]And brought them to the magistrates, saying, These men, being Jews, do exceedingly trouble our city, [21]And teach customs, which are not lawful for us to receive, neither to observe, being Romans. [22]And the multitude rose up together against them: and the magistrates rent off their clothes, and commanded to beat them. [23]And when they had laid many stripes upon them, they cast them into prison, charging the jailor to keep them safely: [24]Who, having received such a charge, thrust them into the inner prison, and made their feet fast in the stocks. [25]And at midnight Paul and Silas prayed, and sang praises unto God: and the prisoners heard them. [26]And suddenly there was a great earthquake, so that the foundations of the prison were shaken: and immediately all the doors were opened, and every one's bands were loosed. [27]And the keeper of the prison awaking out of his sleep, and seeing the prison doors open, he drew out his sword, and would have killed himself, supposing that the prisoners had been fled. [28]But Paul cried with a loud voice, saying, Do thyself no harm: for we are all here. [29]Then he called for a light, and sprang in, and came trembling, and fell down before Paul and Silas, [30]And brought them out, and said, Sirs, what must I do to be saved? [31]And they said, Believe on the Lord Jesus Christ, and thou shalt be saved, and thy house. [32]And they spake unto him the word of the Lord, and to all that were in his house. [33]And he took them the same hour of the night, and washed their stripes; and was baptized, he and all his, straightway. [34]And when he had brought them into his house, he set meat before them, and rejoiced, believing in God with all his house. [35]And when it was day, the magistrates sent the serjeants, saying, Let those men go. [36]And the keeper of the prison told this saying to Paul, The magistrates have sent to let you go: now therefore depart, and go in peace. [37]But Paul said unto them, They have beaten us openly uncondemned, being Romans, and have cast us into prison; and now do they thrust us out privily? nay verily; but let them come them-selves and fetch us out. [38]And the serjeants told these words unto the magistrates: and they feared, when they heard that they were Romans. [39]And they came and besought them, and brought them out, and desired them to depart out of the city. [40]And they went out of the prison, and entered into the house of Lydia: and when they had seen the brethren, they comforted them, and departed. **17**[1]Now when they had passed through Amphipolis and Apollonia, they came to Thessalonica, where was a synagogue of the Jews: [2]And Paul, as his manner was, went in unto them, and three sabbath days reasoned with them out of the scriptures, [3]Opening and alleging, that Christ must needs have suffered, and risen again from the dead; and that this Jesus, whom I preach unto you, is Christ. [4]And some of them believed, and consorted with Paul and Silas; and of the devout Greeks a great multitude, and of the chief women not a few. [5]But the Jews which believed not, moved with envy, took unto them certain lewd fellows of the baser sort, and gathered a company, and set all the city on an uproar, and assaulted the house of Jason, and sought to bring them out to the people. [6]And when they found them not, they drew Jason and certain brethren unto the rulers of the city, crying, These that have turned the world upside down are come hither also; [7]Whom Jason hath received: and these all do contrary to the decrees of Caesar, saying that there is another king, one Jesus. [8]And they troubled the people and the rulers of the city, when they heard these things. [9]And when they had taken security of Jason, and of the other, they let them go. [10]And the brethren immediately sent away Paul and Silas by night unto Berea: who coming thither went into the synagogue of the Jews.

1 THESSALONIANS 2:4—Relations with the community (2:1–3:13), written from Corinth, 50 or 51 CE

Theme	1 THES	Paul
Please God	**2:4** [4]But as we were allowed of God to be put in trust with the gospel, even so we speak; not as pleasing men, but God, which trieth our hearts.	**Gal 1:10** [10]For do I now persuade men, or God? or do I seek to please men? for if I yet pleased men, I should not be the servant of Christ.

1 THESSALONIANS 2:6—Relations with the community (2:1–3:13), written from Corinth, 50 or 51 CE

Theme	1 THES	Jn	Paul
True to God	**2:6** [6]Nor of men sought we glory, neither of you, nor yet of others, when we might have been burdensome, as the apostles of Christ.	**5:41, 44** [41]I receive not honour from men. . . . [44]How can ye believe, which receive honour one of another, and seek not the honour that cometh from God only?	**1 Cor 10:31** [31]Whether therefore ye eat, or drink, or whatsoever ye do, do all to the glory of God. **2 Cor 4:17** [17]For our light affliction, which is but for a moment, worketh for us a far more exceeding and eternal weight of glory;

1 THESSALONIANS 2:9—Relations with the community (2:1–3:13), written from Corinth, 50 or 51 CE

Theme	1 THES	Lk
Preached for gospel's sake	**2:9** [9]For ye remember, brethren, our labour and travail: for labouring night and day, because we would not be chargeable unto any of you, we preached unto you the gospel of God.	**Acts 20:34** [34]Yea, ye yourselves know, that these hands have ministered unto my necessities, and to them that were with me.

1 THESSALONIANS 2:11—Relations with the community (2:1–3:13), written from Corinth, 50 or 51 CE

Theme	1 THES	Lk
Exhorted community	**2:11** [11]As ye know how we exhorted and comforted and charged every one of you, as a father doth his children,	**Acts 20:31** [31]Therefore watch, and remember, that by the space of three years I ceased not to warn every one night and day with tears.

Paul	Other
1 Cor 4:12 [12]And labour, working with our own hands: being reviled, we bless; being persecuted, we suffer it: **1 Cor 9:3–18** [3]Mine answer to them that do examine me is this, [4]Have we not power to eat and to drink? [5]Have we not power to lead about a sister, a wife, as well as other apostles, and as the brethren of the Lord, and Cephas? [6]Or I only and Barnabas, have not we power to forbear working? [7]Who goeth a warfare any time at his own charges? who planteth a vineyard, and eateth not of the fruit thereof? or who feedeth a flock, and eateth not of the milk of the flock? [8]Say I these things as a man? or saith not the law the same also? [9]For it is written in the law of Moses, Thou shalt not muzzle the mouth of the ox that treadeth out the corn. Doth God take care for oxen? [10]Or saith he it altogether for our sakes? For our sakes, no doubt, this is written: that he that ploweth should plow in hope; and that he that thresheth in hope should be partaker of his hope. [11]If we have sown unto you spiritual things, is it a great thing if we shall reap your carnal things? [12]If others be partakers of this power over you, are not we rather? Nevertheless we have not used this power; but suffer all things, lest we should hinder the gospel of Christ. [13]Do ye not know that they which minister about holy things live of the things of the temple? and they which wait at the altar are partakers with the altar? [14]Even so hath the Lord ordained that they which preach the gospel should live of the gospel. [15]But I have used none of these things: neither have I written these things, that it should be so done unto me: for it were better for me to die, than that any man should make my glorying void. [16]For though I preach the gospel, I have nothing to glory of: for necessity is laid upon me; yea, woe is unto me, if I preach not the gospel! [17]For if I do this thing will- ingly, I have a reward: but if against my will, a dispensation of the gospel is committed unto me. [18]What is my reward then? Verily that, when I preach the gospel, I may make the gospel of Christ without charge, that I abuse not my power in the gospel. **2 Thes 3:7–9** [7]For yourselves know how ye ought to follow us: for we behaved not ourselves disorderly among you; [8]Nei- ther did we eat any man's bread for nought; but wrought with labour and travail night and day, that we might not be chargeable to any of you: [9]Not because we have not power, but to make ourselves an ensample unto you to follow us.	**Q-Quelle** Love Enemies: 1 Thes 2:9/1 Cor 4:12/[Mt 5:38-48, 7:12]/[Lk 6:27-36 (QS 9 [Thom 95, 6:2])]

1 THESSALONIANS 2:12—Relations with the community (2:1–3:13), written from Corinth, 50 or 51 CE

Theme	1 THES	Mt	Mk	Lk
Steadfast Righteousness	**2:12** [12]That ye would walk worthy of God, who hath called you unto his kingdom and glory.	**4:18–22** [18]And Jesus, walking by the sea of Galilee, saw two brethren, Simon called Peter, and Andrew his brother, casting a net into the sea: for they were fishers. [19]And he saith unto them, Follow me, and I will make you fishers of men. [20]And they straightway left their nets, and followed him. [21]And going on from thence, he saw other two brethren, James the son of Zebedee, and John his brother, in a ship with Zebedee their father, mending their nets; and he called them. [22]And they immediately left the ship and their father, and followed him. **5:10–11** [10]Blessed are they which are persecuted for righteousness' sake: for theirs is the kingdom of heaven. [11]Blessed are ye, when men shall revile you, and persecute you, and shall say all manner of evil against you falsely, for my sake. **5:20** [20]For I say unto you, That except your righteousness shall exceed the righteousness of the scribes and Pharisees, ye shall in no case enter into the kingdom of heaven. **9:13** [13]But go ye and learn what that meaneth, I will have mercy, and not sacrifice: for I am not come to call the righteous, but sinners to repentance. **18:3** [3]And said, Verily I say unto you, Except ye be converted, and become as little children, ye shall not enter into the kingdom of heaven.	**1:16–20** [16]Now as he walked by the sea of Galilee, he saw Simon and Andrew his brother casting a net into the sea: for they were fishers. [17]And Jesus said unto them, Come ye after me, and I will make you to become fishers of men. [18]And straightway they forsook their nets, and followed him. [19]And when he had gone a little further thence, he saw James the son of Zebedee, and John his brother, who also were in the ship mending their nets. [20]And straightway he called them: and they left their father Zebedee in the ship with the hired servants, and went after him. **2:17** [17]When Jesus heard it, he saith unto them, They that are whole have no need of the physician, but they that are sick: I came not to call the righteous, but sinners to repentance. **10:15** [15]Verily I say unto you, Whosoever shall not receive the kingdom of God as a little child, he shall not enter therein.	**5:32** [32]I came not to call the righteous, but sinners to repentance. **6:22** [22]Blessed are ye, when men shall hate you, and when they shall separate you from their company, and shall reproach you, and cast out your name as evil, for the Son of man's sake.

Jn	Paul	NT	Other
3:5 [6]That which is born of the flesh is flesh; and that which is born of the Spirit is spirit.	**Rom 14:17** [17]For the kingdom of God is not meat and drink; but righteousness, and peace, and joy in the Holy Ghost. **1 Cor 6:9–10** **[9]Know ye not that the unrighteous shall not inherit the kingdom of God? Be not deceived: neither fornicators, nor idolaters, nor adulterers, nor effeminate, nor abusers of themselves with mankind,** [10]Nor thieves, nor covetous, nor drunkards, nor revilers, nor extortioners, shall inherit the kingdom of God. **1 Cor 6:19** [19]What? know ye not that your body is the temple of the Holy Ghost which is in you, which ye have of God, and ye are not your own? **Gal 5:19–21** [19]Now the works of the flesh are manifest, which are these; Adultery, fornication, uncleanness, lasciviousness, [20]Idolatry, witchcraft, hatred, variance, emulations, wrath, strife, seditions, heresies, [21]Envyings, murders, drunkenness, revellings, and such like: of the which I tell you before, as I have also told you in time past, that they which do such things shall not inherit the kingdom of God. **Eph 5:5 (Pseudo)** [2]And walk in love, as Christ also hath loved us, and hath given himself for us an offering and a sacrifice to God for a sweetsmelling savour. **Col 4:11** [11]And Jesus, which is called Justus, who are of the circumcision. These only are my fellowworkers unto the kingdom of God, which have been a comfort unto me. **2 Thes 1:4** [4]So that we ourselves glory in you in the churches of God for your patience and faith in all your persecutions and tribulations that ye endure: **2 Thes 2:14** [14]Whereunto he called you by our gospel, to the obtaining of the glory of our Lord Jesus Christ.	**1 Pet 4:7** [7]But the end of all things is at hand: be ye therefore sober, and watch unto prayer. **1 Pet 5:10** [10]But the God of all grace, who hath called us unto his eternal glory by Christ Jesus, after that ye have suffered a while, make you perfect, stablish, strengthen, settle you.	**Q-Quelle** Beatitudes: 1 Thes 2:12/Col 4:11/2 Thes 1:4/Mt 5:3-12/ Lk 6:20b-23 (QS 8 [Thom 54,68,69])

1 THESSALONIANS 2:13—Relations with the community (2:1–3:13), written from Corinth, 50 or 51 CE

Theme	1 THES	Mt
Faith in Word	**2:13** [13]For this cause also thank we God without ceasing, because, when ye received the word of God which ye heard of us, ye received it not as the word of men, but as it is in truth, the word of God, which effectually worketh also in you that believe.	**13:1–23** [1]The same day went Jesus out of the house, and sat by the sea side. [2]And great multitudes were gathered together unto him, so that he went into a ship, and sat; and the whole multitude stood on the shore. [3]And he spake many things unto them in parables, saying, Behold, a sower went forth to sow; [4]And when he sowed, some seeds fell by the way side, and the fowls came and devoured them up: [5]Some fell upon stony places, where they had not much earth: and forthwith they sprung up, because they had no deepness of earth: [6]And when the sun was up, they were scorched; and because they had no root, they withered away. [7]And some fell among thorns; and the thorns sprung up, and choked them: [8]But other fell into good ground, and brought forth fruit, some an hundredfold, some sixtyfold, some thirtyfold. [9]Who hath ears to hear, let him hear. [10]And the disciples came, and said unto him, Why speakest thou unto them in parables? [11]He answered and said unto them, Because it is given unto you to know the mysteries of the kingdom of heaven, but to them it is not given. [12]For whosoever hath, to him shall be given, and he shall have more abundance: but whosoever hath not, from him shall be taken away even that he hath. [13]Therefore speak I to them in parables: because they seeing see not; and hearing they hear not, neither do they understand. [14]And in them is fulfilled the prophecy of Esaias, which saith, By hearing ye shall hear, and shall not understand; and seeing ye shall see, and shall not perceive: [15]For this people's heart is waxed gross, and their ears are dull of hearing, and their eyes they have closed; lest at any time they should see with their eyes, and hear with their ears, and should understand with their heart, and should be converted, and I should heal them. [16]But blessed are your eyes, for they see: and your ears, for they hear. [17]For verily I say unto you, That many prophets and righteous men have desired to see those things which ye see, and have not seen them; and to hear those things which ye hear, and have not heard them. [18]Hear ye therefore the parable of the sower. [19]When any one heareth the word of the kingdom, and understandeth it not, then cometh the wicked one, and catcheth away that which was sown in his heart. This is he which received seed by the way side. [20]But he that received the seed into stony places, the same is he that heareth the word, and anon with joy receiveth it; [21]Yet hath he not root in himself, but dureth for a while: for when tribulation or persecution ariseth because of the word, by and by he is offended. [22]He also that received seed among the thorns is he that heareth the word; and the care of this world, and the deceitfulness of riches, choke the word, and he becometh unfruitful. [23]But he that received seed into the good ground is he that heareth the word, and understandeth it; which also beareth fruit, and bringeth forth, some an hundredfold, some sixty, some thirty.

1 THESSALONIANS 2:15—Relations with the community (2:1–3:13), written from Corinth, 50 or 51 CE

Theme	1 THES	Lk
Persecutors do not please God	**2:15** [15]Who both killed the Lord Jesus, and their own prophets, and have persecuted us; and they please not God, and are contrary to all men:	**Acts 2:23** [23]Him, being delivered by the determinate counsel and foreknowledge of God, ye have taken, and by wicked hands have crucified and slain: **Acts 7:52** [52]Which of the prophets have not your fathers persecuted? and they have slain them which showed before of the coming of the Just One; of whom ye have been now the betrayers and murderers:

Mk	Lk	Paul
4:1–20	**8:4–15**	**2 Cor 4:4**
1And he began again to teach by the sea side: and there was gathered unto him a great multitude, so that he entered into a ship, and sat in the sea; and the whole multitude was by the sea on the land. 2And he taught them many things by parables, and said unto them in his doctrine, 3Hearken; Behold, there went out a sower to sow: 4And it came to pass, as he sowed, some fell by the way side, and the fowls of the air came and devoured it up. 5And some fell on stony ground, where it had not much earth; and immediately it sprang up, because it had no depth of earth: 6But when the sun was up, it was scorched; and because it had no root, it withered away. 7And some fell among thorns, and the thorns grew up, and choked it, and it yielded no fruit. 8And other fell on good ground, and did yield fruit that sprang up and increased; and brought forth, some thirty, and some sixty, and some an hundred. 9And he said unto them, He that hath ears to hear, let him hear. 10And when he was alone, they that were about him with the twelve asked of him the parable. 11And he said unto them, Unto you it is given to know the mystery of the kingdom of God: but unto them that are without, all these things are done in parables: 12That seeing they may see, and not perceive; and hearing they may hear, and not understand; lest at any time they should be converted, and their sins should be forgiven them. 13And he said unto them, Know ye not this parable? and how then will ye know all parables? 14The sower soweth the word. **15And these are they by the way side, where the word is sown; but when they have heard, Satan cometh immediately, and taketh away the word that was sown in their hearts.** 16And these are they likewise which are sown on stony ground; who, when they have heard the word, immediately receive it with gladness; 17And have no root in themselves, and so endure but for a time: afterward, when affliction or persecution ariseth for the word's sake, immediately they are offended. 18And these are they which are sown among thorns; such as hear the word, 19And the cares of this world, and the deceitfulness of riches, and the lusts of other things entering in, choke the word, and it becometh unfruitful. 20And these are they which are sown on good ground; such as hear the word, and receive it, and bring forth fruit, some thirtyfold, some sixty, and some an hundred.	4And when much people were gathered together, and were come to him out of every city, he spake by a parable: 5A sower went out to sow his seed: and as he sowed, some fell by the way side; and it was trodden down, and the fowls of the air devoured it. 6And some fell upon a rock; and as soon as it was sprung up, it withered away, because it lacked moisture. 7And some fell among thorns; and the thorns sprang up with it, and choked it. 8And other fell on good ground, and sprang up, and bare fruit an hundredfold. And when he had said these things, he cried, He that hath ears to hear, let him hear. 9And his disciples asked him, saying, What might this parable be? 10And he said, Unto you it is given to know the mysteries of the kingdom of God: but to others in parables; that seeing they might not see, and hearing they might not understand. 11Now the parable is this: The seed is the word of God. 12Those by the way side are they that hear; then cometh the devil, and taketh away the word out of their hearts, lest they should believe and be saved. 13They on the rock are they, which, when they hear, receive the word with joy; and these have no root, which for a while believe, and in time of temptation fall away. 14And that which fell among thorns are they, which, when they have heard, go forth, and are choked with cares and riches and pleasures of this life, and bring no fruit to perfection. 15But that on the good ground are they, which in an honest and good heart, having heard the word, keep it, and bring forth fruit with patience.	4In whom the god of this world hath blinded the minds of them which believe not, lest the light of the glorious gospel of Christ, who is the image of God, should shine unto them. **Col 1:6** 6Which is come unto you, as it is in all the world; and bringeth forth fruit, as it doth also in you, since the day ye heard of it, and knew the grace of God in truth: **Q-Quelle** Thanks and Blessings for Disciples: 1 Thes 2:13/[1 Cor 1:6]/2 Cor 4:4/Col 1:6/[Mt 11:25-27], Mt 13:16-17/[Lk 10:21-24 (QS 24, 25)]

1 THESSALONIANS 2:16—Relations with the community (2:1–3:13), written from Corinth, 50 or 51 CE

Theme	1 THES	Mt
Lament over lost souls	**2:16** 16 Forbidding us to speak to the Gentiles that they might be saved, to fill up their sins alway: for the wrath is come upon them to the uttermost.	**21:10** 10 And when he was come into Jerusalem, all the city was moved, saying, Who is this? **21:33–44** 33 Hear another parable: There was a certain householder, which planted a vineyard, and hedged it round about, and digged a winepress in it, and built a tower, and let it out to husbandmen, and went into a far country: 34 And when the time of the fruit drew near, he sent his servants to the husbandmen, that they might receive the fruits of it. 35 And the husbandmen took his servants, and beat one, and killed another, and stoned another. 36 Again, he sent other servants more than the first: and they did unto them likewise. 37 But last of all he sent unto them his son, saying, They will reverence my son. 38 But when the husbandmen saw the son, they said among themselves, This is the heir; come, let us kill him, and let us seize on his inheritance. 39 And they caught him, and cast him out of the vineyard, and slew him. 40 When the lord therefore of the vineyard cometh, what will he do unto those husbandmen? 41 They say unto him, He will miserably destroy those wicked men, and will let out his vineyard unto other husbandmen, which shall render him the fruits in their seasons. 42 Jesus saith unto them, Did ye never read in the scriptures, The stone which the builders rejected, the same is become the head of the corner: this is the Lord's doing, and it is marvellous in our eyes? 43 Therefore say I unto you, The kingdom of God shall be taken from you, and given to a nation bringing forth the fruits thereof. 44 And whosoever shall fall on this stone shall be broken: but on whomsoever it shall fall, it will grind him to powder. **22:1–10** 1 And Jesus answered and spake unto them again by parables, and said, 2 The kingdom of heaven is like unto a certain king, which made a marriage for his son, 3 And sent forth his servants to call them that were bidden to the wedding: and they would not come. 4 Again, he sent forth other servants, saying, Tell them which are bidden, Behold, I have prepared my dinner: my oxen and my fatlings are killed, and all things are ready: come unto the marriage. 5 But they made light of it, and went their ways, one to his farm, another to his merchandise: 6 And the remnant took his servants, and entreated them spitefully, and slew them. 7 But when the king heard thereof, he was wroth: and he sent forth his armies, and destroyed those murderers, and burned up their city. 8 Then saith he to his servants, The wedding is ready, but they which were bidden were not worthy. 9 Go ye therefore into the highways, and as many as ye shall find, bid to the marriage. 10 So those servants went out into the highways, and gathered together all as many as they found, both bad and good: and the wedding was furnished with guests. **23:29–39** 29 Woe unto you, scribes and Pharisees, hypocrites! because ye build the tombs of the prophets, and garnish the sepulchres of the righteous, 30 And say, If we had been in the days of our fathers, we would not have been partakers with them in the blood of the prophets. 31 Wherefore ye be witnesses unto yourselves, that ye are the children of them which killed the prophets. 32 Fill ye up then the measure of your fathers. 33 Ye serpents, ye generation of vipers, how can ye escape the damnation of hell? 34 Wherefore, behold, I send unto you prophets, and wise men, and scribes: and some of them ye shall kill and crucify; and some of them shall ye scourge in your synagogues, and persecute them from city to city: 35 That upon you may come all the righteous blood shed upon the earth, from the blood of righteous Abel unto the blood of Zacharias son of Barachias, whom ye slew between the temple and the altar. 36 Verily I say unto you, All these things shall come upon this generation. 37 O Jerusalem, Jerusalem, thou that killest the prophets, and stonest them which are sent unto thee, how often would I have gathered thy children together, even as a hen gathereth her chickens under her wings, and ye would not! 38 Behold, your house is left unto you desolate. 39 For I say unto you, Ye shall not see me henceforth, till ye shall say, Blessed is he that cometh in the name of the Lord.

Mk	Lk	Paul
11:11–16 11 And Jesus entered into Jerusalem, and into the temple: and when he had looked round about upon all things, and now the eventide was come, he went out unto Bethany with the twelve. 12 And on the morrow, when they were come from Bethany, he was hungry: 13 And seeing a fig tree afar off having leaves, he came, if haply he might find any thing thereon: and when he came to it, he found nothing but leaves; for the time of figs was not yet. 14 And Jesus answered and said unto it, No man eat fruit of thee hereafter for ever. And his disciples heard it. 15 And they come to Jerusalem: and Jesus went into the temple, and began to cast out them that sold and bought in the temple, and overthrew the tables of the moneychangers, and the seats of them that sold doves; 16 And would not suffer that any man should carry any vessel through the temple. **12:1–12** 1 And he began to speak unto them by parables. A certain man planted a vineyard, and set an hedge about it, and digged a place for the winefat, and built a tower, and let it out to husbandmen, and went into a far country. 2 And at the season he sent to the husbandmen a servant, that he might receive from the husbandmen of the fruit of the vineyard. 3 And they caught him, and beat him, and sent him away empty. 4 And again he sent unto them another servant; and at him they cast stones, and wounded him in the head, and sent him away shamefully handled. 5 And again he sent another; and him they killed, and many others; beating some, and killing some. 6 Having yet therefore one son, his wellbeloved, he sent him also last unto them, saying, They will reverence my son. 7 But those husbandmen said among themselves, This is the heir; come, let us kill him, and the inheritance shall be ours. 8 And they took him, and killed him, and cast him out of the vineyard. 9 What shall therefore the lord of the vineyard do? he will come and destroy the husbandmen, and will give the vineyard unto others. 10 And have ye not read this scripture; The stone which the builders rejected is become the head of the corner: 11 This was the Lord's doing, and it is marvellous in our eyes? 12 And they sought to lay hold on him, but feared the people: for they knew that he had spoken the parable against them: and they left him, and went their way.	**11:47–51** 47 Woe unto you! for ye build the sepulchres of the prophets, and your fathers killed them. 48 Truly ye bear witness that ye allow the deeds of your fathers: for they indeed killed them, and ye build their sepulchres. 49 Therefore also said the wisdom of God, I will send them prophets and apostles, and some of them they shall slay and persecute: 50 That the blood of all the prophets, which was shed from the foundation of the world, may be required of this generation; 51 From the blood of Abel unto the blood of Zacharias, which perished between the altar and the temple: verily I say unto you, It shall be required of this generation. **13:34–35** 34 O Jerusalem, Jerusalem, which killest the prophets, and stonest them that are sent unto thee; how often would I have gathered thy children together, as a hen doth gather her brood under her wings, and ye would not! 35 Behold, your house is left unto you desolate: and verily I say unto you, Ye shall not see me, until the time come when ye shall say, Blessed is he that cometh in the name of the Lord. **20:9–19** 9 Then began he to speak to the people this parable; A certain man planted a vineyard, and let it forth to husbandmen, and went into a far country for a long time. 10 And at the season he sent a servant to the husbandmen, that they should give him of the fruit of the vineyard: but the husbandmen beat him, and sent him away empty. 11 And again he sent another servant: and they beat him also, and entreated him shamefully, and sent him away empty. 12 And again he sent a third: and they wounded him also, and cast him out. 13 Then said the lord of the vineyard, What shall I do? I will send my beloved son: it may be they will reverence him when they see him. 14 But when the husbandmen saw him, they reasoned among themselves, saying, This is the heir: come, let us kill him, that the inheritance may be ours. 15 So they cast him out of the vineyard, and killed him. What therefore shall the lord of the vineyard do unto them? 16 He shall come and destroy these husbandmen, and shall give the vineyard to others. And when they heard it, they said, God forbid. 17 And he beheld them, and said, What is this then that is written, The stone which the builders rejected, the same is become the head of the corner? 18 Whosoever shall fall upon that stone shall be broken; but on whomsoever it shall fall, it will grind him to powder. 19 And the chief priests and the scribes the same hour sought to lay hands on him; and they feared the people: for they perceived that he had spoken this parable against them.	**Rom 1:18** 18 For the wrath of God is revealed from heaven against all ungodliness and unrighteousness of men, who hold the truth in unrighteousness; **Rom 2:5–6** 5 But after thy hardness and impenitent heart treasurest up unto thyself wrath against the day of wrath and revelation of the righteous judgment of God; 6 Who will render to every man according to his deeds: **Rom 9:22** 22 What if God, willing to show his wrath, and to make his power known, endured with much longsuffering the vessels of wrath fitted to destruction: **Rom 11:25** 25 For I would not, brethren, that ye should be ignorant of this mystery, lest ye should be wise in your own conceits; that blindness in part is happened to Israel, until the fulness of the Gentiles be come in. **Rom 13:4–5** 4 For he is the minister of God to thee for good. But if thou do that which is evil, be afraid; for he beareth not the sword in vain: for he is the minister of God, a revenger to execute wrath upon him that doeth evil. 5 Wherefore ye must needs be subject, not only for wrath, but also for conscience sake.

1 Thessalonians 2:16 continued on next page

1 THESSALONIANS 2:16—Relations with the community (2:1–3:13), written from Corinth, 50 or 51 CE

Theme	1 THES	Jewish Writings	Other
(*Cont.*) **Lament over lost**	**2:16 (above)**	**Gen 15:16** [16]But in the fourth generation they shall come hither again: for the iniquity of the Amorites is not yet full. **2 Mac 6:14 (Early Jewish)** [14] For in the case of the other nations the Lord waits patiently to punish them until they have reached the full measure of their sins; but He does not deal in this way with us,	**Q-Quelle** Against Pharisees: 1 Thes 2:16/Mt 23:4-36/[Mk 7:1-9]/Lk11:37-54 (QS 34 [Thom 39:1, 89, 102]); Great Supper: 1 Thes 2:16/Rom 9:22/Mt 22:1-14/[Lk 14:15-24 (QS 51 [Thom 64])]; Lament over Jerusalem: 1 Thes 2:16/Mt 23:37-39/Lk 13:34-35 (QS 49)

1 THESSALONIANS 2:17—Relations with the community (2:1–3:13), written from Corinth, 50 or 51 CE

Theme	1 THES	Paul
Endeavored to come	**2:17** [17]But we, brethren, being taken from you for a short time in presence, not in heart, endeavoured the more abundantly to see your face with great desire. **3:10** [10]Night and day praying exceedingly that we might see your face, and might perfect that which is lacking in your faith?	**Rom 1:10–11** [10]Making request, if by any means now at length I might have a prosperous journey by the will of God to come unto you. [11]For I long to see you, that I may impart unto you some spiritual gift, to the end ye may be established;

1 THESSALONIANS 2:18—Relations with the community (2:1–3:13), written from Corinth, 50 or 51 CE

Theme	1 THES	Paul
Hindered	**2:18** [18]Wherefore we would have come unto you, even I Paul, once and again; but Satan hindered us.	**Rom 15:22** [22]For which cause also I have been much hindered from coming to you.

1 THESSALONIANS 2:19—Relations with the community (2:1–3:13), written from Corinth, 50 or 51 CE

Theme	1 THES	Paul
Hope, joy and crown	**2:19** [19]For what is our hope, or joy, or crown of rejoicing? Are not even ye in the presence of our Lord Jesus Christ at his coming?	**2 Cor 1:14** [14]As also ye have acknowledged us in part, that we are your rejoicing, even as ye also are ours in the day of the Lord Jesus. **Phil 2:16** [16]Holding forth the word of life; that I may rejoice in the day of Christ, that I have not run in vain, neither laboured in vain. **Phil 4:1** [1]Therefore, my brethren dearly beloved and longed for, my joy and crown, so stand fast in the Lord, my dearly beloved.

1 THESSALONIANS 3:1—Relations with the community (2:1–3:13), written from Corinth, 50 or 51 CE

Theme	1 THES	Lk
Stay at Athens	**3:1** [1]Wherefore when we could no longer forbear, we thought it good to be left at Athens alone;	**Acts 17:14** [14]And then immediately the brethren sent away Paul to go as it were to the sea: but Silas and Timotheus abode there still.

1 THESSALONIANS 3:2—Relations with the community (2:1–3:13), written from Corinth, 50 or 51 CE

Theme	1 THES	Lk	Paul
Sent Timotheus to comfort and establish	**3:2** [2]And sent Timotheus, our brother, and minister of God, and our fellowlabourer in the gospel of Christ, to establish you, and to comfort you concerning your faith:	**Acts 16:1–2** [1]Then came he to Derbe and Lystra: and, behold, a certain disciple was there, named Timotheus, the son of a certain woman, which was a Jewess, and believed; but his father was a Greek: [2]Which was well reported of by the brethren that were at Lystra and Iconium.	**1 Cor 3:5–9** [5]Who then is Paul, and who is Apollos, but ministers by whom ye believed, even as the Lord gave to every man? [6]I have planted, Apollos watered; but God gave the increase. [7]So then neither is he that planteth any thing, neither he that watereth; but God that giveth the increase. [8]Now he that planteth and he that watereth are one: and every man shall receive his own reward according to his own labour. [9]For we are labourers together with God: ye are God's husbandry, ye are God's building.

1 THESSALONIANS 3:3–4—Relations with the community (2:1–3:13), written from Corinth, 50 or 51 CE

Theme	1 THES	Mt
Christian suffering	**3:3–4** 3That no man should be moved by these afflictions: for yourselves know that we are appointed thereunto. 4For verily, when we were with you, we told you before that we should suffer tribulation; even as it came to pass, and ye know. **2:14–16** 14For ye, brethren, became followers of the churches of God which in Judaea are in Christ Jesus: for ye also have suffered like things of your own countrymen, even as they have of the Jews: 15Who both killed the Lord Jesus, and their own prophets, and have persecuted us; and they please not God, and are contrary to all men: 16Forbidding us to speak to the Gentiles that they might be saved, to fill up their sins alway: for the wrath is come upon them to the uttermost.	**24:6–22** 6And ye shall hear of wars and rumours of wars: see that ye be not troubled: for all these things must come to pass, but the end is not yet. 7For nation shall rise against nation, and kingdom against kingdom: and there shall be famines, and pestilences, and earthquakes, in divers places. 8All these are the beginning of sorrows. 9Then shall they deliver you up to be afflicted, and shall kill you: and ye shall be hated of all nations for my name's sake. 10And then shall many be offended, and shall betray one another, and shall hate one another. 11And many false prophets shall rise, and shall deceive many. 12And because iniquity shall abound, the love of many shall wax cold. 13But he that shall endure unto the end, the same shall be saved. 14And this gospel of the kingdom shall be preached in all the world for a witness unto all nations; and then shall the end come. 15When ye therefore shall see the abomination of desolation, spoken of by Daniel the prophet, stand in the holy place, (whoso readeth, let him understand:) 16Then let them which be in Judaea flee into the mountains: 17Let him which is on the housetop not come down to take any thing out of his house: 18Neither let him which is in the field return back to take his clothes. 19And woe unto them that are with child, and to them that give suck in those days! 20But pray ye that your flight be not in the winter, neither on the sabbath day: 21For then shall be great tribulation, such as was not since the beginning of the world to this time, no, nor ever shall be. 22And except those days should be shortened, there should no flesh be saved: but for the elect's sake those days shall be shortened. **24:15–31** 15When ye therefore shall see the abomination of desolation, spoken of by Daniel the prophet, stand in the holy place, (whoso readeth, let him understand:) 16Then let them which be in Judaea flee into the mountains: 17Let him which is on the housetop not come down to take any thing out of his house: 18Neither let him which is in the field return back to take his clothes. 19And woe unto them that are with child, and to them that give suck in those days! 20But pray ye that your flight be not in the winter, neither on the sabbath day: 21For then shall be great tribulation, such as was not since the beginning of the world to this time, no, nor ever shall be. 22And except those days should be shortened, there should no flesh be saved: but for the elect's sake those days shall be shortened. 23Then if any man shall say unto you, Lo, here is Christ, or there; believe it not. 24For there shall arise false Christs, and false prophets, and shall show great signs and wonders; insomuch that, if it were possible, they shall deceive the very elect. 25Behold, I have told you before. 26Wherefore if they shall say unto you, Behold, he is in the desert; go not forth: behold, he is in the secret chambers; believe it not. 27For as the lightning cometh out of the east, and shineth even unto the west; so shall also the coming of the Son of man be. 28For wheresoever the carcase is, there will the eagles be gathered together. 29Immediately after the tribulation of those days shall the sun be darkened, and the moon shall not give her light, and the stars shall fall from heaven, and the powers of the heavens shall be shaken: 30And then shall appear the sign of the Son of man in heaven: and then shall all the tribes of the earth mourn, and they shall see the Son of man coming in the clouds of heaven with power and great glory. 31And he shall send his angels with a great sound of a trumpet, and they shall gather together his elect from the four winds, from one end of heaven to the other.

Mk	Lk	Paul	Other
13:7–14 [7]And when ye shall hear of wars and rumours of wars, be ye not troubled: for such things must needs be; but the end shall not be yet. [8]For nation shall rise against nation, and kingdom against kingdom: and there shall be earthquakes in divers places, and there shall be famines and troubles: these are the beginnings of sorrows. [9]But take heed to yourselves: for they shall deliver you up to councils; and in the synagogues ye shall be beaten: and ye shall be brought before rulers and kings for my sake, for a testimony against them. [10]And the gospel must first be published among all nations. [11]But when they shall lead you, and deliver you up, take no thought beforehand what ye shall speak, neither do ye premeditate: but whatsoever shall be given you in that hour, that speak ye: for it is not ye that speak, but the Holy Ghost. [12]Now the brother shall betray the brother to death, and the father the son; and children shall rise up against their parents, and shall cause them to be put to death. [13]And ye shall be hated of all men for my name's sake: but he that shall endure unto the end, the same shall be saved. [14]But when ye shall see the abomination of desolation, spoken of by Daniel the prophet, standing where it ought not, (let him that readeth understand,) then let them that be in Judaea flee to the mountains: **13:14–27** [14]But when ye shall see the abomination of desolation, spoken of by Daniel the prophet, standing where it ought not, (let him that readeth understand,) then let them that be in Judaea flee to the mountains: [15]And let him that is on the housetop not go down into the house, neither enter therein, to take any thing out of his house: [16]And let him that is in the field not turn back again for to take up his garment. [17]But woe to them that are with child, and to them that give suck in those days! [18]And pray ye that your flight be not in the winter. [19]For in those days shall be affliction, such as was not from the beginning of the creation which God created unto this time, neither shall be. [20]And except that the Lord had shortened those days, no flesh should be saved: but for the elect's sake, whom he hath chosen, he hath shortened the days. [21]And then if any man shall say to you, Lo, here is Christ; or, lo, he is there; believe him not: [22]For false Christs and false prophets shall rise, and shall show signs and wonders, to seduce, if it were possible, even the elect. [23]But take ye heed: behold, I have foretold you all things. [24]But in those days, after that tribulation, the sun shall be darkened, and the moon shall not give her light, [25]And the stars of heaven shall fall, and the powers that are in heaven shall be shaken. [26]And then shall they see the Son of man coming in the clouds with great power and glory. [27]And then shall he send his angels, and shall gather together his elect from the four winds, from the uttermost part of the earth to the uttermost part of heaven.	**21:9–14** [9]But when ye shall hear of wars and commotions, be not terrified: for these things must first come to pass; but the end is not by and by. [10]Then said he unto them, Nation shall rise against nation, and kingdom against kingdom: [11]And great earthquakes shall be in divers places, and famines, and pestilences; and fearful sights and great signs shall there be from heaven. [12]But before all these, they shall lay their hands on you, and persecute you, delivering you up to the synagogues, and into prisons, being brought before kings and rulers for my name's sake. [13]And it shall turn to you for a testimony. [14]Settle it therefore in your hearts, not to meditate before what ye shall answer: **21:20–27** [20]And when ye shall see Jerusalem compassed with armies, then know that the desolation thereof is nigh. [21]Then let them which are in Judaea flee to the mountains; and let them which are in the midst of it depart out; and let not them that are in the countries enter thereinto. [22]For these be the days of vengeance, that all things which are written may be fulfilled. [23]But woe unto them that are with child, and to them that give suck, in those days! for there shall be great distress in the land, and wrath upon this people. [24]And they shall fall by the edge of the sword, and shall be led away captive into all nations: and Jerusalem shall be trodden down of the Gentiles, until the times of the Gentiles be fulfilled. [25]And there shall be signs in the sun, and in the moon, and in the stars; and upon the earth distress of nations, with perplexity; the sea and the waves roaring; [26]Men's hearts failing them for fear, and for looking after those things which are coming on the earth: for the powers of heaven shall be shaken. [27]And then shall they see the Son of man coming in a cloud with power and great glory. **Acts 14:22** [22]Confirming the souls of the disciples, and exhorting them to continue in the faith, and that we must through much tribulation enter into the kingdom of God.	**Rom 8:17** [17]And if children, then heirs; heirs of God, and joint-heirs with Christ; if so be that we suffer with him, that we may be also glorified together. **2 Thes 2:5–7** [5]Remember ye not, that, when I was yet with you, I told you these things? [6]And now ye know what withholdeth that he might be revealed in his time. [7]For the mystery of iniquity doth already work: only he who now letteth will let, until he be taken out of the way. **2 Thes 2:8** [8]And then shall that Wicked be revealed, whom the Lord shall consume with the spirit of his mouth, and shall destroy with the brightness of his coming: **2 Tim 3:12 (Pseudo)** [12]Yea, and all that will live godly in Christ Jesus shall suffer persecution.	**Q-Quelle** Day of SOM: 1 Thes 3:3-4/Rom 8:17/[Col 1:24]/2 Thes 2:8/[Mt 10:39], Mt 24:17-18, 23, 26-27, 24:28, [Mt 24:40-41]/Mk 13:14-16, 19-23/[Lk 17:22-37 (QS 60 [Thom 3, 51, 61, 113)]; Beatitudes: 1 Thes 3:3-4/Rom 8:17/[Col 1:24]/2 Thes 2:8/[Mt 5:3-12]/[Lk 6:20b-23 (QS 8 [Thom 54, 68, 69])]

1 THESSALONIANS 3:12—Relations with the community (2:1–3:13), written from Corinth, 50 or 51 CE

Theme	1 THES	Mk	Paul	Other
Love one another	**3:12** [12]And the Lord make you to increase and abound in love one toward another, and toward all men, even as we do toward you: **4:9–10** [9]But as touching brotherly love ye need not that I write unto you: for ye yourselves are taught of God to love one another. [10]And indeed ye do it toward all the brethren which are in all Macedonia: but we beseech you, brethren, that ye increase more and more; **5:12–13** [12]And we beseech you, brethren, to know them which labour among you, and are over you in the Lord, and admonish you; [13]And to esteem them very highly in love for their work's sake. And be at peace among yourselves. **5:15** [15]See that none render evil for evil unto any man; but ever follow that which is good, both among yourselves, and to all men.	**9:50** [50]Salt is good: but if the salt have lost his saltness, wherewith will ye season it? Have salt in yourselves, and have peace one with another.	**Rom 12:10** [10]Be kindly affectioned one to another with brotherly love; in honour preferring one another; **Rom 12:18** [18]If it be possible, as much as lieth in you, live peaceably with all men. **Rom 14:19** [19]Let us therefore follow after the things which make for peace, and things wherewith one may edify another. **1 Cor 7:15** [15]But if the unbelieving depart, let him depart. A brother or a sister is not under bondage in such cases: but God hath called us to peace. **2 Cor 13:11** [11]Finally, brethren, farewell. Be perfect, be of good comfort, be of one mind, live in peace; and the God of love and peace shall be with you. **Gal 6:10** [10]As we have therefore opportunity, let us do good unto all men, especially unto them who are of the household of faith. **Eph 4:32 (Pseudo)** [32]And be ye kind one to another, tenderhearted, forgiving one another, even as God for Christ's sake hath forgiven you. **Col 3:12–14** [12]Put on therefore, as the elect of God, holy and beloved, bowels of mercies, kindness, humbleness of mind, meekness, longsuffering; [13]Forbearing one another, and forgiving one another, if any man have a quarrel against any: even as Christ forgave you, so also do ye. [14]And above all these things put on charity, which is the bond of perfectness. **2 Thes 1:3** [3]We are bound to thank God always for you, brethren, as it is meet, because that your faith groweth exceedingly, and the charity of every one of you all toward each other aboundeth;	**Q-Quelle** Parable of salt: 1 Thes 3:12/1 Cor 7:15/[Mt 5:13]/Mk 9:49-50/[Lk 14:34-35 (QS 53)]

1 THESSALONIANS 3:13—Relations with the community (2:1–3:13), written from Corinth, 50 or 51 CE

Theme	1 THES	Paul
Blameless-ness	**3:13** [13]To the end he may stablish your hearts unblameable in holiness before God, even our Father, at the coming of our Lord Jesus Christ with all his saints. **5:23** [23]And the very God of peace sanctify you wholly; and I pray God your whole spirit and soul and body be preserved blameless unto the coming of our Lord Jesus Christ.	**1 Cor 1:8** [8]Who shall also confirm you unto the end, that ye may be blameless in the day of our Lord Jesus Christ.

EXHORTATIONS (4:1–5:25)

1 THESSALONIANS 4:5—Exhortations (4:1–5:25), written from Corinth, 50 or 51 CE

Theme	1 THES	Paul	NT	Jewish Writings
No lust	**4:5** [5]Not in the lust of concupiscence, even as the Gentiles which know not God:	**2 Thes 1:8** [8]In flaming fire taking vengeance on them that know not God, and that obey not the gospel of our Lord Jesus Christ:	**1 Pet 3:7** [7]Likewise, ye husbands, dwell with them according to knowledge, giving honour unto the wife, as unto the weaker vessel, and as being heirs together of the grace of life; that your prayers be not hindered.	**Ps 79:6** [6]Pour out thy wrath upon the heathen that have not known thee, and upon the kingdoms that have not called upon thy name. **Jer 10:25** [25]Pour out thy fury upon the heathen that know thee not, and upon the families that call not on thy name: for they have eaten up Jacob, and devoured him, and consumed him, and have made his habitation desolate.

1 THESSALONIANS 4:8—Exhortations (4:1–5:25), written from Corinth, 50 or 51 CE

Theme	1 THES	Lk	Other
Despising Paul, despises God who gave Holy Spirit	**4:8** [8]He therefore that despiseth, despiseth not man, but God, who hath also given unto us his holy Spirit.	**10:16** [16]He that heareth you heareth me; and he that despiseth you despiseth me; and he that despiseth me despiseth him that sent me.	**Q-Quelle** Whoever hears you hears me: 1 Thes 4:8/[1 Cor 9:1-6]/[Mt 10:40]/Lk 10:16 (QS 23)]

1 THESSALONIANS 4:9—Exhortations (4:1–5:25), written from Corinth, 50 or 51 CE

Theme	1 THES	Jn
Love one another	**4:9** [9]But as touching brotherly love ye need not that I write unto you: for ye yourselves are taught of God to love one another.	**6:45** [45]It is written in the prophets, And they shall be all taught of God. Every man therefore that hath heard, and hath learned of the Father, cometh unto me. **1 Jn 2:20–21** [20]But ye have an unction from the Holy One, and ye know all things. [21]I have not written unto you because ye know not the truth, but because ye know it, and that no lie is of the truth. **1 Jn 2:27** [27]But the anointing which ye have received of him abideth in you, and ye need not that any man teach you: but as the same anointing teacheth you of all things, and is truth, and is no lie, and even as it hath taught you, ye shall abide in him. **1 Jn 4:7** [7]Beloved, let us love one another: for love is of God; and every one that loveth is born of God, and knoweth God.

1 THESSALONIANS 4:10

Theme	1 THES
Increase in love	**4:10** [10]And indeed ye do it toward all the brethren which are in all Macedonia: but we beseech you, brethren, that ye increase more and more;

1 THESSALONIANS 4:14—Exhortations (4:1–5:25), written from Corinth, 50 or 51 CE

Theme	1 THES	Paul
Jesus died & rose for all, even sleeping	**4:14** [14]For if we believe that Jesus died and rose again, even so them also which sleep in Jesus will God bring with him.	**1 Cor 15:3–4** [3]For I delivered unto you first of all that which I also received, how that Christ died for our sins according to the scriptures; [4]And that he was buried, and that he rose again the third day according to the scriptures: **1 Cor 15:12–20** [12]Now if Christ be preached that he rose from the dead, how say some among you that there is no resurrection of the dead? [13]But if there be no resurrection of the dead, then is Christ not risen: [14]And if Christ be not risen, then is our preaching vain, and your faith is also vain. [15]Yea, and we are found false witnesses of God; because we have testified of God that he raised up Christ: whom he raised not up, if so be that the dead rise not. [16]For if the dead rise not, then is not Christ raised: [17]And if Christ be not raised, your faith is vain; ye are yet in your sins. [18]Then they also which are fallen asleep in Christ are perished. [19]If in this life only we have hope in Christ, we are of all men most miserable. [20]But now is Christ risen from the dead, and become the firstfruits of them that slept.

Paul

2 Thes 3:6–12

[6]Now we command you, brethren, in the name of our Lord Jesus Christ, that ye withdraw yourselves from every brother that
walketh disorderly, and not after the tradition which he received of us. [7]For yourselves know how ye ought to follow us: for we
behaved not ourselves disorderly among you; [8]Neither did we eat any man's bread for nought; but wrought with labour and
travail night and day, that we might not be chargeable to any of you: [9]Not because we have not power, but to make ourselves
an ensample unto you to follow us. [10]For even when we were with you, this we commanded you, that if any would not work,
neither should he eat.

Other

Q-Quelle

1 Thes 4:14-17
[14]For if we believe that Jesus died and rose again, even so
them also which sleep in Jesus will God bring with him.
[15]For this we say unto you by the word of the Lord, that we
which are alive and remain unto the coming of the Lord
shall not prevent them which are asleep. [16]For the Lord
himself shall descend from heaven with a shout, with the
voice of the archangel, and with the trump of God: and the
dead in Christ shall rise first: [17]Then we which are alive and
remain shall be caught up together with them in the clouds,
to meet the Lord in the air: and so shall we ever be with the
Lord.

1 THESSALONIANS 4:15–16—Exhortations (4:1–5:25), written from Corinth, 50 or 51 CE

Theme	1 THES	Mt	Mk
Alive in Christ	**4:15–16** [15]For this we say unto you by the word of the Lord, that we which are alive and remain unto the coming of the Lord shall not prevent them which are asleep. [16]For the Lord himself shall descend from heaven with a shout, with the voice of the arch-angel, and with the trump of God: and the dead in Christ shall rise first: **5:1–3** [1]But of the times and the seasons, brethren, ye have no need that I write unto you. [2]For yourselves know perfectly that the day of the Lord so cometh as a thief in the night. [3]For when they shall say, Peace and safety; then sudden destruction cometh upon them, as travail upon a woman with child; and they shall not escape. **5:10** [10]Who died for us, that, whether we wake or sleep, we should live together with him.	**16:28** [28]Verily I say unto you, There be some standing here, which shall not taste of death, till they see the Son of man coming in his kingdom. **24:29–36** [29]Immediately after the tribulation of those days shall the sun be darkened, and the moon shall not give her light, and the stars shall fall from heaven, and the powers of the heavens shall be shaken: [30]And then shall appear the sign of the Son of man in heaven: and then shall all the tribes of the earth mourn, and they shall see the Son of man coming in the clouds of heaven with power and great glory. [31]And he shall send his angels with a great sound of a trumpet, and they shall gather together his elect from the four winds, from one end of heaven to the other. [32]Now learn a parable of the fig tree; When his branch is yet tender, and putteth forth leaves, ye know that summer is nigh: [33]So likewise ye, when ye shall see all these things, know that it is near, even at the doors. [34]Verily I say unto you, This generation shall not pass, till all these things be fulfilled. [35]Heaven and earth shall pass away, but my words shall not pass away. [36]But of that day and hour knoweth no man, no, not the angels of heaven, but my Father only. **26:64** [64]Jesus saith unto him, Thou hast said: nevertheless I say unto you, Hereafter shall ye see the Son of man sitting on the right hand of power, and coming in the clouds of heaven.	**9:1** [1]And he said unto them, Verily I say unto you, That there be some of them that stand here, which shall not taste of death, till they have seen the kingdom of God come with power. **13:24–32** [24]But in those days, after that tribulation, the sun shall be darkened, and the moon shall not give her light, [25]And the stars of heaven shall fall, and the powers that are in heaven shall be shaken. [26]And then shall they see the Son of man coming in the clouds with great power and glory. [27]And then shall he send his angels, and shall gather together his elect from the four winds, from the uttermost part of the earth to the uttermost part of heaven. [28]Now learn a parable of the fig tree; When her branch is yet tender, and putteth forth leaves, ye know that summer is near: [29]So ye in like manner, when ye shall see these things come to pass, know that it is nigh, even at the doors. [30]Verily I say unto you, that this generation shall not pass, till all these things be done. [31]Heaven and earth shall pass away: but my words shall not pass away. [32]But of that day and that hour knoweth no man, no, not the angels which are in heaven, neither the Son, but the Father. **14:62** [62]And Jesus said, I am: and ye shall see the Son of man sitting on the right hand of power, and coming in the clouds of heaven.

1 THESSALONIANS 4:15—Exhortations (4:1–5:25), written from Corinth, 50 or 51 CE

Theme	1 THES	Paul	NT
Alive until Lord comes	**4:15** [15]For this we say unto you by the word of the Lord, that we which are alive and remain unto the coming of the Lord shall not prevent them which are asleep.	**1 Cor 15:51** [51]Behold, I show you a mystery; We shall not all sleep, but we shall all be changed,	**Rev 14:13** [13]And I heard a voice from heaven saying unto me, Write, Blessed are the dead which die in the Lord from henceforth: Yea, saith the Spirit, that they may rest from their labours; and their works do follow them. **Rev 20:4–6** [4]And I saw thrones, and they sat upon them, and judgment was given unto them: and I saw the souls of them that were beheaded for the witness of Jesus, and for the word of God, and which had not worshipped the beast, neither his image, neither had received his mark upon their foreheads, or in their hands; and they lived and reigned with Christ a thousand years. [5]But the rest of the dead lived not again until the thousand years were finished. This is the first resurrection. [6]Blessed and holy is he that hath part in the first resurrection: on such the second death hath no power, but they shall be priests of God and of Christ, and shall reign with him a thousand years.

Lk	Paul	NT	Jewish Writings
9:27 [27]But I tell you of a truth, there be some standing here, which shall not taste of death, till they see the kingdom of God. **21:25–33** [25]And there shall be signs in the sun, and in the moon, and in the stars; and upon the earth distress of nations, with perplexity; the sea and the waves roaring; [26]Men's hearts failing them for fear, and for looking after those things which are coming on the earth: for the powers of heaven shall be shaken. [27]And then shall they see the Son of man coming in a cloud with power and great glory. [28]And when these things begin to come to pass, then look up, and lift up your heads; for your redemption draweth nigh. [29]And he spake to them a parable; Behold the fig tree, and all the trees; [30]When they now shoot forth, ye see and know of your own selves that summer is now nigh at hand. [31]So likewise ye, when ye see these things come to pass, know ye that the kingdom of God is nigh at hand. [32]Verily I say unto you, This generation shall not pass away, till all be fulfilled. [33]Heaven and earth shall pass away: but my words shall not pass away.	**Rom 13:11–12** [11]And that, knowing the time, that now it is high time to awake out of sleep: for now is our salvation nearer than when we believed. [12]The night is far spent, the day is at hand: let us therefore cast off the works of darkness, and let us put on the armour of light. **1 Cor 7:29–31** [29]But this I say, brethren, the time is short: it remaineth, that both they that have wives be as though they had none; [30]And they that weep, as though they wept not; and they that rejoice, as though they rejoiced not; and they that buy, as though they possessed not; [31]And they that use this world, as not abusing it: for the fashion of this world passeth away. **1 Cor 10:11** [11]Now all these things happened unto them for ensamples: and they are written for our admonition, upon whom the ends of the world are come.	**Rev 1:7** [7]Behold, he cometh with clouds; and every eye shall see him, and they also which pierced him: and all kindreds of the earth shall wail because of him. Even so, Amen.	**Dt 30:3–4** [3]That then the LORD thy God will turn thy captivity, and have compassion upon thee, and will return and gather thee from all the nations, whither the LORD thy God hath scattered thee. [4]If any of thine be driven out unto the outmost parts of heaven, from thence will the LORD thy God gather thee, and from thence will he fetch thee: **Is 13:10** [10]For the stars of heaven and the constellations thereof shall not give their light: the sun shall be darkened in his going forth, and the moon shall not cause her light to shine. **Is 34:4** [4]And all the host of heaven shall be dissolved, and the heavens shall be rolled together as a scroll: and all their host shall fall down, as the leaf falleth off from the vine, and as a falling fig from the fig tree. **Dan 7:13–14** [13]I saw in the night visions, and, behold, one like the Son of man came with the clouds of heaven, and came to the Ancient of days, and they brought him near before him. [14]And there was given him dominion, and glory, and a kingdom, that all people, nations, and languages, should serve him: his dominion is an everlasting dominion, which shall not pass away, and his kingdom that which shall not be destroyed.

1 THESSALONIANS 4:16—Exhortations (4:1–5:25), written from Corinth, 50 or 51 CE

Theme	1 THES	Mt	Paul
Lord will descend from Heaven	**4:16** [16]For the Lord himself shall descend from heaven with a shout, with the voice of the archangel, and with the trump of God: and the dead in Christ shall rise first:	**24:31** [31]And he shall send his angels with a great sound of a trumpet, & they shall gather together his elect from the four winds from one end of heaven to the other.	**1 Cor 15:23** [23]But every man in his own order: Christ the firstfruits; afterward they that are Christ's at his coming. **1 Cor 15:52** [52]In a moment, in the twinkling of an eye, at the last trump: for the trumpet shall sound, and the dead shall be raised incorruptible, and we shall be changed.

1 THESSALONIANS 5:1–11—Exhortations (4:1–5:25), written from Corinth, 50 or 51 CE

Theme	1 THES	Mt
Judgment day	**5:1–11** [1]But of the times and the seasons, brethren, ye have no need that I write unto you. [2]For yourselves know perfectly that the day of the Lord so cometh as a thief in the night. [3]For when they shall say, Peace and safety; then sudden destruction cometh upon them, as travail upon a woman with child; and they shall not escape. [4]But ye, brethren, are not in darkness, that that day should overtake you as a thief. [5]Ye are all the children of light, and the children of the day: we are not of the night, nor of darkness. [6]Therefore let us not sleep, as do others; but let us watch and be sober. [7]For they that sleep sleep in the night; and they that be drunken are drunken in the night. [8]But let us, who are of the day, be sober, putting on the breastplate of faith and love; and for an helmet, the hope of salvation. [9]For God hath not appointed us to wrath, but to obtain salvation by our Lord Jesus Christ, [10]Who died for us, that, whether we wake or sleep, we should live together with him. [11]Wherefore comfort yourselves together, and edify one another, even as also ye do.	**7:24–27** [24]For there shall arise false Christs, and false prophets, and shall show great signs and wonders; insomuch that, if it were possible, they shall deceive the very elect. [25]Behold, I have told you before. [26]Wherefore if they shall say unto you, Behold, he is in the desert; go not forth: behold, he is in the secret chambers; believe it not. [27]For as the lightning cometh out of the east, and shineth even unto the west; so shall also the coming of the Son of man be.

1 THESSALONIANS 5:1—Exhortations (4:1–5:25), written from Corinth, 50 or 51 CE

Theme	1 THES	Mt
Judgment day	**5:1** [1]But of the times and the seasons, brethren, ye have no need that I write unto you.	**24:36–45** [36]But of that day and hour knoweth no man, no, not the angels of heaven, but my Father only. [37]But as the days of Noe were, so shall also the coming of the Son of man be. [38]For as in the days that were before the flood they were eating and drinking, marrying and giving in marriage, until the day that Noe entered into the ark, [39]And knew not until the flood came, and took them all away; so shall also the coming of the Son of man be. [40]Then shall two be in the field; the one shall be taken, and the other left. [41]Two women shall be grinding at the mill; the one shall be taken, and the other left. [42]Watch therefore: for ye know not what hour your Lord doth come. [43]But know this, that if the goodman of the house had known in what watch the thief would come, he would have watched, and would not have suffered his house to be broken up. [44]Therefore be ye also ready: for in such an hour as ye think not the Son of man cometh. [45]Who then is a faithful and wise servant, whom his lord hath made ruler over his household, to give them meat in due season?

Paul	Other
1 Cor 4:1–5	**Q-Quelle**
[1]Let a man so account of us, as of the ministers of Christ, and stewards of the mysteries of God. [2]Moreover it is required in stewards, that a man be found faithful. [3]But with me it is a very small thing that I should be judged of you, or of man's judgment: yea, I judge not mine own self. [4]For I know nothing by myself; yet am I not hereby justified: but he that judgeth me is the Lord. [5]Therefore judge nothing before the time, until the Lord come, who both will bring to light the hidden things of darkness, and will make manifest the counsels of the hearts: and then shall every man have praise of God.	Exclusion from the Kingdom of God: 1 Thes 5:1-11/1 Cor 4:1-5/[Mt 7:13-14], [Mt 7:22-23, 8:11-12, 19:30]/[Lk 13:22-30 (QS47, 48); House on a Rock: 1 Thes 5:1-11/1 Cor 4:1-5/ Mt 7:21-27/[Lk 6:46-49 (QS 14)]

Other
Q-Quelle
Day of SOM: 1 Thes 5:1/[Mt 10:39, 24:17-18, 23, 26-27, 28], Mt 24:37-39, 40-41/[Mk 13:14-16,19-23]/ [Lk 17:22-37

1 THESSALONIANS 5:2—Exhortations (4:1–5:25), written from Corinth, 50 or 51 CE

Theme	1 THES	Mt	Mk
Watch	**5:2** [2]For yourselves know perfectly that the day of the Lord so cometh as a thief in the night.	**8:12** [12]But the children of the kingdom shall be cast out into outer darkness: there shall be weeping and gnashing of teeth. **13:42** [42]And shall cast them into a furnace of fire: there shall be wailing and gnashing of teeth. **13:50** [50]And shall cast them into the furnace of fire: there shall be wailing and gnashing of teeth. **22:13** [13]Then said the king to the servants, Bind him hand and foot, and take him away, and cast him into outer darkness; there shall be weeping and gnashing of teeth. **24:37–51** [37]But as the days of Noah were, so shall also the coming of the Son of man be. [38]For as in the days that were before the flood they were eating and drinking, marrying and giving in marriage, until the day that Noah entered into the ark, [39]And knew not until the flood came, and took them all away; so shall also the coming of the Son of man be. [40]Then shall two be in the field; the one shall be taken, and the other left. [41]Two women shall be grinding at the mill; the one shall be taken, and the other left. [42]Watch therefore: for ye know not what hour your Lord doth come. [43]But know this, that if the goodman of the house had known in what watch the thief would come, he would have watched, and would not have suffered his house to be broken up. [44]Therefore be ye also ready: for in such an hour as ye think not the Son of man cometh. [45]Who then is a faithful and wise servant, whom his lord hath made ruler over his household, to give them meat in due season? [46]Blessed is that servant, whom his lord when he cometh shall find so doing. [47]Verily I say unto you, That he shall make him ruler over all his goods. [48]But and if that evil servant shall say in his heart, My lord delayeth his coming; [49]And shall begin to smite his fellowservants, and to eat and drink with the drunken; [50]The lord of that servant shall come in a day when he looketh not for him, and in an hour that he is not aware of, [51]And shall cut him asunder, and appoint him his portion with the hypocrites: there shall be weeping and gnashing of teeth. **25:30** [30]And cast ye the unprofitable servant into outer darkness: there shall be weeping and gnashing of teeth.	**13:33–37** [33]Take ye heed, watch and pray: for ye know not when the time is. [34]For the Son of man is as a man taking a far journey, who left his house, and gave authority to his servants, and to every man his work, and commanded the porter to watch. [35]Watch ye therefore: for ye know not when the master of the house cometh, at even, or at midnight, or at the cockcrowing, or in the morning: [36]Lest coming suddenly he find you sleeping. [37]And what I say unto you I say unto all, Watch.

Lk	NT	Jewish Writings	Other
12:39–40 [39]And this know, that if the goodman of the house had known what hour the thief would come, he would have watched, and not have suffered his house to be broken through. [40]Be ye therefore ready also: for the Son of man cometh at an hour when ye think not. **12:42–46** [42]And the Lord said, Who then is that faithful and wise steward, whom his lord shall make ruler over his household, to give them their portion of meat in due season? [43]Blessed is that servant, whom his lord when he cometh shall find so doing. [44]Of a truth I say unto you, that he will make him ruler over all that he hath. [45]But and if that servant say in his heart, My lord delayeth his coming; and shall begin to beat the menservants and maidens, and to eat and drink, and to be drunken; [46]The lord of that servant will come in a day when he looketh not for him, and at an hour when he is not aware, and will cut him in sunder, and will appoint him his portion with the unbelievers. **17:26–36** [26]And as it was in the days of Noe, so shall it be also in the days of the Son of man. [27]They did eat, they drank, they married wives, they were given in marriage, until the day that Noe entered into the ark, and the flood came, and destroyed them all. [28]Likewise also as it was in the days of Lot; they did eat, they drank, they bought, they sold, they planted, they builded; [29]But the same day that Lot went out of Sodom it rained fire and brimstone from heaven, and destroyed them all. [30]Even thus shall it be in the day when the Son of man is revealed. [31]In that day, he which shall be upon the housetop, and his stuff in the house, let him not come down to take it away: and he that is in the field, let him likewise not return back. [32]Remember Lot's wife. [33]Whosoever shall seek to save his life shall lose it; and whosoever shall lose his life shall preserve it. [34]I tell you, in that night there shall be two men in one bed; the one shall be taken, and the other shall be left. [35]Two women shall be grinding together; the one shall be taken, and the other left. [36]Two men shall be in the field; the one shall be taken, and the other left. **21:34–36** [34]And take heed to yourselves, lest at any time your hearts be overcharged with surfeiting, and drunkenness, and cares of this life, and so that day come upon you unawares. [35]For as a snare shall it come on all them that dwell on the face of the whole earth. [36]Watch ye therefore, and pray always, that ye may be accounted worthy to escape all these things that shall come to pass, and to stand before the Son of man.	**Rev 16:15** [15]Behold, I come as a thief. Blessed is he that watcheth, and keepeth his garments, lest he walk naked, and they see his shame.	**Gen 7:6–10** [6]And Noah was six hundred years old when the flood of waters was upon the earth. [7]And Noah went in, and his sons, and his wife, and his sons' wives with him, into the ark, because of the waters of the flood. [8]Of clean beasts, and of beasts that are not clean, and of fowls, and of every thing that creepeth upon the earth, [9]There went in two and two unto Noah into the ark, the male and the female, as God had commanded Noah. [10]And it came to pass after seven days, that the waters of the flood were upon the earth.	**GThom 21** [21] Mary said to Jesus, "Whom are your disciples like?" He said, "They are like children who have settled in a field, which is not theirs. When the owners of the field come, they will say, 'Let us have back our field.' They (will) undress in their presence in order to let them have back their field and to give it back to them. Therefore I say, if the owner of the house knows that the thief is coming, he will begin his vigil before he comes and will not let him dig through into his house of his domain to carry away his goods. You then, be on your guard against the world. Arm yourselves with great strength lest the robbers find a way to come to you, for the difficulty which you expect will (surely) materialize. Let there be among you a man of understanding. When the grain ripened, he came quickly with his sickle in his hand and reaped it. Whoever has ears to hear let him hear." **GThom 103** [103]Jesus said, "Fortunate is the man who knows where the brigands will enter, so that [he] may get up , muster his domain, and arm himself before they invade." **Q-Quelle** Great supper: 1 Thes 5:2/Mt 22:1-14/[Lk 14:15-24 (QS 51 [Thom 64])]; Day of SOM: 1 Thes 5:2/[Mt 10:39, 24:17-18, 23, 26-27, 28], Mt 24:37-39, 40-41/[Mk 13:14-16,19-23]/Lk 17:22-37 (QS 60 [Thom 3, 51, 61, 113]); Watchful and faithful: 1 Thes 5:2/[Mt 24:42-51]/Lk 12:35-48 (QS 41 [Thom 21:3, 103]. QS 42, 42); Leaven: 1 Thes 5:2/[1 Cor 3:16]/[Mt 13:33]/[Lk Lk 12:11-12 (QS 37 [Thom 44]), 13:20-21(QS 46 [Thom 20, 96])]

1 THESSALONIANS 5:3—Exhortations (4:1–5:25), written from Corinth, 50 or 51 CE

Theme	1 THES	Paul
Judgment	**5:3** [3]For when they shall say, Peace and safety; then sudden destruction cometh upon them, as travail upon a woman with child; and they shall not escape.	**1 Cor 3:15** [15]If any man's work shall be burned, he shall suffer loss: but he himself shall be saved; yet so as by fire. **1 Cor 15:25–28** [25]For he must reign, till he hath put all enemies under his feet. [26]The last enemy that shall be destroyed is death. [27]For he hath put all things under his feet. But when he saith all things are put under him, it is manifest that he is excepted, which did put all things under him. [28]And when all things shall be subdued unto him, then shall the Son also himself be subject unto him that put all things under him, that God may be all in all. **2 Thes 1:8–9** [8]In flaming fire taking vengeance on them that know not God, and that obey not the gospel of our Lord Jesus Christ: [9]Who shall be punished with everlasting destruction from the presence of the Lord, and from the glory of his power; **2 Thes 2:8** [8]And then shall that Wicked be revealed, whom the Lord shall consume with the spirit of his mouth, and shall destroy with the brightness of his coming:

1 THESSALONIANS 5:4—Exhortations (4:1–5:25), written from Corinth, 50 or 51 CE

Theme	1 THES	Paul
Not in dark	**5:4** [4]But ye, brethren, are not in darkness, that that day should overtake you as a thief.	**Eph 5:8–9 (Pseudo)** [8]For ye were sometimes darkness, but now are ye light in the Lord: walk as children of light: [9](For the fruit of the Spirit is in all goodness and righteousness and truth;)

1 THESSALONIANS 5:6—Exhortations (4:1–5:25), written from Corinth, 50 or 51 CE

Theme	1 THES	Mt	Paul	NT	Other
Watch soberly, let no one sleep	**5:6** [6]Therefore let us not sleep, as do others; but let us watch and be sober.	**24:42** [42]Watch therefore: for ye know not what hour your Lord doth come.	**Rom 13:12–13** [12]The night is far spent, the day is at hand: let us therefore cast off the works of darkness, and let us put on the armour of light. [13]Let us walk honestly, as in the day; not in rioting and drunkenness, not in chambering and wantonness, not in strife and envying.	**1 Pet 5:8** [8]Be sober, be vigilant; because your adversary the devil, as a roaring lion, walketh about, seeking whom he may devour:	**Q-Quelle** Watchful and faithful: 1 Thes 5:6/Mt 24:42-51/ [Lk 12:35-48 (QS 41 [Thom 21:3, 103], QS 42, 43])

1 THESSALONIANS 5:8—Exhortations (4:1–5:25), written from Corinth, 50 or 51 CE

Theme	1 THES	Paul	Jewish Writings	Other
Breastplate of faith & love	**5:8** [8]But let us, who are of the day, be sober, putting on the breastplate of faith and love; and for an helmet, the hope of salvation.	**Rom 13:11–14** [11]And that, knowing the time, that now it is high time to awake out of sleep: for now is our salvation nearer than when we believed. [12]The night is far spent, the day is at hand: let us therefore cast off the works of darkness, and let us put on the armour of light. [13]Let us walk honestly, as in the day; not in rioting and drunkenness, not in chambering and wantonness, not in strife and envying. [14]But put ye on the Lord Jesus Christ, and make not provision for the flesh, to fulfil the lusts thereof. **Eph 6:11 (Pseudo)** [11]Put on the whole armour of God, that ye may be able to stand against the wiles of the devil. **Eph 6:14–17 (Pseudo)** [14]Stand therefore, having your loins girt about with truth, and having on the breastplate of righteousness; [15]And your feet shod with the preparation of the gospel of peace; [16]Above all, taking the shield of faith, wherewith ye shall be able to quench all the fiery darts of the wicked. [17]And take the helmet of salvation, and the sword of the Spirit, which is the word of God:	**Is 59:17** [17]For he put on righteousness as a breastplate, and an helmet of salvation upon his head; and he put on the garments of vengeance for clothing, and was clad with zeal as a cloak.	**Q-Quelle** Watchful and faithful: 1 Thes 5:8/Eph 6:14/[Mt 24:42-51]/[Lk 12:35-48 (QS 41 [Thom 21:3, 103], QS 42)]

1 THESSALONIANS 5:11—Exhortations (4:1–5:25), written from Corinth, 50 or 51 CE

Theme	1 THES	Paul
Comfort & edify one another	**5:11** [11]Wherefore comfort yourselves together, and edify one another, even as also ye do.	**Rom 15:2** [2]Let every one of us please his neighbour for his good to edification. **1 Cor 8:1** [1]Now as touching things offered unto idols, we know that we all have knowledge. Knowledge puffeth up, but charity edifieth. **1 Cor 14:12** [12]Even so ye, forasmuch as ye are zealous of spiritual gifts, seek that ye may excel to the edifying of the church. **1 Cor 14:26** [26]How is it then, brethren? when ye come together, every one of you hath a psalm, hath a doctrine, hath a tongue, hath a revelation, hath an interpretation. Let all things be done unto edifying. **Eph 4:29 (Pseudo)** [29]Let no corrupt communication proceed out of your mouth, but that which is good to the use of edifying, that it may minister grace unto the hearers.

1 THESSALONIANS 5:15—Exhortations (4:1–5:25), written from Corinth, 50 or 51 CE

Theme	1 THES	Mt	Paul	Jewish	Other
Render good to all	**5:15** [15]See that none render evil for evil unto any man; but ever follow that which is good, both among yourselves, and to all men.	**5:38–42** [38]Ye have heard that it hath been said, An eye for an eye, and a tooth for a tooth: [39]But I say unto you, That ye resist not evil: but whosoever shall smite thee on thy right cheek, turn to him the other also. [40]And if any man will sue thee at the law, and take away thy coat, let him have thy cloak also. [41]And whosoever shall compel thee to go a mile, go with him twain. [42]Give to him that asketh thee, and from him that would borrow of thee turn not thou away	**Rom 12:17** [14]Bless them which persecute you: bless, and curse not.	**Prov 20:22** [22]Say not thou, I will recompense evil; but wait on the LORD, and he shall save thee.	**Q-Quelle** Love enemies: 1 Thes 5:15/[1 Cor 6:7]/[Col 3:12-14]/Mt 5:38-48/[Mt 7:12]/[Lk 6:27-36 (QS 9 [Thom 6:2, 95], QS 10)]

1 THESSALONIANS 5:18—Exhortations (4:1–5:25), written from Corinth, 50 or 51 CE

Theme	1 THES	Paul
Give thanks	**5:18** [18]In every thing give thanks: for this is the will of God in Christ Jesus concerning you.	**Eph 5:20 (Pseudo)** [20]Giving thanks always for all things unto God and the Father in the name of our Lord Jesus Christ;

1 THESSALONIANS 5:23—Exhortations (4:1–5:25), written from Corinth, 50 or 51 CE

Theme	1 THES	Paul
Be blameless	**5:23** [23]And the very God of peace sanctify you wholly; and I pray God your whole spirit and soul and body be preserved blameless unto the coming of our Lord Jesus Christ.	**2 Thes 3:16** [16] Now the Lord of peace himself give you peace always by all means. The Lord be with you all.

FAREWELL (5:26–28)

2 THESSALONIANS

50 or 51 CE, may be segments of more than one letter

ADDRESS (1:1–12)

2 THESSALONIANS 1:1—Address (1:1–12), written from Corinth, 50 or 51 CE

Theme	2 THES	Mt	Mk
Fellows in Christ	**1:1** [1]Paul, and Silvanus, and Timotheus, unto the church of the Thessalonians in God our Father and the Lord Jesus Christ:	**21:3** [3]And if any man say ought unto you, ye shall say, The Lord hath need of them; and straightway he will send them. **22:41–46** [41]While the Pharisees were gathered together, Jesus asked them, [42]Saying, What think ye of Christ? whose son is he? They say unto him, The Son of David. [43]He saith unto them, How then doth David in spirit call him Lord, saying, [44]The LORD said unto my Lord, Sit thou on my right hand, till I make thine enemies thy footstool? [45]If David then call him Lord, how is he his son? [46]And no man was able to answer him a word, neither durst any man from that day forth ask him any more questions. **24:45–51** [45]Who then is a faithful and wise servant, whom his lord hath made ruler over his household, to give them meat in due season? [46]Blessed is that servant, whom his lord when he cometh shall find so doing. [47]Verily I say unto you, That he shall make him ruler over all his goods. [48]But and if that evil servant shall say in his heart, My lord delayeth his coming; [49]And shall begin to smite his fellowservants, and to eat and drink with the drunken; [50]The lord of that servant shall come in a day when he looketh not for him, and in an hour that he is not aware of, [51]And shall cut him asunder, and appoint him his portion with the hypocrites: there shall be weeping and gnashing of teeth. **25:14–30** [14]For the kingdom of heaven is as a man travelling into a far country, who called his own servants, and delivered unto them his goods. [15]And unto one he gave five talents, to another two, and to another one; to every man according to his several ability; and straightway took his journey. [16]Then he that had received the five talents went and traded with the same, and made them other five talents. [17]And likewise he that had received two, he also gained other two. [18]But he that had received one went and digged in the earth, and hid his lord's money. [19]After a long time the lord of those servants cometh, and reckoneth with them. [20]And so he that had received five talents came and brought other five talents, saying, Lord, thou deliveredst unto me five talents: behold, I have gained beside them five talents more. [21]His lord said unto him, Well done, thou good and faithful servant: thou hast been faithful over a few things, I will make thee ruler over many things: enter thou into the joy of thy lord. [22]He also that had received two talents came and said, Lord, thou deliveredst unto me two talents: behold, I have gained two other talents beside them. [23]His lord said unto him, Well done, good and faithful servant; thou hast been faithful over a few things, I will make thee ruler over many things: enter thou into the joy of thy lord. [24]Then he which had received the one talent came and said, Lord, I knew thee that thou art an hard man, reaping where thou hast not sown, and gathering where thou hast not strawed: [25]And I was afraid, and went and hid thy talent in the earth: lo, there thou hast that is thine. [26]His lord answered and said unto him, Thou wicked and slothful servant, thou knewest that I reap where I sowed not, and gather where I have not strawed: [27]Thou oughtest therefore to have put my money to the exchangers, and then at my coming I should have received mine own with usury. [28]Take therefore the talent from him, and give it unto him which hath ten talents. [29]For unto every one that hath shall be given, and he shall have abundance: but from him that hath not shall be taken away even that which he hath. [30]And cast ye the unprofitable servant into outer darkness: there shall be weeping and gnashing of teeth	**11:3** [3]And if any man say unto you, Why do ye this? say ye that the Lord hath need of him; and straightway he will send him hither. **12:35–37a** [35]And Jesus answered and said, while he taught in the temple, How say the scribes that Christ is the Son of David? [36]For David himself said by the Holy Ghost, The LORD said to my Lord, Sit thou on my right hand, till I make thine enemies thy footstool. [37]David therefore himself calleth him Lord;

2 Thessalonians 1:1 continued on next page

2 THESSALONIANS 1:1—Address (1:1–12), written from Corinth, 50 or 51 CE (*continued*)

Theme	2 THES	Lk
(*Cont.*) Fellows in Christ	1:1 (above)	**12:41–46** [41]Then Peter said unto him, Lord, speakest thou this parable unto us, or even to all? [42]And the Lord said, Who then is that faithful and wise steward, whom his lord shall make ruler over his household, to give them their portion of meat in due season? [43]Blessed is that servant, whom his lord when he cometh shall find so doing. [44]Of a truth I say unto you, that he will make him ruler over all that he hath. [45]But and if that servant say in his heart, My lord delayeth his coming; and shall begin to beat the menservants and maidens, and to eat and drink, and to be drunken; [46]The lord of that servant will come in a day when he looketh not for him, and at an hour when he is not aware, and will cut him in sunder, and will appoint him his portion with the unbelievers.
		19:11–27 [11]And as they heard these things, he added and spake a parable, because he was nigh to Jerusalem, and because they thought that the kingdom of God should immediately appear. [12]He said therefore, A certain nobleman went into a far country to receive for himself a kingdom, and to return. [13]And he called his ten servants, and delivered them ten pounds, and said unto them, Occupy till I come. [14]But his citizens hated him, and sent a message after him, saying, We will not have this man to reign over us. [15]And it came to pass, that when he was returned, having received the kingdom, then he commanded these servants to be called unto him, to whom he had given the money, that he might know how much every man had gained by trading. [16]Then came the first, saying, Lord, thy pound hath gained ten pounds. [17]And he said unto him, Well, thou good servant: because thou hast been faithful in a very little, have thou authority over ten cities. [18]And the second came, saying, Lord, thy pound hath gained five pounds. [19]And he said likewise to him, Be thou also over five cities. [20]And another came, saying, Lord, behold, here is thy pound, which I have kept laid up in a napkin: [21]For I feared thee, because thou art an austere man: thou takest up that thou layedst not down, and reapest that thou didst not sow. [22]And he saith unto him, Out of thine own mouth will I judge thee, thou wicked servant. Thou knewest that I was an austere man, taking up that I laid not down, and reaping that I did not sow: [23]Wherefore then gavest not thou my money into the bank, that at my coming I might have required mine own with usury? [24]And he said unto them that stood by, Take from him the pound, and give it to him that hath ten pounds. [25](And they said unto him, Lord, he hath ten pounds.) [26]For I say unto you, That unto every one which hath shall be given; and from him that hath not, even that he hath shall be taken away from him. [27]But those mine enemies, which would not that I should reign over them, bring hither, and slay them before me.
		19:34 [34]And they said, The Lord hath need of him.
		20:41–44 [41]And he said unto them, How say they that Christ is David's son? [42]And David himself saith in the book of Psalms, The LORD said unto my Lord, Sit thou on my right hand, [43]Till I make thine enemies thy footstool. [44]David therefore calleth him Lord, how is he then his son?

Paul	Jewish Writings	Other
Rom 10:9 [9]That if thou shalt confess with thy mouth the Lord Jesus, and shalt believe in thine heart that God hath raised him from the dead, thou shalt be saved. **Rom 10:13** [13]For whosoever shall call upon the name of the Lord shall be saved. **1 Cor 12:3** [3]Wherefore I give you to understand, that no man speaking by the Spirit of God calleth Jesus accursed: and that no man can say that Jesus is the Lord, but by the Holy Ghost. **1 Cor 15:20–28** [20]But now is Christ risen from the dead, and become the firstfruits of them that slept. [21]For since by man came death, by man came also the resurrection of the dead. [22]For as in Adam all die, even so in Christ shall all be made alive. [23]But every man in his own order: Christ the firstfruits; afterward they that are Christ's at his coming. [24]Then cometh the end, when he shall have delivered up the kingdom to God, even the Father; when he shall have put down all rule and all authority and power. [25]For he must reign, till he hath put all enemies under his feet. [26]The last enemy that shall be destroyed is death. [27]For he hath put all things under his feet. But when he saith all things are put under him, it is manifest that he is excepted, which did put all things under him. [28]And when all things shall be subdued unto him, then shall the Son also himself be subject unto him that put all things under him, that God may be all in all. **Phil 2:5–11** [5]Let this mind be in you, which was also in Christ Jesus: [6]Who, being in the form of God, thought it not robbery to be equal with God: [7]But made himself of no reputation, and took upon him the form of a servant, and was made in the likeness of men: [8]And being found in fashion as a man, he humbled himself, and became obedient unto death, even the death of the cross. [9]Wherefore God also hath highly exalted him, and given him a name which is above every name: [10]That at the name of Jesus every knee should bow, of things in heaven, and things in earth, and things under the earth; [11]And that every tongue should confess that Jesus Christ is Lord, to the glory of God the Father. **1 Thes 1:1** [1]Paul, and Silvanus, and Timotheus, unto the church of the Thessalonians which is in God the Father and in the Lord Jesus Christ: Grace be unto you, and peace, from God our Father, and the Lord Jesus Christ. **Tit 2:13 (Pseudo)** [13]Looking for that blessed hope, and the glorious appearing of the great God and our Saviour Jesus Christ;	**Ps 110** [1]The LORD said unto my Lord, Sit thou at my right hand, until I make thine enemies thy footstool. [2]The LORD shall send the rod of thy strength out of Zion: rule thou in the midst of thine enemies. [3]Thy people shall be willing in the day of thy power, in the beauties of holiness from the womb of the morning: thou hast the dew of thy youth. [4]The LORD hath sworn, and will not repent, Thou art a priest for ever after the order of Melchizedek. [5]The Lord at thy right hand shall strike through kings in the day of his wrath. [6]He shall judge among the heathen, he shall fill the places with the dead bodies; he shall wound the heads over many countries. [7]He shall drink of the brook in the way: therefore shall he lift up the head.	**Q-Quelle** Watchful and faithful: 2 Thes 1:1/[Rom 9:5]/[Mt 24:42-51]/Lk 12:35-48 (QS 41 [Thom 21:3, 103], QS 42); Parable of pounds: 2 Thes 1:1/Mt 25:14-30/Lk 19:11-27 (QS 61 [Thom 41])

2 THESSALONIANS 1:3—Address (1:1–12), written from Corinth, 50 or 51 CE

Theme	2 THES	Lk	Paul
Love one another	**1:3** [3]We are bound to thank God always for you, brethren, as it is meet, because that your faith groweth exceedingly, and the charity of every one of you all toward each other aboundeth;	**9:50** [50]And Jesus said unto him, Forbid him not: for he that is not against us is for us.	**Rom 12:10** [10]Be kindly affectioned one to another with brotherly love; in honour preferring one another; **Rom 12:18** [18]If it be possible, as much as lieth in you, live peaceably with all men. **Rom 14:19** [19]Let us therefore follow after the things which make for peace, and things wherewith one may edify another. **1 Cor 1:4** [4] I thank my God always on your behalf, for the grace of God which is given you by Jesus Christ; **1 Cor 7:15** [15]But if the unbelieving depart, let him depart. A brother or a sister is not under bondage in such cases: but God hath called us to peace. **2 Cor 13:11** [11]Finally, brethren, farewell. Be perfect, be of good comfort, be of one mind, live in peace; and the God of love and peace shall be with you. **Gal 6:10** [10]As we have therefore opportunity, let us do good unto all men, especially unto them who are of the household of faith. **Eph 4:32 (Pseudo)** [32]And be ye kind one to another, tenderhearted, forgiving one another, even as God for Christ's sake hath forgiven you. **Col 3:12** [12]Put on therefore, as the elect of God, holy and beloved, bowels of mercies, kindness, humbleness of mind, meekness, longsuffering; **1 Thes 1:2** [2]We give thanks to God always for you all, making mention of you in our prayers; **1 Thes 3:12** [12]And the Lord make you to increase and abound in love one toward another, and toward all men, even as we do toward you: **1 Thes 4:9** [9]But as touching brotherly love ye need not that I write unto you: for ye yourselves are taught of God to love one another. **1 Thes 5:12–13** [12]And we beseech you, brethren, to know them which labour among you, and are over you in the Lord, and admonish you; [13]And to esteem them very highly in love for their work's sake. And be at peace among yourselves. **1 Thes 5:15** [15]See that none render evil for evil unto any man; but ever follow that which is good, both among yourselves, and to all men.

Other
Q-Quelle
Parable of salt: 2 Thes 1:3/1 Cor 7:15/[Mt 5:13]/[Mk 9:49-53]/[Lk 14:34-35 (QS 53)]; Beatitudes: 2 Thes 1:3/2 Cor 13:11/Gal 6:10/Eph 4:32/Col 3:12/[Mt 5:3-12]/[Lk 6:20b-23 (QS 8 [Thom 54,68,69])]

2 THESSALONIANS 1:4—Address (1:1–12), written from Corinth, 50 or 51 CE

Theme	2 THES	Mt	Mk	Lk
Steadfast endurance	**1:4** [4]So that we ourselves glory in you in the churches of God for your patience and faith in all your persecutions and tribulations that ye endure:	**4:18–22** [18]And Jesus, walking by the sea of Galilee, saw two brethren, Simon called Peter, and Andrew his brother, casting a net into the sea: for they were fishers. [19]And he saith unto them, Follow me, and I will make you fishers of men. [20]And they straightway left their nets, and followed him. [21]And going on from thence, he saw other two brethren, James the son of Zebedee, and John his brother, in a ship with Zebedee their father, mending their nets; and he called them. [22]And they immediately left the ship and their father, and followed him. **5:10–11** [10]Blessed are they which are persecuted for righteousness' sake: for theirs is the kingdom of heaven. [11]Blessed are ye, when men shall revile you, and persecute you, and shall say all manner of evil against you falsely, for my sake. **9:13** [13]But go ye and learn what that meaneth, I will have mercy, and not sacrifice: for I am not come to call the righteous, but sinners to repentance. **18:3** [3]And said, Verily I say unto you, Except ye be converted, and become as little children, ye shall not enter into the kingdom of heaven.	**1:16–20** [16]Now as he walked by the sea of Galilee, he saw Simon and Andrew his brother casting a net into the sea: for they were fishers. [17]And Jesus said unto them, Come ye after me, and I will make you to become fishers of men. [18]And straightway they forsook their nets, and followed him. [19]And when he had gone a little further thence, he saw James the son of Zebedee, and John his brother, who also were in the ship mending their nets. [20]And straightway he called them: and they left their father Zebedee in the ship with the hired servants, and went after him. **2:17** [17]When Jesus heard it, he saith unto them, They that are whole have no need of the physician, but they that are sick: I came not to call the righteous, but sinners to repentance. **10:15** [15]Verily I say unto you, Whosoever shall not receive the kingdom of God as a little child, he shall not enter therein.	**5:32** [32]I came not to call the righteous, but sinners to repentance. **6:22** [22]Blessed are ye, when men shall hate you, and when they shall separate you from their company, and shall reproach you, and cast out your name as evil, for the Son of man's sake,

2 THESSALONIANS 1:5—Address (1:1–12), written from Corinth, 50 or 51 CE

Theme	1 THES	Paul
God's righteous judgment	**1:5** [5]Which is a manifest token of the righteous judgment of God, that ye may be counted worthy of the kingdom of God, for which ye also suffer:	**Phil 1:28** [28]And in nothing terrified by your adversaries: which is to them an evident token of perdition, but to you of salvation, and that of God. **1 Thes 2:12** [12]That ye would walk worthy of God, who hath called you unto his kingdom and glory.

Jn	Paul	Other
3:5 [5]Jesus answered, Verily, verily, I say unto thee, Except a man be born of water and of the Spirit, he cannot enter into the kingdom of God.	**1 Cor 6:9–10** [9]Know ye not that the unrighteous shall not inherit the kingdom of God? Be not deceived: neither fornicators, nor idolaters, nor adulterers, nor effeminate, nor abusers of themselves with mankind, [10]Nor thieves, nor covetous, nor drunkards, nor revilers, nor extortioners, shall inherit the kingdom of God. **Gal 5:19–21** [19]Now the works of the flesh are manifest, which are these; Adultery, fornication, uncleanness, lasciviousness, [20]Idolatry, witchcraft, hatred, variance, emulations, wrath, strife, seditions, heresies, [21]Envyings, murders, drunkenness, revellings, and such like: of the which I tell you before, as I have also told you in time past, that they which do such things shall not inherit the kingdom of God. **Eph 5:5 (Pseudo)** [5]For this ye know, that no whoremonger, nor unclean person, nor covetous man, who is an idolater, hath any inheritance in the kingdom of Christ and of God. **Col 4:11** [11]And Jesus, which is called Justus, who are of the circumcision. These only are my fellowworkers unto the kingdom of God, which have been a comfort unto me. **1 Thes 2:12** [12]That ye would walk worthy of God, who hath called you unto his kingdom and glory.	**Q-Quelle** Beatitudes: 2 Thes 1:4/Mt5:3-12/ Lk 6:20b-23 (QS 8 [Thom 54, 68, 69])

2 THESSALONIANS 1:8–9—Address (1:1–12), written from Corinth, 50 or 51 CE

Theme	2 THES	Paul
Judgment	**1:8–9** [8]In flaming fire taking vengeance on them that know not God, and that obey not the gospel of our Lord Jesus Christ: [9]Who shall be punished with everlasting destruction from the presence of the Lord, and from the glory of his power; **2:8** [8]And then shall that Wicked be revealed, whom the Lord shall consume with the spirit of his mouth, and shall destroy with the brightness of his coming:	**1 Cor 3:15** [15]If any man's work shall be burned, he shall suffer loss: but he himself shall be saved; yet so as by fire. **1 Cor 15:25–28** [25]For he must reign, till he hath put all enemies under his feet. [26]The last enemy that shall be destroyed is death. [27]For he hath put all things under his feet. But when he saith all things are put under him, it is manifest that he is excepted, which did put all things under him. [28]And when all things shall be subdued unto him, then shall the Son also himself be subject unto him that put all things under him, that God may be all in all. **1 Thes 5:3** [3]For when they shall say, Peace and safety; then sudden destruction cometh upon them, as travail upon a woman with child; and they shall not escape.

2 THESSALONIANS 1:8—Address (1:1–12), written from Corinth, 50 or 51 CE

Theme	2 THES	Jewish Writings
Wrath	**1:8** [8]In flaming fire taking vengeance on them that know not God, and that obey not the gospel of our Lord Jesus Christ:	**Ps 79:5–6** [5]How long, LORD? wilt thou be angry for ever? shall thy jealousy burn like fire? [6] Pour out thy wrath upon the heathen that have not known thee, and upon the kingdoms that have not called upon thy name. **Is 66:15** [15]For, behold, the LORD will come with fire, and with his chariots like a whirlwind, to render his anger with fury, and his rebuke with flames of fire. **Jer 10:25** [25]Pour out thy fury upon the heathen that know thee not, and upon the families that call not on thy name: for they have eaten up Jacob, and devoured him, and consumed him, and have made his habitation desolate.

2 THESSALONIANS 1:9—Address (1:1–12), written from Corinth, 50 or 51 CE

Theme	2 THES	Jewish Writings
Punishment	**1:9** [9]Who shall be punished with everlasting destruction from the presence of the Lord, and from the glory of his power;	**Is 2:10** [10]Enter into the rock, and hide thee in the dust, for fear of the LORD, and for the glory of his majesty. **Is 2:19** [19]And they shall go into the holes of the rocks, and into the caves of the earth, for fear of the LORD, and for the glory of his majesty, when he ariseth to shake terribly the earth. **Is 2:21** [21]To go into the clefts of the rocks, and into the tops of the ragged rocks, for fear of the LORD, and for the glory of his majesty, when he ariseth to shake terribly the earth.

2 THESSALONIANS 1:10—Address (1:1–12), written from Corinth, 50 or 51 CE

Theme	2 THES	Paul	Jewish Writings	Other
Christians glorified with God	**1:10** [10]When he shall come to be glorified in his saints, and to be admired in all them that believe (because our testimony among you was believed) in that day.	**Rom 8:17** [17]And if children, then heirs; heirs of God, and joint-heirs with Christ; if so be that we suffer with him, that we may be also glorified together. **Rom 8:23** [23]And not only they, but ourselves also, which have the firstfruits of the Spirit, even we ourselves groan within ourselves, waiting for the adoption, to wit, the redemption of our body. **Rom 11:26** [26]And so all Israel shall be saved: as it is written, There shall come out of Sion the Deliverer, and shall turn away ungodliness from Jacob: **1 Cor 13:12** [12]For now we see through a glass, darkly; but then face to face: now I know in part; but then shall I know even as also I am known. **1 Cor 15:52** [52]In a moment, in the twinkling of an eye, at the last trump: for the trumpet shall sound, and the dead shall be raised incorruptible, and we shall be changed. **1 Thes 1:10** [10]And to wait for his Son from heaven, whom he raised from the dead, even Jesus, which delivered us from the wrath to come. **1 Thes 3:13** [13]To the end he may stablish your hearts unblameable in holiness before God, even our Father, at the coming of our Lord Jesus Christ with all his saints. **1 Thes 4:17** [17]Then we which are alive and remain shall be caught up together with them in the clouds, to meet the Lord in the air: and so shall we ever be with the Lord.	**Ps 89:8** [8]O LORD God of hosts, who is a strong LORD like unto thee? or to thy faithfulness round about thee? **Dan 7:18–22** [18]But the saints of the most High shall take the kingdom, and possess the kingdom for ever, even for ever and ever. [19]Then I would know the truth of the fourth beast, which was diverse from all the others, exceeding dreadful, whose teeth were of iron, and his nails of brass; which devoured, brake in pieces, and stamped the residue with his feet; [20]And of the ten horns that were in his head, and of the other which came up, and before whom three fell; even of that horn that had eyes, and a mouth that spake very great things, whose look was more stout than his fellows. [21]I beheld, and the same horn made war with the saints, and prevailed against them; [22]Until the Ancient of days came, and judgment was given to the saints of the most High; and the time came that the saints possessed the kingdom. **Dan 7:27** [27]And the kingdom and dominion, and the greatness of the kingdom under the whole heaven, shall be given to the people of the saints of the most High, whose kingdom is an everlasting kingdom, and all dominions shall serve and obey him.	**Q-Quelle** Lord's Prayer: 2 Thes 1:10/1 Thes 1:10/[Mt 6:9-13]/ [Lk 11:1-4 (QS 26)]

2 THESSALONIANS 1:11—Address (1:1–12), written from Corinth, 50 or 51 CE

Theme	2 THES	Paul
Prayer for worthy calling	**1:11** [11]Wherefore also we pray always for you, that our God would count you worthy of this calling, and fulfil all the good pleasure of his goodness, and the work of faith with power:	**1 Thes 1:2–3** [2]We give thanks to God always for you all, making mention of you in our prayers; [3]Remembering without ceasing your work of faith, and labour of love, and patience of hope in our Lord Jesus Christ, in the sight of God and our Father;

2 THESSALONIANS 1:12—Address (1:1–12), written from Corinth, 50 or 51 CE

Theme	2 THES	Paul	Jewish Writings
Glorify God in whole person	**1:12** [12]That the name of our Lord Jesus Christ may be glorified in you, and ye in him, according to the grace of our God and the Lord Jesus Christ.	**Rom 9:5** [5]Whose are the fathers, and of whom as concerning the flesh Christ came, who is over all, God blessed for ever. Amen. **Tit 2:13 (Pseudo)** [13]Looking for that blessed hope, and the glorious appearing of the great God and our Saviour Jesus Christ;	**Is 66:5** [5]Hear the word of the LORD, ye that tremble at his word; Your brethren that hated you, that cast you out for my name's sake, said, Let the LORD be glorified: but he shall appear to your joy, and they shall be ashamed.

PAROUSIA (2:1–17)

2 THESSALONIANS 2:1—Parousia (2:1–17), written from Corinth, 50 or 51 CE

Theme	2 THES	Paul
Edification	**2:1** [1]Now we beseech you, brethren, by the coming of our Lord Jesus Christ, and by our gathering together unto him,	**1 Thes 4:13–17** [13]But I would not have you to be ignorant, brethren, concerning them which are asleep, that ye sorrow not, even as others which have no hope. [14]For if we believe that Jesus died and rose again, even so them also which sleep in Jesus will God bring with him. [15]For this we say unto you by the word of the Lord, that we which are alive and remain unto the coming of the Lord shall not prevent them which are asleep. [16]For the Lord himself shall descend from heaven with a shout, with the voice of the archangel, and with the trump of God: and the dead in Christ shall rise first: [17]Then we which are alive and remain shall be caught up together with them in the clouds, to meet the Lord in the air: and so shall we ever be with the Lord.

2 THESSALONIANS 2:2—Parousia (2:1–17), written from Corinth, 50 or 51 CE

Theme	2 THES	Mt	Paul
Do not be shaken	**2:2** [2]That ye be not soon shaken in mind, or be troubled, neither by spirit, nor by word, nor by letter as from us, as that the day of Christ is at hand.	**24:6** [6]And ye shall hear of wars and rumours of wars: see that ye be not troubled: for all these things must come to pass, but the end is not yet.	**1 Cor 14:26** [26]How is it then, brethren? when ye come together, every one of you hath a psalm, hath a doctrine, hath a tongue, hath a revelation, hath an interpretation. Let all things be done unto edifying. **1 Cor 14:32–33** [32]And the spirits of the prophets are subject to the prophets. [33]For God is not the author of confusion, but of peace, as in all churches of the saints. **1 Thes 5:1–2** [1]But of the times and the seasons, brethren, ye have no need that I write unto you. [2]For yourselves know perfectly that the day of the Lord so cometh as a thief in the night.

2 THESSALONIANS 2:4—Parousia (2:1–17), written from Corinth, 50 or 51 CE

Theme	2 THES	Jewish Writings
Opposing God & exalting self	**2:4** [4]Who opposeth and exalteth himself above all that is called God, or that is worshipped; so that he as God sitteth in the temple of God, showing himself that he is God.	**Ezek 28:2** [2]Son of man, say unto the prince of Tyrus, Thus saith the Lord GOD; Because thine heart is lifted up, and thou hast said, I am a God, I sit in the seat of God, in the midst of the seas; yet thou art a man, and not God, though thou set thine heart as the heart of God: **Dan 11:36–37** [36]And the king shall do according to his will; and he shall exalt himself, and magnify himself above every god, and shall speak marvellous things against the God of gods, and shall prosper till the indignation be accomplished: for that that is determined shall be done. [37]Neither shall he regard the God of his fathers, nor the desire of women, nor regard any god: for he shall magnify himself above all.

2 THESSALONIANS 2:7—Parousia (2:1–17), written from Corinth, 50 or 51 CE

Theme	2 THES	Mt	Lk	Paul	NT
Mystery of iniquity	**2:7** [7]For the mystery of iniquity doth already work: only he who now letteth will let, until he be taken out of the way.	**13:36–43** [36]Then Jesus sent the multitude away, and went into the house: and his disciples came unto him, saying, Declare unto us the parable of the tares of the field. [37]He answered and said unto them, He that soweth the good seed is the Son of man; [38]The field is the world; the good seed are the children of the kingdom; but the tares are the children of the wicked one; [39]The enemy that sowed them is the devil; the harvest is the end of the world; and the reapers are the angels. [40]As therefore the tares are gathered and burned in the fire; so shall it be in the end of this world. [41]The Son of man shall send forth his angels, and they shall gather out of his kingdom all things that offend, and them which do iniquity; [42]And shall cast them into a furnace of fire: there shall be wailing and gnashing of teeth. [43]Then shall the righteous shine forth as the sun in the kingdom of their Father. Who hath ears to hear, let him hear.	**Acts 20:29** [29]For I know this, that after my departing shall grievous wolves enter in among you, not sparing the flock.	**Gal 5:10** [10]I have confidence in you through the Lord, that ye will be none otherwise minded: but he that troubleth you shall bear his judgment, whosoever he be.	**2 Pet 2:1** [1]But there were false prophets also among the people, even as there shall be false teachers among you, who privily shall bring in damnable heresies, even denying the Lord that bought them, and bring upon themselves swift destruction. **Rev 19:15** [15]And out of his mouth goeth a sharp sword, that with it he should smite the nations: and he shall rule them with a rod of iron: and he treadeth the winepress of the fierceness and wrath of Almighty God.

2 THESSALONIANS 2:8—Parousia (2:1–17), written from Corinth, 50 or 51 CE

Theme	2 THES	Mt
Revealing the wicked	**2:8** [8]And then shall that Wicked be revealed, whom the Lord shall consume with the spirit of his mouth, and shall destroy with the brightness of his coming:	**24:6–22** [6]And ye shall hear of wars and rumours of wars: see that ye be not troubled: for all these things must come to pass, but the end is not yet. [7]For nation shall rise against nation, and kingdom against kingdom: and there shall be famines, and pestilences, and earthquakes, in divers places. [8]All these are the beginning of sorrows. [9]Then shall they deliver you up to be afflicted, and shall kill you: and ye shall be hated of all nations for my name's sake. [10]And then shall many be offended, and shall betray one another, and shall hate one another. [11]And many false prophets shall rise, and shall deceive many. [12]And because iniquity shall abound, the love of many shall wax cold. [13]But he that shall endure unto the end, the same shall be saved. [14]And this gospel of the kingdom shall be preached in all the world for a witness unto all nations; and then shall the end come. [15]When ye therefore shall see the abomination of desolation, spoken of by Daniel the prophet, stand in the holy place, (whoso readeth, let him understand:) [16]Then let them which be in Judaea flee into the mountains: [17]Let him which is on the housetop not come down to take any thing out of his house: [18]Neither let him which is in the field return back to take his clothes. [19]And woe unto them that are with child, and to them that give suck in those days! [20]But pray ye that your flight be not in the winter, neither on the sabbath day: [21]For then shall be great tribulation, such as was not since the beginning of the world to this time, no, nor ever shall be. [22]And except those days should be shortened, there should no flesh be saved: but for the elect's sake those days shall be shortened. **24:15–31** [15]When ye therefore shall see the abomination of desolation, spoken of by Daniel the prophet, stand in the holy place, (whoso readeth, let him understand:) [16]Then let them which be in Judaea flee into the mountains: [17]Let him which is on the housetop not come down to take any thing out of his house: [18]Neither let him which is in the field return back to take his clothes. [19]And woe unto them that are with child, and to them that give suck in those days! [20]But pray ye that your flight be not in the winter, neither on the sabbath day: [21]For then shall be great tribulation, such as was not since the beginning of the world to this time, no, nor ever shall be. [22]And except those days should be shortened, there should no flesh be saved: but for the elect's sake those days shall be shortened. [23]Then if any man shall say unto you, Lo, here is Christ, or there; believe it not. [24]For there shall arise false Christs, and false prophets, and shall show great signs and wonders; insomuch that, if it were possible, they shall deceive the very elect. [25]Behold, I have told you before. [26]Wherefore if they shall say unto you, Behold, he is in the desert; go not forth: behold, he is in the secret chambers; believe it not. [27]For as the lightning cometh out of the east, and shineth even unto the west; so shall also the coming of the Son of man be. [28]For wheresoever the carcase is, there will the eagles be gathered together. [29]Immediately after the tribulation of those days shall the sun be darkened, and the moon shall not give her light, and the stars shall fall from heaven, and the powers of the heavens shall be shaken: [30]And then shall appear the sign of the Son of man in heaven: and then shall all the tribes of the earth mourn, and they shall see the Son of man coming in the clouds of heaven with power and great glory. [31]And he shall send his angels with a great sound of a trumpet, and they shall gather together his elect from the four winds, from one end of heaven to the other.

Mk

13:7–14

7 And when ye shall hear of wars and rumours of wars, be ye not troubled: for such things must needs be; but the end shall not be yet. 8 For nation shall rise against nation, and kingdom against kingdom: and there shall be earthquakes in divers places, and there shall be famines and troubles: these are the beginnings of sorrows. 9 But take heed to yourselves: for they shall deliver you up to councils; and in the synagogues ye shall be beaten: and ye shall be brought before rulers and kings for my sake, for a testimony against them. 10 And the gospel must first be published among all nations. 11 But when they shall lead you, and deliver you up, take no thought beforehand what ye shall speak, neither do ye premeditate: but whatsoever shall be given you in that hour, that speak ye: for it is not ye that speak, but the Holy Ghost. 12 Now the brother shall betray the brother to death, and the father the son; and children shall rise up against their parents, and shall cause them to be put to death. 13 And ye shall be hated of all men for my name's sake: but he that shall endure unto the end, the same shall be saved. 14 But when ye shall see the abomination of desolation, spoken of by Daniel the prophet, standing where it ought not, (let him that readeth understand,) then let them that be in Judaea flee to the mountains:

13:14–27

14 But when ye shall see the abomination of desolation, spoken of by Daniel the prophet, standing where it ought not, (let him that readeth understand,) then let them that be in Judaea flee to the mountains: 15 And let him that is on the housetop not go down into the house, neither enter therein, to take any thing out of his house: 16 And let him that is in the field not turn back again for to take up his garment. 17 But woe to them that are with child, and to them that give suck in those days! 18 And pray ye that your flight be not in the winter. 19 For in those days shall be affliction, such as was not from the beginning of the creation which God created unto this time, neither shall be. 20 And except that the Lord had shortened those days, no flesh should be saved: but for the elect's sake, whom he hath chosen, he hath shortened the days. 21 And then if any man shall say to you, Lo, here is Christ; or, lo, he is there; believe him not: 22 For false Christs and false prophets shall rise, and shall show signs and wonders, to seduce, if it were possible, even the elect. 23 But take ye heed: behold, I have foretold you all things. 24 But in those days, after that tribulation, the sun shall be darkened, and the moon shall not give her light, 25 And the stars of heaven shall fall, and the powers that are in heaven shall be shaken. 26 And then shall they see the Son of man coming in the clouds with great power and glory. 27 And then shall he send his angels, and shall gather together his elect from the four winds, from the uttermost part of the earth to the uttermost part of heaven.

2 THESSALONIANS 2:8—Parousia (2:1–17), written from Corinth, 50 or 51 CE

Theme	2 THES	Lk	Paul
(*Cont.*) **Revealing the wicked**	**2:8 (above)**	**21:9–14** [9]But when ye shall hear of wars and commotions, be not terrified: for these things must first come to pass; but the end is not by and by. [10]Then said he unto them, Nation shall rise against nation, and kingdom against kingdom: [11]And great earthquakes shall be in divers places, and famines, and pestilences; and fearful sights and great signs shall there be from heaven. [12]But before all these, they shall lay their hands on you, and persecute you, delivering you up to the synagogues, and into prisons, being brought before kings and rulers for my name's sake. [13]And it shall turn to you for a testimony. [14]Settle it therefore in your hearts, not to meditate before what ye shall answer: **21:20–27** [20]And when ye shall see Jerusalem compassed with armies, then know that the desolation thereof is nigh. [21]Then let them which are in Judaea flee to the mountains; and let them which are in the midst of it depart out; and let not them that are in the countries enter thereinto. [22]For these be the days of vengeance, that all things which are written may be fulfilled. [23]But woe unto them that are with child, and to them that give suck, in those days! for there shall be great distress in the land, and wrath upon this people. [24]And they shall fall by the edge of the sword, and shall be led away captive into all nations: and Jerusalem shall be trodden down of the Gentiles, until the times of the Gentiles be fulfilled. [25]And there shall be signs in the sun, and in the moon, and in the stars; and upon the earth distress of nations, with perplexity; the sea and the waves roaring; [26]Men's hearts failing them for fear, and for looking after those things which are coming on the earth: for the powers of heaven shall be shaken. [27]And then shall they see the Son of man coming in a cloud with power & great glory.	**Rom 8:17** [17]And if children, then heirs; heirs of God, and joint-heirs with Christ; if so be that we suffer with him, that we may be also glorified together. **1 Thes 2:14–16** [14]For ye, brethren, became followers of the churches of God which in Judaea are in Christ Jesus: for ye also have suffered like things of your own countrymen, even as they have of the Jews: [15]Who both killed the Lord Jesus, and their own prophets, and have persecuted us; and they please not God, and are contrary to all men: [16]Forbidding us to speak to the Gentiles that they might be saved, to fill up their sins alway: for the wrath is come upon them to the uttermost. **1 Thes 3:3–4** [3]That no man should be moved by these afflictions: for yourselves know that we are appointed thereunto. [4]For verily, when we were with you, we told you before that we should suffer tribulation; even as it came to pass, and ye know.

2 THESSALONIANS 2:9—Parousia (2:1–17), written from Corinth, 50 or 51 CE

Theme	2 THES	Mt
Satan's works	**2:9** [9]Even him, whose coming is after the working of Satan with all power and signs and lying wonders,	**24:24** [24]For there shall arise false Christs, and false prophets, and shall show great signs and wonders; insomuch that, if it were possible, they shall deceive the very elect.

2 THESSALONIANS 2:13—Parousia (2:1–17), written from Corinth, 50 or 51 CE

Theme	2 THES	Paul
Chosen by God from beginning	**2:13** [13]But we are bound to give thanks alway to God for you, brethren beloved of the Lord, because God hath from the beginning chosen you to salvation through sanctification of the Spirit and belief of the truth:	**1 Thes 2:13** [13]For this cause also thank we God without ceasing, because, when ye received the word of God which ye heard of us, ye received it not as the word of men, but as it is in truth, the word of God, which effectually worketh also in you that believe. **1 Thes 5:9** [9]For God hath not appointed us to wrath, but to obtain salvation by our Lord Jesus Christ,

NT	Jewish	Other
Rev 19:15	**Is 11:4**	**Q-Quelle**
[15]And out of his mouth goeth a sharp sword, that with it he should smite the nations: and he shall rule them with a rod of iron: and he treadeth the winepress of the fierceness and wrath of Almighty God.	[4]But with righteousness shall he judge the poor, and reprove with equity for the meek of the earth: and he shall smite the earth with the rod of his mouth, and with the breath of his lips shall he slay the wicked.	Day of SOM: 2 Thes 2:8/Rom 8:17/[2 Cor 7:4]/1 Thes 3:3-4/[Mt 10:39], Mt 24:17-18, 23, 26-27, 28, [Mt 24:37-39, 24:40-41]/Mk 13:14-16, 13:19-23/[Lk 17:22-37 (QS 60 [Thom 3, 51, 61, 113])]; Beatitudes: 2 Thes 2:8/Rom 8:17/ [2 Cor 7:4]/1 Thes 3:3-4/ [Mt 5:3-12]/[Lk 6:20b-23 (QS 8 [Thom 54, 68, 69])]; Assistance of HS: 2 Thes 2:8/1 Thes 3:3-4/ [2 Cor 7:4]/[Mt 10:19-20]/[Mk 13:11]/[Lk 12:11-12 (QS 37 [Thom 44])], Lk 21:14-15

NT
Rev 13:13 [13]And he doeth great wonders, so that he maketh fire come down from heaven on the earth in the sight of men,

2 THESSALONIANS 2:14—Parousia (2:1–17), written from Corinth, 50 or 51 CE

Theme	2 THES	Paul
Called by gospel	**2:14** [14]Whereunto he called you by our gospel, to the obtaining of the glory of our Lord Jesus Christ.	**Rom 5:1–10** [1]Therefore being justified by faith, we have peace with God through our Lord Jesus Christ: [2]By whom also we have access by faith into this grace wherein we stand, and rejoice in hope of the glory of God. [3]And not only so, but we glory in tribulations also: knowing that tribulation worketh patience; [4]And patience, experience; and experience, hope: [5]And hope maketh not ashamed; because the love of God is shed abroad in our hearts by the Holy Ghost which is given unto us. [6]For when we were yet without strength, in due time Christ died for the ungodly. [7]For scarcely for a righteous man will one die: yet peradventure for a good man some would even dare to die. [8]But God commendeth his love toward us, in that, while we were yet sinners, Christ died for us. [9]Much more then, being now justified by his blood, we shall be saved from wrath through him. [10]For if, when we were enemies, we were reconciled to God by the death of his Son, much more, being reconciled, we shall be saved by his life. **Rom 8:29–30** [29]For whom he did foreknow, he also did predestinate to be conformed to the image of his Son, that he might be the firstborn among many brethren. [30]Moreover whom he did predestinate, them he also called: and whom he called, them he also justified: and whom he justified, them he also glorified. **1 Thes 4:7** [7]For God hath not called us unto uncleanness, but unto holiness. **1 Thes 5:9** [9]For God hath not appointed us to wrath, but to obtain salvation by our Lord Jesus Christ,

EXHORTATIONS (3:1–16)

2 THESSALONIANS 3:1—Exhortations (3:1–16), written from Corinth, 50 or 51 CE

Theme	2 THES	Paul
Pray	**3:1** [1]Finally, brethren, pray for us, that the word of the Lord may have free course, and be glorified, even as it is with you:	**Eph 6:19 (Pseudo)** [19]And for me, that utterance may be given unto me, that I may open my mouth boldly, to make known the mystery of the gospel, **Col 4:3** [3]Withal praying also for us, that God would open unto us a door of utterance, to speak the mystery of Christ, for which I am also in bonds:

2 THESSALONIANS 3:3—Exhortations (3:1–16), written from Corinth, 50 or 51 CE

Theme	2 THES	Mt	Paul
Lord will establish & protect	**3:3** [3]But the Lord is faithful, who shall stablish you, and keep you from evil.	**6:13** [13]And lead us not into temptation, but deliver us from evil: For thine is the kingdom, and the power, and the glory, for ever. Amen.	**1 Cor 16:13** [13]Watch ye, stand fast in the faith, quit you like men, be strong. **1 Thes 5:24** [24]Faithful is he that calleth you, who also will do it.

2 THESSALONIANS 3:4—Exhortations (3:1–16), written from Corinth, 50 or 51 CE

Theme	2 THES	Paul
Confidence in God's working	**3:4** [4]And we have confidence in the Lord touching you, that ye both do and will do the things which we command you.	**2 Cor 7:16** [16]I rejoice therefore that I have confidence in you in all things. **1 Thes 4:1–2** [1]Furthermore then we beseech you, brethren, and exhort you by the Lord Jesus, that as ye have received of us how ye ought to walk and to please God, so ye would abound more and more. [2]For ye know what commandments we gave you by the Lord Jesus.

2 THESSALONIANS 3:8–9—Exhortations (3:1–16), written from Corinth, 50 or 51 CE

Theme	2 THES	Mt	Paul	Other
Minister without payment	**3:8–9** [8]Neither did we eat any man's bread for nought; but wrought with labour and travail night and day, that we might not be chargeable to any of you: [9]Not because we have not power, but to make ourselves an ensample unto you to follow us.	**10:8** [8]Heal the sick, cleanse the lepers, raise the dead, cast out devils: freely ye have received, freely give.	**1 Cor 9:18** [18]What is my reward then? Verily that, when I preach the gospel, I may make the gospel of Christ without charge, that I abuse not my power in the gospel. **2 Cor 11:7** [7]Have I committed an offence in abasing myself that ye might be exalted, because I have preached to you the gospel of God freely?	**Q-Quelle** Commissioning the 12: 2 Thes 3:8-9/[Mt 10:1], Mt 10:7-11, [Mt 10:14]/[Mk 6:6b-13]//[Lk 9:1-6]

2 THESSALONIANS 3:8—Exhortations (3:1–16), written from Corinth, 50 or 51 CE

Theme	2 THES	Paul
Labor without charge	**3:8** [8]Neither did we eat any man's bread for nought; but wrought with labour and travail night and day, that we might not be chargeable to any of you:	**1 Thes 2:9** [9]For ye remember, brethren, our labour and travail: for labouring night and day, because we would not be chargeable unto any of you, we preached unto you the gospel of God.

2 THESSALONIANS 3:9—Exhortations (3:1–16), written from Corinth, 50 or 51 CE

Theme	2 THES	Mt	Paul	Other
Example toothers	**3:9** [9]Not because we have not power, but to make ourselves an ensample unto you to follow us.	**10:10** [10]Nor scrip for your journey, neither 2 coats, neither shoes, nor yet staves: for the workman is worthy of his meat.	**Phil 3:17** [17]Brethren, be followers together of me, and mark them which walk so as ye have us for an ensample.	**Q-Quelle** Commissioning of 12: 2 Thes 3:8-9/[2 Cor 11:7]/[Mt 10:1], Mt 10:7-11, [Mt 10:14]/[Mk 6:6b-13]/[Lk 9:1-6]; Commissioning of 70: 2 Thes 3:8-9/[2 Cor 11:7]/[Mt 9:37-38], Mt 10:7-16/[Lk 10:1-12 (QS 20 [Thom73, 14:2], QS 21)]

2 THESSALONIANS 3:10—Exhortations (3:1–16), written from Corinth, 50 or 51 CE

Theme	2 THES	Paul
Work or do not eat	**3:10** [10]For even when we were with you, this we commanded you, that if any would not work, neither should he eat.	**1 Thes 4:11** [11]And that ye study to be quiet, and to do your own business, and to work with your own hands, as we commanded you;

2 THESSALONIANS 3:11—Exhortations (3:1–16), written from Corinth, 50 or 51 CE

Theme	2 THES	Paul
Busybodies	**3:11** [11]For we hear that there are some which walk among you disorderly, working not at all, but are busybodies.	**1 Thes 5:14** [14]Now we exhort you, brethren, warn them that are unruly, comfort the feebleminded, support the weak, be patient toward all men.

2 THESSALONIANS 3:15—Exhortations (3:1–16), written from Corinth, 50 or 51 CE

Theme	2 THES	Paul
Admonish disobedient	**3:15** [15]Yet count him not as an enemy, but admonish him as a brother.	**2 Cor 2:7** [7]So that contrariwise ye ought rather to forgive him, and comfort him, lest perhaps such a one should be swallowed up with overmuch sorrow. **Gal 6:1** [1]Brethren, if a man be overtaken in a fault, ye which are spiritual, restore such an one in the spirit of meekness; considering thyself, lest thou also be tempted.

2 THESSALONIANS 3:16—Exhortations (3:1–16), written from Corinth, 50 or 51 CE

Theme	2 THES	Jn	Paul
God gives peace	**3:16** [16]Now the Lord of peace himself give you peace always by all means. The Lord be with you all.	**14:27** [27]Peace I leave with you, my peace I give unto you: not as the world giveth, give I unto you. Let not your heart be troubled, neither let it be afraid.	**Rom 15:33** [33]Now the God of peace be with you all. Amen.

FINAL FAREWELL (3:17–18)

2 THESSALONIANS 3:17—Farewell (3:17–18), written from Corinth, 50 or 51 CE

Theme	2 THES	Paul
Paul's own handwriting	**3:17** [17]The salutation of Paul with mine own hand, which is the token in every epistle: so I write.	**1 Cor 16:21** [21]The salutation of me Paul with mine own hand. **Gal 6:11** [11]Ye see how large a letter I have written unto you with mine own hand.

1 TIMOTHY

Pastoral epistle, Pseudo-Pauline authorship, early second century [or, by Paul 63–67 CE (MINORITY VIEW)]

ADDRESS (1:1–2)

I TIMOTHY (PSEUDO) 1:1—Address (1:1–2), pastoral epistle, pseudo-Pauline authorship, early second century

Theme	1 TIM	Lk	Paul
Greeting from Paul, an apostle	**1:1 (Pseudo)** [1]Paul, an apostle of Jesus Christ by the commandment of God our Saviour, and Lord Jesus Christ, which is our hope; **2:3 (Pseudo)** [3]For this is good and acceptable in the sight of God our Saviour;	**1:47** [47]And my spirit hath rejoiced in God my Saviour.	**Col 1:27** [27]To whom God would make known what is the riches of the glory of this mystery among the Gentiles; which is Christ in you, the hope of glory: **Tit 1:3 (Pseudo)** [3]But hath in due times manifested his word through preaching, which is committed unto me according to the commandment of God our Saviour; **Tit 2:10 (Pseudo)** [10]Not purloining, but showing all good fidelity; that they may adorn the doctrine of God our Saviour in all things.

I TIMOTHY (PSEUDO) 1:2—Address (1:1–2), pastoral epistle, pseudo-Pauline authorship, early second century

Theme	1 TIM	Paul
Letter to Timothy	**1:2 (Pseudo)** [2]Unto Timothy, my own son in the faith: Grace, mercy, and peace, from God our Father and Jesus Christ our Lord.	**2 Tim 1:2 (Pseudo)** [2]To Timothy, my dearly beloved son: Grace, mercy, and peace, from God the Father and Christ Jesus our Lord. **Tit 1:4 (Pseudo)** [4]To Titus, mine own son after the common faith: Grace, mercy, and peace, from God the Father and the Lord Jesus Christ our Saviour.

EFFECTIVE TEACHING (1:3–20)

I TIMOTHY (PSEUDO) 1:3—Effective Teaching (1:3–20), pastoral epistle, pseudo-Pauline authorship, early second century

Theme	1 TIM	Lk
Stay true to doctrine	**1:3 (Pseudo)** [3]As I besought thee to abide still at Ephesus, when I went into Macedonia, that thou mightest charge some that they teach no other doctrine,	**Acts 20:1** [1]And after the uproar was ceased, Paul called unto him the disciples, and embraced them, and departed for to go into Macedonia.

I TIMOTHY (PSEUDO) 1:4—Effective Teaching (1:3–20), pastoral epistle, pseudo-Pauline authorship, early second century

Theme	1 TIM	Paul	NT
Do not pay attention to myths & genealogies	**1:4 (Pseudo)** [4]Neither give heed to fables and endless genealogies, which minister questions, rather than godly edifying which is in faith: so do. **4:7 (Pseudo)** [7]But refuse profane and old wives' fables, and exercise thyself rather unto godliness.	**Tit 1:14 (Pseudo)** [14]Not giving heed to Jewish fables, and commandments of men, that turn from the truth. **Tit 3:2 (Pseudo)** [2]To speak evil of no man, to be no brawlers, but gentle, showing all meekness unto all men.	**2 Pet 1:16** [16]For we have not followed cunningly devised fables, when we made known unto you the power and coming of our Lord Jesus Christ, but were eyewitnesses of his majesty.

I TIMOTHY (PSEUDO) 1:5—Effective Teaching (1:3–20), pastoral epistle, pseudo-Pauline authorship, early second century

Theme	1 TIM	Paul
Charity out of a pure heart & conscience	**1:5 (Pseudo)** [5]Now the end of the commandment is charity out of a pure heart, and of a good conscience, and of faith unfeigned:	**Rom 13:10** [10]Love worketh no ill to his neighbour: therefore love is the fulfilling of the law.

I TIMOTHY (PSEUDO) 1:6—Effective Teaching (1:3–20), pastoral epistle, pseudo-Pauline authorship, early second century

Theme	1 TIM	Paul
Some became vain	**1:6 (Pseudo)** [6]From which some having swerved have turned aside unto vain jangling; **6:4, 20 (Pseudo)** [4]He is proud, knowing nothing, but doting about questions and strifes of words, whereof cometh envy, strife, railings, evil surmisings, . . . [20]O Timothy, keep that which is committed to thy trust, avoiding profane and vain babblings, and oppositions of science falsely so called:	**Tit 1:10 (Pseudo)** [10]For there are many unruly and vain talkers and deceivers, specially they of the circumcision:

I TIMOTHY (PSEUDO) 1:8—Effective Teaching (1:3–20), pastoral epistle, pseudo-Pauline authorship, early second century

Theme	1 TIM	Paul	Other
Law can be good	**1:8 (Pseudo)** [8]But we know that the law is good, if a man use it lawfully;	**Rom 7:12** [12]Wherefore the law is holy, and the commandment holy, and just, and good **Rom 7:16** [16]If then I do that which I would not, I consent unto the law that it is good.	**Q-Quelle** Concerning Law: Rom 7:12/1 Tim 1:8/[Mt 5:18], [Mt 11:12-13]/[Lk 16:16-17 (QS 56)]

I TIMOTHY (PSEUDO) 1:10—Effective Teaching (1:3–20), pastoral epistle, pseudo-Pauline authorship, early second century

Theme	1 TIM	Paul
Contrary doctrine	**1:10 (Pseudo)** [10]For whoremongers, for them that defile themselves with mankind, for menstealers, for liars, for perjured persons, and if there be any other thing that is contrary to sound doctrine; **4:6 (Pseudo)** [6]If thou put the brethren in remembrance of these things, thou shalt be a good minister of Jesus Christ, nourished up in the words of faith and of good doctrine, whereunto thou hast attained. **6:3 (Pseudo)** [3]If any man teach otherwise, and consent not to wholesome words, even the words of our Lord Jesus Christ, and to the doctrine which is according to godliness;	**2 Tim 4:3 (Pseudo)** [3]For the time will come when they will not endure sound doctrine; but after their own lusts shall they heap to themselves teachers, having itching ears; **Tit 1:9 (Pseudo)** [9]Holding fast the faithful word as he hath been taught, that he may be able by sound doctrine both to exhort and to convince the gainsayers. **Tit 2:1** [1]But speak thou the things which become sound doctrine:

I TIMOTHY (PSEUDO) 1:11—Effective Teaching (1:3–20), pastoral epistle, pseudo-Pauline authorship, early second century

Theme	1 TIM	Paul
Glorious gospel	**1:11 (Pseudo)** [11]According to the glorious gospel of the blessed God, which was committed to my trust.	**Tit 1:3 (Pseudo)** [3]But hath in due times manifested his word through preaching, which is committed unto me according to the commandment of God our Saviour;

I TIMOTHY (PSEUDO) 1:12—Effective Teaching (1:3–20), pastoral epistle, pseudo-Pauline authorship, early second century

Theme	1 TIM	Lk	Paul
Thanks for ministry	**1:12 (Pseudo)** [12]And I thank Christ Jesus our Lord, who hath enabled me, for that he counted me faithful, putting me into the ministry;	**Acts 9:15** [15]But the Lord said unto him, Go thy way: for he is a chosen vessel unto me, to bear my name before the Gentiles, and kings, and the children of Israel:	**Phil 4:13** [13]I can do all things through Christ which strengtheneth me. **Gal 1:13** [13]For ye have heard of my conversation in time past in the Jews' religion, how that beyond measure I persecuted the church of God, and wasted it:

I TIMOTHY (PSEUDO) 1:13—Effective Teaching (1:3–20), pastoral epistle, pseudo-Pauline authorship, early second century

Theme	1 TIM	Lk	Paul
Paul obtained mercy	**1:13 (Pseudo)** [13]Who was before a blasphemer, and a persecutor, and injurious: but I obtained mercy, because I did it ignorantly in unbelief.	**Acts 8:3** [3]As for Saul, he made havock of the church, entering into every house, and haling men and women committed them to prison. **Acts 9:1–2** [1]And Saul, yet breathing out threatenings and slaughter against the disciples of the Lord, went unto the high priest, [2]And desired of him letters to Damascus to the synagogues, that if he found any of this way, whether they were men or women, he might bring them bound unto Jerusalem	**1 Cor 15:9** [9]For I am the least of the apostles, that am not meet to be called an apostle, because I persecuted the church of God. **Gal 1:13** [13]For ye have heard of my conversation in time past in the Jews' religion, how that beyond measure I persecuted the church of God, and wasted it:

I TIMOTHY (PSEUDO) 1:14—Effective Teaching (1:3–20), pastoral epistle, pseudo-Pauline authorship, early second century

Theme	1 TIM	Paul
Grace is abundant	**1:14 (Pseudo)** [14]And the grace of our Lord was exceeding abundant with faith and love which is in Christ Jesus.	**Rom 5:20** [20]Moreover the law entered, that the offence might abound. But where sin abounded, grace did much more abound: **2 Tim 1:13 (Pseudo)** [13]Hold fast the form of sound words, which thou hast heard of me, in faith and love which is in Christ Jesus.

I TIMOTHY (PSEUDO) 1:15—Effective Teaching (1:3–20), pastoral epistle, pseudo-Pauline authorship, early second century

Theme	1 TIM	Lk
Jesus came to save sinners	**1:15 (Pseudo)** [15]This is a faithful saying, and worthy of all acceptation, that Christ Jesus came into the world to save sinners; of whom I am chief.	**15:2** [2]And the Pharisees and scribes murmured, saying, This man receiveth sinners, and eateth with them. **19:10** [10]For the Son of man is come to seek and to save that which was lost.

I TIMOTHY (PSEUDO) 1:17—Effective Teaching (1:3–20), pastoral epistle, pseudo-Pauline authorship, early second century

Theme	1 TIM	Paul
Doxology	**1:17 (Pseudo)** [17]Now unto the King eternal, immortal, invisible, the only wise God, be honour and glory for ever and ever. Amen.	**Rom 16:27** [27]To God only wise, be glory through Jesus Christ for ever. Amen.

I TIMOTHY (PSEUDO) 1:18—Effective Teaching (1:3–20), pastoral epistle, pseudo-Pauline authorship, early second century

Theme	1 TIM	Paul	NT
Charge to Timothy	**1:18 (Pseudo)** [18]This charge I commit unto thee, son Timothy, according to the prophecies which went before on thee, that thou by them mightest war a good warfare; **4:14 (Pseudo)** [14]Neglect not the gift that is in thee, which was given thee by prophecy, with the laying on of the hands of the presbytery. **6:12 (Pseudo)** [12]Fight the good fight of faith, lay hold on eternal life, whereunto thou art also called, and hast professed a good profession before many witnesses.	**2 Tim 4:7 (Pseudo)** [7]I have fought a good fight, I have finished my course, I have kept the faith:	**Jude 3** [3]Beloved, when I gave all diligence to write unto you of the common salvation, it was needful for me to write unto you, and exhort you that ye should earnestly contend for the faith which was once delivered unto the saints.

I TIMOTHY (PSEUDO) 1:19—Effective Teaching (1:3–20), pastoral epistle, pseudo-Pauline authorship, early second century

Theme	1 TIM
Faith & good conscience, some abused	**1:19 (Pseudo)** [19]Holding faith, and a good conscience; which some having put away concerning faith have made shipwreck: **3:9 (Pseudo)** [9]Holding the mystery of the faith in a pure conscience.

I TIMOTHY (PSEUDO) 1:20—Effective Teaching (1:3–20), pastoral epistle, pseudo-Pauline authorship, early second century

Theme	1 TIM	Paul	Other
Hymenaeus given to Satan	**1:20 (Pseudo)** [20]Of whom is Hymenaeus and Alexander; whom I have delivered unto Satan, that they may learn not to blaspheme.	**1 Cor 5:5** [5]To deliver such an one unto Satan for the destruction of the flesh, that the spirit may be saved in the day of the Lord Jesus. **2 Tim 2:17 (Pseudo)** [17]And their word will eat as doth a canker: of whom is Hymenaeus and Philetus; **2 Tim 4:14 (Pseudo)** [14]Alexander the coppersmith did me much evil: the Lord reward him according to his works:	**Q-Quelle** Forgiveness: 1 Tim 1:20/1 Cor 5:3-5/[Mt 18:15, 21-22]/ [Lk 17:3b-4 (QS 58)]

DISCIPLINE (2:1–4:16)

I TIMOTHY (PSEUDO) 2:1—Discipline (2:1–4:16), pastoral epistle, pseudo-Pauline authorship, early second century

Theme	1 TIM	Paul
Prayers, thanks for all	**2:1 (Pseudo)** [1]I exhort therefore, that, first of all, supplications, prayers, intercessions, and giving of thanks, be made for all men;	**Eph 6:18** [18]Praying always with all prayer and supplication in the Spirit, and watching thereunto with all perseverance and supplication for all saints; **Phil 4:6** [6]Be careful for nothing; but in every thing by prayer and supplication with thanksgiving let your requests be made known unto God.

I TIMOTHY (PSEUDO) 2:3—Discipline (2:1–4:16), pastoral epistle, pseudo-Pauline authorship, early second century

Theme	1 TIM
Good & acceptable to God	**2:3 (Pseudo)** [3]For this is good and acceptable in the sight of God our Saviour; **1:1 (Pseudo)** [1]Paul, an apostle of Jesus Christ by the commandment of God our Saviour, and Lord Jesus Christ, which is our hope; **4:10 (Pseudo)** [10]For therefore we both labour and suffer reproach, because we trust in the living God, who is the Saviour of all men, specially of those that believe.

I TIMOTHY (PSEUDO) 2:4—Discipline (2:1–4:16), pastoral epistle, pseudo-Pauline authorship, early second century

Theme	1 TIM	Paul	NT
God wills all saved	**2:4 (Pseudo)** [4]Who will have all men to be saved, and to come unto the knowledge of the truth.	**2 Tim 3:7 (Pseudo)** [7]Ever learning, and never able to come to the knowledge of the truth.	**2 Pet 3:9** [9]The Lord is not slack concerning his promise, as some men count slackness; but is longsuffering to us-ward, not willing that any should perish, but that all should come to repentance.

I TIMOTHY (PSEUDO) 2:5—Discipline (2:1–4:16), pastoral epistle, pseudo-Pauline authorship, early second century

Theme	1 TIM	Paul	NT
One God, one mediator between God & humanity	**2:5 (Pseudo)** [5]For there is one God, and one mediator between God and men, the man Christ Jesus;	**Rom 5:15** [15]But not as the offence, so also is the free gift. For if through the offence of one many be dead, much more the grace of God, and the gift by grace, which is by one man, Jesus Christ, hath abounded unto many. **1 Cor 8:6** [6]But to us there is but one God, the Father, of whom are all things, and we in him; and one Lord Jesus Christ, by whom are all things, and we by him.	**Heb 8:6** [6]But now hath he obtained a more excellent ministry, by how much also he is the mediator of a better covenant, which was established upon better promises. **Heb 9:15** [15]And for this cause he is the mediator of the new testament, that by means of death, for the redemption of the transgressions that were under the first testament, they which are called might receive the promise of eternal inheritance. **Heb 12:24** [24]And to Jesus the mediator of the new covenant, and to the blood of sprinkling, that speaketh better things than that of Abel.

I TIMOTHY (PSEUDO) 2:6—Discipline (2:1–4:16), pastoral epistle, pseudo-Pauline authorship, early second century

Theme	1 TIM	Mk	Paul	Other
God gave self as ransom for many	**2:6 (Pseudo)** [6]Who gave himself a ransom for all, to be testified in due time.	**10:45** [45]For even the Son of man came not to be ministered unto, but to minister, and to give his life a ransom for many.	**Gal 1:4** [4]Who gave himself for our sins, that he might deliver us from this present evil world, according to the will of God and our Father: **Gal 2:20** [20]I am crucified with Christ: nevertheless I live; yet not I, but Christ liveth in me: and the life which I now live in the flesh I live by the faith of the Son of God, who loved me, and gave himself for me. **Eph 5:25 (Pseudo)** [25]Husbands, love your wives, even as Christ also loved the church, and gave himself for it; **Tit 2:14 (Pseudo)** [14]Who gave himself for us, that he might redeem us from all iniquity, and purify unto himself a peculiar people, zealous of good works.	**Q-Quelle** Jesus' witness to John: 1 Tim 2:6/ Gal 1:3-4/[Mt 11:7-19, 21:31-32]/[Lk 7:24-35 (QS 18), Lk 16:16 (QS 56)]; Against Pharisees: 1 Tim 2:6/Gal 1:3-4/ [Mt 23:4-36]/ [Mk 7:1-9]/[Lk 11:37-54 (QS 34 [Thom 39:1, 89, 102])]

I TIMOTHY (PSEUDO) 2:7—Discipline (2:1–4:16), pastoral epistle, pseudo-Pauline authorship, early second century

Theme	1 TIM	Lk	Paul
Paul ordained apostle & preacher	**2:7 (Pseudo)** [7]Whereunto I am ordained a preacher, and an apostle, (I speak the truth in Christ, and lie not;) a teacher of the Gentiles in faith and verity.	**Acts 9:15** [15]But the Lord said unto him, Go thy way: for he is a chosen vessel unto me, to bear my name before the Gentiles, and kings, and the children of Israel:	**1 Cor 9:1** [1]Am I not an apostle? am I not free? have I not seen Jesus Christ our Lord? are not ye my work in the Lord? **Gal 2:7–8** [7]But contrariwise, when they saw that the gospel of the uncircumcision was committed unto me, as the gospel of the circumcision was unto Peter; [8](For he that wrought effectually in Peter to the apostleship of the circumcision, the same was mighty in me toward the Gentiles:)

I TIMOTHY (PSEUDO) 2:9—Discipline (2:1–4:16), pastoral epistle, pseudo-Pauline authorship, early second century

Theme	1 TIM	NT
Women be modest	**2:9 (Pseudo)** [9]In like manner also, that women adorn themselves in modest apparel, with shamefacedness and sobriety; not with broided hair, or gold, or pearls, or costly array;	**1 Pet 3:3–5** [3]Whose adorning let it not be that outward adorning of plaiting the hair, and of wearing of gold, or of putting on of apparel; [4]But let it be the hidden man of the heart, in that which is not corruptible, even the ornament of a meek and quiet spirit, which is in the sight of God of great price. [5]For after this manner in the old time the holy women also, who trusted in God, adorned themselves, being in subjection unto their own husbands:

I TIMOTHY (PSEUDO) 2:10—Discipline (2:1–4:16), pastoral epistle, pseudo-Pauline authorship, early second century

Theme	1 TIM	NT	Other
Women be godly	**2:10 (Pseudo)** [10]But (which becometh women professing godliness) with good works. **5:10 (Pseudo)** [10]Well reported of for good works; if she have brought up children, if she have lodged strangers, if she have washed the saints' feet, if she have relieved the afflicted, if she have diligently followed every good work.	**1 Pet 3:1** [1]Likewise, ye wives, be in subjection to your own husbands; that, if any obey not the word, they also may without the word be won by the conversation of the wives;	**1 ApocJas** "Nothing existed except Him-who-is. He is unnameable and ineffable. I myself am also unnameable, from Him-who-is, just as I have been given a number of names—two from Him-who-is. And I, I am before you. Since you have asked concerning femaleness, femaleness existed, but femaleness was not first. And it prepared for itself powers and gods. But it did not exist when I came forth, since I am an image of Him-who-is . . . And these she produced as she brought down the race from the Pre-existent One. So then they are not alien, but they are ours. They are indeed ours because she who is mistress of them is from the Pre-existent One. At the same time they are alien because the Pre-existent One did not have intercourse with her, when she produced them.' . . . But I shall call upon the imperishable knowledge, which is Sophia who is in the Father (and) who is the mother of Achamoth. Achamoth had no father nor male consort, but she is female from a female. She produced you without a male, since she was alone (and) in ignorance as to what lives through her mother because she thought that she alone existed. But I shall cry out to her mother. And then they will fall into confusion (and) will blame their root and the race of their mother. But you will go up to what is yours [. . .] you will [. . .] the Pre-existent One." . . . "They are a type of the twelve disciples and the twelve pairs, [. . .] Achamoth, which is translated 'Sophia'. And who I myself am, (and) who the imperishable Sophia (is) through whom you will be redeemed, and (who are) all the sons of Him-who-is - these things they have known and have hidden within them. You are to hide <these things> within you, and you are to keep silence . . . James said, "I am satisfied [. . .] and they are [. . .] my soul. Yet another thing I ask of you: who are the seven women who have been your disciples? And behold all women bless you. I also am amazed how powerless vessels have become strong by a perception which is in them." The Lord said, "You [. . .] well [. . .] a spirit of [. . .], a spirit of thought, a spirit of counsel of a [. . .], a spirit [. . .] a spirit of knowledge [. . .] of their fear. [. . .] when we had passed through the breath of this archon who is named Adonaios [. . .] him and [. . .] he was ignorant [. . .] when I came forth from him, he remembered that I am a son of his. . . . When you speak these words of this perception, encourage these four: Salome and Mariam and Martha and Arsinoe [. . .] since he takes some [. . .] to me he is [. . .] burnt offerings and [. . .]. But I [. . .] not in this way; but [. . .] first-fruits of the [. . .] upward [. . .] so that the power of God might appear. The perishable has gone up to the imperishable and the female element has attained to this male element." James said, "Rabbi, into these three (things), then, has their [. . .] been cast. For they have been reviled, and they have been persecuted [. . .]. Behold [. . .] everything [. . .] from anyone [. . .]. For you have received [. . .] of knowledge. And [. . .] that what is the [. . .] go [. . .] you will find [. . .]. But I shall go forth and shall reveal that they believed in you, that they may be content with their blessing and salvation, and this revelation may come to pass."

I TIMOTHY (PSEUDO) 2:11–12—Discipline (2:1–4:16), pastoral epistle, pseudo-Pauline authorship, early second century

Theme	1 TIM	Paul
Advice for women	**2:11–12 (Pseudo)** [11]Let the woman learn in silence with all subjection. [12]But I suffer not a woman to teach, nor to usurp authority over the man, but to be in silence.	**1 Cor 14:34–35** [34]Let your women keep silence in the churches: for it is not permitted unto them to speak; but they are commanded to be under obedience, as also saith the law. [35]And if they will learn any thing, let them ask their husbands at home: for it is a shame for women to speak in the church.

I TIMOTHY (PSEUDO) 2:13—Discipline (2:1–4:16), pastoral epistle, pseudo-Pauline authorship, early second century

Theme	1 TIM	Paul	Jewish Writings
Adam's primacy	**2:13 (Pseudo)** [13]For Adam was first formed, then Eve.	**1 Cor 11:8–9** [8]For the man is not of the woman; but the woman of the man. [9]Neither was the man created for the woman; but the woman for the man.	**Gen 1:27** [27]So God created man in his own image, in the image of God created he him; male and female created he them. **Gen 2:7, 22** [7]And the LORD God formed man of the dust of the ground, and breathed into his nostrils the breath of life; and man became a living soul. . . . [22]And the rib, which the LORD God had taken from man, made he a woman, and brought her unto the man.

I TIMOTHY (PSEUDO) 2:14—Discipline (2:1–4:16), pastoral epistle, pseudo-Pauline authorship, early second century

Theme	1 TIM	Paul	Jewish Writings
Adam's lack of deception	**2:14 (Pseudo)** [14]And Adam was not deceived, but the woman being deceived was in the transgression.	**2 Cor 11:3** [3]But I fear, lest by any means, as the serpent beguiled Eve through his subtlety, so your minds should be corrupted from the simplicity that is in Christ.	**Gen 3:6, 13** [6]And when the woman saw that the tree was good for food, and that it was pleasant to the eyes, and a tree to be desired to make one wise, she took of the fruit thereof, and did eat, and gave also unto her husband with her; and he did eat. . . . [13]And the LORD God said unto the woman, What is this that thou hast done? And the woman said, The serpent beguiled me, and I did eat.

I TIMOTHY (PSEUDO) 2:15—Discipline (2:1–4:16), pastoral epistle, pseudo-Pauline authorship, early second century

Theme	1 TIM	Other
Childbearing	**2:15 (Pseudo)** [15]Notwithstanding she shall be saved in childbearing, if they continue in faith and charity and holiness with sobriety. **5:14 (Pseudo)** [14]I will therefore that the younger women marry, bear children, guide the house, give none occasion to the adversary to speak reproachfully.	**1 ApocJas** "Nothing existed except Him-who-is. He is unnameable and ineffable. I myself am also unnameable, from Him-who-is, just as I have been given a number of names - two from Him-who-is. And I, I am before you. Since you have asked concerning femaleness, femaleness existed, but femaleness was not first. And it prepared for itself powers and gods. But it did not exist when I came forth, since I am an image of Him-who-is . . . And these she produced as she brought down the race from the Pre-existent One. So then they are not alien, but they are ours. They are indeed ours because she who is mistress of them is from the Pre-existent One. At the same time they are alien because the Pre-existent One did not have intercourse with her, when she produced them.' . . . But I shall call upon the imperishable knowledge, which is Sophia who is in the Father (and) who is the mother of Achamoth. Achamoth had no father nor male consort, but she is female from a female. She produced you without a male, since she was alone (and) in ignorance as to what lives through her mother because she thought that she alone existed. But I shall cry out to her mother. And then they will fall into confusion (and) will blame their root and the race of their mother. But you will go up to what is yours [. . .] you will [. . .] the Pre-existent One." . . . "They are a type of the twelve disciples and the twelve pairs, [. . .] Achamoth, which is translated 'Sophia'. And who I myself am, (and) who the imperishable Sophia (is) through whom you will be redeemed, and (who are) all the sons of Him-who-is - these things they have known and have hidden within them. You are to hide <these things> within you, and you are to keep silence . . . James said, "I am satisfied [. . .] and they are [. . .] my soul. Yet another thing I ask of you: who are the seven women who have been your disciples? And behold all women bless you. I also am amazed how powerless vessels have become strong by a perception which is in them." The Lord said, "You [. . .] well [. . .] a spirit of [. . .], a spirit of thought, a spirit of counsel of a [. . .], a spirit [. . .] a spirit of knowledge [. . .] of their fear. [. . .] when we had passed through the breath of this archon who is named Adonaios [. . .] him and [. . .] he was ignorant [. . .] when I came forth from him, he remembered that I am a son of his. . . . When you speak these words of this perception, encourage these four: Salome and Mariam and Martha and Arsinoe [. . .] since he takes some [. . .] to me he is [. . .] burnt offerings and [. . .]. But I [. . .] not in this way; but [. . .] first-fruits of the [. . .] upward [. . .] so that the power of God might appear. The perishable has gone up to the imperishable and the female element has attained to this male element." James said, "Rabbi, into these three (things), then, has their [. . .] been cast. For they have been reviled, and they have been persecuted [. . .]. Behold [. . .] everything [. . .] from anyone [. . .]. For you have received [. . .] of knowledge. And [. . .] that what is the [. . .] go [. . .] you will find [. . .]. But I shall go forth and shall reveal that they believed in you, that they may be content with their blessing and salvation, and this revelation may come to pass."

I TIMOTHY (PSEUDO) 3:1–7—Discipline (2:1–4:16), pastoral epistle, pseudo-Pauline authorship, early second century

Theme	1 TIM	Paul
Character for bishops	**3:1–7 (Pseudo)** [1]This is a true saying, If a man desire the office of a bishop, he desireth a good work. [2]A bishop then must be blameless, the husband of one wife, vigilant, sober, of good behaviour, given to hospitality, apt to teach; [3]Not given to wine, no striker, not greedy of filthy lucre; but patient, not a brawler, not covetous; [4]One that ruleth well his own house, having his children in subjection with all gravity; [5](For if a man know not how to rule his own house, how shall he take care of the church of God?) [6]Not a novice, lest being lifted up with pride he fall into the condemnation of the devil. [7]Moreover he must have a good report of them which are without; lest he fall into reproach and the snare of the devil.	**Tit 1:6–9 (Pseudo)** [6]If any be blameless, the husband of one wife, having faithful children not accused of riot or unruly. [7]For a bishop must be blameless, as the steward of God; not selfwilled, not soon angry, not given to wine, no striker, not given to filthy lucre; [8]But a lover of hospitality, a lover of good men, sober, just, holy, temperate; [9]Holding fast the faithful word as he hath been taught, that he may be able by sound doctrine both to exhort and to convince the gainsayers.

I TIMOTHY (PSEUDO) 3:3—Discipline (2:1–4:16), pastoral epistle, pseudo-Pauline authorship, early second century

Theme	1 TIM	NT
Character for bishops	**3:3 (Pseudo)** [3]Not given to wine, no striker, not greedy of filthy lucre; but patient, not a brawler, not covetous;	**Heb 13:5** [5]Let your conversation be without covetousness; and be content with such things as ye have: for he hath said, I will never leave thee, nor forsake thee.

I TIMOTHY (PSEUDO) 3:7—Discipline (2:1–4:16), pastoral epistle, pseudo-Pauline authorship, early second century

Theme	1 TIM	Paul
Good reputation	**3:7 (Pseudo)** [7]Moreover he must have a good report of them which are without; lest he fall into reproach and the snare of the devil.	**2 Cor 8:21** [21]Providing for honest things, not only in the sight of the Lord, but also in the sight of men. **2 Tim 2:26 (Pseudo)** [26]And that they may recover themselves out of the snare of the devil, who are taken captive by him at his will.

I TIMOTHY (PSEUDO) 3:11—Discipline (2:1–4:16), pastoral epistle, pseudo-Pauline authorship, early second century

Theme	1 TIM	Paul
Bishop's wives	**3:11 (Pseudo)** [11]Even so must their wives be grave, not slanderers, sober, faithful in all things.	**Tit 2:3 (Pseudo)** [3]The aged women likewise, that they be in behaviour as becometh holiness, not false accusers, not given to much wine, teachers of good things;

I TIMOTHY (PSEUDO) 3:15—Discipline (2:1–4:16), pastoral epistle, pseudo-Pauline authorship, early second century

Theme	1 TIM	Paul
Church of living God	**3:15 (Pseudo)** [15]But if I tarry long, that thou mayest know how thou oughtest to behave thyself in the house of God, which is the church of the living God, the pillar and ground of the truth.	**Eph 2:19–22 (Pseudo)** [19]Now therefore ye are no more strangers and foreigners, but fellowcitizens with the saints, and of the household of God; [20]And are built upon the foundation of the apostles and prophets, Jesus Christ himself being the chief corner stone; [21]In whom all the building fitly framed together groweth unto an holy temple in the Lord: [22]In whom ye also are builded together for an habitation of God through the Spirit.

I TIMOTHY (PSEUDO) 3:16—Discipline (2:1–4:16), pastoral epistle, pseudo-Pauline authorship, early second century

Theme	1 TIM	Jn	Paul
Mystery of godliness	**3:16 (Pseudo)** [16]And without controversy great is the mystery of godliness: God was manifest in the flesh, justified in the Spirit, seen of angels, preached unto the Gentiles, believed on in the world, received up into glory.	**1:14** [14]And the Word was made flesh, and dwelt among us, (and we beheld his glory, the glory as of the only begotten of the Father,) full of grace and truth.	**Rom 1:3–4** [3]Concerning his Son Jesus Christ our Lord, which was made of the seed of David according to the flesh; [4]And declared to be the Son of God with power, according to the spirit of holiness, by the resurrection from the dead:

I TIMOTHY (PSEUDO) 4:1—Discipline (2:1–4:16), pastoral epistle, pseudo-Pauline authorship, early second century

Theme	1 TIM	Paul	NT
Some will be given to seductive spirits	**4:1 (Pseudo)** [1]Now the Spirit speaketh expressly, that in the latter times some shall depart from the faith, giving heed to seducing spirits, and doctrines of devils;	**2 Tim 3:1 (Pseudo)** [1]This know also, that in the last days perilous times shall come. **2 Tim 4:3 (Pseudo)** [3]For the time will come when they will not endure sound doctrine; but after their own lusts shall they heap to themselves teachers, having itching ears;	**2 Pet 3:3** [3]Knowing this first, that there shall come in the last days scoffers, walking after their own lusts, **Jude 18** [18]How that they told you there should be mockers in the last time, who should walk after their own ungodly lusts.

I TIMOTHY (PSEUDO) 4:3—Discipline (2:1–4:16), pastoral epistle, pseudo-Pauline authorship, early second century

Theme	1 TIM	Paul	Jewish Writings
False doctrines	**4:3 (Pseudo)** [3]Forbidding to marry, and commanding to abstain from meats, which God hath created to be received with thanksgiving of them which believe and know the truth.	**Rom 14:6** [6]He that regardeth the day, regardeth it unto the Lord; and he that regardeth not the day, to the Lord he doth not regard it. He that eateth, eateth to the Lord, for he giveth God thanks; and he that eateth not, to the Lord he eateth not, and giveth God thanks. **1 Cor 10:30–31** [30]For if I by grace be a partaker, why am I evil spoken of for that for which I give thanks? [31]Whether therefore ye eat, or drink, or whatsoever ye do, do all to the glory of God.	**Gen 9:3** [3]Every moving thing that liveth shall be meat for you; even as the green herb have I given you all things.

I TIMOTHY (PSEUDO) 4:4—Discipline (2:1–4:16), pastoral epistle, pseudo-Pauline authorship, early second century

Theme	1 TIM	Lk	Jewish Writings
God's creation is good	**4:4 (Pseudo)** [4]For every creature of God is good, and nothing to be refused, if it be received with thanksgiving:	**Acts 10:15** [15]And the voice spake unto him again the second time, What God hath cleansed, that call not thou common.	**Gen 1:31** [31]And God saw every thing that he had made, and, behold, it was very good. And the evening and the morning were the sixth day.

I TIMOTHY (PSEUDO) 4:7—Discipline (2:1–4:16), pastoral epistle, pseudo-Pauline authorship, early second century

Theme	1 TIM	Paul
Refuse profane	**4:7 (Pseudo)** [7]But refuse profane and old wives' fables, and exercise thyself rather unto godliness. **1:4 (Pseudo)** [4]Neither give heed to fables and endless genealogies, which minister questions, rather than godly edifying which is in faith: so do.	**2 Tim 2:16 (Pseudo)** [16]But shun profane and vain babblings: for they will increase unto more ungodliness. **Tit 1:14** [4]To Titus, mine own son after the common faith: Grace, mercy, and peace, from God the Father and the Lord Jesus Christ our Saviour.

I TIMOTHY (PSEUDO) 4:8—Discipline (2:1–4:16), pastoral epistle, pseudo-Pauline authorship, early second century

Theme	1 TIM
Godliness profits much	**4:8 (Pseudo)** [8]For bodily exercise profiteth little: but godliness is profitable unto all things, having promise of the life that now is, and of that which is to come. **6:6 (Pseudo)** [6]But godliness with contentment is great gain.

I TIMOTHY (PSEUDO) 4:9—Discipline (2:1–4:16), pastoral epistle, pseudo-Pauline authorship, early second century

Theme	1 TIM	Paul
Godliness is worthwhile	**4:9 (Pseudo)** [9]This is a faithful saying and worthy of all acceptation. **1:15 (Pseudo)** [15]This is a faithful saying, and worthy of all acceptation, that Christ Jesus came into the world to save sinners; of whom I am chief.	**2 Tim 2:11 (Pseudo)** [11]It is a faithful saying: For if we be dead with him, we shall also live with him: **Tit 3:8 (Pseudo)** [8]This is a faithful saying, and these things I will that thou affirm constantly, that they which have believed in God might be careful to maintain good works. These things are good and profitable unto men.

I TIMOTHY (PSEUDO) 4:10—Discipline (2:1–4:16), pastoral epistle, pseudo-Pauline authorship, early second century

Theme	1 TIM	Paul
Labor & suffer for God	**4:10 (Pseudo)** [10]For therefore we both labour and suffer reproach, because we trust in the living God, who is the Saviour of all men, specially of those that believe. **2:4 (Pseudo)** [4]Who will have all men to be saved, and to come unto the knowledge of the truth.	**Tit 2:11 (Pseudo)** [11]For the grace of God that bringeth salvation hath appeared to all men,

I TIMOTHY (PSEUDO) 4:12—Discipline (2:1–4:16), pastoral epistle, pseudo-Pauline authorship, early second century

Theme	1 TIM	Paul
Be an example even in youth	**4:12 (Pseudo)** [12]Let no man despise thy youth; but be thou an example of the believers, in word, in conversation, in charity, in spirit, in faith, in purity.	**1 Cor 16:11** [11]Let no man therefore despise him: but conduct him forth in peace, that he may come unto me: for I look for him with the brethren. **Phil 3:17** [17]Brethren, be followers together of me, and mark them which walk so as ye have us for an ensample. **Tit 2:15 (Pseudo)** [15]These things speak, and exhort, and rebuke with all authority. Let no man despise thee.

I TIMOTHY (PSEUDO) 4:14—Discipline (2:1–4:16), pastoral epistle, pseudo-Pauline authorship, early second century

Theme	1 TIM	Lk	Paul
Received gifts by prophesy & laying on of hands	**4:14 (Pseudo)** [14]Neglect not the gift that is in thee, which was given thee by prophecy, with the laying on of the hands of the presbytery. **5:22 (Pseudo)** [22]Lay hands suddenly on no man, neither be partaker of other men's sins: keep thyself pure.	**Acts 6:6** [6]Whom they set before the apostles: and when they had prayed, they laid their hands on them. **Acts 8:17** [17]Then laid they their hands on them, and they received the Holy Ghost.	**2 Tim 1:6 (Pseudo)** [6]Wherefore I put thee in remembrance that thou stir up the gift of God, which is in thee by the putting on of my hands.

DUTIES TO OTHER CHRISTIANS (5:1–6:2)

I TIMOTHY (PSEUDO) 5:1—Duties to Christians (5:1–6:2), pastoral epistle, pseudo-Pauline authorship, early second century

Theme	1 TIM	Paul	Jewish Writings
Do not rebuke elders	**5:1 (Pseudo)** [1]Rebuke not an elder, but entreat him as a father; and the younger men as brethren;	**Tit 2:2 (Pseudo)** [2]That the aged men be sober, grave, temperate, sound in faith, in charity, in patience.	**Lev 19:32** [32]Thou shalt rise up before the hoary head, and honour the face of the old man, and fear thy God: I am the LORD.

I TIMOTHY (PSEUDO) 5:5—Duties to Christians (5:1–6:2), pastoral epistle, pseudo-Pauline authorship, early second century

Theme	1 TIM	Lk	Jewish Writings
Widows pray	**5:5 (Pseudo)** [5]Now she that is a widow indeed, and desolate, trusteth in God, and continueth in supplications and prayers night and day.	**2:37** [37]And she was a widow of about fourscore and four years, which departed not from the temple, but served God with fastings and prayers night and day. **18:7** [7]And shall not God avenge his own elect, which cry day and night unto him, though he bear long with them?	**Jer 49:11** [11]Leave thy fatherless children, I will preserve them alive; and let thy widows trust in me.

I TIMOTHY (PSEUDO) 5:10—Duties to Christians (5:1–6:2), pastoral epistle, pseudo-Pauline authorship, early second century

Theme	1 TIM	Jn	NT
Widow's rapport	**5:10 (Pseudo)** [10]Well reported of for good works; if she have brought up children, if she have lodged strangers, if she have washed the saints' feet, if she have relieved the afflicted, if she have diligently followed every good work.	**13:14** [14]If I then, your Lord and Master, have washed your feet; ye also ought to wash one another's feet.	**Heb 13:2** [2]Be not forgetful to entertain strangers: for thereby some have entertained angels unawares.

I TIMOTHY (PSEUDO) 5:13—Duties to Christians (5:1–6:2), pastoral epistle, pseudo-Pauline authorship, early second century

Theme	1 TIM	Paul
Do not be idle	**5:13 (Pseudo)** [13]And withal they learn to be idle, wandering about from house to house; and not only idle, but tattlers also and busybodies, speaking things which they ought not.	**2 Thes 3:11** [11]For we hear that there are some which walk among you disorderly, working not at all, but are busybodies.

I TIMOTHY (PSEUDO) 5:14—Duties to Christians (5:1–6:2), pastoral epistle, pseudo-Pauline authorship, early second century

Theme	1 TIM	Paul
Young women marry	**5:14 (Pseudo)** [14]I will therefore that the younger women marry, bear children, guide the house, give none occasion to the adversary to speak reproachfully. **5:22 (Pseudo)** [22]Lay hands suddenly on no man, neither be partaker of other men's sins: keep thyself pure.	**1 Cor 7:9** [9]But if they cannot contain, let them marry: for it is better to marry than to burn.

I TIMOTHY (PSEUDO) 5:17—Duties to Christians (5:1–6:2), pastoral epistle, pseudo-Pauline authorship, early second century

Theme	1 TIM	Paul
Honor elders	**5:17 (Pseudo)** [17]Let the elders that rule well be counted worthy of double honour, especially they who labour in the word and doctrine.	**1 Cor 16:18** [18]For they have refreshed my spirit and yours: therefore acknowledge ye them that are such. **Phil 2:29** [29]Receive him therefore in the Lord with all gladness; and hold such in reputation:

I TIMOTHY (PSEUDO) 5:18—Duties to Christians (5:1–6:2), pastoral epistle, pseudo-Pauline authorship, early second century

Theme	1 TIM	Mt	Mk	Lk
Compen-sation	**5:18 (Pseudo)** [18]For the scripture saith, Thou shalt not muzzle the ox that treadeth out the corn. And, The labourer is worthy of his reward.	**4:17** [17]From that time Jesus began to preach, and to say, Repent: for the kingdom of heaven is at hand. **10:5–15** [5]These twelve Jesus sent forth, and commanded them, saying, Go not into the way of the Gentiles, and into any city of the Samaritans enter ye not: [6]But go rather to the lost sheep of the house of Israel. [7]And as ye go, preach, saying, The kingdom of heaven is at hand. [8]Heal the sick, cleanse the lepers, raise the dead, cast out devils: freely ye have received, freely give. [9]Provide neither gold, nor silver, nor brass in your purses, [10]**Nor scrip for your journey, neither two coats, neither shoes, nor yet staves: for the work-man is worthy of his meat.** [11]And into whatsoever city or town ye shall enter, inquire who in it is worthy; and there abide till ye go thence. [12]And when ye come into an house, salute it. [13]And if the house be worthy, let your peace come upon it: but if it be not worthy, let your peace return to you. [14]And whosoever shall not receive you, nor hear your words, when ye depart out of that house or city, shake off the dust of your feet. [15]Verily I say unto you, It shall be more tolerable for the land of Sodom and Gomorrha in the day of judgment, than for that city. **15:24** [24]But he answered and said, I am not sent but unto the lost sheep of the house of Israel.	**1:15** [15]And saying, The time is fulfilled, and the kingdom of God is at hand: repent ye, and believe the gospel. **6:7–13** [7]And he called unto him the twelve, and began to send them forth by two and two; and gave them power over unclean spirits; [8]And commanded them that they should take nothing for their journey, save a staff only; no scrip, no bread, no money in their purse: [9]But be shod with sandals; and not put on two coats. [10]And he said unto them, In what place soever ye enter into an house, there abide till ye depart from that place. [11]And who-soever shall not receive you, nor hear you, when ye depart thence, shake off the dust under your feet for a testimony against them. Verily I say unto you, It shall be more tolerable for Sodom and Gomorrha in the day of judgment, than for that city. [12]And they went out, and preached that men should repent. [13]And they cast out many devils, and anointed with oil many that were sick, and healed them.	**9:1–6** [1]Then he called his twelve disciples together, and gave them power and authority over all devils, and to cure diseases. [2]And he sent them to preach the kingdom of God, and to heal the sick. [3]And he said unto them, Take nothing for your journey, neither staves, nor scrip, neither bread, neither money; neither have two coats apiece. [4]And whatsoever house ye enter into, there abide, and thence depart. [5]And whosoever will not receive you, when ye go out of that city, shake off the very dust from your feet for a testimony against them. [6]And they departed, and went through the towns, preaching the gospel, and healing every where. **10:1–16** [1]After these things the Lord appointed other seventy also, and sent them two and two before his face into every city and place, whither he himself would come. [2]Therefore said he unto them, The harvest truly is great, but the labourers are few: pray ye therefore the Lord of the harvest, that he would send forth labourers into his harvest. [3]Go your ways: behold, I send you forth as lambs among wolves. [4]Carry neither purse, nor scrip, nor shoes: and salute no man by the way. [5]And into whatsoever house ye enter, first say, Peace be to this house. [6]And if the son of peace be there, your peace shall rest upon it: if not, it shall turn to you again. [7]**And in the same house remain, eating and drinking such things as they give: for the labourer is worthy of his hire. Go not from house to house.** [8]And into whatsoever city ye enter, and they receive you, eat such things as are set before you: [9]And heal the sick that are therein, and say unto them, The kingdom of God is come nigh unto you. [10]But into whatsoever city ye enter, and they receive you not, go your ways out into the streets of the same, and say, [11]Even the very dust of your city, which cleaveth on us, we do wipe off against you: notwithstanding be ye sure of this, that the kingdom of God is come nigh unto you. [12]But I say unto you, that it shall be more tolerable in that day for Sodom, than for that city. [13]Woe unto thee, Chorazin! woe unto thee, Bethsaida! for if the mighty works had been done in Tyre and Sidon, which have been done in you, they had a great while ago repented, sitting in sackcloth and ashes. [14]But it shall be more tolerable for Tyre and Sidon at the judgment, than for you. [15]And thou, Capernaum, which art exalted to heaven, shalt be thrust down to hell. [16]He that heareth you heareth me; and he that despiseth you despiseth me; and he that despiseth me despiseth him that sent me. **22:35–36** [35]And he said unto them, When I sent you without purse, and scrip, and shoes, lacked ye any thing? And they said, Nothing. [36]Then said he unto them, But now, he that hath a purse, let him take it, and likewise his scrip: and he that hath no sword, let him sell his garment, and buy one.

Paul	Jewish	Other
1 Cor 9:8 [8]Say I these things as a man? or saith not the law the same also? **1 Cor 9:14** [14]Even so hath the Lord ordained that they which preach the gospel should live of the gospel.	**Dt 25:4** [4]Thou shalt not muzzle the ox when he treadeth out the corn.	**Did 13:1** But every true prophet who wants to live among you is worthy of his support. So also a true teacher is himself worthy, as the workman, of his support. Every first-fruit, therefore, of the products of wine-press and threshing-floor, of oxen and of sheep, you shall take and give to the prophets, for they are your high priests. But if you have no prophet, give it to the poor. If you make a batch of dough, take the first-fruit and give according to the commandment. So also when you open a jar of wine or of oil, take the first-fruit and give it to the prophets; and of money (silver) and clothing and every possession, take the first-fruit, as it may seem good to you, and give according to the commandment. **Q-Quelle** Commissioning of 12: 1 Tim 5:18/1 Cor 9:14/[Mt 10:1], Mt 10:7-11, 14/Mk 6:6b-13/Lk 9:1-6, [Lk 9:57-62 (QS 19 [Thom 86])]; Commissioning of 70: 1 Tim 5:18/1 Cor 9:14/[Mt 9:37-38], Mt 10:7-16/Lk 10:1-12(QS 20 [Thom 14:2, 73]); Whoever hears you hears me: 1 Tim 5:18/1 Cor 9:14/[Mt 10:40]/Lk 10:16 (QS 23)]

I TIMOTHY (PSEUDO) 5:19—Duties to Christians (5:1–6:2), pastoral epistle, pseudo-Pauline authorship, early second century

Theme	1 TIM	Mt	Paul	Jewish Writings
Do not accuse elder	**5:19 (Pseudo)** [19]Against an elder receive not an accusation, but before two or three witnesses.	**18:16** [16]But if he will not hear thee, then take with thee one or two more, that in the mouth of two or three witnesses every word may be established.	**2 Cor 13:1** [1]This is the third time I am coming to you. In the mouth of two or three witnesses shall every word be established.	**Dt 17:6** [6]At the mouth of two witnesses, or three witnesses, shall he that is worthy of death be put to death; but at the mouth of one witness he shall not be put to death. **Dt 19:15** [15]One witness shall not rise up against a man for any iniquity, or for any sin, in any sin that he sinneth: at the mouth of two witnesses, or at the mouth of three witnesses, shall the matter be established.

I TIMOTHY (PSEUDO) 5:20—Duties to Christians (5:1–6:2), pastoral epistle, pseudo-Pauline authorship, early second century

Theme	1 TIM	Paul
Give deserved rebuke publicly	**5:20 (Pseudo)** [20]Them that sin rebuke before all, that others also may fear.	**Gal 2:14** [14]But when I saw that they walked not uprightly according to the truth of the gospel, I said unto Peter before them all, If thou, being a Jew, livest after the manner of Gentiles, and not as do the Jews, why compellest thou the Gentiles to live as do the Jews? **Eph 5:11 (Pseudo)** [11]And have no fellowship with the unfruitful works of darkness, but rather reprove them. **2 Tim 4:2 (Pseudo)** [2]Preach the word; be instant in season, out of season; reprove, rebuke, exhort with all longsuffering and doctrine. **Tit 1:9, 13 (Pseudo)** [9]Holding fast the faithful word as he hath been taught, that he may be able by sound doctrine both to exhort and to convince the gainsayers. . . . [13]This witness is true. Wherefore rebuke them sharply, that they may be sound in the faith;

I TIMOTHY (PSEUDO) 5:22—Duties to Christians (5:1–6:2), pastoral epistle, pseudo-Pauline authorship, early second century

Theme	1 TIM	NT
Be careful to chose leaders	**5:22 (Pseudo)** [22]Lay hands suddenly on no man, neither be partaker of other men's sins: keep thyself pure. **4:14 (Pseudo)** [14]Neglect not the gift that is in thee, which was given thee by prophecy, with the laying on of the hands of the presbytery.	**2 Tim 1:6 (Pseudo)** [6]Wherefore I put thee in remembrance that thou stir up the gift of God, which is in thee by the putting on of my hands.

1 TIMOTHY (PSEUDO) 5:23—Duties to Christians (5:1–6:2), pastoral epistle, pseudo-Pauline authorship, early second century

Theme	1 TIM	Mt	Mk	Lk	Jn	Paul	NT
Drink wine	**5:23 (Pseudo)** [23]Drink no longer water, but use a little wine for thy stomach's sake and thine often infirmities.	**5:13–17** [13]Ye are the salt of the earth: but if the salt have lost his savour, wherewith shall it be salted? it is thenceforth good for nothing, but to be cast out, and to be trodden under foot of men. [14]Ye are the light of the world. A city that is set on an hill cannot be hid. [15]Neither do men light a candle, and put it under a bushel, but on a candlestick; and it giveth light unto all that are in the house. [16]Let your light so shine before men, that they may see your good works, and glorify your Father which is in heaven. [17]Think not that I am come to destroy the law, or the prophets: I am not come to destroy, but to fulfil.	**4:4** [4]And it came to pass, as he sowed, some fell by the way side, and the fowls of the air came and devoured it up. **4:21** [21]And he said unto them, Is a candle brought to be put under a bushel, or under a bed? and not to be set on a candlestick? **9:49–50** [49]For every one shall be salted with fire, and every sacrifice shall be salted with salt. [50]Salt is good: but if the salt have lost his saltness, wherewith will ye season it? Have salt in yourselves, and have peace one with another. **14:34–35** [34]And saith unto them, My soul is exceeding sorrowful unto death: tarry ye here, and watch. [35]And he went forward a little, and fell on the ground, and prayed that, if it were possible, the hour might pass from him.	**8:16** [16]No man, when he hath lighted a candle, covereth it with a vessel, or putteth it under a bed; but setteth it on a candlestick, that they which enter in may see the light. **11:33** [33]No man, when he hath lighted a candle, putteth it in a secret place, neither under a bushel, but on a candlestick, that they which come in may see the light.	**8:12** [12]Then spake Jesus again unto them, saying, I am the light of the world: he that followeth me shall not walk in darkness, but shall have the light of life.	**Col 4:5–6** [5]Walk in wisdom toward them that are without, redeeming the time. [6]Let your speech be alway with grace, seasoned with salt, that ye may know how ye ought to answer every man.	**1 Pet 2:9** [9]But ye are a chosen generation, a royal priesthood, an holy nation, a peculiar people; that ye should show forth the praises of him who hath called you out of darkness into his marvellous light: **1 Pet 2:12** [12]Having your conversation honest among the Gentiles: that, whereas they speak against you as evildoers, they may by your good works, which they shall behold, glorify God in the day of visitation.

I TIMOTHY (PSEUDO) 6:1—Duties to Christians (5:1–6:2), pastoral epistle, pseudo-Pauline authorship, early second century

Theme	1 TIM	Paul
Honor masters	**6:1 (Pseudo)** 1Let as many servants as are under the yoke count their own masters worthy of all honour, that the name of God and his doctrine be not blasphemed.	**Eph 6:5 (Pseudo)** 5Servants, be obedient to them that are your masters according to the flesh, with fear and trembling, in singleness of your heart, as unto Christ; **Tit 2:9–10 (Pseudo)** 9Exhort servants to be obedient unto their own masters, and to please them well in all things; not answering again; 10Not purloining, but showing all good fidelity; that they may adorn the doctrine of God our Saviour in all things.

TEACHING ON KINGDOM RICHES (6:2–19)

I TIMOTHY (PSEUDO) 6:2—Teaching on kingdom of riches (6:2–19), 63–67 CE

Theme	1 TIM	Paul
Persuade masters to faith	**6:2 (Pseudo)** 2And they that have believing masters, let them not despise them, because they are brethren; but rather do them service, because they are faithful and beloved, partakers of the benefit. These things teach and exhort.	**Phlm 16** 16Not now as a servant, but above a servant, a brother beloved, specially to me, but how much more unto thee, both in the flesh, and in the Lord?

I TIMOTHY (PSEUDO) 6:3—Teaching on kingdom of riches (6:2–19), 63–67 CE

Theme	1 TIM	Paul
Use wholesome words	**6:3 (Pseudo)** 3If any man teach otherwise, and consent not to wholesome words, even the words of our Lord Jesus Christ, and to the doctrine which is according to godliness;	**Gal 1:6–9** 6I marvel that ye are so soon removed from him that called you into the grace of Christ unto another gospel: 7Which is not another; but there be some that trouble you, and would pervert the gospel of Christ. 8But though we, or an angel from heaven, preach any other gospel unto you than that which we have preached unto you, let him be accursed. 9As we said before, so say I now again, If any man preach any other gospel unto you than that ye have received, let him be accursed. **2 Tim 1:13 (Pseudo)** 13Hold fast the form of sound words, which thou hast heard of me, in faith and love which is in Christ Jesus. **Tit 1:1 (Pseudo)** 1Paul, a servant of God, and an apostle of Jesus Christ, according to the faith of God's elect, and the acknowledging of the truth which is after godliness;

I TIMOTHY (PSEUDO) 6:5—Teaching on kingdom of riches (6:2–19), 63–67 CE

Theme	1 TIM	Paul
Withdraw from bad behavior	**6:5 (Pseudo)** [5]Perverse disputings of men of corrupt minds, and destitute of the truth, supposing that gain is godliness: from such withdraw thyself.	**2 Tim 3:8 (Pseudo)** [8]Now as Jannes and Jambres withstood Moses, so do these also resist the truth: men of corrupt minds, reprobate concerning the faith. **2 Tim 4:4 (Pseudo)** [4]And they shall turn away their ears from the truth, and shall be turned unto fables. **Tit 1:4 (Pseudo)** [4]To Titus, mine own son after the common faith: Grace, mercy, and peace, from God the Father and the Lord Jesus Christ our Saviour.

I TIMOTHY (PSEUDO) 6:6—Teaching on kingdom of riches (6:2–19), 63–67 CE

Theme	1 TIM	Paul	NT
Be content in godliness	**6:6 (Pseudo)** [6]But godliness with contentment is great gain. **4:8 (Pseudo)** [8]For bodily exercise profiteth little: but godliness is profitable unto all things, having promise of the life that now is, and of that which is to come.	**Phil 4:11–12** [11]Not that I speak in respect of want: for I have learned, in whatsoever state I am, therewith to be content. [12]I know both how to be abased, and I know how to abound: every where and in all things I am instructed both to be full and to be hungry, both to abound and to suffer need.	**Heb 13:5** [5]Let your conversation be without covetousness; and be content with such things as ye have: for he hath said, I will never leave thee, nor forsake thee.

I TIMOTHY (PSEUDO) 6:7—Teaching on kingdom of riches (6:2–19), 63–67 CE

Theme	1 TIM	Jewish Writings
Possessions do not count in heaven	**6:7 (Pseudo)** [7]For we brought nothing into this world, and it is certain we can carry nothing out.	**Job 1:21** [21]And said, Naked came I out of my mother's womb, and naked shall I return thither: the LORD gave, and the LORD hath taken away; blessed be the name of the LORD. **Eccl 5:14** [14]But those riches perish by evil travail: and he begetteth a son, and there is nothing in his hand.

I TIMOTHY (PSEUDO) 6:8—Teaching on kingdom of riches (6:2–19), 63–67 CE

Theme	1 TIM	Jewish Writings
Food and clothes	**6:8 (Pseudo)** [8]And having food and raiment let us be therewith content.	**Prov 30:8** [8]Remove far from me vanity and lies: give me neither poverty nor riches; feed me with food convenient for me:

I TIMOTHY (PSEUDO) 6:9—Teaching on kingdom of riches (6:2–19), 63–67 CE

Theme	1 TIM	Jewish Writings
Do not be tempted	**6:9 (Pseudo)** [9]But they that will be rich fall into temptation and a snare, and into many foolish and hurtful lusts, which drown men in destruction and perdition.	**Prov 23:4** [4]Labour not to be rich: cease from thine own wisdom. **Prov 28:22** [22]He that hasteth to be rich hath an evil eye, and considereth not that poverty shall come upon him.

I TIMOTHY (PSEUDO) 6:11—Teaching on kingdom of riches (6:2–19), 63–67 CE

Theme	1 TIM	Paul
Follow righteousness	**6:11 (Pseudo)** [11]But thou, O man of God, flee these things; and follow after righteousness, godliness, faith, love, patience, meekness.	**2 Tim 2:22 (Pseudo)** [22]Flee also youthful lusts: but follow righteousness, faith, charity, peace, with them that call on the Lord out of a pure heart.

I TIMOTHY (PSEUDO) 6:12—Teaching on kingdom of riches (6:2–19), 63–67 CE

Theme	1 TIM	Paul
Fight good fight to keep faith	**6:12 (Pseudo)** [12]Fight the good fight of faith, lay hold on eternal life, whereunto thou art also called, and hast professed a good profession before many witnesses.	**1 Cor 9:26** [26]I therefore so run, not as uncertainly; so fight I, not as one that beateth the air: **2 Tim 4:7 (Pseudo)** [7]I have fought a good fight, I have finished my course, I have kept the faith:

I TIMOTHY (PSEUDO) 6:13—Teaching on kingdom of riches (6:2–19), 63–67 CE

Theme	1 TIM	Jn
Jesus gave good confession before Pilate	**6:13 (Pseudo)** [13]I give thee charge in the sight of God, who quickeneth all things, and before Christ Jesus, who before Pontius Pilate witnessed a good confession;	**18:36–37** [36]Jesus answered, My kingdom is not of this world: if my kingdom were of this world, then would my servants fight, that I should not be delivered to the Jews: but now is my kingdom not from hence. [37]Pilate therefore said unto him, Art thou a king then? Jesus answered, Thou sayest that I am a king. To this end was I born, and for this cause came I into the world, that I should bear witness unto the truth. Every one that is of the truth heareth my voice. **19:11** [11]Jesus answered, Thou couldest have no power at all against me, except it were given thee from above: therefore he that delivered me unto thee hath the greater sin.

I TIMOTHY (PSEUDO) 6:15—Teaching on kingdom of riches (6:2–19), 63–67 CE

Theme	1 TIM	NT	Jewish Writings
Doxology	**6:15 (Pseudo)** [15]Which in his times he shall show, who is the blessed and only Potentate, the King of kings, and Lord of lords;	**Rev 17:14** [14]These shall make war with the Lamb, and the Lamb shall overcome them: for he is Lord of lords, and King of kings: and they that are with him are called, and chosen, and faithful.	**2 Mac 13:4** [4]But the King of kings moved Antiochus' mind against this wicked wretch, and Lysias informed the king that this man was the cause of all mischief, so that the king commanded to bring him unto Berea, and to put him to death, as the manner is in that place.

I TIMOTHY (PSEUDO) 6:16—Teaching on kingdom of riches (6:2–19), 63–67 CE

Theme	1 TIM	Jewish Writings
Doxology	**6:16 (Pseudo)** [16]Who only hath immortality, dwelling in the light which no man can approach unto; whom no man hath seen, nor can see: to whom be honour and power everlasting. Amen.	**Ex 33:20** [20]And he said, Thou canst not see my face: for there shall no man see me, and live. **Ps 104:2** [2]Who coverest thyself with light as with a garment: who stretchest out the heavens like a curtain:

1 TIMOTHY (PSEUDO) 6:17–19—Teaching on kingdom of riches (6:2–19), 63–67 CE

Theme	1 TIM	Mt	Mk
Modesty in riches	**6:17–19 (Pseudo)** [17]Charge them that are rich in this world, that they be not high-minded, nor trust in uncertain riches, but in the living God, who giveth us richly all things to enjoy; [18]That they do good, that they be rich in good works, ready to distribute, willing to communicate; [19]Laying up in store for themselves a good foundation against the time to come, that they may lay hold on eternal life.	**5:3** [3]Blessed are the poor in spirit: for theirs is the kingdom of heaven. **6:19–21** [19]Lay not up for yourselves treasures upon earth, where moth and rust doth corrupt, and where thieves break through and steal: [20]But lay up for yourselves treasures in heaven, where neither moth nor rust doth corrupt, and where thieves do not break through nor steal: [21]For where your treasure is, there will your heart be also. **19:23–30** [23]Then said Jesus unto his disciples, Verily I say unto you, That a rich man shall hardly enter into the kingdom of heaven. [24]And again I say unto you, It is easier for a camel to go through the eye of a needle, than for a rich man to enter into the kingdom of God. [25]When his disciples heard it, they were exceedingly amazed, saying, Who then can be saved? [26]But Jesus beheld them, and said unto them, With men this is impossible; but with God all things are possible. [27]Then answered Peter and said unto him, Behold, we have forsaken all, and followed thee; what shall we have therefore? [28]And Jesus said unto them, Verily I say unto you, That ye which have followed me, in the regeneration when the Son of man shall sit in the throne of his glory, ye also shall sit upon twelve thrones, judging the twelve tribes of Israel. [29]And every one that hath forsaken houses, or brethren, or sisters, or father, or mother, or wife, or children, or lands, for my name's sake, shall receive an hundredfold, and shall inherit everlasting life. [30]But many that are first shall be last; and the last shall be first.	**10:23–31** [23]And Jesus looked round about, and saith unto his disciples, How hardly shall they that have riches enter into the kingdom of God! [24]And the disciples were astonished at his words. But Jesus answereth again, and saith unto them, Children, how hard is it for them that trust in riches to enter into the kingdom of God! [25]It is easier for a camel to go through the eye of a needle, than for a rich man to enter into the kingdom of God. [26]And they were astonished out of measure, saying among themselves, Who then can be saved? [27]And Jesus looking upon them saith, With men it is impossible, but not with God: for with God all things are possible. [28]Then Peter began to say unto him, Lo, we have left all, and have followed thee. [29]And Jesus answered and said, Verily I say unto you, There is no man that hath left house, or brethren, or sisters, or father, or mother, or wife, or children, or lands, for my sake, and the gospel's, [30]But he shall receive an hundredfold now in this time, houses, and brethren, and sisters, and mothers, and children, and lands, with persecutions; and in the world to come eternal life. [31]But many that are first shall be last; and the last first.

I TIMOTHY (PSEUDO) 6:17—Teaching on kingdom of riches (6:2–19), 63–67 CE

Theme	1 TIM	Lk	Jewish Writings
Rich be modest	**6:17 (Pseudo)** [17]Charge them that are rich in this world, that they be not highminded, nor trust in uncertain riches, but in the living God, who giveth us richly all things to enjoy;	**12:20** [20]But God said unto him, Thou fool, this night thy soul shall be required of thee: then whose shall those things be, which thou hast provided?	**Ps 62:11** [11]God hath spoken once; twice have I heard this; that power belongeth unto God.

I TIMOTHY (PSEUDO) 6:19—Teaching on kingdom of riches (6:2–19), 63–67 CE

Theme	1 TIM	Mt
Hold to eternal life	**6:19 (Pseudo)** [19]Laying up in store for themselves a good foundation against the time to come, that they may lay hold on eternal life.	**6:20** [20]But lay up for yourselves treasures in heaven, where neither moth nor rust doth corrupt, and where thieves do not break through nor steal:

Lk	Other
6:20	**Q-Quelle**
20And he lifted up his eyes on his disciples, and said, Blessed be ye poor: for yours is the kingdom of God. **12:33** 33Sell that ye have, and give alms; provide yourselves bags which wax not old, a treasure in the heavens that faileth not, where no thief approacheth, neither moth corrupteth. **18:24–30** 18And a certain ruler asked him, saying, Good Master, what shall I do to inherit eternal life? 19And Jesus said unto him, Why callest thou me good? none is good, save one, that is, God. 20Thou knowest the commandments, Do not commit adultery, Do not kill, Do not steal, Do not bear false witness, Honour thy father and thy mother. 21And he said, All these have I kept from my youth up. 22Now when Jesus heard these things, he said unto him, Yet lackest thou one thing: sell all that thou hast, and distribute unto the poor, and thou shalt have treasure in heaven: and come, follow me. 23And when he heard this, he was very sorrowful: for he was very rich. 24And when Jesus saw that he was very sorrowful, he said, How hardly shall they that have riches enter into the kingdom of God! 25For it is easier for a camel to go through a needle's eye, than for a rich man to enter into the kingdom of God. 26And they that heard it said, Who then can be saved? 27And he said, The things which are impossible with men are possible with God. 28Then Peter said, Lo, we have left all, and followed thee. 29And he said unto them, Verily I say unto you, There is no man that hath left house, or parents, or brethren, or wife, or children, for the kingdom of God's sake, 30Who shall not receive manifold more in this present time, and in the world to come life everlasting.	Beatitudes: 1 Tim 6:17-19/Mt 5:3-12/ Lk 6:20b-23 (QS 8 [Thom 54, 68, 69]); Treasures in Heaven: 1 Tim 6:17-19/Mt 6:19-21/Lk 12:33-34 (QS 40 [Thom 76:2])

STERN RECOMMENDATIONS (6:20–21)

I TIMOTHY (PSEUDO) 6:20—Stern Recommendations (6:20–21), 63–67 CE

Theme	1 TIM	Paul
Avoid profane	**6:20 (Pseudo)** [20]O Timothy, keep that which is committed to thy trust, avoiding profane and vain babblings, and oppositions of science falsely so called:	**2 Tim 1:14 (Pseudo)** [14]That good thing which was committed unto thee keep by the Holy Ghost which dwelleth in us. **2 Tim 4:7 (Pseudo)** [7]I have fought a good fight, I have finished my course, I have kept the faith:

I TIMOTHY (PSEUDO) 6:21—Stern Recommendations (6:20–21), 63–67 CE

Theme	1 TIM	Paul
Grace	**6:21 (Pseudo)** [21]Which some professing have erred concerning the faith. Grace be with thee. Amen. **1:6 (Pseudo)** [6]From which some having swerved have turned aside unto vain jangling;	**2 Tim 2:16 (Pseudo)** [16]But shun profane and vain babblings: for they will increase unto more ungodliness.

2 TIMOTHY

Pastoral epistle, pseudo-Pauline authorship, early second century [or, by Paul 63–67 CE (minority view)]

ADDRESS (1:1–5)

2 TIMOTHY (PSEUDO) 1:1—Address (1:1–5), pastoral epistle, pseudo-Pauline authorship, early second century

Theme	2 TIM	Paul
Greeting	**1:1 (Pseudo)** [1]Paul, an apostle of Jesus Christ by the will of God, according to the promise of life which is in Christ Jesus,	**1 Tim 4:8 (Pseudo)** [8]For bodily exercise profiteth little: but godliness is profitable unto all things, having promise of the life that now is, and of that which is to come.

2 TIMOTHY (PSEUDO) 1:3—Address (1:1–5), pastoral epistle, pseudo-Pauline authorship, early second century

Theme	2 TIM	Paul
Prayers	**1:3 (Pseudo)** [3]I thank God, whom I serve from my forefathers with pure conscience, that without ceasing I have remembrance of thee in my prayers night and day;	**Phil 3:5** [5]Circumcised the eighth day, of the stock of Israel, of the tribe of Benjamin, an Hebrew of the Hebrews; as touching the law, a Pharisee; **1 Tim 3:9 (Pseudo)** [9]Holding the mystery of the faith in a pure conscience.

2 TIMOTHY (PSEUDO) 1:5—Address (1:1–5), pastoral epistle, pseudo-Pauline authorship, early second century

Theme	2 TIM	Lk	Paul
Remembering Lois and Eunice	**1:5 (Pseudo)** [5]When I call to remembrance the unfeigned faith that is in thee, which dwelt first in thy grandmother Lois, and thy mother Eunice; and I am persuaded that in thee also.	**Acts 16:1** [1]Then came he to Derbe and Lystra: and, behold, a certain disciple was there, named Timotheus, the son of a certain woman, which was a Jewess, and believed; but his father was a Greek:	**1 Tim 1:5 (Pseudo)** [5]Now the end of the commandment is charity out of a pure heart, and of a good conscience, and of faith unfeigned:

EXHORTATIONS (1:6–2:13)

2 TIMOTHY (PSEUDO) 1:6—Exhortations (1:6–2:13), pastoral epistle, pseudo-Pauline authorship, early second century

Theme	2 TIM	Lk	Paul
Remember God's gifts	**1:6 (Pseudo)** [6]Wherefore I put thee in remembrance that thou stir up the gift of God, which is in thee by the putting on of my hands.	**Acts 6:6** [6]Whom they set before the apostles: and when they had prayed, they laid their hands on them. **Acts 8:17** [17]Then laid they their hands on them, and they received the Holy Ghost.	**1 Tim 4:14 (Pseudo)** [14]Neglect not the gift that is in thee, which was given thee by prophecy, with the laying on of the hands of the presbytery.

2 TIMOTHY (PSEUDO) 1:7—Exhortations (1:6–2:13), pastoral epistle, pseudo-Pauline authorship, early second century

Theme	2 TIM	Paul
God gives Spirit of power	**1:7 (Pseudo)** [7]For God hath not given us the spirit of fear; but of power, and of love, and of a sound mind.	**Rom 5:5** [5]And hope maketh not ashamed; because the love of God is shed abroad in our hearts by the Holy Ghost which is given unto us. **Rom 8:15** [15]For ye have not received the spirit of bondage again to fear; but ye have received the Spirit of adoption, whereby we cry, Abba, Father. **1 Cor 2:4** [4]And my speech and my preaching was not with enticing words of man's wisdom, but in demonstration of the Spirit and of power:

2 TIMOTHY (PSEUDO) 1:8—Exhortations (1:6–2:13), pastoral epistle, pseudo-Pauline authorship, early second century

Theme	2 TIM	Paul
Be not ashamed of testimony	**1:8 (Pseudo)** [8]Be not thou therefore ashamed of the testimony of our Lord, nor of me his prisoner: but be thou partaker of the afflictions of the gospel according to the power of God; **2:3, 15 (Pseudo)** [3]Thou therefore endure hardness, as a good soldier of Jesus Christ. . . . [15]Study to show thyself approved unto God, a workman that needeth not to be ashamed, rightly dividing the word of truth.	**Rom 1:16** [16]For I am not ashamed of the gospel of Christ: for it is the power of God unto salvation to every one that believeth; to the Jew first, and also to the Greek.

2 TIMOTHY (PSEUDO) 1:9—Exhortations (1:6–2:13), pastoral epistle, pseudo-Pauline authorship, early second century

Theme	2 TIM	Paul
Holy calling	**1:9 (Pseudo)** [9]Who hath saved us, and called us with an holy calling, not according to our works, but according to his own purpose and grace, which was given us in Christ Jesus before the world began,	**Eph 1:4 (Pseudo)** [4]According as he hath chosen us in him before the foundation of the world, that we should be holy and without blame before him in love: **Eph 2:8–9 (Pseudo)** [8]For by grace are ye saved through faith; and that not of yourselves: it is the gift of God: [9]Not of works, lest any man should boast. **Tit 1:2 (Pseudo)** [2]In hope of eternal life, which God, that cannot lie, promised before the world began; **Tit 3:5 (Pseudo)** [5]Not by works of righteousness which we have done, but according to his mercy he saved us, by the washing of regeneration, and renewing of the Holy Ghost;

2 TIMOTHY (PSEUDO) 1:10—Exhortations (1:6–2:13), pastoral epistle, pseudo-Pauline authorship, early second century

Theme	2 TIM	Paul	NT	Other
Jesus abolished death	**1:10 (Pseudo)** [10]But is now made manifest by the appearing of our Saviour Jesus Christ, who hath abolished death, and hath brought life and immortality to light through the gospel:	**Rom 16:26** [26]But now is made manifest, and by the scriptures of the prophets, according to the commandment of the everlasting God, made known to all nations for the obedience of faith: **Phil 3:20** [20]For our conversation is in heaven; from whence also we look for the Saviour, the Lord Jesus Christ: **1 Tim 6:14 (Pseudo)** [14]That thou keep this commandment without spot, unrebukeable, until the appearing of our Lord Jesus Christ: **Tit 1:4 (Pseudo)** [4]To Titus, mine own son after the common faith: Grace, mercy, and peace, from God the Father and the Lord Jesus Christ our Saviour. **Tit 2:13 (Pseudo)** [13]Looking for that blessed hope, and the glorious appearing of the great God and our Saviour Jesus Christ;	**1 Pet 1:20** [20]Who verily was foreordained before the foundation of the world, but was manifest in these last times for you,	**Q-Quelle** Watchful and Faithful: 2 Tim 1:10/ Tit 2:13/[Mt 24:42-51]/ [Lk 12:35-48 (QS 41 [Thom 21:3, 103], QS 42)]; Parable of the pounds: 2 Tim 1:10/ Tit 2:13/ Mt 25:14-30/Lk 19:11-27 (QS 61 [Thom 41])

2 TIMOTHY (PSEUDO) 1:11—Exhortations (1:6–2:13), pastoral epistle, pseudo-Pauline authorship, early second century

Theme	2 TIM	Paul
Paul, preacher, teacher, apostle	**1:11 (Pseudo)** [11]Whereunto I am appointed a preacher, and an apostle, and a teacher of the Gentiles.	**1 Tim 2:7 (Pseudo)** [7]Whereunto I am ordained a preacher, and an apostle, (I speak the truth in Christ, and lie not;) a teacher of the Gentiles in faith and verity.

2 TIMOTHY (PSEUDO) 1:12—Exhortations (1:6–2:13), pastoral epistle, pseudo-Pauline authorship, early second century

Theme	2 TIM	Paul	NT
Suffering as a Christian	**1:12 (Pseudo)** [12]For the which cause I also suffer these things: nevertheless I am not ashamed: for I know whom I have believed, and am persuaded that he is able to keep that which I have committed unto him against that day.	**1 Tim 1:10–11 (Pseudo)** [10]For whoremongers, for them that defile themselves with mankind, for menstealers, for liars, for perjured persons, and if there be any other thing that is contrary to sound doctrine; [11]According to the glorious gospel of the blessed God, which was committed to my trust.	**1 Pet 4:16** [16]Yet if any man suffer as a Christian, let him not be ashamed; but let him glorify God on this behalf.

2 TIMOTHY (PSEUDO) 1:13—Exhortations (1:6–2:13), pastoral epistle, pseudo-Pauline authorship, early second century

Theme	2 TIM	Paul
Be faithful	**1:13 (Pseudo)** [13]Hold fast the form of sound words, which thou hast heard of me, in faith and love which is in Christ Jesus.	**1 Tim 1:14 (Pseudo)** [14]And the grace of our Lord was exceeding abundant with faith and love which is in Christ Jesus.

2 TIMOTHY (PSEUDO) 1:14—Exhortations (1:6–2:13), pastoral epistle, pseudo-Pauline authorship, early second century

Theme	2 TIM	Paul
Be faithful	**1:14 (Pseudo)** [14]That good thing which was committed unto thee keep by the Holy Ghost which dwelleth in us.	**Rom 8:11** [1]There is therefore now no condemnation to them which are in Christ Jesus, who walk not after the flesh, but after the Spirit. **1 Tim 6:20 (Pseudo)** [20]O Timothy, keep that which is committed to thy trust, avoiding profane and vain babblings, and oppositions of science falsely so called:

2 TIMOTHY (PSEUDO) 1:15—Exhortations (1:6–2:13), pastoral epistle, pseudo-Pauline authorship, early second century

Theme	2 TIM
Turning away	**1:15 (Pseudo)** [15]This thou knowest, that all they which are in Asia be turned away from me; of whom are Phygellus and Hermogenes. **4:16 (Pseudo)** [16]At my first answer no man stood with me, but all men forsook me: I pray God that it may not be laid to their charge.

2 TIMOTHY (PSEUDO) 1:16—Exhortations (1:6–2:13), pastoral epistle, pseudo-Pauline authorship, early second century

Theme	2 TIM
Mercy for Onesiphorus	**1:16 (Pseudo)** [16]The Lord give mercy unto the house of Onesiphorus; for he oft refreshed me, and was not ashamed of my chain: **4:19 (Pseudo)** [19]Salute Prisca and Aquila, and the household of Onesiphorus.

2 TIMOTHY (PSEUDO) 1:18—Exhortations (1:6–2:13), pastoral epistle, pseudo-Pauline authorship, early second century

Theme	2 TIM	NT
Mercy on Ephesus ministry	**1:18 (Pseudo)** [18]The Lord grant unto him that he may find mercy of the Lord in that day: and in how many things he ministered unto me at Ephesus, thou knowest very well.	**Jude 21** [21]Keep yourselves in the love of God, looking for the mercy of our Lord Jesus Christ unto eternal life.

2 TIMOTHY (PSEUDO) 2:3—Exhortations (1:6–2:13), pastoral epistle, pseudo-Pauline authorship, early second century

Theme	2 TIM	Paul
Endure hardship	**2:3 (Pseudo)** [3]Thou therefore endure hardness, as a good soldier of Jesus Christ. **1:8 (Pseudo)** [8]Be not thou therefore ashamed of the testimony of our Lord, nor of me his prisoner: but be thou partaker of the afflictions of the gospel according to the power of God; **4:5 (Pseudo)** [5]But watch thou in all things, endure afflictions, do the work of an evangelist, make full proof of thy ministry.	**Phlm 2** [2]And to our beloved Apphia, and Archippus our fellowsoldier, and to the church in thy house:

2 TIMOTHY (PSEUDO) 2:4—Exhortations (1:6–2:13), pastoral epistle, pseudo-Pauline authorship, early second century

Theme	2 TIM	Paul
Christian soldier	**2:4 (Pseudo)** [4]No man that warreth entangleth himself with the affairs of this life; that he may please him who hath chosen him to be a soldier.	**1 Cor 9:6** [6]Or I only and Barnabas, have not we power to forbear working?

2 TIMOTHY (PSEUDO) 2:5—Exhortations (1:6–2:13), pastoral epistle, pseudo-Pauline authorship, early second century

Theme	2 TIM	Paul
Strive lawfully	**2:5 (Pseudo)** [5]And if a man also strive for masteries, yet is he not crowned, except he strive lawfully.	**1 Cor 9:25** [25]And every man that striveth for the mastery is temperate in all things. Now they do it to obtain a corruptible crown; but we an incorruptible.

2 TIMOTHY (PSEUDO) 2:6—Exhortations (1:6–2:13), pastoral epistle, pseudo-Pauline authorship, early second century

Theme	2 TIM	Paul
Be fruitful	**2:6 (Pseudo)** [6]The husbandman that laboureth must be first partaker of the fruits.	**1 Cor 9:7–10** [7]Who goeth a warfare any time at his own charges? who planteth a vineyard, and eateth not of the fruit thereof? or who feedeth a flock, and eateth not of the milk of the flock? [8]Say I these things as a man? or saith not the law the same also? [9]For it is written in the law of Moses, Thou shalt not muzzle the mouth of the ox that treadeth out the corn. Doth God take care for oxen? [10]Or saith he it altogether for our sakes? For our sakes, no doubt, this is written: that he that ploweth should plow in hope; and that he that thresheth in hope should be partaker of his hope.

2 TIMOTHY (PSEUDO) 2:7—Exhortations (1:6–2:13), pastoral epistle, pseudo-Pauline authorship, early second century

Theme	2 TIM	Jewish Writings
God gives wisdom	**2:7 (Pseudo)** [7]Consider what I say; and the Lord give thee understanding in all things.	**Prov 2:6** [6]For the LORD giveth wisdom: out of his mouth cometh knowledge and understanding.

2 TIMOTHY (PSEUDO) 2:8—Exhortations (1:6–2:13), pastoral epistle, pseudo-Pauline authorship, early second century

Theme	2 TIM	Paul
Jesus is David's seed, raised from the dead	**2:8 (Pseudo)** [8]Remember that Jesus Christ of the seed of David was raised from the dead according to my gospel:	**Rom 1:3** [3]Concerning his Son Jesus Christ our Lord, which was made of the seed of David according to the flesh; **Rom 2:16** [16]In the day when God shall judge the secrets of men by Jesus Christ according to my gospel. **1 Cor 15:4, 20** [4]And that he was buried, and that he rose again the third day according to the scriptures: . . . [20]But now is Christ risen from the dead, and become the firstfruits of them that slept. **Gal 1:11** [11]But I certify you, brethren, that the gospel which was preached of me is not after man. **Gal 2:2** [2]And I went up by revelation, and communicated unto them that gospel which I preach among the Gentiles, but privately to them which were of reputation, lest by any means I should run, or had run, in vain.

2 TIMOTHY (PSEUDO) 2:9—Exhortations (1:6–2:13), pastoral epistle, pseudo-Pauline authorship, early second century

Theme	2 TIM	Paul
God's word is free	**2:9 (Pseudo)** [9]Wherein I suffer trouble, as an evil doer, even unto bonds; but the word of God is not bound.	**Phil 1:12–14** [12]But I would ye should understand, brethren, that the things which happened unto me have fallen out rather unto the furtherance of the gospel; [13]So that my bonds in Christ are manifest in all the palace, and in all other places; [14]And many of the brethren in the Lord, waxing confident by my bonds, are much more bold to speak the word without fear.

2 TIMOTHY (PSEUDO) 2:10—Exhortations (1:6–2:13), pastoral epistle, pseudo-Pauline authorship, early second century

Theme	2 TIM	Paul
Endure all things for the sake of the elect	**2:10 (Pseudo)** [10]Therefore I endure all things for the elect's sakes, that they may also obtain the salvation which is in Christ Jesus with eternal glory.	**Col 1:24** [24]Who now rejoice in my sufferings for you, and fill up that which is behind of the afflictions of Christ in my flesh for his body's sake, which is the church: **1 Tim 1:15 (Pseudo)** [15]This is a faithful saying, and worthy of all acceptation, that Christ Jesus came into the world to save sinners; of whom I am chief.

2 TIMOTHY (PSEUDO) 2:11—Exhortations (1:6–2:13), pastoral epistle, pseudo-Pauline authorship, early second century

Theme	2 TIM	Paul
Be dead in Christ & live	**2:11 (Pseudo)** [11]It is a faithful saying: For if we be dead with him, we shall also live with him:	**Rom 6:8** [8]Now if we be dead with Christ, we believe that we shall also live with him:

2 TIMOTHY (PSEUDO) 2:12—Exhortations (1:6–2:13), pastoral epistle, pseudo-Pauline authorship, early second century

Theme	2 TIM	Mt	Lk
Suffer & reign with Christ	**2:12 (Pseudo)** [12]If we suffer, we shall also reign with him: if we deny him, he also will deny us:	**10:22, 33** [22]And ye shall be hated of all men for my name's sake: but he that endureth to the end shall be saved. . . . [33]But whosoever shall deny me before men, him will I also deny before my Father which is in heaven.	**9:12** [12]And when the day began to wear away, then came the twelve, and said unto him, Send the multitude away, that they may go into the towns and country round about, and lodge, and get victuals: for we are here in a desert place.

2 TIMOTHY (PSEUDO) 2:13—Exhortations (1:6–2:13), pastoral epistle, pseudo-Pauline authorship, early second century

Theme	2 TIM	Paul	Jewish Writings
God is faithful	**2:13 (Pseudo)** [13]If we believe not, yet he abideth faithful: he cannot deny himself.	**Rom 3:3–4** [3]For what if some did not believe? shall their unbelief make the faith of God without effect? [4]God forbid: yea, let God be true, but every man a liar; as it is written, That thou mightest be justified in thy sayings, and mightest overcome when thou art judged. **1 Cor 10:13** [13]There hath no temptation taken you but such as is common to man: but God is faithful, who will not suffer you to be tempted above that ye are able; but will with the temptation also make a way to escape, that ye may be able to bear it. **Tit 1:2 (Pseudo)** [2]In hope of eternal life, which God, that cannot lie, promised before the world began;	**Num 23:19** [19]God is not a man, that he should lie; neither the son of man, that he should repent: hath he said, and shall he not do it? or hath he spoken, and shall he not make it good?

FALSE TEACHINGS (2:14–4:8)

2 TIMOTHY (PSEUDO) 2:14—False Teachings (2:4–4:8), pastoral epistle, pseudo-Pauline authorship, early second century

Theme	2 TIM	Paul
Do not argue about words	**2:14 (Pseudo)** [14]Of these things put them in remembrance, charging them before the Lord that they strive not about words to no profit, but to the subverting of the hearers.	**1 Tim 6:4 (Pseudo)** [4]He is proud, knowing nothing, but doting about questions and strifes of words, whereof cometh envy, strife, railings, evil surmisings,

2 TIMOTHY (PSEUDO) 2:15—False Teachings (2:4–4:8), pastoral epistle, pseudo-Pauline authorship, early second century

Theme	2 TIM	Paul
Show thyself approved by God	**2:15 (Pseudo)** [15]Study to show thyself approved unto God, a workman that needeth not to be ashamed, rightly dividing the word of truth. **1:8 (Pseudo)** [8]Be not thou therefore ashamed of the testimony of our Lord, nor of me his prisoner: but be thou partaker of the afflictions of the gospel according to the power of God;	**2 Cor 6:7** [7]By the word of truth, by the power of God, by the armour of righteousness on the right hand & on the left, **Eph 1:13 (Pseudo)** [13]In whom ye also trusted, after that ye heard the word of truth, the gospel of your salvation: in whom also after that ye believed, ye were sealed with that holy Spirit of promise, **Col 1:5** [5]For the hope which is laid up for you in heaven, whereof ye heard before in the word of the truth of the gospel;

2 TIMOTHY (PSEUDO) 2:16—False Teachings (2:4–4:8), pastoral epistle, pseudo-Pauline authorship, early second century

Theme	2 TIM	Paul
Vanity is unprofitable	**2:16 (Pseudo)** [16]But shun profane and vain babblings: for they will increase unto more ungodliness.	**1 Tim 4:7 (Pseudo)** [7]But refuse profane and old wives' fables, and exercise thyself rather unto godliness.

2 TIMOTHY (PSEUDO) 2:17—False Teachings (2:4–4:8), pastoral epistle, pseudo-Pauline authorship, early second century

Theme	2 TIM	Paul
Bad behavior increases ungodliness	**2:17 (Pseudo)** [17]And their word will eat as doth a canker: of whom is Hymenaeus and Philetus;	**1 Tim 1:20 (Pseudo)** [20]Of whom is Hymenaeus and Alexander; whom I have delivered unto Satan, that they may learn not to blaspheme.

2 TIMOTHY (PSEUDO) 2:18—False Teachings (2:4–4:8), pastoral epistle, pseudo-Pauline authorship, early second century

Theme	2 TIM	Paul
Do not frustrate the faith of others	**2:18 (Pseudo)** [18]Who concerning the truth have erred, saying that the resurrection is past already; and overthrow the faith of some.	**2 Thes 2:2** [2]That ye be not soon shaken in mind, or be troubled, neither by spirit, nor by word, nor by letter as from us, as that the day of Christ is at hand.

2 TIMOTHY (PSEUDO) 2:19—False Teachings (2:4–4:8), pastoral epistle, pseudo-Pauline authorship, early second century

Theme	2 TIM	Jn	Paul	Jewish Writings
Lord knows each one by name	**2:19 (Pseudo)** [19]Nevertheless the foundation of God standeth sure, having this seal, The Lord knoweth them that are his. And, Let every one that nameth the name of Christ depart from iniquity.	**10:14** [14]I am the good shepherd, and know my sheep, and am known of mine.	**1 Cor 3:10–15** [10]According to the grace of God which is given unto me, as a wise masterbuilder, I have laid the foundation, and another buildeth thereon. But let every man take heed how he buildeth thereupon. [11]For other foundation can no man lay than that is laid, which is Jesus Christ. [12]Now if any man build upon this foundation gold, silver, precious stones, wood, hay, stubble; [13]Every man's work shall be made manifest: for the day shall declare it, because it shall be revealed by fire; and the fire shall try every man's work of what sort it is. [14]If any man's work abide which he hath built thereupon, he shall receive a reward. [15]If any man's work shall be burned, he shall suffer loss: but he himself shall be saved; yet so as by fire.	**Num 16:5** [5]And he spake unto Korah and unto all his company, saying, Even to morrow the LORD will show who are his, and who is holy; and will cause him to come near unto him: even him whom he hath chosen will he cause to come near unto him. **Is 28:16** [16]Therefore thus saith the Lord GOD, Behold, I lay in Zion for a foundation a stone, a tried stone, a precious corner stone, a sure foundation: he that believeth shall not make haste.

2 TIMOTHY (PSEUDO) 2:21—False Teachings (2:4–4:8), pastoral epistle, pseudo-Pauline authorship, early second century

Theme	2 TIM
Be clean, act honorably	**2:21 (Pseudo)** [21]If a man therefore purge himself from these, he shall be a vessel unto honour, sanctified, and meet for the master's use, and prepared unto every good work. **3:17 (Pseudo)** [17]And their word will eat as doth a canker: of whom is Hymenaeus and Philetus;

2 TIMOTHY (PSEUDO) 2:22—False Teachings (2:4–4:8), pastoral epistle, pseudo-Pauline authorship, early second century

Theme	2 TIM	Paul
Flee lust, follow righteousness	**2:22 (Pseudo)** [22]Flee also youthful lusts: but follow righteousness, faith, charity, peace, with them that call on the Lord out of a pure heart.	**Rom 10:13** [13]For whosoever shall call upon the name of the Lord shall be saved. **1 Cor 1:2** [2]Unto the church of God which is at Corinth, to them that are sanctified in Christ Jesus, called to be saints, with all that in every place call upon the name of Jesus Christ our Lord, both theirs and ours: **Gal 5:22** [22]But the fruit of the Spirit is love, joy, peace, longsuffering, gentleness, goodness, faith, **1 Tim 6:11 (Pseudo)** [11]But thou, O man of God, flee these things; and follow after righteousness, godliness, faith, love, patience, meekness.

2 TIMOTHY (PSEUDO) 2:23—False Teachings (2:4–4:8), pastoral epistle, pseudo-Pauline authorship, early second century

Theme	2 TIM	Paul
Avoid foolish questions	**2:23 (Pseudo)** [23]But foolish and unlearned questions avoid, knowing that they do gender strifes.	**1 Tim 1:4 (Pseudo)** [4]Neither give heed to fables and endless genealogies, which minister questions, rather than godly edifying which is in faith: so do. **1 Tim 4:7 (Pseudo)** [7]But refuse profane and old wives' fables, and exercise thyself rather unto godliness. **1 Tim 6:4 (Pseudo)** [4]He is proud, knowing nothing, but doting about questions and strifes of words, whereof cometh envy, strife, railings, evil surmisings, **Tit 3:9 (Pseudo)** [9]But avoid foolish questions, and genealogies, and contentions, and strivings about the law; for they are unprofitable and vain.

2 TIMOTHY (PSEUDO) 2:24—False Teachings (2:4–4:8), pastoral epistle, pseudo-Pauline authorship, early second century

Theme	2 TIM	Paul
Be gentle	**2:24 (Pseudo)** [24]And the servant of the Lord must not strive; but be gentle unto all men, apt to teach, patient,	**1 Tim 3:2–3 (Pseudo)** [2]A bishop then must be blameless, the husband of one wife, vigilant, sober, of good behaviour, given to hospitality, apt to teach; [3]Not given to wine, no striker, not greedy of filthy lucre; but patient, not a brawler, not covetous;

2 TIMOTHY (PSEUDO) 2:25—False Teachings (2:4–4:8), pastoral epistle, pseudo-Pauline authorship, early second century

Theme	2 TIM	Paul
Be meek, acknowledge truth	**2:25 (Pseudo)** [25]In meekness instructing those that oppose themselves; if God peradventure will give them repentance to the acknowledging of the truth; **3:7 (Pseudo)** [7]Ever learning, and never able to come to the knowledge of the truth.	**1 Tim 2:4 (Pseudo)** [4]Who will have all men to be saved, and to come unto the knowledge of the truth.

2 TIMOTHY (PSEUDO) 2:26—False Teachings (2:4–4:8), pastoral epistle, pseudo-Pauline authorship, early second century

Theme	2 TIM	Paul
Pulled from snare of devil	**2:26 (Pseudo)** [26]And that they may recover themselves out of the snare of the devil, who are taken captive by him at his will.	**1 Tim 3:7 (Pseudo)** [7]Moreover he must have a good report of them which are without; lest he fall into reproach and the snare of the devil.

2 TIMOTHY (PSEUDO) 3:1—False Teachings (2:4–4:8), pastoral epistle, pseudo-Pauline authorship, early second century

Theme	2 TIM	Paul	NT
Eschatology: peril in the last days	**3:1 (Pseudo)** [1]This know also, that in the last days perilous times shall come.	**1 Tim 4:1 (Pseudo)** [1]Now the Spirit speaketh expressly, that in the latter times some shall depart from the faith, giving heed to seducing spirits, and doctrines of devils;	**2 Pet 3:3** [3]Knowing this first, that there shall come in the last days scoffers, walking after their own lusts, **Jude 18** [18]How that they told you there should be mockers in the last time, who should walk after their own ungodly lusts.

2 TIMOTHY (PSEUDO) 3:2–4—False Teachings (2:4–4:8), pastoral epistle, pseudo-Pauline authorship, early second century

Theme	2 TIM	Paul
Eschatology: signs	**3:2–4 (Pseudo)** [2]For men shall be lovers of their own selves, covetous, boasters, proud, blasphemers, disobedient to parents, unthankful, unholy, [3]Without natural affection, trucebreakers, false accusers, incontinent, fierce, despisers of those that are good, [4]Traitors, heady, highminded, lovers of pleasures more than lovers of God;	**Rom 1:29–31** [29]Being filled with all unrighteousness, fornication, wickedness, covetousness, maliciousness; full of envy, murder, debate, deceit, malignity; whisperers, [30]Backbiters, haters of God, despiteful, proud, boasters, inventors of evil things, disobedient to parents, [31]Without understanding, covenantbreakers, without natural affection, implacable, unmerciful:

2 TIMOTHY (PSEUDO) 3:5—False Teachings (2:4–4:8), pastoral epistle, pseudo-Pauline authorship, early second century

Theme	2 TIM	Paul
Turn from godlessness	**3:5 (Pseudo)** [5]Having a form of godliness, but denying the power thereof: from such turn away.	**Rom 2:20–22** [20]An instructor of the foolish, a teacher of babes, which hast the form of knowledge and of the truth in the law. [21]Thou therefore which teachest another, teachest thou not thyself? thou that preachest a man should not steal, dost thou steal? [22]Thou that sayest a man should not commit adultery, dost thou commit adultery? thou that abhorrest idols, dost thou commit sacrilege? **Tit 1:16 (Pseudo)** [16]They profess that they know God; but in works they deny him, being abominable, and disobedient, and unto every good work reprobate.

2 TIMOTHY (PSEUDO) 3:6—False Teachings (2:4–4:8), pastoral epistle, pseudo-Pauline authorship, early second century

Theme	2 TIM	Paul
Do not be led into folly	**3:6 (Pseudo)** [6]For of this sort are they which creep into houses, and lead captive silly women laden with sins, led away with divers lusts,	**Tit 1:11 (Pseudo)** [11]Whose mouths must be stopped, who subvert whole houses, teaching things which they ought not, for filthy lucre's sake.

2 TIMOTHY (PSEUDO) 3:7—False Teachings (2:4–4:8), pastoral epistle, pseudo-Pauline authorship, early second century

Theme	2 TIM
Folly is unable to recognize truth	**3:7 (Pseudo)** [7]Ever learning, and never able to come to the knowledge of the truth. **2:25 (Pseudo)** [25]In meekness instructing those that oppose themselves; if God peradventure will give them repentance to the acknowledging of the truth;

2 TIMOTHY (PSEUDO) 3:8—False Teachings (2:4–4:8), pastoral epistle, pseudo-Pauline authorship, early second century

Theme	2 TIM	Paul	Jewish Writings
Corrupt minds refuse truth	**3:8 (Pseudo)** [8]Now as Jannes and Jambres withstood Moses, so do these also resist the truth: men of corrupt minds, reprobate concerning the faith.	**1 Tim 6:5 (Pseudo)** [5]Perverse disputings of men of corrupt minds, and destitute of the truth, supposing that gain is godliness: from such withdraw thyself.	**Ex 7:11, 22** [11]Then Pharaoh also called the wise men and the sorcerers: now the magicians of Egypt, they also did in like manner with their enchantments. . . . [22]And the magicians of Egypt did so with their enchantments: and Pharaoh's heart was hardened, neither did he hearken unto them; as the LORD had said.

2 TIMOTHY (PSEUDO) 3:11—False Teachings (2:4–4:8), pastoral epistle, pseudo-Pauline authorship, early second century

Theme	2 TIM	Lk	Jewish
Delivered from persecutions	**3:11 (Pseudo)** [11]Persecutions, afflictions, which came unto me at Antioch, at Iconium, at Lystra; what persecutions I endured: but out of them all the Lord delivered me.	**Acts 13:50** [50]But the Jews stirred up the devout and honourable women, and the chief men of the city, and raised persecution against Paul and Barnabas, and expelled them out of their coasts. **Acts 14:5, 19** [5]And when there was an assault made both of the Gentiles, and also of the Jews with their rulers, to use them despitefully, and to stone them, . . . [19]And there came thither certain Jews from Antioch and Iconium, who persuaded the people, and, having stoned Paul, drew him out of the city, supposing he had been dead.	**Ps 34:20** [20]He keepeth all his bones: not one of them is broken.

2 TIMOTHY (PSEUDO) 3:12—False Teachings (2:4–4:8), pastoral epistle, pseudo-Pauline authorship, early second century

Theme	2 TIM	Lk	Jn
Christians will suffer persecutions	**3:12 (Pseudo)** [12]Yea, and all that will live godly in Christ Jesus shall suffer persecution.	**Acts 14:22** [22]Confirming the souls of the disciples, and exhorting them to continue in the faith, and that we must through much tribulation enter into the kingdom of God.	**15:20** [20]Remember the word that I said unto you, The servant is not greater than his lord. If they have persecuted me, they will also persecute you; if they have kept my saying, they will keep yours also.

2 TIMOTHY (PSEUDO) 3:14—False Teachings (2:4–4:8), pastoral epistle, pseudo-Pauline authorship, early second century

Theme	2 TIM
Continue in godly ways	**3:14 (Pseudo)** [14]But continue thou in the things which thou hast learned and hast been assured of, knowing of whom thou hast learned them; **2:2 (Pseudo)** [2]And the things that thou hast heard of me among many witnesses, the same commit thou to faithful men, who shall be able to teach others also.

2 TIMOTHY (PSEUDO) 3:15—False Teachings (2:4–4:8), pastoral epistle, pseudo-Pauline authorship, early second century

Theme	2 TIM	Jn
Scriptures bring wisdom	**3:15 (Pseudo)** [15]And that from a child thou hast known the holy scriptures, which are able to make thee wise unto salvation through faith which is in Christ Jesus.	**5:39** [39]Search the scriptures; for in them ye think ye have eternal life: and they are they which testify of me.

2 TIMOTHY (PSEUDO) 3:16—False Teachings (2:4–4:8), pastoral epistle, pseudo-Pauline authorship, early second century

Theme	2 TIM	Paul	NT
Scripture is inspired	**3:16 (Pseudo)** [16]All scripture is given by inspiration of God, and is profitable for doctrine, for reproof, for correction, for instruction in righteousness:	**Rom 15:4** [4]For whatsoever things were written aforetime were written for our learning, that we through patience and comfort of the scriptures might have hope.	**2 Pet 1:19–21** [19]We have also a more sure word of prophecy; whereunto ye do well that ye take heed, as unto a light that shineth in a dark place, until the day dawn, and the day star arise in your hearts: [20]Knowing this first, that no prophecy of the scripture is of any private interpretation. [21]For the prophecy came not in old time by the will of man: but holy men of God spake as they were moved by the Holy Ghost.

2 TIMOTHY (PSEUDO) 3:17—False Teachings (2:4–4:8), pastoral epistle, pseudo-Pauline authorship, early second century

Theme	2 TIM
Be of good works	**3:17 (Pseudo)** [17]That the man of God may be perfect, thoroughly furnished unto all good works. **2:21 (Pseudo)** [21]If a man therefore purge himself from these, he shall be a vessel unto honour, sanctified, and meet for the master's use, and prepared unto every good work.

2 TIMOTHY (PSEUDO) 4:1—False Teachings (2:4–4:8), pastoral epistle, pseudo-Pauline authorship, early second century

Theme	2 TIM	Lk	Paul	NT
God judges living & dead	**4:1 (Pseudo)** [1]I charge thee therefore before God, and the Lord Jesus Christ, who shall judge the quick and the dead at his appearing and his kingdom;	**Acts 10:42** [42]And he commanded us to preach unto the people, and to testify that it is he which was ordained of God to be the Judge of quick and dead.	**Rom 14:9–10** [9]For to this end Christ both died, and rose, and revived, that he might be Lord both of the dead and living. [10]But why dost thou judge thy brother? or why dost thou set at nought thy brother? for we shall all stand before the judgment seat of Christ. **1 Tim 5:21 (Pseudo)** [21]I charge thee before God, and the Lord Jesus Christ, and the elect angels, that thou observe these things without preferring one before another, doing nothing by partiality. **1 Tim 6:14 (Pseudo)** [14]That thou keep this commandment without spot, unrebukeable, until the appearing of our Lord Jesus Christ:	**1 Pet 4:5** [5]Who shall give account to him that is ready to judge the quick and the dead.

2 TIMOTHY (PSEUDO) 4:2—False Teachings (2:4–4:8), pastoral epistle, pseudo-Pauline authorship, early second century

Theme	2 TIM	Lk	Paul
Preach, rebuke, exhort	**4:2 (Pseudo)** [2]Preach the word; be instant in season, out of season; reprove, rebuke, exhort with all longsuffering and doctrine.	**Acts 20:20, 31** [20]And how I kept back nothing that was profitable unto you, but have showed you, and have taught you publicly, and from house to house, . . . [31]Therefore watch, and remember, that by the space of three years I ceased not to warn every one night and day with tears.	**1 Tim 5:20 (Pseudo)** [20]Them that sin rebuke before all, that others also may fear.

2 TIMOTHY (PSEUDO) 4:3—False Teachings (2:4–4:8), pastoral epistle, pseudo-Pauline authorship, early second century

Theme	2 TIM	Paul
Eschatology: turn toward own ways	**4:3 (Pseudo)** [3]For the time will come when they will not endure sound doctrine; but after their own lusts shall they heap to themselves teachers, having itching ears;	**1 Tim 4:1 (Pseudo)** [1]Now the Spirit speaketh expressly, that in the latter times some shall depart from the faith, giving heed to seducing spirits, and doctrines of devils;

2 TIMOTHY (PSEUDO) 4:4—False Teachings (2:4–4:8), pastoral epistle, pseudo-Pauline authorship, early second century

Theme	2 TIM	Paul
Eschat: some turn from truth	**4:4 (Pseudo)** [4]And they shall turn away their ears from the truth, and shall be turned unto fables.	**1 Tim 1:4 (Pseudo)** [4]Neither give heed to fables and endless genealogies, which minister questions, rather than godly edifying which is in faith: so do. **1 Tim 4:7 (Pseudo)** [7]But refuse profane and old wives' fables, and exercise thyself rather unto godliness. **Tit 1:14 (Pseudo)** [14]Not giving heed to Jewish fables, and commandments of men, that turn from the truth.

2 TIMOTHY (PSEUDO) 4:6—False Teachings (2:4–4:8), pastoral epistle, pseudo-Pauline authorship, early second century

Theme	2 TIM	Paul
Ready for heaven	**4:6 (Pseudo)** [6]For I am now ready to be offered, and the time of my departure is at hand.	**Phil 2:17** [17]Yea, and if I be offered upon the sacrifice and service of your faith, I joy, and rejoice with you all.

2 TIMOTHY (PSEUDO) 4:7—False Teachings (2:4–4:8), pastoral epistle, pseudo-Pauline authorship, early second century

Theme	2 TIM	Lk	Paul	NT
Fought for victory in Christ	**4:7 (Pseudo)** [7]I have fought a good fight, I have finished my course, I have kept the faith:	**Acts 20:24** [24]But none of these things move me, neither count I my life dear unto myself, so that I might finish my course with joy, and the ministry, which I have received of the Lord Jesus, to testify the gospel of the grace of God.	**1 Cor 9:24** [24]Know ye not that they which run in a race run all, but one receiveth the prize? So run, that ye may obtain. **1 Tim 1:18 (Pseudo)** [18]This charge I commit unto thee, son Timothy, according to the prophecies which went before on thee, that thou by them mightest war a good warfare; **1 Tim 6:12 (Pseudo)** [12]Fight the good fight of faith, lay hold on eternal life, whereunto thou art also called, and hast professed a good profession before many witnesses.	**Jude 3** [3]Beloved, when I gave all diligence to write unto you of the common salvation, it was needful for me to write unto you, and exhort you that ye should earnestly contend for the faith which was once delivered unto the saints.

2 TIMOTHY (PSEUDO) 4:8—False Teachings (2:4–4:8), pastoral epistle, pseudo-Pauline authorship, early second century

Theme	2 TIM	Paul	NT	Jewish Writings
Crown of righteousness awaits	**4:8 (Pseudo)** [8]Henceforth there is laid up for me a crown of righteousness, which the Lord, the righteous judge, shall give me at that day: and not to me only, but unto all them also that love his appearing. **2:5 (Pseudo)** [5]And if a man also strive for masteries, yet is he not crowned, except he strive lawfully.	**1 Cor 9:25** [25]And every man that striveth for the mastery is temperate in all things. Now they do it to obtain a corruptible crown; but we an incorruptible. **Phil 3:14** [14]I press toward the mark for the prize of the high calling of God in Christ Jesus.	**Jas 1:12** [12]Blessed is the man that endureth temptation: for when he is tried, he shall receive the crown of life, which the Lord hath promised to them that love him. **1 Pet 5:4** [4]And when the chief Shepherd shall appear, ye shall receive a crown of glory that fadeth not away. **Rev 2:10** [10]Fear none of those things which thou shalt suffer: behold, the devil shall cast some of you into prison, that ye may be tried; & ye shall have tribulation ten days: be thou faithful unto death, and I will give thee a crown of life.	**Wis 5:16** [16]Therefore shall they receive a glorious kingdom, and a beautiful crown from the Lord's hand: for with his right hand shall he cover them, and with his arm shall he protect them.

REQUESTS AND FAREWELL (4:9–22)

2 TIMOTHY (PSEUDO) 4:10—Requests and Farewell (4:9–22), pastoral epistle, pseudo-Pauline authorship, early second century

Theme	2 TIM	Paul
Forsaking faith for present world	**4:10 (Pseudo)** [10]For Demas hath forsaken me, having loved this present world, and is departed unto Thessalonica; Crescens to Galatia, Titus unto Dalmatia.	**2 Cor 2:13** [13]I had no rest in my spirit, because I found not Titus my brother: but taking my leave of them, I went from thence into Macedonia. **2 Cor 7:6–7** [6]Nevertheless God, that comforteth those that are cast down, comforted us by the coming of Titus; [7]And not by his coming only, but by the consolation wherewith he was comforted in you, when he told us your earnest desire, your mourning, your fervent mind toward me; so that I rejoiced the more. **2 Cor 8:23** [23]Whether any do inquire of Titus, he is my partner and fellowhelper concerning you: or our brethren be inquired of, they are the messengers of the churches, and the glory of Christ. **Gal 2:3** [3]But neither Titus, who was with me, being a Greek, was compelled to be circumcised: **Col 4:14** [14]Luke, the beloved physician, and Demas, greet you. **Tit 1:4 (Pseudo)** [4]To Titus, mine own son after the common faith: Grace, mercy, and peace, from God the Father and the Lord Jesus Christ our Saviour. **Phlm 24** [24]Marcus, Aristarchus, Demas, Lucas, my fellowlabourers.

2 TIMOTHY (PSEUDO) 4:11—Requests and Farewell (4:9–22), pastoral epistle, pseudo-Pauline authorship, early second century

Theme	2 TIM	Paul
Luke is with Paul. Lauds Mark's ministering	**4:11 (Pseudo)** [11]Only Luke is with me. Take Mark, and bring him with thee: for he is profitable to me for the ministry.	**Col 4:10** [10]Aristarchus my fellowprisoner saluteth you, and Marcus, sister's son to Barnabas, (touching whom ye received commandments: if he come unto you, receive him;) **Col 4:14** [14]Luke, the beloved physician, and Demas, greet you. **Phlm 24** [24]Marcus, Aristarchus, Demas, Lucas, my fellowlabourers.

2 TIMOTHY (PSEUDO) 4:12—Requests and Farewell (4:9–22), pastoral epistle, pseudo-Pauline authorship, early second century

Theme	2 TIM	Lk	Paul
Tychicus goes to Ephesus	**4:12 (Pseudo)** [12]And Tychicus have I sent to Ephesus.	**Acts 20:4** [4]And there accompanied him into Asia Sopater of Berea; and of the Thessalonians, Aristarchus and Secundus; and Gaius of Derbe, and Timotheus; and of Asia, Tychicus and Trophimus.	**Eph 6:21 (Pseudo)** [21]But that ye also may know my affairs, and how I do, Tychicus, a beloved brother and faithful minister in the Lord, shall make known to you all things: **Col 4:7** [7]All my state shall Tychicus declare unto you, who is a beloved brother, and a faithful minister and fellowservant in the Lord:

2 TIMOTHY (PSEUDO) 4:13—Requests and Farewell (4:9–22), pastoral epistle, pseudo-Pauline authorship, early second century

Theme	2 TIM	Lk
Bring cloak from Troas	**4:13 (Pseudo)** [13]The cloak that I left at Troas with Carpus, when thou comest, bring with thee, and the books, but especially the parchments.	**Acts 16:8** [8]And they passing by Mysia came down to Troas. **Acts 20:6** [6]And we sailed away from Philippi after the days of unleavened bread, and came unto them to Troas in five days; where we abode seven days.

2 TIMOTHY (PSEUDO) 4:14—Requests and Farewell (4:9–22), pastoral epistle, pseudo-Pauline authorship, early second century

Theme	2 TIM	Paul	Jewish Writings
Alexander did evil to ministry & will be given according to his works	**4:14 (Pseudo)** [14]Alexander the coppersmith did me much evil: the Lord reward him according to his works:	**Rom 2:6** [6]Who will render to every man according to his deeds: **1 Tim 1:20 (Pseudo)** [20]Of whom is Hymenaeus and Alexander; whom I have delivered unto Satan, that they may learn not to blaspheme.	**2 Sam 3:39** [39]And I am this day weak, though anointed king; and these men the sons of Zeruiah be too hard for me: the LORD shall reward the doer of evil according to his wickedness. **Ps 28:4** [4]Give them according to their deeds, and according to the wickedness of their endeavours: give them after the work of their hands; render to them their desert. **Ps 62:12** [12]Also unto thee, O Lord, belongeth mercy: for thou renderest to every man according to his work. **Prov 24:12** [12]If thou sayest, Behold, we knew it not; doth not he that pondereth the heart consider it? and he that keepeth thy soul, doth not he know it? and shall not he render to every man according to his works?

2 TIMOTHY (PSEUDO) 4:16—Requests and Farewell (4:9–22), pastoral epistle, pseudo-Pauline authorship, early second century

Theme	2 TIM
Prayer for forsaken	**4:16 (Pseudo)** [16]At my first answer no man stood with me, but all men forsook me: I pray God that it may not be laid to their charge. **1:15 (Pseudo)** [15]This thou knowest, that all they which are in Asia be turned away from me; of whom are Phygellus and Hermogenes.

2 TIMOTHY (PSEUDO) 4:17—Requests and Farewell (4:9–22), pastoral epistle, pseudo-Pauline authorship, early second century

Theme	2 TIM	Lk	Paul	Jewish Writings
Supporters in the faith	**4:17 (Pseudo)** [17]Notwithstanding the Lord stood with me, and strengthened me; that by me the preaching might be fully known, and that all the Gentiles might hear: and I was delivered out of the mouth of the lion.	**Acts 23:11** [11]And the night following the Lord stood by him, and said, Be of good cheer, Paul: for as thou hast testified of me in Jerusalem, so must thou bear witness also at Rome. **Acts 27:23** [23]For there stood by me this night the angel of God, whose I am, and whom I serve,	**Phil 4:13** [13]I can do all things through Christ which strengtheneth me.	**Ps 22:22** [22]I will declare thy name unto my brethren: in the midst of the congregation will I praise thee. **Dan 6:23** [23]Then was the king exceeding glad for him, and commanded that they should take Daniel up out of the den. So Daniel was taken up out of the den, and no manner of hurt was found upon him, because he believed in his God. **1 Mac 2:60** [60]Daniel because of his innocence was delivered from the mouth of the lions.

2 TIMOTHY (PSEUDO) 4:18—Requests and Farewell (4:9–22), pastoral epistle, pseudo-Pauline authorship, early second century

Theme	2 TIM	Paul
Lord will deliver from every evil	**4:18 (Pseudo)** [18]And the Lord shall deliver me from every evil work, and will preserve me unto his heavenly kingdom: to whom be glory for ever and ever. Amen.	**Rom 16:27** [27]To God only wise, be glory through Jesus Christ for ever. Amen. **2 Cor 1:10** [10]Who delivered us from so great a death, and doth deliver: in whom we trust that he will yet deliver us;

2 TIMOTHY (PSEUDO) 4:19—Requests and Farewell (4:9–22), pastoral epistle, pseudo-Pauline authorship, early second century

Theme	2 TIM	Lk	Paul
Salute to Onesimus, Prisca, Aquila	**4:19 (Pseudo)** [19]Salute Prisca and Aquila, and the household of Onesiphorus.	**Acts 18:2** [2]And found a certain Jew named Aquila, born in Pontus, lately come from Italy, with his wife Priscilla; (because that Claudius had commanded all Jews to depart from Rome:) and came unto them.	**Rom 16:3** [3]Greet Priscilla and Aquila my helpers in Christ Jesus: **1 Cor 1:16** [16]And I baptized also the household of Stephanas: besides, I know not whether I baptized any other. **1 Cor 16:19** [19]The churches of Asia salute you. Aquila and Priscilla salute you much in the Lord, with the church that is in their house.

2 TIMOTHY (PSEUDO) 4:20—Requests and Farewell (4:9–22), pastoral epistle, pseudo-Pauline authorship, early second century

Theme	2 TIM	Lk	Paul
Erastus at Corinth: Trophimus at Milletum	**4:20 (Pseudo)** [20]Erastus abode at Corinth: but Trophimus have I left at Miletum sick.	**Acts 19:22** [22]So he sent into Macedonia two of them that ministered unto him, Timotheus and Erastus; but he himself stayed in Asia for a season. **Acts 20:4** [4]And there accompanied him into Asia Sopater of Berea; and of the Thessalonians, Aristarchus and Secundus; and Gaius of Derbe, and Timotheus; and of Asia, Tychicus and Trophimus. **Acts 21:29** [29](For they had seen before with him in the city Trophimus an Ephesian, whom they supposed that Paul had brought into the temple.)	**Rom 16:24** [24]The grace of our Lord Jesus Christ be with you all. Amen.

2 TIMOTHY (PSEUDO) 4:22—Requests and Farewell (4:9–22), pastoral epistle, pseudo-Pauline authorship, early second century

Theme	2 TIM	Paul
Blessings of Lord	**4:22 (Pseudo)** [22]The Lord Jesus Christ be with thy spirit. Grace be with you. Amen.	**Gal 6:18** [18]Brethren, the grace of our Lord Jesus Christ be with your spirit. Amen. **Phil 4:23** [23]The grace of our Lord Jesus Christ be with you all. Amen. **Col 4:18** [18]The salutation by the hand of me Paul. Remember my bonds. Grace be with you. Amen. **1 Tim 6:21 (Pseudo)** [21]Which some professing have erred concerning the faith. Grace be with thee. Amen. **Tit 3:15 (Pseudo)** [15]All that are with me salute thee. Greet them that love us in the faith. Grace be with you all. Amen.

TITUS

Pastoral epistle, Pseudo-Pauline authorship, early second century [or by Paul 63–67 CE (minority view)]

ADDRESS (1:1–4)

TITUS (PSEUDO) 1:1—Address (1:1–4), pastoral epistle, pseudo-Pauline authorship, early second century

Theme	TITUS	Paul	NT
Greeting	**1:1 (Pseudo)** [1]Paul, a servant of God, and an apostle of Jesus Christ, according to the faith of God's elect, and the acknowledging of the truth which is after godliness;	**1 Tim 2:4 (Pseudo)** [4]Who will have all men to be saved, and to come unto the knowledge of the truth. **1 Tim 4:3 (Pseudo)** [3]Forbidding to marry, and commanding to abstain from meats, which God hath created to be received with thanksgiving of them which believe and know the truth. **2 Tim 2:25 (Pseudo)** [25]In meekness instructing those that oppose themselves; if God peradventure will give them repentance to the acknowledging of the truth; **2 Tim 3:7 (Pseudo)** [7]Ever learning, and never able to come to the knowledge of the truth.	**Heb 10:26** [26]For if we sin wilfully after that we have received the knowledge of the truth, there remaineth no more sacrifice for sins,

TITUS (PSEUDO) 1:2—Address (1:1–4), pastoral epistle, pseudo-Pauline authorship, early second century

Theme	TITUS	Jn	Paul
Hope in eternal promise	**1:2 (Pseudo)** [2]In hope of eternal life, which God, that cannot lie, promised before the world began; **3:7 (Pseudo)** [7]That being justified by his grace, we should be made heirs according to the hope of eternal life.	**1 Jn 2:25** [25]And this is the promise that he hath promised us, even eternal life.	**2 Tim 1:1 (Pseudo)** [1]Paul, an apostle of Jesus Christ by the will of God, according to the promise of life which is in Christ Jesus,

TITUS (PSEUDO) 1:3—Address (1:1–4), pastoral epistle, pseudo-Pauline authorship, early second century

Theme	TITUS	Paul	NT	Jewish Writings
God's word manifested in preaching	**1:3 (Pseudo)** [3]But hath in due times manifested his word through preaching, which is committed unto me according to the commandment of God our Saviour; **2:10 (Pseudo)** [10]Not purloining, but showing all good fidelity; that they may adorn the doctrine of God our Saviour in all things. **3:4 (Pseudo)** [4]But after that the kindness and love of God our Saviour toward man appeared,	**1 Tim 1:1 (Pseudo)** [1]Paul, an apostle of Jesus Christ by the commandment of God our Saviour, and Lord Jesus Christ, which is our hope; **1 Tim 2:3 (Pseudo)** [3]For this is good and acceptable in the sight of God our Saviour; **1 Tim 4:10 (Pseudo)** [10]For therefore we both labour and suffer reproach, because we trust in the living God, who is the Saviour of all men, specially of those that believe.	**Jude 25** [25]To the only wise God our Saviour, be glory and majesty, dominion and power, both now and for ever. Amen.	**Ps 24:5** [5]He shall receive the blessing from the LORD, and righteousness from the God of his salvation.

TITUS (PSEUDO) 1:4—Address (1:1–4), pastoral epistle, pseudo-Pauline authorship, early second century

Theme	TITUS	Paul	NT
Greeting to Titus	**1:4 (Pseudo)** [4]To Titus, mine own son after the common faith: Grace, mercy, and peace, from God the Father and the Lord Jesus Christ our Saviour. **2:13 (Pseudo)** [13]Looking for that blessed hope, and the glorious appearing of the great God and our Saviour Jesus Christ; **3:6 (Pseudo)** [6]Which he shed on us abundantly through Jesus Christ our Saviour;	**Phil 3:20** [20]For our conversation is in heaven; from whence also we look for the Saviour, the Lord Jesus Christ: **2 Tim 1:10 (Pseudo)** [10]But is now made manifest by the appearing of our Saviour Jesus Christ, who hath abolished death, and hath brought life and immortality to light through the gospel:	**2 Pet 1:1, 11** [1]Simon Peter, a servant and an apostle of Jesus Christ, to them that have obtained like precious faith with us through the righteousness of God and our Saviour Jesus Christ: . . . [11]For so an entrance shall be ministered unto you abundantly into the everlasting kingdom of our Lord and Saviour Jesus Christ. **2 Pet 2:20** [20]For if after they have escaped the pollutions of the world through the knowledge of the Lord and Saviour Jesus Christ, they are again entangled therein, and overcome, the latter end is worse with them than the beginning. **2 Pet 3:2, 18** [2]That ye may be mindful of the words which were spoken before by the holy prophets, and of the commandment of us the apostles of the Lord and Saviour: . . . [18]But grow in grace, and in the knowledge of our Lord and Saviour Jesus Christ. To him be glory both now and for ever. Amen.

PASTORAL EXPECTATIONS (1:5–16)

TITUS (PSEUDO) 1:6–7—Pastoral Expectations (1:5–16), pastoral epistle, pseudo-Pauline authorship, early second century

Theme	TITUS	Paul
Character traits of bishop	**1:6–7 (Pseudo)** [6]If any be blameless, the husband of one wife, having faithful children not accused of riot or unruly. [7]For a bishop must be blameless, as the steward of God; not selfwilled, not soon angry, not given to wine, no striker, not given to filthy lucre;	**1 Tim 3:2–7 (Pseudo)** [2]A bishop then must be blameless, the husband of one wife, vigilant, sober, of good behaviour, given to hospitality, apt to teach; [3]Not given to wine, no striker, not greedy of filthy lucre; but patient, not a brawler, not covetous; [4]One that ruleth well his own house, having his children in subjection with all gravity; [5](For if a man know not how to rule his own house, how shall he take care of the church of God?) [6]Not a novice, lest being lifted up with pride he fall into the condemnation of the devil. [7]Moreover he must have a good report of them which are without; lest he fall into reproach and the snare of the devil. **2 Tim 2:24–26 (Pseudo)** [24]And the servant of the Lord must not strive; but be gentle unto all men, apt to teach, patient, [25]In meekness instructing those that oppose themselves; if God peradventure will give them repentance to the acknowledging of the truth; [26]And that they may recover themselves out of the snare of the devil, who are taken captive by him at his will.

TITUS (PSEUDO) 1:9—Pastoral Expectations (1:5–16), pastoral epistle, pseudo-Pauline authorship, early second century

Theme	TITUS	Paul
Faithful to sound doctrine	**1:9 (Pseudo)** [9]Holding fast the faithful word as he hath been taught, that he may be able by sound doctrine both to exhort and to convince the gainsayers. **1:13 (Pseudo)** [13]This witness is true. Wherefore rebuke them sharply, that they may be sound in the faith; **2:1–8 (Pseudo)** [1]But speak thou the things which become sound doctrine: [2]That the aged men be sober, grave, temperate, sound in faith, in charity, in patience. [3]The aged women likewise, that they be in behaviour as becometh holiness, not false accusers, not given to much wine, teachers of good things; [4]That they may teach the young women to be sober, to love their husbands, to love their children, [5]To be discreet, chaste, keepers at home, good, obedient to their own husbands, that the word of God be not blasphemed. [6]Young men likewise exhort to be sober minded. [7]In all things showing thyself a pattern of good works: in doctrine showing uncorruptness, gravity, sincerity, [8]Sound speech, that cannot be condemned; that he that is of the contrary part may be ashamed, having no evil thing to say of you.	**1 Tim 1:10 (Pseudo)** [10]For whoremongers, for them that defile themselves with mankind, for menstealers, for liars, for perjured persons, and if there be any other thing that is contrary to sound doctrine; **1 Tim 6:3 (Pseudo)** [3]If any man teach otherwise, and consent not to wholesome words, even the words of our Lord Jesus Christ, and to the doctrine which is according to godliness; **2 Tim 1:13 (Pseudo)** [13]Hold fast the form of sound words, which thou hast heard of me, in faith and love which is in Christ Jesus. **2 Tim 4:3 (Pseudo)** [3]For the time will come when they will not endure sound doctrine; but after their own lusts shall they heap to themselves teachers, having itching ears;

TITUS (PSEUDO) 1:13—Pastoral Expectations (1:5–16), pastoral epistle, pseudo-Pauline authorship, early second century

Theme	TITUS
True witness, rebuke for sound faith	**1:13 (Pseudo)** [13]This witness is true. Wherefore rebuke them sharply, that they may be sound in the faith; **1:9 (Pseudo)** [9]Holding fast the faithful word as he hath been taught, that he may be able by sound doctrine both to exhort and to convince the gainsayers.

TITUS (PSEUDO) 1:14—Pastoral Expectations (1:5–16), pastoral epistle, pseudo-Pauline authorship, early second century

Theme	TITUS	Paul	NT
Do not pay attention to untruthful Jewish myths	**1:14 (Pseudo)** [14]Not giving heed to Jewish fables, and commandments of men, that turn from the truth. **3:9 (Pseudo)** [9]But avoid foolish questions, and genealogies, and contentions, and strivings about the law; for they are unprofitable and vain.	**1 Tim 1:4 (Pseudo)** [4]Neither give heed to fables and endless genealogies, which minister questions, rather than godly edifying which is in faith: so do. **1 Tim 4:7 (Pseudo)** [7]But refuse profane and old wives' fables, and exercise thyself rather unto godliness. **2 Tim 4:4 (Pseudo)** [4]And they shall turn away their ears from the truth, and shall be turned unto fables.	**2 Pet 1:16** [16]For we have not followed cunningly devised fables, when we made known unto you the power and coming of our Lord Jesus Christ, but were eyewitnesses of his majesty.

TITUS (PSEUDO) 1:15—Pastoral Expectations (1:5–16), pastoral epistle, pseudo-Pauline authorship, early second century

Theme	TITUS	Mk	Lk	Paul
Pure see purity, defiled see wickedness	**1:15 (Pseudo)** [15]Unto the pure all things are pure: but unto them that are defiled and unbelieving is nothing pure; but even their mind and conscience is defiled.	**7:18–23** [18]And he saith unto them, Are ye so without understanding also? Do ye not perceive, that whatsoever thing from without entereth into the man, it cannot defile him; [19]Because it entereth not into his heart, but into the belly, and goeth out into the draught, purging all meats? [20]And he said, That which cometh out of the man, that defileth the man. [21]For from within, out of the heart of men, proceed evil thoughts, adulteries, fornications, murders, [22]Thefts, covetousness, wickedness, deceit, lasciviousness, an evil eye, blasphemy, pride, foolishness: [23]All these evil things come from within, and defile the man.	**Acts 10:15** [15]And the voice spake unto him again the second time, What God hath cleansed, that call not thou common.	**Rom 4:14–23** [14]For if they which are of the law be heirs, faith is made void, and the promise made of none effect: [15]Because the law worketh wrath: for where no law is, there is no transgression. [16]Therefore it is of faith, that it might be by grace; to the end the promise might be sure to all the seed; not to that only which is of the law, but to that also which is of the faith of Abraham; who is the father of us all, [17](As it is written, I have made thee a father of many nations,) before him whom he believed, even God, who quickeneth the dead, and calleth those things which be not as though they were. [18]Who against hope believed in hope, that he might become the father of many nations, according to that which was spoken, So shall thy seed be. [19]And being not weak in faith, he considered not his own body now dead, when he was about an hundred years old, neither yet the deadness of Sarah's womb: [20]He staggered not at the promise of God through unbelief; but was strong in faith, giving glory to God; [21]And being fully persuaded that, what he had promised, he was able also to perform. [22]And therefore it was imputed to him for righteousness. [23]Now it was not written for his sake alone, that it was imputed to him;

TEACHING AND CHRISTIAN LIFE (2:1–3:15)

TITUS (PSEUDO) 2:1—Teaching and Christian life (2:1–3:15), pastoral epistle, pseudo-Pauline authorship, early second century

Theme	TITUS	Paul
Speak sound doctrine	**2:1 (Pseudo)** [1]But speak thou the things which become sound doctrine: **1:9, 13 (Pseudo)** [9]Holding fast the faithful word as he hath been taught, that he may be able by sound doctrine both to exhort and to convince the gainsayers. . . . [13]This witness is true. Wherefore rebuke them sharply, that they may be sound in the faith; **2:8 (Pseudo)** [8]Sound speech, that cannot be condemned; that he that is of the contrary part may be ashamed, having no evil thing to say of you.	**1 Tim 1:10 (Pseudo)** [10]For whoremongers, for them that defile themselves with mankind, for menstealers, for liars, for perjured persons, and if there be any other thing that is contrary to sound doctrine; **1 Tim 6:3 (Pseudo)** [3]If any man teach otherwise, and consent not to wholesome words, even the words of our Lord Jesus Christ, and to the doctrine which is according to godliness; **2 Tim 1:13 (Pseudo)** [13]Hold fast the form of sound words, which thou hast heard of me, in faith and love which is in Christ Jesus. **2 Tim 4:3 (Pseudo)** [3]For the time will come when they will not endure sound doctrine; but after their own lusts shall they heap to themselves teachers, having itching ears;

TITUS (PSEUDO) 2:5—Teaching and Christian life (2:1–3:15), pastoral epistle, pseudo-Pauline authorship, early second century

Theme	TITUS	Paul	NT
Wives be discreet for the sake of the Word	**2:5 (Pseudo)** [5]To be discreet, chaste, keepers at home, good, obedient to their own husbands, that the word of God be not blasphemed.	**1 Cor 11:3** [3]But I would have you know, that the head of every man is Christ; and the head of the woman is the man; and the head of Christ is God. **1 Cor 14:34** [34]Let your women keep silence in the churches: for it is not permitted unto them to speak; but they are commanded to be under obedience, as also saith the law. **Eph 5:22–24 (Pseudo)** [22]Wives, submit yourselves unto your own husbands, as unto the Lord. [23]For the husband is the head of the wife, even as Christ is the head of the church: and he is the saviour of the body. [24]Therefore as the church is subject unto Christ, so let the wives be to their own husbands in every thing. **Col 3:18** [18]Wives, submit yourselves unto your own husbands, as it is fit in the Lord. **1 Tim 2:11–15 (Pseudo)** [11]Let the woman learn in silence with all subjection. [12]But I suffer not a woman to teach, nor to usurp authority over the man, but to be in silence. [13]For Adam was first formed, then Eve. [14]And Adam was not deceived, but the woman being deceived was in the transgression. [15]Notwithstanding she shall be saved in childbearing, if they continue in faith and charity and holiness with sobriety.	**1 Pet 3:1–6** [1]Likewise, ye wives, be in subjection to your own husbands; that, if any obey not the word, they also may without the word be won by the conversation of the wives; [2]While they behold your chaste conversation coupled with fear. [3]Whose adorning let it not be that outward adorning of plaiting the hair, and of wearing of gold, or of putting on of apparel; [4]But let it be the hidden man of the heart, in that which is not corruptible, even the ornament of a meek and quiet spirit, which is in the sight of God of great price. [5]For after this manner in the old time the holy women also, who trusted in God, adorned themselves, being in subjection unto their own husbands: [6]Even as Sarah obeyed Abraham, calling him lord: whose daughters ye are, as long as ye do well, and are not afraid with any amazement.

TITUS (PSEUDO) 2:9—Teaching and Christian life (2:1–3:15), pastoral epistle, pseudo-Pauline authorship, early second century

Theme	TITUS	Paul	NT
Servants be obedient, pleasing in all things	**2:9 (Pseudo)** [9]Exhort servants to be obedient unto their own masters, and to please them well in all things; not answering again;	**1 Cor 7:21–22** [21]Art thou called being a servant? care not for it: but if thou mayest be made free, use it rather. [22]For he that is called in the Lord, being a servant, is the Lord's freeman: likewise also he that is called, being free, is Christ's servant. **Eph 6:5–8 (Pseudo)** [5]Servants, be obedient to them that are your masters according to the flesh, with fear and trembling, in singleness of your heart, as unto Christ; [6]Not with eyeservice, as men-pleasers; but as the servants of Christ, doing the will of God from the heart; [7]With good will doing service, as to the Lord, and not to men: [8]Knowing that whatsoever good thing any man doeth, the same shall he receive of the Lord, whether he be bond or free. **Col 3:22–25 (Pseudo)** [22]Servants, obey in all things your masters according to the flesh; not with eyeservice, as menpleasers; but in singleness of heart, fearing God: [23]And whatsoever ye do, do it heartily, as to the Lord, and not unto men; [24]Knowing that of the Lord ye shall receive the reward of the inheritance: for ye serve the Lord Christ. [25]But he that doeth wrong shall receive for the wrong which he hath done: and there is no respect of persons. **1 Tim 6:1–2 (Pseudo)** [1]Let as many servants as are under the yoke count their own masters worthy of all honour, that the name of God and his doctrine be not blasphemed. [2]And they that have believing masters, let them not despise them, because they are brethren; but rather do them service, because they are faithful and beloved, partakers of the benefit. These things teach and exhort.	**1 Pet 2:18 (Pseudo)** [18]Servants, be subject to your masters with all fear; not only to the good and gentle, but also to the froward.

TITUS (PSEUDO) 2:10—Teaching and Christian life (2:1–3:15), pastoral epistle, pseudo-Pauline authorship, early second century

Theme	TITUS	Paul	NT	Jewish
Be faithful	**2:10 (Pseudo)** [10]Not purloining, but showing all good fidelity; that they may adorn the doctrine of God our Saviour in all things. **1:3 (Pseudo)** [3]But hath in due times manifested his word through preaching, which is committed unto me according to the commandment of God our Saviour; **3:4 (Pseudo)** [4]But after that the kindness and love of God our Saviour toward man appeared,	**1 Tim 1:1 (Pseudo)** [1]Paul, an apostle of Jesus Christ by the commandment of God our Saviour, and Lord Jesus Christ, which is our hope; **1 Tim 2:3 (Pseudo)** [3]For this is good and acceptable in the sight of God our Saviour; **1 Tim 4:10 (Pseudo)** [10]For therefore we both labour and suffer reproach, because we trust in the living God, who is the Saviour of all men, specially of those that believe.	**Jude 25** [25]To the only wise God our Saviour, be glory and majesty, dominion and power, both now and for ever. Amen.	**Ps 24:5** [5]He shall receive the blessing from the LORD, and righteousness from the God of his salvation.

TITUS (PSEUDO) 2:11—Teaching and Christian life (2:1–3:15), pastoral epistle, pseudo-Pauline authorship, early second century

Theme	TITUS	Paul
Grace for all	**2:11 (Pseudo)** [11]For the grace of God that bringeth salvation hath appeared to all men,	**1 Tim 2:4 (Pseudo)** [4]Who will have all men to be saved, and to come unto the knowledge of the truth.

TITUS (PSEUDO) 2:13—Teaching and Christian life (2:1–3:15), pastoral epistle, pseudo-Pauline authorship, early second century

Theme	TITUS	Mt	Mk
Lord's coming	**2:13 (Pseudo)** [13]Looking for that blessed hope, and the glorious appearing of the great God and our Saviour Jesus Christ;	**21:3** [3]And if any man say ought unto you, ye shall say, The Lord hath need of them; and straightway he will send them. **22:41–46** [41]While the Pharisees were gathered together, Jesus asked them, [42]Saying, What think ye of Christ? whose son is he? They say unto him, The Son of David. [43]He saith unto them, How then doth David in spirit call him Lord, saying, [44]The LORD said unto my Lord, Sit thou on my right hand, till I make thine enemies thy footstool? [45]If David then call him Lord, how is he his son? [46]And no man was able to answer him a word, neither durst any man from that day forth ask him any more questions. **24:45–51** [45]Who then is a faithful and wise servant, whom his lord hath made ruler over his household, to give them meat in due season? [46]Blessed is that servant, whom his lord when he cometh shall find so doing. [47]Verily I say unto you, That he shall make him ruler over all his goods. [48]But and if that evil servant shall say in his heart, My lord delayeth his coming; [49]And shall begin to smite his fellowservants, and to eat and drink with the drunken; [50]The lord of that servant shall come in a day when he looketh not for him, and in an hour that he is not aware of, [51]And shall cut him asunder, and appoint him his portion with the hypocrites: there shall be weeping and gnashing of teeth. **25:14–30** [14]For the kingdom of heaven is as a man travelling into a far country, who called his own servants, and delivered unto them his goods. [15]And unto one he gave five talents, to another two, and to another one; to every man according to his several ability; and straightway took his journey. [16]Then he that had received the five talents went and traded with the same, and made them other five talents. [17]And likewise he that had received two, he also gained other two. [18]But he that had received one went and digged in the earth, and hid his lord's money. [19]After a long time the lord of those servants cometh, and reckoneth with them. [20]And so he that had received five talents came and brought other five talents, saying, Lord, thou deliveredst unto me five talents: behold, I have gained beside them five talents more. [21]His lord said unto him, Well done, thou good and faithful servant: thou hast been faithful over a few things, I will make thee ruler over many things: enter thou into the joy of thy lord. [22]He also that had received two talents came and said, Lord, thou deliveredst unto me two talents: behold, I have gained two other talents beside them. [23]His lord said unto him, Well done, good and faithful servant; thou hast been faithful over a few things, I will make thee ruler over many things: enter thou into the joy of thy lord. [24]Then he which had received the one talent came and said, Lord, I knew thee that thou art an hard man, reaping where thou hast not sown, and gathering where thou hast not strawed: [25]And I was afraid, and went and hid thy talent in the earth: lo, there thou hast that is thine. [26]His lord answered and said unto him, Thou wicked and slothful servant, thou knewest that I reap where I sowed not, and gather where I have not strawed: [27]Thou oughtest therefore to have put my money to the exchangers, and then at my coming I should have received mine own with usury. [28]Take therefore the talent from him, and give it unto him which hath ten talents. [29]For unto every one that hath shall be given, and he shall have abundance: but from him that hath not shall be taken away even that which he hath. [30]And cast ye the unprofitable servant into outer darkness: there shall be weeping and gnashing of teeth.	**11:3** [3]And if any man say unto you, Why do ye this? say ye that the Lord hath need of him; and straightway he will send him hither. **12:35–37a** [35]And Jesus answered and said, while he taught in the temple, How say the scribes that Christ is the Son of David? [36]For David himself said by the Holy Ghost, The LORD said to my Lord, Sit thou on my right hand, till I make thine enemies thy footstool. [37]David therefore himself calleth him Lord; and whence is he then his son?

Lk

12:41–46

[41]Then Peter said unto him, Lord, speakest thou this parable unto us, or even to all? [42]And the Lord said, Who then is that faithful and wise steward, whom his lord shall make ruler over his household, to give them their portion of meat in due season? [43]Blessed is that servant, whom his lord when he cometh shall find so doing. [44]Of a truth I say unto you, that he will make him ruler over all that he hath. [45]But and if that servant say in his heart, My lord delayeth his coming; and shall begin to beat the menservants and maidens, and to eat and drink, and to be drunken; [46]The lord of that servant will come in a day when he looketh not for him, and at an hour when he is not aware, and will cut him in sunder, and will appoint him his portion with the unbelievers.

19:11–27

[11]And as they heard these things, he added and spake a parable, because he was nigh to Jerusalem, and because they thought that the kingdom of God should immediately appear. [12]He said therefore, A certain nobleman went into a far country to receive for himself a kingdom, and to return. [13]And he called his ten servants, and delivered them ten pounds, and said unto them, Occupy till I come. [14]But his citizens hated him, and sent a message after him, saying, We will not have this man to reign over us. [15]And it came to pass, that when he was returned, having received the kingdom, then he commanded these servants to be called unto him, to whom he had given the money, that he might know how much every man had gained by trading. [16]Then came the first, saying, Lord, thy pound hath gained ten pounds. [17]And he said unto him, Well, thou good servant: because thou hast been faithful in a very little, have thou authority over ten cities. [18]And the second came, saying, Lord, thy pound hath gained five pounds. [19]And he said likewise to him, Be thou also over five cities. [20]And another came, saying, Lord, behold, here is thy pound, which I have kept laid up in a napkin: [21]For I feared thee, because thou art an austere man: thou takest up that thou layedst not down, and reapest that thou didst not sow. [22]And he saith unto him, Out of thine own mouth will I judge thee, thou wicked servant. Thou knewest that I was an austere man, taking up that I laid not down, and reaping that I did not sow: [23]Wherefore then gavest not thou my money into the bank, that at my coming I might have required mine own with usury? [24]And he said unto them that stood by, Take from him the pound, and give it to him that hath ten pounds. [25](And they said unto him, Lord, he hath ten pounds.) [26]For I say unto you, That unto every one which hath shall be given; and from him that hath not, even that he hath shall be taken away from him. [27]But those mine enemies, which would not that I should reign over them, bring hither, and slay them before me.

19:34

[34]And they said, The Lord hath need of him.

(Continued)

TITUS (PSEUDO) 2:13—Teaching and Christian life (2:1–3:15), pastoral epistle, pseudo-Pauline authorship, early second century

Theme	TITUS	Lk
(*Cont.*) **Lord's coming**	2:13 (above)	(*Continued*) **20:4–44** [4]The baptism of John, was it from heaven, or of men? [5]And they reasoned with themselves, saying, If we shall say, From heaven; he will say, Why then believed ye him not? [6]But and if we say, Of men; all the people will stone us: for they be persuaded that John was a prophet. [7]And they answered, that they could not tell whence it was. [8]And Jesus said unto them, Neither tell I you by what authority I do these things. [9]Then began he to speak to the people this parable; A certain man planted a vineyard, and let it forth to husbandmen, and went into a far country for a long time. [10]And at the season he sent a servant to the husbandmen, that they should give him of the fruit of the vineyard: but the husbandmen beat him, and sent him away empty. [11]And again he sent another servant: and they beat him also, and entreated him shamefully, and sent him away empty. [12]And again he sent a third: and they wounded him also, and cast him out. [13]Then said the lord of the vineyard, What shall I do? I will send my beloved son: it may be they will reverence him when they see him. [14]But when the husbandmen saw him, they reasoned among themselves, saying, This is the heir: come, let us kill him, that the inheritance may be ours. [15]So they cast him out of the vineyard, and killed him. What therefore shall the lord of the vineyard do unto them? [16]He shall come and destroy these husbandmen, and shall give the vineyard to others. And when they heard it, they said, God forbid. [17]And he beheld them, and said, What is this then that is written, The stone which the builders rejected, the same is become the head of the corner? [18]Whosoever shall fall upon that stone shall be broken; but on whomsoever it shall fall, it will grind him to powder. [19]And the chief priests and the scribes the same hour sought to lay hands on him; and they feared the people: for they perceived that he had spoken this parable against them. [20]And they watched him, and sent forth spies, which should feign themselves just men, that they might take hold of his words, that so they might deliver him unto the power and authority of the governor. [21]And they asked him, saying, Master, we know that thou sayest and teachest rightly, neither acceptest thou the person of any, but teachest the way of God truly: [22]Is it lawful for us to give tribute unto Caesar, or no? [23]But he perceived their craftiness, and said unto them, Why tempt ye me? [24]Show me a penny. Whose image and superscription hath it? They answered and said, Caesar's. [25]And he said unto them, Render therefore unto Caesar the things which be Caesar's, and unto God the things which be God's. [26]And they could not take hold of his words before the people: and they marvelled at his answer, and held their peace. [27]Then came to him certain of the Sadducees, which deny that there is any resurrection; and they asked him, [28]Saying, Master, Moses wrote unto us, If any man's brother die, having a wife, and he die without children, that his brother should take his wife, and raise up seed unto his brother. [29]There were therefore seven brethren: and the first took a wife, and died without children. [30]And the second took her to wife, and he died childless. [31]And the third took her; and in like manner the seven also: and they left no children, and died. [32]Last of all the woman died also. [33]Therefore in the resurrection whose wife of them is she? for seven had her to wife. [34]And Jesus answering said unto them, The children of this world marry, and are given in marriage: [35]But they which shall be accounted worthy to obtain that world, and the resurrection from the dead, neither marry, nor are given in marriage: [36]Neither can they die any more: for they are equal unto the angels; and are the children of God, being the children of the resurrection. [37]Now that the dead are raised, even Moses showed at the bush, when he calleth the Lord the God of Abraham, and the God of Isaac, and the God of Jacob. [38]For he is not a God of the dead, but of the living: for all live unto him. [39]Then certain of the scribes answering said, Master, thou hast well said. [40]And after that they durst not ask him any question at all. [41]And he said unto them, How say they that Christ is David's son? [42]And David himself saith in the book of Psalms, The LORD said unto my Lord, Sit thou on my right hand, [43]Till I make thine enemies thy footstool. [44]David therefore calleth him Lord, how is he then his son?

Paul	NT	Jewish Writings	Other
Rom 10:9 [9]That if thou shalt confess with thy mouth the Lord Jesus, and shalt believe in thine heart that God hath raised him from the dead, thou shalt be saved. **Rom 10:13** [13]For whosoever shall call upon the name of the Lord shall be saved. **1 Cor 1:7** [7]So that ye come behind in no gift; waiting for the coming of our Lord Jesus Christ: **1 Cor 12:3** [3]Wherefore I give you to understand, that no man speaking by the Spirit of God calleth Jesus accursed: and that no man can say that Jesus is the Lord, but by the Holy Ghost. **1 Cor 15:20–28** [20]But now is Christ risen from the dead, and become the firstfruits of them that slept. [21]For since by man came death, by man came also the resurrection of the dead. [22]For as in Adam all die, even so in Christ shall all be made alive. [23]But every man in his own order: Christ the firstfruits; afterward they that are Christ's at his coming. [24]Then cometh the end, when he shall have delivered up the kingdom to God, even the Father; when he shall have put down all rule and all authority and power. [25]For he must reign, till he hath put all enemies under his feet. [26]The last enemy that shall be destroyed is death. [27]For he hath put all things under his feet. But when he saith all things are put under him, it is manifest that he is excepted, which did put all things under him. [28]And when all things shall be subdued unto him, then shall the Son also himself be subject unto him that put all things under him, that God may be all in all. **Phil 2:5–11** [5]Let this mind be in you, which was also in Christ Jesus: [6]Who, being in the form of God, thought it not robbery to be equal with God: [7]But made himself of no reputation, and took upon him the form of a servant, and was made in the likeness of men: [8]And being found in fashion as a man, he humbled himself, and became obedient unto death, even the death of the cross. [9]Wherefore God also hath highly exalted him, and given him a name which is above every name: [10]That at the name of Jesus every knee should bow, of things in heaven, and things in earth, and things under the earth; [11]And that every tongue should confess that Jesus Christ is Lord, to the glory of God the Father. **Phil 3:20** [20]For our conversation is in heaven; from whence also we look for the Saviour, the Lord Jesus Christ: **1 Thes 1:10** [10]And to wait for his Son from heaven, whom he raised from the dead, even Jesus, which delivered us from the wrath to come. **2 Thes 1:1** [1]Paul, and Silvanus, and Timotheus, unto the church of the Thessalonians in God our Father and the Lord Jesus Christ: **2 Tim 1:4 (Pseudo)** [4]Greatly desiring to see thee, being mindful of thy tears, that I may be filled with joy; **2 Tim 1:10 (Pseudo)** [10]But is now made manifest by the appearing of our Saviour Jesus Christ, who hath abolished death, and hath brought life and immortality to light through the gospel: **2 Tim 3:6 (Pseudo)** [6]For of this sort are they which creep into houses, and lead captive silly women laden with sins, led away with divers lusts,	**2 Pet 1:1, 11** [1]Simon Peter, a servant and an apostle of Jesus Christ, to them that have obtained like precious faith with us through the righteousness of God and our Saviour Jesus Christ: . . . [11]For so an entrance shall be ministered unto you abundantly into the everlasting kingdom of our Lord and Saviour Jesus Christ. **2 Pet 2:20** [20]For if after they have escaped the pollutions of the world through the knowledge of the Lord and Saviour Jesus Christ, they are again entangled therein, and overcome, the latter end is worse with them than the beginning. **2 Pet 3:2, 18** [2]That ye may be mindful of the words which were spoken before by the holy prophets, and of the commandment of us the apostles of the Lord and Saviour: . . . [18]But grow in grace, and in the knowledge of our Lord and Saviour Jesus Christ. To him be glory both now and for ever. Amen.	**Ps 110** [1]The LORD said unto my Lord, Sit thou at my right hand, until I make thine enemies thy footstool. [2]The LORD shall send the rod of thy strength out of Zion: rule thou in the midst of thine enemies. [3]Thy people shall be willing in the day of thy power, in the beauties of holiness from the womb of the morning: thou hast the dew of thy youth. [4]The LORD hath sworn, and will not repent, Thou art a priest for ever after the order of Melchizedek. [5]The Lord at thy right hand shall strike through kings in the day of his wrath. [6]He shall judge among the heathen, he shall fill the places with the dead bodies; he shall wound the heads over many countries. [7]He shall drink of the brook in the way: therefore shall he lift up the head.	**Q-Quelle** Watchful and faithful: [Rom 9:5]/Tit 2:13/Mt 24:42-51/ Lk 12:35-48 (QS); Parable of pounds: Tit 2:13/Mt 25:14-30/ Lk 19:11-27 (QS 61 [Thom 41])

TITUS (PSEUDO) 2:14—Teaching and Christian life (2:1–3:15), pastoral epistle, pseudo-Pauline authorship, early second century

Theme	TITUS	Paul	NT	Jewish
Christ's sacrifice for faithful	**2:14 (Pseudo)** [14]Who gave himself for us, that he might redeem us from all iniquity, and purify unto himself a peculiar people, zealous of good works.	**Gal 1:4** [4]Who gave himself for our sins, that he might deliver us from this present evil world, according to the will of God and our Father: **Eph 5:2 (Pseudo)** [2]And walk in love, as Christ also hath loved us, and hath given himself for us an offering and a sacrifice to God for a sweetsmelling savour. **Eph 5:25 (Pseudo)** [25]Husbands, love your wives, even as Christ also loved the church, and gave himself for it; **1 Tim 2:6 (Pseudo)** [6]Who gave himself a ransom for all, to be testified in due time.	**1 Pet 1:18–19** [18]Forasmuch as ye know that ye were not redeemed with corruptible things, as silver and gold, from your vain conversation received by tradition from your fathers; [19]But with the precious blood of Christ, as of a lamb without blemish and without spot:	**Ps 130:8** [8]And he shall redeem Israel from all his iniquities.

TITUS (PSEUDO) 2:15—Teaching and Christian life (2:1–3:15), pastoral epistle, pseudo-Pauline authorship, early second century

Theme	TITUS	Paul
Find favor with all	**2:15 (Pseudo)** [15]These things speak, and exhort, and rebuke with all authority. Let no man despise thee.	**1 Tim 4:12 (Pseudo)** [12]Let no man despise thy youth; but be thou an example of the believers, in word, in conversation, in charity, in spirit, in faith, in purity.

TITUS (PSEUDO) 3:1—Teaching and Christian life (2:1–3:15), pastoral epistle, pseudo-Pauline authorship, early second century

Theme	TITUS	Paul	NT
Obey governing authorities & do good works	**3:1 (Pseudo)** [1]Put them in mind to be subject to principalities and powers, to obey magistrates, to be ready to every good work,	**Rom 13:1–7** [1]Let every soul be subject unto the higher powers. For there is no power but of God: the powers that be are ordained of God. [2]Whosoever therefore resisteth the power, resisteth the ordinance of God: and they that resist shall receive to themselves damnation. [3]For rulers are not a terror to good works, but to the evil. Wilt thou then not be afraid of the power? do that which is good, and thou shalt have praise of the same: [4]For he is the minister of God to thee for good. But if thou do that which is evil, be afraid; for he beareth not the sword in vain: for he is the minister of God, a revenger to execute wrath upon him that doeth evil. [5]Wherefore ye must needs be subject, not only for wrath, but also for conscience sake. [6]For for this cause pay ye tribute also: for they are God's ministers, attending continually upon this very thing. [7]Render therefore to all their dues: tribute to whom tribute is due; custom to whom custom; fear to whom fear; honour to whom honour. **1 Tim 2:1–2 (Pseudo)** [1]I exhort therefore, that, first of all, supplications, prayers, intercessions, and giving of thanks, be made for all men; [2]For kings, and for all that are in authority; that we may lead a quiet and peaceable life in all godliness and honesty.	**1 Pet 2:13–14** [13]Submit yourselves to every ordinance of man for the Lord's sake: whether it be to the king, as supreme; [14]Or unto governors, as unto them that are sent by him for the punishment of evildoers, and for the praise of them that do well.

TITUS (PSEUDO) 3:3—Teaching and Christian life (2:1–3:15), pastoral epistle, pseudo-Pauline authorship, early second century

Theme	TITUS	Paul	NT
All were sinners at one time	**3:3 (Pseudo)** [3]For we ourselves also were sometimes foolish, disobedient, deceived, serving divers lusts and pleasures, living in malice and envy, hateful, and hating one another.	**1 Cor 6:9–11** [9]Know ye not that the unrighteous shall not inherit the kingdom of God? Be not deceived: neither fornicators, nor idolaters, nor adulterers, nor effeminate, nor abusers of themselves with mankind, [10]Nor thieves, nor covetous, nor drunkards, nor revilers, nor extortioners, shall inherit the kingdom of God. [11]And such were some of you: but ye are washed, but ye are sanctified, but ye are justified in the name of the Lord Jesus, and by the Spirit of our God. **Eph 2:1–3 (Pseudo)** [1]And you hath he quickened, who were dead in trespasses and sins; [2]Wherein in time past ye walked according to the course of this world, according to the prince of the power of the air, the spirit that now worketh in the children of disobedience: [3]Among whom also we all had our conversation in times past in the lusts of our flesh, fulfilling the desires of the flesh and of the mind; and were by nature the children of wrath, even as others. **Eph 5:8 (Pseudo)** [8]For ye were sometimes darkness, but now are ye light in the Lord: walk as children of light: **Col 3:5–7** [5]Mortify therefore your members which are upon the earth; fornication, uncleanness, inordinate affection, evil concupiscence, and covetousness, which is idolatry: [6]For which things' sake the wrath of God cometh on the children of disobedience: [7]In the which ye also walked some time, when ye lived in them.	**1 Pet 4:3** [3]For the time past of our life may suffice us to have wrought the will of the Gentiles, when we walked in lasciviousness, lusts, excess of wine, revellings, banquetings, and abominable idolatries:

TITUS (PSEUDO) 3:4—Teaching and Christian life (2:1–3:15), pastoral epistle, pseudo-Pauline authorship, early second century

Theme	TITUS	Paul	NT	Jewish
Changed by God's kindness	**3:4 (Pseudo)** [4]But after that the kindness and love of God our Saviour toward man appeared, **1:3 (Pseudo)** [3]But hath in due times manifested his word through preaching, which is committed unto me according to the commandment of God our Saviour; **2:10 (Pseudo)** [10]Not purloining, but showing all good fidelity; that they may adorn the doctrine of God our Saviour in all things.	**1 Tim 1:1 (Pseudo)** [1]Paul, an apostle of Jesus Christ by the commandment of God our Saviour, and Lord Jesus Christ, which is our hope; **1 Tim 2:3 (Pseudo)** [3]For this is good and acceptable in the sight of God our Saviour; **1 Tim 4:10 (Pseudo)** [10]For therefore we both labour and suffer reproach, because we trust in the living God, who is the Saviour of all men, specially of those that believe.	**Jude 25** [25]To the only wise God our Saviour, be glory and majesty, dominion and power, both now and for ever. Amen.	**Ps 24:5** [5]He shall receive the blessing from the LORD, and righteousness from the God of his salvation.

TITUS (PSEUDO) 3:5—Teaching and Christian life (2:1–3:15), pastoral epistle, pseudo-Pauline authorship, early second century

Theme	TITUS	Paul	Jewish Writings
God's mercy saved	**3:5 (Pseudo)** [5]Not by works of righteousness which we have done, but according to his mercy he saved us, by the washing of regeneration, and renewing of the Holy Ghost;	**Eph 2:4–5 (Pseudo)** [4]But God, who is rich in mercy, for his great love wherewith he loved us, [5]Even when we were dead in sins, hath quickened us together with Christ, (by grace ye are saved;) **Eph 2:8–9 (Pseudo)** [8]For by grace are ye saved through faith; and that not of yourselves: it is the gift of God: [9]Not of works, lest any man should boast. **2 Tim 1:9 (Pseudo)** [9]Who hath saved us, and called us with an holy calling, not according to our works, but according to his own purpose and grace, which was given us in Christ Jesus before the world began,	**Dt 9:5** [5]Not for thy righteousness, or for the uprightness of thine heart, dost thou go to possess their land: but for the wickedness of these nations the LORD thy God doth drive them out from before thee, and that he may perform the word which the LORD sware unto thy fathers, Abraham, Isaac, and Jacob.

TITUS (PSEUDO) 3:6—Teaching and Christian life (2:1–3:15), pastoral epistle, pseudo-Pauline authorship, early second century

Theme	TITUS	Paul	NT
Abundance of Holy Spirit	**3:6 (Pseudo)** [6]Which he shed on us abundantly through Jesus Christ our Saviour; **1:4 (Pseudo)** [4]To Titus, mine own son after the common faith: Grace, mercy, and peace, from God the Father and the Lord Jesus Christ our Saviour. **2:13 (Pseudo)** [13]Looking for that blessed hope, and the glorious appearing of the great God and our Saviour Jesus Christ;	**Phil 3:20** [20]For our conversation is in heaven; from whence also we look for the Saviour, the Lord Jesus Christ: **2 Tim 1:10 (Pseudo)** [10]For whoremongers, for them that defile themselves with mankind, for menstealers, for liars, for perjured persons, and if there be any other thing that is contrary to sound doctrine;	**2 Pet 1:1, 11** [1]Simon Peter, a servant and an apostle of Jesus Christ, to them that have obtained like precious faith with us through the righteousness of God and our Saviour Jesus Christ: . . . [11]For so an entrance shall be ministered unto you abundantly into the everlasting kingdom of our Lord and Saviour Jesus Christ. **2 Pet 2:2** [2]And many shall follow their pernicious ways; by reason of whom the way of truth shall be evil spoken of. **2 Pet 3:2, 18** [2]That ye may be mindful of the words which were spoken before by the holy prophets, and of the commandment of us the apostles of the Lord and Saviour: . . . [18]But grow in grace, and in the knowledge of our Lord and Saviour Jesus Christ. To him be glory both now and for ever. Amen.

TITUS (PSEUDO) 3:7—Teaching and Christian life (2:1–3:15), pastoral epistle, pseudo-Pauline authorship, early second century

Theme	TITUS	Jn	Paul
Justified by grace	**3:7 (Pseudo)** [7]That being justified by his grace, we should be made heirs according to the hope of eternal life. **1:2 (Pseudo)** [2]In hope of eternal life, which God, that cannot lie, promised before the world began;	**1 Jn 2:25** [25]And this is the promise that he hath promised us, even eternal life.	**2 Tim 1:1 (Pseudo)** [1]Paul, an apostle of Jesus Christ by the will of God, according to the promise of life which is in Christ Jesus,

TITUS (PSEUDO) 3:8—Teaching and Christian life (2:1–3:15), pastoral epistle, pseudo-Pauline authorship, early second century

Theme	TITUS	Paul
Finding God's approval, do good works	**3:8 (Pseudo)** [8]This is a faithful saying, and these things I will that thou affirm constantly, that they which have believed in God might be careful to maintain good works. These things are good and profitable unto men.	**1 Tim 1:15 (Pseudo)** [15]This is a faithful saying, and worthy of all acceptation, that Christ Jesus came into the world to save sinners; of whom I am chief. **1 Tim 3:1 (Pseudo)** [1]This is a true saying, If a man desire the office of a bishop, he desireth a good work. **1 Tim 4:9 (Pseudo)** [9]This is a faithful saying and worthy of all acceptation. **2 Tim 2:11 (Pseudo)** [11]It is a faithful saying: For if we be dead with him, we shall also live with him:

TITUS (PSEUDO) 3:9—Teaching and Christian life (2:1–3:15), pastoral epistle, pseudo-Pauline authorship, early second century

Theme	TITUS	Paul
Avoid genealogies & contentious behavior	**3:9 (Pseudo)** [9]But avoid foolish questions, and genealogies, and contentions, and strivings about the law; for they are unprofitable and vain.	**1 Tim 1:4 (Pseudo)** [4]Neither give heed to fables and endless genealogies, which minister questions, rather than godly edifying which is in faith: so do. **1 Tim 4:7 (Pseudo)** [7]But refuse profane and old wives' fables, and exercise thyself rather unto godliness. **2 Tim 2:23 (Pseudo)** [23]But foolish and unlearned questions avoid, knowing that they do gender strifes.

TITUS (PSEUDO) 3:10—Teaching and Christian life (2:1–3:15), pastoral epistle, pseudo-Pauline authorship, early second century

Theme	TITUS	Mt	Paul	Other
Reject heretics after 2 admonitions	**3:10 (Pseudo)** [10]A man that is an heretic after the first and second admonition reject;	**18:15–18** [15]Moreover if thy brother shall trespass against thee, go and tell him his fault between thee and him alone: if he shall hear thee, thou hast gained thy brother. [16]But if he will not hear thee, then take with thee one or two more, that in the mouth of two or three witnesses every word may be established. [17]And if he shall neglect to hear them, tell it unto the church: but if he neglect to hear the church, let him be unto thee as an heathen man and a publican. [18]Verily I say unto you, Whatsoever ye shall bind on earth shall be bound in heaven: and whatsoever ye shall loose on earth shall be loosed in heaven.	**Rom 16:17** [17]Now I beseech you, brethren, mark them which cause divisions and offences contrary to the doctrine which ye have learned; and avoid them. **1 Cor 5:11** [11]But now I have written unto you not to keep company, if any man that is called a brother be a fornicator, or covetous, or an idolater, or a railer, or a drunkard, or an extortioner; with such an one no not to eat. **2 Thes 3:6** [6]Now we command you, brethren, in the name of our Lord Jesus Christ, that ye withdraw yourselves from every brother that walketh disorderly, and not after the tradition which he received of us. **2 Thes 3:14–15** [14]And if any man obey not our word by this epistle, note that man, and have no company with him, that he may be ashamed. [15]Yet count him not as an enemy, but admonish him as a brother.	**Q-Quelle** On forgiveness: Tit 3:10/ Mt 18:15, [Mt 18:21-22]/[Lk 17:3b-4 (QS 58)]; Fruits: Tit 3:10/ Rom 16:17/ [Mt 7:15-20, 12:33-35]/ [Lk 6:43-45 (QS 13 [Thom 45])]

TITUS (PSEUDO) 3:12—Teaching and Christian life (2:1–3:15), pastoral epistle, pseudo-Pauline authorship, early second century

Theme	TITUS	Lk	Paul
Come with Artemas or Tychicus	**3:12 (Pseudo)** [12]When I shall send Artemas unto thee, or Tychicus, be diligent to come unto me to Nicopolis: for I have determined there to winter.	**Acts 20:4** [4]And there accompanied him into Asia Sopater of Berea; and of the Thessalonians, Aristarchus and Secundus; and Gaius of Derbe, and Timotheus; and of Asia, Tychicus and Trophimus.	**Eph 6:21 (Pseudo)** [21]But that ye also may know my affairs, and how I do, Tychicus, a beloved brother and faithful minister in the Lord, shall make known to you all things: **Col 4:7** [7]All my state shall Tychicus declare unto you, who is a beloved brother, and a faithful minister and fellowservant in the Lord: **2 Tim 4:12 (Pseudo)** [12]And Tychicus have I sent to Ephesus.

TITUS (PSEUDO) 3:13—Teaching and Christian life (2:1–3:15), pastoral epistle, pseudo-Pauline authorship, early second century

Theme	TITUS	Lk	Paul
Bring Zenas and Apollos, treat them well	**3:13 (Pseudo)** [13]Bring Zenas the lawyer and Apollos on their journey diligently, that nothing be wanting unto them.	**Acts 18:24–26** [24]And a certain Jew named Apollos, born at Alexandria, an eloquent man, and mighty in the scriptures, came to Ephesus. [25]This man was instructed in the way of the Lord; and being fervent in the spirit, he spake and taught diligently the things of the Lord, knowing only the baptism of John. [26]And he began to speak boldly in the synagogue: whom when Aquila and Priscilla had heard, they took him unto them, and expounded unto him the way of God more perfectly.	**1 Cor 1:12** [12]Now this I say, that every one of you saith, I am of Paul; and I of Apollos; and I of Cephas; and I of Christ. **1 Cor 3:4–6, 22** [4]For while one saith, I am of Paul; and another, I am of Apollos; are ye not carnal? [5]Who then is Paul, and who is Apollos, but ministers by whom ye believed, even as the Lord gave to every man? [6]I have planted, Apollos watered; but God gave the increase. **1 Cor 16:12** [12]As touching our brother Apollos, I greatly desired him to come unto you with the brethren: but his will was not at all to come at this time; but he will come when he shall have convenient time.

TITUS (PSEUDO) 3:14—Teaching and Christian life (2:1–3:15), pastoral epistle, pseudo-Pauline authorship, early second century

Theme	TITUS	NT
Let good works bear fruit	**3:14 (Pseudo)** [14]And let ours also learn to maintain good works for necessary uses, that they be not unfruitful. **2:14 (Pseudo)** [14]Who gave himself for us, that he might redeem us from all iniquity, and purify unto himself a peculiar people, zealous of good works. **3:8 (Pseudo)** [8]This is a faithful saying, and these things I will that thou affirm constantly, that they which have believed in God might be careful to maintain good works. These things are good and profitable unto men.	**Heb 10:24** [24]And let us consider one another to provoke unto love and to good works: **1 Pet 3:13** [13]And who is he that will harm you, if ye be followers of that which is good?

TITUS (PSEUDO) 3:15—Teaching and Christian life (2:1–3:15), pastoral epistle, pseudo-Pauline authorship, early second century

Theme	TITUS	NT
Salutation & grace	**3:15 (Pseudo)** [15]All that are with me salute thee. Greet them that love us in the faith. Grace be with you all. Amen.	**Heb 13:25** [25]Grace be with you all. Amen.

PHILEMON

61 to 63 CE, letter written from prison in Rome

GREETING AND ADDRESS (1–3)

PHILEMON 1—Greeting and Address (1–3), Letter written from prison in Rome, 61–63 CE

Theme	PHLM	Paul
Greeting from Paul, Timothy, Philemon, & fellow laborers	**1** [1]Paul, a prisoner of Jesus Christ, and Timothy our brother, unto Philemon our dearly beloved, and fellowlabourer, **9** [9]Yet for love's sake I rather beseech thee, being such an one as Paul the aged, and now also a prisoner of Jesus Christ.	**Eph 3:1 (Pseudo)** [1]For this cause I Paul, the prisoner of Jesus Christ for you Gentiles, **Eph 4:1 (Pseudo)** [1]I therefore, the prisoner of the Lord, beseech you that ye walk worthy of the vocation wherewith ye are called, **Phil 1:7, 13** [7]Even as it is meet for me to think this of you all, because I have you in my heart; inasmuch as both in my bonds, and in the defence and confirmation of the gospel, ye all are partakers of my grace. . . . [13]So that my bonds in Christ are manifest in all the palace, and in all other places;

PHILEMON 2—Greeting and Address (1–3), Letter written from prison in Rome, 61–63 CE

Theme	PHLM	Paul
Greeting from Apphia, Archippus to church	**2** [2]And to our beloved Apphia, and Archippus our fellow-soldier, and to the church in thy house:	**Col 4:17** [17]And say to Archippus, Take heed to the ministry which thou hast received in the Lord, that thou fulfil it.

PHILEMON 3—Greeting and Address (1–3), Letter written from prison in Rome, 61–63 CE

Theme	PHLM	Paul
Grace and peace	**3** [3]Grace to you, and peace, from God our Father and the Lord Jesus Christ.	**Rom 1:7** [7]To all that be in Rome, beloved of God, called to be saints: Grace to you and peace from God our Father, and the Lord Jesus Christ. **Gal 1:3** [3]Grace be to you and peace from God the Father, and from our Lord Jesus Christ, **Phil 1:2** [2]Grace be unto you, and peace, from God our Father, and from the Lord Jesus Christ.

THANKSGIVING (4–6)

PHILEMON 4–5—Thanksgiving (4–6), Letter written from prison in Rome, 61–63 CE

Theme	PHLM	Paul
Thanks	**4–5** [4]I thank my God, making mention of thee always in my prayers, [5]Hearing of thy love and faith, which thou hast toward the Lord Jesus, and toward all saints;	**Rom 1:8–9** [8]First, I thank my God through Jesus Christ for you all, that your faith is spoken of throughout the whole world. [9]For God is my witness, whom I serve with my spirit in the gospel of his Son, that without ceasing I make mention of you always in my prayers; **Eph 1:15–16 (Pseudo)** [15]Wherefore I also, after I heard of your faith in the Lord Jesus, and love unto all the saints, [16]Cease not to give thanks for you, making mention of you in my prayers;

PHILEMON 6—Thanksgiving (4–6), Letter written from prison in Rome, 61–63 CE

Theme	PHLM	Paul
Thanks makes faith effective	**6** [6]That the communication of thy faith may become effectual by the acknowledging of every good thing which is in you in Christ Jesus.	**Phil 1:9** [9]And this I pray, that your love may abound yet more and more in knowledge and in all judgment; **Col 1:9** [9]For this cause we also, since the day we heard it, do not cease to pray for you, and to desire that ye might be filled with the knowledge of his will in all wisdom and spiritual understanding;

REQUEST TO FREE ONESIMUS FROM SLAVERY (7–22)

PHILEMON 7—Request to free Onesimus from slavery (7–22), Letter written from prison in Rome, 61–63 CE

Theme	PHLM	Paul
Joy & consolation in love	7 [7]For we have great joy and consolation in thy love, because the bowels of the saints are refreshed by thee, brother.	**2 Cor 7:4** [4]Great is my boldness of speech toward you, great is my glorying of you: I am filled with comfort, I am exceeding joyful in all our tribulation.

PHILEMON 9—Request to free Onesimus from slavery (7–22), Letter written from prison in Rome, 61–63 CE

Theme	PHLM	Paul
Prisoner for love of Christ	**9** [9]Yet for love's sake I rather beseech thee, being such an one as Paul the aged, and now also a prisoner of Jesus Christ. **1** [1]Paul, a prisoner of Jesus Christ, and Timothy our brother, unto Philemon our dearly beloved, and fellowlabourer,	**Eph 3:1 (Pseudo)** [1]For this cause I Paul, the prisoner of Jesus Christ for you Gentiles, **Eph 4:1 (Pseudo)** [1]I therefore, the prisoner of the Lord, beseech you that ye walk worthy of the vocation wherewith ye are called, **Phil 1:7, 13** [7]Even as it is meet for me to think this of you all, because I have you in my heart; inasmuch as both in my bonds, and in the defence and confirmation of the gospel, ye all are partakers of my grace. . . . [13]So that my bonds in Christ are manifest in all the palace, and in all other places;

PHILEMON 10—Request to free Onesimus from slavery (7–22), Letter written from prison in Rome, 61–63 CE

Theme	PHLM	Paul
Request for Onesimus	**10** [10]I beseech thee for my son Onesimus, whom I have begotten in my bonds:	**1 Cor 4:14–15** [14]I write not these things to shame you, but as my beloved sons I warn you. [15]For though ye have ten thousand instructors in Christ, yet have ye not many fathers: for in Christ Jesus I have begotten you through the gospel. **Gal 4:19** [19]My little children, of whom I travail in birth again until Christ be formed in you, **Col 4:9** [9]With Onesimus, a faithful and beloved brother, who is one of you. They shall make known unto you all things which are done here.

PHILEMON 13—Request to free Onesimus from slavery (7–22), Letter written from prison in Rome, 61–63 CE

Theme	PHLM	Paul
Onesimus served Paul & gospel	**13** [13]Whom I would have retained with me, that in thy stead he might have ministered unto me in the bonds of the gospel:	**Phil 2:30** [30]Because for the work of Christ he was nigh unto death, not regarding his life, to supply your lack of service toward me.

PHILEMON 14—Request to free Onesimus from slavery (7–22), Letter written from prison in Rome, 61–63 CE

Theme	PHLM	Paul	NT
Free him willingly	**14** [14]But without thy mind would I do nothing; that thy benefit should not be as it were of necessity, but willingly.	**2 Cor 9:7** [7]Every man according as he purposeth in his heart, so let him give; not grudgingly, or of necessity: for God loveth a cheerful giver.	**1 Pet 5:2** [2]Feed the flock of God which is among you, taking the oversight thereof, not by constraint, but willingly; not for filthy lucre, but of a ready mind;

PHILEMON 16—Request to free Onesimus from slavery (7–22), Letter written from prison in Rome, 61–63 CE

Theme	PHLM	Paul
A beloved brother in Christ	**16** [16]Not now as a servant, but above a servant, a brother beloved, specially to me, but how much more unto thee, both in the flesh, and in the Lord?	**1 Tim 6:2 (Pseudo)** [2]And they that have believing masters, let them not despise them, because they are brethren; but rather do them service, because they are faithful and beloved, partakers of the benefit. These things teach and exhort.

PHILEMON 19—Request to free Onesimus from slavery (7–22), Letter written from prison in Rome, 61–63 CE

Theme	PHLM	Paul
Paul's handwriting	**19** [19]I Paul have written it with mine own hand, I will repay it: albeit I do not say to thee how thou owest unto me even thine own self besides.	**Gal 6:11** [11]Ye see how large a letter I have written unto you with mine own hand. **2 Thes 3:17** [17]The salutation of Paul with mine own hand, which is the token in every epistle: so I write.

PHILEMON 22—Request to free Onesimus from slavery (7–22), Letter written from prison in Rome, 61–63 CE

Theme	PHLM	NT
Paul will visit	**22** [22]But withal prepare me also a lodging: for I trust that through your prayers I shall be given unto you.	**Heb 13:19** [19]But I beseech you the rather to do this, that I may be restored to you the sooner.

FAREWELL (23–24)

PHILEMON 23—Farewell (23–24), Letter written from prison in Rome, 61–63 CE

Theme	PHLM	Paul
Say hello to Epaphras	**23** [23]There salute thee Epaphras, my fellowprisoner in Christ Jesus;	**Col 1:7** [7]As ye also learned of Epaphras our dear fellowservant, who is for you a faithful minister of Christ; **Col 4:12–13** [12]Epaphras, who is one of you, a servant of Christ, saluteth you, always labouring fervently for you in prayers, that ye may stand perfect and complete in all the will of God. [13]For I bear him record, that he hath a great zeal for you, and them that are in Laodicea, and them in Hierapolis.

PHILEMON 24—Farewell (23–24), Letter written from prison in Rome, 61–63 CE

Theme	PHLM	Lk	Paul
Signed by fellow workers	**24** [24]Marcus, Aristarchus, Demas, Lucas, my fellowlabourers.	**Acts 12:12, 15** [12]And when he had considered the thing, he came to the house of Mary the mother of John, whose surname was Mark; where many were gathered together praying. . . . [15]And they said unto her, Thou art mad. But she constantly affirmed that it was even so. Then said they, It is his angel. **Acts 13:13** [13]Now when Paul and his company loosed from Paphos, they came to Perga in Pamphylia: and John departing from them returned to Jerusalem. **Acts 15:37–39** [37]And Barnabas determined to take with them John, whose surname was Mark. [38]But Paul thought not good to take him with them, who departed from them from Pamphylia, and went not with them to the work. [39]And the contention was so sharp between them, that they departed asunder one from the other: and so Barnabas took Mark, and sailed unto Cyprus; **Acts 19:29** [29]And the whole city was filled with confusion: and having caught Gaius and Aristarchus, men of Macedonia, Paul's companions in travel, they rushed with one accord into the theatre. **Acts 20:4** [4]And there accompanied him into Asia Sopater of Berea; and of the Thessalonians, Aristarchus and Secundus; and Gaius of Derbe, and Timotheus; and of Asia, Tychicus and Trophimus. **Acts 27:2** [2]And entering into a ship of Adramyttium, we launched, meaning to sail by the coasts of Asia; one Aristarchus, a Macedonian of Thessalonica, being with us.	**Col 4:10** [10]Aristarchus my fellowprisoner saluteth you, and Marcus, sister's son to Barnabas, (touching whom ye received commandments: if he come unto you, receive him;) **Col 4:14** [14]Luke, the beloved physician, and Demas, greet you. **2 Tim 4:10–13 (Pseudo)** [10]For Demas hath forsaken me, having loved this present world, and is departed unto Thessalonica; Crescens to Galatia, Titus unto Dalmatia. [11]Only Luke is with me. Take Mark, and bring him with thee: for he is profitable to me for the ministry. [12]And Tychicus have I sent to Ephesus. [13]The cloak that I left at Troas with Carpus, when thou comest, bring with thee, and the books, but especially the parchments.

Webster's 1828 Dictionary

This glossary is derived from Noah Webster's American Dictionary of the English Language, a dictionary published in 1828, which frequently used Bible verses in the definitions. This is an abridgment of the Webster's 1828. It was created by comparing each word from the Webster's 1828 to a list of words from the King James Bible. If a word from the Webster's 1828 appeared in the KJV, it was included in this glossary.

A

abaddon—to be lost/destroyed Rev. ix.
Abase/abash—confounded or ashamed
abate—pulled down, sunk
abba—father, bishop/prelate
abhor—to despise, hate, reject
abib—produce early fruit
abide/abode—to dwell, wait
abject—cast out
aboard—enter
abominate—to hate [evil]
abortive—before it is complete, immature
abound/abundance—great quantity
abstain—refrain from
abut—contiguous to
accede—give place to
aceldama—field of blood, south of Jerusalem
acquit—set free
adar—Heb calendar, end of February, marks abundance
adder—venomous serpent
adjure—biding oath
ado—difficulty
adulterate—to corrupt
advocate—pleads the case for another, lawyer
affright—sudden fear
afoot—on foot
afore—in front of
agate—on the way
ague—chill and fever
ah—surprise
aha—triumph
alas—sorrow or grief
albeit—as it is
algum—resinous wood
allegory—using figures of speech
alms—tithes
aloes—juice from leaves
aloft—on high, as a ship mast
alway/always—for all time
amerce—penalty softened by mercy
anathema—anathemas, judiciary and abjuratory
anon—soon, immediately
apis—mythology, figure of an ox; zoology, bee
apollyon—destroyer
apostle—on who is sent, follower of Christ Jesus
apothecary—pharmacy
appease—to quiet, calm
appertain—to belong to
appurtenance—an appendage
apt—rightly so
areopagite—member of areopagus
arkite—belonging to the ark
artificer—an artist
assay—to examine
assiduous—to sit and be present
assuage—to lessen
astray—off the right path
asunder—separate
attent—to show attention
aulic—a court
avouched—affirmed

B

Baal—indicates lordship
babe—young child
bdellium—perfume or medicine
beckoned—making a sign
bedstead—support for a bed
beeves—English black cattle
befall/befell—happen to
beget/begotten—procreate
beguile—to deceive
behemoth—monster
behoof—supply a need
belial—unprofitable
belie—to counterfeit
bellow—to make loud cry
ben—fruit or nut for purgatin
bereave—to make destitute
bereft—deprived
beryl—a pale green mineral
beseech to ask with urgency
beset—to surround
besom—a broom to sweep
bestead—to profit or accommodate
bestir—act of stirring
betimes—in season, good time
betroth—truth, to contract
betwixt—between
bewray—to betray
bid—to invite
bier—a death bed for burial
bishop—overseer in church
bite—to fasten on the front of a ship
bleating—sound a sheep makes
bloodguiltiness—guilt of murder
bloody—cruel, murderous
bode—future event
bondservice—slavery
booty—stollen goods
borne—to bear, set boundary
botch—skin infection or bad patch on clothes

bough—tree branch
bourn—a limit, boundary
bramble—prickly shrub
brandish—to wave
brazen—made of brass
brawler—a noisy person
bray—to grind to a powder
breach—to break
bred—educated
breeches—men's pants
brethren—brothers
brigandine—armor of metal scales
brimstone—sulphuric
brothel—house of lewd conduct
bruit—rumor
brute—senseless, rough, bestial
buckler—shield
bul—flounder
bulrush—a rush
burnished—polished

C

Cab—a measure of about 2.9 pints
Cachalot—a whale
Calamus—a reed, pipe, flute
Canker—corroding disease on trees or humans
carnal—unregenerate natural state
carpus—the wrist (not an English word)
catechize—education by asking questions
caul—a membrane in the abdomen; a hairnet
causey—raised path to avoid walking in water
chalcedony—white agate, quartz-like
chamois—a goat
chap—to crack open
chapiter—upper part of a
chaste—no sexual history
chasten/chastise—to punish
chide/chode—to scold
chisleu—Jewish calendar, part November and part December
choler—bile evacuation causing anger
Christ—the anointed
Christian—a believer and witness of Jesus' life and ministry
Chrysolite/chrysoprase—prismatic mineral, green
chub—a river fish
church—collective body of Christians
churl—rude, ill-bred
cistern—receptacle for holding liquids
clad—clothes covering
clamorous—loud words
clave/cleave—to stick to
clef—musical sign
cleft—a split in a rock
clement—mild temper
cloke—loose fitting coat
close—to finish
clouted—poor patch on garment
cloven (cleave)—divided
cockatrice—serpent coming from a rooster egg
cockle—a plant or (2) a shell
coffer—a chest or trunk
colter—a plow's sharp edge
comely/iness—suitable, good proportion
commission—entrusted to do something
commodious—proper place
common—belonging equally to more than one
commotion—agitation
commune—converse together or (2) sexual intercourse
communion—fellowship
compact—closely untied, an agreement
compassion—sympathy and suffering with another
compel—driven with force
comprehend—understand
conceal—to hide
conceit—to form an idea, opinion
conception—to form an embryo in the womb
concision—to cut off, Jewish ritual for baby boys (bris)
concord—union of opinions
concourse—meeting, assembly
concubine—non-married sexual relationship
concupiscence—irregular lust for enjoyment
coney/cony—shooting along
confection -sugary
confederate—allied by a treaty
confound—to throw several things into disorder
congealed—converted into solid state/mass
console—to bring comfort to
consorted—united in marriage
conspire—to plot
consummation—to complete
consumption—eating, passing/wasting away
contemn—to despise; to slight as unworthy
contend—to strive or struggle against
contra—lat., against
contradicting—denying, opposing
contrariwise—oppositely
contrite—bruised, broken
controvert—to turn against
convicted—proven guilty
convocation—calling and
Coptic—Christians in Egypt
copulation—sexual coupling
corban—an offering with life or (2) wicker basket
coriander—seeds with a strong Corinth—a city in Greece
cormorant—black-headed pelican
corpse—dead body
corpulent—excessive flesh
countervail—to show strength against force
coupling—sexual union
court—a hall or chamber
courtier—one who solicits the favor of another, goes to courts of princes
covenant—mutual consent
covert—covered
covet—to wish for
cradle—baby's bed
craft—cunning purposes
crag—break, rough
cram—to press
craw—first stomach of fowls
creak—sharp grating sound
creed—summary of articles professed/believed

cross—two pieces of wood placed across each other, Jesus died on the cross
crossing—passing over a boundary or (2) impediment
crucible—a melting pot
crucify—to subdue and nail to a cross
cruse—a small cup
cubit—the forearm
cumbrance—to obstruct
cunning—unkind motive
cupbearer—person who tasted the king's wine
cuth—to be known, famous

D

dagger—short sword
dainty—delicate, acute sensibility
dale—low place between the hills
dally—delay
dam—a human mother, in contempt
damsel—a young person of noble or genteel heritage
dan—honorable title used by Shakespeare
dandled—danced on one's knee
dare—to venture, with courage
darkly—obscurely, dimly
darling—dearly beloved, favorite
dart—a pointed instrument
dash—to strike down suddenly
daub—disguised, coarsely
dawn—growing light
daysman—a mediator
dayspring—dawn
deacon—a minister, servant
dearth/derth
debase—to criticize
debt—contracted
decked—covered, furnished, adorned
deed—act, agency
deemed—judged
deep—from recesses of heart
defamed—slander
default—failure or omission
defeat—overthrow
defect—mistake
defer—to put off or refer
defile—make impure
defraud—falsify
defy—daring
degenerate—qualities worsen
degree—ranking or space
delicate—delight, fine manners
delightsome—very pleasing
delusion—misleading
den—a cave
denounce—threatening declaration
deposed—degraded or (2) give testimony
deputed—made a substitute
deride—laughing contemptuously
descry—to examine, detect
despite—extreme hatred
destitute—not possessing
detained—to hold back
device—invention
devil—against god, wicked or profane
devise—invention
devote—to consecrate
devour—to eat-up or destroy
devout—reverence for God
diadem—crown
didrachma—Greek money
diet—nourishment or (2) assembly
dignity—worthy
diligence—attentive
dill—plant
disannul—make void (improper use)
discern—to judge aright
disciple—student, follower
discipline—subject to rule
disclose—revealing
discomfited—overcome
discord—disagreement
discreet—prudent
disdained—despised
disgrace—out of favor
dispensation—distribute
disposed—arranged
disputation—argument
distaff—spindle on spinning wheel or (2) female
distill—drops falling gently
divination—foretelling future
divine—Godlike
diviner—agency for god
doctrine—teaching
dodo—large gray & brown bird
doe—she dear or (2) a feat
doleful—sad
dor—Scarabaeus, black beetle
dost—an act by a second person
dote—impaired thinking, to decay
dower—gift
dowry—money paid to family for a spouse
drachma—Greek money
draco—dragon, constellation
draft—to take, adopt
drave—driving
dread—fearful
dregs—sediment of drink or refuse
dromedary—camel
dropsy—watery swelling
dross—rust, waste
drouth—dryness, thirst
dryshod—feet not bathed
dulcimer—musical instrument
dung—excrement
dungeon—deep, dark prison
dunghill—heap of excrement, born meanly
durst—a dare
dwarf—undersized, attendant for a lady or knight

E

earing—small rope in corner of a sail or (2) plowing
earnest—eager

earthy—a heavenly
ease—still
ebony—durable black wood
ed—Saxon word, happy/fortunate
eden—pleasure
edification—to build-up
effected—accomplished
effeminate—womanish, weak
elder—a duck species
eloquent—speaks very well
else—not that mentioned
embalm—to fill dead body with sweet scent
embassador—representative of sovereign
emboldened—encouraged
emerods—hemorrhoids
endamage—to harm
enfeeble—deprive of strength
enlighten—to illuminate
enmity—enemy
enquire—inquire, ask about
enrich—to supply or make rich
ensample—sample
ensign—a mark
ensnare—to imprison
enstamp—impress deeply
ensue—to seek
entail—heir for an estate
entangle—twist
entice—to lead astray
entomb—place body in grave
entreat—a sincere petition
Ephesian—person from Ephesus
ephod—priestly garment
epistle—ancient letter
equity—equal
er—agent, usually male
ere—soon, before
erected—raised
err/error—mistake
errand—to get something
eschew—to shun or avoid
espousals—marriage contract
espy—to see or discover
estranged—withdrawn
eternal—limitless
ether—liquid thinner than air, flammable
eunuch—castrated male
euroclydon—Malta's ferocious wind
evangelist—messenger
ewe—mother sheep
ex—out of
exaction—compelling tribute, fee
examen—examination, swarm of bees
excommunicated—church privileges revoked
execration—cursing
exhort—encourage
expiate—pious appeal for mercy
expiation—atonement for a crime
extinguishment—to put out
extol—to say good about someone
extortion—undue exercise of power

F

fain—glad to avert wrong
fallow—uncultivated
fare—to go or to pass
farewell—to go well
farthing—small copper coin
fashion—to make
fatling—an overfed lamb of cow
fear—anxiety or (2) holy awe
feeble—weak
feign—to reveal falsely
feller—one who knocks down
fellowship—companions brought together
fence—boundary or (2) sword play
fenced—guarded
fend—to keep off or resist
ferret—animal or a tool for iron melding
fervent—ardent or vehement temper
fetch—to get
feud—argument
fever—unhealthy body temperature or (2) passionate
fewness—brevity, smaller
fidelity—loyalty
fillet—a string or rubber band
firebrand—wood on fire
firmament—sky over our heads
firstling—first produce, first thought
fit—a violent bodily disorder
fitly—suitable, proper
flaccid—limber, hanging down
flagon—vessel for pouring liquor
flatter—to appease by praise
flax—a fibrous plant
flay—to skin or strip off
fleece—coat of sheep's wool or (2) to take by stealing
fleet—a flood, creek
fleshhook—ladle for hot pot
flit—to fly or dart along
flock—collection of birds or animals
flog—to beat or strike
flourish—to thrive or glorify God
flue—fireplace opening
flux—passing of liquid
foal—to bring forth a baby horse
fodder—dry animal feed
folly—weak intellect
font—a large basin or (2) printing type
footstool—stool for foot
foraging—looking for food
forbad—forbid
forbear—to stop or (2) be patient with
forbearance—avoid or shun
ford—a watery crossing place
forecast—foresight or scheme
forefront—battle front
foreknowledge—know before
foremost—leading
forepart—beginning
foreship—front of a boat
foreskin—skin over penis

foretell—predict
forewarn—admonish in advance
forfeited—give-up
forged—hammered or (2) counterfeit
forgive—to pardon or treat offended as one not guilty
fornication—unmarried sex, adultery or incest
forsake—abandon
forswear—to deny by oath
forthwith—immediately
forum—tribunal
foster—to nourish
foul—offensive, not fair
fourscore—four times twenty (score)
frank—candid
frankincense—a scent made form inflammable resin
fray—terrifying attack
freeman/woman—not a slave
freewill—voluntary, spontaneous
fret—worry
fro—away, back
froward—turning from
fruitful—very productive
furbish—to polish
furrow—to make a trench
fury—rage, heat of the mind

G

gad—a steel wedge or (2) a walk about
gainsay—contradict
gainsaying—opposing
Galatians—citizens of Galatia, descendents of Gauls
galbanum—blue plant milk
gall—bitter
gallant—splendid
gallows—instrument for punishment
gangrene—mortification of flesh
gape—open mouth to be fed
garner—place to store grain
garnish—to decorate
garrison—troops
gat—to get
gate—entry
gay—merry or (2) ornament
gaze—to fix one's eyes
gazingstock—person held in contempt
gender—born male or female
genealogy—heritage
genesis—beginning
geneva—distilled juniper, gin
genteel—graceful, polite
gentile—pagan who did not worship Hebrew God
gilded—overlaid with gold
gird/girt—spasm or (2) to bind
girdle—belt
glean—to collect grain behind the pickers
glede—vulture
glistering—shining
glutton—over indulgence
gnash—to grind teeth
gnat—a tiny insect
gnaw—to scrape
goad—urge movement
gob—a low word, mouthful
goblet—drinking vessel
God—a supreme being
god—a false idol
godhead—divine nature
godliness—piety
gog—haste, rush
goodliness—beautiful form
goodly—excellently
goods—moveable property
gore—thick blood or (2) to pierce
gorgeous—beautiful
gorget—neck armor for soldiers or ruffle for women
gospel—joyful message
gourd—plant shell used as a vessel
grace—unmerited favor, good will
graff—grave
grant—to give or transfer
greaves—tall-boot armor
Greece—flight of steps
greedy—eager to possess
Greek—language of Greece
grope—seek blindly
gross—bulky, coarse
grudge—unwilling desire
guile—with craft and cunning
gush—rapid flow

H

habergeon—upper body armor
habit—clothes
haft—a handle
hail—frozen rain or (2) exclamation
heinous—hateful
hale—healthy or (2) welfare or (3) to drag (haling)
hallow—sacred
halt—stop
handbreadth—width of hand
handmaiden—female servant
hap—sudden fortune or misfortune
haply—by chance
happiness—pleasure
hardhearted—cruel
hardly—barely, little
hare—rabbit or (2) to frighten, tease
harlot—seller of sex
harness—human & horse armor
harping—dwelling on or (2) buffer on front of ship
harrow—breaks dirt for farmers
harry—to pillage or harass
hart—male deer
hast—Having, thou form
haste—swiftly
hatch—eggs open for creatures or (2) engraving lines or (3) ship opening
haughty—insolent, proud
havock—general devastation
head—chief or (2) top of body

headlong—rashly
headstone—grave marker
heady—hasty, ungovernable
heal—to make whole or healthy
heap—a pile
hearken—to listen or attend to
hearth—brick chimney to warm a room
heath—shrub for brooms
heathen—pagan idol worshipper
heave—to lift
heaven—space where God lives, overhead or in heart Hebrew—tribal group and language
heed—care for
heel—back of foot
heifer—young cow
heinous—improper spelling for wicked act
heir—successor
hell—place of the dead, punishment
helm—defense or (2) ship steering
helmet—armor for head or (2) crest of coat of arms
helve—ax handle
hemlock—poison
hence—in the future
herald—proclaimer
hereafter—future state
hereby—by this
herein—in this
hereof—of this
heresy—error in religion
heretofore—future
hereunto—to this
herewith—with this
heritage—inheritance
Herodians—supporters of King Herod
Heron—bird, near water
hew—to carve
hin—Hebrew measure, English gallon
hind—female red stag or (2) a peasant or (3) backward
hinder—part that follows
hindered—stop
hindermost—the last
hireling—serves for wages
hither—points to a place
hoar—ageing white
hoariness—antiquity
hod—tray for mortar
hold—stop or (2) connect or (3) belief (holding)
holily—sacred
hollow—empty
holpen—help
holy—sacred, pious
hornet—wasp
hosanna—exclamation of praise
hough—thigh
howbeit—however
howsoever—as it will
humble—low
hungred—wanting food
husbandry—breeding
husk—covering of corn, etc.
hymn—song/ode for God
hyssop—fragrant plant

I

ignominy—public disgrace
immortal—exempt from death
immutability—inability to change
impediment—obstruct
impenitent—not contrite
imperious—dictatorial
implacable—not to be appeased
implead—lawsuit
importunity—urgent request
impose—to burden
impotent—weak
impoverish—to make poor
imprecate—to invoke
impudent—wanting modesty
incontinent—uncontrolled sexual appetite
inditing—written dictation
infamy—loss of reputation
infolding—wrapping-up
iniquity—injustice
insurrection—rising against civil authority
intercessor—mediator
interdict—to forbid
intermeddle—to meddle
intermit—to interrupt
interposed—place between

J

Jacinth—a plan
Jah—short for Jehovah
jangling—quarreling
jasper—quartz mineral
javelin—wood spear
jealous—suspicious rivals
Jehovah—a name for God
jeopardy—exposure to hazard
Jesse—large brass candlestick chandelier
jesting—joking
Jew—short for Judah, Hebrew tribe
jewry—Judea region
jezebel—vicious woman
jostle—to run against to push
jot—a point, Hebrew yod
juniper bush with bluish berries
Jupiter—Greek deity
just—proper standard
justice—giving due, honestly
justle—to countermand

K

keeper—guardian
kin/kindred—relationship, family
kind—natural classification
kindle—to set fire, or (2) to bring forth
kindly—of good will
kine—cows, plural
kinsman/woman—consanguine relationship
kite—a name of reproach
knead—pressing ingredients by hand
knop—knob or button

L

lad—to procreate or (2) a young boy
lade—to load or (2) draw water
laid/lain—lay down
lama—god of Asiatic Tartars
lament—mourne
lance—spear
lanch—sliding movement, to throw
landmark—signifier
languish—to wither
lap—loose part on coat
latchet—shoestring
laud—commendation, praise
laver—wash basin
lavish—profuse bestowal
lawyer—law practitioner
leaved—foliage
leaven—fermenting of dough
lees—sediment at bottom of liquor
legion—infantry or (2) great number
lent—40-day prayer & self-deprivation
leper—a person with a skin disease
lest—bad result
leviathan—water monster
Levite—tribe descending from Aaronic priesthood
levy—to raise, collect
lewd—lust for untoward sex
lief—freely loving
liege—feudal vassal
lien—lie or (2) legal claim to land
ligure—precious stone
lintel—side pieces of door frame
lo—look
loathsome—hateful
longsuffering—bearing injuries
lop—to cut off
lothe—to hate
louver—opening in the roof
love—pleasure and delight
Lucifer—name for Satan
lucre—profit
lye—a falsehood

M

mad—disoriented
made—an earthworm
magnifical—grand, splendid
maimed—crippled
malefactor—criminal
malice—harm, without cause
malignity—evil nature
mall—shaded walk or (2) to beat with heavy object
mammon—riches
manger—trough for feeding animals
manifold—number of works
manna—God's bread, Heb., "what is it?"
mantle—coat
mar—to injure
maranatha—Gk, "the Lord comes"
marrow—substance in side bones
mars—myth, god of war
marshal—chief officer or (2) person announcing a dignitary
mart/market—merchant sales
martyr—witness to sacred truth and who usually dies
mattock—weed hoe
maul—beat a person
maw—stomach of brutes
meek—not easily provoked, appropriately humble
meet—qualified or (2) coming together
menstruous—woman's monthly period
mercy—overlooking faults
mesh—net
messiah—anointed
mete—measure, boundary
meteyard—measuring rod
midriff—diaphram
midst—between
midwife—meedwife, woman helping childbirth
might—utmost strength
milch—applied to animals giving milk
mildew—sweet, sticky honey dew or (2) fungus spots due to moisture
mile—1000 paces, 5280 feet.
mill—a thousand or (2) machinery for grinding
millet—a plant
millstone—a heavy stone used to grind grain
mina—weight of monetary unit, $10.50
mind—intention
minding—watching
mine—pit or (2) first person, possession
mingle—mixture
minish—to diminish
minister—on entrusted to do good, serving God or ruler
ministry—religious goals for others
minstrel—singer, performer
miracle—wonder, contrary to course of nature
mire—deep mud
mirth—social merriment
miscarry—lacking success
mite—small insect or (2) piece of money
mock—to deride, imitate with contempt
mollified—appeased
molten—melt
morrow—next day
morsel—improper quantity
mortal—destined to die
mortar—vessel to grind with a pestle
morter—lamp, light
mortgage—grant of estate in fee in exchange for money
mortify—to humble, subdue
mote—small particle or (2) must do
mother—female parent, etymology, from mud
mount—earth mass above the surface or (2) to ascend and ride
munition—fortification
murmur—suppressed complaint
murrain—to die
muse—inspired poetry of (2) deep thought
muster—assemble troops
mutter—imperfect sound of words spoken
muzzle—mouth of a tube or (2) to bind a mouth
myrrh—agreeable smell with bitter taste, medicinal
mystery—profound secret

N

nard—aromatic plant
narrow
narrowed
narrowings—narrow part of a stocking
nativity—birth
naught—nothing
navel—area of severed umbilical cord
nay—no
nazarite—Jew professing purity of life and devotion
neat—a cow (bovine)
necromancer—a conjurer with departed spirits
neigh—whinny of a horse
nether—lower place
nethermost—lowest, hell
nettle—sting
nigh—near
nisan—Jewish calendar, first month of year March
noble—dignified
nod—slight bow of the head or body
noisome—noxious to health
noontide—midday
nor—negative, neither
notwithstanding—independent of contingency
nought—nothing
novice—new, amateur
nun—woman in religious life or (2) bird
nurture—promotes growth, education

O

oath—solemn declaration
obeisance—bow, reverence
oblation—to bear, bring
obstinacy—to oppose
occurrent—incident
odious—hateful
offscouring—rejecting, refuse
offspring—descendents
oft—frequently
og/ogee—architectural molding
omega—last letter of Greek alphabet
omnipotent—unlimited power
onycha/onyx—shellfish
oracle—utterance or sanctuary of a deity
oration—speak
ordain—established order, appointment
orion—constellation
orlop—warship
ospray/ossifrage—sea eagle
outlandish—foreign, not native
outmost—away from middle
outrageous—violent, furious
outspread—to extend
outwent—outgo
overmuch—excessively great
overpast—passed by
overplus—surplus
overreach—beyond
overruling—controlling authority
overseer—superintendent
overshadow—protect
overspread—spread over
overtake—take over

P

pacify—to make peace
pagan -heathen worshipping false gods
parable—a fable for comparison
paradise—garden of Eden, bliss
parcel—divide into parts
parched—dried-up
parchment—dried animal skin used for writing
pardon—to forgive
pare—to cut back
parry—to ward off
partridge—a wild bird
passion—external impressions causing suffering or (2) mental excitement/zeal
Passover—feast of the Jews celebrating God's protection from His wrath
pastor—shepherd of the gospel or a church leader
pate—top of the head, ridicule
patriarch—male family ruler
patrimony—right of inheritance
peck—¼ bushel or (2) low language or (3) bird repeats striking blows
pedigree—preserving blood lineage
peer—one who is equal
pence—penny, small amount
Pentecost—Jewish and Christian solemn festival
penury—poverty stricken
peradventure—by chance
perceive—to observe and know
perdition—utter destruction
peril—hazardous
perish—die
perjured—lie before a court
pernicious—destructive
perpetual—ongoing
perplexed—confused
persecute—to injure or afflict
persevere—to stay in the face of challenges
persuasible—influenced by reasons
perverse/pervert—distorted
pestilent—plague
pestle—a grinder for crushing
petition—to entreat
Pharisee—Jewish elder preserving traditions and laws
philosophy—love of wisdom
piety—practice of reverence
pilgrimage—journey to sacred place
pinnacle—top
pismire—antlike insect
piss—urine
pity—personal suffering for another
plat/plaited—braided
plea/plead—urgent request
pledge—to guarantee
plenteous—abundant
plough/plow—to till soil
pluck—to pull out

plummet—to strike against
plunge—dive into water
pollard—a tree cropped on top
pollux—constellation of the "twins"
pomegranate—a red fruit, with myth of amour & fertility
pomp—showiness
ponder—reflect on
poplar—tree
possession—right to possess or (2) madness of demons
posterity—descendents
potage/pottage—meat boiled in water
potentate—person of power
potsherd—piece of pottery
prating—speaking on trivia
pray—ask, pious request
preach—teach religious message
predestinate—foreordained, unchangeable purpose
prejudice—opinion missing good reason
premeditate—think beforehand
presbytery—overseers
presence—in company of
prevail—trust, gain victory
prey—forcefully seized
pricked—stuck in the flesh
pride—insolent self-esteem or (2) deadliest sin
priest—leadership office in the church
prince/princess—inherited leadership in monarchy
principal—chief
principality—territory
privily/privy—private, secret (clandestine)
proclaim—announce publicly, energetically
procure—to get
profane—unclean, irreverent
profess—open declaration
prophecy/prophet—telling in advance
propitiation—conciliatory
proselyte—to convert
protract—to make longer
proud—arrogant, sinful
provender—meal to live off of
proverb—wise saying
providence—providing or (2) timely care
province—part of a kingdom
provocation/provoke—exciting anger
prudent—using wisdom
pry—inspect carefully
psalm—an emotional, religious song, praise or sadness
publican—tax collector
publish –make publicly known
pulpit—tall desk holding preaching notes
purge—eliminate
purim—Jewish feast celebrating deliverance
purity—without blemish
purloining—stealing
purtenance—belonging to

Q

quaver—trembling voice
quench—fulfill
query—question
quest—seeking
quicken—make alive
quiver—bag for arrows

R

Raca—foolish, contemptible
rafter—roof
rail—a supportive beam or (2) to scoff
raiment—garment
ram—a male sheep or (2) to shove into something
rampart—fortress
rase—to level, remove from the surface of the earth
rash—urgent
ravenous—eager appetite
ravished—violently taken or (2) carnal embrace
reck—to care or notice
reckon—to account or number
recompense—reward
redound—sent, forced back, result or consequence
reed—makes thatch for roofs
reel—to spin or stagger
refuge—shelter
regeneration—new birth in the grace of God
reign—rule by sovereign
rein—leather to steer a horse
religion—binding oath of allegiance to deity
religious—devoted to faith tradition
remission—release, forgive
remnant—the part that remains
remorse—sorrowful
rend/rent—tear or separate
renown—celebrity
reproach—criticize
reprobate—having low values
reproof/reprove—blame
requite—to give good for good or evil for evil
restitution—return to original value
retch—to vomit
reverend—clergy title of respect
riddance—clearing away
rifled—carried away violently
righteous—just, according to divine law
roebuck—small deer
rood—a ¼ acre
rosin—a pine resin
rouse—to wake
royal—kingly, noble, illustrious
rubbish—trash, not believable
rudder—steers ship
ruddy—red color
rude—harsh
rue—regret
ruth—mercy
rye—rough

S

sabaoth—armies
Sabbath—holy day of rest
sackbut—wind instrument
sackcloth—coarse cloth

sacrilege—to profane sacred
saint—a sanctified and holy person
sake—purpose, final cause
salutation—greeting
Samaritan—N. Israel region
sanctify—to set side for divine service
sardius—reddish-yellow stone set in Aaron's priestly breastplate
satan—chief adversary
sate/satiate—to fill or satisfy appetite
satyr—myth, half god, half man
saul—soul
scabbard—sword sheath
scabbed—vile or (2) healing sore
scall—leprosy or scabby
scandal—reproachful situation
scant—limit, less
scarce
scarcely
schism—divided
scholar—student or learned person
science—knowledge
scoff—shun
scorch—burn
score—account, 20 years
scorn—show contempt
scoured—rubbed with rough object
scourge—whip
screak/screech—shriek
scribe—writer, secretary
scrip—moneybag or (2) small certificate
scripture—writing
scroll—rolled parchment/paper
scurvy—disease or (2) vile
scythian—violent, but artistic tribe
seared—cauterized
sect—group who worships
sedition—rebellion, treason
seduce—to entice
see—seat of Episcopal/overseer's power
seemly—suitable
seer—prophet
seethe—boil, swell
selvedge—tightly woven border on cloth
Septuagint—Greek translation of Old Testament
servile—in subjection to another
shall—first person for will+ verb
shalt—second person will+ verb
shambles—flesh market
sheal—to shell
shekel—Jewish money
shepherd—guarder of sheep or (2) pastor of church
sherd—broken piece of pottery
shewing—to show
shibboleth—distinguishes dialect
shittah—precious wood for special tables
shorn—cut off
shroud—burial cloth
shun—reject
sieve—filter
signet—sign of authority
simile—similar
sinew—tendon
sivan—end of May, third month of Jewish year
slew—killed
slothful /sluggard- lazy
smite/smote—hit, killed
snout—long nose, in contempt
snuffers—put out candle
sodden—boil
soder—melted metal to hold pieces together
sodomite—living in Sodom or (2) person committing sodomy
sojourn—wander with temporary dwelling
solace—comfort grieving person
soothsayer—fortuneteller
sop—softened in liquor
sorcerer/ess—user of magic
sottish—foolish
spake—speak
spelt—to divide
spew—vomit
spikenard—plant oil
stacte—liquid myrrh
stanch—to fix
stater—Greek coin
stave—to break or (2) a staff
stedfast—loyal
steward—manager
stewardship—guardian of
stock—post, trunk of a tree
stoop—step
stout—fat
straggle—to stray
strew—to scatter
stricken—to strike
strife—sadness
strove—to achieve
subtil—thin, fine
suet—lard
supple—flexible
sur—above
suretiship—surety
surfeiting—oppressive excess of eating
sware—oath
swine—hog
swoon—faint
sythe—grass cutter

T

Tabernacle—a tent or (2) place of worship
tabor/tabret—a small drum
tackling—harnessing
tale—oral narrative or account of event
tame—domesticated, subdued
tanner—maker of leather
tapestry—woven hanging
tare—a weed or (2) small difference in a measurement
tarry—to wait
tarsus—area below ankle and above foot
tartan—vessel with small mast
tau—last letter of Hebrew alphabet or (2) species of beetle
taught -tight, not slack or (2) educated

taunt—insult
temerity—bold and unafraid
temper—moderate
tempered—adjusted
tempest/tempestuous—storm
temporal—of the world, not eternal
tempt—entice to do wrong
tenet—principle or opinion
tenor—characteristic
teraphim—household deity
terrestrial—of the earth
testament—solemn written instrument
testimony—profession of fact
tetrarch—Roman governor
thee/thou—pronoun or (2) to prosper
thence—from that place, time, or reason
thereat—at that place
thereby—by that place
therefore—as a result, consequently
therefrom—from that place
therein—in that place
thereinto—into that
thereof—of that
thereon—on that
thereout—out of that/this
thereunto—unto that
thereupon—upon that
therewith—with that
thicket—collection of trees
thine/thee/thou—yours
thing—event, action, subject
thirst—eager desire for drink, god, knowledge, etc.
thistle—thorn
thither/hither—to this/that place
thoroughly—without reservation
thou/thee—yours
thrash—beat
thrice—three times
throe—agony
throng—crowd of persons
thrum—weavers thread, twist or fringe
thrust—to push or drive ahead
thummim—Hebrew sign for perfection
thus—example of
thy/thou—yours
thyself—your self
tiara—headdress
tidings—news
tier—rank
tierce—one-third or (2) fencing movement or (3) church liturgy
tillage—preparing land for
timbrel—a drum
tithe—to give a portion of
tittle—small particle
tola—Indian weight
tole—thing to attract a beast
tophet—drum
tottering—uncontrolled movement
tradition—to deliver or (2) doctrine
traffick—commodity trade
trance—mental abandon
transfigured—changed in form
transgress—sin or offend
travail—distress, pain
traversing—crossing
treacherous—faithless
tread—to walk
treason—overthrown government
treatise—composition
tribulation—sorrowful
tributary—subordinate who pays tribute (tax, royalty)
trodden—walked over
trode—footing
troublous—tumultuous
trough—a canoe or water channel
trow—to trust or believe
trump—a musical instrument or (2) winning
tumult—disturbance
twain—two
twice—double, 2 times
twined—wound around
twoedged—two sides
twofold—two times

U

umpire—arbitrator
unaccustomed—not familiar
unadvisedly—indiscreet
unawares—not known
unbelief—distrust
uncertain—not sure
unchangeable—permanent
uncircumcised—foreskin is on penis
uncomely—not suitable
uncondemned—innocent of charge
uncorruptible—without fault
unction—pious anointing
undefiled—pure, not polluted
under—beneath
undertake—to venture
unfeigned—real
unfruitful—without purpose
ungirded—no belt
unlade—to remove
unleavened—without yeast
unloose—free from connection
unmindful—not thinking
unquenchable—continual need
unrighteous—not just
unsatiable—unable to satisfy
unseemly—not fit
unshod—no shoes
unspeakable—warned against saying
untempered—not durable or strong
untoward—awkward, perverse
unwalled—no boundaries
unwittingly—without thinking
unwrought—not made
upbraid—to chide or disgrace
urbane—polite
urim—Hebrew sign of authority

usurer/usury—lending money at excessive interest rate
usurp—seize
utmost—give best effort
utter—speak
utterly—extreme
uttermost—most extreme

V

vagabond—a wanderer
vail—cover
vain—empty
vainglory—pretentious
vale—land between hills
valiant—courageous
vanity—empty pleasure
variable—susceptible to change
vaunt—proud boasting
vehement—forceful fury
venerable—worthy of reverence
vengeance—inflict pain
venison—deer flesh
venom—poison, usually from bite
venture—event involving risk
venus—myth, goddess of beauty and love
verily—really
verity—truth
vermilion—small insect
verse—poem or line of literary composition
vest—to take title or (2) to dress or (3) outer garment
vestry—parochial council or (2) its meeting place
vesture—garment
vex—to irritate
vial—small thin bottle
victual—food ration
vigilant—watchful
vile—bad, mean
vilely—cowardly
vindicate—to correct censure
viol—stringed instrument
virgin—no carnal knowledge or woman not a mother
visage—something seen
vocation—designation of profession, often clergy
vouchsafe—guarantee safety
vow—solemn promise

W

wag—to turn
wages—pay
wail—lament
wait—to attend or serve or (2) to delay
wallow—to roll on the ground
wanton—lewd or (2) wandering
warp—thread, rope for pulling or (2) cow's miscarriage or (3) out of shape
wary—cautious
wast—went
watchtower—watch for danger
way—passage
wayfaring—journey
we—plural pronoun or (2) royal first person
wearisome—tedious
wedlock—to marry
wen—swelling or tumor
wench—young woman or (2) prostitute
wert—was
whelp—a canine (dog) or (2) a contemptuous young man
whence—place or source
whensoever—at some time
where—place
whereabout—about a place
whereas—implies opposition to preceding statement
whereby/wherefore/wherein/whereinto/whereof/whereon/wheresoever/whereto/whereunto/whereupon/wherewith/wherewithal—for this reason
whet—to provoke or (2) sharpen
whilst—while
whit—a tiny measure
whited—whitened
whither/whithersoever—to what place
who/whom/whose—refers to a person
wholly—total or (2) perfect
whoop—a shout
whore—a prostitute
wight—a living being
wilily—by strategy
wilt—to wither
winnowed—sifted or separated from chaff
wit—wise
wither—to lilt, waste away
withholden—withheld
wittingly—knowingly
wont—will not
wot—be aware
wretched—miserable, calamity
writ—a writing
writhe—to distort and twist
wroth—wrath, very angry
wrought—to cause
wrung -wring

Y

Yard—measurement
yarn—thread twisted together
ye—you
yea—yes
yearn—to strain, desire
yester—last
yoke—piece of timber to harness a field animal or (2) servant
yonder—distance

Z

Zeal—passionate

To learn more . . .

Fitzmyer, Joseph A., S.J. *Paul and His Theology: A Brief Sketch*. Englewood Cliffs, NJ: Prentice-Hall, 1989.

Funk, Robert W., ed. *New Gospel Parallels*, Volume One: *The Synoptic Gospels*. Philadelphia: Fortress, 1985.

Funk, Robert W., ed. *New Gospel Parallels*, Volume Two: *John and Other Gospels*. Philadelphia: Fortress, 1985.

The Authorized King James Bible. Nashville: Thomas Nelson Inc (2005), 2005.

R Longenecker, *Ministry and Message of Paul*. Grand Rapids, Zondervan , 1971.

McGrath, Alister E. *In the Beginning: The Story of the King James Bible and How It Changed a Nation, a Language, and a Culture*. New York: Anchor books, a division of Random House, Inc., 2002.

The Greek New Testament. Fourth edition. Munster//Westphalia: Deutsche Bibelgesellschaft, 1993.

The New American Bible. Washington, DC: Catholic Book Publishing Company, 2000.

Throckmorton, Burton H. *Gospel Parallels*. Nashville: Thomas Nelson, 1979.

Webster, Noah. *American Dictionary of the English Language* (1828 facsimile edition).

Scripture Index

Job

Psalms

Proverbs

Ecclesiastes

Wisdom

Sirach (Ecclesiasticus)

Isaiah

Jeremiah

Ezekiel

Romans

2 Corinthians

Galatians

Galatians (*continued*)

Ephesians

Philippians

Colossians

1 Thessalonians

2 Thessalonians

1 Timothy

2 Timothy

Titus

Theme-Subject Index